The Birds of Lancashire and North Merseyside

Lancashire & Cheshire Fauna Society

Lancashire and Cheshire Fauna Society

(Publication No 110)

The Birds of Lancashire and North Merseyside

Illustration by Tony Disley

Steve White, Barry McCarthy and Maurice Jones (Eds)

Hobby Publications

First published in Great Britain in 2008

on behalf of the Lancashire & Cheshire Fauna Society

by Hobby Publications
39 Denmark Road
Churchtown
Southport
PR9 7LL

Typography and page design: The Design Room – www.thedesignroom.org

A CIP reference for this book is available from the British Library.

Printed on 9 Lives 80 recycled paper by Cambridge University Press, Great Britain.

ISBN 978 -1-872839-11-0

This publication should be cited as: White, S.J., McCarthy, B. & Jones, M. (Eds). 2008. *The Birds of Lancashire and North Merseyside*. Hobby Publications, Lancashire & Cheshire Fauna Society. Southport.

CONTENTS

ACKNOWLEDGEMENTS

This, the third Lancashire avifauna, has been produced on behalf of the Lancashire and Cheshire Fauna Society in an attempt to summarise one hundred and fifty or so years of ornithological study and recording in the county. It draws heavily upon the two previous works by Mitchell and Oakes in dealing with the years up the end of the Second World War.

Since that time the main source of information has been the Society's annual Lancashire Bird Reports, together with a host of annual reports and one-off publications that have documented Lancashire's ornithology at a regional or local scale. For up to date information on the numbers and distribution of breeding birds we have been fortunate to be able to turn to the recently published Lancashire Atlas survey.

Behind these books and reports lie uncountable hours of fieldwork by many thousands of birdwatchers who have submitted their observations for publication and have thereby contributed to our present day understanding of Lancashire's birds.

This book can, therefore, have only one dedication – to Lancashire's birdwatching community, to all those who have contributed to local and national surveys, who have assiduously watched their local patch, carried out ringing studies or submitted records of rare birds to the scrutiny of the national or county records committees, and to the bird clubs and others who have ensured that this wealth of information has been preserved for posterity.

We are extremely grateful to the British Trust for Ornithology for provision of ringing data, without which we would have struggled to find very much of consequence to write about the migratory movements and origins of Lancashire's birds.

Just as important has been the provision of data by the local organisers of the monthly Wetland Birds Survey (WeBS) and goose and swan censuses, on which the analysis of population trends of our most numerous waterfowl species is based. We are grateful to the Wetlands Bird Survey partnership (the BTO, RSPB, Wildfowl & Wetlands Trust and Joint Nature Conservation Committee) for permission to use WeBS data.

Photographers and Artists

The final appearance of this book has been enormously enhanced by the inclusion of so many generously contributed photographs and illustrations; all are acknowledged in the text.

In addition to Steve Young and Tony Disley, principal photographer and illustrator respectively, significant contributions have been made by Chris Batty, Chris Galvin, Malcolm Greenhalgh, Dave McAleavy, Mike McKavett, Mike Malpass and Phillip Tomkinson (photographs), and by Nicola Breaks, Phil Jones, David Quinn and Tom Wilmer (line drawings).

All of the photographs were taken within the county with the exception of one or two seabirds which were seen from Seaforth but photographed from the Wirral side of the Mersey Narrows.

The maps in the introductory chapter were produced by Nik Bruce of Lancashire County Council.

The Authors

Like many other county avifaunas, this one has had a long gestation period, beginning in the early 1990s when Maurice Jones brought together a small team including Robert Wilson and David Hindle, with the intention of publishing for the new millennium. The project faltered in the late 1990s and in 2003 the Lancashire and Cheshire Fauna Society took on responsibility for its production.

Draft accounts produced by the first team for rather more than half the species were available and were used as a basis for the updated versions. The second set of initials at the end of each species section indicate the author of the first draft, the first set that of subsequent drafts.

In alphabetical order the authors are: John Bannon (JKB), Stephen Dunstan (SD), Malcolm Greenhalgh (MEG), Bob Harris (RJH), David Hindle (DJH), Maurice Jones (MJ), Barry McCarthy (BM), Steve Martin (SJM), Phil Smith (PHS), Frank Walsh (JFW), Steve White (SJW) and Robert Wilson (RW).

Several of the authors commented extensively on other final drafts and many others contributed additional information and invaluable comments, notably Bill Aspin, Chris Batty, Derek Bunn, Tony Cooper, Derek Forshaw, Peter Hornby, Chris Kehoe, Charlie Liggett, Pete Marsh, Tim Melling, David Sowter, John Wilson, Peter Wilson and John Wright.

Barry McCarthy helped to edit the final text but the ultimate responsibility for all omissions and mistakes is mine.

Steve White, Liverpool, December 2007.

EXPLANATION OF TERMS

Lancashire & North Merseyside

Due to the multitude of boundary changes referred to elsewhere in the introduction, the old county of Lancashire has been much altered and bird-recording areas have changed too. Our present-day recording area consists of the political county of Lancashire (including the unitary authorities of Blackburn with Darwen and Blackpool) together with the four districts of the now disbanded metropolitan county of Merseyside that lie to the north of the Mersey, namely Liverpool, St. Helens, Knowsley and Sefton.

`Unless otherwise specified, references to 'Lancashire' or 'the county' relate to the whole of our recording area – constant reference to 'Lancashire and North Merseyside' or 'the two counties' was felt to be too cumbersome.

Species Status

A summary of status in Lancashire is included below every species' heading.

Lancashire Category A = species reliably recorded in an apparently natural state at least once in Lancashire since 1 January 1950.

Lancashire Category B = species reliably recorded in an apparently natural state at least once in Lancashire before 1950 but not since.

Lancashire Category C = species that, although introduced, now derive from resulting self-sustaining populations (not necessarily within Lancashire).

Lancashire Category D = species that would otherwise occur in Category A except that there is reasonable doubt that they have ever occurred in Lancashire in a natural state. These include birds known to have been ship-assisted where there is a suspicion they may have been aided by people in transit, and British Category C species where it is thought that all Lancashire records relate to escaped or introduced individuals.

Records of species placed in square brackets are regarded as unproven as to identification. They are included only where they have been previously published with more certainty. For the more scarce species, Lancashire totals to the end of 2005 are shown in brackets. Only records accepted by the British Birds Rarities Committee or the Lancashire Records Committee are included. Pre-1950 totals are shown before the comma with post-1950 totals after. A slash indicates that the species is known to have occurred before 1950 but numbers are not known.

Status of Breeding Birds
(based on 1997-2000 survey plus updates)
Rare: breeding in < 7 tetrads or < 11 pairs
Scarce: breeding in < 38 tetrads or < 51 pairs
Uncommon: < 251 pairs
Fairly common: < 1001 pairs
Common: < 5001 pairs
Abundant: > 5000 pairs
Occasional: less than annual
Former: not in last ten years

Status of Passage and Wintering Birds
(based on records during 1981-2005)
Vagrant: < 11 records
Rare: < 26 records
Scarce: < 101 records
Uncommon: < 21 annually
Fairly common: < 201 annually
Common: < 2001 annually
Abundant: > 2000 annually

Standard references

The most regularly referred to texts are not cited in full to avoid lengthy repetition. Full references for the following are contained in the bibliography.

Mitchell (*The Birds of Lancashire.* F.S. Mitchell. 1885, 1892)
Oakes (*The Birds of Lancashire.* C. Oakes. 1953)
Spencer (*The Status and Distribution of Birds of Lancashire.* K.G. Spencer. 1973)
BWP (*Birds of the Western Palearctic.* S. Cramp *et al.* 1977-1994)
Old Atlas (*The Atlas of Breeding Birds in Britain and Ireland.* J.T.R. Sharrock 1976)
New Atlas (*The New Atlas of Breeding Birds in Britain and Ireland: 1988-1991.* D.W. Gibbons *et al.* 1993)
Migration Atlas (*The Migration Atlas: Movements of the Birds of Britain and Ireland.* C. Wernham *et al.* 2002)
Lancashire Atlas (*Atlas of the Breeding Birds of Lancashire and North Merseyside.* R. Pyefinch & P. Golborn. 2001)
Winter Atlas. (*The Atlas of Wintering Birds in Britain and Ireland.* P. Lack. 1986)

All references to breeding bird surveys during 1968-72 relate to the Old Atlas, during 1988-91 to the New Atlas and during 1997-2000 to the Lancashire Atlas.

CBC = Common Bird Census **BBS** = Breeding Bird Survey **WeBS** = Wetland Bird Survey

A SHORT HISTORY OF ORNITHOLOGY IN LANCASHIRE

Defining 'Lancashire'

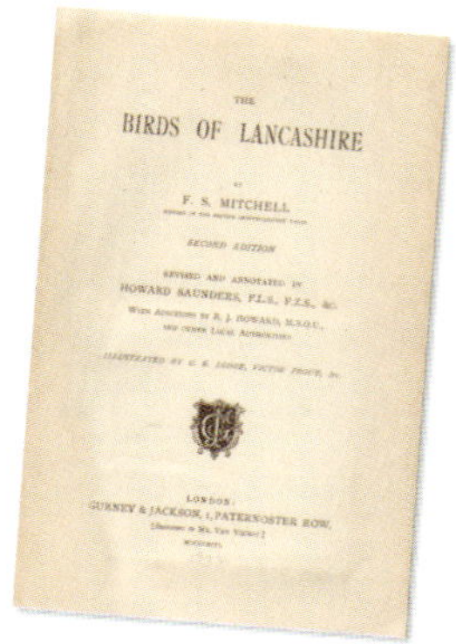

One of the problems faced by anyone interested in Lancashire's ornithological history is the drastic changes to the county structure in 1974, when parts of the County Palatine were hived off to Cumbria and Cheshire and to create Merseyside and Greater Manchester, and fragments of the West Riding of Yorkshire were tagged onto the new Lancashire. The present volume deals solely with the Lancashire of today and Merseyside north of the River Mersey. The consequence is that several great Lancashire bird sites, such as Pennington Flash, the Wigan Flashes, Chat Moss, the black peat moors around Blackstone Edge, much of the Mersey Estuary and Walney and Foulney Islands in Morecambe Bay, which featured often in Oakes's *The Birds of Lancashire*, are not considered here. Neither are many of the observations made by some of the great Lancastrian birdwatchers, such as Frank Horrocks (1912-2003) or Frank A. Lowe (1904-85), who would never have described themselves as 'Greater Mancunians'!

There was some ecological sense in having the 'Over-the-Sands' or Furness part of Lancashire passed over to the new county of Cumbria, for the southern Lakeland Fells, Esthwaite and Coniston Water are part of the Lake District, but that political action did split apart the ecological unit of Morecambe Bay. Conversely, the changes did bring the whole of the Forest of Bowland within Lancashire's remit.

The sudden arrival of parts of Yorkshire into Lancashire has, however, provided some difficulties as far as past records are concerned. Nowhere is this more clearly seen than with Stocks Reservoir, which was in Yorkshire up to the boundary changes of 1974. It is interesting, however, to note that Stocks Reservoir, whose dam trapped the headwaters of the Hodder from September 1930, was first 'discovered' and watched by Lancashire, and not Yorkshire, birdwatchers. Just as the Second World War was ending in August 1945, Clifford Oakes had been looking closely at his pre-1930 Ordnance Survey map. Near to the village of Slaidburn he noticed the name 'Hammerton Mere' printed across an area of moorland and thought that this might indicate a small pool or area of bog that was worth investigation. In those days cars were rare and petrol tightly rationed. Nevertheless Oakes, together with Ken G. Spencer persuaded Arthur Welch, a car-owning Burnley birder, to drive them there to investigate. Their enquiries in Slaidburn led them to Stocks Reservoir and, on 16 August 1945, binoculars scanned the water for perhaps the first time. It was twelve years later, in 1957, when Spencer and Welch (amongst many observers), added Red-breasted Merganser to the breeding birds of Stocks. Incidentally, Hammerton Mere is still shown on the Ordnance Survey map, a short distance to the southeast of the reservoir. The term 'Mere' is misleading in this case, for it is a corruption of 'Moor'.

For the present day birdwatcher these boundary issues may seem irrelevant – a generation has grown up with little sentimental attachment to the old county. However, we must remember that today's records are simply part of the next stage in the ongoing history of Lancashire's ornithology, and that it is only from a long series of records that we can ascertain real increases and decreases in Lancashire's bird populations. But there is more to it. It is beholden on us to remember those who went before us, lest we and our observations are ignored by those who will follow.

Victorian collectors

It would be sad, for instance, if men like Charles Stuart Gregson (1817-99) were forgotten. Gregson was a great collector of all sorts of wildlife. From Formby, where he lived for many years, he claimed to have collected Cirl Bunting eggs, caught and kept alive in a cage a first-winter Lapland Bunting until it moulted into adult male plumage (when no doubt it would have joined his collection of skins), trapped eight Shorelarks in September 1882, 'confirmed' the record of a (shot, of course) White-tailed Eagle from Blundellsands, added Spotted Sandpiper and Slavonian Grebe to his collection of skins and contributed records of the 1863 influx of Pallas's Sandgrouse.

It was, however, in his collecting of Lepidoptera that Gregson's ruthless eccentricity was most manifested (Salmon 2000). He thought that a stand of birch trees might have a population of the Welsh Clearwing, a fairly rare moth. So he had the trees felled and transported to his home for close examination. On another occasion he was out on the dunes and spotted a Clouded Yellow, lacking his butterfly net, he shot it with his twelve-bore!

Character Gregson most certainly was. Reliable, in the opinion of later writers, he most certainly was not. Reginald Wagstaffe noted, in his *The Birds of Southport*, that the Cirl Bunting record 'should be accepted with caution, if at all', considered the Lapland Bunting record 'unsatisfactory', and ignored the White-tailed Eagle record altogether.

Early records

Lancashire's ornithological history extends no further back than the nineteenth century. This is extremely frustrating, for the history more or less begins at the culmination of the taming or alteration of the county's wild habitats through the Industrial and Agrarian Revolutions. What species nested on the heather moors before they became strictly preserved for shooting Red Grouse? What were the unreclaimed mosslands really like? Were species like Red Kite, Ruff, Marsh Harrier, Spotted Crake, Bittern, Twite and Nightjar common in lowland Lancashire in the seventeenth and eighteenth centuries? What occurred on the massive extent of sand dune over which St. Anne's and Fairhaven were quite suddenly built? Little Terns? Sandwich Terns? Questions like these are impossible to answer, simply because no-one went out watching and recording birds so long ago.

We do have a few fragmented records from diarists like Nicholas Blundell and from archives including churchwardens' accounts (Greenhalgh 2004), but they tell only of 'pest' species such as Bullfinches, common species that went into the pot such as Mallard and Teal, and birds of prey that were killed because they had hooked beaks.

Beginnings of systematic recording

Frederick Shaw Mitchell

The first Lancashire county avifauna was Frederick Shaw Mitchell's *The Birds of Lancashire*, published in 1885. Mitchell was born in Bury in 1850, but when still a child his parents moved to Clitheroe. He lived there for 31 years, working in the family business and studying birds in and around the Ribble Valley. There, Mitchell worked with two other Lancashire ornithologists. One, Thomas Altham, lived at Bashall Hall close to the confluence of the Ribble and Hodder. A 'man of his time', Altham was an outstanding finder of birds' nests, and his collection was described as 'fine'. He published nothing. However, he encouraged Mitchell greatly during the writing of his book, and many of his records can be found there.

Robert James Howard (1852-1927) was Mitchell's second close companion who provided both encouragement and records for the first *Birds of Lancashire*. He too was based in the Ribble Valley-Blackburn area (his grave is in Balderstone churchyard). Besides his own birding, Howard bought many bird specimens, which he had expertly set up to provide a splendid exhibition in Blackburn Museum. Today Howard's collection is in the Towneley Museum in Burnley. In 1888, Howard and Mitchell published a slender volume, *The Birds of Stonyhurst*, which included records and observations by them and Thomas Altham from the area around the Hodder-Ribble confluence.

Mitchell's The Birds of Lancashire was as thorough a book as it was then possible to produce, for Mitchell gleaned whatever he could from often quite obscure literature and from a host of correspondents scattered across most of the county. These included J.D. Bannister, Vicar of Pilling from 1825 to 1876, who did much research on the Pilling mosses (*Over Wyre Historical Journal*, Issue 5). Amongst his many records were references to breeding Red Grouse, Golden Plover, Quail, Greater Black-backed Gull and Marsh Harrier; he also mentioned Wryneck occurring at Wyresdale and Stalmine.

There were gaps in Mitchell's coverage, for whilst the east and north of the county were well covered, the coast and its hinterland south of the Lune and north of the Mersey were poorly documented. Nevertheless, Mitchell did produce a foundation on which all subsequent studies have been based. The book contains some fascinating information that is well worth considering even today. For instance, in his introduction Mitchell gave a summary of John Plant's observations of birds in Salford's Peel Park (now in Greater Manchester) from 1850, charting the dramatic impact of urbanisation:

	Species recorded	Species breeding
1850-1860	71	34
1860-1870	42	/
1870-1875	19	8
1876-1880	15	/
1881	13	/
1882	5	2 (Starling and House Sparrow)

If only Mitchell had listed the 71 species seen and the 34 breeding in the park in the 1850s. Would Wryneck and Red-backed Shrike have been among them? Perhaps? Probably? Both did then breed in the county, and the Wryneck was common enough for J. Blackwell to give its arrival date in Lancashire as 6 April for the years 1814-1821 and 9 April for the years 1821-1828, while in 1838 John Scaife had described the Red-backed Shrike, in *The Magazine of Natural History*, as 'by no means a rare bird' in the Blackburn area. He also said of the Whinchat that it was 'abundant in every meadow' – and that is certainly not the case today.

A revised edition of Mitchell's book was published in 1892, the same year that J. Wrigley's slender volume *The Birds of Formby* appeared. The revision was carried out by Howard Saunders. Saunders was one of Britain's great ornithologists and author of the *Manual of British Birds* (1888), a large volume that went through three editions and was in many ways the forerunner of Witherby's *Handbook* and the present *Birds of the Western Palearctic*. A year earlier Mitchell had emigrated with his family to a farm in Alberta. Later they moved to Vancouver Island and there he died in 1929.

The Lancashire and Cheshire Fauna Committee

T.A. Coward

Following Mitchell, the first major influence on Lancashire ornithology was the founding of the Lancashire and Cheshire Fauna Committee (now Society). This organisation was responsible for gathering information on all animal groups in the two counties and producing reports, including the annual bird reports. The Committee's first report was published in 1914 and it includes some interesting records. Here we find a Little Gull, shot off 'Gibraltar Point' near Silverdale on 12 November 1914; it was Lancashire's fourth. . . how things change! The third report, for 1916, included the first recoveries of birds ringed in Lancashire. A Song Thrush ringed by H.J. Moon near Blackpool in June 1913 was recovered at Birkdale the following January, whilst another Song Thrush ringed by Moon at Blackpool in June 1914 was recovered the following January in Co. Clare, Ireland. Of perhaps more interest today was the record of a breeding Wheatear, ringed at St. Anne's on 17 June 1915 by F.W. Sherwood that was recaptured at the same place on 25 May 1916. Urban spread has since wiped out the Wheatear population that bred on the south Fylde dunes.

The Lancashire and Cheshire Fauna Committee appointed referees or recorders who gathered records from correspondents, vetted them and then produced the bird report. In 1914 there were three bird recorders: H.W. Robinson from Lancaster looked to the north of the county, F.W. Smalley to the centre and T.A. Coward to the south.

Of Smalley we know little. Robinson (1875-1941) was a bachelor with enough money not to work but to devote his life to natural history. In his early years he was a keen wildfowler and built up a large collection of bird skins that ended up in Lancaster Royal Grammar School and Kendal Museum. Later he became a keen ringer who, in the thirty years up to 1940, ringed almost 37,000 birds, most of them in this county. Although he wrote no book, he was a prolific writer of notes in magazines, including one in the first ever issue of *British Birds* magazine.

Thomas Alfred Coward (1867-1933) is by far the best known of the trio that produced Lancashire's first bird report. A Cheshire man whose family owned a bleach works in Manchester, Coward was wealthy enough to retire when the business was taken over by a larger combine. Although he acted as Keeper of the Manchester Museum during the Second World War he was a freelance, carrying out an enormous amount of fieldwork in North Wales, Cheshire and south Lancashire as well as travelling widely as far away as the Carmargue, Hungary, Shetland and St. Kilda to study birds. As well as co-editing the county report, he wrote up his observations in a host of magazine articles and several books. His finest work was *Birds of the British Isles and their Eggs*; first published in 1919 this was still in print (in a single volume edited by J.A.G. Barnes) into the 1980s.

Local recording in the early twentieth century

The first half of the twentieth century saw a great increase in bird study in Lancashire that built on the foundation laid down by Mitchell. Several individuals, working their own 'patch', contributed records to the Bird Report and, in some cases, summarised their observations in small books that still make fascinating reading. For instance, C.K. Parker produced *Rossendale Birds* (1928) in which he tells us that 'The Ewood Bridge Sewage Outfall Works is in a large measure responsible for the unusual numbers of species and observations on them recorded for the district. About 1904, or early in 1905, I received permission from the Joint Board to visit the works. . .' By the 1950s birdwatchers across the country were visiting the old sort of sewage farm with its sludge lagoons, but it was the Lancastrian Parker who first realised that sewage works were great bird sites. At Ewood Bridge he watched species formerly considered rare in the county, including Ruff, Curlew Sandpiper and Green Sandpiper, and recorded Spotted Crake, shot there in 1903.

H.P. Hornby was based at St. Michael's-on-Wyre and, besides having earlier records in Mitchell, continued working on the birds in that area well into the twentieth century. His book *The Birds of St. Michael's* (1924) summarised his observations, whilst his large collection of bird specimens was kept in St. Michael's Museum until they were transferred to the Grundy Home Arts Museum in 1955 and later to Fleetwood Museum. Amongst them were two Pallas's Sandgrouse, shot on Rawcliffe Moss in 1880 and a Red Grouse that was possibly the last ever shot on the Over Wyre mosslands.

G.C. Miller worked the countryside around Hoghton Tower and summarised his observations in two appendices to his book *Hoghton Tower* (1948). With the exception of a Cirl Bunting nest at Brindle in 1941 (subsequently disputed by Spencer), his other records of rarer birds were overlooked by Oakes in his *The Birds of Lancashire*. We would today question two records of Woodlark (12 May 1942 and 11 March 1945) and one of a male Isabelline Wheatear at Duxon Quarry on 12 May 1940. However, that of a Great Grey Shrike on 2 April 1940 has more of a ring of truth about it, for he noted that 'a dead House Sparrow, found impaled by the neck on a blackthorn, was probably the victim of this voracious bird.'

J.R. Charnley (1882-1960) was one of the major observers of birds in the Preston-Ribble Estuary area through the first half of the twentieth century. Son of a famous biscuit manufacturer, after his education at Rossall School he was briefly a schoolmaster in Cheshire and then the representative of the British American Tobacco Company in China before returning to his native Preston. By the age of 25 he was given the accolade of being 'Lancashire Naturalist of Note' in the May 1907 issue of the long defunct magazine The Lancashire Naturalist which tells us of his all-round ability as a naturalist; he had, for instance, already published a book, British Butterflies, as well as a short volume called Cockerham Moss. He teamed up with W.H. Heathcote to write The Birds of the Ribble Estuary (1909) and for many years contributed his 'Country Journal' to the Preston Guardian newspaper. Most of Charnley's more important bird records appeared in Lancashire Bird Reports for which, for some years, he was part of the team of recorders.

F.W. Holder

Frederick William Holder (1891-1963) wrote little, but he was one of the county's most important observers in the first half of the twentieth century. He was born and spent all his life living in Southport and, through his marriage to the daughter of a Martin Mere gamekeeper, he had access to not only the coast of what is now North Merseyside but also the extensive mosslands. He was perhaps one of the first watchers rather than collectors of birds. In the 1917 Bird Report he described a southerly migration of Meadow Pipits along the Ainsdale shore on 8 October. In the same report, the recorder T.A. Coward reported that, 'Mr Holder tells me that the normal time for the appearance of the Sanderling on the Lancashire coast from the Ribble southwards is the third week of March, and in autumn the last week in July, and that the birds are common until the end of October.' This was bird study, not mere record bagging.

The 1920 Bird Report included a paper by Holder on the birds of the south-west Lancashire dunes. Amongst the breeding species he recorded were Wheatear, Whinchat, Nightjar, Ringed Plover, Oystercatcher and Redshank. He noted that nesting Shelducks were increasing in the dunes, and that about eight per cent of 300 pairs of terns were Arctic, the rest Common. In the county reports he also recorded several pairs of Dunlins nesting on Martin Mere in 1916, a Twite's nest with five eggs on 30 May 1917 'in heather near Formby,' and a Short-eared Owl's nest with six eggs on 10 May 1917 near Southport. Among many rare or scarce birds he reported a Long-tailed Skua in the Ribble Estuary on 15 May 1917 and a Black-eared Wheatear at Ainsdale on 21 April 1943.

In the light of the present day interest in gulls, one of the most interesting of the rarer birds recorded by Holder was published in the September-October 1920 issue of *The Lancashire & Cheshire Naturalist* under the heading, 'Yellow-legged Herring-Gull, *Larus cachinnans*, Pallas, in Lancashire.' In his short account, he described a gull watched at ranges down to ten yards with Herring Gulls at Freshfield on 10 February 1918. In a footnote to Holder's account, T.A. Coward added, 'I am satisfied that though the bird has only once been actually taken [i.e. shot] in Britain he is correct in his identification.' Nevertheless, because the skin was not procured and other ornithologists thought that it may have simply been an aberrant Herring Gull, the record was never fully accepted.

Many of Holder's records were included in Reginald Wagstaffe's *The Birds of Southport* (1935). After leaving school, Wagstaffe (1907-1983) went to study ornithology at the University of Cincinnati and, on his return, worked in Lancashire museums all his life other than spells in the 1930s at Stockport Museum and from 1941 to 1948 as Curator of the Yorkshire Museum. From 1948 he was Keeper of Vertebrate Zoology at Liverpool City Museum. His knowledge, especially of bird plumages and taxonomy, was so great that he was a member of the British Birds Rarities Committee from 1963-1970. Perhaps his skill was best revealed on 4 January 1969 when he was driving slowly along the tide-line near Formby. He spotted a wing and within seconds, he told me, 'I knew it was from an Ovenbird'!

A forerunner of Wagstaffe's book were joint papers with Holder, including one 'Notes from the South Lancashire Coast' in British Birds (1927-8), Vol 21: 190-194. There we find, under Great Snipe, 'One under observation for twenty minutes in a wet pasture at Marshside, March 19th, 1926.' What a frustrating note!

Walter E. Higham was a bird and nature photographer of national repute who began photography as a schoolboy in 1905 close to his home in St. Anne's, then a quiet seaside resort. In 1945 he published *Birds in Colour* (Collins), but unfortunately the book gave little information about where the pictures were taken, except Oystercatcher (in the Ribble Valley) so we do not know how many were taken in Lancashire.

The second county avifauna

Clifford Oakes (Right) with A. Welch.

By the 1930s knowledge of Lancashire's birds had accumulated to the point that Mitchell's book was grossly out of date and there was a growing demand for a newer county avifauna. In east Lancashire two local ornithologists gathered together the records for their part of the county and, in 1939, *The Birds of East Lancashire* was published. One of its authors was Edmund Battersby who wrote articles for the Accrington Observer. The other was Clifford Oakes (1894-1965), at the time the proprietor of a small café in Burnley who wrote occasionally for the Burnley Express and Burnley News. The two had met when Battersby was out of work during the Depression of the early 1930s, and when Oakes was free of his work they went studying birds, including taking part in some of the first British Trust for Ornithology surveys. In 1937 Oakes took part in the BTO Lapwing survey and wrote: 'My share in this was a road transect comprising Burnley, Whalley, Mytton, Higher Hodder, Red Pump and Bashall Eaves. I covered this route twice each week by bicycle, through the season, watching forty pairs of lapwings from the egg-laying stage to the time when the young ones joined the adult flocks' (*Burnley Express*, 8 January 1938).

The Birds of East Lancashire was a great success and it seemed logical for this to be followed up by a new Birds of Lancashire. However, Oakes appreciated that he would need help from experts on the birds elsewhere in the county (not that he needed much help, for he had already in 1948 published a short account for the RSPB, *A Bird-Watcher in Lancashire*). One possibility was Liverpool's Eric Hardy who published The Birds of the Liverpool Area in 1941. However, that relationship never developed. Instead, Oakes turned to Reg Wagstaffe and R.A.H. Coombes. We have already said that the former was a professional ornithologist based at Liverpool Museum. Coombes was based in the north of the county and had an especial expertise in wildfowl and other coastal birds. However, the joint project was never completed, for his collaborators simply let Oakes down. Ken G. Spencer, who with Arthur Welch had at that time become a close friend of Oakes, suggests that Coombes and Wagstaffe may have considered that the working-class Oakes was not up to the task of completing his share of the book. In any case, Oakes went it alone and completed *The Birds of Lancashire* (1953). A monumental tome, Oakes's book summarised perfectly all the observations that had been collected in lesser books and Lancashire and Cheshire Fauna Committee reports through the first half of the twentieth century.

In east Lancashire Ken Spencer, English teacher and archivist, made a detailed study of the Lapwing, culminating in his book *The Lapwing in Britain* (1953), and took over as Lancashire recorder when Oakes retired in 1957. Many young ornithologists from the late 1950s to the 1970s, the present writer included, received much help and quiet advice from Spencer, whose knowledge of wildlife and its literature remains vast. Just before he retired as county recorder, Spencer produced a short update of Oakes's book in his *The Status and Distribution of Birds in Lancashire* (1973). He also made great contributions to the literature on the birds of east Lancashire in several papers and booklets.

The regional bird clubs and societies

The publication of Oakes's and Spencer's books in 1953 sparked the formation of Lancashire's first bird club, the East Lancashire Ornithologists Club (ELOC), in 1955, when it became one of just 20 such clubs in Britain. Oakes himself became its first chairman; he was followed by Eric Davis in 1965 and Tony Cooper from 1996. Others playing leading roles in the early days included Edmund Battersby, Bill Hale and Len Bouldin. ELOC celebrated its golden jubilee in 2005 and continues to publish an annual report which has several times won national awards in the 'best regional bird report' category.

The Lancaster and District Birdwatching Society (LDBWS) was founded in 1959 with John Barnes as Chairman and Alistair Black as Secretary/Treasurer. The society continues to co-ordinate bird-recording throughout north Lancashire, including small areas in Cumbria, and has produced an annual report since 1959, a check-list of the birds of the area every ten years and a tetrad atlas of breeding birds in 1995. It began with 90 members and currently has around 200.

Eric Ward was the driving force behind the formation of the Rossendale Ornithologists Club (ROC) in 1976. The club gradually evolved from the birdwatching society which Ward had run since the late 1940s at Bacup and Rawtenstall Grammar School, where he taught geography. The ROC continues to produce an annual report, drawing together records from an area that now includes parts of Greater Manchester.

The Chorley and District Natural History Society (CDNHS) was founded by seven local naturalists in 1979, but its roots can be traced back to the publication in 1973 of a *Chorley Bird Report* by Brian Derbyshire and Ken Green and members of the Leigh Ornithological Society, which was at the time the only society recording the birds of the Chorley area. Unlike Lancashire's other bird clubs, the CDNHS's remit and annual reports cover all wildlife within Chorley Borough, together with an extension further east to Belmont Reservoir.

The Fylde Naturalists Society was founded in 1946 and played a leading part in the establishment of the Lytham St. Anne's Nature Reserve in 1968. Between March 1975 and February 1984 they published the *Fylde Naturalist Newsletters*, edited by D. & J Steedon, which included the first *Fylde Bird Reports*. The Fylde Bird Club was founded in November 1982 with the principal aim of achieving some protection for Marton Mere. There were 15 founder members, including Phil Slade, Len Blacow and Stuart Gibson. Since that time Marton Mere has become an important Local Nature Reserve, the club has achieved charitable status and its membership has grown to 110. An Annual Bird Report has been published since 1983 covering a recording area bounded by the Irish Sea, the River Ribble, the River Conder and the A6 road. The club continues to promote local conservation and interest in bird watching.

Freckleton – Lancashire's first 'birding hotspot'

Harry Shorrock and Alan Harrison were both schoolboys when they discovered Freckleton sewage farm as a top quality bird site. Together with Nelson Harwood, a Chesterfield teacher who retired to St. Anne's, they revealed the quality of the inner Ribble around Freckleton sewage farm for scarce and rare migrants, following Parker's example at Ewood Bridge at the start of the century. At first, they generated so many records of scarcer species such as Wood Sandpiper and Little Stint, and rarities like Red-necked Phalarope (1947) and Broad-billed Sandpiper (1950) that some old hands were at least a little sceptical. In October 1952 they located two White-rumped Sandpipers, then known as Bonaparte's Sandpiper, the first Lancashire record of the species. Eventually they persuaded A.W. Boyd (1885-1959), the eminent Cheshire ornithologist and recorder to visit the site (he appeared in top hat and tails on his way to a wedding!) to confirm their identification.

Ken G Spencer

The rise of systematic recording in the mid-twentieth century

The post-war years saw the hesitant beginnings of more methodical ornithological surveys and the gathering of 'data' rather than simply 'records'. Nelson Harwood, for example, published counts of the commoner waders of St. Anne's and Fairhaven Beach during ten visits during December 1953 in Bird Notes from the Fylde Coast (*North Western Naturalist*, June 1954). He also liaised with R.J. Raines in studying diurnal passerine migration in October and November 1951, later published as October Passerine Migration on the South Lancashire Coast (*British Birds*, 1953).

Beginning in the mid-1960s a group of observers, including Malcolm Greenhalgh, Philip H. Smith and John Wilson started to make regular counts of waders and wildfowl around Morecambe Bay and the Ribble Estuary. This was pioneering, for up to then there had been few attempts to quantify large flocks of wildfowl and waders like Knot and Dunlin. Previously most people had used terms like 'very abundant', 'many thousands', or dramatically described what they saw: "Many thousands [of Knot] took wing as the tide turned, and a continuous line of birds some twenty feet deep passed without a break for almost half an hour, flying in the direction of the Lune" (G.R. Edwards on the Wyre Estuary, 16 October 1938). The technique of estimating in tens, then hundreds and then thousands led to the overall estimate of high water wader roosts, wildfowl on estuaries and feeding geese on fields. A comparison

Maurice Jones

of such land-based estimates with the precise counting of simultaneously taken aerial photographs of the same wader roost by Greenhalgh and W.G. Hale indicated that the estimate was remarkably accurate, though often on the low side in flocks of many thousands. This work led to the establishment of the national Birds of Estuaries Enquiry and now continues as the Wetland Birds Survey. The Morecambe Bay data were first published in *Bird Study* and later in *The Birds of Morecambe Bay* (Wilson 1974, 1988) and the Ribble data in Greenhalgh (1971, 1975 and *Wildfowl of the Ribble Estuary*) and Smith and Greenhalgh (1977).

Not one corner of Lancashire has been overlooked by birdwatchers in recent years. Following Parker's pioneering publication of 1926 about Rossendale have come Eric Ward's two volumes, *Rossendale Birds* (1989) and *Rossendale Birds: Millennium Update* (2002), while Peter Hornby's *East Lancashire Ornithologists Club: A members guide* (1994) brought Battersby and Oakes's *The Birds of East Lancashire* up to date. In north Lancashire the Lancaster and District Birdwatching Society has published a series of check lists (Barnes 1959, Hague 1968, Marsh 1979 and Marsh 1989). A similar check list to the birds of the Fylde was produced by Jones (1978), while Pauline McGough published *Birds of Marton Mere* in 2002. South of the Ribble recent important ornithological publications include Barry McCarthy's *Birds of Marshside* (2001), which is a guide to the birds found on this fairly new RSPB reserve, and Philip H. Smith's *The Sands of Time* (1999), an outstanding contribution to the natural history of the Sefton Coast dunes.

In 1979, Maurice Jones, who had begun as one of the small band of birdwatchers at Freckleton and who also made many important observations at Marton Mere, close to his home in Blackpool, and elsewhere in the county, took over as county recorder from Ken Spencer. He continued in this role for 22 years until 2001 (following Ken Spencer's twenty-one year stint), during which time the number of birdwatchers – and thus records – greatly increased. There were also more data coming in from long-term studies like the Birds of Estuaries Enquiry (later the Wetland Birds Survey) and more local reports, including those from the growing number of reserves such as Leighton Moss, Heysham, Seaforth, Mere Sands Wood and Martin Mere. This resulted in a different style of report, crammed with tables and detailed analyses. As the task became ever more onerous in 1984 Maurice wisely made the production of the Lancashire Bird Report a team effort. Steve White, warden at Seaforth Nature Reserve since 1990, took over as bird report editor in 1996 and as county recorder in 2001.

One enigma remains in this brief history – Liverpool's Eric Hardy, who died aged 90 in 2001. Author of *The Birds of the Liverpool Area* (1941) and *Birdwatching in Lancashire* (1979), Hardy ceased sending his records to the Lancashire Bird Report and instead produced the report of the Merseyside Naturalists' Association, which he founded in 1938. He was a familiar figure throughout north-west England, striding out in his long khaki trench coat (he never owned a car) over vast distances, with a rucksack on his back carrying his day's provisions and equipment. He wrote a weekly column in the Liverpool Daily Post for seventy years, earning him a place in the Guinness Book of Records, and through which, together with his weekly broadcasts on Radio Merseyside, he inspired countless people to take an active interest in wildlife.

The birdwatching boom of the late twentieth century

Many factors have helped revolutionise ornithology in Lancashire in the half-century since Oakes's The Birds of Lancashire was published. Firstly, the time available for birding has increased enormously. Up to the 1960s most people worked five and a half days a week, the working day was 8am to 5pm and holidays consisted of two Wakes Weeks, plus Bank Holidays. The advent of the 'leisure revolution' and early retirement in the 1990s dramatically increased the numbers of birdwatchers and the time they could spend on their hobby.

Nowadays it is possible to jump into a car and chase birds wherever we choose, but until the 1960s few had a car, so bicycle, public transport and walking were the only alternatives and people's horizons were more limited. In short winter days in the 1950s and early 1960s, at least three Preston birdwatchers would independently take a pre-dawn Ribble bus to the A6 near Garstang and then trek the footpaths and lanes crossing the Pilling and Cockerham mosses in search of the goose and wader flocks before taking a post-sunset bus back home. Similarly, at least five observers from Blackpool would meet up at the Fowler's Hill bus stop on the A6 to walk the Over Wyre mosses.

Improvements in optical equipment and the spread of knowledge have made previously impossible identification problems soluble. How pleased we were when the Nickel Supra telescope arrived in the early 1960s and roof-prism binoculars in the early 1970s. Yet today we have even more lightweight optical aids, with even more light-gathering power.

One key consequence of access to good quality optics was the development of seawatching, which for the first time allowed the study of migrant and wintering seabirds. By the late 1960s a handful of pioneers, including Andrew Lassey at Formby Point, had begun to uncover hitherto unsuspected offshore riches, and by the mid-1980s seawatching off Seaforth, Formby Point, Blackpool, Rossall Point, Heysham/Morecambe and Jenny Brown's Point had become part of most birdwatchers' routines.

The Mountfort, Hollom and Peterson Field Guide first appeared in 1954, but that gave only the briefest of notes for rare birds. Before then, most would have had T.A. Coward's *Birds of the British Isles* at home and resorted to the public library copy of Witherby's Handbook when necessary. Today we have BWP and a host of field guides and magazines.

Today's telephone and internet information services, pagers and mobile phones mean that whenever a rare bird is found, dozens of birders may arrive on the scene within an hour. Things were a little different a decade or two back. My diary for 17 July 1963 goes as follows: 'In the morning I received a postcard from Harry Shorrock about two Spoonbills he had seen on Sunday at Leighton Moss. I met Peter Taylor and we hitch-hiked to and from Leighton.' Harry had no telephone, so we communicated by post. Peter and I were still at school and could not afford the train fare. We found the Spoonbills, sitting on a dead tree on the Island Pool and then walked along the road and down the Causeway, then the only track across Leighton Moss. There we found what proved to be Lancashire's first Great Reed Warbler calling from the willow fringing the Causeway, and watched it for about fifteen minutes. The following day we wrote to tell Harry of our find. There was not one other birdwatcher at Leighton Moss on that day!

Maurice Jones recounted a similar instance when he and Roy Kendall found a Great Grey Shrike at Leighton Moss on 7 February 1953; they watched it for three hours without seeing another observer. He also illustrated the value of modern communications with the instance of the Stilt Sandpiper that spent over a week in 1967 at Hundred End on the south side of the Ribble. "No observers north of the Ribble knew of the bird's existence," he noted. The postcard system had broken down!

The rise of the conservation movement

Although the RSPB had pioneered protection of breeding terns on the Formby dunes during the 1940s, until 1963 there was not one major bird reserve in Lancashire, nor a Lancashire Trust for Nature Conservation, nor hides at the best birding spots, nor wardens or full-time fieldworkers. In 1964, mainly through the efforts of J.A.G. Barnes and J.A. Black, the RSPB took a lease on Leighton Moss and later purchased what is still the largest reedbed in northern England. As warden the RSPB appointed John Wilson, then a very keen amateur ornithologist and member of a local farming family. Through his labours came the reserve we enjoy today, with its carefully managed reedbeds, hides, ease of access and visitors' centre. He was also influential in the growth of the reserve from the original 400 acres of reedbed to the present 4400 acres that includes the saltmarshes and shore at Hest Bank and Carnforth Marsh (including the Allen and Eric Morecambe pools). In 1964 Leighton Moss had only 365 visitors; by 2004 that figure had grown to around 90,000. John has published papers on Bitterns, Marsh Harriers and Bearded Tits, but Leighton Moss and his work on Morecambe Bay is his lasting legacy.

When the RSPB took over Leighton Moss in 1964 its national membership stood at a few thousand, today there are over a million members. The WWT Centre at Martin Mere opened in 1974 when the Wildfowl Trust membership was 13,000; today the Trust has 124,378 members. Similarly, the Lancashire Wildlife Trust had barely a hundred members in 1974 while today there are over 10,000.

With increasing numbers of birdwatchers and other amateur naturalists came a great increase in new nature reserves, including Seaforth, several on the dunes between Hightown and Birkdale, Marshside, the Ribble Marshes, Mere Sands Wood, Marton Mere (which was once threatened with being in-filled with rubbish), the Lytham St. Anne's dunes, Heysham reserve and bird observatory, and the massive area of foreshore and saltmarsh in Morecambe Bay that is annexed to Leighton Moss. These all have wardens and most have facilities such as hides, picnic areas, car parks, surfaced paths and, at Leighton Moss and Martin Mere, cafes and shops selling binoculars, telescopes, outdoor clothing, bird books and everything else the modern birder might need. Most local authorities in the region have established their own nature reserves, where we can enjoy watching wildlife that is no longer threatened by urban sprawl, pollution or persecution. Few prime bird habitats now lack some form of protection. Most major sites are almost under constant observation, most species with populations of conservation importance or concern are regularly monitored, and the chances of a rare bird being overlooked are close to zero.

All this has not been easily achieved. The great increase in membership of wildlife organisations has strengthened the conservation lobby and helped provide funding for full-time wardens and researchers. As recently as the early 1970s developers destroyed Lancashire's second biggest area of reedbed and willow scrub at Mere Brow, and Hesketh Out Marsh was 'reclaimed' for agriculture, while our largest lowland heathland, Simonswood Moss, was destroyed by peat extraction in the 1980s. Other battles were more successful, including saving Marshside from the threat of housing development and Banks Marsh from succumbing to the fate of Hesketh Marsh.

Today nature conservation has government recognition and the wildlife organisations have more clout and considerably more funding, farming is receiving subsidy for good environmental practice, some areas of mossland that have been drained, arable farmland for at least two centuries are being turned back to their former wild state, and Hesketh Out Marsh is set to be 'reclaimed from agriculture' and reflooded.

The Breeding Bird Atlas of Lancashire

By the end of the twentieth century the changes outlined above had produced a thriving community of skilled, well-equipped birdwatchers with time on their hands, many of them actively engaged in the national surveys organised by the BTO. For the first time, this enabled comprehensive surveys of Lancashire's breeding birds to be carried out.

The fieldwork for the first of these was carried out by the Fylde Bird Club during 1986 to 1990 but delays occurred in publishing the results and it was not until a decade later that distribution maps and a summary were produced (Dunstan & Guy 2000). Shortly after the Fylde survey, the results of the breeding bird survey of north Lancashire were published in 1995 by the Lancaster and District Birdwatching Society as *An Atlas of the Breeding Birds of Lancaster and District* (Harrison 1995).

Inspired by these regional studies, the Lancashire and Cheshire Fauna Society (temporarily 'rebranded' as the Lancashire Bird Club) launched a county-wide survey in 1997. The fieldwork for this involved over 300 observers who surveyed every tetrad in the county and was completed in 2000 with the results published as the *Atlas of the Breeding Birds of Lancashire and North Merseyside*, 1997-2000 (Pyefinch and Golborn 2001). As this book goes to press this survey is about to be repeated during 2008-2011, together with the first county-wide survey of wintering birds. Mitchell and his contemporaries would have been amazed.

Malcolm Greenhalgh
(with special thanks to Ken Spencer, Maurice Jones, Harry Shorrock, Phil Smith and Steve White for valuable information, discussions and advice).

THE BIRDWATCHING SITES OF LANCASHIRE

NORTH MERSEYSIDE AND SOUTH-WEST LANCASHIRE

The Mersey Estuary, Liverpool, Knowsley and St. Helens

The Mersey Estuary is one of the most important sites for wintering birds in Britain, especially for Shelduck, Teal, Dunlin, Black-tailed Godwit and Redshank, but most of its saltmarshes and mud flats now lie outside of Lancashire with just a few kilometres of shoreline between Otterspool and Oglet Bay within the Liverpool boundary. This southernmost section of the Lancashire recording area is dominated by the Liverpool conurbation which still retains good, albeit declining, populations of House Sparrows, increasing numbers of roof-nesting Herring and Lesser Black-backed Gulls and until recently one or two pairs of Black Redstarts, while the Peregrines that colonised the city in the mid-1980s were one of the first urban pairs in Britain. Farmland surrounding Liverpool, Kirkby and St. Helens supports a typical range of breeding species including the county's largest Yellowhammer population and good numbers of Grey Partridges and Corn Buntings.

Woodland cover is low but the last remnants of Lancashire's Willow Tit population hang on in scattered copses. The walled estate of Knowsley Park with its plantation woodlands, grassland and lakes supports the largest diversity of breeding species, including, until the turn of the century at least, Lesser Spotted Woodpecker and Turtle Dove. Within Liverpool, the woods and fields of Croxteth Country Park and nearby Fazakerley also attract an interesting mix of breeding, wintering and migrant species for an urban area.

The sewage farm at Fazakerley used to be a significant birding site but its importance has declined since modernisation, although it still sometimes attracts vast flocks of Swifts, hirundines and Pied Wagtails, and Reed Warblers have colonised its recently created reedbed. Other reedbed habitat occurs in the Sankey Valley in St. Helens and the Rimrose Valley in Sefton, both of which attract their share of scarcer species, including Alpine Swift at the former and Red-rumped Swallow at the latter. Artificial lakes within Knowsley Park and at Prescot Reservoirs, Eccleston Mere and Carr Mill Dam in St. Helens provide the only large open water bodies; they support a range of breeding, passage and wintering waterbirds, including several recent records of scarce ducks, divers and grebes, and the county's largest population of Great Crested Grebes at Carr Mill Dam.

The Sefton Coast

At 2,100ha, the dune system is the largest in England and, although about 40% was lost to various forms of development in the nineteenth and twentieth centuries, much good quality habitat survives, protected by a raft of national and international designations. In 1966 it was estimated that 72 species of birds bred in the dunes and associated scrub, heath and woodland habitats (Felton 1966), the latter dominated by about 250ha of pine plantation which, despite its extent, has limited value for birds beyond sporadically nesting Crossbills. The breeding total has declined to around 67 species currently (Smith 1999); few are particularly notable with the possible exception of Stonechats which have replaced the Whinchats that nested until the late 1970s. Other breeders that have largely or completely disappeared in the last 40 years include Nightjar, Wood Warbler, Spotted Flycatcher, Willow Tit and Cuckoo. These have been replaced by Collared Dove, Green Woodpecker, Reed Warbler, Siskin and Buzzard.

Dunes and pine plantations at Ravenmeols, Formby Point. (Dave McAleavy)

Passage brings good numbers of Wheatears, White Wagtails, warblers and Meadow Pipits, as well as the usual hirundines and thrushes. Relatively few birds winter but increasing numbers of Blackcaps and Chiffchaffs are found in sea-buckthorn scrub at Birkdale. Rarities found in the dunes have included the first British Eleonora's Falcon in 1977, Richard's Pipit, several Barred Warblers, Subalpine Warbler and Lancashire's only Sardinian Warbler in 1992.

Seawatching at Formby Point during late summer and autumn gales may produce Gannets, Kittiwakes, terns, shearwaters, skuas, auks and storm-petrels, while in calm winter weather seaducks, grebes and divers are worth looking for. The greatest prize was a Soft-plumaged Petrel in 1995 but other notable finds have included Cory's, Sooty and Balearic Shearwaters and Forster's Tern. In winter, several thousand Common Scoter sometimes come within sight of land, together with smaller numbers of Red-throated Divers and auks.

The sandy shores are frequented by waders and gulls, the latter sometimes occurring in tens of thousands after a winter shellfish wreck. The Green Beach, an area of recently formed dune and wetland habitats between Ainsdale and Birkdale, attracts large numbers of Snipe and Jack Snipe in winter, while breeding species include Skylark and Ringed Plover. Nearby, Sands Lake at Ainsdale is a notable winter haunt of Tufted Duck.

South of Formby Point the River Alt meanders across extensive sand and silt flats that support internationally important numbers of waders, especially Knot, Bar-tailed Godwit and Sanderling. In winter, noisy skeins of Pink-footed Geese fly out at dusk to roost on Taylor's Bank, north-west of the channel.

The Alt Estuary's flats extend as far south as Seaforth Nature Reserve at the mouth of the Mersey, an area of about 30ha dominated by freshwater and saltwater lagoons. Together with the adjacent Crosby Marine Park and the Mersey Narrows, this is a major bird haunt with 243 species recorded since the 1970s. The site is most notable for the largest spring passage of Little Gulls anywhere in Britain, while, in the right autumn weather conditions, the Mersey Narrows are the best place in the country for close views of Leach's Storm-petrels. About 170 pairs of Common Terns nest on rafts at Seaforth and some of the country's largest roosts of this species assemble in late summer; the site is also notable for a high-tide roost of more than 800 Cormorants. Rarities recorded here include Little Shearwater, Black Kite, Red-footed Falcon, Pacific Golden Plover, Kentish Plover, White-rumped Sandpiper, Buff-breasted Sandpiper, Marsh Sandpiper, Long-Billed Dowitcher, Terek Sandpiper, Bonaparte's Gull, Ross's Gull, Gull-billed Tern, Forster's Tern, Little Swift, Red-throated Pipit, Pied Wheatear, Blackpoll Warbler, White-crowned Sparrow and Song Sparrow.

Until quite recently Black Redstarts nested regularly in the Liverpool Docks but nowadays their outstanding feature is a colony of breeding Kittiwakes.

With some similarities to Crosby Marine Lake, another large coastal lagoon is Southport Marine Lake, which supports a variety of waterbirds, including some of the largest numbers of Mute Swans and Coots in north-west England.

At the northern end of the Sefton Coast, on the shores of the Ribble Estuary, lies Marshside Nature Reserve, 140ha of reclaimed grazing-marsh and neighbouring saltmarsh. This site, with the adjacent golf course and foreshore, is comparable to Seaforth for its bird diversity, with 246 species recorded. Much of the marsh floods in the winter, attracting spectacular numbers of waterfowl, especially Wigeon and Teal, but also Golden Plover, Lapwing and Black-tailed Godwit. Large flocks of Pink-footed Geese are often present in early winter, when storm-driven roosts of gulls can number into the thousands.

The reserve has one of the highest densities of breeding waders in Britain, consisting especially of Lapwing and Redshank. Completely out of the blue was the arrival in 2002 of nesting Avocets which have subsequently established a strong breeding population. Rarities over the past 30 years have included Lesser White-fronted Goose, American Wigeon, Night Heron, Purple Heron, Cattle Egret, Common Crane, Black-winged Stilt, American Golden Plover, Kentish Plover, Baird's Sandpiper, White-rumped Sandpiper, Broad-billed Sandpiper, Long-billed Dowitcher, Lesser Yellowlegs, Marsh Sandpiper, White-winged Black Tern and Savi's Warbler.

The Ribble Estuary

The saltmarshes and sand and mud flats of the Ribble Estuary form another of the most important wetlands for wintering and passage waterfowl in Europe and the most important in Britain after the Wash for its waders, ducks, geese and swans. Sixteen species regularly achieve internationally important totals and the smoke-like flights of waders to and from their high-tide roosts are one of our greatest natural spectacles, attracting birdwatchers from far and wide.

The south side of the estuary has one of the largest extents of saltmarsh in Britain with around 2,000ha (20% of the total intertidal area) (Davidson *et al.* 1991). The run-off of nutrients from the river contribute to the great productivity of the mud flats and their ability to support spectacular numbers of waterfowl. In addition, the grazed saltmarsh provides ideal feeding conditions for wintering Wigeon which have exceeded 100,000 on occasion, by far the largest assembly in the country. They are often accompanied by large flocks of Pink-footed Geese and Whooper Swans. A wide variety of other birds uses the saltmarshes in winter, including large flocks of Skylarks, together with pipits, buntings and finches. These and the waterfowl attract birds of prey, particularly Merlin, Peregrine, Marsh and Hen Harrier and Short-eared Owl.

The Ribble Estuary is also nationally important for breeding birds with large colonies of gulls and Common Terns, most of which are located on the south bank of the river. A 1989 survey counted 20,000 pairs of Black-headed Gulls but subsequent estimates suggest that the colony has declined substantially. However, Lesser Black-backed and Herring Gull numbers have increased during this period and around five pairs of Mediterranean Gulls are now nesting here. There is also an important population of nesting Redshank on the marshes, 231 pairs being recorded in 2003 – a significant reduction on the 400 pairs estimated in 1974. Ruffs breed sporadically and Avocets nested on Banks

Marsh in 2003, but its main claim to fame is as the site of the first successful breeding by Spoonbills in Britain since the seventeenth century in 1999.

The 4700ha Ribble Estuary National Nature Reserve extends onto the northern shores of the river, where the ornithological interest lies mainly in the 6km stretch of saltmarsh between Lytham Main Drain and Dow Brook, Freckleton. The marsh at Warton Bank has developed in the last 50 years and is an important breeding area for Lapwing, Redshank, Skylark and Meadow Pipit, while Reed Bunting, Sedge Warbler, Whitethroat and Linnet breed along the inner bank. In the 1970s Ruffs formed a lek in several years, breeding in 1979, and since 2001 at least one pair of Water Rails has bred. Warton Bank is by far the most important site in Lancashire for wintering Water Pipits and, since 1993, Little Egrets have become regular at Freckleton Naze and Warton Marsh.

Further inland, both Clifton and Lea Marshes have been substantially destroyed but the 50ha of reclaimed grazing marsh at Newton Marsh remain important for wintering wildfowl and its substantial breeding population of Lapwing, Redshank and Skylark and, most notably, two pairs of Black-tailed Godwit. As elsewhere, the once common breeding Yellow Wagtail is now on the verge of extinction.

Crossens Sluice on the south Ribble marshes. (Dave McAleavy)

Access to any part of the Ribble Estuary is difficult and significant numbers of scarcer species undoubtedly pass through unnoticed by birdwatchers. This situation is likely to be improved when the RSPB's plans to return 150ha of reclaimed arable land at Hesketh Out Marsh to estuarine habitats come to fruition. Nevertheless, the list of rarities, especially waders, accumulated in the past 50 or so years is impressive. On the south bank of the river these include Great White Egret, Stilt and Broad-billed Sandpipers, Lesser Yellowlegs and Wilson's Phalarope. In the 1950s before it succumbed to modernisation, Freckleton Sewage Farm on the north side of the estuary was one of the prime birdwatching sites in the county, logging Lancashire 'firsts' such as Little Ringed Plover, White-rumped, Pectoral and Broad-billed Sandpipers and Lesser Yellowlegs, and other rarities like Baird's and Buff-breasted Sandpipers and Long-billed Dowitcher.

The south-west mosslands

Inland of the dunes and estuaries the Lancashire Coastal Plain is dominated by peat mossland, virtually all of which has been reclaimed for intensive arable agriculture and horticulture. Fields are large and hedgerows rare, though there are scattered plantations, largely retained as game cover. These hold some breeding birds, including a few Long-eared Owls and the seriously declining Willow Tit. Sadly, the Turtle Dove seems to be facing extinction here but the jingling song of the Corn Bunting is still heard quite commonly on the mosslands, while a species that is doing particularly well is the Barn Owl, encouraged by the provision of nest-boxes on farms. The largest surviving area of active bog and heathland, at Simonswood Moss near Kirkby, was destroyed in the early 1980s, taking with it the last of Lancashire's breeding Nightjars.

New reed-bed pools at Martin Mere. (John Bannon)

Wintering flocks of Pink-footed Geese, often thousands strong, are a feature of the mossland fields. Keen watchers using a car as a hide may find other goose species in small numbers amongst the Pinkfeet flocks, particularly Russian and Greenland White-fronted, Barnacle, Bean, Brent and Snow. Raptors well represented in winter include Merlin, Peregrine, Hen Harrier and Buzzard, the latter an increasing nester in recent years, while Marsh Harriers regularly summer and have bred. Lapwings and Grey Partridges also breed in good numbers, the latter encouraged by the provision of conservation headlands around fields.

A few traditional mossland sites have been reliable stopovers for small groups of Dotterels in May but several recent years have passed with no records. Passage flocks of 50 or more Whimbrels can usually be found in late April. A fairly recent addition to the agricultural landscape are irrigation reservoirs, one such on Downholland Moss proving attractive to a variety of species, including raptors and waterfowl.

In earlier centuries, the mosslands were punctuated by freshwater meres, the largest of which was Martin Mere, east of Southport. This was drained from the late seventeenth century onwards with the loss of most of its spectacular wildlife. However, in 1973, the Wildfowl and Wetlands Trust established a 150ha reserve at Martin Mere which has effectively recreated some of the habitats associated with the historic landscape. The reserve has become internationally important for wildfowl; in addition to Whooper Swans, the numbers of Teal and Pink-footed Geese are internationally important, while Pintail, Pochard and Shelduck occur in nationally significant numbers.

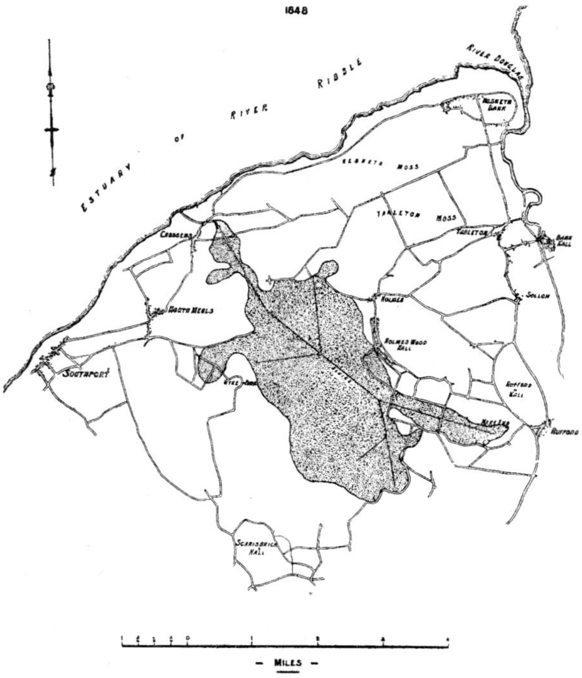

Map of 1848 (from Mitchell), showing the extent of Martin Mere and unreclaimed mosslands (shaded area).

Birds of prey are also a winter and passage attraction with Merlin, Peregrine and Marsh Harrier regular, while several wintering Buzzards are a recent feature. The reserve also regularly holds 100 or more Ruffs, several hundred Snipe and several thousand Lapwings, and it is one of the most reliable sites in the county to see Barn Owls.

Important breeding species include Lapwing, Snipe, Redshank and Tree Sparrow; an extension of the reserve into a former carrot field created a new wetland that attracted three pairs of Avocets to breed for the first time in 2004.

An impressive list of rare and scarce birds has visited the reserve over the years, including Blue-winged Teal, Cattle and Great White Egrets, Kentish Plover, Collared and Black-winged Pratincoles, Wilson's Phalarope, Franklin's Gull and Red-backed Shrike. Temminck's Stint, Pectoral Sandpiper and Green-winged Teal are seen most years.

Nearby Mere Sands Wood, situated on the shoreline of the historic Martin Mere, is a mixture of plantation woodland and excavated sand pits; it supports large numbers of wintering Teal and Gadwall and is one of the county's few breeding sites for Pochard; it previously held a small breeding population of feral Goldeneye. Lesser Spotted Woodpeckers no longer breed but are still seen occasionally. More unusual recent sightings have included the first Lancashire Surf Scoter since 1882 and Arctic Redpoll. Just up the road is the similar but smaller Nuck's Wood, most notable for wintering flocks of up to 100 Gadwall. Farmland in the Martin Mere area is now one of the few remaining regular Lancashire breeding sites for Yellow Wagtail.

THE FYLDE PENINSULA

The interior

The Fylde is essentially a coastal plain (Old English gefilde, meaning plain); the land is very low lying, much of it being below 10m altitude, and with only a minute area exceeding 40m at Ellel Grange and Preesall. It is bisected by the River Wyre into two unequal sections, the smaller northern section generally called Over Wyre.

Much of mediaeval Fylde was covered by low-lying fen and bog and it is probable that woodland cover was always very limited. Mosslands, with deep deposits of peat were predominant in its western third until the mid-eighteenth century. In south Fylde the largest extent of the mossland was in the Marton-Lytham area (originally covering about 25km^2) in which the large kettlehole lake of Marton Mere is located. Marton Mere was partly drained by the mid-1700s, with the adjacent mosslands drained by the early nineteenth century and the mosslands of south Fylde are now entirely obliterated. In Over Wyre the mosses of Stalmine, Pilling, Cockerham and Rawcliffe were huge, covering over 80km^2 (Millward 1955); drainage began in the 1830s but an important, relatively undamaged area of lowland bog habitat remains at Winmarleigh Moss.

Farming is predominantly pastoral north of the Wyre with a mixture of grazing and arable in the south. Many coastal fields in south Fylde still support populations of breeding Lapwing and sometimes Grey Partridge, Skylark, Tree Sparrow, Reed Bunting, Yellowhammer and Corn Bunting.

The farmland of Over Wyre is important for Pink-footed Geese on their migration south and especially in late winter and during the northward passage in spring. Over the years the location of the goose flocks has altered and since the late 1990s they have been concentrated in the vicinity of Eagland Hill and Green Dick's Lane, and in March as far north as Thurnham Moss.

On the inland side of Blackpool, Marton Mere is one of the richest bird sites in Lancashire. Until the mid-1600s it was a large natural lake but by 1741 it had been largely drained and by the 1960s the water surface had been reduced to about 6ha before it was enlarged to 16.5ha in 1973 by the construction of a dam. The site has been watched intensively for 50 years and has yielded a good variety of birds, with 221 species recorded. It is notable as a regular site for wintering Bitterns and is probably the easiest place in the county to see Long-eared Owls in winter. Rarities include Ferruginous Duck, Corncrake, American and Little Bittern, Collared Pratincole, Lesser Yellowlegs, Long-billed Dowitcher, Whiskered and White-winged Black Terns, Red-rumped Swallow, and Cetti's, Savi's, Great Reed and Barred Warblers.

Eastern parts of the Fylde are generally of less ornithological interest as a result of agricultural intensification but Carr House Green Common at Inskip, which has escaped agricultural improvement, yields a steady stream of scarcer migrants, including Yellow-browed Warbler and Wryneck. Two recently worked-out sand quarries at Lightfoot Green and Myerscough support Sand Martin colonies and breeding Little Ringed Plovers. In the extreme east of the Fylde recording area the Rivers Wyre and Brock harbour a few species more typical of the hill streams of western Bowland, such as Goosander, Kingfisher, Common Sandpiper, Grey Wagtail and Dipper,.

Woodland cover is very limited throughout the Fylde. The main concentrations of large trees at Lytham Hall and in the vicinity of Singleton and Ellel Grange are sufficient to support many small rookeries but the Fylde woods are only significant for birds at a purely local scale.

The Cocker Estuary and Cockerham Moss, north Fylde. (Malcolm Greenhalgh)

Coastal areas

The western coastal fringe of south Fylde is almost entirely built up. In the last decade Herring and Lesser Black-backed Gulls have begun to nest on buildings in Fleetwood and north Blackpool, while a pair of Peregrines has been resident in central Blackpool since 1999. In Stanley Park, Blackpool a Grey Heron colony now holds 33 pairs and Nuthatches have recently colonised. The clay cliffs of north Blackpool and Bispham and the dunes of south Blackpool and Fleetwood have been replaced by a 19km concrete seawall. In front of these sterile walls the sandy beaches are almost entirely covered at every high tide, so they are of little value to waders, though large concentrations of gulls may congregate at low tide. Only in the Rossall-Fleetwood stretch do a few Ringed Plovers persist in breeding on a narrow shingle beach between the groynes.

Saltmarsh is expanding between Lytham and Fairhaven, reducing the area of sandy shore but this stretch of coast remains a major site for staging and wintering waders, notably Knot, Dunlin, Black-tailed Godwit and Redshank, while a post-breeding season flock of terns, particularly Sandwich, has been present in recent years seaward of the marsh.

Fairhaven Lake and nearby dunes have yielded a long list of scarce and rare passage and winter visitors, most notably Lancashire's first Ivory Gull and second Dusky Warbler. The site also provides good views of coasting diurnal migrants in autumn.

Between St. Anne's and Blackpool a wide sandy beach is backed by high dunes and, landward of the main road, Lytham St. Anne's Nature Reserve. The beach is particularly notable for wintering Sanderling. In recent years Snow Buntings and Shore Larks have wintered on the beach, while the reserve has the distinction of recording two of Lancashire's four Subalpine Warblers.

The Over Wyre coastline, extending 20km from Knott End to the mouth of the River Conder, is still only lightly urbanised. However, much of the richest coastal marsh between Fluke Hall and Cockerham was embanked and drained in the 1970s. The saltmarsh has recovered to some extent seaward of the embankment and, together with the mud flats, is important for a variety of waterfowl, especially Pink-footed Goose and Curlew. The Pilling Lane Ends area has recorded a number of rarities, notably Glossy Ibis, Pacific Golden Plover, Buff-breasted Sandpiper and Richard's Pipit, while the ringing site at nearby Fluke Hall has regularly held scarce migrants, including a Red-breasted Flycatcher.

Irish Sea inshore waters

The sea off the Fylde coast supports Britain's largest concentration of 40,000 or more wintering Common Scoter on Shell Flat, off Cleveleys. The majority of these are invisible from the shore but seawatchers have regularly seen up to 5,000 birds and occasionally 10,000 from Blackpool. Little Gulls, which winter offshore, appear off Rossall during gales, while Eiders, which used to be seen regularly in nationally significant numbers off Rossall/Fleetwood, have declined markedly in recent years. Scaup, Great-crested Grebe and

Red-throated Diver can all be seen regularly in winter off Blackpool and Rossall Point, often with good numbers of Manx Shearwaters in summer and a similar range of autumn seabirds to those off the Sefton Coast.

The Wyre Estuary

The River Wyre is tidal as far inland as St. Michaels, although the eastern stretch from Great Eccleston to St. Michaels is embanked and of lesser ornithological importance. Key sites are Arm Hill, Barnaby's Sands and Burrow's Marsh on the north side and Skippool Creek and Shard Bridge to Singleton, essentially on the south side of the river. Large numbers of migrant and wintering waders occupy these areas and the Skippool Creek area is noted for its recent rarities – notably Great Knot and three White-rumped Sandpipers.

NORTH LANCASHIRE

The most striking feature of north Lancashire is its great diversity of habitats, ranging from the intertidal sand flats and saltmarshes of Morecambe Bay and the Lune Estuary, through brackish lagoons and reedbed at Leighton Moss, to open water, limestone and sessile oak woodlands and the heather moorlands of Leck Fell. This diversity of habitats is reflected in the variety of bird species. In the past decade 129 species have bred or attempted to breed within the region, a much higher total than in any comparable area of Lancashire. That there is also an excellent diversity in winter is shown by the fact that it is quite possible to see a hundred species during a New Year's Day count.

Intertidal and offshore areas

The vast and fertile intertidal sand flats of Morecambe Bay support internationally important concentrations of waders and wildfowl. The wintering waders, predominantly Oystercatcher, Dunlin, Knot, Curlew and Redshank, spread out at low water to feed on the super-abundant invertebrates then flight to their roost at high tide, a wonderful sight set against the backdrop of the Cumbrian hills. At passage times they are joined by migrant flocks of Ringed Plover and Sanderling. Some wildfowl such as Eider, Shelduck and Merganser feed on the intertidal area but others such as Wigeon and Pintail fly inland to feed.

On spring tides waders congregate at three main roosts on the saltmarshes of Middleton near Sunderland Point, Hest Bank and Carnforth Marsh. The building of rock-armoured groynes as part of the coastal defence work off Morecambe has provided new roosting opportunities, especially for Turnstone and Redshank, while the heliport at Heysham provides an area free of disturbance which attracts thousands of Oystercatcher and Knot to roost, especially on the higher tides.

Morecambe Bay's most unusual breeding species is the Kittiwake which has successfully colonised the gas rigs well offshore. Three sites provide good coverage for watching seabird passage: Heysham Harbour North Wall, Morecambe Stone Jetty and Jenny Brown's Point. Recent dedicated coverage has revealed a regular spring passage of Kittiwakes, Red-throated Divers, skuas and, most notably, Arctic Terns. In autumn, seabirds only occur during a run of very strong onshore winds, also ideal conditions for Leach's Storm-petrel in a good year. Recent rarities include Balearic Shearwater, Long-tailed Skua and Sabine's Gull. The warm water outlet from Heysham Nuclear Power Station also proves attractive to seabirds, especially gulls and terns.

The Lune Estuary and Morecambe Bay saltmarshes and coastal lagoons.

The saltmarshes of the Lune and adjoining fields play host to flocks of Pink-footed Geese especially in late winter but numbers rarely approach those in the Fylde or the south-west. The Lune and Conder Estuaries between Glasson Dock and Conder Green attract large numbers of wildfowl and especially waders at low water. The upper Conder Estuary is one of the few muddy areas on Morecambe Bay and, with the recent creation of a small brackish pool, is good for passage waders such as Green and Wood Sandpipers, Ruff, Greenshank and Spotted Redshank. The colony of Common and Arctic Terns on Colloway Marsh has declined seriously in recent years due to disturbance.

Other saltmarsh breeding birds have also changed, an increase in sheep-grazing causing declines in Redshank and Skylark, but happily this has now been reversed on Carnforth Marsh. The decline in turf production, though, has made some areas less suitable for Lapwing.

To compensate for damaging drainage and reclamation operations undertaken in times past the RSPB bulldozed two shallow brackish lagoons on the inner edge of Carnforth Marsh between 1984 and 1986. With the resulting flooding this has formed a lagoon of about

13ha, now known together with the adjoining saltmarsh as the Eric Morecambe complex, which attracts good numbers of wintering wildfowl, especially Wigeon, Pintail, Shelduck, Gadwall and Teal. Greylag Geese which graze the saltmarsh include numbers of wild birds along with a feral population centred on Leighton Moss.

These lagoons are well used by passage waders both as a feeding and roosting area, especially in late summer when Greenshank, Ruff and Black-tailed Godwit are well represented. In good years Curlew Sandpiper and Little Stint appear in numbers. Breeding birds include a large Black-headed gullery, several pairs of Pochard and Shoveler and an increasing colony of Avocets which first nested in 2001. Irregular breeders have included Mediterranean Gull. Recent rarities include Black-winged Pratincole, Baird's and White-rumped Sandpipers, Long-billed Dowitcher, Wilson's Phalarope, Caspian and White-winged Black Terns and Woodchat Shrike.

Other coastal sites

Important populations of Ringed Plover and Oystercatcher nest on the old slag banks on Carnforth Marsh along with a few pairs of Wheatears at their only lowland breeding site in Lancashire. The coastal strip includes Heysham Nature Reserve and Bird Observatory within the grounds of the nuclear power station. The mixed scrub and small wetland has been a base for visible migration studies and ringing since 1980 and a dedicated band of observers has built up an impressive list of species (236 since 1975), along with an intimate understanding of bird movements along the coast. Rarities include Bee-eater, Richard's and Tawny Pipits, Thrush Nightingale, Melodious, Icterine, Marsh, Dusky and Pallas's Warblers, Golden Oriole, Woodchat Shrike, Serin, Common Rosefinch and Ortolan Bunting. A little further down the coast is the peninsula of Sunderland Point, also good as a migration watchpoint which also attracts many wildfowl and waders at low tide.

Leighton Moss

The 134ha of reedbeds, shallow lagoons and fringing willow scrub at Leighton Moss make up one of Lancashire's most important bird sites with the county's only breeding Bittern, Bearded Tit (colonised in 1973) and Marsh Harrier (from 1987). Spotted Crakes have probably bred there and Garganey nests irregularly at its main Lancashire site, along with nationally important breeding populations of Water Rail, Pochard and Reed Warbler. Wintering wildfowl include significant numbers of Teal, Shoveler, Gadwall and Pochard. The reeds also attract large numbers of roosting Starlings and hirundines. With a list of 265, Leighton Moss and the Eric Morecambe complex have recorded 75% of all species ever seen in Lancashire. Regular passage birds include Black Tern, Osprey and Little Gull, and Spoonbill and Water Pipit are more or less annual in winter. Rarities include American Wigeon, Purple Heron, Little Bittern, Great White Egret, Red-footed Falcon, Black-winged Stilt, Cetti's, Savi's, Aquatic and Great Reed Warblers, Penduline Tit and Golden Oriole.

Reed fen and ditch at Leighton Moss - feeding habitat for Lancashire's Bittern population. (Malcolm Greenhalgh)

A smaller satellite reedbed at Haweswater, part of the Gait Barrows National Nature Reserve, also has breeding Water Rail, Marsh Harrier and Reed Warbler. Further reedbeds have been created in recent years at Barrow Scout and Silverdale Moss.

The Dockacres Complex

The flooded gravel pits of the Keer Valley have now almost all been given over to sailing and angling. The largest, Pine Lake, is deep and usually remains open during cold spells and for much of the winter, attracting large numbers of Coot, Pochard and Tufted Duck, while Great Crested Grebe and Tufted Duck still breed on most of the five meres. They continue to attract migrants such as Black Tern, Little Gull and hirundines but the deeper water and disturbance from fishermen now makes them unattractive to most waders. The Dockacres complex has long been one of the most reliable Lancashire sites for Smew and has notched up two notable county firsts, Pied-billed Grebe and Lesser Scaup, and our most recent Whiskered Tern.

Limestone country

Limestone woodlands and scrub are very much a feature of the Warton Crag and Silverdale area with about 25% of the area covered by woodland. Reserves protecting this habitat include the whole of Warton Crag, managed by Lancashire Wildlife Trust, Lancaster City Council, Lancashire County Council and RSPB, five National Trust properties around Silverdale and Natural England's Gait Barrows. The area has several specialities with good populations of the nationally declining Marsh Tit and Bullfinch being the most important. Hawfinches have several favoured areas, the best known of which is Woodwell in Silverdale; they do, however, seem to be in slow decline. Woodcock are widespread both as a breeding and wintering bird. One success story has been the spread of Buzzards into almost every woodland block. This has been paralleled by the colonisation in the past 25 years of disused quarries by Peregrines and Ravens, and the latter is even showing signs of taking to tree nesting.

The blackthorn, hawthorn and gorse scrub, interspersed with limestone grassland and pavement, has a good population of breeding warblers including Garden and Willow Warblers, Blackcap, Whitethroat and Lesser Whitethroat. Tree Pipits, however, are in decline while, linked to the loss of arable agriculture, the formerly abundant Yellowhammer and Linnet have gone completely, although Linnets still breed in scrub areas along the coast.

The Lune Valley

A different type of woodland, dominated by sessile oak, is found in the Lune Valley. Sites such as Aughton Wood near Crook of Lune and woodlands near Whittington, Cowan Bridge and Wray support breeding birds such as Pied Flycatcher (encouraged by nest-box schemes), Redstart and a rapidly disappearing population of Wood Warbler. Coniferous woodland replaced many of the deciduous woodlands 50-60 years ago but the tables are now being turned and native trees are being planted in several areas. Siskin in small numbers have joined Goldcrest, Coal Tit and Sparrowhawk as regular breeders in this habitat.

With its wide gravel beds and flood-carved sandy banks, the River Lune is important for several species. Large numbers of Sand Martins along with smaller numbers of Kingfishers nest in the banks while Oystercatchers and smaller numbers of Ringed Plover (decreasing) and Little Ringed Plover (increasing) nest on the gravel beds. Faster stretches of the river and its tributaries attract Dippers, Grey Wagtails and Common Sandpipers and Goosanders are now well established residents. Three heronries are located close to the river at Tunstall, Gressingham and near Lancaster.

In recent years spring flooding has become more frequent with, at times, disastrous consequences for nesting birds. This is mainly due to increased drainage in the watershed producing a quick run-off after heavy rain, but climate change may also be partly responsible and the decline of riverside invertebrates, linked to agricultural intensification, is another contributory factor. Many riverside fields are subject to winter flooding and are well used by wintering flocks of Lapwing, Golden Plover and wildfowl especially Teal and Wigeon.

The northernmost of the Lune's tributaries, Leck Beck, cuts through a wooded limestone gorge which supports many typical woodland birds. The bracken covered slopes of Leck Fell, which at 627m is the highest point in Lancashire, give way to heather dominated areas and have breeding Tree Pipit, Merlin, Wheatear, Whinchat, Stock Dove, Stonechat and Ring Ouzel along with a large Red Grouse population. Planted conifer plantations on the fell side are well known for Long-eared Owls.

Farmland

Much of the Lune and Keer Valleys, along with the coastal strip, is now given over almost exclusively to cattle and sheep farming. This habitat has seen the greatest changes in bird populations over the past 40-50 years as agriculture has intensified and become less diverse due to the extensive loss of mixed farming with its arable weeds and crop residues that provided winter food for finches and buntings. In consequence, Yellowhammer, Corn Bunting, Tree Sparrow and Reed Bunting have declined seriously, the first two having almost become extinct as breeding birds, and Linnets, which formerly wintered in large numbers, are now mainly summer visitors in much smaller numbers. Just recently there has been a move to grow maize as a silage crop and the bare ground in spring has provided welcome nesting sites for Lapwing, Oystercatcher and a few pairs of Ringed Plover. When well grown by midsummer the maize fields provide roosting sites for Swallows, Sand Martins and Pied Wagtails and a passage habitat for warblers. Extensive land drainage has destroyed the breeding habitats of Lapwing, Redshank, Snipe, Curlew, Yellow Wagtail, Sedge Warbler and Reed Bunting. The wholesale move from hay to silage, with its much earlier cutting dates, has greatly reduced the breeding populations of Lapwing, Curlew, Redshank and Skylark. Yellow Wagtails have gone from being a common breeding bird, mainly in hay meadows, on almost all farms to fewer than ten pairs in recent years, confined to a few riverside fields along the Lune.

THE FOREST OF BOWLAND

The Forest of Bowland forms the link between north and east Lancashire; its northern areas lie within the recording area of the Lancaster and District Birdwatching Society but most is covered by the East Lancashire Ornithologists Club. A geological outlier of the Pennines, it comprises about 300 square miles of gritstone fells covered with peat moorland and blanket bog. A mosaic of wet pasture and meadows surrounds the fells, each separated by a latticework of drystone walls. The fells are dissected by steep sided cloughs, each with fast flowing streams that converge and flow into the rivers Ribble, Hodder, Wyre and Lune. Ward's Stone, at 560m above sea level, is the highest point in Bowland and is a fairly regular stopover site for spring Dotterel.

The Forest of Bowland is not a forest in the usual sense, in that it is not covered with trees, but it is a forest in the old sense of the word, meaning an extensive tract of open country reserved for hunting, sharing this definition with the Forest of Trawden. There are, however, still plenty of trees in Bowland, with many wooded cloughs and more extensive woodland at Gisburn Forest.

Heather moorland on Hawthornthwaite Fell, Bleasdale in the Forest of Bowland. (Malcolm Greenhalgh)

Moorland fells

The source of the River Hodder in the Forest of Bowland, viewed from Cross of Greet. (Malcolm Greenhalgh)

The Bowland Fells are the single most important site for breeding Hen Harriers in England. They are designated as a Special Protection Area for nesting Hen Harriers and Merlins. Having been persecuted to extinction in Lancashire during the nineteenth century, Hen Harriers reappeared in Bowland in 1969 and now constitute 90% or more of the total English breeding population. Most successful nesting takes place in banks of mature heather on United Utilities' water catchment land.

Merlins share the same heather moorland nesting habitat as Hen Harriers but, being less persecuted, tend to be more widespread breeders in Bowland. These elusive raptors seem to nest comfortably alongside grouse moor management and may even have benefited from gamekeeper protection against egg thieves. Short-eared Owls also nest in the same areas, with their numbers fluctuating widely, dependent on field vole numbers. However, they are not popular on grouse moors due to their habit of supplementing their vole diet with the odd grouse chick. The staple diet of Merlins is the abundant population of Meadow Pipits which nest throughout the grassy and heather moorland areas. Skylarks are also a common prey item, though they avoid the mature heather moors. The pipits also support a strong but declining population of Cuckoos as their main host throughout moorland areas.

The fells also attract small numbers of passage and wintering raptors, most notably occasional records of Rough-legged Buzzard and Golden Eagle.

Peregrines nest in reasonable numbers, mainly because of the availability of quarry ledges and steep-sided cloughs throughout Bowland. Other characteristic birds of the moorlands are Red Grouse, Golden Plover and Curlew. Ring Ouzels and Wheatears nest in the moorland valleys. Both species like rocky, sheep-grazed, grassy areas for feeding, but Ring Ouzels also need rocky slopes with good heather cover close by for nesting; the Langden Valley is the most popular site to connect with this elusive species. Whinchats and Stonechats also have strongholds in Bowland, but presently Stonechats are increasing and spreading while Whinchats are showing a concomitant decline and range contraction.

A much overlooked, but enormously important breeding population, is the colony of Lesser Black-backed Gulls on Mallowdale and Tarnbrook Fells. With around 17,000 pairs it is by far the largest inland breeding colony in Britain. Around 500 pairs of Herring Gulls also nest among this colony.

Farmland

The blanket bog covering the Bowland Fells soaks up rainwater, which gradually drains into the skirt of surrounding enclosed in-bye farmland, then down into the rivers. Where land drainage is not too intensive this leads to damp soil conditions, ideal for breeding waders. Each species requires different heights of vegetation but the common thread is that they all need moist soil conditions. Lapwings are early nesters, and choose short grazed pasture. They can also nest in upland hay meadows which, if unfertilised, have the necessary short sward height during early April. Curlews nest on the moors and surrounding farmland in equal abundance. On the farmland, they prefer to nest in pasture with a longer sward, but will also nest in hay meadows, which by late April provide sufficient nesting cover. With nearly 3,000 nesting pairs, about 8% of the UK breeding population, Bowland is one of Britain's most important sites for Curlew. Of all the wading birds, Redshank appear to be the most sensitive to land drainage; they are now mainly saltmarsh nesters, but Bowland is the inland stronghold in Lancashire. Snipe also need very wet conditions and so are also sensitive to drainage, but will nest in quite small wet flushes running through the fields. Once again, Bowland is one of the county's strongholds for this nesting wader.

Several of the traditional hay meadows around the Forest of Bowland are designated as Sites of Special Scientific Interest, largely for their botanical interest. However, a rich variety of flowers goes hand in hand with extensive farm practices, so these special meadows are also important areas for breeding waders.

Cloughs

Another important habitat is the wooded valleys. The best examples are the ancient deciduous woodlands of Roeburndale, which drain the northern part of the Forest of Bowland into the River Lune, but there are also good examples on the western side along the tributaries of the River Wyre. These are strongholds for the fast disappearing Wood Warbler, now apparently confined to one or two sites in Roeburndale, alongside other characteristic species like Redstart and Pied Flycatcher.

Woodcocks are found in the drier woods in northern Bowland, particularly those along the Ribble and Hodder Valleys. Tree Pipits are found in recent clear-felled areas where a few tall song posts persist, or on areas of rough grassland with a few scattered birches. Coniferous plantations are generally much poorer for birds, but they still have a few characteristic species not generally found in the deciduous woods. These include Coal Tit, Goldcrest and occasionally Crossbill. These plantations are also home to small numbers of both Goshawk and Long-eared Owl.

The River Brennand near Dunsop Bridge in the heart of the Forest of Bowland. (Malcolm Greenhalgh)

Rivers

The four main rivers draining the Forest of Bowland are the Hodder, Ribble, Lune and Wyre, each with many tributaries. They are largely of good water quality, supporting abundant aquatic life, which in turn supports many birds. Found throughout the fast flowing stretches are Dippers and Grey Wagtails, with Kingfishers and Common Sandpipers also occurring on the slower stretches. Sand Martins can be found wherever suitable riverbank nesting sites occur. Similarly, Oystercatchers will nest wherever shingle banks occur, although they are by no means restricted to this habitat. The larger rivers are also home to an increasing breeding population of Goosanders, which were reported nesting in Lancashire for the first time as recently as the early 1970s.

The River Hodder in snow at Higher Hodder Bridge. (Malcolm Greenhalgh)

THE PRESTON AREA

Sandwiched between the recording areas of the Fylde, Chorley and east Lancashire lies the city of Preston. Here the Ribble reaches its tidal limit and the area's ornithology is dominated by the river and its extensive fringing ancient woodlands, and by the newly excavated gravel pits of Brockholes Quarry.

The Ribble forms an important cross-Pennine flyway used by a variety of seabirds and waders during migration periods. The section just downstream of Preston Dock is often the best watchpoint in spring and some large flocks of Common and Arctic Terns and Little Gulls have been seen heading east there in recent years. Upstream of Preston the river banks support breeding Sand Martin, Kingfisher, Ringed and Little Ringed Plovers and Common Sandpiper, while Goosanders, which breed in the woodlands bordering the valley, congregate on the river outside of the breeding season. The deciduous woodlands hold most of the expected breeding species, including sporadically nesting Lesser Spotted Woodpeckers.

Brockholes Quarry's two lakes support a similar range of breeding species as the Ribble itself, together with a number of nesting wildfowl and wetland passerines, including Reed Warbler. Although numbers of wintering wildfowl are increasing, Brockholes is perhaps more important for the variety of species recorded there in winter and on passage. A total of 174 has been recorded there since 1999, many making just brief stops during cross-country flights and including, notably, two first records for Lancashire – Laughing Gull and Semipalmated Sandpiper. Other scarce species include Ferruginous Duck, Black-necked Grebe, Red-throated Diver, Manx Shearwater, Temminck's Stint and Pectoral Sandpiper. However, the site's most important conservation value is as a night-time roost for spring passage Whimbrel; together with Barnacre Reservoir,

Brockholes Quarry, Preston, looking towards the River Ribble and Red Scar Wood. (Tim Mitcham)

which lies to the north of Preston, Brockholes supports the bulk of Lancashire's nationally important passage population which feeds on farmland in the Ribble Valley and the edges of Bowland.

EAST LANCASHIRE

East Lancashire lies to the east of the M6 and within the catchments of the Ribble and its major tributaries, the Darwen, Calder and Hodder. The south and east of the region are traversed by the M65, along which lie the urban areas of Blackburn, Darwen, Accrington, Burnley, Nelson and Colne, while to the north and west of the M65 the region is mainly rural, with Clitheroe and Longridge the only towns of any size.

Pendle Hill from the east. (Malcolm Greenhalgh)

The oldest and lowest of the exposed rocks are of limestone around Clitheroe and Whitewell; elsewhere, millstone grit produces a landscape of escarpments and moorland dissected by steep cloughs, while a series of anticlines has given rise to the major uplands. From west to east these are the Bowland Fells, separated by the Hodder from the Waddington Fells, which are separated by the Ribble from Pendle Hill which in turn is separated from the main Pennine chain by the Calder.

The exposure of the high ground to prevailing south-westerly winds leads to high rainfall. The steep valleys on the upland flanks proved ideal for the establishment of a large number of reservoirs.

Being unsuitable for agriculture, many of the steep slopes in the lower and middle reaches of the Ribble and Hodder Valleys still contain some of the county's finest ancient woodlands. Less steep parts of these valleys are devoted mainly to dairying and livestock rearing, although economic changes have seen an increase in what is sometimes referred to as 'horsiculture'. The climate makes most of the area unsuitable for arable farming and apart from short-lived episodes in the two World Wars, it saw little of the plough. However, a recent development has been the ploughing of pastures in the valley bottoms for the planting of fodder maize. Drainage and reseeding and the change from hay-making to silage have seen major changes in what were once herb-rich meadows, only small fragments of which now remain. Even the upland grasslands have not been immune to these changes. This has led to a considerable decrease in the number of breeding waders and the complete loss of breeding Yellow Wagtails.

Moorlands

East Lancashire is best known for its uplands, which are home to breeding Peregrine, Merlin, Hen Harrier, Red Grouse and Short-eared Owl. Although much reduced in numbers and no longer occurring as widely as before, breeding Ring Ouzels still occur in suitable cloughs. Small numbers of breeding waders such as Snipe, Dunlin and Golden Plover may also be found and the moors east of Burnley now host the only sizeable breeding colony of Twite in the county.

No mention of the east Lancashire uplands would be complete without mention of the annual spring passage of Dotterel on Pendle Hill, the most reliable site anywhere in north-west England for this species. Although a few Red Grouse still remain there, the Twite that used to breed are long gone.

Reservoirs

The main economic uses of the uplands are sheep rearing, water gathering, forestry, game shooting and other recreational activities. Being fed mainly by upland streams, the many reservoirs are nutrient poor and most lack the gently sloping edges which would allow the development of emergent marginal vegetation.

Nevertheless some water-bodies, in particular Stocks Reservoir and the Foulridge complex, may hold quite large concentrations of ducks in winter, including large concentrations of roosting Goosander. In the breeding season, small numbers of Red-breasted Merganser occur on the Hodder and its tributaries, with a spring concentration of up to ten birds at Stocks Reservoir, its only regular Lancashire breeding site. Breeding Goosander are more widespread and virtually all local rivers also hold Grey Wagtail, Dipper and Kingfisher, all three species often being found in urban areas.

Large flocks of Canada Geese are found both at Stocks and in the Foulridge area, although the size of the summer moulting flock at Stocks has decreased. Lack of marginal vegetation and fluctuating water levels mean that few waters are suitable for breeding grebes. Despite these odds, one or two pairs of Great Crested Grebes have been successful at Stocks Reservoir and Barrow Lodge in the last two or three years. Barrow Lodge formerly held two or three breeding pairs of both Great Crested and Little Grebes, but the intensification of fishing there now prevents this. Outside the breeding season, double-figure counts of Great Crested Grebes occur at both Foulridge and Rishton Reservoirs, whereas Little Grebes winter mainly on the Ribble and Calder.

Stocks Reservoir, the premier birdwatching site in east Lancashire and home to breeding Black-headed and Mediterranean Gulls and Red-breasted Mergansers. (Malcolm Greenhalgh)

Breeding waders of the reservoir margins include Redshank, Common Sandpiper, Ringed and Little Ringed Plover. More significant, though, is the colony at Stocks of 1,500 or more Black-headed Gulls, amongst which one or two pairs of Mediterranean Gulls have nested since the late 1990s.

The fluctuating water levels which make the reservoirs unsuitable for breeding grebes do, however, make them attractive to waders, particularly when the exposure of muddy margins coincides with the two main passage periods when almost any species may turn up. Stocks Reservoir is a favoured site; it has had as many as eleven wader species in a single day and Temminck's Stint, Pectoral, Green and Wood Sandpipers have been recorded in recent years.

Common and Arctic Terns also occur at these times; other seabirds are highly unusual but recent records at Stocks and Foulridge include Black-throated and Great Northern Divers, Manx Shearwater, Shag and Arctic and Pomarine Skuas. Other scarce waterbirds recorded at these two sites include Green-winged Teal, Ring-necked and Long-tailed Duck, Smew, Bittern and Red-necked, Slavonian and Black-necked Grebe.

Woodlands

The deciduous woodlands of the river valleys are home to a range of breeding species. Never widespread, Marsh Tit now seems to have retreated to a very few favoured locations in the Hodder Valley, while the decline of Lesser Spotted Woodpecker has been even more dramatic, although odd sightings are still reported from all three main river valleys. While Willow Warbler seems to be holding its own, Wood Warbler, if not already, may soon be extinct as a breeding bird in this area. On the other hand Chiffchaff numbers have increased, and Blackcap and Garden Warbler are common in the breeding season. Although supplemented by winter visitors, Woodcock also breed in suitable deciduous woods. One success story is the great increase in the number of Pied Flycatchers, almost entirely due to the provision of nest boxes in suitable woods.

The coniferous plantations of the uplands are home to Coal Tit, Goldcrest and Chaffinch. Numbers of Siskin have increased in recent years while those of Lesser Redpoll have declined, although the Gisburn Forest still retains probably the largest population in Lancashire. Crossbill numbers depend very much on irruptions and a good cone crop although some are seen every year. These upland plantations are home to a small number of breeding Long-eared Owls, while Tawny Owls are common in both types of woodland. The area around Gisburn Forest and Stocks Reservoir was the last known (introduced) Black Grouse lek site in the county; Isabelline Shrike and Golden Oriole have been recently recorded and it has recently been the most reliable county site for wintering Great Grey Shrikes.

ROSSENDALE

Rossendale is drained into the River Mersey via the River Irwell and its tributaries, which form a dissected plateau with valleys separating blocks of moorland; its highest point is Top of Leach at 474m. Oakes referred to the "Rossendale Highlands" as "a fell system in miniature", a phrase which conjures up a vision of a wild and windswept country with sweeping vistas of steep crag sides and heather covered moorlands. Whilst this may have been the case in days gone by the scene now is one of overgrazed sheep fields and grass moor. The old mills with their attendant lodges and 'goits' have all but disappeared from the valley bottoms to be replaced with steel industrial units and tarmac car parks. This is all to the detriment of Swifts, House Sparrows, Starlings and a number of other once common species that depended on the old stone structures for nest sites. On the other hand, the last twenty years or so have seen an increase in mixed woodland planting and much of this is now coming to maturity.

Whilst Rossendale will never rate highly on the ornithological register it still has plenty to offer. On the high moors to the south can be found nesting Golden Plover, Curlew and Dunlin with the odd pair of Twite, Red Grouse and Merlin. Everywhere on the tops Meadow Pipit and Skylark still breed in good numbers and Wheatears favour the old quarries.

Clowbridge Reservoir at the head of the Limy Valley often attracts passage birds stopping off en route. Many of the reservoirs, in particular Clowbridge, Cowpe, Clough Bottom and Holden Wood, are the summer haunt of Common Sandpipers, while wildfowl and waders provide much winter interest including regular occurrences of small numbers of passage Whooper Swan, Shelduck, Common Scoter and other wildfowl; Cormorants are increasing visitors to fish-stocked waters. Great Crested Grebes have bred on occasions and Little Grebes breed at two or three secluded sites

Kestrels still find nest sites despite the conversion of many farm buildings. Raven, Peregrine and Merlin are rare breeders but there are increasing sightings of Buzzard; Hen Harrier, Hobby, Osprey and Red Kite have been reported occasionally.

Breeding Lapwing, Snipe and Redshank numbers have all declined seriously during the past 25 years, while Little Ringed Plover has a tenuous foothold but Oystercatcher seems to be expanding its range into the area. As elsewhere in the uplands, Whinchats have virtually disappeared, to be replaced by 20 or more pairs of Stonechats. Cloughs and woodlands support a range of common breeding species but Redstart, Tree Pipit and Wood Warbler are, at best rare breeders; Crossbill has bred from time to time. Numbers of Grasshopper Warbler and Whitethroat, however, are increasing. There is only a single small Sand Martin colony along the river Irwell but Dipper and Grey Wagtail are regular along most of the waterways and a few pairs of Kingfisher add colour to the swollen Irwell on a cold spring day. A single heronry which started a few years ago, held seven nests in 2004.

Winter brings large flocks of Redwing and Fieldfare with Brambling confined to a few cloughs where beech predominates. On the high tops migrant Snow Bunting flocks occur from time to time in the quarries and on the open moor. And always the Carrion Crow is never very far away.

THE WEST PENNINE MOORS

The West Pennines cover an area of some 230km^2 dominated by blanket bog moorland with large plateaux rising to 456m at Winter Hill, vegetated mainly with extensive tracts of degraded acid grassland with some wet heath. The area of heather moor is estimated to have halved between 1946 and 1988 as acid grassland has taken over.

Belmont Reservoir in the West Pennine Moors near Bolton, showing the nesting island of the Black-head and Mediterranean Gull colony.

The region is extensively rural with scattered, undeveloped villages where House Sparrows remain common. Land use in the uplands is dominated by water gathering and the vast majority of the area forms part of the United Utilities estate. Sheep farming predominates on the moors with cattle pasture on the moorland edge; some heather moors are managed for grouse-shooting.

A good range of birds breeding on the moorland includes Red Grouse, Merlin, Golden Plover, Dunlin, Curlew, Short-eared Owl, Cuckoo, Stonechat, Whinchat, Wheatear and Linnet. Only a relict population of Twite remains and Ring Ouzel is now only a very occasional breeder with Yellowhammer recently lost from the moorland edge. Peregrine, Raven, Stock Dove, Kestrel and colonies of Jackdaws breed in some abandoned quarries. Hen Harriers winter and pairs regularly linger into spring. In mid-winter the high moors are occupied by Red Grouse, parties of Reed Buntings and the occasional Snow Bunting whilst Golden Plover often start to return to the tops in January.

The high water table produces frequent wet flushes and springs, draining into fast flowing streams with most of the valleys now dammed to create numerous reservoirs, constructed to provide drinking and compensation water for the industrial towns downstream in Lancashire, Greater Manchester and Merseyside. Dipper and Grey Wagtail are common on the upland streams with Kingfisher in places lower down.

The reservoirs hold breeding waders including Oystercatcher, Little Ringed Plover, Redshank and Common Sandpiper, together with breeding Great-crested Grebe, Tufted Duck, numerous Canada Geese and a few Teal, whilst Pintail has bred and Goldeneye summered. Belmont Reservoir supports a large Black-headed Gull colony together with odd pairs of Mediterranean, Lesser Black-backed and Herring Gulls. Large gull roosts assemble on some reservoirs outside of the breeding season, particularly on Lower Rivington, whilst Goosanders roost on several, mainly Delph, Wayoh and Anglezarke, where the once regular flock of Whooper Swans has now disappeared. The ornithological quality of many reservoirs is compromised by recreational pressures, with sailing and other disturbance affecting the distribution and numbers of winter wildfowl and breeding waders respectively.

Upland farmsteads are surrounded by in-bye pastures, many now degraded as rush cover increases. Very few hay meadows remain and improved pastures are now mostly cut for silage/haylage, although many in-bye fields retain breeding Lapwing, Redshank, Snipe and Reed Bunting, often in good numbers, with Grey Partridge still widely distributed. Numbers of Grasshopper Warblers are increasing as they take advantage of the rush-beds; farm buildings often hold large colonies of Swallows whilst Barn Owls have recently recolonised.

Many steep-sided upland valleys are clothed with natural woodlands, typically oak, ash, birch, rowan and holly, often with wet woodland of alder and willow, many now supplemented by introduced beech, sycamore and rhododendron. Upland woodlands, particularly in the Rivington, Anglezarke and Roddlesworth areas, hold typical species such as Pied Flycatcher, Redstart, Tree Pipit, Spotted Flycatcher, Woodcock, Nuthatch, Green Woodpecker and Wood Warbler. Lesser Spotted Woodpecker, Willow Tit and Tree Sparrow are declining towards extinction while there are signs that Buzzard, Goshawk and Hobby are colonising the area.

Extensive conifer and mixed plantations, mainly associated with reservoir surrounds, hold breeding Long-eared Owl, Siskin and Lesser Redpoll with Crossbill in most years and a large heronry in a larch plantation at Entwistle. Woodcock winter in good numbers in plantations and rhododendron thickets. Several massive corvid (mainly Carrion Crow) roosts form in the plantations in midwinter with a large Magpie roost on the county border at Egerton. Finch roosts also occur, although the largest roosts of Brambling have been in rhododendron thickets at Belmont.

Visible migration is often evident through the valleys and along the moor edges, Darwen Moor, for example, and Wheatears and Ring Ouzels commonly linger on the in-bye land. Ospreys are annual on the reservoirs and, if reservoir levels are low, passage waders can be notable both in number and variety.

County rarities are infrequent but have included Lancashire's first Whiskered Tern and Dartford Warbler plus the only Golden Eagle to be photographed in the county.

THE CHORLEY AREA

Sitting between the mosslands in the west and the West Pennine Moors in the east, the area around and including the town of Chorley owes most of its ornithological interest to the River Yarrow. From its source on Anglezarke Moor it works its way through the Rivington reservoir system, passes through Chorley itself, and meanders through the Eccleston and Croston countryside as far as its confluence with the Rivers Lostock and Douglas out on the mosslands.

Around the town of Chorley the Yarrow and its tributary, the Chor, flow through an incomplete circle of ancient semi-natural woodlands which support most of the common woodland species, including Treecreeper, Jay and Great Spotted Woodpecker. Since its arrival in the area around 1980, the Nuthatch is now a common resident species, whilst the elusive Lesser Spotted Woodpecker may still be seen, particularly before the leaves appear in spring when it is quite vocal.

As the river passes between Chorley and Coppull it flows through a former mill site known as Birkacre, whose lodges have been reclaimed to form the focal point of the Yarrow Valley Country Park. The lodges support breeding populations of Mute Swan, Great Crested Grebe, Coot, Moorhen and Mallard. Winter visitors include Tufted Duck, Pochard, Goosander and, increasingly, Cormorant. Rarities have included Ring-necked Duck and Red-throated Diver. Visitors to the park should also have a good chance of seeing Dipper, Kingfisher and Grey Wagtail.

West of Chorley the Yarrow passes through a landscape of pasture and arable farming with hedgerows which provides plenty of avian interest with healthy populations of Linnet, Yellowhammer and Tree Sparrow. Curlew, Lapwing and Oystercatcher are all resident breeding species, and Grey and Red-legged Partridge can still be found. The river itself has one or two Sand Martin colonies along this stretch, and Kingfisher and Grey Wagtail should again be encountered. Whitethroat readily take advantage of bramble patches along the river bank.

At the western end of the borough the Yarrow flows through mosslands around the villages of Bretherton, Croston and Mawdesley to its confluence with the rivers Lostock and Douglas. The mosslands are now mainly arable farmland but still home to Grey Partridge, Corn Bunting and Yellowhammer. Wetter parts have breeding Shelduck, Oystercatcher and Redshank and occasional reedbeds, including those at Croston Marsh and Bretherton Fish Ponds, have breeding Sedge Warblers, Reed Warblers and Reed Buntings. Recently, there have been increasing sightings of Buzzards and after some years of decline, Barn Owls are recovering in the area.

Cuerden Valley Park, in the north of the borough and bordered by the M6 and M65 motorways, is an important site for wildlife. The River Lostock, which flows through the park, is a textbook example of a lowland river with meanders and oxbow lakes. The river and numerous ponds provide good habitats for Water Voles, as well as birds such as Grey Wagtails, Dippers and Kingfishers, whilst the lake has breeding Great Crested Grebe and other waterbirds. Sand Martins, which breed in a nearby sand quarry, regularly feed along the river and over the lake during the summer. Grey Herons have nested in woodland by the lake.

Some areas of reclaimed derelict land have become so important for wildlife that they are now nature reserves. In addition to Birkacre, mentioned above, another part of the Yarrow Valley Country Park, the former waste tip now called Lower Burgh Meadows, has breeding

Grasshopper Warbler, Sedge Warbler, Reed Bunting, Skylark and Whitethroat. These species, together with Willow Tit and Yellowhammer, are also found at the Hic Bibi Nature Reserve at Coppull on the site of a former clay pit and brick works. As well as the rivers, the Leeds-Liverpool Canal (and its Rufford branch), which snakes its way through the area, forms an important wildlife corridor. Withnell Fold Nature Reserve was developed from the filter beds and sludge lagoons of the Wiggins Teape paper mill by the canal. Teal are regular on the lagoons in winter whilst Kingfisher and Water Rail are occasionally seen and two Spotted Crakes were recorded in 1995. A short walk north along the canal brings one to fields known locally as 'Withnell Fold Flashes' which are subject to flooding and may provide sightings of Curlew, Dunlin, Lapwing, Little Ringed Plover, Oystercatcher, Redshank, Snipe and sometimes Green Sandpiper on passage. It has also become a regular stop-off point for good numbers of Whimbrel in spring.

In addition to the reservoirs of the West Pennine Moors, wildfowl interest in Chorley Borough can also be found on several former mill lodges on the moorland fringes, particularly the Healey Lodges below Healey Nab and Heapey Lodges, near the picturesque hamlet of White Coppice. The White Coppice area is also a good place to see Stonechat, Green Woodpecker and Little Owl and summer visitors include Cuckoo, Tree Pipit and Redstart, with Ring Ouzel, Wheatear and Whinchat regular on passage. Further north along the valley of the watercourse, the Goit, Wood Warbler joins more common birds in the woodlands around Brinscall.

The northern boundary of Chorley is formed by the River Darwen at Hoghton Bottoms. This is another river which supports Dipper, Kingfisher and Grey Wagtail as well as a Sand Martin colony. Other birds frequently seen in the locality are Buzzard, Raven, Peregrine, Green Woodpecker and increasingly Barn Owl. Seen only very rarely, but hopefully still resident, is the elusive Hawfinch.

The River Yarrow in Croston village, Chorley. Once heavily polluted, the Yarrow now supports breeding Dippers, a run of Sea Trout and good numbers of Mayflies. (Malcolm Greenhalgh)

Tony Cooper, Bob Ives, Steve Martin, Tim Melling, Jim Ormerod, Phil Smith, Neil Southworth, Frank Walsh, Steve White and John Wilson.

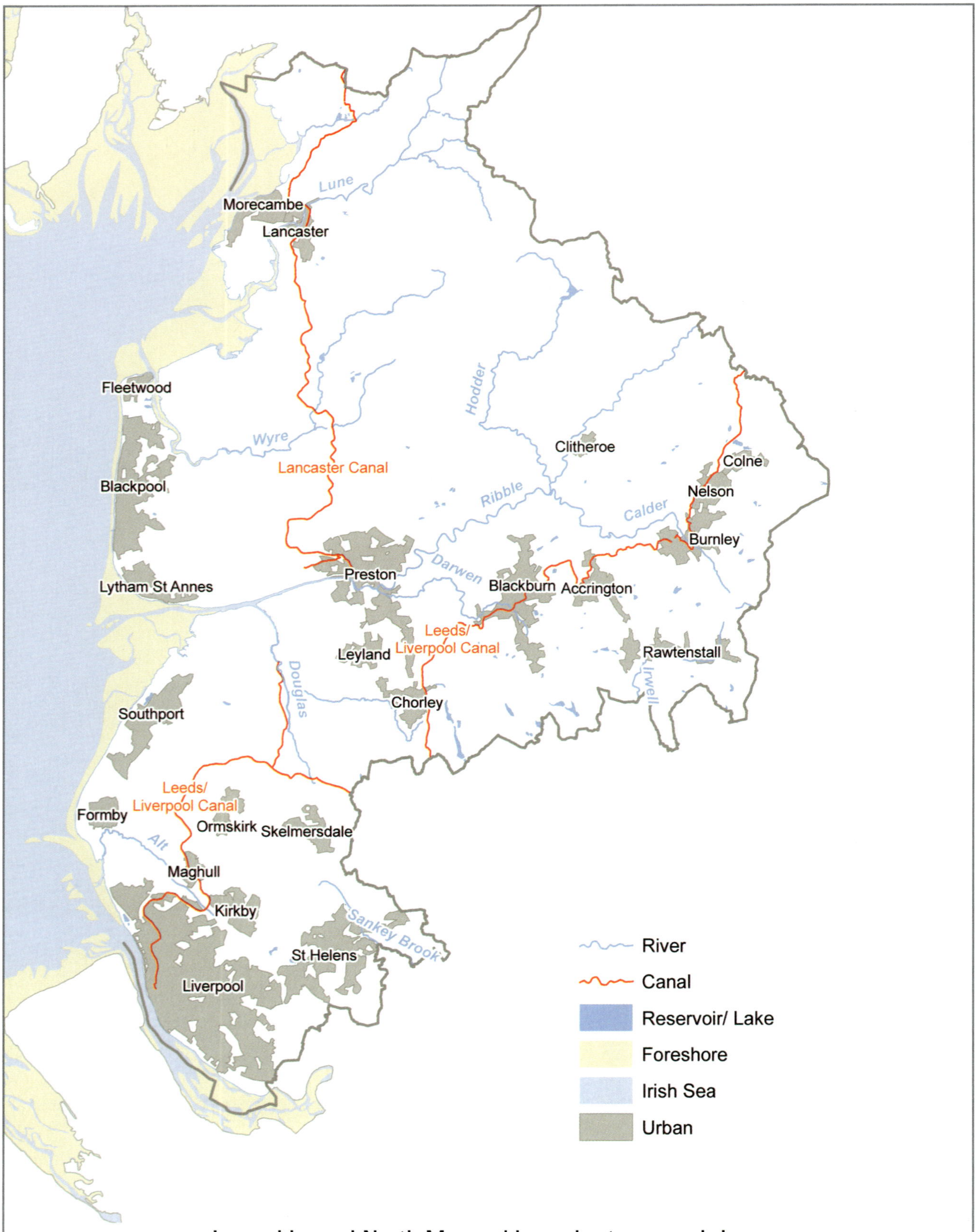

Lancashire and North Merseyside: major towns and rivers

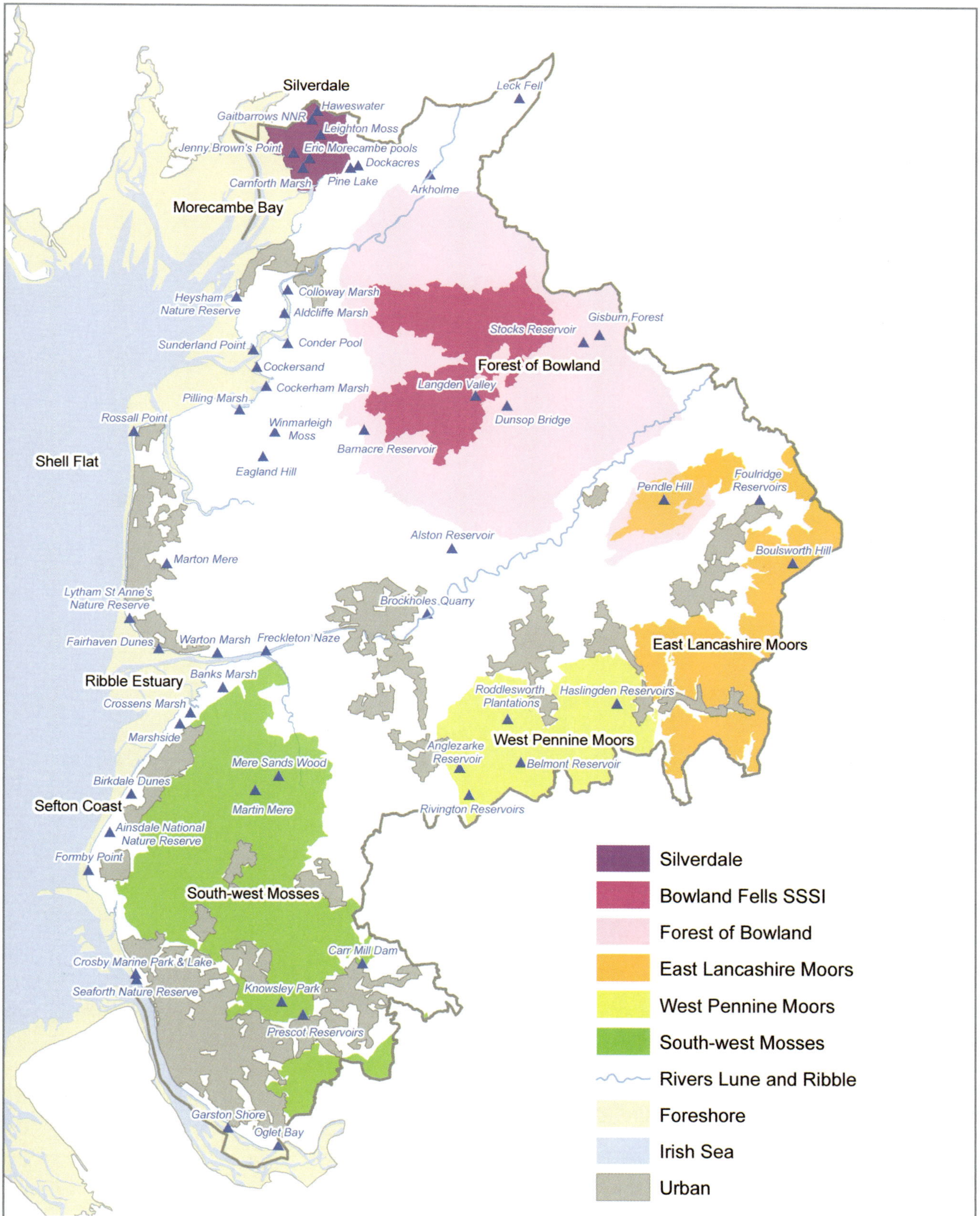

Lancashire and North Merseyside: main birdwatching sites

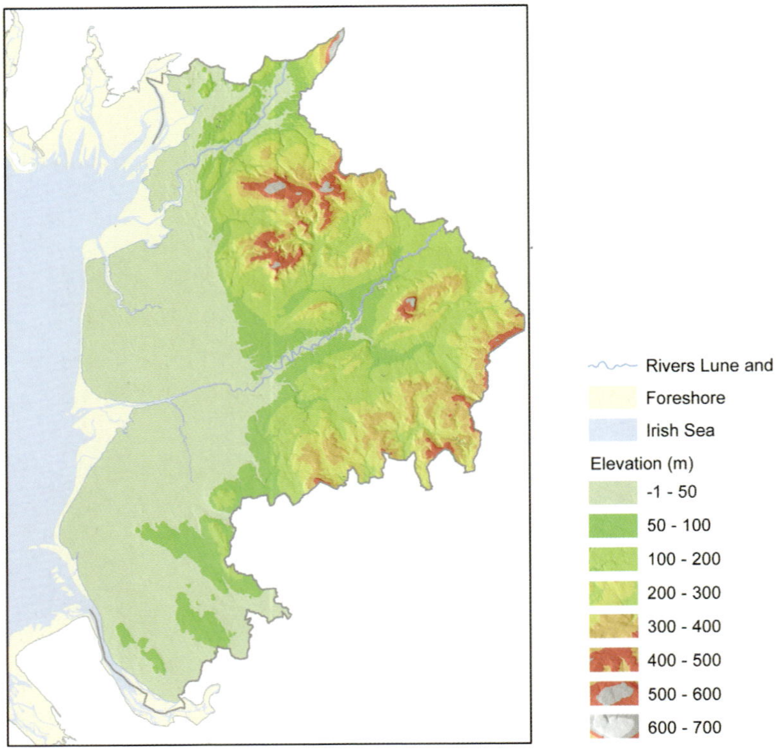

Lancashire and North Merseyside: height above sea level

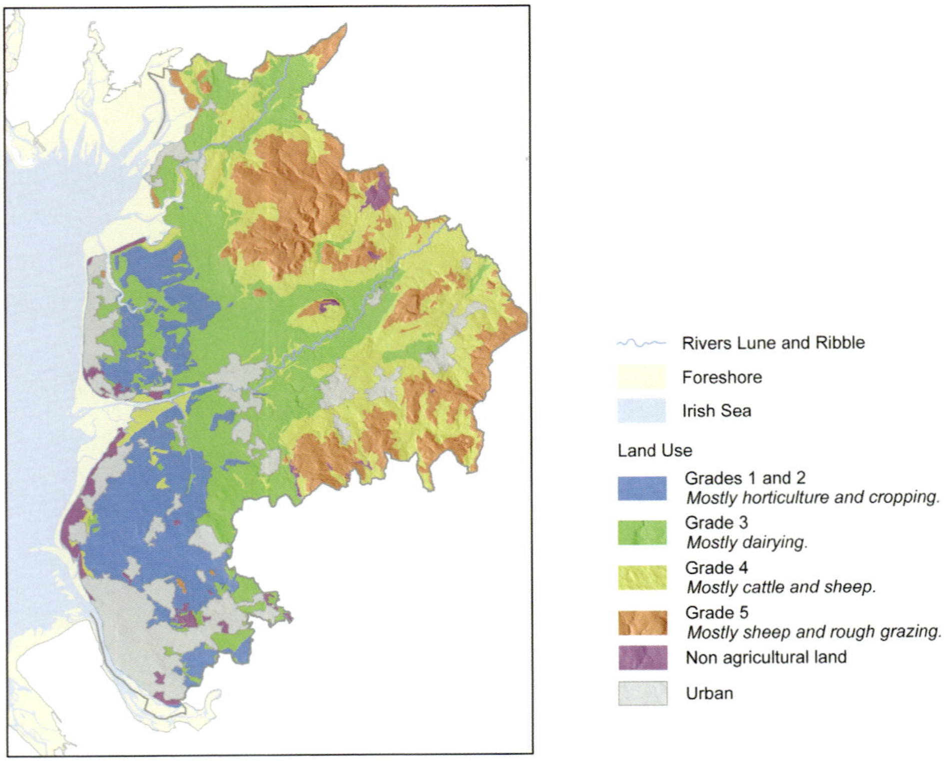

Lancashire and North Merseyside: agricultural land use

The Birds of Lancashire and North Merseyside

MUTE SWAN

Cygnus olor

Lancashire Category A.

Uncommon resident breeder; common in winter.

Both Mitchell and Oakes regarded the Mute Swan as a widespread breeding bird on Lancashire waters but neither gave any indication of numbers or precise distribution, although Oakes referred to groups of 20-30 present all year on the Lune and smaller numbers on the Wyre, Ribble and various 'streams'.

The Lancashire Atlas estimated the breeding population at the end of the twentieth century at around 200 pairs, distributed on canals, lakes and reservoirs throughout the county and largely absent from the south-west mosslands and uplands between the Ribble and the Lune. The breeding population is limited by the species' strongly territorial nature; more than 75% of occupied tetrads support just a single pair and breeding density is highest where there are several discrete waters in areas such as Leighton Moss and the Scorton gravel pit complex.

There seems little doubt that breeding numbers in Lancashire have increased in the last decade or so in parallel with the national recovery after the banning of the use of lead in angling, but there are no earlier county population estimates from which to quantify this. However, a good indication of the resurgence of the Mute Swan during the 1990s is given by the dramatic increase in their breeding distribution in the Fylde from twelve tetrads during 1986-1990 (Dunstan & Guy 2000) to 33 during 1997-2000.

Failed and non-breeding birds congregate in summer at sites which offer a combination of security and ample food for the hazardous period in which their flight feathers are lost. Cavendish Dock in Barrow-in-Furness was for many years the most favoured site in Lancashire; although now part of Cumbria, its catchment area includes a large part of north Lancashire and the Fylde. Weed-cutting operations have drastically reduced the food supply at this site and birds have had to find alternatives. Many shifted to Southport Marine Lake, where average maxima of less than 100 in the early 1990s climbed to well over 200 in August (the main flightless period) in 1996 to 1998 and a peak of 252 birds in the latter year. Other summering sites include Marton Mere and Crosby Marine Lake. More recently, birds have also formed moult flocks on estuarine sites, with three-figure gatherings on both the Ribble and Lune Estuaries. The non-breeding population may total 500 birds, so that the total post-breeding population is probably in the order of 1,000.

Newly hatched Mute Swan cygnets, Seaforth Nature Reserve, May 2004. (Steve Young)

Wintering congregations occur on many of the same sites but also on brackish waters that do not freeze over, saltmarshes and agricultural fields – notably on Aldcliffe Marsh on the Lune where 150 or more are regular – where they frequently join up with groups of visiting Whooper and Bewick's Swans. The most favoured wintering site in Lancashire is Fleetwood Marine Lake. Counts peak at this site during the period November to February, rising from an average of around 50 in the mid-1980s to more than 100 throughout the 1990s with a peak of 256 in February 1999 (Figure 1). The popularity of this site has been underpinned by a funded winter feeding programme of grain and a stream of benevolent visitors with bread. Their dependency on food handouts has been demonstrated in recent years with pairs nesting on the lifeless lake, the cygnets invariably dying off quickly. Birds wintering on Southport (where the largest winter count was 233 in December 2005) and Crosby Marine Lakes are similarly dependent upon supplementary feeding.

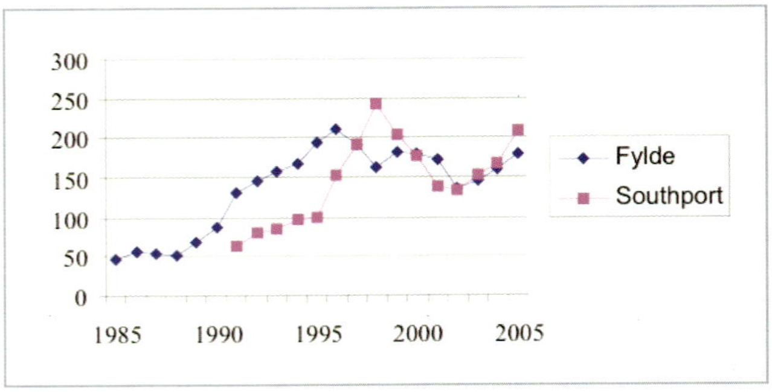

Figure 1. Annual peak counts (3-year rolling means) of Mute Swans at main Fylde sites (Fleetwood Marine Lake, Fairhaven Lake and Glasson Dock), 1982-2005, and Southport Marine Lake, 1989-2005.

Darvic-ringing of birds in Lancashire and neighbouring counties has produced a wealth of information about movements. Care needs to be taken with long-distance recoveries as these often result from rescued birds being released in a different area to that where they were picked up (Migration Atlas). However, for what is often thought to be a sedentary species, young birds in particular can move fairly long distances. A number of birds have moved over 100km from Lancashire into Scotland, north-east England, Yorkshire and north Wales. Others have made the opposite journey, with regular movements into the county from Cumbria, Cheshire, Shropshire and the West Midlands. Birds tend to avoid upland areas and the open sea even during dispersal, and recoveries from the Isle of Man are exceptional. Young birds may wander further afield but they generally return to breed close to the natal area, particular females. Once birds are paired up they are generally highly sedentary, the average recovery distance for a breeding Mute Swan is just 2km from the ringing site (Migration Atlas).

Causes of mortality are well studied; in Lancashire as elsewhere collision with overhead wires is a major factor. Deflectors have been put up at a number of sites throughout the county but this remains a significant problem. Lead poisoning was a problem in the past, and deliberate persecution remains common in urban areas, the confiding nature of many swans making them a sitting target for bored youths with airguns or stones. Entanglement with fishing line and poisoning at supplementary feeding sites add to the problems. Swan rescue groups are estimated to handle more than 5,000 injured birds a year nationally and several are active in Lancashire and surrounding counties, but their precise contribution to maintaining swan numbers is unknown.

Mitchell gave specific status to the 'Polish' Swan, and cited one instance of a 'mixed' pairing with a Mute Swan. This Mute Swan form remains genuinely rare in the county, the only recent report concerning an immature at Barrow Lodge in east Lancashire in 1979.

SD.

This species account was sponsored by Frank Bateson.

BEWICK'S SWAN

Cygnus columbianus

Lancashire Category A.

Common winter visitor from northern Russia.

Bewick's Swan has undergone a striking change of status in Lancashire over the past 150 years, being transformed from a rarity in the nineteenth century (Mitchell reported only one significant occurrence in Lancashire, 24 at Foulridge in March 1857) to an internationally important winter visitor in the late twentieth.

By the middle of the twentieth century Oakes was able to describe the species as a frequent visitor in small numbers. Although he knew of some in the species' present-day heartlands, writing of regular singles on Formby Moss including ten there in 1923, for example, most of his records were in or around what is now Greater Manchester, 17 at Rivington Reservoir in 1923 being a Lancashire example. A note of caution regarding these early assessments of the relative status of Bewick's and Whooper Swans is necessary, however, since, before the availability of high quality optics identification was not straightforward.

Until the middle of the last century Bewick's Swan appears, then, to have been primarily a passage bird, occurring, according to Oakes, mostly in November and March, with 50% of all records in the latter month, and only one record in December, at Hesketh Bank in 1938. A group of five at Cleveley Mere, Scorton from November 1966 to late January 1967 appear to have been the county's first wintering birds. Early spring records, mostly on south-eastern reservoirs, continued to dominate until the late 1960s although flocks began to be seen more frequently on the Ribble marshes. The first really large flock was of 114 at Rake Brook Reservoir near Abbey Village on 18 March 1964.

By the end of the 1970s numbers began to increase so that more than 100 birds were seen each winter with the majority feeding on coastal marshes, a situation which persists to the present day. Annual totals continued to increase steadily throughout the 1980s to more than 300 by 1984/85 and more than 700 by 1989/90 (Figure 1). By the end of the decade a firm pattern was established, with the overwhelming majority of birds feeding during the day on the Ribble saltmarshes – at Hesketh Out Marsh, Hundred End, Marshside and Crossens, Freckleton, Lytham and a few other sites – and on nearby pastures and arable fields, before moving to roosts on the River Douglas and increasingly at Martin Mere, encouraged by the supplementary feeding offered there.

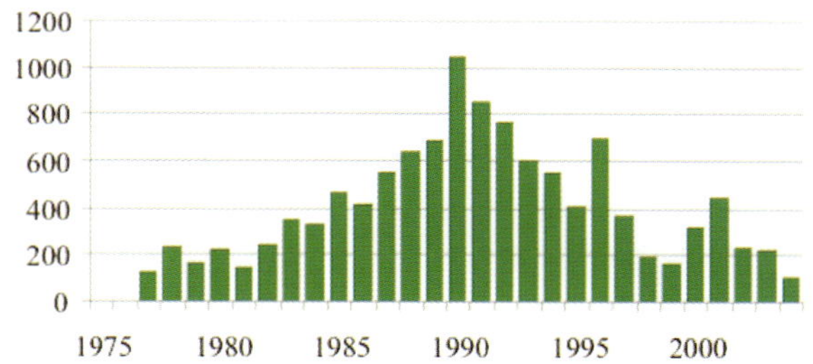

Figure 1. Estimated totals of Bewick's Swans in Lancashire, 1977/78 to 2004/05. [Includes Martin Mere, Ribble and Fylde peak counts plus offshore and inland migrants where there is no definite duplication]

A record 1,046 were at Martin Mere on 13 November 1990 but county totals slipped back a little over the following two winters and then sank to around 350 in 1997/98, to 200-250 in subsequent winters and just over 100 in 2004/05. Two reasons have been put forward for this rapid decline. Firstly, competition with Whooper Swans, whose dramatic increase paralleled the decline of Bewick's during the 1990s; and secondly, a succession of mild winters that allowed more of the western European population to remain in the Netherlands or eastern England. The first explanation, competition from their larger Icelandic cousins, was supported by a study in the late 1980s of agonistic encounters between the two species (J. Brown, unpublished) but it is difficult to see how this alone could have caused so many to abandon Lancashire, especially away from Martin Mere, the main site where the two species mingle.

Climatic amelioration may, then, be a more likely cause, with milder winters in eastern England and continental Europe reducing the need for birds to extend their migration to the west coast. Bewick's Swans, like Pink-footed Geese, have also recently taken to feeding on East Anglian sugar beet, giving them one more reason to desert the county.

Coastal sites to the north of the Ribble also registered more records during the 1980s and particularly the 1990s, but numbers have never approached those further south. The favoured area is north Fylde, particularly in the Pilling area, where the highest count was 116 on 22 January 1995. Birds are a little less frequent further north; they are most regular on Aldcliffe Marsh, where the record flock stands at 65 on 15 February 1998. Sightings of darvic-ringed birds indicate that there is at least some movement between the southern and northern feeding grounds.

The timing of records has changed equally dramatically since the 1960s; Bewick's Swan is now predominantly a wintering bird in Lancashire with the first October arrivals swelling gradually to reach a peak in January (Figure 2). Low numbers in March provide a stark contrast with the earlier situation.

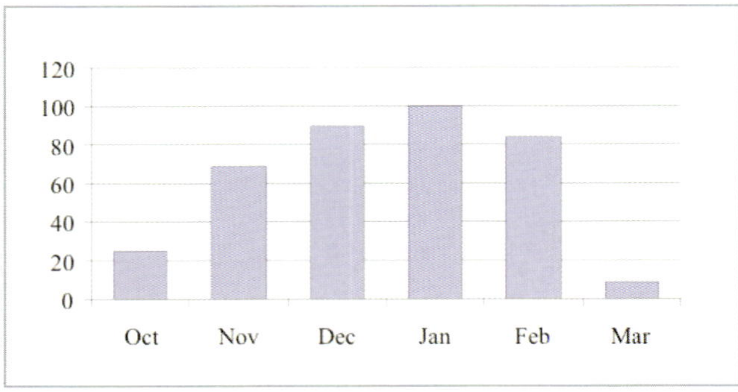

Figure 2. Indices of average monthly peaks (January = 100), Martin Mere, 1987-2005. Source - Swans

The average dates of the first arrivals and final sightings between 1983 and 2002 were 18 October and 17 March respectively, with earliest and latest dates of 2 October and 2 April, although some sick or injured birds have stayed longer, for example singles at Foulridge Reservoir to 27 April 1987 and on Plex Moss until 10 May 2005.

Bewick's Swans are seen in the east of the county most years, usually small flocks taking a brief respite on reservoirs, or overflying migrants. The majority of records have come from reservoirs around Colne, principally Foulridge, Whitemoor and Heckenhurst, but also from a wide scatter of other sites. The largest flocks have been 27 at Foulridge on 27 January 1973, 172 at Heckenhurst on 6 March 1981, 22 at Rivington on 3 March 1988, 80 over Delph and Belmont Reservoirs on 6 November 1997 and 29 on Belmont Reservoir on 22 February 1998. Such birds are occasionally seen in winter but there remains a very distinct bias towards March records. Since most birds have left the Lancashire wintering sites by this time it seems likely that many of these are migrants from outside the county, perhaps from Ireland.

Bewick's Swan, Martin Mere. (Steve Young)

Fairly regular sightings of flocks offshore or flying inland from the coast support the idea of Irish origins for these late birds; most such sightings have been in March. The most notable flocks have included 14 seven miles to the west of the Liverpool Bar lightship in 1970 (undated), 100 going north-east over Leighton Moss on 8 March 1971, 70 east at Formby Point on 1 March 1982, 16 off Morecambe on 3 March 1988, 51 on distant sandbanks off Morecambe on 14 March 1991, 32 well offshore at Heysham on 7 March 1992 with 42 off Jenny Brown's Point the same day and 17 off Rossall Point on the 8th, 17 off Blackpool on 25 March 1992, and 35 over Morecambe Bay on 17 April 1999.

There have been 74 ringing recoveries, all but four involving birds ringed at Martin Mere in winter, and a number of sightings of colour-marked birds. The vast majority have been birds recorded in subsequent winters: three at Slimbridge, singles in the Scottish Borders, Wales, Cambridge and Norfolk, and 46 in the Netherlands. The timing of Dutch recoveries is especially interesting – eleven in January, singles in February and March, 15 in October, 19 in November but none in December. The Netherlands are an important staging site for British birds and it is therefore possible that most of these records relate to migrants. With one exception, all other foreign recoveries come from important staging sites in Germany (three in February, twelve in March, two in April), Estonia (one in late April) and Poland (one in late April). The only breeding season records are one found in mid-May in Arkhangelsk, Russia, a site which is near the western limit of the breeding range but is also an important migratory stopover site on the White Sea, and a female, ringed at Martin Mere in 1991, seen further east on the Pechora Delta in northern Russia in June and July 2000.

SJW.

This species account was sponsored by Charlie Liggett.

WHOOPER SWAN

Cygnus cygnus

Lancashire Category A.

Common winter visitor from Iceland.

The status of Lancashire's wintering Whooper Swans changed dramatically in the last quarter of the twentieth century with estimated annual totals increasing more than thirty-fold since the 1970s, from around 50 a year to more than 2,000, a little less than 10% of the British and Irish wintering population (Figure 1). Unlike the situation of Bewick's Swans this upsurge has been more or less continuous since the 1980s, although numbers may now be stabilising.

This is in stark contrast to the assessment by Mitchell and Oakes that Whooper Swans were 'occasional' or 'irregular' in the nineteenth and early twentieth centuries respectively. Overwintering appears to be a relatively recent phenomenon: most of Mitchell's records involved severe weather influxes, while Oakes reported that birds rarely appeared before the last week of November and were gone by mid-March.

As with Bewick's Swans, the proportion of Whoopers recorded on coastal marshes and the mosslands of the Lancashire Plain has increased significantly since the mid-twentieth century. Oakes believed them to be 'almost unknown in south Lancashire', describing Leighton Moss as their principal haunt. This contrasted with Mitchell, who reported a flock of 27 on the Ribble and 'many' in the Pilling area as early as 1838 and described hard-winter influxes to 'all parts of the coast and mosslands' in 1878-81 (Figure 1).

The majority of 1960s and 1970s records came from inland waters, with the main concentration in the Bolton area. Large flocks in present-day Lancashire included 21 at Foulridge Reservoir in March 1963, and up to 67 at Rivington Reservoir during the winters of 1972/73 to 1978/79. Similar numbers persisted at a number of sites in the east of the county until the mid to late 1990s, for example 67 at Belmont Reservoir in January 1982, 17 at Stocks Reservoir in December 1983, 27 at Walves Reservoir in February 1988, 42 at Coldwell and Croasdale Reservoirs in March 2002, 44 at Belmont Reservoir in April 2003, and an annual flock of up to 27 at Wayoh Reservoir and nearby sites from 1989 that had declined to two birds by 2002.

The species' status in north Lancashire has remained largely unchanged since Oakes's day with flocks of 10-20 seen annually, mostly on the Lune and Kent saltmarshes and surrounding fields or in the Lune Valley between Caton and Kirkby Lonsdale.

The big change has been in the numbers wintering on the Ribble marshes and south-west mosslands, and, to a lesser extent, in north Fylde. Small flocks began to be recorded with increasing frequency in the south-west during the 1970s, and by the early 1980s the pattern of birds feeding primarily on the south Ribble and roosting at Martin Mere had developed. This combination of a variety of rich feeding grounds – on saltmarshes, arable stubbles and grassland – with a secure roost site (and supplementary feeding) close by has undoubtedly been a major factor leading to Lancashire's spiralling numbers.

Adult Whooper Swan, Martin Mere, February 2004. (Steve Young)

Peak counts topped 100 in 1983/84, 400 in 1987/88, 700 in 1994/95, 1,000 in 1997/98 and 1,500 in 2000/01. The largest counts, including 1,083 on 22 December 1998, 1,335 on 22 December 1999, 1,770 in January 2004 and 1900 in January 2005, were all made at Martin Mere, but small numbers of Ribble birds also roost on the confluence of the Rivers Ribble and Douglas and at Freckleton. Feeding areas vary according to food availability but the main sites have been Hundred End, Hesketh Out Marsh, Banks Marsh, Crossens/Marshside, Longton Marsh and, less frequently, Stalmine Moss and Freckleton (where a record Fylde flock of 230 was seen on 6 November 1994). In recent years there has been a considerable increase in large flocks of Whoopers feeding on fields within a short distance of the Martin Mere roost, including 250 at Burscough in 2000 and 500 near Scarisbrick in December 2002. The area at Low Meadows, Rufford has also been an important feeding site, for example 895 there on 31 December 2004.

Numbers in north Fylde, on Cockerham and Winmarleigh Mosses and at Pilling Lane Ends, have never reached these proportions and the largest counts have been 48 in January 1997, 40 in December 1998, 110 in December 2001 and 146 in January 2005.

A coordinated count in January 2005 produced a total of 2,241 in Lancashire: 1980 in the Ribble/Martin Mere area, 110 at Lytham, five at Marton Mere and 146 at Pilling.

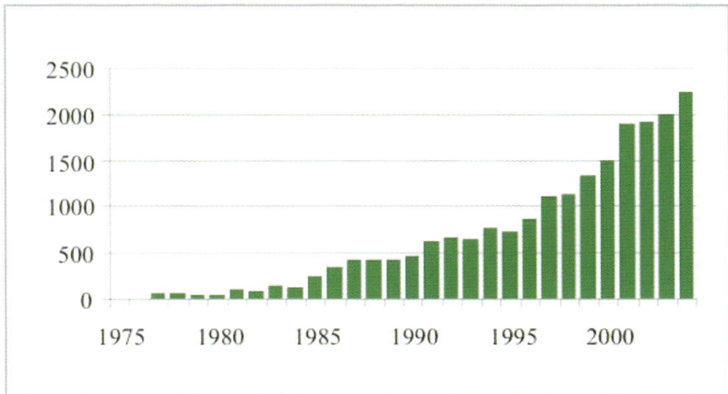

Figure 1. Estimated totals of Whooper Swans in Lancashire, 1977 to 2005. [Includes Martin Mere, Ribble and Fylde peak counts plus offshore and inland migrants where there is no definite duplication]

The recent increase cannot be wholly accounted for in terms of changes in the Icelandic breeding population. Coordinated winter censuses counted 16,700 birds in Britain and Ireland in 1986, rising to 18,000 in 1991, 20,600 in 2000 and 26,366 in 2005, showing an increase in the British and Irish population of around 60% between 1986 and 2005, during which period the Lancashire population rose almost seven-fold. Although occasional birds from the western Russian/Fennoscandian population may visit Britain (Migration Atlas), their numbers are insignificant and none has been proven in Lancashire. The link with Iceland is well-established with more than 100 recoveries of ringed individuals (mostly birds ringed at Martin Mere and recovered on the breeding grounds). Much of this increase must, therefore, have been at the expense of other wintering areas in Britain or Ireland although no single site has shown an equivalent decline.

Although the broad pattern of occurrence of Whoopers is similar to that of Bewick's Swans, there are subtle differences in both timing and distribution, perhaps relating mostly to their different origins.

The average first arrival during 1981-2002 was on 2 October, more than two weeks before that of Bewick's, with the earliest record on 20 September 1988. Most have reached Lancashire by November and, although the peak count usually comes in December, numbers are generally stable throughout the winter (Figure 2). The return to the breeding grounds does not get underway until March with the average last sighting of healthy birds (1983-2002) on 3 April. Icelandic Whoopers do not have the option of breaking their journey to Britain and Ireland and, although there have been some sightings of colour-marked birds making landfall in northern Ireland and Scotland before moving to Lancashire, it is likely that most fly directly between the breeding and wintering grounds, with only short stops to rest along the way.

Having arrived in Lancashire, most Whooper Swans appear to be relatively sedentary, although some colour-marked birds have been recorded moving between Martin Mere and north Fylde in the course of winter. Likewise, they appear to be largely faithful to wintering sites. There is a fairly large number of ringing recoveries and rather more sightings of colour-ringed birds in different winters in Lancashire, southern Scotland and northern Ireland - and rather fewer in southern Ireland and southern England - but it seems likely that the majority of these relate to birds staging during migration rather than shifting wintering grounds.

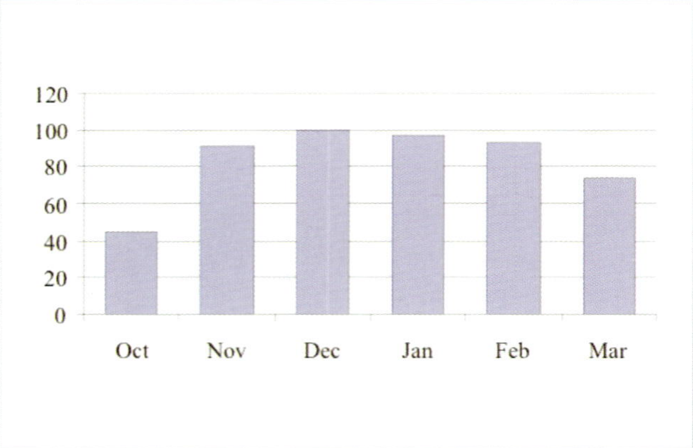

Figure 2. Indices of average monthly peaks (December = 100), Martin Mere, 1987-2005.

Coastal migrants are seen in both spring and autumn most years. Notable flocks have included 40 off Formby Point on 19 November 1986, 54 over Seaforth on 8 March 1991, ten off Rossall Point on 28 October 1991, ten over Lancaster University on 10 March 1992, 72 on the sea off Blackpool on 12 March 1995, 104 over Marton Mere on 18 March 1998 and 35 over Pine Lake, Carnforth on 13 April 2001.

Summering birds are not unusual; most are sick or injured although Martin Mere did have a free-flying flock of around 15 in the late 1970s and very early 1980s. The only recorded breeding was on the south-west mosses in 1983, although perhaps the same pair was present in the Martin Mere area during 1984 and attempted to breed at Mere Sands Wood in 1985. Other summer records include two at Foulridge Reservoir in 1961, one at Foulridge and Barley in 1990, and up to six in the Ribble/Martin Mere area between 1999 and 2001.

SJW.

This species account was sponsored by Charlie Liggett.

BEAN GOOSE

Anser fabalis

Lancashire Category A.

Uncommon winter visitor from northern Europe and Siberia.

There is no indication that Bean Geese have ever been common in Lancashire but they have been recorded annually since at least the late 1960s. Oakes knew of only a handful of records, all from south of the Ribble, but the species was perhaps under-recorded during his time. By the 1970s an average of six birds were seen annually, rising sharply to more than ten a year during the 1980s – perhaps merely reflecting the increased number of observers. The 1990s witnessed low numbers by comparison with an annual average of fewer than four, but the early years of this century have seen a moderate resurgence (Figure 1).

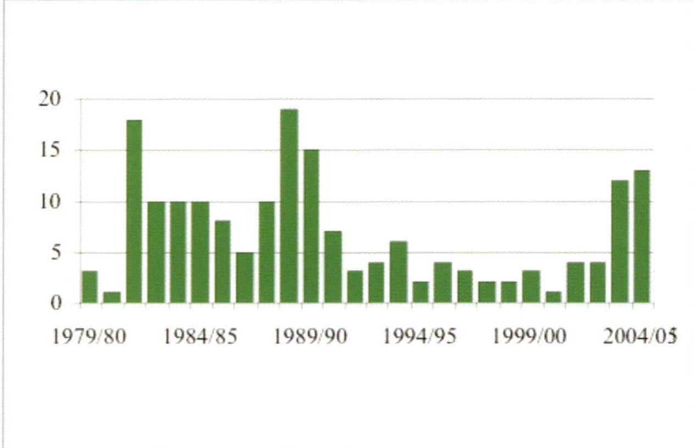

Figure 1. Estimated totals of Bean Geese in Lancashire 1979/80 to 2004/05

Bean Geese are almost always seen in the company of Pink-footed Geese. It is possible that some may arrive with returning Pinkfeet but there is little evidence of this, with just three records in September (earliest 13 September 2002). Records increase a little in October and November but only about a quarter of first sightings are made before December and the main arrival generally occurs from late December to the end of January. This pattern of occurrence is probably best explained by birds moving from other wintering grounds with Pinkfeet in midwinter rather than direct migration to Lancashire.

The vast majority of records are of one or two birds and relatively few obvious family parties are seen. The largest flock seen in Lancashire was of 21 *fabalis* associating with about 30 Pinkfeet near Martin Mere on 16 February 1975. Only two other double-figure flocks have been reported, ten *rossicus* at Marshside on 9 March 1985 and 13 *fabalis* on Aldcliffe Marsh from 9-27 January 1990. Other notable counts have included six *rossicus* at Marshside on 11 January 1986, seven *fabalis* in the Pilling-Cockerham area on 23-25 December 1987 and a family party of two adult and six juvenile *fabalis* on Halsall and Plex Mosses on 22-23 December 1988. No count higher than three has been made since 1990 with the exception of six of undetermined race at Todderstaffe Hall, Singleton on 31 December 2003 and five *fabalis* at Martin Mere in January 2005.

Bean Goose, Martin Mere, March 2003. (Mark Breaks)

Our largest sustained influxes took place in late December 1981 to early January 1982 and the winter of 1988/89, the first involving a likely total of 10-14 *rossicus* and at least eight *fabalis* at widespread sites throughout the south-west mosses and north Fylde, and the second perhaps as many as 18 *fabalis* and one *rossicus* at a similar range of sites.

The geographic spread of Bean Goose sightings within the county reflects that of Pinkfeet with rather more than two-thirds of all records south of the Ribble – overwhelmingly at Martin Mere and Marshside – and most of the rest in north Fylde, mostly in the Pilling-Cockerham area. Apart from the Aldcliffe flock mentioned above, very few have been seen further north: an injured bird at Caton in October 1964, one at Aldcliffe Marsh in January 1993 and a *rossicus* on Colloway Marsh in March 1997. None has been reliably recorded in the east of the county.

Separation of any but classic examples of the two European sub-species, *rossicus* (Tundra) and *fabalis* (Taiga) is far from straightforward. Smith and Forshaw (1988) studied a sample of 91 in the south-west of the county between 1975/76 and 1985/86, concluding that *rossicus* outnumbered *fabalis* by almost 2:1; they also identified three birds that may have been eastern *serrirostris* or *rossicus/serrirostris* intergrades. Records published in the annual county reports tell a rather different story with slightly more *fabalis* than *rossicus* reported, similar numbers assigned to no particular sub-species and a few regarded as intergrades (1974/75-2004/05 = 77, 64, 61 and 11 respectively). However, this needs to be treated with a fair degree of caution since the pattern of reporting has changed significantly over the years. Most birds were simply regarded as 'Bean Geese' until the late 1970s but the proportion of birds identified to sub-specific level has gradually increased, partly due to a better appreciation of key differences but perhaps also to the pressure to claim one or other, since many birders began to regard them as separate species during the 1990s.

Smith and Forshaw speculated that many Lancashire Bean Geese might be birds displaced from continental Europe during hard winters. However, although mid-winter arrivals are the norm, the patterns of occurrence of the two sub-species are subtly different. Fewer than 10% of all *fabalis* arrivals have occurred before December against more than a third of *rossicus*. Since the wintering grounds of *rossicus* are further south than those of *fabalis* – and presumably likely to be affected by hard weather rather later in the winter – this may indicate that some *rossicus* take a more direct route to Lancashire.

SJW.

This species account was sponsored by Jeff Howarth.

PINK-FOOTED GOOSE

Anser brachyrhynchus

Lancashire Category AE.

Abundant winter visitor from Iceland and Greenland.

Pinkfeet have been the commonest geese in Lancashire since at least the middle of the nineteenth century and probably for much longer. Nicholas Blundell of Crosby Hall made a diary entry for 6 February 1708 of a goose-shooting trip to 'Formos-poole' (Far Moss Pool in Little Crosby), a site that continues to be frequented to this day (Forshaw 1982). Mitchell highlighted the south Ribble marshes as the main wintering area and this continued to be the case during the first half of the twentieth century, although Oakes also noted significant numbers in north Fylde, and, to a lesser extent, on the Lune and the (now Cheshire) Mersey. Little is known about numbers during this period; the largest single flock that Oakes knew of was of 2,200 but he suspected that this underestimated the true situation.

By the 1950s annual numbers were estimated at 1,500-4,500, with the Ribble identified as the main arrival site (along with the Humber Estuary) in England (Atkinson-Willes 1963). Figures began to rise dramatically during the 1960s with peak counts of 9,000 in 1965 rising to 11,500 in 1970 and 15,000 by 1973 (Forshaw 1983). This apparently sudden increase was no doubt due in part to increased census effort but it coincided with a more than doubling of the Iceland/Greenland population (BWP.)

Pink-footed Geese, Downholland Moss, January 2007. (Steve Young)

Co-ordinated counts on nine (latterly three) days throughout the winter were initiated in 1977/78 (Forshaw 1978-2006). These provide an invaluable dataset upon which this account is largely based.

Pink-footed Geese regularly move between regions during the winter so it is impossible to judge precisely how many birds appear in Lancashire each year, but these are likely to be significantly underestimated in the following analysis of peak counts. Changes in peak counts over the past 25 years are shown in Figure 1. Numbers continued to rise during the 1970s, breaking the 20,000 barrier in 1979/80 and 30,000 in 1981/82. Peak counts averaged around 25,000 during most of the 1980s but increased to 30,000-35,000 in the early 1990s, and have remained relatively stable since. County-wide totals have exceeded 40,000 birds on three occasions: 41,680 in January 1997, 46,925 in January 2001 and 43,950 on 16 January 2005.

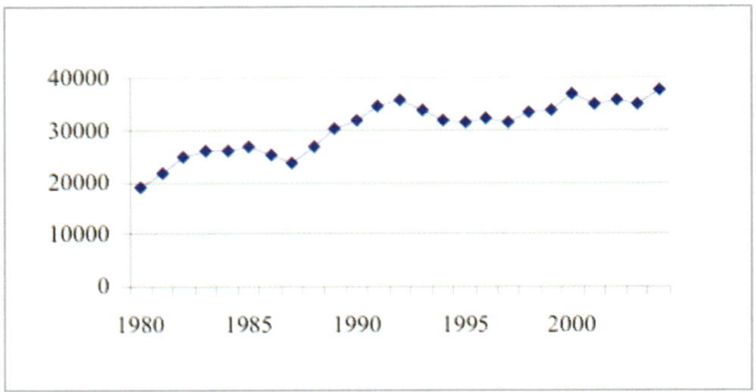

Figure 1. Five-year rolling mean peak counts of Pink-footed Geese in Lancashire, 1978-2005.

The earlier increase coincided with further growth in the breeding population but this alone cannot account for it, since numbers grew nearly three times faster in Lancashire than in Britain as a whole. Lancashire accounted for about 8% of the British wintering population during the 1950s but this rose to 24% in the late 1970s. Since that time, although the peak numbers of Pinkfeet in Lancashire have continued to increase to a five-year mean peak count of 37,668 in 2004/05, they have not quite kept pace with the rise in the national population, of which they have accounted for around 15% since the 1990s. It is possible, therefore, that the county has reached its carrying capacity and may be unable to support further numbers of geese throughout the winter.

The growth in numbers since the 1950s has entailed an equally impressive expansion of range within the county. Most significant has been the dramatically increased use of the Fylde, particularly north of the Wyre, where average annual peaks have increased from 6,500 during the 1980s to 12,000 in the 1990s and nearly 19,000 during 1999/2000 to 2003/04.

In the 1960s and 1970s the favoured Fylde site was north-west of Winmarleigh Moss but this area, together with Rawcliffe Moss, is little used nowadays. The vast majority of geese now feed on a mixture of saltmarsh, pasture, cereal and potato habitats in the Cockerham/Pilling/Eagland Hill area and roost on Pilling Sands. Their range extended during the 1990s to cover an area north to Thurnham and Glasson on the Lune, east to Eagland Hill and west to Stalmine, Hambleton and Cleveleys/Fleetwood, with a roost of up to 6,200 becoming established on Barnaby's Sands on the Wyre. More recently, a regular flock has become established south of the Wyre between Staining, Weeton and Todderstaffe, reaching 3,000 in 2003/04. Notable Fylde totals include 12,885 in October 1987, 15,000 on 13 February 1994 and 26,910 on 16 January 2005 (23,160 roosting on the Lune Estuary and 3,750 on the Wyre).

Numbers south of the Ribble showed steady growth during the 1980s and 1990s with average annual peaks moving from 22,500 to 30,000 during this period, but the first three winters of the twenty-first century witnessed an apparent sharp decline to around 18,000-20,000. It is possible that this may be a result of birds dispersing to new, unmonitored feeding sites, a trend that has been noted since at least the mid-1990s. This south-western range encompasses a huge area of saltmarsh and mosslands, whose outer limits are approximately defined by Southport, Longton Marsh, Croston, Rainford, Knowsley Park, Kirkby, Maghull, Blundellsands and Formby. Despite this expansion, the geese still have a relatively limited number of feeding sites to which they will readily resort, provided they are free from disturbance and contain suitable food. These are thought of as 'traditional' sites, in which the birds have gained confidence over many decades. Nevertheless, some of these sites are now used much less by the geese, particularly the Altcar area and to a lesser extent Downholland Moss, Plex Moss and the area between Martin Mere and Southport. This is believed to be due to agricultural changes, increased disturbance and changes in land use.

Numbers have increased dramatically on the Ribble salt- and grazing marshes, rising from 5,000 or so during the 1970s to more than 10,000 by the mid-1980s and reaching a record 28,000 on 19 November 1989, before reverting to around 10,000 during the 1990s. Favoured sites have been Banks Marsh and, since the mid-1980s, Crossens and Marshside, although there has been a dramatic reduction in the use of Marshside this century. The Ribble birds roosted on Horse Bank off Southport until sand-winning operations shifted them to George's Brow and Banks Sands in the 1970s but they have increasingly roosted at Martin Mere, joining birds that feed on the surrounding farmland. Geese feeding in the Downholland, Altcar, Ince Blundell, Hightown and Little Crosby areas – 7,000 or so in the mid-1990s – roost mainly on Taylor's Bank, off Formby Point.

Although recorded annually in north Lancashire, relatively few Pinkfeet winter there. Favoured areas are Colloway and Aldcliffe Marshes on the Lune, where up to 3,000 – but normally far fewer – have been recorded, usually in late winter. Small numbers are regularly seen with Greylags on Carnforth Marsh. Elsewhere in the county Pinkfeet are essentially passage migrants and are mostly seen in flight.

These changes in numbers, range and distribution have been accompanied by changes in phenology. Oakes described Pinkfeet as mid-winter birds on the Ribble and this remained broadly true for the county as a whole during the 1970s and 1980s, when numbers built up steadily from mid-October to reach a peak in December and declined from mid-February. Since the 1990s the situation has become more fluid; high counts may occur in almost any winter month but the peak is now normally in January, and numbers are far higher than previously in both October and March (Figure 2).

This relatively even pattern of occurrence is particularly marked in the south-west of the county. Until very recently the situation in the Fylde was radically different with very few seen in October and large numbers rarely appearing before January or February, but since the turn of the century more birds have been seen in the early winter months.

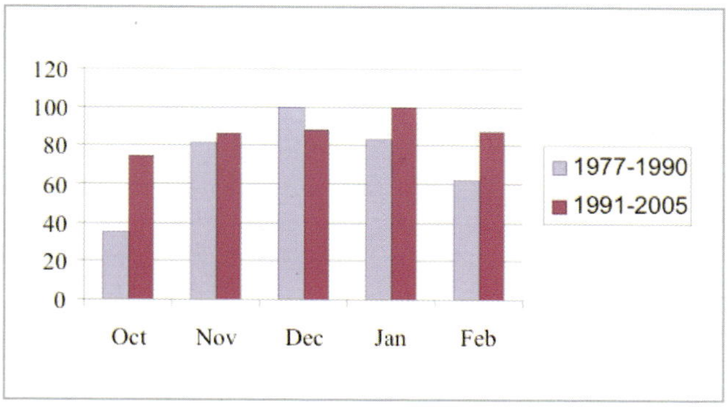

Figure 2. Indices of monthly peak counts of Pink-footed Geese in Lancashire, 1977/78-1989/90 (December = 100) and 1990/91-2004/05 (January = 100).

There have been a few sightings in late August that may have related to wild birds but the first immigrants usually arrive towards the middle of the following month on an average date (1978-2002) of 10 September. Large numbers are rarely seen anywhere during September and 14,000 at Martin Mere on 16 September 2005 was wholly unprecedented.

Sightings of ringed and colour-marked birds provide the most likely explanation for these changing patterns of occurrence. Lancashire is no longer the final winter destination for Pinkfeet but rather a staging post for many birds on their way to and from East Anglia. For the past decade or so, an increasing proportion of the British population has wintered in Norfolk, taking advantage of the remains of sugar beet crops and freedom from disturbance. It appears that many Pinkfeet leave Lancashire during November, or as early as late October in 2005, when Norfolk numbers reach their peak, and return from the New Year onwards. It seems likely that most overflying birds in east Lancashire, where 10-20 flocks of up 1,000 birds are reported annually, are of birds moving to and from Norfolk. The extent of this staging behaviour is not known but its increasing prevalence almost certainly means that the total number of birds using Lancashire in the course of the winter is higher than the peak counts would suggest.

The number of geese in Lancashire depends to a large extent upon the relative availability of good feeding conditions elsewhere. Freezing conditions in Scotland may produce sudden large influxes as in 1984, when several thousand were seen flying south over north Lancashire during 21-26 January, producing a county total of 28,000 at the end of month compared with 11,000 a fortnight earlier. Similar conditions in East Anglia probably produce the same results as birds return early to the milder west coast.

Increasing numbers in Norfolk in recent years reflect the discovery by Pinkfeet of a vast supply of sugar beet residues, but may also be due to a squeeze on food availability in Lancashire due to losses of permanent inland pasture and of cereal stubbles resulting from the switch from spring to autumn sowing. Forshaw (1978-2003; 1998) analysed total goose numbers seen on different field types south of the Ribble. Cereal stubbles supported 28% of 'goose-days' and tend to be favoured early in the winter, while potato remains accounted for 13% and carrots 4%, the latter favoured after frosts have softened them. Winter cereals and grass leys accounted for 5% and 4% of 'goose-days' respectively, but permanent grassland (including saltmarsh, coastal grazing marsh and other permanent pasture), which becomes increasingly important as the winter progresses, is the clear favourite, accounting for more than 40%. No comparable data are available from the Fylde but geese also appear to favour grassland there (M. Jones, *pers. comm.*).

Two distinct populations breed in Iceland and Greenland, and in Svalbard with the former wintering almost entirely in Britain and the latter in Denmark and the Netherlands. All but a handful of recoveries of ringed or marked birds between Lancashire and the breeding grounds refer to the Iceland/Greenland population involving (for BTO-ringed birds) 289 individuals to or from Iceland and to or from Greenland. There is no direct evidence that Svalbard birds have ever occurred in the county but there are four recoveries between Lancashire and the wintering grounds of the Svalbard population: one in Norway in September 1995, eight years after ringing at Martin Mere; one in Holland in November 1987 which had been ringed at Martin Mere in April that year; and one ringed in Holland in January 1981 and shot at Banks Marsh in February 1982. The wanderings of one bird, neck-collared in Denmark in 1994, suggest that interchange between the two populations may be more than accidental. Having been seen in Norfolk in December 1994 it was at Martin Mere in February 1995, moving to Loch Leven later that month before returning to Denmark in April; the bird reappeared at Martin Mere in October 1995 and was last seen in Norfolk the following month.

Neck-collared Pink-footed Goose, Little Crosby, December 2005. (Steve Young)

Flocks of over 1,000 have lingered at Martin Mere and at Pilling towards the end of April in recent years. Injured birds have summered in several years and may have contributed to the small population of feral birds that may turn up almost anywhere in the county. Five pairs were reported breeding in 1991 and up to 40 individuals were regularly reported during the 1980s and early

1990s, mostly believed to have originated from the Scarisbrick estate – but numbers appear to have declined since then with only single figures now reported.

SJW.

This species account was sponsored by the Fylde Bird Club and Graham Clarkson.

WHITE-FRONTED GOOSE

Anser albifrons

Lancashire Category AE.

Fairly common winter visitor from Greenland and northern Russia.

There is no evidence that Lancashire has ever regularly supported a significant wintering population of White-fronted Geese, although 2,000 or so Russian birds frequented the Mersey saltmarshes on the Cheshire side of the river between the 1920s and 1950s. Oakes referred to these birds as having moved from the Ribble to the Mersey but gave no details. Both Mitchell and Oakes regarded the species as uncommon in Lancashire, a status that has remained broadly unchanged to the present day.

Birds from both the Greenland *flavirostris* and Russian *albifrons* populations have been recorded in Lancashire in every winter since at least 1960/61. The majority of sightings consist of single-figure parties, rarely more than ten, of one or other sub-species; Greenland and Russian birds rarely seem to associate together. It is likely that there is some movement within the county during the winter, particularly between the south-west mosses and north Fylde where Whitefronts probably move with the Pinkfeet flocks.

Allowing for such duplication, the average number of annual sightings between 1977/78 and 2004/05 was around 28. Throughout this period Russian birds have outnumbered Greenland Whitefronts by about two to one (on average 23 and twelve respectively per annum), but this preponderance of Russian birds is not the norm in most years; when the two years with major influxes (1987/88 and 1995/96) are taken out of consideration totals of the two sub-species have been more equal (c.340 Russian: c.285 Greenland). Records published prior to 1977/78 are less comprehensive but it appears that the number of Greenland birds has gradually increased since the 1960s, while Russian numbers have been stable or perhaps slightly declined. There is little correlation between the occurrences of the two sub-species: 'good' years for Greenland birds are not necessarily 'good' for Russians.

Significant influxes of more than 40 birds have occurred in roughly one in four years since the 1960s but with no discernible pattern: in 1962/63, 1971/72, 1972/73, 1974/75, 1982/83, 1987/88, 1992/93, 1995/96, 1997/98 and 2003/04. Although there may be a small core that adopt Lancashire as a wintering ground for a number of years it seems that most birds of either race arrive here more by accident than design.

Two winters stand out. December 1987 saw the start of a large national influx of Russian Whitefronts; the first in Lancashire were twelve on Altcar Moss, 20 at Carnforth Marsh and 36 at Marshside on the 5th and 6th. By the end of the month there were about 100 on the south-west mosses (including a flock of 95 at Marshside), 19 at Pilling and 39 on Carnforth Marsh. These numbers held up during January 1988 and the last large count was of 45 in north Fylde on 6 March. The same winter also saw a record influx of Greenland birds, virtually all in the south-west, including 33 on Banks Marsh on 11 December. In all, probably over 200 Whitefronts were seen in Lancashire during winter 1987/88.

Adult Greenland White-fronted Goose with Pink-footed Geese, Heaton Marsh, March 2001. (Mike Malpass)

The winter of 1995/96 brought more than 100 birds into the county, all but two or three of them Russian. Again, the influx began in early December with ten at Martin Mere and seven at Marshside on the first of the month. Ten flew north over Seaforth on the 4th and eleven were in the Leighton Moss area from the following day. More than 50 were distributed between north Lancashire, north Fylde and the south-west in the New Year and the largest single flock of 40 was at Marshside on 3 March.

In the south-west and north Fylde Whitefronts are almost always associated with Pink-footed Geese, sharing the same sites, and the proportion of records in the two areas is broadly consistent with that of Pinkfeet with about twice as many in the south-west. In north Lancashire, however, they are almost always with Greylags; thus until the mid-1970s many were seen on the Lune Valley flood meadows but nowadays almost all records are at Carnforth Marsh. Roughly equal numbers of Greenland and Russian birds occur in the north.

There are only six records in the east of the county: single Greenlands at Stocks Reservoir in January 1983 and February 1996; a Russian with Canada Geese at Rivington in February 1991, with five Russians there and at Belmont Reservoir in February 1992; nine Russians at Altham in November 1993; and a Greenland at Belmont in April 1998. In addition, four feral birds were at Walverden Reservoir in February and November 2003.

The few ringing recoveries give some indication of between-winter movements: a Russian bird ringed at Slimbridge in February 1958 was at Cockerham in October 1959; another Russian ringed in the Netherlands in January 1972 was at Great Altcar in December the same year, and a Greenland bird ringed at the

Wexford Slobs in 1991, which returned there in each subsequent winter, was seen in a party of nine at Martin Mere in November 2001.

SJW.

This species account was sponsored by Chris Honer.

LESSER WHITE-FRONTED GOOSE

Anser erythropus

Lancashire Category AE. (0, 14+).

Vagrant from northern Europe.

The status of the Lesser White-fronted Goose in Lancashire, as in Britain as a whole, is considerably confused due to its popularity in collections, latterly compounded by the now discontinued reintroduction programme in Sweden. Birds that appear amongst the winter flocks of Pink-footed Geese, especially in the company of Russian White-fronted Geese, probably have the best credentials.

A captive-reared first-winter from the Swedish scheme was on Aldcliffe Marsh from 22 November 1991 to 22 April 1992; after leaving Lancashire it moved to Cheshire and Flintshire where it associated with Canada Geese. One at Martin Mere on 19 December 2002 was also considered to be of probable Swedish origin.

The identifications of the following have been accepted by the BBRC and may relate to wild birds: the first was an adult on Downholland Moss from 27 November to late December 1976; this or another was seen at several sites, mostly in Little Crosby and the Altcar Withins area, from 28 December 1977 to 17 January 1978; another adult was at Plex Moss on 18 December 1983 and this was followed by the county's only possibly wild first-winter, at Marshside on 19 January and 15 February 1985.

The last records came in 1991, when at least two adults were seen at a series of sites. The first was found at Martin Mere on 4 October and remained in the area until at least 6 November. A second bird, distinguished by weaker barring on the underparts, appeared at Martin Mere on 27 November; it departed after a couple of hours but what is assumed to have been the same bird was relocated at Little Crosby on 3 December and Cockerham on 8 December.

It is noticeable that, with the exception of one of the1991 Martin Mere birds, arrivals appear to have occurred in mid-winter, perhaps indicating displacement from elsewhere. However, none of the five winters in which these possibly wild birds arrived enjoyed a particularly notable influx of Russian White-fronted Geese.

Records of at least a dozen birds presumed to have been of captive origin have been published between 1987 and 2005 but this is likely to underestimate the true numbers. The most recent include singles at Marshside on 17 April 2002, Preesall from 27 June to 17 July 2002, three on Upper Foulridge Reservoir with Canada Geese and what appeared to be a Lesser White-fronted x Barnacle Goose hybrid on 3 February 2003, an adult at Martin Mere during winter 2003/04, and singles on Southport Marine Lake later in 2004, in the Pilling-Preesall area in 2004-05 and the Leeds-Liverpool Canal in Liverpool on 8 October 2005.

SJW.

This species account was sponsored by Simon Rahilly.

GREYLAG

Anser anser

Lancashire Category ACE.

Scarce feral breeder; wild and feral birds both fairly common in winter.

Mitchell appeared to believe that the Greylag was the commonest of Lancashire's geese during the nineteenth century, describing the Ribble as its main haunt with few seen on the Lune. This seems likely to have been due to confusion with Pink-footed Geese, since throughout the twentieth century wild Greylags were almost entirely confined to north Lancashire, a pattern which persists to this day.

According to Oakes Greylags, numbering some 400-500, were regular visitors to Morecambe Bay between mid-October and early April. He published a record count of 700 on Winmarleigh Moss in December 1939 but these are now known to have been Pinkfeet (K.G. Spencer *pers. comm.*). Oakes published only three records from the south-west: two shot on the Ribble in January 1922, one at Birkdale in January 1938 and six at Freshfield in February 1940. Oakes thought that Pinkfeet and Greylags occurred in similar numbers in north Lancashire until the flooding of Leighton Moss in 1918/19, when Greylags adopted it as a favoured wintering site and became the dominant goose species.

Until the mid-1960s this northern flock was mostly found on Silverdale Marsh but they increasingly frequented the flood meadows of the Lune around Claughton, Arkholme and Melling, while continuing to feed and roost at Leighton Moss and Carnforth Marsh. Use of the Lune Valley began to decline in the mid-1970s with birds eventually becoming virtually confined in winter to Carnforth Marsh, a pattern that has continued to the present day. Peak winter counts have been remarkably consistent throughout this period, varying between 200-400 with an average of just over 300.

On the face of it, then, the status of Greylags in the north of the county has been extremely stable for at least a century – but this is far from clear. To begin with, some national experts have doubted if this wintering flock ever consisted of wild birds; the Winter Atlas, published in 1986, described all birds 'south of a line from the Isle of Man to Teesmouth (as) of feral origin'. This verdict was hotly disputed at the time by Lancashire birdwatchers, who remain convinced that the Silverdale flock continues to contain a significant proportion of wild birds. This was partly on the grounds of the consistency of records going back to the nineteenth century; Scott (1938) described shooting a flock of 500 Greylags at Brogden Marsh on the Kent Estuary in Westmorland, from where birds regularly flighted to Leighton Moss. It was also partly because there were simply too few known feral birds in the region to account for winter numbers. It is conceivable that some originated from the population established in south-west Scotland from northern Scottish stock in the 1930s, but these birds are largely sedentary with average movements of just 10-30km

A crèche of feral Greylags, Knowsley Park, May 2005. (Steve Young)

(Migration Atlas). It therefore seems much more likely that they were genuinely wild birds, probably from the main Icelandic population.

Throughout the 1960s and 1970, however, Greylags were being released by wildfowlers in the region and a feral population became established, initially in south Lakeland but later at Leighton Moss, where the first breeding was recorded at the end of the 1970s. A decade later 20-25 bred annually at Leighton Moss, raising 70-80 young which, together with a non-breeding population of 50-70, could almost account for the wintering population.

By the mid-1990s the county report could only note that wild birds could no longer be safely separated from feral ones although there were still 100 or more whose nervous behaviour suggested that they were wild. Recent studies indicate a further marked behavioural difference, with most wild birds roosting on the Eric Morecambe Pools on Carnforth Marsh and feral birds at Leighton Moss – although there is some small overlap (Wilson 2004). On this basis, it was estimated that 240 wild birds were present in 2003/04.

That wild birds were still visiting the county was confirmed when one ringed in Sutherland on 6 July 1996 was found at Cockerham in January 1997. Then, on 28 February 2004, one appeared at Carnforth which had been neck-collared as a first-winter at Loch Eye in northern Scotland in October 2000 and had been seen in two subsequent winters in both Scotland and Ireland. Although either of these may have been wild Scottish birds the likelihood is that they were Icelandic birds ringed on their usual wintering grounds.

Distinguishing between wild and feral birds elsewhere in the county is an even more difficult task. Ones or twos are reported as 'probably wild' fairly regularly on the south-west mosses and occasionally in north Fylde – usually on the basis of their close association with Pink-footed Geese.

As in the north, the feral population has grown enormously over the past 20 years elsewhere in the county. Breeding by three or more pairs has been recorded at Knowsley Park, Martin Mere, Scarisbrick, Mere Sands Wood, Marshside, Preesall and smaller numbers elsewhere, including one that nested in heather at 300m above sea level on Withnell Moor in 2002, producing a county total of 40-50 pairs. These alone cannot account for the numbers present in the county from late summer. A census in August 1996 recorded 1,020 in Lancashire, out of an estimated national feral total of 30,000. Winter numbers are usually of a similar order with the overwhelming majority in three areas: Martin Mere, Marshside and Southport Marine Lake in the south-west; Wilkinson's Gravel Pit and Nateby in Fylde; and Leighton Moss/Carnforth.

Only one long-distance movement of a ringed feral bird has been recorded: between Holmeswood and Gloucestershire. There are two intriguing controls of birds that may have originated in wild breeding populations in Scandinavia: one ringed in northern Norway in July 1990 and seen at Scarisbrick in January 1993; and one ringed as a pullus in Denmark in June 1994 and seen at Martin Mere during successive winters from 1999/2000 to 2001/02.

SJW.

This species account was sponsored by Charlie Liggett.

SNOW GOOSE

Anser caerulescens

Lancashire Category AE.

Rare winter visitor from North America.

The first published record of a Snow Goose in Lancashire was of an adult blue morph 'near Southport' in October to December 1958. A further 70 records, involving approximately 56 individuals, followed until the end of 2005 but many of these were of birds roaming the county or returning for several successive years. A more accurate estimate of the county total, taking these likely duplications of records into account, is of 33 records involving 47 birds.

There can be little doubt that some of these have been escapes or feral birds; the difficulty lies in knowing how many have been wild. Snow Geese are popular in collections and feral breeding populations have long been established in the Hebrides and more recently in southern England. More than half of all published county records (19) have been reported as feral or escaped. These include our only multiple records: two in the Fylde from 1981 to 1984 (believed to have originated from Blackpool Zoo), three over Marton Mere in August 1986 and eleven at Rossall Point in April 1996.

The origins of the remaining 16 possibly wild individuals are more problematic. All have occurred in the winter months, mostly appearing in December and January, and almost all have been closely associated with flocks of Pink-footed Geese, mostly on the south-west mosses and less frequently in north Fylde. The three records in north Lancashire include a Greater that was shot out of a flock of apparently wild Greylags at Carnforth Marsh in November 1990. At least one has been seen in all but seven years since 1980 but records have declined since the early 1990s. It is likely that several returning individuals have occurred.

In 1996 a white morph adult was tracked as it moved around Britain with wintering Pink-footed Geese; it was seen in the Scottish Borders from early September, then in Lancashire at Downholland Moss and Marshside throughout October and in north Norfolk through December, January and February before returning to Lancashire, flying over Colne on 26 February and then present in the Pilling area intermittently from 28 February until 30 April.

Seven of our records were of blue morph birds and were therefore nominate *caerulescens* (Lesser Snow Goose).

Adult Snow Goose with Pink-footed Geese, Downholland Moss, January 2007. (Steve Young)

It is often extremely difficult to separate races of white Snow Geese in the field, so the published breakdown (3 Lesser, 5 Greater, 1 unspecified) cannot necessarily be taken at face value and it is possible that some birds may have been identified differently by different observers. Nonetheless, taken together with blue morph birds, it does suggest a striking predominance of Lessers (10 out of 15). This ratio is broadly in line with current Canadian population estimates which show Lessers outnumbering Greaters by about 6 million to 600,000. However, Greater Snow Geese are more likely candidates for vagrancy to Britain due to their more easterly breeding range, which includes north-west Greenland, and their migration routes. Blue morph Lessers are relatively common but remain outnumbered by white morph birds; they were largely confined to the eastern Arctic around Baffin Island until recent decades but have since spread into white morph areas.

The pattern of records in Lancashire is thus almost the reverse of what might be expected from the respective breeding ranges and migration routes of the two sub-species: Lessers appear to be as common as Greaters, and blue morph birds more frequent than white morph Lessers. A further problem is that the vast majority of records are of adults, young birds being perhaps the more likely vagrants. Indeed, only one first-winter Snow Goose has ever been reported in the county – at Seaforth in January 2002 and probably the same at Marshside and Martin Mere from May 2002 to the end of the year – and this was almost certainly not wild.

There are no ringing recoveries of wild Snow Geese in Britain but they almost certainly do occur, probably most frequently with Greenland White-fronted Geese with which they are partially sympatric. The best that can be said about the species' Lancashire status is that, although it is probable that wild birds have been recorded, the origin of any individual record remains unproven. Known escapes have been seen fairly regularly in the county but are less frequently reported; most recently they include two or three singles during 2003 on the Lune Estuary, Fairhaven Lake, the south-west mosses and Martin Mere.

SJW.

This species account was sponsored by Frank Bateson.

ROSS'S GOOSE

Anser rossi

Lancashire Category D.

A metal-ringed bird wintered with Canada Geese at Hornby in the Lune Valley in 1961/62. Another was with Pink-footed Geese on the south-west mosses from 5 December 1970 until 17 January 1971 and returned on 8 December 1971, remaining until 8 January 1972, apparently having summered with Pinkfeet. It returned again for the following two winters and was last seen on 12 January 1974.

The most recent records are singles associating with Canada Geese on Eccleston Mere on 31 July 1996, with feral Greylags at Martin Mere from September 2001 to the end of February 2002, with occasional visits to Marshside, and amongst the Pink-footed Goose flocks in the Over Wyre area between 4 February and 17 March 2003. What was believed to be a hybrid Ross's x Lesser White-fronted Goose was at Martin Mere throughout the winter of 2003/04.

SJW.

Adult Ross's Goose with Pink-footed Geese, Pilling, February 2003. (Steve Young)

GREATER CANADA GOOSE

Branta canadensis

Lancashire Category C.

Fairly common feral breeder and common in winter; possibly wild vagrant from Greenland or North America.

The first documented introduction of Canada Geese in Lancashire was in 1810 on the Earl of Derby's Knowsley Park estate (Hardy 1979), which remains a major stronghold. For more than a century their spread was slow and localised, probably restricted to the Liverpool and St. Helens areas until at least the end of the 1930s. Oakes wrote that Canada Geese were almost unknown north of the Ribble in the first half of the twentieth century and seen only occasionally at Rivington. Lever (1977) estimated the Lancashire population at 115-156 birds in 1953, most of which were in Knowsley Park.

All that was to change dramatically during the late 1950s and 1960s when 'surplus' birds from Knowsley and elsewhere in the country were introduced at several locations throughout Lancashire. These introductions were carried out partly by wildfowlers for 'sporting' purposes and partly by the Wildfowl Trust to remove birds from areas where they had become an agricultural pest. Most introductions were poorly documented but it is known they took place at Leighton Moss, Blackpool and Rivington/Anglezarke in 1957 at least.

By the 1970s, breeding populations had become established in the four corners of the county at Wrightington, Fairhaven, the Wyre gravel pits and in north Lancashire, the Lune Valley, the Colne reservoirs and Stocks Reservoir. Post-breeding and winter counts of more than 100 soon began to be registered, including 188 at Hornby on the Lune in 1973, 100 at Foulridge Reservoir in 1976 and 193 at Stocks Reservoir in 1980, while numbers at Knowsley Park peaked at 360 during 1971-85.

By the end of the twentieth century Canada Geese were breeding on virtually all suitable wetlands in Lancashire, with Rossendale the last area to be colonised in 1989. A few pairs even breed high in the uplands up to 500m from reservoirs, for example in Bowland, where several pairs nest in the Tarnbrook gullery, and on Boulsworth Hill. The county's breeding population was estimated at 400 pairs during 1997-2000. Most sites support just a handful of pairs but there are at least three large concentrations: at Knowsley Park, Stocks Reservoir and Belmont Reservoir, the last supporting 43 pairs in 1999. Despite licensed control measures at several sites, including 500 adults culled at Stocks on 2 July 1999 and 2,525 eggs pricked at Belmont Reservoir between 1990 and 2004, there is little doubt that this breeding population continues to increase.

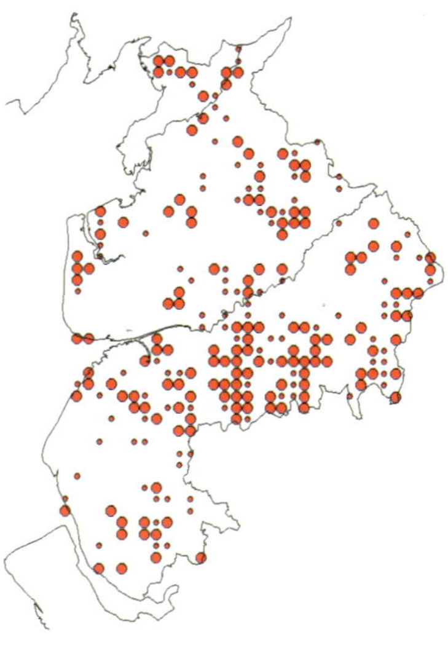

Breeding distribution of Canada Goose, 1997-2000. (Large dots: confirmed. Small dots: possible)

Numbers are probably relatively constant throughout the year but birds are most concentrated, and most easily censused, in late summer when they gather at traditional wetland sites to carry out their post-breeding moult (Figure 1).

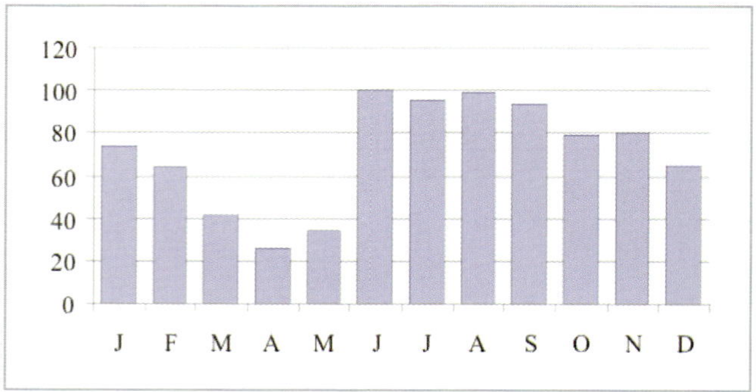

Figure 1. Indices of monthly occurrence, 1990-2005 (June = 100). (Based on counts from main sites tabulated in annual Lancashire Bird Reports)

Stocks Reservoir has long been the most important of these sites, regularly registering peak counts of more than 450, with county record counts of 650 in July 1996 and 700 in June 1998, but numbers have declined somewhat since – with 373 in July 2004 the most this century. Access to Knowsley Park is highly restricted but counts on nearby waterbodies, for example 410 at Eccleston Mere in August 1999, indicate that numbers there may match or even surpass those at Stocks. Foulridge Reservoir also holds large numbers with a peak count of 504 in January 2002; 450 were on Barrowford Reservoir in October 2004. Counts in excess of 100 are now regularly reported from an additional 15-20 sites each year, with the most consistent in recent years being Marshside, Martin Mere, Seaforth, Southport Marine Lake, Wrightington, Fairhaven, Rishton Reservoir, Walverden Reservoir, Rowley Lake, the Belmont area, Leighton Moss and various sites in the Lune Valley.

National censuses located 959 birds in Lancashire in 1991 and 1200-1400 in 1996. Judging by records submitted from the main sites, the county's post-breeding population probably now numbers some 2,000-3,000 birds out of a total population in England and southern Scotland of 82,000 in 2001.

Limited ringing recoveries suggest that Lancashire's Canada Geese are relatively sedentary during most of the year with very few movements of more than 100km recorded, including one from Rivington to Lincolnshire and one from the Ribble to the Netherlands. However, colour-ringing has shown that some of our birds make post-breeding moult-migration flights to the Beauly

Firth in Scotland. Most recoveries, however, involve movements within northern England and show, for example, Stocks Reservoir to be a significant moult site for Yorkshire birds.

It is widely assumed that vagrant, wild Canada Geese turn up in Britain fairly regularly. The case for this in Lancashire was first strongly put forward more than 20 years ago on the basis of a dozen or so records since 1968 of potentially wild Canada Geese amongst wintering Pink-footed Goose flocks (Jones 1983). One or two such birds have continued to be reported almost annually so that by 2003 the total of possibly wild birds stood at 16 records involving some 21 individuals. It is probable that some at least of these have indeed been genuine vagrants, but there is no reason to believe that all solitary or small groups of Canada Geese seen with Pinkfeet are wild.

Although our breeding birds are highly gregarious, some may become isolated after moult migration and, temporarily at least, join up with Pinkfeet. The same may well be true of birds freshly escaped from captivity. Apparently 'wild' behaviour is undoubtedly a necessary feature for recognising vagrants but it is not alone sufficient; even 'tame' birds may take behavioural cues from the majority around them.

Accurate identification of the sub-species is very helpful when considering escape likelihood but is easier said than done. North American ornithologists recognise eleven or so extant sub-species of Canada Goose with relatively disjunct breeding ranges but identification of these away from their known breeding and wintering grounds has rarely been attempted (Delacour 1954).

The whole subject of vagrancy has taken on a keener aspect since the recent decision of the BOU to treat Canada Goose as two separate species, Greater Canada Goose B. *canadensis* (with subspecies *canadensis, fulva, interior, maxima, moffitti, occidentalis* and *parvipes*) and Lesser Canada Goose B. *hutchinsii* (with subspecies *hutchinsii, leucopareia, minima* and *taverneri*). The British breeding population is thought to have originated largely from nominate Greater Canada Goose stock.

Greater Canada Goose, possibly of the subspecies *interior*, with Pink-footed Geese, Crosby, December 2005. (Steve Young)

It is likely that the majority of the apparently wild Canada geese in Lancashire have involved Greater Canada Geese and an attempt has been made to assign a number of these to subspecies. Published reports feature *canadensis, interior* and *parvipes*, while four were classified as *parvipes/taverneri* – subspecies which cross the new divide between Greater and Lesser Canada Goose.

All of these subspecies could potentially occur in Britain as vagrants, although claiming a wild origin for a nominate *canadensis* in the field is impossible due to the British feral population in the main resembling this subspecies. The race *interior*, which now breeds as far north and east as Greenland, is probably the most likely vagrant form of all Canada Geese. However, with atypical feral Greater Canada Geese resembling *interior* and *parvipes*, proving the certain occurrence of vagrant Greater Canada Geese is extremely difficult in the absence of ringing evidence.

Reports of Greater Canada Geese published as possibly wild:

1968	*parvipes/taverneri*, south-west Lancashire, 28 January to 11 February, 2 on 3 February
1969	*parvipes/taverneri*, south-west Lancashire, 9 to 12 February, 4 November to 4 March 1970, same as 1968
1977	*parvipes/taverneri*, Halsall, 29 January
1979	*canadensis*, two with smaller bird, Downholland Moss, 9-24 December
1980	*canadensis*, two, Barton Moss, 8 January
1980	*canadensis*, Plex Moss, 16 & 19 January
1980	*canadensis*, south-west Lancashire, 18-29 December
1982	*canadensis*, Halsall & Little Crosby, 6-7 January
1984	*parvipes*, Martin Mere, November to 6January 1985
1985	*parvipes*, Pilling, 23 January, presumed same Martin Mere
1989	*interior*, three, Marshside, 21-25 December
1990	*interior*, two, Martin Mere, 16-17 January, probably same as Marshside
1991	*parvipes/taverneri*, Martin Mere, 9 January, Pilling at least 24 February to 10 March
1991	*interior*, Jarvis Carr & Pilling, at least 24 February to 10 March
1994	*parvipes/interior*, Martin Mere, one, 9-23 January; two, 10-30 January
1994	*parvipes/interior*, Martin Mere, 13-29 December
1997	*parvipes*, two, various south-west sites, December 1997 to January 1998
1997	'slightly larger' bird with 2 *parvipes*, Marshside, 6 December
1999	*parvipes*, Martin Mere, 9-27 October
2001	*interior/canadensis*, Martin Mere, 23 September to 16 December
2001	'unraced', two, Pilling, 24 November
2001	possible *parvipes*, Pilling/Preesall, 1 & 30-31 December
2002	*interior*, Staynall, Pilling & Cockerham, 12-14 February
2002	*parvipes*, Rossall, 28 January, possibly same as *interior* above
2005	*interior/parvipes*, south-west mosses, December

SJW.

This species account was sponsored by Sue Hayes.

LESSER CANADA GOOSE

Branta hutchinsii

Lancashire Category DE.

Possibly wild vagrant from North America, fairly frequent escapes.

Lesser Canada Goose has only very recently formally been considered a separate species and does not yet appear on the British list. However, there are eight published Lancashire reports of birds belonging to subspecies now considered to be Lesser Canada Goose. Although it is impossible to be certain, it is likely that the majority of the other 20 records of possibly wild birds have been Greater Canada Geese. It is also likely that some Lesser Canada Geese have not been formally recorded as they were considered obvious escapes.

Nor can we be certain that all the birds identified to race were always as claimed, especially given the shifting sands of identification criteria over time. The picture is further blurred by the occurrence in North America of runt Greaters bearing a resemblance to *hutchinsii* (Leafloor *et al.* 1998).

If the records of *minima*, *taverneri* and *leucopareia* were correctly identified then their westerly distribution in North America and the high escape likelihood of, at least, *minima* (of which several escapes are known to have occurred in the county) would mitigate against their acceptance as vagrants in Lancashire.

The subspecies considered to be the most likely vagrant to Europe is *hutchinsii*, of which there are two published Lancashire records, on Plex and Formby Mosses on 14 -28 November 1976, and at Cockerham on 11-28 February 1982. The 1976 bird was submitted to the BBRC in 2006 for consideration, possibly as a first for Britain. Some birds assigned to other subspecies, as well as some unspecified 'small' Canada Geese, may also have been wild *hutchinsii*, but there is also an escape risk with this race.

Lesser Canada Goose of the nominate subspecies, Plex Moss, November 1976. (Maurice Jones)

Published records of birds assigned to race and seen amongst Pink-footed Geese:

1976	*hutchinsii*, south-west mosses, 14 to 28 November
1982	*hutchinsii*, Cockerham, 11 to 28 February
1983	*minima*, Martin Mere and Burscough Moss, 14 to 24 January
1983	*taverneri*, Formby, 13 November to 3 December
1983	*minima*, Eccleston Mere, 3 September to 24 April 1984
1984	*taverneri*, Pilling 11 to 25 March (same as 1983)
1991	*minima*, Martin Mere, 9 January to 6 May
1992	*leucopareia*, Martin Mere, 14 December, Downholland Moss, 22 to 19 December, Plex Moss 26 to 27 December
1995	*minima*, Stanley Park Blackpool
1999	*minima*, colour-ringed escape, Preesall and Blackpool, to at least 2002
1997	*minima*, Pilling, 19 January 2002 *minima*, Pilling, 1 January, same Martin Mere, 15 to 16 January (same as 2001)

Other published records of small birds:

1970	Cockerham, 14 & 21 February
1978	Formby, 7 January
1979	Fylde, 15 March & 1 April
1979	with 2 *canadensis*, Downholland Moss, 9-24 December
1980	Cockerham, 20 December
1987	Over Wyre, February
1991	Marshside, 16-26 November & 14 december
1995	*minima*, escape, Stanley Park Blackpool and Hambleton Marsh
1998	Cockerham, 17 January
1999	*minima*, colour-ringed escape, Preesall & Blackpool, all year, to at least 2001
2000	Martin Mere, October
2001	Marshside, 13 December
2002	*minima*, Wilkinson's GP Preesall, bred with Barnacle Goose, all year
2003	Martin Mere, with Pink-feet, 7 February
2003	Martin Mere, with Pink-feet, 29 October

SJW.

BARNACLE GOOSE

Branta leucopsis

Lancashire Category AC.

Rare feral breeder; wild and feral birds fairly common in winter; wild birds from Greenland and probably mostly from Svalbard.

Few Lancashire species have a more confused status than the Barnacle Goose; genuinely wild birds are outnumbered by the feral breeding population, only part of which has the good grace to winter on the breeding grounds, the remainder mixing with flocks of Pink-footed Geese.

That wild birds do occur is proven by at least 15 recoveries or sightings of ringed birds but just how many do so is less certain. Family parties or single birds (which make up the vast majority of sightings of potentially wild birds) associating strongly with Pink-footed Geese (or Greylags in the north of the county) have the best credentials, along with birds seen on the sea or moving offshore.

The earliest accounts in Lancashire date from the seventeenth century (Willoughby, quoted in Mitchell) while Oakes wrote of 'considerable numbers in Morecambe Bay' during the nineteenth century, becoming much rarer in the first half of the twentieth. He cited just two records in present-day Lancashire: one with Pinkfeet at Martin Mere in February 1934 and 50 at Crossens in December 1941.

Barnacle Geese remained scarce during the 1950s but records began to increase during the 1960s and presumed wild birds have been recorded virtually annually since 1970. This resurgence coincides with that of the population wintering on the Solway, which grew from a low point of 400 in the late 1940s to more than 4,000 in the 1970s.

Assessing numbers is further complicated by movements between sites within winters. Barnacles are known to wander within the three main regions, the south-west, the Fylde and Morecambe Bay, but there is no firm evidence of movements between these areas. For the purposes of the following analysis it is assumed that such interchange is minimal.

Estimated annual numbers averaged more than 25 birds between 1977/78 and 2004/05 but this disguises huge annual fluctuations with most winters producing three or four flocks adding up to a dozen or so individuals. Influxes of 40-60 birds were recorded in 1980/81, 1983/84, 1986/87, 1990/91 and 1991/92. Large numbers were also seen during 1993/94, with 40 at Pilling and twelve at Thurnham on 30 November, and 23 at Marshside and 29 at Martin Mere on 11 December (perhaps the same 52 individuals); at least 33 remained at Marshside to the end of 1993 but almost all had disappeared early in the new year.

With the exception of groups of 20 at Silverdale Marsh on 24 September 1986, Carnforth Marsh in October 1991, Marshside in February 1992 and 74 north over Pilling on 28 September 2003, all other sizeable flocks have been seen on or near the northern coast: 21 at Leighton Moss on 12 October 1980 with 20 there on 25 January 1984; 26 from Jenny Brown's Point on 7 October 1990; and 21 on the River Kent from Halforth on 3 October 2003.

Barnacle Geese with Pink-footed Geese, Marshside, December 1993. (Steve Young)

Around 45% of approximately 700 records since 1960 have occurred on the south Ribble marshes and south-west mosslands, principally reported from Marshside and Martin Mere. The remainder have divided more or less equally between north Fylde (mostly Pilling) and north Lancashire, producing a slight but significant northern bias to their distribution. The only certainly wild birds in east Lancashire were up to eleven, including one Svalbard-ringed bird, at Stocks Reservoir from 12 September to 14 October 1980, a year in which the Solway flock was widely dispersed on arrival due to gales. Singles at Stocks on 30 September 1977 and Whitemoor Reservoir, Colne on 13 April 1978 may also have been wild birds on passage.

The earliest arrivals were eight at Martin Mere on 11 September 1998 but relatively few are seen before mid-October and numbers often peak during mid-winter, coinciding with the movement of Solway birds from Caerlaverock to Rockcliffe Marsh. Most have departed by the end of February while the latest was one flying north with Pinkfeet at Heysham on 16 April 1987.

Records of ringed birds suggest that the vast majority of Lancashire Barnacles come from the population that breeds on Svalbard and winters on the Solway. Fifteen parties are known to have contained birds ringed either in Svalbard or on the Solway, while none has ever been recorded from the larger Greenland-breeding population which winters on the Hebrides and in western Ireland. However, an unringed bird which arrived with, presumably Icelandic, Whooper Swans at Marton Mere on 20 October 1993 may indicate that at least some of this western population may overshoot its regular wintering grounds.

Feral populations

Only occasional birds are seen in north Lancashire, usually with Canada Geese, and the only published breeding records are of one incubating in the Lune Valley in 1977 and a pair in Bowland during 1998-2000. Occasional pairs probably breed in east Lancashire but numbers at the West Pennine stronghold of Belmont Reservoir have been reduced from 13 summering individuals, including three breeding pairs, in the early 1990s to one or two hybridising with Canada Geese this century. In recent years a post-breeding flock of up to 24 has gathered at Stocks Reservoir in late August.

Martin Mere used to house a free-flying breeding flock whose winter numbers increased from about 50 in the late 1970s to a peak of 93 in 1988/89, at which time most were removed to other collections. Only twelve birds were seen there the following winter but numbers gradually increased during the 1990s to reach a new peak of 62 in 2002/03. These birds do not originate from the site – a fact overlooked by many birdwatchers – but form part of the Knowsley Park population; 20-30 at Marshside and other mossland sites in the 1990s are probably part of the same flock.

Another free-flying flock has bred at Blackpool Zoo since at least the mid-1970s and is seen regularly at dusk at Marton Mere, where peak counts increased from 25-30 in 1980s to 50-60 during 1990s. Some presumably wander further afield but few obviously feral birds are seen elsewhere in Fylde.

There is a long-established, but poorly documented, breeding population in Knowsley Park. Some of these birds are probably resident but others certainly wander with 50 or more taking their 'winter holidays' at Martin Mere in recent years. The neighbouring Prescot Reservoirs regularly report 20-40 in late summer and winter and nearby Eccleston Mere has a largest count of 53 in August 2004; 48 near Kirkby in September 2002 probably also came from this population.

The total wintering population is in order of 100-150 birds so, assuming most nest in the county, the breeding population perhaps contains 25 or more pairs.

SJW.

This species account was sponsored by Ron Hothersall.

BRENT GOOSE

Branta bernicla

Lancashire Category A.

Fairly common winter visitor from northern Siberia, Svalbard and North America.

Like all the scarcer species of geese in Lancashire, Brent Geese are most often seen in the vicinity of Pink-footed Goose flocks but they are the least tied to them, being far more coastal in distribution than any other species.

Although the number of published records has increased since the 1960s and 1970s there is no real indication that the status of Brent Geese has changed much since the assessments of Mitchell ('not uncommon') and Oakes ('a sporadic visitor'). On average, around 25 birds have been seen each winter between 1978/79 and 2004/05, but this includes several sizeable influxes and numbers are usually much lower than this. Although the typical sighting is of one or two birds, Brents tend to occur in larger groups more often than similarly scarce species – roughly 60% have been in flocks of six or more birds.

Both the nominate Dark-bellied *bernicla* and Pale-bellied *hrota* subspecies have been recorded annually since at least the end of the 1970s but their patterns of occurrence have differed widely; annual numbers of the two forms show no correlation (Figure 1). About 10% of all records since 1978/79 have not been assigned to sub-species but of the remainder 60% were Dark-bellied and 40% Pale-bellied. These proportions have, however, shown a marked change during the past decade or so: Pale-bellied Brents slightly outnumbered Dark-bellied between 1978 and 1989 but since 1990 almost 70% have been Dark-bellied.

Although Brent Geese have been recorded in most parts of the county, as with other wild geese, records come predominantly from the coast and near-coastal farmland and within this area they show a decidedly northern distribution. Since 1978 there have been approximately 60 records involving about 300 individuals in north Lancashire (mostly on the coast between Heysham and Carnforth Marsh), 80 records of 400 birds in north Fylde (overwhelmingly at Pilling and Cockerham) and 100 records of 250 birds south of the Ribble (mostly at Marshside/Crossens and Martin Mere).

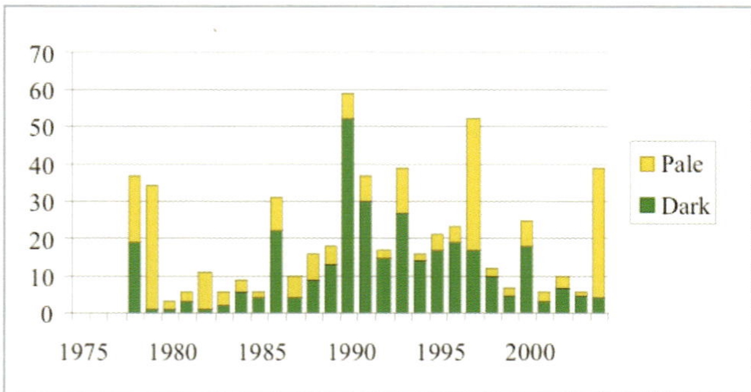

Figure 1. Estimated totals of Pale- and Dark-bellied Brent Geese in Lancashire, 1978/79 to 2004/05.

Pale- and Dark-bellied birds show even more striking differences in distribution, with more than 80% of records in both north Lancashire and north Fylde being dark-bellied, while south of the Ribble numbers of the the two sub-species are roughly evenly split. This pattern reflects their relative abundance (at least in recent years) in our neighbouring counties – Dark-bellied predominate in Cumbria and Pale-bellied in Cheshire and Wirral. It is not obvious why this should be, since it is the reverse of the situation in Britain and Ireland as a whole. Dark-bellied Brents winter primarily in south-eastern and south-western England, with Pale-bellied mostly in Northumberland and northern Ireland. A possible explanation might be found in habitat differences as there is some evidence that Pale-bellied birds are most often found with Pinkfeet in the south-west whilst Dark-bellied are more likely to feed on their own on the Fylde saltmarshes.

Brent Geese with Pink-footed Geese, Marshside, January 1985. (Steve Young)

British wintering Dark-bellied Brent Geese all originate from the central Siberian Arctic, mostly around the Taimyr Peninsula, and their numbers usually peak in January as birds move in from the near continent, a situation reflected in Lancashire where few are seen before the end of November with most records in January and February. The origins of our Pale-bellied Brents is less clear, however. Two distinct populations winter in Britain and Ireland: those from Svalbard predominantly on Lindisfarne and those from high Arctic Canada around Strangford Lough. The Canadian birds stage their migration in Iceland where they presumably mingle with Pink-footed Geese. It therefore seems likely that most Lancashire birds move with Pinkfeet, which might help explain their southerly distribution in the county.

Brent Geese are extremely rare in the east of the county: the only records are six at Hurst Green and Clitheroe (race unknown) in January 1979, two over Rowley Lake (Pale) in January 1989, and singles at Belmont Reservoir (Dark) in April-May 1990, Hurst Green (Pale) in March 1996, Rivington Reservoir in 1997, Altham in 1998 and Brockholes Quarry (Dark) on 15 April 2001; two (Dark) at Wards Reservoir on 1 January 2004, 22 (race unknown) over Belmont Reservoir on 15 February 2004 and one (Dark) at Rishton Reservoir on 28 December 2004.

The largest county flock was of 300 Dark-bellied reported by Oakes at Hundred End on the south Ribble marshes in late January 1929 but nothing nearly comparable has been recorded since. Many of the largest counts have been of coastal migrants, including 32 Pale-bellied south off Heysham on 14 September 1997, 30 Pale-bellied 2km off Ainsdale on 18 November 1979 and 30 off Rossall Point on 27 February 2005. The largest feeding flocks have been 43 Dark-bellied at Cockerham in February 1991 with perhaps 28 of the same flock at Hest Bank and 20 at Pilling that March, and up to 18 Dark-bellied at Pilling in winter 1993/94.

Black Brant (left) with Dark-bellied Brent Goose, Pilling, December 1996. (Steve Young)

The largest influxes came in the winters of 1978/79 (involving about 40 birds, half of which were Pale-bellied), and 1990/91 (more than 50 birds, mostly Dark-bellied). The earliest record was a Pale-bellied juvenile on the sea off Marshside on 7 September 1986.

There is one record, accepted by the BBRC, of an eastern Siberian/North American 'Black Brant' *B. b. nigricans*. This was found with a party of three Dark-bellied Brent Geese at Pilling by Chris Batty on 17 December 1996. It remained in the area, feeding on the saltmarsh close to Pilling Lane Ends car park, until at least 22 February 1997, by which time the group had been joined by a Pale-bellied bird. This was the 73rd record in Britain.

SJW.

This species account was sponsored by Dave Dunlop.

EGYPTIAN GOOSE

Alopochen aegyptiaca

Lancashire Category DE.

The Egyptian Goose was introduced into Britain as early as the seventeenth century but has never become widespread and remains largely confined to East Anglia as a breeding species. The only documented introduction in Lancashire was a pair at Fairhaven Lake in 1973. It is possible that eight seen on farmland on the inner Ribble marshes in January 1977 – which remains the largest flock recorded in the county – may have originated from this pair but there is no firm evidence that Egyptian Geese have ever bred in the county. Certainly, they have never become established here and the majority of sightings may relate to escapes from collections. However, a small population has become established in Greater Manchester in recent years and this may be the source of some records.

Egyptian Geese have been recorded virtually annually in Lancashire since at least 1981, usually in ones and twos at a wide range of wetland sites; the highest annual total was 14 in 1988. A pair was seen with two juveniles at Martin Mere from 31 July 2002 but are not believed to have bred there.

SJW.

RUDDY SHELDUCK

Tadorna ferruginea

Lancashire Category DE.

The status of the Ruddy Shelduck in Lancashire, as in Britain as a whole, is enigmatic in the extreme; occurrences are usually dismissed as being mere escapes, even by those who find them. In 1993 the BBRC, in a review of the Ruddy Shelduck's status in Britain and Ireland, concluded that the species should remain in Category B, reflecting their conclusion that no definitely wild individual had occurred here since the influx of 1892. Two birds were shot in that year in what was then Lancashire: at Hale near Liverpool (Oakes) and 'near Wigan' (Brown & Grice 2005) but none was seen in the present county.

Oakes recorded only a single occurrence within our present borders, a bird at Preston in 1909; he judged this to be an escape from captivity. Since the mid-1960s there have been intermittent records, whose frequency has increased over the years. All but a handful have been on the western side of the county, from Carnforth and the Wyre Estuary to the Ribble, Martin Mere and Seaforth. This in itself is probably of little significance, as it merely reflects the typical distribution of Shelduck with which the Ruddy Shelduck normally associates; one was paired with a Shelduck at Myerscough Quarry during 1999-2001. These visits have been treated with varying degrees of scepticism in the county bird report; two on the inner Ribble marshes from 14 August 1964 to the end of the month with one to 13 September, for instance, were reported as having been accepted by BBRC, with the proviso that they might have been escapes, although observers had stressed the birds' 'wild character'. A female on Banks Marsh from 26 May to 7 June 1979, however, was regarded as 'probably wild', whilst three that flew in from the sea at Blackpool on 16 June 1996 were considered to be of feral origin, due to the date, and one at Martin Mere on 22 December of the same year was judged a certain escape. On some occasions, clearly, the demeanour or location of the bird has been used as the main criterion, in other cases the date – with little evident consistency.

At least one cluster of records stands out as being worthy of special consideration, however. From late June 1994 there was a substantial influx of Ruddy Shelduck, of unknown origin, into northern and north-west Europe; up to 100 were recorded in Denmark and Finland and 40 in Sweden, with a scattering of records in southern and eastern England. On 25 July five visited Crosby Marine Park and Seaforth, six were seen on Longton Marsh on the 29th and there was one at Pilling Lane Ends on 21 August; finally, on 29 August a party of seven flew over Seaforth. Given that virtually all previous occurrences in the county had involved only one or two individuals, such a pattern of records is worthy of note as possibly involving nomadism by wild birds. There is no agreement as to whether these birds originated in the feral populations of western Europe or were genuine wild vagrants from further east (Vinicombe & Harrop 1999).

BM.

This species account was sponsored by N.J. Donnithorne.

SHELDUCK

Tadorna tadorna

Lancashire Category A.

Fairly common resident breeder; common winter visitor.

The Shelduck increased in numbers in Britain and most of its European range in the twentieth century and underwent a huge expansion in range in Lancashire as breeding birds moved progressively further inland.

Mitchell wrote of massive decline during the nineteenth century, describing it as '[keeping] a precarious footing' as a breeding species on Lancashire's sand-dune coasts, and implying that winter flocks of a dozen or so were the largest that might be encountered. Seventy or so years later, the Shelduck's status appears to have been transformed. Oakes considered it to be a common resident on most of the coast, breeding around Morecambe Bay and especially from Longton Marsh on the Ribble southwards to the Mersey Estuary. Breeding was rare only on the south Fylde coast and Oakes made special mention of two pairs that nested there in 1949.

The county's proven breeding range increased by 20% between 1968-72 and 1997-2000 from 20 to 26 10km squares. However, breeding is notoriously difficult to confirm for this subterranean nester unless newly hatched ducklings are seen and, if sites where birds were only known to be present during the breeding season are included, this expansion was more like 40%.

Breeding is no longer confined to sand-dunes and most Lancashire Shelduck now nest at least several kilometres from the coast. Nests are located in thick saltmarsh vegetation, in rabbit burrows and in other cavities along sluices and drainage ditches, as well as in various man-made locations, including up to twelve pairs amongst hay bales in a barn at Hundred End during the 1960s and 1970s (Greenhalgh 1975b). The move inland began during the 1950s and coincided with the onset of myxomatosis which wiped out the rabbit population, so may have been linked to a loss of nest sites on the coast.

A large brood of Shelduck freshly emerged from their rabbit hole, being led to their nursery home on the saltwater pool at Seaforth Nature Reserve, June 2004. (Steve Young)

An estimated 400 pairs nested annually during 1997-2000, almost all of them in the western third of the county with concentrations on the south-west mosslands, inland Fylde, around Morecambe Bay and deep into the Lune Valley. Martin Mere, where they breed in nest-boxes, supports one of the largest mossland populations with up to 40 broods produced in recent years. They remain extremely rare elsewhere but have had a tenuous foothold as far inland as Wood End sewage works near Burnley on and off since the 1960s, and one pair may have bred at Bashall in 2002. Breeding occurred at Roddlesworth in 1966, at Withnell Fold in 2002 and 2003 and at Stubbins on the River Irwell in Rossendale in 2004.

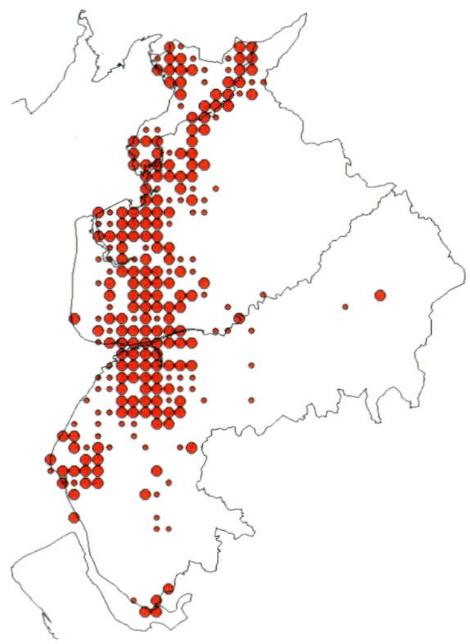

Breeding distribution of Shelduck, 1997-2000. (Large dots: confirmed. Small dots: possible)

Shelduck are unique among breeding wildfowl in Britain in that adults perform a moult migration after the breeding season to the Waddensee on the north German-Dutch coast, joining many thousands from elsewhere in northern Europe. Long ago Mitchell commented on the virtual disappearance of the species from Lancashire in autumn, and Oakes noted reports of eastbound movements. These still persist, although some changes in their pattern have developed in recent years. Most records are of small flocks moving eastward, often flying high and very often in the evening; peak counts have included 50 over Burnley on 8 July 1967, up to 70 over Rossendale on 5 August 1982 and a total of 200 over Rishton Reservoir on 23 July 1988. Some larger flocks were recorded during the 1990s, including totals at Rishton Reservoir of 528 on 19 July 1992 and 217 on 13 July 1994, and up to 350 over Trawden on 18 June 1999. Since the mid-1990s this moult migration pattern appears to have changed significantly. Lancashire-ringed Shelduck have been recovered at a new moulting assembly on the Cleveland coast, and a flock has also become established on the Mersey Estuary which held almost 20,000 birds in July 2003 and may now be the moult site for most, if not all, of Lancashire's Shelduck. There was a flock of 202 moulting Shelduck in

Oglet Bay in June 2001, and small parties heading southwest over Brockholes Quarry on 20 and 22 July 2001 may well have been bound for the Mersey.

Adults begin to return in September and on the Ribble numbers continue to increase towards a late winter peak, while Morecambe Bay usually holds its largest flocks in late autumn (Figure 1).

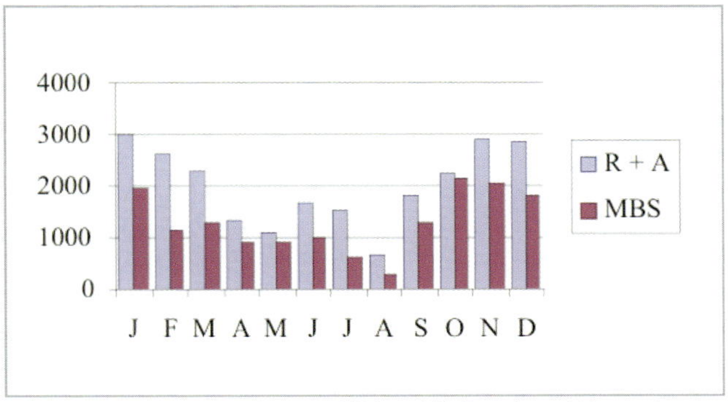

Figure 1. Average monthly peak counts, Ribble and Alt Estuaries and Morecambe Bay South, 1990-2005 (WeBS).

Wintering numbers appear to have increased significantly since Oakes's day, although the picture is obscured by some changes in favoured wintering sites over the years. From the 1960s to the early 1990s many of the highest counts came from the Oglet-Garston area of the north Mersey shore, including 1,235 on 17 December 1971, 6,300 on 12 December 1981 and 1,500 in October 1993. Since the mid-1990s totals there have declined dramatically, probably due to erosion of the mudflats, and birds have moved to the Cheshire shore; 380 at Oglet in February 2002 was the highest count for nearly a decade.

Until very recently the Ribble held the largest numbers, peaking at 6,037 in February 1988, but numbers have declined to an average 3,000 or so in recent years and Morecambe Bay – principally the north Fylde coast between Pilling and Cockerham – looks set to take over as Lancashire's main winter site, with a largest count there of 4,000 in November 2001 (Figure 2). The Alt Estuary holds smaller numbers, including 615 in February 1986 but rarely more than 300 recently.

Since the mid-1990s Martin Mere has gradually acquired the largest inland wintering flock in Britain, peaking at 1,435 in February 2003 and 1510 in February 2005. Wintering Shelduck are comparatively scarce in east Lancashire, with 27 at Dean Clough Reservoir in January 1988 and twelve at Rishton Reservoir on 27 October 1989 the only double-figure counts since the late 1960s. The best estimate of the county's current overall wintering population is around 8,000, about 10% of the British total.

There have been 80 or so recoveries of Lancashire-ringed Shelduck: 47 within Lancashire, eleven elsewhere in England, two in Wales, one each in Scotland and Ireland, eleven in Germany, seven in the Netherlands and one in Denmark. Eleven birds ringed elsewhere in Britain have been recovered here, as well as five European-ringed, all from the German North Sea coast; these were all ringed on the Waddensee during the moult period, and prior to the recent establishment of the Mersey moult site. Four recoveries of Lancashire-ringed Shelduck on the continent in winter indicate that some birds remained abroad after the moult.

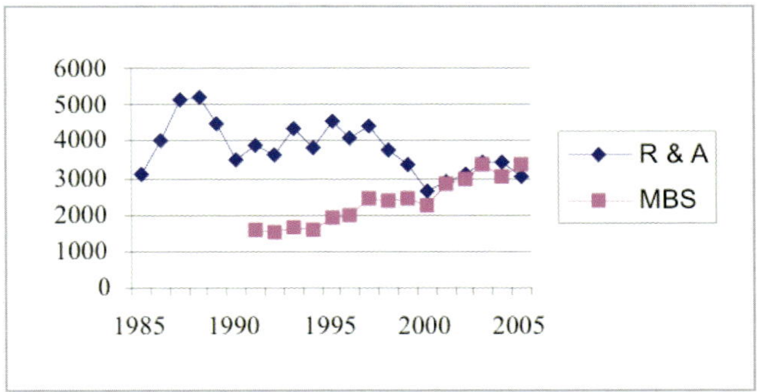

Figure 2. Peak winter WeBS counts (3-year rolling means), Ribble & Alt Estuaries (1982/83 to 2004/05) and MBS (1989/90 to 2004/05).

BM.

This species account was sponsored by Ron Hothersall.

MANDARIN DUCK

Aix galericulata

Lancashire Category DE.

The striking and exotic-looking Mandarin's natural range is in far eastern Asia but a thriving population became established in Britain during the twentieth century, deriving entirely from introductions and escapes from captivity. The New Atlas estimated a total British population of up to 7,000 individuals in the early 1990s, concentrated in south-east England but also in the English Midlands and Scotland.

Feral breeding was recorded in Cheshire during the 1968-72 Breeding Atlas survey, but the first to be reported in Lancashire was on Prescot Reservoirs in February 1976; it is possible, of course that birds had been seen here in previous years but dismissed as mere escapes, and not reported.

Tony Disley

Since the late 1970s there has been an increasing number of Lancashire records, with a clear bias toward the south, centre and east of the county. A small population became established at Ince Blundell, near Little Crosby, in the early 1980s; this was still in existence up to 2000 at least, but was constantly supplemented by additional releases. A second breeding nucleus developed at Martin Mere during the mid-1980s as full-winged Mandarins began to nest outside the collection area; birds from this source bred regularly on the Leeds and Liverpool Canal at nearby Rufford between 1989 and 1998 at least, long after the Wildfowl and Wetlands Trust ceased releases. The general consensus among Lancashire wildfowl experts is that neither breeding pocket can be considered self-sustaining, and it is likely that no more than two or three pairs in total nest successfully in any year.

It is highly probable that most of the sightings of Mandarin Ducks in south and central Lancashire originate from one or other of these ephemeral feral colonies, but where the many visitors to lodges, reservoirs and park lakes in east Lancashire hail from is a matter for speculation. The occurrence of up to seven juveniles at Cliviger, near Burnley on 28-30 July 2000, where four males and a female persisted until at least 2005 but without any evidence of breeding, is perhaps the most intriguing of the recent records.

BM.

This species account was sponsored by Towneley Hall Art Gallery and Museum.

WIGEON

Anas penelope

Lancashire Category A.

Abundant winter visitor from northern Europe and Siberia.

Wigeon breed in open and sparsely-wooded country across the northern Palaearctic from Iceland to the Bering Straits and winter from Britain and Ireland and north-west Africa eastward, mainly along coasts, on muddy estuaries and saltmarshes, as well as in river valleys and by freshwater lakes. An estimated 1.5 million spend the winter in north-west Europe, up to 25% of them in Britain. There is a small British breeding population of some 500 pairs, mainly in Scotland, but the overwhelming majority of British wintering Wigeon migrate from Iceland, Fennoscandia and north Russia. The winter population in north-west Europe as a whole, and in Britain in particular, has increased substantially since the 1970s.

Tony Disley

Wigeon have long been numerous in winter in Lancashire, both Mitchell and Oakes describing the species as common or abundant on the coast but much less frequent inland. Mitchell identified the Lune and Wyre Estuaries as the Wigeon's main resort but by Oakes's time the Ribble Estuary and the south-west mosslands had begun to attract most of our winter flocks, and so the situation remains to the present day.

Wigeon begin to arrive in their Lancashire winter quarters in small numbers in August, although exact arrival dates have become difficult to detect since the mid-1990s due to the establishment of small summering flocks at several regular sites. Numbers build slowly in September then quite rapidly from early October onwards, normally reaching a peak in December (Figure 1). Counts tend to remain relatively high in January and February, before declining rapidly through March and April and only a handful remain in the county after the beginning of May.

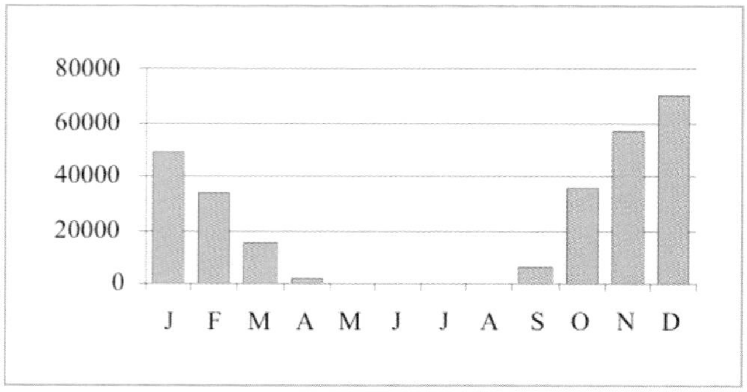

Figure 1. Average monthly peak counts, Ribble Estuary and Morecambe Bay South, 1990-2005 (WeBS).

Peak counts on the Ribble Estuary increased steadily from the early 1970s to the mid-1990s (Figure 2), with landmark counts of 11,655 in November 1983, 30,039 in December 1987, 59,187 in December 1990, 88,612 in November 1991 and an all-time high of 110,278 in December 1994. Since then numbers have declined, ranging from 50,500 to 84,500 in recent winters; nevertheless these still represent about a quarter of all Wigeon wintering in Britain and more than 5% of the total north-west European population. The grazing regime on the Ribble Marshes NNR has been largely directed towards providing sward suitable for Wigeon since the 1980s, and the site now holds nearly three times more birds than the next most important location in Britain, the Ouse Washes.

Within the Ribble area counts on the coastal freshwater marshes at Marshside had remained in the hundreds during the 1980s but increased dramatically to reach 12,000-13,000 since 2000. The bulk of this increase took place after 1997, immediately following conservation work on the RSPB reserve which included extending and deepening scrapes, channels and creeks. Over the same period peak counts at nearby Martin Mere declined

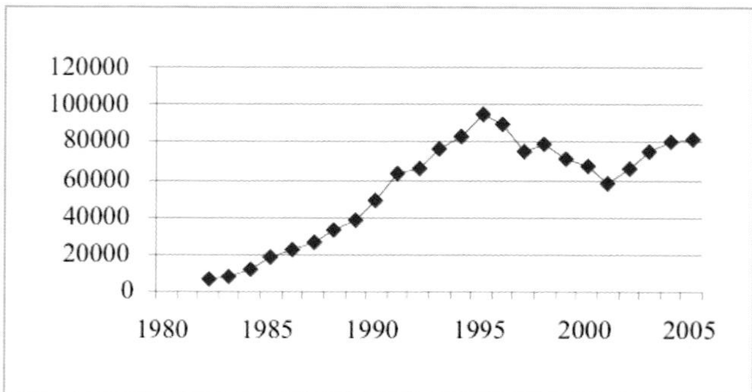

Figure 2. Winter peak counts of Wigeon in Lancashire (three-year rolling means), Ribble Estuary, 1980/81 to 2005/06

substantially from the record 12,700 in January 1994 and the site is no longer even of national importance for Wigeon; it is likely that many Wigeon that had formerly moved inland in rough weather now remain at Marshside.

Nowhere else in Lancashire comes close to matching the Ribble's enormous flocks but the extensive estuarine system between the Lune and the Wyre at the southern end of Morecambe Bay has held fairly substantial numbers since the 1970s. WeBS counts in the Lancashire sectors of the bay averaged 3,700 between 1990 and 2005 and peaked at 5,431 in November 2004. There have been occasional exceptional gatherings at Pilling Lane Ends, including 3,100 in November 1994. Numbers wintering at other coastal sites are much lower, although odd large flocks are occasionally recorded, including 3,000 on the Mersey off Otterspool in January 1994 and 3,500 at Oglet in February 1995.

As in Mitchell and Oakes's days, Wigeon are very much scarcer inland although small parties are fairly regular on many reservoirs in east Lancashire and on the West Pennine Moors. Stocks Reservoir has consistently attracted the highest numbers since the 1970s but two other sites far inland have regularly produced winter counts in the hundreds: the Lune Valley at Arkholme and the Foulridge/Whitemoor Reservoir complex near Colne.

A small part of the Ribble Wigeon flocks, Marshside, November 2003. (Steve Young)

Given our huge winter flocks, and the fact that a small breeding presence has managed to maintain itself in Scotland and the northern Pennines since the late nineteenth century, it is not surprising that occasional nesting has been recorded in Lancashire. Oakes noted probable breeding by a pair at Leighton Moss in 1942 and confirmed nesting there in 1944. Since then one or two pairs have bred at Martin Mere in 1979, 1989 and 1996, and at Stocks Reservoir in 1981. As the wintering population has increased numbers of Wigeon summering here have also grown, providing the prospect of more regular nesting in the future. Most summer records have come from Leighton Moss and the Morecambe Bay Reserve, Martin Mere and Marshside, and totals have increased quite noticeably since 1996, with as many as 50 birds now regularly spending all summer on our coastal and near-coastal wetlands.

There have been eight recoveries of Lancashire-ringed Wigeon, three within the county plus two on the Atlantic coast of France, two in Ireland and one on the River Ob in central Russia. Fifty-three birds ringed in Britain and Ireland have been recovered in Lancashire, 34 from southern England, four from northern England, 13 from Scotland and three from Ireland. Of 28 recoveries of foreign-ringed Wigeon, 15 have come from the Netherlands, six from Iceland, three from Russia, two from Denmark and one each from Belgium and Sweden. The bird on the Ob was ringed at Banks on 24 March 1984 and recovered at Sytomino, 4,495 km to the east on 19 April, having averaged at least 175km per day; all the Icelandic, Fennoscandian and Russian recoveries were during the breeding season, representing the full range of origins of the British wintering population.

BM.

This species account was sponsored by Tony Cooper.

AMERICAN WIGEON

Anas americana

Lancashire Category AE. (2, 22).

Rare winter visitor from North America.

There were only two documented records before the late twentieth century: one shot near Hightown 'several years before 1892' (Wrigley 1892), and a male shot by H.A. Fooks at Leighton Moss in December 1935 (*Field*, 30.10.1936). Spencer commented in 1973 that these two birds '. . . may have been escapes, but their natural occurrence seems at least a possibility'. Our current state of knowledge of the species' pattern of occurrence strongly supports the second conclusion.

There was a 40 year wait for the next, a male found by S.J. Riley, D. Wilkinson and A. Blee at Martin Mere on 23 December 1975 and the first to be identified in the field in Lancashire. It was followed by the only accepted record of a female to date at the same site on 28-30 September 1989.

Male American Wigeon (left) with Eurasian Wigeon, Heysham, 1999. (Tom Wilmer)

And then the floodgates opened. Within ten years the status of American Wigeon changed from national rarity to scarce but annual winter visitor and it was removed from the list of species considered by the BBRC from 2002. In line with the national increase a further 19 records followed in Lancashire up to 2005, all of them of single males with the exception of three males at Martin Mere in March 1990 and two males at Marshside on 25 March 2003. It seems probable that this increase in records is due to a combination of increased observer awareness and improved optical equipment rather than an increase in the breeding population or its propensity for vagrancy.

Eight of the modern records have been at Martin Mere, four at Leighton Moss, four at Marshside, two at Heysham and singles at Seaforth, Pilling, Barnaby's Sands and Marton Mere. It is perhaps understandable that none has ever been found amongst the huge flocks of Wigeon on the south Ribble marshes away from Marshside – they must surely have occurred there, perhaps in fairly significant numbers.

At least one has been recorded in all but four years since 1989, with peaks of four in 1990 and three in 2003. It is most likely that, having arrived in Europe, American Wigeon migrate northward and probably hybridise with their Eurasian cousins each summer. No hybrids have ever been claimed in Lancashire but they would be difficult to pick out – note the very few records of females or eclipse males. A good proportion of the county total are undoubtedly returning birds, and the total number of individuals involved may be as low as ten.

Birds have been found throughout the winter and passage months but arrivals show a rather strange late winter peak (Figure 1).

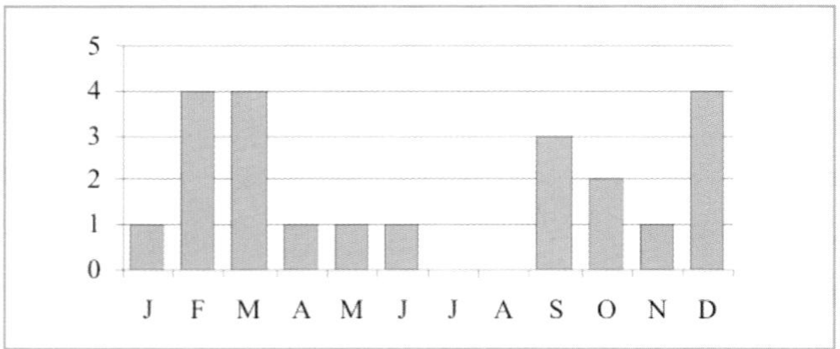

Figure 1. Arrival dates of American Wigeon in Lancashire, 1975-2005

A pinioned female was at Wayoh Reservoir in August and September 1995 and a presumed escaped male was on the Lune at Greta Foot on 10 May 1997 and 29 May 1998.

All records:

<1893 Hightown, one obtained, date unknown
1935 Leighton Moss, male, shot in December
1975 Martin Mere, male, 23 December
1989 Martin Mere, female, 28 to 30 September
1990 Martin Mere, male, 11 February to 24 March
1990 Martin Mere, first-winter male, 20 February to 8 March
1990 Martin Mere, adult male, 4 to 8 March
1990 Seaforth, eclipse male, 15 September
1992 Martin Mere, male, 24 February
1992 Martin Mere, male, 17 to 20 October
1993 Martin Mere, adult male, 22 February to 17 March
1994 Leighton Moss, male, 7 to 19 December
1996 Marshside, male, 27 April to 6 May
1997 Heysham, male, 12 January to 14 February
1998 Leighton Moss, male, 7 November to 19 January 1999
1999 Heysham, adult male, 23 October, also 9 November
2000 Leighton Moss, male, 8 May
2000 Marshside, male, 9 to 15 May, presumed same as Leighton Moss
2000 Pilling, male, 19 September to 6 October
2002 Marshside, male, 3 February
2002 Barnaby's Sands, male, 9 December to 30 March 2003
2003 Marshside, two males, at least 25 March, one 23 March
2004 Marton Mere, male, 1 to 5 June

SJW, MJ.

This species account was sponsored by the Fylde Bird Club and Graham Clarkson.

GADWALL

Anas strepera

Lancashire Category AC.

Scarce breeder; common winter visitor from central and eastern Europe.

The Gadwall was a rare winter visitor to Lancashire in the nineteenth century and Mitchell knew of just four records: two shot near Altcar in April 1865 and singles shot on Grimsargh Reservoir in March 1860, in Morecambe Bay in the winter of 1872/73 and at Singleton on the Fylde on 15 December 1884. Oakes was dubious about both the Altcar and Grimsargh birds. He knew of only one record south of the Ribble (one seen by F.W. Holder and R. Wagstaffe at Ainsdale on 17 March 1926) and one in the Fylde (a female found dead near Carleton on 7 February 1936). However, he documented increasingly regular sightings during the first half of the twentieth century at Leighton Moss, Haweswater and nearby sites, beginning with two females at Leighton on 24 December 1921. By the 1940s pairs were being seen at Leighton Moss with increasing frequency but there was no evidence of any staying throughout the summer.

It is not clear when breeding first took place at Leighton Moss. Marsh (1989) knew of no confirmed breeding as late as 1988, while Rigby (in Pyefinch & Golborn 2001) believed it was likely that a small population may have become established as early as the 1960s, a decade which saw widespread colonisation of Britain by feral birds as a result of large-scale releases for wildfowling purposes (Fox 1988). The first Lancashire releases were believed to have taken place at Leighton Moss sometime during the 1960s and may have continued in the Lune Valley until the present time. A second focus of feral breeding became established in West Lancashire between 1974 and 1986, when a full-winged population was allowed to develop at Martin Mere from captive stock. A final release of a small number of birds took place at Crosby, probably during the late 1980s, so that by the mid-1990s feral breeding populations had become established at three centres in Lancashire, around Leighton Moss, Martin Mere and Mere Sands Wood, and in south Sefton.

The timing of this process of colonisation is well illustrated by the three county-wide atlas surveys; breeding was proven or suspected in just one 10km square during 1968-72, in two squares during 1988-91 but in 15 tetrads in seven 10km squares during 1997-2000, when the Lancashire population was estimated at 25 pairs.

Martin Mere has supported up to five breeding pairs since the early 1990s, while nearby Mere Sands Wood and Nucks Wood each held one or two pairs during the same period. The first successful breeding took place at Marshside in 1995, after which it briefly became the main county site with eight pairs in 2003, declining to three in 2005. Occasional pairs have also nested elsewhere on the outer Ribble, including one on Warton Marsh in 2003. The other main breeding site is at the Leighton Moss/Eric Morecambe complex, where five or six pairs bred annually from the 1990s, rising dramatically to at least 22 pairs in 2004 and 2005. Elsewhere, breeding attempts have taken place in most years in Great Crosby and at Seaforth since 1985, but breeding success has been low. Single pairs have bred at two sites in St. Helens, Prescot Reservoirs and Eccleston Mere – and probably at nearby Knowsley Park – at least sporadically since 1997, and near Brockholes Quarry in 2003.

Breeding distribution of Gadwall, 1997-2000. (Large dots: confirmed. Small dots: possible)

The British breeding population was estimated at 770 pairs in 1990 (New Atlas) and has continued to increase by about 5% per year, largely as a result of the expansion of the feral population, which began with releases in East Anglia in the 1850s, but with additional recruits from the continent (Fox and Mitchell 1988). Rigby thought it likely that some Lancashire breeders away from the original sites were of wild origin but there is no hard evidence for this and the current population size and distribution is compatible with a spread from known release areas.

Nationally, the wintering population has increased by 15% annually in recent years (three times faster than for breeding birds) as the largely sedentary breeding population is joined by continental immigrants. Numbers wintering in Lancashire have increased from about 100 in the late 1980s to 200 or so this century, with the two composite sites of Leighton Moss/Eric Morecambe complex and Mere Sands Wood/Martin Mere/Nucks Wood between them supporting about 90% of the county total. The degree of movement of birds within these sites is not known so these figures, based on peak counts within the composite sites, are likely to be underestimates. The trends in these two areas have been very different with peak numbers declining in West Lancashire during the late 1990s – possibly linked to increasing numbers on the Wigan Flashes in Greater Manchester – and a sharp increase in the north at around the same time (Figure 1). Largest counts include 125 at Mere Sands Wood in October 1988 with 140 there on 8 November 1992, 135 at Martin Mere on 26 November 1985, 100 at Nuck's Wood on 27 November 2005, 193 at the Leighton Moss/Eric Morecambe complex in October 2002 and 297 on the Eric Morecambe complex in October 2005.

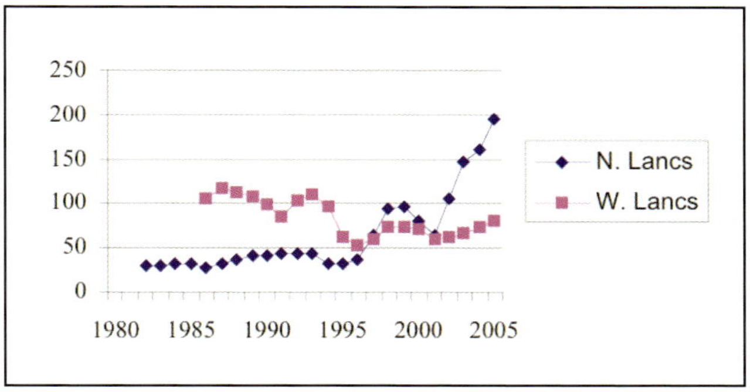

Figure 1, Peak annual counts of Gadwall (3-year rolling means) in West Lancashire (Martin Mere, Mere Sands Wood & Nuck's Wood) 1984-2005 and north Lancashire (Leighton Moss & Eric Morecambe complex) 1980-2005.

Numbers begin to build up at Leighton Moss during August, reaching a peak during October and November before declining as winter progresses, but the main arrival comes a month or so later at the West Lancashire sites where peak counts usually occur during winter (Figure 2).

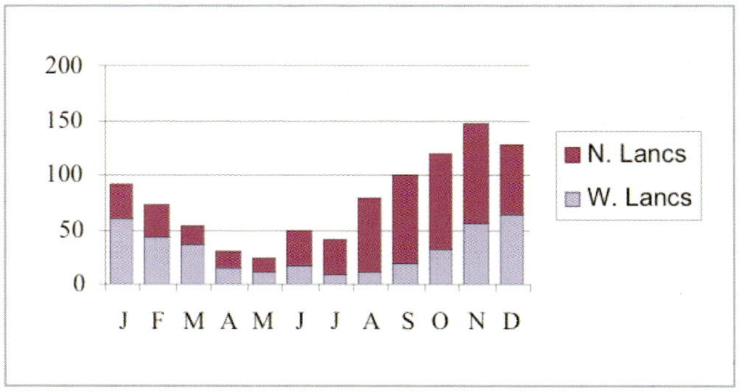

Figure 2. Average monthly peaks of Gadwall in West Lancashire (Martin Mere, Mere Sands Wood & Nuck's Wood) and north Lancashire (Leighton Moss & Eric Morecambe complex), 1996-2005.

Ones or twos turn up occasionally on reservoirs and other waterbodies in central and east Lancashire but six at Lee Green Reservoir in November 2003 and up to 24 at Brockholes Quarry during the winter of 2002/03 were exceptional. Single-figure counts are regular at various Fylde sites, including Marton Mere and the Wyre estuary. Double-figure counts away from the main sites include 13 at Marton Mere in December 1978, 38 at

Marshside in January 1993, 26 at Seaforth in 1995/96 and ten at Prescot Reservoirs in December 2001.

The sole Lancashire ringing recovery involved a female killed at Preesall on 23 November 1983 which had been ringed in Kolmenasva in Estonia on 13 June 1980, 1,723km to the east.

SJW, JKB.
This species account was sponsored by Jacob Clarkson.

TEAL

Anas crecca

Lancashire Category A.

Scarce breeder; abundant winter visitor from eastern and northern Europe.

Almost 200,000 Teal, mainly from Iceland, Fennoscandia and western Russia, spend the winter in Britain (WeBS). This is an exceptionally mobile species in winter, however, and there may be substantial movements within and between wintering areas in response to changes in food availability or weather conditions. In addition, because over 40% of Teal are found in small, widely-dispersed flocks of fewer than 200 birds (Winter Atlas), it is a difficult species to census accurately.

Mitchell and Oakes both regarded the Teal as an abundant winter visitor and uncommon local resident; Oakes considered it to be commoner inland in winter than the Wigeon and listed Leighton Moss and the south-west mosslands, north Lancashire, the West Pennine Moors and north Rossendale as its main breeding areas. He noted that maximum counts on both Morecambe Bay and the Ribble occurred in late September, although sizeable flocks remained all winter at many locations, including in the south-west and on the West Pennine Moors.

Male Teal, Seaforth Nature Reserve, November 2005. (Steve Young)

Teal begin to arrive on their Lancashire wintering grounds from late July and numbers build up substantially during September, much earlier than in the case of Wigeon (Figure 1). In contrast to Oakes's day, nowadays peak numbers at most sites are normally recorded in November or December; about 25% are still present in March and there are usually many stragglers until the end of April. Teal winter on coastal fresh- and saltmarshes as well as on flooded inland water-meadows and by lakes and reservoirs; plant seeds comprise the bulk of the diet and the birds feed mainly in the shallows and at the edges of pools and channels, making them difficult to get to grips with.

Systematic counts in recent decades have revealed quite complex movements, especially within the species' Ribble stronghold. There is an early build-up in numbers during autumn, particularly at Martin Mere where the birds exploit the seed-crop on the freshly-cut marshes; as this supply is consumed many move to Mere Sands Wood or to the Ribble Estuary, concentrating on the flooded grazing marshes at Marshside in late winter, although this pattern may be disrupted by gales and high tides, which drive many back inland.

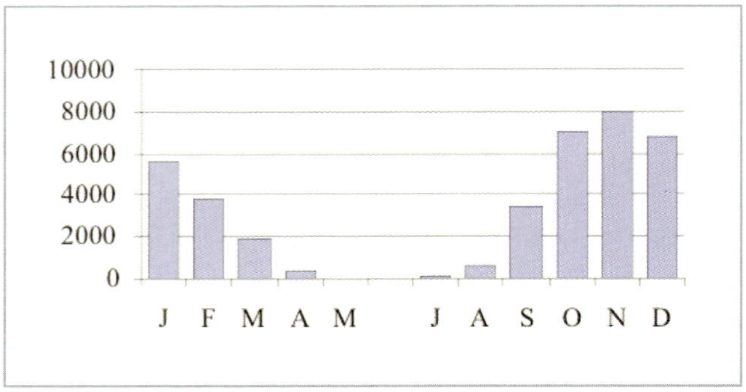

Figure 1. Average monthly peaks counts of Teal in Lancashire, Ribble & Alt Estuaries and Morecambe Bay South, 1990-2005.

Given the mobility of flocks in winter, counts are more difficult to interpret as indicators of population changes than for the more sedentary Wigeon. Peak winter WeBS counts on the Ribble Estuary increased from 2,000 or so in the early 1980s to more than 9,000 at the end of the decade with largest counts of 10,200 in November 1991 and 19,567 in October 2004. Numbers then fell back to between 4,500 and 7,800 annually and have remained at about this level into the present century (Figure 2). Marshside supports a substantial proportion of the Ribble birds with a peak count of 4,840 in December 1998. There is a considerable interchange between the Ribble marshes and Martin Mere, where numbers increased steadily throughout the 1990s to peak at 10,000 in November 2000 and 10,500 in October 2004. Many of these also commute to nearby Mere Sands Wood where the record count was 2,500, also in 2000.

The Winter Atlas described the Mersey Estuary, shared by Lancashire and Cheshire, as hosting some 35,000 birds, by far the largest assembly of Teal in Britain during the winter of 1981/82. Numbers have declined significantly subsequently but the Mersey still held 17,660 birds in October 2001 and remains Britain's second most important site after the Somerset Levels. However,

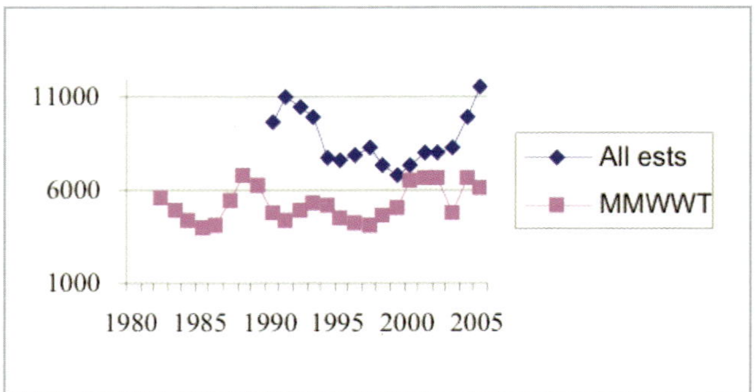

Figure 2. Peak winter counts (3-year rolling means) on the Ribble & Alt Estuaries and Morecambe Bay South (1987/88 to 2004/05) and Martin Mere (1980/81 to 2004/05).

most Mersey Teal now feed and roost on the Cheshire side of the river since the saltmarsh on the Liverpool bank eroded away in the early 1990s as the channel made one of its periodic switches. Recent large counts on the Lancashire side include 6,700 at Oglet-Garston in October 1984, 7,020 in September 1990, 6,600 in October 1991, 2,680 in September 1993, 2,350 in December 1995 and 1,052 in January 2004. Numbers in the Mersey Narrows at Seaforth more than quadrupled during the 1990s – reaching 1,170 in November 2002 – as a small saltmarsh developed there.

Leighton Moss and the Eric Morecambe complex form the most important wintering site in the north with recorded peaks of 1,000 in January 1973 and 1974, 1,600 in December 1980, 1,800 in November 1982 and 2,350 in January 1984, but no count has exceeded 1,000 since the early 1990s. WeBS counts over Morecambe Bay South as a whole peaked at 2,103 in December 1991 and 3,272 in November 2004. However, numbers significantly larger than the WeBS counts have been recorded, particularly in the Pilling-Cockerham area, for example 3,800 on 28 December 2004. After enlargement of the water area at Marton Mere in the 1970s, numbers increased to several hundred, reaching a peak of 1,000 in 2002.

Teal winter very widely inland in Lancashire, albeit in much smaller flocks than on the coastal strip. Stocks Reservoir, in particular, has hosted between 200 and 300 Teal consistently since the early 1980s, and the Belmont Reservoir area has been a regular site since Oakes's time, although peak numbers here have declined from 110 in March 1965, 155 in November 1971 and 135 in November 1995 to fewer than 50 since 1997.

Oakes noted two distinct breeding habitats in Lancashire, with some nesting on coastal and mossland marshes and others by upland streams and pools in the east and north of the county. This pattern has persisted but the population has declined in both lowland and moorland areas in line with the national trend of the last 30 years. Teal bred in 20 10km squares in Lancashire during 1968-72 but in only twelve during 1997-2000, when a total of 32 breeding pairs was confirmed.

Up to ten pairs bred at Leighton Moss in the 1960s but the total had fallen to two or three pairs annually by the late 1970s, and to no more than two in any year since 1998. On the positive side, Martin Mere had its first breeding record in 1989, and since then nesting has been recorded in 1995 and 1996. One pair bred for the first time at Marshside in 2000 and again in 2002, and Eccleston Mere, St Helens recorded its first successful brood in 1997. The situation further inland, however, has become quite bleak, even though two-thirds of the 32 pairs located during the 1997-2000 survey were at upland sites. In the 1970s and 1980s nesting was fairly regular in Rossendale, Bowland, the Lune Valley and, above all, on the West Pennine Moors around Belmont. Six pairs bred on the West Pennine Moors in 1993, raising 38 young; there were six to eleven pairs in the Belmont area in 1990 with six in 1992 and four in 1993, but no more than three pairs in any year since. From 1999 to 2005 there have been no more than seven probable or confirmed breeding pairs recorded in Lancashire in any year, and there has not been a confirmed nesting attempt in Rossendale since 1994.

Mitchell remarked upon the large numbers of Teal captured annually at Hale Decoy on the north bank of the Mersey just south of Liverpool, until 1974 part of Lancashire but now in Cheshire. Many have been ringed there since the 1970s and, together with birds recovered (usually shot) in Lancashire, the total of 72 exchanges with continental Europe gives a clear picture of the origins and migration routes of our wintering Teal. Recoveries involving Fennoscandia (17 Finland, 3 both Sweden and Denmark) and central and western Europe (16 France, 15 the Netherlands, 3 Poland, 2 Germany, one the Czech Republic) predominate, but ten with Russia and one with Latvia point to origins further east, while one from Iceland shows that not all are of continental European origin.

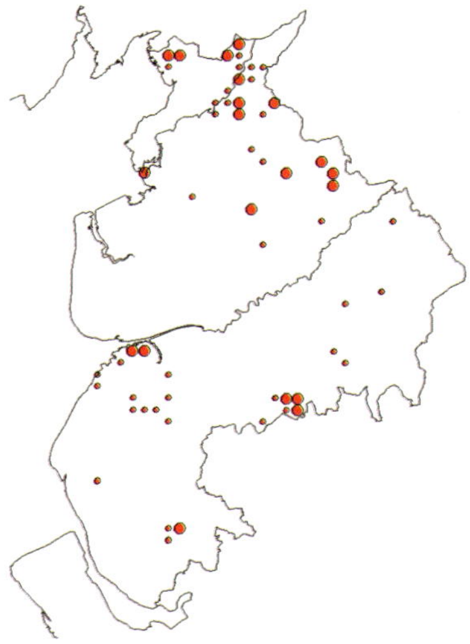

Breeding distribution of Teal, 1997-2000. (Large dots: confirmed. Small dots: possible)

BM.

This species account was sponsored by Michael Franklin.

GREEN-WINGED TEAL

Anas carolinensis

Lancashire Category A. (0, 15+).

Scarce winter visitor from North America.

Green-winged Teal are very closely related to the Eurasian species; females of the two are effectively indistinguishable in the field, and until 2000 the AOU and BOU regarded both forms as races of a single Holarctic species. They are among the most regular and numerous Nearctic vagrants on this side of the Atlantic; most are recorded in Britain and Ireland but there have been occurrences from Iceland south to Morocco and eastwards into central Europe. All Lancashire birds have been found among wintering flocks of Eurasian Teal and many remain on the same lake or marsh for weeks or even months; it is likely that they accompany Eurasian Teal on spring and autumn migrations, as Green-winged Teal frequently reappear at the same site in successive winters.

Male Green-winged Teal, Marshside, March 2007. (Steve Young)

Pete Marsh and his colleagues found the first Lancashire Green-winged Teal at Leighton Moss on 18 April 1979; the bird remained, with a remnant wintering flock of Teal, until 5 May. What was assumed to be the same drake was seen again in March 1980 and on 10 June 1981. Marshside recorded the next, on 6 January 1982, and there was one at Martin Mere during 4-7 November 1984.

Since 1987 one or more have been recorded every year in Lancashire and the presence of several long-staying individuals over the years has made the county one of the best regions in Britain in which to see the species. Two were present together at Martin Mere and Marshside in November and December 1990 and at least three drakes were in the county simultaneously in late 1994; in 2001 and 2002 it was considered that at least four different birds had been recorded.

Marshside and Martin Mere have accounted for the majority of records, which is unsurprising given the large flocks of Teal that winter at both sites. Given their proximity and the frequent movements of Teal between them it is likely that the same individuals have been recorded at both reserves on several occasions in the course of a single winter. Records in north Lancashire and the Fylde have also been fairly regular; there have been sightings of lone drakes at Leighton Moss and/or the Eric Morecambe complex in seven of the winters since 1987, and there have also been records at Cockerham Marsh, Preesall Flash, Pilling Lane Ends and Marton Mere. Seaforth recorded its first Green-winged Teal in January 1995 and another in January 2000; these birds were thought to be separate from the Ribble individuals, and more likely to be associated with Teal wintering on the Mersey. A drake at Stocks Reservoir in late October 2002 was the first for east Lancashire, and is also likely to have been a 'new' bird.

A very conservative estimate puts the minimum number of Green-winged Teal to have occurred in Lancashire to date at around 15 but it could be three or more times that figure.

Drakes have been recorded paired with female Teal at Martin Mere in April and May 1993 and at Preesall Flash in April 2002, while an apparent hybrid male was seen at Martin Mere in January and February 1988. In 2004 Stocks Reservoir held a summering male from 6 June to at least the 21st; it was apparently paired but there was no definite evidence that breeding took place.

BM.

This species account was sponsored by Pat Wisniewski.

MALLARD

Anas platyrhynchos

Lancashire Category ACE.

Common breeder; abundant winter visitor from northern and eastern Europe; frequent releases for shooting.

The Lancashire breeding population of 3,500 or so pairs is augmented in autumn by the release of many thousands reared for shooting; a further influx takes place in winter with the arrival of many Icelandic birds as well as others from north-west Russia, Fennoscandia and the southern shores of the Baltic (Figure 1). Wintering Mallard may be found just about anywhere there is even a small patch of wetland habitat, and the presence of many individuals and small flocks at sites seldom visited by birders makes assessment of the total population difficult, but it is certainly considerably underestimated by the WeBS counts.

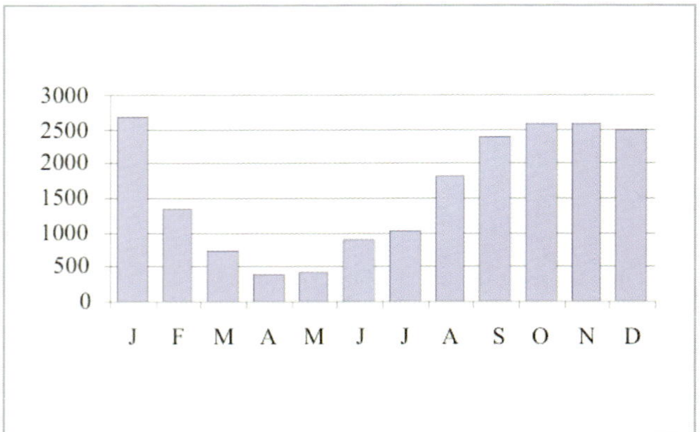

Figure 1. Average monthly peak counts of Mallard on the Ribble & Alt Estuaries and Morecambe Bay South, 1990-2005 (WeBS).

Mitchell described the 'Wild Duck' as a very widely-distributed resident, breeding numerously and seen in large flocks at the coast in winter. Oakes considered the species to be a common resident and winter visitor and the most widespread of our breeding ducks. Post-breeding flocks of up to 200 in Morecambe Bay often swelled to produce midwinter totals of 1,000 or more, while several thousands might be seen on the open coast at Formby Point; winter flocks of up to 200 were frequent on the West Pennine reservoirs, with smaller numbers frequenting Foulridge Reservoir and the Lune Valley.

The status of the Mallard in Lancashire has not changed dramatically since Oakes's time. Numbers at key sites tend to fluctuate substantially during the winter months, and also from

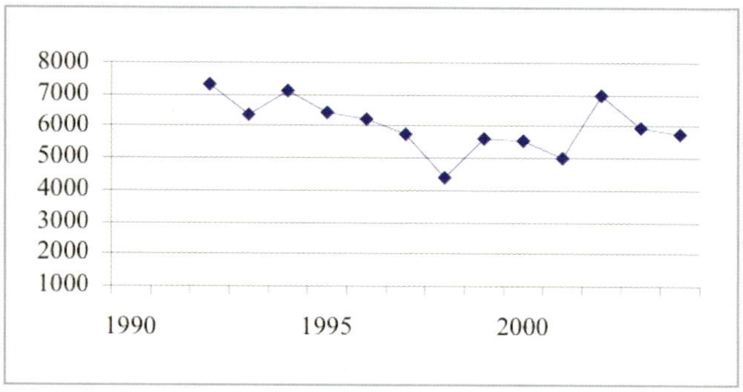

Figure 2. Peak winter counts of Mallard (3-year rolling means) on the Ribble & Alt Estuaries, Morecambe Bay South (WeBS) and Martin Mere (1989/90 to 2004/05).

year to year, although there is evidence of a declining trend from WeBS and other site counts since the early 1990s.

Peak winter counts at the RSPB Morecambe Bay Reserve gradually increased from 526 in November 1978 to 1,590 in November 1985, but went into decline during the 1990s and have remained below 1,000 in all but one winter since 1990. WeBS maxima for Morecambe Bay South have also fallen fairly steadily, from 1,696 in December 1990 to 1,207 in January 2004, with an overall decline of 33% since the mid-1990s, but numbers have remained buoyant in some areas, particularly at Preesall and Pilling, where up to 400 have been recorded on many dates since the mid-1980s. Elsewhere on the Fylde, Marton Mere/Stanley Park Lake showed a pattern of increases during the 1980s and early 1990s from 300 in December 1980 to 700 in January 1991, but peaks have fluctuated around 400 since then.

On the Ribble Estuary and adjacent mosslands the winter picture is equally complex. Ribble WeBS counts grew dramatically from 1,075 in November 1980 to peak at 2,625 in December 1986, but there has been a consistent decrease since then, to 1,861 in December 1990 and 1,445 in November 2005. Elsewhere in the south-west, however, numbers at Martin Mere have remained relatively steady during the 1990s with an average peak count of 3,200 during 1993-2004 and a high of 4,540 in 1995. Some sites that formerly yielded substantial counts, such as Altcar Moss (941 in October 1977)) and Southport's Hesketh Park Lake (880 in November 1991) seem to have vanished from the score sheet altogether.

Male Mallard, Crosby Marine Park, November 2005. (Steve Young)

As in Oakes's day wintering Mallard are common and widespread on Lancashire's inland waters. The West Pennine reservoirs have long been a stronghold; there were 460 at Belmont/Delph Reservoirs in February 1963, 524 at Anglezarke in December 1979 and 1,525 on the combined Chorley NHS area reservoirs in January 1992. In recent years Roddlesworth and Ward's Reservoirs have come to the fore with 417 at the former in January 1996 and 230 at the latter in January 2000. Further north, Foulridge and Stocks Reservoirs have tended to dominate the counts, although Barnacre Reservoir near Garstang has featured strongly with 900 in January 1983, 920 in December 1988, 1,120 in January 1995 and 670 in January 2002. Peaks at Foulridge have included 282 in January 1987 and 314 in October 1994 but have declined since then. At Stocks maxima oscillated wildly in the 1980s: 800 in December 1980, 1,500 in October 1984, 400 in December 1986, and 1,041 in December 1989; since the early 1990s peak counts have fluctuated around 500.

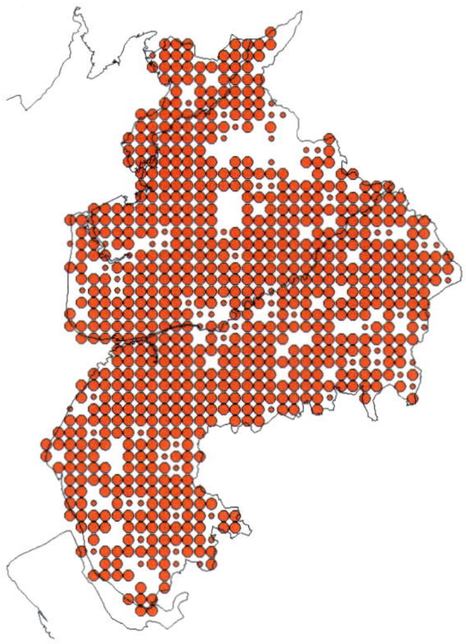

Breeding distribution of Mallard, 1997-2000. (Large dots: confirmed. Small dots: possible)

Mallard breed virtually everywhere in Lancashire and were recorded in 88% of the county's tetrads in 1997-2000 with absences only on the very highest ground of Bowland and the Pennines – although nests are not uncommon on the Bowland fells and on the West Pennine Moors – and some urban areas. They nest in virtually all kinds of waterside vegetation, along ditches and riverbanks and in particular on islands in lowland eutrophic waters, but nests may be found in hollow trees and under boulders, and man-made nest-boxes and baskets are readily adopted. The award for enterprise and daring in Lancashire must, however, go to the female that laid nine eggs underneath stone slabs inside the lion enclosure at Blackpool Zoo in 1982. Under ideal conditions of suitable habitat, plentiful food and protection from disturbance high nesting densities may occur.

At Martin Mere up to 400 pairs bred annually in the early 1990s, 300 of these in the 10ha Waterfowl Gardens (Rigby 1992), but numbers have declined significantly since. Up to 40 pairs at Leighton Moss in the 1960s increased to around 100 in the 1980s and 1990s and, following the pattern noted by Oakes, post-breeding moult assemblies here reached over 2,000 in July and August in the mid-1980s, although numbers have dwindled steadily since to 484 in 2002. An indication of the numbers of breeding Mallard that may be missed by birders in many seasons is provided by a count of 249 pairs on the river Lune upstream of Skerton Weir in 2005.

Mallard are unusual among breeding waterfowl in the length of their nesting season. In Lancashire most ducklings hatch between April and June but it is not unusual to find eggs in the nest as early as the beginning of March, and there are numerous records of females escorting small ducklings as late as August or September, or even, occasionally, in October.

Including birds from Hale Duck Decoy, now in Cheshire, there are 40 records of exchanges between Lancashire and abroad: nine with the Netherlands, five with Germany, 16 with Denmark, five with Sweden, three with Finland and singles with Russia and France. This fits the national pattern in which up to 75% of the British winter population consists of immigrants from northern and eastern Europe.

BM.

This species account was sponsored by Tony Cooper.

PINTAIL

Anas acuta

Lancashire Category AE.

Common winter visitor from northern Europe and Russia.

Winter numbers in Britain have remained fairly stable in recent decades following a substantial increase from the early 1970s to a total of about 25,000 in the mid-1980s (Winter Atlas); 20,052 were recorded by WeBS in December 2000, and the current British winter population is estimated at 27,900.

Mitchell described the Pintail as a winter visitor to Lancashire in small numbers, seldom found far from the coast, while Oakes considered it to be an uncommon but regular winter visitor and passage migrant, rare inland, noting that none had been recorded in east Lancashire between north Rossendale and the Lune Valley. Then as now the main winter concentrations were to be found in the Ribble Estuary, Morecambe Bay and on the Mersey.

The Lancashire wintering population increased steadily during the 1950s and 1960s; by the early 1970s some very substantial flocks were being recorded, and although there has been some decline in the last decade of the twentieth century Pintail remain common winter birds in coastal areas. The first arrivals may be as early as mid-July, but very few are normally recorded before early September; from mid-month numbers increase very rapidly to peak in mid-October at Martin Mere and in December on the estuaries (Figure 1). Most birds remain throughout January and February, but the decline thereafter is usually very quick and few are left by the end of March.

Since at least the 1960s the population has been concentrated from the Ribble Estuary southwards. The floods at Altcar Moss formerly attracted very large flocks, including up to 1,200 on 26 November 1967, 2,950 on 28 September 1973 and 1,050 on 10 October 1981. Martin Mere has held substantial numbers,

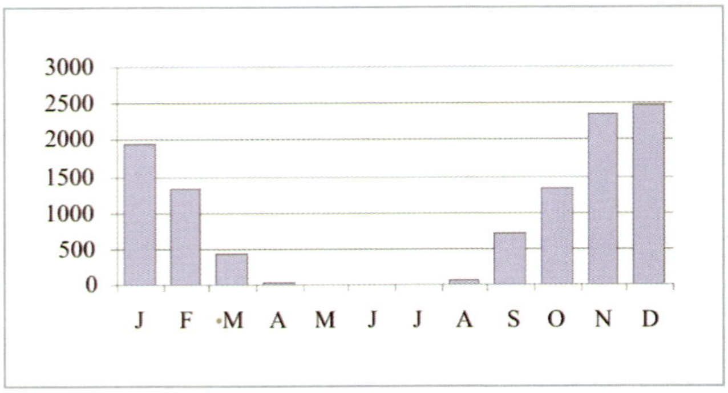

Figure 1. Average monthly peak counts (WeBS) of Pintail on the Ribble Estuary and Morecambe Bay South (1990-2005).

particularly in October and November, as far back as 1978, when 3,000 were present on 5 November. Other large counts there include 4,000 on 19 October 1980, 4,100 in October 1992 and 2,840 in October 1995, but peak numbers have since plummeted with an average of less than 500 during 1996-2005. On the Ribble Estuary proper, average winter peaks rose sharply from around 500 during the 1980s to more than 3,000 during the 1990s, including a record 6,507 in December 1991, but appear to have entered a period of decline since 2000 (Figure 2). It is probable that the spread of saltmarsh vegetation over many of the mudflats may have rendered the area less attractive to Pintail and counts on the shore and saltings at Crossens/Marshside have halved from up to 2,000 in the early 1980s to 1,000 or fewer since. By way of compensation numbers on the freshwater floods at Marshside began to build in the early 1990s and a winter population of up to 300 has since become established with an exceptional 1,190 there in January 2005. Numbers have also increased on the north Ribble shore at Lytham/Fairhaven since the early 1990s, including 2,000 in December 1993 and 2,050 in January 2002.

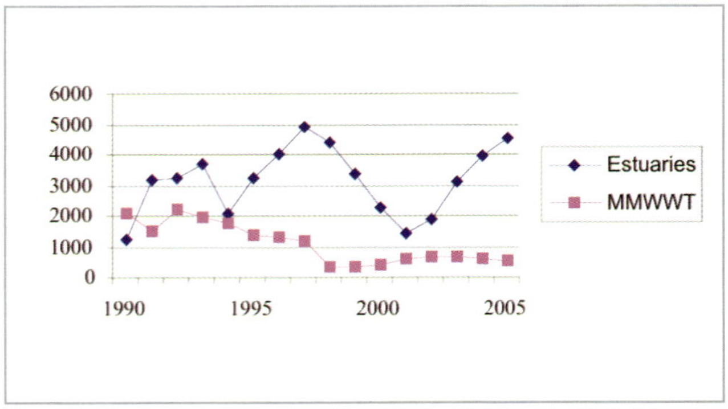

Figure 2. Peak winter counts (3-year rolling means) of Pintail on the Ribble Estuary & Morecambe Bay (WeBS) and Martin Mere (1987/88 to 2004/05).

The Winter Atlas (1986) identified the Mersey Estuary as by far the most important area in Britain for Pintail, with a maximum of 13,800 in January 1983, although most of the flocks tended to favour the Cheshire bank. Nonetheless, there were 1,950 in Oglet Bay in December 1981 and as many as 900 there as recently as October 1991, but peak counts on the Mersey have since spiralled relentlessly downward and the largest recent count in Lancashire waters was a mere 26 at Garston in 1998.

Pintail numbers in the Lancashire sector of Morecambe Bay have generally been lower than on the Ribble since the late 1960s at least. Early counts included 400 at Leighton Moss in October 1972 and 200 at Conder Green in January 1980. WeBS peaks over the whole of Morecambe Bay South averaged around 300 during the 1990s but have increased enormously since 1999, culminating in a record count of 2,454 in December 2003, 2,203 of which were at Jenny Brown's Point. Although there were 1,600 at Pilling Lane Ends–Cockerham Marsh in January 2002 it is the north of the bay which now makes the major contribution to Morecambe Bay totals.

Tony Disley

Coastal movements of small flocks of almost invariably southbound Pintail are a frequent feature of seawatching reports, especially in late autumn. The great majority of records come from the more northerly watchpoints, Heysham, Rossall Point and Blackpool in particular; there have been relatively few reports from Formby Point or the Mersey Mouth. Most movements occur between late September and late November in conditions of strong onshore winds and poor visibility, and are fairly readily explicable as southward passage to wintering areas. One hundred and twenty-one flew south off Heysham on 25 November 1979 and 225 on 6 October 1990; a total of 525 was recorded between 25 September and 26 November 2000, and 430 flew west off Jenny Brown's Point on 10 October 2002. Blackpool reported 220 on 3 November 1991 and 100 on 25 October 2002. It is less easy to account for the occasional records of southbound flocks in late December, January or February, including 120 off Blackpool on 28 December 1995, 219 off Heysham on 10 February 1999 and 278 there on 28 January 2002. These may perhaps have been birds moving from one wintering-site to another.

Oakes dismissed much of inland Lancashire as being devoid of Pintail, but recent data show that, although the species is very much scarcer than either Wigeon or Teal, Pintail are fairly regular visitors in small numbers to many of our inland waters in east Lancashire, Rossendale and the West Pennines. Stocks Reservoir, in particular, has featured winter peaks in double figures since the early 1990s, including 113 in January 2000 and 303 in January 2005.

Pintail is a scarce and sporadic breeding species in Britain. In Lancashire its status is marginal at best; although nesting by wild Pintail has been claimed, several instances of breeding have been attributed to feral stock. The first probable breeding record was on the Ribble in 1961, followed by confirmed nesting at Leighton Moss in 1963, at Mere Brow, near Tarleton in 1970 and twice on the Ribble Estuary during the 1970s. The only other confirmed breeding was a pair at Anglezarke Reservoir in 1999 but doubts about their provenance have arisen with the subsequent discovery that deliberate releases had taken place not far away. Breeding by feral Pintail took place at Martin Mere in 1978 and 1983. Small numbers, usually just ones or twos, have frequently spent the summer in Lancashire, most consistently at established wintering sites such as Leighton Moss, Martin Mere and on the Ribble Estuary.

The majority of recoveries of ringed birds have involved movements within Britain in subsequent winters but there have also been a number of exchanges with continental Europe and Iceland. About half of these were with other wintering or migration sites in western Europe (ten with the Netherlands, two with Denmark and singles with Germany and France), while the remainder came from breeding grounds in Iceland (2), Russia (5), the Baltic States (2) and Sweden (1).

BM.

This species account was sponsored by R.D. Thomson.

GARGANEY

Anas querquedula

Lancashire Category A.

Rare breeder; fairly common passage migrant from North Africa.

The Garganey breeds across the temperate, steppe and Mediterranean zones of the Palaearctic and Britain is at the edge of the breeding range. Consequently, the breeding population of Britain is a fluctuating one, with frequent adoption and abandonment of nesting locations from one year to the next and a cyclical pattern of influx and decline; Ogilvie (2000) suggested a maximum of 160 pairs during the 1990s.

The Garganey was a very rare visitor to Lancashire according to Mitchell; he cited only three nineteenth century records, at Ormskirk, Rufford and Martin Mere, the most recent of these in 1864. By Oakes's time the species had become a good deal more frequent in its visits; following sporadic records in the 1920s there was an increase in occurrences from the mid-1930s, and pairs summered at Leighton Moss in 1942 and 1947. Since then the Garganey has become established as an uncommon spring and autumn migrant and a scarce summer resident; numbers recorded annually have increased steadily since the late 1950s. This may be accounted for in part by greater observer numbers as well as a growing proficiency and confidence in identifying females, juveniles and eclipse males, but numbers of the easily recognised spring males have also clearly increased. Garganey remain, however, strongly attached to a relatively small number of regular sites in Lancashire, all in the coastal west; occurrences further inland, though more frequent than in the past, continue to be sporadic.

Male Garganey, Marshside, May 2005. (Steve Young)

The earliest probable spring migrant recorded in Lancashire (although it may possibly have wintered in Britain) was a male at Martin Mere on 24 February 1995, but there have been many March arrivals and the average first sighting over the past 25 years has been on 29 March. The largest spring flocks consisted of six males and three females at Marton Mere on 15 March 1952 and seven at Fleetwood on 28 March 2003. Nowadays, a sufficiently high number of Garganey are recorded to allow the identification of successive pulses of migration (Figure 1). There is frequently a series of records in late March and early April, followed by a second, larger wave in early May, and often by a third influx later in the month. There appears to be a regular surplus of drakes, with unpaired males, sometimes several together, turning up with paired birds, particularly in May.

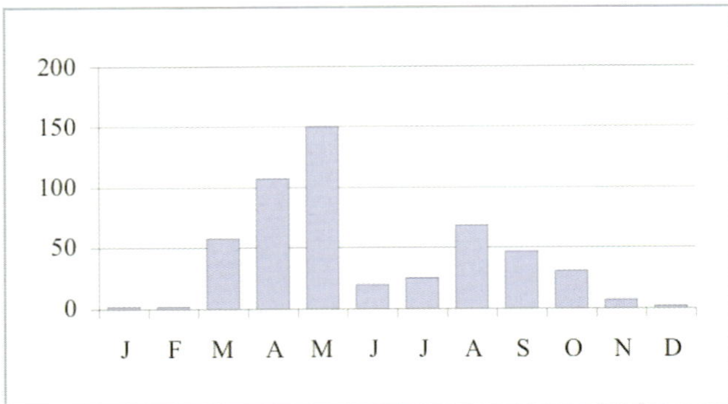

Figure 1. Monthly arrivals of Garganey in Lancashire 1978-2005.

Autumn movements, though usually lighter than those in spring, have also increased over recent decades. Passage is frequently prolonged, with favoured sites recording up to half a dozen eclipse males, females or juveniles between early July and early October. November records are scarce, with only seven individuals since 1978, and there have been only five midwinter occurrences, a bird that wintered at Leighton Moss in 1980-81, one at Mere Sands Wood in January and February 1992, two at Martin Mere in December 1997 and one at Sands Lake, Ainsdale on 5 January 2002. In the last case the bird may well have wintered in the area, as a Garganey was also present at this site on 19 November 2001. Spring records outnumber those during July-October by more than two to one, which, given that the population in autumn is at least twice as large, may suggest a different migration route to that of spring.

Summering by one or more Garganey has been of almost annual occurrence since the mid-1960s. Most records have been at Leighton Moss, but at least one bird spent all or part of the summer at both Martin Mere and Marton Mere throughout the 1990s. Their favoured breeding habitat and reclusive nature make confirmation of nesting difficult, but there have been numerous breeding attempts, several successful. Confirmed breeding by one or two pairs took place at Leighton Moss in 1965, 1996-1998, 2000, 2002 and 2003, and nesting was judged probable there in 1973, 1991, 2001 and 2004. Pairs bred at Weeton, Fylde in 1964 and at Marshside in 1992.

During the 1970s five or six were recorded in a typical year but this average increased significantly during the 1980s and 1990s, to at least 20 annually since 1995. In earlier years there was a clear pattern of 'good' and poor' Garganey years; 1967 and 1974 stand out as above-average seasons. Since the late 1980s, however, there have been no really unproductive years (although totals in autumn are more variable) and an average of more than 30 a year have been recorded in the past ten years, culminating in an unprecedented 59 during 2003 (Figure 2).

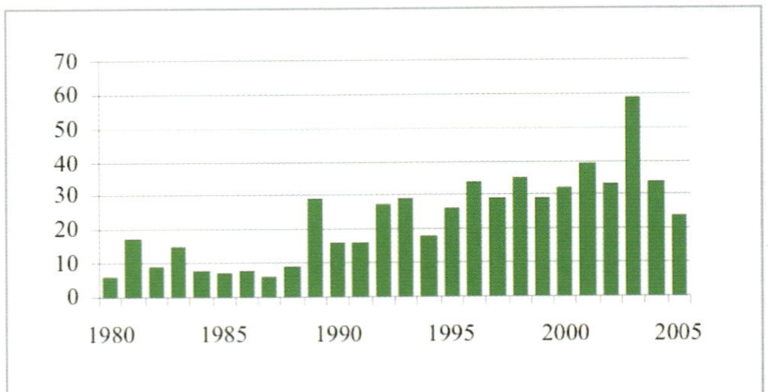

Figure 2. Estimated annual totals of Garganey in Lancashire, 1980-2005

Four well-watched wetlands are responsible for the lion's share of our Garganey records: Leighton Moss and adjacent marshes, Martin Mere, Marton Mere and Marshside, while Mere Sands Wood, Newton Marsh, Seaforth, Fleetwood and the Pilling-Preesall area have also recorded multiple sightings. There have been several records at Stocks Reservoir both in spring and in autumn since 1995, but elsewhere inland records remain exceptional. One was shot at Clowbridge, Rossendale in October 1966 and there were birds at Foulridge Reservoir in spring 1989 and in autumn 1993 and 1996; two pairs were at Dean Clough Reservoir, near Great Harwood on 29 April 1989, and birds were recorded in the Lune valley in spring in 1992 and 2000 and at Abbeystead in October 1994. Brockholes Quarry, on the Ribble upstream from Preston, has attracted an exceptional number of migrant Garganey since 2001, including six together in July 2005.

There has been only one recovery of a ringed bird in Lancashire, a juvenile male trapped in Essex on 4 September 1967 and recovered under unknown circumstances at Longridge nearly four weeks later, a fine example of 'reverse' migration.

BM.

This species account was sponsored by Donald Rusling.

BLUE-WINGED TEAL

Anas discors

Lancashire Category A. (0, 2).

Vagrant from North America.

Two records have been accepted by the BBRC, both of them males. The first was found at Leighton Moss on 6 February 1967 by John Wilson and R.A. Stratton, but it had gone the next day. The second was a little more obliging; found at Martin Mere on 3 September 1992 it remained until the 6th. The bird was moulting out of eclipse plumage and was found while checking the flocks of Common Teal for Garganey, one of which turned up on the following day to allow close comparison.

There is one further documented record, which has never been submitted to the BBRC and therefore does not figure in the national record list: a first-winter male, which was shot by wildfowlers on Hesketh Marsh on the Ribble Estuary on 22 September 1973. The bird was brought to the attention of Mike Ainscough who photographed it and preserved the wings.

An escaped pair was at Mere Sands Wood on 8 February 1987.

SJW, MJ.

This species account was sponsored by Leighton Moss RSPB Wildlife Explorers.

SHOVELER

Anas clypeata

Lancashire Category A.

Scarce breeder; common winter visitor from continental Europe and Russia.

The Shoveler appears to have had a chequered history in Lancashire. Mitchell described it as a scarce winter visitor, but commented that it had been much commoner in the mid-nineteenth century, especially during spring migration, with many shot annually on the Ribble Estuary.

By Oakes's time the species was an increasing breeding resident, nesting at Leighton Moss with smaller numbers elsewhere around Morecambe Bay and in the south-west, and a numerous winter visitor to estuaries and mosslands, though scarce in east Lancashire. There were, however, relatively few references to Shoveler in the county bird reports of the 1960s and early 1970s, giving a probably false impression of low wintering numbers, although a total of 540 at Leighton Moss in September 1971, described as 'exceptional', is in fact higher than any published count anywhere in the county before or since. During the 1950s and early 1960s peaks of up to 400 or 500 were recorded on Morecambe Bay in winter at the Keer mouth, off Hest Bank and occasionally as far south as Morecambe Stone Jetty, these being linked to Leighton Moss birds. This offshore flock decreased rapidly from 1963.

The first comprehensive account in the county report was published in 1978, when peak counts of 24 in February and 66 in December were reported at Marton Mere, 65 in February and 170 in November at Leighton Moss, and 21 at Martin Mere in February with 144 there in October. The presence of a single pair at Marshside in March was considered noteworthy, and two pairs at Whitemoor Reservoir, Colne in December was the only report from an inland site.

Male Shoveler, Seaforth Nature Reserve, November 2003. (Steve Young)

Numbers of wintering and passage Shoveler increased steadily, if unspectacularly, throughout the 1980s. In 1983 Marshside recorded 136 in January, up to 210 were at Leighton Moss in September-October, 87 at Marton Mere in February and 40 at Martin Mere around the same time. Smaller counts were recorded at several other lowland sites, mainly on the Fylde, including Blackpool's Stanley Park, and there were low single figures at Whitemoor, Coldwell and Roddlesworth Reservoirs in spring or autumn. By the early 1990s numbers at the main locations had largely stabilised; peak counts in 1990 included 50 at Marton Mere in March, 140 at Leighton Moss in September, 226 at Martin Mere in October and 123 at Marshside in December.

Wintering numbers remained fairly stable at Martin Mere, Marton Mere/Stanley Park and Leighton Moss/Eric Morecambe complex between 1990 and 2003, with peaks of up to 166 recorded at Martin Mere, an average peak of 120 at the Blackpool sites with an exceptional 413 in 1995, and an average of around 150 at Leighton Moss/Eric Morecambe complex with a maximum of 260 in 2001. Marshside is the only major site where numbers have significantly increased, from 100-120 in the early 1990s to more than 200 this century, with a peak of 393 in 2000.

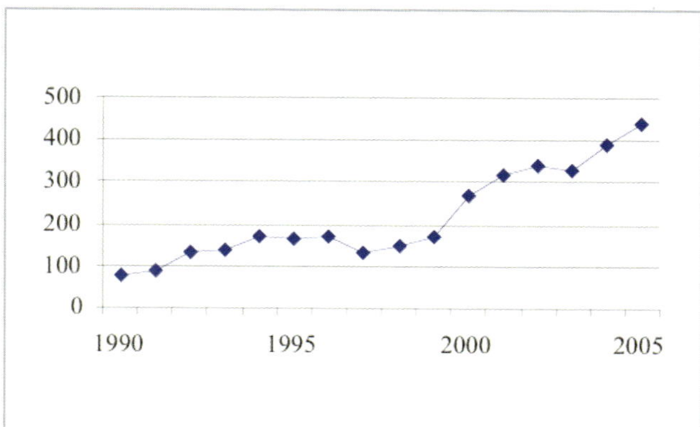

Figure 1. Peak winter counts (three-year rolling means) of Shoveler (WeBS) on the Ribble & Alt Estuaries and Morecambe Bay South (1987/88 to 2004/05).

There are rather consistent geographical variations with regard to the timing of peaks: Leighton Moss tends to record its highest totals early, usually in September, Martin Mere a little later, in October, Marton Mere in November, and Marshside in December; a sequence of movements from north-east to south-west might be a simple explanation for this, although WeBS peaks on Morecambe Bay South and on the Ribble, which include two of the above locations, show no discernible pattern. Another, perhaps more plausible, interpretation is that many of the birds between August and early October are passage migrants.

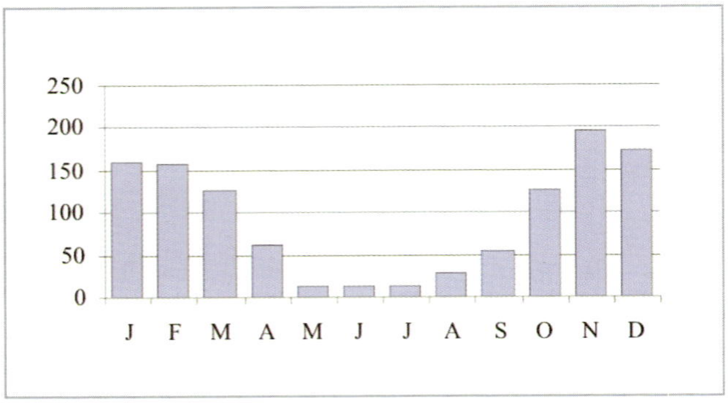

Figure 2. Average monthly peak counts of Shoveler (WeBS) on the Ribble & Alt Estuaries and Morecambe Bay South (1990-2005)

Inland occurrences, both in winter and during passage periods, have generally increased over recent decades, with Foulridge, Whitemoor, Stocks and Dean Clough Reservoirs featuring most prominently, but numbers of Shoveler present at any site rarely exceed single figures.

As in Oakes's day, Leighton Moss and adjacent marshes remain the core breeding location. Numbers there have generally increased over recent decades, from ten pairs in 1964 to about 15 annually between 1967 and 1978, up to 18 by 1980, 15 again for most of that decade, and 20 pairs between 1989 and 1992. Since then, however, the population has declined, to 15 pairs once again in 1996-97, 14 in 2001, nine in 2002, ten in 2003 and 16 in 2004 and 2005. A second major breeding nucleus has become established in the meantime at Marshside; successful nesting by one or two pairs took place in 1983 and up to three pairs bred intermittently until 1995, but subsequent habitat improvements have increased the annual total to around six successful pairs in the late 1990s, nine in 2002 and eleven in 2003, dropping to four in 2005. Fairly frequent nesting by up to three pairs has also been recorded since the late 1970s at Marton Mere (until 1985), Newton Marsh, Freckleton Naze and Martin Mere, while single pairs bred at Mere Sands Wood in 1989 and 1999 and on Aldcliffe Marsh in 2004 and 2005. The 1997-2000 survey estimated a total county population of 35 pairs.

In addition to nesting birds small numbers of Shoveler regularly summer at Martin Mere, Mere Sands Wood and around Morecambe Bay, as well as occasionally on the inner Ribble Estuary, and a pair was present at Stocks Reservoir during the 1998 summer. Given the species' rather restrictive habitat requirements, however, a significant expansion of nesting beyond the established sites seems unlikely unless appropriate habitat management is undertaken.

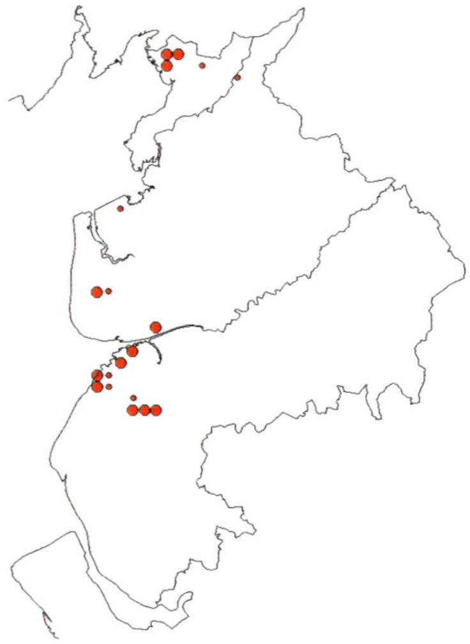

Breeding distribution of Shoveler, 1997-2000. (Large dots: confirmed. Small dots: possible)

There have been two recoveries of Lancashire-ringed birds, a pullus ringed in south-west Lancashire in May 1917 and recovered in the Netherlands in January 1920, and a juvenile male ringed at Martin Mere in July 1986 and shot in western France in February 1989. Only one British-ringed bird has turned up here, a juvenile female ringed at Borough Fen Decoy, Peterborough on 4 March 1990 and shot on Longton Marsh on 6 September, but there have been three recoveries here of foreign-ringed Shoveler, all in the early 1960s – two ringed in North Brabant, Netherlands in the summer of 1960 and shot in the Leighton Moss area in September 1960 and October 1963, and a pullus ringed in Sweden in June 1962 and shot at Hesketh Bank that November.

BM.

This species account was sponsored by the Friends of Marton Mere.

RED-CRESTED POCHARD

Netta rufina

Lancashire Category DE.

If the status of the Ruddy Shelduck in Lancashire is ambiguous, then that of the Red-crested Pochard must be considered downright dubious; our Ruddy Shelducks have at least had the grace to refrain from soliciting food from observers or holding up traffic by walking along a roadway, behaviours manifested by at least two Red-crested Pochards in recent years. On the other hand, there is a substantial wild population of Red-crested Pochards of some 8,000 pairs in Spain, and smaller concentrations in southern France and Germany, a great deal closer to our shores than any equivalent breeding area of the Ruddy Shelduck.

The species is, however, inexpensive and breeds readily in captivity; the ducklings are reputed to be difficult to catch and hence, difficult to pinion (New Atlas), so the probability of escape is high, particularly in Britain, where the species is kept in at least 200 wildfowl collections. Since the 1960s small but well-established breeding populations have developed at the Cotswold

Water Park, on the Gloucestershire-Wiltshire border, and in some London parks (New Atlas).

The first record for Lancashire, a male, was found by John Wilson and others at Leighton Moss on 5 June 1965; it was seen again on 10 August. There were about eight further records of single birds up to 1983, all in the north-west, including a male that wintered at Scorton in 1973-74. The first occurrence south of the Ribble was of a female at Mere Sands Wood in December 1984, described as 'wary' and 'not having originated from nearby Martin Mere'. The rate and geographical spread of records increased in subsequent years. In 1987 there was a male at Seaforth on 8-10 January, apparently during a nationwide influx of at least 15 birds; also in that year the first of several approachable, and often long-staying visitors to east Lancashire turned up at Upper Foulridge Reservoir on 6 December. From 1992, when a female was on Lowerhouse Lodges in February, the Burnley area became the centre of a succession of visitations by both males and females, many of long duration, which continued to at least 2004. Birds were recorded at Rowley Lake in 1994, 1999 and 2000, at Thompson Park Lake in 1995, on the River Calder at Hagg Road in 1996, on Towneley Park Lake in 2001, and again at Lowerhouse Lodges for prolonged periods in 2000. At the last site a tame drake apparently mated with a Mallard in 2001, producing a single hybrid offspring which was also subsequently seen at Gawthorpe, Padiham.

Meanwhile sporadic records of Red-crested Pochards have continued elsewhere, particularly in the Leighton Moss area in 1994, 1995, 2000 and 2002, and on the Upper Lune at Greta Foot in 1998, 2000 and 2002. Records of more than a single bird have been very few; a male, a female and an immature wandered between Preesall Flashes and Marton Mere in August-September 1985, there were two females at Marton Mere in August 1994 and five juveniles at Leighton Moss in August-September 2002. The concentration of these multiple sightings in early autumn is interesting, given that our singletons seem to have occurred randomly, but there remains no real evidence that the species has ever occurred in a wild state in Lancashire.

BM.

POCHARD

Aythya ferina

Lancashire Category A.

Scarce breeder; common winter visitor from central and eastern Europe and Russia.

Pochard breed across the temperate Western Palaearctic and are migratory over most of their range. The breeding populations of Fennoscandia, the Baltic States, Poland and Russia east to the Urals winter in north-west and south-west Europe, while those of western Europe are resident or only partially migratory. An estimated 350,000 Pochard winter in north-west Europe, 59,500 of these in Britain. The breeding population here is of relatively recent origin; nesting was first recorded in Norfolk in 1815 and the 400 or so pairs in Britain are concentrated in east and south-east England.

Mitchell described the Pochard as a winter visitor to Lancashire, not uncommon, though rarer inland; he mentioned no instance of breeding. Oakes considered it to be common in winter, particularly on inland waters in the south and south-east, such as the Anglezarke-Rivington Reservoirs and Eccleston Mere, St. Helens. It was an occasional nester at Leighton Moss, following the first breeding record in 1941. Autumn arrivals commenced in mid-September and peak numbers were attained by November; spring flocks were sometimes large.

Nowadays the species is a fairly numerous winter visitor to many lakes, meres and reservoirs throughout Lancashire; numbers are usually highest on lowland waters, but many inland reservoirs host smaller flocks, and only in Rossendale may the species be considered scarce. Few are found on saltwater in normal winters and only during severe and prolonged spells of freezing weather will appreciable numbers take to the sea.

The Winter Atlas (1986) noted that Pochard numbers in Britain had increased from fewer than 17,000 in the mid-1960s to around 35,000 in the late 1970s and 50,000 by the mid-1980s. This was hardly reflected at all in counts from the main sites in Lancashire. The absence of data from several locations during the period makes comparisons inexact, but peaks at Marton Mere averaged 106 in 1975-79 (maximum 253 in 1978), 116 in 1980-84 and 124 in 1985-89; equivalent figures from Martin Mere were 105, 109 and 128, and for Seaforth 173, 184 and 171. There was a very marginal increase at Stocks Reservoir from 112 during 1980-84 to 119 in 1985-89, while equivalent peaks at Foulridge Reservoir, Colne fell from 53 to 28.

During the 1990s, following deepening of the main mere and provision of grain, the wintering population at Martin Mere increased quite suddenly and dramatically from average annual peaks of around 150 during the 1980s to 492 in February 1992 and a record 1,158 in February 1997, after which peak counts remained in the 750-950 range until dropping to just 583 in 2004 and 475 in 2005 (Figure 1). Numbers at nearby Mere Sands Wood and Nucks Wood have also grown significantly and it seems that these sites serve as refuges for Pochard when disturbed by work at the Wildfowl and Wetlands Trust reserve.

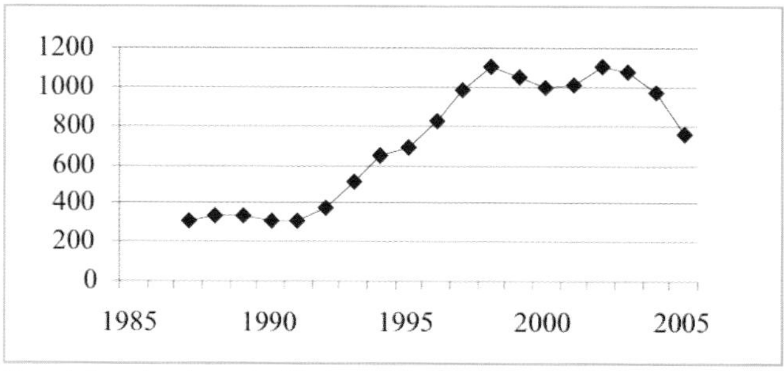

Figure 1. Annual peak counts of Pochard at Martin Mere and Seaforth combined (3-year rolling means), 1985-2005

The north Lancashire population, which moves between various waters in the Dockacres complex and Leighton Moss, depending on disturbance, grew to artificially high numbers during the late 1980s and early 1990s, reaching 460 on Dockacres in November 1992 and peaking at 615 at Leighton Moss in October 1995. This was due to a large-scale programme of grain provision by the shooting syndicate operating at what is now referred to as 'Borwick Waters'. Numbers have declined dramatically there since the mid-1990s.

Male and female Pochard, Seaforth Nature Reserve, February 2004. (Steve Young)

Other large recent counts include 319 at Seaforth in January 2002, but annual peaks of 150 or so are more normal there. Other coastal or near-coastal waters occasionally holding a hundred or more include the marine lakes at Fairhaven and Southport and Thornton ICI reservoir.

Significant numbers have also been found consistently on the West Pennine reservoirs and other waters in the south and centre of the county. Peaks include 375 on Prescot Reservoir in October 1974 and 220 in October 1995, 172 on Anglezarke Reservoir in March 1978, 300 on Wayoh Reservoir in January 1985 and 113 there in January 1995, and 145 on Upper Rivington in January 2003. Notable counts in the Ribble Valley include 145 at Alston Reservoir in February 1996 and 6 at Brockholes Quarry in October 2005.

The main site in east Lancashire is Stocks Reservoir, which regularly supported 150-200 during the 1980s including a record 249 in January 1985, falling to 100-150 since the 1990s. Apart from Stocks, only the Foulridge/Whitemoor Reservoir system has produced appreciable counts, including 105 in March 1964, 172 in February 1980 and 106 in March 1996.

The Lancashire breeding population has expanded steadily since the first records at Leighton Moss in 1941 and 1947. Leighton Moss and the adjacent Eric Morecambe complex remain the core breeding area, with successful nesting virtually annual since the mid-1960s. This population has increased slowly but steadily, with up to ten pairs nesting annually during the 1970s (although five was more typical), an average of six pairs in the 1980s, eight in the 1990s (with twelve in 1997), and eight or nine pairs since 2000.

Since the late 1970s the breeding range has expanded to a further two areas. One pair nested at Marton Mere in 1976 and 1978 but breeding failed to become established there. A small population was founded at Martin Mere in 1987 and up to three pairs have bred there in most subsequent years. Breeding first took place at nearby Mere Sands Wood in 1989 and it too has held up to three pairs almost continuously since. Nucks Wood in Holmeswood, just a few kilometres away from these two sites, has also supported one or possibly two pairs since at least 2002; a pair bred at Whittington Hall Lake in the Lune Valley in 2005. Up to 20 non-breeding birds now summer annually at the main sites, so continuing modest growth in the population seems likely.

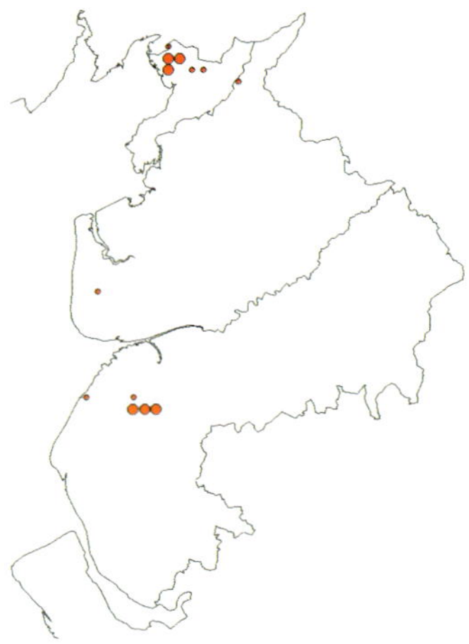

Breeding distribution of Pochard, 1997-2000. (Large dots: confirmed. Small dots: possible)

There have been 21 recoveries of Pochard ringed in Lancashire, all at Martin Mere: five within the county, three in Ireland, six in Russia, two each in Germany, Denmark and Poland, and one in France. Nine birds ringed in East Anglia or the south Midlands have been recovered here, and a male, age unknown, ringed at Lake Engures in Latvia in May 1987 was shot at Preesall in January 1993. The Irish and western European recoveries probably indicate alternative wintering sites, those in central Europe and Denmark birds on passage, and those in Russia and Latvia breeding birds. The longest distance travelled was by a female ringed at Martin Mere on 5 February 1997 and shot at Lake Zakharovo in Russia's Kurgan region, 4490km to the east, around 16 September.

BM.

This species account was sponsored by Fiona Whitfield.

RING-NECKED DUCK

Aythya collaris

Lancashire Category A. (0, 18).

Rare winter visitor from North America.

The earliest record was a male seen in the company of a pair of Tufted Ducks in Knowsley Park on 14 May 1957 by Chris Felton. Since then there have been at least 17 records, all of adult males with the exception of a female at Dockacres and Leighton Moss from 26 October 1990 to 26 May 1991. However, perhaps as few as six individuals have been involved, with two regularly returning birds accounting for the overwhelming majority of records.

Male Ring-necked Duck, Rivington Reservoir, February 1993. (Steve Young)

The most notable of these was the first to be fully documented and reviewed by the BBRC. It was found at Stocks Reservoir on 17 February 1985 and did the circuit of east Lancashire reservoirs and lakes, including Dean Clough, Foulridge, Rowley Lake, Clowbridge, Holden Wood, Wayoh and Short Clough, each winter until last seen at Wayoh Reservoir on 19 August 1995. It was sometimes absent for only a few weeks in summer.

A different male was found at Scorton on 21 May 1994 and what was assumed to be the same bird was at Martin Mere on 1 to 3 June that year. The final record was again in the east at Rivington Reservoir from 3 January to 28 February 2003 and from 8 December 2003 into 2004. This bird was paired with a Pochard and the two spent the summer of 2003 in East Yorkshire.

All records:

1957	Knowsley Park, male, 14 May
1985	Stocks Reservoir, male, 17 February, also other eastern sites to 31 August
1986	Dean Clough Reservoir, male, 11 February, also other eastern sites to 19 April
1986	Stocks Reservoir, male, 18 November to 23 December
1989	Stocks Reservoir, male, 10 January, also other eastern sites to 30 July
1989	Dockacres and Leighton Moss, male, 20 September to 5 November.
1989	Stocks Reservoir, male, 25 September, also other eastern sites to 18 March 1990
1990	Clowbridge Reservoir, male, 17 September, also other eastern sites to 24 January 1991
1990	Dockacres, female, 26 October, also Pine Lake & Leighton Moss to 26 May 1991
1991	Wayoh Reservoir, male 26 November, also other eastern sites to 5 May 1992
1992	Short Clough Reservoir, male, 19 October, also other eastern sites to 19 April 1993
1993	Holden Wood Reservoir, male, 12 September, also other eastern sites to 28 May 1994
1994	Scorton, male, 21 May
1994	Martin Mere, male, 1 to 3 June, presumed same as Scorton
1994	Wayoh Reservoir, male, 15 August, also other eastern sites to 19 August 1995
2003	Rivington Reservoir, male, 3 January to 28 February
2003	Rivington Reservoir, male, 8 December to 5 January 2004

SJW, MJ.

This species account was sponsored by Neil Southworth.

FERRUGINOUS DUCK

Aythya nyroca

Lancashire Category AE. (0, 19).

Rare winter visitor from eastern Europe.

The first record, a male found by Lawrence Eccles and Harry Shorrock on a large flash on the site of the present Heysham Power Station on 17-24 January 1960, was quickly followed by probably the same male together with a female at the same site on 3-22 December 1960. What may have been the male of this pair was again at Heysham on 10 December 1961.

Male Ferruginous Duck, Mere Sands Wood, January 2004. (Chris Galvin)

After a long interval, an eclipse bird arrived at Leighton Moss on 30 August to 1 September 1975 and again on 22 September. A short series of one-day-only males followed further south, at Freckleton on 17 November 1977 and at Seaforth on 15 October 1981 and 24 February 1986.

A female moved between Dockacres and Leighton Moss between 17 October and 31 December 1991, and this or another female was at the same two sites on 25-28 October 1995 and on the Lune at Skerton Weir, Lancaster on 21-26 April 1996, before moving to Leighton Moss on the 28th and remaining there until 1 May.

The next was a male which spent two winters in the Fairhaven/Marton Mere area. It was found at Marton Mere on 14 November 2000 but spent most of the winter - until 18 March 2001 - at Fairhaven Lake. The following winter it was first located at Leighton Moss on 18 September 2001 where it stayed until 19 October before moving to Fairhaven the next day, again spending some time at Marton Mere. This individual was last seen on 8 March 2002. The most recent accepted records were a female at Martin Mere and Mere Sands Wood during the winters of 2002/03 and 2003/04 and a juvenile at Brockholes Quarry on 12-17 September 2004.

There have been several reported occurrences at Leighton Moss in recent years but none has been submitted to the BBRC, which resumed responsibility for assessing records in 1999.

A conservative interpretation of the records, taking into account the likelihood that many have involved returning birds, is that as few as ten individuals may have been seen in Lancashire. Their origins, as with most rare wildfowl, remain a matter for debate, but the occurrence of a coloured-ringed, escaped female on the Dockacres complex in September 2006 confirmed that not all have been wild.

All records:

1960	Heysham, male, 17 to 24 January
1960	Heysham, male and female, 3 to 22 December
1961	Heysham, male, 10 December
1962	Delph Reservoir, female/immature, 14 October, previously Doffcocker Bolton
1975	Leighton Moss, one in eclipse, 30 August to 22 September
1977	Freckleton, male, 17 November
1981	Seaforth, male, 15 to 17 October
1986	Seaforth, male, 24 February
1987	Seaforth, male, 22 January
1991	Dockacres, female, 17 October to 31 December, also Leighton Moss
1995	Leighton Moss, female 25 to 28 October, also Dockacres
1996	Skerton Weir Lancaster, female 21 to 26 April
1996	Leighton Moss, female 28 April to 1 May, same as Lancaster
2000	Marton Mere Blackpool, male 14 to 25 November
2000	Fairhaven, male, 27 November to 18 March 2001, same as Blackpool
2001	Leighton Moss, male, 18 September to 19 October, presumed same as Fairhaven
2001	Fairhaven Lake, returning male, 20 October to 8 March 2002
2002	Martin Mere, female, 13 October to 15 March 2003
2003	Martin Mere, returning female, 20 November to 19 March 2004, also seen at Mere Sands Wood
2004	Brockholes Quarry, juvenile, 12 to 17 September

SJW, MJ.

This species account was sponsored by Joan Watson.

TUFTED DUCK

Aythya fuligula

Lancashire Category A.

Uncommon breeder; common winter visitor Fennoscandia and northern Russia.

Mitchell described the Tufted Duck as uncommon and seen mainly on rivers and inland waters; a pair at Woodfold Park, Blackburn in 1884 was the first breeding record for Lancashire and nesting took place there again in 1891 and 1892. Oakes considered the species to be a scarce and local breeding bird; nesting was recorded near Lancaster in 1922, at Leighton Moss in 1942 and occasionally on the south-west mosslands after 1940. Autumn immigration was noted from mid-October with peak flocks recorded between January and March; numbers in those days appear to have been much lower than at present, however, as these peaks on Wrightington Lakes near Parbold, Rivington Reservoir, Knowsley Park Lake and Eccleston Mere, St Helens seldom exceeded 20 birds. Oakes stated that some Tufted Ducks moved to the coast in hard weather, with 'hundreds' reported on the Ribble Estuary at such times.

Breeding, passage and wintering numbers increased significantly from the 1950s to the 1970s; a flock of 122 was on the Knowsley Park lakes in January 1957 and Spencer (1973) estimated that about 20 pairs bred in Lancashire, although some of these may have been outside our present-day boundaries. The subsequent growth in the breeding population has been steady rather than spectacular; breeding was confirmed in 13 10-km squares during 1968-72, in 16 squares during 1988-91 and in 25 during 1997-2000, when the population was estimated at 125 pairs. These are heavily concentrated in the west, with breeding nuclei around Leighton Moss, Scorton, Marton Mere/Stanley Park, Fairhaven, Mere Sands Wood, Martin Mere and on lakes and reservoirs in Knowsley and St. Helens. There are significant inland outposts at Belmont Reservoir and in the Lune Valley and breeding occasionally takes place at a number of reservoirs in east Lancashire and Rossendale.

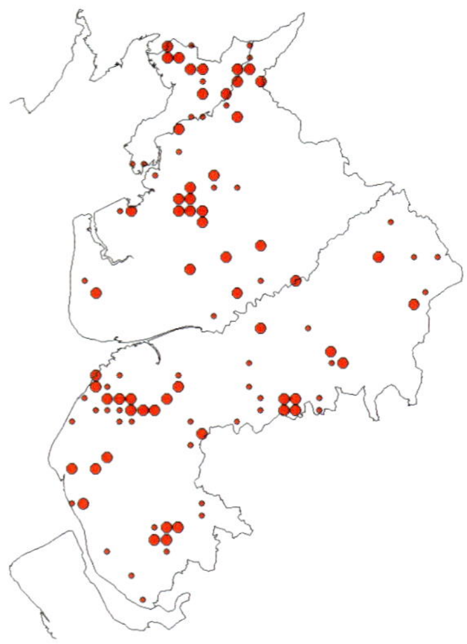

Breeding distribution of Tufted Duck, 1997-2000. (Large dots: confirmed. Small dots: possible)

Outside the breeding season Tufted Ducks tend to concentrate on a relatively small number of waters, again predominantly in the west of the county. The picture is very complex, however, as birds move to-and-fro between adjacent sites, and the different waters also vary in the timing of maximum numbers; some peak in late summer with an influx of moulting birds, others during the main immigration period between late September and November, and yet others in mid- or late winter. Overall, moulting and wintering numbers appear to have increased since the 1970s in line with the national trend but not dramatically, and there have also been periodic local declines.

Relatively few counts of Tufted Ducks in Lancashire exceed 200 birds and there is a slight tendency for the largest flocks to be recorded during late autumn. There were 207 on Prescot Reservoirs in November 1977, 235 there in late October 1982 and 350 in late

September 1995. Two hundred were on the Dockacres complex in November 1992 and there were 215 at Mere Sands Wood in November 1995 and 230 in late September 2002, and 209 at Marton Mere in October 2001. Some substantial flocks, presumably made up of continental moult migrants as well as Lancashire and other British breeders and their offspring, have been recorded in late summer and early autumn; these were particularly evident on Marton Mere in the 1990s, with up to 175 present in August 1993 and July 1994, and more recently at Prescot Reservoirs where over 250 were counted in July and August 2002.

Passage numbers at inland sites are consistently much lower than in the coastal west, but small parties of Tufted Ducks are nevertheless widespread on reservoirs in east Lancashire and on the West Pennine Moors; the species is scarce in Rossendale. The Foulridge-Whitemoor Reservoir complex near Colne has long been the premier resort in east Lancashire: there were 47 at Whitemoor in August 1981, 30 at Foulridge in September 1993, 36 there in July-August 1994 and 24 in August 2001. On the West Pennine Moors, Wayoh Reservoir has regularly attracted large flocks, including 50 in October-November 1985 and 39 in October 1989; there were 109 on Dingle Reservoir, near Belmont in November 1990 and 55 on Upper Rivington in November 2002.

Tony Disley

During the December-March period Tufted Ducks are still to be found in numbers on those waters that feature most prominently in the autumn dispersal/moult period, but there is a subtle difference in distribution, with many of the highest counts in recent decades coming from Leighton Moss and the nearby Dockacres complex and from waters around the Ribble Estuary, in particular Martin Mere, Fairhaven and Southport Marine Lakes, the diminutive Sands Lake at Ainsdale and Seaforth. Two-hundred-and-eight at Martin Mere in February 1996, 252 at Sands Lake in December 1997 with 210 there in December 2005, and 240 at Leighton Moss in December 1999 are the highest winter counts recorded since 1990. Flocks on inland waters are occasionally larger in winter than at other seasons; there were 60 at Wayoh Reservoir in January 1979, 200 there in January 1985 and 44 in December 1990, and winter flocks of twenty-plus have been recorded at Parsonage, Foulridge, Dean Clough and Lee Green Reservoirs in east Lancashire on several occasions since 1990.

The only recent evidence of Tufted Ducks taking to the sea or estuaries in hard weather, as described by Oakes, came in January and February 1963 when 100 were off Morecambe and 17 off Rossall, in January 1982 when widespread small parties were reported, and in February 1991 when 68 were off Formby Point. A few birds are regularly recorded flying past seawatching stations in spring and autumn.

There have been three recoveries of ringed Tufted Ducks in Lancashire: a male, age unknown, ringed at Deeping Lake, Lincolnshire on 22 February 1959 was shot at Burscough on 10 October of the same year, a female, also unaged, ringed at Rostherne Mere, Cheshire on 22 December 1980 was found dead near Ribchester on 11 September 1983, and a juvenile female ringed in Dublin Zoo in August 2003 found at Poulton-le-Fylde on 15 October the same year. Most wintering Tufted Ducks in Britain are from Fennoscandia, the Baltic States and Russia and moult migration birds are also likely to originate in the same area.

BM.

This species account was sponsored by Frank Walsh.

SCAUP

Aythya marila

Lancashire Category A.

Fairly common winter visitor from Fennoscandia and northern Russia.

The status of Scaup appears to have changed very little over the past 150 years. Mitchell described it as 'regular winter visitor' in the nineteenth century, 'occasionally as early as September but usually from October and November'. Its main haunt was in Morecambe Bay where Mitchell described it as 'sometimes plentiful', noting that large quantities were taken with nets in the Arnside and Silverdale area. He considered it rare inland but knew of several that had been shot at Haslingden. Wrigley (1892) described Scaup as common off Formby where they were also regularly taken in dowker nets along with Common Scoter.

Oakes broadly confirmed this picture, viewing Scaup as a 'common winter visitor and passage migrant offshore' and 'scarce inland' during the first half of the twentieth century. However, their distribution appeared to have shifted southward from Morecambe to Liverpool Bay, with rarely more than 50 seen anywhere north of the River Wyre. Although fairly numerous on the northern coasts of Liverpool Bay, the main haunt was between Formby and Crosby where flocks in excess of 300 birds were not unusual.

Coastal numbers appear to have fallen during the 1950s and 1960s (Spencer 1973), a decade or so before a significant national decline was noted. Strangely, there were very few published records of any significance from the Sefton Coast during this period, the two largest flocks both occurring further north: 40 off Morecambe on 10 December 1961 with 100 there during severe weather in January to February 1963, and two separate flocks of around 120 off Rossall Point on 16 January 1963.

Since then annual totals have fluctuated widely but there has probably been little overall change. Up to 50 birds are seen on the coast in an average year, often from a wide variety of sites. Most coastal records are of small groups that remain only for a day or so; some winter flocks linger off Jenny Brown's Point, Morecambe and the Sefton Coast but few do so on the Fylde. Peak counts in Morecambe Bay are generally in the region of 5-15 birds. Recent exceptions have included 20 off Jenny Brown's Point in March 1985 with 29 there on 29 April 2000 and an exceptional 112 on 13 January 2005; up to 32 off Morecambe in winter 1995/96, January to February 2000 and winter 2001/02; and 17 off Rossall Point in early 1986.

Numbers are significantly higher off the Sefton Coast, normally in the range of 20-40 birds but with notable counts of 50 off Formby Point on 19 March 1976 with 58 there on 17 January 1982 and 84 in January 2003, 90 off Birkdale on 2 March 1991 with 40 there in December 1996, and 220 off Southport/Marshside on 8 January 1997 with 45 there in January 2003. However, the largest Lancashire flock in modern times was of 300+ off Blundellsands, Crosby on 21 January 1996.

Female Scaup, Seaforth Nature Reserve, February 2005. (Steve Young)

Scaup are less frequent, more transient and usually less numerous off the south Fylde coast, and numbers have declined significantly there since the 1950s. The only counts of note have been 29 off Blackpool on 26 December 1995 with 65 there in January 2003, and an exceptional 150 off Bispham on 25 January 1997.

Oakes first drew attention to the use of coastal and near-coastal water-bodies, giving an early example of 20 on 16 March 1940 on Southport Marine Lake, where small flocks continue to occur irregularly. The lagoons at Fleetwood, Marton Mere and Fairhaven Lake also attract occasional single figures, but the most frequented site since the 1980s has been Seaforth, which is now the most reliable place in the county to see Scaup, with peak counts of 60 in December 1995 and 73 in January 2002 and January 2005. Seaforth, at least, is used largely as a daytime roost with birds moving away – either to sea or Crosby Marine Lake – to feed at night.

Further inland, records showed a marked increase in the second half of the twentieth century. Spencer (1973) reported 15 records involving 22 birds between 1956 and 1972. More recently, numbers have fluctuated but have averaged around three or four a year. Scaup have been seen on very many inland waters but the most consistent site is Stocks Reservoir, where at least eleven individuals were recorded in 1998 and again in 1999.

Scaup are usually present between late August (very rarely July) and early May but significant numbers are seldom seen before late November and the largest counts are usually made in January and February, often during spells of hard weather which presumably attract birds wintering further north to our milder climate. Two birds have taken up residence and may have bred, but their provenance is highly dubious. The first, a male, was first seen at Dean Clough and Parsonage Reservoirs in 1973 and was present there annually until 1981, although it often disappeared during the summer. Another male was paired with a captive female at Martin Mere throughout 1991 to 1995.

Lancashire is on the southern edge of the main west coast wintering range and the annual variability in Scaup numbers and their probable link with hard weather suggest that many coastal records may be of birds displaced from the main British site in the Solway Firth. The only ringing record is of a bird ringed in Iceland in June 1933 and recovered at Formby in February 1935. This link between Icelandic birds and Britain is well established but wintering birds are also known to originate in Fennoscandia and Russia (Migration Atlas), and it is possible that some inland records during passage periods may relate to these.

SJW.

This species account was sponsored by Ruth Fraser.

LESSER SCAUP

Aythya affinis

Lancashire Category A. (0,2).

Vagrant from North America.

While checking through a large mixed flock of Tufted Duck and Pochard at Dockacres Gravel Pits on 18 December 1994, Bill Aspin and John Wright located an odd-looking first-winter male bird that looked superficially like a Scaup but with a peaked crown. The bird woke briefly, giving a clear view of the bill markings, then obligingly flapped its wings to reveal the crucial upperwing pattern. Identification as a Lesser Scaup seemed the only possibility but it took some time before confusion over a hybrid *Aythya* that had been around for some time could was

Male Lesser Scaup, Myerscough Quarry, October 2005. (Mark Breaks)

resolved – by this time the light was fading and absolute confirmation had to wait for the morning.

On the 19th the bird had resorted to nearby Pine Lake and Pete Marsh managed to get closer views, confirming it as a first-winter male Lesser Scaup. Several hundred birders made the trip to see it but, frustratingly for New Year 'bird-racers' and year-listers, it disappeared on 31 December. However, what was accepted by the BBRC as the same bird reappeared on 5 March 1995 and was seen daily at either Dockacres or Pine Lake until 18 April. This was the ninth record in Britain and Ireland – the first had been recorded in 1987.

The second county record was an adult male at Myerscough Quarry in the Fylde from 6 October to 10 November 2005.

SJW, MJ.
This species account was sponsored by John Wright.

EIDER

Somateria mollissima

Lancashire Category A.

Rare breeder; common winter visitor from Cumbria.

Prior to their colonisation of Walney Island, then in Lancashire but now in Cumbria, in 1949, Eider were rare vagrants. Mitchell linked their occasional occurrence to stormy weather and highlighted just one record – a flock of eleven near Fleetwood in autumn 1882. Oakes added only two records, both on the Alt Estuary, in September 1938 and November 1939.

The Walney colony grew to more than 300 pairs by 1972 but Lancashire records remained scarce throughout the 1970s, averaging fewer than ten birds annually. Most were seen in the Lancashire sector of Morecambe Bay, including a then record count of 18 off Silverdale in September 1974.

Numbers began to grow exponentially from the early 1980s; 1983 saw 30 at Heysham in a gale on 18 January with a further 40 or so records elsewhere during the year, while a total of around 160 the following year included 86 at Heysham on 3 January, again during gale conditions.

The first sizeable count off Rossall Point was made in 1984 but this site has dominated the Lancashire record books ever since, beginning with 360 on 24 April 1985 and followed by a massive 1,800 in December 1989, 2,000 in January 1992 and the county's largest count to date of 2,500 in December 1996. Despite annual fluctuations, numbers seen at Rossall during winter were relatively stable between 1989 and 1997 (Figure 1) but have shown a significant decline since then with 700 in 1998/99 and 684 in 2000/01 the largest peak counts, a mere 52 the most reported in 2002/03, 83 in 2003/04 and 46 in 2004/05. The largest recent counts in this area have been during passage periods: 180 at Rossall on 27 April 2005 and 125 off Knott End on 5 October 2005.

Sizeable flocks have continued to be recorded, usually in windy conditions, further north in Morecambe Bay, including 221 at Heysham on 29 January 1990 and 150 there on 23 December 1991, but here too numbers have declined and 79 off Morecambe in April 1996 with 88 there on 19 December 2005, and 70 off Jenny Brown's Point on 12 May 1997 with an exceptional 970 there on 23 October 2005, are the only counts greater than 50 in the north of the county in recent years. There is little doubt that the same birds are involved in sightings off Rossall Point and Morecambe. Most northern records occur in early autumn and to a lesser extent in spring as birds move through from their wintering grounds off Fleetwood back to Cumbria.

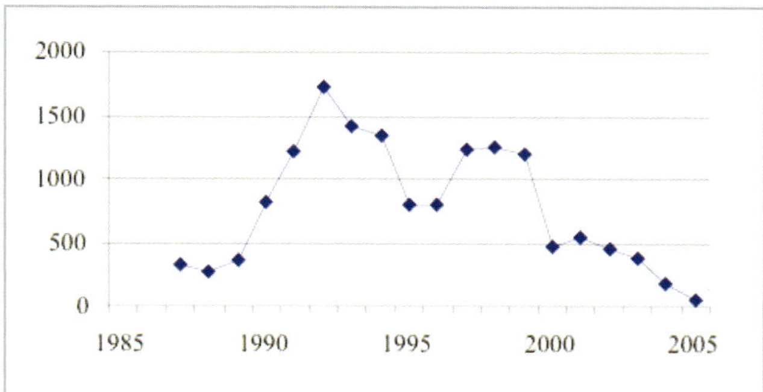

Figure 1. Winter peak counts of Eider (3-year rolling means) off Rossall Point, 1984/85 to 2004/05.

Eider have always been much scarcer everywhere south of Fleetwood although the frequency of records off the southern Fylde coast increased roughly in line with the increase in numbers further north, but most occurrences were of transient birds. The first were two off Blackpool in March 1954, then a tideline corpse at Fairhaven in January 1958, followed by four at St. Anne's in 1960 and annual single-figure counts throughout the 1970s and 1980s, with a notable 96 off Blackpool on 14 March 1991 and 50 off Lytham in March 2004. South of the Ribble, however, there has barely been any change in status since the 1980s. Eider remain less than annual there with eleven south off Ainsdale in October 1982, twelve there in December 1987 and 40 at Formby Point in January 1997 the only flocks of any size.

There is no doubt that the overwhelming majority of the Lancashire coast's wintering Eider originate in Cumbria. Our one ringing recovery of a female ringed at South Walney in 1984 and recovered at Stodday on the Lune in 1992 is hardly conclusive, but British Eider populations, including those in western Scotland, are highly sedentary. It would therefore be surprising if the size of the Lancashire flocks were not closely linked with the species' fortunes in Cumbria. The Walney colony reached a peak of more than 1500 nests in the early 1990s but had declined to 275 by 2002 and 300 in 2004 as a result of increased commercial mussel harvesting, disease and predation.

However, some birds from more migratory populations in Fennoscandia, especially Denmark, and the Baltic are known to visit the east coast of Britain annually, and it is possible that a few may occasionally join the Fleetwood birds. There is no direct evidence for this but the tiny handful of inland records are perhaps more likely to relate to long-distance migrants than to the barely shifting Cumbrian population. The first record in the east of the county was a female at Foulridge Reservoir on 12 January 1964; this was followed by a male and twelve females east over Wood End, Burnley on 24 July 1984, a female which fed on freshwater mussels at Rishton Reservoir on 1-2 November 1993 and three at

Foulridge Reservoir on 3 November the same year. These latter were part of a much larger influx into north-eastern England and the Midlands which had been disoriented by foggy weather and presumably overshot the east coast. The most recent inland bird was a male on Carr Mill Dam, St. Helens on 5 June 2004.

Phil Jones

Small numbers of summering birds began to be noted on the major estuaries from the early 1980s and the first proven breeding attempt was an incubating female on the south Ribble marshes in 1984. It seems likely that a few birds have bred there annually ever since but the only definite records are of one pair in 1993, two or more in 1996, at least three in 1997 and four in 2003. A marked increase at Marshside-Crossens since spring 2003, including eleven males and six females in April 2005, and up to six broods off Lytham in 2003-04, suggest an expanding population. A pair was seen on the Wyre marshes until at least 6 May 1984 but breeding was not thought likely there until 1997 and not proven until 1999. In 2005 one female was seen with young at Glasson and two at Cockersands. Occasional pairs in the Sunderland Point area of the Lune in the 1990s were suggestive of breeding but there is no obviously suitable habitat there and nesting has never been proven; Eider did finally become established as a breeding species in the north of the county when a pair nested successfully on Carnforth Marsh in 2000.

SJW.

This species account was sponsored by Peter Hayes and Pam Lee.

HARLEQUIN DUCK

Histrionicus histrionicus

Lancashire Category D

A male was shot by a Mr. Valender at Crossens during January in either 1916 or 1917, the specimen ultimately residing in Bolton Museum. Oakes regarded the record as genuine but put it in square brackets, believing there was 'a distinct possibility' it was an escape. Spencer likewise regarded the occurrence as 'delicately balanced between 'natural' and 'escape'.' There seems little reason to challenge this view.

SJW

This species account was sponsored by In Focus.

LONG-TAILED DUCK

Clangula hyemalis

Lancashire Category A.

Uncommon winter visitor from northern Europe.

The Lancashire coast is far removed from the Long-tailed Duck's main British wintering grounds off eastern Scotland and the northern isles and it is not surprising that the species has always been uncommon. Its preference for deeper water than most seaducks may also mean that many are missed by shore-based seawatchers.

As with many other seabirds the published record gives an impression of increasing numbers in the final quarter of the twentieth century, but this is most likely to be due to the activities of more and better equipped observers. Both Mitchell and Oakes described Long-tailed Ducks as rare with Oakes dismissing two of Mitchell's three records, leaving one shot at Rishton in 1855 as the first for the county. Oakes himself could add only a further four records within the current county boundaries: one shot at Leighton Moss in November 1934, one seen on Southport Marine Lake in January 1935, two shot at Crossens in October 1941 and one seen off Morecambe in January 1944. A female was at Marton Mere in November 1953 and a male was off Formby in September 1957.

By the end of the 1960s birds were being seen annually, most of them off Morecambe which began to record three or more each winter. However, Spencer, writing in 1972, reported that coastal records outnumbered those inland by only two to one. Long-tailed Ducks have been seen annually in Lancashire since 1963; totals have varied considerably but there is no indication of any consistent trend with records averaging a little over ten a year in each decade since the 1960s (Figure 1). The proportion of coastal records has, however, increased dramatically with about 80% of all birds (1953-2005) seen offshore, 10% on coastal lagoons and 10% further inland.

Above-average influxes have occurred in 1974, 1976, 1989 and 2003 but the largest came in October and November 1991 when approximately 40 were seen along the length of the coast from Morecambe to Formby Point. A further four records involving nine birds in January 1992 completed a record-breaking winter.

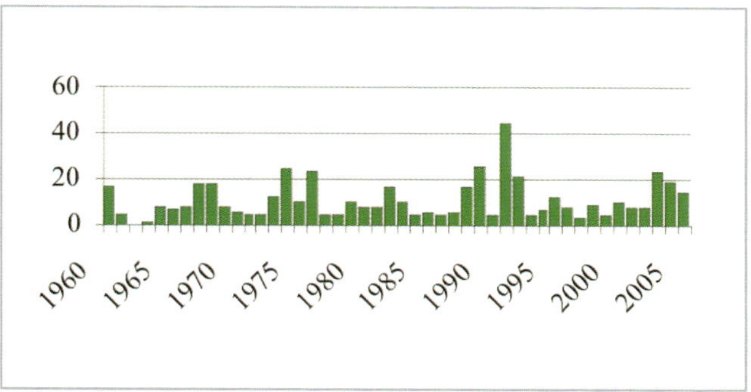

Figure 1. Annual totals of Long-tailed Ducks in Lancashire, 1960-2005

There have been seven summer records between June and September, all involving sub-adult males or 'female/immatures', more than half of which have been on inland waters or coastal lagoons; the longest-staying bird was at Pilling Lane Ends from 16 July to 27 September 1987. The main arrival occurs between mid-October and the end of November (Figure 2) but most late autumn sightings are one-day seawatching records and relatively few birds remain for any length of time; exceptions have included up to seven off Morecambe from 31 October 1959 into 1960 and five there from 8 November 1964 into 1965. Records drop off sharply in December but increase a little in January, partly perhaps due to the 'year-listing effect' but also probably reflecting hard weather movements. These midwinter arrivals appear to stay in the area rather longer than autumn birds, most recently up to eight were off Blackpool from January to March 2004. Perhaps significantly, many of these were amongst flocks of Common Scoter and it is likely that more remain unseen on Shell Flat.

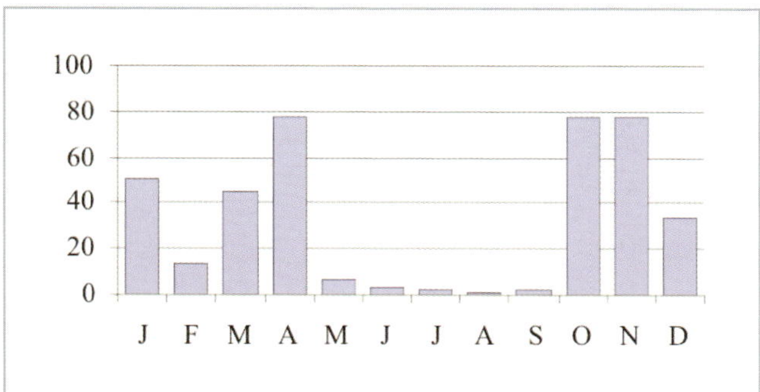

Figure 2. Arrival dates of Long-tailed Ducks in Lancashire, 1957-2005

New arrivals in February are remarkably scarce but a distinct passage movement begins during March and continues into April and occasionally as late as May. The two largest flocks seen in Lancashire have both been in spring: 25-30 off Formby Point on 15-22 April 1974 and 21 off Crosby on 28-29 April 1989.

Coastal occurrences show a marked bias towards the Sefton coast with around 200 reported there, 150 of which were seen from Formby Point. Morecambe is equally predominant in north Lancashire, recording around 90 out of a total of 140 birds; Long-tailed Ducks are distinctly scarce at the northern end of the bay with only four records off Jenny Brown's Point in the last 15 years. The 80 or so records on the Fylde coast have mostly come from Rossall Point but with significant numbers off Blackpool, particularly over the past few years, and a scattering from other seawatching stations.

All the main coastal and near-coastal lagoons in Lancashire – Leighton Moss, Haweswater, the Dockacres complex, the Fleetwood lagoons, Marton Mere, Fairhaven Lake, Marshside, Ainsdale Sands Lake, Southport and Crosby Marine Lakes and Seaforth – have held Long-tailed Ducks over the past two decades, the majority of them female/immatures. In sharp distinction to offshore records, which are overwhelmingly one-day sightings, it is not unusual for birds to linger for considerable periods on these lagoons; examples have included one at Thornton ICI pools from November 1979 to 1 May 1980, up to three at Leighton Moss from November 1980 to 2 May 1981, two at Fleetwood Marine Lake from at least 1 January to 10 May 1992, and one at Seaforth from 16 November to 19 December 1998.

Long-tailed Duck, Crosby Marine Lake, September 2007. (Steve Young)

Long-tailed Ducks have appeared on a total of 25 waterbodies further inland, mostly on the eastern reservoirs and the St. Helens lakes but with two records on rivers – on the Ribble at Balderstone in January 1991 and at Preston in May 2005, and on the Brock at Claughton in October 1991. All have been singles with the exception of two on Rivington Reservoir in October 1960, Sunnyhurst Reservoir in March 1987 and Clowbridge Reservoir in December 1988, and three on Prescot Reservoir November 1983. The timing of inland and coastal arrivals is subtly different. There is little evidence of any significant inland spring passage with just two records in March, and autumn arrivals are four to six weeks later than on the coast. Although the number of records (34) is small this possibly suggests different origins for inland and coastal birds, perhaps with most inland records referring to birds overshooting east coast destinations, a hypothesis supported by the lack of records of adults inland. Without information from ringed birds, however, this has to remain purely speculative.

SJW.

This species account was sponsored by Andrew Cadman.

COMMON SCOTER

Melanitta nigra

Lancashire Category A.

Abundant winter visitor from northern Europe and Russia.

New survey techniques in the opening years of the twenty-first century have completely transformed our knowledge of the distribution and number of Common Scoter in Lancashire's offshore waters – to the extent that the historical record now appears largely redundant. Within the space of three years the best estimate of the Lancashire wintering population had been revised upwards ten-fold.

In the winter of 2001/02 the Countryside Council for Wales began a systematic aerial survey of Liverpool Bay, building on its previous experience in censusing scoter in Carmarthen Bay, which was then believed to be the most important wintering site in Britain. The survey was designed to provide data to inform discussion about proposals to construct several offshore wind farms and was initially intended to be confined to Welsh waters. However, for several years significant numbers of Common Scoter had been sighted by seawatchers in the English sector of the bay – 500 or more off Formby Point and 1,500 or so off Blackpool – both sites where wind farms were proposed.

CCW, with financial backing from the wind farm developers, decided to extend the survey into English waters and flew an exploratory flight off Blackpool on 4 November 2001. The results were explosive: more than 4,000 Common Scoter were found up to 10km off the Fylde coast – and the surveyors felt they had only seen the tip of the iceberg. They were soon to be proven correct. The survey methodology employed involved flying straight line transects and counting the number of scoter in different distance bands in order to estimate numbers in the whole area – it is not feasible to carry out total counts.

The number of birds counted in Lancashire waters during 2001-05 is shown in Table 1. The survey area is divided into three sectors: Shell Flat, the Ribble (roughly Lytham to Southport) and Formby (Southport to the Dee). The overwhelming majority of birds are on Shell Flat with largest counts elsewhere of 1,142 in February 2003 and 1,238 in May 2003 in the Ribble sector, and 3,217 in January 2005 in the Formby sector. By far the largest single count was the 14,002 on Shell Flat in February 2003.

	Jan	Feb	Mar	April	May	Aug	Nov	Dec
2001							4483	
2002	5465	7342	8339	5720		4045	5944	8022
2003	5972	15857			1244			
2004						3485	13344	
2005	12609	9350						

Table 1. Total number of Common Scoter counted in Lancashire sector of Liverpool Bay, November 2001 to March 2005. (Source: Countryside Council for Wales/Wildfowl and Wetlands Trust aerial surveys)

Deriving an accurate picture of the Lancashire winter population from these partial counts is not straightforward but the best estimate is that it lies somewhere between two and three times the peak count (P. Cranswick *pers. comm.*), that is between 31,000 and 47,000 in 2002/03 and 26,000 and 40,000 in 2004/05. Adjusted count data for winter 2004/05 suggested a population in the Shell Flat sector of 28,500 in late autumn (October to November), 31,300 in mid-winter (December) and 26,000 in late winter (February to March) (Anon 2006). On the basis of the Shell Flat counts of 4,045 in August 2002 and 3,485 in August 2004, the late summer moulting population probably consists of some 7,000-10,000 birds.

It is now clear that only a small proportion of the birds offshore – at least on the Fylde coast – regularly come within range of shore-based observers. Nevertheless, concerted seawatching has produced some very large counts in recent years. Landmark counts from Blackpool have been 1,824 in January 1998, 3,146 in September 1999, 3,250 in November 2002, 5,000 in December 2003 and estimates of 10,000 on 27 November 2004 and 15,000 on 8 December 2005; and from Formby Point 811 in January 1998, 1,800 in December 2001, 1,818 in December 2002, 1,229 in November 2004 and an estimated 3,000 in April 2005. Numbers elsewhere are inconsequential. Few are seen from the Sefton coast south of Formby Point, confirming the very low numbers picked up by the aerial survey over the Burbo Bank. There have been just four counts of over 100 in north Lancashire since 1989, the largest 236 in April 2003 – all have been during passage periods and were perhaps birds moving to and from Shell Flat.

Given the difficulties of assessing the numbers of this most marine of our seaducks it is not surprising that the record prior to the late 1990s is patchy; nevertheless, comparisons of shore-based counts suggest that there has been very little change in the status or distribution for at least 100 years. Mitchell referred to the Common Scoter as our 'most abundant coastal duck (occurring) sometimes in flocks of many thousands in Morecambe Bay' and off the Ribble. Wrigley (1892) described an 'immense flock' seen on a boat trip 'which extended from Birkdale . . . to the entrance of the Mersey'. Oakes concurred, saying that the largest numbers were seen 'between the Ribble Estuary and Liverpool'; the largest counts he published were both off Formby Point, 1,200+ on 1 August 1940 and 800-1,000 on 31 October 1942.

The Sefton coast continued to dominate the record book for four decades with notable counts of 3,200 off Formby in late August 1967 (Greenhalgh 1975c) and 5,000 off Ainsdale/Formby on 18 September 1973. No three-figure count off Blackpool was published until 1981 but as seawatching became a more effective proposition numbers rose to 500 in 1985, 1,000 in 1988 and 1,800 in 1992. It seems very unlikely that this was due to any real change in distribution but rather reflects the fact that the Fylde birds are usually much further offshore.

Very little can be added to Mitchell's assessment of phenology: '. . . arrival in mid-July. . . main departure April and May . . . but occasional the whole year'. The aerial surveys suggest that numbers are greatest between December and March with a steady decline during April but still more than 1,000 remaining in May. The largest June and July counts in recent years were 230 off Blackpool in 1999 and 440 there in 2003 respectively, but Mitchell noted 1,000 off the mouth of the Ribble on 7 July 1896. The earliest returning flocks are almost entirely composed of adult males and second-year birds which settle in the area to moult; females and first-winters join them later in the autumn

(Kaiser *et al.* 2006). The largest late summer count was 4,045 between Shell Flat and the outer Ribble in August 2002. Shore-based counts usually increase steadily towards a peak in December and drop dramatically in January, probably due to the main flocks moving further offshore into deeper water as food resources become depleted.

Common Scoter appear to be fairly resistant to 'wrecking' except in the most serious of onshore gales and are rarely recorded in any numbers on coastal lagoons. Two major exceptions were noted by Oakes, involving 'thousands' close onshore at Ainsdale in January 1935 with many on the beaches, and after prolonged gales in December 1941 on the Ribble 'with many casualties' and 30 sheltering on Fairhaven Lake on 29 January 1942. He also wrote that 'during heavy weather birds take refuge on mosslands on all parts of the coast', an event that has not been recorded in more recent times. They are, however, extremely susceptible to oil spillages. This was first noted by Oakes and significant casualties have since been recorded in 1957, 1961, 1965 (when 95 were on Fairhaven Lake on 19 January), 1986 and most recently in January 1994, when a ship leaving the Mersey discharged a glue-like substance which brought 700 or more ashore on the Fylde and Sefton coasts.

'Oiled' male Common Scoter, Ainsdale shore, February 1994. (Dave McAleavy)

Occurrences are annual on the inland reservoirs with an average of around ten birds a year since the 1960s but with larger influxes of 35 in 1994 and 31 in 2003. The largest flocks on reservoirs have included nine at Clowbridge in 1957, 16 at Longridge in 1992, 13 at Entwistle in 1994, nine at Rishton in 1997, ten at Stocks in 1998 and 22 at Prescot in 2003. Although occasional birds turn up inland in midwinter and even in summer, the overwhelming majority of records are in early autumn with a smaller peak in spring, suggesting they relate to overland passage migrants.

Only two foreign-ringed birds have ever been recovered in Britain, both of them in Lancashire: a female ringed in July 1946 in Iceland and recovered at Formby in September 1949; and one ringed on the Gulf of Finland in Estonia in October 1962 and recovered at Formby in December 1964 – suggesting widespread origins for our wintering birds.

SJW.

This species account was sponsored by Stephen Dunstan.

SURF SCOTER

Melanitta perspicillata

Lancashire Category A. (1, 1)

Vagrant from North America.

Lancashire's first was shot by R.H. Thompson at Lytham (presumably offshore) sometime during December 1882. The record was published in *the Zoologist* as a female but subsequent examination of the specimen by McPherson confirmed it as a first-winter male.

It was more than a hundred years before the next record. Given the increasing number of birds found amongst Common Scoter flocks wintering in Britain, which led to its removal from the official national list of rarities in 1990, another Surf Scoter was long overdue in the county. Surely, when one did turn up it would be amongst the huge flocks of Common Scoters off the Fylde coast, Ribble Estuary or Formby Point?

Male Surf Scoter, Mere Sands Wood, October 2002. (Tony Disley)

Well, no! The long wait was actually broken at Mere Sands Wood, an inland site that had never previously recorded any species of scoter. An adult male provided close views as it drifted around the reserve's main lake from mid-morning to dusk on 23 October 2002 (A. Ramsey, M. McCormack, A. Douglas). This was only the twelfth inland record in Britain, only two of which were adult males. It was one of three Surf Scoters reported to have arrived in the country that day and appeared during overcast, rainy weather so perhaps had been migrating overland.

SJW.

This species account was sponsored by Stephen Dunstan.

VELVET SCOTER

Melanitta fusca

Lancashire Category A.

Uncommon winter visitor from northern Europe and Russia.

The British wintering population like that of the Long-tailed Duck is centred on northern and eastern Scotland and, as with that species, Lancashire is a peripheral site for Velvet Scoter. However, small numbers are recorded annually almost always in close association with the huge offshore flocks of Common Scoter.

There is little indication that this situation has changed significantly for at least 150 years. Although increasing numbers have been reported over the past 20 years or so, this is almost certainly due to an equivalent increase in the number of seawatchers and improvements in optics (Figure 1).

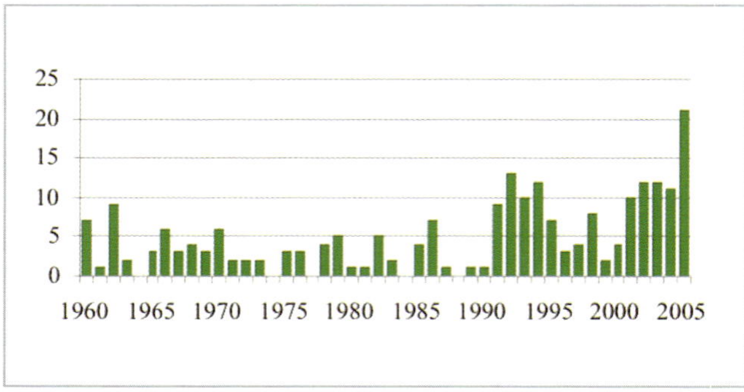

Figure 1. Annual totals of Velvet Scoter in Lancashire, 1960-2005.

Mitchell gave the status of Velvet Scoter as 'infrequent amongst Common Scoter', while Oakes described it as 'fairly frequent but overlooked'. Unsurprisingly, most records prior to the second half of the twentieth century appear to have been of birds found dead or seen or shot close to shore.

Published records averaged just over three birds a year during the 1960s and 1970s, rising to around 4.5 in the 1980s and 1990s. A trebling of the annual reporting rate to almost a dozen in the first six years of this century is largely the result of increased seawatching effort off Blackpool. Around 60% of all sightings are of singles and groups of more than two are infrequent. The largest groups have been four males and four females off Blackpool in February 1992 with eleven males there on 1 March and three males and two females there in late April the same year, four males with two females in January 2005 off Formby Point, five off Rossall Point on 21-22 November 1962, and another five near the Liverpool Bar light on 21 April 1970. Sightings of adult males outnumber those of females and first-winters by 2:1 (n = 144), and, as reported by Spencer (1973), there continues to be some indication that males may arrive on average a month or so earlier than female/immatures.

Female/immature Velvet Scoters, Crosby Marine Park, November 2001. (Steve Young)

Birds have been recorded in every month but are extremely scarce between May and September (Figure 2). Where specified all records but one during July to September have been of adult males, probably associating with the moulting Common Scoter flocks. The latest record of an adult male in spring was on 26 May 1995 at Heysham and the earliest to return on 17 July 1962 at Morecambe. There is a clear peak of sightings during October and November with numbers tailing off during winter before a small rise during March. It is impossible to say whether this indicates that most are passage birds or is simply due to new arrivals moving closer inshore than settled wintering birds and thus being more likely to be picked out by shore-based observers.

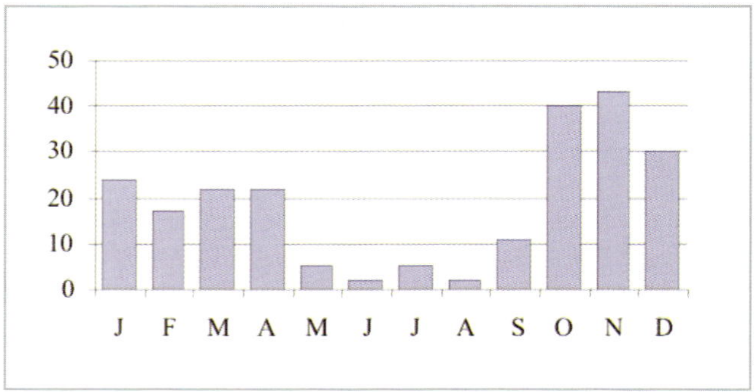

Figure 2. Arrival dates of Velvet Scoter, 1960-2005.

Coastal distribution reflects that of Common Scoter and more than half of all records have been off the Fylde coast, with the remainder split roughly equally between north Lancashire (mainly Morecambe and Heysham) and the Sefton coast (mainly Formby Point).

Very few have ever been recorded away from the sea and most of these have been at coastal locations: a male on the Wyre at Shard Bridge on 12 February 1956, two males at Fairhaven Lake in January 1976, a male at Warton Marsh in December 1978, and four female/immatures on Crosby Marine Lake in November 2001. There have only been two genuinely inland occurrences: three 'probable immatures' on Rivington Reservoir on 12 February 1956 and a first-winter male on the River Ribble near Preston on 21-25 January 1997.

SJW.

This species account was sponsored by Stephen Dunstan.

GOLDENEYE

Bucephala clangula

Lancashire Category AC.

Extinct feral breeder; common winter visitor from Fennoscandia.

One of our most widespread wintering ducks, Goldeneye can be found on almost all inland waters but the largest concentrations occur on the coast, a distribution pattern that appears to have remained largely unchanged for 150 years. Mitchell wrote of 'considerable numbers . . . in the bays and estuaries of the coast' and regular inland records, but he gave no further details for present-day Lancashire. Oakes was more specific, maintaining that offshore flocks seldom exceeded 20-30 birds and that Goldeneye were less numerous than Scaup.

Oakes highlighted Morecambe Bay, particularly the area between Hest Bank and the Lune, as the most important site and this remains the case today, albeit with small changes in locality. Numbers, however, appear to have increased significantly since Oakes's time. Wintering flocks off Morecambe peaked at 139 in 1961 and climbed steadily throughout the decade to reach 215 by

1970. The Morecambe flock – and total numbers in the north of the bay – then declined a little during the 1970s before increasing again to around the 200 mark by the mid-1980s. Winter peaks on WeBS counts have fluctuated since then, but have mostly been in the range of 150-200; some larger counts have been made, including a wholly exceptional 400 in February 1994 and 250 in December 1995. Until recently the largest flocks have concentrated around the rich feeding offered by sewage outfalls; 108 were at the Stodday outfall in February 1978, but the main attraction was the Sandylands outfall in Morecambe until its closure in the mid-1990s. Since then the core range has shifted southward with sites on the south and east of the Lune Estuary now favoured, especially in the Glasson area. Further north, Leighton Moss regularly supports 20-30 birds.

In Oakes's time Goldeneye were regular but never numerous on the coast to the south of Morecambe Bay. Nowadays, relatively few are seen on the Fylde coast and rarely offshore, 25 over the sea at Blackpool in January 2003 and 16 there in January 1987 being exceptional. Marton Mere, the main site, generally reports winter peaks of 20 or so with exceptional counts of 41 in March 2001 and 43 in April 2003. The various lagoons at Fleetwood also regularly hold double-figure flocks, including 43 on the marine lake in 1997 and 30 on the ICI lagoons in 2003.

Apart from Southport Marine Lake, which holds 20-30 in most years and a record 41 during a gale in January 1998, the Sefton coast seldom figured in reports until the creation of the lagoons at Seaforth and Crosby Marine Park in the 1970s. Goldeneye were slow to discover this new site but average winter maxima reached 20 by the mid-1980s and have since increased steadily towards a record 99 in January 2004.

Wild birds have been recorded on the coast in every month of the year but are only present in Lancashire in any numbers for five months, between November and March, with relatively few stragglers during early April and early-returning birds in October. The pattern of records at Morecambe Bay and Seaforth is virtually identical, suggesting there is little or no interchange between these sites (Figure 1). The last to leave in spring are usually first-summers and normally only one or two remain into May. The first arrivals of autumn rarely appear before mid-September and numbers barely increase during October. November and December generally witness a continual build-up but winter peaks rarely occur until January and February, suggesting a move from inland waters rather than inward migration. Certainly, the largest coastal counts are normally made during freezing conditions inland.

First-winter male Goldeneye displaying. (Phillip Tomkinson)

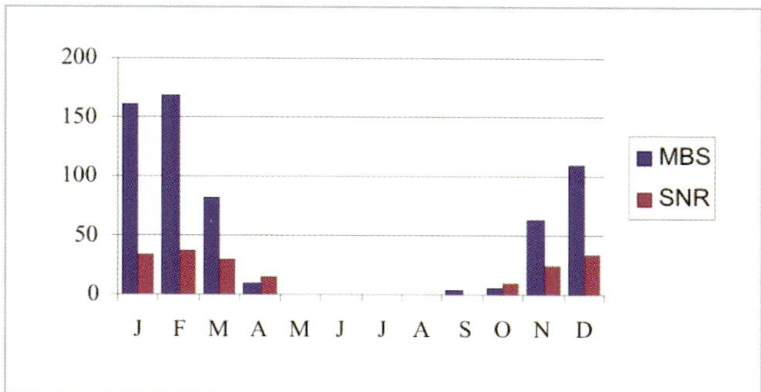

Figure 1. Average monthly peak counts of Goldeneye in Morecambe Bay South and at Seaforth Nature Reserve, 1986-2005.

Small numbers of Goldeneye regularly turn up on almost every inland waterbody, from the park lakes of Liverpool to the largest reservoirs in the east – double-figure counts are more restricted, however. No one inland site has been predominant over the years but several have supported consistently high numbers. The first really large inland count was 97 on Rivington Reservoir in January 1978; 59 were there in December 1991 but recent annual peaks have been in the region of 15-20. Similar numbers were reported from the Longridge reservoirs between at least 1982 and 1997 with a peak count of 62 in February 1993. Noteworthy counts on other still-waters include 37 at Martin Mere in 1996, 41 on Pine Lake in 1999, 41 at Brockholes Quarry in 2002 and 2005, and 40 on Prescot Reservoirs in 2004. Other sites regularly holding double-figures include Stocks, Foulridge, Clowbridge and Belmont Reservoirs.

The Ribble and Lune also support significant numbers. A systematic count of the Ribble located 41 between Preston and Hodder Foot in 2000; other counts include twelve on the Ribble/Darwen confluence in 1996, and 51 at Balderstones in 1985 with 43 there in 1987. The main congregation on the inland Lune is at Skerton Weir in Lancaster, where high counts include 82 in 1988 and 70 in 1994. Further upriver, the largest counts at Arkholme have been 25 in 1987 and 33 in 1992.

The total inland winter population in recent years has probably been in the order of 100 to 150. Together with a coastal population of 200 to 300, the best estimate of the average total is roughly 400 birds, around 1.5% of the British winter population.

Apparently wild birds have summered infrequently, including females at Anglezarke/Rivington in 1975-76 and Whitemoor in 1982 and males at Cockerham in 1995 and Lee Green Reservoir in 2000, but the only possible breeding record was a pair on Delph Reservoir in 1999. Free-flying feral birds at Martin Mere reached a maximum of 40 in the late 1980s and began breeding there 'in the wild' in 1987. They soon colonised nearby Mere Sands Wood, where they were initially encouraged, and up to three pairs bred there in nest-boxes from at least 1988 to 1999, regularly hatching broods but apparently never succeeding in fledging any young. The last remnant of this population were two females at Mere Sands Wood in 2003.

The main European breeding population is in Finland and Sweden and this is thought to be the source of the vast majority of British and Irish wintering birds. There are two ringing records involving Lancashire but only one, a female ringed in Sweden in

May 1976 and recovered on the Ribble at Clitheroe in November 1977, was wild. The other was a (presumably feral) juvenile ringed at Martin Mere on 15 July 1986 and recovered on Lindisfarne, Northumberland on 4 September of the same year.

SJW.

This species account was sponsored by John and Mary Almond.

SMEW

Mergellus albellus

Lancashire Category A.

Uncommon winter visitor from northern Europe and Russia.

The Smew is a relatively short-distance migrant and moves roughly south-west from its breeding grounds in Fennoscandia and north-west Russia into the Baltic and the Dutch North Sea, with the majority of the 350 or so British wintering birds occurring in East Anglia and south-east England. Numbers in western Europe are swelled during hard winters further east and usually peak during December and January.

Oakes accepted only three records: one on the Wyre in January 1886, a pair off Birkdale in January 1928 and a redhead shot at Leighton Moss in December 1931, but Spencer described Smew as almost annual in very small numbers by the end of the 1960s. There have been more than 150 records, mostly of singles, since 1950 although several have involved regularly returning birds. Annual tallies increased from one or two in the 1950s to 1970s to just over four since the 1980s – probably reflecting rising coverage rather than a genuine increase of a species which is undergoing population decline. The largest influxes took place during the winters of 1962/63, with singles at Rivington Reservoir and at Halton on the Lune and seven off Morecambe; 1995/96 when four were in the Leighton Moss/Dockacres area, a different four at Clowbridge Reservoir, two at Prescot Reservoirs and singles at Scorton, Marton Mere, Seaforth, Carr Mill Dam, on the Ribble/Darwen confluence and Dean Clough, Alston and Grimsargh Reservoirs; five at Dockacres in January 2001; and 2001/02 when six were at Martin Mere and singles at Marton Mere, Cockersands and Pine Lake.

There have only been about a dozen records on the sea and, although coastal lagoons – Marton Mere, Fairhaven Lake, Crosby Marine Lake and Seaforth – account for a further 30 or so, the vast majority have been on inland reservoirs and lakes. The main eastern sites other than those mentioned above have been Belmont, Stocks, Foulridge and Lee Green Reservoirs. However, the record book is dominated by occurrences at Leighton Moss and the Dockacres complex, where Smew have been seen almost annually since at least 1990, accounting for more than a third of all Lancashire records. During the period 1990-2003 the 17 or so records of adult males probably related to just two or three returning individuals, and if the same applied to redheads then the county total would be substantially reduced.

Nicola Breaks

Smew are very much late-winter birds in Lancashire with very few seen before mid-November and a clear peak of arrivals during January (Figure 1). Once in the county many remain for several weeks, often into March and occasionally April. The latest were singles at Leighton Moss to 13 May 1970 and Mere Sands Wood to 16 May 1988, and the earliest in autumn on 19 October 1977 at Lee Green Reservoir.

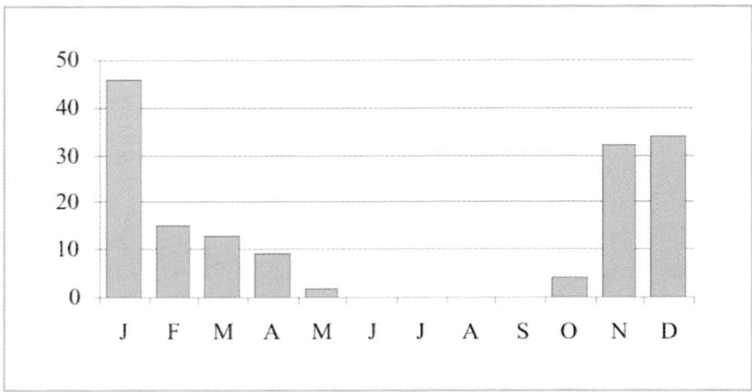

Figure 1. Arrival dates of Smew in Lancashire, 1951-2005.

As in Britain as a whole, adult males are far outnumbered by females and first-winters in Lancashire, with redheads making up more than 70% of all records.

SJW.

This species account was sponsored by June Watt.

RED-BREASTED MERGANSER

Mergus serrator

Lancashire Category A.

Rare breeder; fairly common winter visitor from northern Britain and perhaps Iceland.

The Scottish breeding population increased markedly during the last 20 years of the nineteenth century and the first 20 years of the twentieth, expanding its range southward and first colonising England in 1950 at Ravenglass in Cumbria. Within a few years Red-breasted Mergansers were nesting in Lancashire but, unlike Goosanders which almost certainly colonised later, they have hardly increased since and remain rare breeders. The species has, however, increased dramatically in numbers as a winter visitor over the past half century.

Red-breasted Mergansers seem to have been extremely rare in the county throughout most of the nineteenth century; Mitchell had nothing much to say about the species beyond knowing of a few that had been shot. By the 1950s, Oakes described it as a regular winter visitor in small numbers to Morecambe Bay but scarce and irregular elsewhere; he knew of just one or two records south of the Ribble and none inland in present-day Lancashire.

Breeding was first confirmed at Stocks Reservoir in 1957 and this has remained the most consistent – sometimes perhaps the only – breeding site in Lancashire. Nesting pairs appear to have reached a maximum there of seven between 1978 and 1982 but declined to one to three pairs annually thereafter; many, perhaps most, breeding attempts have been unsuccessful. The Hodder was probably colonised during the early 1960s and one or two pairs have bred at least sporadically ever since; breeding has probably also occurred in the Langden Valley in some recent years. This population is confined to relatively short stretches of the upper Hodder and its tributaries and birds are rarely seen downstream of Dunsop Bridge; it is possible that competition with Goosanders, which breed fairly commonly on the lower reaches of the Hodder and on the Ribble, is one factor in restricting the Merganser population both geographically and in size.

Female Red-breasted Merganser with young, Stocks Reservoir. (Nicola Breaks)

Further north, the first successful breeding was reported at Crook o' Lune in 1974 and one or two pairs probably nested on the Lune until at least 1995 – at Arkholme and Caton and possibly at Skerton Weir in 1991 and Pine Lake in 2000. No reports of breeding on the Ribble have been published in the Lancashire Bird Report since a pair at Ribchester in 1978, but one pair probably bred above Ribchester during the 1997-2000 Atlas survey. The only other nesting attempts have been on the Wyre Estuary in 1978 and 1985, on West Bradford Moor in 1990, and on the Wyre at Marshaw and south of Downham in 2002.

The breeding population was estimated at four pairs in the Lancashire Atlas during 1997-2000 and, although this may be something of an underestimate due to the difficulties of surveying this species, it seems unlikely to be more than six pairs in any one year.

Males generally leave the breeding grounds during June for unknown moulting sites while females mostly depart during September, but sometimes as early as the end of July or as late as mid-October, presumably depending upon the stage of maturity of any young. There is some indication that females and juveniles may head down the main rivers towards the estuaries in late autumn. Few are present in the east of the county or on upland reservoirs between November and January – a pair that wintered at Stocks Reservoir during 2004/05 was unusual – perhaps an average of one a year, although slightly higher numbers can be found closer to the coast on the Dockacres complex. The return to breeding sites, with males almost always arriving in advance of females, sometimes gets underway as early as mid-January but more usually during February and March. Peak counts at Stocks Reservoir almost always occur during April prior to females disappearing to nest and the departure of the males.

Red-breasted Mergansers breeding in Britain are thought to be largely sedentary and it is likely that many if not most of our wintering birds are of Icelandic origin (Migration Atlas), although some visits by Scottish birds cannot be ruled out. Most resort to inshore waters or the outer estuaries of our major rivers, especially the Lune and Wyre. Up to 90% are to be found in Morecambe Bay, a situation that has prevailed since at least the 1960s when the largest flocks were invariably off Morecambe itself, probably attracted by rich feeding opportunities at sewage outfalls. Winter peaks in the region of 200-300 in the early 1960s increased to 390 in November 1966 and 500 in January 1971, which remains the county record. Average peak counts for the bay as a whole fell by almost a half during the late 1970s but remained fairly constant at around 90-100 during the 1980s. A slight upturn at the end of the 1990s, with December counts of 123 in 1997, 112 in 1998 and 101 in 2000, was followed by peaks of just 60-69 during 2001-2003 and 104 in 2005.

Few are seen in Morecambe Bay before September and the main influx occurs in October and November, with numbers usually peaking in December and falling off in the new year (Figure 1); no spring passage peak is discernible from the monthly counts but birds in March and April probably do include some migrants.

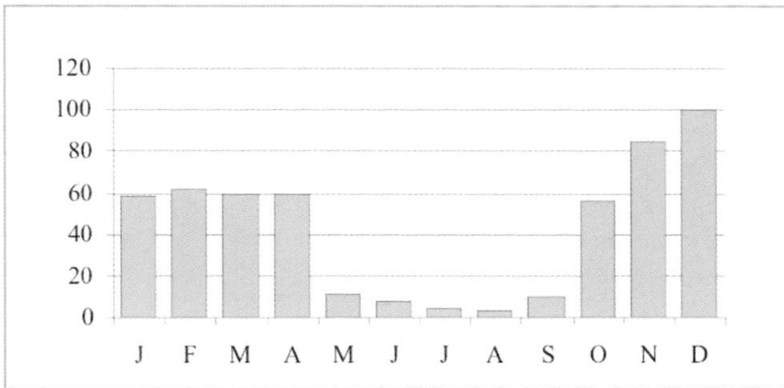

Figure 1. Average monthly peak counts of Red-breasted Mergansers in Morecambe Bay, 1997-2005.

Birds are seen annually but are considerably scarcer on the sea south of Rossall Point and are most commonly seen on passage during April and May and less frequently in October, with a peak count of 40 going north at Formby in April 1980. Notable recent winter counts have been ten off Blackpool in early 1992, 17 off Marshside in November 1995 and twelve at Ainsdale in March 2002. However, coastal lagoons regularly attract significant numbers. The Fleetwood lagoons, especially Fleetwood Marine Lake, regularly supported a flock of 20 or so from at least 1982 to 1998, with a largest count of 41 in November 1996; records at Fairhaven Lake have been less consistent and usually in single or low double-figures, while Marton Mere occasionally holds just one or two with sometimes up to five during spring. On the Sefton coast, Southport Marine Lake regularly held up to eight until the mid-1990s but fewer since. Similarly, Seaforth and Crosby Marine Lake recorded 20 or so annually in late winter during the 1980s and 1990s with a peak of 27 in February 1997 but numbers have fallen to low single figures there during this century.

SJW.

This species account was sponsored by M.E. Pilling.

GOOSANDER

Mergus merganser

Lancashire Category AE.

Uncommon resident breeder; fairly common in winter.

Goosanders first bred in Britain in Perthshire in 1871 and in England in Northumberland in 1941 but the first confirmed Lancashire breeding record was a long time coming – on the lower Lune in 1973 – although nesting had almost certainly occurred before that. Previously the species had been a scarce but increasing winter visitor, described by Oakes as occurring mostly inland but also regular in Morecambe Bay; he believed that one near Southport in 1923 was the only authenticated record on the southern coast since a pair was shot on Formby Moss in 1889.

By 1976 at least 26 females bred on the Lune and further colonisation occurred on the River Bela in 1978, the Hodder and tributaries of the Ribble by 1980 and the upper Wyre in 1982. By the time of the Lancashire Atlas in 1997-2000 the population was estimated at around 100 females and the breeding range extended as far south and east as the Rossendale Irwell at Townsendfold by 1998. The core breeding areas remain the Hodder, the Ribble above Ribchester and its tributaries, the Calder and, above all, the Lune above Skerton Weir, where the population is the most consistently and systematically studied. Numbers of breeding females on the stretch between Skerton Weir and Kirkby Lonsdale (just beyond the county boundary) have fluctuated since the 1970s, averaging a little over 25 between 1989 and 2003 but with higher totals of 31 in 1994 and 36 in 1996. The high density of breeding females on the Lancashire Lune (one per 1.1 km compared with an English average of one per 4.8 km) is partly due to the dozen or so that breed in nest-boxes, suggesting that population expansion may be limited by a lack of natural tree and rock hole nest sites. Information on breeding densities elsewhere is harder to come by but includes 8-11 females on the Ribble between Alston and Jumbles Rocks in 1992.

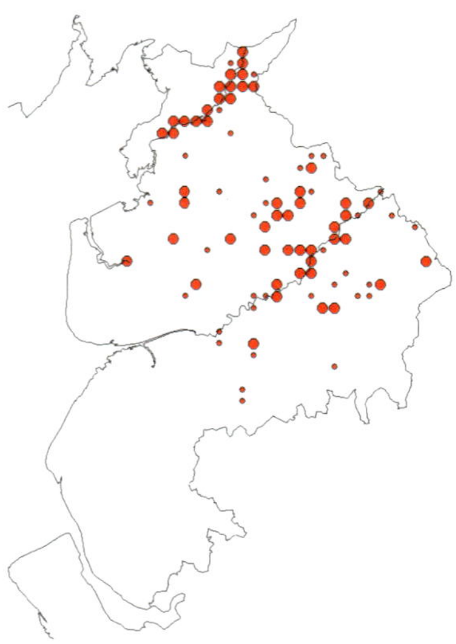

Breeding distribution of Goosander, 1997-2000. (Large dots: confirmed. Small dots: possible)

Eclipse male Goosander, River Ribble, Preston. (Phillip Tomkinson)

Egg-laying on the Lune now begins a week or two earlier than in the 1980s and is mostly completed by late April, at which point the males begin to move away from the rivers – 20 or so adult and immature males are regularly seen moving through the Lune Valley in mid-May with a large count of 53 at Arkholme on 14 May 1994. Females remain on the rivers with their offspring, often ranging as far as 10km from the nest site and sometimes joining up into crèches containing as many as 50 young.

The British population is largely sedentary and rarely winters more than 150km from natal or breeding sites (Migration Atlas), but little is known specifically about the movements of Lancashire birds beyond winter records of single Lune-bred birds at Ribchester and Great Harwood, and of a juvenile in Northumberland. It is therefore not understood to what extent the winter population is composed of local breeders, but winter recoveries of juveniles ringed as chicks in Northumberland (a male) and Norway (a female) indicate some degree of immigration.

Goosanders are very widely dispersed on rivers and reservoirs in winter and most counts are made at communal evening roost sites on eastern reservoirs. The Lune is the only river that has been systematically censused in winter, with an average of 80 birds in January during 1989-1999. Favourite gathering spots are Skerton Weir in Lancaster which held a then record county total of 86 in October 1986, and more recently Leighton Moss which held 54 in November 2002. Comparative survey data for the Ribble have only been published for March 1984 when 28 were located compared with 97 on the Lune catchment. Large gatherings on the Ribble include 20 at Ribchester in 1971, 36 at Preston in 1996 and 50 at Balderstone in February 1985. These figures may considerably underestimate numbers in the Ribble catchment, however, since birds there have a much wider range of alternative sites to resort to than further north.

Since the early 1970s the main roost site in the Ribble area has been the Longridge reservoirs. Peak counts have included 54 in 1974, 65 in 1979 and a record 208 in February 1996 with 96 there that December, but numbers seem to have declined significantly since then – some may have moved to the newly-created lakes at Brockholes Quarry where numbers have grown in recent years. The main Bowland site remains Stocks Reservoir but peak numbers have declined from 40-50 during the 1970s to 20 or less in recent years. All the reservoirs and lakes in east Lancashire have had significant counts at some time in the past 30 years, including 63 at Foulridge (the most consistent site over the years) in 1988, 75 at Whitemoor in 1989, 40 at Clowbridge in 1993 and 56 at Parsonage in 1997. Other eastern sites holding double-figure flocks at least occasionally include Rowley Lake and Jackhouse, Cant Clough, Walverden, Slipper Hill and Rishton Reservoirs. In the West Pennines, Anglezarke and Rivington Reservoirs have supported large flocks from at least the late 1980s with peak counts of 62 in 1997 and 51 in 1999, but the largest counts were at Wayoh Reservoir with 141 in January 1997 and 100 that October, while numbers roosting at Delph Reservoir grew steadily to 54 in 2004/05.

Offshore occurrences of very small numbers are extremely rare and records of 20 redheads off Morecambe in February 1963, for example, may perhaps have referred to Red-breasted Mergansers.

Similarly, few are seen anywhere in the south-west or inland Fylde. Forty-two at Larbreck in eastern Fylde on 17 December 1991 were exceptional, although double-figure counts have been recorded in recent years at Myerscough Quarry. The first in the Fylde were six redheads at Marton Mere in January 1955, where there were just eight further records to the end of the 1990s. There have been just three records at Marshside/Crossens: three in April-May 1983 and singles in November 1998 and winter 2002/03. Birds have been seen at Seaforth in all but four years since 1985 but eight in May 1995 remains the largest count. The situation in West Lancashire was clouded by the presence of up to 20 free-flying birds in the collection at Martin Mere during the 1980s but these never bred and gradually died off in the early 1990s. Since then, records of up to 22 at Mere Sands Wood, two at Downholland Moss irrigation lakes in September 1998 and 14 at Wrightington Lakes in December 2001 may safely be assumed to relate to wild birds.

The midwinter total, therefore, is probably in the region of 350-450 birds, a figure consistent with the county's breeding population plus young, suggesting that any winter visitors are counterbalanced by Lancashire birds moving elsewhere.

SJW.

This species account was sponsored by Cuerden Wildlife Explorers and Watch Group.

RUDDY DUCK

Oxyura jamaicensis

Lancashire Category C.

Scarce feral breeder; fairly common in winter.

The escape or release of unpinioned Ruddy Ducks from Slimbridge, their establishment as feral breeders in Britain in the 1950s and subsequent colonisation of western Europe to the detriment of Spanish White-headed Ducks *Oxyura leucocephala*, provided a major controversy in the late 1990s, when the government began its attempt to eradicate them. No culling had taken place in Lancashire by 2005 but there were signs that numbers were beginning to decline.

The first Lancashire record was a male at Marton Mere on 4-6 December 1968, the year that breeding was first proven in Cheshire near the Shropshire border. No more were seen until a female at Martin Mere on 27-28 September 1975. Ruddy Ducks have been recorded annually since 1977, with three or four a year until the early 1980s and a major expansion by the end of the decade as breeding became regular.

Male Ruddy Duck, Marshside, May 2005. (Steve Young)

The first pair bred 'near Croston' in 1978 but no further records were published until 1983 when a pair bred at Mere Sands Wood and others were prospecting at Marton Mere and Ulnes Walton. Since then breeding has been proven or considered probable on at least 22 sites as the breeding range gradually expanded throughout the 1980s and early 1990s, although some sites appear to have been abandoned quite rapidly. Nesting was first recorded at Leighton Moss in 1984, Bretherton in 1985, Marton Mere and Adlington in 1986, Ulnes Walton and Longton Brickpits in 1988, Fleetwood CEGB and ICI lagoons, Bispham Marsh and Whiston, Merseyside in 1989, Abbey Lakes in Upholland and Preesall Flash in 1990, Street Bridge and Knowsley Park in 1991, Scarisbrick Hall and Arley in 1992, and Pilling and Carr Mill Dam, St. Helens in 1995. No further new sites were colonised until a pair bred at Bracewell Reservoir, Barnoldswick in 2002 and none since, and it appears that the range expansion which appeared unstoppable in the early 1990s might finally have come to a halt.

Ruddy Ducks are extremely secretive when nesting and breeding often goes unnoticed until the young appear, so accurate censusing has always been difficult, but there was a minimum of 15 pairs in 1992 and an estimated 30 pairs during the Lancashire Atlas survey of 1997-2000. Most sites have only ever supported one or two pairs. Exceptions have been Ulnes Walton (3 in 1988), Adlington (4 in 1996), Marton Mere (2-3 sporadically since 1992), Leighton Moss (peak of 5 in 1997-99, 4 in 2000, 3 in 2001-03), Scarisbrick Hall (5 in 1992) and Mere Sands Wood (5 in 1985, 10 in 1986, 4-5 in 1991-97, but reduced to 1-2 in 2000-02 and none in 2003).

Breeding was reported from just six sites in 2002 and only four or five during 2003-05, but this probably understated the true situation – partly, perhaps, due to a reluctance to submit records because of the government cull. Assessing breeding totals was further complicated by the difficulty of gaining access to two key sites, Scarisbrick Hall and especially Knowsley Park, where post-breeding counts suggest a huge expansion in the late 1990s (see below). However, the decline at Mere Sands Wood, Marton Mere and Leighton Moss was well monitored.

Productivity has always been very low in Lancashire with very few young fledging. The reason for this is far from clear, food shortage seems an unlikely explanation since the young feed primarily on chironomid larvae which are abundant. The Lancashire Atlas suggested high rates of predation but gave no supporting evidence. It seems that the county's Ruddy Ducks may always have been a 'sink' population, reliant upon constant supplementation from elsewhere to maintain numbers. If so, they would not have had far to come – numbers in Cheshire have always been far higher than here with 100 pairs already breeding by 1982. Distribution outside the breeding season closely mirrors the breeding range with the largest counts largely confined to key sites in Merseyside, West and central Lancashire and the Fylde, where numbers are high throughout the year. The exception is Leighton Moss where winter records are rare (Figure 1). The first appreciable flock, however, was nine on the River Darwen at Earnsdale on 5 May 1982. Peak site counts include 18 at Leighton Moss in June 1997, 46 at Marton Mere in August 1990, twelve at Martin Mere in April 1992, 18 at Mere Sands Wood in April 1996, six at Seaforth in September 1996 and ten at Sands Lake, Ainsdale in August 2001. County totals rose consistently until the mid-1990s, then declined a little before rising again as a result of high winter counts at Prescot Reservoirs (of birds possibly breeding in Knowsley Park), where county records were set of 63 in December 2002 and 70 in January 2003. However, peak counts at Prescot Reservoirs declined to 21 in 2004 and only three in 2005, so the situation at Knowsley remains unclear.

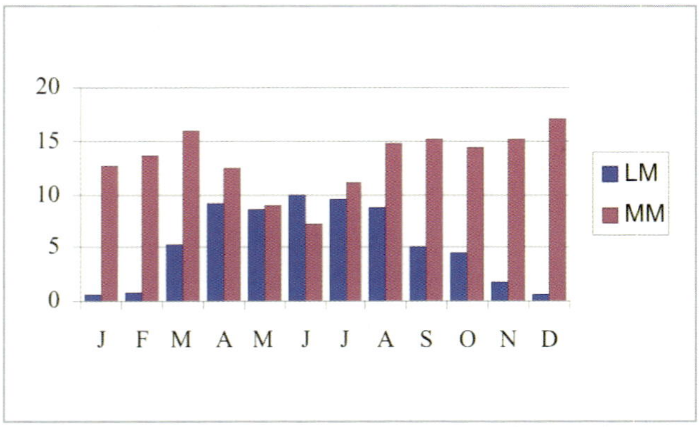

Average monthly peak counts of Ruddy Duck at Leighton Moss (1996-2003) and Martin Mere (1992-2002)

Smaller numbers may turn up on any waterbody within the core breeding range but Ruddy Ducks remain relatively scarce in the West Pennines, east Lancashire and Rossendale, with usually only one or two records a year, probably because of the lack of favoured eutrophic waters. There have been just three records offshore: singles at Rossall Point in February 1984, Blackpool in January 1988 and Heysham in November 1988.

SJW.

This species account was sponsored by the Friends of Marton Mere.

RED GROUSE

Lagopus lagopus scotica

Lancashire Category A.

Common resident breeder.

Once championed as our only endemic bird species, the Red Grouse has long been demoted in status to a sub-species *scotica* of the circumpolar Willow Grouse. It is the classic species of the open heather moorlands of Britain, although it does occur at much lower densities on many grassy upland sheep-walks devoid of heather, where alternative foods like bilberry, crowberry and cotton grass are present.

The indifference shown to the recording of this species, indeed gamebirds in general, by most birdwatchers is offset by the meticulous bag records kept by shooting estates that allow population trends to be monitored accurately.

Red Grouse populations are known to be cyclical, largely due to the build-up of a parasitic nematode worm, particularly prevalent when grouse densities have been high the previous year, resulting in a significant reduction of breeding success. Bag records from the Bowland fells illustrate this classic pattern of boom and bust, here typically taking place over a five-year period (Hudson 1992). An additional problem is the viral disease louping-ill, which is transmitted from host mammals to grouse by the nymph stage of the sheep tick and can cause high chick mortality. It has been suggested recently that the removal of natural predators may exacerbate these cyclical population swings (Davies 2005).

Grouse shooting became increasingly popular from the late 18th century with most grouse moors established as such by the 1840s. The birds were 'walked up' at this time, due to the slow reloading time of the muzzle-loading shotgun, and bags were generally small. With the arrival of the breech-loading shotgun in the 1860s, rapid loading of guns became possible and 'driving' grouse to guns became the vogue for upland landowners. Bag sizes rose dramatically as did the economic value of the moors, the 'glorious twelfth' became a key social event and, over large regions of upland Britain, grouse management replaced sheep rearing as the major land use.

Numbers peaked in the early 20th century, when some 'exceptional Lancashire moors' carried a pair for every two acres (Lovat 1911) but declined steadily following the First World War, due mainly to loss of heather from overgrazing by sheep, spread of bracken, afforestation and an increase in fox and crow populations. The average bag in Britain and Ireland has fallen from some 2.5 million birds prior to the First World War (Leslie 1911) to a mean of 450,000 between 1970 and 1989 (Hudson 1992), a decline of some 82%. The British population is now estimated at 155,000 pairs (Baker *et al.* 2006).

Hunting has been associated with the ancient Forest of Bowland for centuries and the Bowland fells are one of the English strongholds of the Red Grouse. Elsewhere in upland Lancashire, apart from a few managed moors on the South Pennines and West Pennine Moors, only low-density populations occur. The Lancashire Atlas recorded the species in 131 tetrads and estimated the population to fluctuate cyclically between 3,000 and 10,000 pairs. Nearly 30 grouse moors, with an area well in excess of 200 km^2, are currently managed, the vast majority in Bowland, including the outlying Leck, Waddington and Longridge Fells. Some of Lancashire's grouse moors are small, at less than 2km^2, with only part-time keepering. Others are vast, such as the Duke of Westminster's famous Abbeystead Moor in Bowland at over 80km^2, employing six full-time gamekeepers.

The Abbeystead Estate rose to fame in shooting circles on the 'glorious twelfth' of August 1915, when the then owner, Lord Sefton, with seven other guns, accounted for 2,929 grouse in six drives on the Littledale and Abbeystead beats – the all-time record bag for Britain and Ireland. A further 3,042 birds were shot during the following two days on the Mallowdale and Tarnbrook beats, with the bag for the season some 17,078 birds (Gladstone 1930). Abbeystead also holds the record for the largest bag ever made in one season (Oakes 1953). Thereafter, in common with moors countrywide, Abbeystead went into slow decline, so that when the Duke of Westminster bought the estate in 1980 the average annual bag was down to 800. The implementation of intensive management had increased the annual bag to 8,559 by 1989, restoring the estate's status as Britain's premier grouse moor.

A study by the Game Conservancy on a sample of ten grouse moors in Bowland between 1970 and 1989 gave a mean annual bag of 9,222 grouse, equating to 53 shot per km^2 – a marked decline from the average 100+ between 1900 and the 1930s and the 300+ in 1927 and 1933 (Hudson 1992). This decline was linked to a reduction in the numbers of gamekeepers following over-grazing of the heather and serious moor fires during the Second World War (Hudson 1986).

In 1999 the Bowland moors suffered a major population crash, resulting, for example, in only 49 being shot at Abbeystead (down from 2,380 the year before), and these purely for the purposes of research into parasitic worm burdens. Grouse numbers have been slow to recover on many Bowland moors and only by 2003 were stocks high enough for driven shooting to recommence generally. Apart from bag records, meaningful counts from Bowland are few; they include 130+ on Waddington Fell in December 1981, 500 in the Langden Valley in February 1989, 35 at Clougha in October 2002 and a estimate of 1,000 breeding pairs on the moorland sections of the 70km^2 United Utilities Bowland estate in 1982.

In east Lancashire, there are managed grouse moors at Emmott and 'Lancashire' Moor in the south Pennines with a few small ones around Colne. The population on Pendle Hill has declined since a bag of 182 on 12 August 1913 (Spencer 1977), with 80+ in January 1976 and 50 in October 1996 the largest counts in modern times. Grouse are generally scarce in Rossendale, due to the large-scale loss of heather; a fragmented population inhabits the cotton-grass-dominated plateaux, with twelve pairs estimated in 1994.

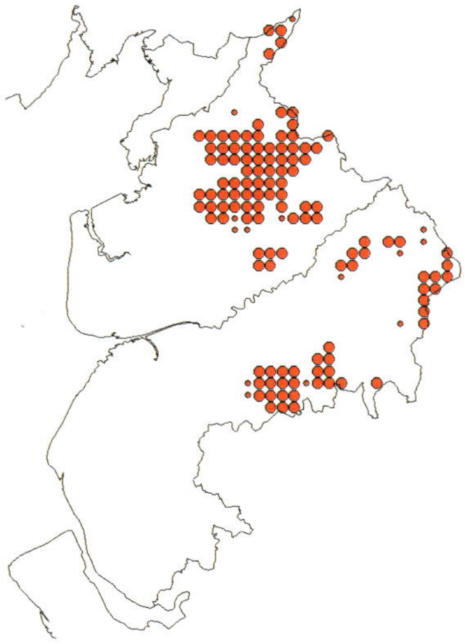

Breeding distribution of Red Grouse, 1997-2000. (Large dots: confirmed. Small dots: possible)

The West Pennine Moors were formerly a collection of productive small grouse moors but, following a 50% loss of heather since the Second World War (Bruce 1991), Red Grouse are now largely confined to the higher plateaux with a current population estimate of 200+ breeding pairs. Several moors are now devoid of grouse, for example on Charter's Moss/Turton Heights, where 60 were shot in 1904 but birds are now absent due to afforestation and overgrazing. Management has also declined, illustrated by the reduction in the number of gamekeepers over the past 100 years from ten to two. Bag figures again amply illustrate the decline: Anglezarke Moor peaked at 1,324 in 1899 and shot the record bag for the West Pennine Moors of 421 on 12 August 1937, but had crashed to under ten birds shot per annum by 1965. In recent years up to 45 pairs (in 1999) have bred on Anglezarke/Withnell Moors, 205+ grouse were seen in the autumn of 2001 with 35 shot on Anglezarke in 2002. Only Darwen Moor has retained any degree of consistency. Here, the annual bag from 1925 to 1955 averaged 600 birds; the moor peaked at 906 shot in 1953 but thereafter went into steep decline. A recent revival in management has resulted in a growing population with, in the last few years, up to 300 shot annually out of post-breeding estimates of over 800 birds. Other recent peak counts from the West Pennine Moors include 120 on Hoddlesden Moss in October 1997, 83 on Winter Hill in July 1990 and 55 on Belmont Moor in August 2002.

Red Grouse were historically present and in some cases managed, on the lowland peat mosses of West Lancashire, north Merseyside and the Fylde. The resident population was, according to Mitchell, boosted by an annual migration from the hills in October and November. The gradual destruction of the lowland mosses led to their protracted abandonment by grouse. Both Simonswood Moss, where birds were (re)introduced by Lord Sefton, and the Over Wyre mosses had lost their resident birds by the early twentieth century, although birds bred annually on Chat Moss (now in Greater Manchester) until 1937 with winter stragglers (possibly from the West Pennine Moors) noted as recently as 1970. Intriguingly, there are records from the Sefton coast of odd birds seen on the Ainsdale dunes during the summers of 1940-1942 and nearby at Formby in 1959.

A rarely witnessed sighting of local migration occurred in late July 2005 when a covey of seven was seen to fly west from Hoddlesden Moss high over Darwen and onto Darwen Moor.

SJM, DJH.
This species account was sponsored by S.J. Martin.

BLACK GROUSE

Tetrao tetrix

Lancashire Category BE.

Extinct breeder, some releases for shooting purposes until late twentieth century.

Black Grouse were originally birds of early successional woodland, inhabiting the transition zone between heath and trees. Following the vast reduction in this habitat in Britain, they now typically occupy a structurally similar mosaic of moorland, rough grazing, young plantations, upland pasture and pioneer (or regressing) woodland and woodland edge.

On moorland, Black Grouse find deep nesting cover in heather, abundant insects for chicks in wet flushes and feed on the seeds and berries of cotton grass, bilberry, heather and crowberry, while unimproved meadows supply rush seeds and herbs. Woodland provides shelter and food from the buds, berries and catkins of rowan, birch, hazel and larch, particularly in winter and early spring. The spectacular communal display ground (lek) requires short vegetation within an open area in the home range of the local sub-population.

Black Grouse have been in decline in Britain for over 150 years due to fragmentation of their core habitats. Overgrazing, unsympathetic forestry planning, agricultural improvement of pasture, drainage and increased predation have resulted in a dramatic and continuing reduction in range and population size; the British population is estimated at 5,000-8,100 lekking males (Hancock *et al.* 1999).

It is almost certain that Lancashire has recently joined a growing list of English counties where the Black Grouse has become extinct. Since the late 19th century populations have been lost in 19 English counties, with relict populations extant only in eastern Cumbria, parts of North Yorkshire, Durham and particularly Northumberland.

Tony Disley

The history of the Black Grouse in Lancashire is clouded by introductions for shooting purposes and there is some doubt that it has ever existed in the county in a truly wild state, at least for a century or more. However, Spencer (1965c) reported a reference to the killing of three 'Heath Cocks' at 'Rowe Moor' on 23 December 1617 (Raines 1848), which he believed to refer to Black Grouse at Rawmoor, close to Slaidburn. Greenoak (1997) cast doubt upon this, arguing that 'Heath Cock' was a local name for both Black and Red Grouse, but extensive research confirms that the term was used exclusively to refer to Black Grouse in Lancashire whereas Red Grouse were called 'Moor Cocks' (K.G. Spencer *pers. comm.*).

Mitchell knew of no wild populations in the present county but reported an introduction at Whitewell in Bowland around 1864 which failed to become established. Oakes referred to an undated introduction by Lord Sefton on the Abbeystead estate. It seems likely that other introductions have taken place unrecorded. There seems to be little reason to disagree with Fitter's (1959) view that 'the very few still to be found in (pre-1974) Lancashire, however, all seem to stem from three introductions during the last century, in Furness, in Lunesdale and on the eastern uplands near Blackburn.'

A highly fragmented population of unknown origin appears to have existed at a very low density for most of the 20th century in parts of Bowland and its periphery. Individuals or small groups were irregularly recorded from Leck Fell in the far north-east, Claughton and Wray on the edge of the Lune Valley to Bleasdale in the west and Easington and Waddington Fells in the south, and many locations in between. Only in the area north of Slaidburn (particularly in the Stocks Reservoir/Gisburn Forest area), Croasdale and in the Tatham/Thrushgill Plantations area does there appear to have been an established breeding population, that, in all probability, was the source of birds seen elsewhere in Bowland.

Mather (1986) reported 13 or more young in the Stocks Reservoir area in 1950 and up to five males were still present there in 1986. The last birds at Abbeystead were seen in 1985 but five were seen in Croasdale in January 1990 with two males and one or two females at a second site in April that year and two pairs at a third. Apart from an unprecedented five on Waddington Fell on 22 September, 1991 signalled the beginning of the end, with only one other sighting –a male at Stocks. Blank years followed years of hearsay until 1997, when females were recorded in two areas with the possibility of a pair at a third site. The rumoured presence of female(s) in 1998 has persisted periodically into the 21st century, with second- or third-hand reports of odd birds seen by gamekeepers.

Records away from Bowland are few and far between. In the south-west, one was reported shot on Rainford Moss around 1890 and a female was present at Formby in November 1917. Even if correctly identified, the provenance of both of these records must be extremely dubious. The only record from the West Pennine Moors concerns a female shot on Darwen Moor on 19 August 1905, whilst in Pendle a small population of unknown origin was present around Twiston Moor in the early 1970s, with the last seen in January 1975.

The continued presence of a Lancashire Black Grouse population would appear a most unlikely proposition, and, given the decline of the species in adjacent areas of Cumbria and Yorkshire, the only possible sources of prospecting birds wandering into Lancashire have probably dried up.

SJM, DJH.

west oak

This species account was sponsored by Westoak Construction Ltd.

RED-LEGGED PARTRIDGE

Alectoris rufa

Lancashire Category CE.

Fairly common resident feral breeder, supplemented by releases.

The Red-legged Partridge is native to the western Mediterranean where it occurs at its highest densities in areas with dry, sandy soils and high summer temperatures. Charles II was the first of several British landowners to attempt unsuccessfully to acclimatise this species when he had birds released in Windsor and Richmond Parks in 1673 (Lever 1977), but it was not until 1770 that a successful introduction took place in Suffolk.

The first known releases in Lancashire were carried out by Sir Thomas Hesketh of Rufford Hall around 1854 and in 1879, with a further introduction by Lord Sefton at Simonswood Moss in 1935. Other releases undoubtedly took place in the early 20th century; one was shot at Mere Sands Wood in 1941 and another appeared at Hag Lodge, Accrington in May 1945. The first confirmed breeding was at Lytham in 1948, though two pairs bred at Golborne Park, which straddles the present Merseyside/Greater Manchester boundary, in 1935. As late as 1973 Spencer commented that the species remained 'insecurely established as a part of the county's avifauna'.

Red-legged Partridge. (Steve Young)

The ability of the Red-legged Partridge female to lay two clutches, one of which is incubated by the male, together with the fact that the young can digest grass and weed seeds soon after hatching, makes it more suited to intense lowland agriculture than the native Grey Partridge. This is reflected in the present British population estimates of 170,000 pairs of Red-legged as opposed to 145,000 pairs of Grey (Mead 2000). The Lancashire population of Redlegs was estimated at 300 pairs in 1997-2000 although, as nationally, continual releases make accurate assessment of the number of breeding birds very difficult. An estimated 800,000 Red-legged Partridges are released each year in Britain, with the number in Lancashire likely to exceed 10,000. Releases in the county have frequently been into unsuitable, often upland, habitats where birds rarely breed and soon die out; the species being widely viewed here as a put-and-take gamebird.

The situation was further confused by the widespread release of Chukar *Alectoris graeca* and Red-legged x Chukar hybrids until this was banned in 1992.

The largest releases occur on the heavily-keepered mosslands of the south-west and the Fylde, where arable farmland provides the most suitable habitat and where, if releases were to cease, the Red-legged Partridge would probably become self-sustaining in small numbers. Small numbers breed annually in the Fylde and many are released annually at Lytham Hall and Over Wyre (4,000 in the latter area in 2003 for example), resulting in a largest count of 195 at Fluke Hall in September 2002. On the equally suitable south-west mosses, large numbers are released on several estates from Tarleton and Bretherton in the north to Parbold in the east and the Altcar estate in the south-west, where up to 400 have been seen as late as 24 November 2000 when most Partridge-shooting would have finished. Other large counts include 100 near Ainsdale in 1996 and on Churchtown Moss in 2005, 58 on Downholland Moss in 2005, 36 on Plex Moss in 1992, 32 at Martin Mere in 1990 and 23 at Little Crosby in 1998.

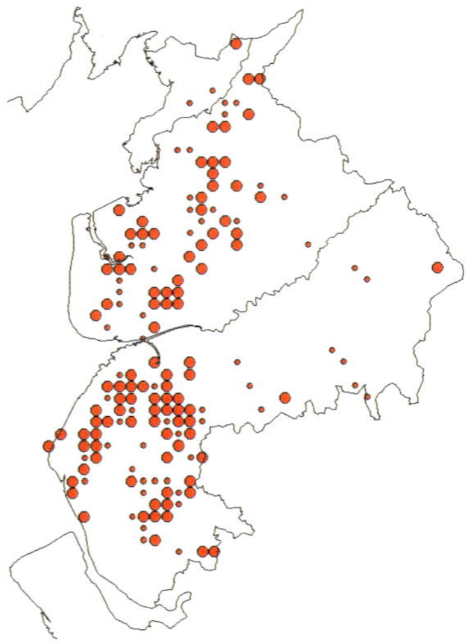

Breeding distribution of Red-legged Partridge, 1997-2000.
(Large dots: confirmed. Small dots: possible)

Habitat away from these county strongholds is largely unsuitable and, due also to the wetter climate away from the coast, breeding is rarely attempted let alone successful. Only in the Lune Valley and to the west of Bowland, particularly in the Scorton, Abbeystead and Oakenclough areas, could breeding be described as regular, although this may be merely a result of the large numbers turned down – 500 released on the Abbeystead estate in 1998, for example. Practically no part of the county is without recent records, due to the constant introductions. Feral populations rarely develop and are invariably short-lived. In the West Pennine Moors around Belmont, for example, gamekeepers released over 1,850 during 1988-2000. A few pairs bred successfully in 1993 and 1999 but none has been seen since 2000. Other recent releases have occurred at five sites in central and southern Bowland, four sites in the Ribble and Hodder Valleys and others at Musbury in Rossendale, at Whitemoor near Colne and at Hoghton Tower, west of Blackburn.

The species is highly sedentary within its main breeding range in Britain but individuals and coveys are sometimes recorded away from known release sites. Examples include 20 at Preston Docks in 1983, one at Sunderland Point in 2003 and singles at Seaforth from April 1993 to February 1994 and again in March 2002. The most bizarre sighting was of one on mudflats at Rossall Point in March 2002, the bird being enveloped by the incoming tide before escaping onto the beach.

SJM, DJH.

This species account was sponsored by Arnold Plant Hire.

arnoldplanthire

GREY PARTRIDGE

Perdix perdix

Lancashire Category ACE.

Very common resident breeder, supplemented by releases.

Lancashire is fortunate still to be able to describe the Grey Partridge as a widespread breeding resident, ranging from locally common on the lowland mosses of the south-west and the Fylde to scarce in the pastoral and upland areas of north and east Lancashire.

Mitchell had little to say beyond describing it as 'a common resident . . . generally dispersed over the whole county', although he pointed to shooting pressure and 'the ceasing of corn-growing' having made it 'comparatively scarce in many districts'. Hardy (1941) stated that it nested in abundance on the mosslands and that a few still nested on the Grand National course at Aintree, which was formerly one of Lord Sefton's best partridge shoots, the beaters driving the birds over Becher's Brook to the guns. For Oakes it was a 'common, well-distributed resident breeding up to 900 feet (300m) on the Pennines, more numerous in corn- and root-fields than grassland, but may be found nesting anywhere from the coastal sand dunes and mosses to the hills'.

Tony Disley

By the 1950s a sharp decline was underway nationally, largely due to the introduction of herbicides into cereal growing and other forms of agricultural intensification, which led to reduced availability of the invertebrates upon which chicks are dependent for their first weeks of life. Chick survival fell from 45% to under 30% between 1952 and 1962 and the British population dropped by 80% in 40 years to an estimated 145,000 pairs by the early 1990s (Tapper 1999). Numbers are believed to have fallen further since, with the BBS recording a 40% decline between 1994 and 2005, and the current population is estimated at 70,000-75,000 pairs (Baker *et al.* 2006).

The Lancashire breeding range has changed little over the years: breeding was confirmed in 48 10km squares in 1968-72, 47 in 1988-91 and 48 in 1997-2000, when Grey Partridges were recorded in 53% of the county tetrads and the population estimated at 2,500 pairs. The Lancashire population has probably fallen in line with national trends but, nevertheless, the county remains a stronghold for the species, certainly within western Britain.

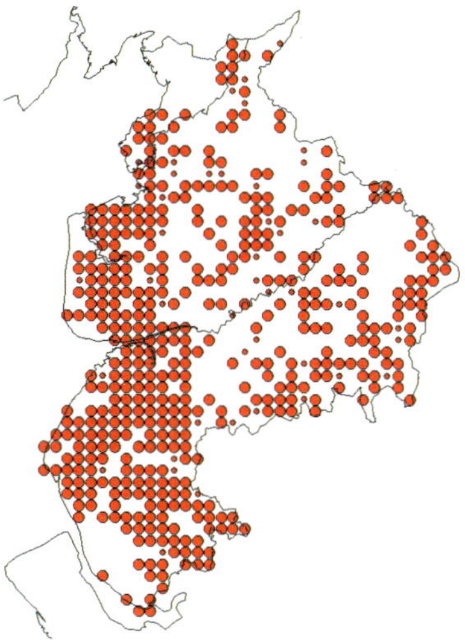

Breeding distribution of Grey Partridge, 1997-2000. (Large dots: confirmed. Small dots: possible)

In part, this may be due to the retention of relatively unmanaged ditch-margins in much of the south-west, but game-management on the larger estates, especially the Altcar, Halsall, Mossborough and Bickerstaffe estates, has also been a crucial factor. On the Halsall estate an average of 4.5 pairs per km^2 was found during 1997-2000 with even higher densities known to be present on the Altcar estate to the south. Countryside Stewardship Schemes involving the introduction of unsprayed, conservation field-headlands increased the number of breeding pairs on the Halsall estate to 112 in 2003. On Croston Moss and elsewhere in the south-west introductions of game-farm reared birds have been undertaken to maintain driven-shooting although Red-legged Partridges are now largely preferred.

Some large concentrations of Grey Partridges have been recorded in the south-west: 107 at Lunt, near Maghull in January 1993, 66 at Hightown in November 1984, 53 on Sollom Moss in October 1995 and 42 at Little Crosby in early 1998, while 90 on Croston Moss in October 1999 were probably released birds in the main. The species remains relatively common on farmland around St. Helens with 96 pairs recorded in the area during 1997-2000.

The other stronghold is the Fylde mosslands where, although declines have been noted, Grey Partridges are still widely distributed and locally common. Winter coveys of 40 at Fluke Hall in November 1998, 38 near Freckleton in December 1998, 45 on Lytham Moss in January 2000 and 24 on Winmarleigh Moss in January 1999 are noteworthy. Releases in the Over Wyre district (of up to 175 birds annually) since 2001 are the probable source of frequent reports of coveys of up to 33 in this area.

In Silverdale the species was described as 'in dire straits' in 2000 and 'precarious' in 2003 and no breeding pairs were found during 1997-2000 – a far cry from the early 1900s when the then drained Leighton Moss was arable land and 'an excellent Partridge shoot' (Reynolds 1989). The picture is a little less bleak further south around the Lune Estuary, where breeding was recorded from five sites on the Overton peninsula in 1998-99 and coveys up to ten strong were seen in the Aldcliffe, Conder Green and Cockersands areas in 2003.

Grey Partridges are present in low numbers throughout most of the largely pastoral landscape east of the M6, where, although absent from some areas of high moorland, they are resident in many upland valleys. Where densities are low, breeding is often under-recorded – in areas of rush pasture for example. They are scarce in the Lune Valley, where two pairs were recorded at Arkholme in 1995; the largest covey reported recently in this area was 25 in 2002, but this followed releases of some 200 birds in both 2000 and 2001.

Breeding was once moderately common and widespread in east Lancashire but is now localised and uncommon, particularly in areas such as Pendle and the Ribble Valley. In 1995 15 double-figure counts were reported and birds were present at 27 localities in 1998, including a covey of 15 at Trawden in November; 81 were seen at eleven localities in 2003, including coveys of 25 at Higher Red Lees and 19 at Waddington. A minimum of ten pairs were located in 1998 in Bowland, where coveys tend to be smaller than elsewhere with 17 at Whitendale in 1993, eleven at Stocks Reservoir in 1997, 15 at Marshaw in 2002 and twelve on Champion Moor in 2003 the recent maxima.

Rossendale saw a marked decline in the early 1980s and, with some fluctuations, numbers have probably declined further since then. Fifteen pairs were located in 1996 and records received from 15 sites in 1999, but in 2005 birds were seen in only seven localities; the largest recent coveys in Rossendale were 14 at Cowpe Moss and 17 at Crown Point in 1997. On the West Pennine Moors birds occur widely at low densities on in-bye pastures and the moorland edge up to an altitude of 325m. They were more numerous before the hard winter of 1963, when whole coveys were found frozen. Thereafter, the species' population has remained relatively stable, albeit temporarily boosted by sporting releases (1,000 in total in six years between 1988 and 1996 at Entwistle and Belmont), after which numbers soon return to 'natural' levels with coveys of up to 25 seen.

Grey Partridges also breed in habitats other than farmland, including coastal dunes and saltmarshes on the Sefton coast and the Ribble Estuary, urban' brownfield' sites, particularly on Merseyside, docklands in Liverpool and Preston, golf courses and areas of rough grassland 'landlocked' by housing and industrial development.

SJM, DJH.

This species account was sponsored by D.S. Martin.

QUAIL

Coturnix coturnix

Lancashire Category AE.

Rare breeder.

Assessment of the true status of the Quail has always been made difficult by its extremely secretive nature and the need to judge numbers according to records of singing males; since males cease singing once mated, most of our records may actually be of (possibly fairly mobile) unmated males rather than breeding pairs.

Mitchell quoted others who described it as common around 1700 and 'as numerous as Larks' in the Pilling area in the first quarter of the nineteenth century, citing game bags at St. Michael's-on-Wyre of 20 and 26 in 1865 and 1866 respectively. He himself noted a dramatic decline from the mid-1870s, ascribing this to increasing use of 'mowing machines, which shave so close to the ground that the sitting birds are invariably destroyed'.

Intriguingly, a note in the second edition of Mitchell's book reported birds being killed 'in every winter month' and found dead on mosslands 'during the hard winter of 1880/81', giving the impression that wintering was thought not to be uncommon. Since the migratory behaviour of Quail was not fully understood at this time, a question mark must hang over these reports for, although wintering in Britain has been known, it occurs only very rarely (BWP). They perhaps indicate that unrecorded releases were taking place at this time; Wrigley (1892) documented one such release in the Formby dunes.

By Oakes's time the Quail was 'a scarce and irregular visitor to South Lancashire; very rare north of the River Ribble'. The last record he knew of in the Fylde – which Mitchell believed to be a county stronghold – was one found dead under telegraph wires at Carleton on 14 May 1929. Hardy recalled a bird calling at Martin Mere in May 1931.

Spencer (1973) regarded Quail as less than annual in occurrence but numbers reported have increased markedly since the 1970s, from an average (median) of three a year during 1978-1989 to nine a year during 1990-2003. Large national influxes prior to the record invasion of 1989 appear not to have penetrated significantly into Lancashire – the highest total reported was six during 1983. The first birds of the 1989 influx were found in Lancashire on 25 May and 'new' males were heard until 12 September, although the bulk of records were in June and July. About 50 were reported, overwhelmingly from the south-west mosslands and the Fylde but with up to five in Rossendale (four of them above 325m) and singles on Heysham Moss and at Clougha and Conder Green.

Double-figure totals were recorded in eight years between 1990 and 2005. Another 'Quail year' occurred in 1997 when ten or more were heard on the Southport and Formby mosses during late May and at least another 25 at a wide range of sites, mostly in the south-west, but also as far apart as Middleton and Coldwell. At least 26 – and perhaps as many as 50 – calling males were heard during July in Over Wyre between Stake Pool, Nateby and Out Rawcliffe.

Quail, probably *japonica* or hybrid, Plex Moss, 2003. (Dave Bickerton)

The geographical distribution of records in more normal years is essentially similar to that of 1989 and 1997, with the vast majority heard in the predominantly arable areas of the south-west and Over Wyre. Quail remain rare in north and east Lancashire, with, in addition to those of 1989 and 1997, totals of just three or four records in the north and 15 or so in the east – out of a county total of more than 300 since 1978. Coastal migrants occurred in the sand dunes at Fairhaven on 13 May 1980 and at Rossall School in June 1988.

Quail rarely appear in Lancashire before May and the majority of calling males are heard during June and July with a few persisting into August and a handful of records in September. There have, however, been a few earlier records – the earliest being one found injured at Accrington on 27 March 1993 – including one flushed at Delph on 1 April and later found dead and preserved in Bolton Museum, one at Burnley on 30 April 1995, one found exhausted after heavy rain at Blackpool on 21 April 1998 and one at Mere Sands Wood on 29 April 2003. The latest were singles flushed at Fairhaven on 15 October 1980 and at Liverpool Airport on 27 October 1985.

The only proven breeding records are of a pair with two young in the Tarleton/Sollom area in 1983 and a pair with four young at Lighthouse Cottages on the Lune Estuary on 26 July 2002.

Until very recently it was taken for granted that all records of quail in Lancashire referred to Common Quail *C. coturnix*, but there are problems with this assumption. Firstly, even ignoring the bumper years of 1989 and 1997, records have been steadily increasing since the late 1970s during a period when Quail numbers have declined sharply throughout most of Europe, to the extent that their status is now classed as 'Vulnerable' (Tucker & Heath 1994). Secondly, some escapes or releases from captivity in Lancashire have been suspected, most notably those on Pilling Moss in 1997 although this was never proven. The two extremely early records at Accrington and Delph mentioned above also seem likely to fall into this category. Finally, Kehoe (2004) argued that a bird photographed at Plex Moss in 2003 showed characteristics of Japanese Quail *C. japonica* and there was a strong likelihood that this domesticated species, which is released for 'sporting' purposes throughout much of Europe, may be hybridising with European Quail and occurring in increasing numbers in northern Europe. Support for this hypothesis comes from the finding that first-generation hybrids, and particularly second-generation back-cross European x Japanese Quail can take on both the migratory behaviour and call characteristics of the former (Deregnaucourt 2004). Large numbers of hybrids are reared and released annually in southern Europe and the future of pure Common Quail in western Europe may be under threat (Deregnaucourt *pers. comm.*).

SJW, DJH.

This species account was sponsored by Derek Gifford.

PHEASANT

Phasianus colchicus

Lancashire Category CE.

Abundant resident breeder, supplemented by releases.

It was originally thought that the Romans had brought the Pheasant to Britain due to depictions of birds on Romano-British mosaics, but no bones have ever been found in British middens. Pheasants were certainly present, if only in captivity, by Norman times and it is likely that they became naturalised shortly after, becoming quite common in parts of Tudor England (Lever 1977, Tapper 1992). The 'Old English' race *P. c. colchicus* – without the white neck ring – from central Asia was the form first introduced, followed by the Chinese Ring-necked Pheasant P. c. *torquatus* and ultimately by several other races and crosses to such an extent that it is thought that no pure *colchicus* birds remain in Britain. Lancashire's claim to fame involves the introduction of the Green (or Japanese) Pheasant *P. versicolor* when the 13th Earl of Derby imported a single male to his famous menagerie at Knowsley Hall in 1841. Selective crossing of this bird with a female Ring-necked Pheasant and selected offspring resulted in nearly pure Green Pheasants, which formed the origins of the many 'melanistic' birds in Britain today.

Male Pheasant, Little Crosby, July 2004. (Steve Young)

With the arrival of the breech-loading shotgun in the 1860s, rapid loading of guns became possible and the sport of driven Pheasant shooting became the vogue for landowners throughout Britain. Subsequent planting of coverts (commonly underplanted with rhododendron) changed the landscape and vast numbers of Pheasants were released, estates competing with each other to produce the largest bags and attract the most influential, hopefully royal, guests. Several Lancashire estates played a part, the most notable being Lord Derby's Knowsley, where bags of over 3,000 a day were obtained before the First World War, and the Croxteth Estate where Lord Sefton and five other guns shot 6,036 in four days in November 1883 including 2,373 at Altcar on 21 November (Gladstone 1930).

Mitchell and Oakes both described the Pheasant as numerous or abundant where preserved, scarce elsewhere, particularly in the south-east of the county. This situation remains largely unchanged today, with the highest densities associated with shooting estates. The Lancashire Atlas estimated the (artificially maintained) breeding population at some 10,000 females in 1997-2000, the only large gaps in distribution being urban Liverpool, Cleveleys/Fleetwood, around Accrington and in eastern Rossendale. Nationally the population is estimated at over 1.8 to 1.9 million breeding females (Baker *et al.* 2006), the BBS showing a growth of 33% during the period 1994-2003.

The range of habitats exploited by Pheasants is wide and varied. While birds are commonly seen feeding in open fields, cover (not necessarily woodland) is required for nesting and roosting. The ideal habitat is a mosaic of tilled land, hedgerows and/or field banks with some woodland. Breeding occurs in the reedbeds at Leighton Moss, a habitat not dissimilar to that occupied in parts of the species' natural range in China, and where a combination of six Pheasant and nine Mallard eggs was found in a Mallard nest in April 1953. Pheasants occur widely in the treeless moorland and upland pastures of Bowland, Pendle and the West Pennine Moors, usually in association with rank heather or *Juncus* rush-beds up to 300m above sea level, although nests have been found as high as 390m in the latter area. There is strong circumstantial evidence to suggest that the presence of large numbers of Pheasants on parts of moorland in the West Pennine Moors is leading to the contraction of the range occupied locally by Red Grouse.

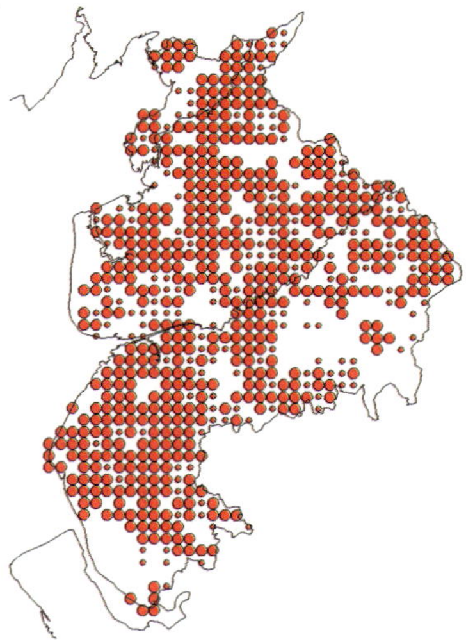

Breeding distribution of Pheasant, 1997-2000. (Large dots: confirmed. Small dots: possible)

Pheasants are largely ignored by birdwatchers, numbers reported being an unrepresentative fraction of those present in the county with, for example, 100 on Plex Moss in 1995, 600 at Belmont Reservoir in 1996 and 1,000 at Eagland Hill in 2002 merely highlighting the scale of local releases. Of more interest are details of self-sustaining populations away from areas of introductions, although no part of the county is immune from periodical recruitment from wandering released birds. For example, small populations remain on the south Liverpool fringe and eight territorial males were at Roddlesworth Plantations in the West Pennine Moors in 2003, a site where no releases have taken place since the 1920s but which lies within 8km of three annual release sites.

SJM, DJH.

This species account was sponsored by Stanton Plant Hire.

RED-THROATED DIVER

Gavia stellata

Lancashire Category A.

Fairly common winter visitor and common passage migrant, probably from Fennoscandia and Iceland.

Although divers as a group are less common off the coast of Lancashire than to our north and south, the low, sleek silhouette of a Red-throated Diver on a murky midwinter sea is a familiar sight to Lancashire seawatchers, as are the characteristic slim profile and flickering wingbeats of migrating birds.

Both Mitchell and Oakes described the Red-throated as our commonest diver, and so it remains to this day, although Oakes reported that it was commoner in Morecambe Bay than further south, a situation that is reversed nowadays. About 1,500 pairs nest in Scotland, but the bulk of the western Palaearctic's population breeds further to the north and east, in Fennoscandia and northern Russia; the entire population winters at sea, predominantly around the coasts of Britain and Ireland, south to the Bay of Biscay.

Birds are recorded from our coast from the end of August in most years, although there are occasional sightings as early as the middle of July; many of the early arrivals are adults, still in full or partial summer plumage. Autumn passage is usually less obvious than movements in spring: 34 off Blackpool on 25 September 1993 and 48 off Formby Point on 23 October 2003 are the highest day totals recorded.

Juvenile Red-throated Diver, Fairhaven Lake, November 2005. (Steve Young)

Parrack (1986) considered that the relative scarcity of Red-throated Divers off north-west England in autumn and winter was due to birds moving south from Scotland favouring the direct route and the sheltered shore of the east coast of Ireland. However, evidence is mounting that birds may not be as scarce in Lancashire waters as previously thought, but rather are widely dispersed and largely out of view from shore. Aerial surveys carried out by the Countryside Council for Wales since 2001 suggest a winter population for the whole of Liverpool Bay of 250 to 1,200 Red-throated Divers (Cranswick *et al.* 2004). Most of these are in Welsh waters but the normal Lancashire population of the bay is believed to be somewhere between 150 and 250, distributed mostly between the Mersey and the Ribble; relatively few are seen over Shell Flat off the Fylde coast.

Shore-based sightings are extremely hit-and-miss and the factors that bring groups of divers into sight of the coast are not fully understood. Most sizeable day-counts, particularly off the Fylde coast, are made up of singles or small groups moving past watchpoints. The location of peak winter counts tends to vary somewhat from year to year, but most of the highest have been off more southerly watchpoints, including 101 off Formby Point on 16 December 2001 and 85 on 26 February 2005. Pride of place, however, must go to Blackpool, with peaks of 86 on 12 January 1991, 71 on 17 December 1995, 137 on 5 January 1997 and 118 on 2 February of the same year. Further north, there were 126 off Heysham on 9 December 1987 and 45 off Rossall Point on 12 December 1997.

Spring passage is often substantial and appears to fall into two phases, the first in March and a second pulse in April and May. Parrack (1986) suggested that the early movements are consistent with the return of Scottish birds to their breeding lochs, whereas the later passage involves Scandinavian birds. The bulk of spring movements are recorded from Blackpool northward, with that site producing by far the largest number of high counts, including 107 on 6 March 1993, 321 on 12 March 1995, 93 on 2 March 1996 and 134 on 19 April 2003. Further south there were 32 off Formby Point on 23 March 1997 and 21 on 20 March 2000. Most of the highest counts in Morecambe Bay have been later in the season, including 35 at Heysham on 4 May 1996 and 23 off Jenny Brown's Point on 23 April 2001; 58 off Heysham and more than 100 off Jenny Brown's Point on 5 April 2005 were exceptional counts for Morecambe Bay at this time of year.

At all watchpoints and in all seasons, peak numbers have increased fairly steadily from the 1960s through to the present but whether this reflects a real growth in numbers or is simply a function of more systematic seawatching with better-quality optics is a matter for conjecture.

Over the years there have been many records of birds, usually singles, on inland waters; Oakes mentioned birds on Stalmine Moss in February 1945 and at Preston in March 1947. Since the 1960s there have been sporadic but widespread occurrences, often of oiled or otherwise stricken individuals, such as the summer-plumaged adult entangled in fishing-line on the Ribble off Clifton Marsh on 28 May 1980. Foulridge and Stocks Reservoirs have seen the highest numbers of inland stragglers, with five and six respectively since 1965; others have been recorded at Prescot, Anglezarke, Black Moss, Lower Rivington and Clowbridge Reservoirs, Brockholes Quarry and on the River Lune. Inland birds have turned up in mid-winter as well as during passage periods, but there is a slight bias towards occurrences in March and April.

BM.

This species account was sponsored by Jack Dixon.

BLACK-THROATED DIVER

Gavia arctica

Lancashire Category A.

Uncommon winter visitor, from northern Europe.

The breeding range of Black-throated Diver closely matches that of Red-throated but its main wintering areas are further to the east in the Baltic, North and Black Seas and it is much scarcer than Red-throated on the coasts of western Britain. Mitchell described it as a rare winter visitor to Lancashire, citing a single record of a bird shot at Lytham during the 1885/86 winter, while according to Oakes it was a very rare coastal vagrant in winter, unknown inland.

Tony Disley

Nowadays it is clear that Black-throated Divers are scarce but annual coastal visitors, with records since the 1960s in all months except June and August. Annual totals averaged just under five between 1978 and 2005 with no clear trend – perhaps surprisingly in the light of increased seawatching – although relatively large numbers were seen annually between 1991 and 1995 and again in 2002-2005. The largest annual totals were fourteen in 2004, ten in 1979 and nine in 1994.

Most are seen singly, and usually loosely associating with Red-throated Divers, either on a winter sea or in migratory flight past a seawatching station. The majority are probably passage migrants, with about 35% of all first sightings occurring in February to April and a further 30% in September to October (Figure 1).

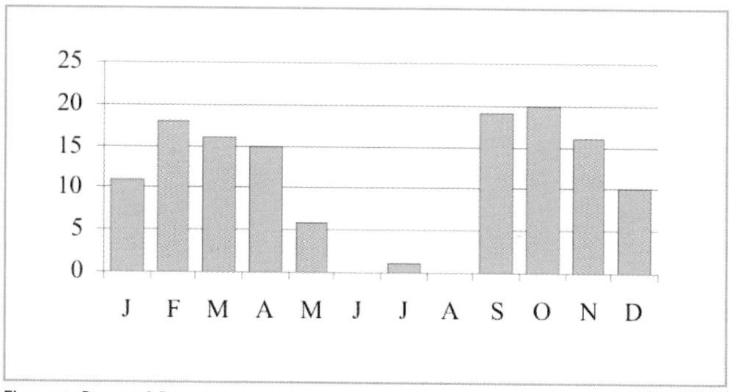

Figure 1. Dates of first sightings of Black-throated Divers in Lancashire, 1978-2005.

Although a small number of autumn birds may remain for some months, winter sightings are less than annual. A large proportion of them are accounted for by the major influx of February 1979, during which large areas of the Baltic froze over, bringing an unprecedented nine birds into the county. Only four of these were recorded on the sea, three off Heysham on 18 March and one at Formby Point on the 4th, the others were relatively long-staying visitors at Seaforth, Southport Marine Lake, Marton Mere, Scorton Lake and Blea Tarn Reservoir, south-east of Lancaster.

During more normal winters records of Black-throated Divers have shown a slight northerly bias: between 1964 and 2005 there were 23 off Heysham-Morecambe, eleven off Rossall Point and 13 off Blackpool. In the south only Formby Point, with some 30 birds during the same period, has featured strongly. Records in the September-October passage period, however, have been heavily concentrated at Formby Point, with 35 since the mid-1960s compared with a mere 14 at all other seawatch sites combined. Spring migrants are slightly scarcer overall but have clearly favoured Blackpool and points further north. One can only speculate to what extent this variation between sites and seasons reflects actual occurrence patterns or seasonal differences in seawatching effort from one location to another.

The dozen or so inland records since the mid-1960s provide too small a sample to permit any generalisations, but winter visits have predominated. One which frequented Marton Mere from 9 Dec 1953 flew off to sea each day to roost. Upland reservoirs have featured strongly, with birds at Anglezarke in February 1986, Churn Clough near Sabden in January-March 1992, Rishton in November 1993, Entwistle in December 1997, Stocks in October 2000 and Holden Wood, Haslingden in late December of the same year. Perhaps the most surprising of all was an adult in breeding plumage on Clowbridge Reservoir, Rossendale on 2 July 1998.

BM.

This species account was sponsored by Mario Chin.

GREAT NORTHERN DIVER

Gavia immer

Lancashire Category A.

Scarce winter visitor from Iceland and Greenland.

Mitchell considered Great Northern Divers to be considerably less scarce than Black-throated, describing them as annual winter visitors in small numbers to the Lancashire coast and also occurring frequently on the larger inland reservoirs. Oakes disagreed as far as inland occurrences were concerned, accepting only one satisfactory record within the present county boundaries, a bird shot on Longridge Reservoir in 1878. He also asserted that coastal records were largely confined to the south-west, with few north of the Ribble Estuary.

The accumulation of data since Oakes's day makes it clear that the Great Northern Diver is somewhat scarcer than Black-throated, with about two-thirds as many records as of the smaller species

Juvenile Great Northern Diver, Crosby Marine Lake, November 2005. (Steve Young)

since the early 1960s. The proportion occurring on inland waters is, however, much higher, vindicating Mitchell's claim of over a century ago.

In the Western Palaearctic Great Northern Divers breed regularly only in Iceland, with a larger population in adjacent parts of the Nearctic, particularly Greenland and north-east Canada. The British and Irish wintering population has a very westerly distribution, as one would expect, from the Northern Isles down the west coast to south-west England. They are, however, decidedly scarce in onshore waters in Lancashire with an average of three records per year between 1978 and 2005 and are, thus, about half as frequent as Black-throated Divers. With the exception of 2003, when an unprecedented 14 were recorded, annual totals since 1978 have varied between none (in three years) and six (in two), and, as with Black-throated, there is no evidence of any trend in the frequency of sightings.

Their pattern of occurrence is subtly different from that of Black-throated, with very few seen during September and a steady build-up from October to reach a midwinter peak in November to January (Figure 1). They appear, then, to be rather more of a winter visitor than passage migrant, but the number of new sightings does rise slightly from February, peaking in May, a month later than for Black-throated – providing evidence of a small spring passage in some years. None has been recorded during June to August.

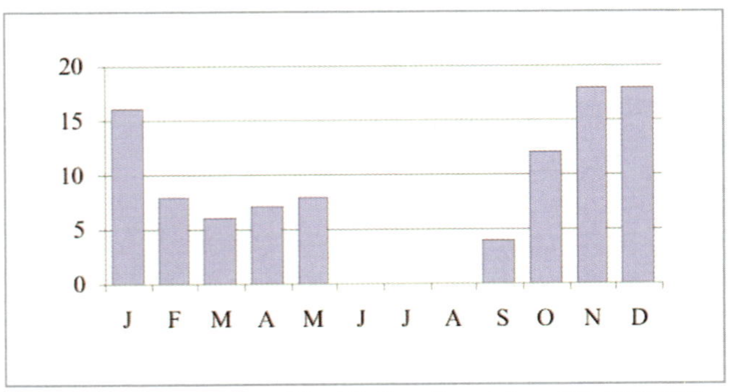

Figure 1. Dates of first sightings of Great Northern Divers in Lancashire, 1978-2005.

The majority of those that have been aged have been juvenile or first-winter birds. Oakes's claim of a southerly bias is partly borne out by more recent data: between 1964 and 2005 eighteen have been recorded in Morecambe Bay, eleven off Rossall Point, 14 at Blackpool and 44 south of the Ribble, the great majority of these off Formby Point.

Given the species' reputation for wintering (and perhaps migrating) further offshore (Parrack 1986) and their origins to our west, it is surprising how many have turned up on inland waters. The proportion of Great Northern records on reservoirs and lakes is twice as great as for Black-throated – at least 16 have been recorded since the early 1960s. The Rivington-Anglezarke Reservoir complex tops the list, with four records, followed by Clowbridge and various waters in the St. Helens area with three, Pine Lake, Carnforth, Foulridge Reservoir and Ogden Reservoir, Haslingden with two apiece, and one at Scorton Lake.

BM.

This species account was sponsored by David Beattie.

PIED-BILLED GREBE

Podilymbus podiceps

Lancashire Category A. (0, 1).

Vagrant from North America.

On 24 May 1997 J.A. Girdley was mixing family duties and birding at Leighton Moss and got into conversation with a couple of relatively inexperienced birdwatchers who mentioned that they had seen an unusual-looking brown grebe at nearby Dockacres Gravel Pits, Carnforth earlier in the day. They pointed to the illustration of Pied-billed Grebe in their field guide and said it resembled that. JAG decided to investigate on his way home - it later transpired that several other birders had heard the same story at Leighton Moss but had decided not to bother!

Immediately on arrival, there was the bird, a summer-plumaged adult on the lake amongst the Coot. It completed a fine year for grebes in the north of the county, where all six species on the British list were recorded.

The bird stayed in the area until 8 June and was seen on and off at Dockacres by very many birders. What was presumably the same individual was subsequently relocated at Skelton Lake, West Yorkshire on 14 June and stayed there until 17 July.

This was the 23rd record of Pied-billed Grebe in Britain and Ireland and, with six occurrences, 1997 was a record year for the species - although it is just possible that five of these were accounted for by this individual making a round trip of England, from London to Northampton, Lancashire and Yorkshire and finally Wiltshire. It remains the only record in north-west England.

Pied-billed Grebe, Dockacres, May 1997. (Steve Young)

SJW, MJ.
This species account was sponsored by Chris Tynan.

LITTLE GREBE

Tachybaptus ruficollis

Lancashire Category A.

Uncommon resident breeder; fairly common in winter.

In 1892 Mitchell described Little Grebes as resident, breeding on a few suitable waters and distributed in small numbers throughout the county in winter. Prior to 1867 there had been only one confirmed breeding record, at the reservoirs attached to Steiner's Printworks at Church, near Accrington. Only four other early regular breeding locations were noted by Mitchell: waters at Rufford, Croston, Woodfold Park in Blackburn and Knowsley Park. Mitchell gave one local name as 'Foot-in-arse' but failed to note which region of the county was responsible for this inelegant epithet.

Oakes reported increasing numbers from the beginning of the 20th century so that by 1953 they were 'a fairly common but local resident', nesting regularly at Leighton Moss, widely separated localities in the Lune Valley, Hurst Green, Clitheroe, Burnley and Knowsley Park, their only site in the south or south-west. Other sites were used sporadically, including dune slacks at Ainsdale (1914), Princes Park, Liverpool (1924-25) and Hesketh Park, Southport (1927). Hardy (1941) noted some additional breeding sites in Merseyside, but it seems unlikely that the county population was much more than 20 pairs in the early 1940s.

Numbers had probably doubled by the 1960s and they were found in 27 10km squares during 1968-72. Their Lancashire range appears to have changed little over the period of the three main atlas surveys, being found in 20 10km squares in 1988-91 (with losses on the Sefton coast, in central Lancashire around Preston, and in Rossendale), and 29 in 1997-2000, when those areas apparently abandoned in the late 1980s had been recolonised. Breeding was confirmed or strongly suspected in 57 tetrads (6%) during 1997-2000 but birds were present in a further 23 tetrads. The current range is mostly south of the Ribble, with the largest concentrations in St. Helens, Sefton and West Lancashire, and with breeding confirmed in only 17 tetrads to the north of the Ribble. A total of 81 pairs was counted during 1997-2000 but the county population was estimated at 125 pairs, indicating a four- or five-fold increase during the second half of the twentieth century.

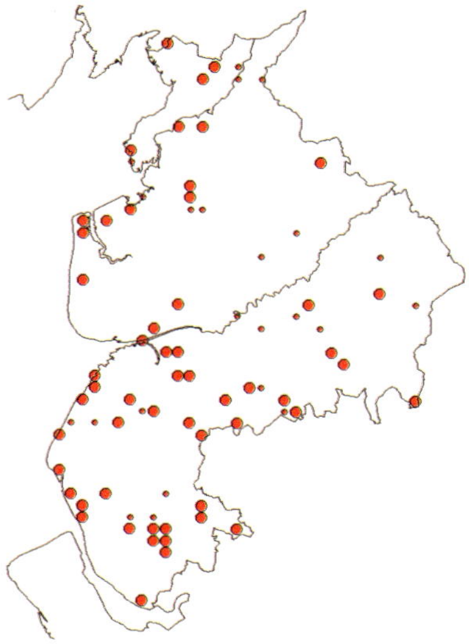

Breeding distribution of Little Grebe, 1997-2000. (Large dots: confirmed. Small dots: possible)

Little Grebes breed throughout the county wherever their preferred habitat of shallow, well-vegetated water exists – on lakes, gravel workings, reed-beds with open water, reservoirs, mill lodges and canals. Most suitable sites – 100 or more in total – have supported one or more pairs at least occasionally during the past 20 years and the population appears to be slowly expanding; reporting rates are low and, although it is difficult to be certain, it seems that a number of new sites were colonised during the late 1990s while some existing sites reported a small increase in breeding pairs. This uncertainty is reflected nationally; BBS data show little change in population size since 1994 but the Waterways Bird Survey shows a 60% decline on linear waterways since the mid-1970s. Breeding productivity in Lancashire appears to be rather low, especially on smaller, more open sites, where human disturbance can be intense and vulnerability to predation is high, and on many reservoirs where fluctuating water levels cause problems. Competition with Ruddy Ducks over breeding territory may also be a factor limiting population expansion.

Most sites hold just a single pair. The only water-bodies supporting more than three pairs in recent years have been Mere Sands Wood (regularly three to five and a maximum of six in 2000-03), Middleton Industrial Estate (three to five since 1993), an unnamed Rossendale lodge (four in 1990-91). Marshside (colonised in 1991), Wrightington Lakes, the Fleetwood lagoons, the Sankey and Rimrose Valleys, Newton Marsh, Brockholes Quarry and a site near Whittle have all held two or three pairs at some time since 1990.

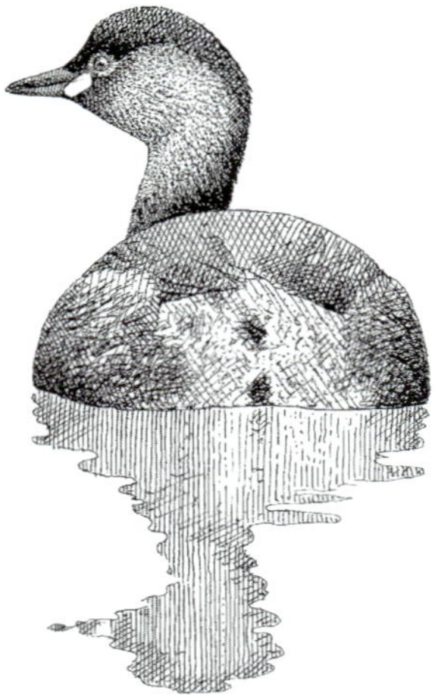

Adult Little Grebe in breeding plumage. (Tony Disley)

Other sites have fared less well. Barrow Lodge near Clitheroe held up to three breeding pairs until the early 1980s when increased angling pressure led to the removal of marginal vegetation. Marton Mere, a former breeding stronghold with up to eight pairs in 1979, raising a maximum 25 juveniles in 1984, is now no longer a breeding site. Why this apparently successful site was suddenly abandoned has been referred to as 'inexplicable'; the last successful fledging of a juvenile here was in 1992 with the last breeding attempt in 1993. Leighton Moss, which always appears to have a couple of pairs present has yet to report positive proof of fledged young.

Although there is some dispersal in late July, mostly of juveniles and probably quite local, this is difficult to distinguish from post-breeding aggregations of birds breeding on the site. For example, Marton Mere held an average of 35 birds in late summer when it was a significant breeding site in the 1970s, with a largest count of 76 in 1978; Dean Clough Reservoir 20 in August 1988, one Rossendale lodge 18 in 1991 and Brockholes Quarry twelve in 2003. Up to ten are recorded regularly at Lee Green Reservoir and 20 or more at Mere Sands Wood.

Adult Little Grebes are highly sedentary and, with many juveniles also remaining on the breeding grounds into winter, there are few purely wintering sites in Lancashire. These include Southport Marine Lake, which holds around 20 in most winters, and Seaforth with usually up to ten and a peak of 20 in November 2000. Few birds are found on running water in winter but single-figure counts are regularly made on stretches of the Rivers Lune, Darwen, Calder and Ribble, particularly when still waters are frozen, for example nine on the Wyre in November 1995. Coastal sightings are exceptional and probably only occur during freezing conditions inland. These include three off Formby Point in February 1978, one off Hest Bank in January 1984, and, most recently, three off Blackpool, two off Fleetwood and one at Formby Point in October 2003.

There are only two ringing recoveries but both give a strong hint that at least a small proportion of the Lancashire population may be long-distance migrants. One of unknown age ringed at Abberton in Essex on 29 October 1956 was found dead in Aintree, Liverpool on the same date in 1958 – a movement of 315km; while a pullus ringed at Kandava in Latvia in June 1983 was shot (it had been thought to be a diving mink) at Pilling in January 1985, having moved a distance of 1653km.

RJH.

This species account was sponsored by Bob Harris.

GREAT CRESTED GREBE

Podiceps cristatus

Lancashire Category A.

Uncommon resident breeder, fairly common in winter.

In 1768 Pennant wrote that the Great Crested Grebe was 'scarce in England', an impression that may have been incorrect due to confusion arising over identification both by name (loon, ducker, gargoose) and recognition – breeding birds were thought to be a different species from those wintering (Harrison and Hollom 1932). By 1831 Montagu stated that 'this bird is indigenous in Britain; it breeds on the meres of Shropshire and Cheshire' and indeed, by 1850, it was well-distributed in small numbers throughout thirteen counties (Harrison and Hollom 1932).

The first documented presence of Great Crested Grebe within Lancashire is found in the Knowsley Hall Game Book, 1807-1818 (Hardy 1979). The three artificial lakes in Knowsley Park provide what is certainly the oldest, and most continuously occupied, breeding haunt within the county (Oakes). Mitchell reported that around 1879 two or three pairs bred there regularly.

The massacre of Great Crested Grebes in the 1850s – when their plumes and 'fur' were used extensively in millinery and in the making of feather muffs – culminated in a national population estimate of 42 pairs in 1860; one or two pairs of which were in Lancashire, almost certainly at Knowsley (Harrison and Hollom 1932). Following the Bird Protection Acts (1870-1880) and natural expansion into suitable habitat, the county has witnessed a slow but steady increase in both distribution and population.

Great Crested Grebe carrying young, Stanley Park, Blackpool. (Phillip Tomkinson)

Prior to 1920 Knowsley Park was the only breeding site in present-day Lancashire, holding one or two pairs. By the 1930s a second site had been added at Walton-le-Dale although breeding there was still irregular. Subsequent surveys indicate a slow, steady increase across the region but changing survey areas and drifting county boundaries mean that we cannot be certain to what extent these reported figures relate to current Lancashire. Hollom (1959) reported 26 pairs in 1946 and 33 in 1954, while Prestt and Mills (1966) increased this to 30-35 pairs at 22 sites in 1966. The last full national census in 1975 reported 81-90 adults at 27 sites, in contrast to Spencer's 39 sites in 1973.

Breeding occurred in 22 10km squares in 1968-72, 19 in 1988-91 and 29 in 1997-2000, indicating a 33% increase in range since the late 1960s. The Lancashire Bird Reports of 1992 and 1993 documented 40-43 breeding pairs, while the 1997-2000 Lancashire Atlas survey found breeding in 66 tetrads, with presence in a further 27; 124 pairs were counted and the population estimated at 140 pairs.

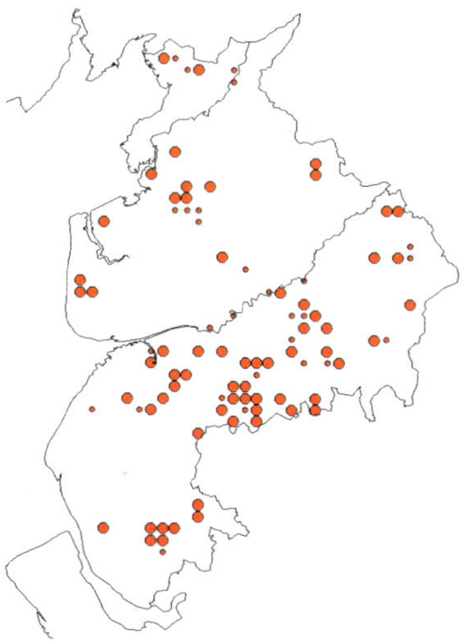

Breeding distribution of Great Crested Grebe, 1997-2000. (Large dots: confirmed. Small dots: possible)

The number of occupied sites is now essentially stable, new breeding sites are few and generally only persist for a year or so, and the number of birds reported annually is fairly constant; it appears that all suitable breeding habitat may now be occupied.

Breeding range is largely determined by the distribution of large water-bodies in the county. Thus, only 25% of breeding sites are north of the Ribble, with the main concentrations at Wyreside Fisheries near Scorton (up to six pairs during the 1990s), Marton Mere (usually three pairs) and the Leighton Moss and Dockacres area. The most important single site is Carr Mill Dam in St. Helens, which was first occupied around 1941 and currently supports up to 14 pairs annually. The reservoirs of the West Pennine Moors support up to 15 pairs in most years, Mere Sands Wood holds six or seven pairs annually, while in the east the Foulridge Reservoirs regularly hold up to three pairs with an exceptional six in 2001.

Breeding success is rarely high – generally fewer than half of all nesting attempts are successful; failures result predominantly from fluctuating water levels, disturbance due to human recreational demands, and predation. Stocks Reservoir, for example, had its first successful breeding for 30 years in 2000 when water levels were unusually high, while breeding by up to four pairs at Barrow Lodge near Clitheroe in the 1970s ceased from 1983 when marginal vegetation was cleared for angling.

Mitchell described Great Crested Grebes as casual winter visitors to most parts of the county with movement to the coast occurring only when inland sites were frozen. Oakes made little reference to winter distribution but it was clear by the 1960s that large numbers were sometimes present on inshore waters throughout the Lancashire coast. The first really big counts were 500 off Morecambe on 25 November 1962, 595 off Formby on 16 March 1969, and, at about the same time, 220 off Squires Gate (Hardy 1979).

Small numbers often remain offshore throughout spring and summer but large numbers only occur there in winter. The Morecambe/Heysham area continues to support nationally important numbers but these have declined somewhat in recent years; the largest recent count was 265 on 23 January 1992 and winter peaks have usually been around 150-200 since then. Relatively few are seen nowadays off the Fylde or Sefton coasts where the largest recent counts are 95 off Blackpool on 1 January 1996 and 96 off Formby in December 1994 with 65 there in March 1999. Numbers wintering on the Mersey Estuary (mostly on its Cheshire sections) became internationally important during the late 1980s, peaking at 277 in October 1992, but declined rapidly from 1998 and now rarely exceed 20.

It is possible that the recent decline on the Mersey and the southern coasts is largely due to increasing numbers wintering inland, probably largely because of a run of ice-free winters. Certainly, the number and proportion of birds wintering inland has increased significantly since the 1960s and birds now remain on many of the main breeding sites year-round. An absence of ringing recoveries, however, means that the origins of the coastal flocks remain a matter for speculation.

RJH.

This species account was sponsored by Bob Harris.

RED-NECKED GREBE

Podiceps grisegena

Lancashire Category A. (/, 90).

Scarce winter visitor from eastern Europe and Russia.

Mitchell knew of seven records between 1872 and 1892 but, apart from one on the Wyre Estuary, it is not known how many were in present-day Lancashire; his remaining six records were from inland sites. Oakes added one record, a bird shot at Stoneyhurst in December 1887, and Hardy (1941) reported singles at Eccleston Mere in January 1939 and Knowsley Park in December of the same year. Further singles were seen off Formby in March 1947 and found dead near Blackpool in the same month. The next was one on the Lune Estuary on 9 January 1955.

Adult Red-necked Grebe in breeding plumage, Knowsley Park, May 2005. (Steve Young)

There have been a further 86 records involving 90 individuals since then. All but four have been singles, the exceptions being twos at Skerton Weir on 5-28 February 1979 with probably the same birds at Carnforth on 11-18 March, at Ogden Reservoir on 17 January 1987, Swinden Reservoir on 16-26 October 1988 and Morecambe on 16 October 1989.

Red-necked Grebes are less than annual in occurrence in Lancashire and there have been 15 blank years since 1958. There have been just two significant influxes: in 1978/79 when 16 were recorded and 1988/89 with ten. (Figure 1). The 1990s saw a marked downturn in average annual totals to less than one per year between 1990 and 2005, compared with three per year during the 1970s and 1980s.

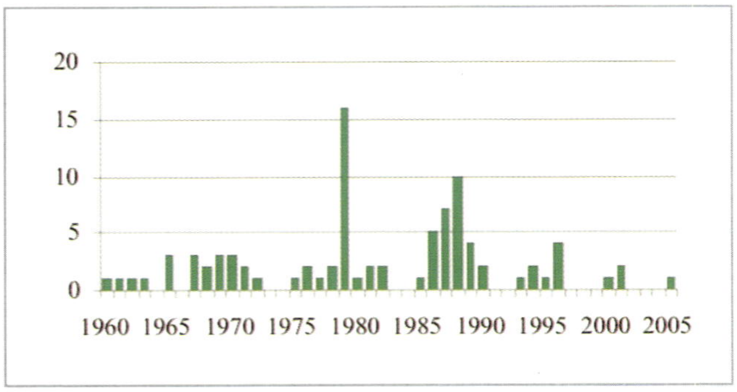

Figure 1. Annual totals of Red-necked Grebes in Lancashire, 1960-2005.

In contrast to Mitchell's day, sightings are principally coastal with more than 50% (47 records) on the sea and a further 20% close to the coast, from Jenny Brown's Point to Seaforth but with a distinct northern bias – Morecambe Bay records outnumber those in Liverpool Bay by almost two to one. Of all the grebes this is the least likely to be seen inland in Lancashire with only 20 or so records, mostly on upland reservoirs. The 1978/79 influx fitted this general pattern with most records on the coast but the period 1985/86 to 1988/89 was unusual with 14 out of 24 individuals occurring far inland.

Red-necked Grebes are migratory, dispersing to coastal waters almost immediately after breeding. A complete simultaneous moult of primaries curtails further movement until September, and Lancashire's earliest autumn migrant was an adult in summer plumage on Rivington Reservoir on 1 September 1986. Figure 2 shows a modest total of records in October-November, with a decline in December; January and February are clearly the months of maximum arrivals, probably as a result of cold weather movements such as occurred in 1978/79 when 14 birds arrived from January onwards. Very few new birds have been recorded in the period March-May; the latest spring records were at Marton Mere and Burwains Reservoir on 25 and 30 May 1987 and at Knowsley Park on 18-20 May 2005.

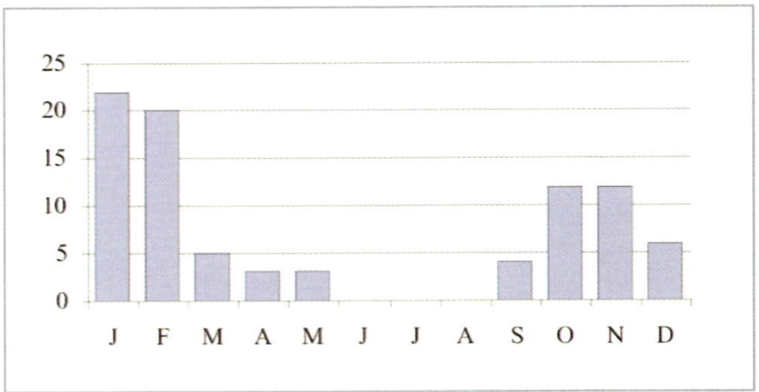

Figure 2. Dates of first arrivals of Red-necked Grebes in Lancashire, 1955-2005.

Although it is difficult to keep track of offshore individuals, it seems that most stays are relatively brief with only about a dozen or so thought to have remained for more than a fortnight. Most inland records are also of a few days duration at most, but with some notable exceptions. During the influx of February 1979 the following all held singles for extended periods of time: Leighton Moss (16 days), Burnley and Stanley Park Blackpool (23 days each) and Haweswater (24 days). Rivington Reservoir hosted a single for 22 days in January 1987 and Guide Reservoir one for 24 days in 1996, while Eccleston Mere in St. Helens holds the longest continuous inland record of 75 days for the period 2 January to 18 March 1988.

The ages of only eleven birds have been published, of which seven were first-winters and four adults.

RJH.

This species account was sponsored by Ribble Bird Tours (01253-407554).

SLAVONIAN GREBE

Podiceps auritus

Lancashire Category A. (9, 130+).

Scarce winter visitor from eastern Europe and Russia.

Mitchell described the Slavonian Grebe as an 'extremely rare winter visitor' and knew of only three records in present-day Lancashire. The first was a first-winter at the mouth of the River Alt in February 1864, followed by singles at Fleetwood in December 1879 and 'near Colne' in the winter of 1880. Oakes added another six records: one shot near Haslingden Grane in 1903 or 1904, a winter-plumaged adult shot at Hightown on 18 December 1903, one near Silverdale on 11 October 1913, two on the Lune at Caton on 28 October 1916 and probably one of these near Lancaster on 15 December 1916. He labelled the species a 'scarce and irregular winter visitor'.

Slavonian Grebe in winter plumage, Seaforth Nature Reserve, February 2005. (Steve Young)

Reported sightings have since increased steadily – with a total of more than 130 between 1950 and 2005 – from an average of just over one a year during the 1960s to 2.5 during the 1970s and 1980s, three in the 1990s and four in the first six years of this century (Figure 1). It is impossible to say to what extent this represents a genuine increase or is simply a result of more and better-equipped observers but, given the species' predominantly offshore occurrence, the latter is likely to be a major factor.

'Slavs' have been recorded annually since 1993 and there have been just four blank years in the past quarter century, in 1971, 1973, 1982 and 1992. Numbers vary relatively little between years and the largest annual totals have been seven in 1991, 1997, 2003 and 2005. Almost all records are of single birds with just eight of twos – including a displaying pair off Morecambe and Jenny Brown's Point from 14 April 2000. Other multiple records are: threes at Heysham on 13 March 1989 and Formby Point on 4 November 1990, and four at Rossall Point on 1 March 1986.

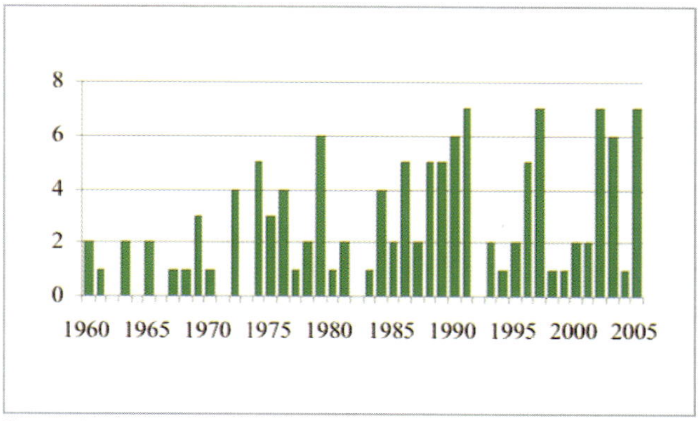

Figure 1. Annual totals of Slavonian Grebes in Lancashire, 1959-2005.

Arrival is on average a month or so earlier than for Red-necked Grebe (Figure 2), with the first typically seen in October and a clear peak of new birds in November and December. The earliest was a juvenile at Prescot Reservoirs on 5 August 2003 and the next earliest on 15 September 1991 at Scorton. New arrivals decline slightly in January and February but these increase in March and April as a small number of migrants pass through the county.

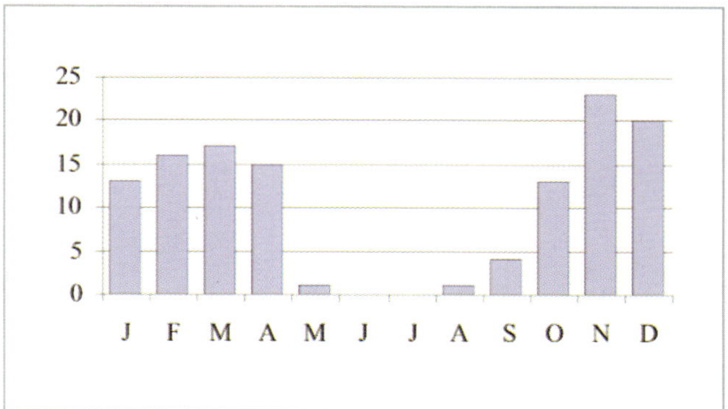

Figure 2. Dates of first arrivals of Slavonian Grebes in Lancashire, 1959-2005.

Although this spring passage takes place both on the coast and inland, almost half of all inland records since 1959 have occurred during March and April, compared with roughly a quarter of those on the sea or coastal lagoons, perhaps indicating some overland movement. However, the overwhelming majority of post-1958 records have been on or near the sea, most of them in late autumn and winter. These are distributed fairly evenly between Morecambe Bay, the Fylde coast and the Sefton coast. The 19 inland records have occurred on a wide range of water-bodies, with only Foulridge and Prescot Reservoirs and Scorton, with two each, registering in more than one year. Other still-water sites are Carr Mill Dam, Mere Brow, Mere Sands Wood, Martin Mere, and Dean Clough, Grimsargh, Longridge, Rivington, Parsonage and Rishton Reservoirs, with just two records on running water, on the Ribble at Preston and Ribchester.

RJH.

This species account was sponsored by Rosie Briggs.

BLACK-NECKED GREBE

Podiceps nigricollis

Lancashire Category A. (7, 115).

Scarce passage migrant; rare winter visitor.

Mitchell knew of just a single record, one killed 'near the Lune mouth, late in March or early April 1886', the specimen ending up at St. Michael's-on-Wyre Museum. There were no further records until Oakes reported an adult captured alive on a pond at Middleton on 28 July 1904. Mr D. D. Pennington (of Birkdale) reported two occurrences at Banks in 1909 and 1910 but gave no details. On 29 January 1937 two birds were seen at the tide edge at Fleetwood (Oakes) and in February 1939 the decomposed remains of a bird were found at the Lune Estuary.

Black-necked Grebes remained an extreme rarity until the 1960s with just two records in the 1950s: singles at Marton Mere on 11 January and Leighton Moss on 21 February 1954. Although several good years were registered from the late 1960s to the end of the 1980s (Figure 1), annual totals continued to average less than 1.5 between 1960 and 1989. The 1990s saw a sharp upsurge, however, with no blank years since 1989 and an average of nearly five annually during 1990-2005; the largest annual totals were ten in both 2003 and 2004.

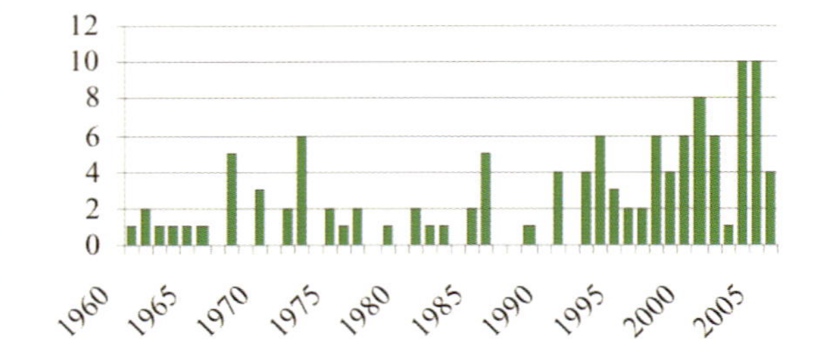

Figure 1. Annual totals of Black-necked Grebes in Lancashire, 1960-2005.

In sharp contrast to both Red-necked and Slavonian Grebes, the Black-necked Grebe is predominantly a passage migrant in Lancashire (Figure 2). Only nine birds have ever been seen in winter (December to February), seven of them on the sea or near the coast and just two any distance inland.

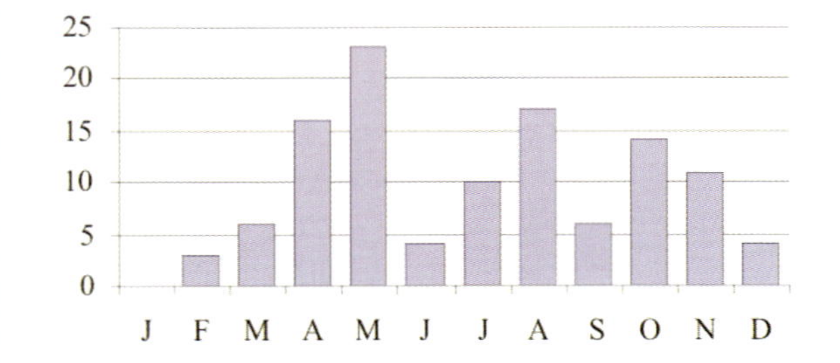

Figure 2. Dates of first arrivals of Black-necked Grebes in Lancashire, 1960-2005.

Spring passage begins at the end of March, increases throughout April and comes to a clear peak in May. In contrast to winter, only two spring records out of a total of 43 have been offshore with eleven a significant distance inland. Breeding birds in Cheshire and Greater Manchester typically arrive in the last week of March, with numbers peaking in late April to early May. They are prone to wander at this time of year, so it is possible that a proportion of Lancashire records relate to these wanderings. However, spring records come from all parts of Lancashire rather than just those areas closest to the breeding areas. They are heavily concentrated at Leighton Moss (14 plus two at the nearby Dockacres complex) and Marton Mere (seven plus four at Myerscough Quarry in inland Fylde), where several recent records have involved apparent pairs, sometimes staying for a week or more.

Tony Disley

Breeding has never occurred in the county but has taken place in recent years at one site in Greater Manchester fairly close to our boundary. The dramatic recent increase in records, fuelled by the increasing population to our south and the presence of apparently prospecting pairs in spring, perhaps indicates that colonisation may be just around the corner.

Post-breeding dispersal starts in July with a first autumn peak recorded in August. A second peak follows in October and November and it is possible that the first peak involves the dispersal of north-west breeding birds, and the second migrants from further afield. However, as in spring, there is little difference in the distribution of records throughout the county between August/September and October/November. The same two sites, Leighton Moss and Marton Mere predominate and about 40% of records are far inland; the only clear difference between early and late autumn is that more birds are seen on or near the coast in the latter period.

RJH.

This species account was sponsored by Ron Hothersall

FULMAR

Fulmarus glacialis

Lancashire Category A.

Fairly common passage migrant; rare in winter.

Until the late nineteenth century St. Kilda was the only known British colony, but by 1988-91 colonies existed virtually all around the coastlines of both Britain and Ireland and by 1998-2002 the British population was estimated at 499,000 pairs, making it one of our commonest seabirds (Mitchell *et al.* 2004). During the 1970s the small eastern Irish Sea population underwent some growth with the consolidation of colonies on the Calf of Man, Anglesey and at St. Bees Head on the Cumbrian coast, but it remains insignificant in national terms, consisting of only around 3,500 pairs (Mitchell *et al.* 2004). The majority of birds do not undertake truly migratory journeys but rather disperse out to sea to more or less all points of the compass, with birds of breeding age returning to the nesting colonies after moulting. So, although numbers seen in Lancashire have increased substantially, Fulmars remain far from abundant.

Mitchell considered the Fulmar to be very rare in Lancashire, recorded only during or after winter gales. One was shot at Fleetwood in December 1881 while another was obtained in unknown circumstances at Blackpool around the same time; another was shot on one of the Rivington reservoirs in December 1883 and a fourth was picked up injured on Formby shore in January 1884. Oakes could find only four further occurrences, inland casualties found near Garstang in the winter of 1889-90 and at Galgate, Lancaster in April 1904, and dead or moribund coastal specimens from Formby in December 1913 and Birkdale in March 1939.

Tony Disley

The growth in systematic seawatching with long-range optics did not begin until a decade or more after Oakes's book was written and since then it has become clear that Fulmars are regular spring and autumn 'migrants' along our entire coastline and occasional visitors in winter.

These winter records make it difficult to pinpoint the start of spring movements back to the breeding colonies, but the first are normally seen in early March and sightings continue on-and-off until the middle of June. The size of movements varies very much from one year to the next; as in autumn, strong onshore winds are usually a necessary condition for substantial numbers of Fulmars to be recorded. Prior to the early 1980s peak counts at all watchpoints were typically below 25 but from then until the mid-1990s there were many records of large movements, although numbers since have fallen back once again to very low levels. The growth in the popularity of seawatching and improved quality of telescopes may well account in large part for the increase in Fulmar records after 1980, but the recent virtual collapse in numbers is less easy to explain, as seawatching effort has in no way diminished.

A movement of 675 off Heysham on 7 June 1987 remains the highest count of Fulmars ever made in Lancashire; 430 passed Blackpool on the same date undoubtedly involving many of the same individuals. Other major spring influxes have included 163 off Heysham on 3 May 1982 and 137 there on 10 June 1991, when 105 were also recorded at Formby Point; a count of 92 at Formby on 25 May 2002 is the highest total since and all other spring counts since 1994 have been of fewer than 40 birds. There are no breeding records in the county, although a bird spent an hour apparently prospecting potential nest-sites around cliffs at Jenny Brown's Point on 26 May 1999.

Occasional movements in July are difficult to attribute. They may involve early autumn dispersals or feeding flocks displaced from breeding areas by brief summer storms; 350 off Heysham on 1 July 1990 is by far the largest such influx on record. Autumn passage tends to be concentrated in the earlier part of the season, and normally peaks between mid-August and mid-September. As in spring, numbers increased markedly in the early 1980s but have declined, though less dramatically, since the mid-1990s. Heysham, Rossall Point, Blackpool and Formby Point have all recorded treble-figure movements: there were 288 off Heysham on 6 September 1990 while 560 there on the 18th is the highest autumn count to date; 143 passed on 14 August 1994 and 150 on 29 August 1997. A hundred were off Rossall Point on 10 September 1987, 285 passed Formby on 28 August 1992 and 198 on 25 August 1995, and 200+ were off Blackpool on 14 September 1997. The movement usually dwindles very rapidly after mid-September, and relatively few are recorded in October; November occurrences are scarce.

As in the days of Mitchell and Oakes, small numbers of Fulmars are occasionally seen in mid-winter, usually during or just after gales; five off Heysham on 6 January 1991 and off Formby Point on 30 December 1994, and seven off Formby on 10 December 2000 are the largest parties recorded to date.

Three dark-morph 'Blue Fulmars', which occur largely in the Arctic, have been fully documented: off Heysham on 22 February 2002, Blackpool on 13 January 2004 and Rossall Point on 12 January 2005, although single birds were reported off Seaforth on 20 October 1986 and at Heysham on 7 June 1987.

Fulmars are robust and powerful fliers, as any seawatcher who has seen birds slicing effortlessly through a September gale will attest; it seems strange, therefore, that the species is unusually susceptible to inland displacement and wrecking. Mortality in storms seems to be high, and prolonged gales almost invariably result in a few dead and dying Fulmars being picked up along the shore, on adjacent saltmarshes, and occasionally, far inland. There have been many records from the interior of the county over the years, but a few will serve as illustrations: one found dead on the Old Coach Road, Rainford on 31 January 1982, an exhausted bird was found at Altham on 25 September 1984, single birds flew over Rowley Lake, Burnley and nearby Padiham after gales on 7 September 1990, and one was on Prescot Reservoirs after a gale on 12 July 1998. Inland visits by Fulmars are not, however, entirely dependent on stormy weather; one flew over Whin Scar Clough,

Burnley, in sunny conditions and light breezes on 24 June 1994 and there have been at least five summer or autumn records since the 1970s of one to three birds flying far up the Ribble Estuary at high tide in calm weather.

There have been six recoveries in Lancashire of Fulmars ringed elsewhere in Britain and Ireland, single birds from eastern Scotland, western Scotland, Fair Isle, the Isle of Man, Anglesey and Co. Wexford, and one from further afield, a bird ringed as a pullus in north-west Iceland on 28 July 1987 and found dead on Cockerham Marsh on 12 February 1988.

BM.

This species account was sponsored by George Lamb.

FEA'S/ZINO'S PETREL

Pterodroma feae/madeira

Lancashire Category A. (0, 1).

Vagrant from Madeira and Cape Verdes.

Barry McCarthy set off for his usual Formby Point watchpoint on the morning of 8 September 1995 more because the force 4-5 north-westerly was likely to make passerine-watching conditions difficult than in real expectation of any major seabird passage. But on his arrival at 08.00 under overcast skies with frequent heavy showers he was happy to discover a substantial movement was underway.

For the next three hours he logged several hundred terns moving south over a rough sea, with a dozen or so Arctic, Great and Pomarine Skuas harassing them. Things quietened down with high tide around 11.00 but at 11.48, now in clear light conditions, he picked up a medium-sized seabird about a kilometre away to the south but coming towards him, travelling fast about three metres above the waves. His view on what it was shifted from Fulmar to Balearic Shearwater until, as it approached closer, it banked and revealed long, slightly swept-back, sooty-black underwings that contrasted starkly with its snow-white underparts. As it swooped down, then banked again, the mousy-grey upperwings and mantle and contrasting grey rump and uppertail came into view. It was a *Pterodroma*! A 'Soft-plumaged Petrel'!

Determining which race (this was before they were split into separate species) had to wait until he got home to compare his notes and sketches with the literature, which confirmed it as one of the two North Atlantic races (now species) on account of its pale rump and lack of a breastband. As with most British and Irish records, insufficient detail was seen to decide which, but it is now assumed that most if not all refer to the relatively common Cape Verde or Fea's Petrel rather than the critically endangered Madeira or Zino's Petrel (Steele 2006).

This was the sixth record of this species group in the UK and the first in north-west England.

SJW.

This species account was sponsored by Barry McCarthy.

CORY'S SHEARWATER

Calonectris diomedea

Lancashire Category A. (0, 2).

Vagrant from Mediterranean and South Atlantic islands.

One was claimed off Rossall Point on 16 August 1986 shortly after a Balearic Shearwater had passed Heysham; it was submitted to the BBRC for evaluation as a first for Lancashire but was not accepted by them.

One seen off Blackpool by Len Blacow on 24 September 1991 therefore became the first county record. The second was seen on a seawatch from Formby Point on 6 August 1993.

SJW, MJ.

This species account was sponsored by Len Knowles.

[GREAT SHEARWATER]

Puffinus gravis

A bird seen near the Crosby lightship in early August 1929 (Canon C.E. Raven. *Musings and Memories*: 67) was published in square brackets by Oakes. The record was reviewed by the county records committee in 1999 and confirmed to be insufficiently described.

SJW, MJ.

SOOTY SHEARWATER

Puffinus griseus

Lancashire Category A.

Rare autumn visitor from southern hemisphere.

This supple and powerful flier is one of the great ocean wanderers; Sooty Shearwaters nest in immense colonies, mainly on remote islands in the southern oceans, and migrate to winter in the North Atlantic and North Pacific during our summer. Birds arrive in numbers off eastern North America in April and May, swing eastwards to the south of Iceland towards north-west Europe in July and pass down our coasts, from Norway to the Canaries, between August and October. Unfortunately, very few seem to find their way through the narrows of the North Channel and into the Irish Sea; the total of Lancashire records is a mere fraction of the massive movements that are regularly recorded off western Ireland, Cornwall or even the English east coast in a single autumn's day. There have been rather more sightings off north-west Wales, the Isle of Man and even from the Irish east coast; it seems that particularly strong onshore winds are required to bring Sooty Shearwaters within range of Lancashire seawatchers.

The first Lancashire Sooty Shearwater was recorded off Blackpool on 12 October 1968. Since then there have been 33 more reports, with noticeable clusters of six during 1972-74, 13 during 1977-79 and six in 1987-88. Since the end of the 1980s, however, reports have dwindled dramatically with autumn singles in 1991, 1993, 2002 and 2005 off Formby Point and one off Blackpool in 1992 the only records. This decline is puzzling, occurring as it did largely after the explosion of interest in seawatching in the early 1980s – it is not reflected anywhere else in Britain or Ireland and suggests, at the very least, that some of the records from the 1970s ought to be reassessed; unfortunately, few are documented. The most likely explanation is that many of the 1970s records, coming as they did at the dawn of the 'seawatching age' and before observers had become fully familiar with skua identification, were misidentifications.

Sooty Shearwater with Manx Shearwaters, off Blackpool. (Tony Disley)

There have been five published spring records, all in May between 1972 and 1975. Since Sooty Shearwaters are very rare in British and Irish waters at this time of year, extreme caution must be exercised in accepting these as genuine. In autumn, two have been reported in July, nine in August, 18 in September and two in October. Most of the early autumn birds have accompanied movements of Manx Shearwaters, usually in strong onshore winds. Later occurrences have tended to be of solitary birds flying rapidly southwards, again over rough seas in westerly gales. All records have been from Rossall Point southwards.

SJW, BM.

This species account was sponsored by John Dempsey.
http://birdblog.merseyblogs.co.uk

MANX SHEARWATER

Puffinus puffinus

Lancashire Category A.

Common passage migrant.

It took nearly 100 years and the development of high-resolution optics for the true Lancashire status of the Manx Shearwater to be resolved. Prior to the 1950s virtually all that was known was derived from tideline corpses and seems to have been widely misinterpreted. Without giving any details, Mitchell described it as an 'irregular winter visitor', while Oakes referred to 'very few winter occurrences', giving only a report of Coward's of seven seen near the Liverpool Bar lightship on 30 January 1931 in support. The only other field observations that Oakes knew of were several small flocks, again seen near the Bar Light, on 3 July 1938, and undated records of 'small parties of unidentified shearwaters' off Formby. He therefore based his analysis of the timing of occurrences almost entirely on records of dead or exhausted birds, concluding they were present in Lancashire waters between April and September, noting that records were more common in spring than autumn.

In one of the early experiments on Manx Shearwaters' homing abilities, a bird caught at the Skokholm colony was released at Northenden, south of Manchester on 23 May 1937 and was recaptured at its breeding site a fortnight later on 6 June, having been seen to fly down the Mersey on release.

The only winter record since Oakes's book was one found at Glasson on 2 December 1972 and, although this was described as freshly-dead, it is doubtful if any Manx Shearwater has ever occurred in Lancashire in a healthy state during winter.

From the 1950s to the 1970s the frequency of records and the number of birds involved increased, though not dramatically; the species did not feature at all in several annual county bird reports during this period. Since the mid-1970s it has become clear that Manx Shearwaters are regularly present offshore, sometimes in large numbers, between April and September; strong onshore winds are normally required to produce high counts, although the largest movement ever recorded here, 1,163 birds off Blackpool on 25 July 1992, took place in calm, sunny conditions.

Few are seen before the middle of April and until very recently movements in spring were typically very light; 50 off Squire's Gate, Blackpool on 9 May 1965 and 45 at Formby Point on 29 May 1972 were the highest counts prior to 1999. Since then, however, there have been several substantial movements in May; 88 were off Heysham on 22 May 1999 and an influx along much of the coastline on 17 May 2000 brought 240 to Heysham and Jenny Brown's Point combined, over 100 off Ainsdale, and 820 moving south at Formby Point. Over 300 were off Jenny Brown's Point in a south-westerly wind on 24 May 2001 and 86 passed Formby on 25 May 2002.

Manx Shearwater, Mersey Narrows, September 2005. (Steve Young)

Since the mid-1980s a pattern of fairly frequent heavy movements in June and July has become established. The earliest of these perhaps include birds moving between breeding colonies in Wales or further afield and favoured feeding areas – including the Irish Sea Front near the Isle of Man and offshore from Walney Island – that are pushed inshore by sudden westerlies. Large post-breeding counts include 425 off Rossall Point on 31 July 1986, 490 at Blackpool on 24 July 1988 and 400 at Formby on 30th June 1999, but movements on 12 July 1998 were exceptional with at least 500 in Morecambe Bay, 216 at Rossall Point, 700 off Blackpool and 520 past Formby Point.

Movements continue throughout August and most have left Lancashire waters by the beginning of September. October records are distinctly uncommon and 80 moving south off Formby Point on 4 November 1979 were quite exceptional. Peak autumn counts over recent decades include 200 off Formby on 16 September 1978, 138 off Blackpool on 19 August 1982, 233 off Rossall Point on 19 August 1985, 274 there on 15 August 1991, 243 at Formby Point on 20 August 1998 and 488 off Blackpool on 12 August 2000.

Manx Shearwaters do not appear to be nearly so susceptible as Fulmars to being driven far inland by gales, or deposited in a dead or moribund condition on the shoreline, presumably due in part to the fact that they are far away in mid-Atlantic during our most violent winter storms. There have, nevertheless, been quite a few casualties over the years, the great majority towards the end of the autumn passage period.

Most inland birds have been picked up dead or exhausted, such as those found at Bacup and Waterfoot, Rossendale in mid-September 1970 and singles at Colne in 1974, Burnley in 1981, Hapton, near Padiham in 1986, St. Helens in 1988, Aintree in 1992 and Chorley in 1998, all in September, and one at Belmont Reservoir on 8 October 2004. Several of these stricken individuals were successfully rehabilitated and released, although what the bird set free on Rivington Reservoir in 1998 made of its liberation can only be guessed at. However, one apparently healthy bird arrived in calm weather at Stocks Reservoir on 18 June 2003 while singles flew over Brockholes Quarry on 17 July and 18 October 2004.

There have been 30 recoveries of ringed birds in Lancashire, 27 of them from Wales and three from Ireland.

BM.

This species account was sponsored by Barry Dyson.

BALEARIC SHEARWATER

Puffinus mauretanicus

Lancashire Category A. (0, 3).

Vagrant from Mediterranean.

The taxonomy of the medium-sized European shearwaters remains a matter of some debate. Until quite recently the two Mediterranean forms, Balearic and Levantine *P. yelkouan*, were treated as sub-species of Manx Shearwater. For a while both were regarded as a single species, Mediterranean Shearwater, but more recently all three forms have been considered to be good species in their own right.

One thing is clear, though, the Balearic Shearwater is one of Europe's rarest breeding birds. The total population was estimated at 3-5000 pairs in 1992 (Hagemeijer & Blair 1997) and is now regarded as critically endangered (Wynn *et al.* 2005). Nonetheless, increasing numbers – 1,000 or more annually (R. Wynn *pers. comm.*) – are seen off southern English coasts in autumn, but it remains decidedly rare in the eastern Irish Sea.

A record of one with Manx Shearwaters off Morecambe on 14 June 1979 was published in the Lancashire Bird Report but the claim was subsequently withdrawn by the observer, having concluded it was a lightly-oiled Manx.

The county's first was found by Pete Marsh and Alan Mackenzie off Heysham on 16 August 1986. It was seen twice at distances down to 400m off the North Harbour wall and at the time was a source of great disappointment since this was before the 'split' and the observers had initially thought, and hoped, that the bird was a Sooty Shearwater, which would have been a first record for north Lancashire. Few other seabirds were seen at Heysham that day – only 47 Fulmars and no Manx Shearwaters.

The two other records have both been at Formby Point: the first flying south offshore on 13 July 1994 (also on a day when no Manx Shearwaters were seen), and the other floundering in the tideline during a north-west gale on 14 September 2004.

SJW.

This species account was sponsored by Pete Marsh.

LITTLE SHEARWATER

Puffinus baroli

Lancashire Category A. (0, 2).

Vagrant from Macaronesia.

On 27 March 1975, local veterinary surgeon David F. Wadsworth, conducting a beached bird survey on Cleveleys beach, picked up a shearwater that seemed smaller than the Manx Shearwaters he had found previously. He contacted Maurice Jones who examined, measured and photographed the bird. The record was accepted by the BBRC as the eleventh for Britain and Ireland. It was identified as an immature female.

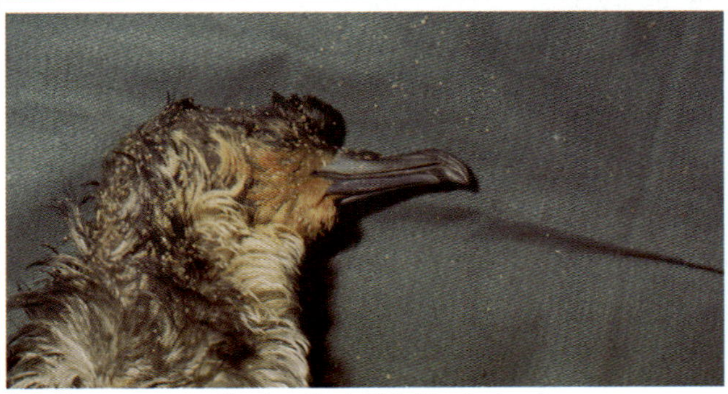

Little Shearwater corpse, Cleveleys, March 1975. (Maurice Jones)

On examination it was found to have been shot – in circumstances that can only be guessed at. The specimen is preserved in Liverpool Museum.

On 1 September 1992 Gavin Thomas caught brief views of a small shearwater flying away from him by the Radar Tower at the mouth of the Mersey at Seaforth. He was almost certain that it was a Little Shearwater but, no doubt bearing in mind that this is one of the most 'rejected' species on the British list, he did not pursue his claim.

Then, early in the morning of 5 September, Chris Kehoe headed to the seawall at Seaforth during strong north-westerly winds. He saw little until at 07.00 four Leach's Petrels and a Fulmar flew out of the river on the ebbing tide and fifteen minutes later two visiting birdwatchers gestured towards a bird coming into the Mersey towards them. As it approached it could only be seen head-on but its rapid, shallow wingbeats and short, flat glides were obvious and it soon showed its profile at a distance of about 400m, revealing small size, short, blunt wings and a white face with prominent dark eye. Obligingly, it then settled on the water, allowing full scrutiny of the face pattern and confirmation of the identification. Soon afterwards, it flew out of the Mersey, past a hide full of oblivious birdwatchers. The record was accepted by the BBRC.

There were several other claimed sightings of the bird subsequently, with the last on 15 September, but none was sufficiently clear-cut for submission to the BBRC.

The taxonomy of the 'Little Shearwater' group underwent significant change in 2005 as a result of DNA studies and birds from the northern and southern hemispheres are now regarded as separate species. All British occurrences are believed to be from the nominate population which breeds off Madeira, the Canaries and Selvagens.

SJW.

This species account was sponsored by Maurice Jones.

EUROPEAN STORM-PETREL

Hydrobates pelagicus

Lancashire Category A.

Uncommon passage migrant and summer visitor.

The nearest breeding colonies to the Lancashire coast are on Sanda off the tip of the Mull of Kintyre, the Calf of Man, Bardsey Island and the Pembrokeshire islands, all of which are relatively small, holding under 200 pairs, with the exception of Skokholm, which holds up to 2,450 (Mitchell *et al.* 2004). European Storm Petrels winter at sea off south-west Africa, leaving breeding areas in British and Irish waters in September and October and returning in late April and May.

Mitchell described the Storm-petrel as a 'winter visitor', seldom seen except during and after gales; numbers were described as substantial on occasion, with many records from far inland, and following easterly as well as westerly gales. Oakes regarded the species as a scarce and irregular storm-driven vagrant in late autumn and winter, but placed less emphasis on inland occurrences.

Until quite recently, the status of the European Storm-petrel in Lancashire had changed little since Oakes's day; it remains considerably scarcer than Leach's Storm-petrel and published records required a written description until 2000. Analysis of occurrences between 1980 and 2005 shows an average annual total of around 28 individuals but with enormous year-on-year variations; there was a clear increase in records between the mid-1980s and early 1990s, but no obvious trend since then (Figure 1).

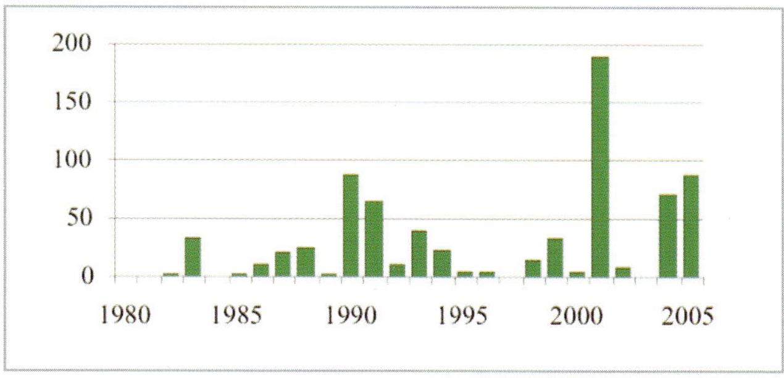

Figure 1. Estimated annual totals of European Storm-petrels in Lancashire, 1980-2005.

During the 1960s and 1970s most of the very few records continued to occur in late autumn, although a scatter of sightings from midsummer onwards heralded the transformation to come. In 1978, a good year, there were five records of single birds in early July and early September, with birds off the Mersey mouth, Formby Point and Blackpool. A major movement, in very wild westerlies, off Seaforth between 16 and 20 October 1983 totalled up to 40 birds, and seemed to recreate the late autumn/'winter' scenarios of Mitchell and Oakes, but this was, in the event, the last noteworthy late-season movement up to the present time.

The small numbers of Storm Petrels recorded during the rest of the 1980s continued to show a predominance of autumn occurrences: a total of 16 between June and August and 44 during September and October; five off Heysham on 29 August 1988 and ten off Seaforth on 8 October of the same year were the highest counts during this period.

European Storm-petrel, River Mersey, Seaforth, July 1990. (Steve Young)

During the 1990s, however, there was a major and sustained shift, both in timing of sightings and numbers of birds involved. Annual totals increased rapidly, and the great majority were recorded in late summer (Figure 2): 88 birds in 1990, 65 in 1991, 39 in 1993, 33 in 1999, an unprecedented 189 in 2001 and 70 in

2004. Peak site counts included eleven off Blackpool on 24 June 1990, ten off Rossall Point on 9 July of the same year and 20 off Seaforth next day, 22 off Heysham on 26 July 1993, up to 170 there during 12-14 July 2001, when double figures were also recorded off Seaforth, and 30 off Seaforth on 22 September 2004. Most of these high counts occurred during, or soon after brief summer gales, but several movements, in 1990 in particular, took place in relatively calm conditions. Between 1990 and 2004 relatively few (fewer than 10%) European Storm-petrels have been recorded after the end of August, compared with 75% between 1958 and 1989.

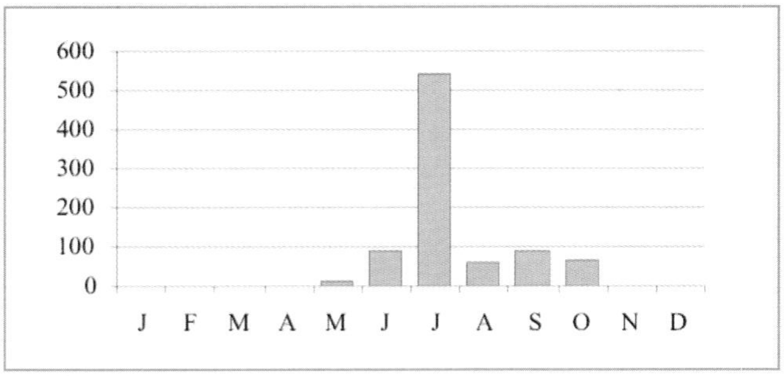

Figure 2. Monthly totals of European Storm-petrels in Lancashire, 1980-2005.

The causes of this change have been a subject for debate and speculation among Lancashire seawatchers. It may be that European Storm-petrels are migrating earlier than in the past, although how that would account for the increase in numbers is unclear. At least some of the birds observed at close range at Heysham in July 2001 were identified as first-summers and it is possible that many Lancashire birds are immatures that are known to wander between colonies before settling to breed at age four or five (Migration Atlas). It might also be the result of an increasing breeding population in the eastern Irish Sea; the estimate of the Skokholm population has recently been increased by 300% (Mitchell *et al.* 2004). It could, however, be that numbers offshore have changed little but that the increased frequency of occasional spells of stormy weather in midsummer over the past decade has brought more birds into view.

The vast majority of sightings are fleeting, although a few sometimes linger in the Mersey Narrows. At Heysham, however, the 'soup' of cooked marine invertebrates emanating from the power station outfalls sometimes attracts feeding birds.

In contrast to the apparent situation in Mitchell's and Oakes's days, there have been just four winter records of European Storm-petrel since the mid-twentieth century – three individuals found dead, on Banks Marsh on 15 December 1958, at Ainsdale on 22 February 1972 and at Tarleton on 6 January 1984, and a live bird off Morecambe on 8 February 1971. The Tarleton bird was also the only one so far found any appreciable distance inland, although a petrel on Holt House Recreation Ground, Colne, for half an hour on 5 August 1984 was probably this species, given the date.

There has been only one ringing recovery in Lancashire, an unaged bird caught at Corsewall Point, Dumfries & Galloway on 19 July 1994 and found in unknown circumstances at Rossall Point on 17 July 2001.

BM.

This species account was sponsored by Barry McCarthy.

LEACH'S STORM-PETREL

Oceanodroma leucorhoa

Lancashire Category A.

Fairly common passage migrant from Outer Hebrides and possibly North America.

A range of geographical and prevailing weather factors have combined to make this bird from the wild North Atlantic islands a regular autumn migrant through the narrows of the Irish Sea. When the winds are favourable, from the birder's perspective if not the birds', scores or even hundreds may be recorded close inshore all along the Lancashire coastline, from Morecambe Bay to the Mersey.

The inaccessibility of its nesting colonies and its nocturnal habits make Leach's Storm-petrel numbers difficult to census, although survey techniques are now fairly reliable. Mitchell *et al.* (2004) estimated a British and Irish breeding population of 48,000 pairs, all but around 2,000 on the St. Kilda complex. Beyond the western Palaearctic, Leach's Storm-petrel is an abundant breeder off the Canadian Maritime Provinces. Birds leave the breeding areas from August onwards and the main arrivals in tropical wintering areas off west Africa are from late November. Large numbers are thought to winter in the Bay of Biscay (Hémery & Jouanin 1988) with a few remaining further north, and occurrences of odd storm-driven individuals on the coasts of Britain and Ireland, including Lancashire, in midwinter are not especially rare.

Autumn passage appears to be concentrated well to the west of Scotland and Ireland; Leach's Petrels are uncommon in the North Sea. In some autumns strong westerlies, especially in September, push large numbers onto the north and west coasts of Ireland from Antrim to Mayo; in these conditions a proportion are driven through the North Channel into the Irish Sea. If the gales continue as birds struggle on southwards, Lancashire seawatchers reap the benefit, as tired birds pass over the surf, and often over the beaches, sometimes for two or three days in succession. Such events require just the right combination of weather and timing, however; in the last 60 years only 1952, 1963, 1970,1978, 1980, 1983, 1987, 1988, 1990, 1994, 1997, 2001 and 2004 can be rated as 'Leach's autumns'. In many other years only a few have been recorded, and even dedicated seawatchers may go for several years without a sighting. This pattern of feast-or-famine appears to be of long standing; both Mitchell and Oakes referred to the species' tendency to occur during or after autumn storms, and highlighted occasional sightings or recoveries of birds far inland.

Major influxes depend on the occurrence of strong westerlies that persist over a period of two or three days at least; it may be that the birds can sustain their southward momentum until prolonged buffeting, and possibly inability to feed, eventually drive many close inshore. Between mid-October and early November 1952 400 dead birds (out of a British total of at least 6,700 casualties) were found along the Lancashire coast and large numbers of flying and distressed birds were seen. In 1978, a typical Leach's autumn, uninterrupted westerly gales veering north-westerly from 11-12 September culminated in counts of 60 off Heysham-Morecambe on the 15th and 41 off Seaforth next day. Later in the month several days of violent storms produced counts of 92 off Heysham-Morecambe on the 29th and 70 off Fleetwood,

80 off Formby Point and 200+ in the Mersey mouth next day, where it was estimated that 'many thousands' were seen during this period (Madge & Alsopp 1978). Birds were carried some way inland by the winds; an immature was killed and a second flew past a car on the M55, 10km inland on the Fylde, on the 29th and another was attacked by a Kestrel as it struggled over Altcar Withins.

Leach's Storm-petrel, Mersey Narrows, September 2004. (Steve Young)

Threats to weary migrants from raptors are not restricted to those driven inland: one was taken, again by a Kestrel, over the waves at Seaforth on 19 October 1983 and another was killed by a Merlin on Crosby shore on 5 November 1996; several have also been seen to be taken by Peregrines, gulls and skuas, including Long-tailed, over the years.

The highest counts of Leach's Storm-petrels in recent decades were made in September 1987. Severe north-westerly gales commenced on the 10-11th and continued until the 15th; birds began to appear close inshore in numbers on the 13th and the movement peaked next day with 140 off Heysham-Morecambe, 392 at Rossall Point, 300+ off Blackpool, 367 off Ainsdale-Formby, and up to 500 in the Mersey mouth. Although some individuals were undoubtedly logged more than once as they passed successive watchpoints, this was a spectacular movement by any standards; all had moved on by the 16th.

The great majority in any year are recorded between the end of August and early October, but there have been a few midsummer records over the years, including singles off Seaforth in mid-July in 1984, 1990 and 1999 – these summer birds are presumably wandering non-breeders. Wild weather between December and February has driven birds onshore, or even inland, in nine winters since the mid-1960s; a total of seven off the Wyre and Lune Estuaries in early February 2002 is the highest number recorded.

The return to the northern breeding areas in April and May seems to be less susceptible to disruption by the weather than the autumn passage; there have been only eight spring records in Lancashire since the mid-1960s, although these have become somewhat more frequent in recent years. One was off Formby Point after gales on 23 April 1979 and one was killed by a Magpie, again in gale conditions, at Carnforth on 3 May 1982. In May 1999 there were singles off Blackpool and Jenny Brown's Point, another at Borwick Lake, Carnforth on the 22nd and a fourth off Heysham on the following day; another was seen from Jenny Brown's Point on 24 April 2001.

Most inland records of Leach's Storm-petrels at any time of year have been within a few kilometres of the coast; single birds at Clitheroe in early November 1952 and mid-November 1966, at Arkholme in the Lune Valley on 27 November 1982 and Rowley Lake, Burnley on 8 October 1988 are the deepest penetrations recorded since the mid-1950s.

It has long been assumed that the numbers seen off the Lancashire and Wirral coasts could not be accounted for by Scottish origins alone and that significant numbers of Nearctic breeders must also be involved in the autumn passage (Migration Atlas). However, the recently revised, and substantially increased, estimate of the St. Kilda population must cast some doubt on this. On the other hand, it is thought that much of the wintering population in Biscay is of Nearctic origin (Hémery & Jouanin 1988) and it is possible that some do move through the Irish Sea in autumn. There have been no ringing recoveries anywhere in Britain of passage birds from either population.

BM.

This species account was sponsored by Ribble Bird Tours (01253-407554).

GANNET

Morus bassanus

Lancashire Category A.

Common passage migrant.

Gannet numbers in Lancashire rose roughly in line with their dramatic increase in the seas off north-west Europe during the twentieth century, which ended with a British and Irish population of 259,000 pairs (Mitchell *et al.* 2004). Our nearest breeding sites are the huge colonies on Ailsa Craig in the Firth of Clyde and Grassholm off south-west Wales (35,825 and 30,688 nests respectively in 1998-2000), and the nearer but much smaller settlements on the Scar Rocks off the Mull of Galloway (1,670 in 1998-2000) and Ireland's Eye in Dublin Bay (147).

Confusingly, Mitchell described the Gannet as a winter visitor, occasionally numerous, which was frequently blown inland during storms. Oakes was less specific as to season but referred to the species as a coastal and inland visitor during heavy weather. Although winter records, and inland casualties, are not unknown nowadays, the Gannet is essentially a summer visitor offshore and a fairly common spring and autumn migrant.

Early birds are occasionally recorded in ones or twos in January and February, but spring movements on our coast normally begin in early March. Spring passage is usually light, although peak counts have increased fairly steadily since the early 1980s; whether this reflects a true increase in numbers or is a function of more diligent spring seawatching is open to debate. There were 25 off Heysham in a north-west gale on 30 April 1982, 41 off Blackpool on 14 April 1985 and 56 off Rossall Point on 10 May 1986; on 10 April 1988 34 passed Blackpool, and there were 49 off Rossall next day. During the 1990s spring peaks increased, including 314 off Blackpool and 120 off Heysham in strong westerlies on 26 April 1992, 73 off Heysham on 6 April and 94 off Rossall Point on 31 May 1993, and 82 off Heysham on 20 May 1996. Three-hundred-and-fifty feeding on fish shoals off Heysham on 15 April 2001 is the highest spring count to date; other large totals include 177 off Blackpool on 26 April 2003, 206 off Formby Point on 7 May 2003 and 230 off Rossall Point on 6 April 2005.

Gannets are seen offshore almost continuously during the summer months, but the true numbers in Lancashire waters can only be guessed at, since most feed far out to sea. Gannets travel considerable distances to feed and it is likely that our summer flocks include adults from both Scottish and Welsh breeding colonies as well as wandering immatures. Small numbers, displaced by winds, are regular, but the largest flocks are seen feeding on shoals of fish, often quite close inshore, in periods of settled weather. These assemblies tend to be largest in Liverpool Bay and off Formby Point in particular: 465 on 16 July 1981, 177 on 10 June 1991, 250 on 20 June 1993, and 287 on 14 June 1998; there were 250 fishing off Blackpool on 9 July 1995 and 219 there on 21 June 1998.

Autumn passage, at first mainly of first-and second-year birds, begins around the middle of July, tends to peak in August or early September, and continues at much reduced levels until early October. In most years the proportion of adult Gannets increases sharply from late August. Up to 50 birds may be logged in an average seawatch during onshore winds; larger counts include 720 off Formby Point on 7 August 1972, 470 there on 16 September 1978 and 384 on 5 July 2005, 311 off Blackpool on 3 September 1983, 200 off Rossall Point on 3 September 1987, 265 off Formby on 31 July 1993 and 384 off Blackpool on 26 August 1996.

In many autumns a few stragglers pass southward in October and early November but there has been no evidence in recent decades of the winter visitations cited by Mitchell.

Both Mitchell and Oakes also emphasised the vulnerability of Gannets to displacement far inland by storms, but between the mid-1960s and 2003 there were only eleven such occurrences, four of them at Martin Mere, in the autumns of 1978 and 2001 and in spring 2002 and 2003. One was at Mellor, Blackburn on 16 October 1967, an immature flew north-east near Longridge on 30 September 1979, there was one at Chorley on 5 September 1983, a long-dead corpse was found at Turton Moor, Darwen on 18 May 1992 and an immature flew south-west over Colne on 14 October 2003. In 2004, however, late September gales produced seven birds inland, four of them in east Lancashire. Perhaps the most interesting inland casualty was an adult recovered at Maghull on 15 May 1991, which had been ringed as a chick in the Channel Islands on 10 June 1984.

There have been an additional 30 Lancashire recoveries of Gannets ringed in Scotland, and one each from Wales and northern England, as well as three recoveries from continental Europe: a pullus ringed on Norway's Lofoten Islands on 11 July 1986 found dead at Blackpool on 13 July 1987, an unaged bird from Livorno on the Italian west coast on 16 April 1989 recovered at Morecambe on 10 July 1990, and a pullus ringed on the Sept-Isles in northern France (the species' mostly southerly breeding site) in July 1988 and found dead at Formby on 7 October 2000.

BM.

This species account was sponsored by Terry Devine and Malcolm Stanley Cooper.

CORMORANT

Phalacrocorax carbo

Lancashire Category A.

Common winter visitor, mostly from Irish Sea colonies.

The distribution of Cormorants in Lancashire appears to have changed relatively little for the past 150 years but their numbers increased steadily throughout the second half of the twentieth century and probably before then. In Mitchell's time they were regarded as 'numerous' only on the Mersey sandbanks with just single figures at other coastal sites, but Oakes added the Lune, Wyre and Ribble to the list of major sites without specifying numbers.

Liverpool Bay remains the species' stronghold, particularly off the Merseyside, Wirral and North Wales coasts. Little is known about the birds' feeding distribution and published counts at sea are few and far between, 350 between Liverpool and the Bar Light in September 1980 and 232 feeding over the Burbo Bank in December 2001 are the exceptions. Just how far Cormorants may range on feeding forays was shown by a bird that was satellite-tracked from Grafham Water to Seaforth in 1996; during its stay it was logged up to 20 km offshore from the Dee Estuary, as far north as south Cumbria and as far inland as either Stocks or Foulridge Reservoirs.

During calm conditions roosts form on the buoys that mark the Mersey Channel and on offshore sandbanks but onshore winds concentrate birds at favoured coastal sites, making the task of censusing them easier. The earliest large published counts were 105 on the Mersey Estuary in April 1963 and 180 at Formby Point in January 1973, but since the mid-1980s the biggest roosts have almost invariably been at Seaforth. Numbers there rose sharply during the late 1980s and again at the end of the 1990s (Figure 1), with average daily counts of 200-300 in winter and with notable counts of 807 in November 1996, 888 in December 2001, 820 in November 2004 and 880 in November 2005. Other recent roost counts on the Sefton coast have included 400 at night in the Mersey Channel in August 1995, 345 at Formby Point in October 2002 and 620 at Southport in December 2003. Although Morecambe Bay (Cumbria and Lancashire sections) is usually cited as the most important coastal non-breeding site in Britain (based upon WeBS), numbers there are far outweighed by those in the English sections of Liverpool Bay on the Dee, Alt and Ribble

Estuaries; indeed, the Seaforth roost alone often surpasses numbers found in the whole of Morecambe Bay.

Until very recently roosts on the Ribble Estuary rarely exceeded 200, but peak WeBS counts averaged more than 400 during 2001-05. Most of these are found on the south bank of the river and there is probably some overlap with Alt Estuary counts at Formby Point and Seaforth.

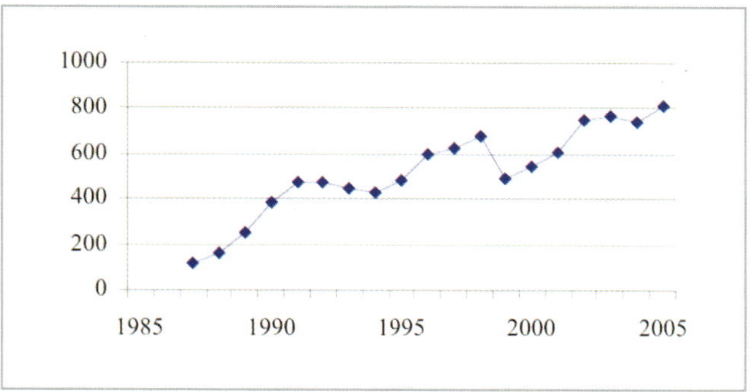

Figure 1. Annual peak counts (3-year rolling means) of Cormorants at Seaforth Nature Reserve, 1985-2005.

Numbers are significantly lower further north and any count of 50 or so is notable on the Fylde coast. These have included 49 at Blackpool in August 1994 and 50+ roosting on the Wyre Light since at least 1978. But these figures understate numbers in the Fylde area since many birds feed and roost within the Ribble Estuary, including 66 at Freckleton in December 1976 with 111 there in September 2001, and up to 166 on the confluence of the River Douglas during the 1990s.

Adult Cormorant, Stanley Park, Blackpool. For many years birds showing this amount of white on the head were recorded as subspecies *sinensis* but the shape of the gular patch confirms this bird as nominate *carbo*. (Phillip Tomkinson)

Numbers in the Lancashire sector of Morecambe Bay have remained fairly stable since at least the 1970s with counts on the RSPB reserve of 100 in December 1973 and 118 in January 1976, and a largest WeBS total of 222 in 1999.

Cormorants are present on the coast throughout the year (Figure 2). The post-breeding build-up is slow to manifest itself, perhaps because most birds remain at sea during relatively calm conditions, but there is a clear peak during October and early November on all sections of the coast. Winter numbers are generally significantly lower as birds presumably disperse to other feeding areas.

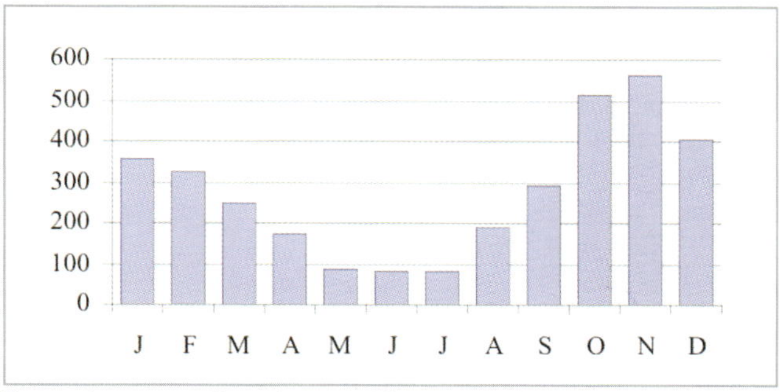

Figure 2. Average monthly peak counts of Cormorants at Seaforth Nature Reserve, 1990-2005.

Cormorants have been seen on inland waters since at least the early part of the twentieth century; Oakes referred to Rivington Reservoir as the main site with 'occasional immatures' at Foulridge Reservoir and Eccleston Mere. The past 20-30 years have seen an increase in numbers at least in line with that on the coast and Cormorants are now regularly recorded on most lakes and reservoirs. Stocks Reservoir has been the best recorded and annual peaks there increased from 13 in 1990 to 67 in September 2002. Other large counts have been 100 at the Dockacres complex in February 1986, 36 at Prescot Reservoirs in 1990, 29 at Rishton Reservoir in 1992, 62 on Dean Clough Reservoir in 1995, 27 at Brockholes Quarry in 2001 and 85 at Martin Mere in March 2004. A tree roost at Scorton, which held 50 or so birds during the 1990s was felled in 2000. Meanwhile, a roost at Alston Wood, Balderstone on the Ribble has held up to 100 birds in recent years.

Given that coastal roost sites switch according to weather conditions, it has never been possible to carry out a county-wide census but a reasonable estimate of the average late autumn to early winter population is in the order of 1,000-1,200, some 4-5% of the British wintering population. The Lancashire sector of Liverpool Bay probably holds internationally important numbers in most years, especially in autumn, but the only coordinated count was of 1,356 during the November 2005 WeBS counts on the Alt and Ribble Estuaries. The coastal breeding population of Britain and Ireland increased from 8,000 to 10,400 pairs between 1969-70 and 1985-87 (Lloyd *et al.* 1991), while the British population was estimated at just over 8,300 pairs in 2000, an increase of 1,300 pairs since 1985-87, but this was almost entirely accounted for by the growth of inland colonies in eastern England (Mitchell *et al.* 2004). The Lancashire coastal population has probably doubled during this period, indicating that proportionately more Cormorants now use the county's offshore waters.

There have been more than 150 recoveries of ringed birds in Lancashire. The overwhelming majority of them have come from Irish Sea colonies, principally in Pembrokeshire and the Solway Firth in Cumbria and Dumfries and Galloway, but with small numbers from Co. Dublin, the Isle of Man, Strathclyde and Anglesey. There have been just two controls from the north-east, from the Firth of Forth and the Farne Islands.

In recent years there has been a handful of sightings – both inland and on the coast – of immature birds colour-ringed at inland sites to the south-east, including Abberton Reservoir, Grafham and Rutland Waters and Besthorpe in Nottinghamshire. Most of these are assumed to be of the continental sub-species *sinensis*; three colour-ringed as pulli in northern France and seen in their first-winter certainly were – two at Seaforth in 1990 and one at Brockholes Quarry in 2004 . Prior to the late 1990s some believed that *sinensis* could be identified on the basis of the amount of white feathering in the head; this is now known to be erroneous but there has been a small number of recent claims based upon the shape of the gular patch. An injured, ringed *sinensis* was resident on Glasson Dock from at least 1999 to 2005. These *sinensis* birds appear to make up a very small proportion of Lancashire's Cormorants, probably less than one in a thousand based on observations at Seaforth but perhaps slightly higher inland. However, if the species is ever to become established as a breeding species in the county it will surely be tree-nesting *sinensis* birds that lead the way.

SJW.

This species account was sponsored by Roy Ekins.

SHAG

Phalacrocorax aristotelis

Lancashire Category A.

Uncommon winter visitor, probably from Irish Sea colonies.

The British and Irish population of Shags is almost three times larger than that of Cormorants, although the former – with breeding populations on the Isle of Man and in North Wales – are marginally less common in the north-east Irish Sea (Mitchell *et al.* 2004). It is therefore somewhat surprising that Shags appear to have always been scarce in Lancashire waters, outnumbered by Cormorants by perhaps as much as 200:1. This discrepancy may, however, be explained by the Shag's general reluctance to wander far from its breeding areas, its aversion to open, sandy coasts and estuaries and our almost complete lack of suitable rocky roost sites.

Mitchell and Oakes both regarded the Shag as a rare winter visitor; Oakes listed only five confirmed records in the first half of the twentieth century, all in autumn or winter and all in Liverpool Bay. Since then records have become a good deal more frequent and also more widely dispersed, both geographically and in terms of season. Only seven were recorded during the 1950s, four of them tideline corpses, but records increased to a mean of four a year during the 1960s. This increased steadily to five in the 1970s and 1980s, six in the 1990s and more than nine during 2000-05 (Figure 1). The largest annual totals have been 13 in 1990, 15 in 1998 and 16 in 2005.

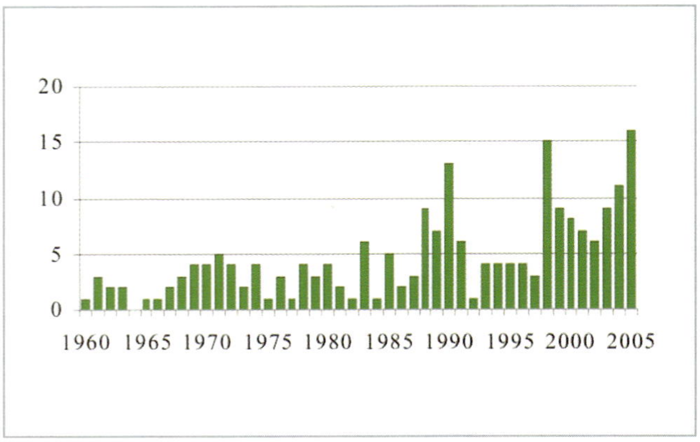

Figure 1. Annual totals of Shags in Lancashire, 1960-2005.

Since at least the late 1970s roughly equal numbers have occurred in northern waters, especially off Morecambe/Heysham, and on the coast south of the Ribble.

Shags have been recorded in every month of the year but they are extremely rare during May to August. Birds generally begin to appear in September and new arrivals peak during October with many lingering throughout the winter (Figure 2). Where the age of the bird has been recorded, juvenile/first-winter Shags have outnumbered adults by about three to one.

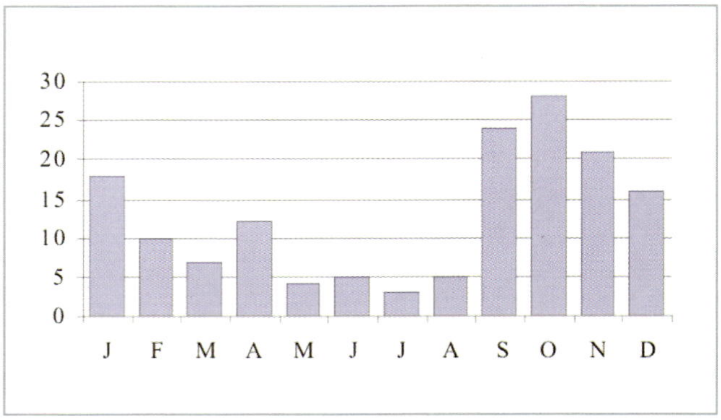

Figure 2. Dates of first arrivals of Shags in Lancashire, 1978-2005.

Over the years quite a few have been found on waters adjacent to the coast, and some of these have remained for days or even weeks. Seaforth and Crosby, Southport and Fleetwood Marine Lakes have all featured repeatedly, and there have been one or two visits to many freshwater sites, including Pine Lake, Marton Mere, the Lancaster Canal and Downholland Moss irrigation ponds. Very few have penetrated far inland in Lancashire, however, despite the occasional tendency of Shags to irruptive wanderings; one such event during the 1984-85 winter brought many, mainly first-year birds, to inland waters throughout the east Midlands and East Anglia but none was recorded in Lancashire. An adult frequented the Ribble east of Preston from September 1989 to March 1990. A first-winter bird on Fishmoor Reservoir, Blackburn on 6-8 November 1996 was the first record for east Lancashire; two years later another first-winter graced Foulridge Reservoir, Colne between 31 October and 2 November 1998.

Juvenile Shag with Flounder, Southport Marine Lake, December 1997. (Steve Young)

There have been 26 recoveries of ringed Shags in Lancashire, 15 from breeding colonies in Wales, four from northern England or the Isle of Man, three from Scotland and four from Ireland.

BM.
This species account was sponsored by
Towneley Hall Art Gallery and Museum.

BITTERN

Botaurus stellaris

Lancashire Category A.

Rare breeder; uncommon winter visitor from western Europe.

We can only guess at the number of Bitterns that must have bred in the county prior to the wholesale drainage of the mosslands in the eighteenth and nineteenth centuries but they were long gone by the time of Mitchell's book in the 1880s. He described them as frequent winter visitors, mostly seen on the relict mosslands and marshes where they had previously bred. Just how regular they were during the nineteenth century is unclear but Mitchell knew of 'a score or so . . . during the last 40 years', which, given the Bittern's elusive habits and that most of Mitchell's records were 'obtained', was possibly a considerable underestimate. The earliest published record appears to be one shot at Poulton Moss, Morecambe on 1 February 1827 (L&CFC Report 1944).

The situation appears to have changed relatively little up the middle of the twentieth century, Oakes describing the Bittern's status as a frequent winter visitor that was regularly shot in the south of the county but less frequently in the Fylde. His records also read as a catalogue of carnage, giving examples of birds shot at Eccleston Mere, St. Helens in December 1890, two on Formby Moss in January 1892, singles at Martin Mere and Scarisbrick in December 1929 and at Preesall in January 1947. He described with satisfaction one that was 'watched' rather than shot at Scarisbrick in January 1939. Bitterns were hunted for a variety of reasons: for sporting trophies, for feathers that were used for trout-fishing flies and even for food. The 1944 L&CFC report mentioned one shot on the Lune Estuary in 1939 which 'was eaten and proved excellent'. Bittern-hunters appear to have been prepared to go to considerable lengths to obtain their quarry. Oakes described one 'deplorable' incident in the winter of 1939/40 at the Leigh Flashes (now in Greater Manchester) of a bird finally shot after being watched for several weeks, 'despite efforts made to protect it'.

Distasteful as this hunting pressure now appears, it is questionable how much it contributed to the Bittern's demise. Loss of wetland habitats must have been the major factor and, when a suitably sized reedbed once more became available at Leighton Moss, the Bittern returned to Lancashire as a breeding species after an absence of perhaps 100 years. Oakes wrote that 'breeding (was) long suspected . . . on (this) mossland near Morecambe Bay', that many had been seen or obtained there in the 1920s and that one was booming during May and June 1941.

Spencer (1973) believed that breeding had been a 'virtual certainty' at Leighton Moss for almost 20 years but the first nest was not found until 1958. Two nests were found in 1961 and the following two decades saw a steady increase in the number of booming males reported, to five in 1964, nine in 1971, eleven in 1977 and a peak of 13 in 1981. During this period breeding by a single pair was also suspected at nearby Haweswater but this was never proven and the last record of a male booming there was in 1981. 'Boomers' declined at Leighton Moss at a rate of one a year between 1981 and 1984 and then more sharply with only six reported in 1989.

By this time the RSPB was investing considerable effort into gaining an understanding of Bittern ecology in order to try to stem the apparently inexorable slide towards extinction, not only at Leighton Moss but nationally. One of the first results of this research was not good news. Males had previously been counted by mapping territories but radio-tracking showed that they were far more mobile than had been thought. New techniques of identifying individual males by voice prints confirmed that earlier population estimates had been too generous, perhaps by as much as 50%. Thus, in 1990 the count of males at Leighton Moss was reduced to four.

The population remained fairly stable for the next five years, actually rising to five males during 1993-95, but sliding to just three in 1996-99, two in 2000 and 2003, and just one booming in 2004 (Figure 1). It remains to be seen whether breeding Bitterns can be retained in north-west England; if not, it will not be through lack of effort, with major reedbed creation schemes being undertaken at Leighton Moss, Martin Mere and the Wigan Flashes in Greater Manchester.

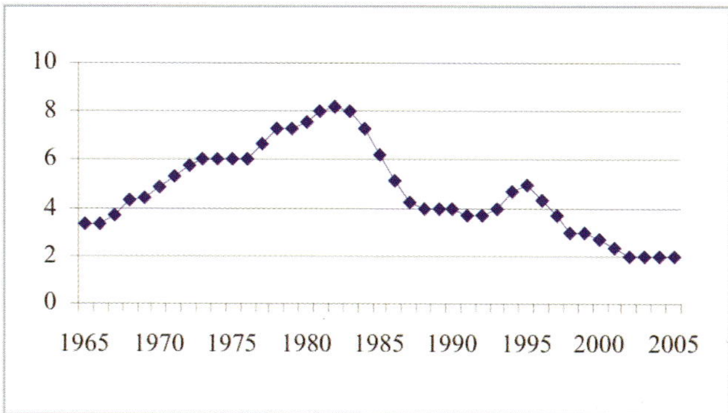

Figure 1. Estimated number of breeding female Bitterns at Leighton Moss (3-year rolling means), 1967 to 2005. (Figures prior to the 1990s have been adjusted downwards by 33% in the light of new census techniques).

The causes of this incipient demise are not clear. No doubt the geographical isolation of the Leighton Moss colony has played an important part, limiting recruitment to the breeding population to Leighton-reared birds. The British breeding population increased from 19 to 33 males between 1992 and 2001 but perhaps East Anglia is just too far away for new birds to make it to Leighton. However, the ageing of the reedbed also seems to be a significant factor, Bitterns appear to be birds of relatively young reedbeds; hopefully when the new reedbeds are created their fortunes will revive.

Breeding success has been hard to monitor. There is no clear relationship between the number of booming males and that of nesting females, for example, although there was only one 'boomer' in 2004, it was thought there were two or three nests. Most recently, three nests were thought to have been successful in both 1995 and 1996, three young were successfully fledged in 1998, two in 2000, two or three in 2002, all possibly by a single female, and four young fledged from a single nest in 2005. Radio-tagging has shown that juveniles disperse from Leighton Moss, usually by August or September. How many have been returning is uncertain, but research in East Anglia suggests that females rarely return to their natal colony. Adults are sedentary and one male is thought to have been dominant at Leighton from at least 1994 to 2000.

It appears that breeding success has been insufficient to replace losses to the breeding population but the underlying causes are not fully understood. A shortage of food, especially eels, seems a likely candidate – over-fishing of elvers at the tidal sluice may have been taking place unmonitored for some years – but eutrophication leading to reduced invertebrate and thus fish numbers may also be implicated (J. Wilson *pers. comm.*).

It is an apparent paradox that numbers of Bitterns wintering away from Leighton Moss have increased significantly over the past decade or so. Spencer knew of only eleven such records in the 25 years prior to 1973. Five more followed in the 1970s, eleven in the 1980s, 20+ in the 1990s and at least 34 in the first five years of this century.

There have been just four winter records in the east: at Stocks Reservoir in 1980, Wayoh Reservoir in 1981, Lomeshaye Marsh, Nelson in 1997 and Belmont Reservoir in 2002 and 2003. The remainder have occurred at a wide range of sites in central and West Lancashire (mainly Mere Sands Wood and Martin Mere), on the Sefton Coast, in St. Helens, on the Dockacres complex and in the Fylde, but the overwhelming majority have been at Marton Mere, Blackpool. This relatively small reedbed site had just two records prior to 1979 but Bitterns have been seen annually since 1988 and the late 1990s saw an enormous increase in numbers, peaking at eight in 2002/03 and seven in 2003/4 (Figure 2).

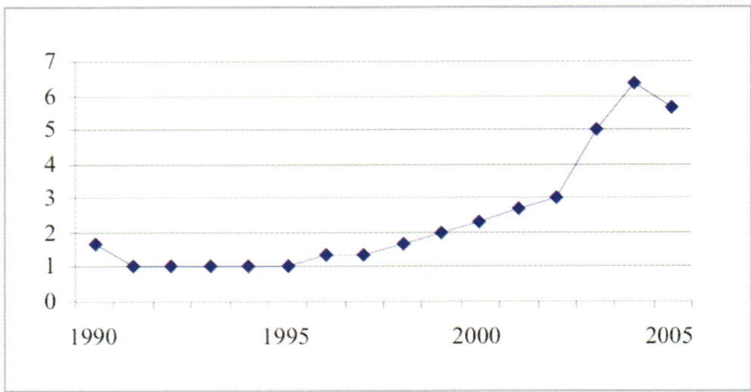

Figure 2. Peak winter counts of Bitterns (rolling 3-year means) at Marton Mere, 1987/88 to 2004/05

Until very recently, when it was confirmed that juveniles left Leighton Moss in autumn, it was thought that most if not all birds seen there in winter were residents. Assessing winter numbers is an impossible task but it is now known that some immigrants occur regularly. Since the late 1990s there have been several sightings of these birds departing in late winter, first flying over the reedbeds giving strange gull-like calls before disappearing high in small groups. Four were observed 'gull-calling' and departing in mid-March 1999, five on 28 March 2001 and three in March 2002. It seems likely that others have left unobserved. The last sightings at Marton Mere are generally in mid- to late March with the latest on 3 April 1996.

National ringing recoveries suggest that wintering immigrants originate in Holland, Belgium, Germany and Sweden but none has been recovered in Lancashire. Early autumn birds are thought likely to be of British origin, perhaps juveniles dispersing from Leighton Moss. Eight such 'passage migrants' have occurred in West Lancashire, the Fylde, Dinckley, Ribchester and Skerton Weir between July and September since 1965, with the earliest at Martin Mere on 15 July 1987. In addition, there have been four August or September arrivals at Marton Mere since 1993. Birds arriving from October onwards are believed to be of continental origin and these probably make up the majority of the wintering

Bittern, Mere Sands Wood, February 1999. (Steve Young)

population, which lingers long after the Leighton birds begin booming in late January and February. There have been just three spring records away from the main sites: at Seaforth and Belmont Reservoir on 11 and 14 March 2002 respectively, and at Martin Mere on 1 April 2003.

SJW.

This species account was sponsored by North Fylde RSPB Wildlife Explorers and in memory of John Reddish.

AMERICAN BITTERN

Botaurus lentiginosus

Lancashire Category A. (1, 1).

Vagrant from North America.

Nationally, American Bitterns were recorded far more frequently prior to the explosion in the popularity of birdwatching than after, with 50 documented occurrences prior to 1958 and just eleven since. North American populations declined significantly during the twentieth century as a result of habitat loss, resulting in fewer vagrants in Britain. Those that do arrive are now much less likely to be detected since the demise of 'collecting' – the overwhelming majority of early records were of birds shot or found injured or dying.

Lancashire's first was no exception: a male shot 'near Fleetwood' on 8 December 1845. The bird was preserved and passed into the collection of Preston Museum, where Spencer examined it and verified the identification, but it has subsequently been destroyed.

American Bittern, Marton Mere, January 1991. (Steve Young)

It was almost 150 years before the next arrived but for the many hundreds of birdwatchers who saw it during its long stay at Marton Mere it proved worth the wait - it was the first 'twitchable' record in Britain for nearly ten years. It was first seen and confidently identified in flight on 24 January 1991 by Derek J. McCullagh but there was a tantalising delay until 2 February, when, in snowy conditions, sufficiently prolonged views of it could be obtained to clinch the identification with certainty (P. Holt, P. Hornby, P.J. Marsh). The bird often proved elusive as it fed in reedy channels and the vegetated margins of the lake but it did show at times in more open areas and few people went away disappointed. It was last seen on 12 May.

SJW, MJ.

This species account was sponsored in memory of Derek McCullagh.

LITTLE BITTERN

Ixobrychus minutus

Lancashire Category A. (0, 4).

Vagrant from southern or central Europe.

Oakes discounted several records published by Mitchell as based on hearsay. He himself recognised five occurrences but four of these were in present-day Greater Manchester, the exception being an undated specimen in the keeping of J. B. Hodgkinson that was shot at Crossens. Spencer also discovered an undated specimen in Manchester Museum, labelled as having been shot in Scarisbrick. Neither appears on the official county list due to uncertainties over their provenance.

The first unequivocal Lancashire record was, therefore, a female found at the western end of Marton Mere by Derek J. McCullagh on 8 August 1956. It stayed until 12 August and was seen by about ten people.

Little Bittern, Leighton Moss, April 1993. (Steve Hunt)

Twenty years later a male was seen in flight at the county's other major reedbed site, Leighton Moss, on 26 May 1976. 'Birdwatchers' had become 'birders' by the time the next arrived – a male, again at Leighton Moss, on 23 April 1993 – and most were not disappointed since, although elusive, the bird stayed in front of Lillian's Hide until 2 May.

In 1997 the focus turned back to Marton Mere when, on 12 June, an adult male began a similar length of stay until the 23rd – though typically elusive, it was seen by many observers and was heard calling from within the reedbed.

SJW, MJ.

This species account was sponsored by Maurice Jones.

NIGHT HERON

Nycticorax nycticorax

Lancashire Category AE. (1, 15).

Rare passage migrant from southern Europe.

Oakes considered the only genuine record to be an adult shot near Blackpool on 14 June 1853, which was recorded, with a description, by J. Bost (*Morris's Naturalist* 1853). A hundred years passed before the next, an adult near Caton, Lancaster on 31 July 1953 (J.A.G. Barnes).

First-winter Night Heron, Ribchester, December 2002. (Mark Breaks)

Then, on 13 April 1980 two first-summer birds were found on Hesketh Golf Course, Marshside. Both remained there until at least the 16th, when one was relocated roosting in pines at nearby Hesketh Park where it remained until the 25th. A juvenile was on the island at Skerton Weir on the River Lune at Lancaster from 25 October to 26 November 1982. The following year produced two records, a second-summer at Hesketh Golf Course on 14-15 May and a juvenile on the Lancaster Canal near Morecambe Golf Course on 17 October. The 1980s closed with an adult on the Ribble between Preston and Ribbleton from 30 April to 5 May 1987.

The 1990s produced singles at Heysham, Marton Mere, Great Harwood and Scorton, and two in flight in the Whitendale Valley, while this century began with a much photographed first-winter on the Ribble at Ribchester and continued with an adult in a garden near Chorley on 27 November 2005.

Although only one definite escaped bird has been recorded in Lancashire, a colour-ringed juvenile at Scorton from November 1988 into 1989, question marks hang over the origins of some records of this species due to the presence of the free-flying flock at Edinburgh Zoo and escapes from elsewhere.

All records:

1853	Blackpool, adult, shot 14 June
1953	Caton, adult, 31 July
1980	Marshside, two first-summers, 13 to 25 April
1982	Skerton Weir Lancaster, juvenile, 25 October to 26 November
1983	Hesketh GC, Southport, second-year 14 to 15 May
1983	Lancaster Canal Morecambe, juvenile, 17 October
1987	Preston and Ribbleton, adult, 30 April to 5 May
1990	Heysham, first-summer, 18 March
1995	Marton Mere, adult/second-summer, 30 June. (Submitted to BBRC 2005).
1996	Great Harwood, adult, 23 April
1997	Whitendale Valley, two adults in flight, 25 May
1998	Cleveley Bridge Scorton, adult, 5 to 7 April
2002	Ribchester, first-winter, 14 to18 December
2005	Anderton, Chorley, adult, 27 November

SJW, MJ.

This species account was sponsored by Susan Metcalf.

SQUACCO HERON

Ardeola ralloides

Lancashire Category B. (1, 0).

Vagrant from southern Europe.

The only record is of an adult shot at Banks in August 1930 by Mr. John Ryding. The specimen passed into the hands of D.D. Pennington and was preserved at Southport Museum (*British Birds* 31: 59). Oakes reported that R. Wagstaffe and J. Clegg had satisfied themselves that the record was genuine while admitting the possibility of it being an escape, which seems unlikely in the light of subsequent knowledge of the species' pattern of occurrence in Britain.

This is one of only three in north-west England, the others were singles shot on the River Eden in Cumbria in June 1845, and present on Walney Island during 6-11 June 2002.

SJW, MJ.

CATTLE EGRET

Bubulcus ibis

Lancashire Category A. (0, 3).

Vagrant from southern Europe.

The county's first was discovered by Graham Clarkson on 25 January 1999 as he drove a minibus full of offenders to a work project at Martin Mere during his work as a Community Service Supervisor. Just before reaching the reserve he glanced over a hedge at Brandreth Barn, Burscough and spotted a medium-sized white bird huddled under one of the farm's horses, sheltering from the driving rain.

Obviously an egret of some sort – but checking further detail wasn't possible due to the nature of his 'cargo'. On arrival at Martin Mere, warden Charlie Liggett was dispatched to confirm the bird's identity.

Cattle Egret, Brandreth Barn, Burscough, February 1999. (Steve Young)

The bird stayed in the area until at least 11 May 1999, often visiting nearby fields where it sometimes followed the plough alongside Black-headed Gulls, regularly roosting at Martin Mere and dropping in to Mere Sands Wood on several days from 19-25 April. But during the early part its stay it was most often seen at Brandreth Barn, in the company of what was to become probably the most photographed horse in Lancashire since Red Rum.

The bird had arrived after several days of strong south-westerlies, as part of a small mid-winter influx into the country, and was in non-breeding plumage. Towards the end of its visit it had nearly completed moulting and the extent and tone of its rufous-brown plumes indicated that it was of the nominate race *ibis* rather than the eastern race *coromandus*, which is widely kept in collections.

Cattle Egret, Brandreth Barn, Burscough, February 1999. (Steve Young)

Remarkably, what was presumably the same bird returned to Brandreth Barn on 4 December 1999, again visiting Martin Mere and Mere Sands Wood before eventually settling at nearby Windmill Farm and finally departing sometime after 3 April 2000.

The county's second also occurred in 2000 but was a much less obliging bird, an adult found at Marshside on 20 July. It was constantly harassed all day by the cattle it was feeding amongst and it came as no surprise that it had disappeared to pastures new after roosting overnight.

SJW, MJ.

This species account was sponsored by Graham Clarkson.

LITTLE EGRET

Egretta garzetta

Lancashire Category AE.

Uncommon passage migrant; scarce in winter.

Little Egrets were a national rarity until the end of the 1980s and were very rare indeed in Lancashire, with the first record coming as late as 1968 on 5 May at Pilling and found by E. Baron, L. Fishwick and A. Jenkinson. Four spring records were accepted by the BBRC between 1970 and 1975, two each at Freckleton and Leighton Moss, followed by further singles at Leighton Moss in June and July 1981, and Cockerham and elsewhere in May 1987.

1989 was the year that changed everything: more than 50 were recorded nationally with Lancashire picking up four, including our first autumn record at Seaforth in August. Little Egrets suddenly ceased to be rare and by 1999 1,000-1,500 were seen annually in Britain. The Lancashire situation has followed this national trend (Figure 1), patchily at first with up to four records usual during most of the 1990s, but with an exceptional eleven in 1995. Then annual totals, allowing for some duplication of records, rose sharply from eight in 1998 to 15 in 2000 and 23 in 2002. By the end of 2003 there had been about 130 records involving 150 or so birds. Most records of feeding or passage birds are of ones or twos, but larger groups have been seen on several occasions, including four on Carnforth Marsh in May 2001, four flying south offshore at Formby Point in November 2004 and five on the Lune and Ribble Estuaries during 2005. In very recent years a regular roost site has become established in a heronry at Ashton Hall near the River Lune which held up to five birds during winter 2004/05 and nine in 2005/06.

The reason for this dramatic change in status lay in the inexorable northward expansion of the breeding range through France during the previous 20 years with Little Egrets becoming established as a breeding species in southern England by 1996.

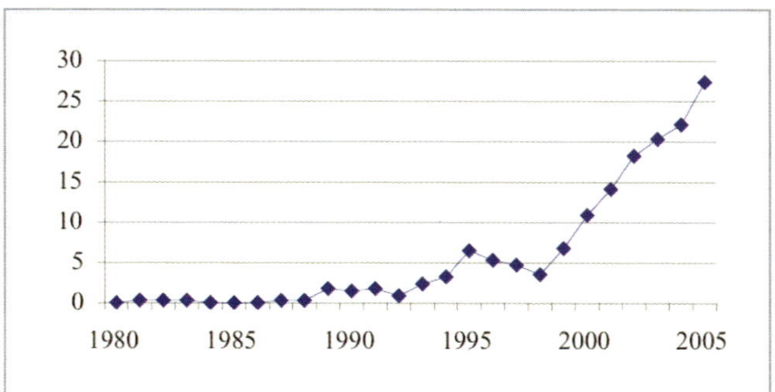

Figure 1. Estimated annual totals of Little Egrets in Lancashire (3-year rolling means), 1978-2005 (excluding known escapes).

Nationally, numbers peak during September and October, swelled by continental birds dispersing northward before retreating for the winter. In Lancashire, however, there have been slightly more records in spring than in autumn, with an annual peak in May (Figure 2). Nationally, 500 or so overwinter but none did so in Lancashire until 2002/2003 when one was at Leighton Moss on 18 December and one remained at Pilling throughout;

four wintered on the Lune and two on the Ribble in 2004/05, with nine on the Lune and three on the Ribble in 2005/06.

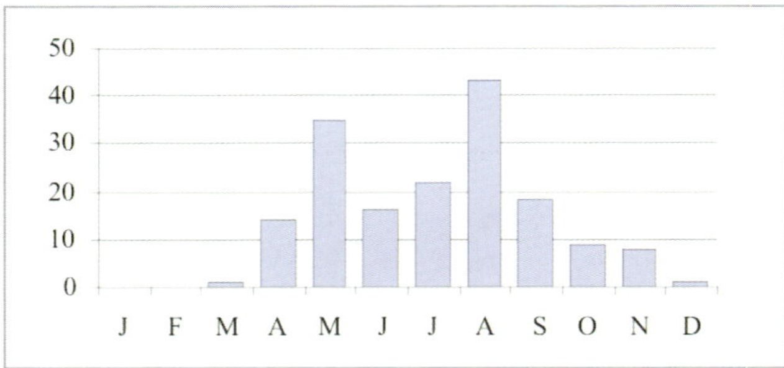

Figure 2. Monthly arrivals of Little Egrets in Lancashire, 1968-2005 (excluding known escapes).

Just under a half of all records have occurred between the south Ribble marshes and the Wyre but the coast between the Lune and Leighton Moss comes a fairly close second. There is only one record on the Lancashire section of the Mersey Estuary, at Oglet Bay in 2002, but Little Egrets are fairly common on the Cheshire side and Seaforth on the Mersey Narrows has seven records. Birds remain scarce any distance inland, although records have become increasingly frequent in the past two years, with a total of about 25 recorded at Martin Mere, Mere Sands Wood, Preston, Brockholes Quarry, Arkholme, Bolton-by-Bowland, Dunsop Bridge, Dean Clough, Belmont, Foulridge and Prescot Reservoirs, and Whinney Hill Tip.

Little Egret, Eric Morecambe complex, August 2007. (Steve Young)

A lone female built a nest and laid at a coastal site in the Fylde in 2002 but the eggs were presumably infertile and were predated. At the time this was regarded as perhaps the first sign of colonisation but this judgement may have been a little hasty; during 2003 it became clear that escaped Little Egrets were turning up in the county with some regularity. At least six were reported to have escaped from Blackpool Zoo, not all of them ringed. Although it was suggested that these were of either the race *nigripes* or *immaculata*, not all had all dark legs and some showed yellow on the toes. A colour-ringed bird at Southport Marine Lake appeared to be an escape from another, unknown source. At the end of 2003 several of these birds were still present on the Ribble but most had disappeared by the end of 2004 and only one remained in 2005. It is not known when the escape situation first arose but it may have exaggerated the apparent increase in wild birds over the past few years.

SJW.

This species account was sponsored by Ron Bedford.

GREAT WHITE EGRET

Egretta alba

Lancashire Category A. (0, 4).

Vagrant from western Europe.

Marshside warden, Tony Baker, was on his way to the reserve on 16 October 2001 when Ken and Rachael Parks phoned to say they had seen what was fairly certainly a Great White Egret on Crossens Marsh on the edge of the Ribble Marshes National Nature Reserve. Since it was virtually on his route he stopped off and, sure enough, there was the bird, 200 metres away alongside the Crossens Sluice – a county first without getting out of the car!

It stayed in the area until at least 21 October but after the initial sighting became less obliging, spending most of its time between Crossens Inner and Banks Marshes, feeding in saltmarsh gullies. The bird put in a brief appearance at Mere Sands Wood on 17 October, where it was seen by just one observer, who did not realise its significance at the time.

This was the 148th record in Britain and Ireland of what used to be a very rare species; its increasing frequency coincides with an expansion of its breeding range into the Netherlands and France.

Great White Egret, Eric Morecambe complex, August 2007. (Steve Young)

It was not long before the second materialised, when what may have been the same individual was seen dropping on to the Plover Field at Martin Mere on 5 January 2002, where it remained briefly before flying off north. Further records followed at the Eric Morecambe Pools on 5 August 2003 and at Lancaster and Leighton Moss from 27 to 30 May 2004. The latter bird had been colour-ringed as a nestling at Lac de Grand-Lieu, Loire Atlantique, France on 28 April 2003 and subsequently wintered around the Gower Peninsula in South Wales during 2004/05. The most recent record was one flying north at Seaforth on 15 October 2004.

SJW.

This species account was sponsored by N.J. Donnithorne.

GREY HERON

Ardea cinerea

Lancashire Category A.

Scarce resident breeder; fairly common in winter.

The first documentary evidence for the presence of herons in Lancashire was provided by the 1085 Domesday Survey of William the Conqueror, which recorded heronries at Knowsley and Crosby – both of which are still extant. Harting (1872, 1873), undertook the next largest survey of all known heronries in Britain and found that many were 'ancient' and located on 'the English Estates'. This was because many of the early heronries were managed – one of the finest spectacles of falconry was considered to be a pair of Peregrines set against a heron. Thus, some of the best kept heronries at the time were administered by estates – Ashton Hall (Hamilton Wood), near Lancaster (established c.1800), Old Park, Ashton-with-Stodday, Lancaster (established c.1805), Formby Hall (pre-1826), Bank Hall, Bretherton (pre-1826), Ince Blundell Hall (pre-1863), Scarisbrick Hall (established 1872), Claughton Hall, Brock Valley (pre-1850), Thurland Castle, Tunstall Hardy (pre-1908 but earlier history obscure), Knowsley Park (since 1085 but not continuous), and later Brockholes (established 1884) and Park Ghyll /Springs Wood, Bolton-by-Bowland (established 1891 but not continuous). Mitchell wrote that the Ashton Hall colony was established from Scottish stock by the Duke of Hamilton but it is not known how widespread such introductions were.

With the decline of falconry from the early 1800s preservation gave way to persecution; nesting trees were felled and birds were harried for eggs, young and skins. Many large colonies were replaced by smaller, dispersed collections of nesting pairs. Mitchell referred to three flourishing heronries – at Scarisbrick Hall, Ashton Hall and Browsholme near Clitheroe. In 1885 Scarisbrick contained 8-10 nests (a static figure for many years), Ashton 25-35 nests and Browsholme, recolonised in 1877, had eight nests at this time. Claughton-on-Brock (Claughton Hall) never held more than six nesting pairs annually but was still surviving in 1892 although tree-felling had reduced the size of the colony.

The BTO's annual heronries census began in 1928 and Oakes was able to paint an accurate picture of active heronries; most were in the north of the county with very few south of the Ribble. The main colonies that existed were at Scarisbrick Hall, Old Park (Ashton-with-Stodday), Keasber Park (Tunstall), Park Ghyll/Springs Wood (Bolton-by-Bowland), Hamilton Wood (Ashton Hall); New England Wood (Tunstall), Ince Blundell, and Claughton-on-Brock. Today only the last four still exist, the rest having been lost, mostly to tree-felling, disturbance or unexplained extinction. Oakes also mentioned breeding at Warton (Fylde) in 1922-23, Whalley and Cliviger in 1944, and former colonies at Leighton Moss, Whittington, Rawcliffe, Redscar, Formby Hall and Kemple End.

There are probably twice as many herons breeding nationally now as in the 1960s; the British population is estimated at 13,430 active nests (Baker *et al.* 2006). BTO data show a 31.5% increase over the period 1994-2003 but this increase appears not to have been reflected in Lancashire (Table 1).

Table 1. Heronries recording more than ten active nests during 1994-2004

Site	Max. nests in last 10 years	Status
Ince Blundell	22	Slow increase
Halsall Moss	16	Static/decreasing slowly
Tunstall	40	Slow increase
Plex Moss	16	Unknown
Claughton	102	Possibly decreasing
Mitton	29	Now extinct, relocated at Winkley Hall Farm
Dutton Hall	20	Unknown
Rimington	11	Unknown
Ainsdale Moss	15	Decreasing
Roby Mill	49	Decreasing
Formby	10	Static/decreasing
Stanley Park	34	Increasing
Entwistle	42	Increasing
Knowsley Park	22	Stable
Low Wood	18	Unknown
Samlesbury	10	Unknown
Downholland Moss	10	Slow decline

Lancashire Bird Reports of 1990-2005 documented another sixteen sites where between five and nine nests were recorded, with a similar number of sites supporting fewer than five. Since 1990 some new colonies have been founded, including at Melling Copse (established 1991, destroyed by storms 2005), Stanley Park, Blackpool (1992), Entwistle (1993), The Snab (1995),Cuerden Valley Park (1995), Bolton-le-Sands (1997), Spring Wood, Whalley (1999), Skerton Weir (2002) and Forton (2003). The first breeding in Rossendale was a single nest between Rawtenstall and Waterfoot in 1999. The Lancashire Atlas recorded 327 active nests during 1997-2000, with notable concentrations in the Ribble and Lune Valleys, and estimated the total population at 350 pairs.

Juveniles disperse in all directions; there have been nine recoveries of Lancashire pulli elsewhere in northern England, eight in southern England and three in Wales. Less is known about adult dispersal but many move towards the coast. Lancashire birds are joined by those from elsewhere during the non-breeding period, with recoveries in the county of 41 ringed elsewhere in northern England, singles from Scotland and Wales and nine from southern England.

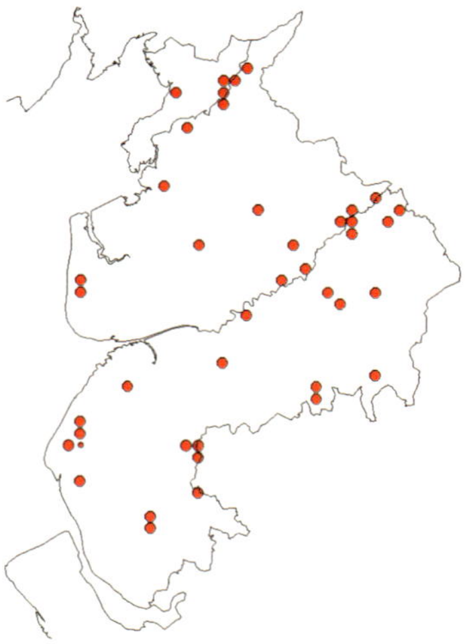

Breeding distribution of Grey Heron, 1997-2000. (Large dots: confirmed. Small dots: possible)

Immigrants from the migratory populations of northern Europe also occur, including two ringed as pulli in Norway and three from Denmark. A pullus ringed at Formby in 1979 and found dead at Downholland Moss in 2003 was the longest lived Grey Heron recorded to date.

Juvenile Grey Heron, Seaforth Nature Reserve, July 2003. (Steve Young)

Movements around the coast are recorded most years during spring and autumn. Usually singles, but up to five birds, have been seen coming in off the sea at Heysham and Blackpool or flying offshore at Blackpool and Formby Point; more than half of the 22 records from the period 1990-2003 were in August and September. There is no consistent pattern to these coastal movements and their origins and destinations can only be guessed at.

Post-breeding and winter gatherings of 20 or more are relatively frequent, especially on estuaries and lowland waters. Notable counts include 47 on Arley Reservoir in February 1993, 54 on the Alt estuary in November 1997, 99 on the Ribble estuary in September 1996, 45 at Freckleton Naze in September 1999, up to 60 feeding on fish-meal at Catforth mink farm in the Fylde in November 2001. During the 1970s up to 39 used to winter regularly at Skerton Weir, Lancaster, and 70 were counted at Leighton Moss during a period of drought in August-September 1976.

SJW, RJH.

This species account was sponsored by Mick Weston.

PURPLE HERON

Ardea purpurea

Lancashire Category A. (0, 11).

Vagrant from southern Europe.

All of Lancashire's Purple Herons have been overshooting spring migrants, arriving within a very concentrated period – 23 April to 18 June.

The first was an adult found by John Wilson (who also saw all the subsequent Leighton Moss records and found several of them) at Leighton Moss on 4 May 1970, remaining until at least the 7th. What was thought by the observer to be a different adult was seen on 8 May but the record was not published by the BBRC. Remarkably, a first-summer bird turned up at Leighton Moss on 18 June the same year and was seen intermittently until the 20th. Also on 8 May 1970, an adult was at Freckleton for one day only – perhaps it was the Leighton Moss bird returning south.

The Freckleton bird remains one of just two records away from Leighton Moss, the other being an adult at Crossens on 9 May 1979.

Leighton Moss has provided a further six accepted records, all but one during the 1970s. A first-summer on 13-15 May 1971 was followed by an adult on 19-25 May the same year. Another first-summer was seen on 15 May 1974 before disappearing until 25 June after which it was seen fairly regularly until 27 July – our only record of a summering bird. The following year produced yet another adult plus first-summer 'double-header', the adult on 4-10 May 1975 and the first-summer on 8-14 June. One or two adults were seen in 1977: one from 30 April to 8 May and another from 24-26 May. It was then nearly twenty years before the latest record, again an adult, from 23 April to 7 May 1996. Their present rarity is no doubt linked to declining populations in southern Europe, especially in France (Hagemeijr & Blair 1997).

It is hardly surprising that Leighton Moss, our largest reedbed, should so dominate the records but the number of multiple records is noteworthy. Although, remarkably, none of these has overlapped it does seem possible that several may have arrived together but were detected separately – it is a large reedbed! Alternatively, this may be an example of birds 'drawing in' their conspecifics.

All records:

1970	Leighton Moss, adult, 4 to 7 May
1970	Freckleton, adult, 8 May
1970	Leighton Moss, first-summer, 18 to 20 June
1971	Leighton Moss, first-summer, 13 to 15 May
1971	Leighton Moss, adult, 19 to 25 May
1974	Leighton Moss, first-summer, 15 May, also 25 June to 27 July
1975	Leighton Moss, adult to 4 to 10 May
1975	Leighton Moss, first-summer, 8 to14 June
1977	Leighton Moss, adult 30 April to 8 May, possibly same 24 to 25 May
1979	Crossens, adult, 9 May
1996	Leighton Moss, adult 23 April to 7 May

SJW, MJ.

This species account was sponsored by Bob Pyefinch.

BLACK STORK

Ciconia nigra

Lancashire Category A. (0, 5).

Vagrant from central or eastern Europe.

The historical pattern of Black Stork records in Britain reflects its changing fortunes as a breeding species in western and central Europe. Sightings – or perhaps more accurately, specimens – were relatively frequent during the nineteenth century and the early years of the twentieth but, as the European population declined, British records plummeted. Numbers then improved from the late 1970s as European breeding areas were slowly recolonised – all Lancashire records come from this period. There seems to be no clear pattern of arrival dates in Britain, with birds likely to turn up at any time between April and October.

Tony Disley

Lancashire's first record was seen flying over Leighton Moss on 27 August 1977 by R.W. Marsh and John Wilson; it appeared the following day at nearby Over Kellet but was not seen subsequently. The next was also at Leighton Moss, an adult that appeared at dusk on 10 June 1989. It was relocated on Carnforth Marsh the following morning and stayed until mid-morning when it flew off high to the north. The following year Leighton Moss made it three in a row with another north-bound 'fly-over' adult on 21 June – what was possibly the same bird was on Sanday in Orkney on 23-24 June.

The Leighton Moss monopoly was finally broken on 18 May 1993 when what was probably an adult was watched for 20 minutes circling over a small wood in Ince Blundell near Crosby on 18 May. However, the latest record was again in north Lancashire; it was found on fields at Ellel, near Lancaster on 23 April 1995 by a farmer, who memorably described it as 'like an Oystercatcher on steroids', and was seen over Blea Tarn Reservoir, Quernmore the following day; what was assumed to have been the same bird was seen at Ennerdale in Cumbria on the 25th.

SJW, MJ.

This species account was sponsored by Danielle Hawker-Bond.

WHITE STORK

Ciconia ciconia

Lancashire Category AE. (0, 29).

Rare passage migrant from southern or central Europe.

The first for the county flew over Marshside on 4 April 1961. It was relocated at Nateby by Horace Kinloch on 6 April and remained there until the 11th, moving to Leighton Moss the same day before re-appearing in Cumbria where it stayed until mid-May.

It was another ten years before the next in May 1971, since when White Storks have appeared in Lancashire with increasing frequency and are now recorded almost annually (Figure 1).

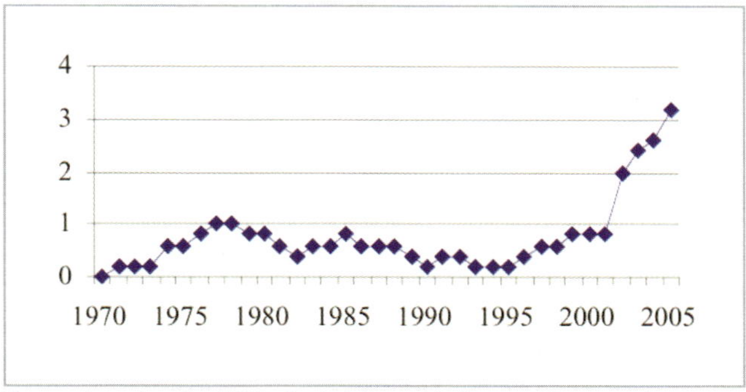

Figure 1. Annual totals of White Storks in Lancashire (5-year rolling means), including known escapes, 1970-2005

Records ceased to be considered by the BBRC in 1980 and the species was dropped from the list of Lancashire 'description species' in 2001. This was not so much because storks had become especially common, and only in part because their identification is straightforward, but rather because the frequency of proven escaped birds had become so high. The origins of most, if not all, of these escaped birds is Harewood House, near Leeds, and it seems likely that most records relate to two birds, only one of them ringed, that regularly wander separately throughout northern England during the summer months before returning to 'captivity' in winter. Records of White Storks in Lancashire are now assumed to be escapes unless proven otherwise.

White Stork, Todderstaffe Hall, Poulton-le-Fylde, 18 May 2002. (Chris Batty)

It is not known when the Yorkshire birds began their travels but it seems likely that at least some of the records in the 1960s and 1970s were of wild birds. A further complication arose following the appearance of one at Scorton on 6 May 1981 which then moved around various sites in the Fylde the following day. What seems likely to have been the same bird was found shot near Lancaster on 31 October; it was ringed and had originated from the Dutch re-introduction scheme. A final twist came in 2004 when the dubious origins of a pair seen at various east Lancashire sites between 30 April and 21 May, and which had earlier attempted to breed in Yorkshire, were revealed – one of them an escape from Belgium and the other released from care in France.

With the exception of one at Marshside on 31 March 1984 (also seen at Preesall the same and following day) which was unringed, all other records until 1999 were seen only in flight and thus could not be checked for rings.

Occurrences have been almost entirely in spring with just one in July and August, two in September and one in October (Figure 2).

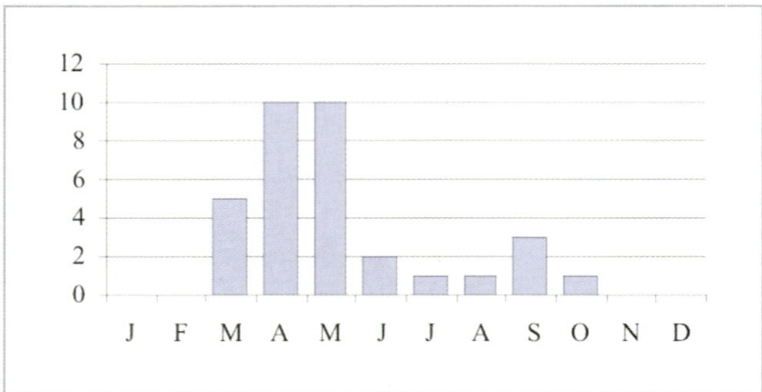

Figure 2. Monthly first sightings of White Storks in Lancashire, including known escapes, 1960-2005

All records:

1961 Marshside, one, 4 April , also Nateby 6 to 11 April & Leighton Moss 11 April
1971 Formby Moss, one, 12 May
1974 Gisburn, two, in September, also Burnley 14 October
1976 Leighton Moss, one, 10 April
1976 Seaforth, one, 15 May
1977 Liverpool, one, 15 September
1979 Cleveleys, one in flight, 4 May
1981 Scorton, one, 6 May, also various sites in Fylde to 7 May
1981 Lancaster, adult, found shot on 31 October, Dutch re-introduction. Possibly same as Scorton bird.
1983 Liverpool, one, 22 October
1984 Marshside, one 31 March, also Preesall, Pilling and Garstang, 31 March to 1 April
1985 Grimsargh, one, in flight, 7 April
1988 Arkholme, one, in flight, 24 April
1988 Lytham Hall, one, in flight, 15 June
1991 Gathurst, one, in flight, 23 March
1996 Galgate, one, in flight, 4 May
1996 Clifton, one, in flight, 2 June
1997 St Helens, one, in flight, 30 March
1999 Lancaster, one, 4 May, also Leighton Moss same day
2000 Marton Mere, escape from Blackpool Zoo, 23 July
2001 Pilling, one 27 March, also Lancaster
2001 Over M55 Fylde, one, in flight, 24 May
2002 Towneley Hall Burnley, one, 9 March
2002 Southport, one, 1 April
2002 Blackburn golf course, one, 3 April
2002 Twiston Moor Pendle, one, 15 April
2002 Brierfield, one, 4 May
2002 Todderstaffe Hall, one, 17-18 May
2002 Martin Mere, ringed escape from Harewood Hall, 17 May, also Tarleton
2003 Barrow Lodge, one, in flight, 1 April, presumed escape
2003 Haydock, one reported, 27 April, presumed escape.
2004 Clitheroe, Cow Ark & Stocks Res, pair, 30 April to 21 May, known escapes
2005 Oswaldtwistle, one in flight, 2 April
2005 Bolton-le-Sands & Lancaster, one in flight 25 July
2005 Much Hoole, one perched on public house, 5 August

SJW.
This species account was sponsored by M. Woods.

GLOSSY IBIS

Plegadis falcinellus

Lancashire Category A. (3, 2).

Vagrant from south-eastern Europe.

Oakes reported two possible sightings in addition to what he regarded as three definite records, all of which occurred before European Glossy Ibis populations began to crash due to the destruction of their wetland breeding habitats and hunting pressure in the second quarter of the twentieth century. More than 300 were recorded in Britain and Ireland prior to 1958 but sightings have been much scarcer since, although there has been something of an upturn since the mid-1980s.

According to Oakes the county's first was shot somewhere 'near Liverpool' sometime 'around 1810' and was described as an 'immature'. The second was shot at Marton Mere, Blackpool sometime during 1859 (Zoologist. 1974: 41-58) and the third was also shot, this time at Garstang during September 1917 and was preserved at Kendal Museum.

First-winter Glossy Ibis, Pilling, October 2006. (Mike Malpass)

The only Lancashire record in recent times was of two birds first seen in the late evening of 20 April 1997 over Long Wood, Pilling by Bob Danson. Perhaps uniquely amongst Lancashire rarity sightings, the finder was up a ladder at the time, checking one of his many nest-boxes! The birds were refound the next day over Pilling Water, flying back to what proved to be their roosting site on the mud flats at Pilling Lane Ends, where they were seen regularly until the 29th, their daytime feeding areas remaining a mystery.

SJW, MJ.

This species account was sponsored by Ribble Bird Tours (01253-407554).

SPOONBILL

Platalea leucorodia

Lancashire Category A. (3, 90).

Scarce passage migrant and summer visitor from western Europe; rare breeder.

The first county record was shot on the Ribble sometime during 1840 by a Mr. Bramley; the specimen was ultimately held at Preston Museum. The second was also shot, at the mouth of the River Alt at Hightown on 28 February 1922; it later passed into the collection at Liverpool Museum. Another, which Oakes did not publish, was on the south Ribble marshes and at Formby during the winter of 1933/34.

None was reported during the 1940s and the first modern record was of up to five 'immatures' at Ainsdale from 6 to 11 October 1958. Two were at Leighton Moss in July 1963 and again in June 1964, and one flew over Blackpool in August 1967. One or two were then seen in most years from 1970 but numbers increased sharply during the 1990s (Figure 1) with, allowing for likely duplication of records, an average of almost four birds annually from 1990 to 2004. There were just two blank years during this period, in 1990 and 2001, and peaks of seven in 1996, 2000, 2002 and 2004.

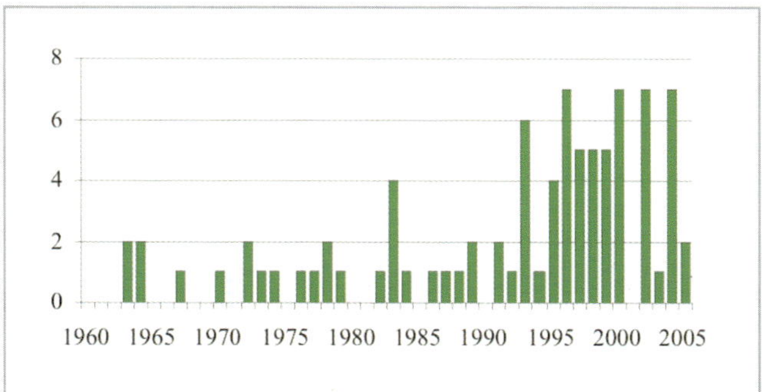

Figure 1. Annual totals of Spoonbills in Lancashire, 1960-2005.

Almost half of all modern records have been at Leighton Moss or the Eric Morecambe complex, and Spoonbills have been seen almost annually there since 1970. Virtually all the others have been on the Ribble marshes, the Sefton and Fylde coasts or at Martin Mere. The only truly inland records have been singles at Wayoh Reservoir on 4 July 1993, Walverden Reservoir on 4 June 2000, Stocks Reservoir on 13 May 2002, Brockholes Quarry on 29 November to 8 December 2003 and Champion Moor on 19 May 2005.

The earliest spring record was at Marshside on 30 March 2002. Birds are occasionally seen during April but most arrivals are in May when many linger throughout the summer, sometimes wandering between sites (Figure 2). There is little indication of any autumn influx – nearly half of the eleven September and October records are accounted for by the 1958 Ainsdale record – but most appear to be juvenile/first-winters.

Although both the early twentieth century records were in winter, there have been just two since, three over Seaforth on 1 December 1997 and the Brockholes bird in 2003 mentioned above. Because of their national scarcity at this time of year, the movements of all these birds could be tracked. The Seaforth birds had been seen previously in Cleveland and later turned up at the RSPB's Conwy reserve; the Brockholes bird had been at Queen Mother Reservoir in Berkshire from 6 to 25 November, at Wilstone Reservoir in Hertfordshire on the 25th and 27th and at Blithfield Reservoir in Staffordshire on the 28th, the day before it arrived in Lancashire. It was later seen on both banks of the Ribble from 24 December to April 2004.

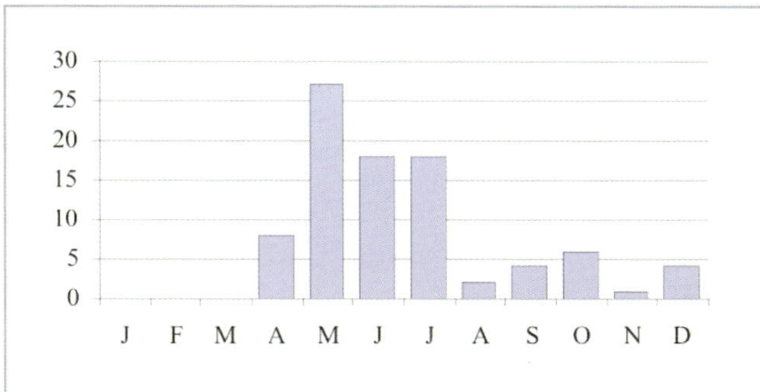

Figure 2. Monthly arrivals of Spoonbills in Lancashire, 1922-2005

A majority of summering birds are first-summers or sub-adults but a number have appeared to be adults in breeding plumage. Nationally, the Rare Breeding Birds Panel reported increasing numbers of birds summering from the 1980s, with many going through the motions of nest-building and three serious breeding attempts – in 1989, 1995 and 1997, the latter at Frodsham on the Cheshire Mersey. Despite the increase in birds summering in Lancashire no breeding attempt had ever been suspected, so it was a major surprise when a pair raised two young on the south Ribble

Spoonbill chicks with unhatched egg still in nest, Ribble Marshes, 1999. (Dave Fletcher)

marshes in 1999 – the first successful breeding in Britain since the seventeenth century. Unfortunately, they have not returned in subsequent years.

The two main western European populations in Spain and Holland both suffered dramatic declines in the 1960s but have since recovered. All of the handful of recoveries of ringed birds in Britain have come from Holland, including a colour-ringed bird seen at Stocks Reservoir on 15 May 2002 and Leighton Moss on the 19th, which had been ringed as a nestling at De Schorren on the Dutch Waddenzee in June 1999. Remarkably, this bird was seen again in 2005 on Champion Moor (close to Stocks Reservoir) on 19 May and briefly at Leighton Moss the same day.

SJW.

This species account was sponsored by John Bannon.

HONEY BUZZARD

Pernis apivorus

Lancashire Category A. (0, 61).

Scarce passage migrant, probably mainly from Scandinavia.

Britain is at the very edge of the Honey Buzzard's breeding range with a breeding population of just 30-50 pairs in 2000 (Ogilvie 2002) compared to 12,000 pairs in France, 500 in the Netherlands and 450 in Belgium. However, many non-breeders may also summer in Britain (Clements 2005). Security concerns led to imprecise mapping of the species' distribution in the New Atlas, but it is clear that confirmed nesting in 1988-91 was confined to southern and eastern England as far north as the Humber, with a discrete, small breeding nucleus in northern Scotland. There is some controversy about recent national population trends (Combridge *et al.* 2003) but it is possible that numbers of Honey Buzzards nesting to our north have increased over the past decade. Certainly, the one or two pairs which bred in Cumbria for a period from the late 1990s may have contributed to the substantial rise in occurrences in Lancashire.

Mitchell referred briefly to records in south Lancashire in the 1830s and near Colne and Burnley in the middle of the century, but Oakes dismissed these on the grounds of a lack of authenticating detail and concluded that there had been no modern records of Honey Buzzards in the county.

Until very recently the species' status in Lancashire has been ambiguous to say the least. The first to be found here was, in fact, a corpse near Chorley on 1 October 1957 and we had to wait nearly 17 years for a report of live bird, a 'probable' seen flying over Leighton Moss on 9 May 1974. Two further reports during the 1970s, over Rossall Point on 8 October 1976 and at Leighton Moss on 1 May 1977, were undocumented, as was a bird at Pendle Hill on 10-11 May 1982. A bird over Skelmersdale White Moss on 11 June 1985, though well-documented, was considered 'inconclusive' by the observer.

A multi-observed bird at Formby Point from 31 May to 4 June 1992 was also not fully documented, nor was one in mid-May 1994 at Blackpool. Only singles at Seaforth on 13 May 1994 and over Heysham and Lancaster on 27 September 1994 met present-day standards of description for this sometimes difficult species. Thereafter, the pace of events quickened appreciably; Honey Buzzards were seen over Little Crosby on 11 May 1995 and Marshside on 2 October 1998, and there were three in 1999: over Seaforth on 16 May and 18 June, and Leighton Moss on 25 May.

Since the end of the 1990s the status of the species in Lancashire has clearly changed from that of vagrant to a rare but almost annual passage migrant. The extraordinary events of September 2000 aside (see below), an average of fewer than five have been seen annually this century. There were three records in 2001: at Heysham on 6 May and yet again at Seaforth on 29 August, while a satellite-tracked Scottish juvenile was monitored over Fleetwood on 17 September and over Ormskirk on the 19th but never seen from the ground. No fewer than eight were recorded in 2002, all in the south-west: spring birds over Fazakerley Reedbed on 18 May and Skelmersdale White Moss on 25 June, and six between 26 August and 21 September, at Marshside, St. Helens, Formby Moss, Lydiate, Fazakerley Reedbed and Cabin Hill, Formby. The last of these, on 21 September, may well have been a satellite-tracked bird that achieved brief if unfortunate media attention; it was logged over Lancashire on the 20th and Cardiff on the 22nd before heading out over the Atlantic to a watery grave some 1,000km from land. There were five records between late April and early October 2003, at Lydiate, Mere Brow, Grimsargh, Fleetwood and Cleveleys, and Brockholes Quarry. Two over Seaforth in May and August 2004 are the latest records.

Juvenile Honey Buzzard with Sparrowhawk, Crosby Marine Park, September 2000. (Steve Young)

Late in September 2000 exceptionally strong south-easterly winds developed quite suddenly over north-west Europe, to such an extent that there were media reports of participants in a balloon-race over north Germany being blown helplessly across the North Sea to an eventual safe landing in eastern Scotland. Scandinavian Honey Buzzards, which had experienced ideal anticyclonic weather during the preceding days that would have facilitated southward passage, were caught up in these winds and unprecedented numbers drifted across the North Sea, to make landfall between Aberdeen and Suffolk from 20 September. Most appear to have come in over the Yorkshire and Lincolnshire coastline, and for the next two weeks Honey Buzzards streamed southwards over east and south-east England; the total number was estimated at 750-1,000 birds. Only a day after the first influx on the east coast two Honey Buzzards were seen over Brockholes Quarry and one over Martin Mere, all on the afternoon of 21 September. By 30 September, when the last three were observed passing over Seaforth, at least 35 and possibly up to 57 birds had been seen in the county. The great majority were recorded over coastal or near-coastal sites, an amazing twelve at Seaforth and eight at Brockholes; five were seen on the Fylde, and only one far inland, over Harden Moor, Rossendale on 22 September. Dunstan & White (2001) suggested that birds moving west from Yorkshire may have used the Ribble Valley as a corridor, and then moved on over south Fylde, the south-west mosslands and the Sefton coast.

Excluding the September 2000 movement, records are divided roughly equally between spring and autumn.

BM, DJH.

This species account was sponsored by Debbie Bannon.

BLACK KITE

Milvus migrans

Lancashire Category A. (0, 4).

Vagrant from southern or central Europe.

As in the rest of the country, many have been claimed but few have been confirmed – this remained close to the top of the list of 'not accepted' species with the BBRC until it was removed from the list of national rarities in 2005.

The first county record was found in the Dunsop Valley, Bowland on 30 April 1989 (A. Dawson, P. J. Marsh & M. Rawcliffe). It was spotted from a moving car – which came quickly to a halt! Watched for ten minutes as it circled the valley, occasionally lost to view, it eventually flew directly overhead before heading off north. It became the 123rd accepted record for Britain and Ireland. What was perhaps the same bird was reported the following day by RSPB staff at Croasdale and Brennand Fell but this record was not submitted to the BBRC.

Black Kite, Seaforth Nature Reserve, April 1994. (Steve Young)

The next two followed in relatively quick succession. The first of these flew over Roughlee, Pendle on 23 May 1992 and the next over Seaforth on 24 April 1994. What was accepted by the BBRC as being the same bird was seen later that morning over Much Hoole, some 20 miles to the north-east. However, these two sightings were reported just 30 minutes apart, the most likely explanation being that one or both sets of observers misjudged the time a little. The last was again a flyover, at Aldcliffe Marsh on 21 June 1999.

SJW, MJ.

This species account was sponsored by N.J. Donnithorne.

RED KITE

Milvus milvus

Lancashire Category AC.

Scarce passage migrant and summer visitor from British introduced populations; rare in winter.

Red Kites bred widely in Britain up to the sixteenth century, but persecution had reduced the population to a relict pocket in mid-Wales by the early twentieth century. This isolated population grew slowly and by 1991 there were 92 territorial pairs, in addition to some 70 unattached individuals (New Atlas). In 1992 reintroduction schemes elsewhere in Britain bore fruit for the first time, when four pairs bred successfully in England and one in Scotland.

Since then reintroduction programmes have proliferated and Red Kites now nest widely in England, Wales and Scotland. Although British Red Kites from both 'old' and 'new' stock are strongly attached to their breeding ranges, juveniles, many of them wing-tagged, have demonstrated a tendency to wander quite widely. In addition, the substantial populations of central and northern Europe migrate through the Low Countries and France to and from wintering areas around the northern Mediterranean; stragglers from these spring and autumn movements were recorded in Britain for many years prior to any reintroductions.

Mitchell wrote that 'the Kite has long been exceedingly scarce, and now only occurs very infrequently'. His only references to nineteenth century sightings within the present county were to a male shot at Inglewhite, near Longridge in September 1868, and occasional undated sightings in Wyresdale and the Bleasdale Fells. He cited the diaries of William Blundell of Crosby in support of the idea that Kites were 'well known' in the seventeenth century, an argument developed by Greenhalgh (2004) on the basis of Nicholas Blundell's notes from the early eighteenth century and other references from the sixteenth century. However, others have disputed this interpretation, arguing that the name 'Kit' was used generically for large birds of prey, including Buzzards (e.g. Mather 1985). Oakes considered the species' history here to be obscure, with the Inglewhite bird the last record.

Red Kite, Newton-in-Bowland, 2004. (Mark Breaks)

The first twentieth century bird was seen at Ainsdale on 21 August 1960; there followed an interval of more than a decade before the next, at Stalmine on 19 September 1971, followed by another at Marshside on 12 April 1979. There were eight sightings during the 1980s, all in the west of the county apart from one at Worsthorne Moor, near Burnley on 6 November 1989. Two birds in spring 1988, at Lytham on 17 March and over Lathom and Bickerstaffe Moss on 3 April were linked at the time with a widespread influx into Britain, presumably of off-course northern European birds returning from winter quarters, but one at Seaforth in October that year was perhaps more likely to have been of Welsh origin.

The surge in Red Kite records began, appropriately enough, in 1992, as reintroduction efforts to our north and south began to pay off; a bird was seen over Sunnyhurst Woods, Darwen on 10 October. There were three records in 1993, one a wing-tagged bird over Brindle, Chorley on 23 August, and two or three more in 1994, one at Marshside on 15 January with probably the same at Martin Mere four days later, and one at Formby on 17-18 April. In 1997 five Red Kites were recorded, and five more in 1999; it may be significant that whereas most of the admittedly few sightings before the reintroduction were in the west, occurrences since have been widespread, with many in upland areas, particularly Bowland and elsewhere in east Lancashire, and on the West Pennine Moors. A bird tracked in east Lancashire in 1999 originated from a release programme at Harewood House near Leeds.

Since 2000 the pace of occurrences has increased still further; in addition to documented records accepted by the county records committee many more have been reported without details, and it appears that some of our visitors wander widely around the region. There were five records at least in 2001, all but one in upland areas; one on Darwen Moor on 30 September was a wing-tagged juvenile from the Black Isle, Inverness, where the species is now numerous. A bird overwintered in the Tarnbrook-Marshaw area of Bowland in 2001/2 and several of the nine or more recorded in 2002 stayed long into the winter. One, a first-winter bird at Altcar Moss from 14 September into 2003 was from a reintroduction scheme in the East Midlands; it was joined by a second bird for at least a month in late autumn. During 2003 a single individual was recorded very widely in Bowland between late March and mid-December and there were two records in the south-west, in March and October. At least ten were seen in 2004, including one that wintered in the Newton-in-Bowland area until early March, and eleven in 2005, including wing-tagged birds from central Scotland and Yorkshire.

The 75 or so Red Kites recorded in Lancashire since 1960 have been seen in all months of the year, but with distinct peaks in March and April and September-October, although summer records have been increasing in recent years.

BM, DJH.

This species account was sponsored by Matthew & Liz Bannon.

WHITE-TAILED EAGLE

Haliaeetus albicilla

Lancashire Category BC. (2, 1).

Vagrant from Scottish introduced population.

Oakes accepted two records published by Mitchell but rejected another. An immature was killed by poachers while roosting in Hodder Hole Wood, Hodderdale in November 1840; it had been seen in the district for several days previously. The specimen passed into the collection of Preston Museum in the mid-twentieth century. Oakes dismissed a report of an immature shot at Blundellsands some time before 1864 by C.S. Gregson (*Nat. Scrap Book* 1864: 16) but gave no reason for doing so. Hugh P. Hornby wrote to Mitchell with details of another, seen flying off a rabbit carcase at St. Michael's-on-Wyre in the last week of October 1875, which he thought was an adult due to the extent of white on the tail.

It was more than 125 years before the next was seen. A dark juvenile flew low over the dam at Stocks Reservoir on 12 March 2003, watched by Roy Taylor and Pete Wilson. It continued over the reservoir, disappearing behind trees but could not be relocated. The bird carried blue wing tags indicating that it was one of ten chicks that had been marked during 2002 from the reintroduced Scottish population.

SJW.

This species account was sponsored by Matthew & Liz Bannon.

MARSH HARRIER

Circus aeruginosus

Lancashire Category A.

Rare breeder; fairly common passage migrant; rare in winter.

It is likely that Marsh Harriers bred regularly in lowland Lancashire prior to the draining of the meres and mosses in the seventeenth and eighteenth centuries, but by the end of the nineteenth century their status had been reduced to that of an accidental visitor. Mitchell recorded that a female had been shot on the nest at Martin Mere around 1870, that breeding had formerly occurred at Pilling and other mosses around Morecambe Bay, and that Marsh Harriers had occurred 'in the rabbit-warrens about Crosby and Formby'. Oakes described the species as a scarce and irregular summer visitor, with a single winter record; a prospecting pair was shot 'by the River Alt' in summer 1932, and single immature birds visited Leighton Moss for varying lengths of time in spring or summer in 1933, 1942, 1946 and 1948 without apparently finding a mate.

From virtual extinction at the turn of the twentieth century, the English breeding population expanded to 15 pairs in 1958 but had been reduced again to a single pair at Minsmere in 1971, after which, due to the banning of organochlorine pesticides and conservation measures, it entered a period of expansion which has continued to the present day, with 200 females nesting currently (Baker *et al.* 2006).

Records of Marsh Harriers in Lancashire became a little more frequent during the 1950s, particularly in spring, and by the mid-1960s two or three were being recorded annually at Leighton Moss in spring, with occasional birds also seen in August and September. Throughout the 1970s the rate of occurrence at Leighton Moss increased further, peaking at six records of immature birds in May and one in autumn in 1979. By this time migrants were also being observed with increasing regularity at other sites in the coastal west, in particular on the south Ribble marshes between Marshside and Hundred End, at Mere Brow, Martin Mere and Altcar Moss; a female at Arkholme on the Lune on 19 May 1979 was the only far-inland occurrence during the 1970s.

In the early 1980s both spring and autumn records proliferated. Adult males began to appear with increasing regularity at Leighton Moss; one present from 19 to 26 April 1983 was seen carrying nest material, and a pair displayed for a time in spring 1984 before moving on. Elsewhere in the county the number and geographical spread of passage occurrences continued to grow and there were numerous instances of birds, mainly immatures, staying through the summer months. Sightings in the Fylde became regular, but most records were from the south-western coastal and mossland sites that had been favoured previously: Martin Mere, Marshside-Crossens-Banks and Altcar Moss.

Male Marsh Harrier, Leighton Moss, June 2006. (Mike Malpass)

In 1987 the long-awaited event took place at Leighton Moss, when a pair nested and fledged three young. Nesting has occurred there in every year since and the number of breeding females has grown, to two in 1989 and 1992, three or four during 1996-99 and three in 2001-2004. In total, more than 100 juveniles have fledged from Leighton Moss since 1987; first flights have become earlier, from mid-July in the late 1980s and early 1990s to the beginning of the month, or even late June, in recent years. A major prey source for Leighton's Marsh Harriers is provided by the ubiquitous Black-headed Gulls that nest on the reserve. In 2004 a male, which had been forced away from Leighton Moss by the territory-holder, nested nearby with a female at Haweswater where they raised four young; a pair nested there again in 2005.

At about the same time that Leighton Moss was recolonised in the mid-1980s, another site mentioned by both Mitchell and Oakes began to attract summering birds. A bird was shot on the mosslands to the east of Formby and Southport in the mid-1980s and ones and twos, mostly immatures, were seen almost annually there during the 1990s. One was seen carrying nest material into a crop on the Altcar Withins in 1996 and display by an adult male and two females was observed in the following spring. A nesting attempt in the same general area failed in 2001 when the crop in which the nest was located was harvested, and it is possible that breeding occurred in 2002. The New Atlas estimated that half of the nest failures in crops are due to human disturbance of one kind or another, compared with only 16% of the failures in reedbeds; an expansion of the latter habitat in our area might produce a significant increase in the Marsh Harrier population.

Passage Marsh Harriers are now widespread. Martin Mere alone reported 15 individuals in 2003 and 22 in 2004 (although there may have been a degree of double-counting involved) and recorded an unprecedented five together on 11 September 2004. The migration periods are prolonged: spring birds are recorded from late March to the beginning of June, and autumn migrants between late July and mid-November, with most seen in August or September. Inland records, formerly very rare, have become virtually annual since the mid-1990s, including sightings over Blackburn, at Cliviger fishponds, Burnley, at Haslingden Grane, Holden Wood and Clowbridge Reservoirs in Rossendale, several sites in Bowland, at Stocks Reservoir in east Lancashire, and at Belmont Reservoir on the West Pennine Moors.

Winter records, which have become commonplace at many sites in East Anglia and southern England, remain rare in Lancashire but show signs of increasing. Since the 1980s records of singles have come from Marshside in January 1995, Leighton Moss in January-February 1996, and Martin Mere in January 1998, with two there in January 2003 and further singles in December 2003 and December 2004, and one at Leighton Moss in January 2005.

There has been only one, not very informative, ringing-recovery: a bird ringed on 18 July 1991 at Martin Mere and recovered at Southport, 10km away, on 22 August the same year.

BM, DJH.

This species account was sponsored in memory of Colin Antrobus.

HEN HARRIER

Circus cyaneus

Lancashire Category A.

Rare breeder; fairly common winter visitor.

In Lancashire the magnificent rolling spring display of the male Hen Harrier can now only be seen on the equally magnificent heather moors of the Forest of Bowland. Courtship display usually begins in Bowland in late March but has occurred as early as February; it may continue until late May or early June.

Hen Harriers appear never to have been common in the county. Mitchell quoted Skaife's opinion that Hen Harriers had been rare in Lancashire in the 1830s but wrote that 'Blue Hawks . . . . still breed occasionally in Upper Wyresdale (i.e. Bowland)' where 'shepherds see the birds about pretty regularly'; he knew of no other breeding locality. Wrigley (1892) cited reports that 'a big blue hawk' used to breed on the south-west mosslands during the 1840s. Mitchell also reported that it was 'known too by the fowlers of Martin Mere and that it had 'been shot in many places near Liverpool' and had

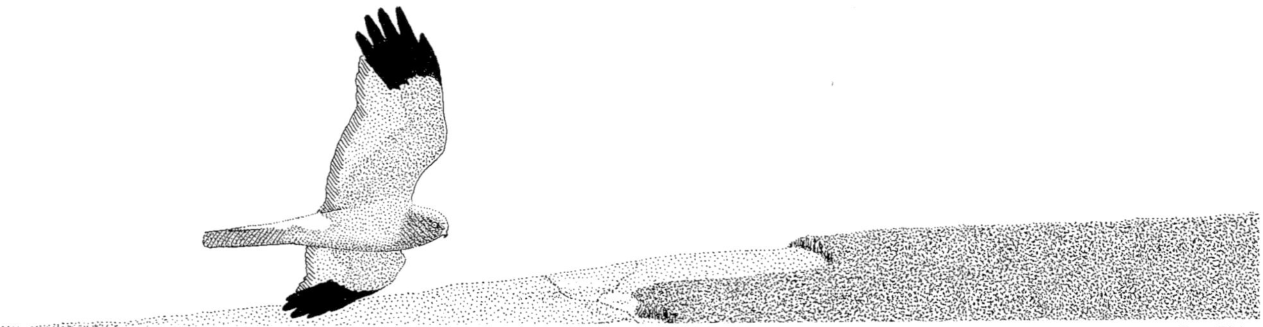

Tony Disley

also been recorded in Rossendale and 'hawking over the stubbles near Goosnargh'.

Mitchell's skeleton description of the breeding and wintering ranges is a familiar one to early twenty-first century birdwatchers but Hen Harriers were lost to Lancashire as a breeding species some time in the nineteenth century. Oakes argued that 'there can be little doubt that the species was generally distributed in north Lancashire during the eighteenth century' but gave no evidence for his assertion. He accepted Mitchell's report of a nest found in Wyresdale in 1876 as 'probably correct' but the only other probable breeding attempts he knew of were on a 'southern mossland' (Chat Moss, now in Greater Manchester) in 1941 and 1943, on habitat that he considered ideal. In Oakes's words the Hen Harrier was essentially 'a passage visitor in small numbers' in the mid-twentieth century. He noted winter occurrences at Cockerham and Simonswood Mosses and other southern mosslands, and on the Crossens saltmarshes.

The first evidence of their return as a breeding species in Lancashire came in 1969 when a nest with three young was found in Bowland. The population appears to have peaked in 1980, when 39 nesting attempts were reported, declining to 20+ in 1990 and reaching a low-point in 1994-95 when there were just six known nesting attempts, before showing a small revival to twelve (involving nine or ten females) in 2003, ten in 2004 and 15 in 2005 (Table 1). The number of young known to have fledged has been highly variable, ranging from six in 1992 and 2000 to 28 in 2004.

Although there have been records in the breeding season elsewhere in Lancashire – including singles in the Forest of Trawden into May 1998 and a pair showing behaviour suggestive of a breeding attempt on the West Pennine Moors until mid-May 2001 – all proven nesting has occurred in Bowland, almost all on the North West Water/United Utilities estates and the Duke of Westminster's Abbeystead Estate. There have also been regular breeding attempts on the neighbouring Bleasdale estate, where one young fledged in 2004.

The British population was estimated at 590 breeding females in 1988-89 (six in England) and 483 in 1998 (19 in England). Lancashire has always accounted for half or more of all breeding attempts in England but the county's contribution to the Hen Harrier's tenuous hold on survival goes beyond that statistic. Throughout the 1990s, the majority of the country's successfully fledged young have come from Bowland – 2004's 28 young were the only ones produced in England that year.

Table 1. Breeding attempts (females) and success of Hen Harriers on the United Utilities, Abbeystead and Bleasdale Estates, 1990-2005. (Source: United Utilities, RSPB, English Nature).

	ATTEMPTS		SUCCESSFUL		FLEDGED YOUNG	
	UU	Abbeystead & Bleasdale	UU	Abbeystead & Bleasdale	UU	Abbeystead & Bleasdale
1990	20	/	11	/	11	/
1991	10	5	4	4	10	10
1992	8	3	2	1	3	3
1993	4	3	1	3	2	7
1994	4	2	2	2	7	4
1995	4	2	3	0	9	0
1996	4	3	4	2	11	8
1997	9	4	6	1	12	1
1998	7	/	6	/	22	/
1999	10	1	7	0	24	0
2000	6	1	4	0	6	0
2001	4	/	2	/	6	/
2002	4	2	3	2	6	4
2003	9	3	3	1	10	2
2004	8	2	6	2	25	3
2005	11	4	9	3	19	4

Although loss of breeding habitat has been a factor in their decline elsewhere in Britain, since their return to Lancashire Hen Harriers have bred exclusively on heather moorland managed for Red Grouse, a habitat which has not changed substantially in either quantity or quality in recent memory. However, overgrazing in some areas and uncontrolled fires have contributed to localised habitat deterioration and, in the case of fire, nest losses. Despite legal protection since 1953 a catalogue of destruction at human hands has contributed to the Hen Harrier's present tenuous state. There can be little doubt that persecution and egg-collecting have been, and probably remain, the main obstacles to their survival; there were 30 confirmed cases of illegal persecution (mainly in Cumbria and Lancashire) between 1990 and 2000 (Brown & Grice 2005). This continuing threat to their survival led English Nature to launch a recovery programme in 2001, while the Association of Chief Police Officers' 'Operation Artemis' in 2004 attempted, with little success in most areas, to get moorland owners to sign up to a code of good practice. Potts (1998) believed that England could support 232 breeding females if persecution ceased. That the Hen Harrier remains a breeding species in England is almost entirely due to the efforts of United Utilities, their tenants and other landowners in Bowland, supported by the RSPB and, latterly, by English Nature. Indeed, in 2004, the English population was entirely confined to Bowland.

Tony Disley

Wing-tagging of juveniles in Bowland has shown that young Lancashire birds regularly move between Bowland, the North Yorkshire Moors, north Pennines and Yorkshire Dales, sometimes making daily flights of over 100km. Many Lancashire birds winter within the county and others parts of northern England but others move further afield; there have been eight sightings of first- or second-calendar-year birds wintering in the south, one in south Wales, three in East Anglia, three in Essex/Kent and one on the Isle of Wight.

Locally-bred winterers are joined by birds from other breeding grounds in Britain and continental Europe. Ringing recoveries and sightings of wing-tagged birds include at least ten from Scotland (Dumfries and Galloway, Islay, Perthshire, Tayside, Ross and Cromarty, and Inverness), and singles from the Isle of Man and the Netherlands. Throughout the 1990s up to a dozen – a mix of Bowland birds and others from northern England and Scotland – wintered in the Lancashire uplands, principally in Bowland and the Stocks Reservoir/Champion Moor area but also in Rossendale, the West Pennine Moors and, less frequently, in the south Pennines. Numbers are almost certainly higher on the coastal marshes and south-west mosslands but it is difficult to keep track of individuals which may wander considerably throughout the winter. Twenty or more have been reported each winter since 1990, mostly from the Ribble marshes and agricultural land around Formby, Southport, Martin Mere, Maghull, Kirkby and Rainford. Other less regular wintering sites include the Wyre and Lune Estuaries and the north Fylde marshes, but the Leighton Moss area is the most frequented site in the north of the county. The best estimate of our wintering population is somewhere in the region of 30-50 birds – out of a British total of more than 2,000 (RSPB).

Hen Harriers are particularly susceptible to shooting at roost sites and none are publicised in the Lancashire Bird Report, although a winter roost of eight birds was reported at a confidential coastal site in 2000.

Although it is often difficult to distinguish them on regular wintering grounds, small passage movements are recorded in spring and autumn in Bowland (especially the Dunsop Valley), the southern hills of the West Pennine Moors and Rossendale, and at coastal sites from Seaforth to Leighton Moss. Evidence from wing-tagging suggests that many of these birds move to and from Scotland (D. Sowter *pers. comm.*). Most wintering birds are found in non-breeding areas from late October to early March, but spring records in April through to mid-May and early autumn records in September occur with some frequency. There has been just one June record in recent years, a ringtail at Leighton Moss on the 23rd in 2003, but July records (most have been at Leighton Moss) are a little more frequent and have included adult males.

SJW, JKB, DJH.
This species account was sponsored by
David Sowter and Christine Mellor.

MONTAGU'S HARRIER

Circus pygargus

Lancashire Category A. (1, 20).

Rare passage migrant from southern Europe.

Although Montagu's Harriers, in their mid-twentieth century heyday, bred as far west as County Cork and Anglesey and north to central Scotland, there is no definite evidence of nesting ever having occurred in Lancashire. However, the first county record, a female shot in the Whitendale Valley by a gamekeeper on 10 June 1889 was reported to have had a brood patch.

Montagu's Harriers have continued to be rare visitors to Lancashire. About 20 have been reported since the Second World War but only a handful of these have been fully documented and it is likely that a number of records actually relate to Hen Harriers.

The first of these was an 'immature' seen at Lytham St. Anne's on the late date of 28-30 September 1958; in the following autumn one was present on a single date at Ainsdale. These records occurred during the period of the species' greatest expansion in Britain, which saw the population grow from 25 pairs in the 1930s to 50 or so in the mid-1950s.

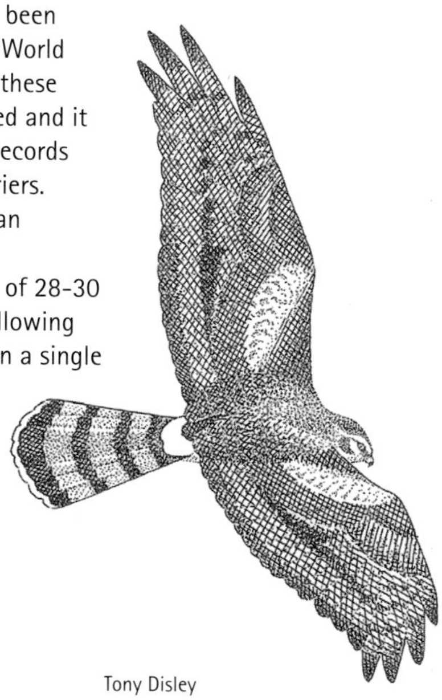
Tony Disley

There were two records of spring migrants in the 1960s, males at Martin Mere on 24 May 1967 and at Leighton Moss on 25 May 1969, while the early 1970s produced three further coastal or near-coastal records, an immature male at Mere Brow from 15 May to mid-June in 1971, an 'immature' at Rossall on 10 September 1971 and an adult male over Crossens Marsh on 30 July 1972. The Mere Brow bird was seen carrying nesting material, which earned it a place in the 1968-72 Atlas as a probable breeder, but there is no evidence that a female was ever present.

Six reports followed during the 1980s, four of these at inland sites: a male at Parbold Hill on the very early date of 11 April 1981, a female in Bowland on 13 June 1987, another female at Belmont Reservoir on 27 June 1988 and a male over Rooley Moor, Rossendale on 23 September 1989. The two coastal reports were of a bird at Carnforth Marsh on 12 May 1980 and a female/immature at Plex Moss on 12 July 1983. The seven occurrences since 1990 were all in the coastal west, apart from a female at Rowley Lake, Burnley on 2 May 1990: males at Marshside on 12-13 June 1992 and 15-16 May 1997 and at Seaforth on 26 May 1994, female/immatures at Marton Mere on 3 May 1995, Rainford on 21 May 2000 and Martin Mere on 18 June 2000, and a second-summer male on Sollom Moss, Tarleton on 20 July 2001 which was also seen at nearby Martin Mere on the 27th.

BM, DJH.

This species account was sponsored by John Bannon.

GOSHAWK

Accipiter gentilis

Lancashire Category BCE.

Rare resident feral breeder.

Goshawks had been exterminated as breeding birds in Britain by the middle of the nineteenth century. In Lancashire, Mitchell cited only a single occurrence in present-day Lancashire, a bird shot near Colne in 1863, although he claimed that birds were still occasionally being shot or caught in Bowland towards the end of the century. Oakes could find no further records, and a bird near Chipping on 30 June 1957 was the first twentieth-century occurrence.

Goshawks began to breed regularly again in Britain in the 1960s; one of these scattered early records was of a pair in the Gisburn Forest in the middle years of the decade. It is generally believed that this recolonisation was due largely, if not entirely, to birds that had escaped from, or been released by, falconers. The Goshawks that began breeding in the 1960s were mainly small, central European birds, whilst those that became established in the 1970s were much larger, paler birds of Finnish stock (Marquiss 1981). There is evidence that these genetic pools mixed as the population grew, producing offspring of varying sizes and plumage tones.

From the outset recolonising Goshawks suffered at the hands of egg-collectors, falconers seeking fledglings, and game-preservation interests. Nevertheless, numbers have grown and their range has expanded considerably; the New Atlas estimated a population of 200 pairs in the early 1990s, mainly concentrated in Wales and the Welsh Marches, the southern Pennines and southern Scotland, and the total is now estimated at 400 pairs (Baker *et al.* 2006).

Casual sightings of Goshawks in Lancashire became increasingly frequent from the mid-1960s; a male was observed displaying near Leighton Moss in April 1967 and by 1978 the species was described as 'regularly present' at one locality. Security considerations have, understandably, clouded the developing picture but it seems clear that breeding by at least one pair was occurring regularly at a locality in Bowland by the early 1980s, with birds present and displaying in at least two other areas. Since then a more-or-less regular breeding presence has become established at sites in the north, east and south of the county; the 1997-2000 Atlas estimated a total of six pairs.

Records are received from all areas of the county nowadays, and at all seasons, at least six annually since 2000. Even allowing for a proportion of misidentifications, and for sightings of escaped birds, it seems likely that the population is at least fairly stable. Goshawks nest in mature trees, usually within extensive stands of coniferous or mixed woodland; this type of habitat is fairly plentiful in Lancashire, as are the favoured prey, pigeons, crows and rabbits. The New Atlas estimated a potential population in Britain of several thousand pairs, so it is likely that the Goshawk will continue to overcome the odds and increase its numbers further in Lancashire.

BM, DJH.

This species account was sponsored by James Beattie and Mike Robinson.

Tony Disley

SPARROWHAWK

Accipiter nisus

Lancashire Category A.

Fairly common resident breeder.

This adaptable raptor has twice demonstrated its resilience in the past century. Relentlessly persecuted by game preservation interests prior to the First World War, and nearly as severely up to the Second, the species benefited from the subsequent decline in large-scale keepering only to fall victim to an even more deadly and insidious foe, the proliferation of organochlorine pesticide use in agriculture during the 1950s. At the top of the food chain, the Sparrowhawk accumulated high levels of these compounds in its tissues, leading to heavy adult mortality as well as brood failure due to eggshell-thinning; by the early 1960s the species had declined to virtual extinction over large areas of eastern and southern England. Following the withdrawal of the substances responsible in the late 1960s the Sparrowhawk has made a steady and apparently complete return to its former numbers.

Female Sparrowhawk, Seaforth Nature Reserve, March 2004. (Steve Young)

Mitchell and Oakes both emphasized the levels of persecution to which the Sparrowhawk was subjected in Lancashire, in spite of which both judged the species to be widespread and not uncommon in well-wooded districts throughout the county. Oakes recorded regular breeding in the Rivington-Anglezarke area and at Rufford, Lathom and Scarisbrick on the south-west mosslands, but considered the species to be commoner further north where nesting took place in denser woodland away from intensive gamekeeping. He cited instances of visits to suburban areas and even city centres, and noted a tendency to resort to coastal marshes and mosslands in winter.

Although the Sparrowhawk's population collapse in Lancashire was not as substantial as that in the arable counties of the east, its fortunes here were at a very low ebb during the 1960s; the relatively few references to the species in the county bird reports of the time emphasise local declines and absences from former haunts. The 1968-72 Atlas mapped the beginning of the recovery, showing presence in 38 of the county's 52 10km squares, but confirmed breeding in only 25 of these.

References to quite rapid recovery became frequent in the bird reports from the mid-1970s, but this was clearly from very low levels, as evidenced by an increase from two nests in the Burnley area in 1978 to eight in 1979 and twelve in 1980. Similar reports of increases in sightings and in breeding numbers during the early 1980s came from the Chorley area, the West Pennine Moors, the Fylde, and north and south-west Lancashire.

By the mid-1990s healthy, even thriving, populations were reported from most areas; the New Atlas (1988-91) recorded presence in 48 of the 52 10km squares and confirmed breeding in 41. The 1997-2000 Lancashire Atlas found the species nesting in 46 10km squares and recorded in 61% of the county's tetrads, concentrated in the lowlands and wooded river valleys. The estimated population of the county is now around 750 pairs, equal to that of the Kestrel; indeed, observers in several regions consider the Sparrowhawk to be the commoner of the two. Nesting is confined to woodland habitats but these may be quite small and Sparrowhawks are common residents of suburban and even urban districts and familiar, if generally unpopular, predators at garden bird-feeders.

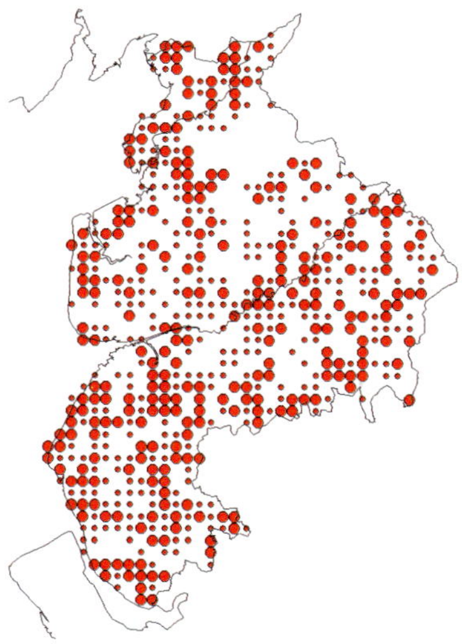

Breeding distribution of Sparrowhawk, 1997-2000. (Large dots: confirmed. Small dots: possible)

Sparrowhawks feed almost exclusively on birds, caught in sudden dashes or after a prolonged chase; small passerines make up the bulk of the diet, but a very wide range of species is taken, especially by the larger female. In Lancashire prey as agile as Sand Martin and Swallow and as bulky as Coot, Moorhen and Grey Partridge has been recorded. Females in particular range freely over open country such as marshes and saltings, especially in winter, and waders including Snipe, Lapwing and Black-tailed Godwit are occasionally taken. Amongst more unusual targets attacked in recent years, mostly unsuccessfully, are Dipper,

Kingfisher, Jack Snipe and Merlin, as well as a day-flying Pipistrelle at Mere Sands Wood in 1989.

The Sparrowhawk population of Britain and Ireland does not migrate, but a degree of post-breeding dispersal, and even some long-distance wandering, seems to be normal. Some continental birds pass through or winter in Britain, many arriving in Scotland direct from northern Europe (BWP). Small-scale movements, usually by high-flying birds are observed fairly regularly at several coastal sites, especially Seaforth, Fairhaven, Blackpool, Rossall Point, and, above all, Heysham. Spring movements occur mainly in April and autumn birds are recorded in September and October. There have been 163 recoveries of Sparrowhawks ringed in Lancashire, 108 within the county and 50 elsewhere in northern England, but two each have turned up in Scotland and in southern England, and one in Wales. Thirty-four birds ringed elsewhere in Britain have been recovered here, 30 from northern England and four from Scotland.

BM, DJH.

This species account was sponsored by George E. Parsons.

BUZZARD

Buteo buteo

Lancashire Category A.

Uncommon resident breeder and passage migrant.

The Buzzard is the most numerous large raptor over most of the western Palaearctic and it is likely that it once bred throughout most of Britain, but by the early twentieth century it had been reduced by human persecution to remnant populations in western England, Wales and Scotland. In Lancashire Mitchell observed that Buzzards had bred in Wyresdale in the 1840s but had since been exterminated as a breeder within the present-day

Buzzard over Knowsley Park, one of the first sites to be recolonised in the south of the county, May 2005. (Steve Young)

county boundaries, although a few were still nesting in south Lakeland and were still being shot or trapped almost annually in Bowland, Wyresdale and in the Ribble and Lune Valleys. There were occasional sightings in winter in coastal areas, especially in the south-west. Although pressure from game preservation interests slackened somewhat during and after the First World War, according to Oakes the Buzzard's situation in Lancashire had hardly improved by mid-century. He recorded attempted nesting 'somewhere in the south' in 1942, but the species remained a rare visitor to the Fylde, the West Pennine Moors and Rossendale, and was only slightly more regular in winter in Bowland and on the south-west mosslands.

The myxomatosis epidemic of the 1950s, which virtually eliminated the rabbit population in many areas, coupled with the effects of pesticide residues up to the 1960s, struck successive blows at the Buzzard's chances of extending its range into Lancashire from neighbouring strongholds in Cumbria and North Wales, but despite these obstacles occasional nesting by a single pair was recorded in the Leighton Moss-Silverdale area from the late 1950s. Progress was exceedingly slow in the early years, however; the 1968-72 Breeding Atlas recorded presence in seven of the county's 52 10km squares, but confirmed breeding in only two, both in the far north. The breeding situation had not improved significantly by the 1988-91 New Atlas, although occasional nesting in the Lune Valley was recorded from 1984 and this had become established by 1988.

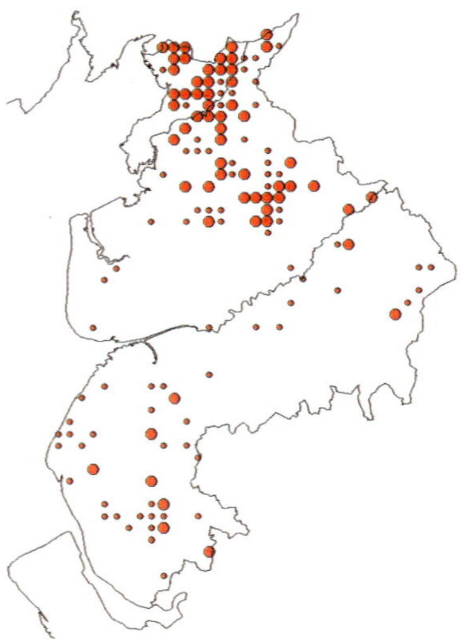

Breeding distribution of Buzzard, 1997-2000. (Large dots: confirmed. Small dots: possible)

There was, however, a gradual increase in the frequency of reported sightings of Buzzards, in all seasons and in all parts of the county, during the 1980s. In 1989 the species was regularly recorded in Bowland and others were reported, mainly in spring or autumn, from Seaforth, Lytham, Darwen Moor, Pleasington, Longridge, Rivington, Worsthorne, Winter Hill and Lancaster, in addition to the by-now regular breeders in the Leighton Moss-Silverdale area and the Lune Valley. From the early 1990s the increase in records and their geographical spread quickened dramatically. Throughout the decade a breeding population gradually became established in west and south-east Bowland and numbers in the Lune Valley expanded and nesting also became regular at several southern sites including Knowsley Park and the south-west mosslands.

The 1997-2000 Lancashire Atlas estimated the population at 70 pairs with breeding confirmed in 19 10km squares and in 59 tetrads, all but nine of which were north of the Ribble. It seems likely that Buzzards recolonised Lancashire from two directions, initially from Cumbria and North Yorkshire, but increasingly from Cheshire, in parts of which the Buzzard was considered to be the commonest species of raptor by 2002. This may soon also be true in some areas of Lancashire as the expansion in breeding range and increase in breeding pairs has shown no sign of slowing during the twenty-first century. Nesting took place for the first time at two locations on the Fylde in 2002, although unconfirmed reports had been circulating from the late 1990s. The populations in the Silverdale area, Lune Valley and Bowland continue to thrive and nesting now takes place throughout Merseyside and the south-west, with eight pairs in Knowsley Park alone in 2004. It seems likely that the county population is now well in excess of 100 pairs.

As breeding has become widespread, numbers seen during passage periods and in winter have grown accordingly. The Lancashire population appears to be largely sedentary but some dispersal, probably mostly by juveniles, does take place. Some birds winter in the hill districts, especially where rabbit populations occur, although severe weather may displace birds to the moorland fringe and lowlands. Sightings of five or six Buzzards together at various locations in central Lancashire, the Fylde and the south-west in autumn are now almost commonplace. On 16 September 2001 there were up to ten together over Brockholes Quarry, and in 2002 up to eleven were seen soaring over Martin Mere, ten over Plex Moss, and eight each at Altcar Withins and at Prescot Reservoir on several dates in autumn, and on 14 September 2003 a party of seven drifted westward over Poulton-le-Fylde. Further counts of ten or more include a flock circling above Tarleton on 1 November 2004 and 14 at Martin Mere on 3 September 2004, and several records at Martin Mere, Marshside, Downholland Moss, Dunsop Bridge and Prescot Reservoirs in 2005. Two indications of just how numerous Buzzards have become at both ends of the county over the past decade were given by the January 2005 winter atlas survey in north Lancashire which located 60 birds in eight 10km squares, and by a total of 27 sightings on the Old Coach Road, Rainford on 3 September 2005.

There have been only five recoveries in Lancashire of British-ringed Buzzards, all ringed as pulli in Cumbria. One ringed at Sedbergh in June 1959 was shot at Birkdale that October, one from Cartmel in June 1960 suffered a similar fate at Newton-le-Willows in September, a bird from Tebay in June 1979 was found dead at Leck Fell in February 1982, one ringed near Kendal in June 1982 was recovered, long-dead, at Hornby on the Lune in the following January, and one from Coniston was found dead near Barnacre in 2001.

BM, DJH.

This species account was sponsored by Marie and Peter Rathbone.

ROUGH-LEGGED BUZZARD

Buteo lagopus

Lancashire Category A. (*l*, 23).

Rare winter visitor from northern Europe.

Rough-legged Buzzards breed across the entire Holarctic tundra zone, in the Western Palaearctic mostly in Fennoscandia and Russia which they desert to winter in central and south-eastern Europe. Autumn migration of birds from Fennoscandia generally takes a southerly or south-easterly route, and thus only relatively few winter in mainland north-west Europe. Even fewer normally reach Britain. The number of Rough-legged Buzzards recorded annually in this country is usually fewer than 20, and these are mainly to be found in eastern coastal areas.

Mitchell classified the Rough-legged Buzzard as a rare autumn migrant in Lancashire and noted that five had been shot during a widespread influx in 1880: on Haslingden Moor, Rossendale on 11 October, at an unknown location three days later, at Waddington Fell, Clitheroe on the 30th, at Formby Hall on 23 November – Wrigley (1892), however, recorded this bird as occurring in 1884 – and near Blackpool in December; the bird at Formby Hall was reported as feeding on trapped rabbits. In the following 70 years only one further occurrence was recorded according to Oakes, a bird shot near Hornby in the Lune Valley in autumn 1915. The next was reported over Freckleton on the unusually early date of 19 September 1954. On 10 October 1961 a bird which had come aboard the SS *Rathlin Head* in mid-Atlantic was taken into care on the vessel's arrival in Liverpool and subsequently released in North Wales. It seems likely, given the predominantly south-easterly migration route of Fennoscandian birds, that this was a 'Rough-legged Hawk' of the Nearctic race *sanctijohannis*, most probably from the population of north-eastern Canada that winters in the eastern USA, from New York south to Virginia.

Possible 'Rough-legged Hawk' in the care of the RSPCA, Liverpool, October 1961. (Merseyside Naturalists Association)

Seven Rough-legged Buzzards were recorded in Lancashire during the 1970s, all in the centre or south-west of the county. Singles were at Halsall Moss on 8 November 1970, Croston Moss on 6-13 November 1971, over Banks Marsh on 22 September 1973, at Grimsargh and by the Alt Estuary (perhaps the same as at Banks) on 13 October 1973, and flushed from Crossens Marsh on 26 March 1977. The last was a bird found poisoned on a rabbit carcase at Mere Brow on 11 February 1979. It is noteworthy that there were no records in Lancashire during the major national influx of 1974-75.

The 1980s saw similar numbers but records displayed a much greater geographical dispersion: one flew over Silverdale on 21 December 1980 and three turned up in late 1981, an immature at Altcar Withins on 6 October, an adult at Lunt, near Maghull on 4 November, and a bird circling over Slyne on Morecambe Bay, mobbed by a Great Black-backed Gull, on 26 December. One at Stocks Reservoir on 18 January 1986 was seen again on 18 February, and one was hunting over Staple Oak Fell above Dunsop Bridge on 3 April 1987.

Phil Jones

The pattern of one-day appearances continued during the 1990s with one notable exception. A first-winter bird first recorded in the Dunsop Valley on 12 February 1996 remained until 2 April, at last affording many Lancashire birders the opportunity to connect with this charismatic species. What was believed to have been the same individual was seen again in the same area from 23 March to 30 April 1997, and returned again on 17 November, staying until 28 March 1998. The other 1990s visitors were short-staying singles: at Abbeystead on 9 December 1990, Silverdale on 22-29 October 1994, Folly Clough, Rossendale on 21 December with perhaps the same in the Langden Valley in January 1995, Martin Mere and nearby Churchtown Moss on 7 and 19 December 1995, Marshside and Banks on 27-30 October 1997 and Leighton Moss on 14 April 1999. The only record since have been singles in Whitendale on 31 March 2003 and Whelp Stone Crag on 6 December 2005, bringing the county tally to 23 individuals since 1954.

All Lancashire records after 1954 have been found either during January-April (eight) or between September and December (18); there have been no ringing recoveries.

BM.

This species account was sponsored by Andy McWilliam.

GOLDEN EAGLE

Aquila chrysaetos

Lancashire Category A. (0, 3).

Vagrant.

Mitchell knew of no records within the current county boundaries and Oakes reported that he could obtain no confirmation of reports at Southport in 1898 or Lunesdale on 3 June 1930, 'published without evidence in the seventeenth Report of the Lancs. and Ches. Fauna Committee (1930, p. 12)'.

The first record for the county was, therefore, a sub-adult found by Keith Woods on 30 May 1983 in Bowland. The same bird was seen again in the Bowland area by Kevin Briggs on 10 July and an immature that was seen and photographed by Roy Rhodes north-east of Belmont on 28 October the same year may have been the same individual.

Immature Golden Eagle, West Pennine Moors, 28 October 1983. (Roy Rhodes)

Another was reported from Bowland, this time an adult, by RSPB staff on 30 April 1987 but no confirming details were ever received and the record therefore cannot be substantiated.

An immature in the Langden Valley late winter 1997 was, however, seen by several observers. It was confirmed as present on 25 March but was reported on several occasions during this period by birdwatchers who had travelled to Dunsop Bridge to see the obliging Rough-legged Buzzard there at the time. An immature bird had been seen over the Yorkshire border at Gouthwaite, a fairly regular winter haunt of the offspring of the then Cumbrian breeding pair, some time previous to the confirmed Bowland bird and it seems likely that it was the same.

An escaped bird was present in Bowland during 2002.

SJW.

This species account was sponsored by Peter Ballentyne.

OSPREY

Pandion haliaetus

Lancashire Category A.

Fairly common passage migrant, probably mostly from Scotland.

Persecution and loss of wetland habitats caused population reductions, and even extinctions, in many parts of northern and western Europe during the nineteenth and early twentieth centuries, but since the Second World War protection in many countries has helped the species to recover and to recolonise old haunts. The Scottish breeding population has grown since the return of the first pair in the mid-1950s, slowly at first under rigorous protection but very rapidly in recent decades.

Mitchell, writing in the years of the Osprey's decline, described the species as an occasional, barely annual, visitor. He stated 'it was known to Dr Leigh (*Nat. Hist. Lanc. etc.* 1700) who reported one shot on the smaller Martin Mere [present-day Marton Mere]' and reported an instance of one that spent several weeks 'in winter' at Knowsley Park in 1881.

Juvenile Osprey, Downholland Moss, August 2004. (Steve Young)

By the early twentieth century the Scottish Osprey population had been extirpated, and Oakes regarded the species as a scarce and irregular passage visitor, with most records in May or October (while claiming, strangely, that Ospreys has been recorded in every month of the year). Among the occurrences he cited were an immature shot at Claughton-on-Lune in May 1927 while carrying a Sea Trout weighing over 1.5lbs, and two others at the same site in May and October 1928, also feeding on Sea Trout. A bird summered at Leighton Moss in 1947, remaining from 12 June until 2 September, and what may have been the same individual returned briefly the following April. Oakes observed that most records had been in the north of the county, with very few seen in the Ribble Valley or in the south.

The pace of occurrences barely increased during the 1950s, as the first recolonisation was acquiring a precarious foothold on Speyside, although there were four sightings, possibly involving just a single bird, in the north of the county in May-June 1957. Four records followed during the 1960s, all in spring and all but one at Leighton Moss; the odd one out turned up at Foulridge Reservoir, Colne in May 1964. Ospreys became significantly more regular and widespread during the 1970s, with a total of 52 records. Leighton Moss continued to attract the lion's share, with up to seven birds in 1970 and six in 1977, but, although most migrants and wanderers tended to favour the Morecambe Bay area and the Lune Valley, there were at least three records apiece in east Lancashire and the south-west.

An average of seven Ospreys were recorded annually during the 1980s but the rate of occurrences accelerated dramatically after 1990 (Figure 1), to an annual average for the decade of 24, coinciding with a further increase in the Scottish breeding population and successful recolonisation of north-west England. In 1999 a pair attempted to breed in England for the first time in recent history, at Bassenthwaite Lake, Cumbria and up to two pairs have done so successfully in the Lake District since 2001.

Ospreys have become regular and not uncommon migrants in Lancashire within the space of less than a decade. There were 65 records in 2000, 43 in 2001, 47 in 2002, at least 50 in 2003 and 2004 and 75 in 2005. The vast majority, in excess of 90%, of records in both spring and autumn are of birds flying directly through and it is largely a matter of chance whether they are seen; true numbers passing through Lancashire are therefore probably significantly greater than the records indicate.

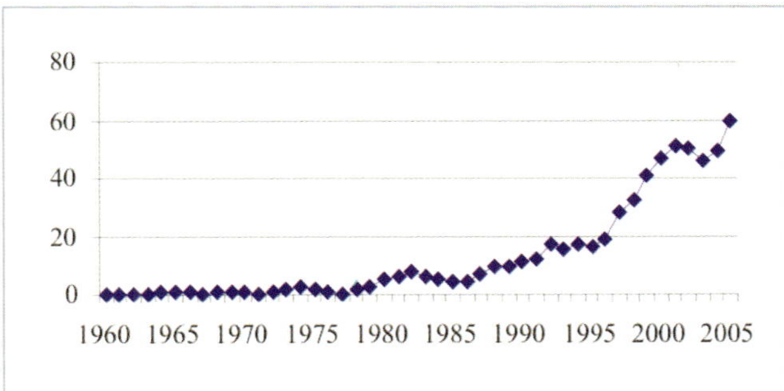

Figure 1. Annual totals of Ospreys in Lancashire (3-year rolling means), 1960-2005.

Small numbers do, however, make stops of a day or so at various waterbodies, behaviour that might be interpreted as prospecting by immature birds; longer stays include singles in 2001 at Leighton Moss and Mere Sands Wood during 2-10 and 15-20 May respectively. The Leighton Moss area remains the most reliable site to encounter fishing birds, but Ospreys are now regularly encountered in the Dunsop Valley, at Stocks Reservoir and other waters in the east and on the West Pennine Moors, as well as on the upper Lune, the Sefton coast and in the Fylde. Nesting somewhere by the well-wooded shore of a reservoir or on one of the major rivers must be at least a reasonable possibility within the next decade.

It is thought that very few Fennoscandian Ospreys migrate through Britain (Migration Atlas) and it is likely that the overwhelming majority of Lancashire records are of Scottish birds.

However, an exceptional ten birds were recorded in the space of ten days from 22 September 2000 during the record influx of Honey Buzzards and it is possible that some at least of these may have been of Scandinavian origin. There has been only one recovery of a wing-tagged Osprey in Lancashire, a bird marked on 20 July 1995 near Aviemore in the Scottish Highlands which visited Leighton Moss on 2 May 1998.

As numbers have increased, first sightings have become progressively earlier during the past 25 years, averaging 6 April with the earliest on 4 March 2005 (Figure 2).

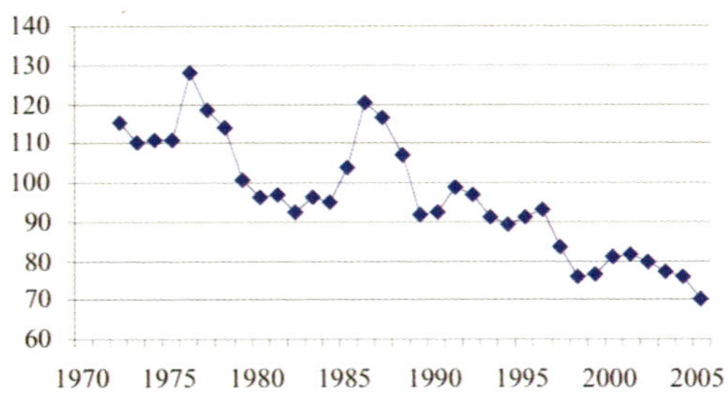

Figure 2. Date of first sighting of Ospreys in Lancashire (3-year running means), 1970-2005. (Day 60 = 1 March, Day 100 = 10 April, Day 140 = 20 May)

Birds have been appearing in March with increasing regularity but the vast majority are seen in April with a moderate passage continuing into May, by which time the majority are presumably non-breeding birds. Nearly 70% of all records have been in spring (Figure 3), suggesting that Scottish Ospreys may take a more easterly route on autumn migration.

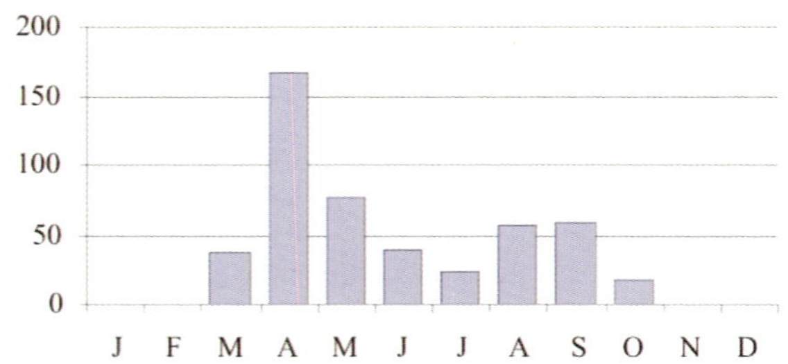

Figure 3. Monthly totals of Ospreys in Lancashire, 1964-2005.

Lengthier stays are far more regular in autumn and have been recorded in the past few years at Leighton Moss, Stocks Reservoir, Brockholes Quarry, St. Helens and Foulridge/Slipper Hill Reservoirs – the last for more than a fortnight from 25 September to 17 October 1999. Most recently a juvenile found at Marton Mere on 14 August 2004 moved to the south-west mosses on the 22nd and remained there until 16 September.

The latest in the county were a juvenile in poor condition at Cleveley Mere, Scorton from 20 October until 27 November 1993 and one seen flying in off the sea at Heysham on 26 October 1999.

BM, DJH.

This species account was sponsored by John Wright.

KESTREL

Falco tinnunculus

Lancashire Category A.

Fairly common resident breeder.

Both Mitchell and Oakes considered the Kestrel to be Lancashire's most numerous bird of prey, found throughout the county and nesting up to 400m altitude on the fells. Oakes reported an increase after the First World War and noted a tendency to move into suburban and even urban areas, particularly on Merseyside. Populations declined over Britain and Ireland as a whole from the mid-1950s, due to the effects of organochlorine pesticides; numbers then recovered in most areas during the 1970s. The long-term trend has been downward with a 37% decrease in the British population between 1970 and 2001 (CBC) and a 18% decrease during 1994-2005 (BBS), and the population is currently estimated at 35,400 pairs (Baker *et al.* 2006).

The Lancashire breeding population appears to have followed the national trend, but county bird reports since the 1980s reflect a very complicated pattern, with reports of declines in some areas, especially in the south, increases in others and a stable situation in several regions. The 1997-2000 Atlas estimated a total of 750 pairs, the same as for the Sparrowhawk, illustrating the reversal of fortunes between the two species since the middle of the last century, which anecdotal reports suggest has continued into the twenty-first.

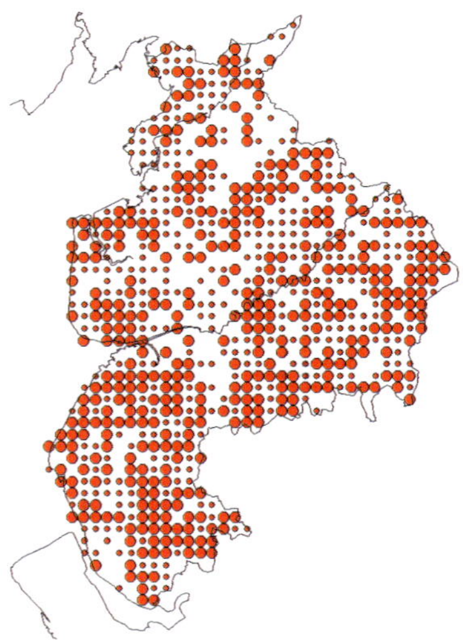

Breeding distribution of Kestrel, 1997-2000. (Large dots: confirmed. Small dots: possible)

Nevertheless, Kestrels still have a widespread breeding range in Lancashire and were present in 79% of the county's tetrads and in every 10km square in 1997-2000. The densest concentrations occur in North Merseyside, the south-west mosslands and parts of east Lancashire.

Most pairs breed in tree-cavities and on cliff-ledges in natural surroundings but they are highly adaptable. Nesting on occupied buildings occurs in many urban areas, including a pair that raised young on a Blackpool cinema every year from 1986 to 1995.

A nest-box programme in the Pilling-Preesall area of the Fylde has attracted up to 13 pairs annually since 1992, fledging a total of more than 400 young by 2005, with a mean of around 3.5 per brood.

Post-breeding gatherings of Kestrels are a notable feature of the species' lifestyle in Lancashire; these may be observed at moorland sites as well as on coastal saltmarshes, particularly on the Ribble Estuary. High counts have included eleven on Haslingden Moor, Rossendale in August 1986, 15 on Pendle Hill in July 1994 and 16 at Belmont in July 2001. The most impressive assemblies have been on the saltings at Marshside and Crossens, where the birds apparently feed mainly on the abundant craneflies, plucked from the tops of sea aster and other saltmarsh plants or taken in flight; peak numbers have varied quite widely, from 33 in September 1979 and 21 in September 1986 to twelve in August 1990, 26 in September 1994 and nine in August 2000, but the general trend has been downward since the late 1990s.

Female Kestrel, Fairhaven, November 2005. (Steve Young)

Lancashire Kestrels have long demonstrated an impressive virtuosity in exploitation of potential prey. Oakes reported sand lizards being taken at Great Crosby and Starlings in flight at winter roosts in east Lancashire. In more recent times birds as large as Lapwing and Snipe have been successfully attacked and Kestrels have been recorded killing a weasel at Delph Reservoir in March 1988, a Leach's Storm-petrel over the surf at Seaforth in October 1988, and a brown rat on Skelmersdale Moss in January 2002. There are several instances on record of other raptors as apparently formidable as female Sparrowhawk and Barn Owl being deprived of their prey by a Kestrel. Scavenging has also been widely observed; Kestrels fed on a Herring Gull corpse on the Wyre Estuary in December 1982 and on a goose carcase at Martin Mere in January 1985, while a female at Trawden fed repeatedly on meat scraps at a refuse-dump in the winter of 1982/83.

Migratory movements, although involving very small numbers, are regularly observed at coastal watchpoints; most records have come from Seaforth, Blackpool, Rossall Point and Heysham. Spring movements occur mainly in late March and April but autumn passage may be protracted, with records between early August and the end of October; around six or seven birds in total in each season has been the norm in recent years. Ringing recoveries indicate a very complex pattern of migration and dispersal. There have been 326 recoveries to date of birds ringed in Lancashire: 154 within the county, 91 elsewhere in northern England, 52 in southern England, four in Wales, 14 in France, two in the Netherlands and singles in Sweden, Germany, Belgium, Spain, Portugal and Morocco. This last easily holds the distance record for a Lancashire Kestrel, a bird ringed as a pullus at Crawshawbooth, Rossendale on 17 June 1991 and recovered 2,375km to the south, in the foothills of the Middle Atlas, on 14 March of the following year.

There have been 82 recoveries here of Kestrels ringed elsewhere in Britain, 65 from northern England, seven from southern England and ten from Scotland, and two foreign-ringed recoveries, from the Netherlands and Finland.

BM, DJH.

This species account was sponsored by Margaret Dempsey and James Galbraith.

RED-FOOTED FALCON

Falco vespertinus

Lancashire Category A. (0, 10).

Vagrant from eastern Europe.

A bird seen near Southport from 26 January to 4 February 1963 was originally accepted by the BBRC but was found to be unacceptable on review in 1990; no winter records have been accepted nationally. The first unequivocal record was of a male, found by S. Woodhouse at Heysham on 17 July 1967.

Spencer published a record of an 'immature' at Southport on 30 April 1972 but he received the details second-hand and it appears not to have been submitted to the BBRC.

There have been eight accepted records subsequently, beginning with a male at Ainsdale on 20 May 1973, a year which marked the first sizeable national influx of birds, and followed by adult males at Leighton Moss on 17-18 May 1974 and at Marshside on 10 May 1979.

First-summer female Red-footed Falcon, Blackpool, June 1992. (Steve Young)

The next was at Ainsdale on 16 May 1981. Nine years then elapsed before another adult male was discovered eating a Lapwing chick at Seaforth on 22 May 1990 and seen later in the day sitting on football goal-posts in nearby Litherland. 1992 brought a record 120+ nationally with Lancashire picking up two of them, both first-summer females, at Marshside on 25 May and on a playing field at South Shore Blackpool from 29 May to 3 June. This was followed by females at Leighton Moss on 27-28 May 1994 and Blackpool on 12 June 2005, with the latter also seen at Middleton on 21 June.

The clustering of arrival dates, with the exception of the 1967 record, from mid- to late May reflects the national pattern.

All records:

1967	Heysham, male, 17 July
1973	Ainsdale, male, 20 May
1974	Leighton Moss, male, 17 to 18 May
1979	Marshside, male, 10 May
1981	Ainsdale, male, 16 May
1990	Seaforth, male, 22 May
1992	Marshside, first-summer female, 25 May
1992	Blackpool, first-summer female, 29 May t0 3 June
1994	Leighton Moss, female 27 to 28 May
2005	Blackpool, female, 12 June, also Middleton, 21 June

SJW, MJ.

This species account was sponsored by Neill Hunt.

MERLIN

Falco columbarius

Lancashire Category A.

Scarce breeder; fairly common winter visitor and passage migrant from Iceland.

Merlins prey on smaller birds of open country across virtually the entire boreal and temperate northern hemisphere. Populations in Iceland, Fennoscandia and northern Russia are migratory but those of Britain and Ireland normally make only altitudinal movements from their moorland breeding areas to winter in coastal and other lowland habitats.

The British breeding population declined steadily during the twentieth century, due to persecution, habitat loss and disturbance. This was accelerated in the 1950s by the effects of pesticide poisoning and the Merlin does not appear to have benefited from the withdrawal of these substances to the same extent as other affected raptor species. The British population was estimated at 1,300 pairs in 1993-94 (Rebecca & Bainbridge 1998).

According to Mitchell, Merlins bred in small numbers on all extensive tracts of moorland in Lancashire; pairs were strongly attached to breeding territories, and most birds moved to the coast in winter. Oakes described the species as nesting fairly numerously in Rossendale and on the moors to the east of Burnley, but apart from Pendle Hill he did not mention Bowland as a breeding area. He believed that birds normally moved down to the coastal plain in August, returning between mid-March and late April, although a few remained all winter on the fells. Spencer (1973) commented that the breeding population of the 1960s was only a remnant of that of the 1920s.

Since the 1960s the breeding status of the Merlin in Lancashire has been shrouded in uncertainty and secrecy; only occasionally has anything like a comprehensive picture of the situation been available. This reluctance to disclose information is

Female Merlin, Marshside. (Mike McKavett)

understandable since, like all raptors, Merlins continue to suffer the attentions of egg-collectors, although thankfully the days of persecution of adults are long gone. The 1997-2000 survey estimated a total population of only 25 pairs but this is likely to have been a significant underestimate – 40 pairs may be more accurate. Trobe (1990) gave map references for 35 Merlin territories in Lancashire, while Pritchard *et al.* (1992) estimated 31 pairs in Bowland alone.

The core breeding area is on the Bowland Fells, with small pockets elsewhere in east Lancashire, in Rossendale and on the West Pennine Moors. Most of the detailed breeding data in recent years derive from the United Utilities estate in Bowland, where in some years breeding productivity has been very encouraging. In 1997 six pairs fledged 15 young, in 1998 eleven pairs managed to raise 28, and 19 young were produced by five pairs in 2002, while 21 fledged from six pairs in 2003, from nine pairs in 2004 and from eight pairs in 2005. Breeding elsewhere in Bowland is seldom reported comprehensively but at least seven pairs nested on the Abbeystead estate in 1992 and at least six pairs in Bowland away from the United Utilities estate in 2004. Regular breeding had ceased on the West Pennine Moors by the early 1960s and was at best occasional until 1992, since when breeding has been annual with seven sites occupied by four or five pairs.

Lancashire Merlins mostly nest on the ground in heather or bracken beds, although tree-nesting in disused crows' nests has been recorded in recent years. Oakes mentioned occasional nesting on the lowland mosses but no such instance has been recorded in more recent decades, although occasional birds are seen in summer at coastal sites, including singles at Hightown on 18 June 1986, Seaforth on 21 June 1993 and Blackpool on 27 June 1998.

Merlins begin to appear in coastal Lancashire from the end of

Tony Disley

July or early August and movements continue at a low level until early November. Southbound migrants are occasionally seen passing offshore from seawatching stations; there were two such in 1995, off Formby Point in September and Blackpool in October, one passed Formby on 26 October 2000 and two were recorded offshore there on 19 October 2001.

Merlins winter regularly in south Fylde, the south-west and around Morecambe Bay. Up to four have been seen at Marshside-Crossens annually since the early 1970s at least, and two or three winter regularly on Carnforth Marsh, Warton Marsh and at Martin Mere. As in Oakes's day a few are reported from upland areas in most winters but whether these are local breeders or their offspring, or migrants from harsher climates, is unknown. Perhaps most likely is that they consist largely of males visiting their territories from time to time rather than remaining all winter.

Ringing recoveries suggest that many of our autumn and winter birds come from other parts of the north of England and from Scotland and Wales, but it is likely that Icelandic birds are also fairly frequent and there is one record of the race *subaesalon*, a juvenile shot at Warton on the Fylde in November 1935 that had been ringed in northern Iceland that July. Some Lancashire breeders have been shown from ringing recoveries to remain within the county during winter but others move greater distances: ten have been recovered in southern England, two in Scotland and one in Wales. One ringed in the nest on the Abbeystead estate in 29 June 1989 was found dead in Brittany on 15 January 1990, and another ringed in the Pennines in July 1995 was similarly recovered near Calais around 15 October 1997. A female ringed in Shetland in 1987 bred in Bowland with a Bowland-ringed male between at least 1989 and 1991.

On migration and on the wintering grounds Merlins display a wider dietary range than on their breeding territories – where they rely heavily on Meadow Pipits – although small passerines such as Skylarks, Linnets and Starlings remain the most commonly-recorded prey. Waders including Dunlin, Snipe and Lapwing are successfully attacked, Leach's Storm-petrels have been chased over the surf on Crosby shore, and a Jay pursued at Sunnyhurst Woods in November 1987. Swallow roosts at Marton Mere regularly attracted one or two hunting birds in several autumns during the 1980s and 1990s. There are several recent records of Merlins 'waiting on' other raptors, especially Hen Harriers, and pouncing on passerines flushed by the less agile harrier; this was observed on Altcar Moss in November 1981, on Hesketh Marsh in January 1988 and at Martin Mere that November. One was seen attacking a Short-eared Owl that had just cached a prey item on Annel Cross Moor in January 2003.

Merlins begin to vacate their Lancashire wintering areas in March and a few northbound coastal migrants are observed in most years in late March and April, especially at Rossall Point and Heysham. All have normally moved on by the end of April, although late migrants are occasionally recorded in the lowlands up to the middle of May.

BM, DJH.

This species account was sponsored by Bob Ashworth.

HOBBY

Falco subbuteo

Lancashire Category A.

Rare breeder; fairly common summer visitor.

The Hobby was a rare visitor to Lancashire until the closing decades of the twentieth century. Mitchell knew of only six records within the present county boundaries but Oakes dismissed all but two of these: a female said to have been shot 'in the act of carrying off a young Pheasant' at Shaw Hill, Chorley in mid-June 1878, and an adult male shot at Blackpool in late November or early December 1885. Both were later examined in collections by R.J. Howard but the choice of prey and the extremely late date respectively make these records seem dubious in the light of more recent knowledge.

Oakes himself added only four records, the first of these reported shot at Marshside sometime in October 1904. However, October records remain extremely unusual in Lancashire and, without a firm date, this no longer seems acceptable as a first for the county, an accolade which therefore probably passes to one at Martin Mere on 17 June 1905 which, according to Oakes, was 'seen attacking birds of thrush size, [and] actually on one occasion striking down a Lapwing before it was shot'. The next was shot at Tatham near Wennington on 12 June 1915 and our first field record followed at Crossens on 9 May 1923.

There were no more records until 1968 but Spencer (1973) reported one or two annually after that date. The situation remained much the same until a slight increase occurred in the late 1970s, with the six reported in 1978 by far the largest annual total to date. An average of four or five were then seen annually during the 1980s, sharply increasing to 15 a year during the 1990s (with a peak of 22 in 1992) and then more than doubling to 40 a year from 2000-05, with a peak of 60 in 2005 (Figure 1).

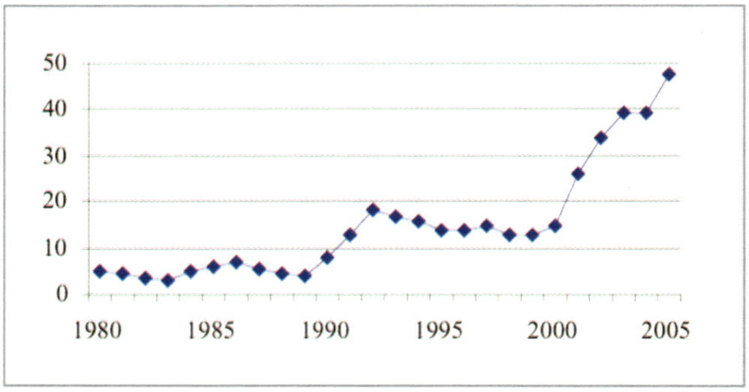

Figure 1. Annual totals of Hobbies in Lancashire (3-year rolling means), 1980-2005.

This roughly tenfold increase in reported sightings in Lancashire accords well with the increase in the British breeding population which was estimated at over 100 pairs in the late 1970s (BWP) and 2,200 pairs at the end of the 1990s (Clements 2001). It was not until the mid-1980s that the Hobby began to advance its range northwards, colonising the central counties of England, where an abundance of gravel pits and sand workings offered a plentiful supply of its favoured dragonfly prey.

Hobby, Hapton, east Lancashire, August 2005. (Bill Aspin)

In 1973 Spencer suggested that 'rumours of nesting might even prove justified' but, despite a huge increase in summer records, it has still not been proven. However, sightings between early June and late July increased from a total of six in 1980-84 to ten in 1985-90, 15 in 1990-94 and 20 in 1995-99. The first strong indications that one or two pairs might be nesting came from the north of the county in 1990, when there were repeated sightings of up to two birds in June and July at Leighton Moss and of singles in the Forest of Bowland. One or two were seen regularly during July 1998 and 1999 at various sites in the Lune Valley and at Leighton Moss and the circumstantial evidence was strong enough by 2000 for breeding to be thought probable somewhere in this area. The following year a pair was seen with two newly-fledged young in the Parbold area during July, and in 2002 two birds were seen daily hunting Swifts and hirundines at Fazakerley Waste Water Treatment Works in north Liverpool from mid-June before bringing two fresh juveniles to the site on 21-22 July. These records certainly indicate that successful breeding had occurred but do not absolutely confirm that nesting took place in the county.

Summer 2003 produced records from what has become a typically wide range of sites, including Brockholes Quarry, Martin Mere, the West Pennine Moors and the Rainford and Prescot areas of St. Helens, but none was reported from areas where breeding was thought to have occurred previously. A regular series of sightings during summer 2004 at both Brockholes Quarry and the south-west mosses also suggested likely breeding, while repeated sightings during the 2005 breeding season suggested that as many as six pairs may have been breeding. The jury is, therefore, still out on whether the Hobby has actually yet colonised Lancashire, although, with nine confirmed and eight probable breeding sites in Cheshire in 2003 this can only be a matter of time.

Records of migrants and summering birds show no clear geographical pattern, occurring in all parts of the county with more or less equal frequency and with clusters probably representing the distribution of birdwatchers rather than that of birds. Hobbies, being largely dependent upon flying macro-invertebrates and hirundines for prey, are late spring migrants and depart early in autumn. Records show a clear peak in July (Figure 2) and there has been only a handful of reliable reports in April (from the middle of the month). Likewise, hardly any have been reported in October and few, if any, of these have fully documented. Between 1974 and 2005 the average date of first arrival was 23 May and the average last sighting 15 September, although spring arrivals have become earlier and final autumn sightings later in recent years.

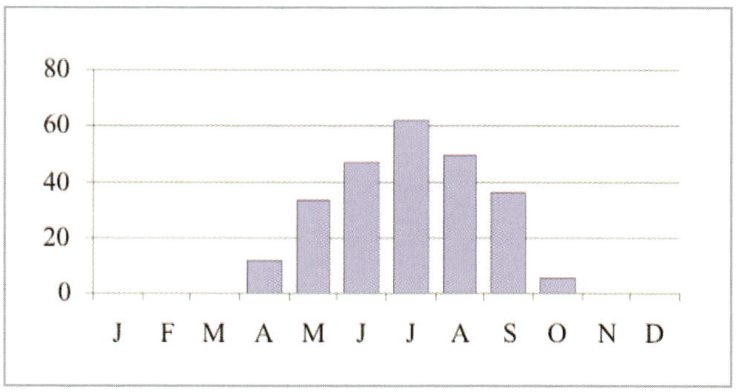

Figure 2. Monthly occurrences of Hobbies in Lancashire, 1974-2005.

Hobby Publications

SJW, JB, DJH.
This species account was sponsored by Hobby Publications.

ELEONORA'S FALCON

Falco eleonorae

Lancashire Category A. (0, 1).

Vagrant from south-eastern Europe.

One of the most remarkable birds ever seen in the county was found at Cabin Hill National Nature Reserve, between Formby and Hightown, by Ken Horton on 8 August 1977. This was not only a first for the county but for Britain too, and, more than 25 years later, the national total has still only reached a mere four records.

The bird, identified as a first-summer on account of the spotting and barring on the underwing and tail, flew around a drying dune slack where Black-headed Gulls and hirundines were hawking insects. On first impression, its overall darkness suggested an Arctic Skua but it quickly proved to be a medium-sized falcon. Fortunately, a Kestrel was also in view, highlighting the larger size, the slow, deep wingbeats and the lack of hovering of the, as yet, unidentified bird.

Having considered all possibilities, Eleonora's Falcon seemed to be the best fit but, aware of its British status, KH returned home to consult field guides. Two features stood out: the slow foraging flight style and dark underwing-coverts. The next morning he returned with three other birders and all were able to get close views of the bird, confirming its identity. At one point it was chased by a Kestrel into a copse and was found perched on a branch and approached to within 50m, revealing fine details of plumage. It then resumed its behaviour of the day before, hawking insects overhead.

Thorough searching in subsequent days drew a blank. In these days of instant communications and huge twitching galleries it seems barely credible that a bird of such outstanding rarity which lingered for two days just outside our main conurbation should have had just four observers. Different times!

Eleanora's Falcon, Cabin Hill National Nature Reserve, August 1977. (Anthea Coppleston. Reprinted from *British Birds*)

SJW, MJ.

This species account was sponsored by Mark Garner.

GYR FALCON

Falco rusticolus

Lancashire Category D.

No Lancashire species has a more uncertain status. Mitchell mentioned a specimen said to have been obtained from a ship coming into the Port of Liverpool some time prior to 1865.

A white morph Greenland bird was reported at Lytham on 6 December 1952 and again on 17 January 1953, but no details were published.

Gyr Falcon, Liverpool, December 1960. (Eric Hardy)

The first fully documented record also arrived by ship; a white phase 'near-adult' brought into the Liverpool docks on 1 December 1960 on board the *Continental Pioneer*, having joined the ship in mid-Atlantic in mid-November. The bird was taken into care by the RSPCA and released in Midlothian on 8 December. Eric Hardy photographed the bird and organised its release, publishing a brief report and photograph in the Merseyside Naturalists Association Report for 1960-62. The report does not make clear whether the bird was taken into care before or after its arrival in Liverpool, but at that time all ship-assisted records were placed in Category D by the BBRC.

The next was a long-staying bird, found at Ainsdale on 18 November 1961, which remained in the area until 29 January 1962 and was seen by many observers. Unfortunately, no details were submitted to the BBRC and this too has to go down as of uncertain provenance.

On the evening of 25 August 1964 at a sludge bed on Lea Marsh, Preston, a heavily-built dark morph falcon flew over, striking a Herring Gull before heading off towards Salwick, not to be seen again. The record was first accepted by the BBRC as a wild bird but it was later learned that a Gyr Falcon had been landed by a trawler at Hull and handed over to the RSPCA who had released it at Bempton Cliffs on 12 August. This was thought to be too much of a coincidence and the Lea Marsh record was reviewed and consigned to Category D.

SJW, MJ.

This species account was sponsored by Graham and Ann Johnson.

PEREGRINE FALCON

Falco peregrinus

Lancashire Category A.

Scarce breeder; fairly common winter visitor.

The recent history of the Peregrine in Britain, and in Lancashire in particular, is a peculiarly fascinating one. Persecution and collecting of eggs and specimens led to some declines during the nineteenth and early twentieth centuries, aggravated by a partially-effective extermination campaign during the Second World War, dedicated to the protection of military carrier-pigeons. Having endured these trials Peregrine populations suffered a near-catastrophic collapse after the mid-1950s due to the effects of DDT and other organochlorine pesticides, and the British population was reduced to a mere 68 pairs by the early 1960s.

Restrictions and eventual bans on the use of the pesticides responsible were followed by a marked population recovery in many countries, resulting in a British population of 1,100 pairs by 1991. This continuing 'super-recovery', as the New Atlas described it, has transformed the species' status in Lancashire.

Mitchell described the Peregrine as a scarce visitor, mainly to the fell country in spring; he cited breeding at Cliviger Gorge, Burnley in the early nineteenth century as the only recent nesting record within the present-day county boundaries. The position had changed little by Oakes's time, although by then Peregrines seem to have become more regular in coastal areas in winter, especially in the south. The nationwide decline of the 1950s and 1960s was less dramatic in northern Britain than further south and throughout this period the Peregrine remained a casual winter visitor to coastal areas, although inland records were relatively rare.

As the recovery gained momentum during the 1970s the rate of occurrences in Lancashire increased slowly; from 1978 up to three birds were present throughout the year in the Leighton Moss-Silverdale area and sightings became fairly regular in the Lune Valley. Both areas are close to the Cumbrian fells, where the residual population was recovering strongly during this time. In 1980 there were press reports of the shooting of a pair in the Lancashire hills, and the pace of occurrences increased very rapidly in the early 1980s; in 1983 up to five pairs attempted to breed, but all were reported to have failed, due either to disturbance or direct persecution.

The breakthrough came in 1984 with confirmed nesting by five pairs which fledged a total of at least three young. One of these pairs nested on the ledge of a bonded warehouse in the Liverpool docks, close to the city centre, and was amongst the first to colonise any urban area in Britain.

Peregrines have bred in every year since and the population has grown steadily to an estimated 35 pairs during the 1997-2000 Atlas Survey. Lancashire lacks the lofty crags and sea-cliffs traditionally used as nest sites by the species in Britain, and its expansion has been partly made possible by a progressive adaptation to man-made habitats. In addition to dock buildings in Liverpool, Peregrines have bred regularly on mill-chimneys in Darwen and Burnley, in an old Carrion Crow's nest on a pylon on the Lune Estuary, on St. John's Church in central Blackpool, a gasometer in Southport and a tower block in north Liverpool, as well as on quarry-sides and quite modest crags in the fell country. The extent of their acceptance of urban environments was exemplified in the early years of this century when three pairs nested in Liverpool with another just across the Mersey in Birkenhead.

Peregrine Falcon, Warton Crag. (Phillip Tomkinson)

However, the bulk of the Lancashire population breeds on low cliffs and quarry-faces and the breeding range is concentrated in the uplands wherever such features occur, in Rossendale, east Lancashire, Bowland and north Lancashire. Ground-nesting has occurred in the South Pennines and in Bowland. The central plain, extending over almost half of the county, has no breeding Peregrines outside of urban areas. In 1997-2000 breeding was confirmed in 31 tetrads but birds were present in a further 39. Some of these are likely to have been birds hunting at some distance from the nest, but many were probably young birds or adults unable to establish a territory. It is likely, then, that the county's pre-breeding population may be significantly in excess of 100 individuals.

The breeding population has probably continued to grow but not all pairs are reported. In 2002 at least 21 breeding pairs were known: up to twelve in Bowland, five elsewhere in east Lancashire, three on the Fylde and single pairs in Liverpool and Southport, but no data were received from several other areas where nesting had occurred in previous years. In spite of positive changes in public sentiment and game preservation practices over recent decades Lancashire Peregrines are still subjected to intermittent persecution and disturbance. County Bird Reports, even since the mid-1990s, have recorded instances of adult birds shot or poisoned and eggs or fledglings stolen or destroyed.

As the breeding population here and in adjacent counties has increased, records of Peregrines in all parts of the county and in all seasons have proliferated. Up to three birds may be seen regularly at several coastal sites, especially in autumn and winter, from Seaforth to Morecambe Bay. They prey on a wide range of wader and wildfowl species, and, on the Ribble Estuary at least, also on Black-headed Gulls. A large female was flushed from a freshly-killed Pink-footed Goose near Preesall in January 2002 and it was thought possible that she had taken the bird; at the other end of the spectrum two were in regular attendance at a large Swallow roost near Ribchester in September 2001.

Birds with established territories are highly sedentary but juveniles and sub-adults may wander large distances. Of the twelve recoveries of Lancashire-ringed pulli, six were recovered elsewhere in northern England, two in Wales and singles in Scotland and Ireland; this last, ringed in east Lancashire on 13 June 1997, was recovered injured in Co. Mayo, 450 km to the west, that December. Although some of these young birds may return to their natal areas, the fact that a majority of recoveries outside of the county have been during summer indicates that many probably become established elsewhere. Fifteen birds ringed as pulli elsewhere in Britain have been recovered here, twelve from northern England, two from southern England and one from Scotland.

There have been no exchanges of ringed birds between Lancashire and continental Europe but it is possible that some individuals from the migratory populations of Fennoscandia and northern Russia do occur in winter. There have been several claims in recent years of birds thought to show characteristics of the race *calidus* which breeds from Lapland east to Siberia but which cannot be reliably identified in the field. However, several records have come from Seaforth in the past ten years of notably large females exhibiting unusual hunting behaviour, either attacking overflying prey from the ground or hanging in the updraft of buildings and launching at passing gulls, ducks and even Cormorants.

BM, DJH.

THE DESîGN ROOM creative graphics — This species account was sponsored by www.thedesignroom.org

WATER RAIL

Rallus aquaticus

Lancashire Category A.

Scarce breeder; fairly common winter visitor from central and eastern Europe.

Mitchell was understandably confused about the status of the Water Rail, describing it as 'much rarer than formerly, but probably now and at all times commoner than supposed, from the extremely retiring nature of its habits'. As there was no evidence to the contrary, he believed, with some justification, that its status was that of a breeding resident. For Oakes it was an 'uncommon and widely distributed resident, breeding regularly in a few localities but better known as a winter visitor from October to March'. Nesting was recorded at Leighton Moss, Tunstall and the Ribble Valley, and suspected on the Formby mosses. Winter records came from Lunesdale, western Fylde, the Formby mosses and Martin Mere, reflecting the present-day distribution.

Leighton Moss has been the county's breeding stronghold ever since it reverted to reedbed and supports more than 95% of the Lancashire population. Until recently, censusing was an exceedingly difficult task since Water Rails are extremely elusive and silent by day during the breeding season. The Leighton Moss population used to be counted by mapping birds calling at dusk in spring. By this method it was estimated that the population reached a low-point of 25 pairs in the mid-1980s after some hard winters, but recovered to 35 in 1988 and 53 in 1994. Since 1995, however, tape-luring has been used and the number of breeding pairs calculated from the number of birds responding to calls.

Recent population estimates have been produced on the assumption that all double and widely dispersed single registrations indicate breeding pairs. Adoption of this methodology effectively doubled the known population to 80 pairs in 1995 and 105 in 1996. Numbers have fluctuated between 88 and 139 since then, but it appears that the Leighton Moss population has been essentially stable throughout the 1990s. The British breeding population was estimated at 450-900 pairs in 1991 and, although it is acknowledged that if tape-luring census techniques were employed more widely this estimate would increase significantly, there is no doubt that Leighton Moss is nationally important for Water Rails, perhaps supporting as much as 10% of the British population.

Breeding pairs are not evenly distributed throughout the Leighton Moss reedbeds but are concentrated entirely in areas where reed grows in water, usually 10-20cm deep. Censuses at nearby Haweswater have confirmed their requirement for wet reedbeds. In 1995 Haweswater was completely dry and no Water Rails were present, but 18 pairs were located when the water table had been raised in 2000; earlier population estimates at Haweswater had been in low single figures.

Breeding is more difficult to confirm at smaller sites, since it seems that Water Rails may remain mostly silent in the absence of calling competitors, and has only been proven conclusively at a handful of other sites in the county, although it has undoubtedly taken place at rather more. One probably important breeding site was the quite extensive reedbed at Mere Brow before it was developed as 'leisure lakes' during the 1970s.

Successful nesting was confirmed at Heysham NR in 1992, when a pair was seen with two young, and again in 1998 when two pairs raised at least four young. It seems likely, however, that at least one or two pairs have bred there since at least 1987 as birds are regularly seen throughout the breeding season. Other proven recent breeding records have come from the Rufford Branch Canal at Sollom in 1999, when someone using a sweep net to survey invertebrates inadvertently scooped up an unfledged juvenile, and at Fazakerley Reedbed since 2001. Any records between late April and July are thought likely to be breeding birds and on this basis breeding was believed probable at Marshside in 1995 and 2001, Marton Mere in 1997 and 2005, in the Rimrose Valley since the mid-1990s, at Warton Bank and Mere Sands Wood from 2001 and Martin Mere in 2004-05. Sightings of an adult with a fledged juvenile at Wood End sewage works on 31 August 1995 and of two adults with a juvenile at Lee Green Reservoir on 11 September may have been local breeders.

The British population is largely resident and probably mostly sedentary although some may make short movements and a few are known to have moved quite long distances (Migration Atlas). Dispersal begins in August and it is likely that the earliest birds turning up at non-breeding sites are fairly local breeders. Those arriving later in autumn are more probably migrants from central or eastern Europe or southern Fennoscandia. The main arrival seems to occur between the end of September and early November. Both Marton Mere and Seaforth show a clear peak during October, indicating that a few birds at least continue their migratory journey, while perhaps the majority settle down for the winter. Records are widely scattered during autumn with birds sometimes appearing briefly in unsuitable habitat, such as singles found dead in the driveway of a house at Blacko on 3 November 1994, on the roof of Bispham Technical College on 11 November 1994 and in St. John's Market in central Liverpool in 2005. Most, however, probably arrive directly at reedbed sites, including Leighton Moss, and remain undetected. There was a conspicuous passage at Heysham in November 1995, coinciding with the arrival of continental Blackbirds and involving two or three influxes of up to five birds.

Water Rail at Marshside. (Mike McKavett)

There are winter records every year in most parts of the county. Crepuscular and daytime calling may reveal their presence in cover at the edge of lakes, reservoirs, inland and coastal marshes, boggy meadows and small ponds. Although records are usually published from up to twenty sites each winter, very many are undoubtedly overlooked; indeed, there is hardly any small patch of wetland habitat anywhere in Lancashire, particularly in the lowlands, that has not reported the species at some time in the past 20 or so years. More unusual sightings include one feeding on pellets put out for domestic ducks in an allotment in Belmont in November 2001 and another on a small garden pond in West Bradford in December 2001.

Water Rails are abundant at Leighton Moss in winter but no attempt has been made to count them, for they remain elusive except when the lakes freeze and they appear at the edge of unfrozen dykes or venturing onto the ice. Marton Mere is the next most important site, with an average of around eight seen each winter from 1995-2005 and a peak of 14 in 1999/2000. Six or seven are usual peak counts at both Heysham and the Rimrose Valley. Most other regular sites, including Wood End sewage works, Lowerhouse Lodges and, more recently, Martin Mere usually hold just one to three, and the only other recent large count was of seven in ditches on Altcar Moss on 11 January 1987. Rather surprisingly, relatively few are recorded on estuarine sites. Marshside is something of an exception with three to five seen in most winters during the 1990s and a peak count of six in freezing conditions in February 1979, but these are mainly on the grazing marshes and very few seem to be flushed from the saltmarshes by high spring tides – in comparison, for example, with the Cheshire Dee marshes. Winter numbers everywhere appear to decline slowly throughout late February and March and few remain into April.

The continental origins of at least some winter visitors are indicated by one ringed at Heysham on 5 November 1990 and subsequently killed by a cat in Vitebsk, Belarus 1,984km to the east on 13 June 1991, and another ringed, possibly on passage, in Holland on 19 October 1997 and found dead at Leighton Moss on 16 February 2002.

SJW, DJH.

This species account was sponsored by Pauline McGough.

SPOTTED CRAKE

Porzana porzana

Lancashire Category A. (/, 84).

Rare breeder; scarce passage migrant from continental Europe.

Mitchell regarded the Spotted Crake as primarily an autumn and winter visitor and stated that 'there (were) few districts in which specimens had not been shot at one time or another'. He reported 'a considerable number' seen or shot near St. Michael's-on-Wyre between September and December, the belief of 'some farmers in the neighbourhood of Martin Mere (that) it was as abundant as the Water-Rail', and that it was 'not uncommon in September near Tarleton'.

Oakes, however, believed only 40 records to have been properly authenticated, more than three-quarters of them north of the Lune (an unknown number therefore in present-day Cumbria). All occurred during the period August to November. He thus disputed Mitchell's winter records and implicitly thought its status much scarcer than Mitchell claimed. The only definite Lancashire records published by Oakes were four 'picked up' at 'a site near Lancaster' in October between 1899 and 1909, specimens obtained at Silverdale on 12 September 1923 and 16 September 1824, singles at Halsall Moss on 2 & 17 November 1925 and 24 November 1935 and an undated record at Haslingden. Most records in the south of the county came from the Formby mosses, where J. Wrigley, writing in 1892, said that the species was often caught in Snipe pantles.

Spotted Crake, Marton Mere, September 1989. (Steve Young)

At least 84 birds were recorded between 1953 and 2005 but, given the species' extremely skulking habits, the real total is likely to have been considerably greater. Seventeen of these occurred during spring and early summer, between March and June, including at least eight records of males calling in the Leighton Moss reedbeds on dates ranging from 27 April (in 1987) and 30 June (in 2000). Although breeding has never been proven, it seems likely that it has at least been attempted at Leighton Moss in recent years. Similarly, Mitchell reported probable breeding at 'a marsh near Preston', where birds were reportedly common and young had been seen prior to the site being drained.

Most records are in autumn, predominantly in August and September (Figure 1), with the earliest arrival on 6 August 2000 at Marshside. Birds regularly linger for a week or more. Just three have been recorded in winter: singles at Tarleton on 23 January 1971, Hightown on 3 December 1971 and Marshside during January and February 1976.

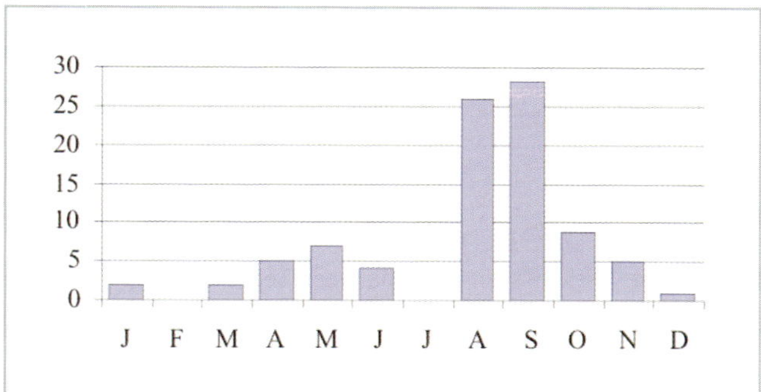

Table 1. Arrival dates of Spotted Crakes in Lancashire, 1953-2005.

Two birds have been recorded together on just six occasions; all other records are of singles. Annual totals have changed little over the past 50 years, averaging 1.1 during the 1960s, 2.5 during the 1970s, 1.7 during the 1980s, 2.0 during the 1990s and 1.6 this century, and records have been less than annual throughout this period. The largest totals were six in 1971 and 1995. The majority of autumn records have not been aged but three-quarters of those that have been were juveniles.

Two sites have between them produced the overwhelming majority of records. Before Marton Mere was enlarged in 1974, open mud patches in the surrounding reed-swamp and intensive watching produced a total of 15 birds between 1953 and 1970, including two together in 1963 and 1966. The only spring record was a single on 23 April 1954. After enlargement, suitable mud areas within the reedbeds were reduced but singles have since been seen in the autumns of 1975, 1978, 1985, 1989, 1996 and 2005, with two in 1995.

Leighton Moss, the other main haunt, has recorded at least 31 birds, one in 1954 and the remainder since 1969.

Birds have also been recorded at the following sites: Seaforth, Hightown, Formby, Marshside, Hundred End, Mere Brow, Mere Sands Wood, Martin Mere, Withnell Fold, Tarleton, Dean Clough Reservoir, Wood End Sewage Works and Lea Green Reservoir in Burnley, the Lune Valley and Heysham.

SJW, MJ.

This species account was sponsored by Maurice Jones.

[LITTLE CRAKE]

Porzana parva

Mitchell reported one shot in the Formby 'whams' in 1875 which ended up in the collection of J. Wrigley, but Oakes regarded the record as unsubstantiated. A record of an immature female at Marton Mere on 31 May 1955 was published by Spencer but was reviewed by the BBRC in 2002 and considered to be insufficiently documented.

CORNCRAKE

Crex crex

Lancashire Category A. (/, c.60).

Extinct breeder; rare passage migrant.

Mitchell described the Corncrake as a common bird but it seems that it was already in decline in Lancashire by the 1880s 'due to its eggs being destroyed by mowing machines'. For at least 50 years, however, Corncrakes appear to have remained widespread. Oakes stated that '30 years ago (in the 1920s) the rasping voice of the Corn-Crake was as well known as the Cuckoo's familiar call'. The 1911 national Land Rail Inquiry concluded that losses were 'scarcely appreciable' in Lancashire.

The decline appears to have begun on the southern plains, accelerating from around 1914, and by the 1940s birds were extremely scarce in present-day Merseyside, West Lancashire and western Fylde, although breeding still took place regularly in the Bolton area and odd pairs nested in the Lune Valley and east of the Fylde plain. Oakes supported Mitchell's view that numbers fluctuated annually, at least in the east, citing 1946 as a particularly good year with, for example, six pairs at Gawthorpe, near Burnley. Oakes also concurred with Mitchell's view that the first birds arrived at the end of April but with few heard calling until May; most left during August with just a few stragglers into October. Wintering birds were supposedly fairly regular during the nineteenth century but there is only one twentieth century record, one shot at Martin Mere on 14 December 1939.

Final extinction was a long drawn-out affair over the next three decades. Probable or possible breeding was reported from Rainford (1952), St. Anne's (1954), Lytham (1955), Whittle-le-Woods (1957), Leighton Moss, Ribchester, Blackburn (all in 1958), at two unspecified locations in 1959, Thornton in Fylde (1960-61), Anglezarke, Balderstone and Darwen (all in 1961), Marton (1965), Colne (1966), St. Michael's-on-Wyre (1969), and Barton near Preston, near Martin Mere, Tarleton, Longton and Goosnargh (all in 1971). These included the last likely breeding records on the Lancashire Plain but a handful of pairs appear to have clung on in east Lancashire and the Lune Valley. One pair is thought to have bred near Clitheroe in 1977 and 'several' males were calling at Coldwell on 8 May 1977 reducing to two by the 25th. Single males were calling and possibly breeding in the Lune Valley during the summers of 1980-82, at a site on the western edge of Bowland in 1983, near Darwen in 1984 and close to the West Pennine Moors in 1987.

It is impossible to say precisely when the last Corncrakes bred in Lancashire since almost all records are of calling males which normally move on once the clutch is completed; the last definite record of successful breeding was as far back as 1952 when two young were reared at King's Moss, Rainford. It seems likely that breeding was at least attempted several times during the 1970s and 1980s, but none has been suspected since then.

There is no doubt about the causes of the extinction. Notwithstanding its name, the Corncrake is essentially a grassland species and the widespread introduction of mechanical mowing after the First World War, causing wholesale loss of nests and chicks, was quickly recognised as the chief culprit. More recently, the problem has been compounded by the conversion of grassland to arable and the replacement of hay meadows by silage leys; little suitable habitat now remains in the county.

From the 1960s onwards an increasing proportion of reports were of short-staying birds, presumably on passage. About 15 were reported in spring or early summer between 1980 and 2003, only two of which stayed for any length of time, at Roddlesworth for at least a week in June 1995 and at Gillar's Green, St. Helens for at least a fortnight in May and June 1998 – neither record produced any evidence of breeding. The earliest were single birds on 11 April 1960 at Hightown, 14 April 1970 at Mere Brow and 15 April 1982 at Plex Moss.

There have been nine autumn records since 1980 with the earliest at Bradshaw Lane, Pilling on 16 July 1997 and the only (barely) 'twitchable' bird at Marton Mere on 30 to 31 October 1996, which remains the latest modern record. Perhaps the strangest record was of one found dead near Liverpool's Pier Head on 22 September 2002, which was believed to have been taken by a Peregrine and is now in the Natural History Museum, Tring.

All modern records:

1980	Lune Valley, male calling during June
1981	Lune Valley, male calling during June
1982	Plex Moss, one, 15 April
1982	Warton, one, 24 April
1982	Lune Valley, male calling during May and June
1982	Whitendale, one, 12 May
1983	Whitechapel, west Bowland, male calling during June
1984	near Sunnyhurst Woods Darwen, male calling from end of May to early June
1986	Banks Marsh, one, 12 October
1987	West Pennine Moors, male calling for five weeks in summer
1988	Warton Crag, one, 14 September
1992	Thurnham, one, 5 June
1992	Crown Point Rossendale, one, 7 June
1992	Martin Mere, one, 21 to 22 September
1995	Roddlesworth, male calling for one week in June
1995	Whitechapel, west Bowland, male calling during summer
1996	Marton Mere, one, 30 to 31 October
1997	Bradshaw Lane Pilling, one, 16 July
1997	Leighton Moss, one 5 September
1998	Gillar's Green St Helens, calling male for at least fortnight from 26 May
2002	Liverpool, one, found dead 22 September
2003	Sefton Meadows Maghull, one, 5 August
2003	Great Plumpton Sidings Fylde, one 15 August

SJW, MJ.

This species account was sponsored by GDP Associates.

MOORHEN

Gallinula chloropus

Lancashire Category A.

Common resident breeder.

There is no indication that the breeding distribution or movements of the Moorhen in Lancashire have altered significantly for at least 150 years. Mitchell described it as 'resident and common, found breeding everywhere in weedy pits and ponds, and frequenting them throughout the winter; when these are frozen, it takes to the running streams'. Oakes concurred, describing breeding as 'common and well distributed from the coast to the hills . . . wherever suitable cover exists; it breeds in sand dune slacks, mossland dykes, reed-grown ponds, lakes, reservoirs, flashes and sewage farms'.

Although some suitable sites have been lost, notably sewage farms and the many marl pits and small field ponds that have been filled in or drained in recent decades, others, such as gravel pits, created wetland reserves and overgrown canals and lodges, have replaced them. The Lancashire Atlas survey of 1997-2000 located Moorhens in 69% of Lancashire tetrads and in every 10km square. The county population was estimated at 3,500 pairs. Their breeding range is almost solid throughout the lowlands, birds are absent only from the most urbanised and heavily wooded areas lacking even the smallest pond and are more sparsely distributed in the eastern half of the county south of the Ribble. With certain exceptions, such as the tarn on Beacon Fell, they are largely absent from the uplands where suitable eutrophic waters are lacking, particularly in central and north-east Bowland and Leck Fell. They do, however, breed on most small ponds in the West Pennine Moors up to 300m above sea level.

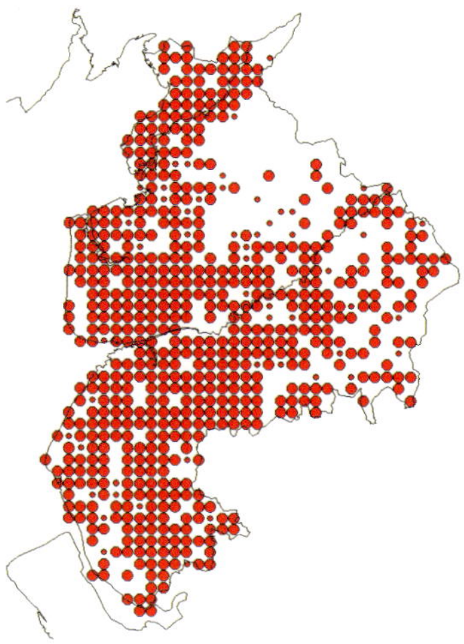

Breeding distribution of Moorhen, 1997-2000. (Large dots: confirmed. Small dots: possible)

Local populations are, however, known to fluctuate. The longest series of data comes from the Waterways Bird Survey of the River Lune from Skerton Weir to Kirkby Lonsdale, where 36 breeding pairs were located in 1981, declining to just 11-13 pairs in 1985-87, partly at least as a result of predation by mink. The population remained at roughly the same low level for several years but, by 1997, had regained its previous strength at 35 pairs, before declining again to 26 in 2003. Breeding densities are much higher on still waters in north Lancashire, particularly at Leighton Moss, where the population is difficult to census but was estimated at 80 pairs in 1985, with 21 pairs on the Eric Morecambe complex in 1993.

Moorhens are locally common in east Lancashire and present all year on the smallest ponds and the largest reservoirs, along suitable rivers and on the Leeds-Liverpool Canal. Counts into double figures are considered noteworthy in this area. In Rossendale they breed on quiet sections of the Irwell and its tributaries, on old mill lodges and at sewage works. One or two pairs are found on most reservoirs on the West Pennine Moors, including eight pairs at Belmont Reservoir in 2001. Moorhens are common on all suitable waters in a wide area around Chorley.

Breeding is extensive throughout the Fylde apart from the peat mosslands. Their adaptability was well demonstrated by successful breeding of a pair on a small ornamental pond on St. Anne's promenade in 1994 and 1995. Fylde strongholds include the Freckleton area, Stanley Park and Marton Mere, Fleetwood and the flashes around Preesall. Moorhens are widespread and numerous in the south-west although large areas of farmland lack ponds and here, as in similar parts of the Fylde, Moorhens are confined to field ditches. The main site is Martin Mere where up to 70 broods were regularly raised during the 1990s and 84 pairs bred in 2002. Marshside supports up to 20 pairs in most years with a record 25 in 1994.

Moorhen carrying nest material, Seaforth Nature Reserve, July 2004. (Steve Young)

Most birds are highly sedentary but some short-distance dispersal takes place in late summer. At most sites winter peaks are similar to or somewhat lower than those of early autumn, suggesting that little immigration or emigration takes place. The exception to this is Martin Mere, where the largest flocks almost always occur in December and January, perhaps attracted by the abundance of free offerings intended for swans. Winter numbers here are the amongst the highest in Britain and grew to record levels in the mid-1990s with counts of 620 in December 1995, 665 in January 1996 and 739 in January 1997. Up to 350 fed on fields adjacent to the Leighton Moss reedbeds in the 1970s, but 125 to 170 was typical in the 1990s, perhaps reflecting increasing mortality due to the expanding Marsh Harrier population; there is little evidence of any migratory movements or winter influxes. Other large late-year counts include 102 at Marton Mere on 27 October 1995 and the same number in hard weather at Marshside/Crossens on 21 December 1992.

Hardy (1941) made reference to night migration, with young birds coming down in central Liverpool in Crosshall Street in August 1931 and St. John's Gardens in August 1932. Spencer (1977) referred to the winter distribution around Burnley being subtly different from that of summer, some haunts being deserted and odd birds turning up elsewhere. He too noted a good deal of nocturnal migration in August and November, with grounded birds in unusual locations more normally associated with Woodcock. He also recorded night movement in March and April.

Although the majority of movements of Lancashire-ringed birds are of just a few kilometres, a few have made longer journeys to or from the county. Nine exchanges with other English counties indicate both southerly and northerly post-breeding movements. They include one ringed at Wood End sewage works on 10 September 1949 and found dead in Northumberland on 10 January 1950, and a juvenile ringed in Shropshire on 19 September 1968 that was shot in Lancashire on 2 April 1972. Our longest distance recovery was a juvenile ringed on 1 November 1972 and found dead at Marton Mere in early April 1974, some 530km from its ringing site in the Netherlands.

SJW, DJH.

This species account was sponsored by Bob Stinger.

COOT

Fulica atra

Lancashire Category A.

Common resident breeder; abundant winter visitor from continental Europe.

As with the Moorhen, the breeding distribution of Coots appears to have been relatively stable throughout the twentieth century. Mitchell described it as 'very local, and whilst breeding numerously in many localities, in others (it) is never seen except as a straggler in winter' – a characterisation essentially repeated by Oakes. Mitchell reported hundreds nesting on the old Martin Mere before it was drained and 'some numbers' at Marton Mere; it was 'plentiful' on ponds between Rufford and Croston and also bred at Knowsley Park, Claughton, Wrightington, Woodfold Park (Blackburn) and Scarisbrick Hall. Oakes knew Leighton Moss as the 'chief breeding site in the county' and reported flocks of up to 300 in July with 'immense numbers' there in winter.

It appears that in the 1940s Coot were nesting commonly at most sites listed by Mitchell – especially in the south-west – but Oakes believed them to be 'unknown except as a rare winter visitor' in south Fylde, parts of the Ribble and Lune Valleys and 'considerable areas of north-east and south-east Lancashire'. In Rossendale, C.K. Parker had only one record of a bird at Ewood Bridge sewage works on 29 October 1911.

This portrayal of the breeding range remained essentially unchanged by the time of the Lancashire Atlas survey in 1997-2000, when breeding Coot were located in roughly a third of the county's tetrads. This range follows that of the Moorhen but their distribution within it is far patchier – especially in Merseyside, parts of central and West Lancashire, and north of the Lune – reflecting the sparser distribution of their preferred nesting habitat on larger, more densely vegetated waterbodies. The most important changes since Oakes's day appear to be the significant colonisation of south Fylde and a smaller increase in east Lancashire south of the Ribble, although breeding remains remarkably scarce in Rossendale.

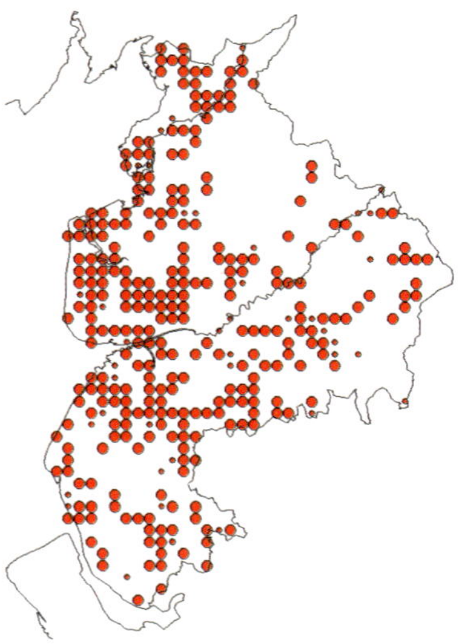

Breeding distribution of Coot, 1997-2000. (Large dots: confirmed. Small dots: possible)

The British breeding population increased by 79% from 1994 to 2005 (BBS) and Lancashire's has probably followed this trend. During recent years there has been some expansion to newly excavated gravel workings and even small field ponds have been exploited. Numbers have increased on all monitored sites, most notably on the Lune Waterways Bird Survey from 15 pairs in the 1970s to 37 in 1997, and at Leighton Moss from 65-75 to 125 pairs (with a further 20 or so pairs on the Eric Morecambe complex) over the same period. Leighton Moss remains the most important breeding site in the county and the increase there is due to the creation of more open water and temporary clearings within the reedbeds.

Two male Coots engaged in familiar armed combat . . .

. . . and one showing a more tender side, preening its mate. (above: Chris Galvin; below: Steve Young)

Spencer (1977) documented the spread of breeding records in east Lancashire from the 1950s: after a single pair at Foulridge Reservoir in 1951, he gave examples of further colonisation of Walverden Reservoir in 1959, Lee Green Reservoir in 1972 and Lowerhouse Lodges in 1976. Breeding pairs remain thinly scattered everywhere in the east, especially north of the Ribble, but their distribution has continued to spread with small clusters on suitable waters in the Blackburn-Accrington-Great Harwood area and around Burnley. From 1967 small numbers began to breed at a few sites in Rossendale but the spread slowed in the 1980s and may now have ceased. Distribution is marginally more solid on the West Pennine Moors but population densities are low – highest on Belmont Reservoir which has supported up to three pairs since the 1990s.

Breeding now takes place in more than half of Fylde tetrads but Marton Mere, where up to ten pairs bred annually during the 1990s, remains their main haunt. Exceptionally, during the mild winter of 1988/89 a bird was incubating eggs at Preesall on 28 December and the pair had two young on 18 January. Coot are found on most suitable waters on the south-west plain and Sefton coast; Marshside, Martin Mere, Mere Sands Wood and Carr Mill Dam hold the highest densities. Numbers and success varied considerably at Marshside during the 1980s, with a maximum of 26 pairs in 1989, but have increased steadily since as a result of water level management to reach 44 pairs in 1999. Martin Mere supported up to 30 pairs during the 1990s but only 15-20 in this century, Mere Sands Wood around ten and Carr Mill Dam up to 15 pairs. Canals are also widely used, notable counts including 94 pairs on a 20km stretch of the Leeds-Liverpool Canal between Liverpool and Maghull in 2005.

After the breeding season Coots, unlike Moorhens, abandon their need for cover and their solitary habits, forming large concentrations on larger eutrophic waters in the lowlands where aquatic vegetation and bank-side grazing is readily available. At both Leighton Moss and Marton Mere the highest numbers occur in late summer, with record counts of 624 in August 2002 and 538 in July 1994 respectively.

A former lake on the site now occupied by Heysham Power Station reported 570 on 7 September 1959. The movement away from the breeding grounds accelerates in late August and early September and leads to a build-up at a number of other sites. Some of these hold their largest numbers for just a matter of weeks, notably Brockholes Quarry (maximum 511 in September 2005) and Fairhaven Lake (maximum 256 on 5 November 1998).

At others, however, notably Martin Mere, Southport Marine Lake and the Pine Lake/Dockacres complex, the flocks continue to increase through to midwinter (Figure 1). These three sites have accounted for the vast majority of birds reported in winter over the past ten years or so, regularly holding more than 2,000 birds between them. The largest counts from these sites are 1,140 in December 2002 at Martin Mere, 1,169 in October 2005 (the largest anywhere in Lancashire) at Southport Marine lake and 765 in December 1996 at the Dockacres complex.

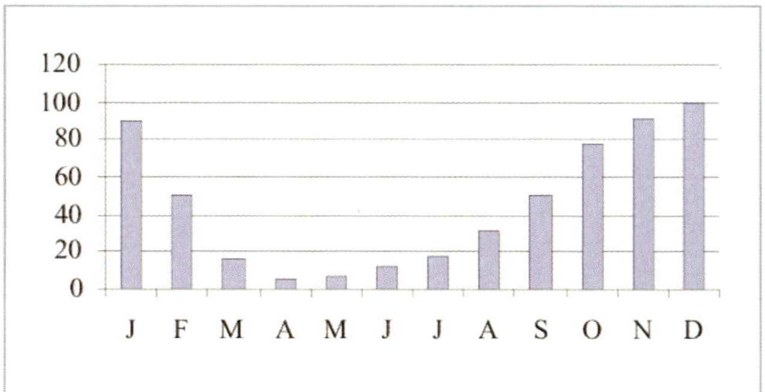

Figure 1. Indices of average monthly peak counts, Martin Mere (1990-2005) and Southport Marine Lake (1998-2005).

Other sites regularly holding 150 or more in recent winters include Prescot Reservoirs (maximum 392 in January 1997), Knowsley Park, Carr Mill Dam, Seaforth/Crosby Marine Park, Ainsdale Sands Lake, Mere Sands Wood, Wyreside Fisheries near Scorton (including 300 in November 1967), Glasson Dock, Fleetwood Power Station, Myerscough Quarry and Blackpool's Stanley Park. Few waters further east support more than 50 autumn or wintering birds, the main exception being Foulridge Reservoir, which had a record 145 on 23 August 1997, while Fishmoor Reservoir recorded 200 in October 2001.

It seems likely that most birds wintering in Lancashire also breed within the county but some immigration does take place, with ten recoveries in Lancashire of birds ringed elsewhere in northern England, and five from southern England (three from Shropshire and singles from Lincolnshire and Essex). One ringed as a chick at Ainsdale Sands Lake in November 2000 was seen at Filey Dams on the Yorkshire coast on 3 March 2004.

SJW, DJH.

This species account was sponsored by David McGrath.

COMMON CRANE

Grus grus

Lancashire Category A. (0, 21).

Rare passage migrant from northern Europe.

Oakes did not include the Common Crane on the Lancashire list, believing that 'most occurrences are undoubtedly due to 'escapes'', including a very tame individual seen near Carnforth for several weeks in the autumn of 1948.

The first accepted record is therefore of four 'near Southport' on 11 November 1961. A further 16 records involving 17 birds have been accepted by the BBRC or the county records committee as probably relating to wild vagrants.

First-summer Common Crane, Pilling, April 2000. (Steve Young)

A large majority of these have been in spring – the earliest in Bowland on 16 March 2002 – with just two autumn records and two winter occurrences (Figure 1). Most sightings have been of birds in flight and few have been seen for more than a day, exceptions being one at Garstang on 23 August to 14 September 1966, two at Pilling on 14-15 April 1987, and singles on a ploughed field at Cockerham on 24 April to 1 May 1992 and at Pilling on 1-18 April 2000.

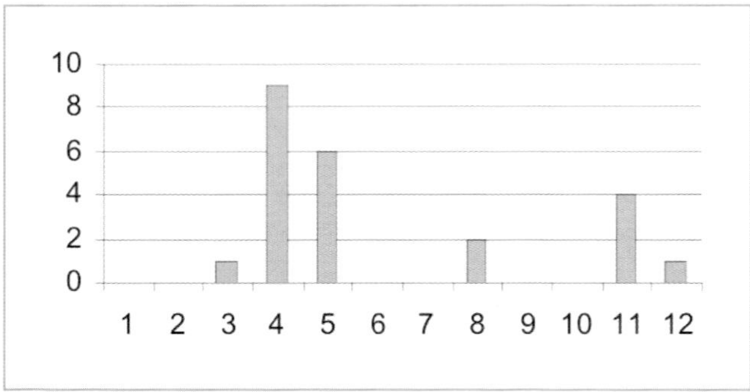

Figure 1. Monthly totals (individuals), 1961-2005

There have also been several records of unidentified cranes, most probably Common Cranes, including two over Pendleton, Clitheroe on 11 August 1974, and singles over Banks Marsh on 26 April 1984, over Cabin Hill on 18 November 1985 and over Lancaster on 29 April 1999. Known escapes include one from Blackpool Zoo in 1983.

All records:

1961	'near Southport', four, 11 November
1966	'near Garstang', one, 23 August to 14 September
1977	Leighton Moss, one flew over, 15 May
1978	Crossens, immature flew over, 7 May
1985	Marton Mere, one flew north, 5 May
1987	Pilling, two, 14-15 April, also at Thurnham on 5 May
1988	Hest Bank & Morecambe Golf Course, one flew over, 19 December
1992	Cockerham, first-summer, 25 April to 1 May
1992	Seaforth, one flew south-east, 14 August
2000	Pilling, first-summer, 1 to 18 April
2000	Carnforth Marsh, displaying pair, 27 April
2001	Lancaster, adult flew north, 20 April
2002	Hyles Moor, Bowland, one, 16 March
2002	Cabin Hill, adult, 9 April, also flew over Marton Mere & Heysham on 10 April
2002	Leighton Moss & Aldcliffe Marsh, one flew over, 5 May
2003	Leighton Moss, one flew over, 10 May

SJW, MJ.

This species account was sponsored by the Fylde Bird Club.

LITTLE BUSTARD

Otis tetrax

Lancashire Category B. (4, 0).

Vagrant from southern Europe.

Mitchell listed an immature male killed at Heaton, near Lancaster around 1840, which was in the possession of W. Fitzherbert-Brockholes of Claughton Hall, near Garstang. Spencer examined this specimen at Lancaster Royal Grammar School in 1960 and confirmed its identity. Mitchell also mentioned a specimen shot at Thornton, near Fleetwood on 15 September 1858. No particulars are available for records claimed at Burscough and Overton (Riddiough 1812, *Naturalist* 1837) but, given the relatively large numbers of Little Bustards that were shot in this country, particularly in the nineteenth century but right up to the middle of the twentieth, there is, perhaps, little reason to doubt them

The number of British records crashed dramatically in the latter half of the twentieth century – there were 150 confirmed records prior to 1958 and fewer than 20 since. The reasons for this were presumably linked to declines in breeding numbers. Although the Little Bustard remains relatively common in Spain, with an estimated 200,000 pairs, there have been large losses (recently showing some signs of reversal) in European Russia, where many British vagrants are believed to originate (Hagemeijr & Blair 1997).

SJW, MJ.

OYSTERCATCHER

Haematopus ostralegus

Lancashire Category A.

Common breeder; abundant winter visitor from elsewhere in Britain, Iceland and Norway.

This apparently highly specialised wader has within the past century demonstrated a remarkable level of adaptability in both diet and breeding behaviour as, throughout Britain and western Europe, breeding populations have been expanding into inland areas since the early 20th century. Up to a million have wintered annually in the Atlantic regions of Europe since the early 1990s, about 315,000 of these in Britain (Rehfisch *et al.* 2003) and more than 40,000 in Lancashire.

Mitchell described the Oystercatcher as commonest around Morecambe Bay but also nesting on the Ribble Estuary and on the Southport-Formby dunes, very common on all coasts in winter but rare inland at all seasons. By Oakes's time penetration inland onto the shingle banks of the Lune Valley was well underway, having begun in the late 1920s; he judged that this had increased significantly since 1939. Oakes concurred with Mitchell that Morecambe Bay was the Oystercatcher's Lancashire headquarters at all seasons; nesting was still occurring on the south Ribble and the south-west dune systems, but it had virtually disappeared from the Fylde as a breeding species although wintering flocks at St. Anne's and Fairhaven were substantial.

Oystercatcher, Eric Morecambe complex. (Phillip Tomkinson)

Studies by Dare (1966) and Briggs (1984) traced the subsequent evolution of the Oystercatcher's breeding behaviour, in north Lancashire in particular. Dare estimated 175-240 breeding pairs, 125-185 of these on the coast, suggesting that inland expansion had been accelerated by the birds' adaptation to a diet of earthworms after estuarine prey had been killed off in the harsh winter of 1962/63. Breeding Oystercatchers spread into the Ribble, Hodder and Wyre Valleys in the 1950s and the Calder in 1968; by the mid-1960s birds in several areas had begun to nest on arable, silage and hay fields, often at a considerable distance from water. Briggs noted that inland breeders returned and laid eggs four weeks earlier than coastal nesters, to take advantage of earthworm abundance in the pre-laying period and cranefly larvae after the chicks had hatched.

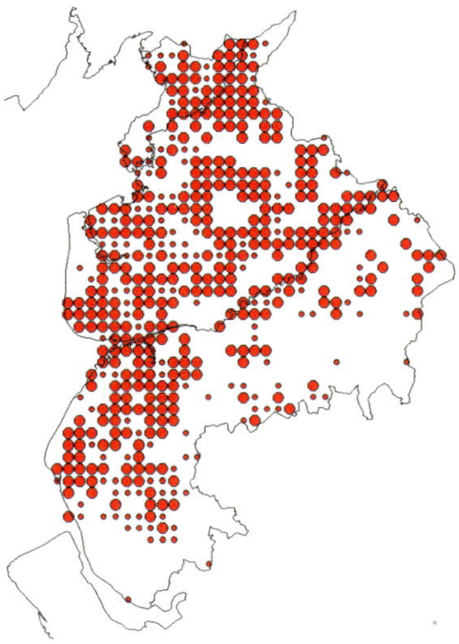

Breeding distribution of Oystercatcher, 1997-2000. (Large dots: confirmed. Small dots: possible)

Farmland-breeding Oystercatchers have been demonstrated to be more productive than riparian nesters, raising up to twice as many young per pair, due mainly to freedom from the risk of flooding, which has, for example, significantly reduced breeding productivity on the Arkholme stretch of the River Lune on many occasions since systematic study began in the 1970s. In 2002, 59 pairs there raised only two young between them and 31 pairs by the river raised a mere nine young in 2005, although pairs in nearby crop fields have reasonably high productivity rates.

The success of Oystercatchers on these new farmland habitats has presumably facilitated the rapid spread of inland nesting since the 1970s; the 1997-2000 Lancashire Atlas Survey estimated a total population of 2,500 pairs, widely distributed across the north, centre and east of the county as well as in the Fylde and the south-west. Only in Rossendale and in urban areas is the species scarce or absent, although a limited adaptation by a few pairs to nesting on the flat roofs of buildings has been evident on the Fylde coast since 1988, and a pair fledged at least one juvenile from the roof of the Jaguar factory at Halewood, south Liverpool in 2005. Most coastal Oystercatchers now nest on reserves; the Eric Morecambe complex recorded an average of 61 pairs annually in the 1980s and 63 in the 1990s, and up to six pairs breed annually at Marshside.

Oystercatchers abandon inland breeding territories in Lancashire in autumn; many move to our own coastline where they join thousands of migrants, mostly from Scotland, the Faeroes, Iceland and Fennoscandia, feeding mainly on cockles on offshore sand-flats.

WeBS winter counts on Morecambe Bay South and the Ribble and Alt Estuaries all showed large increases from the early 1990s; numbers in Morecambe Bay have continued to rise while those on the Ribble and Alt have stabilised this century (Figure 1). The largest counts were 44,560 in October 2002 in Morecambe Bay with 37,874 there in December 2004. Passage numbers on the Alt have been relatively stable during the past 20 years, while those on the Ribble and MBS have shown large fluctuations, but with no clear trend. The average WeBS peaks on Morecambe Bay South during 1990-2005 were 23,921 in winter and 26,395 on passage, whilst the corresponding figures for the Ribble were 17,161 and 12,139, and for the Alt, 2,111 and 1,443. Morecambe Bay as a whole is the most important site for Oystercatchers in Britain, with about 50% of the birds in its Lancashire sector, whilst the Ribble is the fifth most important.

By and large, Oystercatchers have remained faithful to the same roosting-sites over recent decades: Preesall Sands, Fluke Hall and Knott End on Morecambe Bay, the Ainsdale-Birkdale shore and Fairhaven on the Ribble, and Formby Point on the Alt. Some changes have been noted, however. Birds from the north Wirral shore roosted in numbers at Seaforth in the 1980s and early 1990s, peaking at 2,800 in April 1991, but this gathering has all but disappeared in more recent times. For a few years in the late 1990s substantial flocks, often up to 4,000 birds, roosted on Heysham Helipad.

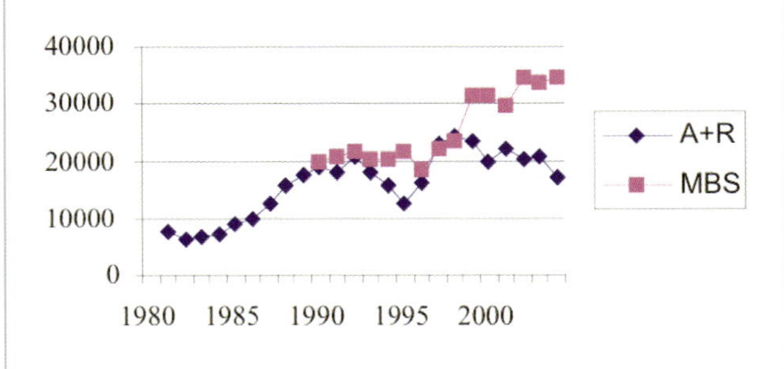

Figure 1. Peak winter counts of Oystercatchers (3-year rolling means) on the Alt & Ribble Estuaries (1978/79 to 2004/05) and Morecambe Bay South (1988/89 to 2004/05).

Peak numbers on the Ribble and Alt occur in winter, on MBS in autumn (Figure 2), which possibly indicates some southward movement in early winter. Early movements in July and early August may involve large numbers of inland breeders making for the coast; later arrivals from late August include a higher proportion of immigrants, which begin moult on arrival and probably move on south once this is completed. Only five out of 31 recoveries of Oystercatchers from Norwegian or Icelandic breeding grounds have been ringed or recovered in Lancashire during the December-February period.

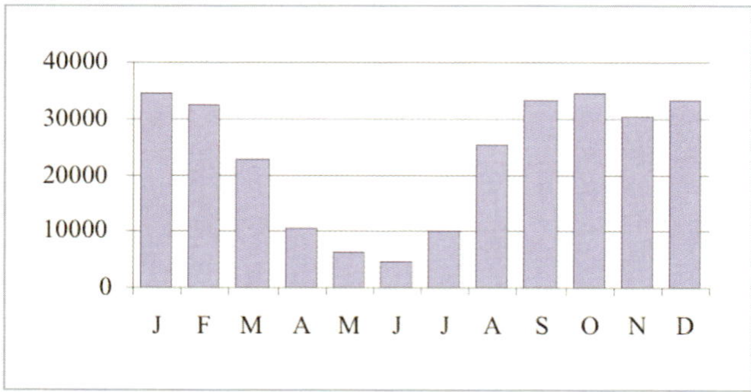

Figure 2. Average monthly peak counts of Oystercatchers on the Ribble & Alt Estuaries and Morecambe Bay South, 1990-2005

Numbers in the recent past have shown spectacular and quite rapid increases and declines due to changes in prey populations. Between 1960 and 1963 cockles virtually disappeared in Morecambe Bay and the Oystercatcher flock fell from some 120,000 to 1,100 (Dare1966). A similar phenomenon on the Ribble saw an increase to over 20,000 during the mid-1970s followed by a temporary collapse to only 8,000 by 1979. More localised increases in marine mollusc numbers regularly produce impressive autumn and winter gatherings at favoured locations; peak site counts over recent decades include 15,000+ at the Eric Morecambe complex on many occasions, 7,000 on Preesall Sands in September 1982, 7,200 at Sunderland Point in December 1985, 10,500 on Ainsdale-Birkdale shore in November 1987, 8,000 at Knott End in September 1990, 6,000 at Marshside in October 2000 and 5,875 at Fluke Hall, Pilling in October 2005.

Inland breeders return from wintering grounds on the Lancashire and adjacent coasts early in the spring, and flocks of 50 or more migrants are frequent at Stocks Reservoir and along the Ribble and its tributaries, with up to 30 at Belmont Reservoir, in March and early April. A notable passage is observed regularly at Arkholme on the Lune, mainly in March, peaking at 734 in 1989, 872 in 1992 and 862 in 2000, and flocks of up to 110 have been seen regularly in March on the Hodder at Burholme in recent years.

Of 441 movements of ringed Oystercatchers to or from Lancashire within Britain 66% have been of less than 100km; 23% have been local, 33% to or from elsewhere in northern England and 26% Scotland, while only 17% have involved Wales and 3% southern England. Movements to and from northern Europe have overwhelmingly involved the breeding populations of Norway (22), the Faeroes (11) and Iceland (9); there are no north-west England recoveries involving the Baltic, Russian or Fennoscandian populations, all of which are confined to the Wash, whilst birds from the Netherlands move to south-east England (Migration Atlas).

BM, MJ.

This species account was sponsored by P.J. Drewery and Lancaster & District Birdwatching Society.

BLACK-WINGED STILT

Himantopus himantopus

Lancashire Category A. (2, 2).

Vagrant from southern Europe.

Oakes gave details of three records, two of which were in our present recording area. One, described as an 'immature', was shot on Freckleton Marsh on 13 December 1928 (*Field*, 21 February 1929). The specimen was held at Preston Museum where it was examined by J.R. Charnley. The other was reported at the foot of Burnslack Fell, near Chipping on 28 October 1944 (*British Birds*: 41: 250). Neither of these records now appears wholly satisfactory: the Freckleton bird is one of just three reported in winter in Britain apart from the recently deceased resident in Norfolk, while the moorland at Burnslack Fell appears extremely unlikely stilt habitat.

In 2006 a pair of Black-winged Stilts nested unsuccessfully at Martin Mere. Two males and a female arrived on 5 May, having been seen in Lincolnshire the previous day. One male departed on 25 May, by which time the pair had completed a clutch of four eggs. These failed to hatch and the nest was abandoned on 23 June; the birds were last seen on 26 June. (Photos: Steve Young)

It was a further forty years before the next was found at Marshside in the morning of 28 April 1984; it remained for only fifteen minutes. Lancashire 'listers' had to wait another nine years before adding the species to their tally, when a colour-ringed female turned up at Leighton Moss on 4 June 1993, remaining on the Eric Morecambe pools on Carnforth Marsh until the 6th. It had been ringed as a nestling at Beauvoir-sur-Mer, Vendée, France, on 16 June 1989 and, after leaving Lancashire, was refound at Shipton-on-Cherwell in Oxfordshire on 8 June.

SJW, MJ.

This species account was sponsored by the Merseyside Partnership Against Wildlife Crime.

AVOCET

Recurvirostra avosetta

Lancashire Category A.

Rare breeder; uncommon passage migrant.

Until the early nineteenth century Avocets bred regularly on the east coast of England from the Humber to Kent but nesting had ceased everywhere by about 1840. There is no indication that they were anything but rare in Lancashire until the last decade of the twentieth century – the Avocet remained a 'description species' until 2000 – and the colonisation of the county in the next few years was as unexpected as it was spectacular.

Mitchell knew of only one record, supposedly shot on the Ribble in 1840, but its provenance is dubious. Oakes added just one more, a very strange report of three found dead on the tideline between Birkdale and Ainsdale on 11 December 1921, but Spencer published records of 'several near Crossens' in the mid-nineteenth century and singles in Morecambe Bay in 1872 and near Fleetwood around 1926.

Widespread coastal flooding as part of military defences during the Second World War allowed the Dutch population to expand, and sporadic nesting began in Essex and Norfolk in 1942. Adopted by the RSPB as its symbol and given heavy protection, the British population has never looked back and reached 800 pairs by 2001.

During the initial period of recolonisation and expansion Avocets made spasmodic appearances in Lancashire. A pair on Hesketh Marsh in early May 1969 was only the third or fourth twentieth century record, but sightings began gradually to increase. There were six records involving seven birds during the 1970s, all on the Ribble Estuary or further south, in April, July and September; in the 1980s five records, also involving seven birds were also confined to southern coastal sites, apart from one at Pilling Lane Ends on 1 April 1983. The first half of the 1990s saw three winter visits by single birds, at Seaforth in November to December 1990, Lytham St. Anne's and various other Fylde locations in February to March 1991, and Freckleton in February 1992. One flying east at Colne on 30 April 1993 was the first record in east Lancashire.

Avocets began nesting at Blacktoft Sands at the mouth of the Trent in the mid-1990s and the population there grew rapidly; this was a significant northward range extension and it is surely not coincidental that the rate of occurrences in Lancashire increased from mid-decade. On 17 March 1996 three Avocets appeared in the Lune Estuary, one remaining until the 21st, and another was at Seaforth on 13 May. One visited the Keer Estuary on 20 May 1997, two were on the Ribble and at Seaforth on 3-4 May 1998, and one spent four months at Leighton Moss and Jenny Brown's Point during June-October. In 1999 two flew north over Seaforth on 2 April, having previously spent some days at Frodsham, Cheshire.

After a brief lull without a record in 2000 the Avocet's status in Lancashire was transformed in 2001, with successful breeding by a pair on the Eric Morecambe complex following a widespread early-year influx. A bird that had wintered on the Mersey just outside our borders turned up at Oglet on 3 February; there were three records in April, one on the Lune Estuary on the 11th, a pair at Martin Mere observed mating on the 17th, and two over Formby on the 27th. In May three were briefly at Marshside on the 3rd and one was at Seaforth in mid-month. The Eric Morecambe complex pair was present from 18 April to 10 August and fledged a single youngster.

Incubating Avocet, Marshside, May 2004. (Steve Young)

The breeding situation was consolidated in 2002. Three pairs on the Eric Morecambe complex raised seven young from at least two broods while two pairs at Marshside RSPB also fledged seven offspring. In addition, there were many sightings of individuals and small parties at other locations between April and October, most of which were assumed to be Leighton Moss or Marshside birds moving to or from the breeding areas; copulation and scrape-making by a pair at Seaforth was observed before the birds moved on to breed at Marshside. There was further numerical and range expansion in 2003: eight pairs at EMP raised three young, two pairs at Marshside fledged seven, while a pair on Banks Marsh was unsuccessful. In 2004 breeding spread to Martin Mere where three pairs nested, while five pairs bred at Marshside and eight on the Eric Morecambe complex, and in 2005 these three sites held three, fourteen and nine pairs respectively. The Avocet is now clearly an established feature of Lancashire's breeding avifauna.

All adults and juveniles appear to leave Lancashire in early autumn, and a bird at Marshside on 4 November 2004 is the latest recorded to date. The first return to a breeding site in spring was also at Marshside, on 10 February 2005, but the main arrival is from mid-March. Inland records remain exceptional, in spite of the growth in the coastal breeding population; two at Belmont Reservoir on 24 April 2002 may have been en route to Marshside, and a single bird flew over Darwen on 17 June 2005.

BM, MJ.
This species account was sponsored by Mary Barritt.

STONE CURLEW

Burhinus oedicnemus

Lancashire Category A. (5, 5).

Vagrant.

Oakes reported a bird shot on Haslingden Moor in the spring of 1879 which passed into the collection of J.R. Charnley: Mitchell omitted this record but according to R.J. Howard there was no reason to doubt it. One was seen near Southport in May 1912 (*Birds of Southport*: 119) and two birds were at Claughton on the Lune on 17 March 1927 (*British Birds*: 23: 310). An immature female that was picked up alive in Knowsley Park on 15 August 1931 had been injured in a collision with overhead wires and died two days later; the specimen is in Liverpool Museum.

Stone Curlew, Knott End, April 2007. (John Jenkins)

There have been five modern records, beginning with one in fields at Moss Edge Farm, Cockerham on 22 November 1975. Another was watched for an hour and a half near White Man's Dam, Knowsley Park on 5 June 1983 and the next was seen by many observers when it spent the day at Jameson Road, Fleetwood on 5 August 1990. Shortly afterwards, another was seen in flight at close range at Oglet Bay on the Mersey in south Liverpool on 27 August. Finally, one was on Withnell Moor on 29-30 June 2004.

SJW, MJ.
This species account was sponsored by the Fylde Bird Club.

COLLARED PRATINCOLE

Glareola pratincola

Lancashire Category A. (1, 4).

Vagrant from southern Europe.

The first British record was shot near Ormskirk in 1807 but there is some confusion about this bird. National records have it as having been shot in October 1807, having been seen earlier that month in Bowness, Cumbria. However, Mitchell quotes Bullock's assurances, apparently referring to the same bird, that it met its end on 18 May 1804 'in the act of taking beetles on the wing, the remains of which were found in its stomach'. The specimen was first collected by the Earl of Derby and subsequently held in Liverpool Museum.

There were no more documented records until a male found at Newton Marsh, Freckleton on 24 May 1974 by M. Ainscough, which remained in the area – also being seen at nearby Clifton – until the 29th and was seen by many people.

The next was at Marton Mere, Blackpool on 30 May 1977, staying until 1 June. Its specific identification remained unresolved for an unprecedented length of time since the bird lacked the typical white trailing-edge to the secondaries of Collared Pratincole, leading to the possibility that it was a Black-winged Pratincole. Later study of photographs of the bird, however, ruled this out and the tail-fork appeared too deep for Oriental Pratincole *G. maldivarum*. The record was reviewed by the BBRC who were eventually able to proclaim it an adult Collared in 2002.

The following year produced a relative long-stayer, this time in autumn. It was on Banks Marsh from 14 to 15 October 1978 before moving to Martin Mere, where it remained until 5 November. Finally, one was seen on farmland near Freckleton on 23 May 2005.

The total European, Turkish and Russian breeding population of Collared Pratincoles consists at best of a little over 20,000 pairs and the species is regarded as endangered in Europe due to the loss of its grassland breeding habitat to cultivation (Hagemeijer & Blair 1997).

SJW, MJ.
This species account was sponsored by John Poland.

PRATINCOLE sp.

Glareola sp.

One was watched by many observers on the saltmarshes near Pilling Lane Ends in the afternoon and evening of 7 July 1997. It was accepted by the BBRC as the fifth record of Collared Pratincole for Lancashire and the 82nd for Britain and Ireland. However, many observers felt at the time that its specific identification was based more on presumption than visible plumage features; indeed, the bird was not submitted to the BBRC as a Collared Pratincole but as 'pratincole sp.'. An apparently short tail and lack of white on the primary tips meant that Oriental Pratincole could not be ruled out. In the light of this, it would be unsafe to accept any specific identification unless further details come to light.

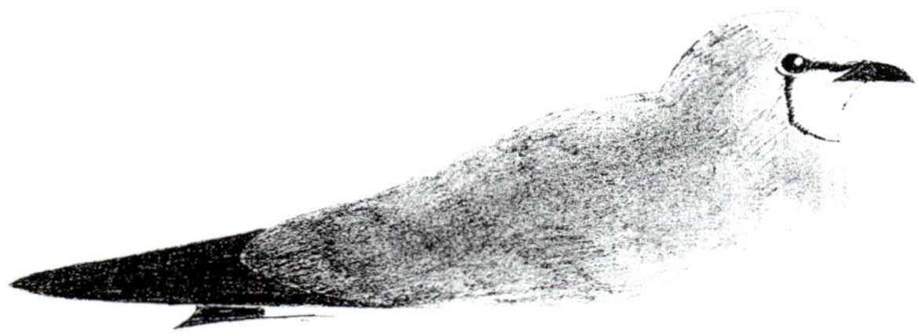

Pratincole, unidentified to species, Pilling, July 1997. (Steve Dodgson)

SJW.

BLACK-WINGED PRATINCOLE

Glareola nordmanni

Lancashire Category A. (0, 2).

Vagrant from south-eastern Europe.

There have been two records of Black-winged Pratincoles in Lancashire but their occurrence in consecutive years and similarities in dates perhaps suggest that just one individual was involved.

The first was a bird in breeding plumage, accepted by the BBRC as a first-summer, which appeared on the Allen Pool at Leighton Moss on 25 August 1996. It was found by Steve Dodgson and Keith Gillon as it roosted with Lapwings on a muddy island but it was not until it flew off, revealing the diagnostic sooty-black underwings and a lack of white on the secondary tips, that its identity became absolutely certain. Fortunately, it was soon relocated on a ploughed field and remained there and on the adjoining saltmarsh for a couple of hours before crossing into Cumbria on the Kent Estuary, adding itself to another county list. In the early evening it returned to Lancashire and roosted on the saltmarsh beyond the Eric Morecambe pools; it stayed in the area until 28 August, regularly commuting between Carnforth Marsh and the Kent Estuary.

Black-winged Pratincole, Martin Mere, August 1997. (Steve Young)

The second was a moulting adult at Martin Mere, first seen a year later – almost to the day - on 22 August 1997. It too was with Lapwings and remained in the fields surrounding the reserve, often giving dramatic overhead performances to the many birdwatchers who went to see it, until 16 September.

The species is a rare breeder in Europe, mainly in the steppe zone from Hungary and Romania eastward. Its European population is put at around 100 pairs and even its Russian heartland supports only 6,500-11,100 pairs (Hagemeijer & Blair 1997) – making the two Lancashire records all the more remarkable.

The Leighton Moss bird was the 31st record in Britain and Ireland and the one at Martin Mere the 32nd; the overwhelming majority have been in southern and south-eastern England. There was one previous occurrence in north-west England, at Inner Marsh Farm, Cheshire on 2 June 1988, and one subsequently, at Grune Point, Cumbria on 17 August to 3 September 2000 – could the latter perhaps have been one of Lancashire's birds returning?

SJW, MJ.

This species account was sponsored by In Focus.

LITTLE RINGED PLOVER

Charadrius dubius

Lancashire Category A.

Scarce breeder; fairly common passage migrant.

Little Ringed Plovers are comparatively recent but highly-successful colonists of Britain; nesting was first recorded in 1938, before which there had been only 13 records anywhere in the country. Breeding became regular from the late 1940s and the species flourished, mainly utilising man-made habitats, particularly the rapidly-expanding network of gravel-pits, to reach 825-1,070 pairs during 1988-91.

The first record for Lancashire was a juvenile at Freckleton Sewage Works on 14-17 September 1958 and the first adult was found at the same site on 13 July 1963, while another adult at Carnforth Marsh in June 1966 was the first record elsewhere.

A single pair bred in the Wigan area, just outside our present-day boundaries, in 1966, and in 1970 Lancashire recorded its first breeding attempts by single pairs at Mere Brow near Tarleton, Croston and Wayoh Reservoir. Nesting again took place at Mere Brow in 1971, when another pair bred near Scorton in the Wyre Valley.

During the 1970s records of Little Ringed Plovers on passage became fairly regular, especially in the south-west; the first in east Lancashire was at Coldwell Reservoir, Nelson in July 1973. By 1982 at least six pairs were nesting annually and passage records had become more widespread, including the first in Rossendale in 1980. There was a major spurt to 15 or 16 breeding pairs in 1984 and up to 17 nested at eleven locations in 1987. Understandable concerns for the security of nests led to many not being made widely known by their finders, especially outside nature reserves, so it is likely that annual totals were underestimated in the early years.

Little Ringed Plover, Seaforth Nature Reserve, July 2005. (Steve Young)

Since 1990 at least 20 pairs have been reported annually, peaking at 38 in 1996, of which 17 were in east Lancashire and six at Martin Mere. Some nests are lost every year through flooding on river gravels and beside reservoirs, or through destruction by vehicles or other human disturbance in the working sandpits and industrial sites on which many choose to nest. Many pairs have laid by mid-April and replacement clutches are frequent, enabling the population to make good the numerous losses of early broods.

The 1997-2000 county Breeding Atlas estimated an average annual total of 50 pairs, based upon a total count of 65 over the four years of the survey. These were dispersed across the county but with concentrations around Belmont Reservoir, in Rossendale, the Mere Brow-Martin Mere area, at Brockholes Quarry and in the Lune Valley.

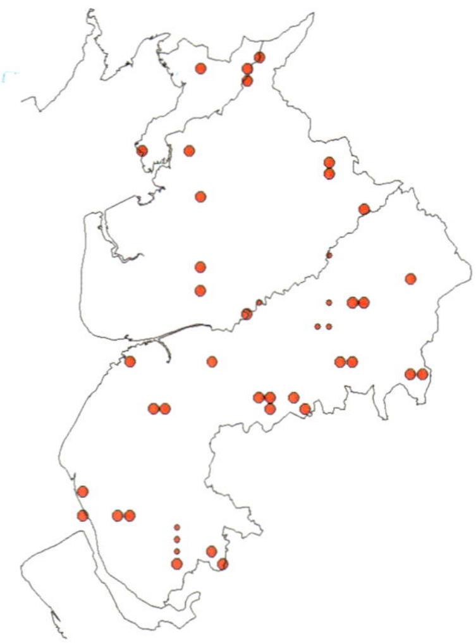

Breeding distribution of Little Ringed Plover, 1997-2000. (Large dots: confirmed. Small dots: possible)

Little Ringed Plovers are among our first spring migrants and arrival dates have tended to become progressively earlier over recent decades. Singles at Arkholme on 12 March 2000 and Brockholes Quarry on 13 March 2004 are the earliest to date, but widespread records in the second half of the month have become the norm since the late 1980s, with average first arrivals on 26 March. Passage continues throughout April and most of May; numbers involved have generally increased, and 21 at Martin Mere on 7 May 1992 is the highest count recorded.

Autumn movements also begin relatively early, with dispersing and passage birds in evidence from the beginning of July. Some substantial parties have been recorded at favoured sites and, as in spring, peak counts have grown steadily from five at Martin Mere in late August 1982 and six at Haslingden Grane Reservoir, Rossendale in September 1986 to 17 at Belmont Reservoir on 7 August 1993, 20 at Anglezarke on 20 July 1996 and 16 at Martin Mere on 7 July 1998. Most birds have departed or passed through by the end of August although there are September stragglers in most years. The average latest date is 15 September and October records are very rare, with one on 15 October 1976 on Clifton Marsh the latest.

There are only seven ringing recoveries, involving five birds, of Little Ringed Plovers in or from Lancashire. Three have involved Brockholes Quarry: a female pullus ringed at Belmont Reservoir on 5 June 1993 was on breeding territory 88km away in North Yorkshire on 14 June 1997, was seen again at Lac de Nomas in south-west France on 4 July 1998 and yet again at Brockholes Quarry on 7 June 2003; a first-summer female ringed at Masham, North Yorkshire on 29 May 1998 was seen at Brockholes Quarry on 27 March 2000; and a female trapped on the nest at Nosterfield Gravel Pits in North Yorkshire on 22 June 2004 was seen at Brockholes on 10 July the same year. A chick ringed at Martin Mere on 7 June 1991 was recovered at Chew Valley Lake, Avon on 31 July 1992, and one ringed as a pullus in Cheshire on 23 July 1995 was found freshly dead at Nateby on 2 September.

BM, MJ.

This species account was sponsored by Tony Disley.

RINGED PLOVER

Charadrius hiaticula

Lancashire Category A.

Scarce breeder, common passage migrant and winter visitor from Iceland and Fennoscandia.

The relatively small breeding populations of Britain, Ireland and north-west Europe are the most southerly in the world; the New Atlas estimated a combined British and Irish total of 10,000 pairs in the early 1990s. Ringed Plovers are classic 'leapfrog' migrants; most Arctic breeders pass through Europe in autumn and spring to and from wintering areas in sub-Saharan Africa and the Middle East, while the north-west European population makes a much shorter journey to winter in Britain, Ireland, south-west Europe and north-west Africa. An estimated 32,400 winter in Britain (Rehfisch *et al.* 2003).

According to Mitchell, the Ringed Plover was the commonest wader of the Lancashire coast, breeding along the entire shoreline and in the lower reaches of all the estuaries; even then, however, the species was beginning to suffer from human disturbance in the vicinity of the burgeoning seaside resorts. Oakes noted that the threat identified by Mitchell had indeed come to pass, greatly reducing breeding numbers on the south-west and Fylde coasts; he considered that the species' stronghold lay between the Wyre Estuary and the northern edge of Morecambe Bay, and stated that passage numbers were also heavier on these northern coasts than further south. By the mid-1940s, however, inland breeding had been recorded in the Wigan area, just outside our present-day borders, and nesting was first proved on the Lune gravels in 1947.

Small colonies had become established on the Lune by the 1960s but in the decades since then the breeding population has become largely confined to a small number of regular coastal and inland locations. The 1997-2000 county Breeding Atlas estimated an annual total of 80 pairs, based on a total count of 86 over the four years of survey. The coastal remnant is largely confined to undisturbed areas, in particular Carnforth Slag Tips, where up to 16 pairs have nested annually in recent years, and the Sefton coast at Seaforth, which held up to ten pairs until very recently, and the shore between Hightown and Southport, where 15 or more pairs regularly breed.

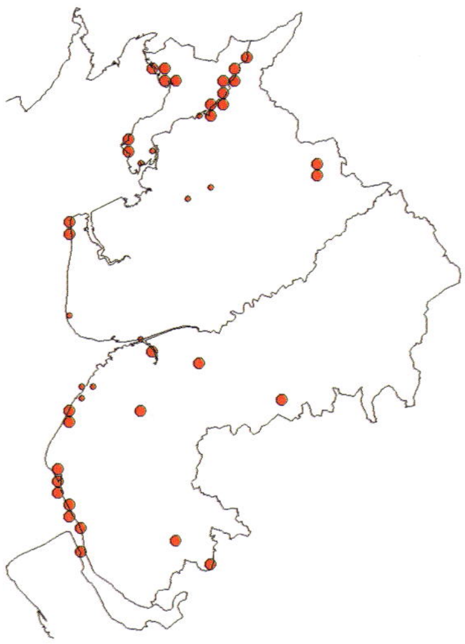

Breeding distribution of Ringed Plover, 1997-2000. (Large dots: confirmed. Small dots: possible)

Although nesting has taken place intermittently at Stocks and Belmont Reservoirs, at Scorton and fairly regularly at Martin Mere since the mid-1990s, until very recently the main inland breeding area continued to be the Lune Valley, in particular the Arkholme area where breeding numbers and productivity have been systematically monitored for over two decades. Up to 25 pairs nested on gravel beds there annually in the 1980s, an increase from only four in the early 1970s. There have been rather fewer since and brood productivity has frequently been very low, due mainly to flooding and trampling by livestock; fifteen pairs in 1996 fledged a total of seven young, nine pairs in 1998 produced twelve, and eight pairs in 2002 failed to fledge a single chick. In 2003 the population at Arkholme fell to four pairs and just three more were located along the entire Lancashire Lune from Skerton Weir to Kirkby Lonsdale, and by 2005 just two pairs bred at Arkholme.

Up to three pairs nested annually in the Liverpool Central Docks from the mid-1990s until the site was destroyed in 2005. Even within protected reserves breeding success is often severely impaired by predation: ten pairs at Seaforth in 2000, for example, managed to fledge only eight young, and seven pairs in the following year just five; the Seaforth population fell to four pairs in 2003 and two or three in 2004-05. These losses have not been compensated for elsewhere, and the county population estimate should now almost certainly be reduced, perhaps to as few as 60 pairs.

Male Ringed Plover sitting tight during a downpour, Seaforth Nature Reserve, June 2004. (Steve Young)

The largely sedentary nature of our breeding Ringed Plovers is indicated by the rather scant ringing data: only two Lancashire-ringed birds recovered outside the county were ringed as pulli; one moved to France in its first winter and the other to North Wales in a subsequent autumn. All of the other 46 birds ringed here were adults, caught during migration periods.

Until very recently a small but fairly stable population of Ringed Plovers wintered in Lancashire, focused on a few coastal sites, in particular Hest Bank in Morecambe Bay and Seaforth and the adjacent Crosby shore, each of which held up to 200 birds throughout the winter months. WeBS counts in Morecambe Bay have plummeted from an average of around 300 in the mid- to late 1990s to less than 100 this century, although this is due in part to birds shifting to a less accessible roost site. Numbers have never been high on the Ribble in winter, averaging 50 since 1980; 180 there in January 2004 was exceptional, while wintering at Seaforth/Crosby shore has virtually ceased since 2000, reducing peak counts on the Alt to around 50 this century. Taken together, wintering numbers on the three estuaries declined by more than 50% between the mid-1990s and the first years of the twenty-first century, although there has been some indication of a small recovery over the past two winters (Figure1).

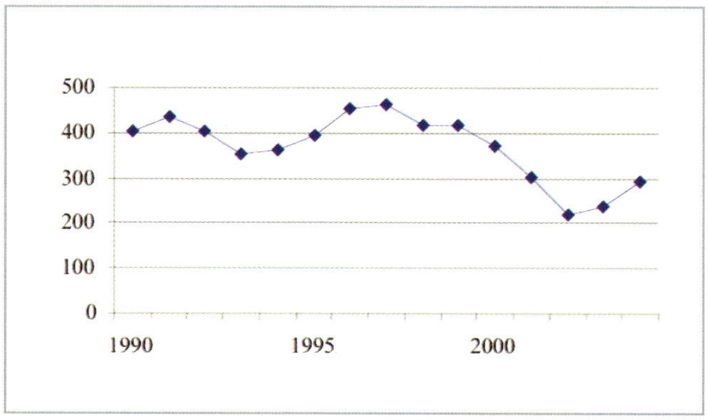

Figure 1. Peak winter counts of Ringed Plovers (3-year rolling means) on the Ribble & Alt Estuaries and Morecambe Bay South, 1988/89 to 2004/5.

However, Ringed Plovers are predominantly passage migrants in Lancashire with the largest numbers occurring in spring (Figure 2). Inland breeders arrive back on nesting territories from early February but spring passage is heavily concentrated on the coast and extends from late March to the end of May. The earliest migrants tend to be British and other north-west European breeders on their short journey back to breeding territories but from mid-April to the end of May a much heavier movement of far northern birds takes place. These spring passage birds are identifiable as the smaller, darker race *tundrae* from the Fennoscandian or Russian Arctic or the dark form of the nominate race from Iceland, Greenland and north-east Canada. There is evidence from ringing that both forms, indistinguishable in the field, pass through Lancashire: one ringed as a chick in northern Finland, within the range of *tundrae*, and recovered on the Ribble that September, and three movements of *hiaticula* to the north-west, one from Greenland and two to or from Iceland. Another Finnish recovery was further south, and more likely to have been *hiaticula*, while other migrants originated in more southerly breeding-grounds, including single pulli from the Dutch and German coasts; other birds from Germany and Denmark, as well as one recovered in Denmark, were ringed as full-grown, and may well have been on passage there.

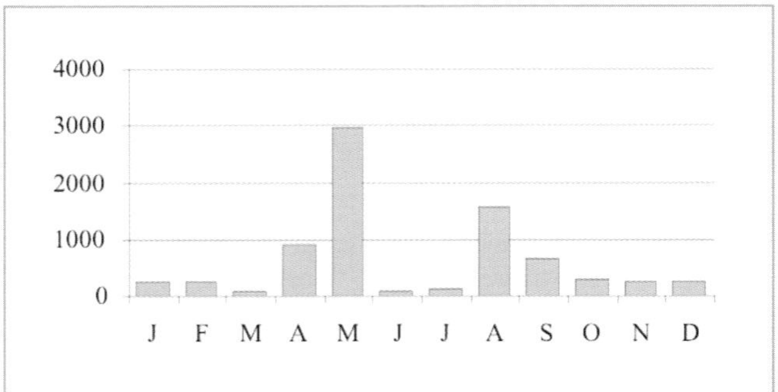

Figure 2. Average monthly peak counts (WeBS) of Ringed Plovers on the Ribble & Alt Estuaries and Morecambe Bay South, 1985-2005.

As in Oakes's time, most of the highest counts from the 1960s to the mid-1980s were on the shores of Morecambe Bay, including 2,400 at Hest Bank in late May 1978 and 1,500 there on 25 April 1982, 1,735 on Carnforth Marsh in May 1979 and 1,000 at Pilling on 13 May 1984. Spring WeBS counts in Morecambe Bay averaged 2,030 during 1990-92, but a dramatic and apparently permanent decline set in from 1993 and 526 in May 1996 is the highest count since then. May WeBS totals, which account for almost 40% of annual totals, averaged just under 2,000 on the Ribble, 900 in Morecambe Bay and 150 on the Alt during 1985-2005.

By the mid-1980s peak counts on the Ribble Estuary began to overtake those further north; there were 2,250 on Fairhaven-Lytham shore on 19 May 1985, and 600 at Marshside with another 500 at Fairhaven on 15 May 1988. Ribble May WeBS peaks fluctuated from 4,000 in 1988 to a low of 493 in 1993, but since then the increase has been steady, to 4,784 in 1999 and 5,432 in 2000. The highest spring count on the Alt Estuary, where numbers have increased steadily since the mid-1990s, was 635 in April 2004. The largest spring counts in east Lancashire are 15 on Whitemoor Reservoir on 17 May 1993 and 36 on Alston Reservoir on 22-23 May 2003.

A modest autumn passage is evident in east Lancashire, Rossendale and on the West Pennine Moors from late July, particularly around reservoir margins. Stocks, Fishmoor, Rishton, Foulridge and Anglezarke Reservoirs feature regularly but counts in double figures are exceptional; they include 40 at Foulridge on 27 August 1962 and 23 there on 10 October 1969, but 13 at Coldwell Reservoir on 16 August 1986, 15 at Stocks Reservoir in late August 1989, and 13 at Fishmoor on 13 August 1997 are the highest autumn totals recorded in more recent decades.

Coastal passage is mainly concentrated in August and early September and is never as heavy as in spring. Large WeBS totals include 510 in August 1990 and 468 in August 1997 in Morecambe Bay; 1,794 in August in 1993, 1,104 in 1994, 1,663 in 1996 and 1,887 in 2002 on the Ribble; and 770 on the Alt in August 2003. Local roosts have occasionally exceeded WeBS totals, notably 1,200 at Marshside on dates in August 1999 and 3,000 on Ainsdale beach in August 2001. Most of these autumn birds are undoubtedly migrants from further north, heading for southern European or African wintering-grounds; ringing recoveries include seven in France (four in winter and three on passage), one in winter in Portugal and singles in Mauritania in November and in Ghana in December, this last the furthest known movement to date of a Ringed Plover from Britain.

BM, MJ.

This species account was sponsored by John Wilson Bateman.

KENTISH PLOVER

Charadrius alexandrinus

Lancashire Category A. (0, 11).

Vagrant from southern Europe.

The only record reported by Oakes was outside our present recording area; he did not accept a report of one at Liverpool on 30 August 1939 (E. Hardy, *Ibis*, July 1940). Another was reported on Hightown shore on 29 July 1951 but this was not published in the Lancashire Bird Report and no further details are known.

The first definite Lancashire record was, therefore, one at Lytham on 19 August 1963 (M. Greenhalgh, N. Harwood, P. Taylor). The next was at Seaforth on 1 February 1975; it roosted with a large flock of Ringed Plovers and was almost certainly the bird that wintered on the Cheshire Dee during 1974/75 and 1975/76.

Phil Jones

A succession of one-day birds then followed in the Southport area: at Marshside on 13 October 1977, 17 December 1979, 23 December 1980 and 17 September 1989; Birkdale on 29 April 1980 and Southport on 17 June 1985. Few details were published concerning these records but at least two birds, a male and a female, were involved.

Kentish Plover, Rossall Point, February 1995. (Steve Young)

The next record in the south of the county was an adult male at Martin Mere on 7 May 1992. Just prior to that a female was found at Rossall Point on 8 March 1992, staying until 1 April. This bird returned to the same site on 11 December that year and became a regular feature there in each winter until last seen on 9 March 1997. It was typically present between November and March and was extremely faithful to the Fleetwood area, being seen elsewhere on just one occasion, at Hest Bank on 19 November 1994 on its first date that winter, just 90 minutes before being seen back at Rossall. What was believed to be the same bird was seen on Walney Island and Sandscale Haws in Cumbria from 3 March to 10 April 1994, having last been seen at Rossall on 26 February. Finally, one was briefly on the shore at Marshside with Ringed Plovers on 4 June 2004.

All records:

1963	Lytham St. Anne's, one, 19 August
1975	Seaforth, one, 1 February
1977	Marshside, one, 13 October
1979	Marshside, one, 17 December
1980	Birkdale, female, 29 April
1980	Marshside, male, 23 October
1985	Southport, female, 17 June
1989	Marshside, one, 17 September
1992	Rossall Point, female, 8 March to 1 April
1992	MMWWT, male, 7 May
1992	Rossall Point, female, 11 December to 9 March 1993
1993	Rossall Point, female, 28 November to 26 February 1994
1994	Rossall Point, female, 19 November to 3 March 1995
1995	Rossall Point, female, 28 November to 21 February 1996
1996	Rossall Point, female, 1 November to 9 March 1997
2004	Marshside, one, 4 June

SJW, MJ.

This species account was sponsored by N.J. Donnithorne.

DOTTEREL

Charadrius morinellus

Lancashire Category A.

Uncommon passage migrant.

The Dotterel's British breeding range is largely confined to the Scottish highlands, with small outposts in southern Scotland and Cumbria. Between 60 and 80 pairs were located during the 1968-72 Atlas survey, increasing dramatically to between 840 and 950 pairs in the 1988-91 New Atlas. There are much larger numbers in northern Europe, including an estimated 17,000 pairs in Norway, 5,000 in Sweden and 2,000 in Finland (Hagemeijr & Blair 1997).

Mitchell's rather fragmentary account illustrated the Dotterel's decline as a passage migrant in Lancashire during the nineteenth century; he recorded that 'hundreds' were shot each May during the 1840s, both in the Pilling-Winmarleigh area of the Fylde and on the south-west mosslands. Though much less numerous than formerly, the species still appeared regularly at mossland sites in spring at the end of the nineteenth century, usually between 26 April and 12 May. However, Mitchell reported few records from the fells, remarking that the species no longer appeared on Pendle Hill. Oakes considered that the Dotterel's misfortunes had continued into the twentieth century, with the annual slaughter on the Fylde and elsewhere having persisted until the 1920s, but discerned a slight recovery in numbers since 1940; he gave 27 April as the average date of first arrival, with most birds seen in the early days of May.

Spring numbers continued at low levels from the 1950s to the mid-1970s, with very few trips reaching double figures. Spencer (1973) reported none larger than four between 1950 and 1972, but there were twelve on Plex Moss between 5 and 12 May 1973. The steady increase in the Scottish breeding population from the late 1970s was reflected in higher numbers and more widespread passage records in Lancashire, and 44 on Pendle Hill on 15 May 1982 was probably the largest trip of the century.

Adult female Dotterel, Pendle Hill, May 2005. (Margaret Breaks)

Since then a widespread pattern of spring records has become established, with virtually annual appearances at a number of upland sites. Pendle Hill is the most widely-known and perhaps the most reliable of these, but annual or near-annual occurrences have been recorded since the early 1990s at Ward's Stone, Hawthornthwaite Fell and Clougha in Bowland, and at Top o' Leach, Whittle Pike, Cowpe Moss, Haslingden Moor, Knowl Moor and Great Hameldon in Rossendale. Records on the West Pennine Moors are more intermittent, with Anglezarke and Haslingden Moors and Winter Hill favoured. Parties of up to ten birds are not uncommon in the uplands and recent May peaks have included 30 on Pendle Hill in 1988 with 28 there in 1993 and 14 in 2002, 15 at Top o' Leach in 1991, 13 at Ward's Stone on 6 May 1996 and 13 on Hawthornthwaite Fell on 9 May 1998 (when 20 were also on Pendle Hill). The average date of first appearance over the past 25 years is 30 April.

Traditional lowland stopping-points, such as Altcar and Formby Mosses, attracted several parties of up to a dozen in late April and early May during the late 1970s and 1980s, but there have been few records since. Plex Moss, to the south-east of Southport, is now the pre-eminent mossland site; it hosted up to eleven in early May 1982, six on 30 April 1990 and near-annual trips since the mid-1990s, including ten in 1998 and 1999 and twelve on 28 April 2002. Spring visits to the Fylde are very infrequent nowadays; two at Eagland Hill on 1 May 1988 and seven there on 29 April 2000 are the only records in recent decades.

Juvenile Dotterel, Pendle Hill. Top, September 2003. (Mark Breaks)

Breeding was reported from Ward's Stone in 1983 (Marsh 1989) and distraction displays have been noted in the Lancashire uplands within the past decade (Brown & Grice 2005).

Dotterels on autumn passage are very much scarcer than in spring. Oakes recorded only two definite records and Spencer added three in the 1960s. Occurrences typically involve one or two juvenile or first-winter birds, and visits during the last 50 years have been quite widespread across the county; most have been at traditional springtime halting-sites. Three on Plex Moss on 8 October 1967 were followed by one on Pendle Hill on 9 September 1988 and an exceptional flock of three adults and nine juveniles there on 25 August 1996. More recently single juveniles were on Pendle Hill on 7-10 September 2000 and 29 September to 1 October 2005, and two were at Clougha on 1 October 2000; a moulting adult was on Hawthornthwaite Fell on 9-10 September 2003 and an adult on Pendle Hill on 8 September 2004. Several have turned up in the Fylde, including two juveniles at Pilling on 16 September 1986 and three there on 28 August 1993, and single birds have been recorded at Crossens, Silverdale, the Cocker Estuary, Walton in Merseyside and Clowbridge, Rossendale; most autumn migrants are recorded in late August or early September. Although a colour-ringed Dotterel was seen on Pendle on 8 May 1990 and another was on Plex Moss on 24 April 1992, we have no information as to the origins or destinations of Lancashire's migrants.

BM, MJ.

This species account was sponsored by the East Lancashire Ornithologists Club and Jonathan Fenton.

AMERICAN GOLDEN PLOVER

Pluvialis dominica

Lancashire Category A. (0, 5).

Vagrant from North America.

The first record was as recently as 1984, when a first-winter was with Golden Plovers at Marshside on 12-13 November (S.J. Riley, J.M. Coates *et al.*). This was followed by a solitary bird of uncertain age on Fleetwood Golf Course on 20 September 1988.

The next was a first-winter amongst a Golden Plover flock at Fishmoor Reservoir, Blackburn on 28 October 1995. It became our first long-stayer, being seen at Fishmoor regularly until 11 November and at nearby Parsonage Reservoir on 1 November. The latest records, both first-winters, were found amongst flocks of Golden Plovers at Marshside, on 27-28 October 1998 and 19 October to 28 November 2003.

First-winter American Golden Plover (centre), Fishmoor Reservoir, October 1995. (Steve Young)

SJW, MJ.

This species account was sponsored by Tim and Janet Davie.

PACIFIC GOLDEN PLOVER

Pluvialis fulva

Lancashire Category A. (0, 2).

Vagrant from Siberia.

The county's first was found by wader counters at Pilling Lane Ends on 22 July 1990 (P.G.D. Morgan, D. Jackson, J. Fletcher). An adult, moulting out of summer plumage, it was then seen daily to 3 August and again on the 8th and 24th.

Pacific Golden Plover, Seaforth Nature Reserve, August 1995. (Andy Pryce)

The second, another moulting adult, arrived from the north with a small flock of Golden Plovers at Seaforth on 1 August 1995 after a week of light easterly winds. It was identified in flight as a 'Lesser' but, although it landed only 60m away, it took an hour before enough features had been pieced together to confirm it as a Pacific Golden Plover. The bird eventually came into full view for about 20 minutes before a raptor spooked it and it flew off with the Golden Plovers.

Pacific Golden Plover, Pilling, July 1990. (Steve Young)

SJW, MJ.

This species account was sponsored by Alex Whitlock.

GOLDEN PLOVER

Pluvialis apricaria

Lancashire Category A.

Uncommon breeder; abundant passage migrant and winter visitor from Iceland and Scandinavia.

Britain and Ireland, with about 23,000 pairs, lie at the southern edge of the Golden Plover's breeding range, with nesting essentially confined to moorland, upland bogs and plateaux in the north and west. Most British birds move to coastal grassland and saltmarshes in autumn, where they are joined later in the year by a significant proportion of the large populations of Iceland, Fennoscandia and Russia. The Winter Atlas estimated a combined winter total of 400,000 to 600,000 birds in Britain and Ireland in the mid-1980s, while Rehfisch *et al.* (2003) estimated the current British wintering population at 250,000.

Mitchell described the Golden Plover as a widespread breeder on the Lancashire fells, wintering in large flocks both in inland valleys and on the coast. Oakes also considered them to be summer visitors to the uplands and common passage migrants and winter visitors. Both agreed that wintering birds tended to arrive in October and depart in March and April. Oakes identified Leck Fell and Roeburndale in the north, and the Ward's Stone-Wolf Hole Crag and Fairsnape Fell-Bleasdale areas of Bowland as main breeding-grounds, with further strongholds further south and east at Pendle Hill, Boulsworth and Worsthorne Moors and in the Thar Hill, Whittle Pike and Turf Moor areas of Rossendale.

Although neither author provided any numerical details it seems clear that the last half-century, at least, has seen a substantial decrease in the breeding population in most areas of Lancashire. The 1997-2000 county Breeding Atlas estimated a total of 130 pairs, effectively concentrated in the Pennines at Emmott, Boulsworth and Worsthorne Moors (about 45 pairs), a more extensive area in Bowland (over 50 pairs), Rossendale (about ten pairs), Pendle Hill (about six pairs) and the West Pennine Moors (up to eight pairs). Golden Plovers prefer to nest on open, flat or gently-undulating acidic bog and heather moor and many of these habitats have been subjected to an ever-increasing pressure of recreational disturbance since the Second World War. Afforestation has also removed much suitable habitat, although this may have been a less significant factor in Lancashire than elsewhere in upland Britain.

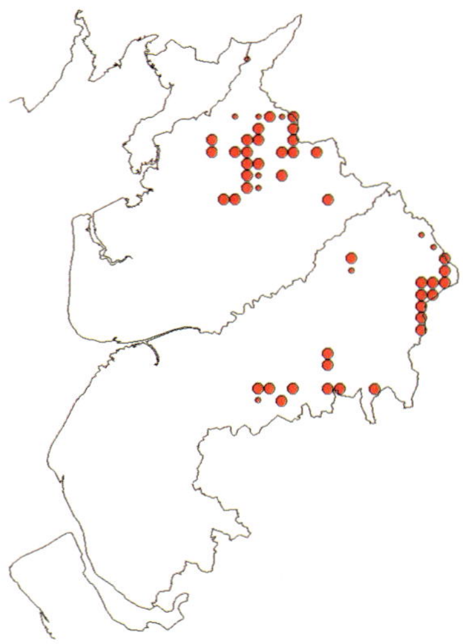

Breeding distribution of Golden Plover, 1997-2000. (Large dots: confirmed. Small dots: possible)

Local post-breeding dispersal and passage movements by birds from further north and east begin on a small scale as early as the beginning of July and gather pace through the autumn, with the major influx of migrants and overwintering birds from northern Britain and Iceland taking place during October and November. Small flocks of up to 200 are fairly regular in Rossendale, east Lancashire and the Lune Valley; some remain all winter if the weather remains mild, often at traditional sites, although several of these flocks, most notably at The Hile, Trawden, Eddisford near

Clitheroe and Upper Foulridge and Parsonage Reservoirs have dwindled or disappeared altogether since the late 1970s.

The great majority of Lancashire's wintering Golden Plovers are to be found on the coast and adjacent mosses. Peak numbers have fluctuated considerably over the years, and the flocks have also favoured a succession of different sites; during prolonged periods of hard weather, in particular, most birds abandon the county altogether for milder quarters further west or south. These factors notwithstanding, the overall winter population has remained fairly stable since the 1950s. WeBS data over the past 20 years show a decrease on the Ribble, with fluctuating numbers on Morecambe Bay and a recent increase on the Alt but the overall county winter population has shown no obvious trend since 1990 (Figure 1). The Golden Plover is not, however, exclusively an estuarine species and the WeBS counts undoubtedly miss a sizeable proportion of feeding birds.

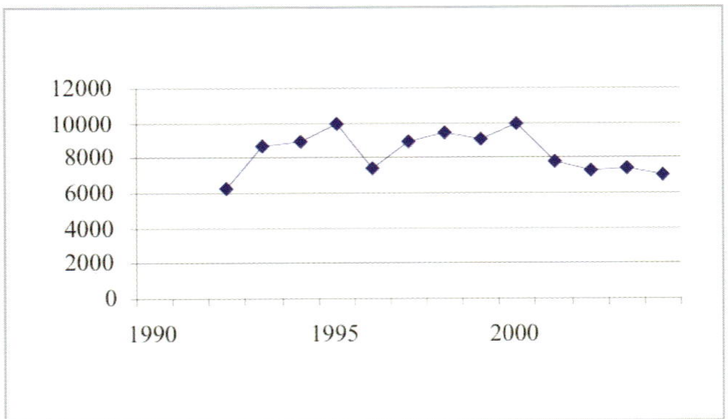

Figure 1. Peak winter counts (3-year rolling means) of Golden Plovers on the Ribble & Alt Estuaries and Morecambe Bay South, 1988/89-2004/05.

In the north, the Pilling-Cockerham area has long been a stronghold; large counts include 3,000 at Fluke Hall in January 1981, 7,000 at Cockerham in November 1982, and 10,500 at Pilling-Cockerham-Bank End on 29 November 2004. The Lune Estuary also sometimes supports large numbers, including 3,000 at Glasson on 13 January 2004, 6,000 on the Conder/Lune Estuary on 31 December the same year and 3,700 on Colloway Marsh on 29 January 2005.

The Fylde shore of the Ribble is also an important wintering area, but with generally reduced numbers in recent decades; there were 8,000 on Newton Marsh in December 1979, 6,000 in December 1982, 4,000 in December 1984, 3,000 in November 1987 and 1,000 in February 1998. In the same area 6,000 were counted at Freckleton in February 1974, 4,000 in December 1981 and 1,150 in November 1995. Flocks on the south side of the estuary at Marshside and Crossens increased during the 1970s and 1980s to an all-time peak of 6,220 in February 1993, but since then the decline has been rapid, to a mere 1,800 in February 2002, although 6,500 there on 25 January 2004 may herald a revival. Numbers are much lower further south and counts of 3,000 at Hightown and Thornton in the 1980s and early 1990s have not been repeated.

Numbers decline rapidly as spring progresses (Figure 2), and by April, when birds begin to acquire breeding plumage, an increasing proportion show characteristics of northern European and Icelandic breeders. There were an exceptional 6,500 migrants at Hundred End in early April 1978 and up to 3,000 were regular at Marshside and 2,000 at Newton Marsh during the late 1980s and early 1990s, but peak passage counts since have been considerably smaller. WeBS passage data, however, show fluctuations from the early 1990s to date but no significant overall trend on any estuary.

Golden Plover in breeding plumage, Seaforth Nature Reserve, May 2003. (Steve Young)

Almost all Golden Plovers leave coastal Lancashire by the beginning of May although a few stragglers occasionally remain until mid-month. Passage numbers inland are normally much lower than on the coast, although the Lune Valley meadows in particular have occasionally seen April flocks of up to 3,000 birds. Further south and east the Trawden-Wycoller area has traditionally attracted flocks in late March and April, including 500 on 20 March 1982, 300 on 7 April 1993 and 210 on 9 April 1999. At The Hile, Rossendale up to 200 were recorded regularly in spring from the early 20th century, increasing to 700 by 1973; there was a steady and rapid decline in numbers thereafter, however, and this spring gathering had disappeared altogether by 1988.

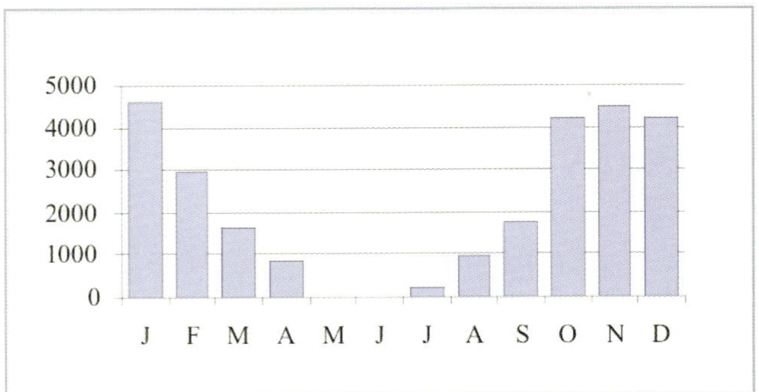

Figure 2. Average monthly peaks of Golden Plovers on the Ribble & Alt Estuaries and Morecambe Bay South, 1985-2005.

It is believed that the majority of Fennoscandian birds that winter in or pass through Britain do so in the east or south-east of the country (Migration Atlas), while Icelandic birds move predominantly to Ireland with some to western Britain. Our wintering population is therefore likely to be composed largely of British and Icelandic birds. There were two recoveries of Icelandic birds in Lancashire in the 1930s and none definitely from Fennoscandia, although one ringed at Heysham on 22 September 1965 and shot near Bologna in Italy in October 1967 may have been of eastern origin.

BM, MJ.

This species account was sponsored by R.D. Thomson.

GREY PLOVER

Pluvialis squatarola

Lancashire Category A.

Abundant passage migrant and winter visitor from arctic Russia.

The Grey Plover breeds on high Arctic, lowland tundra across northern Russia to Alaska and northern Canada, but it is thought that the whole of the British wintering and passage population originates in Russia. A major increase in numbers in north-west Europe in the early 1990s brought the British wintering population to 38,500 (BWP); the current estimate is 52,750 (Rehfisch *et al.* 2003).

Grey Plover in winter plumage, Morecambe. (Mike Malpass)

Mitchell considered the Grey Plover to be not uncommon in winter and on passage, but judged it to be less numerous than previously due to shooting; it was very scarce inland. The position seems to have changed little by Oakes's time, when moderate numbers were recorded on passage, especially in spring and winter; a few birds stayed for the summer, often in breeding plumage. It seems likely that numbers in the early twentieth century were a good deal lower than in later decades, as Oakes described a flock of 200 at Crossens in January 1942 as the largest recorded up to that time. Counts of over a thousand have been fairly regular since the 1960s at favoured coastal sites, and the broad pattern of occurrences in winter and on passage has altered little over the last 40 years, although numbers have changed substantially. The Ribble and Alt Estuaries are both internationally important, both in winter and on passage, while Morecambe Bay South is of national importance; between them these three Lancashire estuaries hold around 16% of the British winter population.

The seasonal pattern is broadly consistent across the three estuaries: a rapid build-up in numbers in August and September to an average mean combined peak of just under 4,000 during 1985-2005, then a gradual decline to about 3,000 by December, probably as some birds move further south, and a steady increase from January to the annual peak of 5,000-6,000 in April and May (Figure 1).

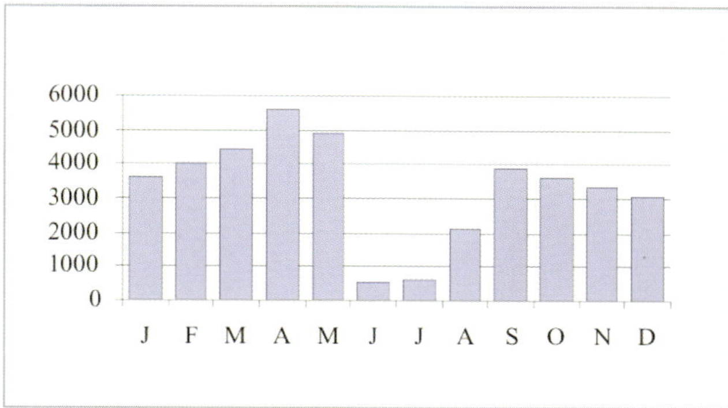

Figure 1. Average monthly peak counts of Grey Plovers on the Ribble & Alt Estuaries and Morecambe Bay South, 1985-2005

Numbers increased at all seasons throughout the 1970s and 1980s but winter and passage counts have shown slightly different trends since the 1990s (Figure 2). Wintering numbers peaked during 1993-96 before falling back towards 1980s levels, while the size of the two passage movements, although fluctuating, has declined by almost a third since 1990. The largest estuarine winter counts are 1,523 in Morecambe Bay in January 1995, 12,856 on the Ribble in February 1997 and 3,340 on the Alt in February 2003; passage peaks on the three estuaries are 2,090 in April 1997, 12,398 in May 1992, and 4,890 in April 2003 respectively.

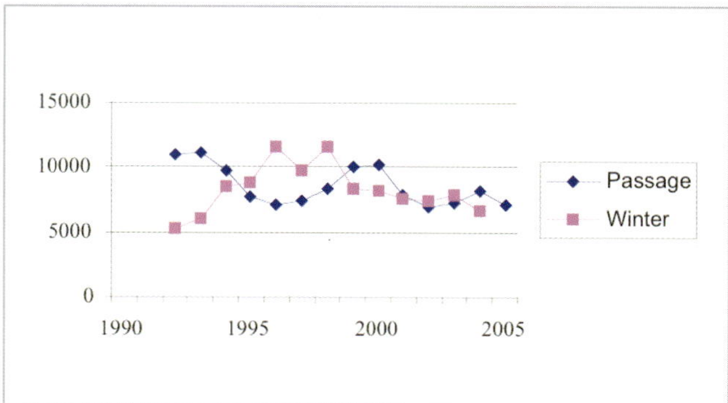

Figure 2. Peak winter and passage counts (3-year rolling means) of Grey Plovers on the Ribble & Alt Estuaries and Morecambe Bay South, 1990-2005.

The main sites in Morecambe Bay are on the Lune Estuary, Pilling-Cockerham and Knott End, although up to 400 have roosted at Heysham in recent years. A flock of 2,500 at Pilling Lane Ends on 25 March 1993 was quite exceptional. On the Ribble Estuary,

Lytham St. Anne's and Fairhaven have hosted substantial numbers of Grey Plovers since the 1950s, including 500 at Fairhaven on 10 April 1959 and 1,069 at four south Fylde roosts combined on 10 December 1983. South of the Ribble, Marshside-Crossens and the beaches from Birkdale to Hightown are pre-eminent, and most of the county's highest counts of Grey Plovers have come from this south-western coastal strip. There were 1,950 at Crossens in October 1973, and 2,510 at Marshside on 27 December 1984 and 3,100 there on 9 January 2001. Numbers at Formby Point on the Alt Estuary have increased very significantly since the early 1980s, when counts of 400-600 were typical, to 1,340 in January 1990 and more than 2,000 on numerous occasions since the late 1990s.

Although spring movements are still in full swing in early May, most birds have moved on by the end of the month. The average 500 or so birds present in June and July are probably mostly non-breeders.

Grey Plovers in breeding plumage, Ainsdale, May 1999. (Steve Young)

During periods of stormy weather Grey Plovers may shelter on farmland a little way inland from their regular roosts, including 800 behind Banks Marsh on 10 February 1974, 468 at Cabin Hill, Formby on 29 October 1981 and 414 there on 4 December 1989, while 58 were huddled on fields at Fluke Hall, Pilling on 26 February 1990. True inland records, however, are as scarce as in Mitchell's and Oakes's days. Most have been recorded at Stocks, Barnacre, Clowbridge, Foulridge, Dean Clough and Parsonage Reservoirs, and the great majority of such visits have been during spring or autumn passage periods and have involved singles, or at most a very few birds.

There have been only two recoveries of Lancashire-ringed Grey Plovers, a first-year bird ringed at Formby Point on 27 February 1987 and found, long-dead, on Hilbre Island at the mouth of the Dee on 6 February 1988, and a bird, age unknown, ringed on the Ribble on 20 August 1986 found injured in south-west Spain on 31 March 1998, which suggests that the winter destination of many Lancashire passage birds is in southern Europe or North Africa.

Two birds dye-marked on the Dutch island of Schiermonnikoog in mid-September 1982 were with a flock of 400 at Pilling on 2 April 1983 – presumably they were on passage on both occasions.

BM, MJ.

This species account was sponsored by R.D. Thomson.

SOCIABLE PLOVER (LAPWING)

Vanellus gregarius

Lancashire Category B. (1, 0).

Vagrant.

The first record for Britain and Ireland was one shot by a farmer from amongst a flock of Lapwings at White Hall, St. Michael's-on-Wyre. The exact date is not known but it was sometime between 1860 and 1866 (Hayhow 1996).

Mitchell first published the record in 1885 as a Cream-coloured Courser *Cursorius cursor* and its true identity was not discovered until 1888 when he published a correction in *The Zoologist* stating: 'It is with mingled grief and joy that I have to advise you, firstly of an error of identification, and, secondly of an addition to the British list.' His excuse was that '. . . with the twenty years' reputation of the specimen as a Courser, and being able only to examine it by candlelight in a crowded case, perhaps I may be forgiven for having been deceived by the superficial resemblance between the two, and for having attributed such discrepancies as I could perceive, to the vagaries of country bird-stuffing.'

The specimen was preserved by a gamekeeper, John Isles, who placed it in a case of birds belonging to another gamekeeper, Joseph Frankland, where it remained for many years with about 60 other birds. It passed into the possession of a farmer, William Frankland and later to Mr. W.H. Doeg of Manchester, who sent it to Henry Seebohm who finally made the correct identification. Seebohm considered the provenance of the bird to be 'perfectly satisfactory' and considered it to be 'about one year old', noting 'there is no sign of the dark streaks on the breast, or the buff streaks on the back so characteristic of young in first plumage; but the black on the crown and the belly, and the chestnut on the thighs are only just beginning to appear.'

Sociable Plovers. (G.E. Lodge in Mitchell, 1892)

The specimen passed into the collection of Manchester Grammar School and ultimately that of Manchester Museum, where it remains today. It is one of only two firsts for Britain and Ireland to have been found in Lancashire – perhaps, following the example of the Elgin Marbles, we should demand its 'repatriation' to Fleetwood Museum! A further 40 records have occurred nationally since but no more have been seen in Lancashire and, with the species now on the verge of global extinction, another seems very unlikely.

SJW, MJ.

LAPWING

This species account was sponsored by In Focus.

Vanellus vanellus

Lancashire Category A.

Abundant breeder and winter visitor from continental Europe.

Spencer (1953) noted that the old local name for the Lapwing was 'Tewit', citing the village of Tewitfield near Carnforth as an example, whereas 'Peewit' was more usual south of the Mersey-Humber line. Lancashire has probably always been a major national Lapwing stronghold but its proportional importance has undoubtedly increased over the past 50 years; as the British population has crashed Lancashire's has declined at a significantly slower rate.

Mitchell described the Lapwing as resident in Lancashire and everywhere abundant, though commoner in the lowlands than on the moors. Oakes agreed, but commented that the population had declined since 1940 due to wartime cultivation of pasture and marginal land; the species remained a very numerous passage migrant and winter visitor.

Spencer (1953) referred to a sharp decline following the severe winter of 1946/47; numbers recovered within four or five years but further local declines were noted by 1953. Since the early 1950s a great deal of data have been accumulated on this species in Lancashire. The picture is complex, and some of the indicators contradictory, but overall there is some cause for concern regarding the species' status, especially as a breeding bird. Lapwings nested in every 10km square in the county in both the 1968-72 and 1988-91 surveys, the latter establishing Lancashire as one of Britain's breeding strongholds. This was confirmed by the 1997-2000 Lancashire survey which found the species to be breeding in all 10km squares and 80% of all tetrads, being absent only from urban areas and the highest moorland tracts.

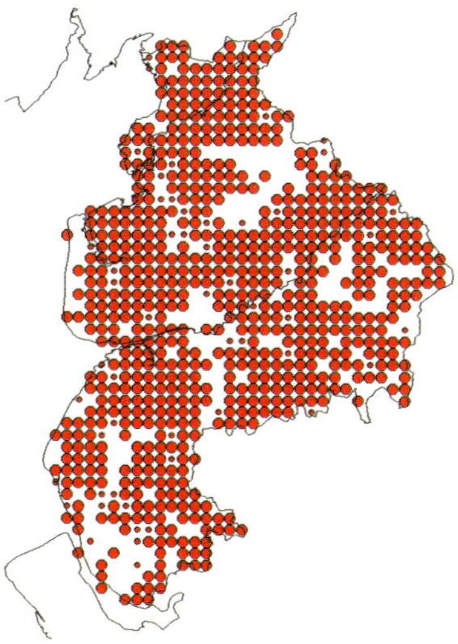

Breeding distribution of Lapwing, 1997-2000. (Large dots: confirmed. Small dots: possible)

Smaller-scale surveys within the county have, however, revealed a complex pattern of local increases and declines as well as major variations in breeding density and success from one habitat type to another.

Most reports of recent reductions in breeding numbers have come from more easterly, upland areas. On The Hile, for example, records from a 100ha CBC plot show a sequence of rises and falls in numbers since the 1960s, but overall a decline in the breeding population from an average of about 40 pairs in the late 1970s and early 1980s to around 14 during 1990-94; breeding ceased altogether after 1998. Less dramatic decreases in numbers have been reported elsewhere in Rossendale.

Tony Disley

Although breeding densities are particularly high on in-bye land on the margins of the uplands in Bowland, the Lapwing has generally fared better in lowland areas and remains widely distributed on both pasture and arable farmland, although modern agricultural practices have taken a severe toll in many areas. The highest densities are found on the wet, grazed fresh- and saltmarshes of our three major nature reserves. Marshside's nesting population has fluctuated widely from 41 pairs in 1984 to 210 in 1993 and 112 in 2002, declining to 81 in 2005. At nearby Martin Mere a similar variation during the 1980s and 1990s saw the population range from 40 to 80 pairs, increasing to a record 131 in 2004. Numbers at Leighton Moss and the Eric Morecambe complex, on the other hand, have remained remarkably stable, averaging 65 pairs in the 1970s, 64 in the 1980s, 66 in the 1990s, and ranging between 52 and 99 since 2000. Unlike in many other parts of Britain, however, the Lancashire population is by no means dependent upon nature reserves, exemplified by the 57 pairs on two farms at Abbeystead in 2003 with similar numbers on one arable farm at Hightown in 2002 and 110 pairs on 25km^2 of in-bye and moorland around Belmont in 1998 (including 33 pairs at Belmont Reservoir).

A systematic survey of breeding Lapwings in 233 randomly-selected 1km squares during 2002-03 estimated a total population in the county of 13,353 pairs (White 2003a). There were substantial regional differences, with Bowland and lowland west Lancashire holding the highest densities (means 7.13 and 7.09 pairs per km^2 respectively) but much lower numbers in the east (2.12 pairs per km^2) and in central Lancashire (1.86 pairs per km^2). Breeding Lapwings showed a marked preference for coastal grazing marshes, followed, in order, by bare ground and stubbles, spring tillage, and upland in-bye pasture; autumn-sown croplands contained by far the lowest breeding densities. The results of this survey compare very favourably with the 8,484 pairs estimated for the whole of north-west England by a BTO-RSPB survey in 1998. These anomalies notwithstanding, it is clear that Lancashire remains a very important area for breeding Lapwings in Britain, holding perhaps 20% of the total English and Welsh population.

Lapwings are extremely faithful to natal sites, as illustrated by long-lived birds ringed as chicks at Seaforth in 1985 and Cockerham in 1987 and found dead at the same locations in 2000 and 2003, respectively.

Post-breeding flocks begin to form as early as June in both upland and coastal areas. Spencer (1953) found that upland flocks usually reached their peak between late June and August. Gatherings at Foulridge, Whitemoor, Parsonage, Stocks, Fishmoor and Belmont Reservoirs are normally in the hundreds, but there were 1,000 at Belmont in July 1982, 1,600 at Whitemoor on 11 September 1995, over 1,000 at Foulridge in July or August in 1994, 1997, 2000 and 2001, and 1,000 in August at Heasandford in 1991 and at Parsonage Reservoir in 1994.

Larger numbers gather at favoured coastal sites at this time of year, including 3,000 on Warton Marsh in late August 1981, 6,000 at Newton Marsh in August 1988, 3,000 at Pilling Lane Ends in September 1993 and at Seaforth in September 1997, and 4,600 at Shard Bridge on the Wyre on 30 August 1998.

British Lapwings are partial migrants; some remain close to their breeding areas in winter, while others may move quite substantial distances. Birds from north-west England and western Scotland migrate mainly to Ireland and to a lesser extent to western France and Iberia – a conclusion largely based on data from birds ringed, almost all as pulli, in Lancashire. There have been 28 such recoveries in Ireland, all during January-March, and 21 in France, 18 in Spain and eleven in Portugal, all in the period from December to February with the exception of one in April and two in July. Two birds have been recovered at the southern limit of the wintering range in Morocco, in December and February. More intriguing are single recoveries in Germany in March and Denmark in April of birds which, judging by the relatively late dates, may have shifted breeding site to the east or north-east.

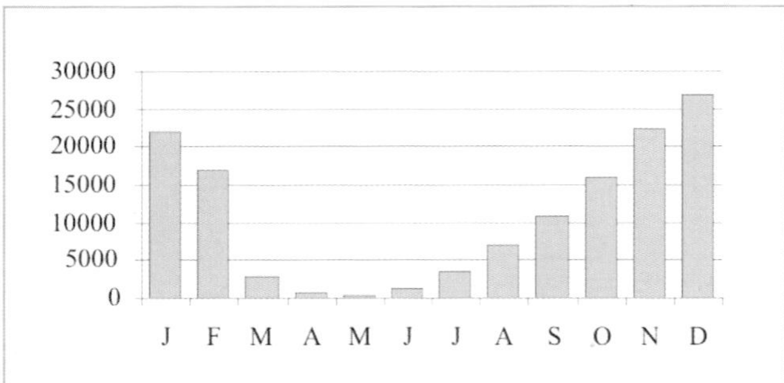

Figure 1. Average monthly peaks of Lapwings on the Ribble & Alt Estuaries and Morecambe Bay South, 1990-2005.

The main arrivals of Lapwings from elsewhere in northern Britain and further afield take place in October and November and numbers increase steadily to reach their peak in most years during December (Figure 1).

Winter flocks inland are normally small, although there were up to 1,000 at Fishmoor Reservoir in December 1995. Since the late 1990s substantial numbers have taken to resting by day on warehouse roofs in Burnley (Spencer 1998), where more than 1,000 were present in November 2001. This habit was first noted in Greater Manchester in 1984 (Calbrade *et al.* 2001) and by 2004 had spread to the Ford Jaguar plant in south Liverpool where 370 were seen. The birds are present from dawn to dusk when they leave for nocturnal feeding sites.

It is in the coastal areas, however, that the vast majority of our wintering Lapwings congregate. Some truly impressive flocks have been recorded, including 15,000 on Cockerham Moss in February 1966, 20,000 on Newton Marsh in November/December 1979, and 12,000 at Martin Mere in December 1980 and between Cockerham and Thurnham in November 1983. There have been no five-figure single-site counts anywhere in the county since 1990 but many thousands still winter on grazing marshes and mosslands from the Lune Estuary to the Alt, including 7,300 at Marshside as recently as December 1998 and 9,500 on the Lune Estuary on 22 November 2002. Winter flocks in excess of 2,000 have also been regularly recorded at Seaforth, Martin Mere, Pilling Lane Ends, the Eric Morecambe complex, Stanah-Skippool, Thurnham, Warton Marsh and Freckleton. Very severe winter weather, as in 1962/63, December 1981 and February 1986, may cause virtually all Lancashire's Lapwings to leave the county in search of milder conditions in Ireland or further south.

Peak winter totals have fallen by more than a quarter on our estuaries since 1990, a decline almost entirely accounted for by a decline of more than 50% in numbers found on WeBS counts on the Ribble following a record total there of 32,590 in December 1990; trends on Morecambe Bay and the Alt have been roughly stable (figure 2).

Figure 2. Peak winter counts (3-year rolling means) of Lapwings on the Ribble & Alt Estuaries and Morecambe Bay South, 1988/89 to 2004/05.

Winter flocks begin to break up in early February in most years and almost all have left the coast by early March; Lancashire breeders are already present on upland territories from the middle of February and territories are occupied by late March at the latest. Eastward movements, presumably of northern European birds, are regularly observed along Darwen Moor and in the Lune Valley in March and April.

Winter immigrants to Lancashire come from a very wide range of areas; ringing recoveries include 31 from elsewhere in northern England and one from southern England, but, surprisingly, none from Scotland. In addition there have been winter recoveries of birds ringed as pulli in western and central Europe and Fennoscandia: four from Norway, two from Germany, and singles from Sweden, Finland, Netherlands and the Czech Republic.

BM, MJ.

This species account was sponsored by Ken Spencer and the Fylde Bird Club.

GREAT KNOT

Calidris tenuirostris

Lancashire Category A. (0, 1).

Vagrant from Siberia.

Lancashire's only record was found by Chris Batty at Skippool Creek and Shard Bridge on the Wyre Estuary on 31 July 2004. The bird was an adult in full breeding plumage and was seen by 20 or so birders before it flew off high to the south-west, towards the Ribble Estuary. Remarkably, it returned to the same sites just over a fortnight later on 16 August, perhaps influenced by the tidal cycle. This time it stayed for two days and was last seen flying off high to the west on the afternoon of the 17th.

This was the third British record, following singles in Shetland in September 1989 and Teesside in October to November 1996.

Great Knot, Shard Bridge, River Wyre, August 2004. (Top: Steve Young. Bottom: Mike Malpass)

SJW.

This species account was sponsored by Chris Batty.

KNOT

Calidris canutus

Lancashire Category A.

Abundant winter visitor from Arctic Canada and Greenland.

The Knot breeds only in the high Arctic. Two populations winter in or pass through western Europe: birds of the race *islandica* from Canada and Greenland spend the winter mainly in Britain, Ireland and the Netherlands, while the nominate race from central Siberia passes through northern and western Europe *en route* to wintering grounds in Mauritania or further south in West Africa.

Tony Disley

The open sandy and muddy bays and estuaries of Britain and eastern Ireland are an important resource at all times of the year. The current British population estimate is 283,000 (Rehfisch *et al.* 2003), and three of the top six winter sites, holding up to 110,000 birds between them, are wholly or mainly in Lancashire.

Except in detail, the status of the Knot in Lancashire seems to have changed little over recent centuries. Mitchell cited a reference in Ray (1678) to large numbers 'on the coast of Lancashire about Leverpool' in February 1671, and described the species as a well known migrant in the late nineteenth century, especially on Morecambe Bay, less common on the Ribble and Mersey, and rarely encountered inland. Oakes considered the Knot to be our most abundant shorebird, although by his day the more southerly estuaries, the Ribble and Alt in particular, had come to predominate, although the species remained abundant on the Wyre and the southern shores of Morecambe Bay. He judged the Knot to be more numerous during spring and autumn passage periods than in winter, and cited several accounts of quite enormous autumn flocks from the 1920s and 1930s, including an estimate by Wagstaffe of 65,000 to 100,000 on Ainsdale shore in August 1925. Peak counts since the middle of the twentieth century, though seldom attaining such heights, have frequently run them close.

Apart from a period of six weeks or so in June and July, Knots are abundant on our coast throughout the year. The two stretches of coastline from Morecambe to the Wyre and from the Ribble to the mouth of the Alt have vied with each other to produce the more impressive counts and there have been clear changes in winter distribution between the estuaries over recent decades. From the late 1960s to the mid-1990s the Ribble and points south tended to hold the highest winter numbers, but since then Morecambe Bay has returned to the lead position.

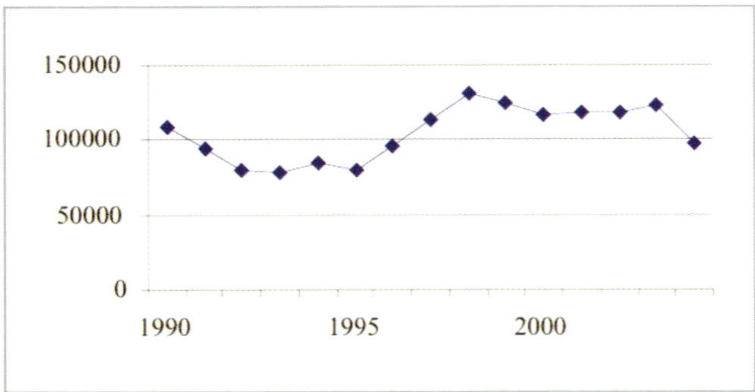

Figure 1. Peak winter counts (3-year rolling means) of Knot on the Ribble & Alt Estuaries and Morecambe Bay South, 1988/89 to 2004/05.

Counts of over 20,000 were quite normal on the Alt from the 1970s to the early 1990s; among the most impressive were 34,000 in January 1981, 46,000 in February 1987 and 51,000 in January 1990. Within the Ribble Estuary the shore from Crossens to Ainsdale has long been a winter stronghold; there were 14,700 at Marshside in February 1982, 30,000 on Southport Beach in January 1986 and 13,000 again at Marshside in January 1996. Winter roosts on the Fylde shore have typically been much smaller but range from a few thousand to 10,000-12,000 in 2003/04. Over the Ribble as a whole WeBS totals showed a steady decline during the 1990s before levelling out in the first years of this century.

Pilling frequently attracted the largest Morecambe Bay flocks from the 1970s to the early 1990s, including 5,000 in December in 1983 and 1994, but sites further north have predominated in more recent years. There were 10,000 at Hest Bank in February 1990 and 11,000 on Carnforth Marsh in February 1996, but since the mid-1990s these birds, and many more, have taken to roosting at Heysham Helipad, where there were 14,500 in February 1997 and over 20,000 in January 1999 and December 2000. Thirty-eight thousand roosted off Ocean Edge, Heysham in December 1998 and 50,000 in late 2000.

Roosting Knot, Heysham. (Phillip Tomkinson)

The northern and southern estuaries also differ in respect of patterns of monthly occurrence, with peak counts on the Ribble and Alt usually occurring during passage periods but during winter on Morecambe Bay (Figure 2).

Massive influxes of autumn immigrants, led by thousands of adults still in breeding plumage, get underway by the beginning of August. On Morecambe Bay the build-up in numbers comes much later than further south; 23,195 in October 1998 is by far the highest autumn WeBS total since the early 1990s, although there were 30,000-40,000 at Pilling in October 1966. On the Ribble, August and September normally produce the highest counts of the year, including 55,000 at Crossens in Aug 1971 with 95,000 there in August and September 1973 and 50,000 in September 1978; 54,000 were at Marshside in September 1983 and August 1984, and 42,000 on 25 October 1987. Since the late 1980s these mega-flocks have been much less frequent; WeBS totals for the estuary over the last decade have fluctuated around 30,000, although 87,370 were present in October 1993. Most autumn peaks on the Alt are well below 5,000, but 18,053 were counted in October 2000 and 22,208 in September 2002.

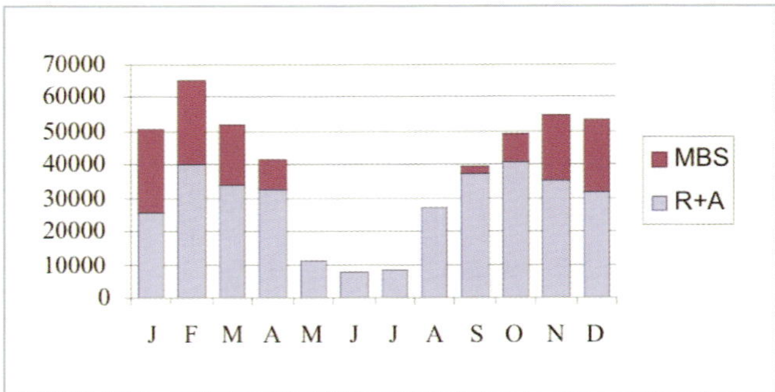

Figure 2. Average monthly peak counts of Knot on the Ribble & Alt Estuaries and Morecambe Bay South, 1985-2005.

Spring flocks on the Alt are normally relatively small with 1,600 in April 2002 the highest recent WeBS total, while the largest spring count on the Ribble was 54,300 in April 1998, and in Morecambe Bay 28,000 at Hest Bank in April 1978.

As in Oakes's day summering Knots, predominantly first-summer birds, are virtually restricted to the coast south of the Ribble. Almost 6,000 were estimated to be on the Ribble during the early 1980s, and this had increased to around 8,000 by the early 1990s, but WeBS totals since have declined to about 3,000. On the Alt, in contrast, there has been a substantial increase in June and July totals: 7,020 in July 1996, 5,145 in June 2000 and 7,261 in July 2002; roosts of up to 5,000 have assembled at Seaforth in some recent summers. Large flocks of first-summers occur roughly every three or four-years in line with the Arctic 'Lemming-cycle'. A strong correlation with numbers of first-summer Bar-tailed Godwit on the Alt raises the possibility that these Knot may be nominate Siberian *canutus*, which share West African wintering grounds with Bar-tailed Godwits (S.J. White unpublished data).

Knot are scarce in inland Lancashire; Oakes cited a single record for the first half of the twentieth century, a bird at Ewood Bridge Sewage Works, Rossendale on 7 September 1914. There were only 23 inland occurrences between 1959 and 1994, mostly of one or two birds, and from most months of the year, at reservoirs such as Foulridge, Whitemoor, Belmont and Stocks. Since 1994 the inland records have increased substantially; there were seven in 1995, three each in 1996 and 1997, and an average of five a year since then. Visits to Stocks Reservoir, and, nearer the coast, to Brockholes Quarry have become almost annual since the late 1990s.

There have been 18 movements of ringed birds between Lancashire and the breeding-grounds of *islandica*: 17 in Greenland and one on Ellesmere Island in north-east Canada, a distance of 4,179 km, together with 54 at their staging-sites in Iceland. Most of these northern records have been in May or June, with just six, all in Iceland, during July or August. Movements between Lancashire and southern Europe are restricted to five in France; together with 95 recorded movements to southern England these may indicate either regular staging in Lancashire or a change of wintering grounds between years. There have been ten exchanges with Norway, where passage birds are known to be *islandica*, but two exchanges with Denmark, twelve with the Netherlands, eleven with Germany and one with Poland – all areas where the two subspecies mingle on passage and in winter – may possibly have involved some *canutus*.

BM, MJ.

This species account was sponsored by Peter Guy.

SANDERLING

Calidris alba

Lancashire Category A.

Abundant passage migrant; common winter visitor from Arctic Siberia and Greenland.

Sanderling breed only on high-Arctic coasts and islands of Canada, Greenland and east-central Siberia. Large numbers pass through Lancashire on passage to and from their west African wintering grounds and smaller numbers winter in the county. The Ribble and Alt Estuaries form the only sites of international importance for Sanderling in Britain, in both winter and spring.

Mitchell described the Sanderling as a regular spring and autumn migrant, mainly on shores from the Ribble southward, and an occasional winter visitor, which was also not uncommon inland. By Oakes's day its status more closely resembled the current position: commoner during spring passage than in autumn, but also numerous in most winters and present in small numbers in summer; it was more frequent at all seasons on southern than on more northerly coasts, but was always scarce inland.

In winter birds are concentrated on the sandy shores of the Ribble and Alt Estuaries, particularly at St. Anne's and from Birkdale southward, where numbers have remained relatively constant for the past 20 years (Figure 1). During the 1970s and 1980s most were found on the Ribble with notable counts of 2,324 in December 1978 and 3,572 in December 1988. Numbers were much lower on the Alt until the late 1990s but have increased significantly since, with high counts of 1,352 in March 1998 and 1,556 in December 2001. Peaks during the same period on the Ribble included 3,655 in March 1995 and 3,004 in March 2002. Winter WeBS counts on Morecambe Bay only occasionally reach 150 birds and 286 in February 1991 is the highest on record.

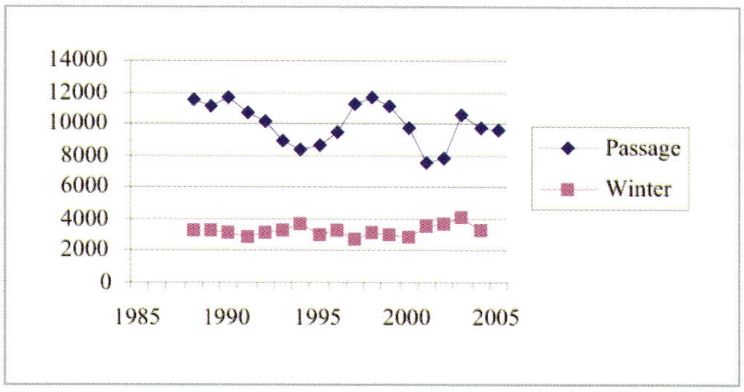

Figure 1. Winter and passage peak counts (3-year rolling means) of Sanderling on the Ribble & Alt Estuaries and Morecambe Bay South, 1987/89 to 2004/05.

Numbers increase a little in March but spring passage reaches a marked peak in May on all the estuaries (Figure 2); these later movements are often concentrated into a brief period, as birds hasten northward to the breeding-grounds, and therefore the largest flocks are perhaps regularly missed by the monthly WeBS census.

The situation in Morecambe Bay has changed substantially in recent decades. Very high numbers were recorded in the Hest Bank-Carnforth Marsh sector during the 1970s, peaking at 5,650 in late May 1981, but declined virtually to zero by the 1990s. On the south shore of the bay, however, spring passage remains substantial; notable counts include 3,130 on Middleton Sands on 23 May 1968, 3,500 at Pilling in late May 1987, 6,150 at Rossall Point on 15 May 1988, 7,000 there on 20 May 1992 and 1,500 on 19 May 2002, but barely exceeded three figures in 2004. However, there has been a shift in recent years to outer bay sites and the species is currently scarce away from Rossall and the Wyre Estuary.

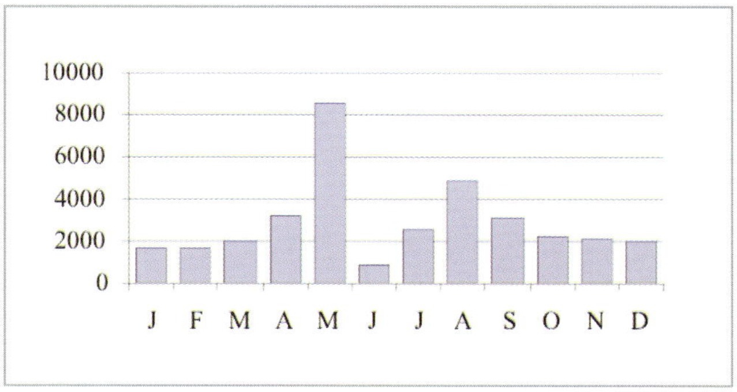

Figure 2. Average monthly peak counts of Sanderling on the Ribble & Alt Estuaries and Morecambe Bay South, 1985-2005.

Combined spring passage totals on the Ribble and Alt Estuaries fluctuated widely during 1985-2005, but with no clear trend; peaks averaged 5,816 on the Ribble and 2,379 on the Alt (but have increased to 4,402 this century). Notable May WeBS counts on the Ribble include 7,100 in 1971, 6,949 in 1988, 8,737 in 1992 and 7,660 in 1996, with spectacular site counts of 7,000 at Crossens on 23 May 1971, 4,200 on St. Anne's Beach on 17 May 1992,

10,000 at Ainsdale on 24 May 1997 and 5,600 at Birkdale on 9 April 2001. The past 20 years have witnessed a steady increase in the size of the spring passage on the Alt, most likely due to accretion of the shoreline south of Formby Point; the Alt birds feed from Crosby to Formby but roost mainly at Formby Point, where the largest flocks include 2,234 in 1987 and 5,047 in 2002.

It is difficult to judge from WeBS data how many Sanderlings spend the summer here, as many June counts catch the tail-end of spring passage while July totals include early-arriving returning migrants, but it is likely that the number is small, fewer than a hundred in most years.

Moulting adult Sanderling, Rossall Point. (Phillip Tomkinson)

Autumn passage begins in early July and continues well into October; peak numbers are usually reached in August or early September. WeBS totals on Morecambe Bay South have been at a low level since the early 1990s, typically no more than 300 birds in August, and there has been a major fall in the published site counts since the 1980s. There were 5,500 at Pilling on 30 July 1972, 4,000 there on 4 August 1981, and 3,500 at Sunderland Point on the previous day; 1,000 were at Rossall Point on 3 August 1986 and 1,270 on 28 July 1991, but no autumn site count has exceeded 800 since.

Ribble totals have also declined but to a lesser extent, from 9,450 in July 1972 and 6,700 on 29 July 1973. Counts of up to 2,000 are still fairly regular at favoured sites, such as St. Anne's Beach and the Birkdale-Ainsdale shore. On the Alt autumn flocks remained remarkably stable until quite recently, with typical peak counts at Formby Point of 1,000 on 2 August 1981, 1,200 on 7 August 1986 and 1,169 in August 1994, but there was a sudden increase to 2,144 in August 2002. WeBS totals for the estuary reached 3,102 in September 2002 and 6,894 in August 2003.

Although Mitchell described the Sanderling as 'not uncommon' inland and Oakes considered it merely 'scarce', neither author cited an occurrence within our present-day boundaries. The first documented inland record was of a single bird at Whitemoor Reservoir, Colne as recently as 29 August 1969. There were eight records in the 1970s, four at reservoirs, three in the Lune Valley and one on the Calder at Altham; all were in May or early June, apart from two October records. During the 1980s there were another six visits, two to the Lune Valley and four at Belmont Reservoir on 18 May 1980. The rate of inland occurrences increased dramatically in the early 1990s and records are now virtually annual, with seven in 1997 – four in spring and three in autumn. In 2000 over 20 visited Brockholes Quarry in May and June and there were eight at Stocks Reservoir during April and May, followed by an unprecedented twelve at Stocks on 28 May 2001. Single-figure totals have been recorded at Martin Mere in most springs since the mid-1990s.

Birds from both the Siberian and Nearctic breeding populations are known to migrate through Britain, although perhaps more of the former spend the winter here, with most Canadian and Greenland birds moving further south (Migration Atlas). Only two Lancashire-ringed birds can definitely be ascribed to either population: one ringed at Marshside in May 1985 and recovered in Greenland the following June, and another ringed on passage in Iceland in June 1974 and controlled at Seaforth on 20 November 1976, probably a wintering bird. Three seen on passage in different years in Lancashire and countries to the east (one in Germany, one in Denmark and one in Sweden) may well have been Siberian, while six ringed in spring or autumn in Lancashire and recovered abroad in different passage seasons (three in France and singles in the Netherlands, Spain and Portugal) were perhaps en route to winter in Africa. The only foreign recoveries in winter are three on Mauritania's Banc d'Arguin and two in Morocco. This admittedly thin evidence suggests that many of our passage migrants winter in Africa and may be of Nearctic origin, but a great deal remains to be discovered about the movements of Lancashire's Sanderlings.

BM, MJ.

This species account was sponsored by P.J. Drewery & Peter Carty.

SEMIPALMATED SANDPIPER

Calidris pusilla

Lancashire Category A. (0, 1).

Vagrant from North America.

In driving rain early in the morning of 25 July 2004, Tony Disley found a small calidrid wader at Brockholes Quarry, Preston which at the time he thought was a drab Little Stint. One other observer, Bill Aspin, looked for the bird and managed to get a minute or so of video recording and a few digital photographs during his five hour stay. It was from this footage, which included a clear shot of the partially-webbed feet, that the true identity of the bird was unravelled the following day. It was aged as an adult and was in breeding plumage. Unfortunately, the bird was never seen again.

Semipalmated Sandpipers, which breed across Alaska and northern Canada, are the most regular of the north American 'peeps' to occur in Britain, with 74 recorded up to the end of 2004, but this was only the second in north-west England, following one at Frodsham, Cheshire in October 1982.

Adult Semipalmated Sandpiper. Brockholes Quarry, 25 July 2004, the lower picture showing the webbing between the toes. (Bill Aspin)

SJW.
This species account was sponsored by Bill Aspin and Tony Disley.

LITTLE STINT

Calidris minuta

Lancashire Category A.

Fairly common passage migrant from northern Russia; scarce winter visitor.

In the late nineteenth century Mitchell described the Little Stint as an uncommon spring and autumn passage migrant. He focused entirely on inland records, including reports of regular spring presence on the moors east of Burnley which in all probability refer to Dunlin. Oakes cited only three acceptable records within our present-day boundaries, one shot on the Ribble Estuary in September 1887, one at Liverpool Sewage Farm on 18 September 1936, and one at Freckleton Sewage Farm on 10 October 1948; the county bird report for 1946 also gave a record from Morecambe on 10 September of that year. With commendable foresight Oakes predicted that the increase in the number of 'capable observers' would show that the Little Stint was a regular if uncommon visitor; it has since become clear that the species is a scarce migrant in spring, much commoner, though in very variable numbers, in autumn, and with fairly regular instances of overwintering.

Most records during the 1950s and 1960s came from regular observation at Freckleton Sewage Farm, where autumn peaks included 19 in September 1953, 38 in September 1957, 60 (all juveniles) on 28 September 1960 – a county record total which was to stand until 1996 – and 30 in September/October 1967. The first record in spring was also at this site, a single bird on 26-28 May 1960.

Spring passage is recorded virtually annually nowadays, although the number of birds involved is small with typically fewer than ten summer-plumaged adults recorded between early May and the middle of June. Coastal and near-coastal locations, especially Marshside, Seaforth, Martin Mere and the Eric Morecambe complex are heavily favoured. The occasional late June birds are perhaps mostly non-breeders, but a few adults on return passage are recorded from mid-July to mid-August in most years, with a higher proportion of these at inland sites than is the norm either for birds in spring or later in the autumn. Since the early 1970s July or August adults have been recorded at Rishton, Belmont, Stocks, Wayoh, Upper Foulridge, Black Moss, Parsonage and Earnsdale Reservoirs, as well as at Greta Foot on the Lune in July 2002. Most southbound adults, however, turn up at a small number of established coastal wetlands where they are joined, or replaced, from late August by a larger influx of juveniles.

The passage of autumn juveniles varies a great deal in size from one year to the next; in recent decades particularly high numbers were present in 1973, 1980, 1981, 1983, 1988, 1993, 1996, 1998, and 2000. Peak site counts have included 42 at Crossens on 27 September 1973 and 21 at the Eric Morecambe complex on 6 September 1988 with up to 30 there in August/September 1993. In 1996 the largest influx so far brought an all-time record 130 to the Eric Morecambe complex during 24-28 September and flocks in double figures to four other coastal sites around the same time; a second movement in late October produced counts of 50 at Martin Mere and 22 at Marshside. At least 208 juvenile birds were reported in 1998, including 42 on Birkdale shore and twelve at Seaforth on 12 September and 36 at the Eric Morecambe complex next day; seven at Whitemoor Reservoir, Colne, also on the 12th. The latter, together with seven at Foulridge Reservoir in mid-September 1995, was an exceptional count for an inland location. Numbers of juveniles at inland sites, mainly by reservoir margins, are invariably much lower than on the coast but records have become more frequent in recent decades; the Foulridge-Whitemoor complex, Stocks, Rishton and Clowbridge Reservoirs have featured regularly, as has Brockholes Quarry in the lower Ribble Valley since the late 1990s.

Adult Little Stint, Seaforth Nature Reserve, June 1992. (Steve Young)

The last autumn stragglers have usually moved on by early November, but since 1960 small numbers of Little Stints have been recorded in many winters, all at coastal sites and mainly on the Ribble Estuary. In 1960/61 there were six at Freckleton Sewage Works; five spent December 1973 at Marshside and up to eight birds wintered there annually between 1977/78 and 1980/81. Such occurrences decreased during the 1980s and there were none in the county between January 1988 and January 1994, when two turned up at Marshside. Since then there have been records in every winter except 1997/98; up to three have been present at Marshside in several winters, but birds have also been recorded at Seaforth, Martin Mere and the Eric Morecambe complex. Three were on Birkdale Beach on 26 December 1995 and more recently the Birkdale-Ainsdale shoreline has become the county's premier wintering-site for Little Stints, with up to six in January 2001 and a record count of 16 from 20 December of that year into January 2002; at least four were again present from December 2002 into 2003, although visits have become more erratic since then.

There have been only two recoveries of ringed Little Stints in Lancashire, both from Norway. One, age unknown, caught in Finnmark on 8 August 1966 was recovered on Longton Marsh on 14 September that year, and a juvenile ringed in More og Romsdal on 2 September 1998 was at Seaforth, 1,135km to the southwest, nine days later.

BM, MJ.
This species account was sponsored by Brian Haynes and family.

TEMMINCK'S STINT

Calidris temminckii

Lancashire Category A. (3, 91).

Scarce passage migrant from Fennoscandia and northern Russia.

The shy and furtive habits of Temminck's Stint may help to account for its exceptional popularity among birders, which can hardly be due to its various plumages, which are the plainest of any of our calidrids. Temminck's Stint favours less extreme Arctic conditions than the Little Stint and breeds across Fennoscandia and northern Russia from the White Sea to the Bering Strait. Although a tiny and precarious breeding toe-hold has existed in northern Scotland since the early 1970s (only one or two pairs were confirmed annually in the 1990s), in Britain Temminck's Stint is essentially a scarce passage migrant, much more regular on the east coast than in the west, and, unlike Little Stint, commoner in spring than in autumn. The species favours freshwater habitats with well-vegetated edges, in which it is wont to skulk; in saltwater locations it tends to frequent muddy creeks and avoids open shorelines and beaches.

Mitchell knew Temminck's Stint as a very rare visitor in spring and autumn, citing only two records: birds shot at Ribbleton, Preston in spring 1864 and on Pilling Moss in 1873. There had been no further occurrences by Oakes's time but since then 91 have been recorded between 1957 and 2005.

The first twentieth-century record was at Freckleton Naze pool on 29 September 1957 and there were four further visits to the nearby sewage works – the famed Mecca for rare waders – during 1959-63. Since the mid-1960s Temminck's Stints have been recorded at many coastal wetlands, from Morecambe Bay to the Mersey mouth. Martin Mere has been the pre-eminent site, by a very wide margin; from the first record of two birds on 25-27 May 1974, no fewer than 29 have been seen there. Other favoured locations over the years have included Marshside (twelve), Seaforth (seven) Leighton Moss (five) and Marton Mere (eight). Although Temminck's Stint is a broad-front, overland migrant across most of its range there have been only four records at inland sites, all in east Lancashire, single birds at Rowley Lake, Burnley on 24 August 1987, Slipper Hill Reservoir, Colne on 25 May 1993 and Stocks Reservoir on 23-26 May 1998 and 13 May 2001.

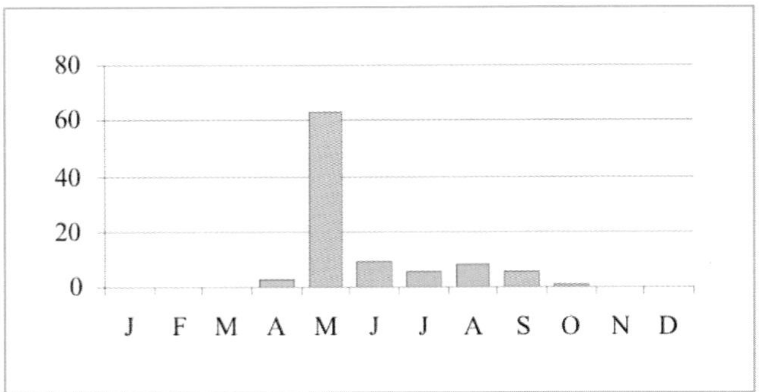

Figure 1. Monthly totals of Temminck's Stints in Lancashire, 1957-2005.

Spring passage takes place between the last days of April and early June but two-thirds of all records have occurred in May. The earliest records were both at Seaforth, on 29 April in 1987 and 2000. Autumn records account for just over 20% of the total, the latest at Freckleton on 11-20 October 1963. All but eight records have involved a single bird, and four at Martin Mere on 24-25 May 2001 is the largest party so far recorded. The rate of occurrence increased from three birds in the 1950s to eight in the 1960s and 17 in the 1970s, but there were only ten birds in the 1980s, none being recorded during 1980-1985. The upward trend resumed with 27 during the 1990s and 28 between 2000 and 2005, with ten in 2001 making that by far our best year to date.

There have been no ringing recoveries.

Tony Disley

BM, MJ.
This species account was sponsored by Tony Disley.

WHITE-RUMPED SANDPIPER

Calidris fuscicollis

Lancashire Category A. (0, 13).

Vagrant from North America.

With eleven records involving 13 individuals, this is one of Lancashire's more regular national rarities; all have been at coastal sites. The first were two first-winters together on sludge beds at Freckleton Sewage Farm on 11 October 1952, found by Harry Shorrock and Alan Harrison amongst a group of Curlew Sandpipers and Little Stints. Maurice Jones and Nelson Harwood arrived later but none of the observers could immediately identify the birds. A few days later they formed a consensus that they were not Baird's but 'Bonaparte's' Sandpipers – if they had been known as 'White-rumped' at the time the identification might have been more straightforward! Both remained until 18 October, with one to the 19th. This was reckoned to be the fifteenth British and Irish record at the time but these included five 'Hastings rarities'.

The next was another first-winter at Southport on 28 September 1963 and what was accepted at the time to be the same bird at Freckleton Sewage Works on 12-14 October, where it became one of the first rarities to be photographed in the field in Lancashire. In the light of our present experience of the average length of stay of vagrant calidrids, and because there seems to have been no positive evidence that just one bird was involved, this was perhaps too conservative an assessment and these might be better regarded as separate records.

A further two first-winters took up residence on a large temporary dredging bed at Lea Marsh, near Preston from 1-5 November 1964 and another, probably first-winter, was at Freckleton on 15 November 1970.

Adult White-rumped Sandpiper, Crosby, July 2007. (Steve Young)

Oddly, after this long run of young birds, all subsequent records have been of adults, which mirrors the national trend. The first of these was at Newton Marsh, Freckleton on 1 September 1981, followed by singles at Conder Green on 14-16 July 1984 and at Seaforth on 19 August the same year. There was then a long gap until one on the Eric Morecambe complex at Leighton Moss from 29 August to 1 September 2001, followed quickly by another at Marshside on 19-20 May 2002 (our only spring record) and one at various sites on the Wyre Estuary from 3 to 11 August 2003. An adult at the same site from 26 July to 3 August 2005 was thought likely to have been this last individual returning.

All records:

1952	Freckleton, two first-winters, 11 to 19 October
1963	Southport, first-winter, 28 September, perhaps same at Freckleton 12-14 October
1964	Lea Marsh, Preston, two first-winters, 1 to 5 November
1970	Freckleton, first-winter, 15 November
1981	Newton Marsh, adult, 1 September
1984	Conder Green, adult, 14 to 16 July
1984	Seaforth, adult, 19 August
2001	Leighton Moss, adult, 29 August to 1 September
2002	Marshside, adult, 19 to 20 May
2003	Wyre Estuary, adult, 3 to 11 August
2005	Wyre Estuary, adult, 26 July to 3 August

SJW, MJ.

This species account was sponsored by Paul Slade and Maurice Jones.

BAIRD'S SANDPIPER

Calidris bairdii

Lancashire Category A. (0, 5).

Vagrant from North America.

The county's first – and Britain's eighth – was a juvenile found on Hutton Marsh on the south bank of the Ribble Estuary by Harry Shorrock and Phil Thompson on 22 September 1963. What was assumed to be the same bird was (re)located on 5 October across the river at Freckleton Sewage Farm, where it remained to the 11th and was seen by many observers. As with the 1963 White-rumped Sandpiper records, we would perhaps be more ready to accept these as separate records nowadays.

Juvenile Baird's Sandpiper, Marshside, September 1982. (J. Clift)

There have been four other accepted records, all of single juvenile/first-winter birds, beginning with one on the Carnforth Marshes at Leighton Moss on 5-6 September 1974. All the others have been on various sites on the Ribble Marshes: at Hesketh Out Marsh on 20 October 1976; Marshside on 19-25 September 1982 and at Marshside again on 12 September 1991.

SJW, MJ.

This species account was sponsored by Maurice Jones.

PECTORAL SANDPIPER

Calidris melanotos

Lancashire Category A. (0, 49).

Scarce passage migrant from North America or eastern Siberia.

Lancashire's first was a juvenile found at Freckleton sewage works by Nelson Harwood and Peter Edwards on 21-26 September 1952. Surprisingly, eighteen more years elapsed before the second, another juvenile at the same intensively-watched site on 20-29 September 1970. A further 15 records followed, at an average of fewer than one a year, to 1998, since when the county total has more than doubled with an average of nearly five annually (including a blank year in 2001) and a peak of eight in 2003 (Figure 1).

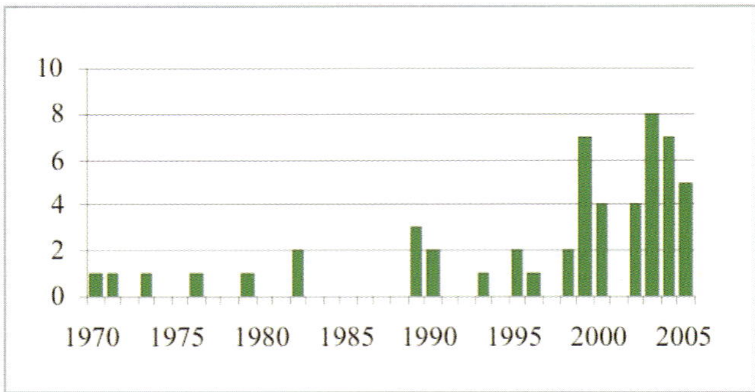

Figure 1. Annual totals of Pectoral Sandpipers in Lancashire, 1970-2005.

As elsewhere in Britain, Pectoral Sandpipers are considerably more common in autumn than in spring (Figure 2). The first spring record was on 6-8 May at Stocks Reservoir in 1990; seven more have followed, mostly during May, on dates between 15 April and 20 May. The average length of stay is about three days but one remained for more than a fortnight at Martin Mere from 15 April to 2 May 2002 and for three weeks at the same site during 2-23 September 2005.

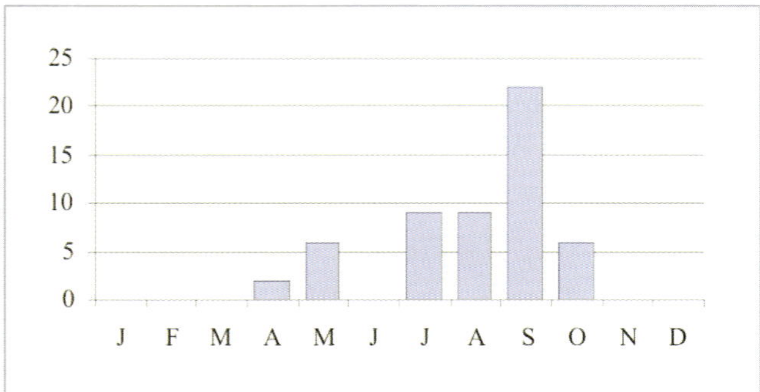

Figure 2. Monthly totals of Pectoral Sandpipers in Lancashire, 1952-2005.

The earliest autumn passage bird was at Stocks Reservoir on 1-12 July 2000 but few have been seen before the last week of July. The passage of adults and juveniles is sharply separated: all July and August records that have been aged are of adults, with the latest on 25 August, while all later records involve juveniles – the earliest on 6 September. About a half of all autumn records have been in September. A record of an unaged bird at Southport on 30 November 1975 was published but, in the light of the extreme rarity of November records in Britain, this now needs to be questioned. Our next latest was a juvenile on Lea and Clifton Marshes on 16-22 October 1976.

Pectoral Sandpiper, Eric Morecambe complex, August 2005. (Phillip Tomkinson)

As with Temminck's Stint, records are extremely evenly distributed throughout the county. Martin Mere and Leighton Moss together with the Eric Morecambe complex, with ten records each, are the most visited sites. There have been two other records in the north of the county, at Kellett Lane TV mast pool on 25-26 July 1990 and two on Conder Pool in July-August 2004. The north and south Ribble marshes (including Marshside) have had a total of ten between them, while another ten have been seen elsewhere in the Fylde. A remarkable eleven have been seen well inland: singles at Anglezarke and Rishton Reservoirs, three at Brockholes Quarry and two on Champion Moor near Slaidburn, and five at nearby Stocks Reservoir. Inland records, including those at Martin Mere, thus account for more than 40% of the county total. With the exception of a few estuarine records whose precise locations were not published, all have been seen on either freshwater habitats or brackish coastal lagoons.

SJW, MJ.

This species account was sponsored by Paul Ellis.

CURLEW SANDPIPER

Calidris ferruginea

Lancashire Category A.

Fairly common passage migrant; rare winter visitor from Siberia.

The breeding grounds of the Curlew Sandpiper on the high-Arctic coastal tundra of Siberia and offshore islands between the mouth of the River Ob and the Bering Strait are the most easterly of any regularly occurring wader in Lancashire.

Mitchell described the species as an uncommon passage migrant in spring between April and the end of May, by which time most were in summer plumage, and in autumn between the end of August and early October. Oakes's account, though more detailed, was essentially similar; he listed six records of spring migrants within our present-day boundaries between 1916 and 1940 (all south of the Ribble) between the early date of 13 March and 25 May. In autumn, there were August records of five at Crossens in 1916 and two at Liverpool Sewage Farm in 1935; he considered September occurrences too numerous to list but cited only two October records, at Southport in 1927 and Freckleton Sewage Farm in 1948. Since then peak counts, particularly in autumn, have increased substantially but otherwise the broad pattern has changed very little.

Curlew Sandpipers are nowadays seen in most springs, but numbers are invariably small; records typically fall in the period between the last week of April and the first week of June, with a marked peak in May. Records come almost exclusively from a few regular coastal and near-coastal sites, mainly from the Ribble southwards; Martin Mere, Lytham, Marshside, Banks Marsh and Seaforth have featured most strongly in the last two decades, and seven at Marshside on 14 May 1998 is the largest party recorded. There have been only four inland occurrences, three at Coldwell Reservoir, Nelson on 3 June 1971 and singles at Stocks Reservoir on 27 May 1992, Alston Reservoir, Longridge on 13-22 May 2003 and Martin Mere on 30 May 2004. In some years a few birds in full or partial breeding plumage are recorded in mid or late June, but whether these are non-breeding first-summers or failed breeders on early return passage is unclear.

Autumn movements normally begin with a small influx of moulting adults, usually single birds, at coastal sites from early July to the beginning of August. The main movement of juveniles gets underway in mid-August and normally peaks in September; in some years there is a second, usually smaller, influx in October. The volume of migration varies greatly from year to year; in 1989 only a single bird was recorded, at Conder Green on 8 October, whereas in 1998 over 230 passed through the county in September alone. During the 1950s and 1960s Freckleton Sewage Farm was the premier site for Curlew Sandpipers, as for many other scarce and uncommon waders; there were 54 there on 5 September 1969, and a then-record flock of 65 was at Conder Green on the 13th. Peak counts since have included 30 at Conder Green on 5 September 1972 and on Clifton Marsh on 3 October 1982, 40 at Pilling Lane Ends on 8 September 1985, 39 at Marshside on 5 September 1988 and 34 there on 13 September 1991, 39 at Lytham on 27 September 1993, 50 at Bank End, Cockerham on 11 September 1998 and a new county record total of 93 on Banks Marsh on the 26th; up to 40 were again on Banks in late August 2000.

Curlew Sandpipers remain scarce in autumn at inland sites. There have been about 30 records since 1970: from Altham and from Stocks, Parsonage, Foulridge and Rishton Reservoirs in east Lancashire, and from Withnell Fold and Belmont, Anglezarke and Wayoh Reservoirs, Brockholes Quarry and Martin Mere in central and south-west Lancashire. Five at Anglezarke on 13 September 1991 and at Foulridge on 6 September 1997, and six at Martin Mere on 17-19 September 2004 are the largest gatherings recorded.

Curlew Sandpiper, Seaforth Nature Reserve, May 1998. (Steve Young)

In many autumns one or two migrants linger well into November, but the species is rare in Lancashire in winter and such records have become more infrequent in recent decades. During the 1960s one to three birds wintered annually in the Lytham-Fairhaven area; there were six in 1960-61, when the last bird remained until 26 April. Single birds were also recorded in winter at Freckleton and Morecambe in the 1960s and one wintered at Freckleton in 1977-78; during the 1980s singles were recorded in five winters at Marshside and one remained at Conder Green from October 1984 to March 1985. There were no confirmed instances of overwintering in the 1990s, although the presence of singles at Pilling Lane Ends and Martin Mere in March 1999 was suggestive; since 2000 individuals have been recorded between December and February at Pilling Lane Ends, Marshside, Clifton Marsh and Martin Mere.

BM, MJ.

This species account was sponsored by Paul Slade.

STILT SANDPIPER

Calidris himantopus

Lancashire Category A. (0, 1).

Vagrant from North America.

The only Lancashire record of what remains one of the rarest of vagrant Nearctic waders – just 27 have been recorded in Britain and Ireland to the present day – was found by R. Kennedy and P. Fearon on a pool at Hundred End, next to Banks Marsh on the Ribble on 27 September 1967. It was a juvenile and remained until 8 October, seen by many observers.

This bird was the sixth record for Britain and Ireland and the first in north-west England.

SJW, MJ.

This species account was sponsored by Jim and Trudy Sines.

PURPLE SANDPIPER

Calidris maritima

Lancashire Category A.

Scarce winter visitor from Arctic Canada and Norway.

The 17,500 Purple Sandpipers that winter in Britain (Rehfisch *et al.* 2003) are found overwhelmingly in the Northern Isles, the Outer Hebrides and on the coasts of eastern Scotland and north-east England. Elsewhere, even in its favoured habitat of rocky, boulder-strewn shores, the species is relatively uncommon. In Lancashire, with its predominantly sandy coastline, it has always been rare.

Mitchell described the Purple Sandpiper, without details, as one of the rarest of our sandpipers, while Oakes considered it to be scarce and infrequent on the Lune Estuary, occasional on the mussel-beds of the north shore of the Ribble and on Morecambe Bay, but very scarce on the Wyre. Since Oakes's day small numbers have wintered more or less regularly at a few locations on the coast, with some evidence of spring and autumn passage. Overall, however, there has been a fairly steady decline in numbers over recent decades which has accelerated since the mid-1990s. Lancashire's Purple Sandpipers, as well as frequenting natural mussel-beds, have also resorted to jetties, training banks, groynes and pier supports.

Since the 1960s the area around Heysham Harbour, especially the old wooden jetty, has been the most reliable county site for Purple Sandpipers. Maxima of 20 were recorded in March 1974 and November 1980, but during most of the 1980s twelve to fifteen was the more typical peak count between late October and April. After about 1992 numbers began to decline sharply; there were maxima of eight in January and six in November/December in 1993 and no more than one or two birds in any winter after 1995. By 2000 regular wintering at Heysham had ceased, although one or two Purple Sandpipers are still seen most years at Morecambe Stone Jetty.

Rossall Point and Knott End at the mouth of the Wyre were a regular wintering resort for Purple Sandpipers from the 1950s, but numbers were always small, normally in low single figures, and none has been recorded in winter since 1998. Further south, a few regularly frequented the Lytham-Fairhaven shore with Turnstones from the 1950s to the 1970s, peaking at eight on 17 February 1969, but the area was abandoned in the early 1980s. Sporadic overwintering occurred at Blackpool, first on the South Promenade during 1984-1990, involving up to eight birds in several years, and from 1992 to 1996 on the supports of the North Pier, where eight were present in the 1992/93 and 1993/94 winters. There were three records at Freckleton Sewage Farm, all in August or September, in 1952, 1969 and 1973. At Seaforth Purple Sandpipers were fairly regular in winter in the late 1970s, with up to a dozen crossing the Mersey from the rocky shores at Egremont to roost with Turnstones. Records, usually of just one or two birds, have become very irregular since the mid-1990s and none has been seen since 2002.

Spring passage back towards northern breeding grounds typically occurs quite late, in April or early May; this had been recorded fairly regularly at traditional wintering-sites, particularly at Rossall Point, where numbers typically peaked in late spring. Migrants continue to turn up, in very small numbers, at locations where regular wintering has ceased, including twelve with Turnstones at Seaforth on 21 April 1995. Similarly, Heysham Wooden Jetty or North Harbour Wall briefly hosted a single passage bird annually during 1998-2003.

Purple Sandpiper, Fleetwood, November 2005. (Phillip Tomkinson)

Autumn movements are usually more widespread, both temporally and geographically, than those in spring; birds have been recorded between July and November in recent decades. A summer-plumaged adult flew around a ship off the Liverpool Bar Light on 13 July 1982 and there were individuals at Blackpool on 13 July 1985 and at Heysham Harbour on 21 July 1989. Records in August and September are not particularly rare, and some of these have been in unlikely locations, typically involving one or two in roosts with Turnstones or other calidrids. One was on the beach at Hightown on 2 August 1971 and there were September records of one or two on Marshside shore in 1975, 1981, 1992, 1999 and

2000; single birds were on Banks Marsh on 2 September 2000 and Fairhaven shore on 28 September 2003.

There have been only two recoveries of Lancashire-ringed Purple Sandpipers, both local, but informative nonetheless. A first-winter ringed at Seaforth on 25 March 1978 was on Hilbre Island at the mouth of the Dee, 25km away, on 22 September of the same year, and a bird ringed at Heysham on 2 April 1977 returned there every winter until 1989, and summered at the site in 1987.

BM, MJ.

This species account was sponsored by Phil Lillywhite.

DUNLIN

Calidris alpina

Lancashire Category A.

Scarce breeder; abundant winter visitor and passage migrant from Iceland, Greenland, Fennoscandia and western Siberia .

Three sub-species of Dunlin appear regularly in Lancashire: *alpina* which breeds in northern Fennoscandia and north-west Russia is an abundant passage migrant and winter visitor; *schinzii* which breeds in the county in small numbers and is also abundant during passage periods and in winter; and *arctica*, which has a total population of only 15,000 breeding in north-east Greenland and which passes through in small numbers en route to and from winter quarters in West Africa. The British wintering population is estimated at 555,800 (Rehfisch *et al.* 2003) and Lancashire's estuaries, with their extensive sand- and mudflats, are all nationally important and the Mersey, Ribble and Morecambe Bay internationally important. Lancashire as a whole supports about 10% of British winter and passage populations.

Mitchell considered the Dunlin to be by far the commonest of our winter shorebirds. He also cited several instances of breeding on coastal mosses earlier in the nineteenth century, but judged that the breeding range had since become largely confined to the uplands, Bowland and the Pendle area in particular. Oakes described both *alpina* and *schinzii* as abundant migrants and winter visitors on the coast, with the latter also regular on passage at inland reservoirs and sewage farms. He reported widespread breeding on the eastern fells, from Parlick and Pendle Hill to the Lancashire Pennines and the south Rossendale moors; nesting persisted on the saltmarshes in Morecambe Bay but had ceased at Martin Mere, a former mossland haunt, after 1916.

Since Oakes's time the breeding range and population has fluctuated to some extent but the broad picture remains fairly similar to that of 50 years ago. Coastal nesting continues, but at a very low level; on Morecambe Bay one or two pairs have bred intermittently at the Eric Morecambe complex since 1984 after the establishment of the RSPB reserve there and consequent reduction in the level of sheep-grazing. Display was observed on Banks Marsh in 1954 and 1968 and territorial behaviour on several occasions since; breeding by at least one pair was confirmed during the 1997-2000 Atlas survey. Inland, six pairs were recorded in Bowland in 1987 and the 1997-2000 survey indicated a population of no more than five pairs. One or two pairs bred annually on Pendle Hill until at least 1970, and occasionally since. The three county 'strongholds' for breeding Dunlin are on the West Pennine Moors, where up to ten pairs have bred in the Belmont area since the early 1990s, the larger plateaux of Rossendale, such as Cowpe Moss, Whittle Pike and Scout Moor, which held at least ten pairs during 1997-2000, and the south Pennines, in particular Boulsworth Hill and Emmott Moor, with at least 15 pairs. The total county breeding population was estimated at 50 pairs in 1997-2000.

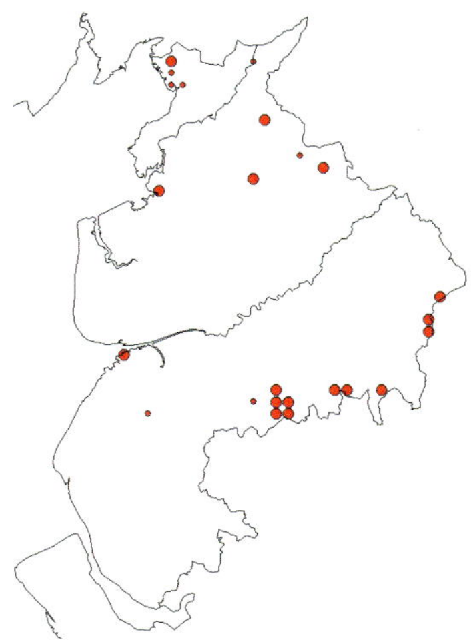

Breeding distribution of Dunlin, 1997-2000. (Large dots: confirmed. Small dots: possible)

Unravelling the movements through Lancashire of the various sub-species is complicated by the difficulties in identifying them in the field, but several decades of ringing data have produced a reasonably clear picture. British and other western European *schinzii* migrate early in the autumn, resulting in a sudden and marked influx into the county during July and August (Figure 1). Their numbers are depleted during September as most move towards more southerly wintering grounds; they are replaced by *alpina* from Fennoscandia and Russia as well as other *schinzii* from Greenland and Iceland *en route* south. It is thought that the majority of wintering birds are *alpina* (Migration Atlas); their numbers remain relatively steady throughout the winter until swelled by the first movements during February. Both forms are intermingled during spring migration, which extends from March to late May, with departing *alpina* being replaced by migrant *schinzii*.

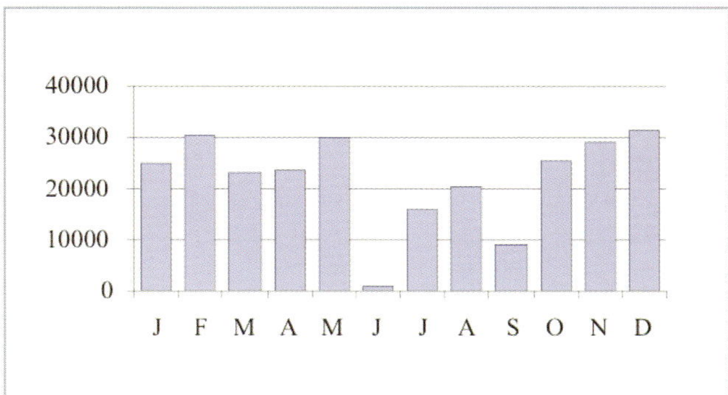

Figure 1. Average monthly peak counts (WeBS) of Dunlin on the Ribble & Alt Estuaries and Morecambe Bay South, 1985-2005.

Post-breeding parties and small groups of migrants are recorded on east Lancashire reservoirs from early July through to October; double-figure counts are exceptional, but include 26 at Foulridge on 17-28 August 1962, 17 at Springs near Belmont on 24 August 1995 and 19 at Stocks Reservoir on 17 August 2003. Dunlin are largely absent from inland Lancashire in winter except, surprisingly, during periods of icy weather when singles or small parties may occasionally be seen by reservoir margins or on riverbanks. Birds pass through in moderate numbers in April and May, coinciding with peak passage on the coast; notable recent counts include 27 at Brockholes Quarry on 13 May 2001, 54 at Stocks Reservoir on 15 May 2002, 82 at Alston Reservoir on 5 May 2003 and 140 at Martin Mere on 18 May 2004.

Wintering numbers on the coast have varied considerably over recent decades, from year to year and from one estuary to another; overall numbers increased throughout the 1990s before falling back this century (Figure 2). However, the county's importance for the species remains indisputable. The Mersey Estuary suffered decreases during the 1980s and early 1990s, followed by a recovery to premier position among British estuaries in winter during 1996-2001; although most Mersey Dunlin frequent the Cheshire shore there were 7,000 at Oglet in February 2002. The Alt supports much lower numbers, on average about 4,000 since 1985 but with larger counts of 6,185 in February 1989 and 12,743 in February 2004.

Figure 2. Winter and passage peak counts of Dunlin (WeBS, 3-year rolling means) on the Ribble & Alt Estuaries and Morecambe Bay South, (1988-2005).

Peak winter counts reached 69,000 on the Ribble in 1973/74 and 98,000 in 1974/75, but fell to an average of 22,000 during 1978-83 and 16,594 in 1986-91. A steady increase during the early 1990s peaked at 45,973 in February 1997 before plunging to 1980s' levels thereafter. Within the Ribble catchment Marshside has attracted the largest roosts over recent decades but no recent count has approached the 52,000 present on 17 November 1974, although 21,000 in December 2002 exceeded the whole estuary WeBS count for that month.

In Morecambe Bay winter peaks normally exceed passage counts by a considerable margin, the largest recent count being 47,928 in December 1997. As on the Ribble, numbers increased sharply during the mid-1990s but have declined to previous levels since 1999. Dunlin numbers wintering on the Alt have remained fairly steady since the mid-1980s and have even shown a small increase in recent years – but this comes nowhere near to compensating for the more than 50% declines on the two major estuaries.

Peak counts on the Alt are usually recorded during spring passage, and there has been a recent increase to a record 11,059 in April 2002. Passage numbers on the two main estuaries have followed much the same trends as in winter (Figure 2). Ribble counts increased hugely from the late 1980s until 1996 before showing a moderate decline and then crashing to an extremely low peak of 12,628 in May 2004. Notable counts include 55,000 in July 1974, 37,485 in April 1985, 39,293 in October 1991, 62,743 in May 1995 and 50,729 in May 2000. Marshside alone recorded 19,500 in September 1996 and 21,000 in September 1997. Passage peaks in Morecambe Bay showed a small upward trend towards the end of the 1990s, during which period the largest seasonal totals recorded were 7,800 in April 1997 and 22,275 in October the same year, but passage numbers have declined severely since then, averaging just under 5,000 this century.

Tony Disley

Very few Dunlin are ringed on their breeding grounds, so a mere 13 out of 341 recoveries of ringed birds in or from Lancashire have been sub-specifically identified. These comprise nine exchanges of *schinzii* within Britain and one with Poland in autumn, and two *alpina* within Britain and one with Germany, also in autumn. There are also very few ringing recoveries that indicate the origins of birds wintering in Lancashire. All 14 were ringed or recovered when abroad during passage periods; birds in Germany, Netherlands and Denmark may have been either *schinzii* or *alpina*, but six in Finland were probably *alpina*. Exchanges between Lancashire and northern and western Europe of birds seen during passage periods paint a similar picture: eight with Denmark, six with Netherlands, five with Germany, two with Norway and one with Poland may have belonged to either subspecies, while three with Finland and three in the Murmansk region of Russia were probably *alpina*.

There have been six passage exchanges with Iceland, one bird found in mid-Atlantic south of Iceland, and one with Greenland, all of which may relate either to the western population of *schinzii* or to *arctica*. One bird, recovered at Sunderland Point on 25 August 1983 was ringed as a pullus on 11 July 1975 at Danmarkshavn in north-east Greenland, within the breeding-range of *arctica*. There are just five movements of ringed Dunlins between Lancashire on passage and abroad in winter: three in Spain, one in Portugal and one in Mauritania. However, regular wintering in southern Europe and North Africa by birds that pass through the county may safely be inferred from four exchanges during passage periods with Portugal, three each with France and Morocco and two with Spain, together with 53 movements to and from southern England. Although most of these are presumed to be *schinzii*, none was definitely proved to be a British breeding bird.

BM, MJ.
This species account was sponsored by Jonathan Fenton.

BROAD-BILLED SANDPIPER

Limicola falcinellus

Lancashire Category A. (0, 8).

Vagrant from Fennoscandia.

The species was added to the county list with one at Freckleton Sewage Farm on 28 September to 7 October 1950 found by Harry Shorrock, Alan Harrison and Nelson Harwood. The next was at Crossens on 16 October 1954; the age of neither of these two birds was recorded.

Broad-billed Sandpiper, Cockersand, May 2006. (Chris Batty)

All subsequent records have been of adults. A sickly bird appeared on a sewage bed at Freckleton on 30 August 1969 and was found dead the next day. Further Ribble records followed at Crossens on 1-4 July 1976 and Banks Marsh on 12-13 June 1985 before two (perhaps a single individual) on the Wyre at the Thornton ICI Pools, Fleetwood on 3-8 June 1986 and 12-21 July 1987. The most recent was again on the Ribble at Marshside on 15 May 1988.

All records:

1950	Freckleton, one, 28 September to 7 October
1954	Crossens, one, 16 October
1969	Freckleton, adult 30 August, found dead 31 August
1976	Crossens, adult, 1 to 4 July
1985	Banks Marsh, adult, 12 to 13 June
1986	Fleetwood, adult, 3 June
1987	Fleetwood, adult, 12 to 21 July
1988	Marshside, adult, 15 May

SJW, MJ.
This species account was sponsored by the Fylde Bird Club.

BUFF-BREASTED SANDPIPER

Tryngites subruficollis

Lancashire Category A. (1, 11).

Vagrant from North America.

Mitchell and Oakes gave details of a male shot on the banks of the River Alt at Hightown in May 1829. It was sent to the Liverpool game market for sale, along with some Snipe, and passed into the possession of the Rev. T. Staniforth of Skipton. Some considerable doubt must be cast over this record since spring records are extremely rare in Britain and because of the lack of supporting details available.

The next three records were, however, better substantiated, all coming from the intensively watched sewage works at Freckleton. The first was found by Nelson Harwood on 19 August 1950 and was seen by several observers during its stay to the 27th. It was published by British Birds as 'probable' and 'square-bracketed' in the Lancashire & Cheshire Fauna Committee report of 1950-56 on the grounds that it was unlikely that a bird that was so rare in eastern USA would ever turn up in Lancashire. Since then, relatively large numbers have been seen in Britain and it is perhaps time for the brackets to come off and for this to be accepted as the first for Lancashire.

Tony Disley

Further unaged singles at Freckleton on 25 September 1955 and 21 August to 4 September 1960 were followed by another at an equally well-watched wader site at Hundred End on the opposite side of the Ribble on 14-15 September 1968. Four were recorded during the 1970s: one at Cockerham on 31 August to 1 September 1973, two were reported near Glasson Dock on 25 August 1979 and a single was on Clifton Marsh less than a fortnight later on 7 September.

It was a further thirteen years before any more appeared but there was a flurry of records during the 1990s; all but one were seen by many observers. These included singles in consecutive years at Pilling Lane Ends: adults on 26 September to 4 October 1992, 18-30 August 1993 and 29 October 1994. It seems likely that these all related to a single returning individual. The most recent occurrence was a first-winter that spent the day at Seaforth on 8 October 1996.

All records:

1950	Freckleton, one, 19 to 27 August
1955	Freckleton, one, 25 September
1960	Freckleton, one, 21 August to 4 September
1968	Hundred End, one 14 to 15 September
1973	Cockerham, one, 31 August to 1 September
1979	Glasson, two, 25 August
1979	Clifton Marsh, one, 7 September
1992	Pilling Lane Ends, adult, 26 September to 4 October
1993	Pilling Lane Ends, adult, 18 to 30 August
1994	Pilling Lane Ends, adult, 29 October
1996	Seaforth, first-winter, 8 October

SJW, MJ.
This species account was sponsored by Harry Shorrock.

RUFF

Philomachus pugnax

Lancashire Category A.

Rare breeder; fairly common passage migrant and winter visitor from northern Europe and Russia.

Though regular in small numbers as a spring and autumn passage migrant in Mitchell's day, the Ruff was much less common than it had been 20 or 30 years previously, when it was taken in large numbers on the Ribble Estuary and when summering and breeding occurred at Martin Mere. As long ago as the late eighteenth century, Pennant (*British Zoology* 1776-77) had recorded Ruff in spring at Martin Mere, while a flightless juvenile was caught at Crossens in the 1840s. Oakes stated that the last breeding attempt at Martin Mere was in 1910 when a clutch of eggs was collected on 20 April.

Lekking has been seen frequently in recent decades, especially at the two major haunts, Marshside and Martin Mere but also at Newton and Warton Marshes on the north bank of the Ribble. However, bearing in mind that gatherings were up to 50 strong (on an unspecified site in spring 1995), at least some of these birds must have been migrants. Nevertheless, breeding has been confirmed fairly regularly on the south Ribble marshes, with three females in 1975, two to four in 1983 and singles in 1969, 1976, 1980, 1982, 1983 and 1987. Females were seen with two newly hatched young on Warton Marsh in 1979 and with three small chicks on the south Ribble marshes in 2002. Breeding was also reported at Martin Mere in June 1989.

Mitchell and Oakes referred to the Ruff as a passage migrant in autumn and, to a lesser extent, in spring. According to both authors birds arrived in late August, peaked in September and declined in October. There were hardly any winter records; indeed, Ruff have only been observed wintering in Britain and Ireland since 1934 with numbers peaking in the 1970s (Migration Atlas). Greenhalgh & Greenhalgh (1971) found that numbers wintering on the Ribble, especially the area around Freckleton sewage farm, began to increase markedly in 1963/64, reaching a peak of 155 in December/January 1967/68. At that time, such numbers were thought to be among the largest in Britain and this area became the Ruff's stronghold in the county from about 1950 to the mid-1970s. In the latter decade, the winter peak was 50, while spring and autumn maxima were 132 and 100 respectively. Nearly all wintering Ruff in Lancashire are males, females tending to migrate further south to winter in West Africa (Migration Atlas).

Old-fashioned sewage-works were also frequented in other parts of the county. Thus, Hardy reported regular sightings during the 1930s at Fazakerley, Liverpool with parties of seven to 14 from October to December in 1937. A similar site at Parbold attracted 24 males and 16 females in mid-April 1958. However, the importance of sewage works was to decline with modernisation.

From the mid-1970s, unprecedented numbers began to appear at the newly developed Martin Mere reserve, perhaps reflecting the decline at Freckleton, and this remains one of the best places to see this species in the county. Over the last decade, mean winter peak counts have been 82 in January and 95 in December, while the spring average maximum is 102 in March (Figure 1). Average autumn numbers tend to be a little lower, ranging from 62 in August to 78 in October.

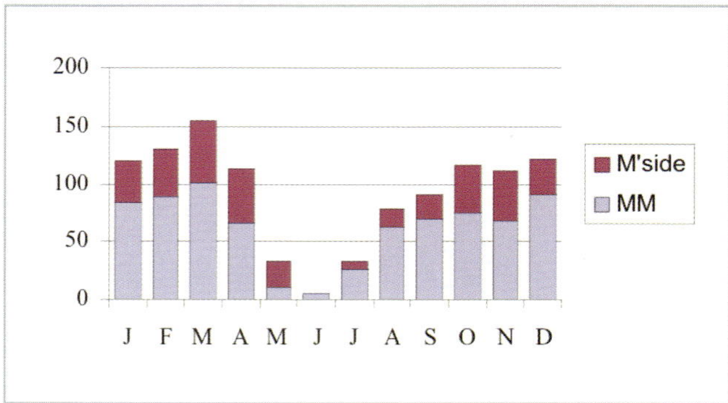

Figure 1. Mean monthly peak counts of Ruff at Martin Mere and Marshside, 1993-2005.

Another major haunt is the south Ribble marshes, with counts of 60 at Banks Marsh in September 1980 and 150 on Hutton Marsh in April 1981. However, the reclamation of 140ha of salt-marsh at Marshside/Crossens in 1974 and its conversion into seasonally-flooded grazing-marsh soon made this the most attractive site for Ruff on the estuary. During the past decade, mean monthly peak counts have included 43 in January, 54 in March, 45 in October and 50 in November (Figure 1). However, McCarthy (2001) pointed to a dramatic decline in numbers, especially in winter, at Marshside in the late 1990s. Thus, the January peak fell from 60 in 1996 to only four in 1998 and five in 2005. Similarly, mean peaks in March and April fell from 28 in 1996 to eleven in 1998 but have increased this century to 62 in April 2004 and 80 in March 2005. These data, especially from Marshside, appear to contradict the idea that spring Ruff in Lancashire are late winterers rather than passage migrants, as ringing returns show that the main spring passage of Ruffs through Europe takes an easterly route (Migration Atlas), suggesting that Lancashire may be an important staging site for birds wintering elsewhere in Britain.

Elsewhere in the south-west, flooded grassland at Great Altcar has been an occasional haunt, with a maximum of 37 birds in April 1981, while small numbers are regularly logged on passage at Seaforth; the site record there is 34 flying south on 28 August 2000. Autumn passage at Seaforth consists almost entirely of juveniles and the same may be true elsewhere, but supporting data are lacking. One at Prescot Reservoir on 16 September 2000 was only the second record for the St. Helens area.

With the demise of Freckleton sewage farm, relatively few Ruff have visited the Fylde in recent decades. However, 14 at Thistleton in December 1979 was noteworthy and as many as 75 were counted at Freckleton Naze in September 2000. Flocks of up to 15 at Blackpool Airport in September 1994 and 14 at Samlesbury Airfield (Preston) in December 1999 and 32 at Eagland Hill in September 2002 were unusual.

Ruff are relatively scarce in east Lancashire, averaging just over four records annually between 1996 and 2005. Spring birds are exceptional but recent records include one flushed from a small pool on Winter Hill on 6 May 1996, two on Champion Moor on 16-17 May 2001 and nine at Stocks Reservoir on 6 April 2002 with two there on the 19th. 1998 was a particularly good year with nine records totalling 30 birds, including ten at Whitemoor Reservoir on 9 September.

Further north, small numbers use the Wyre and Lune Estuaries and the Pilling-Cockerham area. Large counts include 33 in September 1974, 32 in September 2003 and 27 in August 1986, while up to ten are regular in winter. Ruff are also seen on the Eric Morecambe complex; spring peak counts there include 20 in April 1987 and 33 in May 1994, while the autumn maximum is 24 in September 2003.

Due to a dearth of ringing records, the origin of Lancashire Ruff is largely unknown but they probably come from Fennoscandia and western Russia (Migration Atlas). One relevant recovery was of a male ringed in August 1978 at Hale, just over the border in Cheshire, which was found in late June 1979 in Karelia, north-west Russia, presumably on its breeding grounds. Most winter in Africa, especially Senegal and Mali (Migration Atlas), this being reflected by a passage bird at Marshside on 20 April 1985 that had been colour-dyed and ringed in Senegal in mid-February of the same year.

PHS, MJ.

This species account was sponsored by Malcolm Greenhalgh.

JACK SNIPE

Lymnocryptes minimus

Lancashire Category A.

Fairly common winter visitor from Fennoscandia and northern Russia.

The Jack Snipe is a beautifully camouflaged, skulking wader which does not take flight unless almost trodden on; it must always have been under-recorded. Most sightings are of just one or two birds and double-figure counts are exceptional.

Mitchell described it as a very evenly distributed winter visitor, occasionally in 'great numbers' (e.g. at Tarleton), but far less plentiful than the Common Snipe, with records from the third week of September. His earliest was on 21 August 1878, near St. Michael's-on-Wyre.

Oakes regarded the Jack Snipe as a regular autumn and winter visitor in varying but small numbers, with some evidence of a return movement in February. Normally, arrivals took place in the third week of September; exceptionally, a few were recorded in the second week of that month. August records were rare. The largest group known to Oakes was of twelve shot near St. Michael's on 30-31 October 1896. Fewer birds were seen in spring.

This pattern has continued into modern times. The earliest ever claim was one at Leighton Moss on 7 July 2003. More normally, birds arrive from mid- to late September, an early example being one at The Hile on 1 September 1991. Typically, there is a late autumn influx which varies in scale from year to year, perhaps reflecting weather conditions and predator cycles on the breeding grounds (Migration Atlas). The largest arrival in recent years was in November 2001 when 24 were counted at Tagg's Island, Birkdale, on the 25th, eleven at Lytham St. Anne's NR on the 28th and the same number at Marton Mere at the end of the month. This influx must have had a passage element, as numbers remaining into winter 2002/03 were unexceptional, the largest counts being of three at several sites.

Favoured haunts often retain Jack Snipe throughout the winter. For example, there were seven at Seaforth on 9 January 1998 with up to five remaining until March. Numbers reported in the county each winter increased from about 20 in the mid-1990s to 50+ since 2000, the largest totals being 60+ in 2002/03 and 2003/04. Bearing in mind the likelihood of under-recording, especially in some upland areas, actual numbers wintering in Lancashire must be much higher. Our data belie the general impression that the Jack Snipe is declining internationally.

A newly arrived Jack Snipe, Seaforth Nature Reserve, October 1995. (Steve Young)

In spring, birds have been known to linger until early May. Interestingly, Oakes rejected a record for 9 May 1874 in Princes Park, Liverpool, while Spencer thought that the timing of more recent occurrences made that observation 'reasonably credible'. Late sightings include singletons on 6 May 1996 at Marton Mere, 7 May 1976 at Leighton Moss, 7 May 1978 at Cabin Hill and in Rossendale in the first week of May 1997. The latest ever was at Marshside on 18-19 May 1994. This bird was seen making evening display flights – extraordinary behaviour which has hardly ever been observed in Britain.

Virtually any wetland in our recording area may attract a Jack Snipe or two. In the north, Leighton Moss is, not surprisingly, a major haunt. During the 1970s the usual winter peaks here were of 15 to 20 birds, with a remarkable 40 seen on 17 October 1973. More recently, numbers have generally been in single figures. Carnforth Marsh has also been known to produce counts of up to 14 birds, while as many as ten have been recorded at Little Haweswater, Silverdale. The Wyre and Lune saltmarshes are also worth visiting for Jack Snipe, 13 being flushed on a particularly high tide at Hambleton on 10 March 1997, for example.

Before habitat changes took place in 1984, Lowerhouse Lodges were a favoured site for Jack Snipe, with twelve there on 12 November 1983. Sightings have also been made at Pendle Water, between Brierfield and its confluence with the River Calder. Other regular east Lancashire winter localities include Cowpe Moss in Rossendale, Rishton, Dean Clough and Parsonage Reservoirs, and Lomeshaye and Grove Lane Marshes; five were ringed at Barley on 1 November 2003. The largest count in the West Pennine Moors was nine on Oak Field on 31 January 1992.

On the Fylde, Marton Mere and dune slacks at Lytham St. Anne's NR have been reliable localities for this species, the former site particularly before 1974 when the Mere was enlarged. Maxima here have included 20 or more in autumn 1966, eleven in January 1968 and 15 on spring passage in March 1954. Other reports have come from Myerscough Quarry, including 13 on 13 December 2004, and Carr House Green Common, Inskip, where five or six have been recorded at times. Brockholes Quarry, east of Preston, has become a regular haunt in recent years.

Moving to the south-west, a few are seen most winters at Marshside, the maximum being six in 1984. Other localities include Seaforth, Fazakerley Reedbed and Birkdale Green Beach, where five adults were trapped for ringing in 2002 and up to 15 were counted on 16 November 2003. Unexpectedly, seven birds were flushed from the large slack at Cabin Hill NNR on 29 November 2004. Unusual records from the St. Helens area in 2000 were seven at Lea Green Tip on 5th November and four at Sutton Manor Colliery on 12 November, both sites being reclaimed slag heaps. Nuck's Wood, near Martin Mere, is a recently discovered haunt, with up to five present in November 2004; the largest count at Mere Sands Wood was nine on 5 February 2004.

Our Jack Snipe probably breed in northern Fennoscandia and western Russia but there are few ringing data to support this. The only Lancashire recovery is of a bird ringed at Marton, Blackpool, on 14 October 1962, presumably on passage, which turned up at Ballycastle, Northern Ireland on 12 January 1963. However, there are three relevant recoveries of birds handled just over the border at Astley, Leigh. One ringed here on 6 December 1970 was a road casualty near Oulu, Finland on 26 May 1971, presumably on or near the breeding grounds. Another, marked on passage in eastern Flanders on 17 October 1970, was controlled twice at Astley on 23 January 1972 and 2 December 1972, an excellent example of wintering site fidelity. Finally, an individual ringed at Astley on 21 November 1970 was recovered in Portugal on Christmas Day of the same year. The latter example is indicative of a general south-west movement towards France and Portugal of Jack Snipe ringed in Britain in autumn (Migration Atlas).

PHS, MJ.

This species account was sponsored by Paul Thomason & Peter Carty.

COMMON SNIPE

Gallinago gallinago

Lancashire Category A.

Fairly common breeder; common winter visitor from Iceland, Fennoscandia eastern Europe and Russia.

With its beautifully vermiculated plumage, the Common Snipe is one of the most charismatic marshland birds. Sadly, the numbers of this species in Lancashire have fallen markedly in the late twentieth century, reflecting the national 61% decline in the lowlands from 1982-2002 (Wilson & Vickery 2003).

Mitchell described the Snipe as breeding commonly in many localities, such as the valleys of the Ribble, Hodder and Wyre and on moors bounding them, though mostly below 350m. Numbers were augmented by many migrants in winter and no fewer than 260 were shot at St Michael's-on-Wyre in autumn 1872. Hardy listed many breeding sites in the south-west, finding the Snipe an abundant winter visitor to wetlands; he flushed up to 400 off an acre of the flooded Fazakerley Sewage Farm in hard weather.

By Oakes's time, the Snipe was still an abundant nester on the mosslands, common on the plains, especially on the Fylde, and very common on the moors up to at least 400m. He also mentioned breeding in the dune-slacks of the south-west and on the limestone fell-tops in north Lancashire. However, he noted local decreases in some districts 'due to intensive cultivation'. Spencer (1973) recorded the Snipe as a 'widespread nester' and made no mention of a decline. However, the New Atlas found that breeding occurred in only 33 10km squares, compared with 40 in the Old Atlas.

The Lancashire Atlas confirmed breeding in 33 10km squares and presence in 20% of all tetrads. However, Snipe are known to be under-recorded, especially in the eastern uplands, as often the only sign of their presence emanates from drumming and chipping birds at dusk and dawn. The population was estimated at 450 'pairs', with the West Pennine Moors and Bowland being major strongholds. Survey work in 25km^2 of the West Pennine Moors found the density to vary from 19 pairs in the very dry spring of 1990 to 38 in the wetter spring of 1991. As recently as 2002, six pairs bred at Belmont Reservoir and an additional eight at Belmont village. An RSPB survey in 1998 estimated 184 pairs of Snipe on in-bye land in Bowland.

From being common and widespread in eastern Lancashire, Snipe declined to become a scarce and patchily distributed breeder in the 1990s (Hornby 1994). Thus, in a long-term study of a 100ha CBC plot of upland pasture at The Hile, Rossendale, five to seven pairs bred from 1967 to 1990 – except during 1977-1984, when up to 15 pairs were present after a run of mild winters – falling to three pairs in 1991, perhaps due to a cold winter and spring but also a change from dairying to intensive sheep farming, with drainage and liming of 20% of the study area. None bred there in 1993 for the first time in 44 years.

Away from the moors, a few pairs still breed on lowland wetlands, though numbers have greatly declined during the 1980s and 1990s. For example, at Leighton Moss, up to five pairs nested in the 1960s and early 1970s but only one or two in the 1980s and 1990s. Similar declines have taken place at Marshside, from eight in 1983 and twelve in 1993 to two or three at the end of the 1990s and none since 2001; and at Martin Mere from up to 30 pairs in 1988 to below ten in the 1990s, then five in 2003.

On the Sefton Coast dunes as many as six birds were drumming in the area from Hightown to Ainsdale in 1985 but, ten years later, there was only one, at Cabin Hill NNR, and only the occasional pair now nests in the area. In the Fylde, a pair bred on Lytham St. Anne's LNR dunes in 1970 and a few on Warton Marsh in 1979. Breeding was unproven in the Fylde survey of 1988-1991, though one pair bred on the north Ribble marshes during 1997-2000.

Outside the breeding season, Snipe gather in marshes and other wet places and, although many are no doubt overlooked, there is considerable evidence of a decline in wintering and passage numbers over recent decades.

At Leighton Moss, peak autumn passage occurs in September to November with as many as 800 there in October 1971. Lower numbers are present in winter with a small peak in March. Wintering flocks declined to 100 or fewer in the 1980s and there were only about 45 noted from September to December 1997, followed by more respectable counts of 150-225 from early September to December 1998. Smaller flocks are found at the Eric Morecambe complex, for example 77 in late summer 1995; Heysham NR, including 100 in November 2003, and Middleton Industrial Estate, including 200 on 2 December 2001. There was a high count of 369 Snipe at Arkholme in the Lune Valley in November 1978, while a spring gathering of 76 was recorded there on 13 March 1999.

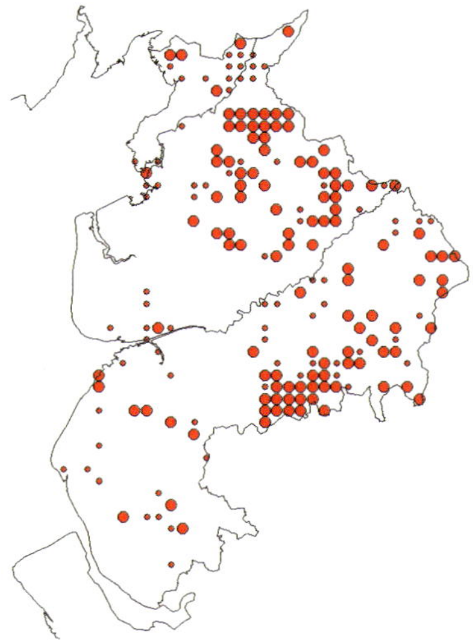

Breeding distribution of Snipe, 1997-2000. (Large dots: confirmed. Small dots: possible)

Favoured haunts in the Fylde include the Freckleton area with as many as 250 present at the Naze Pool in the 1950s, but many fewer in recent years. Other large recent counts have included 222 in February 1995 at Carr House Green Common, Inskip after a very wet winter, 195 in December 1992 at Marton Mere, 134 at Eagland Hill in late autumn 2002 and 259 at Knott End on 14 October 2004.

In east Lancashire counts of 50 or more used to be regular at sites such as Wood End Sewage Works and Lowerhouse Lodges in the 1970s, where single figures are now usual. Low water-levels attract Snipe in groups of 30-60, as in 1995, to the margins of reservoirs, such as Foulridge, Rishton and Dean Clough, though much higher counts were made in the 1960s and 1970s. Grove Lane Marsh, Padiham has been a reliable haunt in recent years with peaks of 69 in February and March 2002 and 96 on 20 November 2004. Wet areas on the West Pennine Moors occasionally produce double-figure counts, including 80 on Cranberry Moss near Entwistle on 7 November 1995, and wintering Snipe are widespread on the in-bye land and lower fells in Bowland.

Impressive counts have been made on the south-west mosslands with Martin Mere being especially favoured, including 500 in July/August 1987 but fewer than 200 by 1994-95. However, this site is still capable of attracting large numbers, for example 480 on 19 September 2003. Large counts at Marshside include 400 in December 1992 and 654 in November 1989, but numbers have slumped since about 1990 (McCarthy 2001); for instance, a peak of just 60 in November 1995. High totals were recorded in wet fields by the River Ribble, south of Preston, in the 1970s and early 1980s, with a maximum of 410 in January 1981, before drainage. Similarly, Altcar Moss held 500 in December 1978 during a period when winter flooding was regular there. Seaforth often holds good numbers late in the year, with 120 in December 1999 and 160 in January 2000; other high Mersey counts include 395 in September at Oglet.

The origins of our passage and wintering Snipe are indicated by 23 exchanges of ringed birds between Lancashire (and Doffcocker Lodge, Bolton just over the border) and continental Europe: five with the former USSR, up to 2,300km to the east; four with Poland and Germany; three with Finland and Holland; two with Sweden and singles with Belgium and Norway. No fewer than 21 have turned up in Ireland between October and February, indicating a strong westerly movement, while five in south-west France, two in Portugal and two in Spain show that some continue southwards.

PHS, MJ.

This species account was sponsored by Jean Roberts.

GREAT SNIPE

Gallinago media

Lancashire Category B. (5, 0).

Vagrant from Fennoscandia and Russia.

The Great Snipe was first described as a species on the basis of a bird shot at Latham around 1787. This type specimen was preserved in the museum of Sir Ashton Lever but was lost when the museum was broken up in 1806.

The species was apparently much commoner in Britain in the nineteenth century and Mitchell knew of over twenty specimens obtained in a period of about twenty years. How many of these were in our present recording area is not known, but H.P. Hornby of St Michael's-on-Wyre is said to have shot several. Oakes gave details of four obtained by Hornby for the St. Michael's Museum which were all shot in the month of September, in 1873, 1879, 1883 and 1917 respectively; the 1917 bird was said to be an adult. These specimens appear to have been lost subsequently but, together with the Latham bird, they are the most plausibly authentic of Lancashire's records.

A further four records were published from our present recording area up to 1948. One was watched in a pasture at Marshside by R. Wagstaffe on 19 March 1926, singles were shot at Leagram on 2 December 1938 and sometime in 1942, and two were seen on marshy land at Higham, near Burnley by P.A. Clancey on 15 February 1948. Spencer added two records: singles seen at Leighton Moss on 20 September 1959 and on the Lune Estuary on 8 November 1959, but the first of these was rejected by the BBRC and the second was not submitted.

There are no other modern records. Identification criteria for Great Snipe have sharpened significantly in recent years and their pattern of occurrence in Britain is now well established, with the overwhelming majority arriving during September; all winter records are now treated with a great deal of scepticism. In the light of this the question should perhaps be asked as to how many of the twentieth century reports were of 'large snipe' rather than Great Snipe?

SJW, MJ.

LONG-BILLED DOWITCHER

Limnodromus scolopaceus

Lancashire Category A. (1, 9).

Vagrant from North America.

In Mitchell and Oakes' time this bird was known as the Red-breasted Snipe, later simply as 'Dowitcher' and later still was split into two species, Long-billed and Short-billed Dowitcher. The early Lancashire records are all assumed to have been Long-billed Dowitchers.

Oakes included a record of one shot 'near Southport' in about September 1873, which went into collection of J.B. Hodgkinson, who later presented it to Preston Museum. Oakes 'square-bracketed' a record of one found by Hodgkinson hanging in a game dealer's shop in Preston in September 1891 on the grounds that its origins were unknown. Hodgkinson had the bird stuffed by a Preston taxidermist and later lent the bird to R.J. Howard.

First-winter Long-billed Dowitcher, Leighton Moss, October 1998. Identification of this bird remained controversial for some time, with some commentators believing it might have been a Short-billed Dowitcher, mostly on account of its very rich plumage tones. (Steve Young)

The first confirmed modern record, a first-winter, was found on 28 October 1951 at Freckleton Sewage Farm (H. Shorrock, A. Harrison, N. Harwood). Another was at the same site from 6 to 10 October 1963 but none was seen during the 1970s.

Our first overwintering bird was found on Banks Marsh on 15 December 1980, was relocated on 6 March 1981 and was seen by many observers until 12 April; first submitted as a 'dowitcher sp.', the BBRC ultimately accepted this bird as a proven Long-billed. An adult that spent a few hours at Marton Mere on the afternoon of 9 September 1989 was the last to be seen in the Fylde.

It was a further nine years before any more were seen but then came a flurry of records. A first-winter was on the Eric Morecambe pools from 5 October 1998 to 1 November and was joined by a second first-winter on 22 October, the latter remaining until 21 April 1999. Another first-winter arrived at Marshside on 19 November 1998 and stayed until 14 May 1999. Echoing the earlier Leighton Moss records, two were found at Seaforth the following year. The first, in almost full juvenile plumage, arrived on 17 October 2000 and stayed until at least the 28th, when two were seen together; the second bird, more advanced in moult, was seen daily until 6 April 2001 and then reappeared in full breeding plumage for one day only on 22 April.

All records:

1873	Southport area, one shot, about September
1951	Freckleton, first-winter, 28 October
1963	Freckleton, one, 6 to 10 October
1980	Banks Marsh, one, 15 December to 12 March 1981
1989	Marton Mere, adult, 9 September
1998	Leighton Moss, first-winter, 5 October to 1 November
1998	Leighton Moss, first-winter, 22 October to 21 April 1999
1998	Marshside, first-winter, 19 November to 14 May 1999
2000	Seaforth, first-winter, 17 to 28 October
2000	Seaforth, first-winter, 28 October to 22 April 2001

SJW, MJ.

This species account was sponsored by the Fylde Bird Club.

WOODCOCK

Scolopax rusticola

Lancashire Category A.

Fairly common breeder and winter visitor from Fennoscandia and Russia.

The elusive Woodcock is one of our most mysterious birds. A woodland wader, it is most frequently observed during crepuscular display flight or silently weaving through the trees when disturbed. Folklore links its migrations with the moon, accounts of the bird carrying its young add to its mystique and it was once even thought that the species' summer months of absence were spent on the moon (Greenoak 1997).

In Lancashire as elsewhere, breeding Woodcock prefer wet deciduous or mixed woodland although conifer plantations and bracken beds are frequently occupied. They favour large woods with frequent clearings and a dense understorey adjacent to worm-rich pastures, where they feed at night on earthworms.

The crepuscular display flight of the male, conspicuous over its breeding territory, provides the easiest way to assess breeding numbers, but counts of roding males, which may mate successively with up to four females, may significantly underestimate the true breeding population.

It is thought that the British population has been in moderate decline for the past 25 years but little is known about trends in the Lancashire population, which was estimated at 300 'pairs' in 1997-2000. The Lancashire breeding range appears to have shrunk a little over the past 30 years, breeding being suspected in 39 10km squares in 1968-72, 24 in 1988-91 and 34 in 1997-2000, when roding males were found in 146 (16%) tetrads. However, the Atlas Survey is known to have been deficient in censusing nocturnal species and both the distribution and population size were almost certainly underestimated.

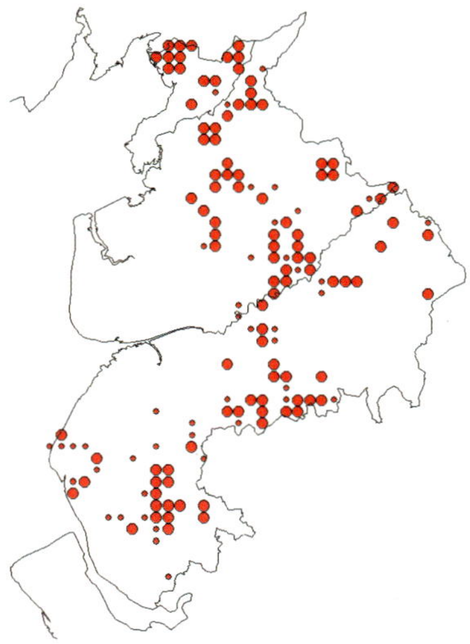

Breeding distribution of Woodcock, 1997-2000. (Large dots: confirmed. Small dots: possible)

Mitchell reported regular breeding during the late nineteenth century, giving Silverdale, Bleasdale, Whitewell, Balderstone, Langho, Sabden and Bashall Eaves as examples of nesting sites. The vogue for woodland planting, mainly as Pheasant covert, assisted range expansion from the mid-nineteenth century and breeding was widespread by the Second World War, with Oakes and Battersby (1939) citing eleven pairs in the Whalley-Clitheroe area in 1934 and Hardy (1941) listing 13 nesting locations in North Merseyside and West Lancashire. Oakes (1953) reported that nesting was regular in Lunesdale and in the upper Wyre and Ribble Valleys, whilst elsewhere in the county breeding status ranged from locally common to scarce and irregular. Hardy (1979) reported 40 'pairs' breeding in the 8 km^2 Knowsley Park in 1957 and 30+ in 1975.

The present-day distribution ranges from Little Crosby and Croxteth Park in the Liverpool hinterland through the south-west mosses, West Pennine Moors, Ribble and Hodder Valleys, the Bowland valleys and fringe, to the Lune Valley and the limestone woodlands of Silverdale. Only the Fylde and large areas of Rossendale and the mosses south of the Ribble Estuary lack breeding birds, presumably due to the lack of sizeable woodlands. Concentrations of roding males include twelve in the Belmont/Delph/Entwistle area in 1989, nine in the Gisburn Forest in 1982, up to eight on Mossborough/Reed's Moss in 2003, seven in the Douglas Valley in 1991, six at Stocks Reservoir in 1998 and five at Rivington in 1998. A survey of the 213ha mixed woodland at Roddlesworth Plantations in 2003 plotted 28 distinct roding circuits, leading to an estimate of ten roding males. Roding activity was observed to start at between five and 20 minutes after sunset and cease at between 25 to 35 minutes after sunset (Martin 2003).

Tony Disley

Although the majority of British breeders are highly sedentary, some do migrate. Extensive ringing of young at Abbeystead, reported by Oakes, resulted in four winter recoveries in southern Ireland, three in Wales and one in Devon. Small numbers seen in non-breeding areas in Lancashire during September may relate to British birds but the population of resident birds is swelled by much larger numbers of immigrants from continental Europe during October and early November, the latter outnumbering the former by about 13:1 in midwinter (Migration Atlas). Extrapolation of the absolute minimum of 600 residents would result in an estimated Lancashire wintering population in excess of 7,800 birds, out of an estimated British winter population of 800,000 (Hirons & Linsley 1989).

Incoming migrants may be temporarily grounded almost anywhere, with Lancashire records from the high fells, suburban gardens, urban parks, town centres, docklands, saltmarshes and even under parked cars and on the roof of Blackpool Tower. Notable 'falls' have included over 50 flushed along the summit of Anglezarke Moor in November 1950. There have been two movements of ringed birds between Lancashire and Norway, one from Germany and two exchanges with Russia, the furthest of these one ringed near Preston in February 1991 and shot near Gorky, 3,000km to the east, on 14 July 1992.

Woodcock are commonly seen in woodlands throughout the county in winter with, for example, over 100 reported in 1991. Multiple sightings include 13 at Mere Sands Wood in February 1999, 12+ at Stocks Reservoir in November 1985, twelve at Marton Mere in January 1984 and occasionally up to 20 in Barrow Scout Wood, Warton. However, the largest counts come from bag-records or reports of birds flushed during Pheasant shoots. Illustrative records include 48 shot in six days at Abbeystead in November and December 1909 (Percy 1986), an annual average of 70 shot in Knowsley Park during 1810-18 and 60-200 after the Second World War (Hardy 1979), 27 shot at Ince Blundell during 1979/80 and 32 on Formby Moss in 1980/81. Beaters have regularly put up day-totals of 30-40 in various woodlands in the West Pennine Moors, including Delph Plantations and Longworth Clough, while more than 50 have been driven from rhododendron thickets at Hill Top, Belmont on several occasions between 1984 and 2001.

SJM, MJ.

This species account was sponsored by Stuart Meredith and T. Pearman.

BLACK-TAILED GODWIT

Limosa limosa

Lancashire Category A.

Rare breeder; abundant passage migrant and winter visitor from Iceland.

This elegant long-billed wader has increased exponentially in numbers in Lancashire during the second half of the twentieth century, reflecting an upsurge in the Icelandic breeding population which has been attributed to climatic amelioration.

Mitchell spoke of small numbers on the Lune Estuary, leaving by the end of October. Singles were shot at St. Michael's-on-Wyre in September 1873 and 1882, and three were seen there on 11 September 1882. He also had one Formby record, but none had been reported in spring.

Oakes knew of records in every month with a well marked spring passage from March to early May and a stronger autumn movement commencing in mid-July and reaching a peak in early September. The spring influx was first noted by T.S. Williams in the Formby area from 1922 to 1926; he estimated just over 100 birds on the flooded Formby Moss in March 1923. There were also occasional sightings of non-breeding birds in June, for instance, a party of nine 'immatures' flushed by F.W. Holder near Martin Mere on 1 June 1920. The largest autumn counts were 80 at Shard Bridge on the Wyre in September 1944 and 145 at Lytham in September 1948, then the county record. The Black-tailed Godwit was irregular on the coast as a wintering bird, numbers usually being small, though a flock of 50 was seen near Fleetwood on 27 January 1947.

The first documented breeding in Lancashire came in 1984 when two chicks were seen on a reclaimed Ribble salt-marsh. Three pairs were present in 1985, one pair rearing two young. In 1988, adults were present during the breeding season on Newton Marsh and nesting, with varying degrees of success, has taken place each year since then to the present day. Chicks hatched in 1996 but were thought to have succumbed to wet weather. Fledging certainly occurred in 1997 and in 2000 three chicks were seen up to a week after hatching. Then in 2003 to 2005 two pairs bred, fledging up to three young each. Egg-collectors took clutches in 1996, 1998 and 1999 but the site has been wardened since 2000. The Newton Marsh breeders are of the continental sub-species *limosa*, rather than Icelandic *islandica* which makes up the bulk of passage and wintering birds in Britain.

The number of birds in Lancashire outside the breeding season has increased enormously since the 1960s. The Ribble Estuary has always been predominant and is the second most important site in the UK, after the Wash, for Black-tailed Godwits both in winter and on passage. Small groups of non-breeding birds are seen during summer – although up to 400 summered at Marshside during the late 1990s – but a trickle of returning adults gets underway at the end of June prior to the main passage from the second half of July. Peak numbers usually occur during August and September, declining on average by a half during October, then usually remaining fairly constant throughout winter before a generally small but distinct spring passage in March and early April (Figure 1).

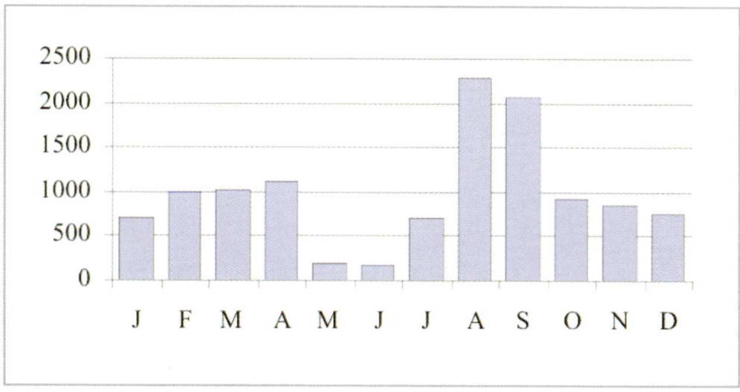

Figure 1. Average monthly peak counts of Black-tailed Godwits on the Ribble & Alt Estuaries and Morecambe Bay South (WeBS), 1985-2005.

Throughout the 1960s and 1970s the largest counts were on the north bank of the Ribble, especially at Lytham and Fairhaven, which had autumn peaks of 1,500 in 1969 and 2,500 in 1976, rising to 4,000, mainly on Warton Marsh in the mid-1980s. Winter numbers also rose during the same period from peaks of 450 in December 1964 to 2,400 in December 1980. In the early 1980s, however, Marshside began to rival the north Ribble sites, registering a maximum autumn count of 2,700 in October 1987 and 3,250 in January 2005. Combined north and south Ribble totals continued to rise throughout the 1990s (Figure 2) particularly in winter, including an notable counts of 4,310 in December 1998 and 1,600 at Lytham alone in February 2000. The size of the spring passage is highly variable (and is often missed by the one-day WeBS counts) but recent high counts have included 1,250 on Newton Marsh in April 1994 and 4,400 at Marshside in April 1998.

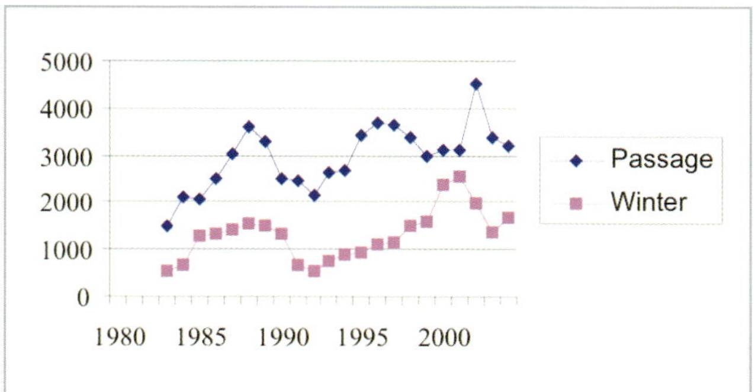

Figure 2. Peak annual counts of Black-tailed Godwits (3-year rolling means) on the Ribble & Alt Estuaries and Morecambe Bay South (WeBS), 1981-2005.

No other Lancashire site comes close to the Ribble Estuary in importance. Numbers using the Wyre Estuary began to increase in the mid-1980s, especially in spring, when large counts included over 500 in 1993, 591 in 1994 and 400 in 1997, with notable autumn counts of 375 in October 1988 and 420 in August 2004; an exceptional 100 birds wintered at Skippool Creek in 2002. Wyre birds occasionally wander as far as Pilling which had a record count of 862 in April 1999. Six hundred and fifty-six were on a flood at Mythop on 28 August 2004. Significant numbers also occur from time to time on the Lune Estuary, including flocks of 200 or so at Bank End, Cockerham on several occasions in autumn and winter 1998 and 2003-2004 and 500 at Cockersands and Glasson in December 2004. Further north, the Eric Morecambe complex is increasingly used, the largest counts being 358 in December 2003 and 660 in April 2005.

Male Icelandic Black-tailed Godwit, Marshside, June 2005. (Chris Galvin)

Although the Mersey Estuary is also internationally important, large numbers are rarely seen on the Lancashire side of the river, exceptions being 131 on the early date of 23 June 2001 which built to 665 by 12 July, and 222 in April 2002. Seaforth is the main site on the Alt but rarely holds more than 100 birds, 750 roosting over the tide on 17 September 1998 being wholly exceptional.

Significant numbers began to appear at Martin Mere during the 1980s. Peaks included 400 on 5 November 1982, 300 in July 1985, 250 in spring 1989 and 320 in October 1988. However, numbers declined to 100 or fewer, mostly in April to July during the 1990s with 380 in April 2005 the only large recent count.

Black-tailed Godwits are scarce in east Lancashire, recorded from many sites but usually as singles or small parties of fewer than ten. Exceptional records were 45 over Stocks Reservoir on 22 April 1998 and 60 at the same site on 28 April 2001. Brockholes Quarry on the Ribble east of Preston began to record significant numbers at the end of the 1990s, especially during spring. Counts of 130 on 31 March 2000 and 305 on 27 April 2001 represent the high points of what appears to be a regular cross-country passage following the course of the Ribble.

Virtually all British wintering Black-tailed Godwits are of the race *islandica* and there are five recorded movements between

Lancashire and their Icelandic breeding grounds. The earliest was ringed on Banks Marsh in August 1985 and recovered at Myvatn in July 1991. Four colour-ringed birds – two ringed in Iceland, and singles ringed in France and on the Wash and also seen in Iceland – have also been sighted in the county since 2001. Seven ringed on autumn passage on the Wash have been recovered at various seasons in Lancashire; these, together with multiple sightings of colour-ringed birds in Britain, Ireland, France and Holland, strongly suggesting that individuals do not use fixed wintering areas or migration routes.

PHS, MJ.

This species account was sponsored by Carol Coupe and John and Mary Almond.

BAR-TAILED GODWIT

Limosa lapponica

Lancashire Category A.

Abundant winter visitor from northern Fennoscandia, western Russia and Siberia.

Rarely seen inland, the Arctic-breeding Bar-tailed Godwit is a long-distance migrant which resorts to large, sandy estuaries both on passage and in winter. Our birds are thought to originate from the Fennoscandian and western Russian breeding population (Migration Atlas). In Lancashire, the Ribble and Alt Estuaries and Morecambe Bay are favoured haunts, being respectively the second, fourth and seventh most important British sites for this species.

The movements of Bar-tailed Godwits in Lancashire have been studied for many years (e.g. Prater 1981; Smith & Greenhalgh 1977; Wilson 1973). The first returning migrants in mid-July are mostly adults, many still in summer plumage. These remain to moult, the Ribble being one of their most important moulting areas in Britain. Later influxes, peaking in September/October, include juveniles and already moulted adults.

Fluctuations in numbers during autumn may reflect movements between estuaries. For example Smith & Greenhalgh (1977) and Wilson (1973) pointed out that a November decline in Ribble birds coincided with an influx to Morecambe Bay, implying a northwards movement. More recently, this trend has been less clear, suggesting that some Ribble birds move elsewhere, perhaps to the north Wirral shore or even to African winter quarters. Winter numbers tend to be more or less stable with a departure in March/April, probably to the Waddensee on the Dutch coast, where birds undergo a partial moult and fatten up for their return migration to the tundra of northern Eurasia (Prater 1981). Some non-breeding first-summer birds in winter plumage remain on our shores for the summer. One hypothesis is that these are birds that have wintered in West Africa and are making a partial return migration. However, there are no ringing data to test this.

Some of the earliest detailed observations of Bar-tailed Godwits in our area were made in the 1920s and 1930s on the south Ribble marshes (Holder & Wagstaffe 1930a). Then the autumn influx rarely exceeded 200, while the winter population from 1921 to 1929 was only 200-300 birds; the largest counts of up to 2,000 (Birkdale on 8 March 1931) were invariably made in March/April. Then as now, summer flocks of 'grey birds' were a notable feature of the Ribble shore, having been first seen by Holder in 1918. He remarked that they spent most of their time in dune-slacks, his highest count being 156 on 1 June 1942 (Oakes 1953). Interestingly, summering Bar-tailed Godwits also roost regularly on freshwater at Seaforth but never do so in winter.

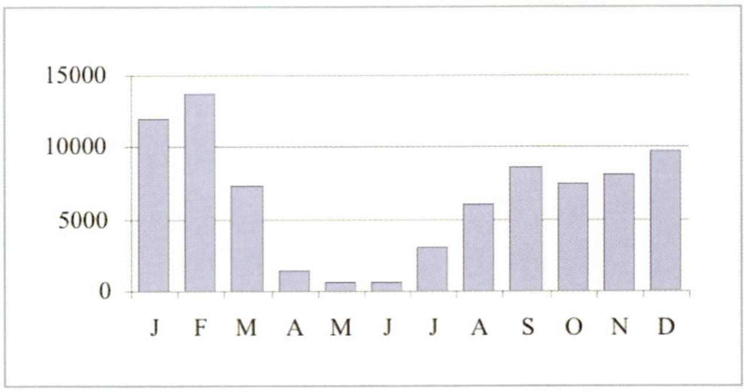

Figure 1. Average monthly peak counts of Bar-tailed Godwits (WeBS) on the Ribble & Alt Estuaries and Morecambe Bay South, 1985-2005.

Beginning in the 1950s, more frequent counts of wader flocks revealed increasing numbers on our coast, with peaks of 2,000 at Ainsdale and 1,000 at St. Anne's during that decade. In February 1963, 2,100 were reported in Morecambe Bay, while 3,000 were at Pilling in September 1967. Smith & Greenhalgh's (1977) maximum on the Ribble was a remarkable 11,600 in August 1973, most being on the south side. In his study from 1967 to 1970, Wilson (1973) reported a winter population of around 7,000 in Morecambe Bay, all but about 550 roosting on the Lune Estuary. His autumn peak was 4,000-5,000 in mid-August.

Breeding-plumaged Bar-tailed Godwits, Crosby Shore, August 2004. (Steve Young)

On the Alt Estuary, Kirby *et al.* (1988) recorded a rapid and spectacular increase in wintering numbers from about 1974 to 1986, reaching nearly 12,000 in the latter year. During the period 1982/83 to 1986/87, the mean winter peak here was 7,077, equivalent to 1.3% of the European and 11.6% of the British population. However, it was suggested that this trend was, in part, due to birds that feed on the Cheshire Dee and north Wirral shore changing their behaviour to roost on Taylor's Bank on the Alt. This supported evidence obtained elsewhere that the Bar-tailed Godwit is a particularly mobile wader, prepared to fly long distances to find a secure roost.

In more recent times, the Morecambe Bay wintering population declined from 6,000-7,000 in the 1970s to 3,000-4,000 in the 1980s, with the Hest Bank roost much less favoured than formerly. A count of 320 there on 22 December 1999 was the highest for some years. The Lune and Wyre, however, retained good numbers with, for example, 4,010 counted at Thurnham on 6 December 1998 and 1,200 at Preesall Sands on 12 October 1997. Up to 1,000 occurred in the Heysham/Sunderland Point area early in 1999, while 830 were counted at Glasson Marsh on 3 January 1999.

On the Ribble, St. Anne's beach, which regularly held roosts of 2,000 or more in the 1970s and 1980s, has become much less used, the highest count for some years being 452 on 15 August 1999. Meanwhile, the south Ribble has gone from strength to strength with 5,300 at Marshside on 9 January 2001 and an exceptional 12,000 at Ainsdale on 19 August 2001.

The Alt population has also remained high, as evidenced by feeding flocks at Formby of 2,400 on 31 July and 2,700 on 16 August 2003. Following much accretion of intertidal mudflats, Crosby shore has become an important feeding area, with 3,000 here on 31 December 2002 the largest of several impressive counts. Summering flocks continue to be a feature of the south-west, including at Seaforth, where between 400 and 700 birds regularly roosted in June during the late 1990s. Another notable flock was of 700 non-breeding-plumaged birds on Warton Bank on 28 June 2003.

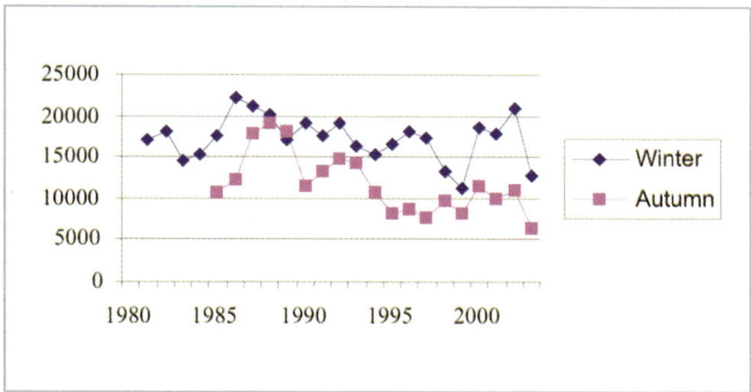

Figure 2. Peak winter and autumn counts of Bar-tailed Godwits (3-year rolling means) on the Ribble & Alt Estuaries and Morecambe Bay South, 1978/79 to 2004/05.

The outstanding international importance of the Ribble and Alt Estuaries for the Bar-tailed Godwit is illustrated by the WeBS counts (Figure 2); combined numbers wintering on the two estuaries have on occasion reached 25,000 birds. Morecambe Bay has declined as a passage location but wintering numbers held up quite well from 1992 to 2003, usually exceeding the qualification level for international importance of 1,000. All the WeBS data show striking fluctuations in both passage and winter counts. BWP suggests that such cycles of abundance are linked to higher nest predation in non-lemming years on the Arctic tundra.

Very small numbers, usually in single figures, are recorded at inland localities. Recent sites have included Belmont, Brockholes Quarry, Martin Mere, Marton Mere, Mere Sands Wood and Rishton, Stocks, Clowbridge, Dean Clough, Barnacre, Sunnyhurst and Wayoh Reservoirs. Two flocks totalling 40 birds were at Belmont Reservoir on 9 September 1979.

There have been relatively few ringing recoveries of Bar-tailed Godwits involving Lancashire. The most interesting are two ringed on passage at Crossens in August 1980 which were retrapped on one of the African winter quarters, in Guinea-Bissau, in March 1988. This may be where some of the 'missing' early-autumn birds from the Ribble go. Most other recoveries have been local. A particularly long-lived bird was one marked at Southport in February 1972 which was found dead at Blackpool 21 years later in January 1993.

PHS, MJ.

This species account was sponsored by Ron Hothersall.

WHIMBREL

Numenius phaeopus

Lancashire Category A.

Common passage migrant, especially in spring en route to Scotland and Iceland.

With its distinctive bubbling call, this smaller, shorter-billed version of the Curlew has long been a familiar passage migrant in western parts of Lancashire, always much more numerous in spring than autumn. Mitchell noted 'considerable flocks' in May, particularly frequenting pastures near the coast, with fewer on the shore itself.

Oakes noted that most Whimbrel passed through Lancashire between 22 April and 15 May, with stragglers until 22 May, and a few remaining into the first eight days of June. Thus, F.W. Holder saw seven at Martin Mere on 1 June 1916. Autumn return began in July, with most sightings in August. Surprisingly, the largest county flock was in autumn, 80 being counted by Holder at Ainsdale on 12 August 1920. Spencer cited early migrants from mid-March and remarked that mid-June records were, by then, almost annual. He also reported two December sightings in 1958.

In more recent decades, the numbers of Whimbrel counted annually in the county have greatly increased, reflecting an international trend which BWP attributes to climatic change and legal protection. As in the past, most are seen in spring, the earliest bird on record being one at Leighton Moss on 11 March 1978 but the average first date over the past 25 years is 15 April.

On the whole, spring passage Whimbrel, as noted by Mitchell, do not particularly favour the coast but usually stop off to feed on damp pastures, cereal fields and, sometimes, ploughed land. Traditional sites include the south-west mosses near Formby, mossland near Nateby, Eagland Hill and Winmarleigh in the Fylde, Red Scar and Elston in the Ribble Valley and the Beacon Fell/Calder Vale area. Some examples of large feeding flocks were 92 on 25 April 1994 at North Moss Lane, Formby with 62 on the nearby Plex Moss two days earlier; 106 at Downholland Moss on 28 April 1992; 200 at Red Scar on 24 April 1993; 122 at Eagland Hill/Nateby on 29 April 1984; 50 on Pilling Moss on 6 May 1976; 100 near the Brock Valley on 3 May 1997 and 180 at Waterside Farm, Fylde on 1 May 2005. Surprisingly large numbers for the coast were 126 on the Morecambe Bay WeBS count in May 2000 and a reserve record of 81 flying over Seaforth on 24 April 2002.

A dramatic development has been the recent discovery of large evening roosts in late April and early May, the first of which was found at Barnacre Reservoir near Scorton where 120 birds were counted on 5 May 1989. In subsequent years, regular visits were made to this site and spectacular numbers were recorded (Table 1), the largest count being 945 on 29 April 1994.

Whimbrel, Seaforth Nature Reserve, May 1995. (Steve Young)

Observations of dusk flights downriver in the Red Scar area of Preston preceded the discovery in 1992 of another roost at Longton Marsh on the Ribble Estuary; the peak here was 761 on 29 April 1996 but access has become difficult in recent years and few counts have been possible. Birds heading for this roost overfly Preston and then fly low over the Ribble channel west of the dock; a small proportion comes in from the north. Windy Harbour at Little Singleton on the Wyre Estuary was identified as a regular roost in 1992 after 223 birds were seen on 5 May. The largest count was of 455 on 1 May 1996 but numbers have declined enormously this century. Finally, Brockholes Quarry on the Ribble east of Preston began to be used in 1999, the highest count there being 401 on 1 May 2003, when 654 were also present at Barnacre, producing a total of 1,055 – an order of magnitude larger than any other known Whimbrel roost in Britain.

These spring assemblies occur essentially simultaneously with the first roosts usually occurring around the third week of April and most birds leaving by the second week of May; the largest numbers are usually present between the last week of April and the first week of May. There is no evidence of any movement of birds between roosts and it is likely that each site is linked to a particular broad feeding area. Combined peak counts in years when all roosts were monitored range from 1,066 to 1,918 but it is likely that more than this use these sites at some time during the spring passage. Spring staging posts are crucial for building up fat reserves to complete the migration back to the breeding areas (Migration Atlas) and the Lancashire farmland where the birds feed is clearly of considerable conservation importance.

Table 1. Peak counts of Whimbrel at spring roosts in Lancashire

	Barnacre Reservoir	Longton Marsh	Windy Harbour	Brockholes Quarry	Combined Peak
1990	491	No count	No count		491
1991	640	No count	No count		640
1992	823	296	223		1342
1993	775	421	No count		1196
1994	945	545	428		1918
1995	668	735	263		1666
1996	409	761	455		1625
1997	651	669	276		1596
1998	847	612	200		1659
1999	476	392	No count	110	978
2000	215	533	118	200	1066
2001	509	No count	88	234	831
2002	236	313	33	186	768
2003	654	No count	32	401	1087
2004	575	No count	28	329	932
2005	553	No count	No count	289	842

A few June records are submitted in most years but it is not clear whether these are late spring migrants, early returning individuals or even summering birds; most are single birds but three were at Jenny Brown's Point on 7 & 9 June 2001.

The timing and extent of the autumn passage is similar to that described by Oakes, numbers being much lower than in spring and tending to favour the coastline and estuaries. Arrivals begin in mid-July, these being mainly failed breeders or females which often desert their young a few days before fledging (Migration Atlas). The bulk of the passage takes place in August and few are seen after early September; the average last sighting since 1978 was 16 September. The largest recent flocks were 45 at Banks Marsh on 13 July 1976, 33 at Parsonage Reservoir on 27 July 1988 and a Morecambe Bay WeBS total of 67 in August 2000.

Winter sightings of Whimbrel remain rare. McCarthy (2001) reported single birds at Marshside on 8 December 1979, 4 November 1982, 31 December 1998 and 1 January 1999.

Very few are seen in eastern parts of Lancashire but sites reporting small numbers of birds in recent years include Altham, Anglezarke, Belmont, Burnley, Coldwell, Darwen Moor, Delph Reservoir, Fishmoor, Foulridge, Great Hill (West Pennines), Higherford, Oswaldtwistle Moor, Parsonage Reservoir., Rishton, Stocks Reservoir and Worsthorne.

The vast majority of British passage Whimbrel breed in Iceland, the Faroes, Fennoscandia and north-west Russia, with Icelandic birds more prevalent in western Britain (Migration Atlas). Two Lancashire (or nearby) ringing recoveries support this: a bird ringed at Husavik, Iceland in July 1929 and recovered 'near Manchester' on 26 April 1931, and an adult female marked in Iceland on 13 June 1997 and read in the field at Brockholes on 24 April 2003. These birds would have been *en route* to or from their winter quarters in West Africa. An individual at Scorton on 25 April 1992 had been colour-ringed on Fetlar, Shetland in June 1987 and was seen there subsequently in summer 1988 and 1989, so some, at least, of our passage birds belong to the Shetland breeding population of 400-500 pairs.

PHS, MJ.

This species account was sponsored by the Fylde Bird Club.

CURLEW

Numenius arquata

Lancashire Category A.

Abundant breeder and winter visitor from continental Europe.

With its remarkable bill and characteristic voice, our largest wader has long been a familiar sight and sound in the Lancashire countryside. In the nineteenth century, the Curlew bred plentifully on the fells. It was also a fairly regular breeder on low-lying mosses, such as Cockerham, according to Mitchell. Hardy recorded it nesting at Simonswood Moss near Liverpool in 1937 with two pairs on Halsall Moss in 1940.

By Oakes's time, breeding also took place on many coastal mosslands in the Fylde and south Lancashire, as well as rough lowland meadows adjacent to hill-country. Spencer cited nesting records throughout Lancashire, though thinly distributed in the west and south-west, and this statement remains broadly applicable today.

In the north, one or two pairs nest in the valley of the River Keer, with one pair on the Morecambe Bay Reserve in most years since 1984. The Waterways Bird Survey found 10-16 pairs in the Lune Valley between Skerton Weir and Leck Beck in the 1980s and 1990s while counts at Arkholme between 1991 and 1995 peaked at 15 pairs.

The Bowland breeding population seems to have increased recently. Thus, in 1982 300 pairs were estimated in 70 km^2 of North-West Water's land in Bowland, a density of 4.3 pairs per km^2, while an RSPB survey of in-bye land in Bowland in 1998 detected a remarkable 2,843 pairs at a density of 6.7 pairs per km^2. Breeding density on moorland tends to be lower, for example 35 pairs nested on $28km^2$ of moorland around Belmont in 2002.

Six pairs of Curlew bred in eastern Fylde in 1984 and three pairs on Winmarleigh Moss in 1983. However, few nest in the western half of the Fylde, although there seems to have been a recent increase in coastal areas, with presence in eight tetrads and breeding in two others (Lancashire Atlas), compared with presence in only five tetrads in the Fylde Atlas.

In eastern Lancashire the Curlew breeds both on moorland and in the larger hay-fields at lower elevations. The Lancashire Atlas found breeding birds to be almost ubiquitous in the Burnley/Colne area. During 1967-1991, between one and three pairs bred on 100ha of upland pasture at The Hile, Rossendale, while in the whole of Rossendale 17-29 pairs bred from the mid-1990s to 2002.

The south-west plain and mosslands support few breeding Curlew. A pair nested at Martin Mere in 1968 and another at Simonswood Moss in 1973. The Old Atlas reported breeding from three 10km squares in the south-west but none was recorded in the New Atlas, nor was breeding confirmed in the Lancashire Atlas.

Overall, the Lancashire Atlas estimated 4,500 breeding pairs of Curlew in 449 tetrads. Although the RSPB estimates a 39% decline of Curlew nesting on lowland grassland in the UK between 1982 and 2002, this does not seem to have been the case in Lancashire, and in the south Pennines as a whole, including areas outside of Lancashire, the population increased by an estimated 108% between 1990 and 2002 (Simm *et al.* 2005).

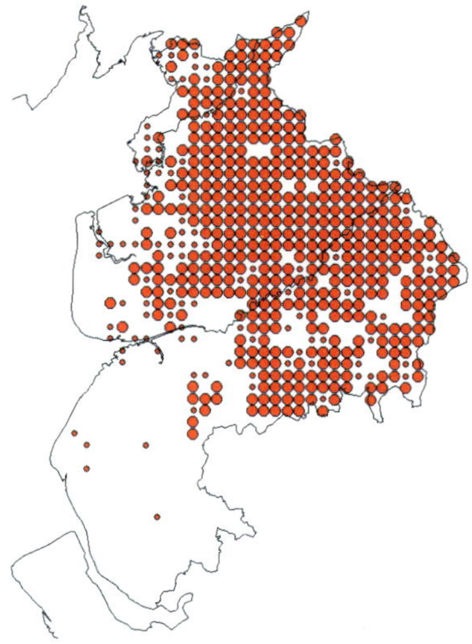

Breeding distribution of Curlew, 1997-2000. (Large dots: confirmed. Small dots: possible)

Movements away from the breeding areas occur mainly during the evenings from the end of June. The moors are deserted in July and, although most birds probably head directly to the coast, others assemble in fields near reservoirs and along rivers. Impressive post-breeding flocks often gather in the Lune Valley, especially near Arkholme, where 2,500 were counted in July 1985. At Simonswood Moss, a strong passage of 500 moving west was noted in the evening of 12 August 1957.

Coastal arrivals also take place from late June onwards. A group of 1,000 on the Keer Estuary on 11 June 1967 may have included some summering birds but numbers increased to 1,900 by the 25th. Further large counts at this site were 5,000 in July 1968, 7,000 in August 1977 and 9,600 in August 1981 but this early influx has declined to about 2,500 in recent years.

Curlew, Eric Morecambe complex. (Phillip Tomkinson)

Peak numbers on the coast are usually seen in August/September, especially on the southern shores of Morecambe Bay, which is the most important passage and wintering area in the UK. High autumn counts include 3,000-4,000 at Cockerham on 20 September 1962, 3,685 on Morecambe Bay Reserve on 14 July 2003, 7,500 at Cockersands on 26 August 2002 and 5,100 at Pilling-Cockerham on 21 August.

Numbers slowly decline until the winter level is reached in late November (Figure 1). Field feeding is a feature at this time with, for example, flocks of 600 at Preesall on 16 November 2001 and 700 near Pilling Lane Ends on 12 December 2003. Morecambe Bay WeBS counts showed the average winter population increasing from about 4,600 in 1995 to 10,400 in 2000, followed by a sharp decline to 4,000-5,000 since 2002. (Figure 2).

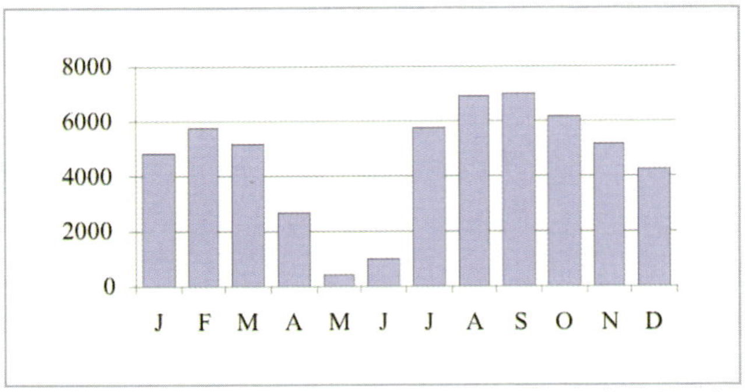

Figure 1. Average monthly peak counts of Curlews on the Ribble & Alt Estuaries and Morecambe Bay South, 1985-2005.

A small spring influx to the coast occurs from mid to late February, reaching a peak in late March or early April (Wilson 1973). Notable recent totals include 5,198 on the Morecambe Bay Reserve in March 2002 and 2,445 at the same site in March 2003. At this time, large numbers of Curlews are moving inland towards the breeding areas. Thus, 1,200 passage birds were noted at Arkholme in the Lune Valley on 12 March 2000 and 800 on 27 February 2002. Many other sites further east record sizeable numbers in early March, the largest recent flocks being 1,000 at Whitemoor Reservoir on 6 March 1997 and 500 by the Ribble at Hurst Green on 1 March 2000. On Morecambe Bay numbers decline rapidly in April and May but there are often summering flocks in June, exceptionally totalling up to 1,500. Trends in WeBS counts during passage periods in Morecambe Bay are similar to those in winter with an increase from 6,500 to 9,000 during the 1990s, and a fall to 5,000-6,500 in the 2000s.

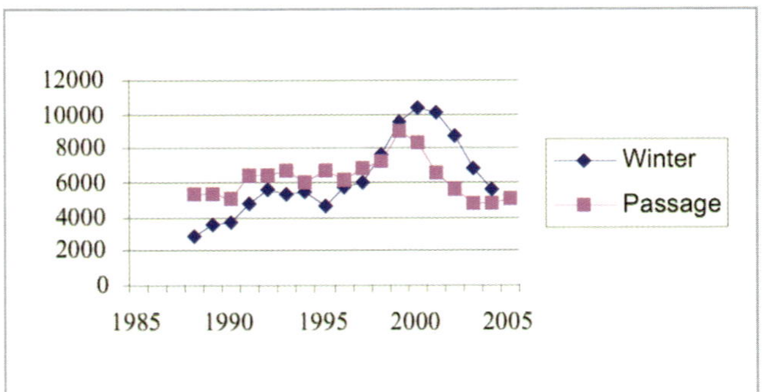

Figure 2. Peak winter and passage counts (3-year rolling means) of Curlews on Morecambe Bay South, 1986-2005.

The Ribble Estuary supports far fewer Curlews, though the pattern of occurrence is similar to that on Morecambe Bay. Smith & Greenhalgh's largest count was of 1,400 in July 1973 and they estimated that the midwinter population was often less than 300. Recent WeBS counts show some increase since the 1970s, with average winter numbers rising from about 350 in 1980 to 2,000 in 1999, followed by a decline to 1,500 or less since 2002. Similarly, average passage totals showed a steady increase from 1981 (200) to 1995 (2,300), after which numbers had fallen to about 1,200 by 2005.

Kirby *et al.* (1988) recorded a winter population on the Alt Estuary of 400-800 during the early to mid-1970s, followed by a decline to about 200 in the early 1980s. Since then, WeBS counts have shown a progressive increase, especially in passage flocks which reached an average peak of 1,400 this century. Mean winter figures were more or less stable at 200-400 in the 1980s, but rose progressively to 1,200-1,400 this century. Inland feeding occurs on the south-west mosslands, such as Altcar Moss, where 200 Curlew were reported at the end of 1999. Completing the picture, around 200 birds are regularly reported at Oglet on the Mersey, both in winter and on passage.

Curlew are mostly migratory; although some British breeders winter close to the breeding area, a majority moves south-west (BWP). There are twelve recorded movements between Lancashire and Ireland and 13 exchanges with Wales but, interestingly, only two with southern England. There are also two winter recoveries in France of birds ringed in Lancashire during the breeding season. A majority of our wintering Curlew are likely to come either from elsewhere in northern Britain – there are 21 recoveries from northern England and one from Scotland – or from Europe. Birds marked locally in winter have turned up in the breeding season in Germany (three), Netherlands (one), Denmark (one), Finland (seven) and Sweden (two). Similarly, of birds ringed abroad and recovered in Lancashire, seven came from Finland, two from Sweden, two from Germany, one from the Netherlands and one from south-west France.

PHS, MJ.

This species account was sponsored by Bernard and Ruth Pollock, Anne Selby and the East Lancashire Ornithologists Club.

SPOTTED REDSHANK

Tringa erythropus

Lancashire Category A.

Fairly common passage migrant and uncommon winter visitor from northern Fennoscandia and Russia.

Spotted Redshanks breed in the boreal zone from northern Scandinavia eastwards across Russia and occur in Lancashire as passage migrants, more numerous in autumn than in spring, and occasionally in winter.

This was apparently a rare species in the nineteenth century, Mitchell detailing only four records: singles shot on the River Alt in October 1864, on the Calder above Whalley around 1873, at St. Michael's-on-Wyre on 22 August 1877 and near Pilling in October

1883. Oakes could add only another three and there were no published records in the county between 1922 and 1957, when one was found on 17 March at Freckleton. Three birds were also seen there in the autumn of the same year. Since then, Spotted Redshanks have been recorded annually in small numbers.

Spring passage typically runs from early April to late May, almost all records being coastal. The largest spring group was six at Marshside on 11 April 1998. Only 16 inland sightings were recorded between 1987 and 2005, all of single birds except for two at Stocks Reservoir on 9 May 1987 and at Martin Mere on 12-13 May 1995.

Female Spotted Redshanks may leave the breeding grounds up to a week before the eggs hatch or when broods are at an early stage, the male being left to cope alone (BWP). In some years this may lead to an influx of birds in their beautiful dusky summer plumage from mid- to late June. Peak counts at this time have included 13 at Hundred End on the south Ribble marshes on 29 June 1969, nine at Leighton Moss on 15-27 June 1970, 23 at Warton Marsh on 27 June 1981 with up to 20 there on 4 July 1982, and 20 at Lytham on 24-27 June 1986. There have, however, been markedly fewer summer records since about 1990.

Autumn passage gathers pace during July and extends to October, the peak usually being in September. Single birds or small parties of up to five are typical, but larger flocks have included 13 on the Cocker Estuary on 30 September 1962, 15 on the Carnforth/Silverdale Marshes on 18 September 1966, eight at Pilling Lane Ends on 30 August 1992, nine on the Morecambe Bay Reserve in October 1996, nine at Banks Marsh on 26 September 1998 with eleven there on 29 August 1999, and ten at Marshside in September 2003 (a site record).

Adult Spotted Redshank moulting into winter plumage with Redshank, Eric Morecambe complex. (Phillip Tomkinson)

As in spring, the majority of autumn records are on the coast, the first modern inland sightings being singles at Great Harwood sewage works from December 1959 to March 1960 and at Laneshawbridge on 8 August 1963. There were only six inland birds in the 1970s, nine in the 1980s and ten in the 1990s, while 19 were recorded from 2000 to 2005 at sites including Brockholes Quarry, Champion Moor, Prescot Reservoirs, Downholland Moss irrigation lakes, Martin Mere, Marton Mere, Mere Sands Wood, Wayoh Reservoir, Withnell Fold and Top o'Leach in Rossendale.

Small numbers of Spotted Redshanks have wintered, usually on the coast, since 1959 at localities such as Banks Marsh, Brockholes Quarry, Colloway Marsh, the Conder and Lune Estuaries, Marshside, Martin Mere, Morecambe Stone Jetty, Morecambe Bay Reserve, and the Wyre Estuary. A remarkable WeBS count of seven birds was made on the Ribble Estuary in December 2001.

PHS, MJ.

This species account was sponsored by the Fylde Bird Club.

REDSHANK

Tringa totanus

Lancashire Category A.

Fairly common breeder; abundant passage migrant and winter visitor from Iceland and continental Europe.

One of our most conspicuous waders, the watchful and noisy Redshank is the marshland sentinel, being the first to warn other species of human approach. In Britain it suffered a marked decline in the early nineteenth century but then increased between about 1865 and 1940 (BWP). In Mitchell's time, therefore, the Redshank was relatively scarce in Lancashire. Oakes, however, described it as a common resident, passage migrant and winter visitor to most coastal areas.

Breeding was first recorded in Lancashire in Rossendale in 1909, while Martin Mere had regular nesting by 1919 and further moorland sites were occupied by 1921. Colonisation continued so that by 1953 breeding areas included Silverdale and Carnforth Marshes, the Lune Valley, Pilling to Cockerham shore, Roeburndale, High Salter Fell, Wyresdale, the Fylde, the Ribble basin, Rossendale, Formby Moss, Lydiate, Sefton and coastal localities in the south. Hardy also mentioned Ainsdale dune heaths, Ince Blundell and the River Douglas meadows. According to Spencer, the Redshank commonly nested on saltmarshes, dunes and coastal fields but avoided dry moorland. Arrival at the breeding areas was a February/March event.

Redshank with Ragworm, Eric Morecambe complex, August 2004. (Chris Galvin)

In the north of the county, the Lancaster Checklist (1969-78) recorded breeding in all 10km squares. The Lune Estuary between Sunderland Point and Lancaster held 99 pairs in 1977, while Sunderland Point to Glasson Dock had 66 pairs. According to a 1985 RSPB survey, this area and the Eric Morecambe complex were in the top ten sites in the country for breeding Redshank, with nest densities of around 100 per km^2. A further 60 pairs bred between Caton and Kirkby Lonsdale in 1977. This part of the Lune Valley has remained an important haunt with 18 pairs at Arkholme during the Lancashire Atlas survey; the Lune Waterways Bird Survey recorded 57 pairs in 2003. With the replacement of heavy sheep grazing by light summer grazing by cattle, the population on the Eric Morecambe complex grew from none in 1981 to 24 pairs in 1989, 15-21 in the late 1990s and 31 in 2005. The Pilling-Cockerham area seems less favoured, perhaps due to reclamation and agricultural improvement in 1979/80. Nine pairs bred there in 1986, while six were found between Pilling Lane Ends and Fluke Hall in 1997. There were eight pairs at Barnaby's Sands on the Wyre Estuary in 1980.

The Forest of Bowland is an important breeding area for Redshank, an RSPB survey in 1998 estimating 261 pairs on wet in-bye pastures. Breeding in Rossendale increased after 1970 with twelve pairs reported in 1987 but, by 1999, they had disappeared. On the West Pennine Moors, up to ten pairs breed on in-bye and wet moorland up to 360m above sea level with a notable concentration around Belmont Reservoir.

Nearer the coast, a National Rivers Authority survey in 1992 yielded 14 pairs along the Ribble and its tributaries between the M6 motorway and Jumbles Rocks. A long-term and detailed research study by W.G. Hale and his students on the south Ribble saltmarshes at Banks located about 400 pairs of Redshanks in 1974; in 1978, 203 nests were found in just $2km^2$ and the mean density between 1975 and 1985 was 115 pairs per km^2. However, this population seems to have declined, as only 186 pairs were found on the south Ribble marshes in 2003. On the north side of the estuary, about 50 pairs nested on Warton Marsh in 1979, while there were 20 at Freckleton in 1993. The wet grazing marshes at Marshside have held up to 38 pairs in recent years, while at nearby Martin Mere, numbers increased from two pairs in 1982 to 20 in 2002.

Although the RSPB estimated a 29% national decline of breeding Redshanks on lowland wet grassland from 1982 to 2002, Lancashire remains a stronghold of this species. Indeed, the Lancashire Atlas estimated as many as 850 pairs in 161 tetrads in 1997-2000. However, saltmarshes and grazing marshes have become increasingly important as drainage, improvement of pastures and silage cutting have led to decreases inland.

Redshanks begin to move away from the breeding grounds in late June, mainly towards the estuaries where the adults undergo a post-breeding moult. The main influx begins in late July and August, peaking from mid-September to October (Figure 1); the latter birds include many of the subspecies *robusta* from Iceland. Many British breeders, previously thought to be a population of nominate *totanus* but now sometimes referred to as sub-species *britannica*, remain here for the winter, while others move south to the Low Countries, France and Iberia, especially first-years which migrate further than older birds (Migration Atlas). Redshanks are site faithful in winter; thus, of 173 ringed in Lancashire, 89 have been recovered locally. Sixteen moved to France and the Channel Islands, eight of which were recovered in winter, six during autumn and two in the breeding season. In addition, one ringed in Lancashire during the breeding season turned up in Portugal in the autumn of the same year. Three birds marked in Iceland while breeding have been recovered in Lancashire, one in winter and two in autumn. Icelandic Redshanks are thought to make up a significant proportion of our wintering population. Thus, Wilson (1973) describes a mid-winter catch of 160 birds on Morecambe Bay, 40% of which were identified as *robusta*.

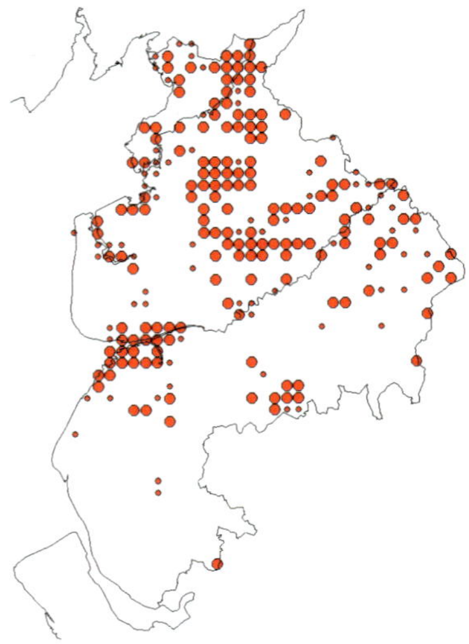

Breeding distribution of Redshank, 1997-2000. (Large dots: confirmed. Small dots: possible)

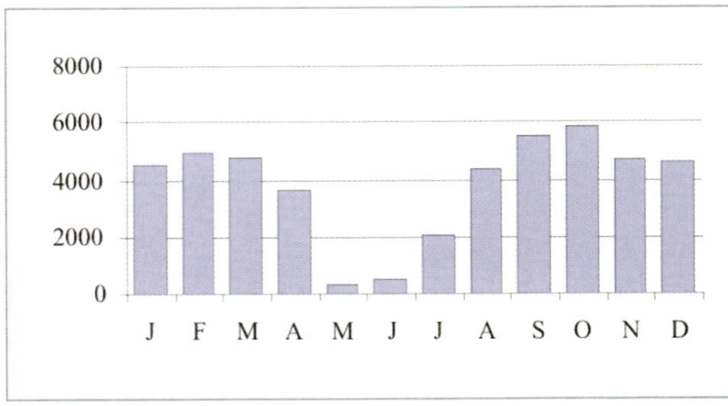

Fig. 1. Average monthly peak counts of Redshank on the Ribble Estuary, Seaforth Nature Reserve and Morecambe Bay South, 1985-2005.

Partly due to mortality and inland feeding as well as counting difficulties (Prater 1981), winter numbers on the estuaries are lower than in autumn. For example, Smith & Greenhalgh (1977) recorded an autumn peak of 5,500 to 6,500 on the Ribble in the early 1970s, followed by a winter population usually under 2,000 and sometimes less than 1,000. Wilson (1973) described a similar trend on Morecambe Bay. Figure 1 shows an average reduction between autumn and winter of 25%. In addition to Prater's explanations, this may be due to some *britannica* moving south. A small spring influx is often seen in March and April, as many as

90% trapped in Morecambe Bay during this period being Icelandic *robusta* (Wilson 1973), which do not leave our shores until late March to early May (Prater 1981).

Both Morecambe Bay and the Ribble Estuary are internationally important for Redshank, as is Seaforth Nature Reserve which is part of the Mersey Narrows SSSI. WeBS counts show that average winter numbers in Morecambe Bay rose steadily from 2,300 in 1990 to 4,000 in 2001/02, peaking at 4,706 in November 2000 (Figure 2), while passage numbers have varied between about 3,000 to 5,600 during the same period, with a maximum of 8,935 in September 1997. Favoured locations include Heysham Stone Jetty, where up to 500 were counted in autumn and winter 2000; a large total of 2,140 was found between Fluke Hall and Bank End on 6 October 2002. Wet fields at Pilling often attract Redshanks in winter, for example 916 on 24 December 1997, up to 600 in recent years on the Wyre at Burrows Marsh and Skippool, and a recently discovered roost at Blackpool's North Shore boating pool which has attracted up to 370 birds since 1996.

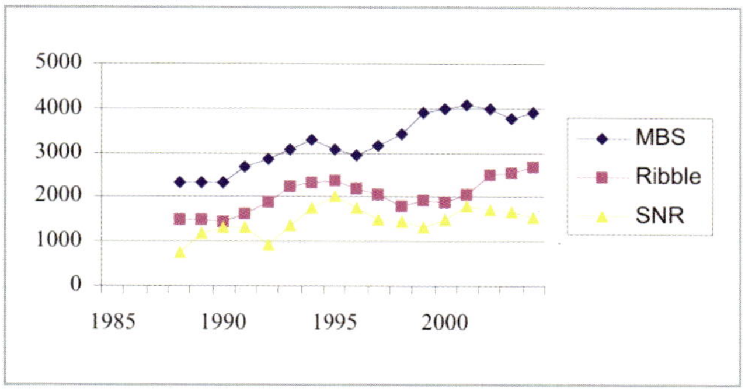

Figure 2. Peak winter counts of Redshank (3-year rolling means) on the Ribble Estuary, Morecambe Bay South and Seaforth Nature Reserve, 1987/88-2004/05.

Winter totals on the Ribble Estuary fluctuated between about 1,500 and 2,500 from 1978 to 2002, peaking at 3,882 in November 2000, while passage numbers showed a steady increase from about 500 to 5,000 during the same period, the peak count being 6,411 in September 1999. Fairhaven is an important roost on occasions, with 1,000 counted there on 9 February 1999. On the south side, Marshside/Crossens is also a major haunt, recent counts including 1,250 in March 2001 and 1,500 on 30 November 2001. An unusual observation on 6 March 1977 was of 1,500 feeding on cockles crushed by cars on Southport beach.

Seaforth counts have regularly exceeded the level for international significance in autumn, winter and spring. There was a steady increase from the late 1970s to about 1996/97, followed by a small decline. Recent peaks include 2,450 in March 1994 and 2,300 in February 2003. Although up to 750 Redshank have been seen feeding at Seaforth in winter, the majority feed on the Cheshire side of the Mersey at Egremont and North Wirral Shore. A decline in 1998 was attributed to construction of sea defences at Egremont which provided alternative roosting sites. The north bank of the Mersey at Garston and Oglet also provides a good habitat for Redshanks, peaking at 1,500 in October 2002.

Very small numbers winter inland. In east Lancashire they are found mainly in the Calder catchment with up to four regularly seen at Altham, Colne Sewage Works and the Foulridge Reservoirs. On the Ribble, the pilot Riverine WeBS Survey of January and February 2000 found 13 on a 7.5km length near Ribchester. They are much rarer higher up the river with four at Smithies Bridge, near Sawley in February 2001 being exceptional.

PHS, MJ.
This species account was sponsored by Malcolm Greenhalgh.

MARSH SANDPIPER

Tringa stagnatilis

Lancashire Category A. (0, 6).

Vagrant from south-eastern Europe.

The first was found by Harry Shorrock, Stan Craig and David Power at Leighton Moss on 14 July 1968 but was not seen subsequently; it was the sixteenth record in Britain and Ireland. Another single was at Martin Mere on 13 September 1974, this one staying for four days until the 16th.

Then, on 3 August 1999, the Lancashire total was more than doubled when, during an exceptional national influx, three juveniles were found on the saltwater pool at Seaforth. They could not be found the next day but two of them returned on the 7th and then moved to the adjacent Crosby Marine Lake on the 8th, where they were seen regularly until 14 August. In the meantime, two arrived at Marshside, some twenty kilometres to the north on 5 August, where they stayed until the 9th with a third bird possibly in the vicinity but separate. The Seaforth and Marshside records were accepted as referring to the same birds but, to add to the confusion, three juveniles had been reported briefly at Swillington Ings in West Yorkshire on 3 August and it had been assumed that these too were the same birds until the timing of the records ruled that out.

Juvenile Marsh Sandpiper, Crosby Marine Park, August 1999. (Steve Young)

The last record was also at Seaforth, an adult on the scrape next to the main hide all day on 22 July 2000 – perhaps it was one of the three from the previous year.

SJW, MJ.
This species account was sponsored by Ribble Bird Tours (01253-407554).

GREENSHANK

Tringa nebularia

Lancashire Category A.

Fairly common passage migrant from Scotland and northern Europe; scarce winter visitor.

Like the Spotted Redshank, this wader often draws attention to itself by its evocative call, but it is usually much more frequent than the former species. There is a small Scottish breeding population (under 1,000), mainly in Sutherland, and British wintering birds probably derive from this stock (Prater 1981). In Lancashire, the Greenshank is primarily a bird of passage in spring and, more commonly, in autumn.

It is clearly much more numerous now than in the nineteenth and early twentieth centuries. Thus, Oakes described it as a regular but uncommon migrant in spring and autumn, though recorded in every month of the year in small numbers. Interestingly, he regarded the species as much more frequent inland than on the coast. His largest recorded party was five at Flixton on 30 August 1944 and he knew of only two winter sightings. By the 1970s occurrences were predominately coastal, east Lancashire being almost entirely avoided, particularly in spring. Late summer Greenshanks were numerous and widespread in most years, with parties of up to 8-10 turning up almost anywhere, and odd ones wintering. Spring numbers were lower, ones and twos being the rule. This pattern is broadly similar today, except that more birds are recorded.

A small group of Greenshanks coming in to land at the Eric Morecambe complex. (Phillip Tomkinson)

Although there is a dearth of ringing recoveries, it is thought that our passage birds breed mainly in Scandinavia and the former Soviet Union and winter in Africa (Prater 1981, Migration Atlas). Returning birds may arrive as early as the middle of March and numbers peak in late April or early May; around 20-30 are seen in an average spring, almost always in ones or twos. Most sightings are on or near the coast; thus, between 1977 and 1989 there were only ten records from sites well inland. From 1990 to 1997, this increased to 18 records of 20 birds, most being from the reservoirs of Stocks, Belmont, the Rossendale area and those around Blackburn and Burnley, as well as Altham, Bolton-by-Bowland and Arkholme. More recently, Brockholes Quarry has become a reliable haunt; indeed, the largest spring party in the last few years was six at this site on 11 May 2000. Other notable inland counts were five at Arkholme on 1 May 1999 and four at Greta Foot on the Lune on 27 April 2003.

As in spring, autumn passage is mainly coastal. It begins in mid-June, peaks in July to September and concludes in November. The first small peak at the end of July consists of adults, while a larger influx at the end of August includes mostly juveniles.

Greenshanks are generally more numerous on Morecambe Bay than on the Ribble, with the Eric Morecambe complex being a major haunt. The record count here was 39 in September 1997 and August 2004. The Lune Estuary is also attractive to Greenshanks, for example 27 on 10 September 1998, and Arkholme in the Lune Valley is similarly favoured, with 16 there in August 1980. The coast from Cockerham to Pilling often supports sizeable flocks, at least 20 being counted on the Cocker Estuary in August 1963 and a similar number at Pilling in 1985. The Shard Bridge area on the Wyre Estuary held up to 21 in late September 2003.

On the north side of the Ribble, Freckleton Naze pool is a well known locality with 16 there on 27 September 1998 and the same number on nearby Warton Bank on 24 August 2002. Banks Marsh on the southern shore held up to 25 Greenshanks in late August and early September 1999. Marshside/Crossens is another regular haunt, the record count here being 27 on 3 September 1988. Further south, the Alt Estuary attracts relatively small numbers, the maximum count at Seaforth being ten on 5 August 1997.

The most productive inland site for Greenshanks during the autumn is Brockholes Quarry, which reported 27 sightings in 2001, the largest group being eight on 19 August, although small numbers are recorded annually on a very wide range of inland waters. The highest numbers are associated with low water levels on the reservoirs, for example in 1984 there was a maximum of 13 at Foulridge from mid-August to early September; twelve were also at Black Moss on 21 August, and up to five at several other sites. A notable late record was of three at Anglezarke on 26 October 2003, while one lingered at the same site until 5 November 2003.

Winter records are usually of singles on the coast at such places as Morecambe Bay Reserve, the Lune marshes, Pilling-Cockerham, the Wyre Estuary, Ribble Estuary and Seaforth. The last mentioned had a bird in six consecutive winters up to 1999/2000. Similarly, at Arkholme, a Greenshank was present for three successive winters from 1978/79 to 1981/82. Exceptionally, three wintered in the Conder Green area in January 1954 and 1955 and at least four at Carnforth Marsh from November to December 1973. East Lancashire winterers included singles at Skirden Beck in January 1991 and Earnsdale Reservoir on 20 February 1993.

Although no breeding record has been fully substantiated in England (Brown & Grice 2005), a clutch of three, taken by N. Yates on Littledale Fell, Caton in May 1937, came into the possession of W.G. Hale in 1977 who confirmed their identification and validated the record (W.G. Hale *pers. comm.*)

PHS, MJ.

This species account was sponsored by Charlie Liggett.

LESSER YELLOWLEGS

Tringa flavipes

Lancashire Category A. (0, 9).

Vagrant from North America.

This Nearctic wader has become a fairly regular visitor to the county in recent years but it used to be a major rarity, with the first record coming as late as 1965; a juvenile found by Malcolm Greenhalgh at Freckleton Sewage Farm on 11 August 1965 and also seen at nearby Clifton Marsh, remaining until 12 August.

The next bird first appeared on a flooded field on the Great Altcar mosses on 28 September 1974 and moved to Martin Mere on the 29th, remaining there until 1 October. What was probably the same individual was in the Freckleton Sewage Farm/Newton Marsh area from 6 October to 16 November. Another fairly lengthy series of blank years was broken by a first-winter, again at Martin Mere, on 18-24 September 1988; what was presumed to be this bird later turned up at Frodsham in Cheshire on the 25th. This was followed by an adult that spent most of the day at Marton Mere, Blackpool on 5 May 1992.

A first-winter on the Eric Morecambe complex on 18 October 1995 was the first record in the north of the county but, after another first-winter at the same site on at least 13 September 1997, all subsequent records have been back on the Ribble.

Separate first-winters were at Marshside from 18 October to 2 December 1997 and at Martin Mere from 28 October to 12 November the same year. One was also seen at Banks Marsh on 19 October and this was joined by another from at least 26 December. Both birds were seen intermittently at Banks – and separately at Marshside and Martin Mere – into 1998 but seemed to split up during late spring and summer, only to 're-find' each other late in the year with at least one remaining until May 1999. This led to them registering as 'possibly breeding' in the Lancashire Atlas survey. Their twenty-month stay made local birdwatchers rather blasé about the species but there was a three year wait for the next: a juvenile on flooded fields near Eagland Hill, Pilling on 12-19 September 2002.

Lesser Yellowlegs, Banks Marsh, February 1999. (Steve Young)

All records:

1965	Freckleton, one, 11 to 12 August, also Clifton Marsh.
1974	Great Altcar, one, 28 September
1974	Martin Mere, one, 29 September to 1 October, presumed same as Great Altcar
1974	Freckleton, one, 6 October to 16 November, presumed same as Great Altcar
1988	Martin Mere, first-winter 18 to24 September
1992	Marton Mere, adult, 5 May
1995	Eric Morecambe complex, first-winter, 18 October
1997	Eric Morecambe complex, first-winter, at least 13 September
1997	Banks Marsh, two first-winters, 18 October to 2 May 1999, also Martin Mere & Marshside
2002	Eagland Hill, Fylde, juvenile, 12 to 19 September

SJW, MJ.

This species account was sponsored by Malcolm Greenhalgh.

GREEN SANDPIPER

Tringa ochropus

Lancashire Category A.

Fairly common passage migrant; scarce winter visitor from northern and central Europe.

The Green Sandpiper is almost exclusively a freshwater wader, usually avoiding tidal and coastal waters (BWP). Birds seen on passage in Lancashire are likely to belong to the northern European breeding population, but information on the origins of British migrants is limited to recovery of a bird ringed in Sweden. (Prater 1981; Migration Atlas).

Mitchell described this species as one of our earliest autumn migrants, having been shot several times in July. He knew of no spring records and indicated its preference for freshwater and absence from coasts. By Hardy's time it was a regular autumn migrant, seen especially at sewage farms, with the main passage from August to September; there were no spring occurrences in Lancashire. Oakes wrote that the Green Sandpiper was a regular visitor in autumn to rivers, mosses and sewage farms, at all times rare on the shore. He cited five spring records and only two sightings in winter, at Marshside on 16 February 1925 and Hacking Bridge on the Ribble on 20 January 1935. His autumn dates were from the first week of July, the largest groups encountered being six at Liverpool Sewage Farm on 11 August 1936 and eight at Wood End Sewage Farm on 1 September 1948.

Since the 1950s the pattern of occurrence has remained essentially similar with a majority of sightings in autumn (mid-June to October), peaking between July and September, after which a few birds remain to winter in the county. Spring passage from late March to late May involves much smaller numbers than in the autumn; birds are never numerous, a typical sighting being of one or two individuals. Recent April records have included parties of three at Wood End (1990) and Arkholme (1994) and two at Arkholme in 2002. Average spring numbers have halved since 1989, from seven to three per annum on average, but it is possible that this is due to greater vigilance in separating wintering birds from migrants. The first birds to arrive in mid-June are adult females which desert the breeding grounds leaving the young to be looked after by the males. Juveniles begin to appear in late July and early August (Migration Atlas).

Green Sandpiper, Seaforth Nature Reserve, August 2001. (Steve Young)

In the north, the most favoured site is now the Eric Morecambe complex, with six there in September 1994, July 1995 and September 1999. The Lune Valley also has good habitat for this species, especially at Arkholme where seven were counted on 5 July 1987. Further downstream, Aldcliffe Marsh is also a notable haunt, the site record being eight in August 2003. The Pilling-Cockerham Marshes are a regular location for Green Sandpipers with seven present on 23 August 1987; Carr House Green Common, Inskip had an exceptional four birds in April 1988.

During the 1960s and 1970s, as many as seven or eight birds could be flushed from Wood End Sewage Works in August or September, while six there on 2 December 1973 was an exceptional winter record. Skirden Beck, a tributary of the Ribble, is another favoured site, nine being recorded on 22 July 1984 and eight on 20 August 1989. However, the attraction of Skirden Beck and the Burnley area has waned in the past ten years and, since the closure or modernisation of the sewage works, any count above two anywhere in the east is now unusual. In Rossendale, spring sightings have included singles at Ewood Bridge Sewage Works on 23 April 1981 and at Ogden Reservoir on 10 May 1996; very surprising was a bird in display flight in Bowland on 23 May 1987.

Nearer the coast, Brockholes Quarry has become a good place to find Green Sandpipers, with five present on 14 August 2001, an autumn passage of more than 20 in 2004 including six on 5 August, and two spring birds on 21 April 2003. Several freshwater sites adjoining the Ribble Estuary are also favoured. Thus, Clifton Marsh produced twelve on 6 September 1956 and Longton Marsh seven on 2 August 1997, while a remarkable 18 were recorded at Hesketh Bank on 1 September 1993. Good numbers have also been seen at Banks Marsh/Hundred End (e.g. six in September 1998) and at Marshside, where at least a dozen birds were logged in autumn 1999 (McCarthy 2001). Not surprisingly, Martin Mere regularly attracts Green Sandpipers, large counts being eleven on 9 July 1994 and ten in August of both 1995 and 1996.

Up to around ten Green Sandpipers now winter annually in the county, the majority of sites being by running water, while passage birds often use still water habitat (Migration Atlas). Since 1989 the main wintering areas have been Aldcliffe Marsh and the Lune from Aughton to Arkholme, Holmere (Carnforth), Skirden Beck, Carr House Green Common, the Wyre at Out Rawcliffe, Altham to Martholme and the Burnley area on the Calder, Syd Brook (Yarrow), Brockholes on the Ribble and Sefton Meadows on the Alt. Their regular occurrence at these places reinforces the opinion that Green Sandpipers are site-faithful in winter (Migration Atlas).

PHS, MJ.

This species account was sponsored by Ross Hughes.

WOOD SANDPIPER

Tringa glareola

Lancashire Category A.

Uncommon passage migrant from Fennoscandia and eastern Europe.

The Wood Sandpiper breeds across the Palaearctic, mainly in the coniferous forest zone and, like the Green Sandpiper, generally avoids seashores and other tidal or marine sites but is less tied to freshwater habitats (BWP). Since 1959, a small population (up to 10 pairs) has bred in the Scottish Highlands but Lancashire birds are likely to originate in Scandinavia and are in transit to or from their wintering grounds in Africa south of the Sahara.

This elegant wader was described by Mitchell as a rare visitor; he cited one shot at Calder Foot on the unusually late date of 18 November 1867 (in more likely Green Sandpiper habitat) and another at Mitton Wood in May 1869. The latter bird was said to have a mate but the claim of a pair with four recently fledged young in the same area was almost certainly an identification error. Two were shot near Cock Bridge on the Calder in August 1879. These were also by running water, a habitat that provides very few modern records, so they may also have been misidentified.

Oakes, who also ranked this species as a rare visitor, could add only one more record for the county – at Carleton, Blackpool on 7 July 1942. After a gap of eight years, the next sighting was on 14 September 1950 at Freckleton sewage farm, followed by a spring bird at Marton Mere on 11 May 1951 and two further spring records at Freckleton in May 1952.

After the early 1950s the status of the Wood Sandpiper in Lancashire changed markedly, Spencer (1973) noting that it had been under-recorded until recently. He had accumulated over 100 records since 1950 and considered the bird annual and widespread, though less common on the whole than the Green Sandpiper. He stated that spring passage was from late March, although in the light of current knowledge, this seems too early. Records peaked in late May to early June, while return migration probably started around 20 June, maximum numbers being seen in August with stragglers until mid-October.

Juvenile Wood Sandpiper, Seaforth Nature Reserve, August 2006. (Steve Young)

During the past 25 years the average dates of first and last records are 4 May and 21 September respectively. The earliest in spring was on 14 April 1983 at Martin Mere, while the latest autumn records are singles at Freckleton Sewage Works to 22 November 1964, and Arkholme from 20 September to 28 October 1978. An unprecedented and never repeated record was of a bird in display song on the River Brock on 14 April 1964.

An analysis of post-1970 records shows that, of 329 records of Wood Sandpipers in Lancashire, only three have occurred on rivers or streams, two at Arkholme in 1978 and one at Skirden Beck in May 1984. This contrasts markedly with the Green Sandpiper which uses both still and running water, the latter particularly in winter.

Increasing observer coverage has led to Wood Sandpipers being reported every year at many sites but particularly at Martin Mere (82 records since 1978), the Eric Morecambe complex (51), and Marshside (25).

An exceptional autumn passage occurred in 1980, with Lancashire's largest flock of 16 on a pool at Freckleton on 6 August out of an estimated total of 30 in the county. Impressive numbers were also seen in 1996, with seven at Martin Mere on 12-13 August and three at Seaforth on 6 August. The autumn influx of 1999 was the most impressive since 1980, large parties including seven on the Eric Morecambe pools from 7-9 August with six remaining to the 18th. Martin Mere also logged seven birds between 4 August and 15 October. Late summer 2003 was on a par with 1999, widespread sightings including four at Martin Mere on 6 August (Figure 1).

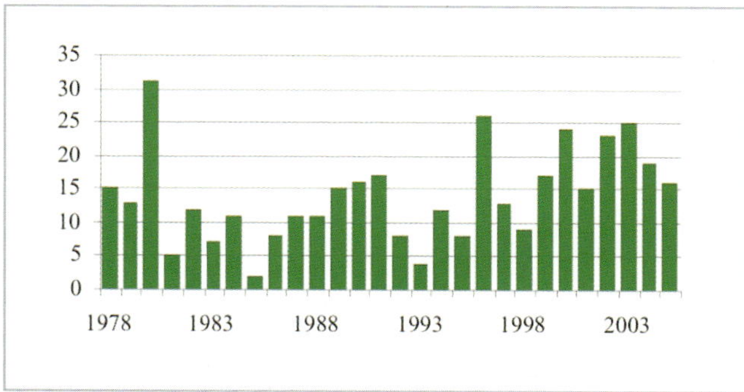

Figure 1. Annual totals of Wood Sandpipers in Lancashire, 1978-2005.

From 1996 to 2005 the number of spring sightings ranged from none in 1998 to ten in 2000 and, in autumn, up to 30 in 1980 and 20 in 1999 and 2004. Both spring and autumn passage periods are highly compressed: more than 80% of spring birds were in May and two-thirds of autumn records in August (Figure 2).

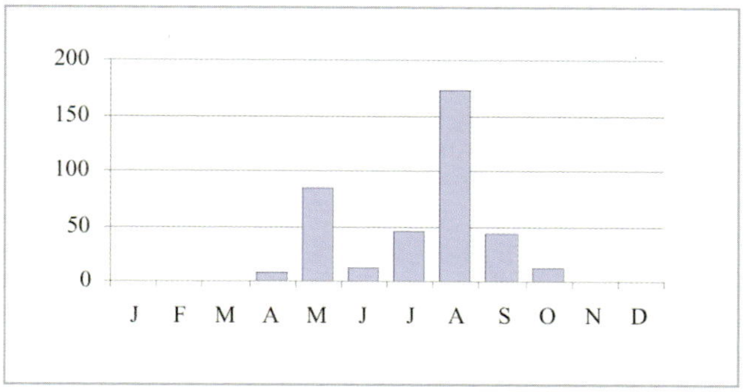

Figure 2. Monthly totals of Wood Sandpipers in Lancashire, 1978-2005.

East Lancashire records are less than annual, the largest party recorded being three at Wood End Sewage Works on 18 August 1980. Other sites far inland reporting single birds have been Abbeystead Lake, Arkholme, Belmont Reservoir, Brockholes Quarry, Champion Moor, Clough Bottom, Clowbridge, Foulridge, Holden Wood, Lee Green, Parsonage, Rowley Lake, Stocks and Upper Coldwell Reservoirs, and Withnell Fold.

PHS, MJ.

This species account was sponsored by Tony and June Money.

TEREK SANDPIPER

Xenus cinereus

Lancashire Category A. (0,1).

Vagrant from Finland or Russia.

The county's only record was found in the late afternoon of 9 June 2000 at Seaforth by Chris Gregson. He had been confined to the hide by continuous rain for some time when a police helicopter flew over low, flushing all the roosting birds. A few minutes later, when everything had resettled, a small grey-brown wader had appeared on the scrape next to the hide about 20m away. Identification at this distance was no problem but the bird quickly disappeared and it was some time before it was relocated, this time at around 200m.

During the ensuing hour it fed on the muddy edge of the saltwater lagoon in a highly distinctive fashion, catching ragworms and scurrying to the water's edge to wash them before eating them. A handful of birders had managed to rush to see it but by the time most arrived the light was fading and the bird had retreated to roost some 300m distant – so that most people's views were of a rather disappointing Common Sandpiper-like blob. Just before dusk it returned very briefly in front of the hide where it was photographed before flying back to roost; it was not seen again.

Terek Sandpiper, Seaforth Nature Reserve, 9 June 2000. (Steve Young)

The Seaforth bird was the 58th record in Britain and Ireland. The first for north-west England had been at Frodsham on the Cheshire Mersey on 27 April 1999 – perhaps it was the same individual.

SJW.

This species account was sponsored by John Wright.

COMMON SANDPIPER

Actitis hypoleucos

Lancashire Category A.

Fairly common breeder; common passage migrant from winter quarters in West Africa.

With its stiff, flickering wing-beats and ringing "swee-wee-wee" call, the Common Sandpiper is a familiar breeder in the northern and eastern parts of our region and a passage migrant almost everywhere. Its typical nesting habitat is shingly river reaches backed by tall herbaceous vegetation but the margins of upland reservoirs are also used. The Lancashire Atlas survey estimated a population in 1997-2000 of about 250 breeding pairs in 102 tetrads, concentrated on the Rivers Lune and Ribble and their tributaries, but also in Bowland and the West Pennines. Breeding Common Sandpipers suffered a 24% national decline between 1970 and 2001; it is not known whether this was due to changes in the quality of breeding or of wintering areas (Migration Atlas) but the Lancashire Atlas attributed declines in some areas to human disturbance.

During the nineteenth century, according to Mitchell, this species was common everywhere in hilly districts, fairly numerous in Rossendale and especially plentiful on the Hodder and its tributaries in Bowland. A few pairs also bred in the south-west; Hardy mentioned Knowsley Park, Wrightington Hall, Rufford and the River Alt near Hightown prior to the 1930s (Williams 1936). Hardy described the Common Sandpiper as a very common spring and autumn passage migrant, arriving in the second week of April and returning from mid-July to October; birds could often be heard calling on night migration over Liverpool. He reported no wintering birds but Oakes cited one at Lancaster on 19 January 1925. Oakes agreed with Mitchell's breeding distribution but added most of the reservoirs of central and south Lancashire. There has been no confirmed breeding in the south-west since Oakes' time, but pairs were present in late May at Mere Brow Leisure Lakes in 1977, at Mere Sands Wood in 1980 and Croston in 1981.

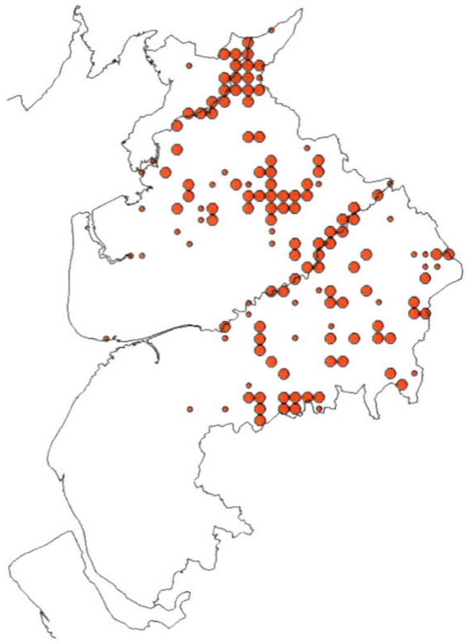

Breeding distribution of Common Sandpiper, 1997-2000. (Large dots: confirmed. Small dots: possible)

In the north, breeding was confirmed on Silverdale shore in 1959 and at Dockacres gravel-pits in the 1980s. The Waterways Bird Survey of the River Lune found between 45 and 68 pairs between Lancaster's Skerton Weir and Kirkby Lonsdale from 1979 to 1993, but only 36 pairs in 2003. The extensive exposed gravels at Arkholme are a particular hot-spot on the Lune, 13 pairs being noted in 1998 and 16 pairs in 2005. However, nests on this part of the river are often washed out by floods in May and early June, so breeding success tends to be low. There seem to have been losses of breeding birds from the small tributaries of the Lune since the 1950s, a problem also noted on some other Lancashire rivers. Nesting occurs on the River Wyre, from Scorton upstream, and on major tributaries such as the Brock. Similarly, despite increasing bank-side disturbance and angling activity, the larger rivers and streams in the Ribble and Hodder catchments are used by Common Sandpipers. In 1997 eight pairs were counted on the Hodder and four on the Ribble between Paythorne Bridge and its confluence with the Hodder. In the same year, twelve pairs were reported from Rossendale; a similar number bred in the region in 2003. Bowland streams supported 22 pairs in a survey area of 70km^2 in 1982, increasing to 33 pairs in 1983. Eleven pairs were found on United Utilities land in Bowland in 2003.

Many of the eastern Lancashire reservoirs are also used for breeding, one stronghold being the Belmont region, where a 25km^2 study area regularly supports eight or nine pairs, rising to an encouraging 13 in 2001; six pairs bred on the margins of Belmont Reservoir in 2005. Stocks Reservoir is another significant haunt, with up to 13 pairs in 1995 and five in 2002.

Departure of females and failed breeders begins when the chicks reach about 14 days old, often in mid-June (Migration Atlas), but arrival as early as 4 June 1997 has been reported at Seaforth; the first juveniles usually appear in the first half of July. The main movement is in July/August, numbers declining though September with a few stragglers in October. Singles or small parties may be encountered in a wide variety of aquatic habitats, both freshwater and maritime, ranging from rivers and reservoirs to estuaries and even the open coast. In the Fylde, the major haunt in July is in the Shard Bridge/Skippool Creek area of the Wyre Estuary, 42 being counted in 1995 and a peak of 67 in July 2003. Also significant is Conder Green, where 15 were seen on 17 July 1997, and other important coastal sites include Freckleton on the Ribble where training walls have attracted up to 32 birds, again in July. Marshside reported a total of 60 birds during the autumn of 1999, with up to six present on several dates.

Seaforth is also a regular stop-over with a high count of 28 on 21 July 1992. Particularly late birds were singles at Conder Green on 1 November 1998 and on the Eric Morecambe complex on 28 November 1998, and two on the Calder at Altham on 18 November 2005.

Common Sandpiper, hunting for flies on the edge of the freshwater pool, Seaforth Nature Reserve, July 1999. (Steve Young)

Good inland sites in autumn include Arkholme on the Lune where 63 were counted along a 5km length as early as 8 June 1996, though these may have been mainly local breeders and their offspring. Stocks Reservoir produced 15 on 16 July 1999 and Prescot Reservoirs a peak count of twelve in 2002.

It is often difficult to tell when the last migrants leave as a few birds have wintered in the county since the 1960s, reflecting the national picture (Prater 1981). Recent winterers have included singles at Altham (26 November 1988 to April 1989, joined by another on 1 January 1989), Martin Mere (3-5 January 1997), River Douglas (23 December 1998), Brockholes Quarry (1998/99; 1999/2000), Mere Sands Wood (12 February 1999), Pilling Lane Ends (25 January 2000), the River Ribble at Samlesbury and Walton-le-Dale, the River Lune at Melling (early 2001) and the River Wyre at Little Singleton from December 2003 to January 2004.

In spring returning birds generally appear in the county from early April, the average date between 1978 and 2005 being the 7th. This compares with an average date of 16 April given by Oakes. The earliest on record were both on 21 March, in 1933 and 1966, but Oakes mentioned an even earlier one on 5 March which he presumed had wintered. Peaking in late April or early May, flock sizes are invariably lower than in autumn but Marton Mere has often attracted sizeable parties, for example 18 on 2 May 1978, 22 on 7 May 1979 and 16 on 3 May 1985. Other large groups included 30 at Arkholme on 26 April 1981, 16 at Skirden Beck on 24 April 1982 and 14 at Belmont on 25 April 1998. Although difficult to quantify, the size of the spring passage appears to have declined significantly since the early 1990s.

The origin of our passage birds is incompletely known but may mainly be northern Britain; the Migration Atlas states that almost all northern migrants are British breeders and that Fennoscandian birds are largely confined to south-east England. There have been three Lancashire recoveries, all in late summer, of birds ringed in the Scottish borders in June or July, and also one from Northumberland, which had been ringed in June. This supports the south or south-westerly movement in autumn proposed by BWP. Similarly, a bird ringed at Hornby on 30 June 1922 turned up near Carmarthen on 16 August in the same year. A colour-ringed bird at Seaforth on 9 August 1996 had been marked at Ladybower Reservoir, Derbyshire. Our only long-distance recovery is of a local breeder, ringed on 17 June 1968, which was found in Morocco on 18 April 1975.

PHS, MJ.

This species account was sponsored by the Fylde Bird Club.

SPOTTED SANDPIPER

Actitis macularius

Lancashire Category A. (0, 3).

Vagrant from North America.

Uniquely amongst Nearctic waders in Lancashire, all three records have been on reservoirs in the east of the county. The first was an adult in summer plumage at Wayoh Reservoir on 19 June 1982 (J.E. Ashworth, C.A. Derbyshire), which later moved to Jumbles Reservoir on the Greater Manchester side of the 'border', remaining there until 6 July.

Next came another adult at Foulridge Reservoir, Colne during 6-10 August 1986 with another adult later the same year at Lower Rivington Reservoir and adjacent filter beds, from 22 November to 11 January 1987.

SJW, MJ.

This species account was sponsored by Brenda Walsh.

TURNSTONE

Arenaria interpres

Lancashire Category A.

Common winter visitor and passage migrant from Arctic Canada and Greenland.

The Turnstone's pattern of occurrence in Lancashire is long-established. Mitchell mentioned a spring passage on the Wyre Estuary but in his time this species was scarce on the Ribble, having, he claimed, previously been common. He made no mention of wintering. Hardy stated that spring migration began in late March or April, extending to mid-May when 'many white-headed (summer-plumaged) birds are seen'. Autumn passage was from early August to November. Oakes added more detail, indicating that after the mid-May peak some birds, including first-years, lingered to the third or fourth week of that month.

According to the Migration Atlas early returning birds are failed breeders, followed by successful adults (the females first) and then the juveniles. The main influx of adults into Lancashire is usually complete by the end of August, while juveniles continue to arrive well into September. Ringing studies on Morecambe Bay found that adults handled in August/September were in wing-moult, later retraps showing that many wintering birds completed their moult in the bay (Wilson 1973), implying that most autumn arrivals remain for the winter (Figure 1). Turnstones are known to be very site-faithful, both between and within winters, but many Canadian and Greenland birds use Britain as a staging area before moving on to winter in France, Iberia and West Africa (Migration Atlas). Later arrivals, including some from Fennoscandia, may replace them.

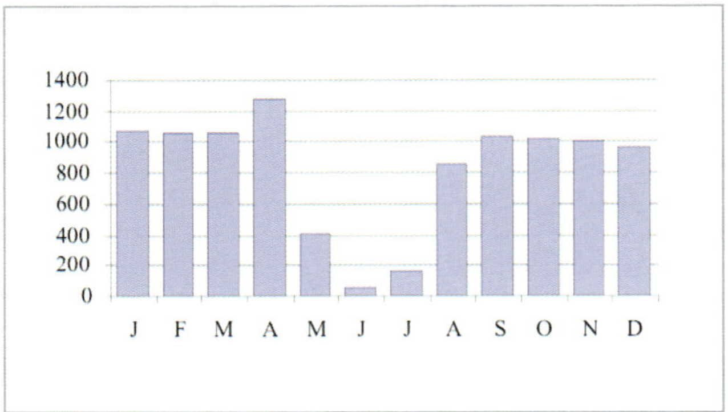

Fig. 1. Average monthly totals of Turnstones on the Ribble Estuary, Seaforth Nature Reserve and Morecambe Bay South, 1985-2005.

In Oakes' time only 40-60 Turnstones wintered in Morecambe Bay. By the late 1960s to early 1970s this had increased to between 900 and 1,600 (Wilson 1973), though not all of these were in Lancashire. WeBS data for Morecambe Bay reveal that a high winter population of over 2,000 in 1990 fell to an average of around 500 this century. A count of 2,337 birds in Morecambe Bay in March 1991 was a record number for Lancashire. A similar trend is evident for passage birds with a steady decline from around 1,400 to 400 during the same period. Morecambe Bay roosts have changed over the years. Thus, Hest Bank to Heysham reported spring peaks of a thousand or more in the early 1980s when some birds switched to Jenny Brown's Point where erosion exposed suitable habitat, up to 200 being found there in November 1984, but increased siltation led to few birds being reported there by 1993. By the latter year, Hest Bank was being used only on the highest spring-tides with an average of only about 20 birds, most having moved to anti-erosion groynes at Morecambe. Nearby Heysham has long been a favoured locality for Turnstones, especially in spring. In 2000, for example, 100 wintered here, peaking at 306 on 3 May; a summering flock of 25 was reported on 21 June 1998. Rossall Point, at the mouth of the Wyre Estuary, is by far the most important Turnstone site on the southern shore of Morecambe Bay, with a exceptional count of 1,010 on 11 May 1985. More recently, winter numbers have been between 200 and 300, with disturbance from dog-walkers leading to the Turnstones roosting on a small island in Fleetwood Marine Lake, where a total of 437 was counted in March 1996.

Smith & Greenhalgh (1977) reported that relatively few Turnstones occurred on the Ribble, perhaps because the only typical feeding area is Church Scar at Lytham. However, they noted that increasing numbers were to be found on Southport beach feeding in tide-line detritus. Their peak count for the estuary was 242 in December 1974, most birds being at Fairhaven and St. Anne's. The Ribble WeBS figures for the period 1978 to 2005 show that winter numbers fluctuated between 48 in 1998 and 523 in 1993, while passage birds increased rapidly from 184 in 1983 to 680 in 1992, before declining to around 250 in the twenty-first century. Lytham is still the main Ribble roost, birds increasingly using small boats moored near the shore as a roost. Recent peak counts there include 440 in August 1995, 380 on 24 August 1998 and 150 in March 2001. The Southport beaches attracted 214 feeding Turnstones on 21 December 1976 and 250 on 6 February 1977. Marshside generally has small numbers throughout the year, an exceptional count being 230 on 25 July 1994.

Until very recently most Alt Estuary birds roosted at Seaforth. High numbers there of about 500 in 1979/80 fell to under 100 in 1985 and a peak of only 24 in July 1987. However, from 1991 a remarkable increase in the winter population took place to an average of about 800 birds between 1994 and 1996; the largest count on the reserve was 1,100 on 5 February 1995. All these were feeding on the Wirral side of the Mersey between Egremont and New Brighton and represented one of the largest and most concentrated populations in Western Europe. However, numbers rapidly declined from 1996 so that, by the turn of the century, wintering numbers were down to about 120; this was attributed to the building of sea-defence groynes at New Brighton which provided alternative roost sites. Seaforth passage figures show somewhat similar trends to the winter data, with an exponential increase to about 730 birds in 1997, followed by a decline to 200 in 2000 and an increase to 400 by 2002. By 2003, no sites for Turnstones in Lancashire qualified as even nationally important.

Fig 2. Peak winter and passage counts (3-year rolling means) on the Ribble & Alt Estuaries and Morecambe Bay South, 1986-2005.

Turnstones rarely occur at any distance from the coast. The first recorded instance seems to have been one at Wood End Sewage Works on 22 May 1950, followed by up to three at Foulridge Reservoir in August 1962, three at Whitemoor Reservoir, Colne on 22 July 1970 and one at Rishton Reservoir on 27 May 1972. In recent years, the majority of sightings have been in spring with Brockholes Quarry, Stocks Reservoir and Martin Mere the most regular sites. Between 1998 and 2005 there were about 62 inland records of 135 birds, the largest parties being nine at Brockholes Quarry on 27 May 2000 and 20 at Martin Mere on 8 May 2004.

Turnstone in summer plumage, Rossall Point. (Phillip Tomkinson)

The view that most Turnstones wintering here are from the Greenland and Canadian breeding population (Prater 1981) is supported by several ringing recoveries. Thus, two birds ringed in Lancashire have been recovered in Greenland during the breeding season, while another locally marked bird turned up on Ellesmere Island in the Canadian Arctic and three Lancashire-ringed individuals have been found in Iceland in May, almost certainly on their way to Greenland or Canada. Similarly, a bird marked on Ellesmere Island was recorded on passage at Seaforth in two consecutive springs. However, Prater also asserted that Fennoscandian (especially Finnish) breeders occur on autumn passage in Britain, moving on to winter in West Africa. Evidence for this in Lancashire includes a bird ringed in Finland in June 1973 which was recovered on Banks Marsh in late August 1985. Also, single Norwegian-ringed birds have turned up at Middleton and Seaforth on autumn and spring passage respectively. The dates for the Finnish bird show that the Turnstone can be long-lived, a fact reinforced by one whose ring was read in the field at Seaforth in summer 1993; it had been marked at the same site in October 1977, when at least a year old, and had therefore survived a minimum of 16 years.

PHS, MJ.
This species account was sponsored by Peter Guy.

WILSON'S PHALAROPE

Phalaropus tricolor

Lancashire Category A. (0, 7).

Vagrant from North America.

The first for the county was on pools at Hundred End, Hesketh Marsh in autumn 1967 (A.S. Duckels, P. Fearon, R.E. Jackson *et al.*). There is some confusion about when it was seen with limital dates given variously as 10 -22 September (Spencer 1973) and 27 August to 17 September (*British Birds* 62: 490).

Another was at the same site on 17 September 1970 and a first-winter followed in fairly close order at Freckleton Sewage Farm on 4-9 October 1973 as this site, which had been the county's wader hotspot for two decades, was in the process of demolition.

A decade later one was at Leighton Moss on 14-15 September 1983 with an adult female there on the Eric Morecambe complex on 24-25 May 1988.

First-winter Wilson's Phalarope, Freckleton Sewage Works, October 1973. (Laurence Eccles)

Since then all records have been back in the south-west, beginning with a juvenile/first-winter at Banks Marsh on 22 September 1990, which was also seen at Martin Mere the same day and again from 27 September to 1 October. The latest record, another first-winter, was also at Martin Mere on 30 September to 3 October 1991.

SJW, MJ.
This species account was sponsored by Maurice Jones and Bob Pyefinch.

RED-NECKED PHALAROPE

Phalaropus lobatus

Lancashire Category A. (3, 22).

Rare passage migrant, probably mainly from Scotland and Iceland.

Mitchell's only statement was that the species was 'said to have been shot on the Ribble' but McNicholl (1883) reported one at Birkdale in 1807.

Oakes listed three records, the earliest a party of three on Ainsdale shore on 23 May 1928. He wrote that the diagnostic characters were noted but mentions only 'white wing markings'; this lack of detail together with the unlikely habitat and the timing, at the height of the passage of breeding-plumaged Sanderling, means that this record cannot be accepted with confidence.

Oakes' second record was a bird in full breeding plumage at Freckleton sewage farm on 5 July 1947, found by Alan Harrison and Harry Shorrock, and the first proven county record. The next, at Leighton Moss on 29 May 1950, was described as 'a very tame bird in full breeding dress. . . under observation at close quarters for nearly two hours'. A record of three at Southport on 15 September 1957 was published in the county report but with no further details.

No more were seen until 1970, since when there have been 22 records, all of singles. Red-necked Phalaropes occurred in 14 years between 1970 and 2005, spread out fairly evenly with no obvious trend. More than one have been recorded in only five years: two in 1989 and 1994, three in 1983 and 1991, and four in 2001. Martin Mere is the favoured site with eight records, while Freckleton, Marshside and Marton Mere have accounted for the majority of the rest. Just two have been found in the east of the county, at Foulridge Reservoir on 9 July 1996 and Wood End Sewage Works, Burnley on 27 May 2002.

First-winter Red-necked Phalarope, Martin Mere, September 1994. (Steve Young)

Records are divided almost equally between spring and autumn (Figure 1) but with May the favoured month, especially the last ten days. The earliest date is 14 May 1994 and the latest 24 October 1983.

All birds up to the end of July whose ages have been recorded were adults, while five out of six after this date were juvenile/first-winters.

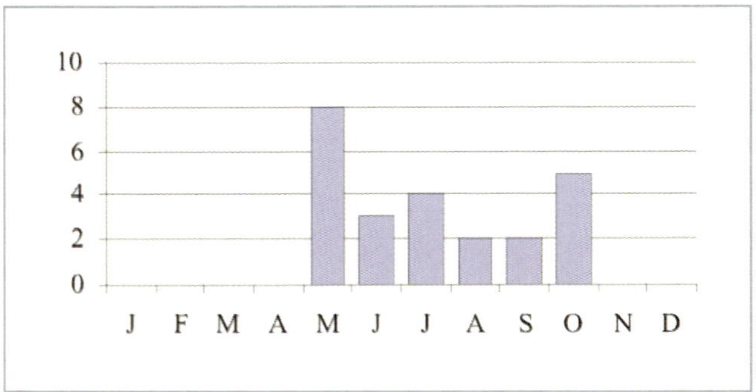

Figure 1. Monthly totals of Red-necked Phalaropes in Lancashire, 1950-2005.

All records:

1947	Freckleton, adult, 5 July
1950	Leighton Moss, adult, 29 May
1957	Southport, three, 15 September
1970	Marton Mere Blackpool, one, 18 August
1974	Freckleton, one, 10 to 16 October
1975	Formby, female, 25 May
1976	Freckleton, one, in flight only, 22 May
1978	Marshside, one, found dead 21 October
1982	Carnforth Marsh, probable female in flight only, 29 May
1983	Fairhaven, first-winter, 13 to 21 September
1983	River Alt inland of Formby, first-winter, 13 to 20 October
1983	Martin Mere, first-winter, 24 October
1989	Marton Mere Blackpool, one, 25 May
1989	Martin Mere, female 30 May
1991	Martin Mere, one, 21 May
1991	Seaforth, first-winter, 17 August
1991	Martin Mere, adult, 3 October
1992	Martin Mere, male, 5 to 9 July
1994	Martin Mere, female, 14 to 17 May
1994	Martin Mere, first-winter, 20 to 25 September
1996	Foulridge Reservoir, female, 9 July
2000	Martin Mere, one, 11 June
2001	Marshside, male, 8 June
2001	Marshside, female 21 to 26 June
2001	Leighton Moss, female, 12 July
2001	Seaforth, male, 29 July to 4 August
2002	Wood End Burnley, male, 27 May

MJ, SJW

This species account was sponsored by the Merseyside Partnership Against Wildlife Crime.

GREY PHALAROPE

Phalaropus fulicarius

Lancashire Category A. (/, 99).

Scarce passage migrant from Greenland and North America.

The Grey Phalarope has an Arctic circumpolar breeding distribution, the nearest populations to us being small ones on the coasts of Iceland (50 pairs) and Svalbard (250 pairs). It migrates to its wintering habitat in tropical and sub-tropical seas almost exclusively by sea routes, being seen inshore or inland only under weather stress, particularly during or after severe onshore gales (BWP). Birds seen in Britain are thought to come from Arctic Canada, Greenland and Iceland, migrating south-east across the Atlantic towards their West African wintering area (Migration Atlas).

In Mitchell's time this species was seen off the coast in spring and autumn and occasionally inland, with one winter record of one shot on the Ribble near Clitheroe at Christmas 1837. Oakes described the Grey Phalarope as a very scarce and irregular visitor to Lancashire. He cited only eight records, all in the period September to November, the first being shot at St. Michael's-on-Wyre in late September 1891. By the 1970s, however, the species was almost annual in autumn but there had been no spring records (Spencer 1973).

Juvenile Grey Phalarope, New Laithe Farm, Newton-in-Bowland, August 2005. (Margaret Breaks)

A total of 99 was recorded from 1950 to 2005, an average of fewer than two per year. Nearly all observations were of singletons, two in a day having been seen on only four occasions, most recently off Seaforth on 10 October 1981. The best decade was the 1980s, when 38 were recorded in the county (Figure 1), the most productive years being 1981 (with eleven sightings), 1987 (seven) and 1988 (six); nearly all were seen during or after autumn gales. Since the 1980s numbers have decreased, following a national trend the reasons for which are not clear, although the Icelandic breeding population is known to have declined (Migration Atlas).

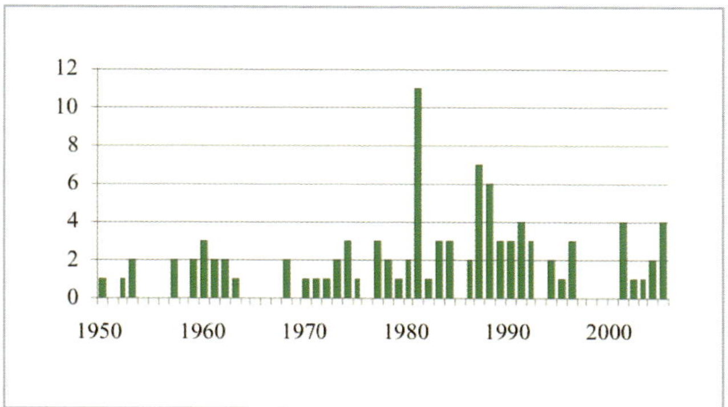

Figure 1. Annual totals of Grey Phalaropes in Lancashire, 1950-2005.

As might be expected, almost all sightings have been coastal, there being only nine at any distance inland (9% of the total). The only inland site with more than a single record is Martin Mere where four have been found, on 28 September 1975, 19 September 1981, 2 October 1991 and 2 October 2001. The others were at Wayoh Reservoir on 20 September 1981, Earnsdale Reservoir on 18 October 1987, Mere Sands Wood on 8-13 October 1988, Longridge Reservoir on 8 September 1992 and New Laithe Farm, Newton-in-Bowland on 27-30 August 2005. Coastal records show a markedly southern bias with more than half of all birds being seen from the Sefton coast, particularly Formby Point and the mouth of the Mersey, more than a quarter from the Fylde coast and just 10% in Morecambe Bay.

As elsewhere in Britain, the majority of Lancashire records are in autumn, with around two-thirds in September and October (Figure 2). The earliest were singles at Newton-in-Bowland on 27 August 2005 and Hightown on 31 August 1970.

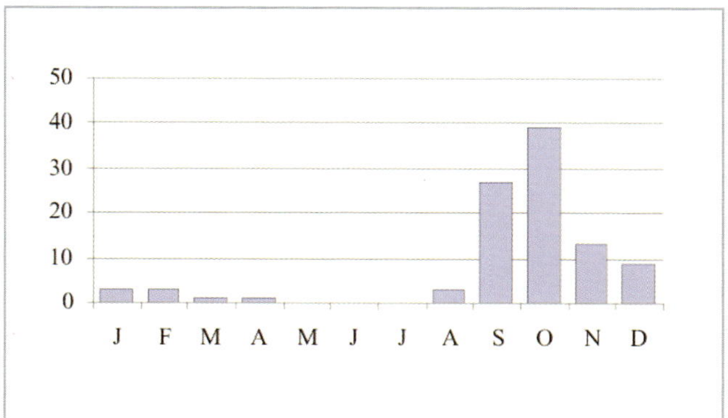

Figure 2. Monthly totals of Grey Phalaropes in Lancashire, 1950-2005.

Of birds that have been aged, nearly all have been juveniles or first-winters. BWP states that this age-group migrates later than the adults and is perhaps more susceptible to bad weather. Interestingly, as many as 15 birds have been recorded between December and February when they should be in West African seas; one can only speculate that these individuals were blown off course in the autumn and had not continued along their normal migration route. Birds returning north usually leave their African winter quarters in March and April. The Migration Atlas states that Grey Phalaropes are even rarer here in spring than in winter, an observation amply supported by the Lancashire data which include only two unambiguous spring records: singles at Ainsdale on 3 April 1977 and Salwick on 21 March 1986. We have no summer records and no birds have been ringed or recovered in the county.

PHS, MJ.

This species account was sponsored by the Breaks family.

SKUAS

Despite huge advances in our knowledge of key structural and plumage features in the past 15 years or so, field identification of skuas can still pose difficult questions; seawatch tallies always look the more authentic for the inclusion of a healthy quota of 'skua sp.' records. The development and wide availability of high quality telescopes during the 1980s transformed seawatching and for the first time allowed scrutiny of distant birds in flight. This, combined with the publication by Lars Jonsson of the first accurate set of plates of the four regular European species in 1987, equipped observers with the means to identify to species a far greater proportion of birds than previously.

Nowadays, reasonably close or prolonged views allow the identification of most adult skuas but juveniles, and especially sub-adults, can still pose significant problems. Seawatching rarely provides second chances and even the most advanced digital photographic technology has yet to resolve all problems. Even the most upright of seawatchers will undoubtedly have been at least tempted to plump for the rarer of alternative explanations of a far-away, dark shape.

Previous generations of birdwatchers had none of our advantages; the earliest records of skuas in the county were of 'collected' birds or tideline corpses. The surge of records of all species which began in the late 1970s is almost certainly mainly a reflection of more, better-equipped and better-informed observers and it is impossible to make judgements about the true status of skuas in our waters much before the mid-1980s.

POMARINE SKUA

Stercorarius pomarinus

Lancashire Category A.

Uncommon passage migrant from Arctic Russia; rare winter visitor.

According to Mitchell one or two Pomarine Skuas were shot in most years in the nineteenth century, all on the coast during September and October. He also mentioned one shot on the Ribble at Samlesbury in October 1879 and referred to several other inland occurrences without giving details. Oakes appears to have been rather sceptical about Mitchell's account and considered only the Samlesbury bird and one 'obtained' at Pilling Moss in 1860 as properly substantiated. He added a further five records: singles killed at Cockersands Light on 28 November 1908 and the Lune Estuary on 11 November 1911, three seen at Ainsdale on 3 June 1917 with one there on 10 July, and one found dead near Rossall on 8 January 1929.

Just two followed in the 1950s, both in 1954 with one at St. Anne's on 17 August and a corpse at Freshfield on 16 October. A further seven records in the 1960s all came in the period 11 August to 3 November, except for a corpse on Cockerham Marsh on 26 November 1961. The 1970s saw a big increase with more than 40 birds reported and numbers rose again to more than 100 during the 1980s, but the 1990s saw only a modest further increase.

On average, about 15 have been seen each year since the 1980s but there are large variations (Figure 1), mostly due to prevailing weather conditions in autumn or the intensity of seawatching effort in spring. The highest annual totals were in 1988 (25), 1991 (35), 2003 (34), 2004 (36) and 2005 (33).

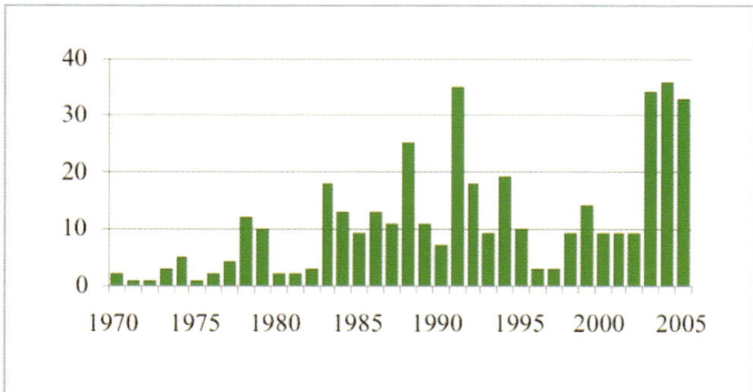

Figure 1. Annual totals of Pomarine Skuas in Lancashire, 1970-2005. [Juveniles and 'immatures' in August and the first fortnight of September, plus all unaged birds are excluded.]

Small numbers of wintering birds lingering into March and perhaps early April sometimes blur the onset of spring passage but the main movement takes place between the third week of April and the end of May, probably peaking in the first or second week of May (Figure 2). Since 1977 there have been around 85 records involving some 165 birds in spring, almost all of which have been seen in Morecambe Bay, principally from Heysham and Jenny Brown's Point, with just 18 records from the Fylde coast and nine on the Sefton coast. Dark morph birds are exceptionally scarce and the overwhelming majority of spring birds have been light morph adults; there are one or two reports of sub-adults, although the possibility that these may have related to adults not yet in breeding plumage cannot be ruled out. One such, at Seaforth from 2-11 May 1987, was the only bird definitely to have spent any significant amount of time in Lancashire waters. All others have been one-day birds, hurrying northward.

Spring 'Poms' were recorded in every year but three between 1983 and 2005. The existence of a regular passage movement through the eastern Irish Sea is now well established, initially on the basis of sightings in the Solway Firth, through which an annual cross-country movement takes place. Although birds have several times been seen flying inland from the Lancashire section of Morecambe Bay, there is no solid evidence that this is a regular event. However, extensive coverage from Jenny Brown's Point during 2003-2005 suggests that 30 or more birds may pass through the bay each spring and this is not entirely weather-related. There is, though, no doubt that Pomarine Skuas usually migrate further offshore than Arctic Skuas.

It is perhaps most likely that a proportion of birds heading north are diverted into Morecambe Bay by moderate to fresh south-westerly and westerly winds. Certainly, numbers in Lancashire are significantly smaller (by about 70%) than in Cumbria; the first time the entire passage reached double figures was in 1992 when 15 birds were recorded with a peak day count of seven at Heysham on 26 April. However, the spring seawatching effort in Morecambe Bay has increased significantly in recent years, culminating in record passage movements of 30 birds past Heysham and Jenny Brown's Point between 16 April and 18 May 2003, 35 between 4 April and 6 June 2004 and 28 between 6 April and 22 May 2005. The largest day-counts were nine off Jenny Brown's Point on 4 May 2004 and at least twelve there on 5 May 2005. It now seems likely that spring passage through Lancashire waters is significantly larger than autumn's, with spring records outnumbering those in autumn by 152 to 22 during 1999-2005.

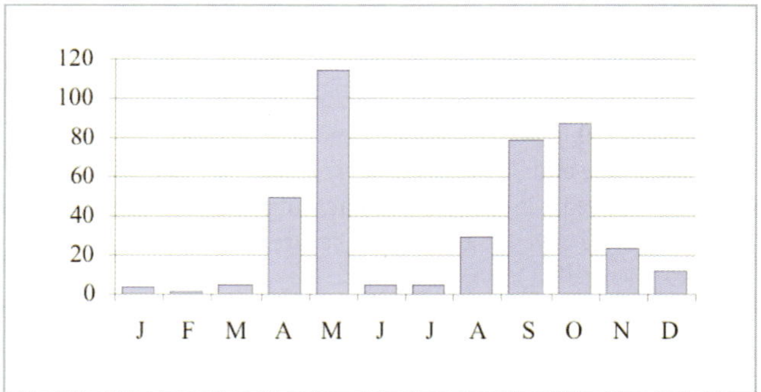

Figure 2. Monthly totals of Pomarine Skuas in Lancashire,1954-2004. [Juveniles and 'immatures' in August and the first fortnight of September, plus all unaged birds are excluded.]

Only a handful have ever been seen in June or July; some have been described as adults, others as sub-adults, but it seems likely that the majority will have been non-breeding second- or third-calendar year birds.

Records of adults increase a little from about mid-August but the bulk of the passage takes place throughout September to mid-to late October. Very variable numbers occur, most records coinciding with westerly gales. This makes it difficult to judge how long individuals stay in our part of the Irish Sea but there is no evidence to suggest that they do so for long – the longest recorded stay of any autumn adult has been a mere two days. This is supported by an almost complete lack of records of feeding birds, contrasting starkly with the behaviour of Arctic Skuas.

In recent years there have been a number of reports of juveniles or 'immatures' during August and early September. These are very difficult to interpret. Pomarine is the latest-breeding of the skuas and the young do not fledge before mid-August (Dementiev and Gladkov 1951); juveniles are very rarely seen in the North Sea – where they are far more abundant than on our coast – much before mid-September and usually not in any numbers before the end of the month. It is possible that some at least of our early records refer to second- or third-calendar year birds but some may have been misidentified. However, it is clear that the autumn movement of juveniles in Lancashire rarely begins before the last week of September and most have been recorded during October. By the end of October the majority of birds are juveniles and the latest record of a definite autumn adult was on 6 November 1999 at Formby Point.

Sub-adult Pomarine Skua, Fleetwood, April 1995. (Steve Young)

The largest day counts have been seven off Blackpool on 6 October 1983; seven on the Mersey at Seaforth on 20 October 1984, at least twelve there on 7-8 October 1988 and another six on 28 August 1994; five off Formby on 16 September 1989; and six at Marshside and Seaforth on 17 October 1991. Although birds are seen most years in Morecambe Bay, autumn records show a strong southerly bias, the reverse of the situation in spring; this is almost certainly simply the result of birds being funnelled towards the Sefton coast and the Mersey by north-westerly winds.

Very small numbers, on average one every three to four years, have been recorded after late November. The period December 1994 to January 1995 produced two juveniles and an adult offshore in the Rossall-Heysham area, a juvenile at Marshside in December and January, and an adult on the inner Mersey at Oglet Bay from 18-25 December. These are the only reports of adults in winter in the county, all others have been juveniles, including presumably five 'immatures' past Fleetwood Pier on 3 December 1999.

The only February record was off Ainsdale on the 26th in 1986 but there have been five records in March, including a second-calendar year bird that remained in the Rossall Point area from at least 22 March to 26 April 1995.

There have been only two authenticated records at any significant distance from the coast: juveniles at Longridge Reservoir from 27 September to 2 October 1976 and at Foulridge Reservoir on 28-29 November 1999.

SJW, MJ.

This species account was sponsored by Phil Lillywhite.

ARCTIC SKUA

Stercorarius parasiticus

Lancashire Category A.

Fairly common passage migrant from Scotland and the Arctic.

Mitchell reported birds being shot between October and April and described the species as uncommon on the coast and rare inland. Their status had become clearer by the time of Oakes's book; he referred to the Arctic Skua as a fairly regular passage migrant in late summer and autumn, frequent on the Fylde coast and further south but scarce and irregular further north. He noted that birds were rare in winter, occasional in spring with a few from mid-July but most in August to September and just a few in October. An exceptional record at that time was of ten at Banks on 9-10 August 1927.

Despite a proliferation of records, the past 50 years have done little to modify Oakes's assessment.

The earliest records, singles at Marshside on 12 March 1985 and on 20 March 2004 at Jenny Brown's Point, may have related to wintering birds. The first clear-cut migrants appear on average (1983-2005) on 14 April. As with most seabirds, the majority are forced onshore by the unpredictable occurrence of westerly winds, but spring records are a little less weather dependent than autumn's and the passage usually peaks during the last two weeks of April and the first half of May, up to a fortnight later than that of Great Skuas. Scottish breeding colonies are usually occupied during April while more northerly breeders do not return until May or even early June (Furness 1987), suggesting that a relatively high proportion of the Lancashire passage may be heading towards Arctic rather than Scottish colonies. This may be borne out by the relatively high proportion of light morph birds recorded (since these are scarce in Scotland but predominate in the high Arctic): 24 (26%) of 93 recorded at Heysham during spring 1989-2003 were pale birds.

Spring numbers of Arctics are, however, considerably higher than of Greats, with about 20 seen annually on average – 68 from Jenny Brown's Point and Heysham in 2004 was an exceptional seasonal total. They also appear to be slightly more gregarious than Bonxies, appearing more regularly in small groups – although most records are of singles. Day-counts above five at any one site are exceptional: they have included eight off Formby on 2 April 1977; 17 off Heysham on 3 May 1982, which included a flock of five; 14 off Jenny Brown's Point on 5 May 2004 and eleven there on 5 May 2005.

More consistent observation at Heysham and Jenny Brown's Point in recent years has added greatly to our knowledge of the spring movement and this, combined with a drop in autumn numbers, means that the Arctic Skua is now primarily a spring species in Morecambe Bay with fewer than 30% of all records occurring in autumn. Although Arctic Skuas are seen in most springs from all the main seawatching stations, records have a distinctly northern bias. Morecambe Bay almost always gets the lion's share and the Fylde coast generally reports more than the Sefton coast – a pattern shared by Pomarine but not Great Skua. The reasons for this are obscure but it may reflect genuine differences in migration routes.

There is, however, little evidence of any inland passage across Lancashire. There have been just three spring occurrences any distance inland: one at Foulridge Reservoir in mid-May 1987, three at Harle Syke, Burnley on 16 May 1994 and one at Stocks Reservoir on 13 May 2002 – intriguingly, this last was flying south-east.

Small numbers are usually recorded in June, presumably a mixture of late migrant adults and wandering sub-adults. There is a significantly higher proportion of inland occurrences in early summer than at other times of the year: singles at Stocks Reservoir on 7 June 1978, Heasandford, Burnley on 1 June 1984 and Mere Sands Wood on 8 June 1986, and two at Water Sheddles Reservoir, Trawden on 13 June 2002.

The first definite returning migrants usually appear from the end of the second week of July and passage usually peaks between late August and the end of September. Birds become rapidly scarcer throughout October and the average last sighting (1983-2004) was on 23 October. November records are rare – about one every three years.

Juvenile Arctic Skua, Mersey Narrows, September 2004. (Steve Young)

Until recent years, autumn passage was significantly heavier than in spring but equally, if not more, variable in size. Combined autumn totals from the two most consistently recorded sites, Heysham and Seaforth, are shown in Figure 1, giving an indication of the trend in records over the past 25 years. Large counts are almost entirely dependent upon autumn gales driving birds that normally pass well offshore into the range of shore-based seawatchers. The virtual absence of equinoctial gales since the mid-1990s has led to a dramatic decline in numbers to 50 or fewer annually; the last double-figure day-counts anywhere in the county were ten on the Mersey at Seaforth on 4 October 1996, 13 off Crosby shore on 1 September 2004 and 14 at Formby Point on 31 August 2005. During the 1980s and early 1990s, up to five a day were typical totals from the main seawatching stations, with peak counts of 10-20 regular. Larger counts included 20 plus 15 'probables' at Rossall on 3 September 1983, 35 off Heysham on 24 September 1991, 23 off Formby Point on 21 September 1993 and 23 off Blackpool on 11 September 1994. Before the downturn, Arctic Skuas were too common to have been fully reported in county reports but estimated totals of 170 were seen in autumn 1990, 150 in 1991 and 215 in 1992.

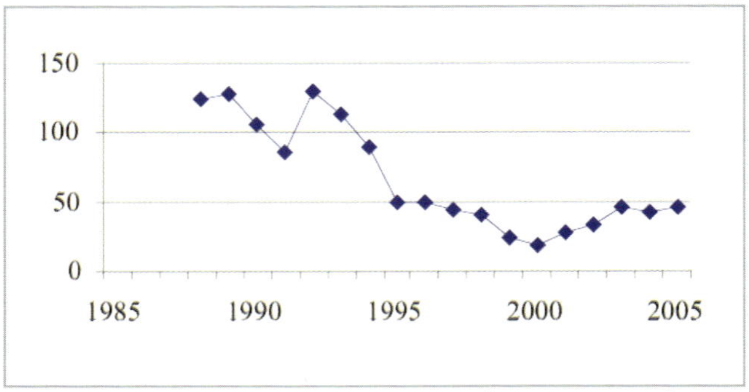

Figure 1. Annual total autumn sightings of Arctic Skuas (3-year rolling means) at Seaforth and Heysham, 1986-2005.

The geographic pattern of records is, as with Pomarine Skua, the opposite of spring; relatively few are seen in Morecambe Bay (particularly in recent years) but sightings are far more numerous in Liverpool Bay. In autumn 2004, for example, the return of autumn gales produced 106 off the Sefton coast, 54 off the Fylde and a mere nine in Morecambe Bay.

Inland records are far more regular than in spring: singles at Rishton Reservoir on 2 September 1973; flying north-east up the Ribble and high over Preston on 29 September 1977; at Eccleston Mere on 12 September 1980; Whitemoor Reservoir on 1 September 1984; Belmont Reservoir on 3 August 1985; Martin Mere on 13 August 1989 (with a remarkable six flying north-west there on 22 August 1989); Springs Reservoir on 27 August 1995 and over Dean Clough Reservoir on 8 October 2004. One became settled on the Altcar Withins, hunting Lapwings, for a week in September 2004. To what extent these records involve birds blown inland from the west coast or cross-country migrants is impossible to say, but the fact that none was seen during the period of decline in coastal records from the mid-1990s to 2003 perhaps supports the former. However, four flying down the Ribble at

Longton Marsh in calm conditions on 11 September 1957 were presumably genuine cross-country migrants.

Records from Seaforth and Heysham indicate that about 40% of aged autumn birds are juveniles (1985-2003, n = 235), but there is much annual variation at both sites. Seaforth adults comprise a high proportion of light morph birds: 37% for the autumn as a whole (1985-2002, n = 99). This rises from 27% in July and August (n = 47) to 45% in September and October, indicating that the proportion of high Arctic migrants increases as the season progresses. This is in stark contrast to the situation in the North Sea where light phase birds are scarce in autumn (Tasker *et al.* 1987).

Despite being by far the commonest skua seen in Lancashire for most of the year, Arctics are decidedly scarce in winter and are recorded far less frequently than Greats or even Pomarines. Counting only those seen between December and February just eight have been recorded: singles near the Mersey Bar Light on 20 February 1974; at Marshside until early December 1977 and on 18 January 1983; off Morecambe on 18-19 January 1983; off Blackpool on 15 December 1993; at Seaforth on 8 January 1995; a juvenile at Morecambe on 18 February 1995 and one at Fleetwood on 3 December 1999.

SJW, MJ.

This species account was sponsored by Seumus Eaves.

LONG-TAILED SKUA

Stercorarius longicaudus

Lancashire Category A. (/, 93).

Scarce passage migrant from Fennoscandia and northern Russia.

Unsurprisingly, all nineteenth century records were shot: an adult near Fleetwood on 20 August 1850 and another adult supposedly on the Ribble in March 1877 – a most unlikely date – the specimen going to St. Michaels Museum. Three birds were shot in Morecambe Bay on 25 October 1859, but it is not known if these were in our present recording area. The first field record was an adult on the Ribble Estuary on 15 May 1916, while the first known juvenile was shot at Bolton-le-Sands on 1 November 1938.

Two records followed in the 1950s: a dead juvenile at Freckleton on 14 October 1952 and an 'immature' (presumably a juvenile) exhausted on the beach between Blundellsands and Hightown on 31 August 1958. Long-tailed Skuas remained extremely rare in the 1960s and 1970s when they were still regarded as a national rarity, with unaged singles at Formby Point on 16-17 August 1967, off Blackpool on 25 October 1969, and an adult off Formby Point on 11 November 1972 with another unaged bird there on 31 August 1973. A juvenile was resting on the beach at Hest Bank on 1 Oct 1978.

An adult at Marshside on 10 May 1979 was only our second spring record – if the 1877 report is discounted – and there have been only two more subsequently, on the Mersey at Seaforth on 17 May 1991 and off Jenny Brown's Point on 9 May 2004. Thus, all spring birds have occurred between 9 and 17 May.

Adult Long-tailed Skua, River Mersey, Seaforth, October 1988. (Steve Young)

Birds were recorded in 16 years between 1980 and 2005 but did not become regular until the late 1980s. As with many seabirds, sightings of which depend upon the 'right' weather conditions at the right time of year, annual numbers vary hugely; the five years 1988, 1991, 1992, 1998 and 2004 between them account for more than 75% of all records since 1980, with an annual average of barely one outside of these years (Figure 1).

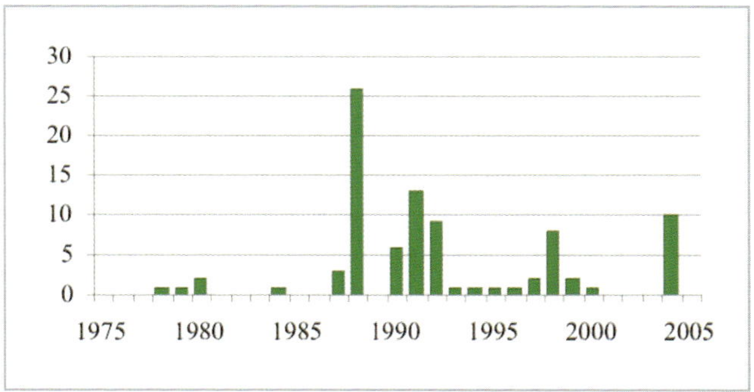

Figure 1. Annual totals of Long-tailed Skuas in Lancashire, 1975-2005.

After two days of strong onshore winds had subsided on 24 September 1988, two juveniles were seen at Rossall Point and an adult at Seaforth and Ainsdale. This alone would have made it an exceptional year but on 7 October force 10 westerly winds battered the Lancashire coast and produced completely unprecedented numbers on the Mersey at Seaforth, doubling overnight the county's historic total. There were at least 30 separate sightings at Seaforth that day with a minimum of twelve birds and probably more than 15 seen; one was also seen at Otterspool in south Liverpool. Most were adults but there were also one light and two dark phase juveniles. The next morning at least four adults, two juveniles and a sub-adult left the river as the wind decreased. A minimum of 17 were seen during the two days but the real total may have been considerably higher. Surprisingly, the only others seen in the county during this period were one at Heysham on the 7th and two there on the 9th.

Nothing remotely comparable has taken place since 1988 but on 20 September 1990 persistent onshore winds again brought at least three adults and two juveniles into the Mersey at Seaforth.

This time, however, they stayed in the area for several days until at least the 24th in relatively calm conditions, possibly encouraged by the easy pickings provided by a massive wreck of Leach's Petrels. The following two years also saw relatively high numbers. At least twelve seen in autumn 1991 between 22 September and 17 October with peaks of at least three on 24 September at Heysham and three on 3 October, and four on 17 October at Seaforth; all the Seaforth birds were juveniles and it is possible they had remained in the area throughout. In 1992 five adults together flew along the shore at Formby on 4 August; these were followed by a juvenile at Formby Point on 30 August and juveniles at Heysham on 31 August and 12 September with an adult there on 7 September.

Juvenile Long-tailed Skua, Mersey Narrows, September, 2004. (Steve Young)

The next significant influx was in 1998 when at least eight, including two adults, were recorded at Seaforth, Formby Point, Rossall Point and Pilling Lane Ends between 14 August and 10 September. Autumn 2004 saw another influx of juveniles with at least three seen off the Fylde coast on 20-21 September and at least five in the Mersey Narrows between 31 August and 23 September.

The earliest autumn adult recorded was on 26 July 1994 and the earliest juvenile on 14 August 1998. October has marginally the most records but 21 out of 35 in that month occurred in 1988, so the passage usually peaks in September (Figure 2). Latest dates for adults and juveniles respectively are 11 November 1972 and 6 November 1999.

None has ever been seen inland and there are no records outside of migration periods.

More than half of all autumn records have been juveniles. Most adults have occurred during main influx years, so that juveniles are rather more regular.

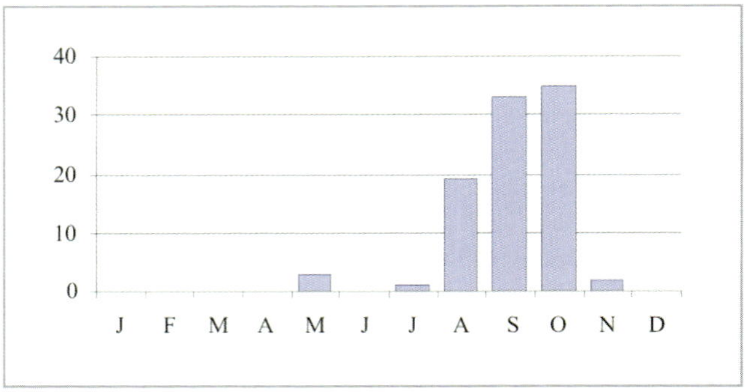

Figure 2. Monthly totals of Long-tailed Skuas in Lancashire, 1952-2005.

SJW, MJ.

This species account was sponsored by John Bannon.

GREAT SKUA (BONXIE)

Stercorarius skua

Lancashire Category A.

Fairly common passage migrant from Scotland and Iceland; scarce winter visitor.

The Great Skua was an uncommon visitor in Mitchell's day; he described it as usually occurring in autumn, sometimes in winter and with odd birds in summer. Oakes could cite only eleven records in our present recording area during the period 1910 to 1950. Seven of these were from what is now Merseyside and four from the Fylde, with six in autumn, four in spring and one in January.

Bonxies continued to be very scarce during the 1960s with an average of only 2.5 seen annually, and barely less so during the 1970s when roughly five a year were recorded. The turning point in the species' fortunes in Lancashire came in about 1977 and the 1980s saw a dramatic increase in records to around 30 a year, remaining at roughly this level during the 1990s and 2000s (Figure 1). No doubt, part of this upsurge can be put down to the increased number of more skilled and better equipped observers but it does to some extent mirror changes in the British breeding population. Great Skuas came close to extinction in the northern isles of Scotland towards the end of the nineteenth century but began to recover in the first decades of the twentieth and boomed during the 1960s (Lloyd *et al.* 1991).

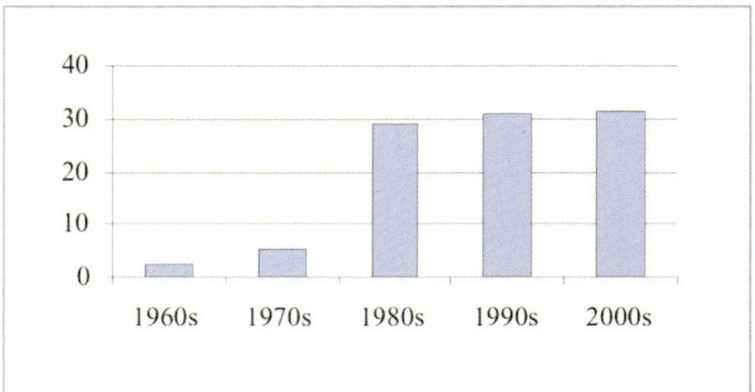

Figure 1. Average annual totals of Great Skuas in Lancashire by decade (1960-2005).

Bonxies are relatively short-distance migrants and begin their return to the breeding grounds during March, but very few are seen in Lancashire waters that early and some of these are perhaps lingering wintering birds. The main passage is concentrated into April and relatively few are seen during May (Figure 2). More surprising is that slightly fewer have been recorded in Lancashire in spring than Pomarine Skuas, perhaps due in part to their stronger flight and lower susceptibility to being blown onshore, their more northerly (rather than north-easterly) migratory direction, or simply because April is not the favourite month for seawatching.

Unlike Pomarine and Arctic Skuas, for which spring records show a marked northerly bias, sightings of Bonxies are spread fairly evenly the length of the coast from Formby Point to the Fylde coast and north to Morecambe Bay. Most records are of single birds, so five off Formby in a gale on 2 April 1977 were exceptional. The only other day counts greater than two all came in 2001: records of three at Heysham on 8 and 17 April and Jenny Brown's Point on 28 May.

Records of singles spiralling high and heading north-east from Silverdale Marsh on 30 April 1979, high east from the Eric Morecambe complex on 12 April 1992 and north, gaining height

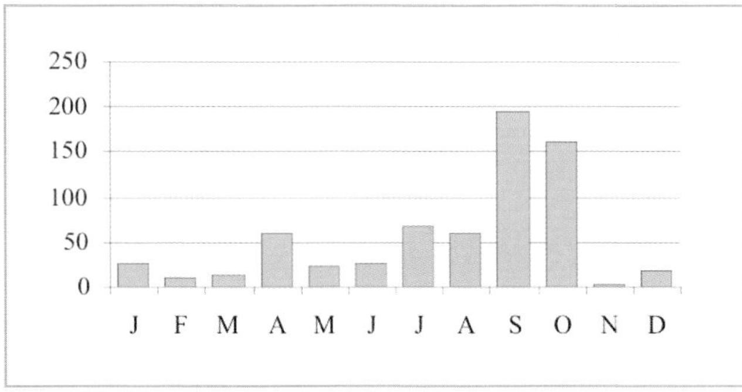

Figure 2. Monthly totals of Great Skuas in Lancashire, 1952-2003

above Morecambe on 21 April 1993 provide the only, somewhat thin, evidence of overland passage. One was feeding on farmland at Marton, Blackpool on 25 March 1948 but there have been no spring records further inland.

We have virtually no information on the age breakdown of birds in any season but it is known that adults (seven years and above) migrate earlier than non-breeding birds (Migration Atlas). It is therefore likely that most of those seen between May and early July – about 50 since 1952 – are immatures.

The autumn return does not usually get underway until mid-July. Like most other seabirds, the size and timing of the passage vary enormously between years, being almost entirely dependent upon weather conditions. The largest seasonal totals have been 58 in 1983 (peak in the first week of September), 42 in 1988 (several peaks from mid-August to early October), 40 in 1992 (peak late August to early September), 43 in 1994 (peak mid-September) and 54 in 2004.

Most sightings are of single birds, occasionally two, and the largest recorded 'flocks' were eight in view simultaneously off Formby on 3 September 1983 and eleven at Heysham on 16 October the same year. Day-counts rarely exceed three or four, even during the most favourable conditions; the county record was 16 at Heysham on 16 October 1983, with other notable counts of eleven at Seaforth on 6 September, eight at both Formby Point and Heysham on 15 August 1990, and nine off Rossall Point on 21 September 2004.

Records become progressively scarcer after the first week of October but November sightings are far from exceptional. As with other skuas, autumn records of Bonxies are considerably more numerous in Liverpool Bay than in Morecambe Bay.

Only two have been recorded inland: singles at Prescot Reservoirs for several weeks in September 1977 and at Habergham Clough, Burnley on 13 August 1986, again providing scant evidence of any cross-country passage.

Birds seen after mid-November are perhaps as likely to be early winterers as late migrants; any appearing from December onwards almost certainly are. Bonxies are remarkably frequent in winter with about 50 seen in the past 30 years between December and February and three during the first half of March.

Strong winds during early 1990 produced a remarkable series of 19 records. Allowing for possible duplication, a minimum of twelve birds was seen between 28 January and 1 March with records from the whole length of the coast from Seaforth to Jenny Brown's Point and three inland, at Martin Mere on 10 February, White Moss, Skelmersdale on 11 February and Upper Rivington Reservoir on 1 March. The only other inland winter records were singles over Edgworth, Darwen on 24 March 1994 and at Clowbridge Reservoir, Burnley on 14 December 2000.

More than half of the world breeding population nests in Scotland, mostly in Shetland and Orkney, and most of the rest in Iceland, and the four recoveries of ringed birds in Lancashire reflect this. All had been ringed as nestlings: a juvenile from Foula, the main Shetland colony, on 11 November 1977 on the Ribble marshes; another Foula juvenile at Seaforth on 18 October 1983; a third calendar-year bird from Foula at Carnforth on 22 March 1990; and an eleven-year-old from Iceland at Blackpool on 1 April 1982.

With the recent speculation that Brown Skuas *S. antarctica* can occur in British waters in winter the specific identification of any large skua at that time of year must now be open to question – we await our first winter corpse with some anticipation.

SJW, MJ.

This species account was sponsored in memory of Frank Lodge.

MEDITERRANEAN GULL

Larus melanocephalus

Lancashire Category A.

Rare breeder; fairly common passage migrant from western and central Europe; uncommon winter visitor.

Nowadays Mediterranean Gulls are taken more or less for granted throughout most of the county, but they were extremely scarce until relatively recently. Their changing Lancashire status reflects the national situation: a vagrant in the 1950s, then showing a sharp increase during the 1960s and 1970s and becoming an established British breeding species in the last decades of the twentieth century.

The first county records were a long-staying first-summer at Formby from 16 April to 24 November 1968 and an adult at St. Anne's on 2 August 1968. Spencer estimated that at least 17 had been seen by 1972, mostly on the Merseyside coast. Records continued to increase, so that by the end of 1992 around 350 had been recorded, averaging five per year in the 1970s, 17 in the 1980s and showing a further sharp rise in the 1990s. By this time the county report could only summarise records but data from Seaforth and Heysham, two of the best-watched sites, suggest that annual totals on the coast may have reached a peak in the mid-1990s, declining a little since then, perhaps reflecting waning observer interest in distinguishing individuals rather than real change.

Certainly, the late 1980s and early 1990s saw a dramatic increase in the geographical spread of records. The first inland records came in 1986 at Rivington and Foulridge Reservoirs and up to ten 'Meds' are now seen annually in the centre and east of the county. Nonetheless, coastal and estuarine records still outnumber inland ones by at least 10:1. Seaforth remains the favoured site with birds present most days but the rest of the Sefton coast is probably equally important, while numbers gradually decline northwards through the Fylde and into Morecambe Bay. The record county day-count was 16 at Seaforth on 13 July 1995.

A small spring movement was first detected at Seaforth during the 1980s and was confirmed on the Fylde coast, particularly Marton Mere, and to a lesser extent in north Lancashire, in the early 1990s. More recently, significant numbers have begun to be seen in east Lancashire but the overall pattern of occurrences remains little changed.

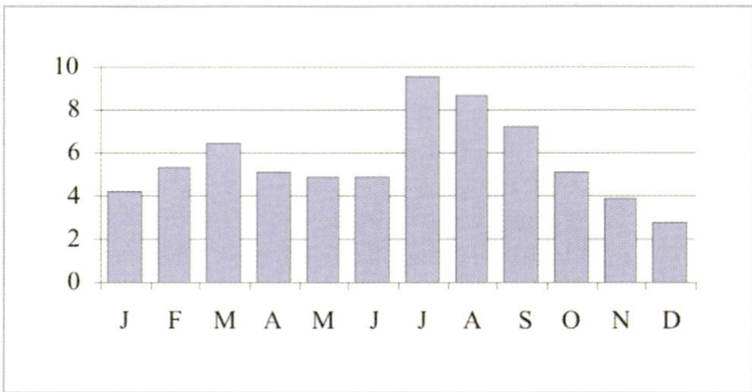

Figure 1. Average monthly totals of Mediterranean Gulls at Seaforth Nature Reserve, 1988-2005.

Adult passage begins in late February but peaks in March; passage adults are rarely seen after the first week of April. Second-summers move a week or so later than adults, sometimes through to early May. Both adults and second-summers often arrive in pairs and courtship displays are regularly seen at coastal sites. Large monthly totals of spring adults and second-summers include 13 at Seaforth in 1997 with ten there in 1989, 1998 and 2000, nine at Marshside in 2002, eight at Marton Mere in 1996 and eleven in east Lancashire in 2002. Total spring passage numbers are probably in the region of 50-100, far more than can be accounted for by locally-breeding birds. There have been two sightings of ringed spring passage adults, one from Holland and one from Belgium, but the destination of most birds remains unknown.

A handful of young birds moves through with the adults, but the majority of first-summers do not arrive until May with the largest numbers often seen during June, many becoming extremely site-faithful; the largest day-count was seven at Seaforth in June 1995. Ringing recoveries indicate widespread origins for these summering first-years: two from Holland, France and Belgium, and singles from Hungary, Slovakia and the Ukraine.

Adult summer Mediterranean Gull, Crosby Marine Park, July 2006. (Steve Young)

Breeding first occurred in Britain in 1968 and numbers have steadily increased to around 100 pairs (Ogilvie 2003). Breeding had been suspected in the huge Black-headed Gull colony on the south Ribble marshes since the 1980s but this was not proven until 2001; five pairs nested there in 2003.

A male held territory at Leighton Moss for part of the breeding season in 1988 and 1989 but the first (unsuccessful) nesting took place at nearby Dockacres in 1990. This pair moved to Leighton Moss but their replacement clutch was probably taken by a Grey Heron. The next definite breeding attempt came in 1997 on the Eric Morecambe complex in 1997, when two young were fledged; the female was Dutch-ringed. A male was paired with a Black-headed Gull at Leighton Moss in 1998 and birds summered in the area during 1999 but there have been no further breeding attempts there.

Breeding was probably attempted at Stocks Reservoir, again amongst Black-headed Gulls, in 1997 and one full pair nested there unsuccessfully in 1998 when a hybrid pair raised one chick. Two pairs bred in 1999 with unknown results and there were two hybrid pairs the next year. 2001 saw access restrictions due to the Foot and Mouth Disease outbreak but in 2002, after this series of false starts, two pure pairs raised one and two chicks successfully, and one or two pairs again nested in 2003 and 2005 and possibly three pairs in 2004. The rapidly expanding Black-headed Gull colony at Belmont Reservoir held three adults during the breeding season in 2004 but breeding was not proven until 2005 when at least one pair nested.

The return passage is far more protracted than in spring. Its timing is blurred by the presence of summering first-years and of adults and juveniles dispersing from local breeding sites but, generally speaking, it begins in early to mid-July and continues to late September/early October. Peak numbers usually occur at the end of July and in early August, the largest monthly totals being 18 at Seaforth in July 1995, 15 there in July 2005 and 16 at Heysham, also in July 2005.

The first juvenile/first-winter was recorded at Formby on 12 September 1983 but up ten are now seen annually, mostly on the coast between Heysham and Seaforth; they begin to arrive in July, usually a little later than adults. The origins of ringed juvenile/first-winters are similar to those of first-summers: six from Belgium, four from Holland, one from Poland and one from the Czech Republic.

Figure 3. Natal colonies of Mediterranean Gulls seen in Lancashire. (Large dots show multiple records)

Numbers decline rapidly in the second half of October, leaving no more than ten wintering. Most of these are adults but a number have been extremely site-faithful between years and it seems likely that many, including all ringed birds, may have first arrived as birds of the year. One apparent example of this was a bird that summered in its second calendar-year in 1995 at Morecambe, returning each winter until 2005 at least and 'acquiring' colour rings at its nest in Poland in 2003. Another is a Czech Republic-ringed juvenile which appeared at Heysham in August 2003, where it has subsequently wintered until at least September 2005.

SJW, MJ.

This species account was sponsored by Stuart Piner.

LAUGHING GULL

Larus atricilla

Lancashire Category A. (0, 1).

Vagrant from North America.

A record of an adult on the Mersey on 3 August 1977 was initially accepted by the BBRC and published as being in Lancashire but was, in fact, claimed from New Ferry on Wirral. It has now been reviewed and rejected by the BBRC.

Given its near monopoly of scarce and rare Nearctic Gulls, it had always seemed a racing certainty that the county's first Laughing Gull would be at Seaforth. That it would actually turn up inland was not widely predicted!

After a record influx into Britain which began in autumn 2005, Lancashire's second Laughing Gull was found at Marton Mere on 9 April 2006. Probably a second-summer bird, it stayed until 16 April, coming to bread and posing for photographers. (Above: Phillip Tomkinson. Below: Steve Young)

John Wright arrived at Brockholes Quarry in Preston early in the morning of 1 May 1999 to find the site shrouded in mist coming off the River Ribble. This quickly cleared to gradually reveal a group of about 20 Black-headed Gulls roosting on one of the islands. To his amazement a medium-sized, dark-backed, hooded gull materialised amongst them, quickly identified as an adult Laughing Gull in full summer plumage.

The news had to be shared with other birdwatchers and, since this was just before the time when everyone carried a mobile phone, five minutes taking a description was all that could be spared before seeking out a phone box. This took a quarter of an hour before finding one in working order and on his return, as the last of the mist was burning off, the gulls were beginning to depart. The Laughing Gull flew off downriver, into the sun, heading towards the Ribble Marshes and the sea – and that was the last anyone saw of it. This was the 101st record of Laughing Gull in Britain and Ireland.

SJW.

This species account was sponsored by John Wright.

FRANKLIN'S GULL

Larus pipixcan

Lancashire Category A. (0, 1).

Vagrant from North America.

An adult-winter was found at Martin Mere on 29 December 1983 and was seen there intermittently until at least 2 January 1984 (D.W. Elmley, M.R. Green, G.H. Halfpenny). The bird usually appeared with Black-headed Gulls in the late afternoon and may have roosted overnight.

What was accepted as the same bird was later seen twice in Cheshire, at Runcorn on 18 January and Frodsham on 27 January 1984. This was only the eighth record of this, the rarest of the Nearctic gulls on the national list, in Britain or Ireland. It was the first to be found in north-west England.

SJW, MJ.

This species account was sponsored by Mark Garner.

LITTLE GULL

Larus minutus

Lancashire Category A.

Common winter visitor and spring passage migrant en route to breeding grounds in Finland.

The Little Gull was an extremely scarce species in Lancashire prior to the 1960s. Mitchell published just three records between 1856 and 1889: at Formby, 'near Preston' and at Rossall Point; and Oakes added a further twelve between 1913 and 1941. Twelve were seen during the 1950s and a further 16 between 1960 and 1964.

The first inkling of change came in 1965 when 21 birds were seen between 17 January and 12 October but the county's first really large flock appeared in February 1968 when 137 were at Formby Point (Lassey 1968).

Smith (1974) recorded a total of 1,086 bird-days on regular visits to Formby Point from 1969 to 1974 and further evidence of the dramatic increase came from Eades on his daily trips from Liverpool to Anglesey as a Mersey Pilot between 1963 and 1976. Just one sighting prior to 1966 was followed by a gradual rise, then a sudden upsurge in both numbers and frequency from 1972 (Eades 1976). Throughout this period most records were in autumn and winter but the largest numbers were generally blown onshore by March gales (Smith 1974) and were probably part of an undetected passage movement. Few were seen during April but small numbers of first-summers in mid-May and early June became increasingly frequent (Smith 1974; Lassey & Greenhalgh 1969). Eades (1976) reported a handful of sightings of adults during March but none at all during April.

All this changed dramatically in the late 1970s. Following the first sizeable, unambiguous passage flock of 36 at Seaforth on 25 April 1977, the status of Little Gulls in Lancashire was wholly transformed. March and April counts on the Alt Estuary increased as a proportion of the county's annual total from 3% during 1969-74 to 54% during 1975-84 (Smith 1987).

Little Gulls over Crosby Marine Lake. (Steve Young)

These developments coincided with the creation of the freshwater lagoon's at Seaforth in the 1970s as part of the expansion of the Port of Liverpool. The timing of the spring passage varies a little from year to year but generally involves an early arrival of up to 100 in late March/early April followed by a larger migratory pulse around the third week of April. As the season progresses the proportion of first-summer birds to adults increases. Few adults remain into May but up to 20 first-summers regularly stay throughout the summer, often engaging in courtship displays.

The magnet that draws the birds is the hatch of chironomid midges. When not feeding on midges over the lagoon the birds return to sea to feed and roost but, as April progresses and the midge hatch grows, more and more time is spent on the lagoon as they make the transition from their winter pelagic diet of small fish and crustaceans to a summer one of freshwater invertebrates (White 1995).

Until 1993 the whole of this passage assembly took place on the freshwater lagoon at Seaforth but in that year the chironomid hatch failed there and the birds decamped to the small model boating lake on Crosby Marine Park. In 1995 the usual work to flush Crosby Marine Lake with seawater failed and the water there became sufficiently fresh to support a large population of midges which the Little Gulls took full advantage of. In succeeding years the birds have tended to alternate between Seaforth and Crosby Marine Lake according to the available food supply.

An adult Little Gull picks a hatching chironomid midge from the water's surface, Crosby Marine Lake, April 2005. (Steve Young)

It is impossible to be certain of the actual number that pass through since it is not known how long individuals stay around. However, the best estimate of total passage size, based partly upon daily fluctuations in numbers and observations of onward migration (White 1995), is that it is between 1.5 and 2.5 times larger than the annual 'minimum passage' (Figure 1). This averaged around 350 between 1985 and 2006 so the average numbers moving through are somewhere between 500 and 1,000. Apparent differences in numbers between years are probably partly accounted for by changes in the timing and magnitude of the midge hatch (which influences how long birds stay), partly by breeding success in the previous year (and therefore the number of first-summers) and partly by weather conditions (which may delay onward migration or cause southern wintering birds to get caught up in the Irish Sea passage).

The largest day-counts are 650 on 19 April 1987, 683 on 20 April 1989 and 700+ on 25 April 2001. Peak counts of adults during 1985-2004 ranged from 82 to 585, those of first-summers from 39 to 231.

It is thought that the main source of these birds is the population wintering off the east coast of Ireland (Madden & Ruttledge 1993), where large numbers have been seen for 20 years or so, including 1,200 on the Arklow Bank in December 2000 (Coveney & Phelan 2001). Evidence is largely circumstantial, however, and is based mainly on the rough equivalence of wintering numbers in Ireland and estimated passage totals at Seaforth, and the timing of their departure from Ireland (Coveney & Phelan 2001) a short while before 'arrival' on this side of the Irish Sea. It is supported by just two recoveries of birds ringed at Seaforth in spring: at Bray, Co. Wicklow in February 1979 and

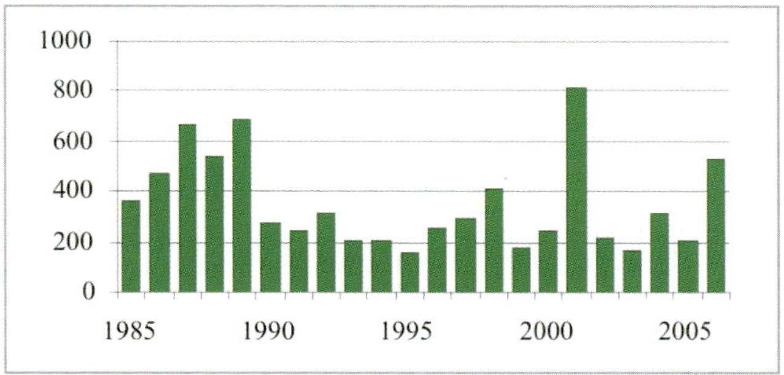

Figure 1. Minimum number of Little Gulls at Seaforth Nature Reserve and Crosby Marine Lake during April, 1985-2006. (The minimum passage is calculated by adding together the largest day count of adults and that of first-summers).

Lough Neagh in September 1984. Two French recoveries of Seaforth-ringed birds – in February 1979 at Finistere, ringed in May 1978, and on 1 April 1991 in the Somme, ringed in September 1980 – indicate either that some of the spring passage originates in the Mediterranean or that there is some interchange between the wintering populations of the Mediterranean and Irish Seas.

There can be little doubt, however, about where they are going. Five birds ringed as chicks in Finland have been seen at Seaforth and one ringed as an adult at Seaforth has been recovered on a Finnish breeding colony. Their route almost certainly takes them across the Pennines to the North Sea and thence into the Baltic. This is supported by the recovery of a bird ringed at Seaforth on 19 April 1986 at Spurn Point, Yorkshire on 17 May the same year but, more importantly, by annual observations of birds leaving Seaforth high to the east and of records of small flocks on many trans-Pennine water-bodies (Messenger 1993). A record of 118 seen at Preston Docks on 29 April 1994, known to have left Seaforth that morning, suggests that the River Ribble may sometimes provide an important migratory flight-line.

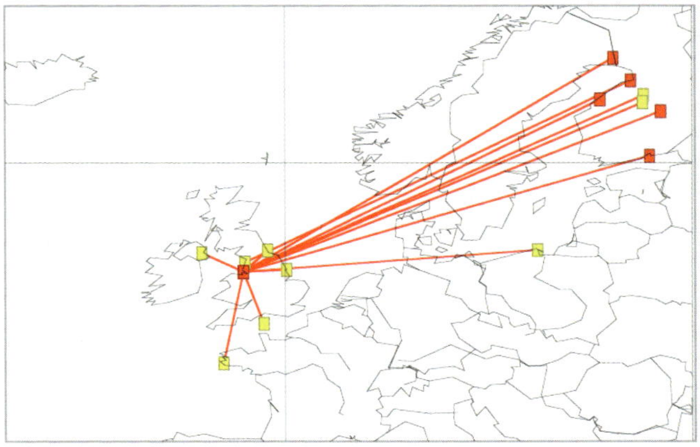

Figure 2. Ringing sites of Little Gulls recovered at Seaforth (red) and recovery sites of birds ringed at Seaforth (yellow).

Few large spring flocks have been seen away from Seaforth/Crosby, the two most notable being 215 at St. Anne's on 17 April 1981 and 162 at Rossall Point on 6 April 1985. Records since then have mostly been of low single-figure groups of adults on passage during April or lingering first-summers during May and June. Leighton Moss and the Dockacres complex are favoured sites with a largest spring count of 23 in May 1990. Small numbers may turn up at any inland waterbody with spring records averaging four annually over the past ten years.

There have only been a handful of breeding attempts by Little Gulls in Britain, so colonisation of Lancashire is very unlikely, although full courtship display by adults has been seen several times at Seaforth and nest-building attempts by first-summers observed at both Seaforth and Leighton Moss.

The autumn passage usually begins in late July and continues through to early October. During the 1970s autumn counts were often the largest of the year; they included 229 feeding on flying ants at Hightown on 25 August 1972, 200 between Seaforth and the Liverpool Bar Light on 15 August 1978 with 270 there on 6 September 1980, and 180 at Seaforth on 1 September 1978. But the last large autumn counts anywhere in the county were of 150 at Seaforth in August 1986, September and October 1987 and 70 in September 1994. Since then the autumn passage has evaporated, peak numbers at Seaforth averaged only 17 during 1995-2005 and relatively few are seen elsewhere; the total passage through the county is probably in the order of 50-100. Inland, numbers are similar to those in spring with an average of around four a year over the last ten years.

The reasons for this dramatic change in autumn are uncertain. Birds used to gather at Seaforth/Crosby to feed as they do in spring but, despite an apparent lack of change in the number of midges hatching, they no longer do so. The best guess is that either they now move directly to their wintering grounds or that these wintering grounds have changed.

By the mid-1980s wintering flocks had become established both in the southern section of Liverpool Bay and off the north Fylde coast. The existence of the first was demonstrated by gale-driven counts at Seaforth of 100 on 14 January 1984, 119 on 24 January 1986, 160 on 9 February 1988 and 135 on 16 February 1990, but winter numbers have rarely exceeded 20 anywhere on the Sefton coast since then.

The northern wintering grounds, however, have proved to be more permanent. The first significant count was of 79 on 28 January 1970 at Rossall Point. Further large, wind-induced counts there have been 200 on 14 February 1987, 100 on 9 January and 2 February 1988, 150 on 24 January 1993, 116 on 3 January 1998 and 100 on 22 January 2002. Birds have been seen with less regularity on both the southern Fylde coast and at Heysham; notable counts include 200 off the southern Fylde coast on 14 February 1987, 110 at Blackpool on 4 January 1991, 126 at Heysham on 10 January 1988 with 244 there on 6 January 1991 and 80 on 12 February 2002. The concentration of these records at Rossall suggested a regular wintering ground somewhere in that area, but its location remained undiscovered until 21 November 2003 when a boat-based team surveying the Common Scoter flocks found more than 200 Little Gulls feeding in flat calm conditions in a relatively small area some 15 km offshore on the northern edge of Shell Flat, south of where it merges with the Lune Deep.

Little Gulls are rare inland in winter, with just five records in the past ten years.

SJW, MJ.

This species account was sponsored by Steve Young.

SABINE'S GULL

Larus sabini

Lancashire Category A. (2, 108).

Scarce passage migrant from northern Canada and Greenland.

Oakes wrote that the first county record was an 'immature' (presumably a juvenile) shot at Morecambe on 21 October 1893. Another 'immature' was shot at the mouth of the River Wyre in November 1911 and was later in the collection of the Rossall School museum.

The first modern records were a juvenile on the beach at Blackpool on 22 September 1950, one at Formby on 25 August 1963 and an adult there on 16 September 1970. Sightings became gradually more frequent during the 1970s as seawatching grew in popularity, with an unprecedented four recorded in 1978. The 1980s produced a series of good seawatching autumns and more than 50 Sabine's Gulls were recorded, the three best years, 1980, 1987 and 1988, accounting for 37 of these – more than a third of Lancashire's total to 2003 (Figure 1).

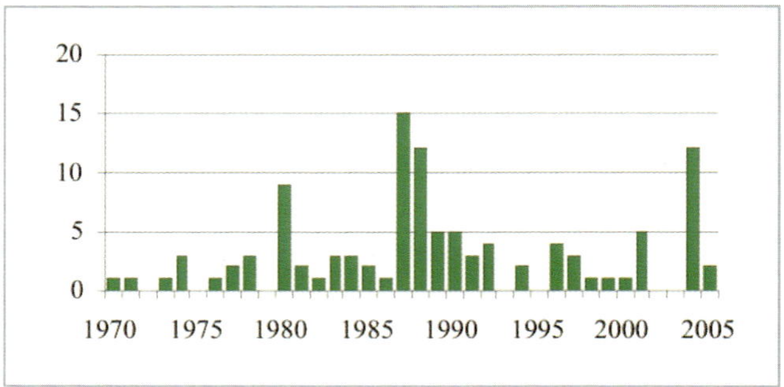

Figure 1. Annual totals of Sabine's Gulls in Lancashire, 1970-2005.

In 1980 passage began on 25 August and continued to 11 October with nine singles recorded from Heysham south to Liverpool. 1987's fifteen records covered a similar span, from 5 September to 21 October; its most notable feature was a gathering of at least six juveniles at Heysham on 14 September, which remains the county's largest day-count. A slightly smaller influx occurred in 1988 between 29 August and 8 October with twelve birds recorded in total at Seaforth and Heysham but none elsewhere.

Another 16 years passed before similar numbers were seen, a total of at least twelve (nine juveniles and three adults) in a brief period of strong onshore winds between 19 and 22 September 2004. At least four were in the mouth of the Mersey for several days, six or seven were seen off the Fylde coast and two off Heysham.

Sabine's Gulls are exceptionally rare in Britain at any time of the year except autumn. Five winter (January and February) and three early spring (March and April) records were published in the Lancashire Bird Report between 1972 and 1990 but serious question marks hang over all these, not least because, as a high Arctic breeding species that winters south of the equator, Sabine's Gulls are late migrants with very few recorded anywhere in the northern hemisphere before early April and even fewer in mid-winter (BWP).

Juvenile Sabine's Gull, River Mersey, Seaforth, September 2001. (Steve Young)

There have, however, been a surprising number of late spring/summer records most of which have probably involved first- or second-summers. One, described as an 'immature', was at Blackpool on 26 May 1972; an 'adult moulting into summer plumage' at Formby Point on 2 June 1977; one in the Mersey Narrows on 2 June 1986; one 'in winter plumage' at Formby Point on 10 June 1991, an 'adult' on 9 June 1994 and another in winter plumage there on 29 June 1996. This last bird was probably the same as one seen at Seaforth on 8 July 1996 and off Freckleton on 8 August. Another winter-plumaged bird arrived at Seaforth on 31 July 1997 and was seen regularly on the Mersey until at least 13 September, probably at Formby Point on 2 September and perhaps on Crosby Marine Lake as late as 23 October the same year.

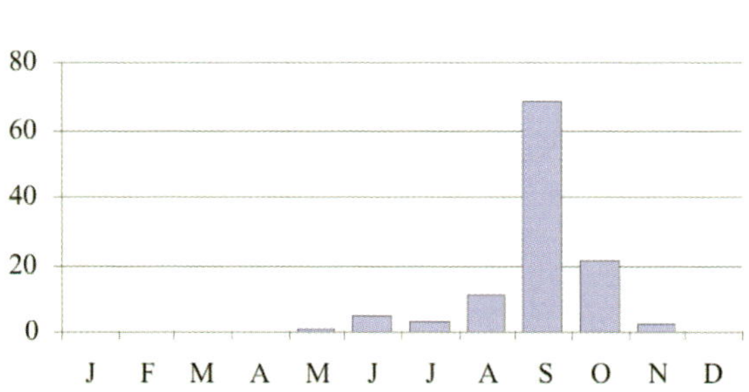

Figure 2. Monthly totals of Sabine's Gulls in Lancashire, 1950-2005.

Virtually all our autumn records have been associated with persistent onshore gales. Most have been seen for one day only but there have been a few occasions when birds have hung on for a few days, for example an adult and a juvenile at Rossall from 5 to 14 September 1987, an adult at Blackpool from 5-23 September 1987, a slightly oiled adult at Heysham from 29 August to 13 September 1988 and two or three juveniles on the Mersey at Seaforth on 13-16 September 2001. The latest autumn dates are of a juvenile at Formby Point on 6 November 1999 and an adult at Fleetwood on 7 November 1994.

More than 60% of all Lancashire's Sabine's Gulls have occurred during September (Figure 2) and all but a handful between the last week of August and the first week of October. Two-thirds of all records have been on the Sefton coast or the Mersey Narrows with 39 off Seaforth alone; Heysham has recorded a dozen or so and the Fylde coast about 27. Virtually none has been seen elsewhere and our only inland record was an adult at Prescot Reservoirs, just a few miles from the Mersey, on 25 August 2001. Juveniles slightly outnumber adults (55:40 of records that were aged), with adults usually occurring a little earlier than juveniles.

SJW, MJ.

This species account was sponsored by Ribble Bird Tours (01253-407554).

BONAPARTE'S GULL

Larus philadelphia

Lancashire Category A. (0, 8).

Vagrant from North America.

There remains some confusion as to which constitutes the first Lancashire record. A first-winter, seen at Morecambe on 4 November 1963 was accepted by the BBRC but the record has subsequently been withdrawn by the observer. Then a first-summer in moult to second-winter was seen from the southern shore of the Mersey Narrows at New Brighton on 21 August 1979. Since the centre of the Mersey marks our boundary with Cheshire it may have flown into Lancashire waters, but it is uncertain if it did. The next was an adult at Seaforth on 23-24 April 1982 during the height of the Little Gull passage; the record was accepted by the BBRC but was disputed by some observers at the time.

Seaforth's first multi-observed bird, an adult moulting into summer plumage, arrived on 6 April 1990. It was part of a record national tally with eleven records accepted that year. It was seen almost daily until the 19th, when it was in almost full breeding plumage. At some point during its stay – perhaps from the outset but definitely from 12 April - it was joined by another moulting adult, which remained until 1 May. Both birds fed on the Mersey and roosted on the reserve, the second being seen several times on the Cheshire side of the river at New Brighton. Another adult the following year was seen at Seaforth on seven occasions between 20 March and 20 April 1991.

Adult Bonaparte's Gull (above centre) with Little Gull and Black-headed Gull, Seaforth Nature Reserve, and (below) feeding on the Mersey, April 1990. (Steve Young)

A further adult in full breeding plumage spent 45 minutes on the freshwater pool at Seaforth on 15 May 1995. This was followed by two first-summer birds also at Seaforth: on 24-25 May 2000 and on 27 May 2001. Seaforth's near monopoly was finally broken when an adult in winter plumage was found on Rowley Lake, Burnley on 25 October 2001, staying for just that day.

SJW, MJ.

This species account was sponsored by John Bannon.

BLACK-HEADED GULL

Larus ridibundus

Lancashire Category A.

Abundant breeder, passage migrant and winter visitor from continental Europe and Russia.

Lancashire currently supports almost 15% of the British and 22% of the English breeding populations of Black-headed Gulls (Mitchell *et al.* 2004) and it appears that the county has always been of considerable importance.

Mitchell documented the shift of one colony from the site of present-day Fleetwood, first to Pilling Moss around 1833 and then to Winmarleigh and Cockerham Mosses after 1876. Oakes reported that this colony supported 10,000 pairs in 1887 but had been deserted by 1913. A long-established colony at a small tarn on the Bleasdale Fells was deserted by 1884.

Oakes gave details of further breeding sites, including a few pairs near Pilling from 1912, up to 35 pairs at a sewage farm near Burnley, 40 pairs at a hill tarn near Burnley in 1948, a small colony at a Liverpool sewage farm in the 1930s, and a colony amongst Common Terns on dune slacks at Formby-Ainsdale that increased from 12 to 200 pairs between 1912 and 1933, declining to six in 1935, and where a handful breed sporadically to the present day. A number of other colonies have been recorded since the Second World War, mostly rather small and sometimes transient. One straddled the present Lancashire/Yorkshire border from at least the 1950s to the late 1970s, shifting between Crow, Boulsworth and Heather Hills and holding 750 pairs in 1958 and 125 in 1975. Other sites have included Musden Head Moor (500 pairs in 1948), a large lake on the site of the present Heysham power station (5-9 pairs in 1959-62), Delph Reservoir (up to 100 pairs in the 1950s with 51 pairs in 1960), small colonies briefly on Darwen Moor and Redmond's Edge in the early 1970s (Martin 2007), Waddington Fell (20-35 pairs in 1977-91), West Bradford Fell (80 pairs in 1991, persisting until at least 1994), Barnacre Reservoir (21 pairs in 1996, now in substantial decline), and occasional pairs at Martin Mere.

Four substantial colonies remained in the late 1990s, two on the coast and two inland. The largest by far is on the Ribble marshes; it became established in the early 1950s, growing to 89 pairs in 1958 and then exponentially to 1,600 pairs in 1968 and 9,000 in the 1970s. The 1989 national survey located 20,000 pairs there, making it the largest coastal colony in Britain. More recent estimates have fluctuated widely, perhaps partly due to methodological inconsistencies: 12,000 in 1996, 8,000 in 1998, 14,300 in 1999 and 8,460 pairs in 2003. Most have always nested on the south bank of the river, principally on Banks Marsh, but Warton Marsh on the north bank held perhaps as many as 1,500 pairs in 1979. Few bred on the north bank during the 1980s but around 2,000 pairs were estimated in 1997, declining to 500 in 1999 and none in 2003. These figures indicate a substantial decline on the Ribble, by perhaps as much as 50% over 15 years, much of which loss is attributable to a combination of competition for nest sites with the growing Herring/Lesser Black-back colony and repeated spring tide flood events that have washed away most first clutches.

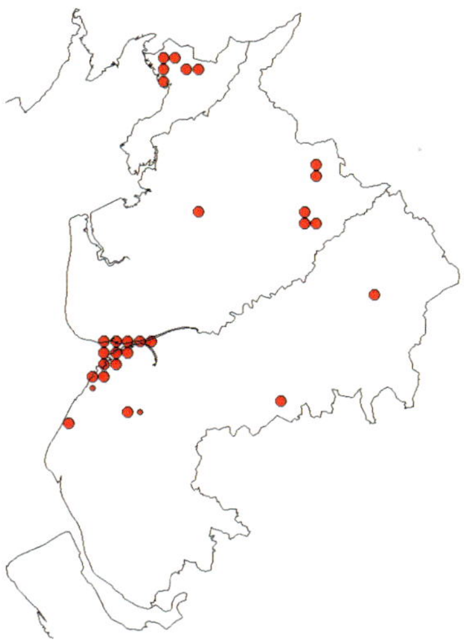

Breeding distribution of Black-headed Gull, 1997-2000.
(Large dots: confirmed. Small dots: possible)

The colony at Colloway Marsh on the Lune Estuary stood at 70 pairs in 1982 and 40 in the late 1980s but was deserted sometime during the 1990s. It is possible that some of these birds relocated to the expanding colony at Leighton Moss and the Eric Morecambe complex, which is now the major northern site. Some hundreds of pairs at Leighton Moss had disappeared by 1955 but the site was recolonised in 1957 and supported over 100 pairs the following year. Numbers grew to 1,000 pairs in 1985 and 1,830 in 1999, declining to 1,183 in 2005. Birds began increasingly to switch from the main reserve to the nearby Eric Morecambe complex on Carnforth Marsh during the 1990s, so that more than 90% nested there at the end of the decade. An offshoot colony was established a few miles away in the Dockacres complex in about 1984; it had grown to 500 or more pairs by 1996 but dwindled to 30 in 2003.

The colony at Belmont Reservoir has held varying numbers intermittently for over 50 years, with peaks of 30 pairs through the 1950s and 1960s, 15 in 1979 and 70 in 1999. Following a reduction in statutory water outflow from 2000 (and hence higher water levels) the colony increased dramatically from just two pairs in 2001 to 810 in 2004 and 1,550 in 2005 (Martin 2007). Numbers have been significantly higher at Stocks Reservoir, where 4,000 pairs were estimated in 1943-44. Similar numbers were reported from 1989 onwards but no proper survey was carried out until the turn of the century, with a partial survey locating 1,418 pairs in 1999 and a full survey 1,580 in 2002; it is impossible to judge whether this apparently large decrease is real or the result of over-optimistic earlier estimates.

Huge numbers of Black-headed Gulls are present in Lancashire during both the breeding season (probably in excess of 50,000 including non-breeders) as well as in winter, making it difficult to monitor the movements of the various populations.

Birds begin to leave their wintering grounds in late February but visible migration usually peaks during March. Lancashire breeding colonies are re-occupied during April, perhaps mostly by birds that have wintered in Britain – recoveries of locally-ringed birds indicate that most stay within 100km of their breeding sites. More northerly and easterly breeders pass through the county more or less simultaneously. Few adults are seen after mid-April but first-summers continue to arrive well into May. No systematic counts of visible migrants have been recorded on the coast but inland records include regular sightings at Arkholme on the upper Lune during March and early April of close to 1,000 a day. Unique amongst major roost sites, numbers usually peak at Martin Mere during late February to April – during spring passage rather than mid-winter.

Autumn return is more leisurely, adults and juveniles begin to arrive in the last week of June and continue to move through to September at least, after which movements are probably more weather-induced than purely migratory. Very large flocks, often running into thousands, regularly exploit the late summer hatching of flying ants, for example 8,000 over Blackpool, Poulton and St. Anne's on 7 August 1983.

The population more than doubles in winter as a mixture of British and foreign breeders settle in. Total numbers in Lancashire, particularly on the coast, are surprisingly poorly documented; they are influenced in part by weather conditions elsewhere in the country and western Europe and in part by local availability of food resources – primarily on rubbish tips, playing fields and parks, tilled land and the coast.

Adult winter Black-headed Gull, Crosby Marine Park, December 2005. (Steve Young)

The first three of these offer a fairly stable food supply year on year and the inland population is relatively constant. Counts located 21,000 inland birds during winter 1963-65 (Spencer 1973) and numbers in east Lancashire alone were estimated at up to 20,000 in the early 1990s (Hornby 1994). Birds primarily feed on tips and roost on reservoirs. Few tip sites are easily accessible and most published data come from roost counts but 18,000 were reported at Whinney Hill, Accrington in January 1998, around 1,000 from Stacksteads, Rossendale in the mid-1990s and 2,000 from Sefton Meadows, Maghull in the early 1980s. The earliest published roost count anywhere in the county was of 6,800 at Whitemoor Reservoir, Colne in December 1961. Other large counts include 10,000 at Stocks Reservoir in January 1983, 9,000 at Foulridge Reservoirs in January 1993 with 8,000 there in winter 1986/87, 13,500 on the three Rivington Reservoirs in January 1993, 9,000 at Martin Mere in December 1995 and 9,000 at Prescot Reservoirs in February 1991. Other counts in excess of 2,000 have come from a range of sites, including Delph (regularly up to 5,000 in the 1980s, maximum of 3,900 since 1995), Clowbridge, Springs, Belmont, Fishmoor, Rivington, Longridge and Alston Reservoirs.

Numbers are rather less predictable on the coast. Generally, most birds feed some distance inland on amenity grassland, tips and agricultural land, flying to roost on beaches and sand-banks in the late afternoon, often stopping off at coastal water bodies such as Marton Mere and Seaforth to bathe beforehand. The coast and inshore waters do not normally offer plentiful feeding opportunities but occasional storm events that 'wreck' enormous numbers of marine invertebrates – principally shellfish and starfish – can attract phenomenal numbers.

In normal years the coastal assemblage certainly numbers more than 50,000, perhaps more than 100,000, spread out between the Mersey and Morecambe Bay. Counts of 8,000 or more have been reported regularly during the past 20 years at Seaforth, Formby Point, Ainsdale to Southport, Marshside, Lytham St. Anne's, Fleetwood to Pilling, the Keer mudflats and other sites in Morecambe Bay. Winter storms can produce much higher numbers: 6,000 were recorded feeding on small fish on the Mersey on 29 November 1973, but it is when huge quantities of shellfish and starfish are washed up on the tideline that numbers really begin to swell, often to the point that they become effectively uncountable. Few of these wreck events have been fully documented; example counts include 15,000 at St. Anne's in February 1996 and 13,900 at Marshside in February 1997. In December 2001 to early March 2002 more than 50,000 were on the Sefton coast, including a count of 13,200 at Marshside, and similar numbers on the south Fylde coast; numbers on the north Fylde coast and the rest of Morecambe Bay went unreported. Other large published counts include 25,000 at Hest Bank in 1982, 10,200 on the Wyre Estuary in November 1984, 13,000 at Rossall in December 1986, 15,000 on the Keer flats in December 1989 with 18,000 there in December 1990, 12,500 at Marshside in December 1993 and 12,000 at Seaforth in November 1998.

Exchanges of ringed birds between Lancashire and abroad are shown in Figure 1. A total of 305 foreign-ringed birds were recovered in Lancashire up to 2002, almost all of them ringed on their breeding grounds. Much smaller numbers (28) ringed in Lancashire (mostly on passage) were recovered abroad. These recoveries confirm that large numbers of birds wintering in Lancashire come from northern and eastern Europe, principally Denmark (64), the Baltic states (53), Norway (51), Finland (50), Sweden (27), Poland (13) and Germany (11). Eight birds ringed as pulli were recovered in their first or second winter on passage or wintering in Morocco (1), Spain (3) Portugal (2) and France (2). Another nestling from Stocks Reservoir was recovered in mid-July in Denmark – the only one to be recovered abroad as an adult.

Figure 1. Exchanges of Black-headed Gulls between Lancashire and abroad by country up to 2002. (Dot size = frequency)

SJW, MJ.
This species account was sponsored by Anne Kingston.

RING-BILLED GULL

Larus delawarensis

Lancashire Category A. (0, 87).

Scarce visitor from North America.

The first British record of this North American gull was on the South Wales coast as recently as March 1973 and the first for Lancashire followed not long after, on 13 April 1979 when an adult was found at Blundellsands on the south Sefton coast by Nick Preston.

This was followed by a first-year at Seaforth on 16 May 1981 but there were no more records until 1986, when the floodgates appeared to open both nationally and locally. Ring-billed Gull was taken off the list of British rarities at the end of 1987 as the BBRC was swamped with submissions, not least from Lancashire – eight records being accepted in 1986 and nine in 1987. An average of just under five were seen annually during the 1990s including another tally of eight in 1991. Since then there has been a small but consistent decrease with only 22 seen between 1998 and 2004, bringing the county total, including an unknown number of returning birds, to 87 (Figure 1). This decline mirrors the national trend and seems to be due largely to fewer arrivals of first-years, perhaps because of changes in autumn weather patterns.

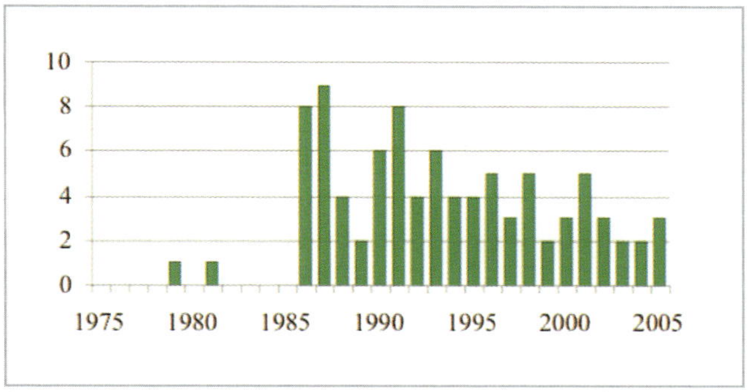

Figure 1. Annual totals of Ring-billed Gulls in Lancashire, 1979-2005 (overwintering birds counted in first year only).

Almost three-quarters (63) of the county's records have been logged on the Sefton coast with 58 of these from Seaforth or the adjacent Crosby Marine Park. The remaining coastal and estuarine records are spread between Otterspool Park in south Liverpool (1), Marton Mere (5) and the Wyre Estuary (5), with just two further north at Cockerham and Heysham. There seems to be little reason for this extraordinarily concentrated distribution other than the number of gull enthusiasts and good gull-watching conditions at Seaforth; if Seaforth's coverage rate was repeated elsewhere the county total would undoubtedly be considerably higher.

The first inland record came early, two at Martin Mere in August 1986. Another two have since been seen at Martin Mere and there have been other records inland at Longridge Reservoir, Preston Dock, Myerscough and Brockholes Quarries, and Eccleston Mere, and two at Fishmoor Reservoir.

Ring-billed Gulls have arrived in Lancashire in most months of the year (Figure 2) but more than 40% of records have been in April or May.

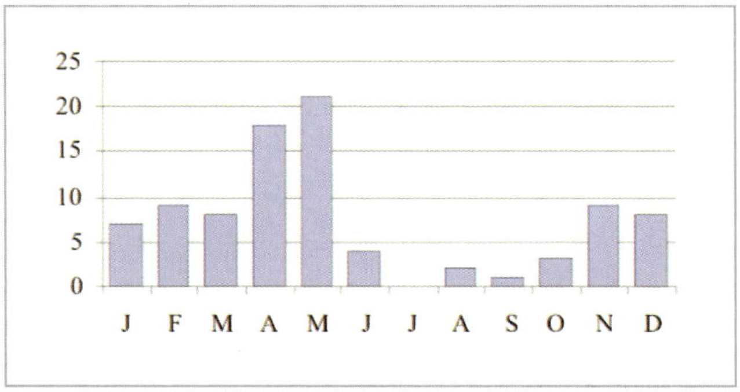

Figure 2. Arrivals of Ring-billed Gulls in Lancashire by month, 1979-2005 (including returning individuals).

At Seaforth at least, spring passage is strongly associated with the northbound movement of Common Gulls, with most Ring-bills being seen during the latter's passage periods. As with Common Gulls, adult Ring-bills tend to arrive earlier than younger birds although there is some overlap; spring adults arrive on average during the first week of April, with second-summers a full month later and first-years towards the end of May and into June. This suggests that, once on this side of the Atlantic, many Ring-billed Gulls follow the spring migrations of Common Gulls, perhaps summering with them. However, evidence has recently emerged of two birds making return journeys between Norway and North America (Fraser & Rogers 2005) and it is possible that some Ring-billed Gulls may make regular transatlantic flights.

There is no evidence that Ring-bills have ever bred in Europe but hybridisation with Common Gulls is a possibility. A first-year at Seaforth from 6 to 25 May 1992 showed mixed characteristics of these two species. It became known during its prolonged stay as the 'thing-billed gull' (Kehoe 1992). Although the record has recently been summarily dismissed as a Common Gull (Olsen & Larsson 2004), the experienced gull-watchers who saw it were in no doubt that it was not.

None has ever been first seen in July and the earliest autumn records were a second-summer at Martin Mere and Marshside in August 1986, an adult at Skippool Creek on 12-13 August 2004, a second-winter at Seaforth from mid-September 1990 and just three at any time during October, none of them adults. There is, therefore, little evidence of autumn passage. Most late arrivals have been during the winter months, distributed fairly evenly from November to February. Both adults and second-winters are as likely to appear in early winter as late; whereas six out of eight first-winters have arrived before the New Year. The earliest first-winter was one at Seaforth on 11 October 1988, shortly after one of the fiercest Atlantic storms of the previous 20 years.

A first-winter found at Seaforth on 22 May 2005 is our longest stayer, being seen at various Mersey sites until 17 February 2006.

Ring-billed Gull, moulting into second-winter plumage, Otterspool, Liverpool, August 2005. (Steve Young)

There have been no ringing recoveries in Lancashire and the only evidence of site fidelity comes from a one-legged adult that wintered at Seaforth in 1996/97 and 1997/98. We know equally little about the wintering grounds of passage birds other than of a first/second winter with distinctive plumage at Seaforth from 19 May to 25 June 1990 that had wintered on the Plym Estuary.

SJW, MJ.

This species account was sponsored by Pete Kinsella.

COMMON GULL

Larus canus

Lancashire Category A.

Abundant winter visitor and passage migrant from Scotland, Fennoscandia and eastern Europe.

The nearest large colonies of Common Gulls are in north-west Scotland and there is no evidence that the species has ever attempted to nest in Lancashire. Small numbers do, however, spend at least part of summer within our major colonies of Black-headed and Lesser Black-backed Gulls on an annual basis – the first documented record being of 20 within the Bowland gullery on 12 June 1956. It is possible that these may eventually prove to be the precursors of future colonisation – small numbers do breed elsewhere in England – but it has been a long time coming. The overwhelming majority, if not all, of these birds have been clearly identified in recent years as first-years and those summering with breeding gulls form only a tiny proportion of those present in the county during the breeding season – Seaforth alone had an average summer peak count of more than 500 between 1985 and 2003.

So, although present in Lancashire all year, the Common Gull is primarily a wintering species – its pattern of occurrence is illustrated in Figure 1 using data from Seaforth, the best-monitored site. Seaforth data indicate that more than 95% of wintering birds are adults, first-winters moving further south.

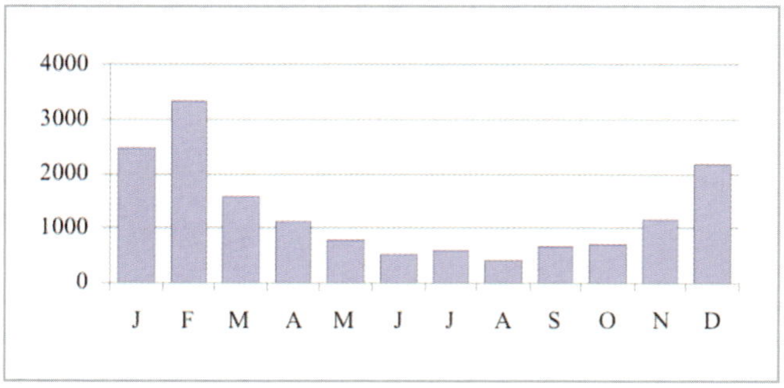

Figure1. Average peak monthly counts of Common Gulls at Seaforth Nature Reserve, 1985-2005.

Mitchell stated that Common Gulls only occurred inland after storms but Oakes described them as less frequent there than other gull species but 'regular in a few districts'. Despite a marked increase in numbers at a few inland sites, first noted at the end of the 1950s, this remains the case – the vast majority winter on or close to the coast.

Wrigley (1892) described them as 'common indeed' in the Formby area, describing the 'average flock' as covering 'an acre of sand'. The first large count to be published was of 6,000 'on the Mersey' on 27 January 1977 and since then the Sefton coast has continued to dominate the record book. The largest roost estimates have come in recent years from Ainsdale-Birkdale: 15,000 at both ends of the year in 1999 and 25,000 on 22 February 2002, on both occasions attracted by shellfish/starfish wrecks. Seaforth/Crosby shore has recorded in excess of 4,000 on several occasions but the only other sites to do so have been Marshside (4,300 in February 1997) and the Keer Estuary (4,500 in January 1991). Large counts have been reported from the Fylde much less frequently – 2,000 at Rossall in December 1985 stand out.

Adult winter Common Gull, Crosby Marine Park, December 2003. (Steve Young)

Except in 'shellfish years', coastal sites are largely used for roosting, most birds feeding some distance inland on farmland, amenity grassland and rubbish tips, flying in to bathe in late afternoon at coastal lagoons such as Marton Mere and Seaforth before roosting on the beaches.

Inland birds also feed on farmland and tips but here reservoirs form the main roost sites. The largest inland winter counts have been 3,125 at Prescot Reservoirs in February 1991, 2,600 on the three Rivington Reservoirs in January 1993, and 2,000 and 2,100 at Stocks Reservoir in the winters of 1989 and 1997. No other site comes close to these numbers although the national gull census of 1993 recorded a combined total of more than 2,000 on just three reservoirs, Foulridge, Longridge and Spade Mill. In Rossendale, however, Common Gulls form only a small proportion of winter gull flocks, with only occasional double-figure counts.

Coastal numbers generally peak during February but it is difficult to say to what extent this is due to continuing winter displacement of birds from the north and east or to the onset of the northward migration. Spring passage gets underway in earnest during March. Few migrant flocks have been recorded on the coast, 1,000 flying north at Heysham on 6 April 1987 being a notable exception, and passage is evidenced most obviously by the gradual increase in the proportion of first-summer birds – counts at Seaforth suggest this changes from less than 10% at the beginning of April to more than 90% by the end of the month.

Migration is often more obvious inland, particularly in areas where birds are scarce in winter. The best-monitored site is the area around Arkholme on the upper Lune, where records suggest that spring passage takes place between the last week of February and the beginning of April; the most notable counts have been 1,500 on 4 April 2002, 1,400 on 25 March 2000 and 1,460 on 18 February 2005. The largest inland spring roost was 5,000 at Stocks Reservoir on 29 March 1995 with 1,000 still present on 3 April.

Adults and a few juveniles begin to return during late July and numbers slowly increase but, apart from at Seaforth, the only records of more than 1,000 in autumn were of 2,100 at Stocks Reservoir on 20 October 2002 and 1,500 at Marton Mere in November 2001.

The total of 108 ringing recoveries outside England up to 1999 (18 of them of birds ringed as full-grown in Lancashire) gives a good indication of the origins of our birds. More than a quarter (34) have been from Scotland but rather more (38) came from Norway, with others from Denmark (13), Finland (12), the Baltic states (4), Germany (3), Holland (3) and Ireland (1).

A possible indication that some wintering birds may originate further to the east comes from observations of several significantly larger, darker-mantled birds at Seaforth and elsewhere during the 1990s. These were originally described as 'showing characteristics of the Siberian race *heinei*' but whether they originate from within the core range of *heinei* or the intergrade zone with *canus* to the east of the White Sea is impossible to determine without a ringing recovery.

Albino or partial albino birds have been reported at Blackpool in July 1981, Seaforth in May 1987, June 1990, April to May 1993 and April to May 2001, and at Rowley Lake in February 1988.

SJW, MJ.
This species account was sponsored by
Clare and David Pollard.

LESSER BLACK-BACKED GULL

Larus fuscus

Lancashire Category A.

Abundant breeder and winter visitor.

The Lesser Black-backed Gull is one of Lancashire's most important breeding species; the Bowland colony is the largest in inland Britain and, together with the Ribble Marshes, supports around 10% of the total population of the western European sub-species *graellsii*.

Up to 1880 a few pairs nested on Pilling Moss and Cockerham Moss held a 'substantial' colony but breeding had ceased by the time of Mitchell's book in 1892. Oakes mentioned two small colonies in north Lancashire, one 'between Carnforth and Arkholme' with 20 pairs in 1922, while Simonswood Moss, near Kirkby, held 95 pairs in 1940 which were reduced to four by 1946 through human interference. One pair bred on Longton Marsh in 1917 but attempts to nest in Rossendale were unsuccessful.

Breeding was first reported in Bowland, at what is now referred to as Tarnbrook Fell, in 1936 when three or four pairs were killed by gamekeepers (Sowter 2002). It is thought that this colony (and that on South Walney) was established as a result of the loss of the colony on Foulshaw Moss (then in Lancashire but now in Cumbria) through fire around 1928. The culling continued on the Lancashire grouse moors until the keepers were called up for the Second World War, when the colony began to expand rapidly and reached around 1,000 pairs by the end of the 1940s, further expanding to 16,000 by 1965 and 25,000 by 1979. Changes in estimated population size from 1965 to 2005 are illustrated in Figure 1, which shows a steady increase until the early 1980s, followed by a sudden, sharp decline in the middle of the decade; numbers began to rise again in the late 1990s, before dropping sharply from 2002. Interpretation of the reasons for these apparent trends is complicated by changes in census methodology over the years but the scale and type of measures employed to control the population has played a major part.

The then Ministry of Agriculture had begun culling birds ostensibly to reduce bacterial contamination of water supplies by 1965, and by 1987 a total of 66,800 birds had been killed. More recently, techniques of deliberate disturbance and egg-removal have been employed to evident effect.

The colony now occupies more than 8.25km^2 on the Abbeystead, Mallowdale and Brennand estates and in 1990 a 1km^2 sanctuary area was set aside, enlarged by 50% in 1994, in which birds could breed unmolested. During the 1990s attempts began to encourage birds to breed in this area through controlled disturbance elsewhere in the colony in an effort to minimise the need for culling. By the end of the 1990s this strategy appeared to be working with a higher proportion of birds nesting within the sanctuary area.

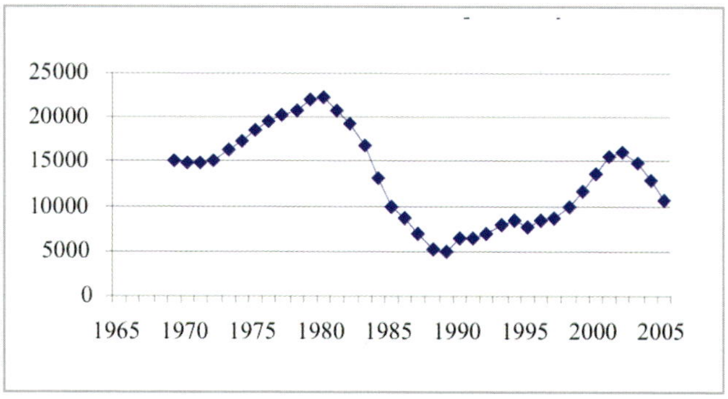

Figure 1. Estimated numbers of breeding pairs (rolling 5-year means) of Lesser Black-backed Gulls at Tarnbrook Fell, 1965-2005. [Some years are interpolated, including 1973-1977]

Breeding was first confirmed on the Ribble marshes in 1973 and the population grew to 520 pairs in 1988, with 2,200 in 1993, 4,100 in 1998 and 3,348 pairs in 2003 – almost all on Banks and Hesketh Marshes, although there were 20 pairs on Warton Marsh in 1979.

Up to eight pairs hung on at Simonswood Moss between at least 1957 and 1972 but the site was destroyed through peat extraction in the 1980s; up to three pairs have bred irregularly on Carnforth Marsh from 1978 to at least 1999. 'Lessers' were present in the Musden Head Moor Black-headed Gull colony in the West Pennines in 1948, and small colonies bred on Anglezarke Moor in the 1920s and Rivington Moor in the early 1930s, but both were removed by gamekeepers. Small numbers also nested in the Black-headed gulleries at Delph and Belmont Reservoirs during the 1950s, with the latter site again hosting summering pairs in the breeding season from 1996 onwards with breeding finally confirmed in 2004.

Lesser Black-backed Gull with begging juvenile, Seaforth Nature Reserve, August 2004. (Steve Young)

Roof-nesting in urban areas was first recorded in 1994 when 18 pairs were found in central Liverpool, one pair at Heysham/Morecambe and seven pairs in Fleetwood/Thornton. These three colonies had increased to 36, 36 and 15 pairs respectively by 2000 while a new colony in Blackpool held two pairs in 1998. In 2005 40 or more pairs also nested on the roofs of the Jaguar factory in Halewood.

The Lesser Black-backed Gull (adults at least) has shifted its wintering range northward since the mid-twentieth century (Barnes 1952). Increasing numbers began to be seen in Lancashire during the 1950s, both on the coast and inland, probably mostly as a result of the opening of landfill sites. Large winter counts during this period of increase included 250 at Laneshawbridge, near Colne on 7 November 1949, 500 at Anglezarke Reservoir in January 1955, 260 at Morecambe in 1969, 580 at Whitemoor Reservoir, Colne in December 1961 and 420 at Carnforth Marsh in December 1974.

Since then the species has not been particularly well recorded, but many of the earlier counts would still be notable today and there is little evidence of any further significant increase in numbers. Coastal numbers have been best monitored at Seaforth, where the average winter peak count between 1985 and 2003 was 650, with maxima of around 1,000 in January 1988 and 850 in December 2001 and no obvious trend up or down throughout this period. As many birds use Seaforth as a transitory stop these peak counts do not account for all of the birds in the general area. Hard weather movements and/or shellfish wrecks can swell numbers considerably – 3,700 on the beaches between Ainsdale and Southport during gales on 9 February 1988 is by far the largest winter count anywhere in the county, while similar conditions in February 2002 produced more than 1,000 birds in the same area.

Data from inland roosts are rather more complete with counts of 100 or so at many eastern sites, up to 400 regularly at Foulridge and Stocks Reservoirs and 300 at Stacksteads Tip, 550 at Rivington Reservoir in February 1988 and 370 at Martin Mere in December 1995. Counts in the Burnley area, however, have declined significantly since the closure of Rowley Tip.

Allowing for gaps in the record, it seems unlikely that more than 5,000 birds, and possibly far fewer, winter in Lancashire. Since the immediate post-breeding population is probably in the order of 75,000, a very large majority of Lancashire breeders must leave the county for the winter. The fact that only 62 (out of a total of 1,031) Lancashire-ringed birds have been recovered in Britain between December and February – with only 22 of these in Lancashire – backs this up.

Lesser Black-backs are far more migratory than Herring Gulls and 40% of all recoveries of Lancashire-ringed birds to 1999 have been made abroad, against only 1% of Herring Gulls. The pattern of recoveries demonstrates a migration route that takes them down the western seaboard of Europe, with some venturing further south to West Africa. Recoveries along this flyway include 122 in France and the Channel Islands, 373 in Portugal, 190 in Spain, 109 in Morocco, six in Western Sahara, three in Algeria, nine in Mauritania, three in the Canaries, two in Gambia and one in Senegal. Two in Mali show that not all are confined to the coasts. Sightings of colour-ringed birds from Tarnbrook, the Ribble Estuary and South Walney confirm this pattern of movement (D. Sowter *pers. comm.*).

Although all age-classes may be present in winter, adults predominate and ringing recoveries show that first-winters on average migrate considerably further – of 26 African recoveries of Lancashire-bred birds south of Morocco/Algeria, 17 have been first-winters and nine second-winter/summers with none older.

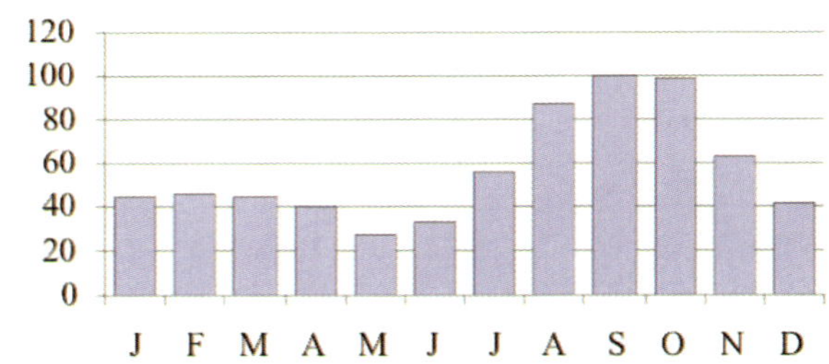

Figure 2. Indices of monthly peak numbers of Lesser Black-backed Gulls at Seaforth Nature Reserve 1986-2004. (September = 100).

There is relatively little movement between Lancashire and the North Sea, with just 19 recoveries of Lancashire-ringed birds in Holland, 13 in Germany, five in Belgium and one in Denmark – almost all of these were sub-adults, ringed as pulli and recovered during the summer months. There are also recoveries in Lancashire during the breeding season of three ringed in Belgium and one in Holland. There have been rather more such sightings of birds colour-ringed in Lancashire since 1998 – ten in Belgium, 25 in northern Germany and 33 in Holland (D. Sowter *pers. comm.*). Very few of these were first-years, several had been reported earlier in southern Europe, and only a handful were resighted anywhere in Britain, suggesting that few exchanges between Lancashire and western Europe are direct.

Recoveries of three ringed as chicks in Norway and two in Iceland indicate that Lancashire is used by long-distance migrants but the scale of this is unclear.

The autumn migration is a protracted affair, extending from mid-July to mid-November. Peak numbers on the coast are considerably higher than in winter as illustrated in Figure 2, which shows the pattern of monthly occurrence at Seaforth, where the average autumn peak count between 1986 and 2003 was about 1,000.

The initial phases of migration are probably often little more than relatively short-distance dispersal to the coast or reservoirs. Such movements may involve large numbers of birds, including the largest roost ever recorded in the county of 4,178 at Formby Point in July 2002 and 1,220 flying over Upholland on 31 July 2000. Other large autumn counts include 1,000 at Stacksteads tip in July 1994, 1,165 on the RSPB Morecambe Bay reserve in July 1995, 1,181 at Rowley Lake on 20 August 1990, 900 at Fleetwood ICI on 11 August 1986 and 1,020 at Martin Mere in September 1995. Early autumn flocks are a mixture of summering immatures and dispersing adults and juveniles, but later in the season probably contain significant numbers of migrants from further north. The Lancashire coast may be an important staging area for birds heading south, including perhaps from Iceland where the population has expanded recently – but there is no ringing evidence for this.

Birds begin to return to the breeding colonies in mid-February but the passage is at its strongest during March and April and significant numbers may still be on the move during May. Notable counts in March have included 1,000 at Seaforth in 1991 and at Stocks Reservoir in 1999, 800 at Stacksteads Tip in 1994, 950 at Foulridge Reservoir in 1995 and 600 at Blackpool in 1999; in April 1,549 at Rowley Tip in 1989, 1,050 at Arkholme in 1995 and 750 at Stacksteads in 1999, while the largest May count was 1,446 at Formby Point in 1994.

Many reports of the nominate race *L. f. fuscus*, which breeds in the Baltic, northern Norway and Finland, were published during the twentieth century. Oakes, for example, referred to twelve at Skerton Weir, Lancaster on 11 January 1922, and claims of singles persisted until as late as the mid-1990s. However, there is only one accepted record of this sub-species in Britain and, given its migration route direct to the south-east Mediterranean and beyond, it seems unlikely to be anything other than a very rare vagrant to Lancashire and probably least likely in mid-winter when most claims have been made.

Dark-mantled birds occurring in Britain are now usually ascribed to the southern Scandinavian sub-species *intermedius* (which was not known about when many early claims of *fuscus* were made) and it is assumed that it is this race to which at least the large majority of Lancashire records refer. Although there are only three ringing recoveries in Lancashire of birds from the breeding range of *intermedius* – all from south-western Norway – in some years at least they appear to make up a significant proportion of winter flocks, perhaps 10% or more, and are probably frequent passage migrants.

SJW, MJ.
This species account was sponsored by David Sowter.

YELLOW LEGGED GULL

Larus michahellis

Lancashire Category A.

Uncommon visitor from southern Europe throughout the year.

The last decade of the twentieth century witnessed an explosion of interest in the identification and status of the Herring Gull complex, resulting in considerable advances in knowledge matched by taxonomic and nomenclatural confusion in equal measure. Until very recently the 'Western Yellow-legged Gull' was treated as a sub-species of Herring Gull *L. argentatus* by the BOU, as a sub-species of 'Yellow-legged Gull' *L. cachinnans* by *British Birds* magazine and as a full species in its own right by other authorities and most birders. Eventually, in 2005 a consensus was achieved to treat it as a full species.

As late as 1986 the Lancashire Bird Report described records of 'yellow-legged Herring Gulls' variously as '*michahellis*', '*cachinnans*' and '*omissus*' (a variant yellow-legged form of *L. argentatus* from the Baltic states).

Resolving the taxonomic issue, however, has not removed all difficulties in identification – Herring Gull-like birds with yellow legs are not always *michahellis*. As well as the risks posed by unusually pale-mantled Lesser Black-backs or the occasional yellow-legged Baltic or British Herring Gull, some records may refer to various hybrid combinations. Nevertheless, a large majority of reported Yellow-legged Gulls are likely to be just that.

Oakes referred to an adult Herring Gull with yellow legs seen by FW Holder at Ainsdale on 10 February 1918, fuller details appearing in the seventh report of the Lancashire and Cheshire Fauna Committee. The first modern record also came from Ainsdale, on 14 February 1977. This was followed by claims of an adult at Martin Mere on 4 August 1979 and singles at Seaforth on 13 January and Lancaster on 23 March 1983.

Birds have been recorded annually since 1985 with more than 350 reported up to 2002, more than 70% of which were at Seaforth and a further 15% from Lancaster. There is no reason to believe that this concentration of records accurately reflects the true distribution in Lancashire, but rather the distribution of the still small minority of birders with the skills, or inclination, to sift through flocks of Herring and Lesser Black-backed Gulls.

As this gull-watching culture has slowly spread, Yellow-legged Gulls have been recorded in small numbers from about 25 additional sites throughout the county, including a dozen or so inland.

The increase in records is best illustrated at Seaforth. Figure 1 shows a steady growth in the estimated number of individuals there from the late 1980s, a sharp increase during the second half of the 1990s before stabilising at around 25 a year at the turn of the century. Throughout this period most Seaforth records have come from just one or two observers (although the individuals concerned have changed over the years), so that survey effort was relatively constant until the reserve's closure in 2004. This suggests that at least part of the increase in records is due to the species becoming genuinely more common in Lancashire – as it has done elsewhere in the country.

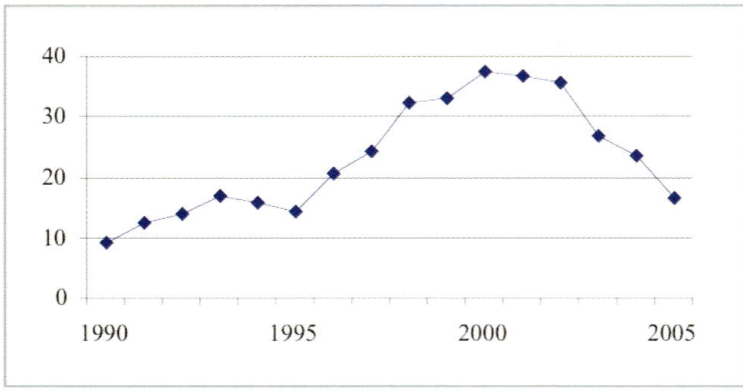

Figure 1. Estimated annual totals (rolling 3-year means) of Yellow-legged Gulls at Seaforth Nature Reserve, 1988-2005.

Within recent decades, as landfill sites blossomed in Britain and northern Europe, Mediterranean *michahellis* have developed a clear moult migration that takes them to these rich feeding areas well to the north of their traditional range, producing a marked late summer peak of records in Britain, particularly in SE England.

Records from Seaforth (Figure 2) reflect this late summer influx but it is not as marked as might be expected and birds are clearly present all year round. The largest monthly totals there have been eight in May 1997, nine in August 2000, eleven in October 1999 and eight that November. There is also a suggestion of a slight increase in spring, perhaps of non-breeding sub-adults moving into the area to summer – a pattern similar to that shown by immature Mediterranean Gulls. Numbers are low during winter with probably not more than half a dozen across the county.

Like other large gulls, some 'Yellow-legs' are known to have returned for several years to favoured sites. The two best documented were one that spent the moult period (July to September) at Bazil Point/Glasson on the outer Lune estuary from September 1992 to at least 2005, and another that spent most of the year at Dockacres between 1996 and spring 2001, when it associated with a Herring Gull. The sedentary behaviour of this latter bird perhaps suggests that it was some form of hybrid.

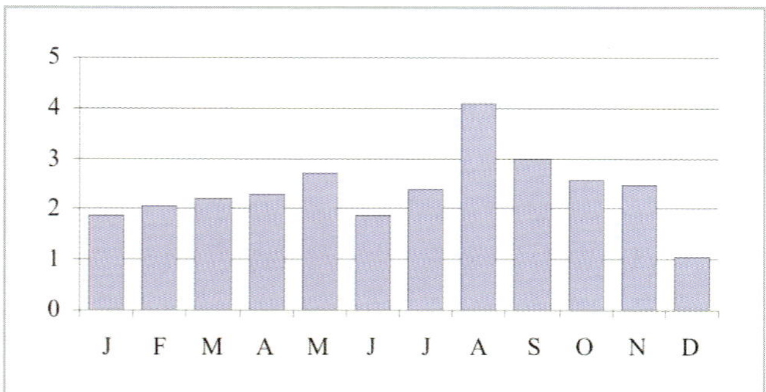

Figure 2. Average monthly numbers of Yellow-legged Gulls, at Seaforth Nature Reserve, 1995-2005.

Almost two-thirds of all records have been of adults or near-adults with a further 30% second- or third-years and less than 10% first-years – just 14 of this latter age-class were identified at Seaforth from 1990 to 2002 and very few elsewhere. Even allowing for the unknown number of returning adults, this apparent age distribution is highly unlikely to reflect reality but simply indicates the difficulties of identifying young Yellow-legged Gulls. As knowledge spreads the proportion of young birds reported will surely increase.

The breeding range of Yellow-legged Gulls has been moving northward in western Europe for several decades and they now breed in small numbers in Britain. It is perhaps just a matter of time before, like Mediterranean Gulls before them, they colonise Lancashire. They may already have done so – it would be next to impossible to pick out the odd bird amongst the Lesser Black-backed colonies. Birds apparently paired with Lesser-black Backed Gulls have been seen on passage at Seaforth in March 1990, February to March 1994, March 1996 and March to April 1998.

Adult Yellow-legged Gull, Seaforth Nature Reserve, September 2005. (Steve Young)

Even the most experienced observers would admit that identification of large white-headed gulls is an imprecise science. Currently, only Yellow-legged Gulls of the Mediterranean sub-species have been identified with certainty and that is the origin of our only ringing recovery, a colour-ringed juvenile/first-winter at Lancaster Tip on 13 September 1999, which had been ringed as a nestling in the Camargue on the French Mediterranean coast and which was seen again at Fishmoor Reservoir from 13 August to early September 2001. It is possible that a proportion of birds occurring in Lancashire might have their origins in one of the Atlantic colonies (sub-species *atlantis*) and the apparent tendency for many birds, especially at Seaforth, to be rather small-looking may support this view. However, there are as yet no confirmed instances of *atlantis* in the UK and other possibilities, such as the perennial problem of potentially similar looking hybrids (for example, between *argenteus* and *graellsii* or *graellsii* and *michahellis*) makes it difficult to see how such a bird could be confirmed without a ringing recovery.

SJW.

This species account was sponsored by Tim Vaughan.

HERRING GULL

Larus argentatus

Lancashire Category A.

Common breeder; abundant winter visitor from western Europe and Fennoscandia.

Herring Gull numbers in Britain underwent a major increase during the middle years of the twentieth century due to reduced persecution and expansion in food resources, principally from rubbish tips and fishery discards. As with other gull species, their association with people is of long standing; McNicholl (1883), for example, wrote of the practice of deliberate feeding of refuse from Southport's fish market to gulls at noon every day.

Mitchell knew of no records of nesting in Lancashire in the nineteenth century and described 'mature birds' as uncommon. The first confirmed breeding record came from Simonswood Moss, near Kirkby, where Hardy (1941) reported two pairs in 1939-41. Herring Gulls first nested in the Tarnbrook Fell Lesser Black-back colony in 1949 and increased to at least 500 pairs by 1967, while in 1969 it was estimated that 20% of the colony were of this species – perhaps as many as 3,000 pairs. Further estimates in the 1970s were in the range of 1,000-3,000 pairs but the percentage of Herring Gulls at Tarnbrook has dropped since then, from 16% in the early 1980s to 2.5% in 1999, representing a decline in numbers from about 2,000 to fewer than 500 pairs (D. Sowter *pers. comm.*).

The Ribble marshes were colonised in 1967 and numbers increased slowly during the 1970s to reach 170 pairs in 1983, then rapidly to at least 750 in 1998 – almost all of them on Banks Marsh but with a handful on the north bank at Warton Marsh. Herring Gulls have never gained a regular breeding toehold anywhere else in the county but up to four bred amongst Black-headed Gulls on Carnforth Marsh and up to three pairs at Stocks Reservoir during the 1990s, when breeding was also attempted at Belmont Reservoir.

Roof-nesting was first noted on a house at Birkdale in 1974 and the habit had become well-established by 1994, when a survey located one pair at Heysham Power Station, a minimum of four at the Thornton ICI plant, seven in Fleetwood and 20 in Liverpool. A further survey in 2000-2002 found 55 pairs on roofs in Blackpool, 79 in the Fleetwood docks area, 30 in Heysham/Morecambe and 25 in Liverpool.

Herring Gulls are our most abundant large gull in winter, regularly occurring in flocks running into thousands. Numbers are greatest after storms when vast quantities of marine invertebrates, especially shellfish and starfish, are cast up onto beaches. At such times counting them accurately is a near impossibility, especially when they are intermixed with Black-headed and Common Gulls.

Adult winter Herring Gull, Crosby Marine Park, February 2005. (Steve Young)

The two largest estimated counts on the Fylde coast were 15,000 at Rossall Point on 26 December 1986 and a mixed flock with Black-headeds of 20,000 at St. Anne's on 3 March 2002. All other counts over 10,000 have been on the Sefton coast. The biggest recorded congregations occurred in January 1985, February 1988, December 1991 to January 1992, January 1993-95, December 1999 to February 2000, December 2000 to January 2001, and January to March 2002. Once attracted to the coast, large numbers often persist for many weeks. The largest estimates have been 100,000+ between Ainsdale and Southport Pier on 22 February 2002 and, on the same stretch of beach, 65,000 on 9 February 1988, 50,000 in January 1985, 40,000 on 1 January 1992 and 30,000 on 22 December 1991, when a further 20,000 were at Marshside.

In less exceptional years total numbers are difficult to gauge but are likely to be in the region of 25,000 to 50,000 on the coast as a whole. Other coastal sites regularly registering more than 4,000 wintering birds include Fleetwood, the Keer Estuary, Formby Point and Seaforth/Crosby shore.

Being almost entirely dependent on rubbish tips, it is not surprising that numbers in the east of the county have fluctuated in line with the availability of this food resource. Herring Gulls were scarce in Rossendale until the 1950s, with just small numbers at reservoirs from late autumn to spring, but from 1953, when a single bird was with Lesser Black-backed Gulls at Stacksteads Tip, numbers rose to 40 in December 1954 and to 120 by the late 1980s and nearly 500 in December 1994. In the Burnley area the maximum count prior to 1939 was just 16 but by the 1970s the winter population averaged about 500 within 10km of Burnley. More recently, during the 1990s, the Foulridge Reservoir roosts were usually around 200-400 with a peak of 500 in December 1995 but counts have declined significantly following the closure of Rowley Tip in 2003. This coincided with an increase in numbers in the Accrington and Blackburn area, where birds feed at Whinney Hill Tip and roost on Fishmoor Reservoir and where peak counts rose from 2,100 in December 2002 to 6,000 in December 2004.

Numbers inland are, however, trifling in comparison to those on the coast. Large numbers are known to roost in winter at

Longridge and Lower Rivington Reservoir but few counts have been published, although they are known regularly to reach four figures at the latter site. The largest flocks reported away from Whinney Hill/Fishmoor have been 2,000 at Lower Rivington Reservoir in December 1986, 3,340 at Prescot Reservoirs in February 1991 with 2,000 there in December 2002; 1,695 at Carr Mill Dam, St. Helens in January 2000; and 1,500 at Rowley Lake, Burnley on 7 February 1998.

Ringing recoveries shed some light on the origins and movements of Lancashire's birds. Of 927 Lancashire recoveries of birds ringed elsewhere in the Britain and Ireland, 229 were from Scotland, 484 from northern England (overwhelmingly from Walney in Cumbria), 178 from Wales, 25 from Ireland and eleven from southern England – with just one foreign-ringed bird from Holland. Recoveries of Lancashire-ringed birds show a broadly similar pattern: 17 in northern England, four in Wales, three in southern England and one in Scotland. A Tarnbrook-bred adult wintering in Denmark is the only recovery abroad.

This paints a picture for the local race *argenteus* of fairly short-distance post-breeding dispersal and winter wandering rather than major migration – more than 90% of recoveries of Lancashire-ringed birds have been within 100 km of the ringing site.

The pattern of monthly occurrences on the coast is illustrated in Figure 1 using data from Seaforth. This shows a clear late winter peak, followed by a gradual reduction in early spring. During May to early July almost all birds are immatures, with adults beginning to return in late July and August and numbers gradually increasing to winter proportions during October.

Although there are no ringing data to support it, some immigration of nominate *argentatus* into Lancashire does undoubtedly occur in winter, probably largely involving birds from the highly migratory colonies in the Norwegian Arctic and eastwards into Russia. Many of these have a highly distinctive appearance and are easily identified in the field. Ringing recoveries show north-east England to be a major wintering site for Arctic *argentatus* (Migration Atlas) but relatively few seem to cross the Pennines.

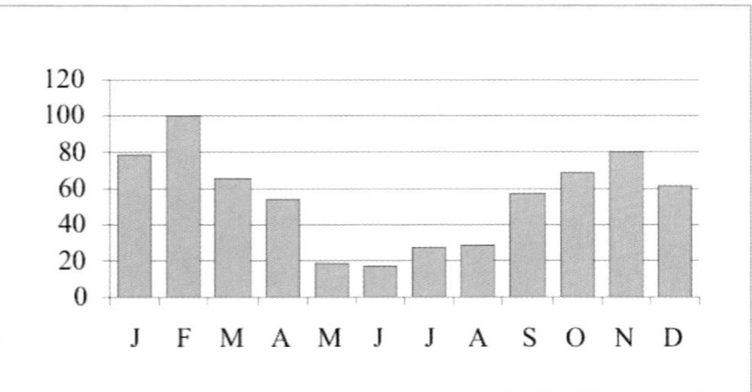

Figure 1. Indices of monthly peak counts of Herring Gulls at Seaforth Nature Reserve, 1986-2005. (February = 100).

The first Lancashire records of nominate *argentatus* were published during the 1980s, closely coinciding with the then burgeoning interest in gulls and the challenge of sub-specific identification, but they must have been occurring earlier. Counts from all the main gull-watching sites became regular during the 1990s; most have been of single birds but ten or more have been seen in a day at Seaforth, Lancaster, and Clowbridge, Foulridge and Fishmoor Reservoirs. Only the more distinctive individuals will normally be recorded so real totals are probably somewhat higher. Unfortunately, few observers have simultaneously recorded *argenteus* numbers so it is difficult to judge the proportion of Arctic birds in our wintering flocks. Informed opinion at Seaforth puts this at about 1-2% in most winters and this is supported by a single count inland of 30 *argentatus* in a flock of 1,500 at Whinney Hill tip in December 1997. Numbers may be substantially higher than this during influxes, however. Counts at Ainsdale/Southport during the shellfish wreck of early 2002 produced estimates of 5,000 *argentatus* amongst 100,000+ Herring Gulls in January and 500 out of 5,000 in February.

Nevertheless, Arctic birds remain a definite minority and it is as a major wintering area for *argenteus* that Lancashire is most notable.

SJW, MJ.

This species account was sponsored by Seumus Eaves.

AMERICAN HERRING GULL

Larus argentatus smithsonianus

Lancashire Category A. (0, 2).

Vagrant from North America.

A first-winter, showing characteristics of the North American race *L. a. smithsonianus*, was found at Otterspool on the Mersey in south Liverpool on 6 March 1994 by Mark Garner and Gavin Thomas; it was assumed to have been the individual seen previously at Neumann's Flash, Cheshire from 26 February to 4 March 1994 which became the first accepted British record. Another first-winter occurred the following year at Seaforth on 26 March. Others have been suspected but, since some Arctic *argentatus* closely match the appearance of some *smithsonianus*, identification of all but the most distinctive individuals is problematic.

Smithsonianus is currently regarded as a race of Herring Gull but it seems that the two taxa are not especially closely related and are likely to be split in the near future (Maclean *et al.* 2005).

First-winter American Herring Gull, Otterspool, Liverpool, 6 March 1994. (Gavin Thomas)

SJW.

CASPIAN GULL

Larus argentatus cachinnans

Lancashire Category A. (0, 1).

Vagrant from central or eastern Europe.

The Caspian Gull is currently regarded as a sub-species of Herring Gull by the BOU, as a race of Yellow-legged Gull by some and as a species in its own right by others. Its field characters were largely unknown until the early 1990s and it was not admitted to the British list until 2003. Records have proliferated since the late 1990s, mainly in SE England and the Midlands, and observers familiar with them can confidently pick out their distinctive appearance, but identification pitfalls do exist and the fact that Arctic Herring Gulls can share certain plumage characteristics may have received too little attention at times. Records in Britain have occurred in all months but with a marked winter peak.

The first whole-hearted claims of Caspian Gulls in Lancashire were of sub-adults at Blackpool on 2 December 1995 and at Seaforth between 19 October and 19 November 1998. Several sightings of birds showing characteristics of Caspian Gull were made at Seaforth and Crosby during 1999: an adult from 18-23 August and adult(s) on 11-27 November. All were submitted to the BBRC but none was accepted.

A further dozen or more Lancashire claims accumulated over the next year or so, mostly from Seaforth or Crosby but also singles at Marshside, Ainsdale, Liverpool Docks, Lancaster Tip and Whinney Hill Tip. One of the best-documented of these was an adult at Seaforth on 6 and 20 October 2001 which was seen by several dozen people, videoed and photographed – unfortunately the crucial outer primaries had been moulted and were regrowing, so the identification could not be clinched.

The first proven Lancashire record was thus a first-winter at Fishmoor Reservoir on 26-27 February 2005, found by John Wright and Bill Berry. As more county birders become familiar with this (sub-)species, records will no doubt proliferate but it seems likely that it will prove to be an occasional rather than a very regular visitor to Lancashire.

SJW.

This species account was sponsored by John Wright.

ICELAND GULL

Larus glaucoides

Lancashire Category A.

Uncommon winter visitor from Greenland.

After the publication of the first detailed identification texts in the 1970s and especially Peter Grant's seminal identification guide in 1982, county birders quickly got to grips with identification issues and differentiating Iceland and Glaucous Gulls is no longer a significant problem.

The same post-Grant surge in interest in gulls did, however, throw up another problem that has still not been resolved and continues to cause something of a headache in distinguishing individuals and thus determining numbers. Before the 1980s almost all Lancashire records were published either as 'adults' or 'immatures' but since then most have been assigned to precise age categories. Definite ageing is difficult for all of the large white-headed gulls (especially older immatures) but it is especially so for Iceland and Glaucous since it is sometimes very difficult to distinguish even first-year from second-year birds in the absence of tell-tale adult-like grey upperpart feathering which many second-winters do not show.

In addition, the published record is full of references to 'first-summers' although it is now thought very doubtful whether any large white-headed gull can be said actually to exhibit such a plumage. None of this would be a serious problem if it were not for the fact that birds ascribed to different age-categories have generally been assumed to be different individuals, raising the likelihood of replication.

All in all, the accounts of Iceland and Glaucous Gulls that follow are, therefore, fraught with uncertainties, particularly in respect of numbers. No attempt has been made to adjust the published record beyond removing a handful of the most obvious duplicate records. It is fairly certain that the frequency of occurrence of white-winged gulls has been overestimated, to what degree it is impossible to say, but the problem is unlikely to invalidate the overall picture presented here.

Iceland Gulls have been consistently outnumbered by Glaucous Gulls in Lancashire by roughly two to one; this reflects the national pattern although Iceland Gulls do seem to be more prone to influxes.

Mitchell knew of no occurrences and Oakes was able to give only two records, a third-winter bird at Lancaster Quay from mid-February to mid-March 1929 and an 'immature' at Formby Point on 8 March 1940. No more were reported until another 'immature' at Southport on 28 December 1958. Records became more or less annual in the 1960s when the first was seen inland, at Kirkby Moss on 2 February 1969. The 1970s saw reports nearly quadruple and this increase continued into the 1980s when an average of six were seen annually. Though still scarce, Iceland Gulls had become established as a regular feature of winter birding. Throughout this period one bird dominated the record books. Having been first seen on the Mersey in 1955, it returned each winter to its favoured spot on New Brighton shore in Wirral, Cheshire (where a 30th birthday celebration was held in its honour). Particularly during its latter years it was seen sporadically just across the river at Seaforth, where the final sighting came on 4 May 1985.

The dramatic change in status was no doubt due in large measure to the increased number of observers but the increased availability of food sources, especially rubbish tips, must also have played a significant role.

Average numbers had steadily increased from the 1960s to the late 1980s but more than doubled during the 1990s before declining a little in the first years of this century (Figure 1). The winter of 1993/94 saw the first really large influx into the county – it remains our largest. After an adult at Darwen sewage works on 5 December about 30 more, mostly first-year birds, were seen up to 5 May 1994, including a county record day-count of three at Fishmoor Reservoir on 31 December. Further influxes of about 20 followed in 1994/95, 17 in 1996/97 and 18 in 2001/02.

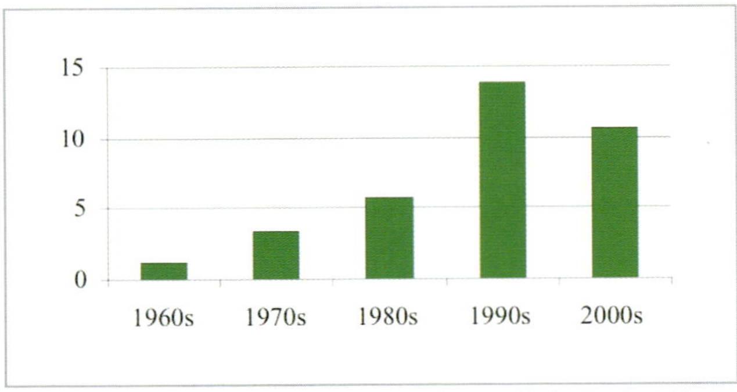

Figure 1. Average annual numbers of Iceland Gulls in Lancashire by decade, 1960-2005. (Includes returning individuals; winterering birds counted in first year only).

Although the majority of Lancashire's Iceland Gulls have been on the coast they have a surprisingly high propensity to occur inland. Almost a third of the 255 records since 1960 for which locations have been published have been inland – virtually three times the proportion for Glaucous Gulls. This possibly reflects a far greater reliance upon landfill sites for feeding than Glaucous Gulls; almost all inland records have been at tips or associated reservoir roosts with favoured localities being Fishmoor Reservoir and Whinney Hill tip (c.44 records) and Rowley Lake and tip (23 records). The loss of many landfill sites during the 1980s and 1990s, particularly in the Fylde and Merseyside, undoubtedly contributed to the decreasing coastal numbers of both white-winged gulls in the late twentieth century.

Coastal records are heavily biased towards the south – with more than 100 reported on the Sefton coast, including 76 at Seaforth, 35 in the Fylde (where some are perhaps associated with the Fleetwood fishery) and 30 or so in north Lancashire – although this is, at least in part, as much a reflection of the distribution of gull enthusiasts as gulls.

Iceland Gulls have been recorded in every month of the year but are primarily December to April birds (Figure 2). There have been seven records in June and one in July, all of young birds, presumably lingering well south of the breeding grounds.

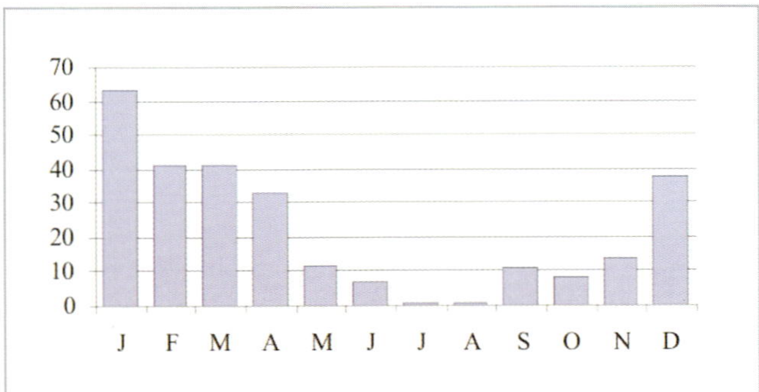

Figure 2. Monthly arrivals of Iceland Gulls in Lancashire, 1960-2005.

Post-breeding birds begin to turn up in small numbers during September to November. Almost all are adults or older 'immatures' – and probably regularly wintering birds; there are only two autumn records of first-years, on 30 October 1995 at Fishmoor Reservoir and 26 November 1994 at Delph Reservoir. The number of new arrivals accelerates during December and peaks in January, and the vast majority of these are first-years. Sightings of new birds decline in February but remain at a fairly constant level until April before tailing off in early May; these are perhaps a mixture of birds forced further south by hard weather and northbound migrants that have wintered further south, with migrants predominating as spring progresses.

Age details of 234 birds have been published since 1960: roughly a third of them as first-years, a third as adults and a third as second-or third-years. The New Brighton bird highlights the possibility that a substantial proportion of records of older birds are regularly-returning individuals that perhaps first arrive as first-years.

Adult 'Kumlien's Gull', Seaforth Nature Reserve, March 1995. (Steve Young)

The taxonomy of Iceland Gulls in regard to the two north American forms, *thayeri* (often regarded as a separate species, Thayer's Gull) and *kumlieni*, remains unresolved. For a short period during the 1980s and 1990s records of *kumlieni* were assessed by the BBRC, who accepted records of adults at Seaforth on 7 January to 6 February 1995 and on 18 February to 15 March the same year, and another adult at Marshside on 5 March 1997. There have been a number of other reports, including a third-winter on Crosby shore on 18 February 1999, and a well-documented third-winter at Fishmoor Reservoir during December 1999. In more recent years, however, doubt has been cast on the practicality of distinguishing all specimens of *glaucoides* from *kumlieni* and interest in sub-specific identification has rather waned.

SJW, MJ.

This species account was sponsored by Pete Marsh.

GLAUCOUS GULL

Larus hyperboreus

Lancashire Category A.

Uncommon winter visitor from the Arctic.

Tony Disley

Mitchell mentioned only one record, an 'immature' with a broken wing at Formby on 8 November 1873, and Oakes could add only one more – at Freshfield in December 1922, with perhaps the same individual being shot at Formby on 2 January 1923. Another four were found during the 1950s – singles at Blackpool, Silverdale, Morecambe and Heysham – but the 1960s saw the beginning of a strong upsurge with a total of 32 recorded.

Since then it has become increasingly difficult to keep an accurate reckoning of annual numbers due to their somewhat nomadic habits causing likely duplication of reports, but published records more than doubled in the 1970s and again in the 1980s. An attempt to estimate annual totals, after stripping out the most likely duplicates, is illustrated in Figure 1. This shows sightings of Glaucous Gulls peaking at an average of 19-20 per year during the 1980s and 1990s before declining sharply to fewer than five during the first six years of the present century, with just two recorded in 2004 and three in 2005. This sudden fall in numbers may be linked to climate change producing a series of mild winters and it may be significant that this apparent change in status of Glaucous Gulls is much greater than that of Iceland Gulls which breed further north. If the trend continues, Glaucous Gulls may before long revert to their former status as county rarities.

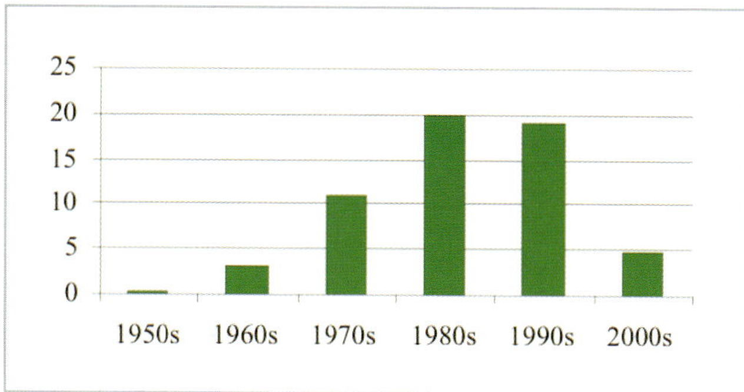

Figure 1. Average annual numbers of Glaucous Gulls in Lancashire by decade, 1950-2005. (Returning individuals counted in each year; overwinterering birds counted in first year only).

Although Glaucous Gulls have been recorded in Lancashire in every month of the year they are essentially winter visitors (Figure 2). Birds are extremely scarce between May and July and almost all have been immatures; the four summer adults have perhaps been sickly individuals.

The autumn return begins in August and there is a steady trickle of new arrivals through to November. The majority of these early birds are adults and a proportion of total records probably relate to a relatively small number of birds returning to favoured wintering sites year after year; the number of first sightings of adults in autumn peaks in September, not rising again before December. First-years are, on the other hand, extremely scarce in autumn, with a total of just eleven seen between late September and November between 1954 and 2005.

About two-thirds of all records have occurred between December and March; numbers peak at the end of winter – first-winters in January-February and adults in February-March. This late influx may be due in part to hard weather in the north pushing birds into Lancashire, but it seems likely that it also reflects the beginning of a passage of birds that have wintered in Ireland or southern Britain. Most adults have moved on by the end of March and only a handful have been recorded during April. Movements of first-years and older non-breeding birds are, however, quite regular throughout April and into early May.

Records of more than 250 winter birds were published between 1970 and 2005 but the number of individuals involved may have been significantly lower than this. Several are known to have returned to the same wintering site year after year, notably two that probably arrived as first-winters at Seaforth in 1991 and reappeared each winter until at least 1999/2000. These two birds probably accounted for the vast majority of sightings of Glaucous Gulls at Seaforth during this period but were in fact seen less than once a fortnight, presumably roaming over a large area and having alternative roost sites. It seems at least possible that the same semi-nomadic behaviour has gone unnoticed elsewhere and that Glaucous Gulls are less common in Lancashire than they appear.

The age break-down of Glaucous Gull records in Lancashire is virtually identical to that of Iceland Gulls: a third first-years, a third older immatures and a third adults (including all records of returning birds). First-year birds of both species have thus been recorded far more often than would be expected from their frequency in the population (full adults should be several times as numerous as first-years). As with Iceland Gulls, it is likely that a significant proportion of Lancashire Glaucous Gulls are birds which have first appeared as first-years and adopted the county as their favoured wintering site in subsequent years.

No one year has ever seen an especially large influx of Glaucous Gulls, the most recorded being 30 in 1988 and 32 in 1998 – about 50% above average for the period. The winter shellfish wrecks that draw huge influxes of Herring Gulls to the coast rarely produce many new Glaucous Gulls.

Coastal records show a marked bias towards the Sefton coast, where about 180 have been reported – 120 of them at Seaforth, against 80 or so on the Fylde coast, including Marton Mere, and 30 in the Lancaster/Heysham/Morecambe area. The largest number seen in any one day was five at Seaforth on 29 March 1990, a likely date for northbound migrants.

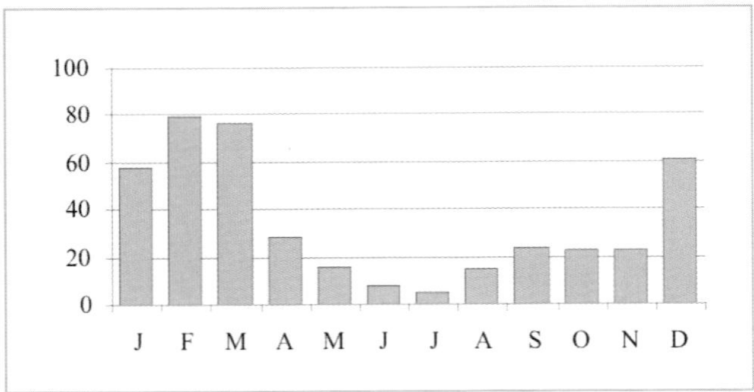

Figure 2. Monthly arrivals of Glaucous Gulls in Lancashire, 1978-2005.

Although coastal rubbish tips do attract Glaucous Gulls – including several Fylde sites in the 1960s and 1970s and Lancaster in the 1980s and 1990s – their often highly sporadic appearances make it likely that many feed offshore, perhaps reliant on fishery discards. Inland, however, tips are just about their only source of food and all records have been either on landfill sites or at reservoir roosts.

The marked coastal bias is emphasised by the fact that none was recorded inland until one at Appley Bridge as recently as 19 March 1983. Since then, however, there have been many more records and latterly the species has become annual inland. In contrast to Iceland Gulls, however, Glaucous Gulls have a predominantly coastal distribution in Lancashire, with about 15% occurring inland – although there has been an indication in recent years that this proportion may be increasing. Favoured localities have been Rowley Tip and Lake, Fishmoor Reservoir and Whinney Hill Tip, Martin Mere and Rivington Reservoir. Inland records are even more skewed towards young birds than on the coast, with almost two-thirds referring to first-years.

Birds considered to be hybrids with Herring Gull have been recorded on about 13 occasions since 1976. These have occurred mostly at Seaforth, with others at Ainsdale, Lytham, Fleetwood, Lancaster and Carnforth. One adult was recorded at Seaforth each winter between 1993 and 1996. Most, however, have been immatures and a perennial problem when attempting to identify young hybrids is the presence of occasional extremely pale immature *argentatus* Herring Gulls that can look superficially hybrid-like.

SJW, MJ.

This species account was sponsored by Malcolm Greenhalgh.

GREAT BLACK-BACKED GULL

Larus marinus

Lancashire Category A.

Rare breeder; common winter visitor from northern Britain and Fennoscandia.

Breeding took place on Pilling Moss early in the nineteenth century but by 1859 shooting and nest destruction had exterminated the colony and Mitchell knew of no other breeding records or sightings away from the coast. No further breeding took place until a handful of pairs became established within the Tarnbrook Fell gullery and later on the Ribble marshes.

The first nest was found in Bowland on 10 May 1949 and a small number of pairs have probably bred there annually since then. Precise figures are hard to establish: Great Black-backs are very much needles in the haystack that is the huge Bowland Lesser Black-backed colony. Nonetheless, two nests were located in 1956 and five in 1967. The number of definite pairs reached a maximum of 15 in 1970 and perhaps as many as 35 in 1972, but large scale culling of gulls has taken place at this site over many years and the number of breeding Great Black-backs appears to have dropped considerably. It was thought that as many as 20 pairs might still be present in the late 1980s but only eight pairs were located in 1999 and there has been little change since (D. Sowter *pers. comm.*).

The species has never become established elsewhere in the north of the county. Single pairs bred on the Lune Estuary in 1969 and the RSPB Morecambe Bay reserve in 1979 and have been present fairly regularly within the Black-headed colonies at Leighton Moss, the Eric Morecambe complex and the Dockacres complex since the 1980s, breeding successfully at the latter site in 2001 and unsuccessfully in 2003. One pair held territory at Arkholme in summer 2000 but no eggs were laid.

The Ribble marshes were colonised fairly recently and rather more successfully. The population grew from a single unsuccessful pair in 1979 to seven pairs in 1998 (six on Banks Marsh and one on Warton Marsh) and six in 2003, after the first successful breeding in 1988. One pair nested unsuccessfully in the Fleetwood Docks in 2002.

Two or more birds have been present in the Stocks Reservoir gullery in most recent summers and have almost certainly attempted to breed but without any evidence of success.

Moderate numbers of young, non-breeding birds are also present during summer, mostly on the coast. Single-site counts of more than 100 are rare; they include 167 at Seaforth on 1 May 1992, 212 at Formby in June 1996 and 105 at Prescot Reservoir on 24 June 1996.

The first adults begin to return in July but numbers rarely rise significantly before September; a roost of 440 at Marshside in August 1997 was highly exceptional. A series of counts at Fleetwood in 1986 illustrates the pace of the build-up: 222 on 7 September grew to 450 by the 21st and over 650 during November, remaining just below this level for the rest of the year.

Coastal roosts appear never to have exceeded 200 in the 1950s or 1960s but some published counts exceeded 300 during the 1970s (e.g. 300 at St. Anne's in October 1978 and 315 at Fleetwood in September 1979) and became fairly regular from the 1980s. Notable counts have been 530 flying to roost at Preesall on 26 November 1983 and 510 on 3 January 1985, 600 at Blackpool on 25 October 1998, 375 at Formby Point in September 2002 and 447 at Seaforth on 13 February 2005. Aggregate flocks along the coast between Formby and Marshside gave totals of 1,227 on 30 November 1981 and 1,200 on 9 February 1988.

Oakes noted an increase inland during the 1940s and this continued during the 1950s and 1960s but numbers were never very high – 18 at Whitemoor Reservoir and 13 at Barrow Lodge, near Clitheroe in December 1961 were record counts at that time – until the late 1960s. Rivington Reservoir recorded 96 in 1966, followed by nearly 300 in 1971 and 200 in 1979 – all in December. Numbers inland rarely match those on the coast but several further large counts include 100 at Rowley Tip, Burnley in December 1983 with 220 there in January 1987 and 177 in January 1988, 197 at Foulridge Reservoir in January 1987, 625 on the Rivington Reservoirs in January 1993, 280 at Alston Reservoir, near Longridge in December 1996 and 140 at Delph Reservoir in December 2000 and 224 at Fishmoor Reservoir on 31 January 2003. Prescot Reservoir, St. Helens often holds three-figure flocks with 850 reported in January 1990. These inland birds are almost totally dependent upon tips for food and the increase in their numbers and shifting distribution reflects the opening and closure of landfill sites; in Rossendale, for example, few were seen before the opening of Stacksteads Tip, after which peak counts grew to 35 in 1994, only to dwindle to almost zero again after its closure in the late 1990s.

A total of 140 birds ringed in Britain and Ireland outside Lancashire have been recovered in the county. Twenty-six of these were ringed in Scotland, where the bulk of the British population breeds; 98 in northern England (mostly Walney Island in Cumbria); 14 in Wales and one each in Ireland and southern England. One bird ringed in the Bowland colony was recovered in winter in Dumfries and Galloway as an adult. All this points to essentially west British origins for our wintering birds but Lancashire recoveries of three first-winters ringed in Fennoscandia (two in Norway and one in Finland) indicate that some come from further afield.

SJW, MJ.

This species account was sponsored by Ron Hothersall.

ROSS'S GULL

Rhodostethia rosea

Lancashire Category A. (0, 4).

Vagrant from north-eastern Siberia.

The county's first, an adult, was found on Birkdale shore on 16 January 1983 by Phil Smith and Derek Forshaw. It was the 35th record in Britain and Ireland.

Amazingly, Phil Smith also found the second. Another adult, it roosted on the causeway at Seaforth during strong gales on 3 January 1988 – about 50 people managed to see the bird that afternoon. The next day saw the return to work after the Christmas holidays and witnessed what was one of the country's first televised 'twitches', but, as business-suited 'truants' strove to avoid the cameras, the star of the show failed to put in an appearance.

Adult winter Ross's Gull (centre) with Little Gulls, Seaforth Nature Reserve, 23 March 1994. (Steve Young)

It seems more than likely that the next two records related to a single bird. An adult was found on the shore near Rossall School on 12 March 1994 and stayed in the Rossall Point/Fleetwood area until the 17th; then, what was assumed to be the same individual spent two hours at Seaforth on 23 March. The following year brought an almost identical replay. An adult was seen briefly at Fleetwood Marine Lake on 24 January 1995 and relocated at Seaforth on the 30th. This then became one of the longest staying Ross's Gulls in the country and was last seen on 15 March. During this time more than 1,000 birdwatchers came to see it but, although predictable, it was never easy. It was seen on the reserve fairly regularly during the day but usually only for short periods before flying off inland to feed. It would then reappear at dusk to roost on the causeway, usually the only gull there, as Seaforth is rarely used as an overnight gull roost.

SJW, MJ.

This species account was sponsored by Steve Young.

KITTIWAKE

Rissa tridactyla

Lancashire Category A.

Rare breeder; common passage migrant and winter visitor.

Mitchell noted that Kittiwakes were present offshore in Lancashire all year round and this remains the case. Significant day-counts (in excess of 100) are almost equally likely to occur in any month of the year, although the largest numbers usually come in early autumn. Despite being by far the most abundant breeding gull in Britain and one of our commonest seabirds (Lloyd *et al.* 1991), Kittiwakes are often difficult to make contact with – ask any bird-race participant! In winter they are almost entirely oceanic; after the breeding season they move into the Atlantic, where they become largely nomadic, and their migratory movements are, therefore, probably less directed than those of most other gull species (Migration Atlas).

Both Mitchell and Oakes regarded inland records as exceptional but these have gradually increased, particularly since the 1980s, so that an average of five or so are seen annually nowadays on various reservoirs and lakes.

Their presence, particularly in winter, is largely determined by the occurrence of Atlantic depressions that gather up and drive them towards the coast. Once offshore they often form large flocks and several hundred may pass a single site in a few hours. The most spectacular such event was on 12 November 2000, when 729 passed Heysham in a single hour. Similar gales in 1984 produced 383 in two hours off Blackpool on 3 January and 600 in a similar period at Rossall Point on the 11th, followed by 390 on the Mersey at Seaforth on the 13th. Another large wreck occurred on 22-23 December 1991, when 484 were logged off Blackpool and 400 off Heysham. The other most notable winter count was 579 off Heysham on 24 January 2001. Despite these huge displacements, remarkably few are seen inland in midwinter.

Kittiwake, Seaforth Nature Reserve, June 1999. (Steve Young)

At the very end of February, Kittiwakes are beginning to move back to their breeding grounds. In recent years some sizeable northbound flocks have entered Morecambe Bay in March and April, sometimes during strong winds but also in periods of poor visibility and even in clear, calm conditions. Thirteen flocks totalling 419 birds flew north off Heysham on 6 April 1993, while in 1995 more than 400 passed in seven flocks between 5 and 25 March. Other significant spring counts at Heysham include 392 on 27 March 1996, 360 on 3 March 2000 and 502 on 4 April 2005. Birds may still be moving through in some numbers during May, the largest counts in recent years being 244 at Formby Point on 17 May 2000, 292 at Heysham on 18 May 2001, when 280 were also seen from Jenny Brown's Point, and 384 there on 5 May 2005.

The long duration of this spring migration presumably reflects a wide range of destinations. Direct evidence of overland passage is restricted to two immatures which soared up above the Keer Estuary and flew east out of sight on 15 May 1966. However, the number of inland records increases somewhat at this time of year, and in the past few years sightings have become regular at Brockholes Quarry on the Ribble at Preston. Taken together, this perhaps indicates some cross-Pennine passage across Lancashire, first suggested by Spencer (1973), to mirror the well-documented movement east through the Solway to our north.

From late May to early July almost all records are of first-years together with a few older, non-breeding birds. The largest, most consistent gathering was on the Mersey from the late 1970s until the mid-1990s with peak June counts at Seaforth of 330 in 1985, 262 in 1990 and 212 in 1991. One theory put forward for this phenomenon was that Kittiwakes (with other seabirds) were feeding upon shoals of small fish drifted into the river at high tide that went 'belly-up' on meeting the out-flowing, heavily polluted Mersey. Certainly, the demise of this congregation coincided with the spectacular improvement of water quality as a result of the efforts of the Environment Agency.

For several summers in the early 1990s adult Kittiwakes appeared to be prospecting for nest sites on the window-ledges of the Liver Building at Liverpool's Pier Head but none has been seen there since 1995. Then, in 1998 two pairs bred successfully 19 km offshore on a Morecambe Bay Central gas platform, the colony increasing to 22 pairs by 2002 (Mitchell *et al.* 2004); whether this can truly be said to be in Lancashire is a moot point. Definite confirmation as a Lancashire breeding species came in July 2005 when 58 pairs were found nesting on the seawall in the Liverpool Docks. Sixty birds had been seen from the Wirral side of the Mersey at the same site during a gale in June 2004 , so it seems likely that the colony may have been established for at least two or three years.

The autumn return usually begins in mid-July; it gathers pace throughout August and continues into September but numbers usually begin to drop from mid-October. During the 1950s two high counts were reported, unprecedented at the time: 520 roosting at Formby Point on 20 August 1956 and 380 on St. Anne's beach on 12 August 1958. The largest counts since have been 700 at Formby in July 1968, with 850 there in July 1972 and 910 on 27 October 2001; 2,000 on the Isle of Man ferry route across Liverpool Bay on 6 September 1980; 680 off Rossall Point on 14 September 1987 (when 500 were also on the Mersey at Seaforth); 560 off Jenny Brown's Point in August 1988; 600 or so at Seaforth in September and October 1988 with 486 there on 19 September 1990; and 700 roosting at Blackpool on 10 August

1990 with 500 there on 10 October 1993. With the exception of those at Formby in 2001, autumn peak day-counts have shown a marked decline since the mid-1990s, probably linked to the 21% decline in the Scottish breeding population between 1985-88 and 1998-2002 (Mitchell *et al.* 2004).

The majority of ringing recoveries relate to the cannon-netting of summering birds at Seaforth and demonstrate their widespread origins. Not surprisingly for such an oceanic species, few Lancashire-ringed birds have been recovered in winter – they include a 16-year-old bird in Italy, singles in France and the Channel Islands and one in the Barents Sea to the east of Svalbard. One was found in a breeding colony on the Faeroes and others in Wales (5), the north of England (6) and Scotland (1). Recoveries of birds ringed away from Lancashire comprise 13 from northern England, six from Scotland, two from Wales, singles from the Isle of Man and Ireland and seven from a single colony in Finistere in northern France.

SJW, MJ.

This species account was sponsored by John C. Wood.

IVORY GULL

Pagophila eburnea

Lancashire Category A. (0, 1).

Vagrant from the Arctic.

The 12th Report of the Lancashire and Cheshire Fauna Committee carried an account of one seen feeding on the corpse of a Teal 'near the Mersey Bar' (an extremely unlikely location to witness such behaviour) on 4 January 1925 by W.H. Riddell. The description was reviewed by T.A. Coward and F.A. Montague, who both felt it probably was an Ivory Gull. Confusingly, what appears to be the same record was published by Hardy (1941) as having occurred on the Mersey Estuary, now in Cheshire, on 4 January 1926 and this is how it appears in the national records.

An adult found at Granny's Bay, Lytham St. Anne's by Keith Sharrock and Peter Smith on 13 February 2002 is thus Lancashire's only record. It was located amongst a very large roost of Black-headed and other gulls which had been attracted to the coast by a large starfish 'wreck'. It initially proved elusive and was not refound until the following afternoon, but on the 15th it was watched by a large and appreciative gallery as it alternated between roosting on the shore and bathing on the adjacent Fairhaven Lake.

Adult Ivory Gull, Fairhaven Lake, February 2002. (Margaret Breaks)

SJW.

This species account was sponsored by Chris Galvin.

LITTLE TERN

Sternula albifrons

Lancashire Category A.

Fairly common passage migrant.

Mitchell believed that the Little Tern had become extinct as a breeding species in present-day Lancashire sometime in the mid-nineteenth century. He identified previous nesting sites in the vicinity of Lytham Lighthouse and between there and Blackpool. His verdict was more than a little premature, however, for at least two colonies survived into the second half of the twentieth century. Charnley wrote in the 1930 Lancashire Bird Report that 'this species has bred for some years on the strip of shingle on the Rossall Shore. It is well looked after by a member of the school staff'. Unfortunately, the colony was abandoned around 1940.

Adult Little Tern with Common Tern, Seaforth Nature Reserve, May 1994. (Steve Young)

Oakes described a nest at Ainsdale, presumably within the larger Common Tern colony, in 1938 as the first in the area for at least 20 years but it seems that there were never more than three pairs here and the last two pairs were seen in 1948 (Smith 1963). A third colony was established around 1928 at Barnaby's Sands on the Wyre Estuary. It supported six pairs in 1934, ten in 1935 and grew to 20 pairs in 1942 but high tides and egg theft reduced these to four in 1944 and one or two in 1948. Nine pairs bred in 1949 and seven chicks were ringed but increased disturbance and commercial shingle extraction caused the gradual desertion of the colony and the last nest was found in 1957 – extinction in Lancashire had finally become a reality.

Oakes described the usual spring arrival date as being between 27 April and 4 May and this remains much the same today with the average first sighting between 1970 and 2005 occurring on 24 April and the earliest at Rossall on 13 April 1991. Spring passage rarely consists of more than two or three records of singles or very small groups which pass quickly through, presumably heading for Cumbrian or Scottish breeding colonies. The largest counts have been 45 off Blackpool on 3 May 1997, 32 off Formby on 15 May 1988 and 42 there on 21 May 1989.

Although most are seen on the coast (particularly in Sefton and the Fylde), inland records average around one a year, including a very early bird at Martin Mere on 15 April 2003. Close to the sea there have been three records at Marton Mere in spring and one in autumn. Most occur on the east Lancashire reservoirs and the only recent inland records in the north of the county have been singles at Arkholme on 23-24 April 1992 and at Wenning Foot, also on the River Lune, on 8 May 2000.

It is difficult to define precisely when the spring passage ends and the autumn return begins since small numbers of what are probably non-breeding birds occur annually in late May and throughout June. However, mid-July usually produces a marked upturn in numbers. Numbers fall quickly during September, and October records are very scarce; two at Southport on 19 October 1963 and one on Crosby Marine Lake on 23 October 2003 are the latest.

Most records relate to singles or small parties, often passing rapidly offshore, fishing as they go, but several sites have recorded larger groups of roosting birds which may stay for several days.

A post-breeding flock that gathered in the Lune Estuary from the 1960s produced notable counts of 145 on 6 August 1960, over 100 in early August 1961 and 1966 and 105 on 1 August 1982. Numbers have been low since 1987 though a count of 40 was made at nearby Pilling on 20 August 1985 and 26 on 9 August 1986. Numbers in the north of the county have plummeted since the 1990s with, at best, one or two a year now being seen in the Heysham area.

Small numbers frequently roost on St. Anne's and Fairhaven beaches, 26 at the latter site on 10 August 1994 being above average as were 24 on 29 July 1995, but eight at Blackpool on 12 August 1996, six there on 19 July 1998 and seven at Lytham on 12 August 2002, 28-31 July 2004 and 28 August 2005 have been the largest autumn counts anywhere on the Fylde coast since.

The Sefton coast registered a sharp increase in records from about the mid-1980s with large counts on the Mersey off Seaforth of 73 on 16 August 1990, of 107 on 1 August 1992 at Formby Point/Hightown with 155 there on the 28th, 90 on 18 August 1994 and 83 on 24 August 1995. As elsewhere in the county, numbers declined sharply in the late 1990s with 18 at Formby/Ainsdale on 28 July 2000 and 21 on 10 August 2003 the largest counts until 72 at Formby Point on 2 September 2004 – but the stretch of coast from Seaforth to Southport is now the only reliable county site for autumn Little Terns.

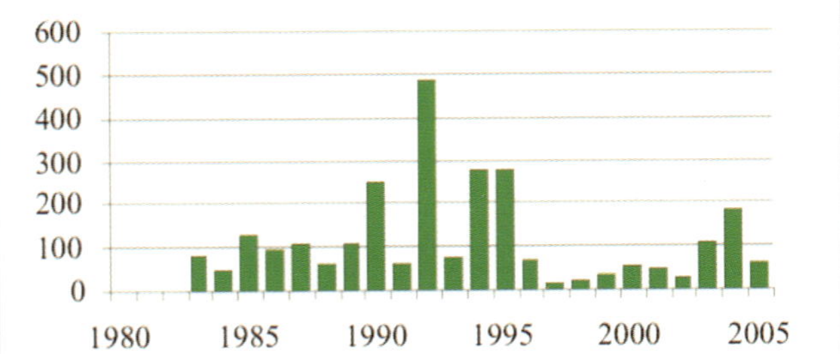

Figure 1. Estimated autumn totals of Little Terns in Lancashire, 1983-2005.

Inland records are much scarcer than in spring: two at Rivington on 22 September 1990, and singles at Foulridge Reservoirs on 17-20 August 1965, Rishton in September 1972, Lowerhouse Lodge on 3 September 1977, Burwains on 26 August 1986, Delph and Belmont Reservoirs on 6-7 July 1997 and Martin Mere on 29-30 September.

Little is known about the origins of Lancashire's birds, the only ringing recovery is of one fund dead at Kellet TV pool in the north of the county in June 2006, which had been ringed as a pullus at Gronant on the North Wales coast in June 2004.

SJW, MJ.

This species account was sponsored by Dave Bickerton.

GULL-BILLED TERN

Gelochelidon nilotica

Lancashire Category A. (1, 2).

Vagrant from southern or eastern Europe.

Mitchell and Oakes referred to a specimen shot at Blackpool in the summer of 1832. The first field record came in 1955 when one was seen on the beach at St. Anne's on 5 September by Nelson Harwood.

The only other was found in a large high-water roost of Common Terns at Seaforth on 30 July 1995. It showed some signs of immature plumage, especially a noticeable secondary bar, so it may have been a second-summer rather than a full adult. After about an hour it flew strongly out to sea but returned shortly afterwards and, despite a battering by the breeding Common Terns, remained around the freshwater pool for the rest of the day. It was seen the following morning but then departed up the Mersey and was seen briefly at Frodsham in Cheshire later that day.

Gull-billed Tern, Seaforth Nature Reserve, 30 July 1995. (Dot Jones)

SJW, MJ.

This species account was sponsored by Dr. Alan Fielding.

CASPIAN TERN

Hydroprogne caspia

Vagrant. Lancashire Category A. (0, 4).

Vagrant from the Baltic or eastern Europe.

Remarkably, all four Lancashire records of the world's largest tern have come from Leighton Moss and the Eric Morecambe complex, a site not generally noted for its terns. All were summer-plumaged birds: singles on 25-26 July and 14 August 1966 (J.A.G. Barnes, P.A. Lassey, J. Wilson), 2-10 August 1973, 13 August 1979 and finally on 16 July 2005.

Caspian Tern, Eric Morecambe complex, 16 July 2005. (Mike Malpass)

SJW, MJ.

This species account was sponsored by Mike Stocker.

WHISKERED TERN

Chlidonias hybrida

Lancashire Category A. (1, 3).

Vagrant from southern Europe.

The first, described as an adult in 'almost full summer plumage', was watched for over an hour at Belmont Reservoir on 24 July 1949 by A. Hazelwood and A.J. Murray. The next was at Leighton Moss on 6 June 1977. Another, in full summer plumage, was found on the evening of 9 June 1983 at Marton Mere, Blackpool. It was seen to fly off, but returned briefly at dawn on the 10th and for a few hours that evening before departing again at dusk.

Whiskered Tern, Dockacres complex, 6 June 1996. (Steve Young)

The latest record, a bird described as 'in second-summer plumage', was at Babydoc gravel pit (now known as Tewitfield fishery), Carnforth on 6 June 1996. It was present from late morning to nine o'clock at night, when it flew off high and was not seen subsequently.

SJW, MJ.

This species account was sponsored by Colin Dixon.

BLACK TERN

Chlidonias niger

Lancashire Category A.

Fairly common passage migrant from western and central Europe.

The Black Tern was described by Mitchell as a rare visitor, as regular inland as on the coast. Oakes's April records mostly related to the Wigan and Leigh flashes (now in Greater Manchester) but he also noted a spring coastal passage mostly in late May and early June and described the autumn passage as smaller and less regular, occurring mostly in September with a few birds into October. Singles at Windy Bank, Rossendale on 22 May and Hurstwood, Burnley on 15 July 1949 were the first records in east Lancashire.

Adult Black Tern, Seaforth Nature Reserve, May 2005. (Steve Young)

Since 1950 Black Terns have been recorded annually in very variable numbers. Spring passage is often urgent with birds staying a matter of hours rather than days before moving on, with the result that numbers are perhaps significantly underestimated. Most influxes are associated with south-east winds in late April and early May as birds are diverted from their usual migration routes across continental Europe. Showery or misty weather conditions then force these high altitude drift migrants to take temporary refuge on inland waters and the coast.

Our earliest were on 11 April 1979 and 13 April 1980 but the average arrival date (1970-2005) was 29 April, while the largest numbers almost always occur during the first two weeks of May.

Estimated spring totals since 1988 are shown in Figure 1. They range between four and 500 with a median of around 25 birds. A handful of often widely separated flocks usually account for the majority of sightings, as in mid-May 1960 when 40 were at Leighton Moss, 25 at Freckleton and 20 at Heysham. The next large count came in 1977 with 90 at Leighton Moss in the evening of 12 May.

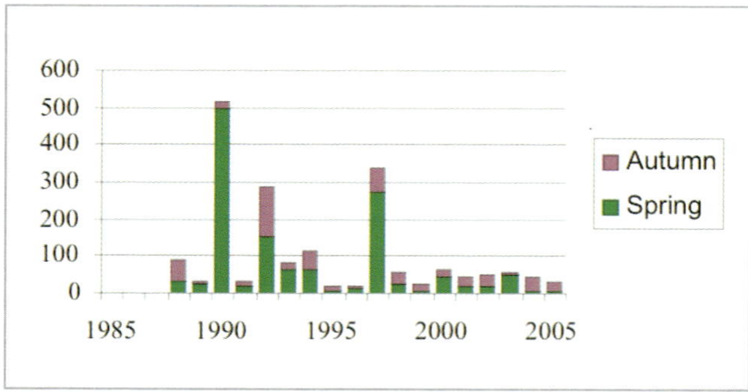

Figure 1. Estimated totals of Black Terns in Lancashire, 1988-2005.

There have been three significant influxes since then. The largest began throughout north-west England on 1 May 1990, when 18 were at Leighton Moss and 13 at Dockacres. Numbers exploded on the following day with 95 at Leighton Moss, 90 at Dockacres, 90 at Foulridge Reservoir, 50 at Eccleston Mere, 40 at Whitemoor Reservoir, 39 at Marton Mere and 35 at Stocks Reservoir and smaller numbers at several other sites. Numbers were much lower on the 3rd but probably included some new birds, including 14 at Forton. Most had gone by the 4th and only ten more were seen that spring. It seems likely that at least 500 passed through Lancashire, almost all some way inland - fewer than 40 were reported from coastal sites.

1992 produced a smaller influx with a total of 152 birds, the largest flock being 32 at Leighton Moss on 14 May. These numbers were surpassed in 1997 when a total of 276 was recorded, most of which were seen on 3 May when 75 were at Leighton Moss, 67 at Stocks Reservoir, 34 at Seaforth and 25 at Freckleton.

Juvenile Black Tern, Seaforth Nature Reserve, August 2005. (Steve Young)

Few are seen after mid-May but the odd bird continues to turn up into June; presumably many of these are non-breeding first- or second-summers.

Autumn passage is much more protracted than in spring, usually beginning in mid-July and stretching through to mid-October, although the main movement normally takes place between mid-August and mid-September. Typically, numbers are a little lower than in spring, averaging around 20 birds per year between 1988 and 2004.

Variation between years is less marked than in spring and only one really large influx has been recorded, in 1992 when at least 138 were seen and the county's share of a nationwide movement included at least 60 at Seaforth and 15 at Foulridge Reservoir on 11 September. Other large autumn counts include 31 at Lea Marsh on the Ribble in August 1964, 61 moving down the Mersey in 90 minutes on 11 August 1975, 28 north off Blackpool in four hours on 16 August 1981, 31 at Dean Clough Reservoir on 8 September 1988 and 30-40 at Seaforth in late August 1997.

The largest autumn counts are almost always made on the coast and on average only about 20% of birds are seen inland in contrast to nearly 45% in spring. As in spring, the largest flocks rarely linger for more than a day but odd ones and twos regularly hang on for a week or more, especially on the coastal lagoons at Seaforth and Crosby or offshore.

Such long-stayers are more often than not juveniles. There have been three exceptionally late records, all involving juvenile/first-winters: on the River Darwen at Walton le Dale on 8 November 1990, on Crossens Marsh on 5-12 November 2000 and at Seaforth from 27 October to 3 November 2001.

SJW, MJ.

This species account was sponsored by the Friends of Marton Mere.

WHITE-WINGED BLACK TERN

Chlidonias leucopterus

Lancashire Category A. (0, 16).

Rare passage migrant from eastern Europe.

The first was an adult at Crossens Marsh on 23 August 1968 found by G.A. Richards. Since then, one has appeared on average every couple of years. Just four records have been of juveniles and 14 of birds in breeding plumage, most of which were described as 'adults', but it seems likely that those seen between late May and mid-July will have been non-breeding birds, perhaps wandering first- or second-summers. Records have been split roughly equally between spring and autumn.

Adult White-winged Black Tern, Seaforth Nature Reserve, July 2003. (Steve Young)

Juvenile White-winged Black Tern, Seaforth Nature Reserve, September 2005. (Steve Young)

All records:

1968	Crossens, adult, 23 August
1969	Leighton Moss, 'immature', 24 August
1969	Freckleton, 'immature', 30 August to 2 September, presumed same as Leighton Moss
1973	Stodday, Lancaster, adult, 21 June to 9 July, also Conder Green, 23 July and Longton Marsh 11-12 August
1977	Martin Mere, adult, 27 May
1977	Clifton Marsh, adult, 20 June, presumed same as Martin Mere
1980	Arkholme, adult, 24 May
1982	Martin Mere, adult, 31 May
1985	Lea Marsh, Ribble, adult, 16 August
1987	Leighton Moss, adult, 1 June
1990	Leighton Moss & Dockacres, adult, 15 July
1993	Marton Mere, adult, to 25-28 June
1993	Seaforth, juvenile to 1-3 September
1993	Seaforth, different juvenile to 11-14 September
2000	Seaforth, adult, 27 May
2001	Martin Mere, adult, 18 June. Also Marshside 19-21 June
2003	Seaforth, adult 14-17 July
2003	Lune Estuary, adult 14-24/8, presumed same as Seaforth
2005	Seaforth, juvenile, 9-14 September, also Crosby Marine Park

All except one, an 'adult' at Arkholme on the River Lune, have been on or close to the coast with multiple records at Seaforth (five), Leighton Moss and Martin Mere (three each). Six have been seen at various sites on the Ribble and two on the Lune, with singles at Marton Mere, the Wyre Estuary and Stodday. The 2003 Lune Estuary bird fed regularly on butterflies.

SJW, MJ.

This species account was sponsored by Andy Bunting.

SANDWICH TERN

Sterna sandvicensis

Lancashire Category A.

Common passage migrant.

All of Mitchell's comments on this species related to the breeding colony on Walney Island, then part of Lancashire. Oakes largely followed suit and the status of the Sandwich Tern in what is now Lancashire was extremely poorly recorded before the boundary changes of 1974 and remained so until the 1980s.

Single pairs were reported by Oakes as nesting, presumably within the Common Tern colony, on the Ainsdale-Formby coast in 1910, 1912 and 1916. There have been no subsequent breeding attempts.

Sandwich are almost always the first terns to be seen in spring, usually arriving a fortnight before the first Common Tern. The average first date between 1970 and 2005 was 28 March, whilst the earliest recorded were at Heysham on 13 March 1990 and an exceptional inland record of three flying south-west over Rowley Lake, Burnley on 17 March 1990.

Small numbers are seen fairly frequently on the coast during April but even double-figure counts are usually infrequent before May; notable exceptions have included 309 on 21 April 2001 off Blackpool, 250 on 25 April 2001 at Heysham and 316 past Rossall on 18 April 2003 with 249 there the next day. Notable May counts have included 144 at Heysham on 1 May 1982, 155 off Blackpool on 5 May 1986, 147 on 6 May 1995, 145 at Formby on 30 May 1992 and 280 there on 3 May 1993. Such large numbers are almost always produced by adverse weather conditions but their timing, when most British breeding birds are well into incubation, raises questions about their destination or origin. There are several possible interpretations. They may be late-moving Scandinavian birds but there is no evidence for any passage movement of these through the Irish Sea. More likely is that they are foraging birds from Cumbrian or Welsh colonies which get caught up in strong westerlies. Alternatively, they may be early failed breeders or late passage, non-breeding sub-adults. The three Lancashire May recoveries of ringed birds do not fully resolve the matter; two originated from Irish colonies and one from Anglesey, while two were full adults and one a third-summer.

Sandwich Tern, Seaforth Nature Reserve, May 2000. (Steve White)

There are similar uncertainties about birds seen in June when large counts have included 270 at Heysham on 7 June 1987 and 235 at Formby on 16 June 1993, but the later the date the more likely records are to be of birds dispersing from the breeding colonies; our three June recoveries were all of adults from Ireland.

The return passage usually gets underway in early to mid-July and is signalled by the arrival of family parties at coastal roosts and the gradual build-up of feeding flocks close inshore.

Numbers normally peak during August but sizeable flocks can sometimes be seen through to mid-September. Some high counts have included 300 at Hightown in early August 1980, 150 at Rossall on 23 August 1987, 200 at Blackpool on 15 September 1991, 325 on St. Anne's beach on 29 July 2000, with 250 at Ainsdale the same day, and 175 at Formby on 13 August 1992. Exceptional numbers were seen off the Fylde and Sefton coasts during 1993, including 240 at Marshside on 17 August, 210 at Formby on 16 July with 255 there on 16 September, and 317 at Blackpool on 11 September. 1995 also brought a sizeable passage with highlights being 184 at Formby on 24 July and 580 there on 24 August; the latter remains the largest ever Lancashire count.

Few birds linger in Morecambe Bay and birds are scarce on passage at Heysham, an exception being 1992 when there were 40 in late August, 75 on 2 September and 60 on the 11th.

Liverpool Bay is the focus of attraction and regularly holds an internationally important post-breeding assemblage although the majority of these are usually in Cheshire, where Hilbre Island regularly records peak counts of 1,000 to 1,500. These birds come from a wide spread of breeding sites as indicated by the six autumn recoveries of ringed birds in Lancashire: a juvenile from Walney Island at Cleveleys on 24 July 1932; an adult from the Farne Islands at Formby in 1984 with an adult from the Sands of Forvie, Aberdeenshire there in 1983 and three from the same colony in 1985.

Numbers seen in the Lancashire sector of Liverpool Bay declined noticeably during the late 1990s but this appears largely the result of an increasing proportion in Cheshire and North Wales waters; an unusual autumn distribution of terns has become apparent in the last ten or so years, with the majority of Sandwich frequenting the southern side of the Mersey and most Commons seen on the north.

Only a few stragglers remain after the first week of October; on average (1970-2005) the last is seen on the 11th. Latest dates are 5 November 1981 at Seaforth and 7 November 1991 at Heysham. There has been just a single winter record in Lancashire, one off Blackpool on 2 December 1994.

Sandwich Terns are rarely seen inland and there is no evidence of any regular overland passage movements. Most records have been of ones and twos but an exceptional eight were over Coldwell Reservoir, Nelson on 19 July 1969, and flocks of seven over the M65 near Blackburn on 18 September 1998 and 34 going north-east near Nelson on 22 July 2000 were reported as this species. Records are divided roughly equally between spring/early summer and autumn. The first published inland record is of an adult and juvenile at Foulridge Reservoir on 18 September 1963 and there have been about 34 additional records to 2005.

SJW, MJ.

This species account was sponsored by N.J. Donnithorne.

FORSTER'S TERN

Sterna forsteri

Lancashire Category A. (0, 2).

Vagrant from North America.

Our first record was an adult in winter plumage at Seaforth on 15 March 1987 (Pete Kinsella, Mark Garner *et al.*). It was seen flying in with large numbers of Black-headed and Common Gulls in the late afternoon. It was quickly located bathing on the freshwater pool, where it was watched for no more than three minutes before it joined a large gull roost and was lost from sight in the failing light. It was presumed to be the same bird that wintered on the North Wales coast every year from 1986 to 1989. This was the 16th record in Britain and Ireland.

The second was watched flying south on a seawatch off Formby Point on 16 August 1992. It too was in winter plumage.

Adult Forster's Tern, Abergele, North Wales, October 1986. The same bird was seen at Seaforth Nature Reserve on 15 March 1987. (Steve Young)

SJW.

This species account was sponsored by Alan Davies.

COMMON TERN

Sterna hirundo

Lancashire Category A.

Scarce breeder; abundant passage migrant from elsewhere in Britain, Ireland, Fennoscandia and western Europe.

Common Terns arrive in numbers in Lancashire from late April. The average date of first sighting between 1970 and 2005 was 12 April and the earliest were two records on the coast on 1 April and one inland at Stocks Reservoir on the 2nd. Birds remain scarce until at least mid-April, however, and the first large influxes are rarely seen before early May. Almost all spring records are of birds at or close to breeding sites, passage birds are rarely seen in any numbers and ringing recoveries indicate that most Common Terns seen in Lancashire in early spring are local breeders. Observations at the Seaforth colony indicate that many birds arrive with their mate of the previous year, a reunion that may have taken place well to the south on the coasts of west Africa or southern Europe – no Lancashire-ringed birds have ever been recovered in spring elsewhere in the UK.

The route taken by passage birds remains a matter of conjecture; there is scant evidence of any substantial offshore spring movement anywhere in Britain away from the Channel coast and it seems likely that most move directly towards breeding colonies at high altitude. The only relevant ringing recovery was of one seen in the Netherlands on 7 May 2003 which was back at its natal colony at Seaforth 19 days later. However, a dozen or so sightings at Seaforth in early spring of birds ringed at Pennington Flash, Leigh suggest that some may gather in Liverpool Bay prior to moving on to their breeding colonies.

Small numbers are seen annually during late April and early May on inland waters. They rarely linger and most are probably taking temporary respite during adverse weather conditions. Such inland flocks rarely rise above single figures; the largest have all been at Foulridge Reservoir – 60 'Commic Terns' on 17 May 1967, 65 on 14 May 1993 and 24 on 25 April 1995. Where these birds are headed is not known but sightings in spring at Seaforth of 28 birds ringed on English and Scottish east coast colonies provide some evidence of a small but regular cross-Pennine passage.

Mitchell described a breeding colony at the original Martin Mere in the late nineteenth century but at the beginning of the twentieth the main site was on the shore between Formby and Ainsdale, where 900 pairs were said to be breeding. Wrigley (1892) noted that they were 'ruthlessly slaughtered . . . by "sportsmen" from Wigan and Manchester". A combination of shooting, egg-harvesting, disturbance, flooding and loss of habitat to development reduced this colony to 350 pairs in 1914, 300 in 1920 and fewer than 80 in 1937, and, despite the efforts of one of the RSPB's earliest wardening schemes, it had effectively disappeared by the late 1940s.

The colony had shifted to the south Ribble marshes by at least 1952, where there was a small colony on Banks Marsh and more than 100 pairs bred on Hesketh Out Marsh in 1954 (Wheeler 1952). During the 1960s pressure from the expanding gull colony on Banks Marsh pushed most terns onto Hesketh Marsh, where 800 pairs bred in 1974 and 1080 pairs in 1976 (M.E. Greenhalgh pers. comm.). The colony then shifted from Hesketh Out Marsh after the erection of flood defence barriers and numbers declined to around 400 pairs in the mid-1980s, rising again as the colony re-established itself along with Black-headed Gulls on Banks Marsh to reach a second peak of 640 pairs in 1988. From about this time the colony again went into decline supporting just 300 pairs in 1993 and around 100 from 1999 to 2003, partly as a result of annual flooding of nests on spring tides and latterly due to competition for nest sites from large gulls.

Our other saltmarsh colony, on the Lune at Colloway Marsh, has been less well studied. It supported 41 pairs in 1954, rising to 195 in 1968 and between 225 and 250 from 1978 to 1983, but by 1986 numbers had declined to 100 pairs and in the 1990s the colony became virtually extinct, suffering, like the Ribble, from a run of high spring tides, exacerbated by disturbance from jet-skiers; seven pairs were present in 2004 but no breeding took place in 2005.

After unsuccessful nesting by a single pair at Seaforth in 1985, breeding rafts were put out on the lagoons the following year and were immediately colonised. The colony reached 20 pairs in 1993 and 129 in 1998. Since then its size has been limited by the number of rafts successfully launched each spring, peaking at 172 pairs in 2005. Despite an abundant food resource, breeding productivity is low with an average of just 0.6 young fledged per pair. This is almost entirely due to losses during incubation caused by the buffeting of rafts during strong winds in early summer. This productivity rate is barely sufficient to maintain the colony but any shortfall is made up by immigrants. Ringing studies indicate that most of the first Seaforth breeding birds came from the Shotton colony on the Welsh Dee. The origins of 121 birds (approximately 25% of the total) that have bred at Seaforth are known, and of these 40% were reared at Seaforth, 28% at Shotton and 18% on the Ribble; more surprisingly, five have come from east coast colonies, five from inland sites in the English Midlands, one from Anglesey and one from Zeebrugge in Belgium.

Breeding elsewhere has been limited and sporadic: one pair at Barnaby's Sands on the Wyre in 1956, one probable pair at Leighton Moss in 1975, one or two pairs at the Scorton gravel pits from 1991 to 1994 and single pairs at Mere Sands Wood in 1997, Martin Mere in 2001 and Jumbles Reservoir in 2002.

Courtship-feeding Common Terns, Seaforth Nature Reserve, July 2004. (Chris Galvin)

Common Terns rarely begin breeding before three years of age and very few first-summer birds have ever been reliably recorded, but most return to breeding colonies as second-summers (White & Kehoe 2001). Young birds are more or less indistinguishable from adults (White & Kehoe 2001) so little was known about their movements until 'ring-reading' of birds in the field began at Seaforth in the early 1990s. Second-summer birds begin to arrive at Seaforth in the first week of June, a full six weeks after the adults. By the end of June more than half the birds present may be immatures engaging in courtship displays. Seaforth-bred birds are joined by birds from all over Britain and Ireland (Figure 1); most only stay for a week or so, presumably moving on to investigate other colonies. In late June and early July there are usually 200 or so non-breeding birds present at Seaforth and it is likely that at least four times that number pass through.

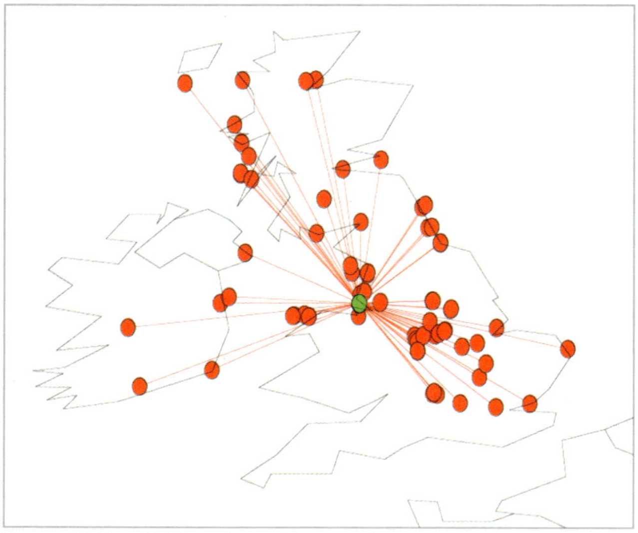

Figure 1. British and Irish natal sites of immature Common Terns seen at Seaforth during 1994-2003.

The return movement is far more conspicuous and protracted than in spring. Beginning from about mid-July, it usually peaks in late August and the first week of September with most birds gone by the end of that month.

The largest roost counts have been 4,100 at Formby on 25 August 1971, 3,000 there on 23 August 1975 and 29 August 1983, 5,000 at Ainsdale on 31 August 1976, 1,200 at St. Anne's on 14 August 1988, 1,200 at Heysham on 15 August 1989 and up to 2,000 at Seaforth during August-September 1990-1995 with 2,250 there in 1992.

Despite another large count of 2,166 at Formby Point on 20 August 2005, when a further 650 were at Seaforth, there appears to have been a genuine and continuing decline in the post-breeding assembly in Liverpool Bay since the end of the 1970s (peak counts at Seaforth averaged only 1,065 between 1996 and 2005), although numbers remain of international importance and amongst the largest in Britain.

Since the late 1990s Common Terns have become progressively scarcer away from Merseyside, with Heysham recording just single-figure peaks since the turn of the century and the Fylde coast registering a dramatic decline with the last sizeable roosts at St. Anne's being 150 on 18 August 1993 and 185 on 30 July 2004.

Some impressive offshore movements have been recorded, including 779 in an hour at Formby on 19 September 1979, 2,123 in 2.5 hours off Blackpool on 2 September 1990, 1,600 there on 27 August 1992 and 1,200 on 14 August 1993. Many of these may have been weather induced movements rather than truly migratory ones but, unlike in spring, there is real evidence of a coastal passage movement.

Birds are recorded at inland waters with a similar frequency to spring, usually only in ones and twos; larger autumn flocks include 16 at Rowley Lake, Burnley on 10 August 1989 and 34 at Rishton Reservoir on 11 September 1992. Evidence of a cross-country passage in autumn is well established. A total of 126 birds has been seen at Seaforth bearing north-east coast rings, seven of them during the year of ringing.

Figure 2. Natal sites of Common Terns ringed abroad and seen at Seaforth, 1994-2003.

Liverpool Bay supports one of the largest post-breeding gatherings in Britain and draws in birds from all parts of the compass in autumn; in addition to those from the north-east, sightings at Seaforth include 61 from the English midlands, East Anglia and south-eastern England, 25 from Anglesey, 18 from the west of Scotland, and 58 from Ireland, together with 47 from other parts of Europe, including many from Fennoscandia (Figure 2).

Some birds remain well into October – many are probably immigrants from further north – but there have been no three-figure counts after the first week of October. November records, especially from Seaforth and Heysham, mostly involve sick or injured birds, and the only truly winter report was of an 'immature' off Formby Point on 29 January 1967.

The western European Common Tern population is known to winter off the west coast of Africa (Migration Atlas) and this is confirmed by 16 recoveries of birds ringed or seen at Seaforth or on the Ribble in eight countries between Mauritania and Ghana, mostly in Senegal, Guinea and Sierra Leone. More unusual have been two recoveries in recent years of Lancashire-ringed birds in southern Africa, the wintering grounds of the Fennoscandian population: one in Namibia and one near Cape Town.

SJW, MJ.

This species account was sponsored by Barry Guise.

ROSEATE TERN

Sterna dougallii

Lancashire Category A.

Scarce passage migrant, mostly from Ireland.

All of Mitchell's and most of Oakes's records came from Walney and Foulney Islands near Barrow, former breeding sites that are now in Cumbria. According to Oakes there was no evidence that the species had ever bred in present-day Lancashire but he did publish six reports of one to three birds during mid-May to mid-August from the vicinity of the Ainsdale/Freshfield ternery between 1916 and 1941.

The number of published records gradually increased: two on St. Anne's beach on 13 July 1955 and one at Knott End on 22 July 1956 were followed by five records from Formby in the 1960s in May, July and August, two or three at Knott End on 19 August 1965 and singles at St. Anne's on 19 July and 9 August 1969.

Roseate Tern, Seaforth Nature Reserve, June 1995. (Steve Young)

Another 28 records involving 37 birds were published during the 1970s and 1980s. The earliest were two at Formby on 25 April 1984 but most were in May, with two in June and autumn records in July-August and two in September. During this period there was another record from Leighton Moss on 2 June 1974 and one inland on the River Lune at Arkholme on 21 May 1978, but most records came from Formby, the River Mersey and the Ribble Estuary with odd ones further north on the Fylde coast and at Heysham.

There were a further 39 records involving 50 or more birds between 1990 and 2005, almost all of which were fully documented. Their pattern of occurrence was markedly different to the earlier period (Figure 1), with just two in May and three in August and the remainder in June and July.

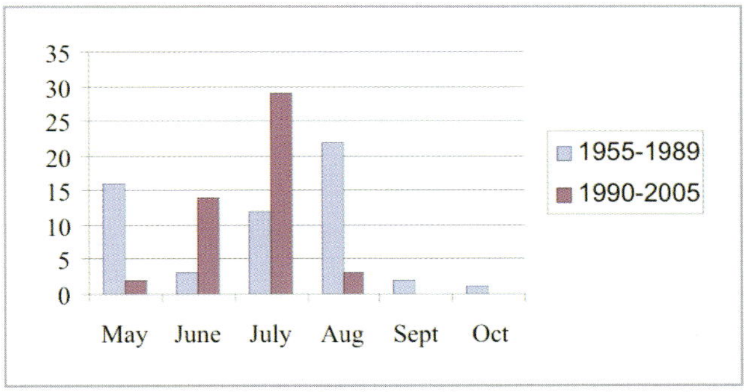

Figure 1. Monthly totals of Roseate Terns in Lancashire,1955-1989 and 1990-2005.

A large majority were at Seaforth, which recorded up to eleven birds annually but with blank years in 1993, 2003 and 2004. The remainder were one at Heysham on 15 May 1990, singles flying south at Formby on 24 July 1995 and 30 July 2003, an injured bird at Marton Mere on 10 June 2001, and singles at Fairhaven on 31 July 2004 and Formby Point on 15 August 2004 and 3 August 2005.

Ringing details are known for eight birds seen at Seaforth; all were ringed as nestlings. One, on 19 August 1987, was either a second-or third-summer from Anglesey, while six of the remainder, between 1995 and 2002, were second-summer birds ringed at Rockabill in Dublin Bay. Several of these records have involved apparently mated pairs and mating behaviour has been observed on several occasions and token nest-building twice, but none of this has ever looked like a serious breeding attempt. The female of one such pair, present for one day in July 1997, proved to be a six-year-old from Rockabill, the only definite adult of breeding age recorded at Seaforth.

The picture suggested by these post-1990 records is of non-breeding birds attracted to the Seaforth Common Tern colony, where they may linger for a day or two, 'practising' the rituals of courtship, before moving on. In stark contrast to the earlier reports, there is no evidence of any spring passage or post-breeding dispersal.

After coming close to extinction in Britain and Ireland at the end of the nineteenth century, numbers grew to about 3,000 pairs in the 1960s before going into rapid decline to 2,400 in 1969-70, 500 in 1988 and 790 in 1999-2000 (Lloyd *et al.* 1991; Mitchell *et al.* 2004). The vast majority nested, as now, on the east coast of Ireland, but the Anglesey colonies supported around 250 pairs until the late 1960s, dwindling to single figures during the 1990s, and one or two pairs hung on in Cumbria until 1969. The changing pattern of occurrence in Lancashire over the past 50 years reflects the virtual extinction of Roseate Terns in the eastern Irish Sea.

SJW, MJ.

This species account was sponsored by Kenny Dummigan.

ARCTIC TERN

Sterna paradisaea

Lancashire Category A.

Rare breeder; common passage migrant en route to Scotland and northern Europe.

The historical status of the Arctic Tern in Lancashire is extremely difficult to unravel. Knowledge of current identification criteria enabling its separation from the Common Tern did not become widespread until the 1980s. Until then most references to passage terns in Lancashire Bird Reports described them as 'Common/Arctic' or 'Commic' Terns; very few records of specifically identified Arctics away from the breeding grounds were published before the 1980s. In the light of current knowledge, earlier reports of large flocks are now assumed to relate to Commons but this rests on the untestable assumption that no major changes in the relative status of the two species have taken place in the last 100 years or so.

Problems of identification are less severe on the breeding grounds, but nonetheless real. All available evidence indicates that the proportion of Arctic Terns within the county's major tern colonies has always been small – probably rarely more than 10% and more usually less than 5%. Lancashire lies towards the southern limits of the breeding range although slightly more substantial numbers nest in Anglesey to the south and Cumbria to the north.

Most of Mitchell's text related to breeding on Walney Island, now in Cumbria. The best documented colony in the early twentieth century was on the shore between Ainsdale and Freshfield, but even here data are fragmentary. The first proven breeding was in 1910 and in 1920 48 pairs were estimated out of the total 300 pairs, but, in the light of subsequent records, this seems likely to have been rather generous. Three pairs nested in 1938, eleven in 1947 and 16 in 1948; the last breeding records there were of single pairs in 1959 and 1962 as the colony succumbed to increased disturbance.

Oakes mentioned irregular nesting on the north Fylde coast with one brood reared in 1946, and breeding on Longton Marsh in 1917. One pair bred at Longton Marsh in 1964 and nesting may have occurred subsequently at this inaccessible site. Throughout the second half of the twentieth century Lancashire's main tern colony was on the south Ribble marshes, initially on Hesketh Out Marsh but later on Banks Marsh as the former site was claimed for agriculture. A bird was seen carrying food in 1961 and between three and ten pairs nested regularly from 1970, peaking at perhaps as many as 20 pairs in 1984 and 1985 but with only low single figures since the 1990s.

The proportion of Arctics at our other main tern colony on Colloway Marsh on the Lune appears always to have been slightly greater than on the Ribble. Single pairs were reported in 1966, ten in 1968-69, 15 in 1972 and 1980 and ten in 1986. Increased disturbance, especially by jet-skiers, caused the colony to be largely abandoned during the 1990s but one or two remained in 2002 and 13 pairs attempted nesting in 2004.

Oakes mentioned that Arctic Terns arrived later than Commons and this remains true. Our earliest record was at Heysham on 1 April 1994 but average first arrival (1970-2004) is on 16 April, four days later than for Common Tern.

Our knowledge of the northbound passage has been added to enormously recently. Numbers increased exponentially between the 1970s and 1990s – almost entirely due to the diligent watch kept at a single site, Heysham. The first reported spring flock in Morecambe Bay was of 28 off Morecambe on 13 May 1983, followed by 62 at Heysham on 26 April 1988 but no really big movement was noted until 1991, when 419 went past Heysham in four flocks on 23 April, with up to 54 on several dates through to 29 May.

Subsequent large day-counts at Heysham include 300+ on 12 May 1992, 250 on 4 May 1993, 517 in one hour on 3 May 1996, 653 on 9 May 1997, 224 in 45 minutes on 3 May 1998, 323 on 11 May 1998, 500 on 3 May 2000, 362 on 7 May 2000, 100+ on 23 April 2001, 338 on 25 April 2001, 271 on 6 May 2001, 387 5 May 2002, 386 on 3 May 2004 and 736 on 24 April 2005 with a record 963 the following day.

From these it seems clear that a large annual passage movement takes place through Morecambe Bay, mostly during a three week period from the last week of April. Total numbers can only be guessed at; a minimum of 2,670 was seen from Heysham and Jenny Brown's Point in spring 2000 and 2,083 in 2005, but it is likely that only a proportion of the passage is ever observed. Birds are usually seen in compact flocks passing offshore in the morning (at Heysham) or evening (at Jenny Brown's). Weather conditions undoubtedly play a considerable role in determining the numbers brought within range of observers, with misty conditions often producing the largest numbers. At times, flocks have appeared to have come from inland, including 109 at Morecambe on 27 April 1989, but rather more have been seen to move inland, including 187 from Heysham 12 May 1997, 73 on 30 April and 141 on 3 May 2000; it is believed that most birds migrate in a north-easterly direction, mainly following the course of the River Keer.

This passage has been recorded off Rossall and Blackpool, including a count of 206 north in ten parties at the latter site on 23 April 1994, 453 on 17 April 2003 and 455 on 25 April 2005. It is much less evident in Merseyside, where the largest spring counts rarely exceed 20 (220 off Formby on 7 May 2005 being exceptional) – suggesting perhaps that coastal migrants move directly from North Wales into Morecambe Bay.

Overland passage has occasionally been observed directly. Since 1994 migration watches on the River Ribble at Preston have recorded many small parties moving upriver before rising high over Preston and heading east or north-east. Five flocks containing 64 birds were seen to do this on 30 April 1995 but this was put into perspective on 25 April 2005 when 1,030 were recorded in four hours. In recent years, small numbers have been noted further east on the Ribble at Brockholes Quarry, Preston, including 16 on 6 May 2000.

However, the existence of a regular movement can be inferred by the annual sightings of small, often only single-figure, flocks on inland waters, usually brought down by rainy conditions. Oakes noted twelve at Wrightington on 22-23 May 1947, while more recent counts have included 31 at Foulridge Reservoirs on 30 April 1988, 17 there on 2 May 1990, eleven at Withnell on 20 May 1993 and 40 at Stocks Reservoir on 6 May 1998. It is an open question as to how many of these refer to birds moving east across the Pennines and how many are drifted in our direction from more easterly routes.

There are no spring recoveries of ringed birds in Lancashire, so the destination of passage birds remains unknown but very substantial colonies exist in western Scotland, the Northern Isles and north-east England and 'our' birds may be heading to any of these or even towards Scandinavia.

The power station outfalls at Heysham regularly hold feeding birds during June and early July; counts include up to 70 on 17-30 June 1993 and 40 throughout June 1997. It is likely that many are foraging breeding birds from the Lune and Cumbrian colonies but others are probably wandering non-breeders. Seaforth regularly attracts small numbers of immature birds, presumably first- or second-summers, during June, many of which are in winter plumage.

Juvenile Arctic Tern, Crosby Marine Park, November 2005. (Steve Young)

Birds are relatively scarce in Morecambe Bay after early July, onshore gales being required to push them into the Heysham/Morecambe area. Large counts include 300 on 4 September 1987, 100 on 2 September 1988 and 100 on 9 July 1990.

Relatively few are seen amongst the build-up of Common Terns on the Sefton and Fylde coasts, but, in contrast to Morecambe Bay, records are more numerous here than in spring, particularly during onshore winds in late summer and early autumn. Significant counts include 108 at Ainsdale on 11 July 1942, and 70 on 2 September 1945; 85 at Formby Point on 14 August 1981, 70 on 28 August 1992 and a strong passage in 1994 with 136 on 18 August, 44 the next day, and 85 on 26 August; and 63 off Blackpool on 23 July 1994. The largest counts since then were 225 off Formby Point on 30 August 2003 and 360 there on 9 August 2005.

One or two birds are seen annually at inland reservoirs, typically during early August to mid-September. The largest numbers have been at Rishton Reservoir, Blackburn with 14 on 18 September 1991 and 28 bird-days in the period 8 August to 13 September 1992.

A few birds, almost all juveniles, linger offshore into October, typically to mid-month. Late records have included three at Heysham on 23 October 1988 and singles at Seaforth and Marton Mere on 26 October 1996 and at Formby on 29 October 1989. The latest were at Heysham to 2 November 1995 and 12 November 2005.

There have been two recoveries of ringed birds in Lancashire which hint at the possibly diverse origins of passage birds. One found dead on the Mersey on 3 October 1977 had been ringed as a nestling in Northumberland on 7 July 1964, while a juvenile found dead at Crosby on 15 September 1967 had been ringed on 11 August at Schades Oer Umanak on the west coast of Greenland.

SJW, MJ.

This species account was sponsored by Barry Guise.

GUILLEMOT

Uria aalge

Lancashire Category A.

Common passage migrant and winter visitor.

Guillemots are a familiar, if never common, staple of autumn seawatching on the Lancashire coast – or at least they used to be. However, the past few years have witnessed a dramatic decline in sightings of a species that had been taken for granted, and Razorbills are now by far the most numerous auk in Lancashire waters, especially in Liverpool Bay. The reasons for this are obscure. The British and Irish population of Guillemots increased by 32% between 1985-88 and 1998-2002 and they remain our most abundant breeding seabirds with an estimated population of about a million pairs (Mitchell *et al.* 2004); our nearest large colony at St. Bees Head in Cumbria increased from an average of 4,200 individuals in the mid-1990s to over 8,000 in 2002 (Blackledge 2002).

All previous authors suggested that the Guillemot has long been fairly common in Lancashire. Mitchell noted large flocks from February to May in outer Morecambe Bay (now mostly in Cumbria), with a few in late summer and an increase through the autumn to winter period. Dead or dying birds were washed up after stormy weather, otherwise birds were generally seen some distance from the shore. Oakes also reported regular sightings and described Guillemots as locally common, especially in Morecambe Bay and the Formby Channel. The earliest arrivals he knew of were off Sunderland Point on 3 August but few were seen before mid-September, when Guillemots were often numerous off the Mersey Mouth with a few penetrating the river as far as Liverpool Pier Head. Although he did not specify precise numbers, Oakes wrote of 'considerable flocks recorded in spring on Morecambe Bay from early March until the last week of April' and occasionally into May. He noted that 'oil-clogged' birds were frequent throughout the year.

These assessments of the Guillemot's patterns of seasonal occurrence from the late nineteenth to the middle of the twentieth century accord reasonably well with the record of the following 40 or so years, with the largest numbers seen during autumn passage and following winter gales.

Summer records are few and far between – unsurprisingly, given the lack of any substantial breeding colonies in our immediate vicinity and the tendency of birds to feed close to breeding sites – although one did spend the summer in Heysham Harbour in 1989. Substantial post-breeding flocks do sometimes build up offshore, for example an exceptional 500 in an unspecified area of Morecambe Bay in June 1960 and 330 near the Liverpool Bar light in August 1976, but the largest more recent summer counts have been 50 off Blackpool in June 1981 and 56 off Formby in June 1991. An adult was seen feeding a half grown young off Blackpool on 28-29 July 1985.

Guillemot, Crosby Marine Park, September 2006. (Steve Young)

Movements down the coast get underway in early autumn but the passage is usually most pronounced during late September and October, with the largest numbers always dependent upon strong onshore winds. Notable counts have included 320 off Heysham on 26 September 1987, 1,230 south in three hours off Blackpool on 10 October 1992 and 2,150 from the same site on the same date in 1993, and 438 past Formby Point in less than an hour on 31 October 1971. Most autumn peak counts have been considerably smaller, however; although 100 or more used to be the norm, for the past decade or so peaks have usually been about 30-40.

A decline in numbers began to be apparent in the mid-1990s. The last three-figure autumn count was 290 past Ainsdale on 13 October 1992 and there were just a handful of double-figure counts between 1994 and 2005, by which time Guillemots were so scarce that virtually every record was published in the annual county report.

Few overwinter close to shore; Heysham regularly recorded 20-30 until 1989 but since then low single figures have been the norm, with 20 on 24 February 1997 the one exception. Hardly any are seen from the Fylde or Sefton coasts even during winter storms and recent boat and aerial surveys confirm that few are present offshore, the largest counts being 34 between the mouth of the Mersey and the Liverpool Bar Light on 15 February 2002 and 30 over Shell Flat in January to March 2003. Storms regularly produce large numbers of tideline corpses, for example 39 at Ainsdale-Birkdale on 13 March 2000 and 15 at St. Anne's during September 2003.

Large spring movements have always been sporadic and the largest recent counts have been 65 off Formby Point on 12 May 1991 with 39 there on 17 May 2000, 124 at Heysham on 15 April 2001 and 22 off Blackpool on 9 April 2003.

Inland records were noted by Oakes but such occurrences are rare. All have been singles: at Dean Clough Reservoir on 30 December 1974, Mere Sands Wood on 7 November 1985, Leighton Moss, Rivington Reservoir, Preston Dock and Pine Lake after storms in February 1990 and Cuerden Valley Park on 17 January 1993.

There have been Lancashire ringing recoveries from around Britain and Ireland, mostly from Irish Sea breeding colonies: six from Scotland, three from northern England, eleven from Wales and 15 from Ireland. Although sub-specific identification in the field is almost impossible, the vast majority of Lancashire birds are likely to be British-breeding *albionis* but there have been several records ascribed to northern *aalge*, including one ringed and identified on the basis of plumage colouration and biometrics at Heysham in February 1993.

SD, MJ.

This species account was sponsored by Tony Riden.

BRÜNNICH'S GUILLEMOT

Uria lomvia

Lancashire Category D.

An adult was found dead on the tideline near the Morecambe Stone Jetty by Keith Hague on 15 April 1960. Whether it had ever been alive in Lancashire waters is, of course a matter for speculation.

Brunnich's Guillemot, Liverpool, January 1965. (Merseyside Naturalists Association)

Eric Hardy published details and a photograph of an adult which came into Liverpool on the liner *Carinthia* on 10 January 1965 but this was described as injured, so had almost certainly been cared for by the ship's crew, thus ruling out its acceptance even by today's more relaxed rulings on 'ship-assisted' records.

SJW, MJ.

This species account was sponsored by The Merseyside Naturalists Association, in memory of Eric Hardy.

RAZORBILL

Alca torda

Lancashire Category A.

Common passage migrant and winter visitor.

The Razorbill was formerly much the scarcer of the two regular auk species in Lancashire but, beginning in the late 1980s, that has slowly reversed as Guillemot sightings have declined and those of Razorbills have increased. This has been particularly noticeable during the autumn passage but also to a lesser extent in spring. The British and Irish breeding population, at 216,000 individuals, is about a fifth as large as that of Guillemots, although it too increased significantly between 1985-88 and 1998-2002 (Mitchell *et al.* 2004).

Tony Disley

Mitchell regarded the Razorbill as 'plentiful from early autumn until May' but noted that it was only seen 'a mile or two away from the land . . . except in heavy weather, when many are washed up dead.' He gave no real indication of its abundance in relation to Guillemot. Oakes was even less forthcoming, merely noting that it was sometimes numerous offshore and frequently met with as a shoreline casualty; he believed it to be more regular in Liverpool Bay than further north.

Relatively few records were published from the late 1950s until the late 1970s. An indication of the recent upsurge in numbers is reflected in the fact that twelve on 19 February 1978 and 20 on 27 February 1979 off Formby Point were considered notable. These were however soon eclipsed by 90+ among a larger number of unidentified auks from Formby on 21 September 1979, the first evidence of a marked autumn passage.

Throughout the 1980s annual totals varied between six and 24, except for 35 in 1988 (but these included 15 corpses on Fylde and Ainsdale tidelines). An increase in seawatching from the mid-1980s was no doubt partly responsible for the rise in sightings that followed. Following 132 off Blackpool on 9 October 1993 there were an unprecedented 1,590 on the 10th, then 250 on the 14th and 189 on the 19th.

This October peak has been repeated in subsequent years, the most notable counts from the Fylde coast being 1,193 past Blackpool on 16 October 1994, 550 past Rossall on 21 October 2000 and 536 from Blackpool on 3 October 2002. Large counts have also lately come from Formby Point, though these often include a large number of 'auk sp., presumed Razorbills' seen at distance. In 2001 the largest counts were 350 plus 362 auk sp. on 19 October, and 296 plus no fewer than 1,037 auk sp. on the 27th. In 2002 89 Razorbills and 891 auks presumed to be this species moved past Formby on 5 October.

Significant spring passage was first noted in 1996, with 70 off Rossall on 5 April, 76 from Blackpool on the 14th and 77 there on 27 May. More recent counts include 40 off Heysham on 16 April 2001 when 269 were also seen off Blackpool, and 155 off Blackpool on 13 April 2003.

Winter sightings have also increased but not nearly as much as during passage periods, with around three per winter being the norm since 1990. Larger counts include six at Heysham on 4 December 2001, ten off Blackpool on 16 December 2001 and twelve between Seaforth and the Liverpool Bar light on 15 February 2002.

Inland records continue to be extremely rare with just four in the past half century, all but one of which – a single on Anglezarke Reservoir on 18-19 November 1980 – occurred after violent storms in February 1990: at Dolphinholme, Anglezarke and Lowerhouse Lodges, Burnley.

An curious record concerned a small juvenile seen with six adults off Heysham on 3 September 1969; it is unusual for a bird of this age to be seen so far from breeding grounds.

Recoveries of ringed birds show a wide spread of origins within Britain and Ireland: six from Scotland, two from northern England, four from Wales and five from Ireland.

SD, MJ.

This species account was sponsored by Peter Stevens and Heather Skaife.

BLACK GUILLEMOT

Cepphus grylle

Lancashire Category A. (1, 45).

Scarce passage migrant; rare winter visitor.

The Black Guillemot is a wonderful sight in summer with dapper pied plumage set off by red legs and gape. However, birds in any plumage are a rare occurrence in Lancashire and few allow close study as they are generally seen relatively briefly on seawatches. By the end of 2005 there had been only 46 records, all of them of singles with the exception of two off Formby Point on 23 October 1994 and a remarkable four together off Rossall Point on 12 January 2005.

Mitchell described it as a 'rare winter visitor to the coast' but published no specific records and the first definite Lancashire occurrence was published by Oakes, an 'immature' female captured alive at Hare Tarn near Carnforth on 18 February 1914, which remains our only inland record.

There was then a 40 year gap until the next records, at Freckleton in September 1954 and Marshside in September 1955, and a further 30 years before our fourth, a long-stayer off Rossall on 2 to 24 November 1985. Since then birds have been recorded in 17 out of 21 years and there has been no real indication of any upward or downward trend. It seems likely that the apparently sudden growth in records from the mid-1980s had more to do with the upsurge in seawatching than to any real increase. Annual totals are usually just one or two but there were six records (probably involving four individuals) in 1996.

Tom Wilmer

Except for one at Cockersands on 22 August 2002, all records since 1985 have come from the main seawatching stations: 24 off the Fylde coast (Blackpool & Rossall Point), ten off the Sefton coast (Formby Point & Ainsdale) and nine off Heysham/Morecambe.

Virtually all have been one-day birds lingering briefly offshore or passing seawatching stations. Longer-stayers have included first-winters at Heysham Harbour and outfalls on 25 September to 7 October 1995 and 16-23 March 1996. The lack of a rocky shoreline anywhere on the Lancashire coast undoubtedly limits its attraction for Black Guillemots.

This Black Guillemot was in the Heysham area from April to June 2006, apparently prospecting for a nest site. Unfortunately it was on its own, although it did display to a Feral Pigeon at one time! In 2007 it appeared to have found a mate and was prospecting nest sites. (Jean Roberts)

Black Guillemots are generally sedentary throughout their circumpolar range, but particularly so in the southern extremes like Britain where frozen seas are not a problem. The median distance for recoveries of British ringed birds is a mere 10.5 km (Migration Atlas). The nearest breeding colonies to Lancashire are on Anglesey, the Isle of Man and at St. Bees Head in Cumbria, the only English breeding site which currently holds around seven pairs. These Cumbrian birds regularly winter as far south as Walney Island, and some Lancashire records probably relate to birds dispersing from this colony. Similar numbers breed on Anglesey and around 150 pairs on the Isle of Man, which is perhaps the major source of our birds.

Although birds have been recorded in all months of the year they are exceptionally scarce during winter with just eight records from November to April (Figure 1). Small numbers have occurred from May onwards but the overwhelming majority have been seen between August and October with a very marked peak in September, which has accounted for more than a quarter of all records.

Fewer than a third of published records were aged but of these a clear majority were juveniles or first-winters, as might be expected of a sedentary species with limited dispersal.

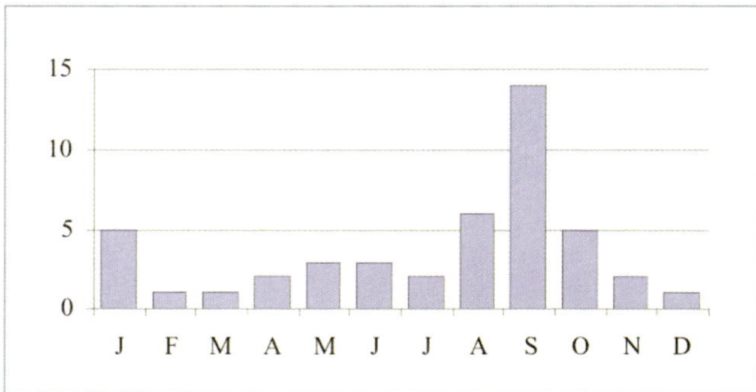

Figure 1. Monthly totals of Black Guillemots in Lancashire, 1954-2005

SD, MJ.

This species account was sponsored by Roy Drinkwater.

LITTLE AUK

Alle alle

Lancashire Category A. (/, 80).

Scarce winter visitor from the Arctic.

During periods of strong north westerlies in winter there is one sight that ardent Lancashire seawatchers hope for, a diminutive Little Auk 'jinking' over the waves. Unfortunately, the experience most birders will have had of the species in the county will have involved a dead or dying bird on a marine lake or other atypical habitat.

The Lancashire status of the Little Auk has probably changed little over the past 100 years or more, although sightings of live, healthy birds have increased significantly since the seawatching 'revolution' of the 1980s. Mitchell and Oakes both described it as a rare winter visitor. Oakes documented several wrecks in the early years of the twentieth century; birds were reported the length of the coast from the Mersey to Morecambe Bay in early February 1912 with at least 15 seen near Lancaster and several inland, including one at Clitheroe. Singles at Formby in January 1916 and

December 1938 and at Banks in November 1928 were followed by another widespread wreck during November and December 1938, including casualties at Formby and Ormskirk. One of five or six flying over Hesketh Marsh on 8 November 1948 struck an overhead wire and later died.

Six were recorded during the 1950s: off Formby Point on 9 October 1951, at Walton Sewage Works in November 1952, taken into care and rehabilitated from a Poulton-le-Fylde garden in January 1953, dead in a Freshfield garden in December 1954, in a Walton garden November 1955 and alive in a Burnley cemetery in December 1959.

Things then went very quiet with just two records, singles at Formby Point in October and December 1967, for the next 20 years, after which sightings became more frequent. The average number seen per winter since the early 1980s is a little over 2.5 (Figure 1) but there have been notable influxes of eight in 1983/84 and 1987/88 and ten in 1990/91. The record total of 13 seen during 2003/04 was heavily skewed by inclusion of at least ten seen in flat calm conditions over Shell Flat during a boat survey of Common Scoters on 21 November 2003.

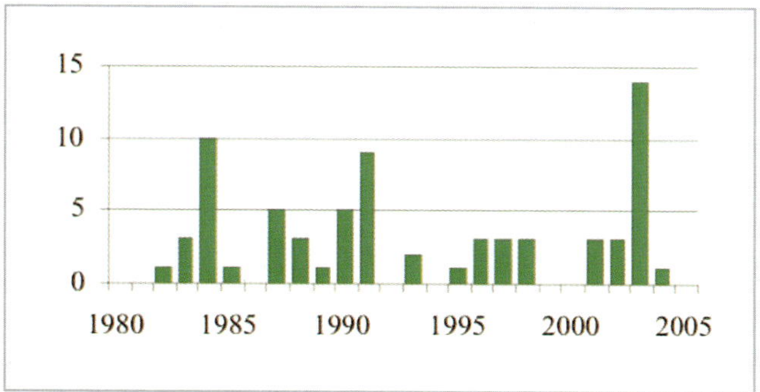

Figure 1. Annual totals of Little Auks in Lancashire, 1980-2005.

With that exception, recent records are strongly concentrated in the months of December and January, and only one live bird has been noted outside the period October-February, at Heysham on 4 March 1979 (Figure 2).

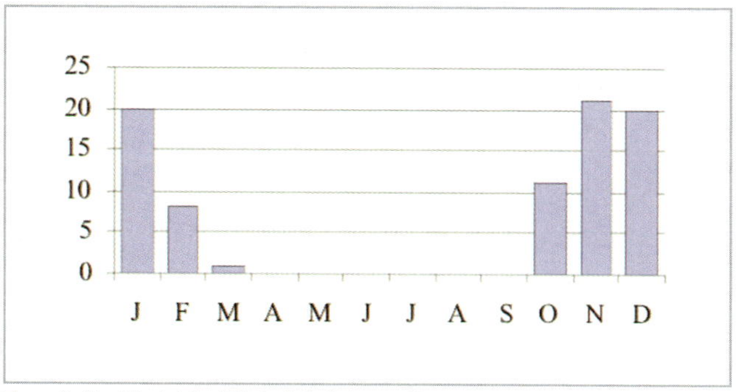

Figure 2. Monthly totals of Little Auks in Lancashire, 1950-2005.

The majority of sightings have been at the usual seawatching stations on the Sefton and Fylde coasts and Morecambe Bay but several have been found 'wrecked' near the coast and there has been a handful of records further inland: singles at Clitheroe in February 1983 and November 1990, Chorley in November 1990, Wiswell Moor and Coldwell Reservoir in December 1990, and Withnell Fold in November 1995. With the exception of the Withnell Fold bird, these inland records have all occurred when birds have also been seen on the coast, so it seems more likely that they were blown inland from the Irish Sea than overland from the North Sea.

Virtually all Lancashire records have come during or in the aftermath of strong onshore winds.

This Little Auk, released on Sands Lake, Ainsdale in November 2001, narrowly escaped death on this occasion, but, like most Little Auks wrecked in Lancashire, succumbed to natural causes shortly afterwards. (Steve Young)

SD, MJ.
This species account was sponsored by Sarah Dempsey.
http://birdblog.merseyblogs.co.uk

PUFFIN

Fratercula arctica

Lancashire Category A.

Scarce passage migrant.

For such an abundant breeding species Puffins are remarkably scarce off the Lancashire coast, partly because there are few sizeable colonies within striking distance but mostly due to their rapid dispersal from the breeding sites to their oceanic wintering areas. It is a very difficult bird to catch up with in the county; virtually all records have been brief views on seawatches and only two apparently healthy birds have stayed longer than a single day – at Formby Point on 18-19 September 1979 and Heysham on 17-18 May 2001.

Mitchell devoted just three lines to the species, describing it as occurring offshore in autumn and winter and often being washed up dead; Wrigley (1892), for example, wrote of 'dozens washed up dead on the (Formby) shore' in the winter of 1879. Oakes added a little detail, stressing storm-driven occurrences and documenting what appears to have been a major wreck in late April 1947 during which nine corpses were found near Blackpool alone.

The next two Lancashire records were also tideline corpses: at Fleetwood in September 1951 and Blackpool in July 1952. Since then birds have been seen at an average of around two annually in most years since the advent of quality optics and the growth in popularity of seawatching in the late 1970s. Throughout this period almost all records have been of singles with occasional twos and a highest day-count of three off Blackpool in May 1997. Oddly, there appear to have been rather more multiple records in the 1950s to 1970s, including reports of 17 off Formby Point on 28 September 1968 and seven on 28 September 1977, both in south-westerly gales. A total of 16 records involving 50 birds was published between 1951 and 1981 in contrast with 41 records of 52 birds from 1982 to 2005. All records of apparently healthy birds have come from the seawatching hotspots of Heysham, Jenny Brown's Point, the Fylde coast and Formby Point.

There are two clear seasonal peaks, coinciding with movements towards breeding colonies in spring during April and May and autumn dispersal in September (when almost a third of all records have occurred) to November (Figure 1). At least six of the ten winter records between December and February are known to have been found dead or oiled and it seems likely that others may have been sickly. The largest recent wreck was in January 1984, when three corpses were found on north Lancashire beaches and a live bird was seen off Blackpool.

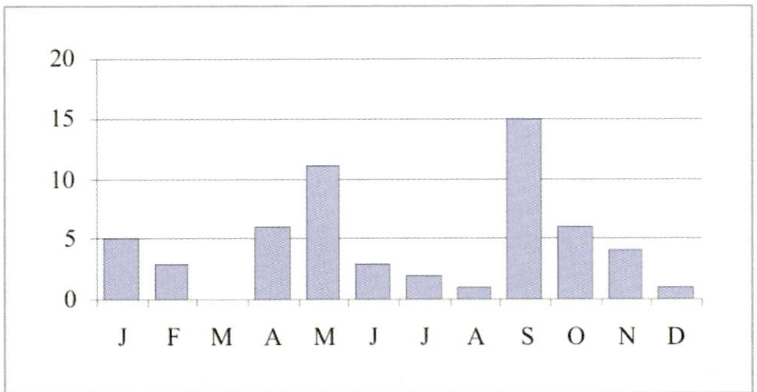

Figure 1. Monthly totals (records) of Puffins in Lancashire, 1952-2005.

Both Mitchell and Oakes wrote of wrecked birds turning up some distance inland, including twentieth-century records near Garstang and at St. Michael's-on-Wyre in spring, and at Great Eccleston, Fylde in October 1926. Spring 1947 produced several inland records, including at Pendleton, Clitheroe on 24 April and Carnforth on 9 May. The only recent inland record was one found dead at Borwick near the Cumbrian border on 28 January 1984.

There have been four Lancashire recoveries of ringed birds, all found dead on the Fylde coast and ringed on Welsh islands: one on Skomer, two on Skokholm and one on Puffin Island, Anglesey.

SD, MJ.
This species account was sponsored by Bernadette Bickerton.

PALLAS'S SANDGROUSE

Syrrhaptes paradoxus

Lancashire Category B. (33+, 0).

Vagrant from central Asia.

Mitchell and Oakes provided fascinating details of the influxes into Lancashire of this Asiatic desert species in the invasion years of 1863, 1888 and 1890. A repeat performance seems highly unlikely since the global population has contracted markedly.

1863.

Several were 'obtained' in Morecambe Bay, near Lancaster, from the last week of May to the end of June. The ovaries of the females contained eggs in various stages of development (*Zoologist.* 1863).

Two males were shot out of a flock of about 15 on the Scarisbrick estate. The birds were feeding in a field of spring oats and flew off in a northerly direction.

1888.

Eight were on mossland one mile north of St Michael's-on-Wyre on 20 May. Two males and two females were shot at this location on 21 May. Two males and one female were shot out of a flock of seven on St Michael's Moss on 1 June and a female was shot there on 7 June.

Singles were seen in flight on Tarleton Moss on 25 May and 3 September. Three males were shot out of a flock of 20 at Rawcliffe Moss on 3 June.

1890.

Two birds were shot out of a flock of five at Winacre Farm, Martin Mere towards the end of the year. Oakes states that these may have been 'relics' of the 1888 invasion, though there were occurrences in several counties including Yorkshire and Lancashire during 1890 (*Handbook of British Birds*, Vol. 4: 149).

SJW, MJ.
This species account was sponsored by In Focus.

FERAL PIGEON

Columba livia

Lancashire Category C.

Abundant resident breeder.

The Feral Pigeon, descended from the wild Rock Dove, is a common breeding resident, thoroughly urbanised in the towns and cities of Lancashire and North Merseyside. Earlier authors generally ignored this feral form and thus it is not possible to give a full account of its history in the county. However, it is unlikely, though not impossible, that its wild ancestor ever bred in our area. It is often thought that many Feral Pigeons are 'lost' racing pigeons but in 1997 the large seafront population at Morecambe was carefully checked for rings, as part of a Hawk & Owl Trust study into raptor impact on racing stock, and no ringed birds were found.

During the 1997-2000 survey Feral Pigeons were recorded in 48% of the county's tetrads. They breed in all towns and large villages and also on many lowland farms, but are absent from extensive upland areas. Nests, which are frequently just a few scraps of vegetation, are invariably placed on man-made structures and breeding is generally densest in the larger conurbations. Nesting occurs on church towers, public buildings, museums, factories, warehouses, supermarkets, railway stations and residential properties.

In central Liverpool populations fell with the closure of the south docks but in recent times have increased in suburban areas, perhaps partly as a result of discarded fast food and partly due to the deliberate feeding of wild birds in gardens and public parks. Data from Liverpool suggest that there are about 30 pairs per occupied tetrad, a figure which is certainly equalled in the centre of Lytham, while a 1km BBS square at Blackpool Pleasure Beach had 130 birds in 2003. The county population was estimated at 10,000 breeding pairs, but, given the lack of interest in this species exhibited by birdwatchers, this may well be an underestimate. There is also a large non-breeding population. There is little evidence of population change, though in Rossendale the species appears to be spreading into gardens and onto playing fields, while maintaining its population in urban centres. Reproduction may start at less than one year old and the permanent pair bond, together with the production of 'pigeon milk', enables breeding to take place at any time of the year. In Lytham and Liverpool nesting regularly occurs in January, and occasionally in December.

Feral Pigeons, Sefton Park, Liverpool, May 2005. (Steve Young)

The Feral Pigeon is non-migratory, taking a wide variety of artificial foods, many of which are intentionally provided by man. However, in autumn many urban pigeons spend time gleaning nearby stubble fields. The largest flock seen at stubble was one of 450 near Eagland Hill in December 1989, and flocks of around 150 are regularly seen at other Over Wyre sites. A flock of 200 was seen on stubble near Speke in south Liverpool in September 1992.

The largest recorded feeding congregation is at Martin Mere where counts of 1,030 were made on 12 March 1998, 800 in January and December 1996 and 725 in November 1995. These high numbers are clearly due to the availability of feed put out for the captive wildfowl collection. Elsewhere, counts of 500 have been made at Seaforth Docks and at Oglet in south Liverpool. A winter census carried out in 1998/99 between Liverpool Pier Head and Speke yielded a total of 2,340 birds in flocks of 11 to 240. Feeding flocks of 100-200 are probably not uncommon but few birdwatchers take note of them. Numbers can also be large in medium sized towns. A count of 300 was made at Southport Marine Lake in 2003 and a population of 300 was recorded in Blackpool town centre in 1998, although a pair of Peregrines has recently reduced their numbers. Stable populations exist in many smaller conurbations with, for example, around 70 recorded in Bacup town centre in 1995, while 40 were roosting at Clitheroe Royal Grammar School in 1992. In St. Anne's a flock of over 100 birds regularly suns itself on the roofs of the shops which form the town square, and a suburban garden in Lytham regularly hosts up to 40 birds and at least 80 exploit the food thrown out by the public for ducks at Fairhaven Lake.

Fouling of public buildings and open spaces has led many local authorities to attempt to reduce Feral Pigeon populations, but this has generally been thwarted by a combination of generous provision – both deliberate and unwitting – of food by the public, and the species' spectacular reproductive potential.

JFW, DJH.

This species account was sponsored by Frank Walsh.

STOCK DOVE

Columba oenas

Lancashire Category A.

Fairly common resident breeder.

Until the last quarter of the nineteenth century Stock Doves were frequently confused with Feral Pigeons and even Woodpigeons and, partly as a result, very little is known of their status in Lancashire before 1870. Mitchell noted a remarkable increase in the Ribble, Hodder and Wyre Valleys around 1877 and mentioned sites in Bowland, Pendle Hill and near Blackburn. Before 1870 their distribution seems to have been essentially coastal, with outposts in upper Wyre and especially in south Lancashire, where the use of rabbit burrows as nesting sites was important.

In the twentieth century the breeding range continued to expand and Oakes considered it a common but rather local resident, much attached to rough hilly country but a much scarcer breeder on the cultivated plain. Nest sites were found in woodlands, quarries, cliffs, exposed tree roots on river banks, derelict farm buildings, masonry bridges and rabbit holes. Spencer pointed out that the extensive evacuation of hill farms in the interests of reservoir construction resulted in the creation of ready-made nesting sites. Hill farms, at least in Bowland, were also being abandoned for economic reasons during the Depression years, with the sheep-walks being amalgamated into ever larger units. The great increase in the establishment and abandonment of quarries also provided a source of secure nest sites.

The population began to decline nationally from about 1950. This has usually been attributed to pesticide use and was most problematical in the intensive arable areas of eastern England but probably also affected the Lancashire population, especially on the southern plain. It was also reflected in a population decline in the east (Hornby 1994). Numbers began to recover nationally in the late 1960s and increased by 87% between 1970 and 2001 (CBC) and by 30% between 1994 and 2004 (BBS). At the beginning of the 1970s Spencer confirmed that the population had declined significantly throughout Lancashire but Stock Doves were probably breeding in 47 10km squares in 1968-72. This range increased to 49 squares in 1997-2000, with breeding confirmed in all but three of these and in almost a third of the county's tetrads.

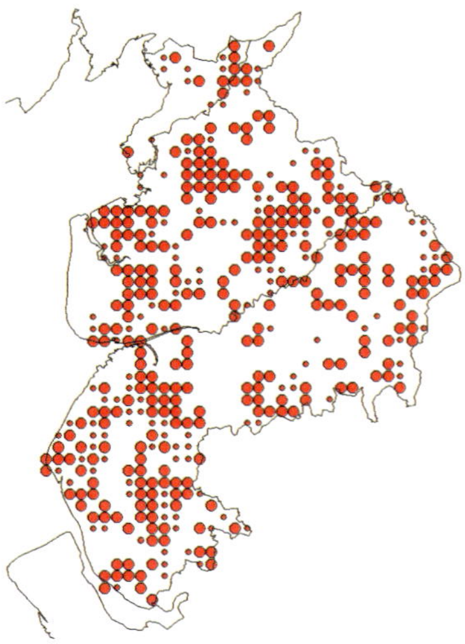

Breeding distribution of Stock Dove, 1997-2000. (Large dots: confirmed. Small dots: possible)

Habitat and nest site preferences vary between regions; in the lowlands most nests are in tree-holes or ivy-covered trees, while on the moorland edge, barns, especially those away from farmhouses, and derelict farm buildings are used. Breeding in rabbit burrows no longer seems to occur. Their flexible choice of breeding site gives Stock Doves a larger overall Lancashire range than the much more numerous Collared Dove, although their distribution within that range is much patchier, and birds are largely absent from most of the uplands, western Fylde, Chorley and district and north of the Lune except on the river's upper reaches. Unlike its close relatives, the Stock Dove largely avoids urban areas although a few pairs are found in urban parks.

It is likely that the main limiting factor to their spread is a lack of suitable nest sites. Provision of nest-boxes in the Pilling-Preesall area increased the local population from three pairs in 1992 to 37 pairs in 2003, fledging over three young per pair. Unlike Collared Doves, they are not attracted to supplementary feeding sites in this area, indicating that food shortage is not a problem. Nest-box schemes have also been established at Arkholme, Lytham Hall, Belmont and Mere Sands Wood. Only limited information on breeding densities away from Over Wyre is available, but an intensive study of farmland in south Liverpool and Knowsley during the 1990s yielded an average density of 2.5 pairs per tetrad (P. Slater *pers. comm.*). The Lancashire population was estimated at 850 pairs in 1997-2000.

Stock Dove, Little Crosby, June 2005. (Steve Young)

British Stock Doves are highly sedentary birds; the median recovery distance of birds ringed in the UK is 6km (Migration Atlas). Only seven out of a total of 28 ringing recoveries to or from Lancashire have involved movements outside the county (six exchanges with northern England and one to the south); only 14 have been further than 10km and none more than 100km. Some dispersal from the breeding grounds does, however, occur during autumn. Oakes stated that most birds left the coastal dunes between August and October, reappearing in March, while Spencer wrote that Stock Doves deserted east Lancashire for the winter, returning in February. Very few passage flocks have been recorded; they include 24 at Leighton Moss in October 1986, and in October 2005 seven over Laund Hey, Rossendale on the 2nd, three over Caton Moor on the 9th and over Fairhaven on the 27th, and twelve south over Seaforth on the 29th.

Autumn and winter flocks rarely exceed 100 and Hornby (1994) regarded counts above 20 in east Lancashire as exceptional, though Oakes & Battersby (1939) made reference to winter influxes there with totals of up to 200 recorded at Mitton. More recently, 150 at Parsonage Reservoir in November 1995 was exceptional. The highest winter densities are in areas of mixed farming on the Fylde and the arable land of the south-west. The largest counts include 200 on Cockerham Moss in October 1960 and Halsall Moss in November 1964, 400 at Martin Mere in December 1980, 200 at Churchtown, Southport in December 1985, 345 on Halsall Moss in December 1982, 400 at Skelmersdale White Moss in January 1992 and 500 in large concentrations of pigeons on the south-west Lancashire mosses in January 1995. During the early 1980s a large flock frequented the Ribble saltmarshes at Crossens with a maximum of 445 in February 1984, but within a decade this habitat was rarely frequented. North of the Ribble at Warton Marsh flocks of 120 occurred in the winters of 1989 and 1990 but have subsequently declined to occasional flocks of 20 or so. In recent years most three-figure counts have come from Over Wyre, with Eagland Hill being especially favoured; there were 230 there in November 2002, when a flock of 200 was also briefly at Myerscough Quarry.

JFW, DJH.

This species account was sponsored by Bob and Diane Danson.

WOODPIGEON

Columba palumbus

Lancashire Category A.

Abundant resident breeder.

The Woodpigeon is one of the commonest non-passerine birds in Lancashire, with an estimated population of 25,000 breeding pairs in 1997-2000. It has bred in all 10km squares in the county since at least 1968-72. It was already common in England in the first half of the nineteenth century (Holloway 1996) and increased during the fourth quarter of the century due largely to an increase in green crops, especially clover, which provided winter food (Parslow 1973). Mitchell considered it a universally distributed resident in Lancashire, occurring in flocks of thousands and very destructive in both spring and autumn in arable areas.

Oakes reported it to be very common and well distributed despite persecution, which intensified during World War II, because of the damage it caused to agriculture and its value as a source of non-rationed meat. After the War the Woodpigeon was still regarded as a pest and regularly attracted the attention of shooting parties. Indeed, shoots were still being organized in Bowland by Ministry of Agriculture personnel in 1954. Even in the 1990s Smith *et al.* (1995) reported that 97% of farmers shot Woodpigeons to protect their crops.

Nationally, colonisation of urban areas has been going on for over 100 years, and Spencer (1977) recorded how the species became increasingly common and suburban in east Lancashire after 1964, following colonisation of coniferous woodlands. Hardy (1941) reported occasional breeding in Sefton Park, Liverpool. Since that time Woodpigeons have become common there, with 15 pairs on this 1km^2 site (Slater 2001; P. Slater *pers. comm.*). More recently birds have become increasingly frequent in suburban gardens in south Fylde and West Lancashire, observations which are in line with national trends (Toms 1997-2004).

Woodpigeon, Little Crosby, May 2005. (Steve Young)

A rich and abundant diet enables the species to produce crop milk which facilitates the feeding of young throughout an exceptionally protracted breeding season. Instances of early urban breeding include an unseasonal pair nesting in Townley Park, Burnley on 24 December 1964.

The national population declined due to agricultural changes in the late 1960s and early 1970s but the introduction of oil-seed rape in the mid-1970s (Inglis *et al.* 1990) contributed to an increase of 87% from 1970 to 2001 (CBC) and 12% during 1994-2004 (BBS). In 1988-91 the New Atlas showed that breeding was most abundant in areas of North Merseyside, West Lancashire and the Fylde where intensive arable farming is concentrated. In 1997-2000 breeding was confirmed or considered possible in 92% of Lancashire tetrads, being absent only from open coastal habitats and treeless, heather and grass moors – north-eastern Bowland being the only substantial unoccupied area.

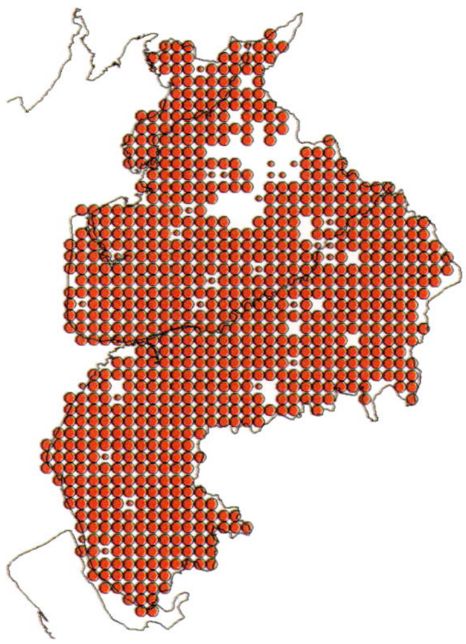

Breeding distribution of Woodpigeon, 1997-2000. (Large dots: confirmed. Small dots: possible)

The Woodpigeon is essentially a woodland species occurring in both coniferous and deciduous woodlands, of whatever size. However, Lancashire lacks really large forests, with the exception of Gisburn Forest, and most birds feed mainly in surrounding farmland. Nesting occurs in woods, rural parklands, gardens and now regularly in urban and suburban street trees. When trees are in short supply overgrown hedges are chosen, usually over 4m tall, though nests much lower down are occasionally found. Nesting on man-made structures remains very unusual in the county but has been recorded on a building in Towneley Park and in a hole on a Rossendale viaduct. In addition birds have been noted calling from high buildings in Liverpool city centre but nesting there has not been confirmed.

The seasonal availability and patchy distribution of food sources – mainly agricultural crops and particularly oil-seed rape – largely determines the seasonal movements of flocks. Coastal passage occurs annually but involves relatively few birds. Spring passage is rarely noted, the largest recent coastal movement being 273 north over Seaforth on 30-31 March 2004. Seven years of intensive autumn migration watching at Fairhaven produced a maximum annual total of 3,516 in 2003, with the next highest being 146. Heysham and Seaforth also regularly record small numbers moving south, with an exceptional 1,910 at Seaforth on 29 October 2005. Inland movements may be more substantial; 3,490 over Darwen Moor on 3 September 1992 and 4,470 south over the western fringes of Bowland on 17 November 2003 are by far the largest reported in recent years.

By late autumn huge numbers may gather. The highest November counts occurred in the south-west in 1986 with 30,000+ going to roost near Carr Mill Dam on the 28th and 5,000 at MMWWT on the 17th with a similar number at Bretherton/Croston during the month. November counts of 2,500-5,000 have been reported in five of the last 25 years, while similar numbers have occurred in December in 13 years, perhaps indicating increased concentration rather than increased numbers. The largest December counts include 5,000 on flood meadows at Hoscar and a further 5,000 at Eccleston in 1979, 5,000 at Shirdley Hill in 1981 with 'huge numbers' also seen on Altcar and Churchtown Mosses, up to 10,000 on Churchtown Moss in 1982, 6,000 at Mere Sands Wood in 1988 and at Bowkers Green, Aughton in 1998. Unusually large numbers concentrated in the West Pennine Moors in 2002 with 'huge numbers' feeding on beech-mast at Anglezarke and Rivington and 12,500 reported over Darwen Moor on 3 December. Large movements often precede or coincide with the onset of cold weather.

The largest winter concentrations have occurred in January, usually feeding on the south-west coastal plain, especially in the Churchtown/Scarisbrick area. The largest counts include 10,000 on Churchtown Moss in 1980, 32,000 at Bickerstaffe in 1988, while on 6 January 1995 up to 65,000 were estimated at Plex Moss, 15,000 in the Churchtown/Scarisbrick area and 6,000 at Martin Mere. Numbers frequently decline quite rapidly, suggesting that most leave for breeding areas by February, though in March 1992 5,000+ were still at Rufford in mid-March, an unusually late date for such a large number.

Few very large winter concentrations have been reported from the Fylde, perhaps because of the predominance of pasture – an exception being 5,000 at Pilling on 19 February 2005 – and relatively few are seen in the east, where the largest recent count was 1,500 feeding on beech mast in the Cliviger Valley on 21 January 1996.

Most recoveries have involved movements within Lancashire but there have been 20 exchanges with other counties with northern England, ten in the south and one with Wales. Only three of these have been further than 100km, the longest being one ringed as a pullus in Liverpool in August 2001 and found dead in Devon in February 2002. Our only foreign recovery was a pullus ringed in July 1975 and shot in Calvados in northern France that November.

JFW, DJH.

This species account was sponsored by Simon Glinn.

COLLARED DOVE

Streptopelia decaocto

Lancashire Category A.

Common resident breeder.

The dramatic range expansion of the Collared Dove north-westwards through Europe from around 1930, which brought the species to the channel coast of France by 1950, has been well documented. Nevertheless, breeding was not reported in Britain until a pair was found in Norfolk in 1955, two years after Oakes compiled his avifauna. Colonisation of south-eastern and eastern Britain was rapid, and by 1958 breeding extended up the east coast as far as Aberdeenshire and, although the Pennines clearly provided a significant barrier, pairs of Collared Doves bred in Formby and Ormskirk in 1961. The arable fields of south-west Lancashire and North Merseyside proved optimal habitat and subsequent population growth was explosive. By 1964 there were at least 57 pairs breeding in Lancashire south of the Ribble and two roosts in Formby each held up to 120 birds (Smith 1963), while another in Hesketh Park, Southport reached a peak of 220 birds in December (Hudson 1965).

North of the Ribble a single bird was at Lytham in May 1962, two were at Marton Mere in May 1963 and two were at Fleetwood in July 1963, with three there in November 1963. Twenty arrived in Lytham in 1964 and three pairs bred. One found dead in Lytham that December had been ringed in Holland the previous year, which indicates the possible origin and long range irruption of these colonists. Further north a pair bred at Leighton Moss in 1964 but the species was otherwise unrecorded north of the Wyre. However, by 1968 Collared Doves were well established in Morecambe and by 1970 had been recorded in all coastal 10km squares in the county.

The first in east Lancashire was recorded at Barrowford on 23 April 1966. Another followed at Higherford in June 1968 but breeding was not proven until 1974 at Nelson when other pairs were suspected at Brierfield and Barrow near Pendle. A small breeding population was firmly established in the east by 1975.

Coastal populations south of the Ribble were notably large, even by national standards. In February 1970, during a bout of very cold weather, a gamekeeper at Formby claimed a feeding concentration of 2,000-3,000 in a Pheasant covert. Although this could not be confirmed by local birdwatchers, who were denied access, they were impressed by the large numbers of Collared Doves flighting back and forth (Hudson 1972). Coastal populations north of the Ribble also grew rapidly and by autumn 1965 the Lytham flock was 60 strong.

By 1970 the Collared Dove had colonised the east coast of Britain northwards to the Orkneys and the species had occupied the Isle of Man, Islay, the Outer Hebrides, and coastal areas of Ireland. However, records remained few and far between in inland Lancashire north of the Ribble and in east Lancashire as a whole, though the species continued its spread into new localities, albeit at a much slower rate than earlier. The Preston area was occupied between 1969 and 1973 and a flock of 40 birds was counted at Midge Hall in the latter year. Expansion continued, with in-filling near the coast and extension into central and east Lancashire, initially along the main river valleys. This eastwards extension was quite slow and patchy; Collared Doves only reached the Rossendale area in 1975 and first bred there in 1979 (Ward 2002).

By the end of the century almost all of lowland Lancashire was occupied and in 1997-2000 breeding was confirmed in three-quarters of the county's tetrads. Distribution remains extremely patchy in the eastern half of the county south of the Ribble and Collared Doves are absent from almost the whole of Bowland and the north-east. Their grain-dominated diet leads to a close association with man and Collared Doves are commonly seen at garden bird-tables, in suburban parks and in the heart of the conurbations. In the east of the county they are largely restricted to such areas (Hornby 1994) but in the west the open countryside is more hospitable and, although arable farmland is preferred, breeding is virtually ubiquitous. Notable concentrations are attracted wherever grain is available, around barns, silos and Pheasant rearing pens, for example.

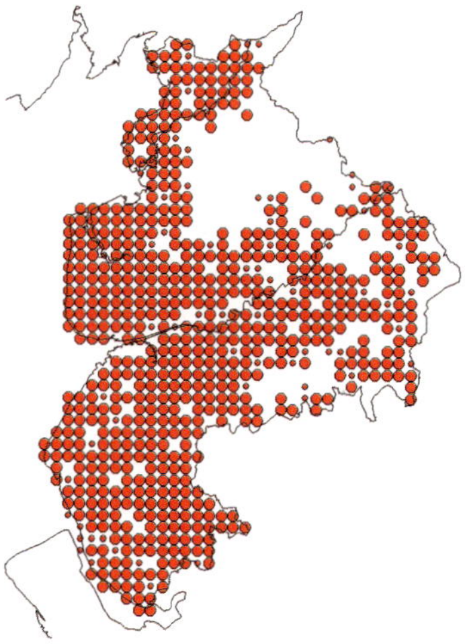

Breeding distribution of Collared Dove, 1997-2000. (Large dots: confirmed. Small dots: possible)

One major factor in the rapid spread of the Collared Dove is its prolonged breeding season, and consequent high potential productivity. In Britain the Collared Dove is known to breed in all months, and in our area, although most nesting occurs between March and September, breeding activity is also regularly recorded in January and February and sometimes in October. Nests are almost always in trees or tall hedges, with ornamental conifers frequently chosen. However, occasionally man-made structures are used as nest supports, most notably when in 1989 a pair nested on South Pier, Blackpool.

Information on breeding densities in Lancashire is limited but not particularly well-favoured suburban areas on the Fylde have 16 to 32 breeding pairs per km^2, while in east Lancashire some occupied tetrads support only a single breeding pair. The Lancashire Atlas gave an estimated breeding population of 3,250 pairs. The national population increased more than threefold between 1970 and 2001 (CBC) and by 41% between 1994 and 2004 (BBS), but recent trends in Lancashire are unclear. Although there have been widespread anecdotal reports of declining numbers in our area as a whole, the species was considered still to be expanding its range in Rossendale as recently as 1994, though this had ceased by 2000 (Ward 2002).

Outside the breeding season the species is highly gregarious with flocks of 30-40 commonplace at autumn and winter food sources on the lowland plains and at communal roosts. However, flocks exceeding 30 are exceptional in east Lancashire (Hornby 1994), while in Rossendale flocks of only ten or twelve were mentioned by Ward (2002). By comparison, in the Fylde flocks of 100 or so are reported most years. Nevertheless, numbers appear to be declining. The highest count recorded in the Fylde was a flock of 250 at Marton Mere in 1988, with the highest count in recent years 170 at Medlar in 1998 (and this was exceptional). Counts in the south-west regularly exceeded those further north with a maximum of 400 at Sefton Park in 1992, and other counts exceeding 300 at Ince Blundell in 1991, and Hillhouse, Formby in 1981 and 1982. However, the only Lancashire count above 200 during the last ten years was of 239 at Hy Fly Hatcheries, Preesall on 5 December 2004 and, though Collared Doves have not generally excited the interest of birdwatchers, this relative lack of recent large autumn/winter flocks, perhaps signals a real decline in population size.

Collared Doves, Little Crosby, December 2004. (Steve Young)

The Collared Dove, despite its range expansion which came about with long-range movements mainly by immature birds, is considered to be basically a resident bird. Lancashire ringing recoveries largely reflect this. Although there have been seven recorded movements of more than 100km, most of these occurred in the 1970s during the period of rapid expansion in northern Britain. There have been ten exchanges with other counties in the north of England and three with the south, plus two to Scotland and one to Ireland, the longest distances being Lancashire-ringed birds to County Tyrone (305km) and Aberdeen (426km).

Nationally there is a tendency for a post-breeding season movement in a north-westerly direction in August but at the regularly watched coastal sites such as Seaforth, Fairhaven, Lytham St. Anne's NR and Heysham there is a southwards movement, (or coasting eastwards, in the case of Fairhaven) in September and October. The number of birds involved is low most years, with the largest autumn totals at Fairhaven of 53 in 1991 and 87 in 2004.

There is also some evidence of a small northward movement through our area in April, for example four at Heysham NR on 20 March 2005 and a total of 66 migrants over Fairhaven between 20 March and 2 May the same year. Our only ringing recovery confirming these movements was of one ringed in Norfolk in January 2003 and found dead in Aughton in September the same year.

JFW, DJH.

This species account was sponsored by Brenda Walsh.

TURTLE DOVE

Streptopelia turtur

Lancashire Category A.

Rare breeder, probably extinct; scarce passage migrant.

This highly attractive migratory dove is now a very local and rare breeder on the mosslands of south-west Lancashire and north Merseyside. It seems destined to become extinct as a breeder within 100 years of having first colonised our area.

Mitchell described it as a rare and occasional summer visitor with no known breeding record; most reports to that date had been of birds shot on migration in May, June, August and September. During the nineteenth century the Turtle Dove had spread fairly rapidly from south-east England in a north-westerly direction, colonising Cheshire in the 1860s and 1870s and being well established there by 1900. Although occasional breeding had been signalled from as far north as Carlisle it had not been recorded breeding in our area (Holloway 1996).

It is thought that nesting may have occurred in 1904 (Spencer 1973) but the first proven breeding was at Lytham in 1910; one of the best-documented early nesting records was from Lytham Hall in 1919. The species spread and consolidated south of the Ribble in the period 1920-1950; according to Oakes the Turtle Dove was restricted as a breeder to the area south and west of a line from Marton Mere through Rufford and Parbold to Knowsley, though in that area it was well established and had become a fairly common summer visitor. It is virtually certain that this statement should have referred to Martin Mere, not Marton Mere, and would then have reflected the situation which pertained until about the mid-1980s. Thus Lancashire has long been at the extreme north-western limit of the breeding range. The principal breeding habitat is overgrown hedgerows, scrub and small copses adjacent to low lying, light sandy arable lands. Stands of sapling birch and hawthorn on the mossland periphery are especially suitable for nesting, and increased drainage and cultivation of these areas have inevitably had an adverse impact on the species' fortunes.

At the time of the Old Atlas (1968-1972) a total of 21 10km squares were occupied with breeding confirmed in 16, almost all south of the Ribble apart from a single confirmed breeding record in the Winmarleigh area. That survey period probably coincided with the absolute peak of Turtle Dove numbers in north-west Europe which subsequently suffered a sharp decline. The New Atlas (1988-91) reported a major reduction in range to seven 10km squares with breeding confirmed in just two, a trend reflected throughout northern England. This decline was probably due to a combination of adverse factors including agricultural intensification on the breeding grounds, which resulted in greater use of insecticides and herbicides, reclamation of rough ground, nitrogen enrichment of poor soils and a major change from hay-making after grasses and herbaceous plants have seeded to silage cuts before seed production, all leading to a reduction in the variety and availability of weed seeds.

Turtle Doves were located in eleven 10km squares in Lancashire during 1997-2000 but breeding was thought likely in just five, this apparent increase since 1988-91 being almost certainly illusory and due to the more comprehensive coverage of the later survey. Breeding was considered probable or proven in just eight tetrads, all south of the Ribble, and it was thought that the total population was no more than five pairs at any time during the period.

Breeding birds can be extremely elusive and not all those found are reported; nevertheless, records published in the annual county reports give an indication of the rapidity of the recent decline. Smith (1963) reported a 'colony' of 12-20 pairs on Halsall Moss during the 1960s and a minimum of 16 pairs bred on these mosslands east of Formby and Southport in 1982 with birds reported from 14 potential breeding sites in the south-west in 1984. Post-breeding gatherings of 30 at Kirkby Moss on 4 August 1976 and 19 at the same site on 11 August 1983 bear witness to a thriving breeding population in the Simonswood Moss area (a site that was destroyed by peat extraction in the late 1980s), which seems unlikely ever to be repeated. Indeed, by 1986 reduced numbers were reported for the first time and 'an apparent decline' was again reported in 1988.

Turtle Dove, south-west mosslands. (Mike McKavett)

The number of south-western sites from which Turtle Doves have been reported in the breeding season has continued to decline markedly during the past decade and most records probably now refer only to overshooting spring migrants. The most recent reports of probable breeding were at Croston Moss in 1993, Churchtown, Southport in 1995, in or near Mere Sands Wood, the Altcar Withins, Knowsley Park and St. Helens until around 1999, and regularly at Haskayne Cutting where the last known nesting in the county occurred in 2001. The total number of birds reported anywhere in the county declined to six in 2001 and just two in

2004 (both in Merseyside and seen for one day only) and 2005 (one briefly at Heysham on 15 May, the other arriving in poor condition by ship into the Seaforth Docks). Extinction as a breeding species may not yet have arrived but it cannot be far off.

Away from the low-lying mosslands of the south-west any occurrence is notable, although the Lancashire coastal plain north of the Ribble used regularly to yield records. There were nine records in both the Fylde and Lancaster areas (including the Bowland fringe) during 1984-1993, with eight and seven respectively during 1994-2003. Fylde records comprise singles in March and April, ten in May, seven in June, one July, six September, two in October and November and three in December. Thus, assuming the March bird was wintering, there have been six winter records, most of them with flocks of Collared Doves. The most recent was at Whyndyke Farm, Blackpool on 1-5 December 2003 with 80 Collared Doves, maintained by very heavy provision of black sunflower seed. Of 17 dated records from the Lancaster area, 13 were in May-June, two in August and singles in September and October. Just outside the Fylde, one was at Broughton in June 1996.

The Pennine fringe in south Lancashire has produced occasional records such as two at Rivington in 1985 and one at Sunnyhurst Wood, Darwen from 14 May to 15 June 1984. East Lancashire with its higher rainfall, cooler summers and heavier soils is not favoured and there have been few records there. The first was found dead in early autumn 1964; the remainder were passage birds which stayed for one day only, all during May to early July with the exception of one at Rishton on 4 September 1993. The most recent was at Great Harwood on 9 July 2002. Rossendale has had three May records, in 1968, 1988 and 1995, and an exceptionally early one on 21 April 2003.

The identity of a bird which arrived at Seaforth after prolonged south-easterlies on 19 May 1992, remaining until the 24th, was never resolved. Initially it was thought to be a Turtle Dove but its vinaceous-brown head, breast and mantle and slate-blue back and rump suggested Oriental Turtle Dove *Streptopelia orientalis* of the western race *meena*.

JFW, DJH.

This species account was sponsored by Chorley & District Natural History Society.

RING-NECKED (ROSE-RINGED) PARAKEET

Psittacula krameri

Lancashire Category CE.

Probably extinct breeder; frequent escapes.

A small population became established in Sandfield Park, Liverpool around 1970 and almost certainly bred there for a number of years before dying out in the early 1980s. It is likely that one or more pairs have bred elsewhere since then but there is no definite evidence of this and no proof that any new self-sustaining population has become established. The most likely candidate is a group of six or so that were seen regularly in gardens in Skelmersdale from at least 2001 to 2005, but reports of these birds have almost all been second-hand and there is no evidence that any juveniles have been seen. Similarly, a flock of five seen near Lydiate on 25 April 2004 may have been a family party.

Ring-necked Parakeet at feeding station, Little Crosby, January 2004.

Singles have been recorded annually since at least 1970 with up to six a year since the mid-1990s; most are presumed to be escaped cage-birds.

SJW.

This species account was sponsored by Simon Jackson.

CUCKOO

Cuculus canorus

Lancashire Category A.

Uncommon breeder and summer visitor.

As the twentieth century came to a close Cuckoos had become decidedly hard to find in many parts of lowland Lancashire and increasingly scarce in much of the uplands. The British population began to decline in the latter half of the twentieth century and fell by 43% during 1970-2001 (CBC), accelerating to 29% during 1994-2005 (BBS).

In Mitchell's day the Cuckoo was 'universally distributed' in Lancashire, equally common on dunes, mosses, hills and moors. There was no suggestion by Oakes of any significant change in numbers or distribution, but by 1973 Spencer noted that the Cuckoo, though still widespread and fairly numerous, was generally agreed to be in decline.

This contraction in both range and numbers has continued inexorably ever since, to the extent that the 1997-2000 county Breeding Atlas estimated a population of no more than 250 'pairs'.

Apart from a few pockets such as the Pilling area of north Fylde, a strip of the south-west mosslands from Rufford to Knowsley, and the dunes of the Sefton coast, the great majority of breeding Cuckoos are nowadays to be found on the moors. The healthiest populations are in the uplands, where Meadow Pipits are the almost invariable hosts – in Bowland, in particular on the Abbeystead and United Utilities estates, and on the West Pennine Moors.

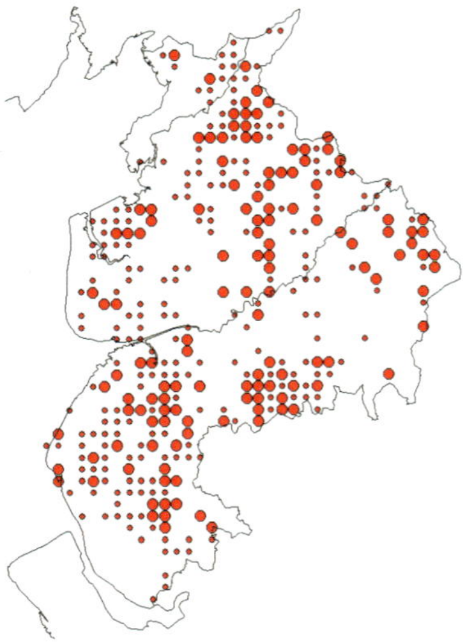

Breeding distribution of Cuckoo, 1997-2000. (Large dots: confirmed. Small dots: possible)

Mitchell listed the main host species in order of frequency as Meadow Pipit, Skylark, Dunnock, Yellowhammer, Whinchat, Pied and Yellow Wagtails, and Sedge Warbler. Both on the coast and in the hills Meadow Pipits continue to be the main host species, followed by Dunnock and Sedge Warbler, with Blackbird and Reed Bunting very much minority choices. In contrast to Mitchell's and Oakes's times Skylarks appear no longer to be parasitised to any extent although a well grown Cuckoo was found and photographed in a Skylark's nest on the edge of Longridge Fell during spring 1969.

Various causes for the decline have been proposed, including falls in the populations of main host species, especially Meadow Pipit and Skylark, and decreases in abundance of the Cuckoo's favourite food, hairy caterpillars, due to climatic and agricultural changes. Meadow Pipit numbers have also fallen in recent decades over much of lowland Lancashire, in some areas quite sharply. They remain numerous in Rossendale, however, where Cuckoos are now decidedly scarce after a decline dating back at least to the mid-1970s.

In line with the severe decline in our breeding population the number of Cuckoos on spring passage published in the county bird report has also fallen significantly, even since the mid-1990s. Although the comparison is rather a crude one, during 1991-95 a mean of 89 birds were reported in April and May while the corresponding figure for 1999-2003 was 61. The major reduction has generally been in May records although 70 were reported in 2004. Autumn migrants, almost all nowadays in July and August, have been so few during the last decade that a similar comparison would be pointless. Most autumn birds are reported from upland areas and there have been no more than three coastal or near-coastal records in any year since 1992. Cuckoos on autumn passage were fairly regular at Heysham until the early 1990s but none has been recorded there since August 1999.

Male Cuckoo, Grizedale Valley, Bowland. (Mike McKavett)

Mitchell gave 27 April as the average date of first arrival, while for Oakes it was 25 April, with very few occurring before mid-month. However, the median date of first arrivals in the county between 1976 and 2005 was 18 April, significantly earlier than that given by either Mitchell or Oakes. Whether this was a real change or merely reflected higher rates of reporting is unclear. The earliest spring Cuckoo was at Martin Mere on 23 March 1990, but as in Oakes's time very few are seen or heard before late April.

The main passage, if such it can be called nowadays, still begins in the last week of April. Spring passage has been very thin on the Sefton and south Fylde coasts since the early 1990s, but it is normally a little more lively on northern shores, from the Wyre to Morecambe Bay. A steady stream of twelve birds flying east over Anglezarke Moor in half an hour on 30 April 1983 was quite exceptional.

Most adults leave for their African winter quarters in July or early in August, while juveniles linger to late August and September. The latest Cuckoos on record are single juveniles at Spenbrook on to 29 September 1975, and, on the coast, at Heysham on 27 September 1992. Since the mid-1990s dates of last sightings have become significantly earlier and single birds in the Dunsop Valley and on Downholland Moss in 2004 are the only September records since 1996; median last dates were 4 September during 1975-1989 and 28 August during 1990-2005.

There have been only two recoveries of Cuckoos ringed in Lancashire, a female pullus ringed on Hightown Dunes on 31 May 1992 and retrapped on Hilbre Island, Wirral on 23 May 1993, and another pullus ringed at Crosby on 8 June 1989 and found dead on the railway line between Hall Road and Hightown stations on the 27th.

BM, DJH.

This species account was sponsored by Rosslyn Colderley and family.

BARN OWL

Tyto alba

Lancashire Category A.

Uncommon resident breeder.

By all accounts Barn Owls were common and widespread in Britain until the 1960s; a survey in 1932 recorded a population of 12,000 pairs in England and Wales alone. A long-term decline, which began in the middle of the twentieth century, was attributed to the effects of pesticides and to changes in agricultural practices that reduced rodent populations as well as removing roosting and nesting-sites, and increasing road mortality (Bunn *et al.* 1982). The 1988-91 New Atlas recorded a 43% decrease in occupied 10km squares compared with 1968-72, a decline that was virtually country-wide across Britain.

Tony Disley

Mitchell described the Barn Owl as very generally distributed 'in limited numbers' in Lancashire, though subject to persecution by gamekeeping interests. Oakes reported a steady increase in rural areas from the 1930s, and noted that the species had also re-established itself in many urban districts. The Fylde, where it nested 'at almost every farmstead and in many of the old ruined windmills' and the south-west mosslands were the Barn Owl's strongholds, but the species was described as scarce only in Rossendale; an indication of its local abundance is given by a record of eleven hunting over a single field on the southern mosslands in daylight in December 1945. Oakes also noted a common choice of nest-site 'under thatched roofs which have been reinforced with corrugated iron'.

Spencer (1973) suggested that 'the Barn Owl was nowhere very rare in Lancashire' but its fortunes in Lancashire from the 1960s may be simply summarised: the species has virtually disappeared from north and east Lancashire, Rossendale and the West Pennine Moors, and only the Fylde and the south-west retain healthy populations.

The process was fairly relentless, though gradual; the 1968-72 Atlas recorded breeding in 43 10km squares and presence in another three; by the 1988-91 New Atlas breeding pairs were located in only 13 squares, with presence in five more, a reduction in range of 62% in 20 years. Barn Owl breeding productivity is subject to marked short-term fluctuations, associated with weather patterns in spring as well as with cyclical variations in abundance of Short-tailed Voles, but the decline in Lancashire, as elsewhere in Britain and Europe, is clearly due to more sustained environmental changes. These are probably complex; by now the effects of pesticide poisoning can probably be taken out of the equation, but there has been a general 'tidying' of the countryside, with removal of hedges, old barns and sheds, a reduction in rodent numbers and increased mortality from road casualties.

Disturbance and nest-robbery have also played their part. A small population that existed in the Gisburn Forest, where they hunted the rides, in the 1960s was augmented by a programme of nest-box provision in derelict buildings from 1965 to four pairs in 1969. The population was, however, lost by the end the 1970s, probably mainly as a result of high levels of nest-robbery and disturbance following publication of details in the Liverpool Daily Post (D. Bunn *pers. comm.*).

The story is, however, not one of unrelieved gloom. Barn Owls have made a sustained comeback in the south of the county since the 1980s. Breeding was confirmed in 23 10km squares during 1997-2000 and presence in a further seven, and the population estimated at 130 pairs. These were found in 148 tetrads, 16% of the county, and were almost entirely confined to the west with concentrations in the Pilling-Cockerham area and parts of south Fylde, and especially on the south-west mosslands throughout North Merseyside and West Lancashire and parts of South Ribble.

One factor aiding their continued success here may be that the normal field-boundary in these areas is a ditch rather than a hedge; ditches and their rough margins are more likely to have survived the drive for agricultural intensification. However, in both stronghold regions the Barn Owl population has been greatly aided by the widespread provision of nest-boxes, thanks to the sustained work of local bird-ringers and the cooperation of farmers. The species has taken readily to these; even so, breeding success has varied enormously from one year to the next over the decades. In 1994 a population of 25-30 pairs was estimated for the south-west, an increase from the 1960s, in contrast to the national trend. Up to four pairs breed annually to the west of Chorley, at the edge of the mosses; this represents a recolonisation during the 1990s, mainly due to the erection of nest-boxes by local ringers and farmers.

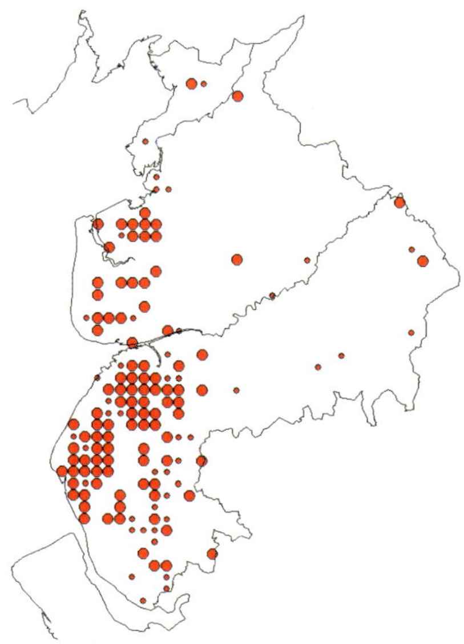

Breeding distribution of Barn Owl, 1997-2000. (Large dots: confirmed. Small dots: possible)

The county Atlas showed breeding in two tetrads in the Lune Valley in 1997-2000, but otherwise Barn Owls are only occasional visitors to north Lancashire, with virtually annual records at Leighton Moss up to the late 1990s, and a few seen at Heysham. In the east intermittent breeding continues, with three pairs fledging young in 1991; since then one or two pairs bred in the Darwen area in 1992 and a pair fledged four young from two clutches at Hurstwood, Burnley in 2001, while at least two pairs bred in east Lancashire in 2005. In Rossendale single pairs bred in 1982 and 1983, and two or three in 1985, but since then the species has been no more than a casual visitor to the region. Barn Owls are little more than vagrants on most of the West Pennine Moors; one near Belmont in November-December 2003 was the first recorded in that area for ten years and was followed by successful breeding in 2004 and 2005, for the first time since the early 1960s.

Dark-breasted individuals, showing the characters of the central and eastern European race *guttata*, are rare visitors in winter; one was on Cockerham Moss in January 1961 and 1962 and there were records at Churchtown, Southport in November 1989 and at Marton Mere in February and March 1990.

The nest-box programmes in the Fylde and the south-west have seen hundreds of pulli ringed since the 1960s; to date 253 Lancashire-ringed Barn Owls have been recovered, 210 within the county, 18 elsewhere in northern England and seven in southern England. Four have travelled over 100km from their birthplaces on the south-west mosslands to an early death: one ringed on Plex Moss on 5 July 1974 was found, long dead, near Bedford on 6 November, one ringed near Martin Mere on 14 June 1989 was recovered dead near Colchester, Essex on 1 November, a bird from Homer Green, near Maghull on 25 June 1992 turned up dead near Staverton, Gloucestershire on 24 January 1993, and one from Holmes, near Tarleton on 7 July 1999 was also picked up dead near Slimbridge in the same county on 11 December. Twenty Barn Owls ringed elsewhere in Britain have been recovered here, 17 from northern England, one from Wellington, Shropshire and two from Dumfries and Galloway in south-west Scotland.

BM, DJH.
This species account was sponsored by Tony Duckels and Sheila Howarth.

SCOPS OWL

Otus scops

Lancashire Category D.

One arrived in the Liverpool Docks on 27 March 1959 aboard the MV *Silverdene*, having come on board in the Red Sea. On arrival it flew off the ship into a warehouse where it was caught by Eric Hardy who later released it at Helsby in North Cheshire. It was reported to have flown around the train compartment on its way from Liverpool. (*MNA Bird Report* 1958/59).

At the time all ship-assisted rarities were disregarded but there is no indication that this bird was in any way assisted by the ship's crew and nowadays such a record might stand a far better chance of gaining admission to Category A.

Scops Owl, Liverpool, March 1959. (Eric Hardy)

JKB, SJW.
This species account was sponsored by The Merseyside Naturalists Association, in memory of Eric Hardy.

[HAWK OWL]

Surnia ulula

One seen in the Bleasdale fells near Chipping on 13 September 1959 was originally accepted by the BBRC (BB 53: 446) but, on review in 1999, it was felt that the racial identification was not fully resolved and that the possibility of escape could not be ruled out.

SJW, MJ.

LITTLE OWL

Athene noctua

Lancashire Category C.

Fairly common resident breeder.

Little Owls are not native to Britain; the first attempted introductions, in Yorkshire in the 1840s, failed but subsequent efforts in Kent in the 1870s and Northamptonshire in 1888-90 took hold. After 1900 the species expanded its range and population dramatically and by 1920 Little Owls were breeding in most parts of England and Wales south of a line from the Humber to the Mersey. More recent data indicate that the British population has been roughly stable since the 1970s (CBC, BBS).

Mitchell's claim of one near Ormskirk a few years before 1863 was dismissed due to lack of detail by Oakes, who regarded a bird seen at Rawtenstall, Rossendale on 8 April 1917 as Lancashire's first. In the subsequent decade records proliferated: at Banks in February 1920, Formby in April 1921, Bretherton, Chorley and Wennington in the Lune Valley in 1922, Clitheroe in June 1923, St. Michaels-on-Wyre in April 1924 and Winmarleigh and Wharles, also on the Fylde, in 1925. By the late 1940s Little Owls had bred at Sabden, Longridge Fell, Burnley and Rawtenstall, and according to Spencer (1973) the colonisation of Lancashire was complete by 1957, with the species especially common among the disused quarries and dry-stone walls of the east.

Since the 1960s Little Owls have steadily filled in most of the gaps in their Lancashire range; the species is widespread in rural areas, both in the lowlands and on the moorland edge where open country is interspersed with hedgerows and small copses. They regularly hunt by day, perching on stone walls or buildings from which they locate their mainly invertebrate prey. They nest in hollow trees and crevices in old buildings, dry-stone walls and quarry-sides; Little Owls take readily to nest-boxes and these have significantly boosted the population in several localities. The 1997-2000 county Breeding Atlas estimated a total of 400 pairs, which may be something of an underestimate since birds were located in 400 tetrads (43%) although breeding was confirmed in only 298. Little Owls are scarce or absent only in parts of the higher fells and in urban and suburban areas.

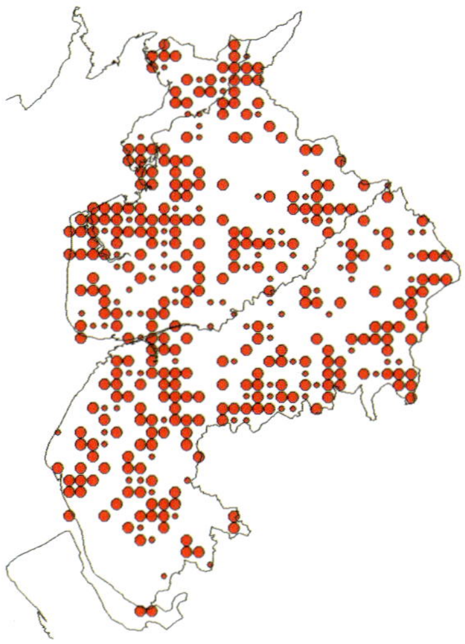

Breeding distribution of Little Owl, 1997-2000. (Large dots: confirmed. Small dots: possible)

Little Owls were scarce in the north of the county until the early 1970s, but are now widespread in the Ribble Valley and parts of Bowland, and especially in the Lune Valley. Nest-boxes at Arkholme were temporarily removed in 1999 as the occupants were taking a heavy toll of Ringed Plover, Redshank and Lapwing chicks. The Fylde and the south-west hold the densest populations with, for example an estimate of 50 breeding pairs in the mosslands of Sefton and nearby areas of West Lancashire in 2005. Little Owls are fairly evenly distributed across the Fylde, with the highest concentrations Over Wyre.

Little Owls tend to suffer local population losses due to felling of nesting trees and the modernisation of old barns and sheds, and the value of nest-box programmes in maintaining and increasing numbers is well illustrated by the success of a project in the Pilling-Preesall area of the north Fylde. The population there fluctuates fairly widely, but an average of 18 pairs bred annually over the ten years 1994-2003; in 1998, the peak year, all but one of 28 breeding pairs made use of nest-boxes. Little Owls are widespread in east Lancashire, Rossendale and the Chorley area; the species was described as 'almost common' in east Burnley in 1997, although a local decline was noted on the West Pennine Moors in 2000. The Rossendale Ornithogists' report described the Little Owl as 'thriving' in that region in 2004, with breeding season records from 21 locations, all in quarries or on moorland edge.

Little Owl, Champion Moor, 2001. (Mark Breaks)

Little Owls are not great wanderers, and of 20 recoveries of birds ringed in Lancashire 18 have been within the county and the other two elsewhere in northern England. Only one has been known to travel more than 100km, a bird ringed at Little Crosby on 14 December 1958 and found freshly dead in North Yorkshire on 26 April 1960; there has been only one recovery in Lancashire of a bird ringed elsewhere in northern England.

BM, DJH.

This species account was sponsored by Bob and Diane Danson.

TAWNY OWL

Strix aluco

Lancashire Category A.

Common resident breeder.

Having recovered from persistent persecution by gamekeepers until the early twentieth century and escaped the worst effects of pesticide poisoning in the 1950s and 1960s, the Tawny Owl is found throughout Britain in all but the most mountainous regions. The 1988-91 New Atlas estimated a national total of 20,000 pairs.

Mitchell emphasised the relentless persecution to which the species was subjected in the nineteenth century and described the Tawny Owl as a scarce, local and decreasing resident, although it is likely that the complete dearth of records from the south of the county to which he referred was due to lack of coverage rather than to genuine absence. At any rate, by Oakes's time this was the most numerous and widespread of our owls, having greatly increased in numbers since the 1920s; this he attributed to legal protection as well as to 'the decline of superstition and the spread of rational ideas.'

The status of the Tawny Owl in Lancashire appears to have changed little in the last half-century, at least in terms of its range. It remains our most common, widespread and familiar owl. The 1997-2000 Breeding Atlas estimated a population of 1,000 pairs, although this may now be a little on the high side. They are distributed across the entire county (in 51% of tetrads) with the exception of city centres and the highest fells, although the species has bred above 250m in Bowland. Just about every stretch of wooded or semi-wooded habitat, at least in the lowlands, has its resident pair, or pairs, of Tawny Owls, provided there are suitable nesting-sites. They take readily to nest-boxes, including those intended for Barn Owls.

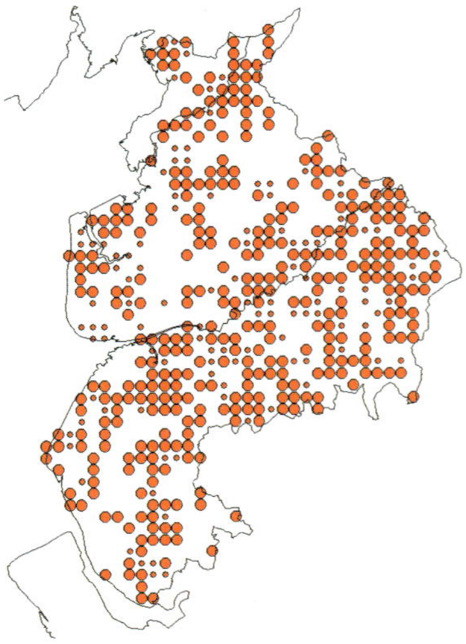

Breeding distribution of Tawny Owl, 1997-2000.
(Large dots: confirmed. Small dots: possible)

Breeding pairs compete with, and dominate, Long-eared Owls and it is likely that Tawnies have driven the scarcer species from many traditional woodlands on the south-west mosslands. Breeding densities may be significantly enhanced by the provision of boxes; in the Pilling-Preesall area of the Fylde up to 14 pairs have taken advantage of such a programme every year since 1987. Other notable population clusters include up to eight pairs in Witton Country Park, Blackburn in the 1980s and around Darwen Moor in the early 1990s, and up to twelve pairs in the Formby/Ainsdale pinewoods and four each at Leighton Moss and Mere Sands Wood in more recent years. In autumn juveniles disperse from their natal area and at this time may be seen or heard in localities where breeding does not take place, including docklands and city centres.

As with all nocturnal species, accurate monitoring of Tawny Owl populations is difficult but many observers have reported significant local declines over the past decade, including in south Fylde and the Ribble Valley.

The Tawny Owl's adaptability is illustrated by numerous instances of unusual and even apparently eccentric behaviour. Oakes related that in the spring of 1948 Spencer watched a pair evict Rooks from a newly-built nest in a Burnley rookery; they subsequently bred in the nest, surrounded by breeding Rooks.

A pair at Arkholme in 1996 predated the adults and young of no fewer than eight Jackdaw nest-boxes (although in 1998 a pair deserted, following harassment by Jackdaws). Ground nesting has been recorded on at least three occasions in plantations in the West Pennine Moors and a ground-nesting pair at Slaidburn in 2002 successfully raised two young. Duckels (Lancashire Atlas) reported a pair that nested in a hole in a stream-bank near Inglewhite during the 1960s and early 1970s which included in its diet Bullheads fished from the stream. Other unusual feeding behaviours included a female that thrashed rhododendron bushes in Witton Country Park ten successive times on 30 June 1983 in order to flush out roosting passerines, and a bird near Stocks Reservoir in 1987 which was observed feeding on a Rabbit road-kill.

Tawny Owl, Martin Mere, April 2005. (Steve Young)

There have been 166 recoveries of Tawny Owls ringed in Lancashire, 148 within the county and the other 18 elsewhere in northern England; only one travelled more than 100km from its birthplace, a bird ringed as a pullus at Pilling Hall on 13 May 1996 and found dead near Longtown, Cumbria exactly a year later. Five birds ringed elsewhere in Britain have been recorded here, four from northern England and one from Wales.

BM, DJH.

This species account was sponsored by John and Mary Almond and Berwyn Morris.

LONG-EARED OWL

Asio otus

Lancashire Category A.

Scarce breeder; uncommon winter visitor from northern Europe.

Although British Long-eared Owls are mainly resident, apart from dispersals of young birds after fledging, the populations of most of Fennoscandia and northern Russia migrate south or south-west in late autumn. A variable proportion of these reach Britain and Ireland, where they tend to form roosts of varying sizes in thorn or willow-scrub as well as in conifers. Most of these immigrants are found in eastern Britain but some penetrate further west; the Winter Atlas (1986) estimated a combined winter population of Britain and Ireland of 10,000-35,000 birds.

Mitchell described the Long-eared Owl as a very local resident, more widespread in autumn and winter due to immigration. He identified Knowsley Park and Rufford in the south-west, Winmarleigh and Claughton in the north of the county, and Whitewell and Longridge Fell in the Ribble and Hodder Valleys as recent or current breeding locations.

In Oakes's time the species remained a local breeder although he described it as common in a few areas, particularly north Fylde, where up to twelve pairs bred in a single locality in the Stalmine-Pilling-Cockerham area. Long-eared Owls were also well distributed in south Fylde and on the south-west mosslands, where up to five pairs had nested in a single wood near Southport in 1915-16. Nesting was regular in parts of east Lancashire, in particular the Burnley, Clitheroe and Longridge areas, and around Rivington on the West Pennine Moors, but the species was scarce in the Lune Valley and did not breed in Rossendale. Probable immigrants were described as occasionally common in the south-west in winter. As recently as 1957 there was an estimate of seven to ten pairs breeding in the pinewoods between Hightown and Ainsdale; in 1963 nesting was recorded in at least five coverts on the mosses inland of Formby (Smith 1963).

Ten years later, however, Spencer's (1973) assessment of the species' status in Lancashire was markedly pessimistic; the population was 'sadly diminished', with its last stronghold on the mosses between the Ribble and Mersey. This situation is reflected in the 1968-72 Atlas, which showed breeding in twelve 10km squares and probable nesting in one other, only four of these north of the Ribble.

Since then, with due allowance for the difficulty of censusing breeding Long-eared Owls, the population appears to have stabilised, albeit at a much lower level than in Oakes's day. The New Atlas found breeding or presence in 16 10km squares, whilst the 1997-2000 county Atlas recorded confirmed or possible nesting in 37 tetrads, also in 16 10km squares, and estimated a total population of 30 pairs. These are heavily concentrated in North Merseyside and the south-west mosslands, where they nest in even quite small game covert woodlands within the arable areas. There are also a few outlying breeding clusters in Rossendale, the Burnley area, the West Pennine Moors, the Lune Valley and Grindleton Forest, and possibly at Gisburn Forest and Longridge Fell. Since 2000 nesting by one or two pairs has been recorded annually in the Leck Fell area in the north-east, where gamekeepers have reported their presence for at least 15 years.

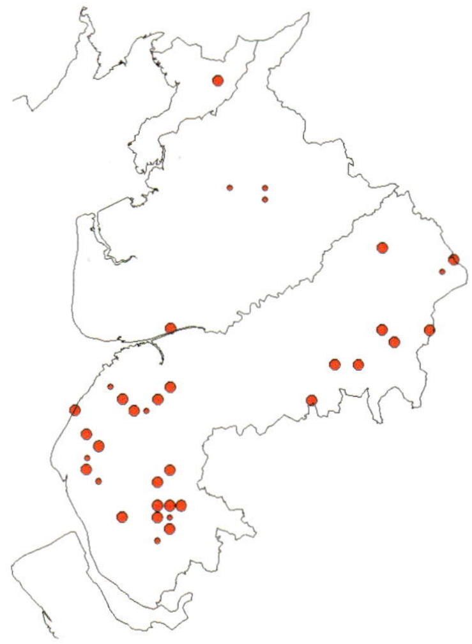

Breeding distribution of Long-eared Owl, 1997-2000. (Large dots: confirmed. Small dots: possible)

Over the years winter roosts of Long-eared Owls have been discovered in many parts of the county; some of these have been maintained over successive winters, although numbers of occupants have varied. Roosts tend to form in November, reach a peak in December-January and dwindle in early spring, with the last birds frequently lingering on until early in April. As native Long-eared Owls tend to establish territories very early, often in January, it is likely that many, if not all, of the inhabitants of Lancashire winter roosts are immigrants from northern Europe; this conclusion is supported by a single ringing-recovery, an unaged bird ringed near Prescot on 22 February 1976 and found freshly dead in Kristianstad, southern Sweden, on 20 June 1977.

Long-eared Owl at winter roost, Marton Mere, February 1997. (Steve Young)

A roost just south of Preston was occupied in successive winters from at least 1974 until 1979, peaking at up to eight birds on several occasions, and up to three roosted annually on White Moss, Skelmersdale during 1979-84. The county's longest-established roost of recent decades has been in existence at Marton Mere in most winters since 1990. Numbers have fluctuated widely: there were two in November 1988, up to six in 1990/91, eight in November-December 1998, up to five in 1999/2000, two in 2000/01 and up to six in 2003/04 and 2004/05. Other significant, though normally smaller, gatherings have been located at Leighton Moss in many winters since 1980, at Martin Mere since 1991, at Rimrose Valley, Crosby since 1997, and in the Croston-Bretherton area, Chorley in 1998-99. How many others go undiscovered at sites unfrequented by birders may only be guessed at.

There has been very little direct observation of migrant Long-eared Owls in Lancashire. Perhaps the most noteworthy are two records in 1991, of singles at Heysham on 29 October and at Seaforth two days later; the latter arrived with flocks of migrant thrushes. Since then individuals have been seen at Heysham in autumn 1999 and at Formby Point on 10 October 2002.

In addition to the bird in Sweden mentioned above, eight Long-eared Owls ringed as pulli in Lancashire since 1916 have been recovered, all dead – five within the county and singles in West Yorkshire, Leicestershire and Dorset. In addition, three birds ringed as pulli in neighbouring counties have been killed or found dead here since the 1960s – from Rochdale and Leigh in Greater Manchester and from Risley Moss, near Warrington.

BM, DJH.

This species account was sponsored by John Bannon.

SHORT-EARED OWL

Asio flammeus

Lancashire Category A.

Scarce breeder; uncommon winter visitor.

The status of the Short-eared Owl in Lancashire appears to have changed substantially since Mitchell's day. He described the species as predominantly a winter visitor to coastal dunes and mosses and a scarce breeder suffering from persecution. Apart from a nest on Pendle Hill in 1877 he emphasised breeding on mossland heaths in the Fylde and around the Ribble Estuary, and Oakes named these as Cockerham, Winmarleigh, Pilling, Martin Mere, Tarleton and Halsall.

By Oakes's time breeding was restricted to the uplands, with fairly regular nesting recorded at Ward's Stone, Parlick and Fairsnape Fells in Bowland, and further east and south at Boulsworth Hill, in Rossendale, and on Brinscall and Anglezarke Moors. He cited only a single instance of lowland nesting in the twentieth century, at Ainsdale in 1916. In Oakes's opinion the published records overemphasised the species' preference for coastal wintering; in addition to regular presence on Winmarleigh and Formby Mosses, Banks and Crossens Marshes and Sefton Meadows, he described the Short-eared Owl as frequent in winter on the Rossendale moors as well as in the Darwen and Entwistle areas.

Since the 1950s the breeding fortunes of the Short-eared Owl have undergone both highs and lows; county bird reports in 1964, 1982 and 1987 referred to losses due to human persecution, but this appears to have diminished in recent years. The 1997-2000 survey estimated an average total of 30 pairs. Most were in Bowland, where they nest on both the open moorland and in young plantations. Although Meadow Pipits, Skylarks and various small rodent species are taken, the main prey of breeding Short-eared Owls is the Short-tailed Vole and breeding productivity varies widely according to that species' abundance. 1996 was a 'vole year' and up to 20 pairs bred in Bowland, with up to 30 young fledged from eleven monitored nests. Voles were abundant again in 2003 and 2004, resulting in 19 probable pairs in 2003 and 23 in 2004 on the United Utilities Bowland estate alone, but this total slumped to just three pairs in 2005.

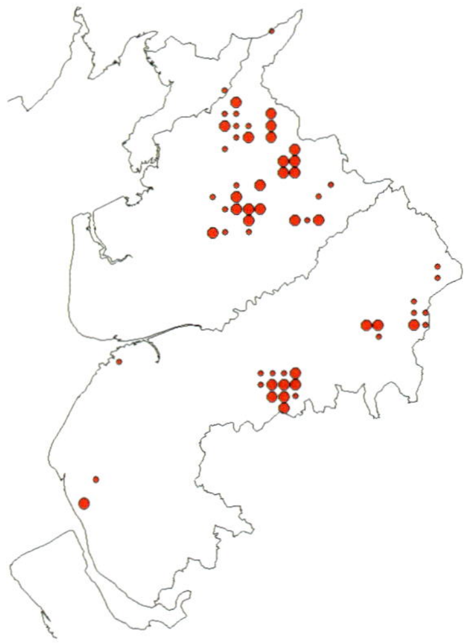

Breeding distribution of Short-eared Owl, 1997-2000. (Large dots: confirmed. Small dots: possible)

Breeding also occurs elsewhere in east Lancashire and there are small populations on the West Pennine Moors, where up to five pairs breed in the Belmont area, and in Rossendale, with one or two pairs in most years.

Sporadic nesting is still recorded on coastal mosses and saltmarshes. A pair attempted to breed on Plex Moss in the late 1950s; in 1982 a pair bred on Sefton Meadows, although one of the adult birds was subsequently shot, and fairly regular breeding has taken place there until the present day. Successful nesting by up to two pairs took place on coastal set-aside at Hundred End during the late 1980s, a pair summered near St. Helens in 2003 and a pair fledged three young in the Altcar area in 2005.

Passage and dispersal bring birds to the coast from late July or early August in most years; one flying in from the sea at Heysham on 6 October 1995 and singles there on 14 October 1996 and at Seaforth three days later were almost certainly on passage.

Short-eared Owl hunting over Marshside Out Marsh. (Mike McKavett)

While there have been some changes in the wintering sites favoured by Short-eared Owls over the years, the same locations tend to recur again and again in the bird report. It is likely, however, that the total number of birds wintering in coastal Lancashire has decreased since the late 1980s. Oakes referred to seven on Winmarleigh Moss in December 1940 and there were up to 24 in a single roost at Warton Crag in February 1979; since then sites further south and west have tended to predominate. There were twelve on the Wyre Estuary in December 1981 and January 1982, and nine there in December 1985 and in January 1989; ten were present on Clifton Marsh in March 1986 and in December 1988. More recently Warton Marsh and Marton Mere have dominated Fylde counts; there were ten at Warton in October–November 2002, up to six at Marton Mere and nearby mosses in December in 1990 and 1996, and four there in January 2003.

The saltings and mosses between the Ribble and the Mersey have historically constituted the Short-eared Owl's main wintering area, and the stretch between Hundred End and Marshside is the jewel in that particular crown. Up to 17 were on Banks Marsh on 17 October 1982 and 15 at Hundred End in December 1988, twelve at Marshside-Crossens in December 1978, eleven in December 1981, ten in December 1995 and, after nearly a decade of low counts, up to 14 in December 2003. Other impressive gatherings in the south-west include twelve at Otterspool in March 1979, often hunting under floodlights, eight there in November-December 1992 and 14 at Sefton Meadows in December 2005.

In a recent return to the situation of the 1950s, substantial numbers have again been overwintering in the uplands since the late 1990s probably as result of successive mild winters; this may help to account for the corresponding decline in numbers at most coastal sites. Six were present on Champion Moor in December 2000 with up to eight there in 2002/03, when another seven were on Twiston Moor.

Although most Short-eared Owls have vacated coastal wintering grounds by the end of March, and most Lancashire breeding birds have returned to the fells by this time, singles and occasional small parties are recorded in the lowlands until the middle of May, including seven over Kirkby Moss on 9 April 1989 and eight on Skelmersdale White Moss on 16 April 1992.

There have been five recoveries of birds ringed as pulli in upland Lancashire: birds shot in their first winter at Lytham St. Anne's in November 1953 and in West Yorkshire in August 1975, and three found dead, one close to its birthplace near Slaidburn in August 1954, another in Kent in February 1958 and the third near Burnley in November 1998. One bird ringed as a pullus beyond our borders has been recovered here, from Howarth, West Yorkshire on 14 May 1996 and found dead near Colne on 15 June. Although there are no recoveries from further afield, data from elsewhere in Britain suggest that a substantial proportion of Lancashire's wintering Short-eared Owls are from Fennoscandia, eastern Europe as far as Russia, and Iceland.

BM, DJH.

This species account was sponsored by John Wright.

[TENGMALM'S OWL]

Aegolius funereus

Mitchell and Oakes referred to a specimen said to have been shot near Preston, probably close to Penwortham, in the summer of 1851. It was bought by Mr. W. Felkin and later passed into the collection of Nottingham Town Museum, where it was examined by Alfred Newton.

The unlikely date, extreme rarity of this species in Britain and uncertain provenance of this bird mean that the species cannot be regarded as having occurred in the wild in Lancashire with any certainty.

SJW, MJ.

NIGHTJAR

Caprimulgus europaeus

Lancashire Category A.

Extinct breeder; rare passage migrant.

The extinction of the Nightjar as a breeding species was a long time coming, but the process that began some time in the middle of the nineteenth century finally reached its unhappy conclusion in the 1980s. Mitchell noticed a decline in the lowlands during the 1880s, writing 'it was once common on all the South Lancashire mosses, but is now only found on the more secluded ones, and where the character of these is suitable, and clumps of timber dot the heathy spaces, it breeds regularly'. He had little else to say but implied that breeding still occurred on northern fells and possibly sand-dunes.

Nationally, a reduction in range had become evident before 1930 as the species began to withdraw from many northern and western areas, and by the end of the 1970s the population was largely confined to heaths and forestry plantations in East Anglia and southern England. Just after the Second World War Oakes noted further declines in parts of the southern mosslands and the Fylde and extinction in Rossendale by 1917, but was still able to describe the Nightjar as 'a widely distributed summer resident, found in moderate numbers in one or two districts but nowhere really common'. Modest but regular breeding clusters remained in the Warton Crag-Silverdale area; the lower Lune Valley around Halton, Caton and Quernmore; Cockerham and Winmarleigh Mosses; and the Ribble Valley around Longridge Fell, Kemple End and Pendle.

Tony Disley

The bulk of the population was found, however, in the south-west, where Oakes described Nightjars as 'well established and fairly numerous', even increasing, in the young coastal pinewoods of Formby and Ainsdale, nesting mostly amongst the conifers and occasionally in the dunes. He noted a decline elsewhere on the south-western mosslands but wrote of nesting 'sparingly' near Kirkby, Bickerstaffe and Rufford.

The half-century since Oakes's book has seen the Nightjar population dwindle inexorably to extinction; nowadays it is no more than a rare passage migrant, less than annual in occurrence. The Warton Crag population, which contained up to 20 pairs in the early 1950s, had declined to two or three by 1960, by which date the Lune Valley pocket had also been reduced to a mere two pairs on the hills above Quernmore. Nightjars bred annually on the western edge of Blackburn at Billinge Hill and Witton Park until the early 1960s, and churring males were present regularly on Longridge Fell. However, a survey of all known east Lancashire haunts in 1972 failed to record a single contact (Spencer 1973), although intermittent records of males in song continued at Longridge until the mid-1970s.

The Nightjar's last breeding foothold was in the coastal pine plantations and heaths of the south-west. Good numbers bred in the Sefton Coast pinewoods between Cabin Hill and Ainsdale in the post-war years, Smith (1963) counting up to twelve pairs at Ainsdale alone in 1957. Three males were churring at Formby Point in 1968 (Lassey 1968) but the area had been deserted by 1970 according to Spencer, probably as a result of the maturation of the woodlands. However, breeding by one or two pairs persisted on Simonswood Moss, near Kirkby until 1980 after which this extensive heathland was destroyed by peat-extraction.

Since then, although there have been some suggestive breeding season records, nesting has not been confirmed. There were one or two birds at Ainsdale on 30 May 1981 and a male was in song at a mossland site in 1982, but the 1981 BTO survey recorded none in upland Lancashire. A bird flew over Warton Crag on 14 June 1987 and a male spent two days at Earnshaw Reservoir in July 1991; in 1992 a female was recorded at Jumbles Reservoir on the West Pennine Moors on 17 July and there were two birds at Grindleton Fell, north of Clitheroe earlier in the month, with a male churring there on the 14th. Two were present at a site in the south-west in early summer 1995, and in perhaps the most intriguing of all these recent occurrences a male was seen near Sabden on 31 May 1998 and a female or juvenile was found dead in the same area on 7 September. The most recent record involved reports of one or more birds on Royal Birkdale Golf Course and at Ainsdale NNR on several dates in late May and June of 1999, but no further details were received.

Nightjars continue to occur in Lancashire as spring passage migrants, but visits have grown steadily less frequent over the last two decades; most records have been in the south-west or the Fylde and typically involve a very brief encounter with a single bird. Since 1985 passage birds have been recorded at Martin Mere on 27 April 1986, over Darwen Moor on 26 May 1987, over Formby on 16 May 1988, on Hesketh Golf Course, Marshside on 16 May and at Marton, Fylde on 1-2 June 1999; a female flew each evening at Aintree Racecourse on 18-20 May 2001, one was found in a garden at Garstang on 11 June 2002 and another was at Gait Barrows on 1 June 2004.

Autumn records are exceedingly rare: one was shot at Belmont on 2 September 1904 and corpses were found at Martin Mere on 3 October 1973 and at Woodvale on 16 September 1975; one was hawking insects at dusk at Newton Marsh on 3 October 1974. A brief view of one flying over Marshside on 26 September 1981 is the most recent occurrence.

BM, MJ.

This species account was sponsored by Stuart W. Campbell.

SWIFT

Apus apus

Lancashire Category A.

Common breeder; abundant passage migrant.

The status of the Swift in Lancashire appears to have altered little since the days of Mitchell and of Oakes. For the former it was a common and widely-distributed summer visitor, while Oakes emphasised its abundance in built-up areas, even in the hearts of manufacturing towns, where mill buildings and chimneys were favourite nesting-sites, although it was also common in smaller rural towns and villages. April records were exceptional, and the average date of first sighting in east Lancashire was given as 9 May; passage continued into the first week of June. Southward movements began in mid-July and were largely completed by mid-August, with September birds scarce and later records very exceptional.

Our earliest arrivals have been in the first days of April: one in Skelmersdale on the 1st on 2004, two over Whalley on 4 April 1990 and one over Barrowford Reservoir, Nelson on 4 April 2002. Widespread sightings of individuals and small parties from around 25 April are now the norm and the average date of first arrival during 1978-2005 was 20 April.

Up to 200 were over Marton Mere on 30 April 2003 but in most years the main passage does not get underway until the first week in May and continues intermittently until early June. Spring movements are usually most evident during sustained periods of southerly or south-easterly winds, although adverse wind conditions combined with heavy rain may occasionally produce very large gatherings over reservoirs, marshes and other water-bodies. Most of the larger movements have been recorded on the coast, including 500 at Marton Mere on 11 June 1983 and 5 June 1992, 1,250 over Marshside in four hours on 11 May 1993, 1,200 there on 24 May 1993 and 1,800 in four hours on 11 May 1995, and a thousand moving south in heavy rain at Seaforth on 20 May 2002. There are, however, also many records of impressive flocks at inland locations: 500 passed over Foulridge Reservoir, Colne on 7 June 1987 and 400+ on 19 May 1993, 500 over Arkholme in the Lune Valley on 10 May 2000, 1,100 over Haydock Racecourse in two hours on 1 May 2003 and 1,000 over Ewood Bridge Sewage Works, Rossendale, on 18 May 2003.

As elsewhere in Britain, we have little detailed knowledge of the Swift's breeding behaviour or population in Lancashire. Mitchell mentioned nesting in stone-quarries at Longridge in the 1880s and Oakes referred to similar behaviour at Hoghton and in Rossendale at over 500m altitude. An unusual variation recorded by Oakes involved three pairs that nested annually in a Sand Martin colony near Preston in the 1940s, making use of tunnels from which the rightful inhabitants had been evicted. Nowadays the majority almost certainly nest in houses but larger buildings often support the largest colonies, in church towers in Lancaster, for example.

The 1997-2000 Atlas survey confirmed breeding in 34% of the county's tetrads, concentrated in urban areas; only in the higher parts of Bowland and the Pennines, and in lowland districts without extensive conurbations such as inland Fylde and the south-west mosslands, is the species absent or scarce. The total breeding population was estimated at 2,000 pairs. Urban regeneration and house modernisation have certainly taken their toll, one example being losses of nest sites due to the wholesale demolition of cotton mills in east Lancashire in the last quarter of the twentieth century.

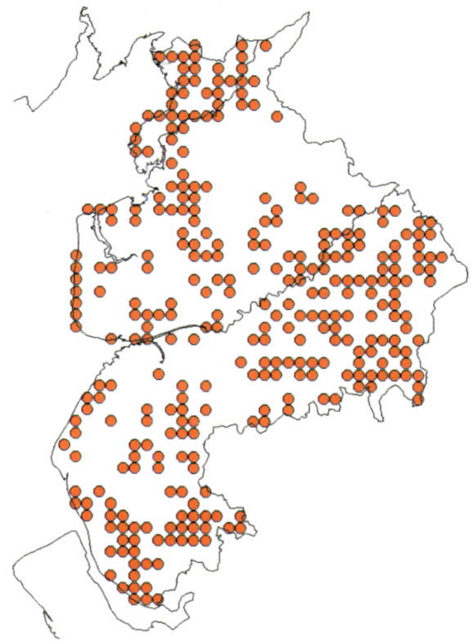

Breeding distribution of Swift, 1997-2000. (Large dots: confirmed. Small dots: possible)

Powerful and rapid flyers, Swifts are often observed in midsummer, occasionally in large numbers, feeding on insect-swarms over moorland and wetland locations far from their main breeding-areas. Three hundred were over Rivington Reservoir on 18 June 1981, 500 over Winter Hill in June 1985, 700 fed on midges and gnats over Marshside on 26 June 1992 and there were 600 over Marton Mere on several dates in June 1994; an enormous flock of up to 5,000 fed on black clouds of insects at Fazakerley Reedbed in June 1998 during a very wet summer, and 1,000 flocked over Clowbridge Reservoir, Rossendale in mid-June 2000.

Eggs are laid from late May and incubation normally takes about three weeks; the young fledge in another six weeks on average and are on the wing by late July or early August. Both adults and young birds are on their way south very soon afterwards; in cold, wet summers, however, as in 1965, 1977, 1978, 1985, 1998 and 2002 fledging, and consequently migration, may be considerably later in many areas.

It is likely that many non-breeders and failed pairs are on the move by early July, but autumn passage normally peaks between the third week of that month and the third week of August. Some very large movements have been recorded, although many birders feel that Swifts 'just disappear' in August in most years. Thirteen hundred passed over Burscough on 26 August 1982 and there were 500+ over Tarleton on 22 July 1986, 800 over Seaforth on 4 August 1988 and 3,000 there on 11 August 1992, 3,000 at Martin Mere on 14 August 1992, up to 2,000 again at Seaforth in early August in 1993, 1995 and 1996, 1,000 over Rufford Moss on 4 August 2001 and 2,000 over Clowbridge Reservoir on 27 July 2003.

Swift, Seaforth Nature Reserve, May 2006. (Chris Galvin)

A scattering of individuals and occasional small parties are usually recorded during September, but, as in Oakes's day, October Swifts are scarce with no more than one or two reported in most autumns. Prolonged wet summers, however, are occasionally followed by an exceptional crop of late migrants, as juveniles fledge late. In 1978 up to 86 were on the Altcar Withins on 3 October and 80 at Lytham on the 7th, and there were single stragglers at Bootle on 8 November and at Warton, Carnforth, on the 12th. In 1985, after another miserable summer, three Swifts passed over Nelson on 6 November. There have been four other November records, at Blackpool on 14 November 1984 and nearby at Layton the next day, Fairhaven Lake on 7 November 2003, Sankey Valley, St. Helens on 5 November 2005 with one at Stalmine the following day, but the latest was of one flying south along the coast at Rossall on 4 December 1963.

There have been 90 recoveries of Swifts ringed in Lancashire, 67 within the county, 16 elsewhere in northern England, one each in southern England and Wales, one each in eastern France and south-west Spain, two in Morocco and one in the Republic of Congo; this last, ringed at Marton Mere on 25 June 1986 was shot near Kinshasa on 17 February 1992. Fifty-five birds ringed elsewhere in Britain have been recovered here, 50 from northern England, three from southern England and two from Wales.

BM, DJH.
This species account was sponsored by Chris Hawkins.

ALPINE SWIFT

Apus melba

Lancashire Category A. (1, 3).

Vagrant from southern Europe.

Mitchell and Oakes gave two records, of which one was in our present recording area: a bird killed near Preston in August 1879 which passed into the collection of Mr. P. Sefton of Baxenden and later into the Towneley Museum, Burnley.

There have been a further three accepted records. Our first modern record was found by Dave Owen in the Sankey Valley Park, St. Helens on 2 April 1985. There have been two subsequent singles: over the River Brock, near Claughton on 4 June 1990 and at Caton in the Lune Valley on 25 May 1992.

An earlier record at Whalley on 10-11 July 1964 has recently come to light; it was not submitted when first received in 1969 but has now been sent to the BBRC for adjudication.

SJW, MJ.
This species account was sponsored by Ribble Bird Tours (01253-407554).

LITTLE SWIFT

Apus affinis

Lancashire Category A. (0, 1).

Vagrant from North Africa.

The only record is of one found at Seaforth by Chris Kehoe in the late afternoon of 22 May 1984 as a sudden heavy shower brought in large numbers of hirundines and Swifts to feed over the freshwater pool. The bird fed low over the lagoon for some 30-45 minutes but had disappeared by the time other birdwatchers arrived.

The record was accepted by the BBRC as the sixth for Britain and Ireland. It remains the only record in north-west England.

SJW, MJ.
This species account was sponsored by Sam Pyefinch.

KINGFISHER

Alcedo atthis

Lancashire Category A.

Uncommon resident breeder.

The Kingfisher still suffered persecution in the late nineteenth century on account of the demand for its brilliant plumage for use in the millinery trade and the manufacture of fishing-flies. Mitchell considered it numerous, however, on all secluded streams. That the species may well have been commoner than it is today is suggested by Mitchell's tally of nine pairs in 1883 in a small area around Clitheroe where he lived. He listed the Wyre, Ribble, Cocker and Hodder as rivers with noteworthy populations but the Kingfisher was mainly a winter visitor to the south of the county; many moved to coastal areas in autumn.

When Oakes wrote his avifauna the Kingfisher had been hit hard by two very severe winters in rapid succession, in 1939/40 and 1946/47, but he was optimistic that a quick recovery was likely; he cited the same favoured rivers as Mitchell, with the addition of the Darwen, and noted several instances of breeding in the coastal west since 1930, including at Salwick, Marton and Lytham on the Fylde, and at Waterloo, Sefton and Lydiate in the south-west, as well as possible breeding at Formby Hall in 1936. Kingfishers were regular or occasional winter visitors to the Liverpool parks, Eccleston Mere and Carr Mill Dam in St Helens, and to tidal gutters at Crossens and Banks.

After a series of generally favourable winters during the 1950s Lancashire's Kingfishers were virtually wiped out by the long, hard freeze of 1962/63. In the spring of 1964 only one confirmed breeding pair was recorded in the county bird report – in the Preston area. Even as late as 1967 only a very slight recovery was evident, although a pair bred at Appley Bridge. The Kingfisher's breeding biology is, however, well-adapted to population recovery, with up to eight in a clutch and three broods in a season when food is abundant, and Spencer considered that the species was once again fairly common in the county by the early 1970s. More recent but less prolonged cold spells in early 1979 and 1981/82 had a less dramatic impact; although breeding was not recorded in the Chorley NHS area in 1982, up to five pairs bred in the following year.

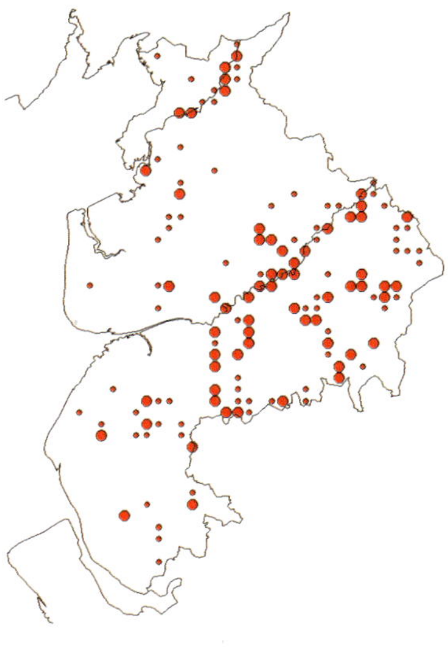

Breeding distribution of Kingfisher, 1997-2000. (Large dots: confirmed. Small dots: possible)

The present-day breeding distribution of the Kingfisher appears to differ only in detail from that outlined by Oakes. Changes to watercourses, involving straightening and shaping of banks, human recreational disturbance and the effects of agricultural and industrial effluents on fish-stocks may have had local detrimental effects, but, in compensation, a general improvement in water-quality in and near urban and industrial areas, especially in the east, has led to recolonisation of stretches of waterways previously abandoned. The Kingfisher, as a regular and fairly numerous breeder is, however, effectively confined to the north, east and centre of the county; nesting in the Fylde and the south-west is, as in Oakes's time, annual in small numbers.

Kingfishers were recorded in 136 tetrads (15%) in 1997-2000, their range virtually unchanged since 1968-72. The population was estimated at 100 pairs but this may have been a little conservative.

In the north the species is well-established on the Lune, Keer, Greta and Conder. The total population was estimated at 15 pairs at the end of the 1990s when an average of two to three pairs bred on the Lune with an exceptional six pairs in 1993 (Harrison 2000), but the Lune population increased to six pairs in 2002 and twelve in 2003. A pair bred on Carnforth Marsh in 1993 but this has not been repeated; breeding by one or a few pairs is regular in the Scorton area along the Wyre and on its tributary, the Brock.

The Ribble Valley and east Lancashire make up the Kingfisher's heartland; breeding takes place along virtually the whole length of the main river and its main tributaries, the Hodder, Calder and Darwen, accounting for perhaps as much as three-quarters of the Lancashire population. Kingfishers benefited from the clean-up of the Irwell system in Rossendale from the 1960s; the Limy and Whitewell, as well as the main river, have recorded confirmed or probable breeding since the mid-1970s, nesting took place in the Waterfoot area in 1977 and the species has nested regularly below Rawtenstall since 1980.

Kingfisher, Leighton Moss, September 2005. (Mike Malpass)

The Preston area is the Kingfisher's stronghold in central Lancashire, with regular or frequent nesting on the Ribble upstream of the city, and occasional breeding at Penwortham and in Avenham and Haslam Parks. Further south and east, in the Chorley area, breeding has occurred in recent years on the Douglas-Yarrow system, on the river Lostock at Farington and elsewhere around Leyland, and in Longworth Clough at Belmont.

In the south-west breeding Kingfishers remain scarce; single pairs nested at Mere Sands Wood in 1991 and 1998 and at Martin Mere in 1991 – and probably at both sites on and off since – and on the Leeds and Liverpool Canal at Lathom, Burscough and Halsall in several years since 1987. In the St. Helens area, after several years of presence in the breeding season, nesting was reported from Carr Mill Dam in 2002-05 and Eccleston Mere in 2003-05. Kingfishers have become regular nesters in the Fylde; breeding occurred in dykes on Lytham Moss and at Wesham in the 1950s, at

Poulton in 1977, 1978 and 1997, and on Woodplumpton Brook since 1970 and annually during 1984-87. Currently used sites include the River Brock west of the A6 and the Wyre near Churchtown and St. Michael's.

Although many birds remain within the breeding range all year, juveniles tend to disperse after fledging and many are recorded in autumn and winter on coastal and mossland waters around Morecambe Bay (particularly Leighton Moss and the Eric Morecambe complex) and throughout the Fylde and the south-west; canals, drainage ditches and sluices, urban park lakes, tidal creeks and even docks are visited. Early coastal arrivals sometimes occur during July but more usually from August to October. Many are transient occurrences, with birds remaining for a day or two before moving on, so the total number of Kingfishers involved in these dispersals is impossible to estimate with any confidence; some birds may become faithful to regular wintering-sites, however, as in the case of a bird at Seaforth and adjacent docks during 2000-05. Almost all Kingfishers leave the lowlands in early spring, presumably to return to traditional breeding areas.

Seven ringed Kingfishers have been recovered in Lancashire; four of these were local birds, none of which had moved further than 17 km. A juvenile ringed at Shipley, West Yorkshire on 28 June 1936 was found dead at Barley, near Pendle on 13 December 1937, another ringed in Barbondale, south Cumbria on 4 August 1931 was found dead on the River Lune at Lancaster on 31 October, and a first-winter ringed at Hale, Cheshire on 6 November 1988 was recovered, long dead, in St. Helens on 20 April 1989.

BM, DJH.
This species account was sponsored by Peter Ballentyne.

BEE-EATER

Merops apiaster

Lancashire Category A. (2, 5).

Vagrant from southern Europe.

A full page of Oakes's book is devoted to an account of the first Lancashire record published in *British Birds* 40: 180; this concerned two birds that frequented suburban gardens containing beehives at Ainsdale from 8 October to 7 November 1946.

In 1984 a bird flew over Anchorsholme Park, Cleveleys in the afternoon of 1 August; that evening it was seen perched not far away at Bispham Marsh before flying off north. The same bird was seen at Leighton Moss on the evening of 5 August and at Heysham Harbour and Middleton on the 8th.

The next two records were of birds seen and heard calling in flight, two at Hoghton, near Preston on 16 May 1988 and one at Lancaster on 29 September 1991. Finally, one was watched for several hours at Ainsdale NNR, perched and hawking insects over the dunes, on 16 May 2001. Unfortunately, this was during the height of the Foot and Mouth Disease crisis and only reserve staff could gain access.

SJW, MJ.
This species account was sponsored by Jan Stinger.

ROLLER

Coracias garrulus

Lancashire Category A. (2, 2).

Vagrant from southern Europe.

Two of the four records given by Mitchell and Oakes were in our present recording area. One was shot at Marsden Heights, near Burnley on 25 August 1848, and another at Blackpool in May 1868.

It was almost a century before the next was found at Ainsdale on 6-7 June 1963 by Peter Carah. The second modern record was a juvenile seen briefly in Watson Road Park, Blackpool on 30 September 1982 before flying off south; it was almost certainly the bird seen previously near Bassenthwaite Lake in Cumbria on 25-29 September.

SJW, MJ.
This species account was sponsored by Jan Stinger.

HOOPOE

Upupa epops

Lancashire Category A. (10, 42).

Rare passage migrant from southern and central Europe.

Mitchell listed about thirteen records in our present recording area. Oakes accepted seven of these as authentic and added singles at Wyresdale Park, Scorton in late October 1900, Tarleton Moss in 1905 and Southport on 14-15 October 1937.

Hoopoe, Halton, Lancaster, October 1998. (Steve Young)

There was then nearly a 20 year wait before the next, when, in the space of two years, three were seen on the Fylde. Singles were shot at Marton in 1954 and at Weeton in September or October 1955, and one was in a Blackpool garden from 3 to 8 October 1954. Hoopoes were then recorded in most years up to 2003 and with increasing frequency from around the mid-1980s. All records have been singles.

There have been 30 spring records since 1955, mostly between the middle of April and the middle of May but with extreme dates of 3 April 2001 at Billinge (Merseyside) and 11 June at Parbold in 1973 and Charnock Richard in 1997. Most of the twelve autumn records have been between mid-September and mid-October (Figure 1), with the earliest on 10 September 1986 at

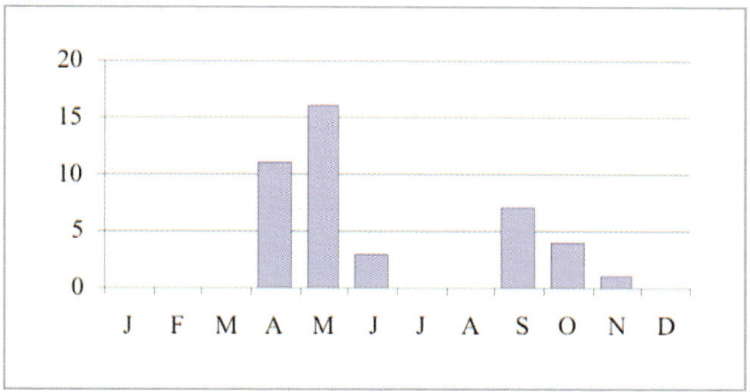

Figure 1. Monthly totals of Hoopoes in Lancashire, 1955-2005.

Crawshawbooth and the latest on 6 November 2001 in Fulwood.

Most have been one-day birds and the longest stayers were the 2001 Billinge bird which lingered until 7 April and one at Halton, Lancaster on 10-23 October 1998.

The vast majority of records are from the south-west, Fylde and central Lancashire, inland to Chorley, Preston and Scorton, with relatively few in the north. Further east, birds have been found at Salesbury, near Ribchester on 11 May 1981, Cant Clough Reservoir on 8 April 1984, Crawshawbooth on 10 September 1986, and Whitewell Bottoms, Rossendale on 5 May 1995 with probably the same bird at Clough Bottom on the 14th. Remarkably few appear on the coast – Heysham, Fleetwood, Lytham St. Anne's and Seaforth having just one record each, for example.

SJW, MJ.
This species account was sponsored by Maurice Wilby.

WRYNECK

Jynx torquilla

Lancashire Category A. (/, 44).

Rare passage migrant from continental Europe.

It is difficult for modern Lancashire birdwatchers to comprehend that Wrynecks once bred commonly in the county. Mitchell cited a local name, 'lang-tongue', indicating that it must have been a familiar sight to many and Riddiough (1812) described it as breeding commonly in the Ormskirk area. It seems that breeding numbers had begun to decline before the 1850s and by the end of the nineteenth century Mitchell described the Wryneck as 'being represented only by an odd specimen here and there, shot or picked up dead'.

Mitchell implied that its breeding distribution was fairly widespread but the only localities he mentioned were Frenchwood near Preston, Wyresdale and Stalmine, together with details of a nest with seven fresh eggs found in the trunk of an old wild apple tree at Winmarleigh in the second week of June 1883. This is the last published breeding record in Lancashire, though a nest of six eggs was found (and collected!) at Heaton Park, Manchester on 1 June 1912.

Wryneck, Seaforth Nature Reserve, September 2006. (Steve Young)

Oakes published records of singles at Heysham on 3 September 1908, at Overton on 2 October the same year and at Yealand Conyers on the early date of 28 March 1948. The 1950s produced just two records and the 1960s three, but since then there has been an average of just over one a year. All records have been of singles and there has never been any significant influx; the highest annual totals have been three in 1981, 1986 and 1996.

Spring occurrences are rare with just four in addition to the 1948 record, the earliest at Hesketh Golf Course, Southport on 1 May 1981 and the latest at Leighton Moss on 11-19 June 1980. The earliest in autumn was trapped on 22 August 1970 at Leighton Moss; most arrive during September (Figure 1), with the latest at Cockersands on 19 October 1995.

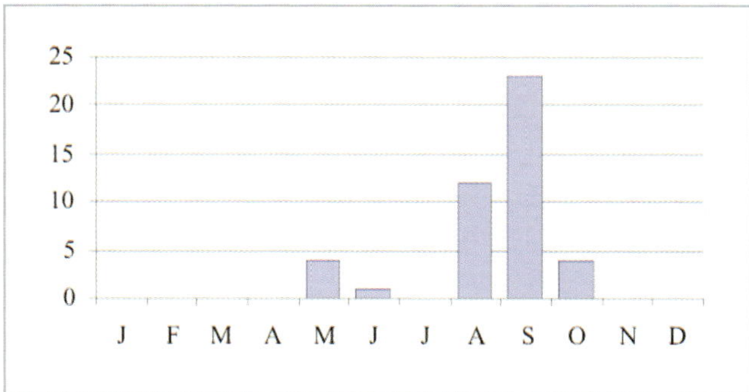

Figure 1. Monthly totals of Wrynecks in Lancashire, 1958-2005.

Like Hoopoes, Wrynecks can turn up almost anywhere, an extreme example being one found in a basement garage of Preston police station on 22 August 1973. A total of 16 has been recorded inland, in the Chorley and Preston areas, Bowland, east Lancashire, Rossendale and at Inskip. However, they appear to show a slightly stronger affinity for the main coastal watchpoints with six recorded at Formby Point/Hightown and five at Heysham.

SJW, MJ
This species account was sponsored by Bill Curtis.

GREEN WOODPECKER

Picus viridis

Lancashire Category A.

Fairly common resident breeder.

Green Woodpeckers feed on the ground, mainly on adult ants and their pupae; accordingly, they prefer open woodland with clearings, and edges adjacent to farmland, heaths and scrub. Such habitat is rare in the Lancashire Plain and Green Woodpeckers have probably always been scarce in the west and south-west.

A steady northward expansion of the national breeding range that began in the 1920s has continued steadily and the British population increased by 115% during 1970-2001 (CBC) and by 31% during 1994-2005 (BBS) – a trend which has been reflected in Lancashire.

Mitchell described the Green Woodpecker as having been common in Lancashire in the early eighteenth century but rare in the 1880s, with regular nesting only in the Preston area and odd records elsewhere in well-wooded districts. By the 1950s, however, the species had become a widely-distributed though local resident, following an increase in numbers since about 1930 according to Oakes. It was particularly well-established in the north, in the Lune and Ribble Valleys; the increase in the south of the county had been much less marked, and breeding had yet to be recorded in the Fylde. Spencer (1973) noted a further period of expansion in the 1940s and 1950s, which had been halted and in places reversed, by the 1962/63 winter; although Green Woodpeckers were still numerous from the Ribble Valley northwards, they were very scarce further south.

The 1997-2000 survey estimated a total Lancashire population of 200 pairs; birds were recorded in 172 tetrads, or 18% of the county, but in only three tetrads in the western third of the county south of the Lune.

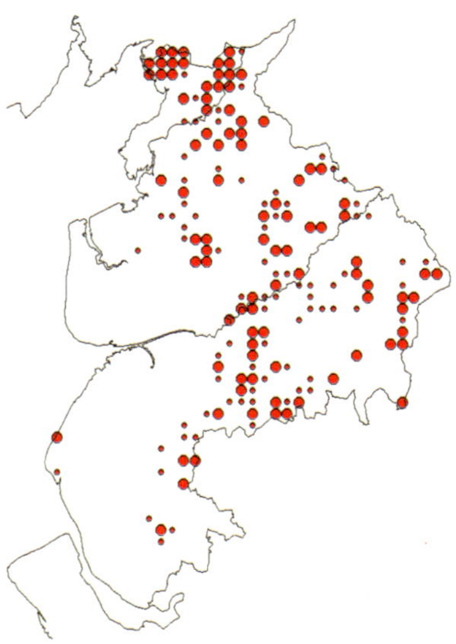

Breeding distribution of Green Woodpecker, 1997-2000. (Large dots: confirmed. Small dots: possible)

North Lancashire remains the stronghold. Green Woodpeckers are most common in the Silverdale-Warton-Yealand area, in the Keer Valley east to the Lune, and along the river upstream of Arkholme, where up to three pairs have bred annually since the 1970s. Casual visits to Heysham have been virtually annual since 1996. The species is also a widely-distributed and regular breeder in the wooded valleys of north Bowland as far south as Dunsop Bridge, Whitewell and the Gisburn Forest, but is less regular on the western edge of the fells, in Grizedale and the Wyre and Brock Valleys. In the Ribble Valley breeding is more or less regular from the northern and eastern outskirts of Preston to Longridge, the Pendle area and Blackburn; further east, several pairs breed in the Burnley area, particularly at Cliviger, Hurstwood and Wood End. A marked range expansion into Rossendale began in the early 1980s; a bird at Stubbins in late 1981 was the first in the area for several years, and nesting was recorded in Lumb Vale and the Irwell Valley in 1986. In 1989 a pair bred at Crawshawbooth and further expansion was observed from the early 1990s, with more-or-less annual breeding at Musbury Vale, Hare Clough, Whitworth, Grane and Healey Dell; presence was recorded at twelve locations in the region in 2002.

Tony Disley

From Leyland south to the West Pennine Moors the population of Green Woodpeckers has fluctuated considerably in recent decades. They were described as 'increasing' in the late 1970s and present at 16 sites in the Chorley NHS region in 1984, but by 1989, when confirmed breeding was recorded only at Brindle, no pairs were present in Roddlesworth Plantations where there had been three in 1986. Further declines were reported in the Rivington area in 1992, but by 2000 they were described as reoccupying former haunts, and birds were present at ten locations in the region in 2002; two pairs again nested at Roddlesworth in 2003. The Belmont/Delph/Entwistle area was (re)colonised in 1985 with up to three pairs annually since.

Apart from a small, isolated outpost in the Formby-Ainsdale pinewoods – which dates from at least the early 1980s and where the numerous links golf courses probably provide a crucial feeding resource – Green Woodpeckers are at best scarce and irregular nesters on the south-west plain. Occasionally a series of sightings raises hopes of range expansion, but these almost invariably peter out without a result. There were occasional records at Billinge Hill Quarry, near Rainford in 1984 and 1987, at Mere Sands Wood in 1985-86 and at Hilldale, Parbold in 2001. Only in the Knowsley Park and St. Helens area is there evidence of a possible breeding foothold, with increasingly frequent sightings, especially at Prescot Reservoirs, since 2000. On the Fylde, at least intermittent nesting occurred at Lytham Hall from the early 1950s to the mid-1960s; since then birds have been recorded there in 1978, 1982, 1984, 1986-87 and 1988-89, with breeding considered possible in 1987. Elsewhere in the area Green Woodpeckers are merely scarce and irregular visitors, recorded between 1980 and 2003 at Ribby Hall (several times), Marton Mere, Singleton, Bispham Marsh, Rawcliffe Hall, Ingol, Blackpool and Freckleton Naze.

Green Woodpeckers occasionally turn up at coastal migration watchpoints, particularly at Heysham, while Seaforth recorded its first in April 2003, but given the species' highly sedentary habits there is no reason to suspect that these are other than locally-based wanderers.

BM, DJH.

This species account was sponsored by Brian Hugo.

GREAT SPOTTED WOODPECKER

Dendrocopos major

Lancashire Category A.

Common resident breeder.

The Great Spotted Woodpecker has provided one of the major avian success stories of the late twentieth century. Nationally, it has undergone major changes in distribution in recent centuries, having withdrawn entirely from Scotland and northern England in the eighteenth and early nineteenth centuries, but recovering all the ground lost in an expansion that began around 1870 and continued throughout the twentieth century. The British population grew by 185% during 1970-2001 (CBC) and by 120% during 1994-2005 (BBS) – all available evidence suggests that the Lancashire population has at least equalled these increases.

Mitchell's account gave an impression of general scarcity although he listed Ormskirk, Knowsley, Roddlesworth, Redscar, Witton Park, Whalley, Claughton and unspecified locations in Bowland as places where breeding had been recorded during the nineteenth century. By Oakes's day a substantial population increase and range extension had certainly taken place; he described the Great Spotted Woodpecker as 'well distributed' and 'present in almost every suitable woodland north of the Ribble, while its scarcity in some southern districts is merely in proportion to the cover available'. The densest populations were found along the lower Ribble Valley between Red Scar and Mitton Bridge, but breeding took place in all the Ribble woodlands to the county boundary and the species was common in the Wyre Valley and parts of the Fylde. The Lune Valley, however, had been colonised only recently and the species was scarce in the Silverdale area; in the south, a post-war increase was noted in the Kirkby-Knowsley area and recent breeding had been recorded at Formby Hall, Ince Blundell, Scarisbrick and Haydock. In the centre and east of the county the bird was present in urban parks in Blackburn and Burnley, and in the Wrightington and Rivington areas; local movements were regularly observed in winter.

There appears to have been no major Lancashire range extension since the 1950s but, although some local declines have been reported periodically, the overall population has increased significantly as gaps within the range have been infilled and breeding densities increased. The 1997-2000 survey estimated a total population of 900 pairs, breeding in 62% of the county's tetrads. Only the highest, most treeless tracts of Bowland, some arable farming areas in the lowlands and densely built-up urban areas were without breeding Great Spotted Woodpeckers.

The most conspicuous expansion has been in Rossendale; only two or three breeding pairs were confirmed in 1981-82 but by 1991 nesting was recorded in seven locations and by 1994-95 Great Spotted Woodpeckers were described as breeding in all suitable woodlands and still spreading. Colonisation of less optimal habitats may have been facilitated by the species' adoption of garden feeders. In 2002-3 three pairs bred in Staghills Wood and nesting was confirmed in up to five other locations.

In east Lancashire Great Spotted Woodpeckers were reported to be increasing in the Burnley area in 1991; in 1998 five pairs bred at Stocks Reservoir and breeding occurred in virtually every stretch of woodland of any size in the region during 1997-2000. The species is widespread in the north, and since Oakes's time has become common in the Silverdale area; at Arkholme, after a decline to two pairs in the 1970s, four pairs nested in 1995-96 and five annually since 2000. Great Spotted Woodpeckers are also well-distributed, and locally numerous, in the Chorley area, with evidence of a general increase since about 1990; in 2003 a survey of Roddlesworth Plantations (a site also mentioned by Mitchell) located 16 territories, and up to 28 pairs bred in the Anglezarke-Rivington woods in 2002-05.

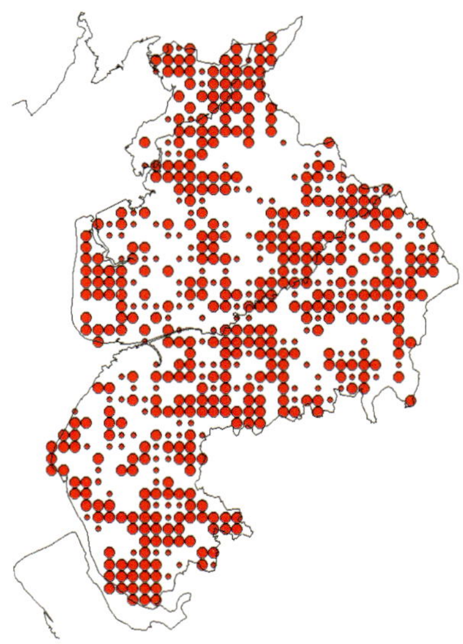

Breeding distribution of Great Spotted Woodpecker, 1997-2000.
(Large dots: confirmed. Small dots: possible)

The lack of extensive tracts of woodland in the Fylde has not deterred expansion there, and the 1997-2000 survey confirmed breeding in 36 tetrads. In the south-west, where at least 15 pairs were estimated to be nesting in 1987, thirteen bred in south Liverpool alone in 1994 and 2002, and up to five pairs nest annually in Mere Sands Wood. There are at least six pairs in the Ainsdale-Formby pinewoods, and breeding on or near Hesketh Golf Course, Marshside has been annual since 1993.

Great Spotted Woodpecker, Little Crosby, November 2004. (Steve Young)

British Great Spotted Woodpeckers belong to the subspecies *pinetorum* and are highly sedentary. Of 14 recoveries of Lancashire-ringed birds, only one had moved further than 10 km from the original site, while just one ringed elsewhere in northern England has been recovered here. Scandinavian populations are, however, subject to periodic autumn eruptions and significant influxes into Britain were recorded in 1949 and 1962; most were seen on the east coast, but small numbers have reached Ireland at such times, and it is highly likely that Lancashire sees a proportion of these visitors. In most autumns a few birds, apparently on passage, are recorded at coastal watchpoints, often moving with tits, thrushes and other migrant passerines. In recent years most have been seen at Heysham, Rossall Point-Fleetwood, Marshside-Crossens and, especially, at Fairhaven, where 14 were recorded between late September and mid-November in 1990, and 20 between 23 September and 5 November in 2002. There were seven late-autumn records at Heysham in 1995 and nine in 2004. The largest single movement was 13 flying north-east with Redwings at Marshside on 9 October 2004; two clinging to the seaward wall of the lighthouse cottage at Cockersands on 22 October 2004 were fairly certainly migrants.

The only clue to the origins of at least some of these coastal birds is provided by an individual trapped at Heysham in late November 2001 which had a wing-length consistent with the nominate Scandinavian subspecies.

BM, DJH

This species account was sponsored by Bill Curtis.

LESSER SPOTTED WOODPECKER

Dendrocopos minor

Lancashire Category A.

Rare resident breeder.

Lancashire's Lesser Spotted Woodpeckers have probably always been close to the edge of their national breeding range and, together with the outpost in Cumbria (Stott *et al.* 2002), our small population now forms the most north-westerly in Britain. It is, therefore, fragile and highly sensitive to factors affecting populations in the core range. Breeding has probably never been anything other than very scarce in the county but the past 100 years or so have seen a moderate increase followed by a more recent downward spiral.

The Lesser Spotted Woodpecker was a very rare resident in Lancashire in the late nineteenth century; Mitchell knew only of records from Red Scar, Preston and from Feniscowles, near Blackburn, and confirmed breeding at Claughton-on-Brock in 1883. Oakes noted some spread and increase in the population since 1900, citing confirmed or probable nesting at Read and Haydock in 1944 and near Preston in 1947, with others present at Mitton Wood, on the Brock and at Hoghton Bottoms since 1936. Spencer (1973), commenting that proof of breeding was difficult to obtain, considered that pairs had bred in at least a dozen locations at some time since 1950, while odd birds could turn up almost anywhere in autumn or winter.

Since the 1970s the picture has been broadly consistent across the three core breeding areas, Chorley/Blackburn, north Lancashire and the Ribble Valley: regular confirmed or probable nesting at a small number of sites, with fairly frequent reports of breeding-season presence at other locations and odd, one-off breeding records elsewhere. Overall, however, there is strong evidence of a decline in numbers since the late 1990s.

This conforms closely to the national picture; numbers increased appreciably over much of the British range in the 1970s, probably due to the increase in insects and larvae provided by dead and dying trees following the spread of Dutch elm disease, but from the early 1980s, as the elms disappeared from the landscape, numbers returned to their former level. The decline in the British population was estimated at 81% during 1966-1999 (CBC) but the species is now so scarce that no national survey can monitor current trends; the national population is estimated at 1,400-2,900 pairs (Baker *et al.* 2006). The reasons for the national crash are poorly understood but two main hypotheses have been advanced: competition with and nest-predation by the increasing population of Great Spotted Woodpeckers, and changes in the abundance of dead wood and dead-wood invertebrates (Fuller *et al.* 2005). There have, however, been few if any obvious changes in the extent or management of broad-leaved woodland in Lancashire for several decades, so, if the problem is one of habitat quality, it is a subtle one.

There were breeding season sightings in 54 tetrads (6%) during the 1997-2000 Lancashire survey but breeding was only thought to be proven or probable in 18 and the population was estimated at 40 pairs. However, only ten sightings were reported all year in 2002, eleven in 2003, six in 2004 and eight in 2005. Although this may in part be due to an understandable reluctance to disclose what may turn out to be their final breeding sites in the county, there is general agreement that extinction may not be far away.

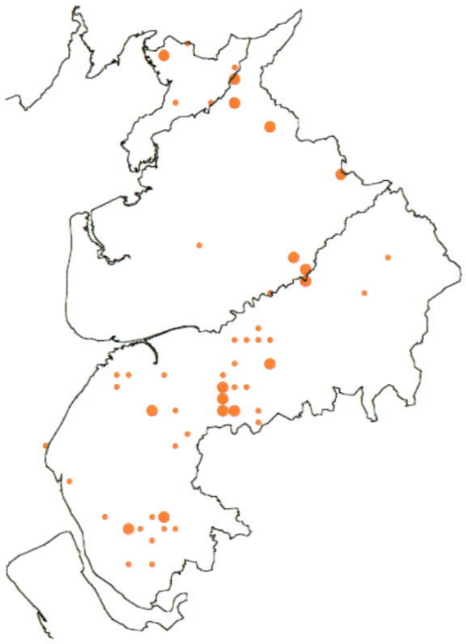

Breeding distribution of Lesser Spotted Woodpecker, 1997-2000. (Large dots: confirmed. Small dots: possible)

Since the 1980s at least the Chorley-Leyland area, especially the Yarrow Valley woodlands, has been the Lesser Spotted Woodpecker's Lancashire stronghold. Two or three pairs bred annually in Worden Park, Leyland in the early 1960s and nesting became established in the woods to the south and west of Chorley during the 1980s. In 1985 presence was recorded at Brinscall, Leyland, Chorley, Hoghton Bottoms and Yarrow and Anglezarke Reservoirs; by 1990 at least four pairs were breeding annually in the Chorley NHS region, and five confirmed plus one probable nesting pair were recorded in 1996. The species was reported to have occupied several new sites, including Gillibrand, by 1998, and in 2000 Lesser Spotted Woodpeckers were recorded there and at Duxbury, Withnell Fold, Birkacre, Astley Park, Burgh Hall Wood, Adlington, Shaw Hill and Brinscall. Although breeding was not confirmed at any site, it is likely that most if not all these breeding-season reports involved territorial birds. Since 2001 a marked decrease in reported sightings suggests that at least a temporary local decline may be underway; suspected breeding only was reported in the Heskin-Eccleston area of Chorley in 2004.

In the north of the county intermittent breeding took place in the Silverdale-Leighton Moss area in the 1960s and 1970s, and fairly frequent records during the 1980s and less regular sightings since suggest that a small breeding population may persist there. In 1978 three pairs bred at Arkholme on the Lune with one or more there annually until 1996 but, apart from a single pair at Melling in 2000, breeding has not been confirmed in the Lune Valley since. South of Lancaster, nesting was recorded intermittently at Scorton and Street Bridge on the middle Wyre between the early 1960s and the early 1990s; since then occasional sightings, most recently of a male at Ellel Grange in spring 2003, again raise the possibility of a continuing breeding foothold.

In Mitchell's and Oakes's days the Preston area was a breeding nucleus for Lesser Spotted Woodpeckers, and between the 1960s and mid-1990s confirmed or probable nesting was reported from the Broughton area, Grimsargh, Samlesbury, Red Scar and Penwortham; further north, in the Brock Valley at Claughton, Bilsborrow and Waddecar breeding was considered likely in the early-to-mid 1990s, and infrequent sight records have persisted, although reports from the Preston area generally have dwindled dramatically since the early 1990s.

Further east, breeding season records have come from the Ribble Valley and along its tributaries, in particular at Mitton Wood, Witton Country Park, Read, Ribchester, Whalley, Clitheroe, Bolton-by-Bowland, Blacko and Altham, with many scattered records elsewhere, both within and outside the breeding season. East Lancashire may now contain the majority of the county's dwindling population of Lesser Spotted Woodpeckers and supported the only confirmed breeding record – at an undisclosed site – in 2005. In Rossendale, however, there have been only three recent records: single birds at Haslingden in November 1983, at Stacksteads in September 1996 and King's Hillock Wood in February and March 2005.

In the Fylde and the south-west Lesser Spotted Woodpeckers are at best intermittent and increasingly scarce breeders. Lytham Hall was an established nesting-site between 1951 and 1991, with two pairs present in some years. Breeding was recorded at Cockerham in 1972 and at Salwick in 1982; increasingly frequent spring records led to the species being described as 'becoming established' in the 1987 county bird report, with confirmed or probable nesting at Lytham, Poulton, Ribby Hall and Out Rawcliffe. Since then, however, sightings at all times of year have decreased dramatically and there have been no instances of confirmed breeding in the region since 1991.

Lesser Spotted Woodpecker, Mere Sands Wood, February 1987. (Steve Young)

In the south-west a pair bred in Croxteth Country Park in 1974; annual nesting here and at Knowsley Park has been considered probable since then, and the species bred in Sefton Park, Liverpool in the 1980s, when nesting was also considered likely at Ince Blundell and Crosby Woods. The species was discovered in the Mere Sands Wood-Rufford area around 1983 and nesting by a single pair was virtually annual at the former site between 1986 and 1996, but has become increasingly irregular since; breeding probably took place in 2001, but there have been no confirmed records subsequently. Nesting was thought probable at Scarisbrick Hall in 1986 and 1994, and was confirmed at Lathom, near Burscough in 1989.

Autumn and winter records of Lesser Spotted Woodpeckers are widespread, though scarce and unpredictable; birds have occasionally been recorded far from known breeding areas, as at Formby Point in April 2000, and individuals occasionally turn up at bird-tables and feeders in urban and suburban areas.

BM, DJH.
This species account was sponsored by Mike Robinson and John Wright.

WOODLARK

Lullula arborea

Lancashire Category A. (/, 1).

Vagrant from southern Britain or continental Europe.

Mitchell described the Woodlark as a formerly common resident breeding bird in many parts of Lancashire and blamed the incessant pursuit by professional bird-catchers for its increasing scarcity. Twenty or so years previously (c.1860), it was noted as plentiful near Liverpool and Prescot, in Wyresdale and at Samlesbury. However, Coward in the 1921 LCFC Report described Mitchell's contention that Woodlarks were once plentiful as "of uncertain foundation" and noted the common confusion with Tree Pipit.

Oakes glossed over the issue of breeding in the county but if Woodlarks had indeed been regular breeders during the nineteenth century they would have been on the very edge of the their British breeding range in Lancashire. This had contracted into southern and south-eastern England by the twentieth century but began to expand again during the 1990s as a result of a long run of warmer winters and the availability of more suitable breeding habitat, especially in clear-felled conifer plantations. By the early years of this century they were established as regular breeding birds in Yorkshire and it is perhaps just a matter of time before we (re)gain the Woodlark as a breeding species.

Very few Woodlarks have been reported in Lancashire during the past 100 years and hardly any have been fully substantiated. One was reported feeding with Greenfinches on spent hops at Livesey, near Blackburn on 13 December 1890 and another near Nelson on 17 December 1928 (BB 22: 210) but Oakes thought that the evidence was inconclusive. Further reports include one feeding amongst oat-straw spread for cattle at Wennington on 25 January 1945, one flying south at Formby on 12 October 1956 and three feeding in fields there on 16 October that year.

There have been only two records in the last thirty years. One was reported on Kirkby Moss on 20 January 1974 but not published in the Lancashire Bird Report, while another flew south, calling, over Heysham on 23 March 1996 – this latter remains our only fully-documented record.

SJW, MJ.
This species account was sponsored by Sarah Louise Jones.

SKYLARK

Alauda arvensis

Lancashire Category A.

Abundant breeder and passage migrant.

Mitchell described the Skylark as 'universally distributed' and 'one of our commonest birds'. He devoted most of his account to describing how 'thousands are sent to markets, caught on the mosses and sand-hills' through the use of various traps, noting one bird-catcher's haul of 95 dozen in a fortnight on Tarleton Moss in 1890/91.

Breeding birds remained abundant and almost ubiquitous in Oakes's day 'from within a few yards of high-water mark on the low-lying parts of the coast to the tops of the high moors', and apparently uncommon only in the upper Lune Valley. Their calamitous decline in the last quarter of the twentieth century in the wake of agricultural intensification must, then, have seemed unthinkable to an earlier generation of birdwatchers. Nationally, 55% disappeared between 1975 and 1994 (Chamberlain & Crick 1999) and the species underwent a further 13% decline from 1994 to 2005 (BBS).

For some time those studying the fate of the Skylark thought these losses were largely confined to lowland agricultural areas, where the main cause has been the switch from spring to autumn-sowing of cereals, but it is clear that, in Lancashire at least, an equally severe decline has been taking place in the uplands, where dramatically increased levels of sheep-grazing are probably the major culprit. The situation on The Hile, where numbers shrank by 75% in less than 20 years, was probably representative of similar upland sites (see Figure 1). Higher stocking rates have also been implicated in similar declines on saltmarshes, particularly in north Lancashire, even on land under conservation management. Long runs of data are largely lacking but Marshside, where breeding pairs have declined from around 120 in 1983 to 20 in 2005, is perhaps typical.

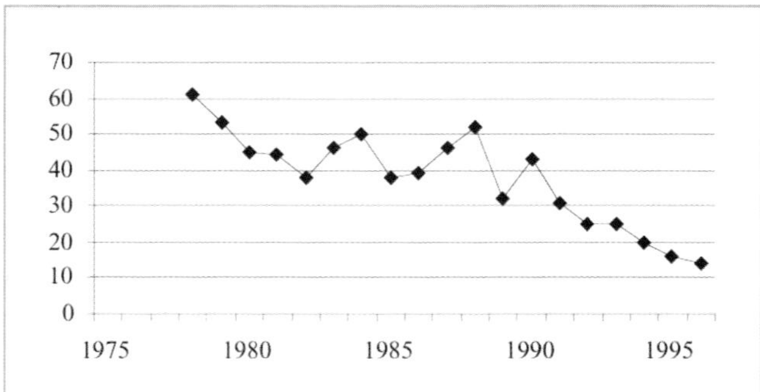

Figure 1. Number of breeding Skylarks (pairs) on The Hile CBC plot, Rossendale, 1978-96 (E. Ward)

These population declines are not yet reflected in changes in broad-scale distribution; Skylarks bred in all 10km squares and 75% of the county's tetrads during 1997-2000 and were absent only from urban areas, predominantly heather moorland and heavily wooded locations. Almost 5,000 singing males were counted during the Lancashire Atlas survey and a population of at least 8,000 pairs was estimated. Breeding densities were highest in the south and west Pennine uplands (an average of 10.6 counted per tetrad), and the south-west mosslands (11.4 per tetrad), and lowest in the Ribble and Lune Valleys and Bowland; densities varied enormously with the top two tetrads holding 88 and 120 singing males. Skylarks are beginning to be lost, however, from the more marginal areas of the breeding range; in north Lancashire, for example, they had disappeared from 20% of tetrads between 1986-93 and 1997-2000, a range contraction of about 15%, although some areas still hold moderate densities – 8 pairs per km^2 on Caton Moor, for example.

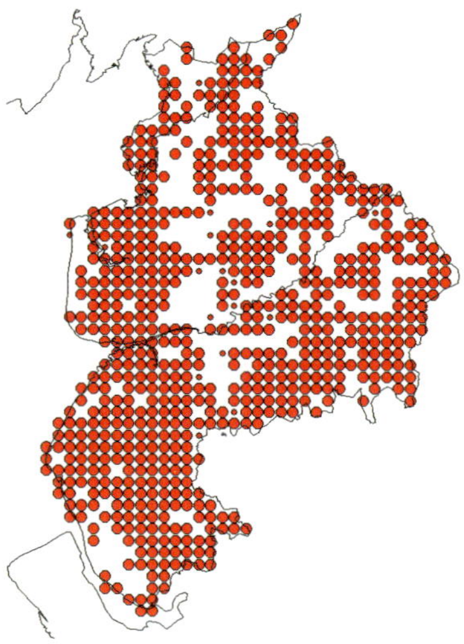

Breeding distribution of Skylark, 1997-2000. (Large dots: confirmed. Small dots: possible)

Birds begin to leave the upland areas in early July and few remain after the end of September; some September birds may be on passage. Southbound migrants begin to appear at all the main watchpoints in early to mid-September and passage continues until mid-November. The peak movement invariably occurs in October when birds are seen most mornings; notable recent counts include 450 south at Heysham in one hour on 10 October 1988, 600 at Seaforth on 15 October 1990 with 800 there on 6 October 1991 and 500 on 8 October 1995, 630 at Marshside on 10 October 1993 and 354 at Marton Mere on 14 October 1995. All these were, however, put into the shade by the 1,550 that flew east in 30 minutes over Fluke Hall, Pilling in the company of exceptional numbers of Redwings on 9 October 2004 (Roberts & White 2006). Large autumn movements are also occasionally picked up further inland, for example 300 at Martin Mere on 28 October 1995.

Numbers seen on coastal visible migration watches vary enormously between years but have declined significantly in the last decade. Day-counts of 1,000 or more were regular at Marshside during the 1970s and 1980s but are usually in the low hundreds nowadays (McCarthy 2001). Minimum autumn totals at Seaforth ranged from 100 (in 1999) to 2,750 (in 1990) during 1990-2004 and declined by almost 75% during this period, from an average of 1,560 in 1990-95 to 475 in 2000-05 (Figure 2). Heysham totals appear rather more stable, averaging around 200 during 1993-2003.

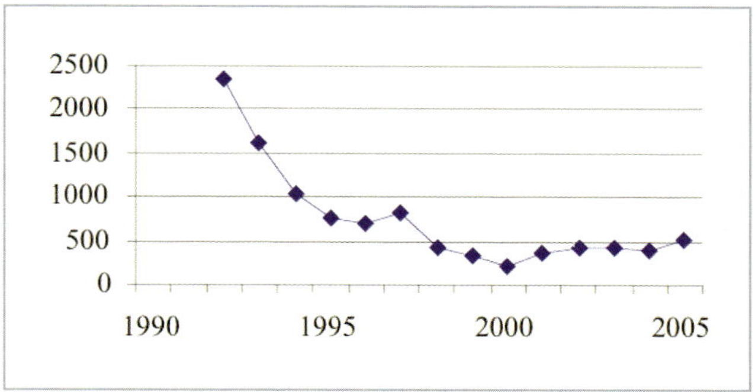

Figure 2. Estimated totals of autumn passage (September to November) Skylarks (3-year rolling means) at Seaforth Nature Reserve, 1990 to 2005.

From November to February only small numbers are usually recorded in the eastern half of the county and double-figure winter flocks are fairly unusual, the largest in recent years being 30 at Parsonage Reservoir on 31 December 1996.

The vast majority winter on farmland in the south-west and the Fylde, and especially on coastal saltmarshes. Flocks of 100 or more are regularly noted on the outer estuaries of the Lune, Wyre, Ribble and Mersey, with notable recent counts including 400 at Barnaby's Sands in January 1993, 1,200 on Rawcliffe Moss in February 1994 and up to 2,000 at Marshside/Crossens in 1995/96 – when 1,000 were also on the north bank of the Ribble at Warton Marsh – and again in January 1998, and 427 at Oglet in December 1995. As at other seasons, winter numbers have greatly declined, exemplified by Marshside/Crossens, where 6,000 were seen on the saltmarshes as recently as February 1986 but with 400-600 the norm since the late 1990s.

Large farmland flocks have included 300-600 at various Over Wyre sites in 1984, 1993 and 2000, 400 at Martin Mere in February 1997 and 1,000 in the Rufford area in December 1996. Severe spells of winter weather may result in large movements, including vast numbers at Crossens in January and February 1979, many small parties totalling 500 birds on St. Anne's beach on 14 December 1981 and an offshore passage of 90 in three hours at Blackpool the same day.

Singing male Skylark, Southport. (Mike McKavett)

The return to the upland areas may begin in mid-January in mild winters, but more usually from the first week of February, with peak arrivals during the second half of March. Recurrence of cold weather may cause flocks to re-group locally and there may be some larger scale movements, for example 1,200 flying west in snowy conditions over Leighton Moss on 22 March 1980. Coastal passage in spring has always been much lighter than in autumn and has likewise declined during the past 10-15 years. The largest recent count was 360 at Marshside on 21-22 March 1993 and most watchpoints rarely record more than daily single figures these days. Small numbers are also recorded inland at this time of year – 80 at Towneley on 7 March 1995 were exceptional, but it is unclear if this was a cold weather or passage movement.

The majority of the English population belongs to the nominate race which breeds throughout most of northern and central Europe but birds breeding in north-west England, Scotland and Ireland are subspecies *scotica*. It seems likely that most migrant Skylarks moving through Lancashire are also *scotica* but smaller numbers of *arvensis* from continental Europe may be involved in some late autumn movements. It seems likely that the large movement with Redwings over Pilling on 9 October 2004, for example, may have involved continental *arvensis*.

Ringing recoveries shed no light on this; there have been no recorded movements of ringed birds between Lancashire and abroad. Of 35 recoveries of Lancashire-ringed Skylarks just six have been further than 10km and only two more than 100km: a pullus recovered in winter on Anglesey three years later in 1976, and an adult ringed on 20 January 1967 and recovered in Warwickshire on 30 March the same year. Only one bird ringed outside of the county has been recovered in Lancashire; this was from northern England.

SJW, RW.

This species account was sponsored by John Bannon.

SHORELARK

Eremophila alpestris

Lancashire Category A. (*I*, 74).

Scarce winter visitor from Fennoscandia.

The only one of Mitchell's records in our present recording area related to eight birds captured in gin traps set for Skylarks on the coast at Formby in early September 1882. The specimens were later examined by T.A. Coward. The date of this record is exceptional, with no modern record occurring before 14 October. In December 1899 one was shot at Oxcliffe near Lancaster and two were reported shot at Ainsdale in 1908.

After one at Ainsdale in December 1920 no more records were published until a single on Fairhaven shore from 8 December 1963 to 13 March 1964. At least 35 records involving an estimated 73 birds followed between 1963 and 2005 (Figure 1). Shorelarks were seen in most years between 1963 and 1983 but in only eleven between 1984 and 2005, with the period 1984-93 being a particularly lean spell. Five or more were recorded in just four years, 1966 (8), 1976 (6), 1980 (10) and 1998 (11).

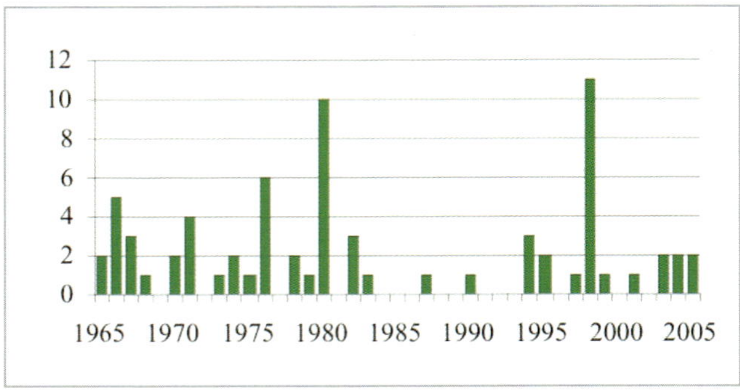

Figure 1. Annual totals of Shorelarks in Lancashire, 1965-2005.

The vast majority have been on the southern coasts where they feed in sparse vegetation or, more usually, along the strandline.

Notable concentrations include five at Fairhaven during winter 1966/67, four at Ainsdale from 1 December 1971 to 2 February 1972, five at Seaforth on 6 February 1976 with six there on 31 October 1980, and four on Hesketh Out Marsh from 9 November 1980 to 22 March 1981. The species is remarkably scarce on the coast north of Blackpool, with two at Rossall Point on 13 February 1970 and singles at the Carnforth slag tips on 15 January 1968, 19 February to 1 March 1975, 2-9 April 1997 and 22 November 1998 the only records.

Shorelark, Starr Gate, Blackpool, December 2003. (Steve Young)

The first inland record was near Stocks Reservoir on 23 February 1987, followed by one with Snow Buntings on Pendle Hill on 16-17 December 1990 and another there on 29-31 October 1994. There were two at Moss Quarry, Whitworth in Rossendale on 26-27 January 1995 and, finally, one at Fazakerley Reedbed, Liverpool on 16 December 2001.

All recent records fall within the period mid-October to the end of March with the exception of one on the Carnforth slag tips on 2-9 April 1997 (Figure 2). New arrivals are distributed fairly evenly between October, November and December and probably about a third settle in for the winter. Only two have been first recorded during January and both may have been local movements, but the ten 'new arrivals' in February perhaps indicate dispersal from more distant locations. All British records are believed to refer to the subspecies *flava* which breeds in Fennoscandia and western Russia.

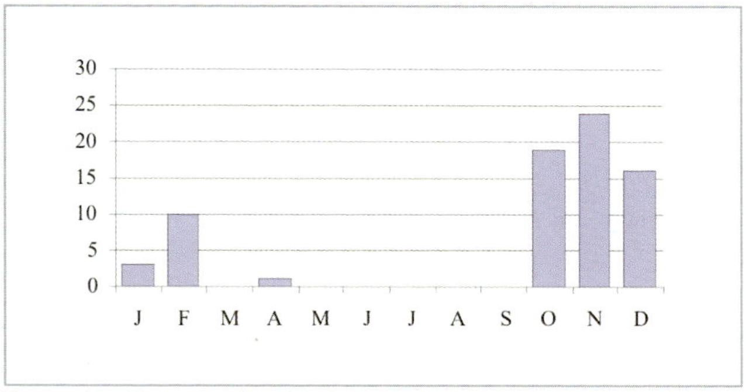

Figure 2. Monthly totals of Shorelarks in Lancashire, 1963-2005

SJW, MJ.

This species account was sponsored by Margaret Shields.

SAND MARTIN

Riparia riparia

Lancashire Category A.

Common breeder and passage migrant.

Both Mitchell and Oakes described the species as a common though localised summer visitor. In Oakes's time the main breeding colonies were along the courses of the Ribble, Lune and Wyre and their tributaries, and on the Irwell. He mentioned one colony that nested in a quarry at 600 feet (200m) asl and two miles from water 'in the eastern fells'. Breeding had not been recorded for some years in north Rossendale and breeding Sand Martins were rare in the Fylde and the south-west, although one colony persisted in the banks of the peat-cuttings on Formby Moss, where three colonies had existed in the late nineteenth century (Wrigley 1892), until at least 1921 and ten pairs nested in sand dunes at Cloven-le-Dale, Formby in 1923.

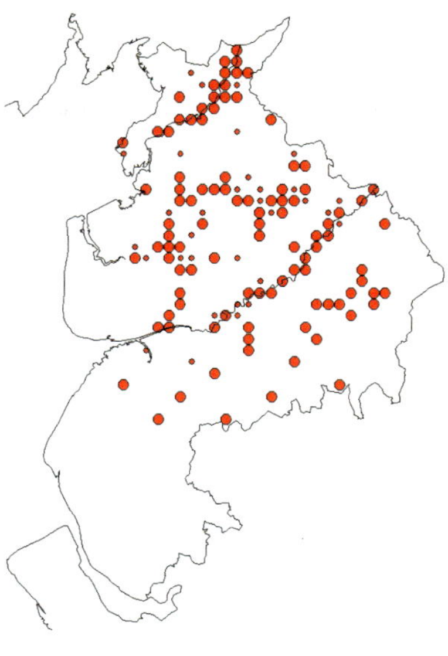

Breeding distribution of Sand Martin, 1997-2000. (Large dots: confirmed. Small dots: possible)

Sand Martin populations are subject to periodic, apparently cyclical, increases and declines, attributed mainly to rainfall levels in the wintering areas. A general increase in numbers in Europe in the mid-1960s was followed by a severe population crash during 1968-72; partial recovery in the late 1970s was followed in turn by a slump in 1983-84, a strong recovery in the late 1980s, another severe decline in 1991-92 and a return to relatively robust population levels after 1994. Numbers have, however, not recovered to pre-1968 levels.

Broadly speaking, the Lancashire population appears to have followed these national trends, although purely local factors such as riverbank erosion and modifications, the development of new sand-pits, flooding and spring weather have also been influential. However, the Lancashire breeding range declined by roughly 20% (from 35 to 28 10km squares) between 1968-72 and 1997-2000, when occupied nest-holes were found in 132 (14%) tetrads and the population was estimated at 3,500 pairs. With recent declines on the Lune at least, this is probably fewer than 3,000 now. The general distribution, however, remains very similar to that of Oakes's day.

Although artificial sites, especially working sand quarries, play an increasingly important role, a large majority of Lancashire's Sand Martins still nest in natural riverbank sites.

The River Lune is by far the most important breeding site for Sand Martins in the county and the population (including on a short stretch in Yorkshire) has been monitored since the late 1970s, showing three distinct peaks in 1981-83, 1989-90 and 1995-96, each larger than the one preceding (Figure 1). The highest total was 2,695 nest-holes in 1996. The largest colony lies immediately above and below the viaduct at Arkholme; it has been afflicted by periodic flooding, as well as by Mink predation, but held 1,203 nests – almost half the Lune total – in 1996; the colony had declined to 746 pairs in 2005.

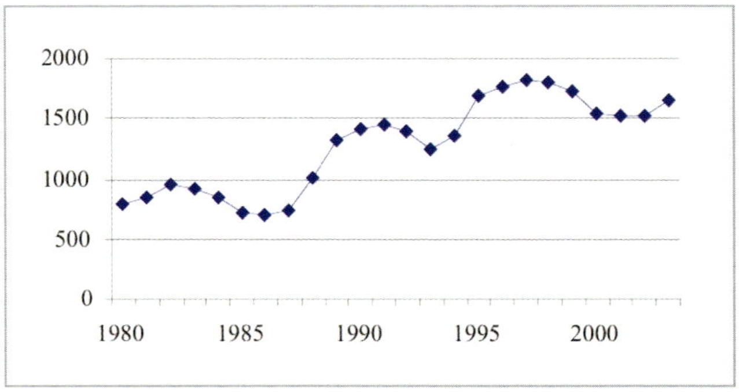

Figure 1. Occupied nest-holes (5-yr rolling means) of Sand Martins on the River Lune (Skerton Weir to Kirkby Lonsdale), 1977-2003 (2001 estimated due to Foot & Mouth Disease)

Further south, a National Rivers Authority survey along the Ribble from Preston to Brockhall in 1992 located 290 nests in 13 colonies, with 50 in each of the two largest at Samlesbury and Ribchester; this, however, followed a general population slump in 1991. The 1997-2000 atlas survey found Sand Martins nesting more or less continuously along the length of the Ribble from Preston to the Yorkshire boundary. A colony at an active sand quarry at Lightfoot Green, Fulwood grew to 160 nest-holes between 1995 and 2004 as a result of suspension of operations during the nesting season, while Brockholes Quarry held 106 pairs in 2004.

Colonies elsewhere in east Lancashire, as well as in the Rossendale and Chorley regions, are generally smaller than those further north, and equally vulnerable to riverbank or sand-extraction works, flooding and other hazards. Sixty-five pairs nested in the banks of the Calder at Read in 2004 with another 40 pairs nearby at Altham-Martholme. The latter stretch of river recorded a major increase in breeding numbers in 2005, with three colonies totalling 183 nests. The main Rossendale colony is on the Irwell at Stubbins but birds have also bred at Townsendfold in recent years. Many of the smaller colonies over the years have made use of pipes and other man-made cavities, particularly in the Burnley area and in Rossendale.

In the Fylde breeding Sand Martins are virtually confined to the middle Wyre around St. Michaels and Churchtown, where 100 pairs bred in 1990 and 32 in 1997, although 350 nested at Myerscough Quarry in 2000, falling to 36 by 2003 after landscaping works.

The species is a very scarce and irregular nester in the south-west and colonies are invariably very small; there were occasional records from the Hundred End-Hesketh Bank area in the 1980s and early 1990s and from Lydiate in the 1980s, but very few since at any site.

Oakes gave 30 March 1947 as the earliest arrival date, with peak passage between 10 April and 20 May, while Spencer (1973) cited 12 March 1961 as the earliest. This was trumped by one at Leck Beck on the upper Lune on 4 March 1977 and again at Leighton Moss on 24 February 1990. First arrivals have become progressively earlier over the past 25 years and 12 March is now the median first date.

Spring passage is very variable in size but the main movements are normally recorded between early April and the middle of May. Significant roosts usually build up in the reedbeds at Leighton Moss during this period, including 1,000 in mid-May 1979, 5,000 in late April 1994 and 1996, and 4,000 on 3 April 2001. Other notable movements and roosts include an early 200 at Arkholme on 20 March 1993 and a similar number at Foulridge Reservoir, Colne on 13 May 1995, 60 per hour in an eight-hour period at Heysham on 11 April 1996, 500 at Marton Mere on the 23rd, and 200 at Lower Rivington Reservoir on 13 April 2000 and at Parsonage Reservoir, Blackburn on 11 May 2002.

Sand Martin at roost, Pine Lake, April 2002. (Mike Malpass)

Coastal movements in autumn usually begin in early July and continue intermittently until mid-September, with the highest counts usually around Morecambe Bay and on the Fylde coast. Peak numbers at Leighton Moss are normally reached during August, including 5,000 in 1973, 1980 and 1981 and 3,500 in 1994 and 2000; a roost of 15,000 there on 12 September 1989 was exceptional both in size and the lateness of the date. Other noteworthy counts include 3,700 at Fleetwood Power Station on 4 September 1989, 350 south at Seaforth on 25 July 1995 and 500 at Marton Mere two days later, 5,000 again at Marton Mere in late July 1996 and 3,000 there on 11 August 2000. Inland passage is typically very much lighter, with 400+ over Skelmersdale White Moss on 1 September 1982, 100 at Wood End Sewage Works, Burnley on 23 August 1987, 200 at Altham-Martholme on 7 September 1997 and 100 at Foulridge Reservoir on 21 August 1999 among the highest counts in recent decades.

Most local breeders and migrants have departed by the middle of September, with last sightings usually around the end of the month or in early October. The average last date in the county in the past 25 years is 3 October, and the latest ever were three at Scarisbrick Hall near Southport on 29 October 1972.

There have been 174 recoveries of Sand Martins ringed in Lancashire, 15 within the county, 39 in northern England, 99 in southern England, four in Scotland, two in Wales, six in France, three in Spain, one each in Malta and Norway, and four in Senegal; the overall pattern provides a useful indication of the migration route our birds take, as well as where many of them spend the winter. The Senegal recoveries are of particular interest: two birds ringed at Churchtown, Fylde in June and August 1990 were controlled in Djoudj National Park on 25 March 1991 and 11 February 1992, respectively, and two ringed at Caton on the Lune on 25 June 1992 were also recovered in Djoudj, one on 28 November 1992 and the other on 8 January 1993.

One hundred and eighty-nine Sand Martins ringed elsewhere in Britain and Ireland have been recovered here, 36 from northern England, 148 from southern England, two each from Wales and Scotland and one from Ireland. There have also been four recoveries of birds from further afield, all on the Lune, one from Belgium and two from France, and a first-winter bird ringed in Djoudj on 6 February 1993 and controlled at Caton on 11 July.

BM, RW.

This species account was sponsored by Brian Haynes and family.

SWALLOW

Hirundo rustica

Lancashire Category A.

Abundant breeder and passage migrant.

This most familiar of our hirundines suffered a substantial decline in the early 1980s but this has been reversed in recent years, with an overall increase in Britain of 11% between 1970 and 2001 (CBC), and of 32% during 1994-2005 (BBS).

Mitchell and Oakes both described the Swallow as a common summer visitor to Lancashire. Mitchell's date of first arrival was

10 April, although the 17-18th was more usual. By Oakes's time there were a few records in late March, with an exceptional occurrence, which remains our earliest ever, of one at Blackpool on 5 March 1918, although he gave 12 April as the average first date.

The Swallow remains a common and widespread breeding species in Lancashire; the New Atlas Abundance Map shows the densest population across a broad swathe of the centre of the county, from the Longridge and Ribchester areas south to Tarleton and Ormskirk. The 1997-2000 survey estimated a total of 10,000 territories in 90% of tetrads with only the highest Bowland and Pennine fells and some heavily built-up areas of Liverpool and the Fylde coast devoid of breeding Swallows. This population estimate was perhaps a little optimistic and 8,000 may be more realistic. Almost all nest in farm outbuildings, sheds, garages and porches, as well as beneath bridges and culverts, although one or two pairs bred in a cave on Silverdale Marsh in the 1980s and 1990s, and a single pair in an underground air-raid shelter at Hightown in 1985. A pair nested successfully in a shooting-hut in Bowland at an exceptional 400m altitude in 2004.

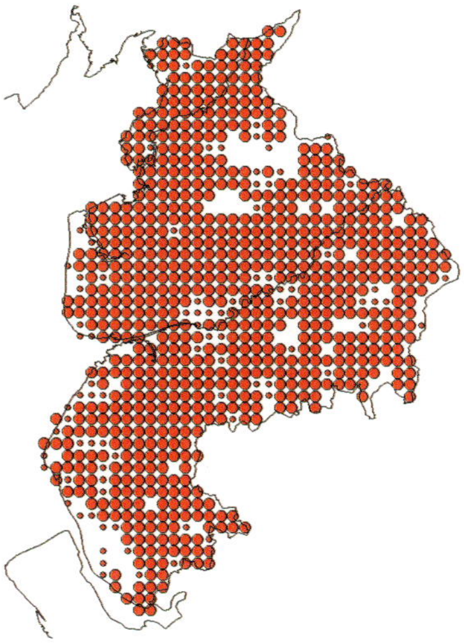

Breeding distribution of Swallow, 1997-2000. (Large dots: confirmed. Small dots: possible)

Most colonies are small; two or three pairs is typical, and many nest singly. Observations at monitored nesting-sites in the Pilling-Preesall area show that slightly over 50% of pairs are double-brooded with a small proportion triple-brooded; it is not unusual to find unfledged young still in the nest in September, especially following a wet summer as in 1985, and fledging in early October has occasionally been recorded.

Although most Swallows reach Lancashire between mid-April and mid-May, as in Mitchell's and Oakes's days, there has been a tendency for an increasing proportion of migrants to appear progressively earlier over recent decades; widespread records in the second half of March have been virtually annual since the mid-1980s, and a bird at Seaforth on 10 March 1997 is the earliest to date, apart from the 1918 Blackpool bird. The average first arrival during the past 25 years was on 27 March.

Visible migration varies greatly in scale from one year to the next; it is likely that most Swallows pass quickly and unnoticed at higher altitudes in warm, dry spring weather, whereas cold, wet conditions with adverse winds may produce substantial low-level movements at both coastal and inland locations. A thousand passed north at Marshside on 12 and 13 May 1980 and a similar number on 10 May 1981, with several hundred recorded over Heysham on the following day, 500+ at Arkholme on 21 April 1985 and 300 at Foulridge Reservoir on 30 April 1988. May 1993 saw an exceptional passage, including 250 north per hour at Heysham on the 10th, 1,100 over Marshside on the 11-12th and 600 at Foulridge on the 13th. An oddity of the spring passage at Seaforth is that the overwhelming majority of spring migrants always move south, perhaps overshooting birds re-orientating towards north Wales.

Juvenile Swallows, Little Crosby, June 2006. (Steve Young)

A thousand Swallows were roosting nightly at Leighton Moss by 23 April 1996 and there were 2,500 there on 9 May 1997, with 1,000 at Foulridge two days later; more recently roosts at Leighton Moss have again exceeded 1,000 on several dates in May. Small-scale movements of Swallows continue into June in some years, particularly over inland reservoirs and sewage works.

Post-breeding roosts begin to form at favoured locations by the middle of July in most years and the first juveniles are often on the move by the end of the month. The largest recent gatherings in the past were in reedbeds at Leighton Moss, Marton Mere and in the Fleetwood area. Up to 10,000 were fairly usual at Leighton Moss from mid-August during the 1980s and early 1990s, with a peak of 15,000 in mid-September 1989, but smaller roosts have become the norm there in more recent autumns. The peak count at Marton Mere reached 8,000 in late August and September on several occasions between the late 1960s and the early 1980s, but numbers grew significantly thereafter, to 10,000 on 31 August 1983, 18,000 on 2 September 1990, and 15,000 in late August 1994 and early August 1995. Since the late 1990s, however, the roost has seldom held more than 2,500 birds. Fleetwood Power Station attracted 16,000 roosting Swallows on 4 September 1984 and there were 10,000 on Fleetwood Marsh on 17-18 August 1993. These large Fylde roosts have largely disappeared as birds have taken to roosting in maize over a wider area, including 4,000 in one field at Singleton in August 2004. 5,000 roosted at Middleton Industrial Estate, Heysham in August and September 2002.

As traditional coastal roosts have declined in size new congregations of migrant Swallows have appeared at inland locations, among the largest 5,000 at Padiham on 31 August 1991, 10,000 at Gressingham in the Lune Valley on 19 September 1996 and in maize fields at Ribchester in mid-September 2001, 5,000 at Ribchester in mid-August 2003 and another 5,000 in the Brockholes-Samlesbury area in mid-September the same year.

Visible migration of Swallows in autumn is normally much heavier than in spring, noteworthy movements include 1,500 over the Wyre Estuary in 50 minutes on 24 August 1983, 2,000+ south at Seaforth on 30 August 1991 and 1,500 there on 23 August 2000, 1,000 over Eagland Hill, Pilling on 10 September 1994 and 2,000 over Darwen Moor edge in an hour three days later, 3,000 at Marshside on 16 September 1997, 5,000 over Belmont on 21 September 1997 with 1,275 south-east in three hours over Heysham the same day, and 1,146 over Caton Moor on 1 August 2004.

The main passage is normally over by the end of September but small parties of stragglers are widely reported through October and occasionally more substantial flocks are recorded, including 1,200 roosting at Marton Mere on 2 October 1987. November Swallows are virtually annual nowadays with three or four records in a typical year since the late 1990s. Spencer (1973) noted three December occurrences, in 1957, 1963 and 1970, and a single January bird, at Freshfield on 9 January 1964. Further December records, mainly around Morecambe Bay or in the Fylde, have occurred in 1984, 1985, 1986, 2000, 2002, 2003 and 2004. The average last record over the past 25 years has been 14 November.

Recoveries of two juveniles at Gressingham in August 2005 which had been ringed earlier in the year in Glamorgan and Staffordshire indicate that some of our autumn birds are reverse migrants.

There have been more than 400 recoveries of Lancashire-ringed Swallows in Britain and Ireland, 34 of them from abroad. Of these, eleven have been in South Africa, where most British Swallows spend the winter; these include the first bird to be recovered there under Witherby's original ringing scheme, a pullus ringed at Lytham on 3 July 1915 and found dead near Grahamstown in the Eastern Cape on 6 February 1916. There have also been seven recoveries in France, four in Spain, one each in Belgium, Italy and Finland, four each in Morocco and Algeria, and one each in Nigeria and Congo. The 132 recoveries in Lancashire of birds ringed outside the county have all been British-ringed.

BM, RW.

This species account was sponsored by Frank Walsh.

HOUSE MARTIN

Delichon urbicum

Lancashire Category A.

Common breeder and passage migrant.

There was no significant change in the British breeding range between the 1968-72 and 1988-91 atlases but CBC data suggest a population decline of 32% between 1970 and 2001, while the BBS indicates an increase of 38% during 1994-2005.

Mitchell considered the House Martin to be as common in Lancashire as the Swallow but believed that competition with House Sparrows was leading to local population declines – which were more likely a result of industrial pollution reducing numbers of aerial invertebrates (Brown & Grice 2005). Oakes, however, judged House Martins to be much less numerous overall, although locally abundant. House Martins were generally scarce and local in Merseyside and south-west Lancashire in Oakes's day, more numerous a little further east in the Billinge, Chorley and Parbold areas and most common in the Fylde. The Lancashire range has remained unchanged since 1968-72, with House Martins found in all 10km squares, but the 1997-2000 survey, which confirmed breeding in almost 60% of the county's tetrads, showed a distinct concentration in the western half of the county. Unsurprisingly, House Martins were absent from most of the higher areas of Bowland and the Pennines and many of the south-west mosslands, where human habitations are scarce, but were also very scarce in some urban areas, notably the Liverpool conurbation and much of the Fylde coast.

A total of 4,000 pairs was estimated in 1997-2000. No earlier population estimate exists but, in an extensive study of an area of 1,368km^2 in east Lancashire, Bouldin (1968) recorded an average of 2,609 nests during 1960-67, which suggests that a substantial population decline has taken place.

However, House Martins have extended their range into some areas of the county where they had been uncommon, most dramatically in Rossendale where widespread breeding became established only in the early 1980s. Local variations in colony sizes are frequently reported; new building developments provide

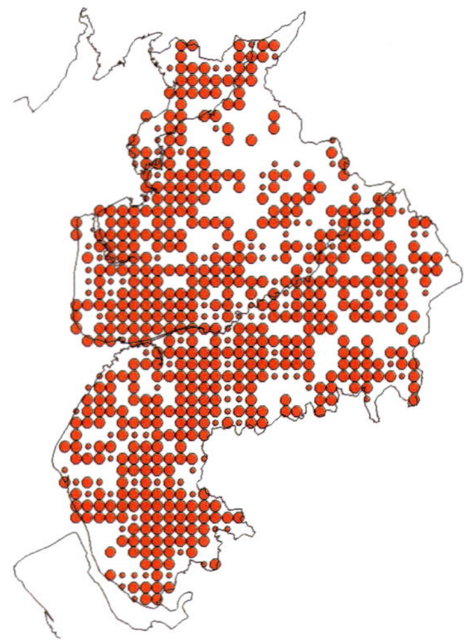

Breeding distribution of House Martin, 1997-2000. (Large dots: confirmed. Small dots: possible)

nesting opportunities, balanced by losses of established colonies due to renovations or demolitions, as in the case of Heath Charnock Hospital in Chorley, where up to 50 pairs regularly nested until it was knocked down in 1994. An annual survey of nesting House Martins within a 25km radius of Accrington between 1958 and 1967 found that overall numbers remained fairly consistent but individual colonies fluctuated considerably in size over the years. The number of colonies there varied from 567 to 620 over the ten years, and the total number of nests from 2,580 to 3,026. Most colonies were small; over 60% contained fewer than four nests and only 3% held more than 30 (Bouldin 1968). Most colonies that have been censused over any appreciable period in more recent decades show considerable year-on-year variations in size; at Rossall School between ten and 19 nests were recorded annually during 1988-96, while in Belmont Village the population has been counted annually since 1996, with the number of nests varying between 41 (1998) and 21 (2005).

Juvenile House Martin, Seaforth Nature Reserve, August 2006. (Steve Young)

According to Oakes odd birds were recorded from mid-April but arrivals in strength did not normally occur until the end of the month or even the first week of May. The onset of spring migration now appears to be a little earlier, with the first appearing on average on 3 April over the past 25 years, but the main passage still takes place from the last week of April to the third week of May. Spencer published an extremely early record at Garstang on 17 March 1963, since when there have been seven further March occurrences, all in the last week of the month and four of them since 2000 when 'early springs' began to be taken for granted.

Most of the spring passage passes unnoticed but heavy, if brief, surges of migration do sometimes occur in suitable weather conditions. Noteworthy counts include 300 at Marshside on 12 May 1980, 'many hundreds' over Hightown on 10 May 1981, up to 300 over Darwen on 11 May 1992, 200 at Seaforth on 30 May 1993, 550 at Marshside on 11 May 1995, 400 at Arkholme on 11 May 2000, and 250 over Ewood Bridge Sewage Works, Rossendale on 22 May 2002. Movements have normally ceased by the second week of June, although a very exceptional 300 moved over Ewood Bridge on 9 June 1990.

Many, perhaps up to 60%, of Lancashire House Martins are normally double-brooded and, as in Oakes's time, reports of nearly-fledged young – presumably replacement broods – in the nest at the end of September are not uncommon, and this has occasionally been observed as late as mid-October and exceptionally on the 25th in 2004 at Glasson.

The beginning of autumn passage is rather unpredictable: occasionally, movements are observed from early July but more normally towards the middle or end of the month; exceptionally, passage does not commence until the middle of August.

In most years the heaviest movements take place between early August and late September. Oakes mentioned regular impressive passage movements in the Ribble Valley, including occasional flocks of over a thousand at Ribchester. More recently, counts in excess of 300 birds have been frequent, movements of up to 500 not particularly uncommon, and significantly higher numbers recorded occasionally. A thousand House Martins flew over Altham Sewage Works on 29 August 1980, there were 1,250 at Martin Mere on 18 August 1989, and 960 in just over two hours going north over St. Anne's and Blackpool shore on 29 September 1991. At Seaforth over 500 flew south in a matter of minutes on the morning of 20 September 2002, and 800 passed there on 28 August 2003. Small parties of late migrants are usually fairly widespread in the first half of October and occasionally more substantial flocks are recorded even later, including 160 south at Hightown on 29 October 1981, 45 at Whalley on 12 October 1991, 40 at Shortclough in Rossendale on 5 October 1997 and at Warton (Fylde) on 2 October 1998, 103 over Roby Mill on 7 October 1997 and 65 at Crossens on 3 October 2004.

Although the average last sighting over the past quarter of a century has come on 1 November, records in that month have become less frequent since the 1970s and 1980s – when they were virtually annual – and the most recent was of four at Heysham on 3 November 2000. A few House Martins have, very exceptionally, lingered into winter; one was at Formby Point on 7 December 1968 and two at Conder Green on 21 January 1980, whilst two birds at Caton in the Lune Valley in the bitter weather of late December 1981 and early January 1982 roosted by night in one of the previous season's nests.

There have been 57 exchanges of ringed House Martins between Lancashire and other parts of Britain, the most interesting being one ringed at Stodday, Lancaster on 31 August 1909 and recovered in Surrey on 29 October that year. An unaged bird ringed at Formby on 15 June 1983 was recovered in unknown circumstances in Algeria near Bechar in the Saharan Atlas on the unexpected date of 15 July 1984; it may, of course, have been long-dead.

BM, RW.

This species account was sponsored by Frank Walsh and Ron Hothersall.

RED-RUMPED SWALLOW

Cecropis daurica

Lancashire Category A. (0, 3).

Vagrant from southern Europe.

Despite a significant increase in Britain as a whole, this remains an extremely rare species in north-west England with just four occurrences in Cheshire, one in Cumbria and three in Lancashire.

The first was watched flying low through the dunes at Ainsdale on 4 May 1968 by Harry Shorrock. The next was found feeding over the Leeds-Liverpool Canal in the Rimrose Valley in Litherland, near Liverpool on 25 June 1996. It remained at the northern end of the valley until late the following afternoon, feeding with House Martins and periodically disappearing into the nearby housing estate where the martins were nesting.

Red-rumped Swallow, Rimrose Valley, Litherland, 25 June 1996. (Steve Young)

The most recent record occurred in what became a major 'invasion' year nationally in 2004. Found as it fed over Marton Mere on 18 April, it was present for less than two hours in the morning before returning at dusk.

SJW, MJ.

This species account was sponsored by Maurice Jones.

RICHARD'S PIPIT

Anthus richardi

Lancashire Category A (1, 30).

Rare passage migrant from Siberia.

Both Mitchell and Oakes accepted a record of a bird on the banks of the River Wyre near Fleetwood in June or July 1869. It was described as "flying in and out of gorse bushes on the banks of the river...almost 'plumb' up into the air, calling something like a Skylark... then darting into the next thick bush". Neither this behaviour nor the date – there is only one published modern British record in either June or July – inspire confidence.

The next published record was of one found by J. Carter on a ploughed field at Carleton, Blackpool on 24 December 1946. This was followed by one at Freckleton Naze on 29 September 1957.

A ten-year gap then ensued until another was found at Hundred End on 8 October 1967. A further 24 records involving 29 birds have been published since then but there must be some doubt about one at Hightown on 28 August 1971, an extremely early date in the light of subsequent experience – the earliest record on Fair Isle, for example, being a full fortnight later on 10 September.

More than half have occurred since 1992, roughly in line with the national picture. British records showed a marked upturn from the late 1970s and the species was removed from the list of national rarities in 1982. All records have been of singles with the exception of twos at Rossall in 1968, Pilling Lane Ends in 1992, Heysham in 1994, Fleetwood Golf Course in 1994 and Coal Clough near Burnley in 2004.

Richard's Pipits are less than annual in Lancashire and multiple records have only been recorded in 1968 (4), 1992 (3), 1994 (4), 1995 (5) and 2003 (4). Nationally, about 100 birds are recorded annually; the largest influx came in 1994, when 338 were recorded in England, and Lancashire's share was six birds, two of which were not discovered until early 1995.

Richard's Pipit, Lytham Moss, April 2007. (Stuart Piner)

There have been just three records any distance inland: at Carr House Green, Inskip on 15–17 April 1989, at Parsonage Reservoir on 14–16 October 2003 and Coal Clough Wind Farm on 1–19 December 2004; the remainder have been on or close to the coast.

Most Richard's Pipits arrive in autumn, almost all of them in October (Figure 1), reflecting the national situation in which the vast majority are seen between the last week of September and the third week of October. Average arrival dates in Lancashire appear to be a little later than nationally, perhaps indicating some movement across country after landfall on the eastern coasts.

There have been four winter records since the 1946 Blackpool bird: singles in 1995 at Pilling Lane Ends from 8 January to

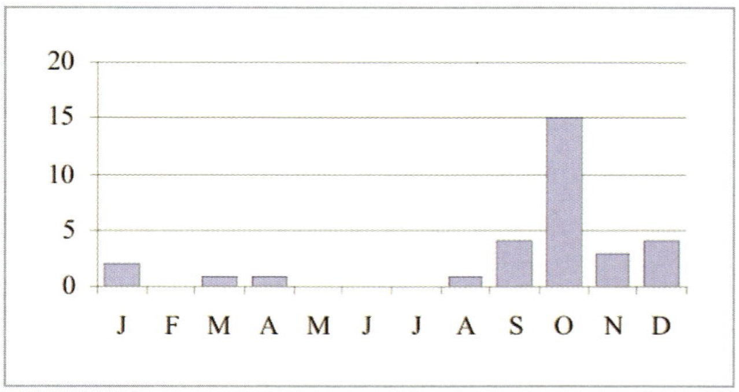

Figure 1. Monthly totals of Richard's Pipits in Lancashire, 1946-2005.

4 February, at Marshside on 16 January, at Rossall Point on 2-6 December and the two at Coal Clough in December 2004 . Completing the picture are two spring records of singles at Blackpool Airport from 26 March to 29 April 1983 in addition to the Inskip bird mentioned above.

All records:

1946	Carleton, Blackpool, one, 24 December
1957	Freckleton Naze, one, 29 September
1967	Hundred End, one, 8 October
1968	Hundred End, one, 14 October
1968	Rossall, one to two, 22 October to 4 November
1968	Freshfield, one, 6 to 8 November
1971	Hightown, one, 28 August
1971	Hightown, one, 26 September
1983	Blackpool, one, 26 March to 29 April
1988	Altcar Rifle Ranges, one, 15 October
1989	Carr House Green, Inskip, one, 15 to 17 April
1992	Pilling Lane Ends, two, 27 September to 3 October
1992	Heysham, one, 18 October
1994	Heysham, two, 9 October
1994	Fleetwood, two, 17 October
1995	Pilling Lane Ends, one, 8 January to 4 February
1995	Marshside, one, 16 January
1995	Leighton Moss, one, 25 October
1995	Marshside, one, 1 November
1995	Rossall Point, one, 2 to 6 December
2000	Heysham, one, 7 November
2003	Parsonage Reservoir, one, 14 to 16 October
2003	Crossens, one, 19 to 22 October
2003	Crosby Marine Park, one, 24 October
2003	Heysham, one, 24 October
2004	Coal Clough Wind Farm, two, 1 to 19 December

SJW, MJ.
This species account was sponsored by Tony Myerscough.

TAWNY PIPIT

Anthus campestris

Lancashire Category A. (0, 3).

Vagrant from southern or central Europe.

Tawny Pipit ceased to be considered a national rarity when it was removed from the list of species considered by the BBRC in 1982 and, although numbers appear to have declined during the 1990s, around twenty a year remains the British average. However, the records show an overwhelming bias towards southern and eastern coasts and the species remains a major rarity in north-west England.

The first was watched for twenty minutes on the golf course at Rossall Point, Fleetwood in the early morning of 29 May 1985 by Ian Gardner.

Our only other records have both come from Heysham. The first was a 'fly-over' at 09.55 hrs on 4 September 1996, logged by observers familiar with the species' call. It flew low to the south-east, a flight-line consistent with arrival from Walney Island, across Morecambe Bay in Cumbria, where one had been seen shortly before. The second was more obliging; it was found in the power station compound in the late morning of 16 May 2001 and was watched through the boundary fence by many observers until it disappeared that evening. It was identified as a male on the basis of a single parachute display flight.

Tawny Pipit, Heysham, May 2001. (Steve Dodgson).

SJW, MJ.
This species account was sponsored by Alan Draper.

TREE PIPIT

Anthus trivialis

Lancashire Category A.

Uncommon breeder and passage migrant.

Mitchell described Tree Pipits as 'fairly plentiful in all wooded districts' and 'generally distributed over the whole of the county'. Oakes, however, considered them to be 'decidedly local, owing to [their] habitat requirements', but common in the Ribble Valley, on the western side of the Rossendale hills and in parts of north Lancashire. He gave typical arrival and departure dates as 14 April and the first week of September respectively.

National CBC data showed a slow downward drift from 1970 to 1987, then a decline of more than 60% by 1995 and 27% between 1994 and 2005 (BBS). The Lancashire breeding population appears to have followed this national trend, at least until recently. The breeding range fell from 26 to 16 10km squares between the sample surveys of 1968-72 and 1988-91, rising to 18 in the complete 1997-2000 Lancashire Atlas survey, when males were located in 77 tetrads (8%) – all but twelve in the eastern half of the county – and the population was estimated at about 100 singing males. Numbers have continued to fall during the early years of this century and the county population may soon drop as low as 50 pairs.

If such a scarce species can be said to have a Lancashire stronghold it is in the moorland edge woodlands of the West Pennine Moors, where breeding was confirmed in almost all tetrads in SD61 and the southern part of SD62 during 1997-2000 and where some 33-50% of the county population is probably located. The main site for the past 15-20 years has been the Roddlesworth Plantations, where there were 38 singing males in

1980, reducing to 27-28 in 1988-90 and 14 in 2003. Other woodlands holding significant numbers of territorial males since the mid-1990s include Lead Mines Clough (maximum eight), Belmont (maximum seven) and Rivington/Anglezarke (maximum twelve). Further east in Rossendale numbers are much lower and breeding has only occurred at a handful of sites since the early 1980s, including Haslingden Grane, Stubbins, Crawshawbooth and Deeply Vale, where two or three pairs in 2000 was the last published breeding record. Indeed, two birds at Calf Hey Reservoir on 30 March 2005 were the first in Rossendale since 2000.

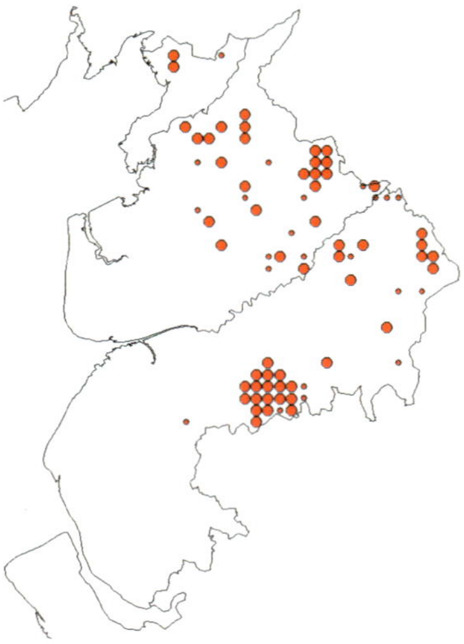

Breeding distribution of Tree Pipit, 1997-2000. (Large dots: confirmed. Small dots: possible)

The Bowland valleys, particularly those opening out into the Lune valley to the north and throughout the Hodder Valley in the south, still retain regular breeding populations. Favoured sites on the Hodder in the past ten years or so have included Longridge Fell, the Langden Valley, Beacon Fell, Dunsop Bridge but principally the Gisburn Forest/Stocks Reservoir area, where clear-felling has produced suitable habitat. Further south, another cluster of records east of Colne and Earby was published in the Lancashire Atlas but little suitable habitat exists in this area and the records perhaps related to passage migrants.

Tree Pipit, Grizedale Valley. (Mike McKavett)

Although described as locally abundant in the Lancaster area in 1959 and still common in the 1980s, there has been a considerable decline during the 1990s, for example five pairs at Warton Crag in 1990 had declined to a single pair in 1996-2005.

Throughout the middle reaches of the Ribble and in the Darwen and Calder Valleys birds are very thinly scattered at only a few sites, where numbers were considerably reduced by the mid-1980s and breeding probably only occurred sporadically by the mid-1990s.

Tree Pipits had ceased to breed anywhere in south-west Lancashire, north Merseyside or the Fylde by 1997-2000. Oakes mentioned occasional nesting at Formby, Rufford and Parbold and breeding occurred at Knowsley Park at least in the 1960s and in Formby into the 1980s. Breeding has never been proven in the Fylde although there have been several breeding season reports from the Lytham area, including birds at Preesall and Ribby Hall in 1987.

The earliest ever spring arrival was a single at Knott End on 17 March 1957 and the earliest inland at Stocks Reservoir on 20 March 2003. The average first arrival during the past quarter century has been on 5 April but numbers usually peak in the last week of April and the first week of May, with very few after the third week of May.

Passage is rarely conspicuous inland and difficult to monitor on the coast, where few birds are ever seen on the ground – recording relies almost entirely on detecting flight calls. Numbers vary greatly between years but nevertheless there has been a clear downward trend over the past 20 years or so. Heysham's best spring was in 1983 with a peak day-count of 60 on 30 April and ten or more on a further seven dates, but the largest total spring passage there since 1990 was just 27 in 1996, with an average of barely more than a dozen records. Marshside records are more variable, perhaps because of less consistent coverage; the highest total was 25 in 1998 and the largest day-count 15 on 12 April 1993, but spring totals have never exceeded single figures since 2000. Migrants are seen annually at other watchpoints on the Sefton and Fylde coasts – with a notable tally of 32 at Rossall Point in spring 1998, including 19 on 27 April – and further inland, for example ten over Downholland Moss on 24 April 2003.

The first autumn passage birds may occur as early as mid-July – the earliest at Heysham was on 19 July 1994 – but the main movement comes between mid-August and the first week of September, with stragglers to the end of the month. October records are scarce, the latest being singles inland at Whitewell on 8 October 1985 and on the coast at Formby on 18 October 1967. As in spring, there are large fluctuations between years, since 1990 at Heysham, for example, ranging between six in 2003 and 179 in 1991 with a median total of around 20. Most published Fylde records come from Fairhaven which reported its highest autumn total of 149 and day-counts of 40 and 41 in 1984, but numbers have declined significantly here too, with a largest recent count of six on 9 September 2002. Various Merseyside sites, notably Seaforth and Fazakerley, also regularly produce small autumn totals but concerted observation can produce surprises such as the twelve recorded over Sefton Park in south Liverpool in autumn 1995.

Our only ringing recovery is of one returning to its natal site at Padiham in 1948, so the origins of migrants remains unknown. However, it is probable that the larger, late autumn movements involve continental birds, which are known to arrive annually on the east coast (Migration Atlas).

SJW, RW.
This species account was sponsored by Derek Cook.

MEADOW PIPIT

Anthus pratensis

Lancashire Category A.

Abundant breeder and passage migrant; common in winter.

The familiar 'Mipit' is one of Lancashire's most numerous breeding species, a common winter resident and one of our most abundant and conspicuous visible migrants – it is also one of our least studied and understood birds.

Mitchell considered it probably the county's commonest bird and most widespread breeding species, 'breeding numerously everywhere, from the sand-hills just above high-water mark to the tops of the loftiest hills, and equally so on the most cultivated and the most waste lands.' He believed Meadow Pipits to be largely resident unless severe weather moved them 'in bleaker districts'.

By the middle of the twentieth century, however, Oakes was aware of the complexity of the Meadow Pipit's status, describing it as 'a common resident, an abundant passage migrant in spring and autumn, and to some extent a summer visitor'. Breeding distribution was little changed from Mitchell's day, covering the whole county from dunes and coastal mosses to the highest fells.

National CBC data showed a decline in numbers beginning in the early 1980s and this was reflected in a small reduction in breeding range between the Old and New Atlases. However, the population appears to have stabilised with the BBS showing a small decline of 6% between 1994 and 2004.

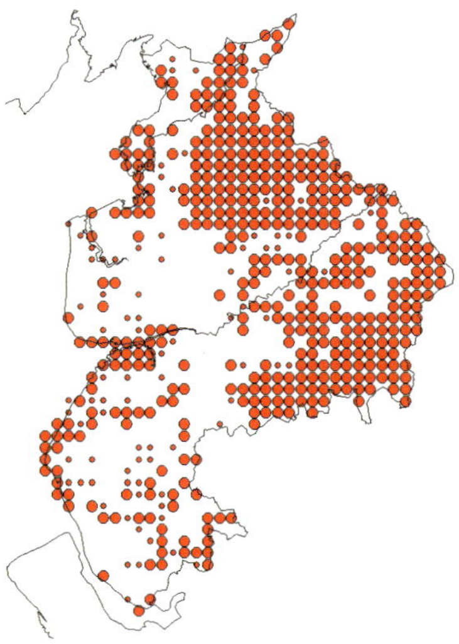

Breeding distribution of Meadow Pipit, 1997-2000. (Large dots: confirmed. Small dots: possible)

The 1997-2000 Lancashire survey confirmed breeding in every 10km square but it was evident that huge distributional changes had taken place in the previous half century. Meadow Pipits had withdrawn almost entirely from lowland agricultural areas and in the western third of the county bred commonly only on coastal dunes and saltmarshes. Their distribution in the east remains almost continuous on moorland and in young plantations in Bowland, the West Pennine Moors, Rossendale and the south Pennines, but is much sparser in the extreme north-east and a broad swath either side of the River Ribble. Very few nest anywhere in inland Fylde, where breeding is restricted to dunes and saltmarshes, or other areas of the central Lancashire plain, but a reasonable scattering of pairs remains in some areas of West Lancashire and inland Merseyside, favouring rough grassland and ex-industrial sites – very few, if any, breed on intensively farmed land.

There are few systematic surveys from which to judge recent population trends although a recent survey of the south Pennines, including areas outside of Lancashire, estimated a decline of 29% between 1990 and 2002 (Simm *et al.* 2005). The CBC site at The Hile, Rossendale – on an area of upland pasture – registered a relatively stable population from 1973 to 1990, fluctuating between 23 and 29 pairs, but this dropped to around 17 to 21 pairs during the early 1990s, ten in 1996 and six in 2002. Numbers have also declined on the Sefton coast: at Marshside from up to 36 pairs during the 1980s to a dozen or so in the 1990s but recovering to 18 in 2002; and at Seaforth – partly due to increased rabbit-grazing reducing nesting cover – from 20 pairs to just one between the late 1980s and late 1990s. Average breeding densities were estimated at more than 50 pairs per square kilometre in Bowland during the early 1990s (Harrison 1995), while a 1km square on Darwen Moor held 31 pairs in 2003 and another in Alden, Rossendale 70 pairs in 2004. Densities elsewhere are considerably lower, however, and the county population was estimated at 16,000 pairs during 1997-2000 based upon an estimated average of 30 pairs per occupied tetrad ($4km^2$).

Meadow Pipit, Hightown, May 2005. (Steve Young)

Birds begin to move away from upland breeding grounds from about mid-August with very few remaining by late October. Recent ringing evidence suggests that there is a tendency for the earlier birds to be mainly juveniles and the later birds mainly adults (P.J. Marsh, C. Bell pers comm.). Large numbers are observed on autumn passage, especially at coastal localities where Meadow Pipits almost always make up the largest part of visible migration.

The main movement takes place between mid-September and mid-October and, as in Oakes's day, the largest numbers occur in the south of the county – average autumn totals at Seaforth are at least four times higher than Heysham's with Fylde coast counts somewhere in between. Heysham's best recent autumn was in 1998 when 4,016 flew south between 15 August and 2 October. Day-totals in excess of 1,000 were seen at Seaforth in all but two years during 1990-2005 and more than 2,000 in all but six. The largest counts there have been 7,000 on 25 September 1991, 7,000-10,000 on 8 October 1995, and 6,000 during late September in 1998, 2000 and 2003. These southbound flocks move on a fairly broad front and several hundred are regularly seen in the Rimrose Valley, a couple of kilometres to the north-east of Seaforth, but the really big numbers always hug the shore, until veering west towards the North Wales coast or else continuing due south towards south Wirral.

Notable counts elsewhere on the coast include 986 at Fairhaven on 23 September 1990, 1,200 at Heysham on 25 September 1991 with 1,400 there on 18 September 1997, 2,800 at Marshside on 8 October 1995, 4,000 at Marton Mere on 14 October 1995 with 3,416 there on 29 September 2000, and 2,800 at Rossall Point on 21 September 1998 with 4,834 there on 27 September 2003.

Autumn totals at Seaforth, which average around 6,000 but range from about 3,000 to 15,000, are usually much greater than at other coastal sites, where large seasonal totals include 2,760 at Fairhaven in 1991 and 4,016 at Heysham in 1998, when 12,000 also went through at Rossall. Coastal movements almost always occur in the early morning and, at Seaforth, big flocks are rarely seen much after 10 a.m. except on days of exceptional passage. Overcast conditions sometimes ground up to 1,000 birds but most move on within an hour or so and no large build-up of migrants has ever been recorded on the Lancashire coast.

Inland passage is less thoroughly monitored and probably takes place over a broad front; the largest recent day-counts have been 1,810 over Billinge Hill, St. Helens on 23 September 1989, 6,000 over Darwen Moor on 29 September 1998, 1,200 at Garstang on 30 September 2000, 1,975 over Caton Moor on 21 September 2003 and 1,156 over Laund Hey, Rossendale on 24 September 2005.

Passage ceases fairly abruptly in mid-October and any birds seen after mid-November can be regarded as wintering. Very few remain in the uplands during the winter months, mostly single-figure flocks in more sheltered locations – twelve on the summit of Pendle Hill in December 2000 were unusual. Larger inland flocks may be encountered at sewage works, examples being 100 at Chorley in January and December 1979 and 150 at Ewood Bridge in January 1981. Elsewhere, inland flocks are usually below 20, exceptions include 56 at Sawley in December 1982, 45 at Read in December 1992, 50 at Stocks Reservoir in December 1993, 50 at Martin Mere on 25 November 1997 and 40 at The Hile in January 1999. Numbers are higher along the coast, especially on the Wyre, Ribble and Mersey saltmarshes, mostly in flocks of fewer than 25 but occasionally 50-100 birds. Wintering numbers are probably significantly under-reported but a reasonable guess at the county population would be in the order of 2,000-5,000.

Birds may return to the moors as early as late January if the weather is favourable, though 50 at the edge of Haslingden Moor on 14 February 1987 and 40 at The Hile on 31 January 1989 and 11 January 1999 were early for such numbers. In severe weather the return may be delayed until the second half of March but small-scale movement on the coast and in the lowlands normally begins in mid-February. Spring passage is usually most intense between mid-March and mid-April and, as in autumn, is most noticeable on the coast, where daily northbound movements of 300 or more are fairly frequent.

Larger recent day-counts include 1,500 at Leighton Moss in April 1994, 1,000 at Heysham on 7 April 1990 and 13 and 27 March 1991 with 1,500 there on 6 April 1998 and 1,244 on 2 April 2005, 1,000 at Rossall Point on 29 March 1998 with 2,078 and 3,500 there on 20 & 29 March 2001 and 3,632 on 13 April 2004, 7,480 at Blackpool on 4 April 1992, 2,500 grounded by rain at Marshside on 12 April 1993 with 1,200 there on 30 March 2000, and 2,000 at Seaforth on 4 and 5 April 1992.

For such an abundant bird, ringing recoveries are decidedly few: just 23 ringed in Lancashire and five from elsewhere. These offer some clues about southerly migratory routes and winter destinations; one was recovered in mid-Wales in winter and seven recovered or ringed in southern England (three in winter, four on passage). Unfortunately, none of these was a definite Lancashire breeder but five Lancashire pulli have been recovered in the main wintering grounds of British birds in southern Europe (three in France and two in Portugal), and singles ringed on migration have been recovered in Belgium and Spain. However, no ringing recoveries shed any light upon the origins of birds wintering in or on passage through the county, and these remain a matter for speculation. Perhaps the majority of autumn migrants are nominate *pratensis* from northern England and eastern Scotland, but it seems likely that *whistleri* from Ireland and western Scotland also pass through in considerable numbers. The major question mark remains how many *pratensis* breeding in Greenland, Iceland or Scandinavia – all of which are known to pass through Britain – are involved in the west coast passage. A juvenile ringed at Spurn in East Yorkshire on 8 October 2003 and controlled on Caton Moor on 10 October 2004 was perhaps of Scandinavian origin.

SJW, RW.

This species account was sponsored by Bob Stinger.

RED-THROATED PIPIT

Anthus cervinus

Lancashire Category A. (0, 2).

Vagrant from Fennoscandia or northern Russia .

The first county record was found at Seaforth by Chris Kehoe, John Dempsey, Gavin Thomas and Steve White on 25 May 1992, after several days of sustained light, south-easterly winds; it was one of 21 found in England that month. On arrival it bathed and preened before moving to the rubble mounds where it burst into full song for several minutes. After 90 minutes it disappeared off to the west.

The second bird, also at Seaforth, was much less obliging; it flew over calling on 29 April 1995. There are very few April records nationally, with most spring birds arriving in mid- to late May.

A very high proportion of British records come from the geographical extremities of Shetland and Scilly. Red-throated Pipits are extreme rarities in north-west England with none yet seen in Cumbria and just five in Cheshire – all in Wirral, preserving the Merseyside monopoly.

Male Red-throated Pipit in breeding plumage, Seaforth, May 1992. (Steve White)

SJW, MJ.

This species account was sponsored by Mark Farrar.

ROCK PIPIT

Anthus petrosus

Lancashire Category A.

Fairly common passage migrant and winter visitor from Fennoscandia.

Mitchell reported breeding 'near Heysham' in the nineteenth century but Lancashire's lack of any significant stretches of rocky coastline means that Rock Pipits are unlikely ever to have been anything other than extremely rare and sporadic breeders. Oakes confirmed occasional nesting on Walney Island (now in Cumbria) but our nearest populations are now in northern Cumbria and north Wales. Both Mitchell and Oakes described it as a scarce but regular winter visitor to the coast, citing Fleetwood, Cockerham, the Ribble Estuary, Ainsdale and Formby as examples.

Rock Pipit, Morecambe, 2002. (Mike Malpass)

Neither Mitchell nor Oakes reported any significant passage movement but nowadays Rock Pipits have become familiar as autumn, and to a lesser extent spring, migrants as well as winter visitors. Most are recorded along the coast although some movement takes place along the major rivers, especially the Ribble and Calder. Autumn arrivals generally begin between the last week of September and the first week of October. Earlier records include one at Heysham on 25 August 1996, one at Seaforth on 28 August 1996 and three at Cockersands on 30 August 1980. Most records of autumn passage birds are in October and early November, usually of single birds but occasionally in low single figures. The majority of records at the main coastal watchpoints are of birds flying south calling but ones and twos do sometimes linger for a day or so. The largest day-totals in recent years are ten at Cockersands on 27 October 1991 and eight over Seaforth on 23 October 1996 with five there on 29 September 2002; a report of 60 at Hightown on 29 October 1981 is thus an order of magnitude higher than any other autumn count in Lancashire and therefore perhaps questionable.

Autumn records are scarcer inland but birds are seen most years, especially from late October into November. Most are of singles and the largest recent count was three at Rishton Reservoir from 7-21 October 1999.

The autumn migration has been best recorded at Seaforth but even here the species is almost certainly significantly under-recorded, records being largely dependent upon the presence of sharp-eared observers. Average dates of the Seaforth passage (1990-2005) are 27 September to 15 November with peak numbers usually in mid-October. Autumn totals during the same period have ranged between three and 28 with an average of 15. Rather lower numbers than these are regularly recorded at Heysham (including 13 in autumn 1995), Marton Mere (including four on 17 October 1974) and Marshside (including ten in autumn 2000), and sporadically at other coastal sites. There is no reason to believe that Seaforth is an especially favoured site, so it seems likely that at least 200 and perhaps as many as 500 Rock Pipits pass through Lancashire during autumn.

Wintering numbers are usually significantly lower. Although occasional singles are seen inland and on sandy shores, the only significant and regular concentrations are found on the saltmarshes of the Lune, Wyre and Ribble Estuaries. During the 1970s and 1980s most were seen on the south Ribble marshes of Banks, Crossens and Marshside, with notable counts of 49 on Crossens saltmarsh in December 1974, 35 there in February 1977 and 35 between Crossens and Marshside in December 1982. Numbers plummeted on the south Ribble from the mid-1980s with no double-figure peaks recorded until 18 in December 1991 and twelve in February 1995, and single figures only since January 1996.

Up to five wintered annually at Lytham jetty from 1979 to 1998. Elsewhere on the north Ribble the situation is less certain, since very few counts have ever been published – eight at Warton Bank on 18 February 1999 being an exception – but at least small numbers have been seen regularly in recent winters although it is clear that they are outnumbered by Water Pipits, at least at the Warton Bank hotspot.

Reports from north Fylde have increased significantly since the mid-1980s, when twelve at Pilling on 31 January 1981 and five at various sites in late 1985 were the largest published counts. Ten or so were seen regularly at Stanah during the early 1990s, up to seven at Hambleton in the mid-1990s, 24 on the Wyre marshes (including 14 on Barnaby's Sands) on 26 December 1995, 15 on the Wyre marshes in January 1998 and 20 at Burglar's Alley Marsh, Thornton on 23 February 2003 with 13 there that December. A systematic count of the Wyre Estuary saltmarshes in December 2004 produced a total of 76 birds. A similar survey of the Lune Estuary saltmarshes in January 1992 located 30 birds and up to 13 have been recorded on Aldcliffe Marsh in most winters since 1999, and up to 15 at Sunderland Point during 1994-95. More recent estimates for north Lancashire suggest up to 55 birds with 35-40 of these on the Lune and the remainder on the RSPB or Middleton saltmarshes. Estimates from WeBS counters, who have access to private coastal stretches, tentatively suggest about 25 birds along the coast between the Lune and Wyre, mainly on the saltmarshes. Most late autumn records inland come from reservoirs but the only definite wintering birds were singles at Colne sewage works every year from 1993/94 to 1996/7 and one – with a Water Pipit – at Cant Clough Reservoir in January and February 2004.

Overwintering birds begin to move out by late February and their numbers are largely depleted by mid-March. A small spring passage, rarely involving more than two or three birds at any one coastal site, occurs most years – four at Seaforth on 30 March to 2 April 1988 were exceptional. Extreme dates at Seaforth (1990-2005) are 18 February and 11 April but average dates are 13-23 March. Later spring records were singles at Ford, Liverpool on 2 May 1967, Penwortham in May 1986 and Marshside on 26 May 1995. There have been four recent summer occurrences: singles at Seaforth from June to October 1986 and on 6 June 1987, and at Clifton Marsh on 10 July 1979, and two at Marshside on 7 June 1980.

Two sub-species occur in Britain: nominate *petrosus* which breeds on rocky shores throughout the country and *littoralis* from Fennoscandia and the Baltic. Until very recently it was common currency that the vast majority of Lancashire records referred to *petrosus* and that *littoralis* occurred principally as a scarce spring passage migrant with less than annual occurrences reported, mostly from Seaforth but also from Sunderland Point, Hambleton and Marshside. This arose mainly from the fact that the two sub-species are indistinguishable until late winter when some *littoralis* begin to attain a distinctive breeding plumage (which in turn renders them confusable with Water Pipits). However, *petrosus* is known to be exceptionally sedentary and ringing studies indicate that the only significant dispersal within Britain involves birds (formerly known as *kleinschmidti*) that move from Shetland to Orkney and north-east Scotland. Continental *littoralis*, on the other hand, is mainly migratory and large numbers are known to winter on the English east coast, mostly on saltmarshes (Migration Atlas). A combination of habitat preference, migratory behaviour and the relatively large numbers of passage and wintering birds, have led most observers to believe that the overwhelming majority of Lancashire records are in fact *littoralis*. This is supported by the one ringing recovery, a first-winter ringed in Sweden (and therefore *littoralis*) in October 1994 and found dead at Little Singleton, Fylde in February 1998, and a sighting of a Scandinavian colour-ringed bird at Bank End Point on 27 February 1998.

It is possible that some *petrosus* do occur, perhaps from north Cumbria or western Scotland, and two or three regular birds on the rocky shore at Morecambe and occasional ones and twos amongst the rocks and seawalls in the Heysham Harbour/Head area are perhaps the best candidates.

SJW, RW.

This species account was sponsored in memory of Gail Bunker.

WATER PIPIT

Anthus spinoletta

Lancashire Category A.

Uncommon winter visitor from western or central Europe.

Our understanding of the status of Water Pipits in Lancashire changed radically during the last years of the twentieth century when the number of published records rose from an average of fewer than four per year between 1968 and 1997 to more than 27 between 1998 and 2003, leading to the species being taken off the list of county birds requiring written descriptions in 2002. This may, to some extent, have been a result of increased interest and knowledge of identification criteria following the split from Rock Pipit in 1986, but the increase is almost wholly accounted for by records from a single site, Warton Bank on the north Ribble marshes, which have challenged long-standing assumptions about the British wintering areas of Water Pipits.

Mitchell published just one record – three birds at Fleetwood in October 1843 – but he regarded this as 'insufficiently verified'. Oakes made no mention at all, but Spencer knew of 17 records within the old county boundaries between 1962 and 1972 and regarded their occurrence as 'probably annual'. However, he spoke of a 'preponderance of April sightings', a time of year when some Scandinavian Rock Pipits (whose possible occurrence in Lancashire was not considered much before the mid-1980s) become confusable in plumage with Water Pipits. Now that our views on the frequency of occurrence of *littoralis* Rock Pipits have been so dramatically revised, many records before the 1990s, particularly in early spring, must be thrown into some doubt.

To add to the confusion, it was widely believed that Water Pipits did not winter on saltmarshes and were extremely scarce in north-west England (Winter Atlas), and it is possible that some birds escaped attention before the Warton Bank situation was finally resolved at the end of the 1990s on the basis of concerted observation and photographic evidence. Lancashire birders learned a great deal about the Rock/Water Pipit complex from this (sometimes heated) debate and, although many issues remain to be resolved and occasional records continue to be contentious, we can be reasonably confident that almost all records of both species have been correctly assigned since about 1995. Earlier coastal records are much less certain.

Two sites stand out prior to the late 1990s. Up to seven birds regularly wintered at Altham sewage works until its closure in 1989. Occasional singles continued to be recorded on adjacent stretches of the River Calder until 1992 but none has been seen there subsequently. Until very recently Leighton Moss was rightly considered *the* place to see Water Pipits in Lancashire; one or two are known to have wintered there virtually annually since at least 1968, with three reported in November 1978. Other non-estuarine sites recording occasional wintering or passage birds include Belmont, Cant Clough, Clowbridge, Coldwell, Dean Clough, Foulridge, Parsonage, Stocks, Sunnyhurst and Wayoh Reservoirs, Colne and Wood End sewage works, Martin Mere and Scorton. The only recent wintering record in the uplands is of one ringed at Cant Clough Reservoir in March 2003 and returning for three subsequent winters.

More than 40 records from Crossens and Marshside have been published since 1974 but numbers seem to have declined somewhat in recent years. Peak counts include four in October 1978, five to eight in April 1984 and three in April 1996 and March 2002. A complete lack of records from other south Ribble marshes perhaps reflects minimal survey effort there.

Water Pipit, Leighton Moss, March 2004. (Phillip Tomkinson)

Estuarine records north of the Ribble remained extremely scarce until very recently with just one or two from various north Ribble, Wyre and Lune saltmarsh sites but all this changed with the discovery of the north Ribble population at Warton Bank in the mid- 1990s. This site is largely inaccessible and observations are mostly restricted to spring tide periods when birds are forced off the marsh (Dunstan 2004). The first record to be published was a single on 2 May 1992 but intensive study during the winter of 1997/98 produced a staggering peak count of 19 birds on 30 March. Similar numbers were recorded between 20 February and 21 March 1999 and subsequent peak counts have been eleven in March 2000, seven in February 2001, 15 in February 2002, eight in March 2003 and twelve in March 2004. Actual numbers may be somewhat greater than these counts suggest; 25 or more Water/Rock Pipits are seen regularly and it is known that Water Pipits predominate on this site.

Spurred on by these findings on the Ribble, recent survey work has also uncovered regular smaller numbers on the Wyre and irregular ones and twos on the Lune marshes, at Hambleton, Fleetwood Marsh, Aldcliffe and Colloway.

Very little is known about the ecology of this saltmarsh population, in particular where they feed and what they feed on. It is possible that it is associated with freshwater flushes on the upper marsh at Warton Bank (as appears to be the case with a similar but smaller wintering population at Neston on the Cheshire Dee), but access restrictions prevent more detailed study.

The earliest published record is of one on 29 September 1992 at Stocks Reservoir. However, the earliest at Warton Bank was on 25 October 1992 with more arrivals during November, but peak counts are always at the end of February or during March, after which numbers decline rapidly. The latest at Warton Bank was on 2 May 1992 and inland at Coldwell Reservoir on 5 May 1991. The March peak may suggest a small spring influx but it may simply be an artefact of good conditions for observation. Alternatively, birds that were previously spread widely across the marshes may come together prior to migration. Like so much concerning all of Lancashire's saltmarsh pipits, much study remains to be carried out.

SJW, MJ.

This species account was sponsored by the Fylde Bird Club.

YELLOW WAGTAIL

Motacilla flava flavissima

Lancashire Category A.

Scarce breeder; fairly common passage migrant.

For more than a hundred years the Yellow Wagtail was a common breeder throughout most of the lowlands of Lancashire. Mitchell believed it to be most frequent on cultivated land, 'breeding oftenest in corn, hay, and fallow fields', and least common 'between the Lune and Morecambe Bay'. He listed four different local names, indicating that it was a familiar bird of the countryside. Oakes confirmed Mitchell's summary of distribution, describing it as 'rather local in the . . . Silverdale area and one or two south-western districts' but very common on the plains 'especially in the Fylde' and abundant 'on many mosslands 'particularly . . . on the partially reclaimed lands at Tarleton and Hesketh Bank'. He described meadows as the favoured nesting habitat. Just how numerous it must have been in the mid-twentieth century is demonstrated by Oakes's lyrical words: 'there are few sights more heartening in the spring than the flocks of brilliant male Yellow Wagtails on cultivated fields or the river margins'.

It is now many years since anyone saw a flock of Yellow Wagtails in Lancashire.

A small contraction in national range was first noted in the 1930s (BWP) and population declines were picked up by the Waterways Bird Survey during the 1970s and by the CBC in the 1980s; national populations fell by an estimated 67% during 1977-2001 (CBC) and by 33% between 1994 and 2005 (BBS). The English population on wet grasslands declined by 65% between 1982 and 2002 and that of NW England by 84% during the same period (Wilson & Vickery 2005). Population size and range in Lancashire have shrunk so rapidly over the past 20 or so years that Yellow Wagtails seem to be in serious danger of local extinction.

The scale and timing of the decline is well illustrated by distributional changes between the Old and New Atlases. In 1968-72 Yellow Wagtails bred in 44 10km squares in Lancashire but this fell to 24 squares in 1988-91, a decline in range of almost 50%. These losses were concentrated in the eastern areas of the Fylde and the western edge of Bowland. By the time of the Lancashire

Atlas in 1997-2000 the breeding range had contracted to 16 squares, a further 33% decline in less than ten years. During this period breeding had ceased completely in the Fylde – the last published records were at Pilling in 1994 and Freckleton in 1995. Breeding was confirmed in just 43 tetrads (less than 5% of the county) and was largely confined to just three 10km squares (SJ49, SD40 and SD41) in a narrow belt of farmland on the mosslands from Knowsley north to the Ribble. The county's population was estimated at 70 pairs during 1997-2000 but is certainly smaller than this now – perhaps considerably fewer than 50 pairs.

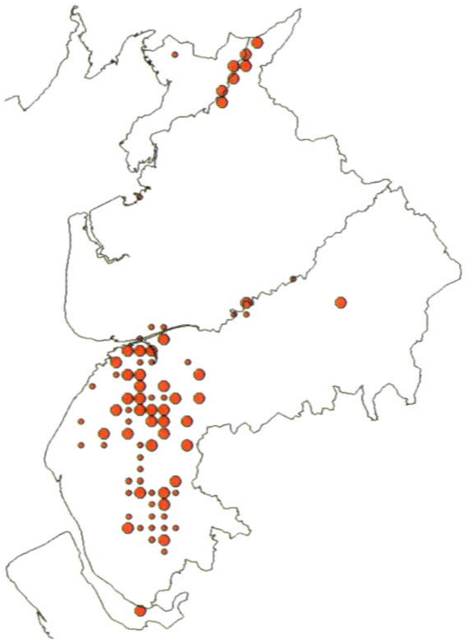

Breeding distribution of Yellow Wagtail, 1997-2000. (Large dots: confirmed. Small dots: possible)

The main reasons for this near demise undoubtedly lie in the range of agricultural changes that has affected so many farmland birds, the most significant of which have probably been the almost complete loss of mixed farms and, in particular, the virtual disappearance of extensive, damp pastures. Yellow Wagtails now breed in just two habitats in Lancashire: some remain in traditional riverine situations but the vast majority are found on the 'improved' mosslands of the south-west, apparently favouring fields in horticultural – especially carrot – rather than cereal production. Here, extensive networks of drainage ditches provide many of the large invertebrates on which they depend. In recent years favoured sites have included areas around Rufford, Ormskirk and Rainford. Few sizeable concentrations appear to remain and the largest reported recently was ten pairs in the Old Coach Road area between Kirkby and Rainford in 2003. Their range extends north to Tarleton and east to Parbold and Eccleston with just one or two pairs in south Liverpool. One or two pairs bred on Hesketh Marsh during the late 1990s but these may now have disappeared. None now regularly breed to the west of the Leeds-Liverpool Canal although one pair was suspected in 2003 at Downholland Moss and breeding by single pairs was confirmed there, and at Altcar Withins, in 2005.

In north Lancashire breeding is now entirely restricted to sites adjacent to the River Lune between Claughton and the Yorkshire boundary. The Waterways Bird Survey of 32km of the Lune between Skerton Weir and Kirkby Lonsdale found that breeding pairs were increasing until 1982 but declined from an average of 28 during the 1980s (35 in 1982) to 14 in 1993 and a maximum of eight during 1997-2000. The favoured area is around Arkholme which continued to support three pairs until at least 2003. Elsewhere in the north a small population at Leighton Moss became extinct after 1979. A 1977 survey of the six coastal 10km squares in the Lancaster district found birds breeding in 37 tetrads and estimated a population of 80-100 pairs but by 1994 the distribution had declined to 17-21 tetrads and by 1997-2000 to just seven, all on the upper Lune.

The Lancashire Atlas confirmed just two other breeding sites in the county: near Walton-le-Dale on the Ribble and by the River Calder at Altham to Martholme, where one or two pairs bred up to 1997 and one pair until 2004. The last known breeding elsewhere in east Lancashire was at Trawden in 1992 and Laneshawbridge in 1997. The most recent published breeding record in Rossendale was at The Hile in 1978.

Oakes gave the average date of first arrival in south Lancashire as 13 April. Nowadays (1978-2004) it is a little earlier on 9 April, although sometimes as late as the 19th; the earliest ever was a male at Arkholme on 24 March 1996. The main movement, however, usually occurs between the last week of April and mid- to late May.

Yellow Wagtail, Seaforth Nature Reserve, April 2007. (Steve Young)

Passage numbers have crashed during the past 20 years. Large numbers were recorded through Marton Mere during the 1950s and 1960s, with the largest roost of 75 on 2 May 1954. These large spring movements continued into the 1970s and early 1980s, for example 32 moving through Arkholme in an hour on 28 April 1978, 300 at Marshside on 3 May 1978, 50 north at Otterspool on 23 April 1979, 60 at Padiham on 2 May 1979 and a flock of 37 at Leighton Moss on 26 April 1981. However, these are now distant memories; day-counts nowadays rarely exceed single figures and the largest recent records include 65 at Seaforth on 26 April 1987 and 38 at Foulridge on 27 April 1989. Marshside is fortunate if it records a spring total of more than ten nowadays, while Seaforth has slumped from an average of 75 bird-days in 1986-90 to ten in 2000-2004 and Heysham totals from 38 in 1983 to three or fewer since 1996 (Figure 1).

Occasional birds, probably mostly first-summers, continue to arrive at coastal sites during June but the autumn passage usually starts in mid-July and peaks in late August to early September. Numbers have followed the same dismal trend as in spring. Earlier peak counts included 70 at Marton Mere in September 1955 and 1956, 100 at Lea Marsh on 21 August 1964 , 117 at Freckleton on 16 August 1971, 100+ at Banks on 1 September 1980, 40 at Marton Mere on 23-24 August 1981, 150 at Preesall on 4 September 1981, 40 at Skerden Beck on 17 August 1983 and 100 at Seaforth on 9 September 1989. In contrast, the largest day-counts since the 1980s have been 50 at Seaforth on 25 & 30 August 1991, 40 there on 4 September 1995 and 15 on 28 August 2003. Seaforth's autumn totals have plummeted from an average 700 bird-days in 1986-1990 to 25 in 2000-2005, while Marshside's highest total since the 1980s was 42 bird-days in 1999. Autumn totals at Heysham have not reached double figures since 1990. Most birds have moved through by the end of September and October records are generally few and far between. The latest was one at Seaforth on 11 November 1995.

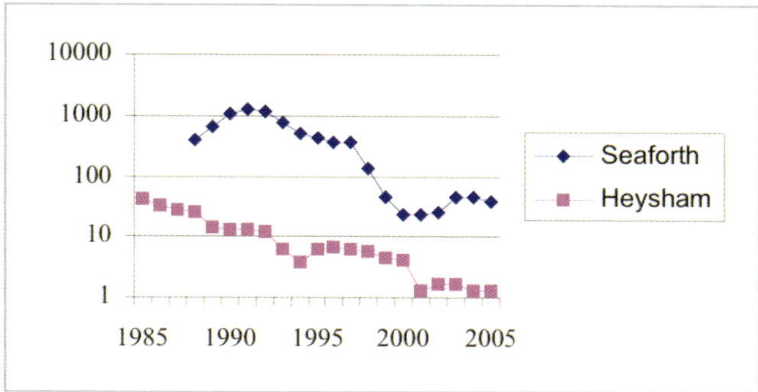

Figure 1. Annual bird-days of Yellow Wagtails (3-year rolling means; log scale) at Heysham and Seaforth Nature Reserves, 1985-2005.

There have been four recoveries of Lancashire-ringed birds in southern Europe, all of them in autumn (singles in France and Spain and two in Portugal) and one in spring in Morocco, but none on their sub-Saharan wintering grounds. The timing of autumn migration is illustrated by two within-year recoveries: singles ringed on 17 August to France on 12 September 1978, and on 22 July to Portugal on 15 September 1957.

It is likely that some October and November records are of continental, nominate *flava* birds but these 'female-types' are difficult to confirm at this time of year; birds strongly suspected to have been of continental origin include singles at Skerton Weir on 7 November 1981, Seaforth on 30 September 2001 and Heysham on 19 October 2001.

Blue-headed *flava* males do, however, occur with some regularity, especially in spring. None of Oakes's records were in the present county and, while Spencer reported a further four birds to 1957, no sites were specified. The first definite record, therefore, was a male at Cabin Hill on 21 May 1975. A further 33 records of males (including those described as resembling *beema*, whose actual identity remains unknown) have been published between 1977 and 2005, the earliest at Marshside on 17 April 2003 and the latest, also at Marshside, on 28 September 1997. Most have been on the Fylde and Sefton coasts, with Marshside, and particularly Seaforth, having the lion's share in the past ten years.

Male Blue-headed Wagtail, Seaforth Nature Reserve, May 2005. (Steve Young)

A single male bred successfully at Halford on the Lune Estuary in 1991 and one at Whittingham in the Lune Valley in June 2001 was later seen in the company of a presumed female *flavissima* and may have bred. In addition, birds with a resemblance to *beema* bred on Freckleton and Warton Marshes from 1956 to 1986.

There have been five records of birds showing characteristics of Grey-headed *thunbergi* males. Four have been at Seaforth or Crosby Marine Park: on 26 April 1984 (a very early date for this sub-species), 27 May 1987, 9 May 1992 and 1 July 1999, and one on the Eric Morecambe Pools on 14 May 1992.

One showing all the characteristics of Black-headed *feldegg* was seen by several observers at Seaforth on 25 April 1987; it was pended by the BBRC at the time but was resubmitted in 2005; a decision is awaited.

SJW, RW.

This species account was sponsored by Margaret Dempsey.

CITRINE WAGTAIL

Motacilla citreola

Lancashire Category A. (0, 1).

Vagrant from western Russia or Siberia.

Although not the only rarity to be found during a Lancashire bird race, this was without question the most exciting. One of the Fylde Bird Club teams (P. Bainbridge, A & L Parnell) dropped into Newton Marsh, Freckleton on 4 May 1997 in order to 'tick off' a Garganey that was known to be present and hoping to see Yellow Wagtail. One team member thought they'd succeeded in this when he got a glimpse of yellow on a bird that dropped down on the edge of a pool, frustratingly out of view. Another disagreed – he'd seen the bird as being grey and white.

A closer approach brought the bird into view, revealing it to be a female Citrine Wagtail, thus resolving the initial confusion between Yellow and Pied Wagtail.

The bird remained around this pool until 7 May, fortunately close enough to the road to allow many birdwatchers to enjoy views of it on this private site.

Female Citrine Wagtail, Newton Marsh, May 1997. (Steve Young)

More than 100 Citrine Wagtails had been seen previously in Britain and Ireland but the majority of these were in the Northern Isles and at various east coast sites. Most are first-winter birds in autumn although spring records have also increased recently; this remains the only record in north-west England.

SJW, MJ.

This species account was sponsored by Peter Ross.

GREY WAGTAIL

Motacilla cinerea

Lancashire Category A.

Fairly common breeding resident and passage migrant.

The past 150 years have seen remarkably little change in the status of the Grey Wagtail in Lancashire. Its riverine habitat has, of course, remained intact and detrimental changes in water quality appear not to have affected its numbers or distribution significantly.

According to Mitchell, in the nineteenth century it bred 'on most of the secluded and rocky streams in the northern parts of the county' and moved to 'the towns and villages' in winter, but was 'seldom seen near Liverpool or other low-lying districts'. Oakes was more explicit, saying it nested 'plentifully . . . along the entire range of Pennine hills and intersecting valleys . . . and confluent streams of the Lune, Greta, Wenning, Roeburn, Brock, Wyre, Calder, Hodder, Ribble, Darwen and Irwell', as far west as Preston on the Ribble and on moorland streams up to 600' (200m)'. He noted that 'the number of birds which successfully breed in south-east Lancashire [mostly now in Greater Manchester] is remarkable in view of the amount of disturbance and pollution which prevails.'

This could serve almost equally well as a description of the current distribution. During 1997-2000 Grey Wagtails bred in roughly a third of Lancashire tetrads, overwhelmingly in upland areas in the eastern two-thirds of the county. Greenhalgh put forward two reasons for this long-term stability in the Lancashire Atlas. Firstly, The Grey Wagtail is less dependent upon clean water than other riverine species such as Dipper, being able to switch from the mayflies and caddis-flies of unpolluted streams to midges and other flies which thrive elsewhere. Their numbers are, however, constrained by the availability of suitable nest-sites; on the Ribble, Hodder and Lune catchments more than 80% of nests were located on natural, vertical rock faces with the remainder in tree roots or built-structures. This undoubtedly limits their spread onto lowland watercourses but the past two decades have seen increased colonisation of West Lancashire and Merseyside.

National population data indicate that Grey Wagtail numbers can be significantly reduced by hard winters and take some years to recover. Strangely, Oakes believed that the severe weather of 1946/47 had little impact upon the Lancashire population, but that of 1962/63 certainly did. This may go some way to explain the apparent increase in the county breeding distribution at the 10km square level between 1968-72 and 1988-91 from 29 to 31 squares. A further increase to 37 squares in 1997-2000 is perhaps partly explained by limited expansion into the lowlands but also by the recent run of mild winters which have allowed population growth. Nationally, Grey Wagtail numbers decreased by 30% between 1970 and 2001 but increased by 75% between 1994 and 2005 (BBS). These trends are reflected in data from the Waterways Bird Survey of the Lune, which show an average of 25 pairs in the three years to 1976 declining to an average of 14 pairs during the 1980s and 14 in the 1990s before reaching a new high of 20 pairs in 2003.

Nicola Breaks

A survey of the Lancaster and north Bowland area in 1983-85 found densities of 0.2 pairs per km on the Conder, Langden Beck, Dunsop and Croasdale catchments, 0.4 on the Keer and Lancaster Canal, 0.5 on the Lune, 0.6 on Leck Beck and the Wenning, and 0.8 in the Wyre catchment (Harrison 1995). Other surveys found ten pairs on the Hodder between Doeford Bridge and the Ribble confluence, eight pairs on the Ribble between Paythorne and the Darwen confluence and nine pairs on the Lancashire sections of the Irwell in 1997, and nine pairs from Hodderfoot to Doeford Bridge in 2000.

A total of 384 breeding pairs was counted during 1997-2000 and the county population was estimated at 500 pairs.

Breeding is not entirely restricted to upland rivers and streams. Many eastern reservoirs, for example Rowley, Rishton, Parsonage, Belmont, Delph and Anglezarke/Rivington, also support small numbers, while a pair has bred at the newly created Brockholes Quarry since 2002. The distribution in the south-west lowlands has slowly increased since the late 1980s and 20 or more pairs now breed annually, most of them on the Leeds-Liverpool Canal from

Liverpool's Stanley Dock, through Burscough to Appley Bridge. Others have bred at Netherley sewage works in south Liverpool, Newton-le-Willows, St. Helens, Carr Mill Dam, Fazakerley sewage works, Formby town centre, and our only coastal pairs at Crosby Marine Park since 2001 and at Southport Marine Lake and Blackpool Pleasure Beach in 2005. A few pairs breed on the Wyre, Brock and other streams west of the A6. One pair nested successfully in hanging baskets at Witton Country Park in 2003.

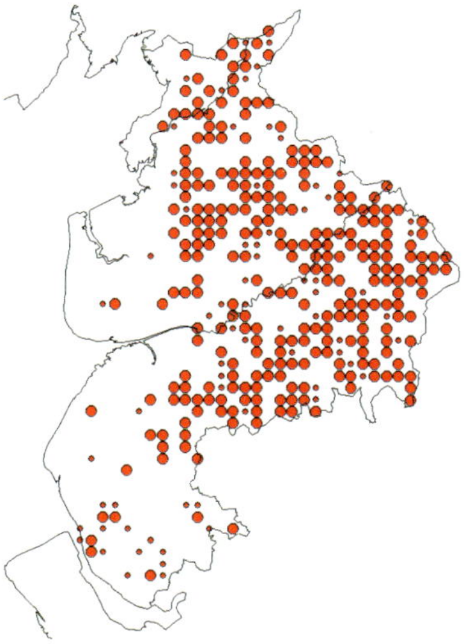

Breeding distribution of Grey Wagtail, 1997-2000. (Large dots: confirmed. Small dots: possible)

Many birds desert the breeding areas after nesting, heading towards the lowlands and coast for winter. However, the mostly mild winters since the 1990s appear to be encouraging more birds to stay within the main breeding range. Eastern sewage farms have always attracted their fair share, for example 30 at Ewood Bridge, Rossendale in January 1992 with ten there in March 1993, and 6-8 at Colne in 1993-95. Odd birds also remain scattered throughout the middle and lower reaches of the main rivers, occasionally in small concentrations, for example four on the Ribble at Calderfoot in 2000 and five on the Calder between Altham and Martholme in 2003. It is difficult to judge how many winter in the lowlands or on the coast, since concentrations large enough to be reported rarely occur. Nevertheless, records of up to five are received annually, especially from the Fylde, and birds are increasingly regular in urban areas, including Blackburn, Burnley, Chorley, Southport, Lytham, Blackpool and Liverpool, where they sometimes occur well away from water, often taking insects from roof tops in the manner of Pied Wagtails. Winter roosts are poorly recorded but recent examples include 15+ in Sefton Park, Liverpool in the late 1980s, 20 in Knowsley Park in 1989, and eleven with Pied Wagtails at Banks in 1992. Although dramatically under-recorded in winter, available data point to winter numbers considerably lower than the expected 2,000 or more post-breeding population; the majority of Lancashire's breeding birds, therefore, probably leave the county.

The return movement to upland breeding areas sometimes begins in late January but more usually during February and March and occasionally in early April. A high count was twelve at Dunsop Bridge on 7 April 1990. Very small numbers are recorded along the coast, mainly in March but occasionally from February to early May. Spring totals at any one site rarely exceed three but recent exceptions include ten at Heysham and seven at Seaforth in 1999, and 24 at Marshside in 2000.

Although post-fledging dispersal may begin during the second half of June most family parties are seen from mid-July onwards. Single-figure groups are normal and ten on the Ribble at Gisburn on 20 August 1984, eleven at Rowley Lake on 16 September 1989 and 17 on the Calder at Altham to Martholme on 13 August 2003 were notable. Larger roosts sometimes form, 70-100 in conifers near Calf Hey Reservoir, Haslingden on 15 August 1979 being exceptional.

Southbound passage usually begins in mid-August and continues until November, with most movement in September. It is most visible on the coast. Autumn totals at Heysham averaged 160 during 1991-2003 with a maximum of 320 in 2000. Slightly lower numbers are recorded at the other main watchpoints, Rossall, Fairhaven, Marshside and Seaforth. Most day-counts are in single figures but notable recent records include 35 at Marshside on 8 October 1995, 49 at Heysham on 5 September 1999 with 42 there on 10 September 2000, 43 at Fairhaven on 9 September 2002, 50 at Seaforth on 11 September 2002 and 49 at Blackpool on 7 September.

There are two recoveries linking Lancashire in autumn or winter and Scotland in the breeding season, both on Tayside, but none that indicate more southerly wintering sites of Lancashire breeders or passage migrants.

SJW, RW.

This species account was sponsored by Peter Hornby.

PIED WAGTAIL

Motacilla alba yarrellii

Lancashire Category A.

Abundant resident breeder.

The Pied Wagtail is a widespread breeding bird throughout Lancashire and, although never abundant anywhere, is probably our most common 'waterbird', frequenting a variety of wet habitats, and is a familiar sight on pastures, around farm buildings and in urban parks and similar open spaces such as golf courses. It also breeds in a wide range of other habitats from moorland (except for heather-dominated areas) to sand dunes.

Mitchell had very little to say about its numbers or distribution beyond 'resident and common, breeding everywhere', but he did note that Lancashire's Pied Wagtails are primarily migratory 'though there are few districts where a pair or two may not be seen the year round'. Oakes's account was a little more comprehensive. He described it as 'a partial resident, a summer visitor and a passage migrant . . . common in most parts from the coastal sand dunes to derelict moorland farms'. Its breeding distribution was, however, uneven, being sparse in the Fylde except on the Pilling and Cockerham mosslands, scarce or absent from parts of the south-west where densities were higher on the coast than inland, although 'most buildings on agricultural land have nesting pairs'.

Very little appears to have changed in the intervening years. The 1997-2000 survey recorded breeding in 658 Lancashire tetrads with possible breeding in a further 115, representing 83% of the county. It is largely absent from the highest parts of Leck Fell, north-east Bowland, the south Pennines and West Pennine Moors, and in the Fylde from western urban areas and north of the Wyre. Heather moorland, heavily wooded areas and saltmarshes are also largely avoided. Breeding is sparse within all urban areas and in the inner districts of the Liverpool conurbation, the species is largely restricted to dockland and derelict industrial areas.

Nest sites are almost always in man-made structures, including farm out-buildings, dry-stone walls, quarries, slag heaps, greenhouses and factory yards and buildings. More exotic nest sites include the log-flume ride at Blackpool Pleasure Beach, the entrance to Blackpool South Pier and inside the birdwatching hide at Stocks Reservoir.

The Lancashire population was estimated at 4,000 pairs in 1997-2000 but this was probably an underestimate, and the true figure may well be in excess of 6,000 pairs. The Lancaster and District Atlas estimated a total of 1,400-1,500 pairs within its nine 10km square survey area, based upon known breeding densities during 1983-85. These ranged from 0.4 pairs per square km in the Langden Beck and Dunsop catchments and other areas to 2.4 pairs in the Lune catchment; while CBC data from Halton Park indicated 8 pairs per square km on grazed pasture and surveys on Carnforth Marsh recorded 14 pairs per square km. Numbers can fluctuate enormously within a short period of time; for example the Carnforth Marsh population varied between 21 and 31 pairs during 1995-99.

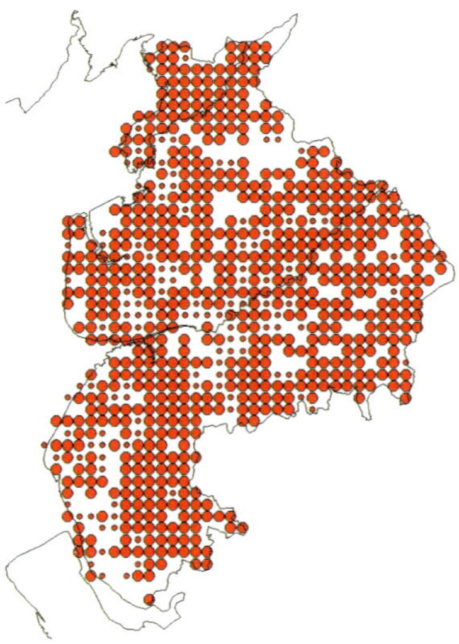

Breeding distribution of Pied Wagtail, 1997-2000. (Large dots: confirmed. Small dots: possible)

Hard winters can also take a heavy toll but this has rarely been recorded in Lancashire, apart from a report of much reduced numbers in the north-east during 1982. Nationally, numbers have increased overall by 52% between 1970 and 2001 and by 21% between 1994 and 2005 (BBS), but the Waterways Bird Survey showed a 49% decrease on riverine habitats between 1975 and 1998. Data from the Lune WBS show a fluctuating population of between 66 and 90 pairs between 1980 and 1994 but numbers have declined over the past ten years (Figure 1). No comparable information is available for other areas of the county or for other habitats, with the exception of CBC data from The Hile in Rossendale, where none bred prior to one pair in 1984, rising to three pairs in 1989 and four in 1994.

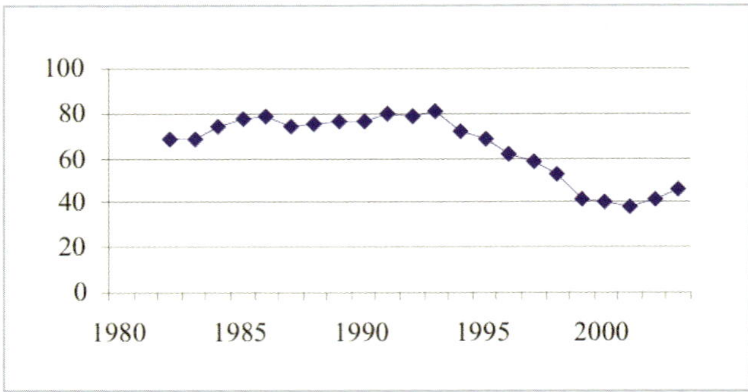

Fig. 1. Numbers of pairs of Pied Wagtail (3-yr rolling means) on the River Lune (Skerton Weir to Kirkby Lonsdale, 1980-2003.

Although some birds remain in the vicinity of their nest site throughout the year, including in the more sheltered upland areas, most disperse to more favourable lowland sites from late July through to late October, many moving out of the region altogether, joining the passage of birds from further north. Even inland river valleys are mostly deserted in winter unless some favourable habitat, such as a sewage works, is present.

Sizeable roosts may form during late summer, for example 100+ at Lee Green Reservoir on 29 July 2002 and 250 at Banks on 7 August 2002, but the largest movements usually take place during September and October. Leighton Moss recorded its largest ever roost, estimated at 1,000, during September 1980, reducing to 600 in October, but peaks of up to 450 are more normal. Other notable autumn roosts include 280 near Nelson on 13 October 1967, 350 at Banks Marsh on 1 September 1980, 200 at Ewood Bridge sewage works on 12 November 1980, 300 in central Burnley on 31 October 1988, 1,000 in central Preston on 21 September 1994, 300 at Colne sewage works on 22 September 1995 and 250 in Blackburn town centre in October 2003.

Visible migration is regular but rarely spectacular. Inland, it has been best recorded near Darwen Moor, where several hundred are seen most autumns, and on the Lune at Arkholme, where day-totals include 187 on 26 August 1980 and 275 on 30 September 2002. Autumn totals at Heysham include 678 in 1993 and 1,389 in 1995, but are usually lower. Estimated totals at Seaforth – where numbers usually peak during September – include 1,000-1,500 in 1991, 1995 and 2003, but as elsewhere in the county, these were spread relatively evenly throughout the season. Large day-counts of overflying or temporarily grounded birds are unusual; they include 150 on four separate dates at Marshside between 27 August and 26 September 1993 with 350 there on 8 October 1995, 200 at Heysham on 9 October 1994 with 268 there on 11 October 1995, and 300 at Seaforth on 25 September 1991 and 8 October 1995. Various sites on the Fylde coast regularly produce peak counts of 50-100.

Juvenile Pied Wagtail, Seaforth Nature Reserve, September 2003. (Steve Young)

Some autumn roosts persist in smaller numbers throughout the winter, notably Leighton Moss which regularly holds 100-150 during December to February. Others, especially in urban areas, increase in size, for example from 400 at Victoria Hospital, Blackpool in October 2002 to 500 during December. Other large urban winter roosts, many of them persisting for a considerable number of years, have been recorded in Burnley, Preston, Blackburn, Chorley, Lancaster and Liverpool. Elsewhere, the largest recent roost counts have been 700 in a factory at Crossens in December 1971 and 400 at Fazakerley Reedbed since the late 1990s. Birds regularly congregate around favourable feeding sites such as sewage farms and wherever livestock are kept; large waterbodies are also favoured, although 106 at Stanah ICI reservoir in January 1994 were unusual.

Spring passage begins in late February but usually peaks between mid-March and early April, a few arriving as late as mid-May at sites well inland. Numbers are lower than in autumn, and although counts of 50 or more occur at sewage works daily totals are usually below 20. High counts elsewhere include 178 an hour moving upstream at Arkholme on 3 March 1993 and 165 an hour there on 24 March 1996, 250-350 regularly roosting at Leighton Moss with a maximum of 500 on 22 April 1988, and 96 moving through Rossall Point on 15 March 1984. Daily counts at Heysham and elsewhere along the coast usually total fewer than 20, rarely more than 50, however 300-400 at Heysham on 3 April 1987 were exceptional. Large roosts may occur at this time of year, such as 100 at Belmont on 18 March 1990 and 400 in Chorley town centre on 7 March 1996.

The majority of Pied Wagtails ringed in Lancashire and subsequently recovered have been juvenile/first-winters so their natal areas are not known. However, two ringed as pulli have been recovered in the following winter on the Atlantic coast of Spain, and others (some of which may have been nominate *alba*) have been recovered or ringed in France (seven), Spain (three), Portugal (two) and Morocco (one), either in winter or on passage. Interestingly, these exceed the total of eleven recovered or ringed in southern England during the same seasons, perhaps indicating that a large proportion of Lancashire migrants leave the country. The origins of 30 passage migrants are known, 16 in Scotland and 14 elsewhere in northern England, suggesting a substantial movement through Lancashire from the north.

SJW, RW.

This species account was sponsored by Ron Hothersall.

WHITE WAGTAIL

Motacilla alba alba

Lancashire Category A.

Common passage migrant en route to Iceland.

It is likely that a very large proportion of White Wagtails breeding in the Faeroes, Iceland and Greenland pass through Britain and Ireland on passage but there is little evidence that any substantial numbers of continental birds, which follow a south-east migration route in autumn, do so (Migration Atlas). In the absence of any ringing recoveries it is not possible to be certain, but it seems highly probable that the overwhelming majority of Lancashire's spring birds are indeed headed north-west or north.

Mitchell devoted considerably more space to the White than the Pied Wagtail, concluding that the former 'occurs much more frequently . . . than is supposed'. However, he seems to have based these conclusions almost entirely upon specimens and had little to say about patterns of occurrence, although he appears to have been aware that it occurred only on passage. Oakes gave the timing of the passage as from late March to early May and considered migrants to be fairly numerous, but the largest flock he knew of was 30 at Crosby on 24-28 April 1941.

Northern White Wagtails are long-distance migrants and winter further south than *yarrellii*, mostly in Africa and often south of the Sahara (BWP). Although one of our earliest sub-Saharan spring migrants, they occur significantly later than *yarrellii*. The earliest records are a matter of dispute; there have been claims of birds as early as mid-February but, since few pass across the Straits of Gibraltar before the end of February (Migration Atlas), such early records would require detailed documentation. The average first arrival at Seaforth (1986-2005) was 1 April although odd birds have appeared as early as the middle of March. Passage at Seaforth rarely begins in earnest before the second week of April and peaks soon after – on average on the 21st (1986-2005) – with very few remaining into the second week of May.

Male White Wagtail, Seaforth Nature Reserve, April 2004. (Steve Young)

As Oakes noted earlier, the heaviest passage takes place on or close to the coast. Over the past 20 years or so this appears to have become more and more concentrated on the Sefton coast but sizeable counts have been made further north. Early examples include 50 on the Keer Estuary on 24 April 1962 and 60 roosting with Yellow Wagtails at Sunderland Point on 29th-30 April 1965 and 42 at Leighton Moss in April 1980. Peak day-counts in north Lancashire seem to have declined somewhat, rarely reaching double figures during the 1990s, but hundreds are seen there during the course of spring, for example 50 through Aldcliffe Marsh between 12 April and 4 May 2002. Notable records on the Fylde coast include 70 at Marton Mere on 2 May 1954, 120 at Fleetwood power station on 22 April 1986, 350 at Lytham on 19-22 April 1979, 55 on Clifton Marsh on 26 April 1996 and 28 at Pilling on 17 April 2002.

Numbers are considerably higher south of the Ribble. During the 1990s Marshside rarely recorded more than 100 bird-days in spring with peak counts usually in the low teens, 200 on 29 April 2001 being exceptional. However, day totals of more than 100 were regular during the 1980s, including 200 on 20 April 1981 and 150 on 20-21 April 1987. The focus has since shifted further south on the Sefton coast, which had been identified by Oakes as the prime site. Large counts on the dunes include 120 at Birkdale on 27 April 1998 with 200 there on 18 April 2003, but birds are found (but rarely recorded) everywhere between Southport and Crosby Marine Park. The passage is best monitored at Seaforth, where up to 1,000 bird-days are recorded annually, probably involving up to 300-400 individuals most years but with peak counts of 250 on 23 April 1989 and 150 on 26 April 2003.

Significant numbers also pass through the near-coastal mosslands in the west, where notable recent concentrations have included 47 at Preesall on 27 April 1994 and 60 on Plex Moss on the 30th. Further inland, most records come from sewage works and reservoirs and less frequently from stretches of river, particularly the Ribble. Just ones and twos are normally involved and 100 roosting in *Juncus* near Entwistle on the very late date of 29 May 1988 was completely exceptional. More recent counts include ten at Foulridge Reservoir on 25 April 1996, 22 through Brockholes Quarry in spring 2002 and ten at Alston Reservoir on 19 April 2003.

The size and timing of the autumn passage is far less clear. It is possible that some pass unnoticed within overflying flocks of Pied Wagtails and birds are far less easy to identify in autumn than in spring. However, detailed scrutiny of grounded *alba* wagtails at several sites suggests that White Wagtails are genuinely scarce in Lancashire at this time of year. Autumn totals at Seaforth rarely exceed 20 with similar numbers at Marshside and far fewer further north. The main movement appears to occur from late August to the end of September. Low single-figure counts are the norm, the only recent exception being 20 dispersed over a large area of farmland in the Old Coach Road area of St. Helens on 6 September 2003. Very few have ever been seen in north Lancashire in autumn.

Our only ringing recovery was a female ringed in Gloucestershire on 14 April 1981 and found dead at Fleetwood a week later on 21 April.

SJW.

This species account was sponsored by Dave McAleavy.

WAXWING

Bombycilla garrulus

Lancashire Category A.

Fairly common winter visitor from Fennoscandia and Russia.

Waxwing numbers in Britain fluctuate wildly between years; occasional large influxes occur, with irruptive behaviour driven by increased population size and limited food availability in their normal wintering areas, the most recent being in 1946/47, 1965/66, 1988/89, 1990/91, 1991/92, early 1996, 2000/01 and 2004/05. The pattern of these influxes is well established, with first arrivals usually in eastern Scotland and north-east England and a gradual dispersal south and west as food resources become depleted. They feed entirely upon berries and, if supplies of their favourite rowan or hawthorn are not available, turn instead to a wide variety of cultivated species such as cotoneaster. Nowadays, the largest concentrations of berry-bearing trees are found in urban areas and most Waxwings are seen ranging through suburbia and increasingly in town centres.

Some Waxwings are seen in Lancashire in most winters, in the 50 years since 1956 there have been just twelve winters when none was recorded. Half of these blank years fell between 1979/80 and 1983/84 and there have been just two since then, in 1987/88 and 2001/02. However, outside influx years, numbers rarely reach double figures, averaging about half a dozen per winter since 1990. All records have occurred between October and April. Oakes published one at St. Michael's-on-Wyre during the first week of July 1933 but this was discounted by Spencer (1973) as uncorroborated.

Even during 'Waxwing winters', Lancashire totals never approach those on the eastern side of the country but, nevertheless, there have been several notable influxes. By far the greatest numbers occur in north and east Lancashire, with smaller numbers in central Lancashire and relatively few on the central and southern-western plain in the Fylde, South Ribble, West Lancashire or Merseyside. Why this should be so is unclear. Certainly these latter areas lie on the western edge of the county but their urban areas do not lack berry-bearing trees; perhaps it is their generally low levels of tree cover that discourage Waxwings from exploring them.

Once arrived, Waxwings are usually highly nomadic, sometimes dispersing into a number of quite small flocks and sometimes congregating around plentiful food supplies before moving on when these are depleted. This makes it extremely difficult to assess total numbers and those illustrating the account of the main invasion years that follow are probably on the conservative side.

Mitchell noted that 'many specimens were obtained [in Lancashire] in the winters of 1828/29, 1849/50, 1863/64. 1866/67, when large arrivals took place all over the kingdom. The whole of the Lancashire examples were taken in the months of December and January'. Oakes reported further large influxes in 1894/95, 1911/12 and 1932/33, noting that most occurred 'in northern districts'. He documented fully what he described as 'by far the most important visitation' during the very severe winter of 1946/47. After the first at Cockerham on 1 December numbers built rapidly with separate flocks of 150 and 200 in the Carnforth area by 23 December and up to 80 in Clitheroe from the end of December, with a scattering of smaller groups in Parbold, Cleveleys, Preston and elsewhere, most departing during February. It seems likely that more than 500 birds were involved, more than 90% of which were seen north of the Ribble.

The next invasion came in 1965/66, when at least 260 individuals were noted. The first sizeable flocks were seen very early with 30 on Warton Crag on 6 November and a similar number at Turton at about the same time. The largest flock recorded was 145 at Warton Crag on 10 November, reducing to 95 on the 12th with just one left by the 21st. Elsewhere, there were a number of mostly single flocks, chiefly around Garstang, Preston, Leyland and the Ribble Valley. A smaller influx took place during 1970/71 when birds were reported from at least 20 localities in all parts of the (then) county with the largest flock of 52 in Carnforth. Another lesser influx in 1974/75 saw small numbers in many parts of north and east Lancashire and the Ribble Valley, with maxima of 40 at Brierfield and about 94 at Warton Crag in December.

More than a decade then elapsed before the next Lancashire Waxwing winter began on 2 November 1988. Numbers peaked during mid-December with 94 at Warton (Carnforth) and 30 at Salterforth near Barnoldswick. The likely total was more than 350 birds and the last were seen on 15 April at Leyland. The winters of 1990/91 – which began very early with three at Crawshawbooth on 31 October – and 1991/92 each produced up to 100 birds, mostly in the east, but with no really large flocks.

The late 1990s and early years of the present century brought ever shorter gaps between successive large influxes. A very late invasion began in early January 1996 and ended with the county's latest record in Darwen on 17 April. Again, around 350 individuals were seen with the largest regional flocks 73 in Nelson, 55 in Burnley, 33 in Clitheroe, 28 in Blackburn, 37 in Crosby and nine in Lytham. Just one appeared in Rossendale and, unusually, few were seen in the north of the county. The winter of 1996/97 produced about 50 birds, while, starting on 13 December, 2000/01 again saw total numbers in the region of 350-400, including peaks of 113 in Burnley, 66 in Blackburn, 38 at Heysham, 14 at Lead Mines Clough, Chorley, 18 in Liverpool and 16 in St. Helens. The next influx began in January 2002 and involved perhaps as many as 200 birds through to March 2003, with largest flocks of 15 in Claughton in the Lune Valley and elsewhere in the Lancaster area, 40 in Darwen town centre, 15 in Burnley, six in Chorley and 17 in Southport.

Finally, what was certainly the best winter since 1946/47, probably involving considerably more than 500 birds, got underway on 29 October 2004. By the end of the year it had produced flocks of 165 in Burnley and 42 in Nelson on 2 December, 120 at Barrow and 55 in Clitheroe the next day, 250 in Burnley on the 8th, 50 in Preston on the 22nd, 25 in Morecambe on the 21st, 40 in Chorley on the 24th, and 50 in Blackburn on the 28th rising to 180 on 1 January 2005. Significant numbers began to work their way through to Merseyside in the second week of January, peaking at a county record of 320 in Liverpool on the 23rd. The initial concentration in the east of the county and the birds' gradual spread westwards were notable features and, for the first time, sightings of colour-ringed birds gave a clear indication of the speed of the cross-Britain movement. Two ringed at Inverurie near Aberdeen on 30 October were first seen in Barrow on 3 and 5 December, and two different birds from the same catch in Burnley on 10 and 11 December, one of which was later seen in Warrington and then in Buckinghamshire in January 2005.

A different bird ringed at Inverurie on 31 October 2004 was seen in Liverpool on 23 January 2005 and then on 26 January 380km away in Exeter, while one ringed at Westhill, Aberdeen on 7 November 2004 was seen in Preston on 21 January 2005. The only other recovery in the county was one ringed in Aberdeen on 6 November 1970 and found dead in Liverpool on 1 March 1971.

Waxwing, Liverpool, 23 January 2005. This colour-ringed bird was part of the largest influx of recent years; it was ringed at Inverurie near Aberdeen on 31 October 2004 and was seen again in Exeter, 380km south-west of Liverpool, on 26 January. (Steve Young)

SJW, RW.

This species account was sponsored by Maureen Rimmer.

DIPPER

Cinclus cinclus

Lancashire Category A.

Uncommon resident breeder.

The Dipper is predominantly a sedentary resident of clean, shallow, turbulent spate streams with unstable gravel- or boulder-strewn beds supporting large densities of their chief foods, the larvae of stoneflies, mayflies and caddisflies, and Minnows.

Dippers are usually absent from the middle and lower reaches of our larger rivers, where the flow is placid and meanders over a bed of silt, sand or compacted gravel. Thus on most of the Lancashire Lune and Ribble they are very scarce breeding birds whereas many Lune and Ribble tributaries have territories from the open moor down to the confluence. During the 1997-2000 survey, for instance, Dippers were not recorded breeding on the Lune adjacent to Wenning Foot, but nested along most of the Wenning and its two tributaries the Roeburn and Hindburn. Similarly, on the Ribble the species was recorded at only three sites but bred along almost the entire length of the Hodder and its tributaries, the Loud, Langden, Dunsop and Croasdale.

A similar pattern can be seen on the Wyre system. Dippers do not breed on the slow reaches below Garstang, but they do so commonly upstream of Garstang and on the Brock and Calder (Bleasdale). It seems, however, that the Dipper has disappeared from some of the smaller Wyre tributaries since the 1960s, for in 1962-3 there were five pairs on Sparting and Westfield Brooks, but none was recorded here during 1997-2000.

Oakes noted that 'in Rossendale the species is less common than formerly but still breeds in some of the upper valleys, including several locations on the Anglezarke uplands'. This decline on streams south of the Ribble that were badly affected by pollution in the late nineteenth and through the first half of the twentieth century is slowly being reversed as a consequence of the cleaning up of sources of pollution, modernisation of sewage works and riverine habitat improvement. The Dipper now occurs along the upper reaches of the Lostock, Yarrow and Douglas, the Darwen downstream of Blackburn, on the Calder and its tributaries above Whalley, the upper sections of Eagley and Bradshaw Brooks and along the upper Irwell and its tributaries in Rossendale. It has recently been recorded in spring on the formerly grossly polluted Douglas downstream of Gathurst. On the Darwen and Yarrow the return of the Dipper followed the development of a diverse clean-water insect community including six species of stoneflies and seven species of mayflies (M. E. Greenhalgh unpublished). The Lune population, however, declined by more than 50% during the 1990s – from eleven pairs during the late 1980s to just four in 1998.

Dippers have been recorded breeding by upland reservoirs, including Stocks, Upper Rivington, Anglezarke and Delph, where a pair has bred most years since 1999 in an open-fronted nest-box. They usually feed on inflowing streams that have much higher densities of insect foods than the reservoirs themselves. However, birds have been recorded on several occasions at Belmont and Delph Reservoirs 'floating on the surface of the water and diving like a Little Grebe'; they were probably feeding on the fry of Three-spined Sticklebacks, as was one feeding close to the shallow outfall of Parsonage Reservoir on 26 September 2004.

Dipper, River Brock. (Phillip Tomkinson)

Dippers invariably have two broods that may disperse quickly after fledging but few move any great distance; just four out of 23 recoveries have involved movements out of Lancashire, all to neighbouring counties. One in the Sankey Valley in St. Helens on 28 August to 29 November 2002, had dispersed a distance of at least 25 km (the nearest breeding streams are on the West Pennine Moors).

Then, beginning usually in November though some years as early as mid-October, male Dippers begin to set up territories, which they proclaim by singing and defend by ousting other males, with the result that many are forced from the breeding streams in autumn. Some take up vacant territories or may colonise streams that were formerly polluted. However, like surplus Red Grouse, the majority simply appear to disappear. Just occasionally one or two are recorded away from breeding streams: for instance, singles at Upholland on 13 October 1983; in Sefton Park, Liverpool in the early 1980s; on the Rivers Calder and Brun in Burnley town centre since 1988; Nelson town centre on 15 February 1994 and Pine Lake on 30 October 2001. The St. Helens area has been most favoured with records of ones or twos in at least six winters since 1988, mostly in the Sankey Valley, and two summer records, both in the Sankey Valley, from 21 June to 30 August 1984 and on 21 June 1997. A notable roost of nine birds was found under a motorway bridge at Scorton on 9 October 1989.

Oakes noted that Lancashire Dippers 'are normally resident on territories throughout the winter, but hard frost may compel them to seek easier conditions on lowland rivers far removed from their usual habitat'. While Dippers on some northern rivers do move downstream, sometimes as far as the coast, in very hard weather (Tyler and Ormerod 1994) there is little evidence of similar movements in Lancashire. In fact, the lower reaches of our larger rivers do not provide any better feeding in icy weather than the upper reaches where Dippers breed. If they did then Dippers would presumably breed there. Furthermore, in icy weather Dippers are not seen on the Lancashire shores, and they are unlikely to be overlooked there! In hard weather Dippers on the Hodder at least are less obtrusive and are easily overlooked as they seem to prefer feeding amongst cover (under overhanging trees and in sheltered inlets) rather than out in the open. Even in the arctic conditions of February 1963 Greenhalgh (unpublished) found that Dippers on the Brock and Sparting Brook remained on territory and that there was sufficient open water where birds could feed on both streams mainly on case-less caddis and stone-clinger mayfly larvae. In this respect it is important to note that, in the winter months, the populations of the larvae on which Dippers feed are reaching their peaks and that the size of many species of larvae (especially the larger stoneflies and 'stone-crawling' mayflies) are approaching their maximum prior to their spring emergence.

The 1997-2000 survey suggested a county Dipper population of about 200 pairs but this figure is likely to grow significantly as river habitats are improved and more streams cleared of pollution.

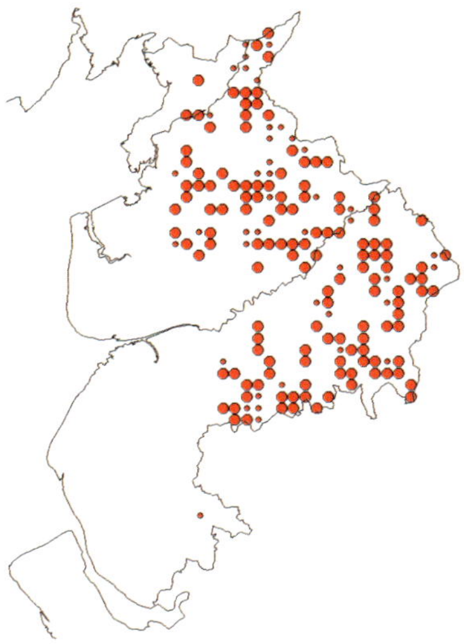

Breeding distribution of Dipper, 1997-2000. (Large dots: confirmed. Small dots: possible)

There is just one record of the nominate continental sub-species 'Black-bellied Dipper', at Skerton Weir on the River Lune in Lancaster from 20-27 November 1988 – the first for north-west England. All other records are assumed to relate to the British sub-species *gularis*.

MEG, RW.

This species account was sponsored by Margaret Dempsey.

WREN

Troglodytes troglodytes

Lancashire Category A.

Abundant resident breeder.

The Wren is probably Lancashire's most numerous and widespread breeding bird; although commonest in woodland with a dense scrub layer, nesting occurs in a great range of habitats including farmland, hedgerows, parkland, urban parks, suburban gardens, hillside ravines and even open moorland up to 450m where some shelter is afforded by walls or buildings.

Its population was estimated at 75,000 pairs during 1997-2000 but this was based upon national rather than regional breeding densities, about which little is known away from a handful of sites. With an annual mortality rate of about 60% (BWP) balanced by a huge potential reproductive rate, populations are extremely volatile and hard winters often lead to large temporary reductions. For example, breeding pairs at Billinge Wood, Blackburn and at Leighton Moss fell from 46 to 24 and 75 to 50 respectively between 1981 and 1982; while the winter of 1990/91 reduced numbers from 113 to 81 pairs at Leighton Moss, from 95 to 53 at Sunnyhurst Woods, Darwen and from 40 to 14 at Duxbury Woods, Chorley. Prolonged series of relatively severe winters, such as occurred between 1978/79 and 1990/91, can depress population levels over the medium term but numbers bounce back relatively quickly.

Wren, Little Crosby, March 2003. (Steve Young)

The national population is thought to have increased by 24% during 1994-2005 (BBS). Despite a further check caused by another hard winter in 1995/96 – which reduced numbers at Duxbury from 32 to 21 and at the Ribchester CBC site from 22 to 13 pairs, and led to a 40% decline in numbers on north Lancashire CBC plots – the impression almost everywhere in Lancashire was that by the end of the century the population was as high as anyone could recall. At Mere Sands Wood, for example, the number of singing males fell from 24 to 10 between 1990 and 1997 but rebounded to a record 49 in 1999 and 58 in 2003, while the Leighton Moss population had recovered to 106 pairs by 1999.

The Lancashire Atlas survey recorded breeding Wrens in 97% of the county's tetrads during 1997-2000; they were absent only from the highest ground in some parts of north-east Bowland and the south Pennines, a situation which appears to have changed little, if at all, since Mitchell's day.

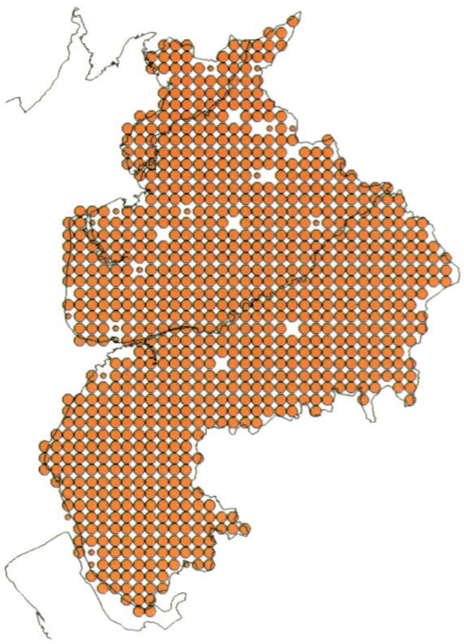

Breeding distribution of Wren, 1997-2000. (Large dots: confirmed. Small dots: possible)

Although most of the Lancashire population is probably highly sedentary, a combination of juvenile dispersal and a move from higher, more exposed areas, brings Wrens into an even wider range of habitats in winter, including reedbeds and saltmarshes and a handful of sites such as Seaforth and Lytham St. Anne's Nature Reserves, where they do not breed. They remain highly dispersed, however, and the largest winter counts reported in recent years were 35 at Marshside – where 20 was an average peak during the 1990s – on 29-30 December 2000, and 34 at Newton Marsh on 15 January 2002.

A small spring passage is reported most years at coastal sites during March and early April. The largest recent daily counts have mostly come from Marshside, including 15 on 15 March 1998, 16 on 1 April 1999 and 14 on 12 March 2002. Heysham usually only records single-figure aggregate totals of definite spring migrants.

Autumn movements are much larger and are also sometimes detected inland, for example 20 in a single bush at the edge of Darwen Moor on 11 November 1990 and 40 along a length of dry-stone wall there on 20 October 1991. A coastal passage takes place between mid-September and early November, usually peaking in mid-October. Large recent autumn totals include 150 through Heysham in 1988, 204 bird-days at Marshside on ten dates in 1993 and 272 bird-days at Marton Mere the same year. Overnight falls are rarely spectacular but double-figure counts are annual the length of the coast. The largest include 45 at Marshside on 20 October 1992 with 55 there on 10 October 1993 and 38 on 17 September 1998.

Nationally, the median distance between ringing and recovery sites is less than 1km (Migration Atlas) and only five Lancashire-ringed birds have been recovered outside the county. These do include, however, two long-distance movements: a juvenile ringed at Read on 4 July 1980 (so, presumably a fairly local bird) and found dead in Bognor Regis in January 1982, and one ringed at Heysham during a fall of Willow Warblers on 23 April 1994 and found dead in Cheltenham on 13 April 1995. The breeding areas of some of our wintering and passage birds is hinted at by one ringed in Fife in July 1997 and controlled in Garstang in September that year, and two movements between Lancashire and Cumbria.

Lancashire lies near the southern boundary of the breeding range of the subspecies *indigenus*, a race endemic to northern Britain and Ireland but only very subtly different from the widespread nominate race of southern Britain and most of mainland Europe. In the absence of evidence from ringing it is hard to know whether nominate *troglodytes* has occurred in the county, either as a wanderer from southern Britain or a winter or passage migrant from the continent. Since many Scandinavian birds depart in autumn, some moving as far south as Spain, at least occasional visitors from this area would be expected.

SJW, RW.

This species account was sponsored by N.J. Donnithorne.

DUNNOCK

Prunella modularis

Lancashire Category A.

Abundant resident breeder.

Mitchell described the 'Hedge Sparrow' as 'common, wherever there is any cover, throughout the whole county . . . it is very tame and sociable, keeping with the fowls about the barns'. Oakes had little to add, noting that breeding occurred 'up to an altitude of 1,000 ft (300m)' and that it was most abundant in 'woodland . . . and hedgerows near coppices' but less numerous 'in the hedgerows of open country'.

On the surface, little has changed since the 1950s. The Dunnock remains widespread, common and taken for granted by most birdwatchers. Lancashire population trends are not known but national numbers declined during the 1970s and 1980s culminating in the smallest ever known population in the mid-1990s, resulting in its appearance on the Amber List of Species of Conservation Concern. Happily, it seems to have undergone a moderate resurgence since then for, although its population in 2001 was 36% lower than in 1970, numbers increased by 22% between 1994 and 2005 (BBS).

Unfortunately, there are insufficient data available to judge overall population trends in Lancashire. The population at Billinge Wood in Blackburn increased, with some fluctuations, from 19 to 41 'pairs' from 1979-1985; at Leighton Moss after 1964 numbers reached a maximum of 40 after the mild winter of 1977/78 and a minimum of 21 after the cold winter of 1985/6, but quickly recovered to 30-36 'pairs' from 1987-1999; at nearby Warton Crag numbers fell from nine 'pairs' in 1989 to three in 1998; while the population on the Mount Vernon CBC plot in north Lancashire remained stable at seven pairs throughout the 1990s. Taken together, these results seem to indicate that the county population has remained roughly stable for the past 20 years, recovering quickly from any winter losses; there is no evidence of any major decline during the 1970s to mid-1990s.

Dunnock, Liverpool, March 2005. (Steve Young)

The county population was estimated at 30,000 'pairs' in 1997-2000 but, as with all our commonest species, this was based upon knowledge of national rather than local breeding densities. Breeding was recorded in 89% of the county's tetrads in 1997-2000. Like Robins and Wrens they were absent only from the highest areas of Bowland, Leck Fell and the south Pennines, but much scarcer than either of these species throughout the uplands, reflecting a lack of dense scrubby vegetation which they require for nesting. Dunnocks breed commonly in urban areas, even where minimal suitable habitat exists.

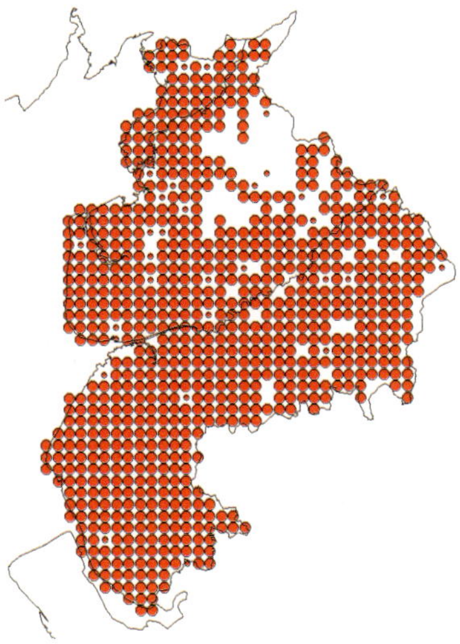

Breeding distribution of Dunnock, 1997-2000. (Large dots: confirmed. Small dots: possible)

The two sub-species that breed in Britain and Ireland – *hebridium* in Ireland and western Scotland and *occidentalis* in the rest of Britain – are largely sedentary, their movements almost entirely limited to short-distance post-juvenile dispersal, usually measured only in hundreds of metres (Migration Atlas). Throughout its Lancashire range wintering numbers are rarely much different to those of summer. Only three out of 94 birds ringed in Lancashire and subsequently recovered had crossed the county boundary, and just six birds ringed elsewhere have been recovered in Lancashire. All of these involved movements of at most a few kilometres.

Nevertheless, apparent influxes are reported at coastal sites in most years, particularly in autumn, and these have long been reported as involving at least some passage migrants. The highest spring counts occur in late March and early April, a period which coincides with the height of song activity when Dunnocks are most conspicuous. It is therefore possible that the spring passage is largely illusory but ringing work at Heysham has established that small numbers of new birds do appear, typically fewer than ten each spring.

Numbers at coastal watchpoints are significantly higher in autumn. Birds that appear during late July and August are widely assumed to be locally dispersing juveniles but the status of birds involved in the main movement, which takes place from September to early November, is less clear. Large recent counts include twelve at Seaforth on 13 October 1990 (before the species bred there), 15 at Marshside on 31 October 1993 and 27 at Marton Mere on 7 November 1997. Seasonal totals from Marton Mere include 225 bird-days between September and mid-November 1993 but how many individuals may be involved and what proportion of them are genuine migrants remains a matter for speculation. At Marshside, for example, it is felt that there is no evidence of any passage or irruptive movements (McCarthy 2001). Monitoring movements inland is far more difficult but Martin Mere, for example, regularly reports autumn influxes, and one at 370m on the summit of The Hile in Rossendale on 26 October 1998 was certainly not a local bird.

The strongest evidence of autumn migration comes from Heysham where small numbers of newly arrived, unringed birds are seen regularly during September, followed by low-weight birds – often associated with falls of thrushes – in October. Annual Dunnock totals on visible migration watches are small. They include one flying off with Meadow Pipits at Rossall Point on 23 September 1998, but most come from Heysham, including eight between 16 September and 17 October 1992, six in off the sea before flying south on 16 September 1993, two in off the sea on 5 October 1994, 18 south on 25 September 1998 and six on 18 September 2002.

Trapping has so far yielded no information on the origins or destinations of these probable passage migrants but it is possible that some October birds are nominate *modularis* from Fennoscandian, central European or Russian populations, which are highly migratory and are known to arrive annually in small numbers in the northern isles and on the English east coast (Migration Atlas).

SJW, RW.

This species account was sponsored by Pauline McGough.

ROBIN

Erithacus rubecula

Lancashire Category A.

Abundant resident breeder, common winter visitor from continental Europe.

Mitchell's description as 'resident, abundant and nesting everywhere' is as apt today as it was in the nineteenth century; Robins bred in at least 95% of Lancashire tetrads during 1997-2000. Breeding takes place in most habitats except the barest high moorland, saltmarsh and densely built-up areas without green spaces. The species thrives in close proximity to man, often nesting in outbuildings as well as garden hedges, walls and even discarded appliances. Mitchell described a pair nesting inside a dead cat in 1881 as showing evidence of their 'manners becoming demoralized . . . in the vicinity of large towns'!

The Lancashire Atlas estimated the county population at 50,000 pairs, but this was simply as a proportion of national numbers. Population size appears relatively constant over the long term but, as an overwhelmingly sedentary species, Robins are susceptible to prolonged cold winters. Breeding pairs on five CBC plots in north Lancashire fell by more than a third after severe weather in 1995/96 (Harrison 2000) but numbers had almost recovered to 1995 levels by 1998. Nationally, CBC and BBS results show increases of 43% from 1970-2001 and 17% from 1994 to 2005 respectively, and there is no reason to believe that the Lancashire population has behaved any differently.

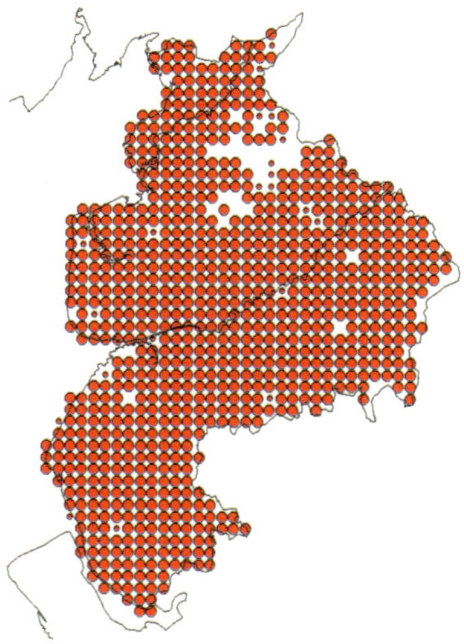

Breeding distribution of Robin, 1997-2000. (Large dots: confirmed. Small dots: possible)

Most nesting takes place between mid-March and June, beginning a week or so later in the uplands, but in mild conditions the breeding season may begin earlier, as, for example, when one pair successfully raised a brood near Gisburn in February 1998. Nationally, Robins are highly site-faithful with fewer than 5% nesting more than 20km from natal or previous breeding sites (Migration Atlas) and ringing data suggest a similar situation in Lancashire.

Spring movements are most noticeable as breeding territories that were deserted in winter, mostly in the uplands, become re-occupied. Coastal passage is scarcely perceptible. Small numbers (usually 10-20) of unringed, and presumably new, birds are trapped at Heysham in March and April most years, but the only other passage movements reported in recent years were nine at Seaforth on 20 March 2000 and three at Rossall Point on 19 March 2005. The only ringing record of a spring movement involves a first-winter from Mere Sands Wood on 19 March 1998 to the Calf of Man ten days later.

Juveniles begin to disperse shortly after fledging but rarely move any distance before completing their post-juvenile moult after three months or so; dispersal from the breeding grounds, when it does occur, may be prolonged with some adults and many juveniles departing as late as October (Migration Atlas). Many of the later migrants may, therefore, be of British origin. Nationally, fewer than 10% move more than 10km (Migration Atlas) and only ten Lancashire-ringed birds, not all ringed as pulli, have been recovered outside of the county during winter; 121 out of 150 such recoveries have been made less than 10km from the ringing site.

Robin, Little Crosby, March 2005. (Steve Young)

However, even a small proportion of such an abundant species can produce quite sizeable passage movements. Most are seen at the main coastal watchpoints but short-lived autumn influxes of up to 50 birds are detected regularly at some well-monitored inland sites, notably Mere Sands Wood and Martin Mere. Coastal passage takes place from mid-August to mid-November but is heavily concentrated in September and October. An average of 90 migrants have been ringed at Heysham annually since 1994, many more presumably escape the nets. Similar numbers probably move, usually unmonitored, through various other sites, 378 bird-days at Marton Mere in September to mid-November 1993 and 402 at Marshside during the same period being examples. The largest recorded 'fall' was on 19 September 1992 when more than 100 were at Heysham, 200 in Otterspool Park in south Liverpool, 18 at Marshside, 40 at Seaforth and Martin Mere, and large numbers on the Morecambe Bay gas rigs – and no doubt many more elsewhere. Other large day-counts include 82 at Marshside on 26 September 1993, 70 at the same site on 11 October 1994, 74 at Heysham on 17 September 1998, 66 in Fleetwood on 29 September 1998 and 53 at Marton Mere on 14 September 2000. Ringing recoveries show that a majority of these coastal migrants probably originate in northern England or Scotland. No bird ringed in Lancashire has been recovered abroad but birds ringed on autumn passage at Heysham and Leighton Moss have been found in Gwent, Dyfed, Buckinghamshire and Oxfordshire. However, a first-winter ringed in the Netherlands on 20 October 1997 was recovered at Dunsop Bridge in May 1998, indicating that at least some Lancashire birds do leave the country.

British breeding Robins are of the race *melophilus* but some migrants, especially in October and November, may be continental birds of the race *rubecula*. Grey, orange-breasted birds are regularly reported from Heysham and elsewhere. There are no Lancashire recoveries of continental birds but first-winters ringed on the Isle of May on 24 September 1986 and controlled just 27 hours later at Heysham, a distance of 240km; at Fife Ness on 12 October 1988 and controlled at Heysham three days later; and in Fife on 18 August 1996 and recovered in Lancaster on 4 March 1997, suggest Fennoscandian origins involving *rubecula*. However, one ringed as a first-winter in Litherland in December 1998 and recovered the following July in Dundee, where it was likely to have been breeding, casts some doubt on this.

Winter distribution patterns are similar to those in the breeding season although most birds have left the more exposed uplands by the end of October. At most sites it is impossible to distinguish winter visitors from residents once the passage has finished, but winter numbers on the coast are almost everywhere greater than during the breeding season and Seaforth, where Robins have only bred once, regularly supports a winter population of around 20.

SJW, RW.

This species account was sponsored by R. Wilson.

THRUSH NIGHTINGALE

Luscinia luscinia

Lancashire Category A. (0, 1).

Vagrant from eastern Europe.

Thrush Nightingale, Heysham, September 1993. (Pete Marsh)

One, tentatively aged as an adult, was trapped and ringed at Heysham NR on 25 September 1993 by Paul Cammack and Pete Marsh. After its release it adopted the species' usual skulking habits and was seen briefly on just a couple of occasions by a handful of observers that day but not subsequently.

This was the 103rd record in Britain and Ireland but remains the only one seen in north-west England.

SJW, MJ.

This species account was sponsored by Heysham Nature Reserve.

NIGHTINGALE

Luscinia megarhynchos

Lancashire Category A. (0, 5).

Vagrant from southern Britain or Europe.

Mitchell and Oakes both mentioned a bird seen and heard at Whittingham in June 1871, but considered the details inconclusive. The first Lancashire record was therefore a singing male at Formby on 30 May 1965 (R. South and C.K. Williams). The next was watched feeding in full view by a group of Cheshire birdwatchers on Fairhaven dunes on 29 October 1966.

All subsequent records were in the Formby-Southport area, beginning with one at Freshfield on 15-19 April 1967, then another singing male at Crossens on 20-24 May 1980, which was heard at nearby Banks a few days later.

In the three years 1982-84 what was assumed to be a returning bird was singing from sea buckthorn thickets on Massam's Slack on the Ainsdale National Nature Reserve. During this period its earliest arrival was on 28 April; during 1982 it sang well into June but it was last heard on 18 May 1984. There was no evidence of any female being present but quite why this bird showed such apparent site fidelity with no prospect of breeding remains a mystery – it certainly deserves full marks for persistence.

The Ainsdale bird remains the last to be heard in the county; the final record was of a first-summer male which was trapped and ringed at Freshfield Dune Heath, Formby on 28 May 1991.

Although the British breeding range of the Nightingale has contracted in recent years and is concentrated in the south-east of England, it is still surprising just how rare it is in Lancashire – we have had more spring records of Bluethroat. The location of all records in such a small area is also difficult to explain and such a concentration is not shown by any other vagrant species in the county.

SJW, MJ.

This species account was sponsored by Tim Mitcham.

BLUETHROAT

Luscinia svecica

Lancashire Category A. (0, 10).

Vagrant from southern Europe and Fennoscandia.

The first record was a female found by Lawrence Eccles on 6 September 1958. It was initially published as being 'near Sunderland Point' but was, in fact, on the site of the present power station at Heysham.

The next four records were all at Marshside: a female on 5 May 1973; a male of the white-spotted, southern race *cyanecula* on 13 March 1977; a male of the nominate red-spotted race on 18 June 1978; and finally, after a gap of nearly twenty years, another white-spotted male on 6 April 1995.

Also in 1995, sometime in early May, a red-spotted male was found in a poor state at a primary school in Bacup and was taken into care but later died. This is the only county record away from the coast.

The next was a red-spotted male in the rubble mounds at Seaforth on 16 May 1997; this was followed by singles on waste ground in Peel Park, Blackpool on 1 October 1997 and near the Eric Morecambe Pools at Leighton Moss on 11 November 1998.

White-spotted Bluethroat. (Tony Disley)

The latest came in late May 2003 when a non-birdwatcher in Ingol, Preston heard a dull thud on his back door early one morning and discovered a dazed, probably female, bird sat on his doorstep. It recovered and later flew off.

The sub-species *cyanecula* is by far the scarcer of the two in Britain, with an average of about two a year, so the two Marshside records are notable. Spring white-spotted *cyanecula* birds are 'overshoots' from southern European breeding areas and arrive several weeks before *svecica* pass through on their way to northern Europe – typically in March and April with red-spotted *svecica* appearing in May.

The ratio of spring to autumn records in Lancashire is approximately in line with national figures which have shown a large shift from autumn to spring occurrences since the 1960s. Although Bluethroats have been recorded nationally with increasing frequency over recent decades only 0.5% of English records have been in the north-west (Brown & Grice 2005).

All records:

1958	Heysham, female, 6 September
1973	Marshside, female, 5 May
1977	Marshside, white-spotted male, 13 March
1978	Marshside, red-spotted male, 18 June
1995	Bacup, red-spotted male, unknown date in May, Died in care.
1995	Marshside, white-spotted male, 6 April
1997	Seaforth NR, red-spotted male, 16 May
1997	Blackpool, one, 1 October
1998	Leighton Moss, one, 11 November
2003	Ingol, Preston, female, unknown date in late May

SJW, MJ.
This species account was sponsored by John Dempsey.
http://birdblog.merseyblogs.co.uk

BLACK REDSTART

Phoenicurus ochruros

Lancashire Category A.

Rare breeder; scarce passage migrant from western and central Europe.

Mitchell regarded Black Redstarts as rare winter visitors and mentioned three records, in south Liverpool sometime in the 1840s and 1850s and at Lytham in 1892, but Oakes regarded the first two of these as unconfirmed. He added eight records: singles at Formby (2), Darwen, Marshside and Southport between 1921 and 1926, at Hornby in 1940 and on moors east of Chorley in 1947, and a singing male at a war-damaged site in Liverpool from 14 June to 11 July 1949 – perhaps our first breeding record.

Breeding was not confirmed until 1977 when two or three pairs nested in the Canning and Albert Docks in central Liverpool but it seems highly likely that it had occurred previously. At least one pair bred at the same site from 1978 to 1981 but two fledged young in 1979 were the only proof of success. As the southern docks began to be redeveloped in the 1980s the birds appear to have shifted territories but these were never properly pinned down until a pair was found with three fresh juveniles on the Salisbury Dock, north of the Pier Head in July 1994. In the intervening period males had been heard singing from a variety of city centre sites in summer but without any evidence of breeding. It is possible that a pair bred in the same area until at least 1998 when a female was seen with two dependent young on the nearby Huskisson Dock in early September; regular sightings of a male and female at Seaforth in May to July 1987 may also have related to these birds. However, although these Central Docks were surveyed annually from 2000-2003 no Black Redstarts were seen. Confirmation that birds were still at least prospecting for nest sites in Liverpool came in 2003 when a singing first-summer male and a female were seen in March on the derelict Post Office building in the city centre.

Female or first-winter Black Redstart, Carnforth, February 2006. (Mike Malpass)

The only other confirmed and successful breeding in Lancashire took place at South Shore, Blackpool in 1997 and in Blackburn in 2000, but it has been strongly suspected elsewhere. Females were seen with single juveniles near Hala, Lancaster in early August 1991 and on Pendle Hill from 12 August to 19 September 1995, and fairly regular records in and just after the breeding season in the Pendle Hill area to 2003 are highly suggestive. There have also been several records of apparently unpaired males on territory, including at a Burnley factory from 28 May to 16 June 1984, in Nelson from 7-9 June 1987, Preston Dock on 16 June 1987, Heysham Power Station between May and mid-July 1988 and at Sherfin near Haslingden for two weeks in June 1989. The presence of an adult female on the West Pennine Moors around Belmont in May 1995 and juveniles there in August 1999 and August 2000 suggest breeding nearby.

Breeding birds make up only a small fraction of annual totals, however. Passage and wintering records increased steadily during the 1970s and averaged ten a year between 1980 and 2005, with larger influxes of 18 in 1987, 20 in 1988, 25 in 1995 and 20 in 1996 (Figure 1).

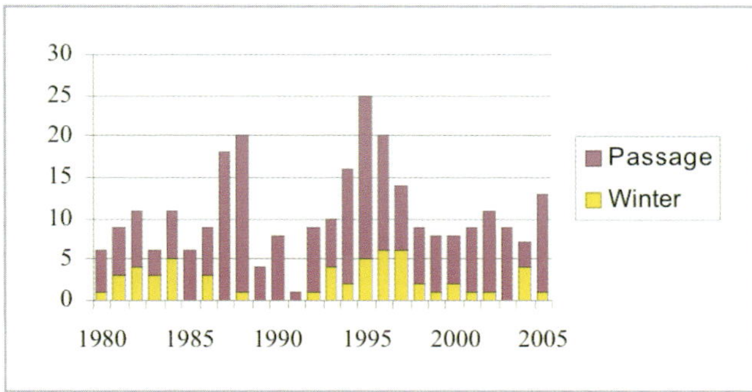

Figure 1. Total numbers of wintering and passage Black Redstarts in Lancashire, 1980-2005.

Wintering has occurred in all but six years since 1978 at an average of two records a year – eight during 1996/97 was exceptional. Records usually involve just one or occasionally two or three birds and are almost always at coastal sites, with most coming from Rossall Point, Heysham, Lytham St. Anne's and Marshside. Most inland winter records have been of short duration but exceptions have been a first-winter male at Rainford from 16-23 January 2000, a female/immature on Pendle Hill from 15-30 December 2000 and a male at Earby from 30 December 2002 to 18 March 2003.

Although it is sometimes difficult to separate them from wintering birds, the first spring migrants may appear as early as mid-February. Passage continues through to late May but is at its strongest from late March to mid-April (Figure 2). Records are predominantly coastal and distributed fairly evenly at many sites between Seaforth and Heysham, but occasional birds are noted inland, particularly in north-east Lancashire and the Burnley area. An average spring seldom produces more than one or two migrants; eight in 1987 and six in 1988 and 1998 were exceptional.

June and some July records may relate to undiscovered breeding attempts or wandering first-summers but a male at Mere Sands Wood on 13 July 1986 was perhaps on return passage. The autumn movement rarely gets underway much before October, however, and usually peaks during November, after which a handful of birds stay on for the winter. Birds are about twice as numerous as in spring, three or four records being a typical tally with eight in 1996 and 2005 our largest 'influxes'. As in spring, the vast majority of records come from the well-watched coastal migration stations from Morecambe Bay to the Mersey. Also as in spring, singles are the norm, so four at Squires Gate, Blackpool on 23 October 1988 and at Heysham Power Station on 27 October 1996 were exceptional.

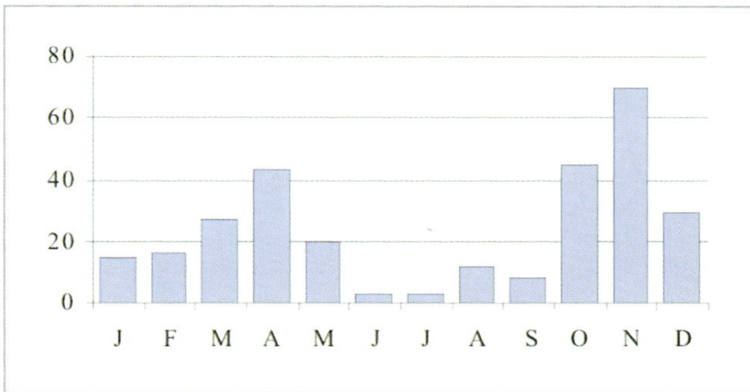

Figure 2. Monthly totals of Black Redstarts in Lancashire, 1963-2005 (excluding breeding birds).

Inland sightings of autumn migrants are few and far between and most have occurred in Rossendale, Bowland and the West Pennines: at Rivington in September 1964, Crawshawbooth in November 1971 and again in November 1996, Waddington Fell in November 1983, Knowsley Industrial Estate in September 1993, Dunsop Valley in October 1997, Musbury in August 1999, Winter Hill in August 2000, Clowbridge Reservoir in November 2000, Whitendale in September 2002 and Newton Fell in August 2003.

SJW, MJ.

This species account was sponsored by David and Jill Player.

REDSTART

Phoenicurus phoenicurus

Lancashire Category A.

Common breeder and passage migrant.

The Redstart is primarily a bird of open broadleaved woodland, particularly oak, preferred locations being on valley sides and in moorland edge cloughs. On east Lancashire farmland it regularly nests in scattered, old hawthorns or alders along streams or field boundaries. Holes in trees and walls are utilised as breeding sites, although nest-boxes are used at several Lancashire sites.

Mitchell described the Redstart as 'almost universally distributed but nowhere very common', while Oakes noted that 'though rather more restricted in distribution than formerly it is still a common bird in north and mid-Lancashire'. National CBC data showed a significant decline between 1964 and 1973, attributable to droughts in the wintering grounds of the Sahel. Numbers have since recovered; the CBC index increased by 50%

during 1988-1991 while the Breeding Bird Survey registered a further national increase of 34% between 1994 and 2002.

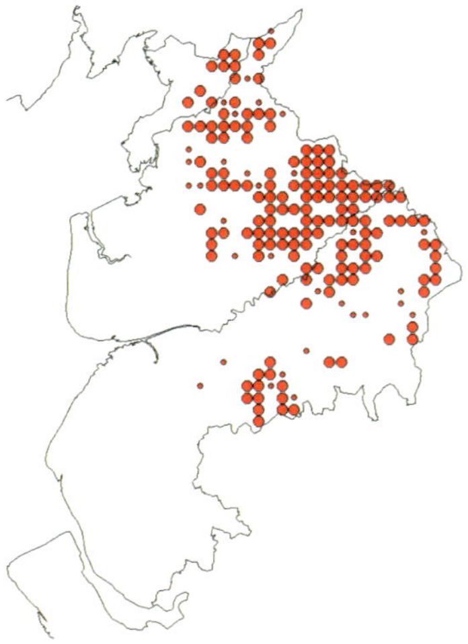

Breeding distribution of Redstart, 1997-2000. (Large dots: confirmed. Small dots: possible)

The Lancashire population was not fully surveyed prior to the atlas project in 1997-2000 and it is not possible to trace previous changes with any precision but these are likely to have mirrored the national situation. The breeding range does appear to have contracted during the 1970s and early 1980s. Redstarts were breeding in 28 10km squares in the county during the Old Atlas survey (1968-1972), declining to 21 in the New Atlas (1988-1991), but losses seem to have been concentrated in marginal areas, particularly around Silverdale, West Lancashire and Merseyside. These areas have not been recolonised and breeding Redstarts are now completely absent from the west of the county and only occasional pairs breed in Rossendale. Numbers also declined in many parts of the lower Ribble, Darwen and Calder Valleys, for example at Witton Country Park, Blackburn where breeding pairs fell from five or six during the 1960s to only an occasional pair from the late 1970s. However, breeding was confirmed in 152 tetrads in 21 10km squares during 1997-2000, so the decline in range appears to have halted.

County bird reports gave a rather (probably unjustified) gloomy impression of breeding numbers during the 1990s with typically fewer than 100 pairs reported but the Atlas survey located 389 pairs during 1997-200 and estimated a total population of around 800 pairs. Lancashire densities of around 40 pairs per occupied 10km square are thus significantly lower than the national estimate of 70 pairs (New Atlas).

Reasonable numbers can be found in the higher reaches of the Lune Valley and south of the Ribble eastwards to Clitheroe, but the highest densities, in the region of 7-10 pairs per occupied tetrad, are on the fringes of the West Pennine Moors, particularly the Rivington/Anglezarke area, and in the Forest of Bowland (SD64, SD74 & SD75).

Sites that have been regularly monitored in recent years show no clear trend in breeding numbers. In the south, the Rivington/Anglezarke area held twelve pairs in 2002 but only five in 2003, while numbers at Roddlesworth dropped from nine pairs in 1996 to three in 2003. In the north, the Downham/Twiston area, north of Pendle Hill, reported five singing males in 1996, rising to 25 in 1999 then twelve in 2002 and 2002. Numbers in one area around Stocks Reservoir apparently declined from twelve singing males in 1998 and 2002 to six in 2003, while the population on another part of the United Utilities estates in Bowland increased from ten pairs in 1995 to 15 in 2002 and 19 in 2004, falling to ten in 2005. Monitoring of nest-boxes in six woods in the Lune Valley, however, showed a steady increase from six pairs in 1989 to ten in 1992, followed by a sharp decline to four pairs in 1997 and just one in 1998.

There are only three March records: on the 28th at Formby in 1968, the 29th at Marshside in 1981 and the 31st at Whitendale in 1983. The average first arrival date in the past 25 years is 11 April and most birds are probably back by the second week of May. The timing of the return (measured by first dates) has not changed significantly during the past quarter century. Although first sightings are generally on the coast, this is probably largely due to greater observer coverage; the vast majority of birds undoubtedly return straight to the breeding sites. The coastal spring passage is invariably light with rarely more than 20 reported in total from the main watchpoints of Seaforth, Marshside, Blackpool and Heysham. Daily totals rarely exceed two at any one site; most larger counts have been at Heysham, including five on 24 April 1995 and 21 April 1996 and seven on 23 April 1998, when four were also at Blackpool. Occasional coastal records during late May and early June probably mostly involve first-summer birds. Almost all spring passage birds are British breeders (Migration Atlas) and, although some coastal migrants may be heading towards Cumbria and Scotland, some may be local breeders – as indicated by a record of a male ringed on Hilbre Island on the Cheshire Dee on 14 April 1988 and recovered at Whitewell, near Clitheroe, on 19 May the same year.

Male Redstart, New Laithe Farm, Newton-in-Bowland. (Phillip Tomkinson)

Autumn movement begins in July but most early birds may be dispersing juveniles, for example one ringed in the nest at Bashall

Eaves in May 1981 and recovered 27km to the south-west at Astley Park, Chorley on 22 August. The main movement takes place between early August and early September with late September and October records coming mainly from the coast – at the same sites as in spring. The total size of the autumn coastal passage is much the same as in spring but there are significant differences between sites – at Heysham, spring records outnumber those in autumn by almost two to one (1995-2003) and at Marshside by more than four to one, while at Seaforth more than twice as many occur in autumn (1985-2003). The latest inland record was at Chipping on 2 November 1989, and on the coast at St. Anne's on 10 November 1982. Few are seen after mid-September, however, and the average last date over the last 25 years is 9 October. The peak migration time for both British and continental birds is during September so, in the absence of any relevant ringing recoveries, the origins of migrants are unknown, but it seems likely that at least some later birds are of continental origin.

Recoveries of Lancashire-ringed Redstarts conform to the general pattern of movements of British birds, which stage in Iberia and north Africa before some cross the Sahara. One was recovered in Morocco (in April), two in Spain (September and October), one in Portugal (October) and one in Kent (August). All Lancashire records relate to the nominate race which breeds throughout Europe; no claims of eastern *samamisicus* have been pursued.

SJW, RW.

This species account was sponsored by Roger Dewhurst.

WHINCHAT

Saxicola rubetra

Lancashire Category A.

Uncommon breeder; fairly common passage migrant.

The Whinchat is a local summer visitor which breeds in the upland regions in the east, also occurring as a double passage migrant. It is a bird of damp, rough grassland which is often found on moorland edges and also in young conifer plantations, railway embankments, heathland and waste areas. Tall vegetation such as gorse, bracken, large umbellifers as well as fences and posts are used as song perches.

Mitchell considered the Whinchat to be common everywhere except in Rossendale and around Accrington, singling out the Fylde, where it was described as abundant. He appears to have believed moorland to have been a secondary habitat compared with cultivated land in the lowlands. By Oakes's time the situation was reversed. Breeding pairs were numerous in the eastern hills although moderate populations were still widespread in the lowlands, on the Sefton and Fylde coasts, the mosslands and 'waste' land fringing the southern cultivated zone. The lowland population was, however, in decline, probably in large part due to the large-scale conversion of grasslands to arable and cultivation of previously 'waste' land during the Second World War. Prior to 1939 six pairs bred in just one part of the older dunes at Lytham St. Anne's but dune nesting seems to have ceased there by 1950 due to building and increased disturbance.

As agricultural change continued apace during the 1960s, Whinchats had effectively withdrawn from the lowlands with just a few pairs hanging on by 1968-72 (Old Atlas). Most of these were on the Sefton coast between Crosby and Formby, where up to 22 pairs bred during the 1970s. This population was in steep decline by the end of the decade and last nested on the dune coast and at nearby Sefton Meadows in 1980, being 'replaced' by Stonechats; the last breeding record on the Sefton coast was at Marshside in 1982. By the time of the New Atlas in 1988-91 Whinchats were completely absent from the Lancashire lowlands. They made an unexpected comeback during the Lancashire Atlas survey when a single pair bred in Liverpool from 1997-2002 in rough grassland at Fazakerley Waste Water Treatment Works. Another interesting example of opportunism occurred in the early to mid-1980s, when up to four pairs colonised a recently vacated smallholding site at Towneley prior to its redevelopment as a golf course.

Male Whinchat, Seaforth Nature Reserve, May 2004. (Steve Young)

The afforestation of parts of the uplands during the 1960s and 1970s probably boosted populations at first by providing additional suitable breeding habitat, but mature conifer plantations leave no space for Whinchats. The intensification of grazing and switch from hay to silage during the 1980s and 1990s was perhaps a greater threat, however. The upland breeding range shrank by at least 25% between the Old and New Atlases and by a further 15% between 1988-91 and 1997-2000, with breeding season presence in 27 and 23 upland 10km squares respectively. These broad-brush changes may conceal larger declines at the local level, since in most areas suitable habitat on the moorland edge is fairly scattered – the Lancashire Atlas confirmed breeding in just 57 upland tetrads, just 6% of the county as a whole and around 10-15% of the upland area.

A total of 100 pairs was counted during 1997-2000 and the Lancashire population was estimated at 150 pairs. National surveys have never gained sufficient coverage of the uplands to monitor relatively scarce species well, but the BTO Breeding Bird Survey estimated a 15% decline in Whinchat numbers between 1994 and 2002. Anecdotal evidence and limited published records suggest this may be something of an underestimate in Lancashire and the population may now be as low as 100 pairs.

The county stronghold is in Bowland, especially in an area of about 25 km^2 within squares SD64, SD65, SD66 and SD74, which between them supported about 80 pairs in 1997-2000. Particularly favoured areas in central Bowland include the Langden and Brennand Valleys, Whitendale, Croasdale Fell and the Lamb

Hill/Catlow Fells area, where populations were said to have run into treble figures in the 1970s. There were 71 pairs on the United Utilities estate in this area in 1982, but numbers had fallen to 43 in 1986, 34 in 1991, 24 in 1995 and 19 in 2005, indicating a long-term decline since the 1970s. Small numbers occur in south and south-west Bowland, particularly north of Chipping, but the population is well below the 31 pairs recorded in 305 acres there in 1957 with, for example, just four pairs on Saddle End in 2004.

Other significant clusters were found during the Lancashire Atlas survey on the West Pennine Moors area (about 15 pairs) and between Clitheroe and Earby (about 25 pairs), with a thin scattering of breeding sites to the south and east of Burnley. Just two pairs were confirmed breeding north of the Lune and two in the Leck Fell area.

There has been a considerable decline in numbers in east Lancashire since the mid-1960s, when many sites in the Burnley area held up to four pairs and an exceptional 30 pairs bred in the Thursden Valley alone (Hornby 1994). The Thursden Valley supported only an occasional pair during the 1990s, with just scattered pairs at other Burnley sites. Rossendale has witnessed a sharp decline since the 1980s with just 4-6 pairs located during the Lancashire Atlas survey in two areas – around Holden Wood Reservoir and The Hile.

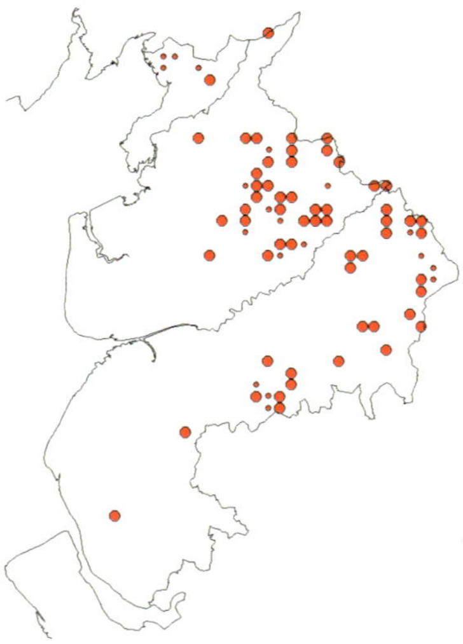

Breeding distribution of Whinchat, 1997-2000. (Large dots: confirmed. Small dots: possible)

Whinchats are one of our later migrants and the first spring arrivals are usually during the second half of April, on average on 20 April over the past 25 years. The earliest was near Clitheroe on 20 March 1976. There is no discernible difference between arrival dates at inland or coastal sites. Numbers peak at the end of April and during the first half of May, tailing off by the end of the month with infrequent records into June. Most sightings are of ones or twos, an inland record of nine at White Moss on 5 May 1978 being exceptional. Larger numbers are more regular all along the coast, the highest counts being 44 at Marshside on 9 May 1982, 31 there on 11 May 1993 and 22 on 6 May 1997, 23 on Aldcliffe Marsh on 4 May 1992 and twelve at Fleetwood on 9 May 1998. Marshside is by far the best coastal site with an average spring total of about 25 since 1991 compared with ten or so at Heysham and Marton Mere; numbers have declined dramatically at Seaforth from 10-15 in the late 1980s and early 1990s to five or so more recently (Figure 1).

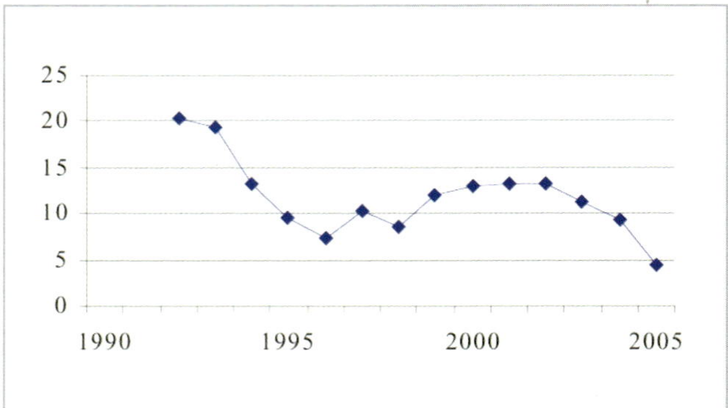

Figure 1. Estimated totals (3-year rolling means) of autumn migrant Whinchats at Heysham and Seaforth Nature Reserves, 1990-2005.

Return passage begins as early as the first week of July but more usually towards the end of the month, peaking between mid-August and mid-September. Although most sightings are of ones and twos, higher numbers are occasionally recorded inland, especially around the eastern reservoirs, with high counts of ten at Cant Clough at the end of August 1995, 16 at Clowbridge on 24 August 1997 and nine at Belmont on 31 August 1997. Autumn totals at inland sites are often at least as large as on the coast, for example 26 in Rossendale and 14 at Belmont in 2002. Fourteen at Rishton Reservoir on 17 August 1993 is the largest published count further north.

The largest count on the coast was 20 at Cabin Hill on 15 September 1985 but double-figure counts have been exceptional. Autumn totals are generally significantly lower than in spring: both Marshside and Heysham have averaged around four since the early 1990s with even fewer at Marton Mere, and none of these sites has logged more than single-figure totals during the same period. Seaforth, and probably other sites on the Sefton dune coast, is the exception, with an average of about eight per autumn and double-figure totals up to 17 in seven of the past 15 years.

A few birds pass through as late as the second half of October, mostly on the coast. The average final date in the past 25 years is 18 October and the latest were singles inland at Plunge on 2 November 1988 and on the coast at Marshside on 12 November 1979. Although there is no evidence from ringing, it is likely that some at least of these late birds are continental migrants. This is supported by the recovery of a bird ringed as a juvenile in Lancashire in September 1966 in Algeria the following April, far to the east of the north African recovery sites of all known British birds (Migration Atlas).

The only other recoveries of Lancashire birds (both pulli) outside the county were in April in Staffordshire and France in September.

SJW, RW.

This species account was sponsored by Adam Graham.

STONECHAT

Saxicola torquatus

Lancashire Category A.

Uncommon resident breeder and passage migrant.

Until very recently Stonechats appear to have nested predominantly in coastal habitats in Lancashire. Mitchell described the main breeding areas as the Sefton and Fylde dune coasts and the shores of Morecambe Bay. Confusingly, McNicholl (1883) regarded the Stonechat as a casual visitor to the Birkdale and Ainsdale dunes in contrast to the fairly common Whinchat. Mitchell also believed them to have been relatively common on 'wastes where gorse grows freely' and quoted J.F. Brockholes who described it as abundant within a ten mile radius of Liverpool city centre – presumably including drier mosslands to the east. Upland breeding sites in the mid-nineteenth century included Accrington and Bacup but Mitchell believed numbers had declined inland. Oakes described Stonechats as rather scarce and local, most numerous along the dunes of the Fylde coast and further south – so scarce that he would not identify specific sites. Harsh winters in 1939/40, 1940/41 and 1946/47 severely depleted numbers and led to a significant reduction in distribution.

Spencer (1973) estimated the breeding population at around 30 pairs 'in a good year' (although some of these may have been in present-day Cumbria), with about five pairs inland. In 1977 20 pairs nested inland with at least twelve in west Bowland. Harsh weather in early 1978 produced another setback which seems to have affected inland breeders most severely; it was another 20 years before numbers there began to recover. National numbers continued to decline until at least the late 1980s (Marchant *et al.* 1990), but recent years have witnessed a major resurgence with an increase of 227% between 1994 and 2005 (BBS). The Lancashire population has followed these trends; breeding was confirmed in seven coastal 10km squares in the Old Atlas, declining to five in the New Atlas and rising to 16 squares (just four on the coast) during 1997-2000.

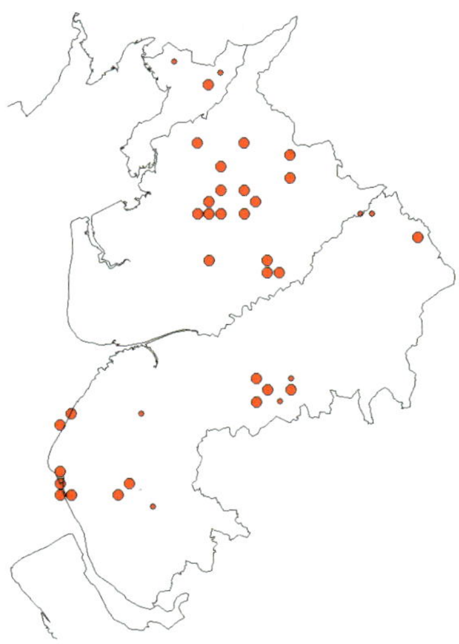

Breeding distribution of Stonechat, 1997-2000. (Large dots: confirmed. Small dots: possible)

Breeding Stonechats disappeared from the Fylde coast after the winter of 1946/47 until 1952. Up to three pairs bred there during the 1950s but none nested between 1962 and 1967 when two pairs returned (Clarke 1981). The main breeding location during the 1970s was Lytham St. Anne's NR with two or three pairs, declining to one or two pairs in the 1980s. None bred after 1989 until single pairs at Blackpool Airport in 2002, Lytham St. Anne's NR in 2004 and Fairhaven Dunes in 2005.

Small numbers persisted on the Sefton Coast during the 1950s to 1970s but numbers grew rapidly from one pair in 1970 to 14 in 1978, after which the population fell back to the 6-8 pairs which still persist, mostly now breeding between Crosby and Formby. Rising numbers during the 1970s coincided with the local extinction of Whinchats.

Male Stonechat, Seaforth Nature Reserve, March 2005. (Steve Young)

Up to two pairs bred at Heysham during the 1960s and 1970s and singles at Halton Park in 1975 and Leighton Moss in 1977, but there was no further breeding on the northern coast until a pair at Middleton in 2003. As elsewhere, the northern inland population appears to have grown throughout the 1970s, with five pairs at Clougha Fell and one at Marshaw in 1975 and twelve pairs in north-west Bowland in 1977, with known breeding also at Longridge and Waddington Fells. It was virtually wiped out by the winter of 1978/79 with none reported in 1979/80 and just one in 1981, and there were no further records of confirmed breeding until 1994 when a pair nested on Catlow Fell, near Stocks Reservoir. For the next few years two or three pairs were suspected to be breeding but 1999 saw the beginning of a nearly exponential increase, particularly in Bowland. This was best monitored on the United Utilities estate where ten territories were located in 1999, 24 in 2000, 39 in 2002 and 46 in 2005.

The cycle has been similar elsewhere in the uplands, in east Lancashire, Rossendale and the West Pennine Moors area, where until very recently most records of breeding came from the period 1975-78, including at Longridge and Waddington Fells, Worsthorne, Sabden, Pendle Hill, Haslingden, the Plunge Valley, Turton/Darwen Moor and in the Anglezarke-Rivington area, with a maximum of about six in 1976/77. There were occasional records during the period 1987-92 but breeding was confirmed in the White Coppice-Anglezarke-Rivington area from 1993 and on Belmont and Darwen

Moors from 1996, rising to a total of eight pairs on the two latter sites in 2003. The total population on the West Pennine Moors was thought to be in excess of 30 pairs in 2004.

None was recorded in Rossendale during 1997-2000 but there were four pairs in 2003 and five pairs in the Grane Valley alone in 2004 with pairs reported from a further eight sites. The area east of Burnley remains sparsely colonised, however, with just a single pair found during 1997-2000 rising to three pairs in 2004.

The Lancashire population was estimated at 60 pairs during 1997-2000 but is probably closer to 150 pairs now. There is little doubt that increased survival over a series of mild winters since the mid-1990s is the driving force behind this recent expansion. As late as 1996 very few records of wintering away from the Sefton or Fylde coasts were reported but by 2000 records came from at least 20 sites, mostly inland. Various Sefton coast sites held a total of 35 in 2001/02 and there have been recent counts of four or more at Harrisend Fell, Hawthornthwaite Fell, Great Hameldon, the Stocks Reservoir area, Dunsop Valley, Darwen Moor, Belmont, Cockersands, Fazakerley and several sites in Rossendale, with lower numbers at very many more. A total of 48 were reported in east Lancashire in late 2004. Many more go unreported and the winter total is probably around 200. Stonechats are partial migrants with part of the population medium-distance migrants and the remainder sedentary; it is likely that most wintering birds remain close to their natal or breeding sites.

Juvenile Stonechat, Hightown Dunes, May 2005. (Steve Young)

Spring passage of those birds that have migrated south normally begins in mid-February, continuing through to early or mid-April but is always heaviest during March. Aggregate numbers vary enormously, especially on the coast, with the highest totals 35 at Marshside and 34 at Marton Mere in 1994, 43 at Marton Mere in 2000 and 36 at Marshside in 2002. Most records are of ones or twos and the only large 'falls' were seven at Pilling Lane Ends, nine at Martin Mere, five at Heysham and ones and twos at nine other coastal sites on 26-27 February 2003, 50 or more between Marton Mere, Lytham St. Anne's NR and Fleetwood ICI on 13-15 March 2000, and 14 on Lytham St. Anne's NR on 7 March 2001.

First-brood juveniles may begin to disperse as early as June but the first autumn records more usually occur in late July or early August, with the main passage between mid-September and late October and small numbers seen regularly until late November. Until very recently autumn totals rarely broke single figures, 20 through Heysham in 1988 being a notable exception. Numbers have increased in line with the expansion of the inland breeding population. Several large single-day counts occurred in 2003 with twelve on Pendle Hill on 5 September and at Birk Bank on the 17th and 18 at Clougha on the 27th, while twelve were at Clowbridge Reservoir in September 2001. Coastal totals have shown much less change with up to ten seen at various coastal watch-points north to Heysham since the early 1990s and largest tallies at Marshside of 20 in 1994 and 22 in 1999.

Most ringing recoveries relate to birds returning to natal sites or making very short movements between years with just two definite migrants both ringed in Cumbria: juveniles from Hodbarrow to Leighton Moss in 1991 and from Sellafield to Formby in September 1992. With the exception of our one 'Siberian Stonechat', all Lancashire records are believed to relate to the sub-species *hibernans* although the possibility that some continental *rubicola* have occurred on passage cannot be discounted.

SJW, RW.

This species account was sponsored by John Bannon.

'SIBERIAN' STONECHAT

Saxicola torquata maura

Lancashire Category A. (0, 1).

Vagrant from Siberia.

A female or first-winter was seen and photographed on Downholland Moss on 26 December 1983 by Mike Pennington. This was the 68th record in Britain and Ireland of this distinctive, pale-rumped eastern form that some regard as a candidate for a 'split'. At the time it was the latest ever seen nationally, with just one previous December record and most in September and October in the Northern Isles and eastern England. It remains the only record in north-west England.

SJW, MJ.

This species account was sponsored by Craig Howarth.

WHEATEAR

Oenanthe oenanthe

Lancashire Category A.

Fairly common breeder; common passage migrant from northern Britain, Iceland and possibly Greenland.

The breeding distribution of Wheatears has undergone substantial change during the past 100 years or so. Mitchell regarded them as local in distribution and 'most common on the moors and fells' but also 'found breeding on the whole range of the coast sand-hills from Liverpool northwards' and inland 'where large tracts of "moss" form a solitude which suits their retiring habits'. He singled out Winmarleigh Moss as a site where breeding birds were plentiful but provided only a very sketchy picture of the upland distribution, while noting local declines, for example around Blackburn, due to 'the enclosing of commons and waste lands'.

Mossland breeding continued into the mid-twentieth century, Oakes describing Wheatears as holding their own on several mosses – he reported nesting in peat stacks – and re-establishing themselves on others, but he specified no sites. Nesting seems also to have continued fairly frequently on the dunes, deep in rabbit burrows, but Oakes blamed increasing urbanisation for a decrease on the Fylde and Sefton coasts. They were already in decline on the Sefton dunes in the 1930s and none nested after 1955.

Male Wheatear at Belmont. (Tony Disley)

Precisely when the last pair bred on the mosslands is unclear but none has been reported for at least 20 years. Apparent pairs have summered on the Sefton Coast on a handful of occasions in the past 15 years but successful breeding has never been considered likely; one pair bred near Pilling in 1972 with possible breeding at Knott End in 1994 but nesting on the Fylde dunes probably ceased by the 1940s.

Breeding was confirmed in just five lowland 10km squares in 1968-72 but by 1988-91 this was reduced to just one at a single site, the long-established colony on Carnforth slag tips. Up to nine pairs bred there during the 1980s, declining to four or five in the 1990s and a perilous two during 1998-2004.

In the uplands the Wheatear is a bird of open, short grass habitats, where it uses dry-stone walls, rock outcrops and quarries as nest sites. Breeding takes place over much of the upland area but is concentrated in Bowland in the north, and the West Pennine Moors and Rossendale in the south. The range has scarcely changed since 1968-72, breeding having been confirmed in 24 upland 10km squares in the Old and New Atlases and 23 in the Lancashire Atlas. There has, however, probably been a more considerable contraction in distribution at a more local level, for example a decline was noticed east of Burnley from around the mid-1980s and suspected elsewhere.

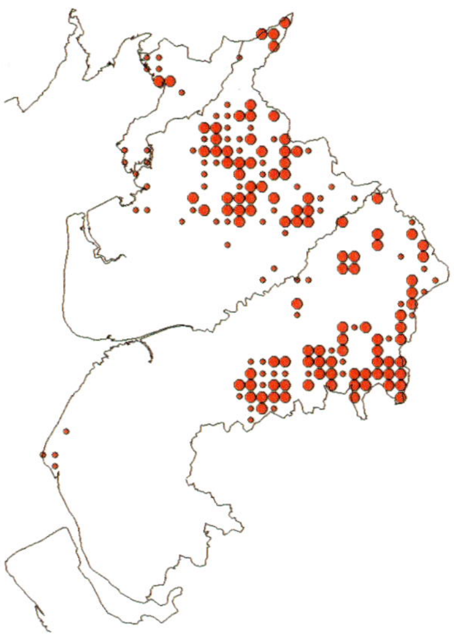

Breeding distribution of Wheatear, 1997-2000. (Large dots: confirmed. Small dots: possible)

The Lancashire population was estimated at 375 pairs in 1997-2000 with probably a little over a third of these in Bowland and most of the remainder on the West Pennine Moors eastwards to Rossendale. Nationally, numbers declined by 36% between 1994 and 2005 (BBS), while a survey of the south Pennines, including areas outside of Lancashire, estimated a 46% decline between 1990 and 2002 (Simm *et al.* 2005).

Regular censuses on the United Utilities Bowland estate indicate a steady decline in numbers since at least the early 1980s. Forty pairs were recorded in 1983, followed by 30 in 1995 with an additional nine males and three females. Repeat surveys in 2002, 2003, 2004 and 2005 found 27, 18, 16 and 22 territories respectively. Around five pairs also breed annually on Pendle Hill, one or two pairs on Longridge Fell and a thin scattering of pairs east of Burnley at Cant Clough, Sheddon Clough, Swinden Reservoir and the Thursden Valley.

Rossendale is the second most important area and Wheatears were described as widespread there in 1978 and reasonably numerous a decade later (Ward 1988). Quarries provide a favoured habitat, supporting 17 pairs in 1982 and eleven in 1992. Significant local declines have been noted, for example from four pairs at Clowbridge Reservoir in 1989 to an occasional one in the late 1990s. Overall, though, numbers appear to be steady but with sometimes marked annual fluctuations, for example breeding was recorded at 17 sites in 1996, six in 2002 and eleven in 2003.

Numbers on the West Pennine Moors area appear to have peaked in the early to mid-1970s, with comments regarding increasing scarcity being made during the period 1978-82. Small numbers breed on Anglezarke and Rivington Moors, four pairs being recorded in 1993. Numbers around Belmont fluctuated between one and five pairs during the period 1990-96 but grew to eight in 1998 and six in 2002 before falling to three in 2005.

Wheatears are usually highly faithful to both breeding and natal sites (Migration Atlas), illustrated by a nestling ringed in June 1915 at Fairhaven and recovered at the same site in late May the following year.

The Wheatear is always one of our first spring migrants. Our earliest was at Pilling Lane Ends on 26 February 2003 – the previous earliest was on 1 March 1975 on Carnforth Marsh – and the earliest inland on Darwen Moor on 8 March 1997. According to Oakes the average first arrival in the county was on 19 March, while in the past 25 years it has been 11 March. The first birds are usually seen a few days later inland, for example on 22 March at Belmont during 1993-2002 but often not until towards the end of the month in Rossendale.

The main coastal passage usually gets underway in the third week of March, peaking during April, but numbers remain high until early May with occasional first-summers seen through to June. The earliest arrivals are almost always adult males, followed a week or so later by females and first-summer birds. No one site stands out; birds are regularly dispersed the length of the coast and on the coastal plain, most often on recently ploughed land. Large day-counts include 75 at Seaforth on 5 May 1978, 37 at Martin Mere on 6 May 1992, 54 at Heysham on 15 April 1996, 57 on Plex Moss on 22 April 1996 with 46 at Marshside the following day, 141 at four sites in Fleetwood on 23 April 1998 when 35 were also at Marton Mere, 80 on Aldcliffe Marsh on 30 April 2001 and 40 on Colloway Marsh on 24 April 2003. Numbers further inland are generally lower but some quite large concentrations do occur, for example 50 on Boulsworth Hill on 8 May 1989, 30 at Dean Clough Reservoir on 1 May 1994, 50 at Great Hameldon on 27 April 1996 and 50 at Clowbridge Reservoir on 23 April 2002. An exceptional 163 bird-days were counted at Belmont between March and May in 1995 and 184 in the same period in 1999.

Observations at Seaforth suggest an average length of stay of 1.5 to 2.5 days, indicating an average spring total there of 200 individuals between 1986 and 2005 with perhaps as many as 350 in 1992. Two other regular coastal watchpoints, Marshside and Heysham, record rather fewer with averages of around 175 and 200 bird-days respectively during the 1990s. Seaforth totals have declined by more than a third since the mid-1990s but it is unclear if this is the case elsewhere. It is impossible to assess the total size of the passage through the county accurately but it is probably at least in the low thousands.

A ringing study on the Hightown Dunes and at Seaforth during the 1990s (J. E. Taylor unpublished) showed that the first adult male Greenland Wheatears *Oe. oe. leucorhoa* (assessed according to wing length) usually arrive around 12-14 April and that by the last week of April virtually no nominate *oenanthe* males are present. The situation is less clear with females but respective timings are probably about a week or so later than for males. On this basis it is estimated that about 45% of the total spring passage on the Sefton coast has consisted of *leucorhoa* since the mid-1980s, considerably more than would be suspected from field observations. The same study indicates that spring males consistently outnumber females by 3:2.

Male Greenland Wheatear, Seaforth Nature Reserve, August 2007. (Steve Young)

There is only one ringing recovery showing the natal origin of a spring passage bird, a juvenile ringed on the Calf of Man on 30 July 1996 and trapped at Blundellsands on 25 March 1997. We therefore know next to nothing of the destinations of either *oenanthe*, which range as far as the Faroes, or *leucorhoa* which probably head for both Iceland and Greenland. An adult ringed at Ainsdale on 31 March 1972 and recovered in Morocco in September 1973 confirms the known wintering area of British birds.

The first dispersing juveniles are sometimes seen on the coast at the end of June but the main migration is rarely underway before mid-July and almost always peaks between mid-August and mid-September. The average last sighting is on 1 November but late November records are reasonably frequent, and the latest singles at Rossall on 26-27 November 1985, Sunderland Point on 24 November 1985, Marton Moss on 23 November 1960, and inland at Whitendale on 20 November 1998.

Numbers everywhere are considerably lower than in spring. Estimated totals through Seaforth since 1985 averaged about 100 individuals but no other site regularly records nearly as many. The largest seasonal totals (bird-days) include 555, representing 275-300 individuals, at Seaforth in 1986, 180 at Heysham in 1997, 188 at Fleetwood in 1998 and 111 at Belmont during August 1999. Peak day-counts include 40 at Hightown on 30 September 1975, 70 at Seaforth on 26 Aug 1985, 23 on Turton Moor on 21 August 1988, 19 at Parsonage Reservoir on 16 August 1988, 25 on Pendle Hill on 22 August 1999 and 21 at Heysham on 9 September 2002.

A possible explanation for the lower numbers in autumn is that a greater proportion of *leucorhoa* migrate directly to Iberia across the sea (Migration Atlas). Adults are trickier to distinguish in the field in autumn but first-winters are usually distinctive and, although the Sefton coast ringing study has not yet come up with conclusive results, a fairly high number of birds at Seaforth are believed to be *leucorhoa* – probably a majority from mid-September. The recovery of birds ringed as nestlings in the Fylde in 1912 and recovered in France on 8 September 1912, and at Sabden in 1948 and also recovered in France on 30 August 1948 illustrate the relatively early migration of British birds.

SJW, RW.

This species account was sponsored by John Bannon.

PIED WHEATEAR

Oenanthe pleschanka

Lancashire Category A. (0, 1).

Vagrant from south-east Europe or Asia.

On the morning of 27 October 1997 Steve White and Chris Sharratt watched a wheatear drop down onto a wall at Seaforth NR. It had been a fortnight since the last 'Northern' Wheatear had been seen on the reserve and it deserved some scrutiny. But before it could be 'scoped' it flew, revealing an extensively white tail, suggesting either Pied or Black-eared Wheatear, and giving the impression of a dark throat and underwings. Before long it was relocated, thoroughly scrutinised and pronounced as a first-winter male Pied.

It stayed around a rabbit warren for the rest of the day, allowing close approach as it perched on the mounds. This behaviour nearly led to its downfall as a Sparrowhawk swooped within centimetres, causing it to retreat down a rabbit hole for some time.

First-winter male Pied Wheatear, Seaforth Nature Reserve, 27 October 1997. (Steve Young)

This was the 38th record for Britain and Ireland. Most have occurred on the east and southern coasts and this remains the only one in north-west England; 1997 was a particularly good year with three other records around the country. Late autumn dates are the norm.

SJW, MJ.

This species account was sponsored by Tim Vaughan.

BLACK-EARED WHEATEAR

Oenanthe hispanica

Lancashire Category B. (3, 0).

Vagrant from southern Europe.

Oakes gave details of our only records to date. Two males, 'probably of the western race [*Oe. h. hispanica*]' were seen on a potato field near Lytham, in the company of many male Common Wheatears on 18 to 22 April 1940 by R.H. Fisher and J.W. Sutcliffe (BB 34: 109). A black-throated male, also of the western race, was seen at very close range by F.W. Holder in the dunes at Ainsdale on 21 April 1943 (BB 37: 36).

If correctly identified, the Lytham record would be the only multiple occurrence in Britain.

SJW, MJ.

DESERT WHEATEAR

Oenanthe deserti

Lancashire Category A. (0, 2).

Vagrant from North Africa or south-west Asia.

Both records to date have come from the Fylde. A first-winter female was found at Rossall Point, Fleetwood on 5 November 1991 by D. Rusling and R. Scholes. It hardly strayed from its initial location and was seen along the shore and on the adjoining golf course until the 19th.

The second, a first-winter male was found along the northern edge of Blackpool Airport on waste ground close to Morrison's supermarket on 11 November 1994 . Like the first, it moved little and was seen daily until the 21st.

First-winter male Desert Wheatear, Blackpool, November 1994. (Steve Young)

These were the 39th and 47th records in Britain and Ireland and the second and third for north-west England, after one on South Walney in November 1986. Late autumn or early winter arrivals are the norm and most aged records have been of first-winters. Most British records are probably of the nominate sub-species, originating in central Asia rather than North Africa.

SJW, MJ.

This species account was sponsored by the Fylde Bird Club.

RING OUZEL

Turdus torquatus

Lancashire Category A.

Scarce breeder; uncommon passage migrant.

Lancashire's Ring Ouzels require very specific breeding habitat, nesting only above 250m in undisturbed rocky moorland cloughs, gullies and derelict quarries, generally with scattered trees and frequently close to in-bye pasture or other closely grazed grassland. This combination of features is far from common and it seems unlikely that the species has ever been anything but a scarce breeding bird in the county. Mitchell believed that a few pairs bred on the Manchester and other mosslands, but Oakes maintained there was no evidence for this; certainly there has been no indication of breeding away from the high fells in living memory.

Their remote and scattered habitat makes Ring Ouzels difficult to survey but there is some evidence that the British population has been in decline since at least the 1970s, a change which has been reflected in Lancashire. The UK range declined by 27% (753 to 549 10km squares) between the two national atlas surveys and around 40% of tetrads occupied in 1988-91 had been deserted by 1999 (Wotton *et al.* 2002).

Reasons suggested for this include competition for breeding territories from Blackbirds and Mistle Thrushes as a result of climate change, allowing the latter two species to breed at higher altitude; afforestation; disturbance from human leisure activities, particularly fell-walking; and agricultural 'improvements'. Problems on migratory stopover sites or wintering grounds, including depletion of junipers in Morocco, may also play a part.

Mitchell described them as fairly plentiful along the Yorkshire border (Bowland was then in Yorkshire), regularly found nesting on Haslingden Moor and Hapton Scout, and common on Withnell and Anglezarke Moors with a few pairs on Pendle Hill. There had been some apparent decline by Oakes's time, when the Ring Ouzel was described as local in the Anglezarke area, although still plentiful on several north-eastern fells including Stiperden, Boulsworth, Pendle, Parlick and Fairsnape.

Spencer (1973) noted that Ring Ouzels were moderately well distributed around Pendle Hill and east of Burnley between Deerplay Moor and Trawden during the early 1970s. Around six to eight pairs bred in Rossendale during the 1980s, principally near Cliviger, Haslingden Grane, Musbury Tor and Alden in the west, and the Plunge Valley, Cowpe Valley and Lee Quarry areas in the south.

The Lancashire breeding range shrank by almost 25% from 20 10km squares (confirmed in all) to 16 (confirmed in 8) between 1968-72 and 1988-91 and showed a further small decline to 15 (confirmed in 9) squares in 1997-2000. The increasing difficulty in obtaining confirmation of breeding perhaps indicates that the scale of the decline both in distribution within this range and population size has been greater than previously thought.

Bowland remains the county stronghold but the Lancashire Atlas survey located five pairs breeding in Rossendale, 3-5 pairs in the Trawden area, three pairs around Pendle Hill, one or more in the upper Lune Valley, and a possible breeding pair in the Leck Fell area. Breeding has not been confirmed in Rossendale since 2000.

Since the late 1990s, birds have been present in several years at sites in the West Pennine Moors, with breeding confirmed in 2000 (for the first time since 1979) and considered probable in 2002. Nesting was also regular in the Saddle End-Greenough Clough area near Chipping until at least the mid-1970s. A few pairs breed in north-west Bowland, in the upper reaches of Littledale and Roeburndale.

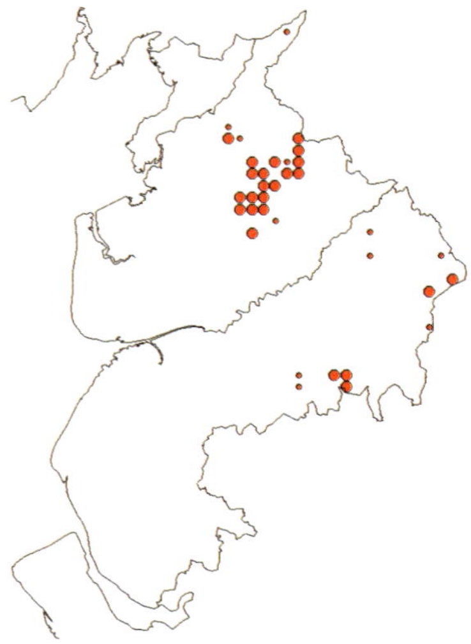

Breeding distribution of Ring Ouzel, 1997-2000. (Large dots: confirmed. Small dots: possible)

Most of Lancashire's birds are found within SD65 and adjacent areas. This Bowland population is centred upon the United Utilities estate, where numbers appear to have taken a sharp fall since the mid-1990s. Thirty pairs were estimated in 1983, 35 in 1989 (12 in the Langden Valley, seven in Whitendale, four on Croasdale Fell and four elsewhere) and 34 in 1995 (12 in the Langden Valley, six in the Hareden Valley, three in Whitendale, six on Croasdale Fell and seven elsewhere). By 1999 the population had fallen to 19 pairs and systematic surveys in 2002-2005 found only 16, 15, 14 and 12 definite or probable pairs (P. Wilson *pers. comm.*). Even allowing for possible differences in survey technique, this points to an almost 75% decline in the space of a decade. The total Lancashire population was estimated at 35 pairs in 1997-2000, representing about 0.5% of the British and 2% of the English population (Wotton *et al.* 2002). Twenty pairs might be a more accurate figure now; Ring Ouzels are clearly in serious trouble. The reasons for this are not known but an intensive study begun in 2003 has tentatively uncovered low levels of nest survival (P. Wilson *pers. comm.*).

Oakes reported the earliest arrival as 26 February (year not published) but this was perhaps an over-wintering bird. The next earliest records were in the Rimrose Valley, Merseyside on 11 March 1999 and the Langden Valley on 14 March 1997. First sightings have become significantly earlier over the past 25 years, on average on 24 March.

The earliest birds both inland and on the coast are usually single males and many may be back on territory by the end of the month. There is increasing evidence of a regular passage movement through the breeding areas from the end of March to mid-April. Sizeable groups are seen occasionally on Pendle Hill, including eight on 23 April 1989 and seven on 19 April 1995, and also in Rossendale and on the West Pennine Moors. Birders unfamiliar with Bowland, who went looking for the Rough-legged Buzzard in the Dunsop Valley in early April 1997 expressed surprise at finding six Ring Ouzels there, but such numbers remain regular in the area. Two colour-ringed birds seen in Bowland in March 2004 and believed to have been ringed in the Grampians provide the strongest evidence that a proportion of early spring records on the fells are migrants moving through.

Spring records on the coast and, less frequently, the lowlands further inland also peak in early April but may extend into early May; they have averaged eight a year since 1995, usually singles at all the main watchpoints from Seaforth to Heysham. One of the best coastal passages was on 11-15 April 1980, when 14 were seen along the Merseyside coast between Marshside and Seaforth. Birds moving through Lancashire in late April and May perhaps include some Fennoscandian migrants but are more likely to be British first-summers – the only ringing evidence is of one ringed as a pullus in Pendle and shot in the French Pyrenees the following year, presumably on return migration, on 28 March 1935. One at Cabin Hill on the unusual date of 10 June 1990 was presumably a non-breeding bird.

Pre-migratory dispersal takes place from late July, initially within the breeding range but later further afield to lower altitudes. Migration begins in late August and continues throughout September into October. Two ringing recoveries give an indication of the timing of the migration: a pullus ringed at Sowerby Bridge in West Yorkshire in May 1954 and found 23km away at Trawden on 15 September the same year; and another ringed in the nest in Lancashire in May 1976 and found in Navarre in north-east Spain on 15 September that year. Migrants may make brief stop-overs on the moorland fringes to take advantage of rowan berries and other food resources, for example, 13 at Whitendale on 17 October 1995, annual records on in-bye land near Darwen Moor with eleven there with Fieldfares and Blackbirds in October 1999, and ten through Belmont in 2002.

Male Ring Ouzel, Seaforth Nature Reserve, March 2002. (Steve Young)

Coastal migrants are recorded in very small numbers in most years, rarely before the end of September and more often in October. Records after mid-October are more likely to be Fennoscandian than British migrants. Certainly, one with the massive Redwing movement over Marshside on 9 October 2004 seems likely to have been of continental origin, and many autumn migrants at Heysham coincide with falls on the east coast and are associated with other Scandinavian migrants. A handful have remained into winter: at Lytham on 4 December 1966, Lytham St. Anne's NR on 31 December 1969, in a garden at Hare Appletree, near Clougha (two) in December 1976, Sabden on 14-19 January 1985, Marton Mere on 8-14 December 1986, in a Burnley garden from 29 November to 7 December 1993, Sunderland Point on 29 January 1996 with one in Silverdale at about the same time (these were cold-weather displacements from an unknown source), Earby from mid-February to the end of March 1996 and, most recently, near Darwen Moor on 11 December 2000.

SJW, RW.

This species account was sponsored by John Bannon.

BLACKBIRD

Turdus merula

Lancashire Category A.

Abundant breeder and winter visitor from continental Europe.

The Blackbird is one of the most widespread and abundant of Lancashire's birds, present all year in a wide variety of habitats, including broadleaved and mixed woodland, parkland, urban parks and gardens and farmland wherever there is sufficient cover of trees or bushes. In towns and cities, where there are few trees, Blackbirds utilise the tops of buildings and street lights as singing posts, relying on man-made structures for nest sites if required. Nests are also found in moorland cloughs, isolated farmsteads up to 300m above sea level and quarries at heights of 350m; Oakes reported a nest at 1,400' (427m) at Haslingden. Several pairs breed in moorland bracken-beds and deep heather up to 350m above sea level on the West Pennine Moors on – and in some cases at higher altitudes than – sites formerly occupied by Ring Ouzels.

In mild winters nesting occasionally takes place very early. The most remarkable records are of a pair feeding young in Blackburn town centre on 7 February 1985 and on the same date in 1988. Others include pairs feeding young at Skippool on 16 February 1983, a female with nest material at Freckleton on 20 January 1990, a half-completed nest in Rossendale on 5 January 1992, and a pair feeding young near Colne on 13 February 2002. Males in full song during December and January are reasonably frequent.

There has been no obvious change in breeding status in recent years, with pairs breeding in virtually all areas of suitable habitat. The Lancashire Atlas located Blackbirds in 870 (93%) of the county's tetrads in 1997-2000, with breeding proven everywhere except the higher moorland of Bowland, Leck Fell, south-east Lancashire and the West Pennine Moors. We have no comprehensive data on breeding densities but, in general, numbers increase towards the west, with the highest densities occurring in urban areas. The county population is estimated at 45,000 pairs, based upon average national densities.

Blackbirds are probably at least five times as abundant as Song Thrushes in Lancashire but this was not always so. Mitchell regarded Song Thrushes as normally the more numerous although Blackbirds had overtaken them by the late nineteenth century due to their higher survival rates during severe winters. Blackbirds were clearly the more common species by the middle of the twentieth century (Oakes) and Spencer thought that the breeding population was twice as large as that of Song Thrushes.

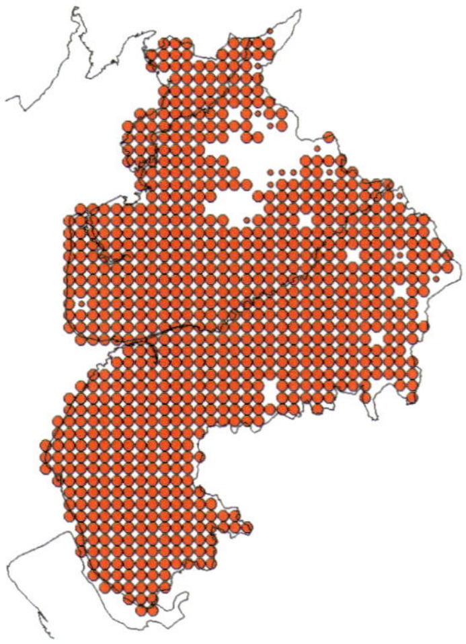

Breeding distribution of Blackbird, 1997-2000. (Large dots: confirmed. Small dots: possible)

The British woodland and farmland population showed a steady decline according to the CBC between 1974 and 1991 but the more representative BBS indicates a 22% increase between 1994 and 2005. Information from several well-monitored sites, including Leighton Moss, Warton Crag, Broughton and Mere Sands Wood, suggests that the Lancashire population has broadly followed the national trend.

Male Blackbird, Little Crosby, February 2004. (Steve Young)

Ringing recoveries show the Lancashire population to be overwhelmingly sedentary; juveniles and adults very rarely disperse more than 10km and more often less than 1km, and most return to breed close to natal sites. However, more birds from NW Britain, including Lancashire, are migratory than elsewhere in the country (Migration Atlas). There are no recoveries of Lancashire pulli in continental Europe, and almost all movements over 20km have been to Ireland. Irish recoveries are becoming less frequent and perhaps originated in cold weather movements (Migration Atlas).

There is no evidence of any significant passage of British birds through Lancashire and any early early autumn movements are probably no more than fairly local dispersal. The autumn passage of continental Blackbirds may begin as early as late September but almost always peaks between mid-October and mid-November. Precise timing varies from year to year but ringing totals at Heysham (1997-2003) indicate that roughly 15% pass through during September, 40% in October and 45% in November. Much of this migration takes place at night and Blackbirds do not usually figure very highly in counts of visible migrants. Passage movements are more generally registered as sudden increases at coastal and inland sites which hold Blackbirds year-round, and it is likely that many smaller-scale movements are missed. Large day-counts include 200 at Loveclough, Rossendale on 7 November 1981; 150 at Heysham on 22 October 1991 with 250 there on 23 October 1993 and 100 on 6 November 2003; 150 at Red Scar Wood on 17 December 1992; 100 at Eccleston Mere, St. Helens on 3 October 1993; and 238 at Marton Mere on 25 November 1994.

It is not known how many autumn arrivals remain for the winter but the proportion doing so almost certainly increases during November and few movements are noted after mid-December with the exception of occasional hard-weather influxes. These late influxes are rarely of any great size; one example was a total of 148 on a 14km transect near Carnforth on 11 December 1983 compared with a normal winter population of 60. Few sites record winter peaks of more than 25, indicating that birds are highly dispersed. Recent larger counts include 100 in Childwall Woods, south Liverpool in February 1990, 145 at Marton Mere in December 1994, 50 regularly at Leighton Moss in the mid- to late 1990s, 40 or so at Mere Sands Wood in the late 1990s, 30+ at Belmont in December 2001, 60 on the Birkdale dunes in January 2003, 65 at Morecambe in February 2003 and 100 at Bispham on 26 December 2004. Blackbirds' preference for urban areas is well demonstrated by the large counts made around Christmas in recent years on the aptly-named 'Blackbird Walks' in the Marton Mere and Stanley Park area of Blackpool – including a phenomenal 523 on 27 December 2000.

A high proportion of passage and wintering birds are of foreign origin. There have been 75 movements of ringed birds between Lancashire and continental Europe: 24 involving Norway, 17 Sweden, 4 Finland, 10 Denmark, 9 Germany, 10 Holland and 2 Belgium. All of those ringed or recovered in Lancashire were outside the breeding season, while almost all those ringed or recovered abroad were either in the breeding season or on passage. The exceptions were two wintering (not in the same year as in Lancashire) in Denmark, two in Belgium and two in the Netherlands – all countries where Blackbirds are only partially migratory. Many Lancashire recoveries of birds ringed elsewhere in Britain probably also relate to continental breeders, for example one ringed at Spurn on 11 October 1988 and recovered at Clifton on 23 November the same year. Other wintering birds, however, are short-distance migrants from the north, for example one ringed at Formby on 29 December 1980 and recovered in Brampton, Cumbria on 18 April 1981.

Spring passage is usually virtually undetectable with rarely more than single-figure counts registered. 'Fall' conditions, however, sometimes produce larger numbers; recent examples include 30-40 at Heysham in fog on 14 March 1991, with similar numbers there on 15 March 1993 and 17 March 1999, and 30 at Marton Mere on 11 March 1999.

SJW, RW.

This species account was sponsored by Ron Hothersall.

[DARK-THROATED THRUSH]

Turdus ruficollis

Spencer published a record of one at Lytham St. Anne's on 24 November 1971 but with no further details. Another male at Bolton-le-Sands on 2 & 7 February 1996 was widely reported but, as with the earlier record, it was never submitted to the BBRC. Both were thought to have related to the sub-species *atrogularis* 'Black-throated Thrush'.

FIELDFARE

Turdus pilaris

Lancashire Category A.

Abundant winter visitor and passage migrant from continental Europe, probably mostly from Norway.

Mitchell described Fieldfares as present in Lancashire between October and May, 'though seldom later than April', with both arrival and departure dates about a fortnight later than Redwings.

Oakes gave the expected arrival date 'in northern districts' as 18-25 October, a week to ten days later than for Redwing. He described Fieldfares as common on mosslands, including Pilling and Cockerham, and noted their attraction to the Formby asparagus fields, on whose berries they fed. Return migration began in early March but was heaviest between 25 March and 24 April; notably late records were at Littledale, near Lancaster on 13 May 1933, Haslingden on 15 May 1909 and Carleton, near Blackpool on 7 June 1945.

These days first arrivals are generally at the end of September, a week to ten days later than Redwings, but significant numbers are rarely seen before the second week of October. Despite their relatively late arrival there have been a number of very early occurrences, including singles near Ribchester on 28 August 1969, at Cabin Hill on 31 July 1974, Oswaldtwistle on 25 August 1976, Rossall on 3 August 1983, Formby on 28 August 1983, a remarkable twelve birds at Chapel Hill, near Rawtenstall on 12 August 1990 and one with Mistle Thrushes at White Greet on 7 August 2005. Since fewer than 1% of continental birds move more than 50km from their nesting site before the end of September (Migration Atlas), it is possible that these early records may relate to the small British breeding population which is spread thinly in Scotland and northern England from Northumberland and Durham southwards to Derbyshire and Staffordshire. This population has declined from about 20-25 pairs at the end of the 1980s to 2-6 in 2001 (Ogilvie 2003), so the fact that there have been no August records since 1990 may be a reflection of this; however, odd birds continue to be reported during mid-September.

Fieldfares are quite capable of withstanding the arctic winter as long as food supplies hold out (Norman 1994) and both arrival dates and numbers are influenced by the availability of berries in Scandinavia. Most autumns, however, see two relatively distinct pulses of migration into Lancashire: in mid-October and from the end of October to mid-November. As with all thrushes, much of this migration takes place at night but records of daytime flights have proliferated in recent years as visible-migration-watching has become more popular.

Large movements are now regularly detected both inland and on the coast. Representative counts include: 3,000 going north-west over Billinge Hill on 2 November 1986 with 1,186 north-west over Calf Hey, Haslingden, 950 over Leighton Moss and 200 at Preesall the same day; 2,594 south-west over Heysham in five hours and 1,500 west over Carnforth in 20 minutes on 11 October 1988; 2,000 over Burnley on 26 October 1990; 2,510 south over Belmont with 906 at Warton Crag and several thousand elsewhere on 16 October 1999; 4,541 at Heysham, 3,900 at Seaforth, 1,750 at Marton Mere with several thousand elsewhere on 5 November 2000; 5,000 south-east over Brockholes Quarry on 16 October 2001; 2,780 south over Seaforth, 2,257 over Fairhaven, up to 1,800 over two Blackpool sites and 494 over Heysham on 13 October 2003; and 4,000 east over Marshside on 9 October 2004.

Large, usually transitory roosts can build up throughout the migration period, normally in inland woodlands. Examples include 3,000 at Leighton Moss in late October 1983; 2,700 at Longridge on 18 November 1984; 1,200 at Longworth Clough on 29 October 1989; 2,000 near Slaidburn and 1,500 in the Trough of Bowland on 15 November 1989; 1,500 at Whinscar Clough, near Burnley on 31 October 1990; 2,000 at Roddlesworth on 18 October 1993; 1,000 at Catford, 1,000 at Rowley Lake, 900 at Eccleston and 500 at Wheelton on 4 November 1998; and 1,200 at Abbeystead on 14 October 2003.

Fieldfare, Liverpool, December 2005. (Steve Young)

Newly arrived birds frequently feed on the berries of rowan, hawthorn, whitebeam and yew. When these food sources are exhausted they either move on or resort to open farmland. Relatively few large flocks are reported in late November to early December but it is not clear to what extent this is because birds are widely dispersed or because most migrants pass through the county fairly rapidly.

The number and size of flocks vary considerably from winter to winter according to weather conditions. During most winters groups of 100 or so are reported from up to a dozen locations with larger flocks of up to 300 at a further handful, but prolonged frosts force birds off farmland and concentrate them wherever berries remain available or frost-free conditions prevail. The largest congregations rarely occur before the New Year and probably involve birds already wintering in the county together with immigrants from further afield. The largest winter concentrations have included 800 between Nether Kellet and Halton on 21 January 1978; 1000 at Altham on 15 December 1978; 800 at Whalley in December 1988; 1,000 at Rufford on 3 January 1995; 1,400 at Belmont on 1 January 1996 with 800 at Leighton Moss, 500 at Trawden and 500 at The Brex over the next fortnight, and 800 at Roddlesworth in February; 850 on Longridge Fell on 11 January 1998; and 700 on the Birkdale dunes on 8 January 2003. Fieldfares sometimes frequent gardens during hard weather, though they are less inclined to do so than Redwings. Sometimes they resort to more unusual sources of food, for example the berries of sea buckthorn on coastal dunes. An exceptional gathering of 500 was noted feeding on windfalls in a Silverdale apple orchard on 19 January 1985.

During spells of severe weather further movements may take place, the most spectacular example being on 22 January 1984, when a heavy passage was reported throughout Lancashire. Several locations produced counts of over 1,000, including 1,500 over Anglezarke in three hours, 2,000 over Heysham and 4,500 moving south-west over Carnforth. Further large midwinter movements include 450 south over Cuerden Valley Park on 2 January 1996, 410 west over Heysham on 27 January 1996 and 700 over Brownside on 20 February 1997. The British and Irish population in 1981/2 to 1983/4 was estimated to be in excess of a million (Winter Atlas); the Lancashire population was around 5,000 which, taking into account annual fluctuations, has probably not changed greatly in the ensuing 20 years.

Pre-migratory movements into the county often become evident in late February but migration does not get fully underway until mid-March, continuing to mid- to late April. In contrast to autumn, very few spring migrants are seen on the coast but flocks of 100 or more are seen annually at a very wide range of inland sites. Larger counts include 885 roosting in Gisburn Forest on 13 April 1978, 3,000 at Laneshaw Bridge on 29 March 1981, 1,000 at Stocks Reservoir on 25 March 1983, 1,000 at Hornby on 12 April 1983, 800 at Inskip on 8 April 1984, and 600 at Abbeystead with 800 in Whitendale on 13 March 1998.

Late spring records are almost annual, usually ones and twos but with an exceptional 30 at Leyland on 15 May 1967. More recently there was one at Hurstwood on 2 June 1973, a male in song in Bowland on 11 June 1987, two at Kelbrook on 30 May 2000, and one was seen, apparently summering with Ring Ouzels, on 7 August 2005 at White Greet in Bowland. The most intriguing records relate to six in the Musbury area, near Haslingden in July 1986 and a party of six including two juveniles in the same area on 7 September of the same year. Another two were also recorded at Musbury on 26 June 1995.

Most movements of ringed birds between northern Britain and breeding areas abroad involve Norway, while Swedish and Finnish birds have mostly been recovered in south-eastern England (Migration Atlas). Lancashire recoveries largely conform to this with four exchanges with Norway, two with Finland and one with Sweden. There have been four recoveries in France outside the breeding season in subsequent years of birds ringed in Lancashire in autumn or winter, which may indicate either onward migration or a change in wintering grounds. However, one ringed at Carnforth on 3 December 1962 and found dead in Co. Wexford on 29 January 1963 confirms that relatively long distance midwinter movements do take place during hard weather.

SJW, RW.

This species account was sponsored by John Butterworth.

SONG THRUSH

Turdus philomelos

Lancashire Category A.

Common resident breeder.

The Song Thrush remains widely distributed throughout most of Lancashire wherever there is a reasonable amount of deciduous or mixed tree cover, including parkland, urban parks and gardens, copses on farmland and in the vicinity of farms where there are tall trees. Population crashes in the aftermath of hard winters have been documented in the county since the middle of the nineteenth century, but numbers appear always to have recovered quickly until a long-term decline set in during the 1970s.

Mitchell described it as 'resident and common everywhere, even in the neighbourhood of the largest towns.' He spoke of the 'terrible havoc' caused by the winters of 1878/79 and 1879/80, when birds 'left the Ribble valley entirely' in 1878 and 'hundreds, [perhaps] thousands' were on a warren on the Formby dunes in 1879; typically, however, numbers were said to be back to normal by 1883 or 1884. Similarly, Oakes noted a recovery in 1948 following the devastating winter of 1946/47.

National CBC data showed a 33% population decline in woodland and almost 66% on farmland between 1975 and 1994. Numbers have stabilised since then and, although the overall decline remains more than 50% since 1970, the BBS showed a 18% increase between 1994 and 2005. Monitored sites in north Lancashire illustrate the timing and scale of this downturn and subsequent resurgence. Populations at Halton Park and Thurnham fell by 40% between 1971 and 1978, and by 75% at Williamson Park between 1973 and 1986. The 25 pairs at Leighton Moss fell to nine in 1987 but increased slowly to 14 by 1992 and 18 by 1999, while at Warton Crag numbers grew from three pairs in 1989 to 13 in 2001 and 2005. Similar trends were reported throughout this period from the Lune and Ribble Valleys, the Fylde, east Lancashire and the Chorley area.

The Lancashire Atlas survey began after a prolonged freeze in January and February 1997 which significantly depressed numbers, but by its conclusion in 2000 many surveyors were reporting a revival. Song Thrushes were located in 782 tetrads (84%) within a range essentially similar to that of Blackbirds, but the breeding distribution was much more uneven, especially in Rossendale and parts of east Lancashire, the West Pennine Moors, West Lancashire and North Merseyside. This patchy distribution is explained in part by the willingness to breed at higher altitude – Oakes reported nesting of Song Thrushes at altitudes up to 250m (700') and there is no evidence that this has changed. In the lowlands the main factor affecting distribution is probably linked to Song Thrushes' dependence on earthworms and their reliance upon pastures and other short-sward grasslands including lawns.

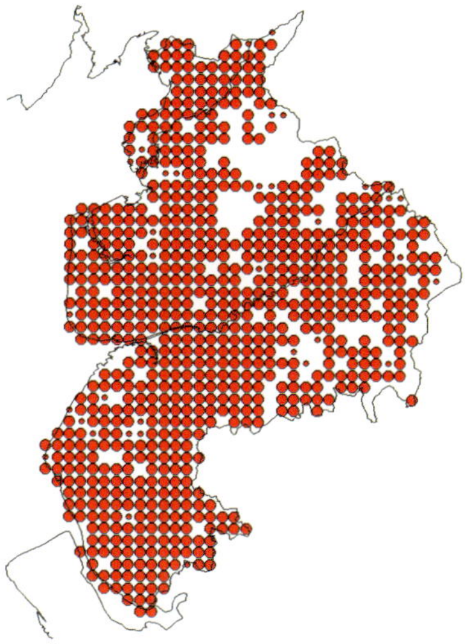

Breeding distribution of Song Thrush, 1997-2000. (Large dots: confirmed. Small dots: possible)

Just under 3,000 pairs were counted in the Lancashire Atlas survey, producing a population estimate of 10,000. Average densities varied enormously, increasing in general towards the west. Two or fewer pairs were counted in 65% of occupied tetrads while only 8% supported more than ten. The highest densities were found in Silverdale (with an average of 13 pairs per tetrad), the upper Lune and lower Ribble valleys, parts of West Lancashire and the suburban fringes of the Liverpool conurbation (especially Blundellsands and south Liverpool). Twenty-six territories were mapped in 213ha at Roddlesworth Plantations in 2003.

Odd birds are reported in song during January most years and occasionally as early as the end of November. Oakes reported a pair on eggs in Lancaster on 17 December 1908 and Mitchell one in Liverpool on 26 January 1859, but breeding does not usually get underway much before the beginning of March.

Spring passage along the coast may begin in late February and continues until late March, but daily counts rarely exceed four or five; most migration probably takes place at night and goes unnoticed. Larger counts of birds assumed to have been migrants include 20 at a roost near Stakepool on 25 February 1989, twelve at Roughlee on 8 March 1996, ten at Heysham on 17 March 1999, 13 at Mere Sands Wood on 15 March 2000 and twelve at Marton Mere on 30 March 2000.

Autumn passage is more conspicuous but, as in spring, most movements are probably nocturnal; day-counts of grounded birds are seldom large but hundreds probably pass through various coastal sites. Some birds begin to move away from the hillier areas of Lancashire from mid-September and the first arrivals on the coast that month probably include some of these and others from elsewhere in northern Britain, for example one ringed as a nestling in Northumberland and controlled at Heysham the same autumn. The largest recent early autumn counts include 50 at Marshside on 29 September 1981, 22 in the Burnley area on 28 September 1993, 21 over Roby Mill on 16 September 1999 and 19 at Marton Mere on 28 September 2003.

Most Lancashire birds are sedentary – about 85% of recoveries of Lancashire-ringed birds were less than 10km from the ringing site. A small proportion do, however, move longer distances; winter or passage recoveries include ten in Ireland, four in southern England and one in Wales, together with three in Spain and two in France. There have been no foreign recoveries since 1976 and seven of the Irish recoveries were before 1946, a pattern which is repeated nationally and, together with other evidence, has led to the suggestion that British Song Thrushes are not truly migratory but only move any significant distance in response to severe weather (Migration Atlas).

Song Thrush. (Phillip Tomkinson)

October is by far the most productive month; estimated totals through Heysham, for example, are usually four to five times higher than in September. The largest recent day-counts at the main sites have been 21 at Fairhaven in 1990 (22nd), 35 at Marshside in 1993 (24th), 27 at Marton Mere in 1996 (29th), 49 over Roby Mill in two hours in 2000 (9th), 22 at Netherley Sewage Works, south Liverpool in 2002 (14th) and an unprecedented 150 at Heysham on 10 October 2002 (just after huge falls on the north-east coast of England), with several counts of 50+ to the first week of November. On the day of the huge Redwing movement on 9 October 2004 just 15 were reported at Marshside and 25 at Freehold, Lancaster.

November totals are considerably lower and few are seen after the middle of the month. Oakes and Spencer believed many of these late migrants to be *hebridensis* from the Western Isles but there is no ringing evidence to support this. Nowadays, it is thought that many, if not a majority of, October and November birds are continental *philomelos* – on the basis of colouration, frequent association with and similar volatile behaviour to Redwings and the very large numbers sometimes seen on the English east coast at this time of year. Ringing evidence to back this up is, however, limited; there have been only ten autumn recoveries of Fennoscandian birds and six from Holland or France anywhere in Britain (with none in Lancashire) but rather more from Holland in winter, including one found dead in Blackpool on 3 April 1997.

Wintering birds are probably well-dispersed and double-figure counts are unusual anywhere. The few exceptions are almost certainly the result of hard weather movements; they include 20 at Heysham on 31 December 1995, 14 at Marshside on 27 January 1999 and 15 on the Birkdale dunes on 8 January 2003. A count of 40 alongside 523 Blackbirds on the Blackpool 'Blackbird Walk' on 27 December 2000 was quite exceptional; the following year the same trip registered six Song Thrushes and 115 Blackbirds, probably giving a fair indication of respective wintering numbers in the county.

SJW, RW.

This species account was sponsored by Susan Metcalf.

REDWING

Turdus iliacus

Lancashire Category A.

Abundant winter visitor and passage migrant from Fennoscandia and Iceland.

Mitchell believed that numbers had fallen in some areas during the course of the nineteenth century, which he attributed to the effects of severe winters. Redwings were found 'in considerable numbers' in most parts of the county but 'only occasionally in Rossendale, arriving usually in the latter half of October 'but in mild seasons in the earlier half'. Wrigley (1892) related one unusual incident: 'When skating on the (Formby) slacks in the severe winter of 1890-91, G. Rheam and the writer ran down scores of redwings and fieldfares, which were so weak as to be scarcely able to get out of the way.'

In Oakes's day Redwings were similar in status and distribution to Fieldfares but arrived some ten days earlier with the main arrival in the first three weeks of October. Northward movement usually began in mid-March and the latest Oakes knew of was one at Marton on 3 May 1939.

Nowadays, they usually arrive in late September or early October. The earliest were singles at Nelson on 7 September 1995, Southport on 8 September 1970 and two over Rowley Lake, Burnley on 8 September 1990. The average first arrival during 1983-2005, was 23 September but large numbers are rarely seen before early October, and more normally from mid-October to early November.

Redwing, Liverpool, January 2005. (Steve Young)

Much migration takes place at night when it is impossible to keep track of numbers or flight direction, a report of 'enormous numbers' passing over the Lancaster area on the nights of 8 & 9 October 1989 being typical. It is therefore quite possible that the majority of passage birds pass through the county undetected and unreported. For many years the East Lancashire Ornithologists' Club has begun its October meetings by gathering outside, listening to Redwings calling overhead, often revealing substantial westerly movements.

Daytime counts have shown a dramatic increase over the past 10-15 years, almost certainly due to the burgeoning interest in visible-migration-watching in the last years of the twentieth century rather than to any real change in the ratio of nocturnal to diurnal movement. Significant passage movements usually come in short pulses lasting for just a single day, normally between the second week of October and the first week of November. Inland, large flocks may be encountered almost anywhere and it is likely that they move across country on a relatively broad front, not appearing to follow any particular line. Coastal flocks almost always move broadly south and appear to keep within sight of the shoreline, generally producing larger concentrations than inland. Weather conditions within the breeding range are almost certainly the main determinant of the timing of migration, with birds waiting for calm, usually anti-cyclonic, weather before heading west into Britain. Optimum conditions for observing their passing in Lancashire are light southerly to easterly winds with low cloud cover, forcing the birds into low-level flight.

Peak day-counts at most sites are normally just a few hundred but much larger concentrations occur periodically. The first large published count was of 3,240 flying south-west over Heysham in five hours on the morning of 11 October 1988. Similar numbers have been recorded with some regularity since, mostly but not exclusively at coastal watchpoints. These have almost always been seen from dawn until late morning but occasionally past midday. The largest counts include 3,725 south across the Kent Estuary in 1.5 hours on 29 October 1989, 2,000 over Martin Mere on 14-15 October 1993, 6,000 over Darwen Moor on 12 October 1997, 2,484 over Heysham on 15 October 1999, 4,100 over Seaforth on 5 November 2000 (with 2,185 over Heysham, 550 over Marton Mere and 200 over St. Helens the same day), 5,000 south-east over

Brockholes Quarry on 16 October 2001, 1,700 over Healey Nab on 9 October 2002 and 1,525 over Seaforth on 13 October 2003 (with 1,387 over Heysham, 1,485 over Fairhaven, and 300-450 over Marton Mere, Lowerhouse Lodges and Jackhouse Reservoir the same day).

There is probably a degree of duplication between counts at coastal sites as birds head south, as the 2003 records suggest. The large number of smaller flocks, most of which go unnoticed or unreported, add to the difficulty of estimating the total number of birds passing through the county during autumn – but, on the basis of data published since the early 1990s, somewhere in the region of 10,000-20,000 might be a reasonable estimate.

The events of 2004 were, then, without precedent. On 9 October an estimated 40,000 flew over Fluke Hall, Pilling and a similar number were seen over Southport town centre and Marshside. Flight direction at both sites was east-north-east and very few were seen anywhere else on the coast, giving the impression that the birds were coming off the Irish Sea. The following day large numbers were seen in south-east Lancashire, initially moving east before diverting north on meeting the Pennines. These included 10,000 at Anglezarke and 'large numbers' at Haslingden. Coastal counts on the 9th – all moving east or north-east – included 4,500 at Fleetwood, 3,000 at Pilling and 6,000 in two hours over Lancaster University. The total for the two days was certainly more than 100,000 (Roberts & White 2006).

Sizeable temporary roosts sometimes build up during the autumn passage; 2,000-3,000 have occasionally been recorded at Leighton Moss with a maximum of 5,000 on 6-8 October 1984, but no autumn gatherings of any size have been reported since 500 at Whin Scar Clough in late October 1990.

Most birds pass straight through the county, and wintering numbers are relatively low. During normal winters flocks of up to 50, occasionally 100, are found scattered throughout much of the county. Very rarely flocks of several hundred or more are encountered, including 1,200 between Nether Kellet and Halton (a distance of 3km) on 21 January 1978, 640 at Witton Country Park on 22 January 1983, 600 at Clayton-le-Dale, near Blackburn on 23 December 1983, 1,000 at Mere Sands Wood on 24 December 1985 and the same number near Whalley on 21 December 1988. Winter peaks since then have been considerably lower, including 500 at Leighton Moss in November to December 1991, 500+ feeding on beechmast in Lever Park, Rivington on 3 March 2001, and 400 at Marles Wood on 23 February 1997, at Rufford in January 1998 and at Yealand Redmayne in March 2002. Winter roosts often form in rhododendron or conifer plantations; they may build up substantially, increased by cold weather influxes as in January 1984, when 1,000 were in a plantation at Billington near Blackburn and 1,500 at Formby Hall, and in late January and February 1986 when 1,000 roosted at Lancaster University. The British and Irish population in 1981/2 to 1983/4 was estimated to be in excess of a million, of which around 10,000 were in Lancashire (Winter Atlas) but the usual county population seems to be rather smaller nowadays.

Visible movements sometimes occur during severe weather; the last very severe winter in 1962/63 is known to have led nationally to large-scale movements and high mortality of Redwings (Dobinson & Richards 1964) but it was not fully documented in Lancashire. More recently, there were marked southerly movements at a number of locations in December 1981 including 500 low over St. Anne's beach in an hour on the 14th. Other cold weather movements include a sudden influx of 1,000 at Eccleston Mere on 21 January 1984 with 1,500 moving south west near Carnforth and 2,000 over Heysham the following day. Milder winters since the 1990s have reduced the frequency of these displacements but a cold snap in December 1995 produced 300 at Rishton, near Blackburn and 350 at Leighton Moss. Severe conditions may cause many to leave the county, as in 1979 when birds ringed in Lancashire were recovered subsequently in Wales, Ireland and France.

Spring passage is much less marked than autumn's, mostly occurring between mid-March and mid-April. As in autumn, much movement takes place at night and goes unrecorded. The majority of sightings are of fewer than 20 birds, although flocks of up to 60 are occasionally seen, particularly in March. Flocks of 200 at Clayton-le-Dale on 12 April 1983, 375 at Barnoldswick on 30 March 1984, 200 at Fence on 18 March 1985 and 575 east over Arkholme on 26 March 1995 were unusual. Very few remain after mid-April but stragglers can linger into late May, and song is occasionally heard, for instance one at St. Anne's on 31 May 1997. There are two summer records: one at Blackpool on 13 June 1998 and five flying north-west over Crawshawbooth on 24th July 1995.

Both sub-species of Redwing are seen in Britain in winter and on passage. Icelandic *coburni* winter in Scotland, Ireland, western France and Iberia but there are no ringing recoveries involving either England or Wales (Migration Atlas), suggesting that they may be relatively uncommon in Lancashire. Oakes published details of one picked up dead in Burnley on 24 November 1945 which was identified on the basis of biometrics; Spencer (1973) noted a total of seven occurrences but did not list them.

National ringing data suggest that a large majority of nominate *iliacus* seen in Britain breed in Finland and western areas of the old Soviet Union, with only 5% and 14% of recoveries involving Norwegian and Swedish birds respectively (Migration Atlas). Foreign recoveries of Lancashire-ringed birds broadly support this with three to Finland (one ringed in spring, two in winter) in the breeding season. Recoveries in subsequent winters in Greece, Italy and Georgia also imply eastern origins, as does our only foreign-ringed recovery, a first-winter ringed at Helgoland on 11 October 1980 and controlled at Altham on 31 January 1981. Scandinavian birds do certainly occur, but evidence from ringing is limited to two recoveries of Lancashire winterers in Norway.

There have been several recoveries of birds ringed on passage on the English and Scottish east coast, including at least four within a single autumn/winter: from Spurn, Northumberland, Fife and Fair Isle. Eleven have been recovered on staging or wintering grounds in south-western Europe, seven in France, three in Portugal and one in Spain. Just one of these movements was within a single season, ringed at Clifton Hall in October and shot in Portugal in January. All the remainder were ringed in Lancashire in winter and recovered abroad in subsequent winters, consistent with them being *iliacus*, adults of which migrate further than first-winters while *coburni* do the reverse.

SJW, RW.

This species account was sponsored by John Butterworth.

MISTLE THRUSH

Turdus viscivorus

Lancashire Category A.

Common resident breeder.

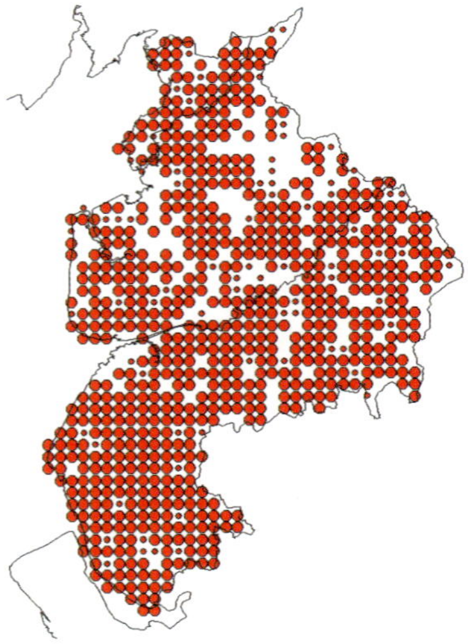

Breeding distribution of Mistle Thrush, 1997-2000. (Large dots: confirmed. Small dots: possible)

The status of the Mistle Thrush appears to have changed little during the 130 years since Mitchell described it as breeding evenly throughout the county – but it was not always so. The species undertook a dramatic colonisation of Britain and Ireland from the early years of the nineteenth century; previously limited to south of a line from the Gower Peninsular to the Wash, it had colonised all of England by the 1850s (Old Atlas). None of this was referred to by Mitchell, so perhaps colonisation of Lancashire had occurred before the living memory of late nineteenth century ornithologists.

Mistle Thrush, Liverpool, December 2005. (Steve Young)

Breeding was confirmed in all 10km squares in the county during the national atlas surveys of 1968-72 and 1988-91 and the Lancashire survey of 1997-2000, and no significant changes in distribution within the breeding range were reported during that period. The population has fluctuated, however, and marginal breeding areas have probably been deserted temporarily, largely as a result of hard winters. Oakes reported that birds were very scarce after the winter of 1946/47 but it seems that they recovered quickly. Localised changes in distribution and breeding densities have undoubtedly occurred in response to changing habitats and the development of new opportunities. Oakes quoted one example, an increase in the Formby area due to the increased cultivation of asparagus on whose berries birds fed. More generally, the widespread planting of native and exotic berry-bearing shrubs in towns and cities in the latter half of the twentieth century has helped Mistle Thrushes consolidate their hold in many urban areas.

Relatively open habitats are favoured but choice of breeding area is extremely catholic – woodland edges, parkland, urban parks, suburban gardens, recreational areas, derelict industrial sites and farmland with copses, scattered trees and hedgerows. Breeding took place in 770 tetrads (83%) in 1997-2000. Their range was broadly similar to that of Song Thrush and they were absent only from the high fells and saltmarshes, but distribution was much patchier along the Fylde coast and Over Wyre, and in the Preston and Blackburn areas.

Trees provide the usual nest site but birds are not averse to using man-made sites such as window ledges, roofs and the insides of buildings. More unorthodox nest sites in the county have included an open-backed van and a steel girder in a factory loading-bay. Nests have been located in upland quarries and on dry-stone walls beyond the tree-line where Oakes reported nesting up to 300m (1,000') above sea level. Breeding usually starts at the beginning of March but nest-construction in mid-February is not unusual and pairs with young at Lytham St. Anne's in January 1997 and Southport in January 2005 were presumed to have nested in November.

Mistle Thrushes hold much larger territories than Blackbirds or Song Thrushes and breeding densities are consequently lower. Exceptionally, nests may be very close together, for example within 5m at Arkholme in 1985, 12m on a Burnley building in 1987 and 7m at Rawtenstall Cemetery in 1993. Average territory size on CBC plots in north Lancashire during 1988-94 were 37.6ha and 25.6ha on Mount Vernon Farm and Warton Crag respectively. Assuming an average density of 4-5 pairs per occupied tetrad (400ha), the county population was estimated at 3,000 pairs in 1997-2000. Nationally, numbers are believed to have declined by 36% from 1970-2001 but the population has been stable since 1994 (BBS), a situation that appears to be reflected in Lancashire where most sites have reported only small fluctuations since the early 1990s.

Adults and young form small post-breeding flocks, usually assembling in July, sometimes as early as June, and breaking up by November. These groups can be encountered almost anywhere but often where plentiful berries are available, especially bilberry on moorland but also rowan,whitebeam or yew. They generally number fewer than 30 birds but larger autumn gatherings have included 80 at Skirden Beck on 19 September 1981, 100 on Anglezarke Moor on 22 September 1985, 70 or more at Salterforth, near Colne, on 9 September 1993, 86 at Oakenclough on 13 September 1996, 80 at Halewood on 19 August 2002, 60 at Clougha from the end of June 2003 and 60 at Rivington on 8-18 September 2003.

As autumn progresses some move towards the lowlands and the coast and it becomes difficult to distinguish localised movements from genuine migration. Notable movements have included 50 moving through Heasandford, near Burnley on 8 October 1980, 201 flying from the east in small flocks at Fazakerley in north Liverpool on 17 September 1998 and 56 over Leagram Mill, Little Bowland on 24 August 2003. By October sizeable flocks become considerably scarcer inland but have included 40 at Sunnyhurst Wood on 8 October 1990, 38 at Rishton Reservoir on 26 October 1992, 42 at Cliviger on 15 October 1998 and 40 at Thrushgill on 12 October 2002.

Small numbers of presumed migrants, rarely more than single figures in a day, are noted at coastal sites between mid-September and mid-November in most years. Autumn passage has been monitored most consistently at Heysham, where annual totals of birds flying south-west or temporarily grounded average 30-40 but with 129 in 1985; and at Fairhaven where 85 were seen on 16 days between 30 September and 11 November 2003. Daily numbers at Heysham rarely exceed ten but larger counts include 24 on 19 September 1985 and 48 on 10 October 1996. Visible migration watches at Fairhaven logged 18 on 13 October 1985, 12 on 15 October 1990 and 37 on 7 November 2003. Peaks elsewhere include 13 over Marshside on 24 September 1993 with 25 on 9 October 2004, 24 at Marton Mere on 24 September 2001 and 35 over Seaforth on 12 October 2003.

The vast majority of British Mistle Thrushes are essentially sedentary with a median recovery distance of ringed birds of less than 1km (Migration Atlas), a fact confirmed by Lancashire ringing recoveries. More than 80% of recoveries of birds ringed in the county have been within 9km of the ringing site, and only three have left Lancashire (two recovered in northern England in winter and one in Wales in the breeding season, none further than 100km). Only five ringed anywhere else in Britain have been recovered in Lancashire: one ringed as a nestling in Strathclyde (352km) in 1953 and found at Fleetwood on 27 March 1954, one ringed as full-grown in Burton-on-Trent in January 1955 and recovered at Abbeystead on 13 June the same year, and three from elsewhere in northern England. Continental birds are thought to migrate through or winter in Britain in small numbers (Migration Atlas) and it seems likely that late autumn passage in Lancashire, particularly when associated with passage of Icelandic and Scandinavian thrushes, includes some of these – but confirmation through ringing is lacking.

As with other British thrushes, spring passage is rarely detected, a total of three at Heysham on 16-17 March 2002 being typical. An extraordinary record of more than 50 at St. Helens RUFC ground on 12 April 2000 seems likely to have involved migrants; if so, they surely cannot have been British birds.

Many birds become extremely territorial in winter, defending food resources vigorously against other thrushes. Flocks of any size are unusual between December and February, examples include 28 at Lytham Hall on 24 December 1988, 40 at Billinge Hill on 18 January 1992, 20 at Belmont on 20 December 1992, 25-40 at several Chorley sites in 1992 and 1993, 128 at Mere Brow on 1 January 1996, 71 at Rufford on 8 December 1996, 20-25 regularly at Leighton Moss in the 1990s, 20 at Musbury on 9 December 2000 and 30 at Ince Blundell on 30 December 2000.

SJW, RW.
This species account was sponsored by the Friends of Marton Mere.

CETTI'S WARBLER

Cettia cetti

Lancashire Category A. (0, 9).

Vagrant from southern Britain or western Europe.

The county's first Cetti's Warbler was first heard at Marton Mere by Harry Andrew on 17 October 1990 and its identity was confirmed on 4 November by Maurice Jones; it stayed until at least 24 March 1991. A calling bird was also heard at Marton Mere on 26-27 November and 4 December 1994 but it was never seen. What may have been the same bird appeared again on 9 October 1995 and stayed until 8 April 1996. There was then a three year gap before the next was found at Marton Mere on 13 November 1998. This one remained into the New Year and probably the same bird returned on 28 December 1999 (staying until 10 February 2000) and again on 13 October to 13 December 2000. It seems likely that at least two individuals were involved in this series of six records at Marton Mere.

Two of the three other Lancashire records were at Leighton Moss: a male which was first seen on 28 October 1995, then trapped and ringed on the 30th, remaining to 8 March 1996, and this or another on 27 Oct 1996 and perhaps other dates. The latest was one at Fazakerley Reedbed, Liverpool from at least 11 February to 3 March 2005.

Cetti's Warbler, Marton Mere, March 2007. (David Moreton)

All records:

1990	Marton Mere, one, 17 October to 24 March 1991
1994	Marton Mere, one, 26 November to 4 December
1995	Marton Mere, one, 9 October to 8 April 1996
1995	Leighton Moss, one, 28 October to 8 March 1996
1996	Leighton Moss, one, 27 Oct at least
1998	Marton Mere, one, 13 November to early April 1999
1999	Marton Mere, one, 28 December to 10 February 2000
2000	Marton Mere, one, 13 October to 13 December
2005	Fazakerley Reedbed, one, 11 February to 3 March

SJW, MJ.

This species account was sponsored by Maurice Jones and the Friends of Marton Mere.

GRASSHOPPER WARBLER

Locustella naevia

Lancashire Category A.

Uncommon breeder and passage migrant.

Lancashire's Grasshopper Warblers frequent damp mossland, perhaps with great tussock sedge, reed canary-grass and scattered alder or willow, along the edge of reedbeds, in overgrown mossland ditches. They are also found in newly planted woodland where there is suitable ground cover such as bramble, grasses, nettles and willowherb, until these are shaded out by growing trees. Such areas become suitable again when mature trees are felled and removed, as has happened in the Gisburn Forest. Another habitat is provided by well-established dune systems with plentiful ground vegetation and scattered bushes. Recent developments have involved birds nesting in oil-seed rape and linseed fields, as at Bretherton in the 1990s, and dense rush-beds on upland in-bye up to 350m above sea level on the West Pennine Moors.

Singing male Grasshopper Warbler, Hightown Dunes, May 2005. (Steve Young)

Mitchell described the Grasshopper Warbler as 'not uncommon in suitable locations, but nowhere more common and numerous than in the Ribble Valley, with many pairs breeding near Clitheroe'. Oakes cited five locations in the Ribble Valley and four in Bowland, and singled out Leighton Moss as a particularly favoured breeding site; he noted a lack of fidelity to breeding sites which were frequently abandoned for several years before being recolonised.

Breeding is notoriously difficult to monitor but it is thought that numbers increased strongly in England during the 1960s before declining sharply since 1970 (Brown & Grice 2005). BBS data, however, suggest a large recovery of 50% between 1994 and 2005, an increase which appears not to have been reflected in Lancashire. The county breeding range has shrunk by about 25% over the past 30 years: birds were located in 42 10km squares during the 1968-72 atlas survey, falling dramatically to 19 in 1988-91 but rising again to 32 during the 1997-2000 Lancashire Atlas survey. This recorded Grasshopper Warblers in 89 tetrads (10% of the total), spread thinly across most of the county, but with notable absences from the Lune and Ribble Valleys and the uplands. Breeding was confirmed or thought probable in just 36 tetrads involving 59 pairs, but the county population was estimated at 150 pairs.

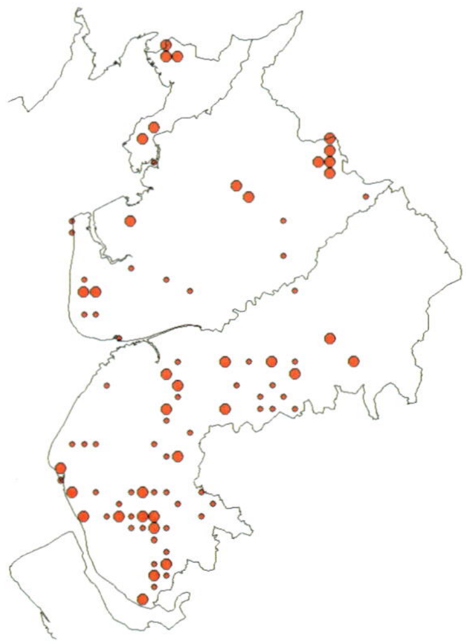

Breeding distribution of Grasshopper Warbler, 1997-2000. (Large dots: confirmed. Small dots: possible)

Roughly two-thirds of possible breeding birds were found south of the Ribble, with the most obvious concentrations on the fringes of the Liverpool conurbation, St. Helens and the Sefton Coast south of Formby. Most of the remainder breed wherever there are suitable wetlands in a broad swathe from Martin Mere east to the western fringes of Rossendale. Recently the largest cluster, of up to six males, has been in dune scrub between Blundellsands and Hightown.

As elsewhere in the county, breeding sites in the south-west and central mosslands come and go. Mere Brow, near Tarleton was formerly the outstanding site, with up to 15 pairs in the late 1960s, but most suitable habitat was destroyed in the 1970s to create the leisure lakes. The Bretherton/Croston area remains a relative stronghold with up to ten males recorded during the 1990s. Various sites on the West Pennine Moors have all held one or two pairs in recent years, including Roddlesworth, Belmont, Rivington and White Coppice. Breeding is at best sporadic in Rossendale and the few records have been mostly from Haslingden Grane, Crawshawbooth and between Clowbridge and Crown Point.

Very few breed between the Ribble and the Lune, apart from a handful on the Fylde – most regularly one or two pairs at Marton Mere and Winmarleigh and Cockerham Mosses – and in the Langden Valley, but there is a large cluster around Stocks Reservoir and the Gisburn Forest. Large-scale felling created much new habitat here during the 1990s and eleven territories were occupied in 1995, but these had fallen to two in 2003 as suitable habitat gave way to maturing woodland.

Only two locations north of the Lune hold Grasshopper Warblers, the Heysham area, where three pairs bred on Heysham Moss in 1992 and breeding has been suspected at Middleton in recent years, and Leighton Moss. Long-term monitoring at Leighton Moss revealed a dramatic increase in occupied territories, from an average of about ten during the early to mid-1970s to a peak of 24 in 1980, as a result of extensive coppicing of willow. Numbers then went into gradual decline, falling to six territories in 1990 and only one or two since 2003.

The first birds usually arrive during the second half of April, on average on the 17th in the past 25 years. One grounded in fog on Silverdale Marsh on 9 April 1975 is our earliest record. The main arrival comes during the last week of April and the first ten days of May, tailing off after mid-May. Most records refer to single reeling males, occasionally more, and come generally from breeding or potential breeding locations.

Once males have ceased singing, Grasshopper Warblers are essentially undetectable to field observers and our knowledge of post-breeding dispersal and passage in Lancashire is extremely poor. Most autumn records come from known or potential breeding sites, including males reeling as late as 26 September near Darwen in 1995, 16 August at Clowbridge Reservoir in 2001 and 19 August at Stocks Reservoir in 2002, making it difficult to distinguish migrants from lingering summer residents. The average last record at Leighton Moss between 1976 and 1996 was 27 August.

Only four presumed migrants have been trapped at Heysham, the most recent on 29 September 1996. Few are seen after late August but recent records include singles at Rossall Point on 26 September 1987, Fleetwood on 16 September 1989, Marshside on 17 September 1993, Leighton Moss on 24 September 1997, Lee Green Reservoir on 25 September 1997, Seaforth on 19 September 1999 and Downholland Moss on 10 September 2004. The latest records were at Freshfield on 2 October 1968 and Hightown on 4 October 1981.

SJW, RW.
This species account was sponsored by Maurice Wilby.

SAVI'S WARBLER

Locustella luscinioides

Lancashire Category A. (0, 5).

Vagrant from southern Europe.

Not surprisingly, all records have been of singing males and all appeared during the national peak arrival period of mid-April to late May. The first was watched briefly at Marshside on 28 April 1977 by Barry McCarthy. Two years later there were two in the Leighton Moss reedbeds, a bird with no tail from 20 April to 1 May 1979 in reeds just to the south of the 'Osprey' island which arrived during southerly winds, and a fully-tailed bird at least one mile away on the eastern edge of the reserve from at least 25 May to 7 or 8 June. These two sightings were 'lumped' as the same bird by the BBRC. After a long gap, another well-watched singing male was at Leighton Moss from 14 April to 24 June 1991.

The final twentieth century record came with one at Marton Mere, Blackpool on 27 May 1995 and there was then another lengthy wait before Leighton Moss produced its fourth on 9-23 May 2003.

The number of Savi's Warblers breeding in southern and eastern England declined steadily during the last decades of the twentieth century – when all but the most recent of Lancashire's records occurred – from around 30 possible pairs in the late 1970s to fewer than ten by the turn of the century. The number of non-breeding migrants fluctuated widely during the same period, becoming sufficiently common for the species to be removed from the list considered by the BBRC in 1982, only to become markedly scarcer and be reinstated to the BBRC list in 1999.

Male Savi's Warbler, Leighton Moss, May 2003. (Steve Young)

All records:

1977	Marshside, male, 28 April
1979	Leighton Moss, male, 20 April to 1 May
1979	Leighton Moss, possibly new male, 25 May to 7 June
1991	Leighton Moss, male, 14 April to 24 June
1995	Marton Mere, male 27 to 28 May
2003	Leighton Moss, male, 9 to 23 May

SJW, MJ.

This species account was sponsored by the Fylde Bird Club.

AQUATIC WARBLER

Acrocephalus paludicola

Lancashire Category A. (0, 1).

Vagrant from eastern Europe.

One was caught and ringed on the Main Dyke at Leighton Moss on the interface of reed and iris/dock areas on 19 August 1979 by Tim Jorgenson and John Wilson. The bird had a very marked crown stripe and a number of Sedge Warblers were on hand for comparison, so both observers were immediately certain of the identification. JW had recently returned from a trip to Poland to see Aquatic Warblers!

Unfortunately, although the ringing details were submitted to the BTO, no description was sent to the BBRC. Aquatic Warbler was regarded as a national rarity at the time and all records were assessed by the BBRC until 1982. Consequently, the Leighton Moss bird does not appear in the national record list but its validity is not in doubt.

SJW, MJ.

This species account was sponsored by Dr. Alan Fielding.

SEDGE WARBLER

Acrocephalus schoenobaenus

Lancashire Category A.

Common breeder and passage migrant.

The Sedge Warbler was described by Mitchell as breeding numerously in suitable lowland localities in the latter half of the nineteenth century. Oakes described it as 'well established in its main haunts', which included Leighton Moss, the south-west and Fylde mosses and the Preston area. However, he intimated that its numbers had declined by the middle of the twentieth century, noting that, due to drainage and reclamation of wetlands, it had become scarce on the Fylde coast, the Kirkby mosses and around Clitheroe, was declining in south-east Lancashire and was scarce around Longridge and rare in the Lune Valley.

The national population declined dramatically during the 1970s and 1980s as a result of drought in the African wintering quarters, which was at its worst in 1982 and 1983. The magnitude of the decline was well illustrated at Leighton Moss, where the number of breeding pairs fell from 138 in 1982 to a low of 88 in 1985. Populations then fluctuated until 1992 when there was a new low of 66 pairs, followed by a progressive increase to 98 pairs in 1996 and 106 in 1999, but the potential fragility of this resurgence was illustrated by another decline to 74 in 2001, possibly caused by encroaching reed and increased wetness of the reed-beds producing less suitable breeding habitat. These changes are in line with national trends. CBS data showed a 66% decrease between 1968 and 1985 but numbers had recovered to 1970 levels by 2001 and have remained fairly stable since then.

These population changes were reflected in changes in distribution reported in the three atlas surveys in Lancashire, with breeding confirmed in 41 10km squares in 1968-72, declining dramatically to 30 squares in 1988-91 but recovering to 37 in 1997-2000, when possible breeding was reported in a further three squares. The 1997-2000 Lancashire Atlas recorded breeding Sedge Warblers in 234 tetrads, roughly a quarter of the county. The county population was estimated at 3,000 pairs in 1997-2000 but monitoring of a number of key sites points to a possible decline since around 1995-96, against the reported national trend.

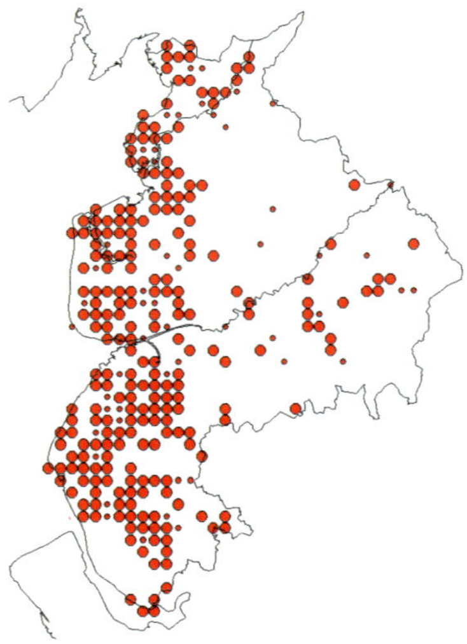

Breeding distribution of Sedge Warbler, 1997-2000. (Large dots: confirmed. Small dots: possible)

Sedge Warblers are common breeders in the western third of the county. They show a wider choice of breeding habitat than Reed Warblers, favouring the drier parts of reedbeds and the zone between willow and alder as at Leighton Moss, ditches, dykes and scrub-fringed watercourses. Drier situations such as rough ground with abundant ground cover in the way of brambles or nettles are also chosen, and in recent years fields of oil-seed rape have been utilised. At the 75ha Lytham Moss CBC plot, in the five years between 1987 and 1995 whenever some land was planted with oil-seed rape, more than half of all territories were located in this crop. There are also records of nesting in Marram (for example at Fairhaven in the 1960s), tall privet and a fig tree covered with bramble and rank grass.

Oakes' description as 'the warbler of the plains' still holds good today. Sedge Warblers are widespread in North Merseyside, both along the coast and on the mosslands. Important coastal breeding sites include the banks of the Mersey in south Liverpool, the dunes near Hightown, and Marshside. Further inland, the main sites are the Rimrose Valley, the Leeds-Liverpool Canal, and Carr Mill Dam and the Sankey Valley in St. Helens. Many sites have shown a steady decline in numbers since the mid-1990s, for example Marshside from 31 pairs in 1995 to eleven in 2003 and the Rimrose Valley from 30 pairs in the late 1990s to fewer than ten in 2003; similar declines have been registered in the Sankey Valley.

Much the same habitats are occupied in the lowlands of West and central Lancashire. Mere Sands Wood and Martin Mere hold significant concentrations, though also showing signs of recent decline, for example from 44 pairs at Martin Mere in 1995 to 26 in 2003 and 36 in 2004. The wetlands at Mere Brow were considerably reduced in importance by development in the 1970s, while the Leeds-Liverpool Canal between Rufford and Tarleton supported 24 pairs in 1988, confirming the attractions of this habitat. Well-established breeding locations in the Chorley area include Bretherton, Croston, Birkacre, Withnell Fold, Ulnes Walton and Hic Bibi.

The most important Fylde site is Marton Mere; records published in the county report indicate a decline from 25 to a dozen or so pairs since the mid-1990s but up to 40 singing males are regularly recorded in May and it is thought that a relatively constant 20 pairs have bred during this period (McGough 2002). Carr House Green Common, Inskip held 21 pairs in 1995 and other important sites include the Fleetwood lagoons, Stanah, the Preesall Flashes, and the drained mossland dykes between Lytham Moss and Bryning near Wrea Green.

Centres of population in north Lancashire away from Leighton Moss include the Eric Morecambe complex, which held 20 pairs in the late 1990s, Haweswater, the Lune Estuary, and Heysham where 20 pairs breed regularly. Inland breeding is largely confined to the banks of the Lune, with up to 20 pairs between Lancaster and Kirkby Lonsdale, notably at Arkholme where they have taken to nesting in Japanese knotweed.

Birds are much less common in the hillier districts of east, north-east and central Lancashire with breeding confined to valley sites where small amounts of suitable habitat have survived, such as Witton Country Park, Lowerhouse Lodges, and Lomeshaye, Grove Lane and Whitebirk Marshes. They are also regular at Altham and Wood End Sewage Works, but only occasional at Ewood Bridge where they were frequent before modernisation in 1968. The surrounds of reservoirs may also provide suitable habitat as at Lee Green, Rivington, Anglezarke and Wayoh Reservoirs. A male singing at 230m above sea level near Abbeystead on 13 May 2002 and a breeding pair at 260m above sea level at Belmont Reservoir in 2004 were unusually high.

Our earliest records are 27 March 2003 at Leighton Moss and 29 March 1997 at Marshside. First arrivals have become earlier during the past 25 years and the average date is now 14 April, although most birds appear at the end of April and in the first half of May. One at Wood End Sewage Works, Burnley on 19 April 2003 is the earliest record in the East Lancashire Ornithologists Club area but one at Folly Tip, Rossendale on 8 April 1997 was considerably earlier.

Spring passage is heavily concentrated at wetland sites, with few records away from potential breeding habitat. This makes it difficult to separate migrants from newly-arrived breeding birds. Passage is best monitored at Heysham, where good numbers are ringed in most springs, including 118 in 1995, 120 in 2000 and 136 in 2001. Reedbed sites such as Marton Mere, Martin Mere and the Rimrose Valley regularly report more singing males in mid-May than remain to breed; presumably some are moving through. The largest falls in recent years have been 50+ at Heysham on 13 May 1991 and 30-40 there on 12 May 1993, but similar falls are more widespread, including 30 at Marton Mere with 32 at nearby Heron's Reach on 1 May 2000.

Sedge Warbler, Hightown Dunes, May 2005. (Steve Young)

Autumn passage is more leisurely than in spring, beginning in mid-July and continuing through to mid-September with reduced numbers into early October, but peak counts almost always occur in August. Numbers are lower than in spring but birds are more regularly encountered away from breeding sites and occasionally in dry habitats. Daily counts rarely exceed ten, although 20 were in a Fleetwood reedbed on 20 August 1989. Seasonal ringing totals at Heysham are usually less than 50 but 1992 saw 50 trapped between 8-31 July with a further 29 to September. Notable falls there include 25-30 on 24 August 1990 and 40 trapped at Middleton Industrial Estate on 8 August 2002. Few are seen after mid-September; the average last date in the county is 30 September. Three at Marton Mere in the second week of October 1979 were notable, and the latest record is a single at Leighton Moss on 25 October 1978.

Most locally-ringed birds, almost all ringed as juveniles, move south-west through Dorset, Gloucestershire, Avon, Devon, Cornwall and south Wales or south-east to Sussex, Hampshire and Essex (a total of 64 in southern England and seven in Wales). There have been controls from many parts of France (24), Spain (3) and Portugal (1), mostly in the same year that they were ringed. More than twenty of these (all ringed in July to September) were controlled within a fortnight, suggesting that some were already on migration in Lancashire. Notably rapid journeys include singles from Fleetwood to Dorset in five days in 1989, from Heysham to Sussex in four days in 1991, from Mere Sands Wood to Suffolk in three days in August 1998, from Leighton Moss to Glamorgan in three days in August 2005, from Leighton Moss 705km to northern France in eleven days in September 1996, and from Marton Mere 1,151km to northern Spain in eleven days in 1953.

Only one has been recovered in the sub-Saharan wintering grounds, 4,356km distant in Senegal in December 1992, but another was recovered on its return journey in Morocco in May 1995. Remarkably, this is the only spring recovery of any bird ringed in Lancashire anywhere in a direct line from the wintering grounds. Similarly, none ringed in southern England or southern Europe in spring has been recovered in Lancashire – all 31 such recoveries (four of them from France) had been ringed in previous autumns – suggesting that the return from Africa is rapid and direct while the outward journey involves more stopovers. The one exception was caught on Bardsey on 14 May 1985 and trapped at Heysham on the following day.

Movements between Lancashire and northern Britain are rather fewer, but sufficient to illustrate the likely breeding grounds of our passage migrants. They involve 24 birds to or from other sites in northern England and 13 to or from Scotland, all of them ringed or controlled between April and August. These include a juvenile ringed at Loch Spynie in Grampian on 27 August 2000 and controlled at Leighton Moss a week later on 3 September and one from the small colony on Graemeshall Loch on Orkney. Two other recoveries are more intriguing: one ringed on 15 May 2001 at Heysham and controlled in Luxembourg on 14 August the same year, and a juvenile ringed at Haydock on 20 August 1984 and controlled near Merano in northern Italy on 1 May 1985, suggesting it was heading towards an eastern breeding site. Sedge Warblers usually migrate quite early in the autumn but a bird ringed at Heysham on 4 October 1994 and controlled at Kenfig Pool in south Wales on 12 October the same year was an exception; it would have been interesting to know its origin.

SJW, RW.

This species account was sponsored by John Gramauskas.

MARSH WARBLER

Acrocephalus palustris

Lancashire Category A. (0, 5).

Vagrant from western or central Europe.

The first was seen and heard in song by Tony Duckels and Phil Smith in the Hightown Dunes on 6 June 1971. A juvenile was caught at Heysham on 19 Oct 1985 and retrapped there on the 22nd but was never seen in the field; it remains our only autumn record. The bird was carrying a Dutch ring but, unfortunately, it had been ringed in Holland as a Reed Warbler. The biometric details and photographs taken at Heysham convinced the Dutch of their mistake.

Heysham's second was a male singing from 0900 to 1600 hours in a dense willow copse on 15 May 1990. The song seemed to bear more resemblance to Blyth's Reed Warbler but a late afternoon sighting at very close range included a clear view of the well-spaced primary tips on a long wing, clinching the identification.

Our most remarkable record came from Folly Tip, Rossendale on 13 June 1997. It was seen throughout the day but its identity was not absolutely confirmed until it was trapped, ringed and photographed in the evening.

A couple of years later another bird turned up inland, this time at Fazakerley in north Liverpool on 16 June 1999. It was seen briefly at close range but mostly in flight between feeding sites in Japanese knotweed and hawthorn. However, it sang persistently throughout the morning, showing a huge range of mimicry, and many brief glimpses revealed the long primary projection although the precise spacing of the primaries was never properly seen.

SJW, MJ.

This species account was sponsored by Richard Charles.

REED WARBLER

Acrocephalus scirpaceus

Lancashire Category A.

Fairly common breeder and passage migrant.

The Reed Warbler was described as rare and local by Mitchell. He knew of no regular breeding haunts but reported breeding by one or two pairs at Goosnargh in 1878 and at Sefton Meadows. Oakes believed that nesting had become even rarer by the end of the nineteenth century but that migrants were still fairly frequent. F.W. Holder found a nest 'in the Southport area' (Crossens-Banks) in 1916 and three pairs were present at the same site in a linear reedbed in 1949. One was singing 'on a northern mossland' (Leighton Moss) in 1923 and breeding was confirmed there in 1934 and during the 1940s. The very fact that Oakes felt obliged to safeguard the confidentiality of this site emphasises just how rare breeding was in the middle of the twentieth century. Oakes also implied that breeding took place at Fleetwood in 1949 and 1950 and, in the addenda to his book, he reported a pair in June 1951 at Marton Mere, where one to three pairs bred most years throughout the 1950s and 1960s. Hardy (1979) added Martin Mere, Mere Brow, Hightown (until the late 1950s), Kirkby and Eccleston Mere to the list of early twentieth century breeding sites.

'Many' were described as singing at Leighton Moss in 1959 (Barnes 1960) but colonisation accelerated with the formation of the RSPB reserve in 1964. Before this, almost 80% of the reed was burnt each winter in an attempt to retain open water for wildfowling, thus severely limiting suitable breeding habitat.

For many years, Leighton Moss remained the only breeding site of any significance in the county. During 1968-72 the Old Atlas survey found Reed Warblers breeding in just seven 10km squares in Lancashire, three of which represented Leighton Moss and nearby sites such as Haweswater, which was probably first colonised in 1959. The other sites were around Fleetwood and in St. Helens. These areas were reconfirmed as breeding sites during 1988-91 when breeding occurred in only four 10km squares, and it appeared that Leighton's near-monopoly of the species, at the north-western limit of its range, might remain as permanent a feature as for Bittern, Marsh Harrier and Bearded Tit. However, the early 1990s saw a rapid expansion of the Lancashire breeding distribution, the consolidation of existing small colonies and the establishment of new ones, so that by 1997-2000 Reed Warblers were breeding in 50 tetrads and 19 10km squares, a nearly tenfold increase in range in less than a decade.

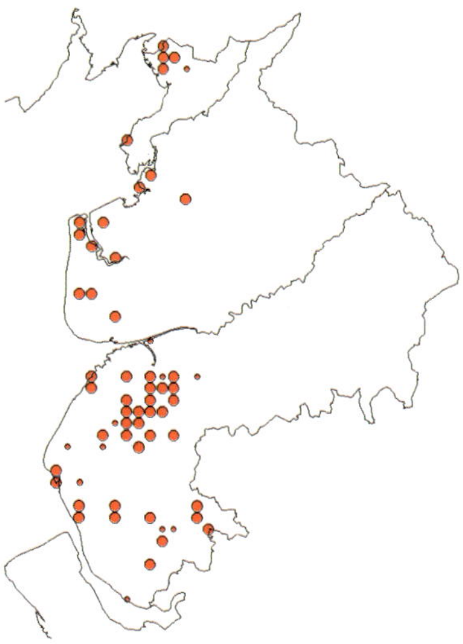

Breeding distribution of Reed Warbler, 1997-2000. (Large dots: confirmed. Small dots: possible)

The British population underwent a significant expansion from the 1980s and increased further by 43% from 1994-2005 (BBS). A growing national population no doubt fuelled the changes in Lancashire but the creation of new reedbed habitat provided the opportunity. These distributional changes have yet to produce an equivalent increase in population size. The Leighton Moss population is thought to have remained relatively constant at around 400 pairs throughout this period, although censusing such a large colony is fraught with difficulty. The breeding productivity of the colony is often high – a massive 838 out of 1,008 birds trapped in 2002, for example, were juveniles. The whole Lancashire population was estimated at 450 pairs during 1997-2000, emphasising the continuing dominance of Leighton Moss, but this was perhaps a slight underestimate and the true figure is probably closer to 500 pairs.

Elsewhere in north Lancashire, Haweswater appears to have been the next site to be colonised – as early as 1966, but most new colonies became established during the 1990s. Nesting probably first occurred at Heysham in 1990, growing to three pairs in 1997; the Eric Morecambe Complex has held two or more pairs since 1992, Pine Lake five pairs in 1993, Cockersands one or more since 1999 and Aldcliffe Marsh up to six pairs in the past five years. It seems likely that most of these colonies were established by Leighton Moss birds but there is evidence from ringing that some move to more distant breeding sites, for example singles probably breeding in Northumberland in 1996 and 1999.

Significant numbers occur in the Fylde, especially at Marton Mere where numbers increased after 1974 when the mere was enlarged and where 15 or more pairs now breed annually. During the 1990s up to five pairs nested at Preesall Flashes and several pairs at Jameson Road, Fleetwood, and breeding also occurred at Stanah, Conder Green, Pilling, Moss Side near Lytham and Myerscough Quarry. West Lancashire and adjacent areas support by far the largest cluster of breeding sites in the county, most of which were established during the early to mid-1990s. Martin Mere and Mere Sands Wood are the largest with 18 and 20 pairs respectively in 2002. Other sites supporting low single-figure populations, not always annually, include several stretches of the Leeds-Liverpool Canal, Croston Moss, Bretherton fish ponds, Ulnes Walton, Birkacre, Withnell Fold, Downholland Moss irrigation lake and several reedy mossland ditch systems. Further north, Brockholes Quarry was colonised in 2002 and remains the only site in the Ribble Valley.

Reed Warbler, Mere Sands Wood. (Phillip Tomkinson)

North Merseyside is similarly dominated by two sites: the Sankey Valley in St. Helens and the Rimrose Valley in Litherland, where up to twelve pairs nest. Half a dozen or so pairs breed on the Sefton Coast at both Marshside and Tagg's Island, Birkdale. A couple of pairs nested on the Sugar Brook alongside the East Lancashire Road in Fazakerley for much of the 1990s but the colony expanded onto the adjacent Fazakerley Reedbed when it was created in the latter years of the decade – this remains Liverpool's only site.

Reed Warblers are rare in the hillier eastern half of Lancashire and there have been no breeding records. There have been a few records of singing males making brief stops during spring passage, including May records at Rowley Lake in 1989 and Lowerhouse Lodges and Whitebirk Marsh in 2002. Autumn occurrences are even rarer and the only recent record was of two at Lee Green Reservoir from 29 July to 4 August 2001.

Spring arrival can be a protracted affair but mainly takes place from late April to mid-May, although occasional birds may not arrive until late June. Late arrival is illustrated by one ringed at Scotman's Flash, Wigan on 30 May 2003 and caught at Mere Sands Wood on 22 June that year, one ringed at Kenfig, Glamorgan on 25 June 1988 and controlled at Heysham on 10 August 1988, and one ringed as a breeding male at Barrow-in-Furness in 1986, controlled at Heysham on 23 May 1987 and subsequently back at Barrow on 13 June the same year. The earliest records were on 7 April at Leighton Moss in 2002 and Marton Mere in 2005. The latest first arrival at Leighton Moss is 27 April, while the average for the county, invariably at Leighton Moss or Marton Mere, over the past 25 years has been 18 April.

Unsurprisingly, since Lancashire still lies close to the north-western limits of the breeding range and very few Scandinavian birds are thought to pass through Britain in spring (Migration Atlas), there is very little evidence of any through passage and spring records away from breeding sites are exceedingly rare.

Autumn passage gets underway in late July and continues throughout August, with much reduced numbers in September and stragglers into October. The average last date in the county is 9 October, but there have been a handful of later records including at South Shore, Blackpool on 7 November 1982, Clifton Hall on 14 November 1993 and Leighton Moss on 1 November 2002. The latest, however, was one of the latest ever British records, one trapped and ringed at Marshside on 16 December 1984.

As in spring, most probable migrants are seen at reedbed sites and are difficult to detect. However, birds do turn up away from breeding habitat with more frequency than in spring, including almost annual singles at Seaforth since the late 1990s and one at Otterspool, south Liverpool on 13 September 1992. Significant totals of likely migrants are sometimes ringed, such as 25 at Jameson Rd, Fleetwood in August and September 1989. Early arrivals are likely to be dispersing juveniles; there are no such records in Lancashire of birds ringed outside the county but one that moved from Leighton Moss to West Yorkshire between 1 and 21 July 2000 illustrates this behaviour. There have been 60 movements recorded between Lancashire and other parts of the north of England (and one to Scotland), and it is likely that most of our migrants originate there, but some come from further afield, for example a juvenile ringed in southern Sweden on 2 August 1997 and controlled at Leighton Moss three weeks later on 24 August.

The migration routes of Lancashire birds are much better understood. Twenty-three Lancashire-ringed birds have been recovered in the south of England in autumn (most in August to September) plus four in spring (April-May), and 20 ringed in the south in autumn have been recovered in subsequent years in Lancashire. From southern England birds take a markedly westerly route across France and Iberia into north Africa before arriving at their West African wintering grounds. The nine recoveries of Lancashire birds in France and the Channel Islands (two in May-June and seven in August-September), two in Spain (in May and September) and two in western Morocco (one in November, one unknown) fit well with the national picture. The potential speed of migration is illustrated by one ringed at Leighton Moss on 22 August 1995 and controlled 705km away in Finistere in northern France a week later. None has been found in the wintering grounds. The oldest known Lancashire bird was ringed at Leighton Moss on 7 August 1994 and controlled there on 26 May 2004.

SJW, RW.

This species account was sponsored by Alan Creaser.

GREAT REED WARBLER

Acrocephalus arundinaceus

Lancashire Category A. (0, 3).

Vagrant from southern Europe.

All three records have, unsurprisingly, been of singing males at the county's two major reedbed sites. One was heard from the causeway at Leighton Moss on the rather in-between date of 17 July 1963 (M.E. Greenhalgh, P. Taylor). It was never seen but was accepted by the BBRC as the 39th record in Britain and Ireland; the Lancaster and District Checklist, however, described this record as 'not accepted at the county level, an unsatisfactory situation' (Harrison 2000). Another very elusive bird was found by John Wilson in the same area at Leighton Moss in June 1991, where it was seen on the 4th and heard briefly on the 8th and 13th.

The latest bird, at Marton Mere on 21 May 2003, was far more obliging, singing consistently and providing patient watchers with close and prolonged views during its stay to the 29th.

Great Reed Warbler is a major rarity outside south-east England, East Anglia and the northern isles; the only other record in north-west England was trapped at Red Rocks in Cheshire in May 1975.

Male Great Reed Warbler, Marton Mere, May 2003. (Steve Young)

SJW, MJ.

This species account was sponsored by the Fylde Bird Club.

ICTERINE WARBLER

Hippolais icterina

Lancashire Category A. (0, 5).

Vagrant from Scandinavia or central Europe.

Mather (1986) published a record of a pair nesting in eastern Bowland (then in Yorkshire) in 1970. He based this upon a second-hand report from observers who had first identified the birds as Wood Warblers but then decided they were Icterine, apparently on the basis of an unusual song, larger bill and pinkish eggs. The lack of corroboration or detailed description, however, makes this record impossible to accept (Doherty 1992). None has ever bred in England (Brown & Grice 2005).

Two records were published in 1984. The first (unaged) was at Cabin Hill NNR on 27 July 1984 and the second, described as a 'worn adult', at Fleetwood Golf Course on 12 August; neither description was completely convincing in the light of current knowledge. Although Icterine Warblers have been recorded in Britain this early they are very rare – there are just ten or so July records out of a total of more than 3,000. It seems likely that any seen at this time of year would be birds that had arrived in spring rather than new arrivals, and thus adults.

The first 'twitchable' record was a first-winter at Seaforth on 27 September 1992, and this was followed by another first-winter at Mount Park, Fleetwood on 24 September 1998 and another watched for just a few minutes at Heysham NR on 5 September 2005.

First-winter Icterine Warbler, Seaforth Nature Reserve, 27 September 1992. (Steve Young)

SJW, MJ.
This species account was sponsored by David and Jackie Moreton.

MELODIOUS WARBLER

Hippolais polyglotta

Lancashire Category A. (0, 2).

Vagrant from southern Europe.

One was reported at Fairhaven Marine Lake on 19 August 1972 but no details were published so even its age is unknown. A juvenile/first-winter was trapped at Haskayne Cutting on 28 August 1972 by Stuart Thomas; unfortunately no description of this bird can be traced other than of basic biometrics, but its wing length certainly ruled out Icterine. Another was claimed at Marshside on 24 August 1976 but another observer disputed the identification.

Tom Wilmer

There was no doubt about the next two records, however. The first was a first-winter, trapped at Heysham on 17 August 1988 by Tom Wilmer and reported in the field the following day and on the 24th. The second, also a first-winter and also trapped by Tom Wilmer on 6 September 1996, was seen just prior to its capture and these views, combined with the prevailing north-easterly wind and the time of year, suggested an Icterine, but the biometrics clearly proved otherwise.

First-winter Melodious Warbler, Heysham, 6 September 1996. (Pete Marsh)

SJW, MJ.
This species account was sponsored by Tom Wilmer.

BLACKCAP

Sylvia atricapilla

Lancashire Category A.

Common breeder and passage migrant; fairly common winter visitor from central Europe.

The Blackcap's status has changed markedly since Mitchell's day when it was described as evenly distributed throughout the county, but nowhere common with only one or two pairs in any one district, and rare in the Liverpool area. Oakes sketched a distribution essentially similar to the Garden Warbler's but believed Blackcaps to be generally less common, giving the Ribble Valley between Red Scar and Ribchester and north-east of Garstang to Calder Fell as exceptions.

The relative abundance of these two warblers has dramatically reversed since the 1950s; while Lancashire's Garden Warbler population appears to have remained relatively stable, Blackcap numbers have risen enormously. Nationally, a steady increase from the 1950s was followed by a rise of 155% between 1970 and 1998 (CBC) and 61% during 1994-2005 (BBS). The broad Lancashire range changed little between 1968-72 and 1997-2000 with breeding confirmed in all 10km squares, but within that range there has undoubtedly been a large amount of infilling, for example to the west of Blackburn since 2001.

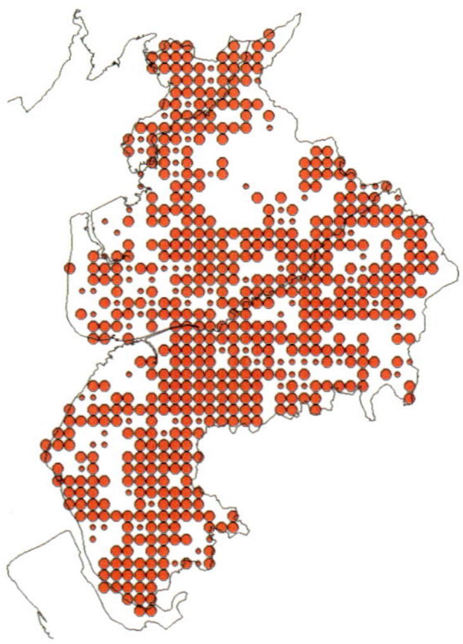

Breeding distribution of Blackcap, 1997-2000. (Large dots: confirmed. Small dots: possible)

Habitat requirements are less demanding than those of the Garden Warbler and Blackcaps have adapted readily to smaller habitat patches even in urban areas. It is not quite ubiquitous but was located in 70% of the county's tetrads in 1997-2000 and was absent only from the highest ground, the most urbanised areas and featureless farmland. Breeding is widespread in all suitably well-wooded parts of Lancashire, but patchily distributed in coastal areas south of the Lune, north Fylde (both sides of the Wyre), the south Ribble marshes, the south-west mosslands and parts of east Lancashire, and largely absent from northern areas of Bowland.

Female Blackcap. Liverpool, February 2005. (Steve Young)

The combined population of the RSPB sites of Leighton Moss, the Morecambe Bay reserve and Warton Crag remained relatively stable at around 20-25 pairs throughout the 1990s, but numbers at Warton Crag doubled from an average of six in the 1990s to eleven in 2000-04, a density of roughly one pair per 2ha. Few other sites have been so well monitored, but average numbers at Mere Sands Wood rose from 12.8 pairs in 1990-94 to 18.4 in 1995-99, and the population of Roddlesworth Plantations increased from five pairs in 1990 to twelve in 2003. Such increases in the range of 40-100% are probably fairly typical, although populations at some sites have remained quite stable, for example eight and ten pairs at Lytham Hall in 1987 and 2002 respectively. No significant decline has been reported anywhere.

Increasing densities have been matched by localised range extensions. Oakes considered Blackcaps to be virtually extinct as a breeding species in Rossendale but they colonised rapidly throughout the 1970s and 1980s and by 2000 were breeding on at least 20 sites. A similar increase was noted in many parts of north Merseyside during the same period and Blackcaps are now familiar nesters throughout the Liverpool conurbation.

Oakes knew of no records of birds wintering in Lancashire but Spencer, writing in 1973, referred to a few occurring in most winters since 1959. Nationally, in response to generally milder winters and increased availability of food in gardens, winter records increased from an average of 22 during 1945-54 to 380 during 1970-77 and more than 3,000 in the late 1980s (BWP). It seems likely that Lancashire followed the national trend, albeit a little later than in the south and east of the country; published records increased from just one in 1989/90 to 32 in 1996/97. Ringing studies on the Birkdale dunes, where Blackcaps feed mostly on sea-buckthorn berries, suggested a wintering population there of 40 or more in 2000 and 2003, while a detailed survey in the Lancaster & District Birdwatching Society area located birds at 21 sites in 1995/96. Most records come from gardens, where it is certain that birds are significantly under-reported, and the real winter population is almost certainly more than 100 and may be considerably larger.

It is known that most wintering British Blackcaps originate in continental Europe; only one ringed British breeder has been confirmed as wintering. The vast majority appear to come from western and central Europe (Migration Atlas), but the only winter ringing recovery in Lancashire was of a juvenile ringed 1517km away in Slovenia on 13 September 1999 and recovered near Garstang on 24 January 2000. Another juvenile ringed at St. Ives, Cornwall on 3 November 1993 and controlled at Ingol ten days later also seems more likely to have been of continental origin than a British reverse migrant.

The increased phenomenon of over-wintering causes difficulties in determining the exact date of first arrivals and the end of autumn passage. Some wintering birds have remained until at least the first week of April. Generally, spring passage lasts from late March until mid-May, with a peak in late April and early May. The average date of first arrivals in the period 1976-95 at Leighton Moss, where observer coverage is high, was 3 April. Most records involve just one or two birds and the largest day-total was eight trapped on 23 April 1998 at Heysham, where spring ringing totals ranged between five and 27 and averaged 16 during 1993-2003.

Juveniles begin to disperse from breeding areas during July and it is likely that most movements involve fairly local birds until at least mid-August. Passage movement at Heysham is usually strongest between late August and late September but a second peak often occurs during October, including a record fall of 15 on 30 October 1993. An average of 60 birds were ringed there each autumn between 1993 and 2003 and the likely total moving through probably regularly exceeds 100. No other coastal site comes close to the Heysham counts. Single-figure totals are the norm at Marshside and Marton Mere with six the record day -count at the former and eleven at the latter.

Ringing recoveries shed some light upon the origins of birds moving through Lancashire in autumn, with two ringed elsewhere in northern England and two in Scotland, and seven recoveries of Lancashire-ringed birds in northern England in subsequent years. Sizeable influxes at the same time as arrivals of presumed Scandinavian Blackbirds have been noted several times at Heysham, and it is possible that some, if not most, October arrivals originate in continental Europe although hard evidence is lacking.

Remarkably, the only autumn recovery of a Lancashire-ringed bird anywhere to our south was one ringed on 12 September 1976 and recovered 17 days later onboard a ship in the Bay of Biscay, although seven ringed during autumn in southern England have been recovered in Lancashire during subsequent years. Four birds ringed in the county during autumn have, however, been recovered in north African wintering areas, three in Algeria and one in Morocco, the absence of recoveries in Iberia perhaps suggesting 'leap-frog' migration by at least a proportion of northern British breeders.

SJW, RW.

This species account was sponsored by Paul Thomason.

GARDEN WARBLER

Sylvia borin

Lancashire Category A.

Common breeder; fairly common passage migrant.

Mitchell quoted Montagu's 1802 *Dictionary of British Birds* to the effect that the first British Garden Warbler had been discovered in Lancashire towards the end of the eighteenth century, a claim later disputed by Newton who argued it was known previously from a specimen in Yorkshire. Since the date of neither record was published, Lancastrians can draw their own conclusions. Uncertainty still reigned over its status in Lancashire towards the end of the nineteenth century; by Mitchell's account it was commoner than Blackcap around Clitheroe and Garstang, comparatively numerous in the Hodder Valley near Stonyhurst and well distributed around Blackburn, but rare in all other parts. Most of this confusion had been resolved by the mid-twentieth century. Oakes confirmed that Garden Warblers were more numerous than Blackcaps in 'some northern localities, notably so at Melling, near Carnforth, and further south in the Lune valley' and in the Whalley-Clitheroe district. The species' core breeding range also encompassed Silverdale, parts of Bowland and much of the Ribble Valley, but it was only local or occasional in the Fylde and the south-west.

The British population has fluctuated over the past 40 years, reaching a peak in 1964, declining until the mid-1970s, recovering until the 1990s then stabilising during 1994-2005 (BBS). The Lancashire breeding range declined from 28 10km squares in 1968-72 to 20 in 1988-91, reflecting the national decline during this period, but had almost doubled to 39 squares by 1997-2000, suggesting that the population may have returned to 1960s' levels against the national trend. Breeding was confirmed in 202 tetrads during 1997-2000 and suspected in a further 95, giving a maximum potential range covering a third of the county. The population was estimated at 2,000 pairs. Casual reports and those from well-monitored sites suggest that regional populations have been at worst stable and at best undergone further expansion this century.

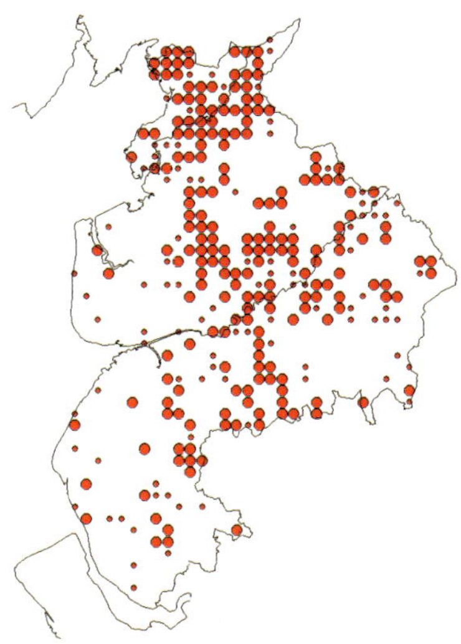

Breeding distribution of Garden Warbler, 1997-2000. (Large dots: confirmed. Small dots: possible)

Unlike all other warblers, with the exception of the much rarer Wood Warbler, breeding is heavily concentrated in the eastern two-thirds of the county, particularly within a roughly 20km band extending from the fringes of the West Pennine Moors, northwards through Bowland to the Lune Valley, wherever the favoured dense scrub and bramble habitat is found.

Garden Warbler, Stocks Reservoir, 2005. (Mark Breaks)

The densest populations are found in north Lancashire, in Silverdale and the Lune Valley between Lancaster and the Yorkshire border. Warton Crag supports one of the highest densities of breeding Garden Warblers in Britain, the 25.5ha owned by RSPB holding 14-21 pairs throughout the 1990s, rising to 26 in 2001 but falling to 15 in 2005. The population at nearby Leighton Moss fluctuated between five and 15 pairs during the 1980s and 1990s – largely in response to habitat management – while five pairs at Arkholme in 2000 were considered a good total. Although largely absent from the central areas of Bowland, significant breeding clusters are found on its western and southern fringes, particularly in the Scorton-Bleasdale area, east to Chipping and Bashall Eaves; Mitchell's assertion that Garden Warblers were more numerous in the Garstang area than Blackcaps was considered still to hold good in 1984.

Birds are widely but locally distributed throughout the Ribble Valley, reflecting the limited availability of suitable habitat. Breeding sites extend from Lower Penwortham on the Ribble to Witton Country Park on the Darwen, Gisburn Forest on the Hodder and Spring Wood, Whalley and Read along the Calder. Breeding pairs are very thinly scattered in the east due to a lack of suitable habitat, but larger concentrations have occurred including five singing at Heasandford in 1993 and seven or eight at Foulridge in 1991. The Chorley-West Pennine Moors area supports good populations with increased numbers reported since the early 1980s. The main sites are Anglezarke/Rivington, Birkacre/Duxbury Park in the Yarrow Valley, Withnell Fold, Roddlesworth, Belmont and Wayoh, each of which supports three to ten pairs.

Throughout the rest of the county Garden Warblers are decidedly scarce. In Rossendale breeding occurs at a handful of sites on the Greater Manchester boundary, while nesting was confirmed in just four tetrads in the Fylde during 1997-2000 (two on the Wyre Estuary and two near Myerscough), ten in north Merseyside (six of these in St. Helens), and similar numbers in West Lancashire. Lytham Hall held up to five singing males in the 1950s but development caused local extinction by the 1970s.

Spring passage usually begins during the last ten days of April – on average on the 21st during the past 25 years – although arrival has become progressively earlier during the 1990s. Witherby *et al.* (1938-41) published a record of one on 3 April 1937 but this may not have been within the present county boundary and was questioned by Oakes. The earliest documented record is one at Warton Crag on 14 April 1993. The peak of passage usually comes during the first half of May, with scattered records until late May and occasionally into June. Arrival is as early at inland breeding sites as on the coast, where most sightings relate to singles, so four at Heysham on 7 May 1989, five there on 5 May 1995 and four at Cabin Hill, Formby on 14 May 1989 can be regarded as exceptional 'falls'. Spring totals at the main coastal watchpoints rarely exceed single figures with recent maxima of 14 at Marshside in 1998 and ten at Heysham in 1999.

Although dispersal is often recorded from mid-July, the main autumn passage usually takes place during August and early September and occasionally continues to the end of the month and into October, when it is likely that at least some birds are migrants from continental Europe (Migration Atlas). As in spring, most sightings, both inland and on the coast, are of singles but larger day-counts include four at Marshside on 11 August 1996 and six at Heysham on 22 September 1999. Seasonal totals include 16 at Heysham in 1996 with 24 there in 1997 and seven through Marshside in 1996. October records are fairly regular and the average last sighting is on 23 October. Later records include singles at Martin Mere on 25 October to 8 November 1987, at Heysham on 13 November 1995 and at Fluke Hall on 6 November 2005. There have also been four records of apparently over-wintering birds. One was feeding on sea-buckthorn berries at Fairhaven from 1-12 December 1960, another on sloes in a Longton garden on several occasions in late December 1995 and, most recently, one was ringed in the Birkdale dunes on 23 November 2005 with another feeding on apples in a garden at Ainsdale on 29 November to 6 December 2005.

The overwhelming majority of Lancashire records undoubtedly relate to the nominate race which breeds throughout western Europe and Scandinavia but it is possible that some records are of the Russian race *woodwardii* which has occurred in England.

An extraordinary proportion of our few ringing recoveries demonstrate unexpected migratory movements. Our only spring recovery was of a (presumably overshooting) female ringed at Hightown on 9 May 1985 and recovered in Cornwall eight days later. Four of the remaining six records involve within-autumn reverse migration by British or continental birds: juveniles from Oxfordshire on 20 June 1980 to Lancaster on 6 August; Hampshire on 21 August 1994 to Pilling on 3 September; from Kent on 6 September 1997 to Wennington on 25 September; and a juvenile from the Pas de Calais on 12 August 1990 to Heysham on 26 August.

SJW, RW.
This species account was sponsored by David and Jill Player.

BARRED WARBLER

Sylvia nisoria

Lancashire Category A. (1, 16).

Vagrant from central or eastern Europe.

First-winter Barred Warbler, Marton Mere 24 October 2004. (Phillip Tomkinson)

Oakes reported one shot near Fleetwood on 20 August 1898. There have been a further 16 records, all of single first-winter birds in autumn. The first twentieth-century record was at Fairhaven on 11 September 1961. Unsurprisingly, all have been found at well-watched coastal sites, with the notable exception of one found dead at Hoghton, between Preston and Blackburn, on 18 November 1972. This was an unusually late bird; all others have occurred between August and October (Figure 1), reflecting the national pattern which shows a clear peak in the last ten days of August.

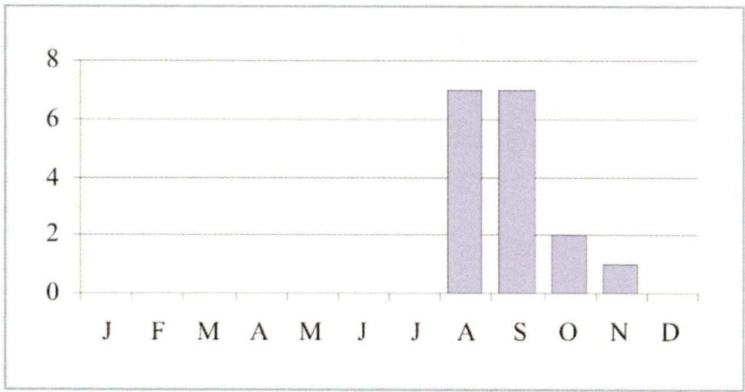

Figure 1. Monthly totals of Barred Warblers in Lancashire, 1898-2005.

All have been one-day birds with the exception of one at Fairhaven on 12-14 September 1985 and one at Blackpool's South Shore which stayed for nearly a fortnight from 1-12 October 1997. More than a quarter have been trapped by ringers: at Hightown in 1981, the Heysham birds in 1983 and 1997 and those at Freshfield Dune Heath (Woodvale) in 1988 and 1999.

All records:

1898	Fleetwood, one shot, 20 August
1961	Fairhaven, one (unaged), 11 September
1967	Crossens, first-winter, 16 September
1970	Leighton Moss, first-winter, 24 August
1972	Hoghton, one (unaged), freshly dead 18 November
1975	Rossall Point, first-winter, 12 September
1975	Heysham, first-winter, 13 September
1978	Freshfield, first-winter, 25 August
1981	Hightown, first-winter, trapped 6 September
1983	Heysham, first-winter, trapped 18 August
1985	Fairhaven, first-winter, 12 to 14 September
1988	Freshfield Dune Heath, first-winter, trapped 23 August
1997	Heysham, first-winter, trapped 30 August
1997	Lytham St. Anne's NR, first-winter, 28 September
1997	Blackpool, first-winter, 1 to 12 October
1999	Freshfield Dune Heath, first-winter, trapped 27 August
2004	Marton Mere, first-winter, 24 October

SJW, MJ.
This species account was sponsored by the Fylde Bird Club.

LESSER WHITETHROAT

Sylvia curruca

Lancashire Category A.

Fairly common breeder and passage migrant.

Because of its short song-period, which may last no more than two weeks, Lesser Whitethroats can easily be overlooked and their local status is prone to confusion, but there is little evidence to suggest that their Lancashire distribution has altered enormously for the past hundred years or so.

Mitchell was at pains to dismiss a statement published in *Ibis* in 1865 that Lancashire was one of a handful of counties in which the Lesser Whitethroat did not breed. He stated that it nested in all suitable localities around Clitheroe, was common in the Chipping area and present further west near Haighton and Grimsargh, believing, however, that it was very rare elsewhere.

Oakes confirmed that breeding continued in the mid-twentieth century at all the sites mentioned by Mitchell and added Cabus (near Garstang), Pilling, Whalley, Ribchester, Elston and Hoghton, highlighting the Ribble Valley as the main stronghold. Its status at that time is probably best described as widespread but uncommon although some local breeding clusters were of reasonable size, like the six or so pairs between Whalley and Stoneyhurst. Oakes believed breeding to be probable in Silverdale and at Leighton Moss but knew of only two sites in the south-west, Aughton (near Ormskirk) and Formby Hall.

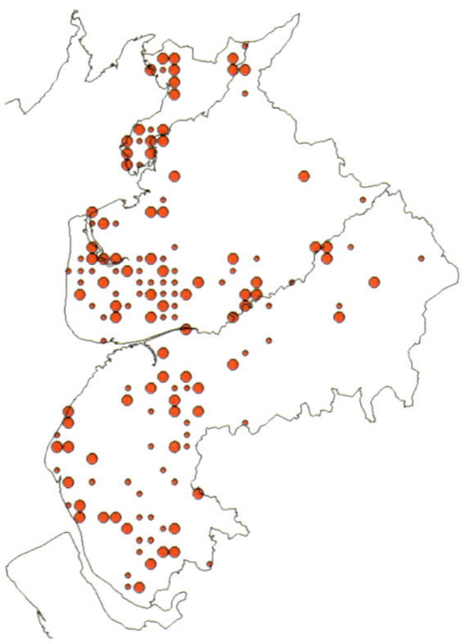

Breeding distribution of Lesser Whitethroat, 1997-2000.
(Large dots: confirmed. Small dots: possible)

By the 1970s it had become clear that Lesser Whitethroats had an essentially western distribution in Lancashire and that the highest densities were to be found in north Lancashire. It is not clear whether this represented a genuine shift in range since Oakes's time or merely a filling in of gaps in knowledge.

The national population is subject to regular fluctuations but the period between the Old and New Atlases, 1968-1991, saw a significant range extension which was reflected in the Lancashire distribution increasing from 21 to 27 10km squares. Nationally, numbers decreased by 35% between 1994 and 2005 (BBS), but the Lancashire distribution showed a marked increase to 37 10km squares during 1997-2000, perhaps partly as a result of the intensive efforts put into the Lancashire Atlas survey and partly reflecting normal fluctuations for a species at the edge of its breeding range. Lesser Whitethroats were found in 152 tetrads (16% of the county) but breeding was only confirmed in slightly more than half. Almost two-thirds of these registrations were in the western third of the county which accounted for 75% of the breeding pairs. The county population was estimated at 250 pairs.

Some of the highest densities occur in parts of north Lancashire where Lesser Whitethroats occur in three distinct clusters – in Silverdale, around Heysham and on the eastern upper Lune. Breeding was first proven on Warton Crag in 1954 and the limestone areas around Silverdale are particularly favoured wherever there is sufficient scrub. Numbers have declined on the RSPB sites of Leighton Moss, the Eric Morecambe complex and Warton Crag from around twelve pairs in the 1980s to roughly six in the past few years. The main cluster nowadays is around Heysham, Morecambe and Lancaster where perhaps 30 or more pairs breed at an average density of about one per square kilometre; the most productive sites in recent years have been Heysham NR and Aldcliffe with about six pairs each. Elsewhere in the north, Lesser Whitethroats are thinly scattered in the Lune Valley and south of Lancaster including Hornby, Melling, Arkholme, Scorton and Garstang.

The Fylde population has expanded significantly since the 1970s when breeding was largely restricted to the north Ribble area around Freckleton Naze and Lytham Hall. In 1997-2000 a total of 44 breeding pairs was located in 17 tetrads – almost all south of the Wyre – and, taking unconfirmed breeders into account, the population might have been as high as 75 pairs. Breeding locations vary to some extent from year to year, the more regular sites including Skippool, Stanah, Knott End, Preesall Flashes, Marton Mere, Weeton, Kirkham, Freckleton Naze and Warton Bank.

Breeding is much more thinly spread in West and central Lancashire, mostly in a fairly narrow corridor roughly between Chorley and Skelmersdale. As a species which rarely breeds above 200m, it is generally absent from the hillier areas in the east of the region, where it is confined mostly to the valley bottoms, although occurrence was recorded in young conifer plantations on Beacon Fell in the 1950s and below Saddle Fell during the 1960s. It has always been at the edge of its range in east Lancashire with just a thin scattering of breeding pairs, mainly in the Ribble and Hodder catchments north of Pendle Hill, but also occasionally in the Burnley and Colne areas.

The most important area for Lesser Whitethroats in North Merseyside is the dune system between Birkdale and Formby, where several pairs usually breed. Birds also occur at a handful of sites on the edge of the conurbation, including south Liverpool, Halewood, Tarbock, Knowsley and the Rimrose Valley, but they are remarkably scarce in the eastern parts of St. Helens.

Like other Sylvia warblers, Lesser Whitethroats are relatively late migrants, with an average first arrival in Lancashire for the past 25 years of 23 April but a week later on 1 May at Leighton Moss in the north of the county. For many years our earliest was one at Wray in the Lune Valley on 16 April 1944 until a male at Marton Mere on 13-22 April 2005. The main passage is from the end of April until mid-May, with some late arrivals in early June. Single birds are usual and they occur at widespread locations; few are seen away from potential breeding habitat but not all are proven to go on to breed. In 1995, for example, there were spring records from 25 sites but breeding was only reported from 14. Small numbers are seen most years at the main coastal watchpoints: 16 unringed birds, and therefore possible migrants, were trapped at Heysham from 1-24 May 1995 and 14 to mid-

May 2000 with a record count of 14 singing males there on 14 May 2005, while Marshside recorded a total of six from 3 May to 1 June 1997.

Post-breeding dispersal may begin as soon as early July but more usually towards the end of the month. Autumn passage is, if anything, somewhat less pronounced than in spring, with rarely more than single-figure county-wide totals reported in any year. A record 54 were ringed at Heysham in autumn 1995, 40 of them to mid-August were probably local breeding birds but the remainder to 8 September were thought to be migrants.

Numbers usually peak between mid-August and early September and sightings become rather scarce towards the end of the month – with an average last sighting on the 19th – and decidedly rare after that. Late records include singles at Marton Mere on 26 October 1989, in Blackpool on 6 November 1989, 18 October 1993 and 15 October 1999, in Burnley on 29 October 1995, at Crook o' Lune on 23 November 1999, Jenny Brown's Point on 16-17 November 2000, and two in Crosby on 30 September 2000; the latest was one at Lytham St. Anne's NR on 2-23 December 1998.

Male Lesser Whitethroat, Marton Mere. (Phillip Tomkinson)

Some birds later in the autumn presumably originate from well to the east, perhaps far enough away to be from populations previously recognised as '*blythi*', though this race now considered synonymous with *curruca*. Two records have been published as such: the Blackpool bird of October 1993 and one trapped at Heysham on 23 September 1996, while the Jenny Brown's Point bird also showed sandier than normal upperpart colouration.

SJW, RW.

This species account was sponsored by Neil Southworth.

WHITETHROAT

Sylvia communis

Lancashire Category A.

Common breeder and passage migrant.

Mitchell's description as 'one of the commonest of the summer migrants, breeding numerously' could stand for today, except that he went on to say that the only area he knew of where it bred 'in but small numbers' was Furness (now in Cumbria). Intriguingly, this implies a considerable presence in the eastern half of the county, which is certainly not the case today. Oakes was slightly more precise about its breeding range, describing it as very local in the south-east (now mostly in Greater Manchester) and in 'north-eastern industrial areas', but 'elsewhere a common nester from the Mersey northwards, being especially numerous in the Fylde, at Pilling and Cockerham, and in the valleys of the Ribble and Lune'.

This approximates to the present situation but, as elsewhere in Britain, Lancashire's Whitethroat population has undergone huge fluctuations since the 1950s. The Sahel drought of the 1960s led to a 75% decline nationally between 1968-69 with further smaller decreases until 1974, after which there were several ups and downs but an overall upward trend since the mid-1990s with the BBS showing a 27% increase between 1994 and 2005. Little of this is reflected, however, in broad-brush distributional changes in Lancashire. Whitethroats were found in 50 10km squares in 1968-72, declining to 45 in 1988-91 and 47 in 1997-2000, but these small changes are almost certainly simply the result of losses outside the main range. The Lancashire Atlas confirmed breeding in half of the county's tetrads during 1997-2000 with possible breeding in a further 6%.

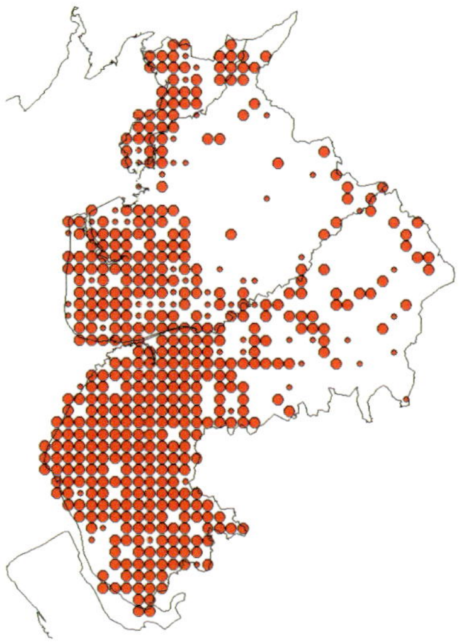

Breeding distribution of Whitethroat, 1997-2000. (Large dots: confirmed. Small dots: possible)

The breeding range is largely similar to that of Lesser Whitethroat, with a heavily western bias, but the distribution is much more solid almost everywhere within this range. In the western third of the county Whitethroats are absent only from the most urbanised areas, saltmarshes and a scrubless area between

Cockerham and the Lune; elsewhere Whitethroats breed in abundance wherever favoured open areas of scrub and tangled ground vegetation are to be found.

A county population of 5,000 pairs was estimated in 1997-2000. Some of the highest densities occur in North Merseyside, particularly on the Sefton Coast and nearby inland sites. Site censuses during the 1980s included 38 males per 100ha on the Birkdale dunes in 1981. Despite some fluctuations numbers appear to have increased significantly at several key sites, particularly during the early years of this century. Numbers breeding at Hesketh Golf Course and Marshside/Crossens rose from 10-12 pairs during the 1970s and early 1980s to an average of 19 during the 1990s, 24 in 2000, 34 in 2001 and 38 in 2004. Similarly, breeding pairs in the Rimrose Valley increased from ten or so during the late 1990s to about 40 in 2004, when 24 pairs also nested in 35ha at Freshfield Dune Heath with 29 there in 2005.

Whitethroat, Hightown Dunes, May 2005. (Steve Young)

There are many breeding sites in south Liverpool, some on derelict industrial land, including 25 pairs in the Oglet area in 2005. Similar densities are found around Kirkby and in St. Helens and throughout West and central Lancashire to the south and west of Preston. Representative counts include 17 pairs at White Moss, Skelmersdale in 1990 and 30 in the Sankey Valley in 2001.

Whitethroats are widespread in the Fylde, particularly in the west and to the south of the Wyre. Several Wyre Estuary sites support regular populations, including 25 singing males at Jameson Road, Fleetwood in 2001. Marton Mere usually holds ten or more pairs and similar numbers can be found at Lytham Moss and Carr House Green Common, Inskip, with single figures at many other sites.

There are relatively few on the western fringes of Bowland between Lancaster and Preston, most being found around Scorton and Garstang, where a significant increase was noted in the mid-1990s. Habitat is generally unsuitable throughout the Ribble, Hodder and Calder Valleys, with their mosaic of mature woodland, pasture and severely trimmed hedges. Several sites around Chorley and the West Pennine Moors support a handful of breeding pairs.

In north Lancashire the species is fairly common on the limestone around Silverdale, with about eight pairs at Warton Crag throughout most of the 1990s. There are good numbers at coastal locations, particularly the Morecambe Bay reserve, where there were eight pairs in 1996, and at Heysham where 16 pairs bred in 1989, 13 in 2000 but only six in 2001. The species is also common along both sides of the Lune Estuary, for example eleven males at Aldcliffe in 1991, but uncommon in much of the Lune Valley due to lack of suitable habitat.

Whitethroats are almost entirely absent from Bowland and were never common breeders anywhere in east Lancashire even before the 1969 collapse – but they remain thinly distributed at a small number of suitable sites on lower ground, mainly in the Calder catchment but also in the Ribble and Hodder Valleys. Breeding has been confirmed since 2003 at Lee Green Reservoir and since 2002 at Lowerhouse Lodges. Whitethroats bred regularly in Rossendale along the Irwell Valley in the 1950s and 1960s but the 1969 crash led to a complete absence of records from 1970-75 before Ewood Bridge was recolonised in 1976; their range has since spread to Crawshawbooth, Waterfoot, Bacup and the Plunge Valley.

The first spring arrivals are usually in mid-April, the average date in the past 25 years being the 20th. The earliest were singles at Heysham on 9 April 1944 and Ribchester on 6 April 1965. However, the main arrival usually comes at the end of April and in the first week of May, but sometimes as late as the middle of May. Since breeding is so widespread it is almost impossible to differentiate passage birds, new arrivals and those settling down to nest, but the average passage period at Seaforth (1996-2003), where none bred until 2004, is from 26 April to 21 May. Several sites, including Marton Mere, Marshside, Freshfield Dune Heath and the Rimrose Valley, regularly report mass arrivals, with numbers of singing males quickly declining as birds presumably move through.

Post-breeding dispersal begins in July and most sites usually report accelerating departure by the end the month. Ringing studies at Heysham indicate that substantial numbers of immigrants begin to arrive in mid-July, probably mostly juveniles, and that most local birds have left by mid-August. Numbers usually peak there sometime in August (with notable influxes of 25 on 13 August 1994 and 10 August 2000, and 40 on 5 August 2002) and few are seen after the second week of September. The average passage period at Seaforth is from 23 July to 25 September. Small numbers of migrants are seen throughout the county: a strong autumn passage in the Chorley area in 1996 included counts of eleven at Adlington Park and eight at Birkacre. The average final sighting is on 29 September but October records are not unusual – mostly on the coast but including one at Crawshawbooth on 2 October 1995 – the latest being singles at Seaforth on 20-23 October 1990 and at Bamber Bridge on 26 October 1945.

It is likely that most movements in early autumn involve fairly local birds since true migration usually begins in late July for juveniles and in August for adults (Migration Atlas). Relatively little is known about the origins of these longer distance migrants, since there have been few movements of ringed birds between Lancashire and areas to our north: one from the Isle of Man, ten to or from northern England, and one ringed in Dumfries and Galloway on 27 July 1996 and recovered in Burnley on 26 August that year. Remarkably, of eight recoveries of Lancashire-ringed birds to our south only four have been in southern England, two in the midlands (Shropshire and Leicestershire) and two on the south coast in Hampshire and Devon. The four foreign recoveries were recovered in western France (two), Spain and Portugal, all during September except for one in France in early November. This relative lack of British recoveries perhaps indicates that many birds leaving Lancashire fly non-stop to southern Europe.

There have been no recoveries of Lancashire birds in the wintering grounds of the Sahel or west Africa but one ringed in Senegal, possibly on passage, on 15 March 1993 was recovered in Morecambe on 1 May that year – a distance of 4,345km. Two other within-spring recoveries in the county suggest a possible coastal migration route: one in 1988, ringed on Bardsey Island on 1 May and recovered at Lytham St. Anne's on 7 May; the other in 1959, ringed on Skokholm on 25 May and recovered in Skelmersdale on 13 June. The latter was a first-summer bird, perhaps typical for late spring migrants.

SJW, RW
This species account was sponsored by Barry Dyson and Berwyn Morris.

DARTFORD WARBLER

Sylvia undata

Lancashire Category A. (0, 1).

Vagrant from southern Britain or southern Europe.

Our only record was found by Steve Martin on his BBS square on grouse moorland on Darwen Moor on 3 May 2003. It was a male in full plumage and was singing regularly throughout its stay to at least 17 May, and on at least one occasion was seen gathering nest material. Unfortunately, it was in the middle of the grouse breeding season and the landowner was understandably reluctant to grant access to more than a handful of people.

The British breeding population has increased dramatically over the past decade or so, largely due to a succession of mild winters, and reached a peak of almost 2,000 pairs in 2000. However, Dartford Warblers are still almost wholly confined to southern England with the nearest (small) population to Lancashire in Glamorgan. It seems most likely that the Darwen Moor bird was an overshooting spring migrant, perhaps a first-summer bird, but its length of stay must give some hope that the species may eventually colonise the county if climate change continues at its present rate.

SJW.
This species account was sponsored by S.J. Martin.

SUBALPINE WARBLER

Sylvia cantillans

Lancashire Category A. (0, 4).

Vagrant from southern Europe.

All four records have been spring males and have occurred during the May to early June peak arrival period for this southern European 'overshoot'. The first was trapped and ringed in the dunes at Hightown on 22 May 1966 by Tony Duckels, Dave Lowe and M.P. Dye. It was only the 25th record in Britain and Ireland of what is now a much more frequently reported species. The bird was seen in the same area by many observers from the 24th to the 27th.

The 1980s produced two records of singles: at Lytham St. Anne's N.R. on 27-28 May 1985 and in scrubland at Freeman's Wood, Lancaster on 9 May 1989.

Remarkably, the most recent on 13 June 2001 was again at Lytham St. Anne's N.R. and found by the same observer as in 1985. It proved to be extremely elusive and was seen on just three brief occasions as it skulked in dense sea-buckthorn.

All records:

1966	Hightown, male, trapped 22 May, present to 27 May
1985	Lytham St. Anne's NR, male, 27 to 28 May
1989	Lancaster, male, 9 May
2001	Lytham St. Anne's NR, male, 13 June

SJW, MJ.
This species account was sponsored by Maurice Jones.

Dartford Warbler, Darwen Moor, May 2003. (Tony Disley)

SARDINIAN WARBLER

Sylvia melanocephala

Lancashire Category A. (0, 1).

Vagrant from southern Europe.

A first-summer male was trapped during a Constant Effort Site ringing session on 28 May 1992 in scrubland adjacent to RAF Woodvale in Formby by J.D. Fletcher, D. Ogle and G. Langley. The site is now part of the Lancashire Wildlife Trust's Freshfield Dune Heath reserve, but at the time it was owned by the Ministry of Defence and access was strictly controlled. After discussions with Sefton Council's Ranger Service, the bird was released in scrub on the Lifeboat Road dunes at Formby Point in order that as many birdwatchers as possible could see the bird. Unfortunately, after release it behaved in a manner typical of *Sylvia* warblers – it skulked in deep cover, calling frequently but rarely showing itself for more than a few seconds. It stayed until at least 31 May.

Male Sardinian Warbler, Freshfield Dune Heath, 28 May 1992. (Dave McAleavy)

This was the first record in north-west England and only the 29th in Britain and Ireland, and, up to this time, very few had been 'twitchable'.

SJW, MJ.

This species account was sponsored by Sylvia Sloan.

GREENISH WARBLER

Phylloscopus trochiloides

Lancashire Category A. (0, 1).

Vagrant from north-east Europe.

Our only record was found in sycamore and sea buckthorn scrub at Crosby Marine Park from the Seaforth NR side of the fence on the morning of 15 September 1994 by Pete Kinsella. A small number of other birders arrived soon after but it never showed properly again, although it was heard calling for an hour or more and what may have been the same bird was seen in flight several times.

SJW, MJ.

This species account was sponsored by Dr. Alan Fielding.

PALLAS'S WARBLER

Phylloscopus proregulus

Lancashire Category A. (0, 4).

Vagrant from Siberia.

Pallas's Warblers have occurred in Britain with increasing frequency since the 1980s, perhaps reflecting a westwards range extension in Siberia, and the first in Lancashire was long awaited. One was claimed on the Springfield Nuclear Energy plant at Salwick on 29 April 1983 but was rejected by the BBRC, perhaps in part because it would have been the first spring record in Britain.

The first accepted record was found by D.A. Scott and J.A. Wolstencroft on 23 October 1989 in the quarry area at Jenny Brown's Point, Silverdale, where it remained until the 26th – still the only one to stay more than a day in Lancashire. By the end of 1989 more than 500 had been recorded in Britain and Ireland and the species was taken off the official 'rarity list'.

Two of our remaining records turned up at apparently unlikely locations in Blackpool, providing just rewards for local patch birders. The first was in a small urban park garden in Gynn Square on 29 October 1994, where more than 70 people managed to see it, and the second in a row of poplars and adjacent small gardens close to Blackpool Football Club's Bloomfield Road ground on 1 November 1997.

Sandwiched in between these two came another in the north of the county, at Heysham on 5 November 1995. It was found in sycamores alongside the railway line/golf course at nine in the morning and remained there for about 90 minutes before flying off with a flock of Long-tailed Tits.

Pallas's Warbler, Hightown Dunes, December 2006. (Steve Young)

SJW, MJ.

This species account was sponsored by the Fylde Bird Club.

YELLOW-BROWED WARBLER

Phylloscopus inornatus

Lancashire Category A. (0, 59).

Scarce passage migrant from Siberia.

Remarkably, our first two records were both found in urban Fylde – the first in a garden in St. Anne's on 21 October 1957 by J.V. Morley. The second, on 16-17 October 1984, was quite extraordinary; it had found its way into a house adjacent to the railway bushes near Blackpool Pleasure Beach and the householder summoned a local birdwatcher to identify it. The bird was caught and photographed in a large glass jam jar before being released in Watson Road Park where it was seen again next day.

First-winter Yellow-browed Warbler, Heysham, October 2005. (Reuben Neville)

A further 57 individuals have been recorded since, with the only blank years being 1987 and 1991. Ten of these were trapped by ringers. The highest annual totals were seven in 1988, which saw a record national influx with more than 700 recorded, and 2005 when twelve were recorded in Lancashire during another record national influx. In more usual years, one to four records have become the norm (Figure 1). National numbers increased steadily to around 200 a year from the 1950s – leading to its removal from the list of species considered by the BBRC in 1962 – and rose dramatically between 1984 and 1988 before settling to an average of 300 or so since the 1990s.

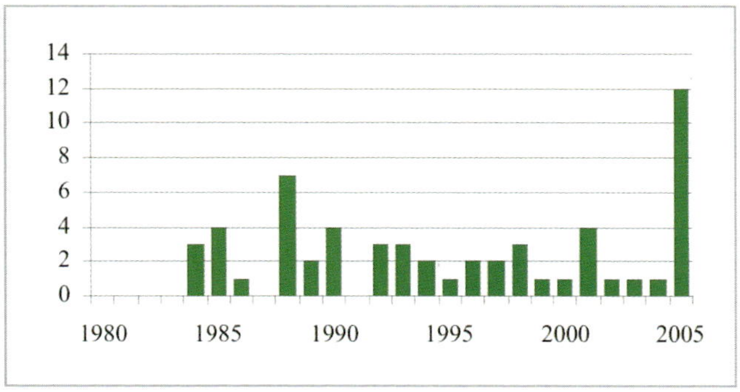

Figure 1. Annual totals of Yellow-browed Warblers in Lancashire, 1980-2005.

There have been two winter records: at Carr House Green Common, Inskip from 15 December 1984 to 5 January 1985, and in gardens in Childwall in the south Liverpool suburbs from at least 22 February to 11 March 1998.

Few Yellow-browed Warblers have ever been found in Britain in spring, so a singing male in Skelmersdale on 26 April 2004 was a quite exceptional record.

Autumn passage begins on average during the second week of September and peaks between the end of September and mid-October; birds become scarce after the end of October. The earliest record in Lancashire was on 1 September 1989 at Heysham and the latest autumn birds on 8 November 1993 at Fence, near Burnley and on 5-13 November 2005 in Haslam Park, Preston. Significantly more have been discovered in October than September (Figure 2), again reflecting the national pattern.

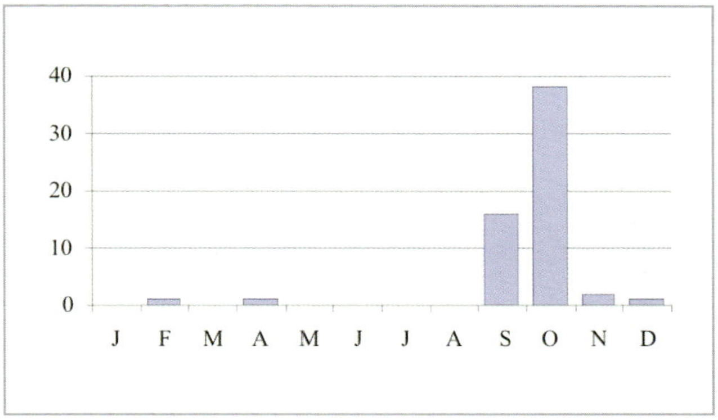

Figure 2. Monthly totals of Yellow-browed Warblers in Lancashire, 1957-2005.

Twenty-two records have been in the north of the county; 16 of these were at Heysham and include Lancashire's only multiple occurrences – three on 26 September 1985 and two on 15 September 1989 – with others at Jenny Brown's Point, Leighton Moss, Aldcliffe and Morecambe. The remainder have been divided fairly evenly between the Sefton coast (14 between Seaforth and Marshside), the Fylde coast (13 from Lytham to Pilling) and inland. The apparent northern bias is perhaps largely a function of the intensive ringing effort at Heysham.

The number of records inland is rather surprising. In addition to the four mentioned above, a further six have occurred: one trapped at Homer Green in Merseyside on 29 September 1984 and singles at Wrightington on 22-24 September 1988, Nelson on 28 October 1995, Fazakerley in north Liverpool on 4 October 1999 and 26-28 September 2001 and Newton-in-Bowland on 8-12 October 2005.

SJW, MJ.

This species account was sponsored by the Breaks family and Dave McAleavy.

DUSKY WARBLER

Phylloscopus fuscatus

Lancashire Category A. (0, 2).

Vagrant from Siberia.

On 4 November 1994, after a night of south-easterly winds and a morning of slow but steady numbers of migrants in the mist nets, a first-winter bird was trapped at midday in the alder copse at Heysham N.R. by Tom Wilmer and others. The bird was photographed and released and was seen briefly in the field later that day. The following night was still and clear and thrushes were heading into the sky soon after dusk, presumably accompanied by the Dusky Warbler which was not seen again.

It was the 143rd record in Britain and Ireland but the overwhelming majority of these have been in the Northern Isles or on the east coast – this was the first in north-west England although another was trapped in Cheshire in November of the following year. Nationally, 1994 was the best ever year for this Siberian vagrant, with a total of 21 birds recorded.

Our second record was found in scrub in the Fairhaven dunes on 23 October 2003. It was far more obliging than the first, calling continuously and showing regularly as it fed on a circuit of willows until 24 October. 2003 was another bumper year nationally with 23 records, the second best ever. Late October into November is the typical arrival date for this species.

Dusky Warbler, Fairhaven dunes, 23 October 2003. (Chris Batty)

SJW, MJ.

This species account was sponsored by Maurice Jones.

WOOD WARBLER

Phylloscopus sibilatrix

Lancashire Category A.

Scarce breeder and passage migrant.

Mitchell ranked the Wood Warbler as Lancashire's second most numerous *Phylloscopus* warbler, less common than Willow Warbler but 'much more plentiful than the Chiffchaff'. It appears to have been a widespread breeder in the late nineteenth century 'wherever wooded heights occur' and was thus rare in Rossendale, what is now Merseyside and elsewhere in the south of the county. Mitchell described it as common between Preston and Pleasington and near Padiham, occasional on Whalley Nab, and rare but regular around Haighton near Preston. It bred annually in woods at the foot of Pendle Hill but 'Longridge Fell and the wooded banks of the Hodder are its favourite habitat, and there it may almost be called numerous'.

Oakes added some more flesh to Mitchell's outline of breeding distribution, describing the 'essential' habitat conditions as 'oak, beech and sycamore woodlands, with or without undergrowth of bracken and preferably on sloping ground . . . old parklands with massive trees [being] particularly favoured'. He summarised its mid-twentieth century status as: fairly common in Silverdale; thinly distributed in the upper Lune Valley and Roeburndale, but with a number of pairs near Caton and other woods east of Lancaster at the foot of Clougha Fell; widespread in Wyresdale, wooded ravines of the eastern fells and throughout the Ribble Valley from Preston to the Yorkshire boundary; and rare in Rossendale, the central plain and the south-west. Barnes (1959), however, wrote that it was 'much less numerous [in north Lancashire]' than Oakes believed and there were few probable breeding records in Silverdale (including at Yealand and Warton Crag) during the 1950s.

Fifty years later, the Lancashire Atlas of 1997-2000 revealed a very different picture. Little change was evident at the 10km square level, with breeding confirmed in 16 squares during 1968-72, 23 in 1988-91 and 16 in 1997-2000, but Wood Warblers were located in only 64 tetrads in 1997-2000 and confirmed as breeding in just 36 (less than 5%). The total population was estimated, perhaps optimistically, at 100 pairs. There has been a major decline nationally since the early 1990s with the BBS showing a fall of 65% between 1994 and 2005, making the Wood Warbler one of Britain's most rapidly declining species. Although impossible to quantify, there is little doubt that this trend has been reflected in Lancashire and, if unchecked, the Wood Warbler may soon be regarded as a rare breeder in the county. Their decline has accelerated this century and Lancashire's Wood Warblers appear to be on the edge of extinction with a population of (probably considerably) less than 50 pairs – even on the most optimistic reading, fewer than ten pairs were reported in 2005. There have been no obvious changes in the breeding habitat sufficient to account for this decline, so its causes must presumably lie elsewhere.

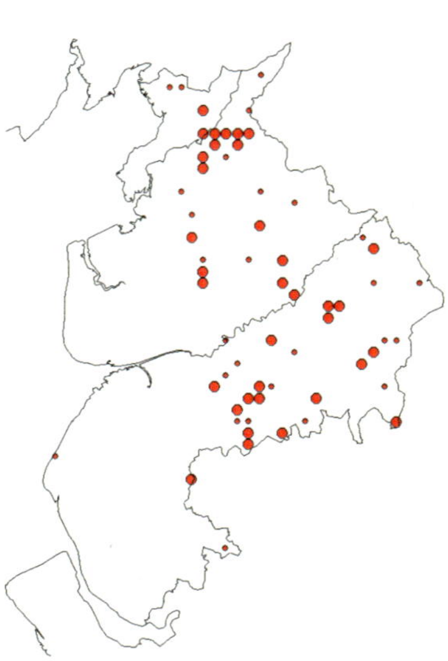

Breeding distribution of Wood Warbler, 1997-2000. (Large dots: confirmed. Small dots: possible)

More than half of the population is concentrated in two breeding clusters, in the Lune Valley and the fringes of the West Pennine Moors.

In north Lancashire most are found in sessile oak woodland throughout the Lune Valley, but especially in the tributary valleys of Littledale and Roeburndale. A survey carried out in the LDBWS area as part of the 1984 BTO Wood Warbler survey located 58 singing males in 20 Lancashire tetrads, while the Lancaster and District Atlas survey (1986-91) of the same area found birds in 34 tetrads, suggesting a significant increase in distribution. This had, however, dramatically reversed by 1997-2000 when singing males were located in just 19 tetrads with breeding thought probable in eleven; none was confirmed as breeding in Silverdale or in northern Bowland except around Dunsop Bridge and in Roeburndale. A further survey of north Lancashire in 2005 located just one singing male, in Roeburndale.

Wood Warbler, Grizedale Valley. (Mike McKavett)

The other main cluster lies in scattered woodlands in Chorley and the West Pennine Moors, including in recent years Sunnyhurst Wood, Roddlesworth Plantations, Wheelton, Brinscall, Rivington, Black Coppice and the Yarrow Valley. These sites are quite different in character to the northern sessile oak woodlands, at Roddlesworth, for example, Wood Warblers breed mainly in beech and mixed woodland areas. The population trend in this area since the early 1990s is unclear. Surveys at Roddlesworth, for example, revealed twelve singing males in 1990, nine in 1995 and seven in 2003, while Sunnyhurst Wood, Darwen held two or three pairs during 1990-2002. Other sites have been monitored less thoroughly but sporadic counts have included eight males at Rivington in 1989 and six at Brinscall in 1996 falling to just two pairs in 2005. The number of sites reporting breeding has, however, certainly declined since the late 1990s.

Wood Warblers can still be found in fluctuating numbers in the valleys west of Bowland, including upper Wyresdale, Scorton, Grizedale, and the Brock Valley. The upper Hodder Valley also remains an important area, and Moor Piece near Bashall Eaves, which has held up to three pairs in recent years, has become one of the county's favoured sites to see Wood Warblers – although only unmated males were seen here in 2004 and 2005. Elsewhere in east Lancashire breeding sites are scarce but small clusters were found in 1997-2000 around Sabden-Read and Clowbridge. Breeding has always been sporadic in Rossendale but was reported from five sites in 1991, falling to two or three in 1997-2000 and none in 2003.

Lancashire's most southerly recent breeding site was at Dean Wood near Appley Bridge but none has been reported there for several years. Nesting has never been confirmed in the Fylde and, although males were present late into the season at Lytham Hall in 1988 and at Fairhaven in 1990, breeding is unlikely to have occurred. One or two pairs bred at Formby until the mid-1980s and one pair at Hollins Hey in St. Helens in 1988, but all sightings in the south-west in the past ten or more years undoubtedly refer to migrants.

The earliest spring bird was one at Kew Wood, Southport on 14 April 1979 but the average arrival date over the past 25 years is 22 April. Clear-cut passage birds are relatively scarce and most early records are of males singing on the breeding grounds in the last week of April through to mid-May. Coastal passage is light with an annual average total since 1990 of just two or three records at a variety of sites between Liverpool and Leighton Moss; slightly heavier influxes involving eight birds were recorded in 1999 and nine in 2002.

Autumn sightings are less than annual and Wood Warblers are significantly rarer on the coast than Yellow-browed Warblers. Only eleven August or September records were reported during 1990-2005 and most of these were at inland sites close to the breeding grounds. All were singles with the exception of five in a mixed *Phylloscopus* flock at Rivington on 1 September 1991. The only coastal or near-coastal migrants in recent years have been at Heysham on 30 August 1993, Eccleston Mere on 13 September 1996, Liverpool on 15 August 1998 and Downholland Moss on 12 August 2003. The average last sighting is 24 August and the latest was at Formby on 26 September 1967.

SJW, RW.

This species account was sponsored by David. J. Pack and Mike Robinson.

CHIFFCHAFF

Phylloscopus collybita

Lancashire Category A.

Common breeder and passage migrant, fairly common winter visitor from continental Europe.

Chiffchaffs were rarely seen or heard in Mitchell's day and he had himself 'never come across it in 15 years of pretty close observation'. The only breeding sites he was able to publish were in the Hodder Valley, near Clitheroe and Burnley, at St. Michaels-on-Wyre, Leagram and Goosnargh. Oakes confirmed it as the rarest of our breeding leaf-warblers, describing it as locally numerous in Silverdale but very restricted in range elsewhere. He cited Wennington as the only known breeding site in the Lune Valley – although a survey in 1956 located 14 singing males there – and knew only of small numbers in the Ribble Valley east to Chipping and Leagram, around Formby and on the surrounding mosslands.

These descriptions of Lancashire status just 50-60 years ago seem scarcely credible today when Chiffchaffs are widespread in suitable habitat over most of the county. Although fluctuations in the national population, including marked troughs in 1976 and

1984 attributable to the Sahel drought, were doubtless reflected in Lancashire, there is no evidence of any large-scale, dramatic change in national distribution over the past 35 years. Chiffchaffs were found breeding in 41 Lancashire 10km squares during 1968-72, 35 in 1988-91 and 46 in 1997-2000. However, it seems likely that breeding numbers increased significantly in Lancashire during the 1960s and 1970s, leading to colonisation of many previously unoccupied sites. In east Lancashire, for example, Chiffchaffs were first recorded at Spring Wood and Stocks Reservoir in the late 1970s and have remained regular there ever since.

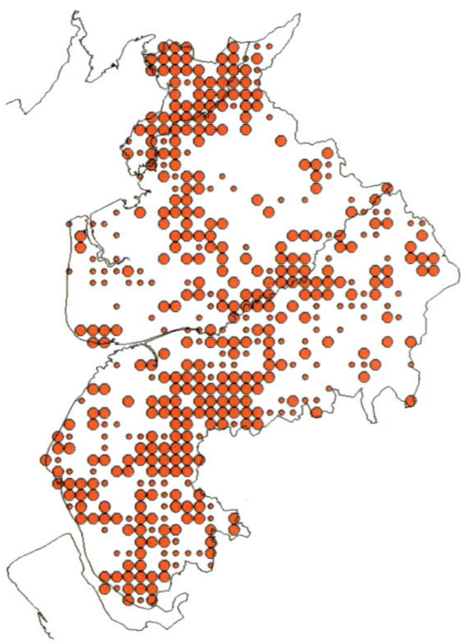

Breeding distribution of Chiffchaff, 1997-2000. (Large dots: confirmed Small dots: possible)

The breeding distribution overlaps almost entirely with that of the Willow Warbler, but Chiffchaffs are only about a quarter as numerous with an estimated population in 1997-2000 of 5,000 pairs. However, in some areas these proportions may be almost reversed, for example in south Liverpool in 2005 where 60 pairs of Chiffchaffs held territory on 30 sites compared with 26 pairs of Willow Warblers on twelve sites.

Anecdotal reports suggest that numbers have risen since the early 1990s but perhaps not as greatly as the 30% national increase reported by the BBS between 1994 and 2005. Birds were found in 474 tetrads during the Lancashire Atlas survey with breeding confirmed in 330 (36% of the county). Most were found in mature deciduous or mixed woodland and scrub with adequate, often thick, ground cover for nesting, but also in some urban parks, large suburban gardens and on farmland with copses or overgrown hedges. The largest breeding concentrations are found in north Lancashire, the middle reaches of the Ribble Valley, Chorley, eastern areas of West Lancashire and surrounding the Liverpool conurbation.

In north Lancashire Chiffchaffs are common in Silverdale and throughout most of the Keer and Lune Valleys and there is evidence of significant in-filling of the breeding range between the LDBWS (1986-91) and Lancashire Atlas (1997-2000) surveys. Breeding pairs are thinly distributed on the western fringes of Bowland between Lancaster and Preston and throughout the Ribble Valley, particularly in well-wooded areas between Preston and Ribchester, and in the Darwen Valley around Blackburn and Darwen. Seven pairs bred in the Roddlesworth Plantations in 2003. Small numbers are also present above Ribchester, in parts of the Hodder Valley and along the length of the Calder and its tributaries. Most records from Rossendale, where Chiffchaffs used to be decidedly scarce but appear to be increasing, are from the Stubbins area and Crawshawbooth.

Another almost solid breeding area exists between Chorley and Skelmersdale, east towards Ormskirk, but birds are more scattered in most of West Lancashire and the north Merseyside mosslands where woodland is sparser. Old country house parklands in Little Crosby, Ince Blundell and particularly Croxteth and Knowsley all support moderate populations and breeding is regular at many sites in south Liverpool.

Two areas stand out where Chiffchaffs remain thin on the ground: the high ground of Bowland and much of east Lancashire and Rossendale; and the western half of the Fylde, where breeding was confirmed in just nine tetrads in 1997-2000, mostly in the Lytham area.

Over-wintering has been reported increasingly throughout the county since the late 1950s. Most reports refer to singles but a remarkable series of records came from the Sefton Coast in recent years, including at least three at Hesketh Golf Course in December 1995, 20 or so in the Formby area at both ends of 2000 with perhaps as many as 40 there in early 2001 and up to six regularly in the Birkdale dunes this century. Prior to this, county totals were about 10-20 each winter, many of which were in gardens and parks. As with Blackcaps, wintering birds are undoubtedly significantly under-reported and the average Lancashire total is perhaps 50 or more.

A fairly high proportion of winter records have been reported as showing characteristics of the Fennoscandian sub-species *abietinus* but the majority appear to be nominate *collybita*. This fits well with the national pattern but there have been no recoveries of British birds ringed as pulli so exact origins are not known, although it is likely that most wintering *collybita* are of continental origin (Migration Atlas). There are two winter recoveries of ringed birds in Lancashire: a male recovered at Formby in January 1996 had been ringed at Birkdale on 11 June 1994 and was perhaps a very late migrant headed further north but may have been a local breeder; while a juvenile found dead in Barnoldswick in January 1997 had been ringed in Belgium on 6 September 1996 and may either have been a western European *collybita* or have come from further east.

Records of singing males in late February and early March may relate to wintering birds and the onset of spring passage is hard to determine but probably occurs in mid-March – the average first date at Leighton Moss during 1976-95 was 17 March. Most spring birds are seen in breeding habitat, making it difficult to judge either the size or timing of through-passage, but the main movement on the coast runs from late March and throughout April, with occasional birds until late May. Single-figure day-counts are the norm and 14 a short way inland from Formby on 30 March 1958 were exceptional. Spring totals during the 1990s averaged about 40 at Heysham and 30 at Marshside.

Wintering Chiffchaff, Crosby Marine Park, December 2005. (Steve Young)

Some local dispersal occurs during June to mid-July, for example a juvenile ringed on 8 June 2000 at Formby and trapped in the Rimrose Valley three weeks later, but migration proper usually gets underway in mid- to late August and is usually at its height during September. Average ringing totals at Heysham during 1999-2005 were three in August, 18 in September and seven in October. Birds continue to move through during October and into November when they merge with arriving winterers. Large day-counts are exceptional, the largest in recent years being 15 at Heysham on 22 September 1994 and ten at Marshside on 26 September 1999, but an unprecedented fall of around 250 *Phylloscopus* warblers on Parbold Hill in misty conditions on 25 August 2001 included many Chiffchaffs. Autumn totals are about twice as high as in spring at Heysham, but, surprisingly, somewhat lower at Marshside.

Ringing recoveries shed little if any light on the origins of Lancashire's autumn migrants but from mid-October the number of birds reported as showing characteristics of *abietinus* increases significantly. One ringed in Orkney on 29 October 1990 and trapped at Heysham on 25 November was most probably Scandinavian. An exceptional number of such birds were reported at Heysham in 1993, including five on 13 November. It is likely that a large proportion of late autumn migrants are Scandinavian *abietinus* together with western and central European *collybita*. Although several *tristis* have been reported, none has been fully documented and, in the light of current knowledge (Dean & Svensson 2005), there is no evidence that this race has ever been recorded in Lancashire.

Within-autumn recoveries of birds ringed in Lancashire include two in southern England and one in south Wales, while one ringed on Guernsey in April 1997 was controlled at Heysham on 22 October that year. Our only foreign recoveries were one ringed at Forton on 20 July 1991 and controlled in Senegal in January 1992, and another ringed at Heysham in August 2003 and controlled at Leighton Moss in July 2004 and again in Morocco in November 2004.

SJW, RW.

This species account was sponsored by R. Wilson.

[IBERIAN CHIFFCHAFF]

Phylloscopus ibericus

Meticulous notes were taken by Henry Finch of a bird singing for half an hour in Abercromby Square in central Liverpool on 29 April 1992. Two song types were noted. The predominant one was rendered as 'da da da da weet weet weet weet ter ter ter ter ter ter' with the last phrases described as a rapid trill, and the other as 'weet weet weet weet deda deda deda'. These bore close resemblance to tapes of Iberian Chiffchaff and the record was originally published as such in the Lancashire Report. However, when Iberian Chiffchaff was given full species status the BBRC required that the bird be seen as well as heard. Unfortunately, although a small passerine was seen where the song was coming from, this was not definitely the singer.

A second candidate was found by Ed Smith in Skelmersdale on 19 April 2004 where it remained until 2 May. Although the opening phrases of its song resembled that of Common Chiffchaff, it ended with a rapid trill during which the whole bird quivered like a Wood Warbler. Some plumage and structural features, especially the bright green/yellow rump and undertail, also marked it out as very unusual, but it was its positive response to tapes of Iberian Chiffchaff song (and indifference to that of 'Common'), that convinced most of its several hundred observers that it was Iberian. However, when sonograms of the song were examined it was found to be composed entirely of Common Chiffchaff notes, although the structure was quite different (White 2005).

The Skelmersdale chiffchaff, April 2004. (Steve Young)

SJW.

WILLOW WARBLER

Phylloscopus trochilus

Lancashire Category A.

Abundant breeder and passage migrant.

'Abundant everywhere' was Mitchell's description, a view only slightly qualified by Oakes's 'abundant . . . breeding almost everywhere in the lowlands from the sand dunes and salt marshes of the coast to the fringe of the moors . . . [to] just over 1000ft (300m)'.

Not much of these accounts needs to be amended with respect to the present breeding distribution. Willow Warblers were recorded in 808 tetrads during the 1997-2000 survey with breeding confirmed in 740 (80% of the county). They were absent only from the most heavily urbanised areas of Liverpool, the south Fylde coast, Preston and some east Lancashire towns, from the south Ribble saltmarshes and the very highest ground in north-east Bowland and the south Pennines. Willow Warblers are found almost anywhere where there are trees with some understorey, at sea level in the Formby pine woods and as high as the upper parts of tree-lined cloughs on the moorland edge, but, unlike Chiffchaffs, they prefer young woodland, scrub and mossland with birch, willow or alder.

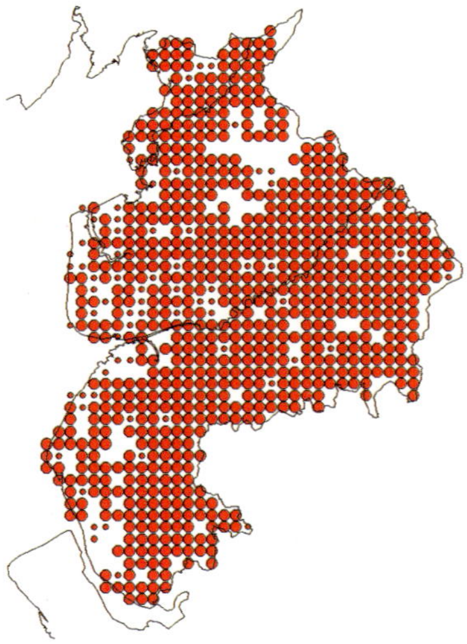

Breeding distribution of Willow Warbler, 1997-2000. (Large dots: confirmed. Small dots: possible)

The 1997-2000 Lancashire population was estimated at 20,000 pairs but this was calculated solely as a proportion of the British population. National CBC data showed numbers remaining fairly constant until a sharp decline at the end of the 1980s was followed by a partial recovery. Current estimates are that the British population has been relatively stable during 1994-2005 (BBS).

Information on population trends in Lancashire is restricted to a handful of well-monitored sites, mostly in the north, and anecdotal impressions from observers elsewhere. The Leighton Moss population fell by a third from an average of 76 pairs to 50 between 1985-89 and 1991-95 with a peak of 82 in 1989 and a low of 43 in 1991. Nearby Warton Crag showed a similar, perhaps larger, decline during a similar period from 54 pairs in 1989 to 26 to 34 pairs during 2000-05; a total of 86 pairs bred on the RSPB Silverdale reserves in 1999. Also in the north, breeding pairs on the Mount Vernon CBC plot fell from 26 in 1984 to 19 in 1989. Although these declines have been brought about to some extent by changes in habitat management, they do suggest significant losses in the north.

Elsewhere in the county judgements on population trends rely upon fragments of hard information. The Roddlesworth Plantations population, for example, fell from 66 singing males in 1990 to 46 in 1995, while at nearby Sunnyhurst Wood numbers declined from 30 to 18 males in the same period. Most regional reports have highlighted continuing declines during the 1990s but none have been quantified and there has been a recent suggestion that losses in the western and southern lowlands may be to some extent balanced by gains in east Lancashire. The main support for this comes from the Stocks Reservoir/Gisburn Forest area where breeding pairs are reported to have increased significantly during the 1990s. Sample counts include 70 singing males in one part of the site on 5 June 1999 and 22 along a 2km transect in 2003. Numbers were also reported to be increasing in Rossendale during the early years of this century.

Willow Warblers arrive in the county some two or three weeks after Chiffchaffs with an average first date during the past quarter century of 31 March. First arrivals come a little later in the north (on average on 9 April at Leighton Moss during 1976-95) and in the east (12 April in the Burnley area: Spencer 1977). Our earliest was one at St. Anne's Cemetery on 19 March 1990. The main movement is, however, rarely underway before mid-April and continues until mid-May, although ringing totals at Heysham during 1999-2005 suggest that numbers passing through in April outnumber May birds by more than three to one. Coastal records vary hugely between springs, falls being largely dependent upon weather conditions. The largest day-count by far was of 300-500 at Heysham on 11 May 1993 when a more moderate 35 were at Marshside. Other big Heysham counts include 100 on 29 April 1995 and on 17 & 21 April 1996. Marshside spring totals have averaged about 100-150 since the early 1990s but 345 were seen in 1998; the largest day-count there was 66 on 12 April 1993.

Willow Warbler, Seaforth Nature Reserve, April 2002. (Steve Young)

Juveniles begin their southerly migration in the second half of July with adults following a fortnight or so later, having completed their post-breeding moult (Migration Atlas). The main coastal passage takes place during August; ringing totals (1999-2005) indicate that roughly equal numbers pass through Heysham during July and September, with more than twice that number in August. Autumn totals at both Heysham and Marshside tend to be lower than in spring. The largest day-counts at Heysham include 75 on 3 August 1982 and 200 on 22 August 1984 with 350 the following day, but numbers have never approached these levels since. Marshside's best autumn total was 214 in 1996, which included its highest autumn count of 32 on 11 August; further south, the highest count at Seaforth was 30+ on 2 August 1998. Single-figure counts are recorded regularly at a wide range of inland sites but only two large falls have ever been recorded: 'several hundred' at Longworth Clough on 21 August 1991, and 250 *Phylloscopus* warblers, mostly Willow Warblers, on Parbold Hill on 25 August 2001, when 40 were also at Heysham. Numbers reduce considerably towards the end of September but there are October records in most years and the average last sighting over the past 25 years came on 13 October. Later records include singles at Marton Mere on 30 October to 2 November 1966, Astley Park, Chorley on 9 November 1990 and, our latest, at White Moss on 18 November 1989.

The vast majority of migrants are undoubtedly nominate *trochilus*, probably overwhelmingly from Britain but with some from southern Scandinavia or western Europe. A number of records of birds showing characteristics of the sub-species *acredula* which breeds in northern Sweden, Norway, Finland and Russia have been reported, however. Oakes published the first, a male 'obtained' near Burnley on 26 April 1947, subsequently held in York Museum. Another was claimed with Redwings in Rossendale on 22 October 1988, but most have been seen or trapped at Heysham, including six ringed there on 19 September 1992. However, the key differences in colouration and wing length between the two sub-species are subtle and clinal (Svensson 1992) and, although it is highly likely that birds from within the range of *acredula* have occurred, there is no ringing evidence fully to substantiate this; two ringed on passage in Shetland and controlled in Lancashire may be the best candidates.

There have been a number of exchanges of ringed birds between Lancashire and areas to the north – 32 with northern England (mainly Cumbria) and 13 with Scotland, including one ringed at Heysham on 7 May 1989 and found dead in Highland Region five days later, and one ringed in Lothian in August 1997 and controlled at Heysham on 26 April 2001. A male ringed at Heysham on 26 April 2001 and controlled on Orkney on 12 May that year may have been breeding there but was perhaps on its way to Scandinavia.

The 28 exchanges of ringed birds between Lancashire and southern England have almost all been both ringed and recovered on passage, with roughly equal numbers in spring and autumn in both areas. There are no records of Lancashire birds in the sub-Saharan wintering grounds but two have been recorded on passage in the Channel Islands, one in France, one in Spain and two in Morocco.

SJW, RW.

This species account was sponsored by David J. Pack.

GOLDCREST

Regulus regulus

Lancashire Category A.

Common resident breeder and winter visitor from continental Europe.

The Goldcrest is best known to most Lancashire birders as a passage migrant and winter visitor but it appears always to have also been a fairly common breeder. Mitchell gave the impression that nesting probably occurred wherever there was 'spruce-fir'. He named only a handful of sites in present-day Lancashire: 'Chipping and all down the Hodder', Longridge Fell, 'wooded districts bordering the Fylde' and areas 'near Accrington and Blackburn'.

Like Mitchell, Oakes noted the heavy impact of severe winters on breeding numbers, singling out 1916/17, 1939-42 and 1946/47. He described a much larger breeding range in the middle years of the twentieth century, encompassing the Lune Valley, Silverdale, Cabus and Barnacre to the east of Garstang, the Ribble Valley and north-east Lancashire, where he gave Haighton, Chipping, Hurst Green, Stonyhurst, Mytton, Downham, Huntroyde, Ogden Clough and Towneley as breeding localities. Breeding was much scarcer south of the Ribble and the only sites he could name were Scarisbrick, Formby Hall and the Formby/Ainsdale pine woods, although a reference to Horwich (now in Greater Manchester) probably referred to the Rivington area. He knew of no breeding records in the Fylde.

Goldcrest, Seaforth Nature Reserve, May 2004. (Steve Young)

The Lancashire Atlas survey of 1997-2000 did little to alter this view of the overall range of the Goldcrest but fleshed out the detailed distribution, surprising many observers as to just how widespread breeding is. Birds were found in the breeding season in 401 tetrads (43% of the county). The county population, which was thought to be at a high level during the survey years, was estimated at 5,000 pairs. They occur primarily in large conifer plantations or mixed woodland, nesting in a variety of tree species, mainly spruce but including pine, larch, yew and ornamentals, habitats which are mainly found in the Lune Valley, Silverdale,

Bowland, Bleasdale, Rossendale, the West Pennine Moors, the Sefton Coast dunes and Knowsley Park and surrounding areas of St. Helens. However, even rather sparse areas of woodland such as occurs in Liverpool's Victorian urban parks can hold a pair or two, and breeding was confirmed in suburban gardens in Southport during the survey. Although numbers are low in such marginal habitats, Goldcrests are absent only from areas of treeless moorland and farmland. They remain extremely scarce in the Fylde, where they were found in only nine tetrads in 1997-2000.

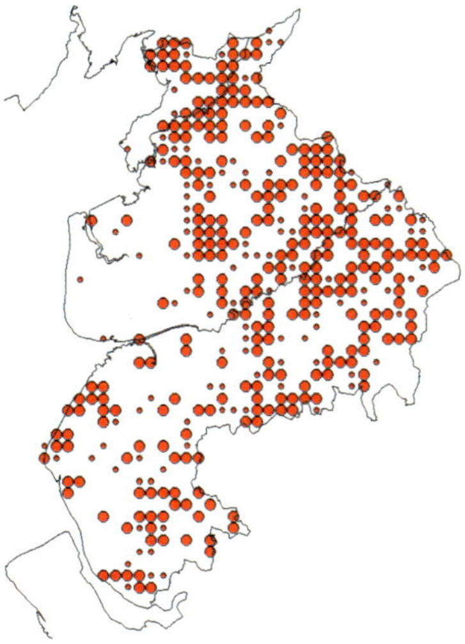

Breeding distribution of Goldcrest, 1997-2000. (Large dots: confirmed. Small dots: possible)

There have been several hard winters since Oakes's book, notably 1962/63, 1978/79 and 1985/86, all of which undoubtedly checked the breeding population. Hard evidence of the size of this impact is limited but figures from Williamson Park in Lancaster give an illustration: five breeding pairs in 1978 were reduced to none in 1979, while the population fell by 75% between 1985 and 1986 but had recovered fully within two years. Another cold spell in 1990/91 led to low breeding numbers at several sites including Leighton Moss and Mere Sands Wood and the total loss of eleven pairs at Sunnyhurst Wood in Darwen. An unbroken succession of mild winters has followed since then, and it is likely that the high populations found during 1997-2000 have further expanded, perhaps in line with the 71% national increase reported by the BBS between 1994 and 2005.

Some local movement may be detected in July but autumn passage more generally begins in late August, with the main movement between mid-September and the end of October, tailing off by mid-November. Large build-ups have taken place at several inland sites, for example 100+ in the Roddlesworth Plantations on 18 September 1990 and 1 November 1992, 75 at Winmarleigh Hall on 5 September 1993, 80 at Dean Clough on 14 October 1997 and 'very large numbers' in misty conditions on Parbold Hill on 25 August 2001. Numbers vary considerably depending on the severity of the previous winter and the year's breeding success (Figure 1). The largest autumn totals in recent years at Heysham and Marshside, the two best-monitored coastal sites, have been 600 in 1997 and 275 in 1995 respectively.

Ringing studies at Heysham in recent years indicate that on average roughly equal numbers pass through in September and October. The largest coastal falls include 80 in the Formby/Ainsdale pinewoods on 21 October 1956, 75 at Fluke Hall on 18 October 1982, 100 at Lytham Hall during October 1988, 200 at Heysham

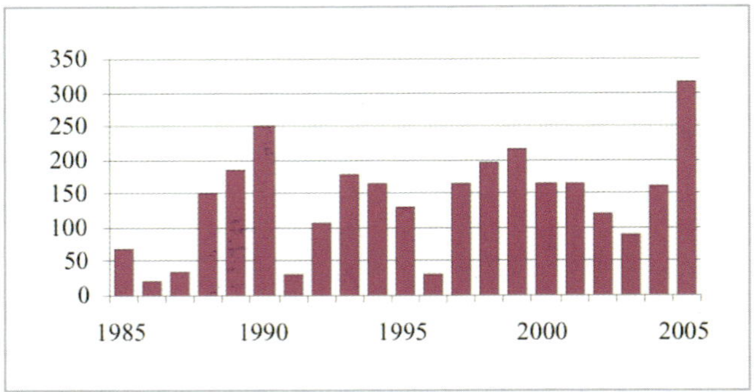

Figure 1. Annual ringing totals of Goldcrests at Heysham Nature Reserve, 1985-2005.

on 15 September 1989 and 100 there on 25 September 1997, 150 at Jenny Brown's Point on 29 October 1995 and 63 at Marshside on 5 October 1997.

It is likely that most early birds are of British origin but ringing evidence is restricted to a few late summer and early autumn movements of birds from Cumbria and the Calf of Man, where the main passage is thought to consist of northern British birds (Thorpe & Sapsford 1992). It has long been assumed that a large proportion of migrants from late September onwards are of continental origin but the evidence for this is also largely circumstantial, based mainly on the arrival of significant numbers in Lancashire some days after large falls of migrants on the east coast, and supported by just two recoveries – one ringed in Norway on 3 October 1989 and controlled in Liverpool on 5 November 1989, and another ringed in Latvia on 21 September 1998 and found dead at Lytham on 6 October that year.

We have little idea of how many coastal migrants move further south or of their ultimate destinations. Although there have been eleven movements of ringed birds between Lancashire and southern England, only three have definitely been wintering in the south. One ringed at Heysham on 18 October 1997 and controlled on Anglesey the following day illustrates the speed of movement. Although the majority of ringing recoveries conform to the expected north-south or east-west autumn migratory direction, some of Lancashire's Goldcrests exhibit a strange propensity to move in the 'wrong' direction. A juvenile ringed in Preston on 7 October 1990 and found in the Netherlands on 15 November that year may have been either a British bird wintering abroad or a re-orientating Scandinavian one, while one that moved from Heysham on 27 September 1997 to Spurn on 15 October that year defies easy explanation. But the strangest of all was one ringed, presumably on spring passage, in Denmark on 9 April 2001 and trapped at Heysham on 2 May the same year.

Goldcrests disperse widely in winter, frequenting deciduous woodland, hedgerows and suburban gardens, often in the company of mixed tit flocks. Numbers often remain fairly high in nesting areas, including coniferous plantations in the east and north-east, though it is not certain how many of these are resident. Some ringed in the autumn do stay for the winter, for example one ringed at Pilling on 3 October 1992 and retrapped there on 27 February 1993. Most winter records are of low single figures but larger concentrations do occur in some winters. Leighton Moss, for example, held around ten during most winters during the 1990s but 40 were there at the end of 1999. Other larger counts include 70 in willow beds near Rivington on 31 January 1991, 45 at Mere Sands Wood on 29 January 1991, 50 at Wayoh Reservoir on 18 December 1993, 70 in the Southport area on 24 December 1995 and 25 in the Delph plantations on 3 January 2000.

Some return movement may begin in late February but the main spring passage takes place in March and early April with a few stragglers during May. The total passage through coastal watchpoints, although generally smaller than in autumn, is amongst the largest of our warblers. Notable totals include 200 through Heysham between 13 March and 9 April 1995, even larger numbers there between 14 March and 3 April 2005 when 208 were ringed and 190 through Marshside in spring 1999; large falls include 100 at Heysham on 28 March and 3 April 1988 with 150 there on 29 March 1998. Day-counts on the Sefton and Fylde coasts, however, rarely exceed 20 or so.

SJW, RW.
This species account was sponsored by
Ian and Diana Wrapson.

FIRECREST

Regulus ignicapillus

Lancashire Category A. (1, 142).

Scarce winter visitor from western or central Europe.

Oakes regarded the claim that a pair had bred near Lancaster in 1927 as unproven and he himself found our first record, a male in the Cliviger Gorge, Burnley on 9 September 1943. This was followed by one in a St. Anne's garden on 2 November 1957 – following a Yellow-browed Warbler there on 21 October! – and a further five singles during the 1960s.

Male Firecrest, Seaforth Nature Reserve, March 2006. (Steve Young)

The number of records rose gradually during the 1970s and 1980s (Figure 1) and Firecrests have been reported annually since 1980, with a total of 135 between 1971 and 2005. The largest annual totals were nine in 1990, eleven in 1998 and twelve in 2003; an average of six have been seen annually over the past ten years compared to just over two a year during the 1970s and 1980s. It is impossible to judge whether this reflects a genuine increase in occurrences or simply more and better-equipped observers. Firecrests can be extremely unobtrusive, particularly in winter, and many must be missed even at well-watched sites – about a quarter of all post-1970 records have been caught by ringers.

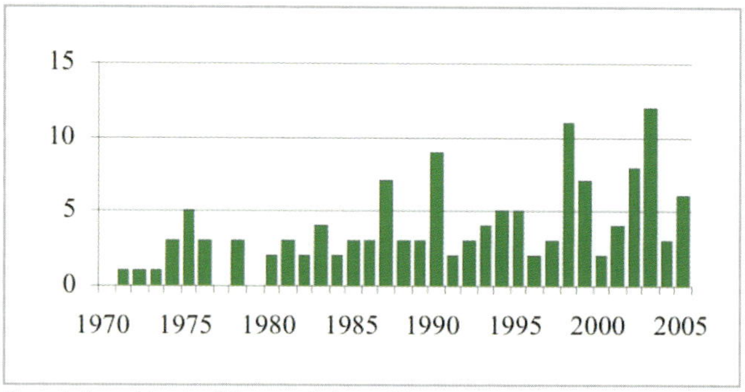

Figure 1. Annual totals of Firecrests in Lancashire, 1970-2005.

Most records are of one or two birds but there were up to three at Silverdale in winter 1974/75, three at Formby on 14-16 March 1978, at least three in the Heysham area in September-October 1990, and six were trapped at two adjacent sites in Formby in December 1998.

The earliest autumn bird was one at Jenny Brown's Point on 7 September 1999 but arrivals show a clear peak in October and especially in November (Figure 2), several weeks later than in Britain as a whole (Migration Atlas) and perhaps indicating that birds make their way gradually across the country from southern and eastern coasts. They are thus one of our latest winter visitors and birds continue to be found during December and January. Although there are a number of records of birds remaining throughout the winter, for example twos at Marton Mere in 1998/99 and 2002/03, and at Martin Mere in 2002/03, most records are of much shorter duration.

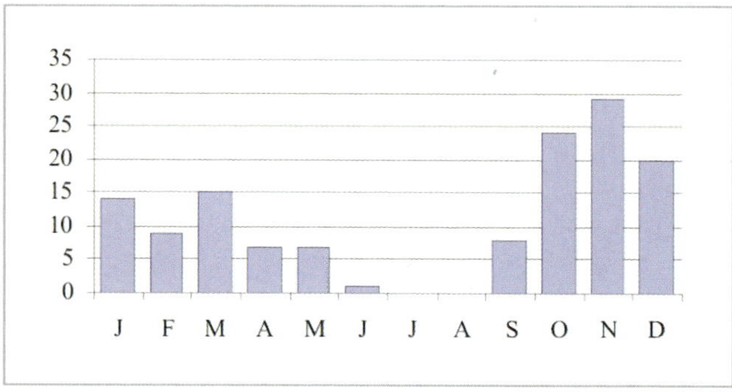

Figure 2. Monthly totals of Firecrests in Lancashire, 1953-2005.

A smaller second peak of new arrivals in March signals the start of a barely perceptible spring passage which extends into May, with the latest on 26-27 May 1995 at Seaforth. Our only summer record was a male trapped at Freshfield Dune Heath on 17 June 1990. This bird had a fully-developed brood-patch and was almost certainly breeding in the locality; it was thought likely that it may have been displaced by the felling of pines at nearby Formby Hall, a site where many Firecrests have been trapped over the years.

Two-thirds of all records have been at coastal or near-coastal sites – notably at Heysham and Formby. The eleven records in east Lancashire include one singing at Crawshawbooth on 1-2 May 1990 and two singing at Folly Clough on 16 April 1995.

There is just one ringing recovery: a female trapped at Portland Observatory on 12 April 2004 and found freshly dead in Maghull on 31 December 2004.

SJW, RW.

This species account was sponsored by In Focus.

SPOTTED FLYCATCHER

Muscicapa striata

Lancashire Category A.

Fairly common breeder and passage migrant.

Spotted Flycatchers are among the latest summer visitors to arrive on European breeding-grounds and among the first to leave in autumn. The first spring migrants are occasionally recorded in Lancashire in the last week of April and the earliest to date was at Lumb Vale, Rossendale on 17 April 1979. The average first sighting during the past 25 years has been on 1 May and peak passage normally occurs around the middle of the month. Coastal migration usually occurs later with, for example, an average first date of 15 May at Heysham during 1988-99, suggesting perhaps that these passage birds may be heading further north while Lancashire birds return directly to their breeding grounds. A few stragglers are still on the move at coastal watchpoints in early June. Most records involve one or very few birds, but larger counts include seven at Heysham on 1 June 1985 and eleven there as recently as 28 May 1998. A widespread influx on 11 May 1993 brought six to Marton Mere, 22 to the Fleetwood area and at least a dozen to Marshside, and an unusually heavy passage continued intermittently until the end of the month. Occasional influxes aside, there is clear evidence of a steady decline in passage numbers at most coastal sites since the mid-1990s.

Mitchell described the Spotted Flycatcher as a common breeder throughout Lancashire and even abundant in particularly suitable areas; birds were seldom seen before mid-May or after the end of August. The species' status had changed little by Oakes's time, when it was well-distributed and fairly common, especially in the Silverdale area, north Fylde, the Ribble Valley and at Formby, Aughton, and Knowsley in the south-west. He recorded breeding in urban parks in Liverpool, Preston, Blackburn, Burnley and Lancaster.

The decline had not yet begun when Spencer (1973) described the Spotted Flycatcher as widespread and numerous; in 1964-65 a pair bred in Winckley Square in the centre of Preston, and nesting was recorded there in Avenham Park as recently as 1983. Also in that year, however, a decline in numbers was noted in the Penwortham area and such reports recurred with increasing frequency between 1985 and 1995. In 1988 decreases in breeding numbers were reported from Leighton Moss, Roddlesworth Plantations and Sunnyhurst Woods, Darwen; during this period, however, some local recoveries were also observed. The population at Roddlesworth, for example, increased from nine pairs in 1989 to 13 in 1990, and the species was described as 'abundant' at Marshaw, Bowland in 1993. By the mid-1990s, however, local observers and regional reports were recording significant falls in numbers both of breeding pairs and of birds on migration. Continuing declines were reported from Rossendale and the Darwen area in 1995, and only three pairs nested at Roddlesworth Plantations in 2003.

Spotted Flycatcher, New Laithe Farm, Newton-in-Bowland. (Phillip Tomkinson)

Populations over much of western and central Europe have declined dramatically since the 1970s (Tucker & Heath 1994); in Britain this has amounted to a collapse, with a decrease of 85% between 1966 and 1999 (CBC) and a further 26% between 1994 and 2005 (BBS). Breeding success remains relatively unchanged and it is thought that the causes of the decline are likely to lie in the wintering grounds or passage areas, or perhaps with post-breeding food shortages on the breeding grounds (Fuller *et al.* 2005).

Although the species requires perches from which it makes sallies after insect prey it is otherwise versatile in its choice of nesting-habitat, from woodland clearings, glades and edges to parkland, gardens, farmyards and other man-made environments. Spotted Flycatchers are relatively tolerant of human proximity and will readily nest against the walls of houses and farm buildings where trellises or climbing plants are provided. All such habitats are widespread in Lancashire and the evident very large decline in numbers had not yet resulted in an equivalent reduction in breeding range by the time of the Lancashire Atlas. Breeding was confirmed in 48 10km squares in 1968-72, 41 in 1988-91 and 38 in 1997-2000, when the population was estimated at 600 pairs and birds were present in 275 tetrads (30% of the county).

By the end of the twentieth century Spotted Flycatchers had effectively disappeared from the coastal areas of the south-west and Fylde, and elsewhere breeding pairs were very thinly spread, with the largest concentrations in the north and east, along the valleys of the Lune, Wyre, Ribble and Hodder. Since 2000 the breeding situation in much of Lancashire has deteriorated further; in Rossendale, for example, a total of eight pairs in 1999 and 2000 fell to three in 2001 and one in 2002, when not a single breeding pair was reported from the south-west. One possible pair in St. Helens during 2003-05 was the only evidence of breeding in North Merseyside.

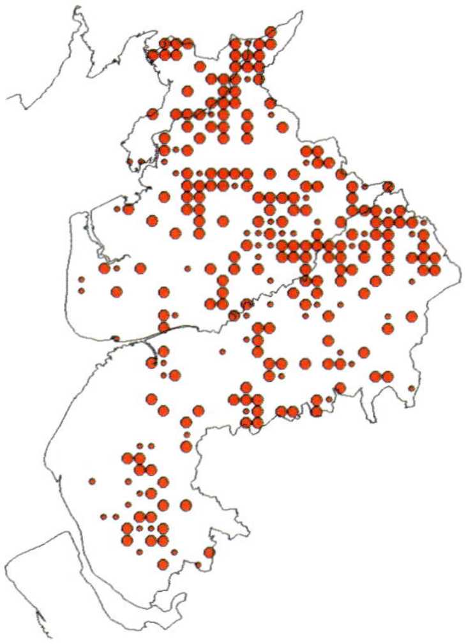

Breeding distribution of Spotted Flycatcher, 1997-2000. (Large dots: confirmed. Small dots: possible)

The Lancashire Atlas map may no longer represent the current situation at all closely, and it seems clear that the once-common Spotted Flycatcher is in a very perilous state as a Lancashire breeding species with its population perhaps declining by more than 50% since the atlas survey.

Autumn movements may begin in late July, but most migrants are recorded between mid-August and mid-September; the average last date is 4 October but very few are normally seen in that month. Nothing in recent decades has come close to the 60 birds recorded by Oakes at Towneley, Burnley on 16 August 1933 or even the 20-30 there on 1 August 1939. Migrants are recorded very widely, at both inland and coastal locations, and peak counts more recently have included nine at Fluke Hall, Pilling on 23 September 1980, eight at Rowley Lake, Burnley on 28 August 1988 and 15 at Heysham on 19 September 1992 and at Beacon Fell on 4 September 2002. There has been a general decrease in numbers recorded at Heysham NR since the mid-1990s, but autumn 2002 was described as the worst to date, and only one bird was seen there in 2003 with two in 2004. The latest inland migrant was at Folly Tip, Rossendale on 7 November 1996, and there have been two November records on the coast: on the 15th at Formby in 1959 and the 1st at Heysham Moss in 1986. Given their early departure from the breeding grounds it is likely that at least some late migrants are of continental origin.

There has been only one recovery of a Spotted Flycatcher from Lancashire, a juvenile ringed at Hightown on 21 August 1976 and found dead in Belfast on 23 June 1979.

BM, RW.

This species account was sponsored by Marie and Peter Rathbone.

RED-BREASTED FLYCATCHER

Ficedula parva

Lancashire Category A. (1, 8).

Vagrant from central or eastern Europe.

Clifford Oakes found the county's first in a woodland clearing at Mitton Hall, north-west of Whalley, on 4 October 1945. The bird was observed sufficiently well to identify it as an adult male. Autumn adults remain relatively scarce in Britain and all subsequent Lancashire records have been first-winters.

The first of these was seen at Formby Point on 31 October 1952 but six of the other seven were found in the Fylde, including a notable series of five in Blackpool. The Blackpool birds spanned nearly a quarter of a century but remarkably all but one were found by the same observer, Ed Stirling, beginning with one in his own back garden (which contains a single sycamore!) in the evening of 26 October 1978. This was followed by another in a garden at Layton on 23-24 October 1983, then singles in Watson Road Park on 2-4 October 1984, in bushes alongside the railway behind Blackpool Pleasure Beach on 31 October 1984 and, finally, at the same site on 2 October 2001.

Red-breasted Flycatcher, Fluke Hall, 12 October 1996. (Barry Dyson)

The two other records came from Formby Point on 14 October 1990 and Fluke Hall, Pilling on 12 October 1996 – perhaps oddly, the latter is the only Lancashire bird to have been trapped and ringed.

The peak autumn arrival period of Red-breasted Flycatchers in Britain is from late September to mid-October but the average date for Lancashire birds is a little later than this, perhaps suggesting cross-country movement after landfall and a short stay on the east coast.

All records:

1945	Mitton Hall, adult male, 4 October
1952	Formby Point, first-winter, 31 October
1978	Blackpool, first-winter, 26 October
1983	Layton, Blackpool, first-winter, 23 to 24 October
1984	Watson Rd. Blackpool, first-winter, 2 to 4 October
1984	Blackpool South Shore, first- winter, 31 October
1990	Formby Point, first-winter, 14 October
1996	Fluke Hall Pilling, first-winter, 12 October
2001	Blackpool, first-winter, 2 October

SJW, MJ.

This species account was sponsored by N.J. Donnithorne.

PIED FLYCATCHER

Ficedula hypoleuca

Lancashire Category A.

Uncommon breeder and passage migrant.

Populations of Pied Flycatchers over most of Europe appear to be stable (Hagemeijer & Blair 1997) but the long-term trend in Britain is less clear. Following an increase from the 1950s, much of which was attributed to the widespread use of nest-boxes, the 1988-91 New Atlas estimated a total British population of 35,000-40,000 pairs, heavily concentrated in the wooded upland valleys of Wales and northern England; more recently, however, a 30% decrease in numbers was detected between 1994 and 2005 (BBS).

In Mitchell's day Pied Flycatchers appear to have been very local breeders in Lancashire, having declined in numbers since mid-century. He mentioned the Gisburn Forest and the Burnley and Preston areas as former breeding localities, but could cite only three instances of nesting since 1870 – at Whalley, Clitheroe and Rufford. Oakes could find no breeding records between one at Halton-on-Lune in 1895 and three to the east of Preston, at Hoghton, Riley Green and Red Scar, during 1939-46.

Since 1960, however, the population has grown quite spectacularly, encouraged by the introduction of nest-box schemes in suitable wooded habitats in several regions of the county. These have contributed hugely to a range expansion in Lancashire from six 10km squares in 1968-72 to 15 in 1988-91 and 17 in 1997-2000, when the population was estimated at 100 pairs, confined entirely to upland woods in the north, east and centre, usually along river valleys and stream-beds.

Breeding distribution of Pied Flycatcher, 1997-2000. (Large dots: confirmed. Small dots: possible)

In the north the first boxes were erected in Roeburndale, in the upper Lune Valley, in 1966, and further schemes were later initiated at Claughton and Arkholme. Six pairs bred in north Lancashire between the Wyre and the Lune in 1968, increasing to 29 by 1985, 44 in 1988 and at least 60 in 1990; there has been a slight decrease since then, but some breeding pairs have taken to natural nest-sites.

In east and central Lancashire successful nest-box programmes have produced small but apparently healthy populations in the Hodder Valley at Whitewell since 1977, at Moor Piece, Calder Vale, the Brock Valley – where breeding was first recorded in a natural hole in 1954 – and more recently on the United Utilities Bowland estate. Eleven pairs bred at Whitewell in 1991, eight in the Brock Valley in 1999 and up to five pairs annually at Moor Piece during 2000-03 and 18 pairs in 2005. Breeding was first recorded in Rossendale, at Baxenden, in 1978, where two pairs bred in 1984 and six in 1991, and intermittent nesting has continued at Grane, Crawshawbooth, Stubbins and in the Limy Valley.

There has also been some success with nest-boxes in the West Pennine Moors, particularly in the Rivington/Anglezarke area where schemes were initiated in 1983, following breeding on two occasions in a natural site at Rivington in the 1970s. Two pairs bred in 1984, nine in 1992 and twelve pairs raised young at six sites in 1997, but numbers declined to four successful pairs in 2004. In the Roddlesworth Plantations, breeding in boxes began in 1974 when two pairs nested, peaking at six in 1991 and 1992 before declining to one in 1998 with no confirmed breeding since. Up to four pairs bred in nest-boxes at three sites around Belmont from 1993 to 1995 but only a single pair intermittently since, as has the occasional pair in nest-boxes at Turton Bottoms.

Pied Flycatcher, New Laithe Farm, Newton-in-Bowland. (Phillip Tomkinson)

The only record of nesting on the Fylde was in a box at Salwick in 1994 and, apart from the instance at Rufford mentioned by Mitchell, nesting has never been recorded in the south-west, although a male held territory at Mere Sands Wood for over a week in spring 1995.

As in Oakes's time, spring migrants begin to arrive in mid-April – on average on the 17th during the past 25 years – although the main passage does not normally begin until the last week of the month; it peaks in the first half of May and movements have usually ceased well before the beginning of June. The earliest arrival was one at Leighton Moss on 12 April 1994, but early birds are just as likely to be observed at inland breeding-locations as at coastal watchpoints.

Autumn movements begin in the middle of July, but most birds are recorded between mid-August and mid-September with the average last sighting in the past 25 years on 23 September. There are October records about every other year, but very few have been seen after mid-month. In contrast with spring, relatively few autumn migrants are recorded inland; coastal or near-coastal hot-spots include Heysham, Watson Road Park in Blackpool – due in part no doubt to daily observer coverage – and, more recently, Fazakerley woods in north Liverpool. The latest inland migrant was at Sabden on 17 October 1953, and the county's latest ever in Watson Road Park on 1-3 November 2001.

The fact that the overwhelming majority of Lancashire's breeding Pied Flycatchers utilise monitored nest-boxes has produced a wealth of ringing data over the last 40 years. Young birds, particularly females, show little fidelity to natal areas in subsequent years, exemplified by pulli controlled later while nesting in Scotland, Cumbria, County Durham, Northumberland, North Yorkshire, Shropshire and Dyfed. The most remarkable movement was by a male, ringed in the nest at Wray in the Lune Valley on 9 June 1990 and found nesting at Lingen in north-west Germany on 28 June 1991, but other first-summer birds have been recovered in the breeding season in the Netherlands, Belgium and Denmark. Recoveries have also shown, however, that birds ringed as adults are highly likely to return to Lancashire breeding-sites in subsequent years. Lancashire-ringed juvenile Pied Flycatchers have been recovered on autumn passage in north-west Spain (two), Portugal and south-west France and in the following spring in Italy. There have been 20 recoveries here of birds ringed elsewhere in Britain, 15 from northern England, four from Wales and one from Scotland.

BM, RW.

This species account was sponsored by Marie and Peter Rathbone and in memory of Keith Woods.

BEARDED TIT

Panurus biarmicus

Lancashire Category A.

Rare resident breeder.

This reed-swamp specialist has its only Lancashire stronghold within the extensive reedbeds of Leighton Moss where it has established a thriving colony since 1973. Autumn dispersal from this site accounts for at least some of the reports from Marton Mere, where the species is a very scarce autumn and winter visitor. The species is very rare elsewhere in the county.

The first sightings, followed by eventual colonisation, resulted from a marked increase in Bearded Tits in the United Kingdom during the 1960s and 1970s, itself linked to the massive expansion of the Dutch population following the creation of huge areas of reedbed during the early years of the reclamation of the polders. This increase and the range expansion of the British population led to autumn irruptions and these produced the first Lancashire records in 1965.

The first Lancashire record was of a flock of nine, found by Maurice Jones, circling then moving north at a height of 100 feet (30m) over Formby Point on 10 October 1965, followed by a single bird at Marton Mere on 22 October and two there the next day. Subsequent reports at Marton Mere were of a male and three females irregularly from 25 October 1965 to 4 January 1966 and up to five until the end of February. Four birds were caught (2 males & 2 females) at Marton Mere that winter and one of the females had been ringed on 23 September 1964 on the Dutch polders, establishing the link to the large Dutch population. The first for Leighton Moss were part of the same irruption: five from 5 November 1965 until 15 March 1966. There was an isolated record of two heard at Marton Mere on 30 October 1966.

There were no further sightings until 29 October 1971, when two were seen over North Shore, Blackpool and then five at Leighton Moss on 13 November 1971. Some of the Leighton Moss birds remained all winter and two females stayed throughout the spring and summer of 1972. The following winter four were seen at Leighton Moss on 24 October 1972 and ten on 12 November and at least four were still present on 20 March 1973.

The first successful breeding came in 1973 at Leighton Moss, when a brood of recently fledged young was seen being fed by the parents. Subsequent population changes are shown in Figure 1.

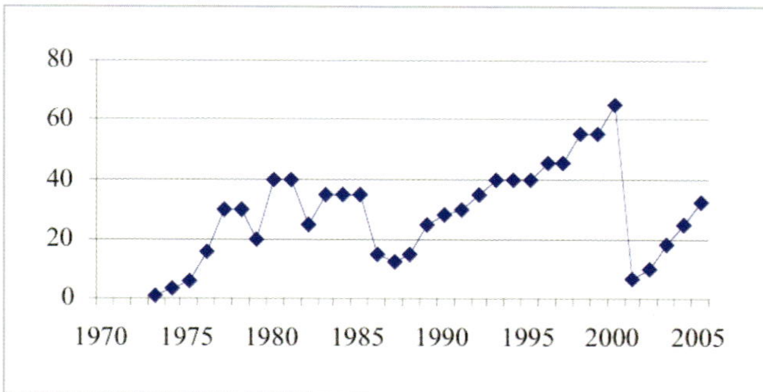

Figure1. Numbers of breeding pairs of Bearded Tits at Leighton Moss, 1973-2005.

The declines in 1979, 1982 and 1986-88 were linked to spells of cold weather, especially periods of snow cover, which denied Bearded Tits access to their main winter diet of reed seed. With a succession of mild winters the population increased to a record 65 pairs in 2000, when 275 young were ringed. This was followed by a catastrophic crash to only seven pairs in 2001, thought to be due to an unusually prolonged period of very high water levels from October to December (which submerged the reed litter, a favoured feeding site) followed in late December by a period of heavy snow cover. It was touch and go whether the population would survive but it has prospered in succeeding years to reach 25 pairs in 2004, when at least 75 young were fledged. Survival rates have also returned to previous levels: at least 34% of 2002's fledglings survived to 2004, while the adult survival rate over the same period was 54%. Thirty-two pairs bred in 2005.

Since 1997 reed 'wigwam' nest-boxes have been used, partly to attract birds to nest in the wetter areas of reed but also to help in the intensive research study which has included periods of ringing activity from 1975-79 (383 ringed) and 1992-2005 (1,881 ringed). Winter recoveries from the early period of ringing were singles in Bolton in October 1978, Coventry in March 1980 and four caught together at Blacktoft Sands in Humberside in January 1980. The Blacktoft records were particularly noteworthy since, as well as three birds marked in July 1979, a bird ringed at Leighton Moss in July 1975 was in the same flock. Despite the greatly increased numbers that have been ringed and colour-ringed since 1992, apart from the records from Martin Mere detailed below, only one other bird has been reported away from Leighton, a nestling ringed in May 1994 and caught while breeding at Billingham in Cleveland the following May.

Tony Disley

Irruptive behaviour has, however, been witnessed regularly at Leighton Moss. Birds fly in groups low over the reeds calling excitedly and then fly high, some being seen to leave, although most drop back into the reedbeds. This behaviour occurs mainly from late September to early November and is especially intense during periods of settled, fine weather. Perhaps surprisingly, it became less evident as the population increased in the late 1990s, an observation supported by fewer sightings away from Leighton in this period.

Irrupting birds have been recorded at nearby Haweswater but, since the consolidation of the population at Leighton Moss, most records elsewhere in the county have come from Marton Mere. The first was a ringed pair (not from Leighton Moss as no ringing had then taken place) from 30 November 1973 until 27 March 1974. One or two followed in late October 1979, a pair in December 1988, then no more until singles in November 1993 to February 1994 and September to November 1994. In 1995 there were five early in the year with one still present on 1 April and one to three from 18 November to the year's end. Colour-ringed birds from Leighton Moss were seen in both 1994 and 1995. Finally, a pair was present from November 1998 to February 1999.

Other records include a single heard over the Alt Estuary in misty conditions on 16 October 1973, two females at Preesall on 6 November 1977, two at Martin Mere on 26 November 1977 with one there on 3 December, and singles at Mere Brow on 14 December and Marshside on 18 December 1977. There was a ringed male at Barrow Lodge near Whalley on 3-4 November 1978, six at Martin Mere on 15 April 1981, one at Wood End Sewage Works, Burnley on 22 November 1981, a pair crossing Aldcliffe Marsh on 22 October 1982, two at Pine Lake, Carnforth on 18 October 1991 with ten there briefly the next day, and seven on Morecambe golf course on 16 October 1994. Most recently, singles were at Pilling Lane Ends on 16 September 2001 and Martin Mere in mid-October, and two at Fazakerley Reedbed in north Liverpool from November 2004 to March 2005.

SJW, RW.

This species account was sponsored by Maurice Jones and John Wilson.

LONG-TAILED TIT

Aegithalos caudatus

Lancashire Category A.

Common resident breeder.

Mitchell described the Long-tailed Tit as generally but locally distributed in Lancashire; it was least numerous in the east, although common in both the Ribble and Wyre Valleys. Oakes considered it to be less common than the Marsh Tit, numerous only between the Lune and the Ribble and scarce or absent in the Fylde and the south-west; in the latter area he could cite only two twentieth-century breeding records, at Churchtown, Southport in 1912 and Rufford in 1927. Small parties were widespread in winter, including at Darwen, Rivington and Belmont, where the species did not breed. Spencer (1973) described the Long-tailed Tit as still local south of the Ribble but Smith (1963) recorded the first definite breeding in Formby in 1957 after which a small population became established.

The Long-tailed Tit became one of the avian successes of late twentieth-century Britain, with a population increase of 52% between 1970 and 2001 (CBC) but remained stable during 1994-2005 (BBS). The Lancashire population was undoubtedly increasing throughout this period but its fastest period of growth appears to have been during the late 1980s and 1990s. The county breeding range has increased by 33% in the past 30 years, from 36 10km squares in 1968-72 to 39 in 1988-91 and 48 in 1997-2000, when breeding was confirmed in 498 tetrads (53% of the county) and the population was estimated at 3,000 pairs. The largest concentrations are found in the Ribble Valley, the Chorley area, the central lowlands from Preston north to Lancaster on the western fringes of Bowland, and in north Merseyside. Breeding pairs are widespread in urban and suburban areas throughout the county and only in the higher fell country, parts of the coastline and the interior of the Fylde can the distribution be described as sparse.

This range extension has been best monitored in east Lancashire. Until the 1950s there was a small population which was largely confined to the Ribble catchment. Oakes's first record elsewhere was a family party at Towneley in 1932 and a breeding pair was found at Simonstone near Padiham in 1957 (Hornby *pers. comm.*), but flocks of 30 in the Burnley area during the winters of 1960/61 and 1961/62 suggest that more were breeding in other parts of the east. The hard winter of 1962/63 provided a major set-back to this small population and breeding was not proven again until 1972 at Wood End. Several pairs bred at nearby Towneley in 1982 and by 1992 breeding was widespread; in 1998 the species was described in the county bird report as the success-story of the decade in the Burnley area.

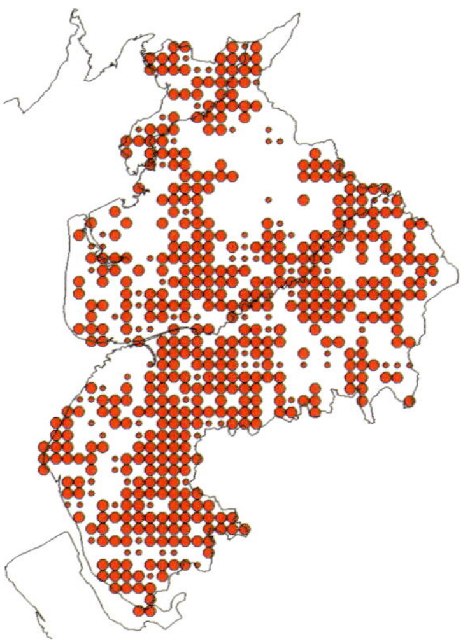

Breeding distribution of Long-tailed Tit, 1997-2000. (Large dots: confirmed. Small dots: possible)

Isolated pairs were recorded in south Liverpool from the late 1980s but by 1998 Long-tailed Tits were virtually ubiquitous, breeding within a kilometre of the city centre. Their breeding distribution now runs more or less continuously from Knowsley and St. Helens north to the Ribble and east to the West Pennine Moors. By the late 1980s breeding was taking place in the Irwell and Limy Valleys in Rossendale and this expansion has continued, although distribution remains patchy.

Long-tailed Tits bred at Lytham Hall in the 1950s and 1960s but the species was a very scarce breeder elsewhere in the Fylde, although there were regular sightings in the Cockerham-Winmarleigh area in winter at least. Significant expansion into western Fylde did not occur until the late 1980s and 1990s and the breeding distribution there is still uneven.

Long-tailed Tits tend to nest either in gorse and other bushes at low levels or quite high up in mature trees; the latter preference may have facilitated their expansion into urban and suburban parks and large gardens. A number of other factors appear to have contributed to this species' remarkable population increase, in particular a series of relatively mild winters since the late 1980s and an increasing tendency to exploit supplementary food sources at garden feeders and bird-tables at all times of the year. This had been observed since 1980 at least, but from the early 1990s became a regular and frequently-noted phenomenon in all regions of the county.

Long-tailed Tit, Little Crosby, March 2005. (Steve Young)

The increase in the breeding population has been accompanied by a significant growth in the size of post-breeding and winter flocks. These begin to assemble as early as June and move in noisy, cohesive parties from copse to copse and garden to garden until the flocks break up in early spring, a highlight of inland birding during the winter months. In the 1960s and 1970s flocks of 30 or 40 birds were scarce enough to warrant particular notice and few were seen prior to the late 1980s, although 70 were recorded at Formby in January 1979. More typical of this period were 30+ at Scorton in November 1966, up to 30 at Lower Healey, Chorley in October 1980 and at Stocks Reservoir in December 1985, and 35 at Skelmersdale in August 1988. More recent flocks have included 80 at Roddlesworth Plantations in November 1989 and 70 there in January 1995, 70 at Sunnyhurst Woods, Darwen in October 1991 and 60 there in December 1995, 78 at Fazakerley in August 1997 and 90 at Mere Sands Wood in September 2002.

Although spring migrants have been virtually undetectable in Lancashire (there was some evidence of very slight passage at Heysham in March and April 1999, and a more sizeable movement there in spring 2002), late autumn passage at coastal watchpoints is fairly regular and the number of birds involved has increased markedly since the late 1980s. Eight at Freckleton on 18 October 1973 were considered noteworthy at the time, but in November 1981 fourteen were ringed at Hightown and 40 were ringed at Heysham during 21-22 October 1983. 1990 brought Heysham its highest autumn total so far, with 80 birds ringed; 31 were seen there on 21 October 1995 and 36 were trapped between 6 September and 26 October in 1999. Large counts of overflying and grounded migrants have continued to be made annually, most notably in 2000 when up to 50 a day were seen at Heysham in October and more than 100 on the 13th; further substantial movements were observed at several coastal sites in the autumns of 2002, 2003 and 2004.

There have been 25 recoveries of Lancashire-ringed Long-tailed Tits, 17 within the county, seven elsewhere in northern England, and one in Scotland, a bird ringed at Heysham on 25 September 1993 and controlled near Edzell, Grampian on 13 November. Four birds ringed elsewhere in northern England and one from southern England have been recovered here.

BM, RW.

This species account was sponsored by Barbara Beattie.

BLUE TIT

Cyanistes caeruleus

Lancashire Category A.

Abundant resident breeder.

This most familiar species has been virtually ubiquitous in Lancashire for at least 150 years. The Blue Tit is an abundant resident of broad-leaved and mixed woodland, coppices, parks and gardens, widespread in suburbs and even inner cities provided that suitable nest-holes are available, and is very accepting both of nest-boxes and of garden feeders.

Tony Disley

Both Mitchell and Oakes knew the Blue Tit as Lancashire's commonest and most widespread tit; Mitchell noted that the species had made use of artificial nest-boxes as long ago as 1832. Oakes observed that they were more nomadic in autumn and winter than Great Tits, and Spencer (1973) noted that dispersal was often conspicuous in late September and October; he judged that the species' breeding population outnumbered that of the Great Tit by three to one.

The British population grew by 19% between 1970 and 2001 (CBC) and by 24% during 1994-2005 (BBS). The New Atlas estimated 3.3 million territories in Britain and Lancashire's proportion of these was estimated at 40,000 in 1997-2000, when Blue Tits were present in 94% of Lancashire tetrads and were absent only from the highest Bowland fells and small areas of the south Pennines.

Population levels in Lancashire appear to have remained essentially stable throughout the 1950s and 1960s, rising during the 1970s and continuing to increase, albeit with intermittent fluctuations, until the late 1990s, a pattern shown broadly consistently in records from several regularly-monitored locations. At Leighton Moss 28 pairs bred in 1982, 34-37 during 1983-87 and 43-45 during 1988-90, declining to the high thirties for most of the 1990s but increasing again to 47 pairs in 1999. In the Pilling-Preesall area a systematically monitored nest-box programme peaked at 109 pairs in 1997; brood productivity data show considerable fluctuations, but averaged 5.45 fledged per nest in the 1980s and 5.61 in the 1990s. Seventy-five pairs at Sunnyhurst Woods, Darwen in 1988 increased to 82 in 1989 and 93 in 1990, but fell to 77 in 1991, a year of poor breeding success by Blue Tits across the county. Fifteen pairs at Mere Sands Wood in 1991 increased to 23 by 1996, 62 in 1997-98 and 77 in 1999.

In the first years of the new century, however, there have been some indications of falling numbers and declining breeding productivity. A marked decrease in numbers at feeders, as well as in the breeding population, was reported in Rossendale in 2001 and 2002, while in the Pilling area nest-box occupancy fell dramatically, from 95 pairs in 1999 to 48 in 2000 before recovering to 85 in 2002 and 65 in 2005. However, fledging rates declined significantly there during 2000-2005, to fewer than five juveniles per nest. At Mere Sands Wood nest-box occupancy has averaged 53 per annum since 2000, a marked reduction on the late 1990s. This very recent development may, however, be merely another short-term fluctuation; the Warton Crag CBC population, for example, has varied from 5-22 pairs during 1989-2005 with no clear trend.

Post-breeding dispersal, often in company with Great and Long-tailed Tits, is widely observed from late June to mid-August. Noteworthy post-breeding totals include over 60 at Black Coppice, Chorley on 10 July 1990, 33 juveniles trapped at Heysham in July and August 1991, 70 at Sunnyhurst Woods on 14 August 1992 and 108 at Mere Sands Wood on 24 July 1993.

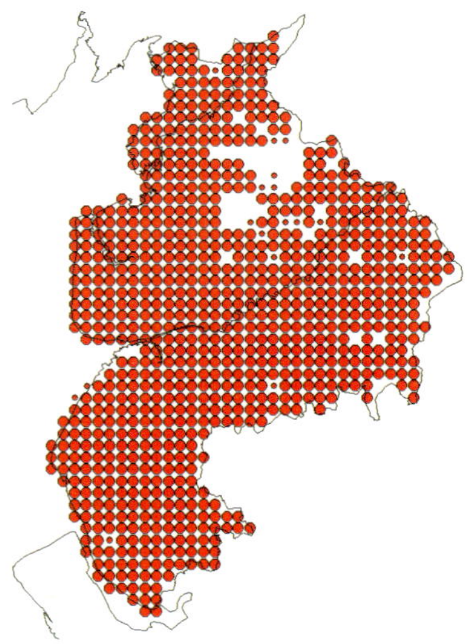

Breeding distribution of Blue Tit, 1997-2000. (Large dots: confirmed. Small dots: possible)

Much heavier passage, consisting mainly of southbound migrants, is frequently recorded at both coastal and inland sites between early September and the middle of November, but such movements are much more evident in some autumns than in others. A major influx in September-October 1957 saw numbers of Blue Tits frequenting vegetation on traffic-islands in central Liverpool; more recently, large-scale irruptions have been recorded in 1983-85, 1987-88, 1993 and 1996. A late September influx in 1983 brought 300 to Heysham, a heavy passage of 96 birds in two hours at Lytham St. Anne's NR on 2 October, and up to 100 passed daily at Hightown Dunes in early October, while 50 were on the move at Fluke Hall, Pilling as late as 12 November. In 1996 the heaviest passage to date at Heysham produced counts of 150 on 2 October, 100+ on the 7th and further movements later in the month and in early November, with a total of 319 ringed. Inland, there were 200 at Reedshaw Moss Plantation on 13 October 1985 and 100 at Sunnyhurst Woods on 25 September 1993. Since the 1996 influx autumn movements have usually been very light; 48 at Marshside on 17 September 1998 with 40 there on 23 October 2003, and 70 eastbound, overhead migrants, also at Marshside, on 9 October 2004 have been the largest counts.

During the winter months flocks of 20 to 30 Blue Tits are quite widespread and much larger gatherings are occasionally reported, including up to 250 at Leighton Moss in the winter of 1966/67, 150 at Wycoller Dene on 11 December 1982, up to 100 at Clifton Hall, Fylde in November-December 1987, up to 50 at a factory bird-table at Hoddlesden, Darwen in February 1991 and 72 at Fluke Hall on 9 January 1996. Spring movements, as with many other passerine species that are conspicuous on autumn passage, are normally very slight or undetectable; a few passed through Heysham between late March and early May in 1992.

There have been more than 500 recoveries of Lancashire-ringed Blue Tits, around 450 within the county, 51 elsewhere in northern England, five in southern England and one in Wales. The longest journey on record was undertaken by a pullus ringed near Burnley on 16 June 1967 and controlled in Sussex on 16 October 1968. There have been 47 recoveries in Lancashire of Blue Tits ringed elsewhere in Britain, 42 from northern England, four from southern England and one from Wales. No claims have ever been made in Lancashire of the nominate continental race and it seems likely that even the largest autumn movements are comprised of birds of the endemic British sub-species *obscurus*.

BM, RW.

This species account was sponsored by Joyce Riley and in memory of Patricia Anne Jones.

GREAT TIT

Parus major

Lancashire Category A.

Abundant resident breeder.

Great Tits are most numerous throughout Britain in lowland areas and have adapted successfully to live in urban parks, gardens, cemeteries and orchards as well as coppices and hedgerows on farmland. Most populations have remained relatively stable in recent decades. The New Atlas estimated 1.6 million territories in 1988-91 and there had been no significant change in range or numbers since 1968-72. More recently, however, a significant population increase has been reported, 51% between 1970 and 2001 (CBC), and 44% during 1994-2005 (BBS). Great Tit numbers have, therefore, been increasing roughly twice as fast as those of Blue Tit.

Mitchell described the Great Tit as a plentiful resident at all seasons. Oakes's very brief account concurred; the species bred throughout lowland Lancashire and up to 250m above sea level on the fells, and was a regular nester in suburban areas. In winter Great Tits joined other tits, Treecreepers and Goldcrests in roaming through woods and copses. Spencer (1973) noted that some passage was discernible in early October.

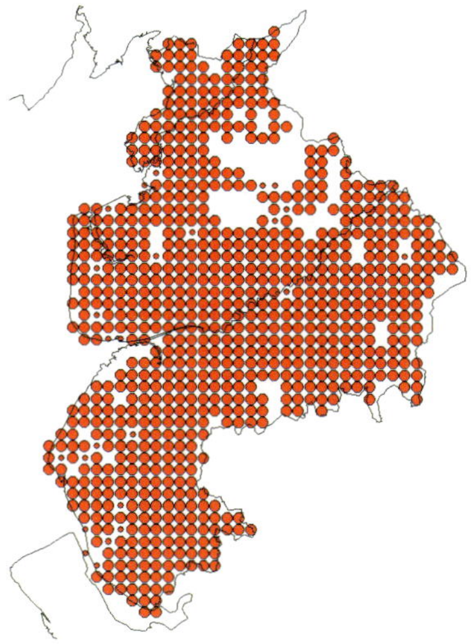

Breeding distribution of Great Tit, 1997-2000. (Large dots: confirmed. Small dots: possible)

The Lancashire breeding population appears to have increased significantly, if not spectacularly, since the 1970s, although occasional local setbacks due to hard winters have been reported such as a decline from 39 pairs in Billinge Wood, Blackburn in 1981 to 25 the following year. Two developments may have facilitated this growth in population, increasing use of garden bird-tables and nut-feeders throughout the year, and an increase in the provision of suitable nest-boxes in many parts of the county. At Leighton Moss the Great Tit population has remained remarkably stable, averaging 33 pairs annually in the 1980s and 31 in the 1990s. At Mere Sands Wood, however, the erection of nest-boxes increased the population from eight pairs in 1991 to 15 in 1996, 25 in 1997-98, 31 in 1999 and an average of 25 pairs during 2000-2005. During the mid-1990s a nest-box programme also led to substantial population growth in the Belmont area from 29 to 37 pairs. More recently, at Arkholme, nest-box occupancy has increased from six pairs in 1998-99 to nine in 2002 and 21 in 2005. Elsewhere in the Lune Valley woodlands 14 nest-box pairs in 2000 increased to 27 in 2003, while in upland woods on the United Utilities Bowland estate six pairs of Great Tits made use of boxes in 2002 and 24 in 2003. The county's most consistently-monitored nest-box scheme, in the Pilling-Preesall area, saw an average occupancy of 14 pairs annually during 1988-92 increase to 42 in 1993-99 and to 53 pairs since 2000; brood productivity, though showing some year-to-year variation, has not changed significantly, averaging 4.5 fledged young per pair during 1988-2005.

The breeding range is essentially similar to that of the Blue Tit. Breeding was proven or suspected in 88% of Lancashire tetrads in 1997-2000, when Great Tits were absent only from large areas of Bowland and smaller districts on the West Pennine Moors and the south Pennines, from the most heavily urbanised areas of Liverpool and Blackpool, and the south Ribble and Lune marshes. The population was estimated at 20,000 pairs, half that of the Blue Tit.

Post-breeding parties, usually accompanied by other tit species, are widely recorded from mid-June onwards; numbers are normally small and 40 at Mere Sands Wood on 25 June 1988 and at Darwen Moor edge on 14 August 1996, and 20 at Lee Green Reservoir, Burnley on 12 June 1998 are among the most noteworthy. Later in the autumn modest movements are occasionally recorded, mainly at coastal watchpoints; these usually coincide with significant Blue Tit passage, although numbers rarely approach those of the smaller species. There were very few Great Tits in the widespread coastal tit movements of September-October 1983. A more significant influx in late September and October 1985 resulted in 35 birds trapped at Heysham out of a total 70 recorded, and there was a small influx at Rossall Point on 28-29 September, another 15 there on 27 October, and 29 at Fairhaven on the 13th. In 1986 17 Great Tits were caught at Heysham in the first half of October and 20 were trapped at Fluke Hall, Pilling during October 1987. Since the early 1990s coastal passage in autumn appears to have dwindled; increased ringing totals at Heysham since the late 1990s have been attributed almost entirely to the growth in the local breeding population due to the provision of nest-boxes. Up to 20 Great Tits at Marshside on 26 September 1999, 18 September 2002 and 16 October 2003 are among the highest coastal counts in recent years.

Tony Disley

Small groups of Great Tits wander about, again usually with other tit species, during the winter months, although larger flocks are occasionally recorded. There were 70 at Mitton Wood, Whalley on 11 January 1981, 50 at Clifton Hall, Fylde on 14 November 1987, 36 at Mere Sands Wood on 22 February 1999 and 20+ at Marton Mere on 4 December 2003. The only evidence of possible spring passage involved small numbers of unringed birds at Heysham in February and March of 1993 and 1994.

There have been 185 recoveries of birds ringed in Lancashire, 170 within the county, ten elsewhere in northern England and five in southern England. The furthest known journeys were undertaken by a first-winter female ringed at Knott End on 20 October 1985 and controlled at Holme Pierrepoint, Nottinghamshire on 6 April 1986, and a first-winter male from Euxton, Chorley on 2 January 1989 controlled at Ingleby Greenhow, North Yorkshire on 30 April. There have been only five recoveries here of Great Tits ringed elsewhere in Britain, three from northern England and two from southern England, a bird of unknown age ringed at Colchester, Essex on 14 February 1965 recovered on Plex Moss, Formby on 12 May, and another caught at Ringstead, Northamptonshire on 1 September 1984 and controlled at Knott End on 8 March 1986. Although a few irruptions of nominate continental breeders into England have been recorded (Brown & Grice 2005), none has been reported in Lancashire and it seems likely that all known records relate to the sub-species *newtoni*.

BM, RW.
This species account was sponsored by N.J. Donnithorne.

CRESTED TIT

Lophophanes cristatus

Lancashire Category A. (0, 1).

Vagrant from northern Europe.

One was found in Lytham Parish Church wood on 24th October 1964 by Nelson Harwood. It arrived with an influx of Coal Tits after a prolonged period of northerly winds. This record was considered retrospectively by the county rarities committee in 1999, and added to the county list at that time. Notes taken at the time were sufficient for the record to be accepted but not detailed enough to assign the bird to sub-species.

The Scottish population is highly sedentary but occasional birds were recorded outside the breeding range as far south as Stirling and Perth during the 1980s. There were a number of records of nominate *cristatus* from northern Europe in England and one of the southern European race *mitratus* during the nineteenth century, but few were seen anywhere in England during the twentieth century, the most recent being one in Northumberland in August to September 1984.

SJW, MJ.
This species account was sponsored by Ribble Bird Tours (01253-407554).

COAL TIT

Periparus ater

Lancashire Category A.

Common resident breeder.

Mitchell described the Coal Tit as a local breeding resident which was more widespread in autumn and winter. The species' status had changed little by Oakes's time; he identified the region from the Wyre to Longridge Fell and the Ribble Valley as the main breeding area. Coal Tits were also resident in the south-west, particularly in the Formby-Ainsdale pinewoods, but the species was scarce as a breeder in the Fylde, in Rossendale and on the West Pennine Moors.

Between the 1950s and early 1990s the situation changed only slowly as new breeding areas were gradually colonised; a steady increase was noted in Rossendale from the early 1980s and nesting was first recorded at Arkholme in the Lune Valley in 1982. There were some setbacks due to severe winters: in 1979 the population at Leighton Moss fell from three pairs to one, and did not recover until 1983, and the 1981/82 winter reduced numbers at Billinge Wood, Blackburn from 35 to 23 pairs but the population had recovered to 36 pairs within a year. In the Fylde, a pair bred at Salwick in 1987 and nesting was fairly regular at Lytham Hall and Stanley Park, Blackpool in the early 1990s; in the south-west, four or five pairs nested annually in Mere Sands Wood during the same period.

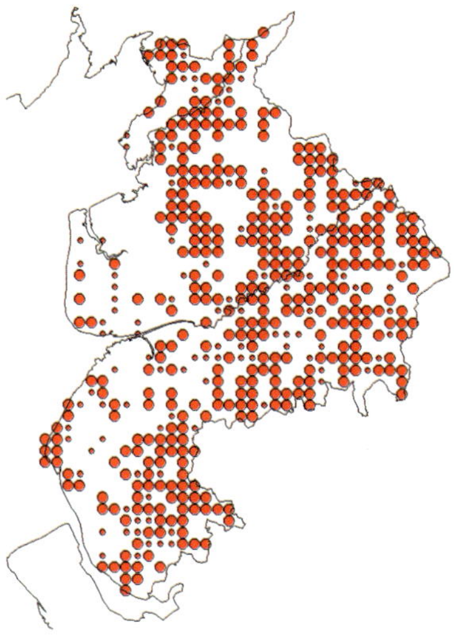

Breeding distribution of Coal Tit, 1997-2000. (Large dots: confirmed. Small dots: possible)

Nationally, Coal Tits suffered severely in the prolonged hard winter of 1962/63, but the population more than regained its numbers in the subsequent decade. This was assisted by mild winters and the increase in suitable habitat provided by conifer afforestation programmes, particularly in upland areas, a trend reflected in Lancashire. The British population increased by 23% between 1970 and 2001 (CBC) and by 35% during 1994-2005 (BBS). Anecdotal evidence suggests that Lancashire's birds showed similar increases but these did not register in any substantial change of range: Coal Tits were found in 48 Lancashire 10km squares during 1968-72, 42 during 1988-91 and 47 during 1997-2000. However, Coal Tits were present in 52% of Lancashire tetrads during 1997-2000 when the population was estimated at 5,000 pairs.

The population is most densely concentrated in the eastern two-thirds of the county and Coal Tits are absent only from the unwooded areas of the Fylde, the south-west mosses and the highest moorlands. Most are found in conifer plantations but the species is also widespread in clumps of mixed woodland, urban and suburban parks and cemeteries, and even in large gardens with a few conifers. Since 2000 the Coal Tit appears to have consolidated its breeding position further; up to eight pairs now breed annually at Mere Sands Wood and it continues to expand its range in Rossendale.

Tony Disley

Post-breeding dispersals are widely reported from eastern areas from late June onwards, when small parties frequently associate with Goldcrests and other tit species. Flocks were described as very numerous in early autumn 1983, and there were up to 30 at Ogden Plantation on 10 August 1987, 30 at Delph Plantations on 19 September 1992 and 25 at Moor Piece on 25 September 2005.

More widespread and often much heavier movements are recorded in late autumn in some years at both inland and coastal sites. A major influx in 1957 was mainly confined to Rossendale, where a flock of up to 70 flew south-west over Bacup on 4 October. At Heysham, where at least a few southbound migrants are recorded annually, there was an exceptional passage in 1985 with two main arrivals, in late September and mid-October; up to 600 Coal Tits in total were recorded, with a peak of 70 on 29 September. Meanwhile, 40 passed at Rossall Point on 28 September and a similar number at Hightown next day, while up to 50 were recorded at Fairhaven on the 30th. It is believed that these migrants were mainly if not exclusively British in origin, as there was no evidence of an influx of continental birds into the country prior to or during the period of movement.

Further widespread movements were recorded in September-October 1989 when 60 passed at Heysham on 29 September, and a total of 110 birds was ringed on the Fylde in October and early

November. In 2003 Heysham's heaviest passage since 1985 saw 111 flying south on 2 October; on the same day 60 passed in an hour at Belmont and an unprecedented 15 at Seaforth.

In contrast to autumn, spring movements are almost undetectable; a few birds are occasionally recorded at Heysham NR in March or early April.

Flocks of Coal Tits are often widespread in winter, and these have grown larger in recent decades. In several regions, most notably Rossendale and east Lancashire, parties of Coal Tits have demonstrated an increasing attraction to garden feeders since the mid-1990s, where they display a particular appetite for sunflower seeds; birds are frequently observed caching these in crevices in walls and trees. This adaptation may stand the species in good stead in future severe winters.

There have been 30 recoveries of Coal Tits ringed in Lancashire, 27 within the county, two elsewhere in northern England and one in Wales, and three recoveries here of birds ringed in northern England. All of these presumably refer to the British race *britannicus* and there is as yet no firm evidence that the nominate continental race has ever occurred in the county. It seems likely, however, that some late migrants are of continental origin and the influxes of late October 1964, which produced our only record of Crested Tit, together with those of 1989 and 2003 probably contained nominate birds.

BM, RW.

This species account was sponsored by Frank Walsh.

WILLOW TIT

Poecile montanus

Lancashire Category A.

Scarce resident breeder.

Willow Tits favour wetter habitats than Marsh Tits and are usually found in damp, even swampy, woodland and thickets where they excavate their own nest-holes in rotten tree-trunks, stumps or posts. Suitable wet woodlands of birch, willow and alder were once plentiful on the south-western and Fylde mosslands and it seems likely that Willow Tits must have been widespread and common throughout much of the Lancashire Plain at least until the final extensive draining of the mosslands began in the nineteenth century. However, the Willow Tit's status in Lancashire before the 1950s is shrouded in mystery. Its existence here was unknown in Mitchell's time, but Oakes's account, some fifty years after its separation from the Marsh Tit, is fragmentary and provides little information on either numbers or range, apart from a reference to its absence from the eastern Ribble Valley and that it appeared to be well distributed 'west of Bolton'. His description of a party of twelve 'identified beyond doubt' on call at Silverdale in January 1946 must be treated with a great deal of caution, coming as it does from the Marsh Tit's long-standing county stronghold.

By 1973, however, Spencer was able to describe the Willow Tit as the Marsh Tit's replacement south of the Ribble, with some overlap in ranges along the lower reaches of that river, and with a few breeding records in the north. The 1968-72 Atlas recorded their presence in 18 10km squares in Lancashire, with breeding confirmed in all of them, from the Preston, Leyland and Chorley areas across the south-west mosslands to Merseyside; breeding was also confirmed to the north-east of Preston in the lower Ribble Valley. Comments in the county Bird Report around this time emphasise the species' local abundance: in 1965 it was 'a very numerous breeder on the southern mosslands' and 'the typical tit of the Leyland mosses'. Outside the core area, however, nesting was local and sporadic even then. Breeding was recorded on Heysham Moss in the 1960s, but not subsequently, and a pair bred at Quernmore in 1971. On the Fylde there was an unsuccessful breeding attempt in the elder understorey of a pine plantation at Winmarleigh in 1962, and a pair held territory at Lytham in 1972 and bred at Freckleton Naze the same year. A pair bred at Staghills in Rossendale in 1978.

In most of Europe populations have been fairly stable for at least four decades but the past 20 years or so have witnessed a dramatic decline in Britain – by 74% between 1966 and 1999 (CBC) and 65% during 1994-2005 (BBS). The Willow Tit was clearly in grievous trouble at the turn of the 21st century. The New Atlas recorded a 9.8% range reduction between 1968-72 and 1988-91 and estimated 25,000 Willow Tit territories in Britain, concentrated in the English Midlands, Wales and Yorkshire, but the main impact of a virtual population collapse has been felt since the early 1990s and was barely registered by the New Atlas.

Tony Disley

In Lancashire range contraction appears to have begun in the Preston area in the mid-1970s although up to three pairs bred at Penwortham until 1983; nesting ceased at Longton after 1979 and in the Alston-Tunbrook area in the early 1980s. During this period the population in the south-west remained healthy; in 1982 three pairs bred at Mere Sands Wood and there were no fewer than nine pairs in two copses on Altcar Moss. Breeding was reported from 15 areas in the south-west in 1987, including Halsall, Formby, Kirkby and Simonswood Mosses; in south Liverpool Willow Tits bred regularly at Speke and Halewood and in Croxteth and Calderstones Parks during this period, and the species was described as numerous in the area as recently as 1992. During the 1980s and 1990s Willow Tits may even have extended their range in the Chorley/West Pennine Moors area with breeding considered regular at Coppull, Birkacre, Yarrow Valley, Rivington, Roddlesworth, Wayoh and near Belmont. The 1997-2000 atlas survey recorded breeding in ten tetrads in this area.

Odd instances of possible or confirmed nesting continued to be recorded elsewhere in the county in the 1980s and early 1990s; a pair was present all year at Rawcliffe Hall in the Fylde in 1985-86, and breeding was reported from the Darwen area at Eccleshill during 1984-90 and at another site in 1991. Pairs were present at Scorton on the Wyre in April 1983, at Fair Oak near Dunsop Bridge in spring 1988 and at Higher Hodder Bridge in April 1989; a single bird was at Clowbridge Reservoir, Rossendale, in June 1991.

By the early 1990s, however, shadows were gathering over the Willow Tit in Lancashire, as elsewhere in Britain. The New Atlas recorded presence in only 13 10km squares in Lancashire, a range contraction of more than 25% since 1968-72, and breeding was confirmed in only nine of these.

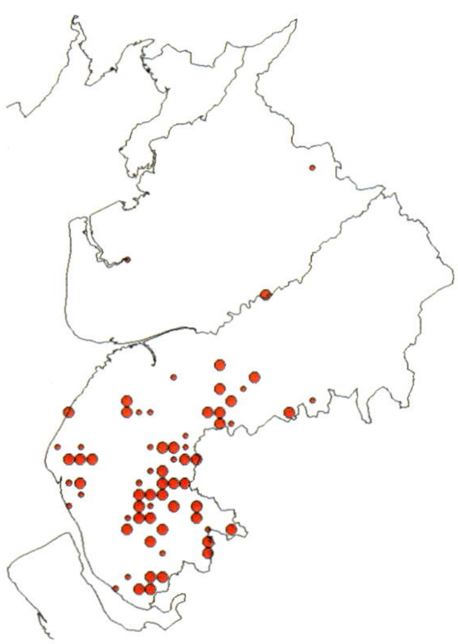

Breeding distribution of Willow Tit, 1997-2000. (Large dots: confirmed. Small dots: possible)

The species had effectively disappeared from the Ribble Valley, the Preston area and two squares on Merseyside, but it was 1995, when breeding ceased at Mere Sands Wood, before the deteriorating situation in the south-west was highlighted in the county bird report. A survey in 1997 of 17 sites in the Southport-Formby area, all of which had held breeding birds in 1978, located only a single pair. The decline has continued inexorably ever since. The most recent comprehensive survey, the 1997-2000 Lancashire Atlas, estimated a total of 100 pairs, heavily concentrated on the mosses inland of Southport and Formby and around Skelmersdale, St. Helens and Halewood; 39 of the 49 territories located were confined to just six 10km squares.

It is beyond doubt that the Willow Tit's situation has deteriorated further in the new century. The Sefton coast has been almost entirely abandoned, and after the 1997 high-point the species is now rare in the Chorley area – a single bird at Duxbury in January 2003 was that region's only record all year – and is possibly extinct in the West Pennine Moors with no sightings since 2002. Since 2000 the species is believed to have become extinct in Knowsley (C. Felton *pers. comm.*) and confirmed breeding has been reported only in St. Helens (from the Sankey Valley, Rainford, Carr Mill Dam and Bold Moss), and from Blundellsands and Skelmersdale White Moss, although it is likely that some at least of the scattered sightings elsewhere in the now virtually-defunct stronghold of the south-west represent surviving pairs. The county population may now be as low as 50 pairs.

The reasons for the Willow Tit's catastrophic recent decline are not fully understood, but favoured hypotheses include a reduction in food supplies caused by lack of woodland management, competition from Blue and Great Tits which may take over nest holes, and increased predation, especially by Great Spotted Woodpeckers (Fuller *et al.* 2005). Evidence for any of these is lacking in Lancashire although all three competitor bird species increased significantly during the 1990s, coinciding with the onset of the demise of the Willow Tit.

Records outside the breeding season from areas where the Willow Tit was either scarce or absent as a breeding bird were fairly widespread from the 1960s through to the 1980s, but have become very infrequent since. Birds were occasionally observed in roaming tit flocks and garden visits were not unusual, including several to central Southport in February 1987. More recent records of dispersing or wandering individuals include one by the Wyre above Scorton on 2 January 1989 (where singles had been seen in January 1967 and March 1969), one ringed at Pilling in October to December 1992, one or more present at Stocks Reservoir in successive winters from 1992 to 1994, one trapped at Pilling Lane Ends on 18 September 1994, birds in Rossendale at Calf Hey in January 1995, Stacksteads in January 1996 and Haslingden in November 2003, two at Rawcliffe Hall in January 1998, one at Lee Green Reservoir, Burnley, from July 2000 to the year's end and one at Cottam brickworks in winter 2004/05 and 2005/06.

Instances of Willow Tits clearly on passage are very few; singles at Freckleton sewage works on 22 August 1965, at Heysham on 11 April 1966 and 6 August 1988, at the Alt Estuary in August 1971, and an adult and a juvenile at Seaforth before flying south on 2 June 1995 may qualify in this category. There has been only one recovery of a Lancashire-ringed Willow Tit, a first-winter bird ringed at Formby on 19 October 1988 and controlled at Great Altcar, 8km away, on 21 April 1991.

All British birds belong to the endemic race *kleinschmidti* and there is no evidence that the northern European race *borealis* has ever occurred in Lancashire.

BM, RW.

This species account was sponsored by Steve Riley.

MARSH TIT

Poecile palustris

Lancashire Category A.

Fairly common resident breeder.

The range of the Marsh Tit lies entirely within the western Palaearctic, from southern Scandinavia, Britain and western Europe to the Volga; it is a mainly sedentary inhabitant of deciduous woodland and forest, especially oak and beech. Populations are relatively stable in most of its European range but declining in Fennoscandia and the Baltic (Hagemeijer & Blair 1997) as well as in this country. The British population fell by 56% between 1970 and 2001 (CBC), but appears to have increased by 33% during 1994-2005 (BBS). The 1988-91 New Atlas recorded a 17% reduction in national distribution since 1968-72, and estimated 60,000 Marsh Tit territories, concentrated in southern and eastern England and south Wales; the contraction in range had been particularly marked in northern England.

Mitchell's account must be treated with caution, since prior to 1900 the existence of the Willow Tit as a separate species had not been recognised, and all records were reported as Marsh Tits. He described the species as fairly plentiful in the Preston and Chipping areas; a nest was found by the Hodder near Clitheroe in 1876. Oakes identified the Silverdale-Yealand Conyers area as the Marsh Tit's Lancashire stronghold; elsewhere in the north the distribution was patchy, and the species did not breed at all in the Fylde. He described it as common in the Ribble Valley from Red Scar and Samlesbury on the outskirts of Preston to Read, and ubiquitous in the woods and coppices between Ribchester and Clitheroe, though rare east of Burnley. There were few confirmed nesting records in the south-west, although Marsh Tits were described as occasional in winter in the Southport, Formby and Rufford areas. Spencer (1973) noted breeding in the Darwen Valley but described the species as otherwise scarce south and east of the Ribble.

Since the early 1970s the species has held on to, and may even have consolidated, its core breeding area in north-west Lancashire; elsewhere, however, there has been a gradual but unremitting decline. As in Oakes's day the Marsh Tit is relatively common in the limestone woodlands around Silverdale, Yealand Conyers and Warton, where the abundant shrub layer of hazel, ash and hawthorn appears to provide ideal habitat. The species has been under-recorded in this general area and population trends are difficult to discern. Leighton Moss suffered a decline from 13 pairs in 1980 and 1985 to ten in 1989 and six or seven during the 1990s, while Warton Crag held up to seven pairs between 1989 and 2004 at an average density of 0.16 pairs per hectare. Other CBC surveys between 1989 and 1999 in this area found average densities of 0.42 pairs per hectare in Grubbins Wood and 0.58 in Potts Wood, some of the highest recorded in Britain.

The 1997-2000 Lancashire survey confirmed that breeding occurred throughout the Silverdale area in a solid block of eleven tetrads. If the population densities cited above are representative then it seems likely that Silverdale alone supports a population of 250-300 pairs. The county population was estimated at 375 pairs during 1997-2000 but this was suspected to be something of an underestimate. Elsewhere in the north, Marsh Tits are local and sparsely distributed in the Lune Valley, particularly at Arkholme and in Aughton Wood; continued breeding further up the Lune in SD67, where none were located during the Lancashire Atlas survey, has recently been confirmed (P.J. Marsh *pers. comm.*). South of Lancaster nesting appears to have ceased in the Scorton area since 1999. In the Fylde, Marsh Tits bred very locally in the Lytham area up to the1970s but none has been seen there since 1989. Birds were present at Thurnham Hall until the early 1990s, and three pairs bred at Ellel Grange in 1999 but breeding had ceased by 2000-2001 at this, the species' last Fylde site.

Breeding distribution of Marsh Tit, 1997-2000. (Large dots: confirmed. Small dots: possible)

There was little change in the breeding range at the 10km square scale between 1968-72 (when birds were located in 24 squares) and 1997-2000 (21 squares), but the distribution away from Silverdale has contracted significantly. Breeding was confirmed in just 15 tetrads outside north Lancashire during 1997-2000 and the indications are that these losses have continued.

In east Lancashire Marsh Tits were described as widespread though scarce breeders throughout the Ribble, Calder and Hodder woodlands as recently as 1986. Up to seven pairs nested in the

Whitewell area in the 1980s, occasionally in nest-boxes, and breeding-season presence was recorded fairly regularly around this time at Higher Hodder Bridge, Spring Wood, Whalley, Ribchester, Alston and Mitton Wood. By 2000, however, a major decline throughout the region was all too evident and, although odd pairs bred in new localities, such as Moor Piece and Stocks Reservoir, most former nesting sites had been abandoned. Occasional sightings at Whitewell and Doeford Bridge, however, indicate continued presence in this stretch of the Hodder Valley. Breeding has never been recorded in Rossendale, although singles were reported at Calf Hey in May 1997 and Helmshore in April 1998.

Occasional individuals or pairs have been reported from several sites within the current or previous breeding range of Willow Tits in the Chorley area and West Lancashire over the past 25 years but their identification has never been fully substantiated.

Marsh Tits are recorded more widely during the autumn and winter months, although such visits have become more infrequent in many areas as the breeding range has fragmented and contracted. Visits to garden feeders are, unsurprisingly, regular in the Silverdale area. There were many sightings throughout the Ribble and its tributary valleys during the 1970s and 1980s, with a few birds turning up further afield, as at Padiham and Burnley in November 1974, Great Harwood in August 1979, and Hapton in October 1983. Since the early 1990s such occurrences have become rare, although there were single birds at Nelson in November 1993 and at Broadley and Whitworth, Rossendale, in the 2000/01 winter.

Sightings outside the breeding season were particularly frequent in coastal Fylde during the 1970s and 1980s; there were five at Fluke Hall on 12 September 1983 and several birds wintered in the Blackpool area in the mid-1980s. Since 1990 only five have been recorded, at Hambleton in October-December 1991, Marton Mere in October 1991, Cleveleys in December 1993, Salwick in December 1997 and Swillbrook in September 2000.

Apart from reports of singles at Ainsdale in January 1981 and near St. Helens in late 1982 there have been no records in the south-west since the late 1950s, and, since both these records (and those mentioned by Oakes) occurred within the range of Willow Tits at time when these were common, there must be considerable doubt that Marsh Tits have ever occurred in the south-west.

Marsh Tits are very scarce at coastal migration watchpoints. One was at Rossall Point on 15 October 1981 and a major influx of tit species in autumn 1985 produced Heysham's first records, with three birds ringed; others were recorded at Fairhaven on 5 October and at Rossall on the 23rd. Heysham Moss and Nature Reserve recorded three in September–October 1994, a first-winter bird was ringed at Heysham NR on 26 April 1998, and two were on Heysham Moss in late 2003. Inland, single Marsh Tits moved with parties of Goldcrests on Darwen Moor edge on 19 December 1995 and in mid-November 1998. There have been no ringing recoveries.

Lancashire lies at the boundary of the distribution of the nominate race and that of *dresseri*, which breeds throughout southern England (BWP).

BM, RW.

This species account was sponsored by Tony Cooper.

NUTHATCH

Sitta europea

Lancashire Category A.

Fairly common resident breeder.

In Mitchell's day the Nuthatch was exceedingly rare in Lancashire and he published only two records, in Wyresdale in the 1860s and at Waddow Hall, Clitheroe in 1880. By Oakes's time the species was only slightly less scarce, with records at Churchtown, Southport and Martin Mere in the 1920s and at Appley Bridge, Wennington, Waddow Hall and elsewhere in the Clitheroe area, and Towneley, Burnley since 1942. None of these involved confirmed breeding but by the early 1970s Spencer (1973) identified the Clitheroe, Southport and Liverpool areas as holding single breeding pairs. The 1968-72 Atlas recorded confirmed nesting in only one 10km square in Lancashire and presence in nine others, but Nuthatches were shown to be widely distributed immediately to our south in Cheshire and to the north-east in North Yorkshire, with a smaller and more dispersed population in south Cumbria.

By 1988-91 Nuthatches had expanded their Lancashire range threefold and were breeding in 20 10km squares and present in a further eight. Newly-colonised areas were spread throughout the county but concentrated in east and north Lancashire and Merseyside, suggesting that birds had infiltrated from all three neighbouring counties. The pace of occupation has accelerated in more recent years: the 1997-2000 survey recorded breeding in 37 10km squares and presence in another three. Only in the Fylde, the south-west outside of North Merseyside and in Rossendale is it still an uncommon and irregular nesting species. The Nuthatch has been one of the British avifauna's major successes of the late twentieth century, with an increase of 115% during 1970-2001 (CBC) and 71% between 1994 and 2005 (BBS). In Lancashire this has been even more spectacular with the population increasing by at least a factor of 20 from the 1960s to reach an estimated 500 pairs in 1997-2000.

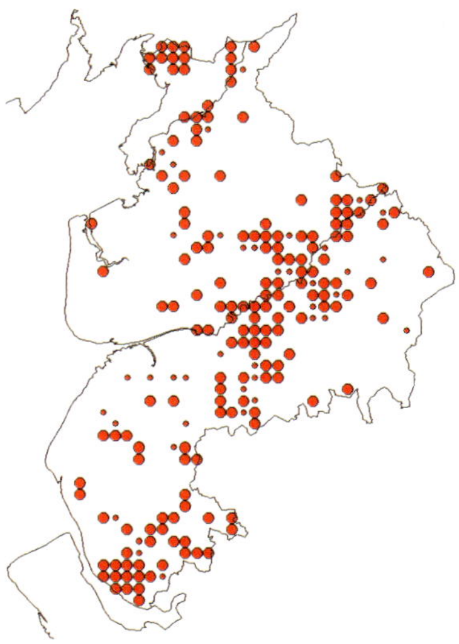

Breeding distribution of Nuthatch, 1997-2000. (Large dots: confirmed. Small dots: possible)

In the north there were only ten records between the 1944 Wennington bird and 1984, although these included breeding in a nest-box at Whittington, also in the Lune Valley, in 1975. In 1985-86 a pair bred in Roeburndale, and in 1989 several years of regular presence in the Silverdale area culminated in breeding records at Eaves Wood and Woodwell. A survey of the L&DBWS area suggested a total population of twelve pairs from the late 1980s (Harrison 1995), but by 1997 there were at least 30 pairs in the Arnside-Silverdale area alone (Harrison 2000). Breeding first took place at Leighton Moss in a nest-box in 1993, and by 1995 Nuthatches were nesting in Wyresdale. Two pairs bred at Arkholme in 1995 and by 2003 at least three pairs were resident there. Nuthatches are now widespread in the Warton-Silverdale area, with nine pairs on Warton Crag alone in 2002.

Further south, isolated sightings in the Preston area in the 1960s and 1970s were followed by a slower colonisation than elsewhere, but by the end of the 1990s there were several pairs in the woods along the Ribble between Penwortham and Samlesbury; by 1991 breeding was taking place in the Brock Valley, where five pairs bred at Myerscough College in 2002. In east Lancashire, closer to the North Yorkshire population and where breeding footholds had probably existed since the 1940s, the expansion was dramatic. Breeding by a pair at Huntroyde in 1973 was followed by a steady increase in the vicinity and by 1978 up to ten pairs were nesting in the Read-Simonstone-Padiham area, increasing to 13 in 1983 and 18 in 1984. Meanwhile Nuthatches were spreading into all suitable woodlands in the Ribble, Darwen and lower Hodder Valleys. Continuing increases were reported throughout lowland east Lancashire during the 1990s; in 2000 four pairs were located in 3km of riverine woods between the Lower and Higher Hodder Bridges and in 2002 twelve pairs bred in Witton Country Park, Blackburn and eight at Bolton-by-Bowland.

Nuthatches remain scarce in Rossendale, however, probably due to a lack of suitable mature woodland. The first records were at Redisher in February 1978 and Ewood Bridge in March 1981; a pair bred at Helmshore in 1988-89 and again in 1994, but since then only Healey Dell has produced records on a regular basis. The first Nuthatch in the Chorley area since the 1942 Appley Bridge record was near Leyland in December 1965; birds were present at Hoghton, Cuerden, Eccleston and Duxbury Woods during 1978-80. Breeding was first recorded at Duxbury in 1983; two pairs nested there in 1985 with another at Shaw Hill, and Nuthatches were described as regular in the Leyland area by 1984. By 1990 at least seven pairs were breeding in the Chorley NHS area, increasing to at least ten in 1992, twelve in 1995 and at least 15 in eight locations in 1997. The more southerly parts of the region were colonised from the late 1980s, and by 2000 there were at least 14 pairs in the Rivington/Anglezarke area, rising to at least 21 pairs in 2004.

In the far south the Mersey and Manchester Ship Canal appear to have served for a while as a deterrent to northward expansion by the substantial Nuthatch populations of Wirral and north Cheshire. Although occasional sightings in Liverpool had been recorded since the late 1950s probable nesting was not reported until 1974, and confirmed breeding, by a pair in Calderstones Park, until a decade later. Once established, however, the bridgehead expanded steadily; by the mid-1990s there were three pairs in Sefton Park and up to 15 in Croxteth Country Park. The population of the former site had increased to five pairs by 2002, when a pair also nested in Prince's Park. Further east, increasingly frequent records around St. Helens after 1994 were followed by breeding at Eccleston Mere and Prescot Reservoirs in 2001-2.

Nuthatch, Little Crosby, February 2004. (Steve Young)

On the south-west mosslands the advance of the Nuthatch has been much more halting, due to a lack of suitable woodland habitat. A pair bred at Scarisbrick Hall, inland of Southport, in 1967 and nesting has been regular in the Rufford area since 1981, but frequent visits to nearby Mere Sands Wood in the 1990s did not result in a breeding presence there. Nuthatches bred again at Scarisbrick Hall in 1997-98 and probably nested in the Botanic Gardens at Churchtown and near Ormskirk in 2001.

A similar scarcity of extensive tracts of broadleaved trees or riverine woodland corridors in the Fylde has also hampered the Nuthatch's colonisation of that area. The first record was at Lytham Hall in April 1962, followed by a fifteen-year interval until the next at Thornton in October 1977, and by a further nine-year gap before two were recorded at Preesall and singles at Lytham and Singleton in 1986. The first proven breeding record, at Weeton in 1987 was followed by pairs at Clifton Hall in 1993 and Hackensall Wood, Knott End, in 1997. The pace of events appears to have quickened in more recent years; a single pair at Ingol Golf Course in 1999 increased to three in 2000, when a pair also bred at Ellel Grange.

Very few Nuthatches have ever been seen away from breeding areas in Lancashire; a recent example was one at Seaforth on 1 September 2003, 5km away from the nearest breeding site. There has been only one recovery of a Lancashire Nuthatch, a pullus ringed in Dean Wood, Rivington on 16 June 1991 which was found dead after striking a window 8km away near Bolton on 14 July.

BM, RW.
This species account was sponsored by Keith and Nadine Deacon.

WALLCREEPER

Tichodroma muraria

Lancashire Category B. (1, 0).

Vagrant from southern Europe.

The first British record was one shot at Stratton Strawless, Norfolk on 30 October 1792; eighty years on, the second was shot at Sabden in east Lancashire on 8 May 1872. Mitchell described the event: it was seen by mill-hands at a cotton mill, drawing attention to itself by its crimson-banded wings, and after some time was shot by Edward Laycock, who took it to Mr. W. Naylor of Whalley. The specimen was badly damaged and its sex could not be determined. It came into Mitchell's possession and later passed to Mr. J. Whittaker of Rainworth Lodge, Nottinghamshire, after whose death it was acquired by Mansfield Borough Council.

Wallcreeper. (G.E. Lodge in Mitchell, 1892)

SJW, MJ.
This species account was sponsored by Sarah Louise Jones.

TREECREEPER

Certhia familiaris

Lancashire Category A.

Common resident breeder.

The current fortunes in Britain of this woodland specialist are unclear; BWP noted an increase, but more recent evidence is ambiguous with the CBC indicating a population decline of 17% between 1970 and 2001 and the BBS and increase of 23% during 1994-2005. In Lancashire there is little indication of any significant change in range or numbers for the past 30 or more years.

Mitchell described the Treecreeper as a local and uncommon resident which had decreased over much of the county, including the Ribble and Hodder Valleys and the Preston and Liverpool areas. Its fortunes appear to have improved greatly by Oakes's time and he considered it common around Silverdale and from the Lune Valley south to the Ribble and beyond, to Rufford and Rivington. It was only an occasional breeder in the vicinity of Formby, Scarisbrick and Knowsley, and was essentially a winter visitor to most of the south-west and to the Fylde. Spencer (1973) described the Treecreeper as breeding throughout the county in suitable wooded areas and found even more widely during the winter months.

Distribution appears to have changed very little since the 1960s; Treecreepers were found in 48 10km squares in both 1968-72 and 1997-2000, when breeding was considered likely in 381 (41%) tetrads and the county population was estimated at 1,500 pairs. Treecreepers appear to be resident wherever there is sufficient woodland habitat and there is no clear geographical pattern to their Lancashire distribution, although they are absent from the treeless moorlands of the Pennines and Bowland, from much of the Lancashire Plain and the south-west mosslands, and from most coastal habitats.

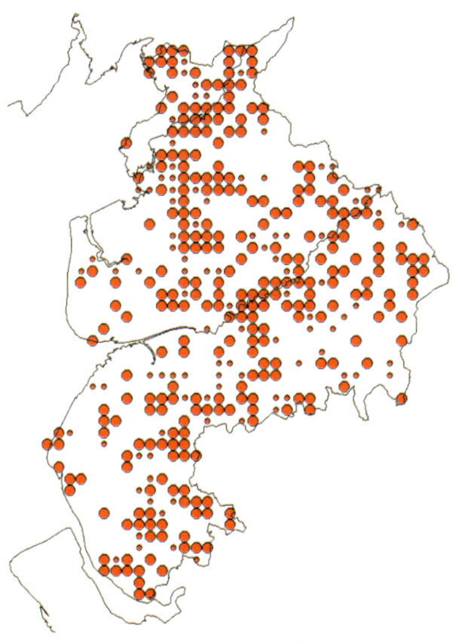

Breeding distribution of Treecreeper, 1997-2000. (Large dots: confirmed. Small dots: possible)

The highest densities are found in the well-wooded Lune, Wyre, Ribble, Hodder, Calder, Darwen and Yarrow Valleys. Breeding pairs are very thinly distributed in Rossendale and especially in the Fylde, although a pair has bred in Blackpool's Woodland Gardens since 1990 and up to four nested at Ingol Golf Course and two in Stanley Park, Blackpool in 2000. Treecreepers appear to have made little use of specially-designed nest-boxes in Lancashire, although there was some success with these at Crawshawbooth, Rossendale in the 1970s and a pair nested in a box in Roeburndale in 1991. There are occasional records of pairs nesting in sheds and other structures, including wooden angling-huts at Ogden Reservoir, Rossendale and at Arkholme in 2002.

Treecreeper, Little Crosby, December 2003. (Steve Young)

Only minor changes in populations at monitored sites have been recorded: at Leighton Moss three pairs in the 1960s had increased to six by 1978 and remained around that level during the 1980s and early 1990s, increasing briefly to eight pairs in 1985 but since the mid-1990s three or four pairs has been the norm. Two pairs at Mere Sands Wood in 1991 declined to one in 1993 but recovered in 1996-97; at least three pairs bred there in 1999 and up to four annually since.

Post-breeding dispersal occasionally produces a very small number of records at coastal migration watchpoints between July and early November. During the exceptional passage of tit species in September-October 1985 seven Treecreepers were trapped at Heysham, the first records for the site. In subsequent years annual visits by a few birds have become the norm there; typically one or two are ringed in July and two or three in late autumn. Elsewhere, odd birds have been recorded at Fairhaven, Warton Bank, Marshside and Oglet since 1980, and at least ten were in Formby Hall Woods in late autumn 1983. One or a few Treecreepers are occasionally recorded with mobile tit flocks in mid-winter, including five in Stanley Park on 11 December 1983, at least 15 in the Roddlesworth Plantations on 5 January 1990 and singles at Marton Mere and Martin Mere in early December 1995. Some have adapted to using garden nut-feeders, for example in the Blackburn area since 2001.

There has been only one recovery of a Lancashire-ringed Treecreeper, a bird ringed at Lancaster on 21 November 1999 and found freshly dead locally on 16 January 2000. Far more interesting is the record of a bird ringed at Spurn Point on 18 September 1983, in an autumn of heavy tit migration and after falls of Goldcrests on the east coast, and found freshly dead 200km to the west at Garston in south Liverpool a fortnight later on 3 October. This is the most travelled by far of only five recoveries of more than 20km in Britain and seems highly likely to have been a continental bird of the partially migratory race *familiaris*, the British sub-species *britannica* being highly sedentary (Migration Atlas).

BM, RW.
This species account was sponsored by
Bernard and Ruth Pollock.

PENDULINE TIT

Remiz pendulinus

Lancashire Category A. (0, 1).

Vagrant from central or eastern Europe.

The county's only record was found, not surprisingly, at our largest reedbed at Leighton Moss on 11 November 2004. Several birders were watching a Bittern from Lillian's Hide when the Penduline Tit appeared in the same field of view, feeding on a reedmace seed-head. It was first 'called' by Brin Best but then Steven Grimshaw, who had been filming the Bittern, realised that he had accidentally caught the Penduline Tit on video. The bird showed distantly on and off during the afternoon but was not seen subsequently.

SJW.
This species account was sponsored by John Donnelly.

GOLDEN ORIOLE

Oriolus oriolus

Lancashire Category A. (3, 20).

Rare passage migrant from continental Europe.

Mitchell reported a female shot at Quernmore near Lancaster around the 1820s but Oakes did not consider this record genuine.

Male Golden Oriole, Burnley, 6 June 1946, found and painted by Philip A. Clancey, who lived in Burnley after the Second World War before moving to take up a post at York Museum. He subsequently moved to South Africa and became Director of the Durban Museum where he wrote and illustrated 'The Birds of Natal and Zululand'.

Oakes himself recognised three acceptable records, including a pair near Chipping for several days in the summer of 1870, which moved to the vicinity of Leagram Hall, where the male was shot. An adult male was seen and heard in an oak wood north of Burnley on 6 June 1946 and another male was seen at Bleasdale on the unusual date of 19 November 1946.

The next was a male on the Martin Mere estate, near Mere Brow, from 17-19 June 1951. Breeding took place in the Rusland Valley (then in Lancashire but now in Cumbria) between 1959 and 1961.

There have been a further 17 records since then but the Golden Oriole remains one of Lancashire's most enigmatic species. Only one of these more recent records has remained at any site for more than a day, indeed most have been seen rather fleetingly, often in flight, or heard in song without clear views being obtained. Add to this the fact that few have been seen by more than a single observer and one has a recipe for speculation, but it needs to be borne in mind that transience seems to be a feature of migrant Golden Orioles wherever they occur.

Adult male Golden Oriole, Leighton Moss, November 2005. (Steve Young)

One possible exception involved a series of records of first-summer males on three separate dates between 22 May and 16 June 1992 at Heysham Moss, Ainsdale and Martin Mere, which may perhaps have related to a single individual. Our only definite 'long-stayer' was an adult male at Leighton Moss on 16-19 November 2005.

All records are published in the table, showing that most have been on or near the coast with just four in east Lancashire: two at Rivington and singles at Whin Scar Clough and Stocks Reservoir.

Figure 1 shows a strong clustering of records in May and June with one in late July and two in April. This shows a close fit with the national pattern but the 1976 Liverpool record is amongst the earliest in Britain and is perhaps suspect for this reason.

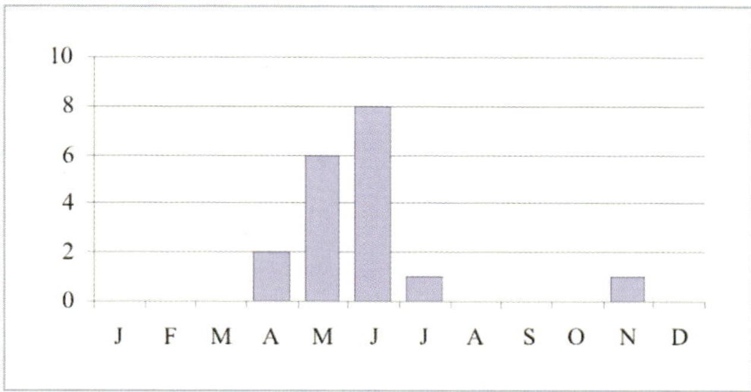

Figure 1. Monthly totals of Golden Orioles in Lancashire, 1951-2005.

All records:

1870	Chipping, pair in summer
1946	Burnley, male, 6 June
1946	Bleasdale, male, 19 November
1951	MMWWT, male, 17 to 19 June
1964	Leighton Moss, male, 28 May
1970	Mere Brow, female, 12 May
1971	Mere Brow, male, 7 June
1971	Alt Estuary, male, 13 June
1973	Southport, male, 24 April
1976	Liverpool, male, 16 April
1978	Thornton near Crosby, male in flight, 20 May
1984	Formby Point, male, heard only, 7 May
1985	Rivington, singing male, 5 to 10 June
1990	Whin Scar Clough, female, 1 June
1992	Heysham Moss, first-summer male, 22 May
1992	Ainsdale, first-summer male, 25 May (possibly same as Heysham)
1992	MMWWT, first-summer male, 16 June (possibly same as Heysham)
1996	Cabin Hill NNR, female, 2 June
1997	Rivington, singing male, 21 May
2000	Marton Mere, female in flight, 14 May
2000	Fazakerley, male in flight, 28 July
2003	Stocks Reservoir, singing male, heard only, 14 June
2005	Leighton Moss, adult male, 16-19 November

SJW, MJ.

This species account was sponsored by Sheila Mary Cooper and in memory of Mrs. Hilda Sharples.

ISABELLINE SHRIKE

Lanius isabellinus

Lancashire Category A. (0, 1).

Vagrant from central Asia.

Discovered by Nick Mason while carrying out a wildfowl count at Stocks Reservoir on 5 November 1996, the county's only record could only initially be identified as a shrike of a species unknown to the observer. Detailed notes enabled probable specific identification over the phone and this was confirmed the following morning in the field by Tim Melling.

The bird was a first-winter and initially thought to have been a male of the western sub-species *phoenicuroides* ('Turkestan Shrike'). However, a review of the record by Tim Worfolk (2000. *Dutch Birding* 22: 6.) argues that it was more likely to have been of the eastern race *isabellinus* ('Daurian Shrike').

Isabelline Shrike, Stocks Reservoir, November 1996. (Steve Young)

The bird was extremely confiding and spent most of its stay – until 11 November – in a small group of hawthorns, making frequent sallies to take caterpillars and other insect prey from the ground. It also took many small passerines, including Great Tit, Blue Tit, Robin and Goldfinch. Unexpectedly, it was also seen eating hawthorn berries – BWP does not list vegetable matter as having been previously recorded in the diet of Isabelline Shrike.

This was the 46th record of Isabelline Shrike in Britain and Ireland and the first in north-west England. The overwhelming majority of previous records have come from eastern and south-western coastal locations, so this inland record was especially remarkable.

SJW, MJ.

This species account was sponsored by Sylvia Pyefinch.

RED-BACKED SHRIKE

Lanius collurio

Lancashire Category A. (/, 13).

Extinct breeder; vagrant from continental Europe.

For a twenty-first century birder, to read Mitchell's account is to visit a long-lost world. Although decreasing, the Red-backed Shrike was still a regular breeding species in Lancashire, arriving in mid- to late May and departing in mid-September. He mentioned breeding sites at Bootle, Rainhill (1860), Farington, Penwortham, Midge Hall (between Preston and Southport), Haighton (1872), Broughton (1875), Goosnargh (1878), Knott End (1882), Rivington, Clitheroe (1860) and Colne (for several years in a bramble-filled clough). Skaife (*Magazine of Natural History*, 1838) stated that it was by no means a rare bird near Blackburn, several specimens being obtained each year. In 1850 Red-backed Shrikes bred throughout England and Wales, as far north as south Cumbria and north Yorkshire but by 1920 most of northern England had been abandoned and by 1950 the species had fallen back south of a line from the Wash to South Wales.

Oakes, however, published only two records in the period 1909 to 1938 and both were outside our present recording area. It seems likely, then, that the Red-backed Shrike became extinct as a breeding species in Lancashire towards the end of the nineteenth century.

Tony Disley

There have been thirteen modern records between 1966 and 1997, involving fourteen individuals – three females, five males and six first-winters. The earliest of these was a male at Formby on 10 May 1969 and the latest a first-winter at Lea Marsh near Preston on 30 September 1971. Records are divided fairly evenly between spring and autumn with most in May and September (Figure 1). This date range is similar to the national pattern, which shows clear peaks at the end of May and the beginning of September. Nationally, however, birds are roughly twice as common in spring as in autumn.

All were on the western side of the county, mostly at well-watched coastal migration sites. All were one-day birds with the exception of a female at Formby Point on 18 May 1978 which was subsequently seen at Ainsdale NNR on the 20th, and a juvenile at Martin Mere from 23 September to 3 October 1981. The only multiple record was of two juveniles at Heysham on 28 September 1992.

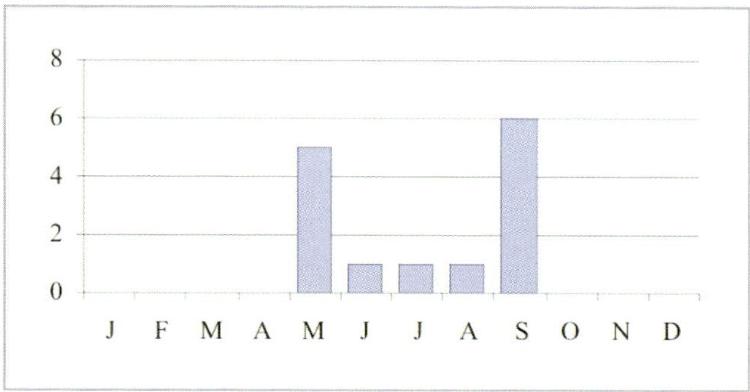

Figure 1. Monthly totals of Red-backed Shrikes in Lancashire, 1966-2005.

All modern records:

1966	Brock Valley, female, 14 May
1969	Formby, male, 10 May
1970	Formby Moss, first-winter, 5 September
1971	Lea Marsh Preston, first-winter, 30 September
1977	Leighton Moss, male, 7 June
1978	Formby Point, female, 18 May. Also Ainsdale NNR 20 May
1981	MMWWT, first-winter, 23 September to 3 October
1984	Seaforth NR, first-winter, 28 August
1985	Fleetwood, female, 16 May
1989	Blundellsands, male, trapped 24September
1992	Heysham, two first-winters, 28 September
1996	Marshside, male, 16 May
1997	Fazakerley, male, 8 July

BM, SJW, MJ.

This species account was sponsored by Dave Hardaker.

GREAT GREY SHRIKE

Lanius excubitor

Lancashire Category A. (/, 100+).

Scarce winter visitor and passage migrant from Fennoscandia.

Mitchell's description of the nineteenth century status of Great Grey Shrike as 'rare [but occurring] too often to make its captures worth detailing' is far from illuminating. Oakes, however, believed it to have become a 'very rare vagrant' during the first half of the twentieth century and he published just three records from our present recording area: singles shot near Chorley on 20 March 1880 and at Bretherton in February 1890, and one seen on the extremely unusual date of August 1882 near Preston.

Oakes' view is a little baffling in the light of the species' current status, which fits rather better with Mitchell's, and Spencer (1973) considered that Oakes had over-rated the species' rarity, given that at least 60 had been recorded (within the pre-1974 borders) in the two decades since the publication of Oakes's book. On the other hand, it seems unlikely that very many of this often-conspicuous and site-faithful species would have been overlooked in an era when specimen collection was still actively pursued. The Great Grey Shrike may, however, have been significantly scarcer in the early twentieth century than it became subsequently.

Great Grey Shrike, Stocks Reservoir, 2003. (Mark Breaks)

On average, about two have been seen annually in the county since 1953 and during the 1970s records were frequent enough for only a summary of occurrences to be published in the county report. Birds have been seen in 17 winters since 1977/78, usually just one to three but with five in 1966/67 and 1982/83, and four in 1988/89. Our records are not sufficiently complete to identify any trend since the 1950s but it does appear that sightings have become rather less regular since the 1970s and particularly since the mid-1990s. This is in line with national records which appear to have declined significantly from around 1995. This trend has also been noted since the 1980s in the main wintering grounds of the Fennoscandian population in central Europe and is believed to have been partly a result of an increasing proportion of birds wintering within Sweden rather than to any change in population size (Hagemeijer & Blair 1997).

The earliest records have both been at Fairhaven on 6 October in 1972 and 1979 and most arrive between October and mid-November, although a handful remain unfound until later in the winter (Figure 1). The latest sighting was at the Eric Morecambe complex on 27 April 1993.

More than 100 records have been published since 1953 but the number of individuals involved is considerably lower, probably not many more than 40. Only about a third of records (18 since 1977) clearly relate to passage migrants, mostly at coastal watchpoints. Most of the remainder have stayed in the county for at least part of the winter and several have returned in subsequent winters. The longest staying of these have been in the Silverdale and Leighton Moss area between 1960/61 and 1964/65, at Lytham from 1962/63 to 1967/68, Clitheroe/Downham from 1964/65 to 1966/67 and Formby from 1967/68 to 1970/71. More recently one was at Stocks Reservoir during winter 2002/03 and 2003/04, and probably again in spring 2005.

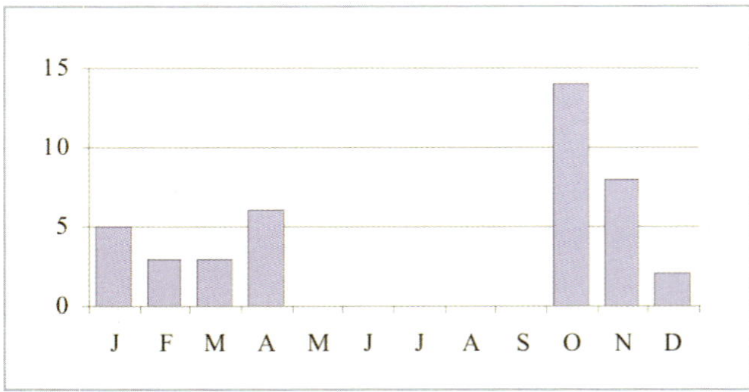

Figure 2. Monthly totals of Great Grey Shrikes in Lancashire, 1978-2005.

Records have shown no clear geographical pattern since the 1960s and have been spread more or less equally between north and east Lancashire, the Fylde and central and southern Lancashire and North Merseyside.

SJW, BM, RW.

This species account was sponsored by Roy Kendall.

WOODCHAT SHRIKE

Lanius senator

Lancashire Category A. (0, 4).

Vagrant from southern Europe.

Mitchell gave two records, both considered insufficiently detailed by Oakes. One was said to have been killed by a cat near Lancaster according to the manuscript of the Rev. J.D. Bannister. The second was reportedly shot at Walton-le-Dale in 1870 and stuffed by Mr R Entwistle of Bolton (*Manchester City News*, 1875).

Female Woodchat Shrike, Marshside, May 2007. (Steve Young)

During his days as a teacher at Rossall School, Andrew Cadman regularly walked the school grounds in the early morning before beginning work, and on 1 June 1978 he found Lancashire's first confirmed Woodchat Shrike on a fence post there. It soon flew off east towards the old Fleetwood power station/ICI pools site and was not refound. Around four hundred Woodchat Shrikes had been recorded in Britain and Ireland at the time of the Rossall bird and the species was taken off the BBRC rarities list at the end of 1981 – but it has not become noticeably more common in Lancashire.

The next record was also in the Fylde, a first-winter bird in hawthorns on the dunes north of Fairhaven Lake on 29-31 August 1987. The focus then shifted to the north of the county. First came an adult at Heysham Power Station on 30 April 1988 and then, after a long wait, a juvenile in a hedgerow north of the Eric Morecambe Pools at Leighton Moss on 28 August 1999 – a bird which stayed all day to be enjoyed by many visitors.

SJW, MJ.

This species account was sponsored by the Fylde Bird Club.

JAY

Garrulus glandarius

Lancashire Category A.

Common resident breeder.

Mitchell had this to say about the plight of the Jay in the latter part of the nineteenth century: 'every year decreasing in numbers; its propensity for emptying Pheasants' eggs causing it to be mercilessly destroyed by the game-keeping fraternity. It is very shy and wary, and seldom falls to the gun; poison being the chief element in its extermination' – an implied prophesy of impending extinction which, as Oakes pointed out, fortunately did not come to fruition. Oakes himself spoke of 'incessant persecution' in the first half of the twentieth century which, together with woodland felling, had caused further shrinkage in distribution, in spite of which 'the species (was) not only holding its own but actually increasing in a few localities'. He described the core breeding range as central Lancashire, from Preston eastwards into the Ribble Valley and south to Rufford and the Roddlesworth/Anglezarke/Rivington plantations. Birds were scarce in the Fylde and east Lancashire.

The latter years of the last century saw a gradual expansion but at a slower rate than for either Carrion Crow or Magpie, all these species no doubt benefiting from less intensive game-keeping after the Second World War. The Jay has a less catholic diet than the latter species and is more restricted to oak woods but the species is found in most deciduous woodlands in Lancashire, even where there is only a small proportion of oak. The range increased from 42 10km squares in 1968-72 and 41 in 1988-92 to 49 in 1997-2000, when the county population was estimated at 2,000 territories in 446 tetrads (48%), more than two-thirds of which were south of the Ribble.

In the north Jays breed chiefly in the Silverdale-Yealand area and between the Keer and the Lune Valleys, but in recent years they have become more regular in the Lune Valley itself. Birds have been long-established in the larger wooded areas of the Ribble, lower Hodder, lower Calder and Darwen Valleys and between Preston and Garstang. A significant expansion of range was noted in east Lancashire from about the mid-1970s, when birds became established in Towneley and many other small areas of woodland where they had previously been rare or very uncommon in the breeding season. The Briercliffe area was colonised in 1984. The first record in Rossendale was at Lumb Vale in 1968, with all records until the mid-1970s confined to the area between Irwell Vale (where nesting was confirmed in 1976) and Stubbins Vale.

They have continued to spread, reaching as far up the Lumb Valley as Clough Bottom Reservoir by 1992, and by 2003 all the Rossendale valleys were occupied.

The Jay is a well-established breeding bird in all suitable parts of Chorley, which, together with adjacent areas of West Lancashire and Blackburn with Darwen, forms the species' county heartland. It is particularly prevalent in the Duxbury-Birkacre woodlands, in Cuerden Valley Park and the plantations on the western fringes of the West Pennine Moors. In the sparsely-wooded Fylde, two or three pairs bred at Lytham Hall from at least the 1950s and their range increased from three to 29 tetrads between 1986-1990 (Dunstan & Guy 2000) and 1997-2000.

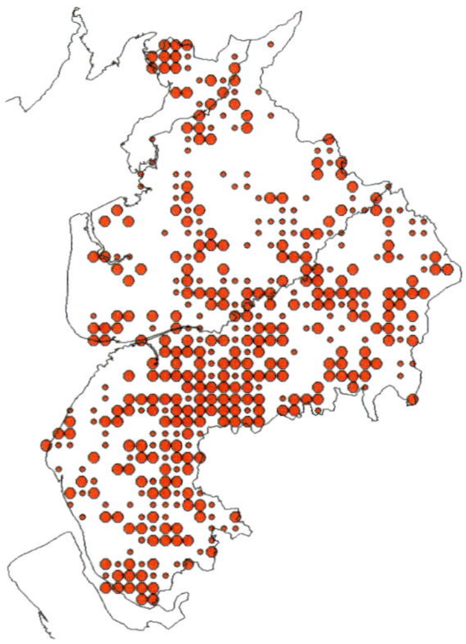

Breeding distribution of Jay, 1997-2000. (Large dots: confirmed. Small dots: possible)

Jays were scarce in North Merseyside until the 1980s, away from well-established sites such as Croxteth and Knowsley Parks. They have slowly spread throughout the south Liverpool parks and St. Helens, and, having colonised the Sefton coast pinewoods in 1977, have become increasingly widespread to the north of the conurbation.

Jays are more widespread outside the breeding season, when they may be encountered in much more open situations. Normally, only occasional birds are seen during autumn passage at coastal sites, although there were marked influxes/movements in the autumns of 1983, 1993, 1996, 2001 and 2005. National influxes are triggered by the failure of continental acorn crops and, in 1983 and 2001 at least, westward movements were accentuated by the failure of the crop in Britain.

In 1983 the first sightings were flocks of 29, 31 and 34 moving south over Walton Hall Park, Liverpool from 11-18 September, followed by a small movement over Burnley on the 23rd. Then came a heavy influx in north-east Lancashire and the Anglezarke-Rivington area in October and 30-40 at Penwortham in the same month. Over 50 stayed all winter at Calderstones Park, Liverpool, and many small groups were encountered in the Fylde from mid-October, including twelve at Freckleton and 19 at Preesall. A total of 71 were reported in the Fylde in October with up to 30 remaining in December and 18 in February 1984; this compared with a total of 26 winter birds in the previous 30 years, with never more than two together (Leeming 1985).

A much less spectacular influx occurred in 1993 but several areas recorded birds for the first time in a decade. Most were on the Fylde coast, where at least 35 non-resident birds were seen from 16 September to 20 November, with others at widespread locations in north and north-east Lancashire and North Merseyside, the largest group being 13 at Sefton Park, Liverpool in late September. 1996 brought another notable influx: at least 45 were in the Rivington area on 22 October, while more than 80 individuals were reported at 31 sites in the Fylde during October, and Marshside recorded an unprecedented seven between 26 September and 20 October. The largest count was 60+ in the Silverdale-Woodwell area on 1 January 1997 with 32 at Astley Park, Chorley on the 4th, both areas with established breeding populations.

Jay, Stanley Park, Blackpool. (Phillip Tomkinson)

The next major influx began in September 2001, when Jays began to be reported from unusual sites, including singles at Seaforth and Lytham Moss on the 23rd and 24th and three over Lancaster on 25th. A total of 216 was seen at 35 sites in the Fylde with the main influx occurring from 11-14 October (Walsh 2002). At least 22 passed over Heysham from 4-28 October and birds flew over Seaforth on four dates. The most recent movement occurred between 21 September and 25 October 2005 and included peak counts of 13 over Fairhaven, 22 separately over the Rimrose Valley and Seaforth, and 13 at Heysham.

There are just 19 recoveries of ringed Jays to or from Lancashire; all have involved local movements except for three exchanges with other northern counties. The origins of the large national influxes have never been confirmed through ringing but it is likely that continental birds of the nominate race are involved as well as the British sub-species *rufitergum*.

JFW, RW.

This species account was sponsored by Ian and Diana Wrapson.

BLUE JAY

Cyanocitta cristata

Lancashire Category D.

One was found by Gordon and Brenda Milward on their garden feeders at Thornton near Crosby on 5 June 2003. It was videoed during its 30 minutes stay before it flew off to the west. Remarkably, the bird was relocated on 7 June, again on feeders, in a garden at Hillside, Southport.

There is no doubt about the identification nor the authenticity of these records but there will inevitably be considerable debate about the bird's origin. On the plus side, Thornton is only a few miles distant from the Seaforth Docks with their history of north American 'stowaways'. The Blue Jay's range is almost wholly restricted to north America with its strict export controls and the species is not believed to be regular in captivity.

The record has been submitted to the BBRC but, as a potential first for Britain, the ultimate decision will be taken by the BOURC.

Blue Jay, Thornton, Merseyside, 5 June 2003 (Gordon Milward)

SJW.

MAGPIE

Pica pica

Lancashire Category A.

Abundant resident breeder.

The Magpie has long been a common species in our area; Mitchell mentioned that it bred in all districts and that its abundance was in inverse proportion to the intensity of persecution by gamekeepers and farmers. Even in those days flocks of up to 60 congregated in winter on coastal fields manured with shell-fish. Oakes referred to it as a very familiar species which had extended its range within Lancashire considerably since the 1930s. He described it as 'common in all parts of the county (with the exception of) the Formby-Aughton area', breeding on moorlands at 1150' (350m) asl and forming regular winter roosts in plantations at over 1000' (300m) asl. Oakes also noted a recent move into urban areas stating that 'in recent times the bird has commonly nested in city outskirts and now visits gardens in Manchester and Liverpool where previously it was never seen'.

Nowadays, Magpies are firmly established as an urban species and this has undoubtedly contributed significantly to the doubling of their British population since 1970 (CBC/BBS). By 1997-2000 they were breeding in every lowland area of Lancashire and were recorded in 89% of the county's tetrads, being absent only from the largely treeless and well-keepered moorlands. The only sizeable areas from which Magpies were missing as a breeder were Bowland and the surrounding uplands (where they were absent from 60 tetrads), and to a lesser extent parts of the West Pennine Moors. A relaxation of persecution in some areas has probably also influenced their expansion but in some areas, especially on grouse moors, control measures through Larsen-trapping and shooting continue to keep numbers in check.

Many people's perceptions of the recent increase in Magpie numbers is coloured by their more than proportionate expansion in urban areas due to their readiness to exploit new feeding opportunities, including garden bird feeders, discarded fast-food and refuse tips. Increasing occurrence in urban areas was noted in north Lancashire from the 1940s, in Rossendale, Formby and Southport in the 1950s, and east Lancashire from the mid-1960s. Lancashire examples of Magpies with unusual feeding habits include birds taking live fish from a garden pond in the Chorley area in 1982 and from Marton Mere in 2002, and removing metal foil caps of milk bottles in Trawden in 1983 and in Fairhaven in 1990. Their predilection for nestlings is often exaggerated (Gooch *et al.* 1991) but that they can wreak local havoc is amply attested by the report of a family of Magpies raiding Swallows' nests and taking 70 eggs and 35 pulli in the Pilling area in 1989.

Tony Disley

The Lancashire population was estimated at 12,000 pairs in 1997-2000 but this was not much more than an educated guess. Studies in Sheffield found breeding densities of around 20 pairs per km^2 on the urban fringe and up to 32 pairs in the urban area (Birkhead 1991). Smaller scale surveys in Lancashire have yielded lower densities: 9-11 pairs per km^2 in Waterfoot and Stacksteads in Rossendale in 1977, and 17.5-19 in Ansdell and Fairhaven in 2001 (J.F. Walsh *pers. comm.*), with average territory sizes of 10ha and 5.6ha respectively. No studies have been carried out in rural Lancashire and it is not known how typical the Rossendale or Fairhaven densities are for urban areas, but it seems likely that average county densities are likely to be at least five per km^2 and the total population in excess of 15,000 pairs.

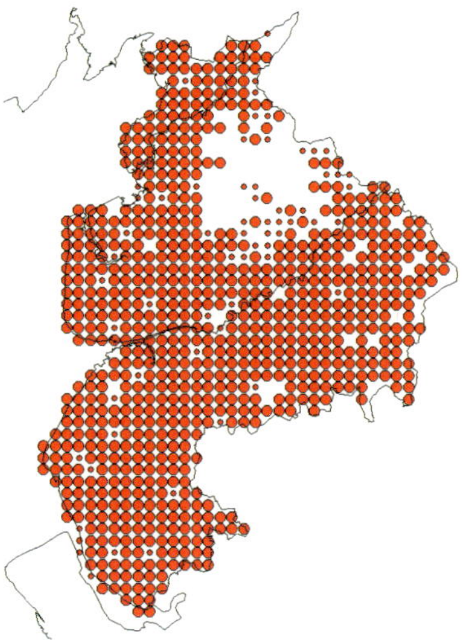

Breeding distribution of Magpie, 1997-2000. (Large dots: confirmed. Small dots: possible)

At high densities, competition for nest sites with other Magpies and Carrion Crows has led to some unusual choices, including barn beams and quarry ledges as well as the floodlights of Blackpool Football Club in 1988. The use of electricity pylons was first recorded in the 1950s and in 1999 a pair bred 35m up on a gantry in the Seaforth Docks. In 1990 a pair built their nest in the roof-space of a deserted moorland farm above Belmont.

Outside the breeding season feeding birds are commonly seen in groups of up to 20 but usually fewer than 40 individuals. However, roosting congregations may be much larger – especially during December and January cold spells – even though some paired birds stay close to their nest site for most of the year. One of the best-monitored roosts is at Blackpool Zoo where monthly peaks during 1998 included 354 in January, 264 in late February, 110 in September and 257 in November. The highest count there was an estimated 450 in hard weather at the end of December 1995, which appears to be one of the largest recorded in Britain (Birkhead 1991; Brown & Grice 2005). In 2000 a team of experienced observers counted around 350 entering the Blackpool Zoo roost in both winter periods, gathering after feeding at Stanley Park, Marton Mere, two adjacent golf courses and the surrounding suburban housing estates.

All types of copses and woodlands are used for roosts, ranging from willow scrub at Leighton Moss and Royal Lytham Golf Course to coniferous plantations at Dean Clough Reservoir. For many years during the 1980s this latter site consistently hosted one of the largest roosts in the county with a maximum of 285 recorded in January 1988 and 255 in November 1989. Other large roost counts have included 250 at Lower Rivington Reservoir in January 1985 with around 160 there in 1996, and 205 at Egerton (a few metres over our boundary in Greater Manchester) in December 2000 with 200 there in January 2003. In the last 20 years winter roosts of over 100 have been reported from nine other sites: Cuerden Valley Park in 1987, Eccleston Mere in 1989, Burnley in 1990, Childwall in 1992, Lee Park Golf Course in 1993, Whitworth in 1998, Royal Lytham Golf Course in 1999 and 2000, and 190 in the Rimrose Valley in November 2003.

Although the Magpie is highly sedentary small movements are occasionally noted, most obviously at coastal sites such as Heysham, Rossall, Fairhaven and Seaforth between late September and late October. Daily totals do not normally exceed ten, but occasionally movements of up to 30 birds are reported. Of 68 recorded movements of ringed birds only 13 have been further than 10km, with just five exchanges with neighbouring counties and one remarkable bird, ringed in June 2002 in Northumberland and found dead at Stalmine in May 2003.

JFW, RW.

This species account was sponsored by Frank Walsh.

NUTCRACKER

Nucifraga caryocatactes

Lancashire Category A. (0, 1).

Vagrant from Siberia.

The very large influx into Britain in autumn 1968, when more than 300 were seen, led to one or two birds being found in the county, neither of which was seen by any birders. One was at Stalmine, near Preesall from 26 September to 12 November. It fed on apples in an old orchard and was photographed at very close range with a box camera by C. Stirzaker – it was also seen by J. Porter but later searches in the area, in very poor weather, proved fruitless. Maurice Jones examined the photograph and verified the record. What was accepted by the BBRC as probably the same bird was seen at Rossall School on 3 October by a groundsman, who relayed the description to Andrew Cadman.

It is assumed that the Lancashire records refer to the irruptive Siberian race *macrorhynchos*, colloquially known as 'Slender-billed Nutcracker', as they occurred in an irruption year and nominate central European race is essentially sedentary.

SJW, MJ.

This species account was sponsored by Richard Charles.

CHOUGH

Pyrrhocorax pyrrhocorax

Lancashire Category A. (1, 6).

Vagrant from Irish Sea colonies.

Mitchell merely stated that the Chough was 'occasionally, but very rarely seen on the coast, generally after heavy weather and probably storm driven from the Isle of Man or North Wales'.

Oakes thought that Mitchell's statement may have been based in part on a reference in Byerley's 'Fauna of Liverpool' to an undated bird at Crosby; this individual was said to have been preserved by Mather. Oakes added no further records.

A bird picked up dead at Litherland by J. Clegg on 12 April 1976 was, therefore, the first conclusive county record; it had been ringed on Bardsey Island in June 1975. Another two followed in rapid succession, the first on Royal Birkdale golf course after a severe gale on 16 Nov 1977, and this or another at Heysham Head on 17-18 November 1977.

The next was seen and heard in flight south of the Liver Building in central Liverpool on 23 July 1978 and perhaps the same bird was at Otterspool Tip, Aigburth and in the city centre from 23 April 1979 and throughout 1980. A long-dead corpse was found in the dunes at Formby Point on 30 May 1995 and, finally, one was seen at Jack Scout, Silverdale on 10 January 2005. What seems likely to have been the same bird then appeared at Preesall on 12 August 2005 and was subsequently seen at several Fylde coast sites until 3 October.

Choughs are not notable migrants but they do show some post-juvenile dispersal. In addition to North Wales, our nearest breeding colonies are on the Isle of Man, which may have been a source of some of the more recent Lancashire records.

Chough, Knott End, August 2005. (Chris Batty)

SJW, MJ.
This species account was sponsored by Sue Bedford.

JACKDAW

Corvus monedula

Lancashire Category A.

Common resident breeder.

The Jackdaw is now a locally common breeding resident with an estimated county population of 5,000 pairs in 1997-2000, but it appears to have been considerably scarcer during the nineteenth century. Mitchell regarded breeding as widespread but only in small numbers, although he did detect a slight increase in many parts of the county. By the middle of the twentieth century Oakes reported further increases, highlighting nesting on limestone crags at Leck Fell, woodland colonies in Pilling and Formby, breeding in a quarry in Hoghton and on buildings everywhere. It was, however, inexplicably almost entirely absent from Rossendale's many quarries and cliffs.

The past 50 years have seen a continued spread and infilling throughout Lancashire, and, although some gaps in distribution remain, breeding was thought likely in 62% of tetrads in 1997-2000. Jackdaws are commonest in east and north Lancashire and scarcest in central and southern areas and arable areas of the Fylde, West Lancashire and Merseyside. The indications are that Lancashire has broadly followed the national trend which saw a further population increase of 40% during 1994-2005 (BBS).

The limestone quarries of north Lancashire provide ideal sites for large colonies; those at Warton Crag and Trowbarrow, for example, are estimated to total some 300 to 400 birds. They also nest on cliffs in the Lune Valley as well as up to a dozen pairs each in Goosander nest-boxes and in farm buildings at Arkholme.

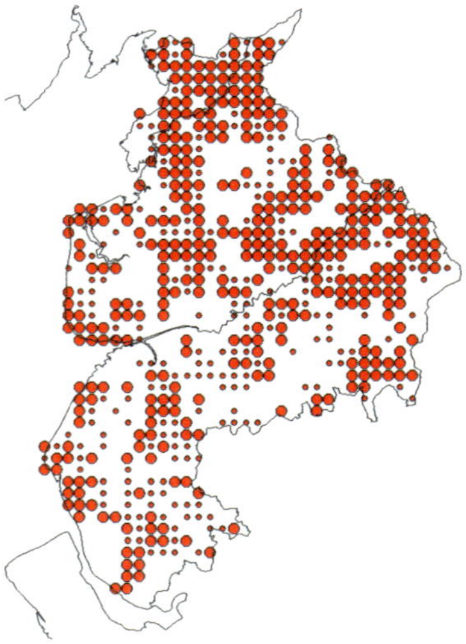

Breeding distribution of Jackdaw, 1997-2000. (Large dots: confirmed. Small dots: possible)

Spencer (1977) commented that the species' status and distribution in the Burnley area was much as it had been in 1939, though sandstone quarries were rarely occupied. It remains locally but widely distributed throughout the Ribble Valley where 100 were prospecting for nest sites in chimney pots in Clitheroe in March 2001. In Rossendale, the only site mentioned by Parker (1928) was St. Mary's Church, Rawtenstall but there was a spread up the Irwell Valley during the 1950s and numbers were still increasing steadily in 1993; a colony on Ilex Mill chimney, which held 20 pairs in 1964, had doubled in size by 2002.

Colonies formed in a few of the millstone grit quarries in the Chorley/West Pennine Moors area, including 21 pairs in two quarries at Withnell in 1995 rising to 40 pairs since 2000. The colony in Hoghton Tower quarry that once held up to 100 pairs is now very much reduced, due mainly to growth of scrub. In central Chorley and nearby Adlington, 16 pairs bred in churches in 1998.

Increases were being reported throughout North Merseyside in 1994; perhaps as many as 100 pairs now breed in the Sefton Coast woodlands and smaller numbers are regular in south-east Liverpool. The Fylde population is centred chiefly around Knott End and Preesall (where 24 pairs bred in Parrox Hall in 2002), Thornton, Poulton, Blackpool and St. Anne's. North of Garstang a sizeable but uncensused colony exists at Ellel Crag Quarry.

Jackdaws feed in a wide variety of habitats, including grazing land, rough pasture, stubble fields, freshly ploughed land and tips; they also scavenge around farms and other habitation during freezing weather. Substantial flocks of 1,000+ winter on the Fylde mosslands, the largest being 2,000 at Winmarleigh in December 1974, 2,000-2,500 at Eagland Hill in December 1993 and February 1997, and 2,000 at Pilling in February 1997 and 2002. Large counts south of the Ribble include 1,000+ on Mawdesley Moss in January 2000, 800 on Croston Moss in January 1999, 600+ on Much Hoole Moss in February 1997 and 500 at Adlington Hall in December 1989.

Considerable numbers also gather at winter roost sites, often in the company of Rooks and Carrion Crows. The largest recent regional counts include: on the Fylde, 560 at Singleton in October 1988 and 1,450 Over Wyre in September 1998; in Bowland, 500 in the Gisburn Forest in March 2002; in the West Pennine Moors, 800 at Upper Rivington in November 2003 and 700 in the Entwistle Plantations during the 1980s and 1990s; in St. Helens, 1,000 at Eccleston Mere in November 1998 and 300 on Reed's Moss in December 2003; and in Sefton, 420 in the Ainsdale/Formby Pinewoods in October 2003 and 550 in the Rimrose Valley during September 2003. Jackdaws are also noted, in company with Rooks, flying from their roosts on Wirral over south Liverpool in the morning to winter feeding sites in the city's hinterland, returning in the evening.

Jackdaw, Little Crosby, June 2005. (Steve Young)

British breeding Jackdaws are largely sedentary, in sharp contrast with populations in northern and eastern Europe. Some continental birds are known to migrate to eastern England (Migration Atlas) but, although it is possible that some reach the west coast, there is no evidence of this in Lancashire – all 44 recoveries of ringed birds have either been within Lancashire or involved exchanges with neighbouring counties. Recoveries include one found dead at a roost near Pilling on 16 April 1986, almost 19 years after it had been ringed as a nestling on Walney Island on 31 May 1967.

Migratory movements do occur on the coast, however, particularly in autumn. In 1983 700 flew south over St. Anne's on 21 October with two flocks totalling 1,000 coming in off the sea there the following day, and 350 over Fleetwood on 5 November. Other large counts on the Fylde include 1,100 south over Fairhaven on 13 November 1989 with 800 on 17 October 2003, and 700 over Marton Mere on 21 October 1995. Smaller numbers are also seen most years at Heysham, Seaforth and other Liverpool sites, and occasionally inland, a total of 829 south over Seaforth on five dates during mid-October 2001 and 476 there on 17 October 2003 being notable.

SJM, RW.

This species account was sponsored by Brenda Walsh.

ROOK

Corvus frugilegus

Lancashire Category A.

Abundant resident breeder.

Unlike many other farmland birds, Rooks seem to have been largely unaffected by modern agricultural changes and their Lancashire numbers appear to have changed little for more than 100 years, with small declines in some areas offset by increases in others. Mitchell described them as 'abundant and increasing, both on arable and grazing lands, and only falling off in numbers where suitable trees for nesting begin to get scarce', while Wrigley (1892) described them as 'universally common' in the Formby area.

Sixty years later Oakes's view was little different: 'a very common resident, well distributed everywhere but decidedly more abundant . . . throughout the north'. He noted the loss of many rookeries to road developments but these seem simply to have relocated. A partial census of the county was carried out by the BTO in 1945 and Oakes's summary of the results showed 18 rookeries in Lunesdale with a total of 1,336 nests; 2,200 nests in 39 rookeries in a 315 square mile area of the Fylde, central and north-west Lancashire; and 1,762 nests in 140 square miles of north-east Lancashire. He also reported smaller colonies at Broughton, Rivington, Turton, Aughton (Merseyside), Maghull, Lathom and Woolton in south Liverpool.

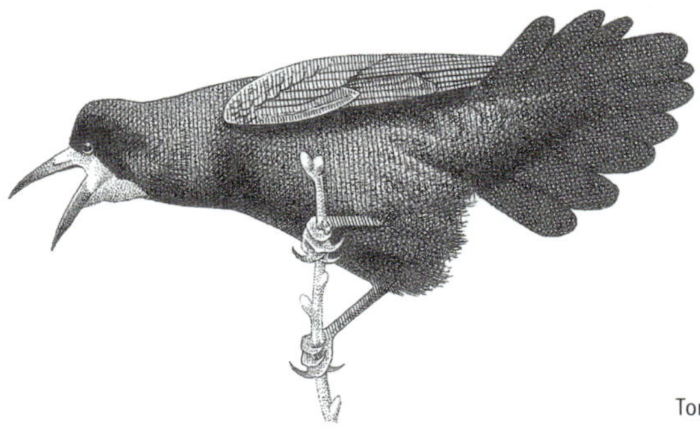

Tony Disley

Many of the largest 1945 rookeries referred to by Oakes have since fragmented: Arkholme down from 508 to 168 in 2002, Woodford Hall from 283 to 52 in 1997, Simonstone Hall near Padiham from 277 to 29 in 1997, Wrightington from 237 to 160 in 1996 and Westby from 200 to 129 in 2003. Nationally, numbers increased by 40% between 1975 and 1996 but were stable between 1994 and 2005 (BBS). The total Lancashire population appears to have roughly conformed to the national trend but with distinct regional differences.

Nest numbers decreased in north Lancashire (part of which is now in Cumbria) by 36% during 1958-67 but then increased by 65% during 1975-1985 and a further 20% by 2002. The number of rookeries has more than doubled since 1975 while average rookery size has barely changed, from 25 nests in 1975 to 26 in 1985 and 23 in 2002.

In east Lancashire numbers grew from 4,500 in 1962 to 6,204 in 192 rookeries in 1986. Spencer referred to tree-felling in 1949 at Ormerod House, Burnley ending a colony that stretched back to at least 1802, and the rookery at Woodfold Park, Blackburn was reduced from 283 to 52 in 1977 due to the same cause. Censuses in Rossendale showed a significant increase from 357 nests in 1945 to 901 in 1979, but numbers have declined by an almost equal amount to 436 in 1997. The Crawshawbooth rookery, which had 62 nests in 1995, dates back to at least 1845.

An annual census of rookeries has been carried out in the Chorley area since 1978, showing an increase from 154 nests at 7 sites in 1978 to 324 nests in 11 rookeries in 1984, reaching a maximum of 421 at 9 locations in 1998 with numbers stabilising since at 400 nests at 8 sites in 2003. The largest rookeries are at Croston, which has grown from 45 nests in 1981 to 162 in 2003, and at Wheelton which increased from 15 in 1980 to 130 in 1983, declining to 69 nests by 2003.

There were 2,293 nests in 37 rookeries in the Fylde in 1982 and the situation was little changed in 2005 when 2,335 nests were located in 47 rookeries. The 1982 survey found 621 nests in 13 rookeries in south-west Fylde (Steeden & Steeden 1982, 1984); by 2003 this population had grown to 810 nests in eight rookeries and by 2004 there were 931 nests in nine rookeries, few of which had been extant in 1982. These included Queensway on Lytham Moss, which held 148 nests in 1982, 140 in 1996, 253 in 2003 and 330 in 2004, making it the largest known in the county and one of the largest recorded in England since 1975 (Brown & Grice 2005). The Warton Hall rookery had 15 nests in 1982 and 110 in 2003, while the Bradkirk Hall rookery increased from nine nests to 103 in 2004.

In Merseyside and West Lancashire numbers decreased from 688 in 17 rookeries in 1937 to 341 nests in 1962 (Hardy 1941, 1979). Just seven rookeries remained in North Merseyside in 2000, mostly in St. Helens and Knowsley with just two in south Sefton and none in Liverpool. The largest Liverpool site at Woolton declined from some 200 nests in 1945 to 28 in 1978 and became extinct soon after.

Culling can significantly affect numbers and distribution at a local level. Rook shooting (with catapults) was recorded at the Ince Blundell, Crosby rookery as early as 1704, and, although it has reduced in recent years, persecution continues with, for example, 19 nests containing well-grown young shot out at Preesall in 1989, 50 adults shot from the Turton rookeries the same year, and young shot at Greta Foot in the Lune Valley in 2002.

The Rook is a catholic feeder utilising both arable land and pasture throughout the year. The highest numbers are reported in autumn and winter, including 800 at Cogie Hill, Wyre in January 1983, 800 on Rawcliffe Moss in January 1997 and 540 on Lytham Moss in September 1998. They also feed on tips throughout the county, such as 400 on White Moss, Skelmersdale in February 2002 and at Freckleton in 1986. Slurry spread on grazing land can attract sizeable numbers, for example 785 at Adlington Hall in November 1997. Flock sizes appear to have diminished in central Rossendale; 400-500 were regular during the 1950s and 1960s but only 250-300 in the 1990s. Curious habits include feeding on peanuts in the backyard of a Nelson house in November 1987, rowan berries near Trawden in September 1992 and on unripe acorns in the West Pennine Moors.

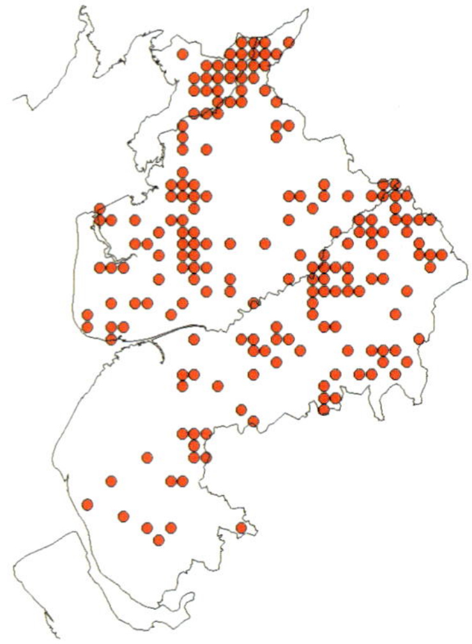

Breeding distribution of Rook, 1997-2000. (Large dots: confirmed. Small dots: possible)

Large roosts form in winter, when the populations of several rookeries often join with Jackdaws and/or Carrion Crows in communal gatherings. Simonstone Hall, a long-established roost that dates back to at least 1928 (Parker 1928), still draws birds in from as far away as Rossendale. Oakes stated that this roost held up to 1,600 birds but that this was eclipsed by up to 3,000 at Woodford Hall. In recent years the largest roost has been 1,800 at Salwick in the winter of 2000, with 600 in the Roby Mill rookery in 2000 and 400 in the Maghull rookery in August 1983. Several large roosts form in mid-winter on the West Pennine Moors – which is surprising as the area is home to only a few small rookeries – including 800 in the Entwistle Plantations in 1986 and 1989, with 600 in 2002, all in hard weather. Elsewhere on the West Pennine Moors, 500 roosted at Upper Rivington and 300 at Roddlesworth in November 2003.

A regular winter spectacle is the twice-daily flight of several hundred Rooks across the Mersey and over Liverpool from roosts in Wirral to feeding grounds on the edge of the conurbation.

British Rooks are highly sedentary with a median recovery distance of 4 km; of 15 ringed in Lancashire only two have been recovered outside the county, both in northern England. However, small movements are seen most autumns at coastal watchpoints, notably 85 over Rossall on 13 October 1995, 150 over Lytham on 21 October 1983, 280 over Fairhaven on 19 October and 110 south at Seaforth on 12 October 2003. Whether these represent movements of British birds or migrants from continental Europe (which are known to occur on the English east coast) is impossible to say.

SJM, RW.

This species account was sponsored by N.J. Donnithorne and Frank Walsh.

CARRION CROW

Corvus corone

Lancashire Category A.

Abundant resident breeder.

Carrion Crows have undergone a major change in fortunes since Mitchell's time; he described the species as 'getting scarcer every year, especially where there is any game-preserving'. Oakes noted an increase during 1939-45, when the amount of 'keepering was substantially reduced, with new territories near Wennington in Lunesdale and in Roeburndale. Fair Oak and Burnslack Fells were described as 'strongholds' and breeding had expanded into Bleasdale and Wyresdale but remained scarce in the Fylde and the south-west. However, his assumption that a lack of cover would prevent the Carrion Crow from becoming numerous anywhere south of the Ribble has subsequently proven to be incorrect. Since then the story has been one of increases throughout the county, particularly marked during the 1960s and 1970s, and although nationally the BBS showed an increase of 12% between 1994 and 2005, the Lancashire population has probably stabilised at an estimated 12,000 pairs.

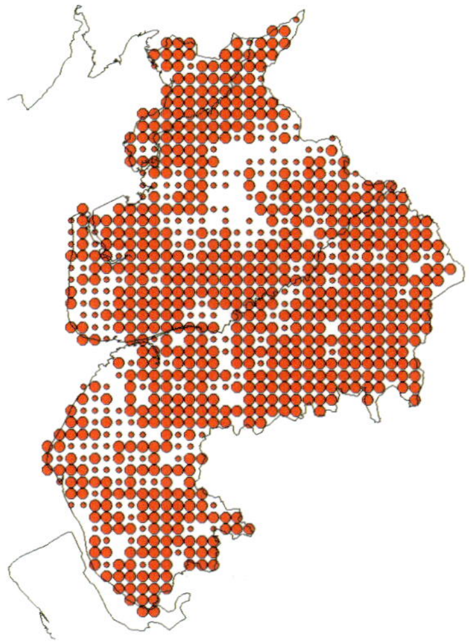

Breeding distribution of Carrion Crow, 1997-2000. (Large dots: confirmed. Small dots: possible)

Tony Disley

This population increase has resulted in greater competition for traditional tree nest sites and a wide range of often unusual alternatives has been utilised, including posts in the Lune Estuary in 1967 and Carnforth Marsh in 1984 and slag-heap cliffs at Carnforth. There are a number of records of nests on electricity pylons, including three pairs in Rossendale in 1982, plus a nest on the 'Big One' roller-coaster in Blackpool in 1996. A ground nest was found on the summit of a moorland hill above Belmont in 1995.

Carrion Crows were found in all Lancashire 10km squares in the surveys of 1968-72, 1988-91 and 1997-2000, but their distribution has increased within that range to include 93% of the county's tetrads in the latest period, when they were absent only from the most urbanised areas and the higher moorlands, especially in Bowland.

Their spread appears to have been more or less continuous since the 1950s. They were described as having increased markedly in the 20 years to 1959 in north Lancashire, and as common and widespread there by the 1980s. Though evidently unknown as a nesting bird in east Lancashire as recently as the 1930s (Oakes and Battersby 1939) and still uncommon in 1950, they had become familiar and widespread residents by the mid-1970s. Breeding landmarks included the first nesting at Wood End, Burnley in 1951, Clowbridge around 1953, Towneley in 1958 and central Burnley by 1967 (Spencer 1977). In Rossendale the Carrion Crow was only an occasional visitor until becoming regular from the 1950s, with two breeding pairs between Edenfield and Townsendfold in 1959, and expanding rapidly in the 1970s. Colonisation of the West Pennine Moors during the 1950s was followed by a rapid increase during the next 20 years. By the late 1970s, large communal winter roosts of up to 500 had formed at Upper Rivington, Roddlesworth and particularly at Entwistle Plantations, where a staggering 1,800 Carrion Crows (plus 800 Rooks and 700 Jackdaws) roosted during hard weather in December 1986. Persecution continued however, with keepers reporting killing over 1,300 (many shot at the Entwistle roost) between 1984 and 1988.

Elsewhere, numbers increased on the Sefton coast and south-west mosslands during the 1990s, although keepers still restrict numbers. Breeding had occurred in Liverpool at Wavertree, Sefton Park and Mossley Hill by the 1970s. The Fylde experienced a gradual increase during 1955-75 and breeding was confirmed in 69 out of 129 tetrads in 1986-90.

Large flocks have become commonplace at all times of year. During the breeding season, flocks of subordinate, non-breeding birds may be attracted to rich feeding locations generally outside the territories of local breeding pairs; two examples were 100 on Waddington Fell in June 1985, attracted by a large hatch of craneflies, and 200 at Ewood Bridge Sewage Works in June 2002. Other large summer flocks, probably including post-breeders and their offspring, were 200 in the Plunge Valley, Rossendale in August 1984 and 300 near Darwen in July 1990.

The catholic tastes of the Carrion Crow enable it to use a variety of feeding sites in winter – on refuse tips, manured fields, winter stubble, sewage farms, moorland, saltmarshes and along the shoreline. The largest congregations include 600 on stubble near Pilling in 1983, up to 600 at Horncliffe Tip in 2002 and 300 at White Moss Tip, Skelmersdale in 2003. Enormous roosts can build up during winter, particularly in the West Pennine Moors and western Rossendale where numbers consistently total over 2,000 at six major roost sites, including a regular 700 at Entwistle in 1997-2000 and 600 at Calf Hey plus 650 in the Delph Plantations in November/December 2003. Elsewhere, the largest reported recently were 350 at Myerscough in January 1999.

Carrion Crow, Croxteth Park, Liverpool, February 2004. (Steve Young)

Most birds are sedentary and there have been only nine movements of ringed birds to or from Lancashire of 10km or more, one of them to Wales. Spring passage on the coast is barely noticeable but autumn passage, usually just single-figures daily, is regular and usually peaks in late October. Large movements include four counts of 52-73 over Fairhaven from 20-27 October 1990, and 62 over Heysham on 2 October 1988.

SJM, RW.

h&cplanthire

This species account was sponsored by H&C (Plant Hire) Ltd.

HOODED CROW

Corvus cornix

Lancashire Category A.

Rare winter visitor.

The Hooded Crow breeds in Scotland, Ireland and the Isle of Man and, although largely sedentary, some movement does take place and these western breeding areas seem the most likely source of records in Lancashire, where it has occurred as a scarce winter visitor and passage migrant for many years. However, small numbers from Fennoscandia also occur down the east coast of England (Migration Atlas) and it is possible that some may penetrate westwards into the hill country in the east of our area, but there is no evidence for this. Until its last decade most twentieth century records referred to single birds on one date, but recently a handful have taken up residence in the south-west and in coastal Fylde.

Mitchell reported Hooded Crows as being relatively frequent during the early part of the nineteenth century but much rarer in the 1880s, when they seldom occurred before October and rarely inland. He quoted Leigh's *Natural History of Lancashire*, published in 1700, describing 'Sea-Crows' as 'common upon the sea-coasts' where they preyed upon mussel-beds by dropping stones on them. This suggests a northerly distribution in the county since mussel-scars do not occur with any frequency on the sandy southern coasts. Mitchell also described them as 'very common' on Martin Mere before it was largely drained in 1849-50. Evidently birds were common enough in the nineteenth century to have acquired a local name, 'Manx Crow', probably accurately reflecting their origins.

Although 'Hoodies' remained uncommon in the first half of the twentieth century they turned up with considerable regularity – annually between 1921 and 1947 according to Oakes. Most records published by Oakes were on the Sefton coast and the south-western mosslands, including Martin Mere, Formby Moss and Halsall Moss, with a notable six birds at Formby Hall on 15 January 1921. Much smaller numbers were seen fairly regularly further east – mostly in what is now Greater Manchester – but Oakes's only inland winter records in the present county were at Aughton near Ormskirk, Rawtenstall and Nelson.

The south-west mosslands and the Sefton and Fylde coasts have continued to be the most favoured areas since Oakes's time. Birds have been reported annually since 1978, with the exception of 1982 and 2005, at an average of about three records a year. However, the number of definite new arrivals is significantly lower as many have taken up residence for a number of years, often interbreeding with Carrion Crows. Their numbers are further exaggerated by individuals wandering over quite large areas and, at a reasonable guess, new birds are probably significantly less than annual in occurrence.

Tony Disley

Numbers are much lower in north Lancashire where there have been just six or seven records, all on or near the coast, since 1978, the most interesting being a pristine pink bird feeding on mussels at Heysham on 18 April 2002. Similar low numbers have been seen in the eastern uplands, mostly in the West Pennine Moors area and in Rossendale, including an early record at Rivington in December 1953. Singles at Clitheroe in December 1985, Stocks Reservoir in April 1992 and Thrushgill in 2004 represent the north-easterly limit of Lancashire records.

A large majority of records occurs between October and April but increasing numbers have been reported during the summer months in the past 20 years or so. It is not clear to what extent this predominance of records during winter and passage periods represents a genuine influx into or movement through the county, or a local seasonal movement towards well-watched mosslands where they are more likely to be seen. However, records on the coast are heavily biased towards passage periods, especially from late March to April, perhaps indicating some movement back to the main breeding range.

There are no proven recent records of pure pairs breeding in Lancashire, but Oakes monitored a nesting pair at Stocks Reservoir in 1945 which failed when one was shot; he also believed that a record, published by Mitchell, of seven at Leagram Hall near the Yorkshire border on 15 August 1876 may have been a family party.

However, breeding almost certainly took place on the Formby/Southport mosses during the early 1990s. Two birds, described at the time as pure Hooded, seen there in the company of three hybrids in January 1992 seem likely to have been a family group. If so, one or other of the breeding birds must surely have been a hybrid. What were probably the same birds became resident in the area and probably bred annually until at least 1995 but hybrids – and perhaps pure birds – continued to be seen on these western mosses and at Marshside until at least 2002. One paired with a Carrion Crow in the Rufford-Holmeswood area during winter 2002/03 may have been one of their offspring, although it too was described as a Hooded Crow. A Hooded bred with a Carrion Crow at Ansdell in 2002 and their offspring probably accounted for a series of records on the Fylde coast during 2001-05. Another Hooded x Carrion pair nested in Walton in north Liverpool in 1997 and 1998. The only other hybrids reported in recent years were singles at Earnsdale Reservoir in October 1991 and Dingle, south Liverpool in July 2005.

SJW, RW.

This species account was sponsored by N.J. Donnithorne.

RAVEN

Corvus corax

Lancashire Category A.

Scarce resident breeder.

In the past decade the status of the Raven has changed from that of a rare to a scarce breeding bird in Lancashire, and it is now regular at both coastal and inland sites. The species suffered considerably in the past from persecution by gamekeepers and farmers and was considered extremely rare by Mitchell, though it was still sometimes seen in Pendle, Bowland and, uncommonly, on the coast. Nesting in Mitchell's time was reported from Wyresdale and on Thievely Pike, Cliviger. During Oakes's time Ravens remained rare, with records confined to upland areas in Bowland and east of Burnley, and along the coast. An unusual record at that time was a pair seen flying north-east over Leyland on 2 March 1941.

During the period 1951-70 most records continued to come either from Bowland or along the coast, and all related to one or two birds. There were coastal sightings at Cockerham Moss, Ansdell, Formby Moss and Formby Point and from the area between Leighton Moss and Carnforth. The only inland record was at Cliviger in February 1957.

Tony Disley

Very few were reported during the 1970s and 1980s. Birds were seen at Hightown on 25 April 1971, Leighton Moss in November 1973 and January 1976, Rivington in November 1976, Eaves in central Fylde in December 1976 and Arkholme in September 1978, followed by sightings from the Bowland area in February 1980 and November 1981, Rossendale in May 1980 and October 1986, Jenny Brown's Point in September 1984 and Leighton Moss in February 1985.

Breeding was confirmed in one 10km square during the 1968-72 survey, with birds present in a further three squares, but none was confirmed in 1988-91 and birds were seen in just two squares. There has, however, been an upsurge in records since 1987 as colonisation took place on two fronts – from Cumbria and North Yorkshire in the north and east and North Wales and Cheshire in the south.

There was an unsuccessful breeding attempt in the Langden Valley in April 1987, when the eggs were destroyed, but Ratcliffe (1997) reported another, successful, Bowland nest in 1987. Breeding was also suspected in the Langden Beck area in 1993 (Harrison 1995) and was confirmed on Calder Fell in 1995.

There has been a great increase in sightings in the Silverdale area during the winter months, probably initially birds from Whitbarrow Scar in Cumbria, but more recently also as a result of breeding in Lancashire quarries. By 1995 Ravens were regular in winter at Leighton Moss in most months and breeding was confirmed at three sites in the Silverdale area in 1997-2000.

On the West Pennine Moors, breeding was first confirmed in quarries at Withnell in 1993, with the resident pair(s) since occupying similar sites at Hoghton Tower and just over the border in Bolton; post-breeding flocks of seven and ten were seen in 2002. Further south-west, a pair nested at a working quarry near Parbold in 1996. Sightings also began to increase in east Lancashire during the 1990s, in the Rossendale, Burnley, Nelson and Colne areas, and by 1997-2000 up to nine scattered pairs may have been breeding. For the first time since Mitchell's day, in 2000 a pair bred successfully in the Cliviger Valley, rearing four young. A pair established itself in a quarry at Clitheroe during the 1990s, having ousted the previously resident Peregrines.

Colonisation from the south began later, at the end of the

1990s, and was quite different in character with birds nesting on buildings within the conurbation rather than in quarries. Records of birds flying over Seaforth increased markedly during the early 1990s but the first attempted breeding came in 1999 on Liverpool's Anglican Cathedral, where three young were raised the following year. It may not be too fanciful to imagine that these birds had themselves been reared on the roof of that other great cathedral in Chester (only 25km away as the Raven flies). Disturbance of the nest site led to desertion in 2001 but different pairs bred successfully on gasometers in Southport and in St. Helens that year. The Southport pair lost their territorial battle with Peregrines in 2002 but two young were fledged from a lighting gantry in the Seaforth Docks and there were numerous sightings in the St. Helens area. The following year, however, one of the Seaforth birds disappeared and its mate left the area, and, with just occasional sightings in Southport, Liverpool and St. Helens, it appeared that the colonisation of Merseyside had come to a halt. The only other instance of urban breeding in Lancashire was a pair that has nested on an electricity pylon in Penwortham since 2002, which may have been responsible for much of the sharp increase in sightings in the Fylde during 1999-2004.

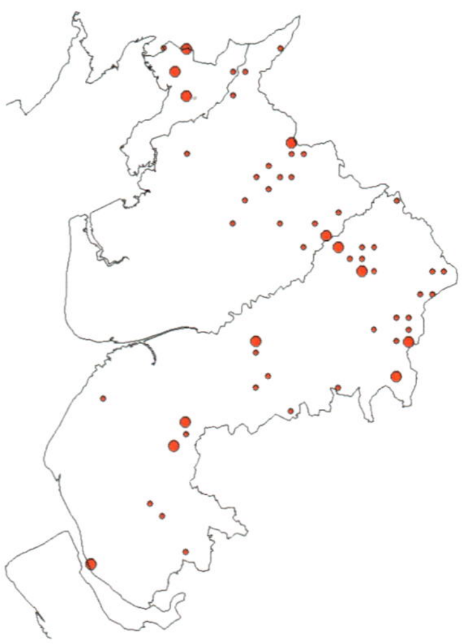

Breeding distribution of Raven, 1997-2000. (Large dots: confirmed. Small dots: possible)

According to Ratcliffe (1997) eight pairs bred in Lancashire in 1995, though only the Hoghton record was submitted to the county report. The 1997-2000 survey estimated a population of 20 pairs. The number of published breeding records has decreased since then to around six a year, but it is clear that the species is under-reported, perhaps in some cases to protect nest sites from destruction.

JFW, RW.

This species account was sponsored by Brenda Walsh.

STARLING

Sturnus vulgaris

Lancashire Category A.

Abundant breeder, passage migrant and winter visitor from Europe and Russia.

The Starling's European range expanded both to the north and the south between the mid-nineteenth century and the mid-twentieth but since then declines have affected both the British breeding population and our wintering birds from Fennoscandia, central Europe and Russia.

Mitchell described the Starling as an increasing resident, common everywhere and often forming immense flocks in winter. According to Oakes numbers had greatly increased in the early twentieth century and the Starling was an abundant and widespread resident and winter visitor. He listed Ellel Grange and Morecambe in the north, Rossall and Blackpool in the Fylde, and Rainford, Childwall, Aigburth and Wavertree in the south-west as former winter roosting-centres; more recently Silverdale, Wrightington and Tarleton held the highest numbers, although all were eclipsed by the more than a million roosting at Barley-in-Pendle between 1943 and 1947.

The British breeding population was estimated at 1.1 million pairs during 1988-91, following a marked population decrease since the 1960s; more recently continuing reductions have been reported, of 66% between 1970 and 2001 (CBC) and 21% from 1994 to 2005 (BBS). There is, however, little detailed evidence of change in the Starling's breeding status in Lancashire since the 1950s. The 1997-2000 survey showed the species to be one of our most widely-distributed residents, breeding in nearly 90% of the county's tetrads and found everywhere except in the highest and most exposed fell-country of Bowland and the Pennines; a total of 15,000 pairs was estimated but this was not based on known densities. However, in line with the national trend, many observers have reported strong impressions of declines in many regions since the 1980s, particularly in urban and suburban areas.

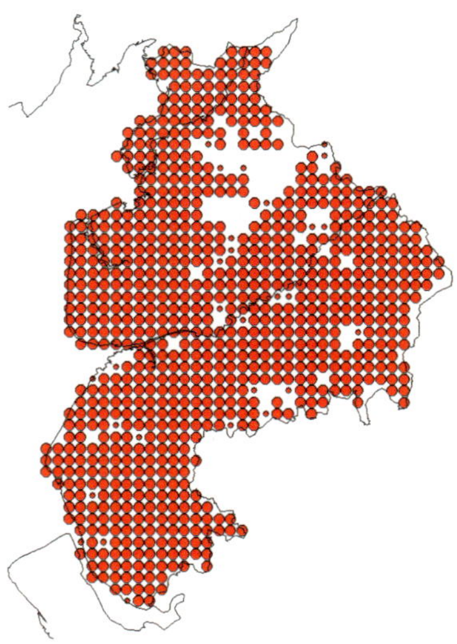

Breeding distribution of Starling, 1997-2000. (Large dots: confirmed. Small dots: possible)

As soon as the young fledge, normally from mid-May, flocks gather and frequent newly-cut grassland, saltmarshes, pastures, moorland and tips, wherever there is an abundance of invertebrate food, especially cranefly larvae. These flocks swell as summer progresses and more adults join them; there were gatherings of up to 2,000 in mid-June in Bowland in 1983 and on Darwen Moor edge in 1992, 2,500 (almost all juveniles) at Marton Mere in June 2001 and 4,000 on moorland at Clowbridge Reservoir, Rossendale in June 2003.

Starling roost, Leighton Moss. (Phillip Tomkinson)

By July and August roosts at favoured sites are already substantial, although these have become less impressive since the early 1990s. Up to 25,000 were present at Leighton Moss in late June in 1980 and 1981, 20,000 in July 1994 and 25,000 in August 1988; 25,000 were also at Thornton, Fylde in August 1983 and up to 100,000 were estimated to be in Broadwater Wood, Fleetwood during July and August in 1984 and 1985. More recently peak counts at this time have generally been rather lower: 2,000 at The Hile, Rossendale in late July 1991, 3,000 at Marton Mere in August 1995, 18,000 in August at Leighton Moss in 1999 and at Marton Mere in 2002; counts of 50,000 at Stocks Reservoir on 7 August 1998 and 26,000 at Warton Marsh on 22 July 2001 are exceptional. Large numbers fed on ants in the rubble mounds at Seaforth during the 1990s, including a flock of 7,000 in late July 1999.

Continental migrants begin to appear from mid-September and passage takes place at coastal watchpoints, and less regularly inland, until the middle of November. Numbers vary considerably from year to year, but large counts of overflying birds include 4,723 at Fairhaven on 27 October 1991 and 3,500 at Heysham on 3 November 1994 with 2,493 there on 30 October 1995. Coastal counts have been generally lower since the mid-1990s with 1,400 at Heysham on 7 November 1998 and 769 at Fairhaven on 8 November 2003 among the highest. Large movements at inland locations have also become more infrequent in recent years. Seventeen hundred passed over Barnoldswick in just 15 minutes on 7 November 1983, 1,034 moved through the Grane Valley, Rossendale on 6 November 1989 and 4,500 flew over Darwen Moor edge on 11 November 1990; 2,300 fed on in-bye land at Belmont in November 1994 and 3,000 flew west there on 7 November 1999. More recently, 2,000 over Parsonage Reservoir on 15 October 2003 has been the only four-figure count reported.

Between October and March some enormous roosts have been recorded, many of these reforming over successive winters. An assembly in conifer plantations at Beacon Fell, north-east of Preston, held up to a million birds at its peak in the mid-1960s, and a roost at Dean Clough, Blackburn reached an estimated 700,000 in the late autumn of 1959; up to 250,000 roosted at Haslingden Grane during the 1960s and 1970s. The Leighton Moss reedbeds host the county's most durable roost; peak numbers are normally present in autumn, declining in mid-winter and building up again later. Up to 180,000 were estimated in September 1971, with peaks of 50,000-70,000 during most of the 1970s and 1980s. Many of these birds moved to the old Central Pier at Morecambe in 1984 but, after this burnt down in 1991, the Leighton roost built up again to 25,000-30,000 in most winters and up to 45,000 in December 2001.

Starling flocks are regularly pursued by birds of prey but attacks by mammalian predators like this Stoat are much less frequent. Seaforth Nature Reserve, September 2006. (Steve Young)

Other noteworthy gatherings of Starlings have included 70,000 south over Martin Mere to an unknown roost on 8 November 1981, up to half a million on Hesketh Marsh in January-February 1985 and a long-established roost at the Royal Ordnance Factory at Euxton, Chorley which grew from 50,000 in February 1990 to 250,000 in winter 1991/92, 800,000 in February and December 1993 and 900,000 in February 1994, declining to half a million in February in 1996 and 1997. A roost of 50,000 or so remained active at least to the end of the 1990s. Large roosts of 50,000 or more in Liverpool city centre and 10,000 or so in the Liverpool docks were regular during the 1980s but had completely vanished by the mid- to late1990s.

Since the turn of the century maximum roost totals across the county have decreased dramatically and up to 20,000 at Stocks Reservoir in late 2000, a similar number at Sand Villa, Pilling on 18 October 2003 and 35,000 in the Pilling-Cockerham area on 12 March 2005 are among the largest recent gatherings reported.

Eric Hardy reported a most extraordinary mortality event when birds returning to a roost in Speke on 15-16 January 1959 were brought down into a heavily-oiled River Mersey during thick fog. He recorded a drop in roosting numbers of 20,000 during the two days and considered 10,000 casualties to be 'not unreasonable', having personally counted 2,000 corpses washed up on the shores of the river.

Hard-weather movements are occasionally observed in mid-winter, including 2,400 south at St. Anne's on 22 January 1984 and 3,084 off Blackpool on 14 January 1985. There is little evidence of coastal movements in spring.

Exchanges of ringed Starlings between Lancashire and northern Europe by country.

There were 1,533 recoveries of Starlings ringed in Lancashire up to 2003 and 351 recoveries within the county of birds ringed elsewhere. Most movements have been within Britain and Ireland but there have been 257 exchanges with continental Europe. These are divided roughly equally between Fennoscandia (17 Finland, 14 Norway, 41 Sweden, 44 Denmark) and central and eastern Europe (30 Germany, 9 Poland, 46 Baltic States, 22 former Soviet Union) with a further 24 with the Netherlands, six with Belgium and two with France.

BM, RW.

This species account was sponsored by Mike McGough.

ROSE-COLOURED STARLING

Sturnus roseus

Lancashire Category A. (0, 6).

Vagrant from south-east Europe.

According to Mitchell Rose-coloured Starlings were fairly regularly seen – or rather shot – in Lancashire. He quoted claims from Lathom (General History of Birds, 1821) that 'one or more Pastors has been killed, almost every season, about Ormskirk', from Byerley of one shot near Liverpool around 1840, and David Mitchell that 'examples had occurred near Lancaster in four successive years'.

Oakes considered almost all of Mitchell's records unacceptable due to inadequate detail; those that he did judge to be satisfactory were all outside our current recording area.

The first unequivocal county record was an adult at Formby on 9-14 August 1963 in the garden of Mrs. E.M Butler. It was initially published in the county report as "probably an escape" but Spencer (1963) cast some doubt on this; certainly, the timing of the record fits well with the species' now well established pattern of occurrence in Britain. Another adult was found at Formby on 2 August 1979.

Adult Rose-coloured Starling, Warton, Carnforth, June 2002. (Mark Prestwood)

Although Rosy Starlings were seen in Britain with increasingly regularity throughout the 1980s the bulk of sightings were in south-west England, and no more were seen in Lancashire until a juvenile at Skelmersdale on 17 October 1990.

Another decade passed without further records; then came a flurry of occurrences at the beginning of the twenty-first century. All were adults and all were in back gardens: in St. Anne's on 6 July 2001; in Warton, near Carnforth on 15 June 2002 and in Birkdale on 19 August 2002.

All records:

1963	Formby, adult, 9 to14 August
1979	Formby, adult, 2 August
1990	Skelmersdale, juvenile, 17 October
2001	St. Anne's, adult, 6 July
2002	Warton, Carnforth, adult, 15 to 16 June
2002	Birkdale, adult, 19 August

SJW, MJ.

This species account was sponsored by Andrew Cadman.

HOUSE SPARROW

Passer domesticus

Lancashire Category A.

Abundant resident breeder.

As elsewhere in the country House Sparrows were taken for granted and effectively ignored by birdwatchers in Lancashire until the realisation dawned in the late 1990s that the British population was experiencing a serious crisis. The CBC indicated a 65% decline on farmland between 1970 and 2001 but even more worrying were reports of their disappearance from urban areas throughout the country. Apart from some small-scale studies no attempt was made to census House Sparrows in Lancashire until the very end of the twentieth century, with the result that we have no baseline data from which to monitor the changes.

Although it is strongly suspected that the Lancashire population has declined in line with the national trend, House Sparrows remain widespread and numerous and it is not yet possible to detect any changes in the broad-scale breeding distribution.

Mitchell's brief account described the House Sparrow as resident and exceedingly abundant everywhere in Lancashire; he noted that large numbers nested in trees in the Fylde and in the Southport area. Oakes repeated the observation regarding tree-nesting (confirmed at Marton Mere in the 1950s), and described the House Sparrow as numerous everywhere except on isolated farmsteads, and flocking in large numbers on farmland from June onwards. In 1973 Spencer described the species as abundant and widespread, noting that migration was sometimes perceptible at coastal watchpoints in October.

House Sparrows were reported as breeding in all of Lancashire's 10km squares in all three atlas surveys since 1968 and in 1997-2000 were present in 85% of the county's tetrads. They are absent only from the highest ground of Bowland, the West Pennine Moors (where they disappeared from farm buildings during the early 1990s) and the south Pennines, where human settlements are sparse.

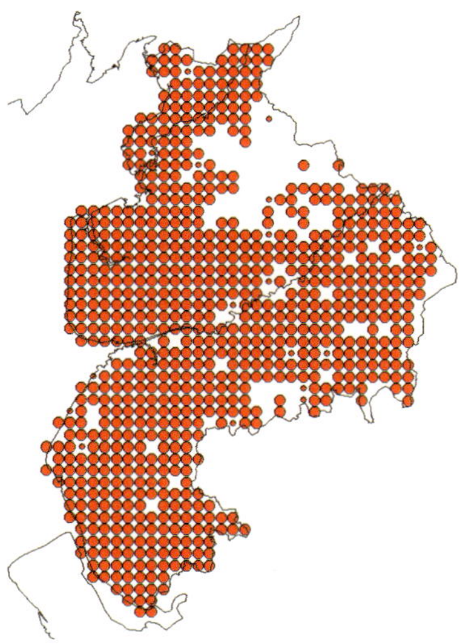

Breeding distribution of House Sparrow, 1997-2000. (Large dots: confirmed. Small dots: possible)

County bird reports from the 1950s to the late 1980s made virtually no mention of the House Sparrow's breeding status, which appears to have changed little, or been taken for granted, during this period. In 1989, however, a decline in numbers was noted in Rossendale and in Liverpool in 1994. By 1995 reports of local population declines began to appear with increasing frequency: in the Kirkby area in 1995, at Heysham, Crosby and Over Wyre in 1996, and throughout the Fylde in 1997. Continuing reductions in Rossendale were reported in 1998, and in the Burnley and St. Anne's areas in 1999. Monitored nesting at Arkholme showed an increase from 13 pairs in 1994 to 17 in 1995, but the population there declined to twelve pairs in 1999, ten in 2000, and four in 2002. Meanwhile, in the Pilling-Preesall area a monitored population of 15 pairs in 1996 fell to 14 in 1997-98, twelve in 1999 and seven or eight in 2000-01.

These population trends were not universal, however; in 2000 House Sparrows were described as still common in the Belmont area, and as increasing there in 2002-03, and more widespread recoveries appeared to be underway as the new century began. The breeding colony at Pilling-Preesall grew to 19 pairs in 2002 and 29 in 2005, supplementary winter feeding playing no small role in this revival.

The complexity of the House Sparrow's breeding situation is well, if inconclusively, illustrated by a survey of North Merseyside in 2001-02 which censused breeding House Sparrows in 88 randomly selected 25-hectare squares. No consistent relationship was found between breeding density and a range of environmental variables, such as tree-cover, age of housing and areas of roadway, commercial buildings or derelict land. The survey found an average of 52-71 pairs per km^2, with the lowest densities in commercial and residential areas of inner Liverpool and St. Helens and highest numbers in the outer suburbs and estates; Southport recorded a high population, whilst that of nearby Formby was very low. The total population of north Merseyside was estimated at 11,400 pairs. If similar densities occur throughout urban Lancashire this would imply a total urban population of around 30,000 pairs in Lancashire and north Merseyside (White 2002).

However, densities elsewhere are not known, with the exception of a smaller-scale study in south Fylde in the late 1990s which reported a much lower average density of up to ten pairs per km^2. The population of the village of Forton was estimated at a minimum of 350 individuals in 2004. Rural House Sparrows remain largely unstudied in Lancashire but, although densities are certainly lower in the countryside, an estimate of a further 10,000 pairs seems reasonable.

The widespread tree-nesting commented upon by both Mitchell and Oakes appears largely to have ceased, although three pairs bred in adjacent bushes at Hesketh Golf Course, Marshside in 1990 and a pair nested in a hedgerow at Barley in 2000.

The large post-breeding and winter flocks noted by Oakes were still very much in evidence until the early 1990s. Most were recorded in coastal or near-coastal areas and included 400 at Peel, near Blackpool in September 1983, 200 on Clifton Marsh in August 1986, 350 on Skelmersdale White Moss in late August and September 1988, 278 at Martin Mere on 12 December 1989, and 200 at Seaforth in July 1992. Since the mid-1990s three-figure counts have become less frequent, but up to 200 were present at Fazakerley Reedbed in July-August 1998 and at Hambleton in September 2003, and there were 220 at Altcar Withins in October 2000. A feeding-station set up at Heysham in the mid-1980s was overrun by House Sparrows and consequently abandoned; since its re-establishment in November 1993 very few of the species have been recorded there.

Inland flocks have usually been much smaller, but 140 were at Sunnyhurst Woods in November 1990, up to 150 were in a supermarket car-park in Blackburn in December 1991 and there were 200 at Myerscough in autumn 2005; one farmland feeding station at Eagland Hill held 157 on 8 August 2004. Groups of up to 60 visited gardens in Burnley in October 1992 and January 1995 and 65 in Belmont regularly since 2000.

Small numbers of House Sparrows are occasionally recorded on autumn passage at coastal watchpoints, mainly at Heysham and on the Fylde. Forty-five passed south at Fairhaven on 25 October 1983, 134 on 1 October 1988 and 22 on 17 October 1990; at Heysham ten were recorded on 4 November 1984 and three flocks totalling some 25 birds on 18 August 1996. Numbers have dwindled at all sites in more recent years, and a single bird at Heysham on 12 October 1999 was the first migrant recorded there since 1996.

House Sparrows are normally highly sedentary; of 58 Lancashire-ringed birds recovered to date all but one was within the county, and none had moved more than 10 km. There have been three recoveries here of birds ringed elsewhere in northern England.

Up to two House x Tree Sparrow hybrids were resident in gardens at Belmont from 2003-05.

BM, RW.

This species account was sponsored by John Bannon.

TREE SPARROW

Passer montanus

Lancashire Category A.

Fairly common resident breeder.

Tree Sparrow populations are peculiarly subject to sudden and dramatic decreases, followed by equally rapid recoveries. In Britain high numbers from the 1830s to the 1930s were followed by a sharp decline after 1950, when populations in western Britain fell significantly and Tree Sparrows became extinct for a time in Ireland. A strong recovery from the early 1960s was again succeeded by a steady decline from about 1978, reflected in a 20% reduction in range in Britain between the 1968-72 and 1988-91 Atlases, experienced mainly in south-west and north-east England, Wales and Scotland. The New Atlas (1993) estimated 11,000 territories in Britain but more recent data indicate continuing declines. The CBC showed an overall loss of 94% between 1970 and 2001 but this was based upon a geographically unrepresentative sample and may be something of an exaggeration. The boom-bust cycle seems to have resumed in the last decade, however, with a 23% increase in population during 1994-2005 (BBS).

Mitchell described the Tree Sparrow as a very local resident in Lancashire, breeding most regularly in the 'neighbourhood of Manchester' but also near Chipping and Preston and in the Hodder Valley. By Oakes's time the known distribution had increased greatly but his description of it was consistent with Mitchell's: Tree Sparrows were 'widely distributed' in the south-west, 'sparingly' so around Burnley and in Rossendale, but 'more common' in the Blackburn and Preston areas. Breeding was unknown in north Lancashire although winter flocks had been seen there, while birds were thought to 'be absent from the Fylde plain at all seasons'.

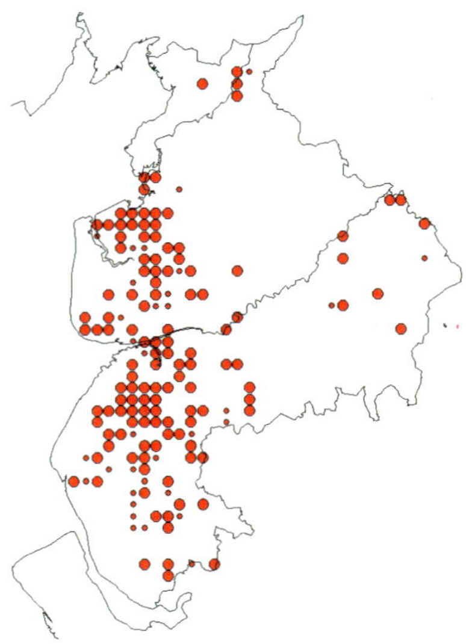

Breeding distribution of Tree Sparrow, 1997-2000. (Large dots: confirmed. Small dots: possible)

There is reason to doubt that either of these accounts accurately reflected the true status of Tree Sparrows, however. At a time when the national population had begun to fall sharply, Spencer (1973) considered that numbers in Lancashire had increased in recent decades and Tree Sparrows were a widely distributed breeding bird, a view confirmed by the Old Atlas survey in 1968-72 when breeding was confirmed in 48 Lancashire 10km squares.

The range had declined to 43 10km squares by 1988-91 but breeding was not confirmed in six of these, probably indicating that more significant local losses had been incurred. By 1997-2000 the full extent of the decline since the 1960s was apparent, with a 40% reduction in range to 29 10km squares and birds found in 157 (17%) tetrads, located overwhelmingly in the western third of the county south of the Lune. Breeding was suspected in just eight tetrads in east Lancashire and four in the north (three of them on the upper Lune). Up to 75% of the county population was concentrated in two areas: the mosslands of West Lancashire and Over Wyre.

Tree Sparrow. (Chris Galvin)

A range of agricultural changes are implicated in the decline but loss of winter stubbles and suitable nest sites were probably the most critical. Throughout the county Tree Sparrows have responded well to the provision of nest-boxes, especially where this has been combined with supplementary winter feeding. Populations have been brought back from the brink of extinction in many areas and it is noticeable that the largest continuing losses are in the south-west, the old heartland of the species, where conservation effort has been least. One recent exception has been at Hundred End, where 24 pairs inhabited nest-boxes in 2005.

The Tree Sparrow was a very common breeder in the south-west in the 1960s and was still fairly widespread in the late 1980s. By the mid-1990s, however, colonies had become smaller and fewer; the South-West Lancashire Ringing Group commented in 1994 that very few were then being ringed, whereas over a hundred birds had formerly been caught every year. Numerous small breeding clusters have persisted, however, and the 1997-2000 survey located 159 pairs (out of a county total of 462) in just three 10km squares concentrated on the mosslands inland of Southport. A nest-box scheme at Martin Mere attracted 20 pairs in 1998 and 18 in 2004, and two pairs used boxes at Mere Sands Wood in 2000-04. Elsewhere in the south-west the species is barely clinging on around Hightown and in Knowsley and St. Helens.

Colonies are widespread in the Fylde, especially in Over Wyre where the population has survived the cyclical ups and downs since the 1960s. Tree Sparrows were already locally common there in the 1970s but decreases became apparent from the mid-1980s and the population reached a low point around the mid-1990s. However, the recovery since then has been dramatic, attributable to a considerable extent to a combination of supplementary feeding and the provision of nest-boxes. In 1986 72 pairs made use of nest-boxes in the Pilling-Preesall area; the total had declined to 45 pairs in 1991 and to 38 in 1994. A steady recovery, to 56 pairs in 1996 and 94 in 1998, has gathered pace in more recent years, reaching 102 pairs in 2000, 115 in 2002 and 155 in 2005.

Elsewhere in the county, however, the picture is generally one of steady decline rather than mere cyclical fluctuation, with the species gradually falling back into smaller and increasingly isolated pockets, sustained in some areas by a combination of winter feeding and nest-box programmes.

Many colonies have disappeared around Chorley and Preston in the last decade but the species still breeds in reduced numbers in several widely scattered colonies. In the West Pennine Moors they retain a precarious foothold in a couple of small colonies west of Anglezarke. Thirty pairs breeding in nest-boxes in Roddlesworth Plantations in 1972 were reduced to three by 1992, with no breeding since.

In east Lancashire widespread breeding was recorded to the east and west of Burnley until around 1990 but by 1995 a virtual population collapse had restricted breeding Tree Sparrows to two tiny remnants, at Walverden Reservoir and in the Altham-Martholme-Great Harwood area along the River Calder. Very recently feeding and nest-box provision have substantially increased breeding numbers in the latter area, from two pairs in 2000 to eleven in 2003. Smaller populations may also survive near Calderfoot and at Ribchester.

In Rossendale the first regular breeding presence was recorded at Deeply Vale in 1957 and a small colony persisted there until 1992. From the 1960s the population in the region increased and spread with the establishment of colonies at Ravenshore, Lumb Vale, Plunge and Crawshawbooth, but a decline from the early 1980s saw all abandoned by 1993; a single bird at Buckhurst in 1999 is the only record since then.

Tree Sparrows also increased and spread in north Lancashire during the 1960s and by the mid-1970s the species was well-established in the Lune and Conder Valleys, in the Lancaster and Galgate areas, and around Silverdale. In a now-familiar scenario a decline during the 1980s and early 1990s eliminated most colonies, and left a very fragmented residual population by 1995, with a few pairs along the Lune, at Over Kellet and at Dockacres. Since then a nest-box scheme at Arkholme has maintained the local population at around eight or nine pairs, and a similar programme at Cockersands attracted nine pairs in 2000. A formerly more widespread population stretching from Middleton to Lancaster refuse tip has been limited to four or five pairs at Heaton village in recent years, utilising winter feeders and probably responsible for records on the Aldcliffe maize field during autumn.

The size and distribution of post-breeding and winter flocks has closely mirrored the fortunes of the breeding population over the last 40 years. The largest numbers are normally present in the south-west and the Fylde. By far the highest count was of 1,000 birds on Churchtown Moss on 24 January 1981 but gatherings of

300-400 were occasionally recorded in both regions from the 1960s to the mid-1980s. Since then flocks of over a hundred have been the exception, although 300 were present on Hesketh Marsh on 6 October 1988, 140 on Kirkham Marsh in March 1991, 120 at Eagland Hill, Pilling in December 1993 and on Hesketh Marsh in November 1994, 100+ on Bickerstaffe Moss in October 1995 and up to 200 at Over Wyre feeding-stations in winter during 2002-04.

Elsewhere in the county flocks have dwindled dramatically as breeding populations declined or disappeared. This is well illustrated by the situation at Wood End Sewage Works, Burnley, where a post-breeding flock of 250 on 16 August 1984 contrasts with later maxima of 70 in July 1990 and only nine in August 1991. In the mid-1980s autumn gatherings of up to 70 Tree Sparrows were not unusual in the Altham-Martholme area and 50 were present there as recently as August 1992, but a party of seven at Martholme in September 1997 was the highest count anywhere in east Lancashire that year. The recent partial recovery in breeding numbers in this locality was, however, reflected in a count of 40 Tree Sparrows at Harwood Bar feeding-station in December 2003.

In the Chorley area 120 were at Cuerden Valley Park in November 1991 and 150 in October 1992, but 50 in September 1993 is the highest total recorded there since then; there were 92 at Bretherton in January 1998 and 60 at Withnell Fold in September 2001. In the north, small numbers of Tree Sparrows winter around Morecambe Bay and the Lune Estuary; a hundred at Cockersands in December 2000 probably originated from local nest-box schemes as well as from the nearby Pilling concentration.

Autumn movements at coastal sites were occasionally quite substantial in the 1960s and 1970s; 132 moved south at Ainsdale on 20 October 1968 and several hundred were recorded at Fairhaven in a typical autumn prior to the mid-1970s. Aggregate totals at Fairhaven have dwindled greatly since then, to 60 per autumn in the mid-1980s and fewer than 20 in the mid-1990s; four there in September-October 2003 were the first recorded for several years. Twenty-four flew over Seaforth on the 13th and 30 on 17 October in 1990, but very few have been seen there since; small numbers were recorded between late September and mid-November in 1998, and three on 17 October 2003. Similarly, only a handful of Tree Sparrows has passed through Heysham since 1990, although there were 25 at Sunderland Point on 14 October 1995 and a few there on 27 October 1998. Inland, small movements were occasionally observed on Darwen Moor edge until the mid-1990s, including a total of 75 in October- November 1991, but there have been very few since.

The origins of these migrant or dispersing Tree Sparrows remains essentially unknown, as there have been no recoveries here of birds ringed outside Lancashire, and the species is essentially sedentary in Europe. Of 31 recoveries of Lancashire-ringed Tree Sparrows all but two have been found locally and only three had travelled further than 10km from the ringing-site. The most recent exception was a pullus ringed at Out Rawcliffe in 2004 and killed by a cat in Tadcaster, North Yorkshire in March 2005.

BM, RW.

This species account was sponsored by Bob and Diane Danson and the Fylde Bird Club.

CHAFFINCH

Fringilla coelebs

Lancashire Category A.

Abundant resident breeder, passage migrant and winter visitor from continental Europe.

The status and distribution of Lancashire's breeding Chaffinches appear to have changed very little for at least 150 years. Mitchell described it as 'everywhere common' and Oakes as 'abundant ... and probably the most numerous small passerine with the exception of the Starling'.

The Lancashire Atlas survey found Chaffinches in 92% of the county's tetrads and 'guesstimated' the breeding population at 60,000 pairs, making it our second most common species after Wren. It is found in all types of woodland, including conifer plantations where it can be numerous, breeds on farmland wherever there are hedgerows or a few trees and may also be found high up moorland cloughs where there are at least a few scattered trees or shrubs.

The breeding range is virtually continuous over most of the county but is more fragmented on higher ground as in Rossendale, where it is mainly restricted to conifer plantations. Chaffinches are very thinly spread, and often absent, from the treeless fells of Bowland and the saltmarshes of the Ribble and the north Fylde coast. Surprisingly for so common a bird not noted for its shyness, the Chaffinch is almost totally absent as a breeding species in the Liverpool conurbation, even in the large Victorian parks, and on the Fylde coast between Lytham and Fleetwood. In stark contrast to Greenfinches and to a lesser extent Goldfinches, Chaffinches appear largely to have failed to adapt to suburbia and its garden-feeding opportunities.

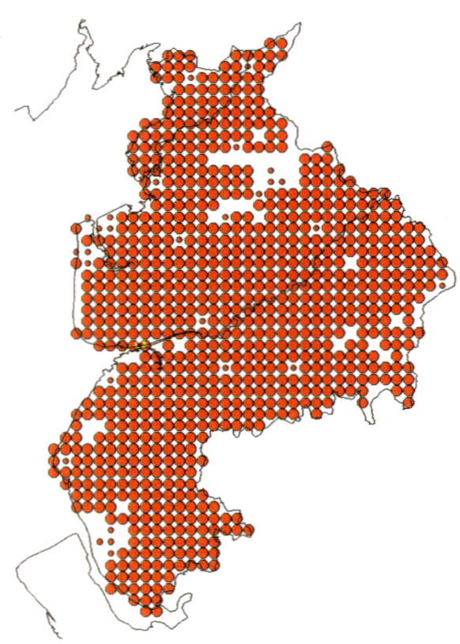

Breeding distribution of Chaffinch, 1997-2000. (Large dots: confirmed. Small dots: possible)

Numbers were thought to be at a national low point during the period 1960-62, perhaps because of the effects of organochlorine use. They recovered over the next few years to 1969, and increased by 29% between 1970 and 2001 (CBC) and by

15% during 1994-2005 (BBS). Little is known about population trends in Lancashire but serious declines noted in parts of east Lancashire during the early 1960s and an increase in Rossendale from the late 1970s both reflected national trends.

During the winter months birds often stay in the locality where they were reared, even in the hillier parts of north-east Lancashire and Rossendale. Although they feed mostly on grain or beech-mast when available they also exploit *Spartina* on saltmarshes, exposed grass and mud around reservoirs, sewage filter debris, bird tables and, increasingly, peanut feeders. The largest feeding flocks are found in the arable areas of the Fylde and the south-west. These occasionally exceed 300, with 500 being reported from Glasson in November 1981, Lytham Marsh in December 1991 and Rainford in December 1993. Groups of 1,000 birds were noted at Pilling in January 1981 and in the Kirkby-Simonswood Moss area in January 1989. More recent large lowland counts have included 270 at Bretherton in 1996, 200 at Warton Bank in 1997, 250 on Plex Moss in 1999, 300 at Mossborough Hall, Rainford in January 2001, 700 on White Moss, Skelmersdale in February 2001 and 230 at Pilling in 2002.

Male Chaffinch, Little Crosby, February 2004. (Steve Young)

Flocks of up to 100 birds are fairly common in the hillier parts of Lancashire but counts of over 200 are unusual. The largest have been 300 at Altham in February 1981, 400 at Hurst Green in February 1991, 300 at Newton-in-Bowland in January 1999, and several flocks of 100-200 feeding on beech mast in east Lancashire, at Grove Lane plantation and Brierfield, and at Rivington in December 2002. Few flocks in Rossendale number more than 50, the largest report being 100 at Ewood Bridge Sewage Works in November 1986.

Large roosts of 500 or more sometimes build up in winter, the largest being 1,560 at Delph Plantations in January 1985 with 950 there in February 1987, and 1,100 at Singleton Hall, Fylde in February 1994. Ringing data indicate some movement between winter roosts, for example between Clifton and Lytham Hall. Such movements are probably related to changing locations of food sources.

Spring passage occurs mainly between mid-March and mid-April but often passes largely unnoticed, totals ringed at Heysham giving perhaps the best indication of its timing (Figure 1). Only small numbers are usually recorded on visible migration watches, 68 moving east over Fairhaven on 21 April 1984 being exceptional.

Autumn passage is considerably larger and more obvious. Movement through the coastal watchpoints usually gets underway in the second half of September, with average peak day-counts (1990-2003) that month of about 250 at Fairhaven but only 50 or so to the north at Heysham and to the south at Seaforth. The largest September counts during this period have been 416 on the 28th in 1985, 420 on the 30th in 1995 and 398 on the 30th in 2002, all at Fairhaven.

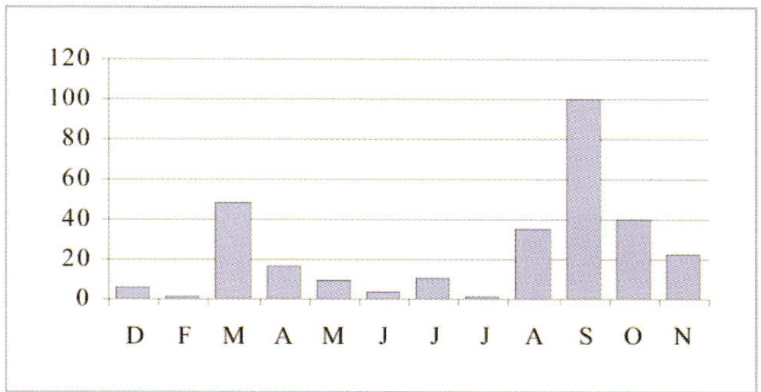

Figure 1. Monthly indices of Chaffinches ringed at Heysham Nature Reserve, 1999-2005. (September = 100).

It seems likely that the earliest movements mostly involve dispersing British birds. This is supported by observations at Heysham that suggest that birds fly predominantly north to south in September but come mostly from the east during October, suggesting a continental origin for the later birds. Visible migration totals at Heysham rarely exceed 1,000 in October and 900 there on 23 October 1989, 985 over nearby Hest Bank in 75 minutes on 28 October the same year, and 1,351 over Crag Bank on 22 October 2005 were exceptional day-counts for north Lancashire. Further south such numbers occur in late autumn with far more regularity. Notable counts include 904 over Fairhaven on 13 October 1990 with 1,528 on 4 November 2003; and 2,000+ over Seaforth on 23 October 1996 with 1,000 there on 18 October 1997 and 19 October 2001. An estimated 12,000 visible migrants were logged at Fairhaven in October and November 2005, including 2,221 on 14 October and 2,004 on the 27th.

Figure 2. Movements of ringed Chaffinches between Lancashire and NW Europe.

Significant but smaller numbers are also counted regularly inland, for example a total of 1,620 over Billinge Hill, St. Helens between 18 September and 17 November 1987 and 2,235 over the Darwen Moor watchpoint between June and December 1993. The largest day-count in recent years was of 700 going south-east over Brockholes Quarry on 16 October 2001.

The vast majority of ringing records are of Lancashire- or other British-ringed birds moving very short distances, confirming their sedentary nature. Thirteen birds ringed in Lancashire have been recovered abroad, all of them ringed during winter or passage periods. Their recovery sites fall into two broad regions: five birds to Denmark, Norway and Sweden; and eight to Holland, Belgium and Germany (Figure 2). The Scandinavian recoveries have all been during the breeding season, while those in continental Europe have been during winter or passage periods. The seven recoveries of foreign-ringed birds in Lancashire are consistent with this pattern, with three ringed in Norway and Sweden during the breeding season, and four in Holland and Belgium ringed in late autumn. This confirms that many of our wintering birds originate in Scandinavia (nationally about 50% do) and perhaps most passage migrants as well. Intriguingly, there are two within-winter movements between Lancashire and continental Europe: one from Heysham on 22 November 1994 to Holland on 6 April 1995, the other from Holland on 17 October 1981 to Blackpool on 16 January 1982. These suggest that some, presumably Scandinavian, birds may regularly shift wintering sites within one season as well as alternating them between years.

SJW, RW.

This species account was sponsored by Bob Pyefinch.

BRAMBLING

Fringilla montifringilla

Lancashire Category A.

Common winter visitor from Fennoscandia and northern Russia.

Bramblings breed abundantly in coniferous, broadleaved and mixed woodland and forest from Fennoscandia across north Russia and Siberia. All populations are migratory and autumn movements begin in late September and continue until mid-November, their extent strongly dependent on food availability, especially of beech-mast. The Winter Atlas (1986) estimated that the total number of Bramblings wintering annually in Britain and Ireland varies from 50,000 to 2 million birds.

To both Mitchell and Oakes Bramblings were winter visitors, very numerous in some years but scarce in others, and present from late October to early April; Mitchell emphasised the species' affinity for mossland stubbles and coastal habitats. Sizeable influxes were recorded in 1880/81 when large numbers were present at St. Michaels-on-Wyre, in 1911/12, 1920/21, 1928/29 when hundreds arrived at Martin Mere on 11 January, 1933/34, 1939/40, and 1947/48 which featured high numbers in the Burnley and Clitheroe areas from late October. Oakes also noted evidence of spring passage in March and early April.

The status of the Brambling appears to have changed very little over the last half-century. Autumn movements, quite light in most years, are typically recorded at both coastal and inland sites between early October and mid-November, the birds often moving in the company of Chaffinches; the earliest on record is one at Marshside on 13-14 September 1999.

Male Brambling, Little Crosby, March 2002. (Steve Young)

Among the more notable coastal movements were 250 south over Formby Point in 45 minutes on 25 October 1965, several hundred at Fairhaven during late October 1973, a total of at least 500 at Heysham in October-November 1985 with a peak of 245 on 20 October, 142 there on 30 October 1995, and 200 at Fluke Hall, Pilling on 18 October 1992. More recently, peak counts have tended to be lower but 2005 was an exception with notable counts of visible migrants on 27 October of 211 at Fairhaven, 63 at Heysham, 52 at the Rimrose Valley and 38 at Seaforth, and 58 over Lytham St. Anne's NR on the following day.

Inland, significant visible autumn movements have included 24 south over Billinge Hill on 18 October 1986, 17 through the Grane Valley on 8 October 1989 and 40 at Fern Isle Wood, also in Rossendale, on 26 October 1997, and a massive 870 in just two hours at Marshaw, Bowland on 20 October 2002 at the leading edge of an exceptional winter influx.

Over the years substantial winter flocks have been recorded in all parts of the county from upland plantations and beech-woods to coastal saltmarshes, mossland stubbles and even urban parks and cemeteries. In most years total numbers are small, and flocks scattered, but there were major influxes in 1978/79, 1980/81, 1983/84, 1984/85, 1992/93, 1995/96 and 2002/03. The winters of 1980/81 and 2002/03 deserve special attention.

An enormous influx into Liverpool in January-February 1981 saw a roost at Stockton's Wood, Speke increase from 10,000 on 31 January to a peak of 16,300 on 6 February; during February there were flocks of 500-2000 Bramblings at Calderstones Park, Childwall Hall Woods, Allerton Golf Course, Woolton Woods and Black Wood, Childwall. At least 560 were killed by traffic along a Speke roadway that month, having become sick and disoriented after drinking a mixture of salt and anti-freeze on recently-gritted roads. Elsewhere, 400 were present at Ribby Hall, Fylde in January and February, 330 at Whalley Nab and 230 at Simonstone in February, 100 at Stubbins, Rossendale in mid-February and 250 at Altham in March; birds remained widespread until mid-April, with four at Altham on 8 May the latest recorded.

In late autumn 2002 a large influx into the east of the county led to exceptional flocks feeding on beech-mast throughout the winter, including a roost of 1,700 at Belmont in November that still held 300 in January, 450 at Dunnow Hall, Slaidburn and up to

100 at Bacup in December, 500 at Whitewell and 300 at Sunnyhurst Hey Reservoir, Darwen in January, and 400 at Barrowford in February. Only very small numbers penetrated to the coastal west, the lure of upland beech-mast apparently proving irresistible.

As in Oakes's day, the main spring passage comes in March and early April. This is virtually imperceptible at coastal watchpoints but small parties are typically recorded at inland locations where few had been present during the preceding winter. Exceptional counts include 200 at Tarleton on 9 April 1967, 100 at Barnacre Reservoir, Garstang on 15 March 1986 with 120 at Cockerham on 20 April and 230 at Rivington on the 13th-23rd, 40 at Martin Mere on 8 April 1994 , up to 40 at Dunnow Hall in April 2001 and 25 at Mere Sands Wood on 25 March 2002.

A few singing males have been recorded among late stragglers over the years and a bird at Mere Sands Wood on 28 May 2000 is the latest spring migrant thus far. The only summer record is of a bird at Crawshawbooth, Rossendale on 28 July 1987.

There have been 26 recoveries of Bramblings ringed in Lancashire, eight within the county, three elsewhere in northern England, six in southern England, two each in the Netherlands, Sweden and Finland and one each in Denmark and Italy. This last, an unaged male ringed at Scarisbrick on 30 November 1975, was shot at Carcare near Genoa three years later, to the day. Three birds ringed elsewhere in Britain have been recovered here, two from northern and one from southern England, and there have been three European-ringed recoveries, two first-winter males from Norway recovered in the Liverpool area in the early 1980s and a first-summer ringed in Sweden on 23 April 1992 and found freshly dead at Halsall on 1 April 1993.

BM, RW.
This species account was sponsored by Marie and Peter Rathbone.

SERIN

Serinus serinus

Lancashire Category A. (0, 3).

Vagrant from southern Europe.

There have been three records, all since 1990, reflecting increasing numbers nationally; the species ceased to be considered a national rarity in 1982.

What was probably a first-winter male was the first. It was seen and heard flying south over Heysham NR on 8 October 1990 by Pete Marsh and Tom Wilmer before dropping into bushes near Ocean Edge, where it was watched briefly before flying off south-east.

The other two records were fly-overs, picked up on call but seen sufficiently well for their identity to be confirmed – at Martin Mere on 27 May 1993 and at Ainsdale NNR on 24 June 1994.

SJW, MJ.
This species account was sponsored by Pete Marsh.

GREENFINCH

Carduelis chloris

Lancashire Category A.

Abundant resident breeder.

Mitchell described the Greenfinch as a common resident throughout the county in the nineteenth century which tended to vacate the more exposed areas in winter. That the species' dietary adaptability is no recent phenomenon is demonstrated by his observation that birds fed on discarded hop-seeds at a Blackburn brewery in hard weather. To Oakes this was an abundant breeding species, which moved in flocks during the winter months to waste land and stubbles, particularly in coastal areas; spring passage was noticeable in March and April at both coastal and inland locations. The Greenfinch's status had not changed appreciably by the early 1970s, when Spencer (1973) commented that winter flocks on arable land included many birds from Yorkshire and elsewhere in northern England.

The British population has continued to increase – by 22% between 1970 and 2001 (CBC) and by 43% during 1994-2005 (BBS) – and the Greenfinch remains an abundant breeding species in Lancashire. Its breeding range has remained unaltered since at least 1968-72 and the 1997-2000 Atlas survey estimated a total of 12,000 pairs, found in 84% of the county's tetrads and distributed throughout in plantations, woodland, coppices, dense hedgerows, large gardens, parks and churchyards. Only in the treeless parts of the Bowland and Pennine fells and on saltmarshes is the species absent, although it is relatively local though widely-distributed in Rossendale. Changes in agricultural practices that have reduced the availability of weed-seeds and insects in summer and stubbles later in the year have not had a detrimental effect on Greenfinch numbers; many have moved to newer crops, such as oilseed rape, maize and sunflowers, or have abandoned farmland altogether to feed at bird-tables and feeding-stations.

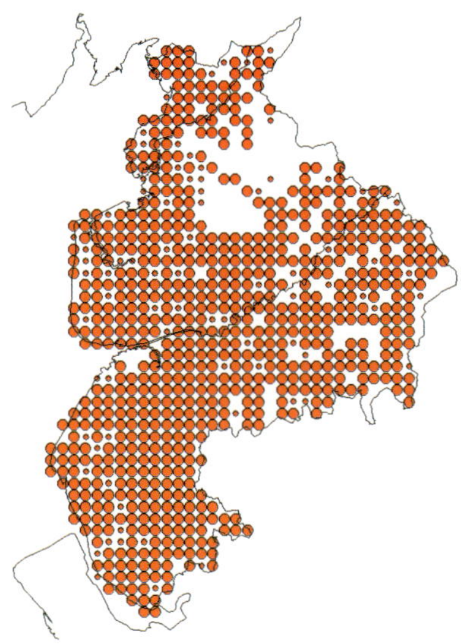

Breeding distribution of Greenfinch, 1997-2000. (Large dots: confirmed. Small dots: possible)

Post-breeding flocks begin to assemble in July and gatherings of up to 50 birds are widespread in early autumn. Over the years concentrations have grown and dwindled at various locations but there is evidence of a general increase in flock size since the late 1980s. Large early-autumn moulting flocks, numbering several hundred birds, frequented the Hightown-Crosby dunes during the 1970s but had disappeared by 1982. Among other notable coastal counts have been 300 at Glasson Dock on 31 July 1980, 200 at the Eric Morecambe complex in late summer 1992, 400 at Black Lane Head, Pilling on 29 July 1995 and 750 on oilseed rape fields in the same area on 8 August 1999. Inland, there were 75 at Barrow Lodge, Whalley on 17 August 1984, 50 in the Limy Valley above Crawshawbooth on 6 August 1985, 200 at Foulridge Lower Reservoir, Colne on 24 August 2002 and 200 at Martin Mere on 20 August 2005.

Larger flocks build up from September onwards. Again the coastal west tends to see the most impressive gatherings, of which the most spectacular was a flock of 3,000-3,500 feeding on stubbles at Cogie Hill, Fylde on 19 September 1992. There were 700 at Martin Mere on 26-27 September 1995, 200 at Marshside in late October 1998, 250 at Reed's Moss, St. Helens, in late September 2000 and 220 on Lytham Moss on 9 October 2002. Two hundred fed on sunflower heads at Myerscough College on 30 October 2003, while in 2005 500 were in a sunflower field at Bradshaw Lane, Pilling on 22 September, 300 at Fleetwood and 600 at Birkdale on 19 October and 353 in the Rimrose Valley on the 27th .

Further inland, a hundred were present at Hoddlesden, Darwen and 60 at Barden Lane, Burnley in October 1990, 80 in a Belmont garden in October 2000 and 45 at Broadly Fold, Rossendale in November 2000.

Winter flocks and roosts reflect the autumn pattern, both in distribution and size, with the largest in the south-west and the Fylde. Gatherings of up to 200 are quite widespread, but there were 900 at Hundred End on 6 February 1971, 450 at Fleetwood Marine Lake during the 1984-85 and 1985-86 winters, 200 at Singleton, Fylde in January 1990 and at Little Crosby in February 1991, 50 at Walverden Reservoir, Burnley in December 1995, 200 at Delph Reservoir in December 1997 and 300 at the Old Coach Road, Rainford on 7 December 2003.

As in Oakes's time, small numbers of migrants are occasionally recorded at coastal watchpoints in March and April, including 40 at Heysham between mid-March and mid-April in 1989, 33 there between 4 March and 11 April 1997 and 35 in March and eleven in April 1999. Small movements are also observed at inland sites, especially in east Lancashire and Rossendale during this period; 34 were recorded over Darwen Moor edge in March and 24 in April 1998.

Passage in late autumn is frequently conspicuous, particularly along the coast, although numbers involved vary considerably from year to year. One hundred and nineteen flew south at Fairhaven on 15 October and 140 at Seaforth on 20 October 1990, 70 at Heysham on 14 October 1995, 60 there 3 October 1998, and 75 on 22 October 2000.

Passage numbers have continued to climb this century. In 2002, 2,064 passed over Fairhaven between 22 September and 19 November and 200 were ringed at Heysham and 174 at Greenhalgh Castle Tarn, Garstang during the autumn. October 2003 produced another heavy, widespread coastal movement: 80 were caught at Heysham on 11 October, 100 passed through Seaforth on the 13th and 200+ at Fairhaven next day, and there were 146 at Rossall Point on the 19th with 83 there on the 26th. 2,550 flew over Fairhaven between 12 September and 10 November 2003 but this was overshadowed by a massive total of 7,029 there between 6 September and 19 November 2005 with a peak of 618 on 29 October.

Male Greenfinch, Little Crosby, March 2004. (Steve Young)

Heysham visible migration data suggest a combination of north to south and east to west migrants and this is reflected in the ringing recoveries from a wide range of sites east of the Pennines from Northumberland to Nottinghamshire, together with a small proportion of young birds of local origin, especially females, that move south in autumn as far as the Midlands.

There have been more than 650 recoveries of Greenfinches ringed in Lancashire, nearly 500 of them within the county, 120 elsewhere in northern England, 20 in southern England, eleven in Wales and five each in Scotland and Ireland. One hundred and sixty-four birds ringed in northern England have been recovered here, as well as 44 from southern England, 21 from Wales and one from Ireland. These conform closely to the national pattern with north-south movements predominating in autumn, with fewer east to west. There have been no recoveries in or from continental Europe.

One of the strangest recoveries ever received by the BTO involved a Greenfinch ringed at Warton on 18 February 1960, the ring of which was found at Arkholme on 7 July 1991 with a metal detector.

BM, RW.

This species account was sponsored by Les Ward.

GOLDFINCH

Carduelis carduelis

Lancashire Category A.

Common resident breeder.

The Goldfinch was exploited almost to extinction in Britain for the cage-bird trade in the nineteenth and early twentieth centuries but legislation in 1933 outlawing commercial trapping, followed by further measures in 1954 directed against private bird-catching, were followed by a steady increase in the population. The New Atlas (1993) noted recent range expansion into northern Scotland and estimated 220,000 Goldfinch territories in Britain; more recently a 35% increase has been recorded between 1970 and 2001 (CBC) and 35% between 1994 and 2005 (BBS).

Mitchell's account reflects the plight of the Goldfinch in Lancashire at the height of the bird-catchers' depredations; he described the species as resident but on the verge of extinction, citing only a handful of sporadic breeding records in the Blackburn, Chipping and Liverpool areas. Oakes noted a recent recovery following the 1933 Act but considered the Goldfinch to be still very scarce and local with a total of fewer than ten confirmed breeding records in 1946, in the Parbold-Rufford area, Liverpool and the Lune and Ribble Valleys. Small flocks were encountered fairly widely in autumn and winter but by more recent standards these were small indeed, including 15 at Hurst Green in November 1945 and 30 on Merseyside in November 1946. Further legislation in 1954 prohibited the keeping of wild-caught birds and finally laid the basis for the species' recovery. Breeding was confirmed in 47 10km squares during 1968-72 and by 1973 Spencer was able to describe the Goldfinch as well-established throughout the county, with flocks in excess of 100 birds fairly widespread in autumn and winter.

The species has continued to flourish since the early 1970s; breeding data are sparse and intermittent, but Goldfinches were described as increasing in Rossendale and in the Liverpool and Southport areas in 1978, common throughout the Burnley area in 1985, increasing around Darwen in 1989 and Rossendale's commonest finch in 1993. The 1997-2000 survey uncovered a distribution essentially similar to, but sparser than, that of the Greenfinch with breeding confirmed in 70% of the county's tetrads and an estimated population of 3,500 pairs. As with Greenfinches, Goldfinches were absent from barren and treeless areas of the uplands and the coast, but were much less commonly found in urban areas than the larger species.

Goldfinch, Seaforth Nature Reserve, June 2004.

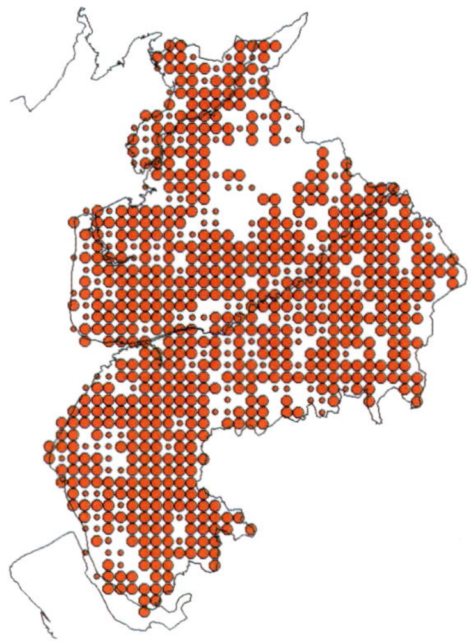

Breeding distribution of Goldfinch, 1997-2000. (Large dots: confirmed. Small dots: possible)

The nesting season extends from April to August but by the beginning of that month mixed flocks of adults and juveniles begin to assemble in areas where knapweed, ragwort or thistles are plentiful; these are augmented by passage birds in September and October. Peak counts of 100-150 were typical at this time from the late 1960s to the mid-1990s but exceptional gatherings included 250 at Foulridge Reservoir in September 1969, up to 200 at Penwortham in August 1983, 300 at Rivington Moor edge in October 1985, 165 on thistles at Hightown on 29 September 1987, and 140 on knapweed at the Eric Morecambe complex in August 1992.

Since the mid-1990s the size of many autumn flocks has increased significantly; 350 fed on thistles at Marshside on 1 October 1996 and there were up to 450 there in mid-September 1998 and later in the month in 2000; 500 were at Seaforth on 15 August and flocks of 300 and 150 at Belmont Reservoir on 29 September in 1997, 300 at Hurstwood Reservoir, Burnley on 8 October 2001 and 400 at Clowbridge Reservoir, Rossendale on 29 September 2002.

Most European Goldfinches, including those breeding in Britain, move south or south-west in autumn to the Mediterranean region, where food plants continue to produce seed during the winter months; substantial numbers, however, also remain in the breeding areas. Passage movements are recorded at coastal watchpoints, and less regularly inland, in September and October. These vary considerably in size from one year to the next but numbers do not appear to have increased in line with the growth in autumn feeding-flocks in recent years. At Heysham up to 70 per day passed through between early September and early October in 1982; 60 were recorded there on 17 October 1985, 77 on 13 October 1990, 42 on 16 September 1996 and 80 on 30 September 2000. At Fairhaven 32 flew south on 29 October 1983, parties of up to 40 Goldfinches passed on several dates in October 1990, and 55 on 27 and 28 September 1992. A hundred passed through Seaforth on 25 September 1991 and 45 at Lytham St. Anne's on 27 September 2003. Inland, 411 were recorded moving through the Grane Valley, Rossendale between August and November 1989 and 1,490 bird-days were recorded at a watchpoint on Darwen Moor edge between July and late November in 1991 and 1,105 in September 1998.

Over 80% of British Goldfinches leave in autumn for winter quarters in Belgium, western France and Spain (BWP) and it is noticeable that winter flocks in Lancashire, particularly in inland areas, are normally much smaller than those in autumn. Prior to the early 1990s counts of 30 or more were fairly infrequent but in recent years winter peaks have increased considerably; observers in several regions have attributed at least some of this growth to the adaptation by many Goldfinches to a diet of peanuts and sunflower and niger seeds at bird tables and feeding-stations. There were 200 at Martin Mere on 8 February 1992, 100 at Eccleston Mere, St. Helens in January 1993 and 300 at British Aerospace, Warton on 22 December 1998. Inland, 200 fed on alder seeds at Waterfoot in January 1986, there were 80 near Burnley on 3 December 1992, 45 at Musbury, Rossendale in February 1999 and 50 at Rowley Lake, Burnley on 14 November 2003.

Small groups of Goldfinches are recorded on spring passage in April and early May at both inland and coastal sites. Thirty passed through Witton Country Park, Blackburn in mid-April 1967, 27 at Shrugg's Wood, Leyland on 6 April 1986, 25 at Alders Folly, Rossendale on 7 April 1991 and 90+ at Cuerden Valley Park during 4-12 April 1994. As in autumn, most movements are observed at well-watched coastal locations: 45 passed at Heysham on 21 April 1984 and 52 on 2 May 1995; twenty were recorded at Lytham on 5 May 1986, 54 at Rossall Point between 23 April and 4 May 1992, 187 there between 7 April and 9 May 1998 and 16 on 18 April 2003, when 80 also flew north at Marshside.

There have been eight recoveries of Goldfinches ringed in Lancashire, four within the county and two each in northern England and Scotland. Three birds ringed elsewhere in Britain have been recovered here, two from Cheshire and one from Surrey. There has been only one recovery from continental Europe, an unaged male ringed in Belgium on 22 December 1991 and found freshly dead at Fulwood, Preston on 27 February 1993.

BM, RW.

This species account was sponsored in memory of Patricia Ann Jones.

SISKIN

Carduelis spinus

Lancashire Category A.

Uncommon resident breeder, common passage migrant and winter visitor from Fennoscandia.

Mitchell was able to publish just a single breeding record, six pairs that were reported to have summered and raised young in the Lancaster area in 1836 after several hundred had wintered. Otherwise, he described the Siskin as a winter visitor but gave no real indication of numbers, although the 1836 record implies that significant invasions must have occurred. Little seems to have changed by the middle of the twentieth century; Oakes referred to Siskins as 'regular and comparatively common winter visitors' to 'one locality . . in south Lancashire' but 'rare and irregular elsewhere (although) often overlooked owing to its tree-top feeding habits'. He published just a handful of winter records from Hoghton, Samlesbury and Duxon Hill between 1939 and 1943, as well as a party of 20 at Formby Hall in February 1936. Breeding first occurred 'at a southern haunt' (which Oakes hesitated to name but was perhaps the Formby-Ainsdale pinewoods) in 1939 and again in 1947.

Siskins expanded their range and numbers in Britain following the spread of commercial conifer plantations from the mid-twentieth century and their range increased by 85% between 1968-72 and 1988-91. Writing in 1973, Spencer could add no further breeding records in present-day Lancashire (although two pairs nested near Belmont in 1961) and largely confirmed Oakes' assessment of winter status. By 1988-91, however, the breeding range had expanded to 17 10km squares from three in 1968-72, and by 1997-2000 had almost doubled again to 30 squares. The 1997-2000 Atlas survey estimated a total of 200 pairs, all in conifer plantations or mixed woodlands and widely spread in 72 tetrads, but concentrated in the uplands with outlying pockets elsewhere, including the Sefton coast and the Lune Valley.

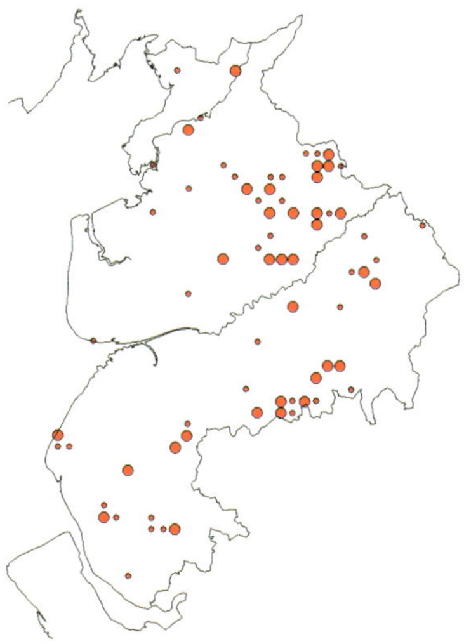

Breeding distribution of Siskin, 1997-2000. (Large dots: confirmed. Small dots: possible)

The process of colonisation of Lancashire is not well documented but dispersing juveniles seen in the Burnley area in 1982 may have come from a relatively close breeding site, and from the mid-1980s there was a marked increase in breeding-season records. Siskins were displaying at Stocks Reservoir in 1985, and from the early 1990s confirmed and probable nesting records proliferated. In 1992 Siskins bred in Lord's Lot Wood in the lower Lune Valley, there were up to six pairs at Haslingden Grane, Rossendale, at least two at Ainsdale NNR, and at least three pairs probably nested in Bowland. By 1995 nesting was regular in Bowland, the Gisburn Forest, Belmont (6 pairs in 2002) and Roddlesworth and Delph Plantations, and was becoming established at Haslingden, in the Wayoh-Entwistle area, and in the Ainsdale-Formby pinewoods.

There appear to have been no significant recent changes in the size of the British population although there are sometimes large fluctuations between years; certainly, there is no hard evidence of any decline in Lancashire, although Siskins are now reported less frequently than a decade ago at garden feeders.

Post-breeding movements, usually small, are recorded from late June, mainly at inland locations adjacent to the core breeding-areas, although there were two at Heysham on 29 June 1991; an exceptional flock of 50 was at Clough Bottom Reservoir in east Lancashire in July 1997.

Autumn passage proper may extend from mid-August to late November; timing and numbers involved vary considerably from year to year but substantial movements of Siskins have become more regular since the early 1990s, especially at coastal watchpoints. Noteworthy counts include 100 at Formby Point on 18 October 1972, 50 at Lytham St. Anne's on 2 November 1983, 87 at Fairhaven on 13 November 1984, 62 at Heysham on 28 September 1985 and 90 on Warton Crag in mid-September 1988.

Autumn 1993 was exceptional, with a minimum of 802 passing through Heysham between 17 September and 28 November and 265 at Seaforth during roughly the same period; there were 283 over Fairhaven on 18 September alone and 85 there on 5 October. Inland, 860 bird-days were recorded at Darwen Moor edge between July and December. Significant autumn passage of Siskins was also observed in 1994, 1996, 1997, 2001 and 2002. Outstanding recent counts include 192 at Heysham on 27 November 1996, 102 there on 20 November 2001 and 143 on 10 October 2002, 150 at Leighton Moss on 3 October 1999 and 83 at Lytham on 13 October 2002. Inland, there were 100 at Rawtenstall on 4 October 1996, 50+ at Garstang and at Brinscall on 1 October 2000 and 85 over Caton Moor on 4 October 2002.

Male Siskin, Little Crosby, April 2002. (Steve Young)

Winter flocks of Siskins have become larger and more widespread since the 1970s; small parties were observed feeding on peanuts at feeders, especially in the east, as long ago as 1973. Flocks of up to 35 were widely reported in Rossendale and also around Burnley and at Roddlesworth Plantations during January-March 1978, and there were up to 100 at Eccleston Mere, St. Helens in December 1981; 150 fed in alders at Scorton in December 1983 and there were 200+ at Formby Hall in January 1986 with flocks of up to 150 in Rossendale until April of that year. Up to 200 Siskins spent the 1991-92 winter in Roddlesworth Plantations, similar numbers were recorded at Stocks Reservoir in February 1996, and there were 180 in Delph Plantations in February 1997 and 170 at Belmont in December 2000.

Spring movements are often protracted, although numbers seldom approach those of autumn; passage begins in early March in some years and may continue until the end of May. There is evidence of a general increase in the volume of migration at both coastal and inland locations in recent years. Prior to about 1990 spring totals at most coastal watchpoints rarely exceeded 100, but more recent counts have included 33 at Seaforth on 18 March

1990, 225 at Rossall Point between 19 March and 12 May and 58 at Heysham in March and April 1998, 30 at Formby Point and 48 at Heysham on 8 April 2000 and 53 at Marshside next day. Small parties are widespread inland in March and April, the largest being 200 at Langden Beck on 23 March 1991 and 60 at Belmont in May 2004.

There have been 68 recoveries of Siskins ringed in Lancashire, six within the county, 20 elsewhere in northern England, five in southern England, 33 in Scotland and singles in Wales and Ireland. Two birds have been recovered on the continent, a first-winter male ringed at Euxton, Chorley on 5 March 1989 controlled in Limburg, Belgium on 31 October and another male from Kemple End, Clitheroe on 3 April 1995 found dead near Trondheim, Norway on 10 June 1998. Fifty-two Siskins ringed elsewhere in Britain and Ireland have been recovered here, seven from northern England, 26 from southern England, eight from Scotland and one from Ireland. There have been three foreign-ringed recoveries, unaged females ringed in Belgium on 24 September 1993 and 28 March 1995 and controlled, respectively, at Lancaster on 16 January 1994 and Heysham on 27 November 1996, and another female ringed at Caen in northern France on 1 April 2002 and controlled at Over Kellet on 9 April 2004.

BM, RW.

This species account was sponsored by Jill Blackburn.

LINNET

Carduelis cannabina

Lancashire Category A.

Common resident breeder.

Marked population declines associated with changes in agricultural practices have been recorded in recent decades in Britain, Ireland and much of north-west and central Europe. The New Atlas estimated 520,000 territories in Britain in 1988-91 with only a 4.6% decrease in range since the original 1968-72 survey, but a more recent assessment has estimated a decline of 51% in the British Linnet population between 1970 and 2001 (CBC) and by a further 7% during 1994-2005 (BBS).

In Lancashire, Mitchell described the species as most plentiful in coastal areas but also numerous on inland mosses. He reported decreases in numbers since the mid-nineteenth century in the Fylde, Rossendale and the Burnley and Blackburn areas, at least in part due to widespread trapping for the cage-bird trade. Oakes considered the Linnet to be a common and widespread resident, particularly abundant on the coastal plain both north and south of the Ribble; gorse-clumps and hedgerows were favourite nest-sites. Oakes saw little evidence of autumn passage, although winter flocks were numerous in both coastal and inland regions, up to 250m above sea level. Spencer (1973), however, described the species as uncommon in winter in the east of the county.

Changes in the Linnet's Lancashire breeding status since the 1970s are unclear. At the 10km square level there was no change in distribution between 1968-72 and 1997-2000, when breeding was confirmed or suspected in 634 tetrads (68%) and the Lancashire population was estimated at 5,000 pairs. Only in densely-wooded lowland areas, urban districts and on the highest fells are breeding Linnets absent. They are particularly common in the south-west, the Fylde and the lower Lune Valley, but colonies are also widely distributed in parts of east Lancashire, Rossendale and the West Pennine Moors, where Linnets have increased notably in former Twite habitat along the moorland edge since the early 1990s with, for example, 50 pairs now breeding on the West Pennine Moors.

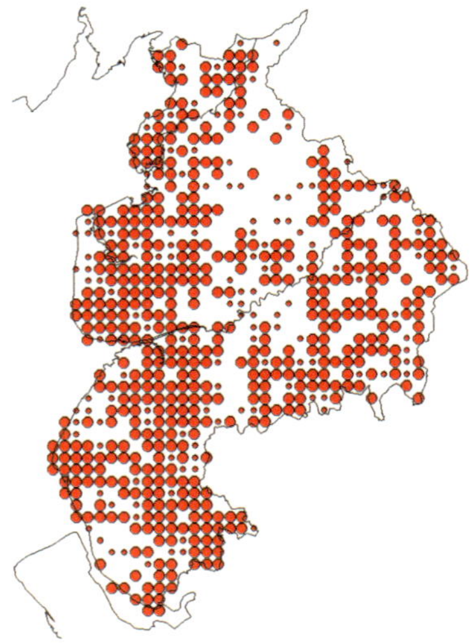

Breeding distribution of Linnet, 1997-2000. (Large dots: confirmed. Small dots: possible)

On the negative side, however, there is evidence of substantial thinning in numbers of breeding Linnets at some regularly-censused localities. At Marshside-Crossens around 30 pairs nested annually in the late 1970s and 1980s, both in the relict dunes and on the saltmarsh but by 1992 the population had fallen to about twelve pairs and by 1999-2002 to four or five, although eight pairs bred in 2003 and nine in 2004, reflecting a slight but general recovery in the south-west. At Heysham there has been a similar collapse from 20 pairs in 1987 to five since the late 1990s, attributed in part to predation of nests by Magpies; numbers at Leighton Moss and the Eric Morecambe complex, however, have remained stable at 15-20 pairs since the mid-1960s.

Male Linnet, Hightown Dunes, April 2005. (Steve Young)

Post-fledging dispersals begin in July, merging into more general passage from early August through to late October. In addition, altitudinal movements are seen in Rossendale and east Lancashire as most Linnets vacate those regions in late autumn. Most of the large early-autumn flocks and roosts are recorded in the coastal west; up to 750 were regularly present at the Eric Morecambe complex between the 1960s and the late 1980s but totals have been much lower since. Other noteworthy gatherings include 300 at Bretherton on 20 August 1983 and at Billinge Hill Quarry on 7 August 1990, 1,000 at Cogie Hill, Pilling on 15 August 1993 and 400 at Nateby, also in the Fylde, in mid-August 2002. Flocks further east are usually smaller, although there were 110 at Earnsdale Reservoir, Darwen in late August 1987, 300+ at Dean Clough Reservoir in August 1996 and 100 at Foulridge Reservoir in August 2002.

Even larger flocks and movements have been recorded in September and October, although the size of these has clearly diminished since the mid-1990s; most of the higher counts have been in the Fylde or the south-west. There were 440 in a roost at Preesall in September 1983, 500 at Seaforth on 6 October 1991 and near Pilling on 19 September 1992, 700 on Churchtown Moss, Southport on 24 September 1993 and 400 near St. Helens in October 2000. Inland Lancashire normally sees the largest flocks in September, including 250+ at Stocks Reservoir on 25 September 1983 and 120 at Parsonage Reservoir, Blackburn in September 1991 with 100 there in September 2003.

Passage of Linnets at coastal watchpoints is very variable, and concentrated mainly between mid-September and mid-October; 83 passed at Fairhaven on 5 October 1984 and 244 during 26-29 September 1992. Heysham totals include 70 on 13 October 1990 and 95 on 4 October 1992; 198 moved south over Rossall Point between 21 September and 22 October 1992, and there were 250 at Sunderland Point on 9 September 1999. Inland observations occasionally produce very large aggregate counts; for example 2,019 were recorded over Haslingden Grane, Rossendale during August-November 1989 and 2,630 bird-days were recorded at Darwen Moor edge between August and December in 1995.

During the winter months Linnets are largely confined to coastal areas, where flocks of 50-100 are not unusual, although there is some evidence of a decline in flock sizes over recent decades. There were 700 at Hesketh Bank in December 1970, 400 were at nearby Banks Marsh on 23 December 1982 and 1,200 at Marshside on 19 January 1985. Since the late 1980s 400 at Marshside and 1,000 at Stanah, Fylde in December 1996 with 300 at Lytham Marsh the same month, 300 at Old Coach Road, St Helens on 6 January 2001 and 500 at Gale Moss, Chorley in February 2002 are among the highest counts recorded. In eastern areas even single-figure parties are unusual in winter, and a total of 62 at three sites in Rossendale during early December 1995 was particularly noteworthy.

The return of Linnets to inland breeding areas usually takes place between late March and mid-April; along the coast a variable passage is recorded between late March and early May. Heysham recorded its highest totals of visible northbound migrants of 830 between 31 March and 7 April 1990, with a peak of 400 on 1 April, and 566 between 19 March and 9 May 2005; by contrast, only 38 were recorded there between 7 and 23 April in 1994. A total of 452 flew north at Rossall Point between 28 March and 30 April 1998 and there were 170 on Lytham Moss on 9 April 2002.

There have been 72 recoveries of Lancashire-ringed Linnets, 43 within the county, seven in northern England, five in southern England, nine in France and eight in Spain; these last indicate where at least a proportion of locally-bred birds spend the winter. Fifteen birds ringed elsewhere in northern England have been recovered here.

BM, RW.

This species account was sponsored by Frank Walsh.

TWITE

Carduelis flavirostris

Lancashire Category A.

Rare breeder; fairly common winter visitor from Western Isles and South Pennines.

Twite bred 'as commonly on the south Lancashire mosslands as in more elevated districts' in the late nineteenth century according to Mitchell, although the only lowland site he actually mentioned was 'mosses near Preston'. It is unclear exactly when lowland breeding ceased. Oakes reported a nest found in heather by F.W. Holder on Formby Moss in 1916 as the last known in that area – although Smith (1963) reported nesting there as late as 1930 – and final breeding on Chat Moss, now in Greater Manchester, in 1940. Drainage, agricultural improvement and peat-cutting undoubtedly hastened the Twite's demise throughout the lowlands.

Mitchell described breeding birds as numerous in the uplands near the then Yorkshire border and plentiful near Blackburn, but declining around Colne and on Pendle Hill. Oakes identified a more extensive breeding range, from the south Pennines west through Rossendale to the Anglezarke Moors, and as far north as Pendle Hill. He described breeding birds as locally common but most of the sites he mentioned are now in Greater Manchester, exceptions being Stiperden, Anglezarke, Haslingden Grane and Pendle.

Surveying breeding Twite is a complex task and there were no reliable estimates of the size of the Lancashire population before the 1990s. However, there can be no doubt that the past 20 years or more have witnessed a drastic reduction in numbers, although the breeding range changed little until the beginning of this century. Birds were present in 16 10km squares during 1968-72, 17 during 1988-91 and 14 during 1997-2000, but within this range there were many local extinctions and previously large aggregations have shrunk to one or two pairs, exemplified by the declining number of 10km squares where breeding was proven during the three survey periods – 14, 12 and 10 respectively. A mere 27 nesting pairs were located during 1997-2000 but the Lancashire population was estimated at 40 pairs. These were found in 17 tetrads, at an average density of 0.6 pairs per km^2, at the lower end of estimated densities in the south Pennines of 0.4-3.5 pairs/km^2 (McGhie *et al.* 1994). The south Pennine population, including Yorkshire, was thought to contain some 200-400 pairs in the early 1990s (Brown *et al.* 1995), while estimates of the British population fell from 65,000 pairs in 1988-92 to 10,000 (600-800 in England) in 1999 (Langston *et al.* 2006).

The catastrophic decline in the Lancashire population was best monitored on the Hile CBC plot in Rossendale, where numbers fluctuated between eight and eleven pairs during 1967-73, rising to 17 in 1975 but followed by a steady fall to one or two pairs from 1987 with the last in 1995. This probably typifies what happened throughout most of the county with the result that by the early years of the twenty-first century just one substantial breeding site remained.

The main Lancashire stronghold has probably always been in the area east of Burnley and Nelson on the moors around Hurstwood, Worsthorne, Boulsworth Hill and Trawden, where small breeding clusters of five or more pairs were well-distributed during the 1970s (Spencer 1977). A survey carried out by the East Lancashire Ornithologists Club located 31 pairs on two sections of Boulsworth Hill in 1967, 20 pairs on part of Hameldon Hill in 1968, a total of 46 pairs east of Nelson and 25 pairs in the Burnley area. However, by the early 1990s most moors supported only one or two pairs, five being exceptional (Hornby 1994). These east Lancashire sites were resurveyed in 2004 and 2005 when most colonies had become extinct and only a very few pairs were hanging on (A. Raine *pers. comm.*).

An RSPB survey in 1990 located seven pairs on Emmott Moor, Trawden, five near Trawden Forest, five around Boulsworth Moor, one on Deerstone Moor, two in the Hameldon-Entwistle Moor area and single pairs at Hurstwood, Worsthorne and Stiperden, making 22 pairs in total. About a dozen pairs were found in this area during 1997-2000, but very intensive surveys of one moorland site east of Burnley near Cant Cough Reservoir located 18+ pairs in 2002, 20 in 2003 and 25 in 2005 (A. Raine *pers. comm.*). It therefore seems likely that the 1997-2000 survey missed a significant number of pairs in this area. However, this east Burnley population appears to be the only one in the county that is holding its own, so the current Lancashire population is probably no larger than 30 pairs.

Elsewhere it is a different picture, on Heald Moor south-east of Burnley, for example, the population fell from ten pairs in 1993 (White & Kehoe 1993) to extinction by the end of the 1990s.

Rossendale has experienced a similar decline. Twite were locally common in the mid-1970s and still widespread in the mid-1980s but all sites experienced declining numbers. In addition to The Hile, the population on Haslingden Moor fell from 17 pairs in 1968 to one or two by the late 1980s; the situation at Cowpe Moss and Clowbridge has been essentially the same. The early 1990s saw a temporary resurgence with ten pairs at Lee Quarry in 1992; twelve pairs nested in a fenced-off tree-planting area at Facit, near Whitworth in 1993, which were reduced to two or three in 1994 after fire had damaged the site. Only eight pairs were thought to have bred in the whole of Rossendale during 1997-1999, but only two breeding sites remained in 2003 and breeding was not confirmed in either 2004 or 2005, although a handful of sightings during the breeding season suggest that one or two pairs may still be present.

It has been much the same story further west. On the West Pennine Moors numbers have declined from over 30 pairs in the early 1980s to fewer than ten during 1997-2000, with a remnant three or four in 2003. The 'stronghold' on Darwen Moor fell from ten or more pairs in 1983 to just one in 2003-2005. One pair is thought to have bred on Withnell Moor in 2004.

Pendle Hill was always the favourite site for birders wanting to add Twite to their year-list; they were relatively common (but apparently never censused) here during the 1980s but dropped to fewer than five pairs by 1999, just one or two at the turn of the century and are now extinct. Twite have always been surprisingly scarce in the rest of Bowland, despite the abundance of apparently suitable moorland habitat. In the mid-1970s a pair nested in west Bowland and there were three pairs on Marshaw and Chipping Fells. There have been occasional records from Burn, Salter and Croasdale Fells. One pair bred at Abbeystead during the LDBWS survey of 1986-91 and another near Ward's Stone in 1997-2000.

Lancashire Twite nests are usually situated in old bracken, heather or dry-stone walls but some also use crevices in slopes, cliffs and quarries. Until recently it was not thought that loss of nesting habitat was a major factor in their decline. However, recent research suggests that mature stands of bracken may be a critical nesting requirement in Lancashire and may have declined significantly (A. Raine *pers. comm.*). Also implicated is the relatively recent intensification and simplification of upland agriculture, with the loss of arable fields, overgrazing of the in-bye, conversion of hay meadows to improved leys and early cutting of silage crops leading to reduced availability of grass- and other seeds on which Twite depend. In order partially to compensate, supplementary feeding stations have been set up in various parts of the United Utilities' south Pennine estate.

Post-breeding flocks start forming in July and become widespread on the moorlands and reservoir edges in August, most birds moving away during September and October. There have been huge reductions in the size and frequency of such flocks. Examples include declines from up to 300 at The Hile in the mid-1970s to 100 during the 1980s and just 20-40 in the early 1990s, and 300 at Belmont Reservoir in 1974 to 50 in 1990, with 25 in September 1997 the last sizeable flock there. The largest recent Rossendale gatherings have been 70 near Lee Quarry in September 1995 and 55 at Musbury in September 1999. Flocks of 100 or more were fairly regular throughout the breeding range until the early 1980s, including over 400 at Habersham Eaves near Burnley on 10 September 1967. Prior to the establishment of a feeding station at Cant Clough Reservoir the largest recent post-breeding flock was 60 in August 1994, but nowadays the site attracts much larger numbers with a maximum of 250 on 5 October 2003. Ringing studies have shown that birds from breeding sites throughout the south Pennines gather together and wander the uplands during this period (Raine *et al.* in prep. [1]).

Oakes wrote that the uplands were never entirely deserted during winter, noting that flocks of up to 40 could be encountered, while Spencer (1977) described winter flocks around Burnley as 'not unknown, both on high ground and low, but they are irregular'. Three hundred on rough pasture at The Hile in January 1974 is our largest known winter flock. The number induced to leave is probably largely determined by weather conditions and available food resources and the recent establishment of winter feeding stations has enabled more to remain, for example up to 80 in recent years at Cant Clough.

It is difficult to separate passage migrants from wintering birds, although 22 coming in off the sea at Formby Point on 23 October 2003 were certainly new arrivals, as were two with

Linnets at Brockholes Quarry on 13 April 2004. Up to 200 feeding in Pheasant pens near Preesall in April 2003 were perhaps more likely to have been local winterers moving to a new feeding area.

Colour-ringed Twite, Heysham. (Phillip Tomkinson)

Spencer (1973) noted the disparity between numbers breeding and wintering in Lancashire (at this time the former were much higher than the latter, a situation which is now reversed) and wrote that it was clear that 'many birds are elsewhere'. Ringing studies in the early 1990s established that many south Pennine birds winter on English east coast saltmarshes from Lincolnshire south to Kent – where they appear during October and remain until March – although there have also been a handful of recoveries on the North Sea coasts of the Netherlands, Belgium and France. Extensive colour-ringing in Lancashire and other south Pennine areas since 2003 initially confirmed this pattern, but sightings during winter 2003/04 caused some doubt as to whether the whole population undertakes this south-easterly autumn migration (see below).

Oakes was aware of 'small parties occasionally [wintering] in one or two coastal districts' but it has been apparent for some time that our coastal saltmarshes hold quite large numbers. Hardy (1941) described them as frequent in winter on the saltmarshes near Southport. They can be difficult to pick out amongst other finches and small passerines and their precise wintering sites undoubtedly vary from year to year according to food availability. Flocks of 50 or more have been detected along the whole length of the coast but are more regular and numerous on the Ribble Estuary and the southern shores of Morecambe Bay. Larger flocks include 200 between Fleetwood and Stanah on 2 February 1984, 200 at Oglet on the Mersey in 1985, 80 on Cockerham Marsh and 100 at Cockersands in 1991, 60 at Thurnham in 1993, 150 at Pilling in 1992 and 80 in 2002, 107 at Marshside in 1997, 98 at Banks in 1999, 94 at Cockersands in 2000, 50 at Bolton-le-Sands in 2002, 60 at Stodday and 40 at Glasson in 2003, 120 at Heysham on 14 March 2003 and 86 at Aldcliffe and 90 on a Pilling farm feeding station in February 2005.

Ringing studies at Heysham and the Duddon Estuary in Cumbria over the past few years have indicated that wintering Twite are fairly mobile within Morecambe Bay and that the number of individuals using a site is probably two or three times greater than the peak count (P.J. Marsh *pers. comm.*). The Lancashire coastal population may therefore be in excess of 500 birds.

Until very recently their origins remained a mystery since it was thought that all the south Pennine population moved south-east. It seemed as if the problem had been solved in 2003 when two Heysham-ringed birds were found on Sanda, off the Mull of Kintyre in the breeding season, together with two movements in the opposite direction and exchanges further north with Eigg, Staffa, Oronsay and South Uist (the latter population is treated as a separate race *bensonorum*, distinct from the main British race *pipilans* by BWP). Briefly, it appeared that there was a simple answer: Lancashire breeders moved to the east coast while Hebridean birds moved to the Lancashire coast.

But then in winter 2004 and 2005 came several controls of colour-ringed south Pennine birds on the south Ribble marshes. Further confirmation that at least some south Pennine birds winter on the west coast came when a West Yorkshire nestling was seen in North Wales in 2004/05. Fractions of the south Pennine breeding population thus appear to migrate either west or south-east in autumn, while some remain in the breeding area. The reasons for this apparently arbitrary choice of wintering area remain a mystery.

On the basis of further controls of ringed birds, it now seems likely that the wintering populations of Liverpool and Morecambe Bays are largely separate, with the former consisting predominantly of south Pennine breeders, and the latter mainly of Hebridean birds (Raine *et al.* in prep [2]).

Without yet challenging this general conclusion, ringing studies have, however, produced evidence of some mixing of these populations. For example, two birds ringed at Heysham in 2002/03 were seen at Donna Nook in Lincolnshire in February and December 2004, and several ringed in the Pennines have now been seen in Morecambe Bay and on the Lune. The Lincolnshire controls confirm that not all Twite are loyal to particular wintering grounds, a conclusion supported by the control of a bird ringed on the Ribble in 2004/05 and seen at Heysham in 2005/06. Clearly, much remains to be discovered about the now apparently complex movements of British Twite between breeding and wintering areas.

SJW, RW.

This species account was sponsored by Peter Hornby and David Sowter.

LESSER REDPOLL

Carduelis cabaret

Lancashire Category A.

Fairly common breeder; common passage migrant and winter visitor.

Until 2001 the Lesser Redpoll was regarded as a race of Common Redpoll *Carduelis flammea* but most Lancashire birdwatchers have always recorded the two sub-species separately and we can be confident that the overwhelming majority of 'Redpoll' records refer to Lessers.

Mitchell described the Lesser Redpoll as a regular breeder in small numbers, particularly in the higher reaches of the Ribble and Hodder Valleys; birds were more widely distributed in winter when it was regularly seen in mixed-species flocks. The known range had expanded by Oakes's time, when he described it as a common and increasing resident in most districts. There seems to have been a widespread increase in numbers during the 1930s and 1940s, but Oakes singled out the Formby/Ainsdale pinewoods, the Kirkby to Rufford area and 'the country east of Preston to the Yorkshire border' for special mention. Breeding was also well established in the Fylde but scarce in Rossendale and the Bolton area. The largest autumn and winter flocks were found in the south-west, particularly in the Hightown-Southport-Rufford-Croston area, wherever birch and alder grew.

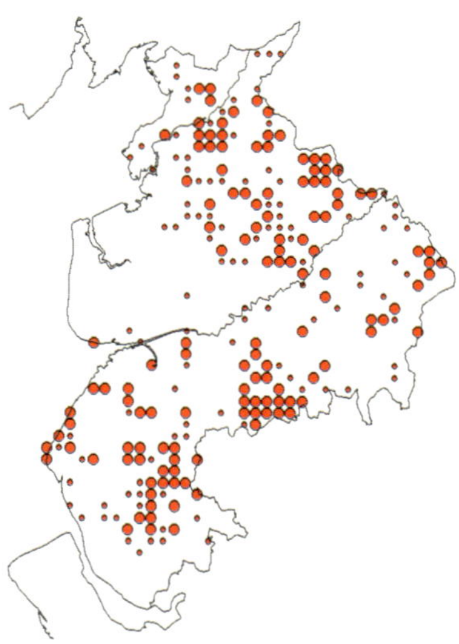

Breeding distribution of Lesser Redpoll, 1997-2000. (Large dots: confirmed. Small dots: possible)

Spencer (1973) considered that the range expansion had continued and the 1968-72 Atlas confirmed breeding in every 10km square in Lancashire except one in the far north-east, where presence was recorded. By 1997-2000 breeding was confirmed in just 33 10km squares with birds present in a further nine, indicating a roughly 33% decrease in confirmed range. The 1997-2000 Lancashire population was estimated at 700 pairs located in 237 tetrads (25%) but concentrated in the east between the Ribble and the Lune, on the fringes of the West Pennine Moors and in the St. Helens area. The British population went into decline at some time during the 1970s and decreased by 89% between 1970 and 2001 (CBC) and by 40% during 1994-2004 (BBS). Lesser Redpoll populations appear to have peaked at different times across the main regions of the county, but a general pattern of contraction and decline was observable by the mid-1980s.

In north Lancashire the species was widespread and fairly common between 1968 and 1988 but declined sharply in subsequent years; at Leighton Moss up to eight pairs bred annually in the 1970s, around four in the 1980s, only a single pair in 1991, and nesting had ceased there by 1995. In the east a decline was reported from the late 1970s and numbers continued to fall until the late 1980s but have now stabilised at low levels. Breeding pairs are often concentrated in conifer plantations, as on Waddington and Longridge Fells, in the Stocks Reservoir area and the Dunsop Valley. There was a marked range expansion in Rossendale – where there had been only occasional nesting records in the Irwell Valley in the 1950s – from the mid-1960s until about 1980, facilitated by widespread planting of birches, alders and willows on derelict land. Decreases were noted from the mid-1980s, although Lesser Redpolls still bred regularly along the Irwell, around Haslingden and in the upper Limy and Whitworth Valleys in 1990; a virtual population collapse after 1993 saw only isolated breeding pockets remaining by the century's end.

Lesser Redpolls appear to have maintained their position best on the West Pennine Moors and in south-east Chorley, although local declines elsewhere have been balanced to an extent by small recoveries and by range expansions, particularly in the south of the region. Six pairs, for example, bred in Roddlesworth Plantations in 1988, two or three during 1990-96 but a survey in 2003 located ten breeding pairs there. Nine pairs bred in birch and conifer woodlands around Belmont in 2004.

There have been many fluctuations in local populations in the south-west, but the fortunes of breeding clusters on the Merseyside coast and in West Lancashire have generally declined over the past 30 years or so. At Hesketh Golf Course, Marshside, the population grew from an initial colony of two pairs in 1984-86 to a peak of 12-15 in 1992, before declining steadily to extinction by 1999. The area between St. Helens and Ormskirk, however, remains a relative stronghold. Lesser Redpolls are now scarce and irregular breeders in the Fylde following a major contraction in range since the 1970s; just one pair bred during 1997-2000, at Lytham.

Post-breeding flocks begin to form in July although autumn movements do not peak until September-October; there is clear evidence of an overall decrease in passage numbers since at least the early 1990s. Large autumn flocks include 300 at Roddlesworth Plantations in October 1970, 150 feeding on meadowsweet near Clitheroe from July to October 1979, 100 at The Hile on 18 August 1987, 80 at Skelmersdale White Moss in October 1988 and 150 at Longworth Clough, Belmont in August 1989. More recent flocks include 80 at Stocks Reservoir in September 1997 with 100 there on 23 October 2001, and 40 feeding in alders at White Coppice, Chorley on 20 October 2002.

Coastal passage has become thin and intermittent in recent years. A substantial movement at Heysham and Fairhaven in September-October 1985 peaked at 24 at the latter on 20 October. Other visible migration counts include 56 at Seaforth on 13 October 1990, and 139 at Heysham during September 1996 with 20 in October that year, 21 over Caton Moor on 14 October 2005 and 34 over the Rimrose Valley on 16 October 2005. It is, of course, impossible to distinguish Lesser from Mealy Redpolls in flight but it is likely that almost all early migrants are Lesser Redpolls while later movements may involve a few Mealies.

In winter, small flocks, nowadays seldom larger than twenty birds, are widely distributed at favoured inland locations, in particular in the Stocks-Gisburn Forest area and in the woodlands at Roddlesworth and around Belmont. Larger counts include 100 at Gawthorpe, Burnley on 8 February 1979 with 200 at Heskin, Chorley that December, 150 at Brinscall in February 1985 and 200 at Belmont in December 1995. Since the mid-1990s 100+ at Heapey, Chorley on 23 December 1998 and 60 at Roddlesworth in November 2003 were amongst the largest gatherings reported until a larger influx in winter 2004/05, which saw 70 at Holden Vale, Rossendale and 100 at Stocks Reservoir in January, and 100 at Longridge Fell and 55 at Leighton Moss in February.

Unusually, coastal passage is often more conspicuous in spring than in autumn and there is no hard evidence of a recent decline in numbers; migration extends from late March to late May with a peak in late April or early May. Recent ringing evidence indicates that all or nearly all spring birds are Lessers. Heysham recorded totals of 220 between 17-27 April 1987 and 243 between 19 April and 17 May 1998, with 75 on 14 May 1992, 113 on 3 May 2000 and 87 on 17 April 2003 the highest day-totals. Small parties are also regularly seen overflying Fylde and Sefton coastal watchpoints; 83 flew over Fairhaven on 21 April 1984, 53 at Rossall Point on 12 May 1998 and 60 at Marshside on 18 April 2003. Flocks of up to 30 birds are also widely reported from inland sites, including 60 at Wayoh Reservoir on 31 March 1991, 70 at Rowley Lake, Burnley on 2 April 1992 and a similar number at Mere Sands Wood four days later, 48 at Arley, Chorley on 8 April 1992 and 50 in the Dunsop Valley on 1 May 1997.

There are only three Lancashire ringing recoveries of definite Lessers, all involving local movements, but most if not all 'Redpoll sp.' recoveries were ringed in summer or early autumn and probably also relate to Lessers. Fifteen of these involve exchanges with northern England and nine with the south, while two were recovered later in their year of ringing in Belgium and one in the Netherlands.

Lesser Redpoll (right) with Mealy Redpoll (left), Heysham, May 2006. (Mark Breaks)

BM, RW.

This species account was sponsored by Jonathan Fenton.

MEALY (COMMON) REDPOLL

Carduelis flammea

Lancashire Category A.

Scarce passage migrant and winter visitor from Fennoscandia.

Mitchell wrapped this species in square brackets but cited reports of several having been captured at Mellor, Blackburn in winter during the 1860s. Oakes also considered this record to be inadequately described but suspected that 'the Mealy Redpoll occurs oftener than the published records suggest'. He felt compelled, however, to regard it as a rare winter visitor and published just two records: seven at Leighton Moss on 23 March 1930 and one shot near Burnley on 23 February 1947. Spencer (1973) maintained that the species had been known to old Lancashire bird-catchers as uncommon, but not really rare, and that there had been at least eight confidently-identified records within the pre-1974 county boundaries, extending from 7 September to 23 March.

Common Redpolls have been recorded with certainty in fifteen years since 1973, the great majority of occurrences involving one or at most a few birds accompanying Lesser Redpolls or occasionally Siskins. Most have been in north and east Lancashire, with fewer visits to Rossendale and the Chorley region, fewer still to the south-west, and just five in the Fylde between 1955 and 2003. Most are seen in mid- or late winter, and autumn records have been very few; there were two at Read on 28 October 1981, two at Rowley Lake, Burnley on 12 November 1988, a total of six at Heysham in early November 1995 (precursors of that winter's major incursion) and two at Earnsdale Reservoir, Darwen on 27 October 2002. Spring records, in the absence of a midwinter influx, are also exceptional; in 1983 a total of 13 was present in east Lancashire – at Padiham, Hapton and Dunsop Bridge – in late April and early May, and in 2002 there were single birds at Marton Mere and at Sunnyhurst Hey Reservoir, Darwen, in late March.

The winters of 1985/86 and 1995/96 stand out as occasions of significant irruptions of Mealy Redpolls into the county. Eleven with Lesser Redpolls at Rowley Lake in mid-December 1985 were followed by ten accompanying Siskins at Ainsdale NNR on 7 January 1986, two at Habergham Clough, Burnley on the 13-14th, one at Scorton on the 19th and up to seven in the Aldcliffe-Stodday area near Lancaster in mid-February. The largest influx to date began in December 1995 and some were still present at several locations into April 1996; small parties were widespread in December, from Leighton Moss and Morecambe to Burnley, Rishton and Belmont in the east and centre of the county and

Mere Sands Wood and Eccleston Mere in the south-west. Numbers peaked in January-February 1996, when there were 60 at White Coppice, Chorley, 40 each at Rowley Lake, Whin Scar Clough and Delph Plantations, and up to 150 at Mere Sands Wood; smaller parties were widespread, particularly in Rossendale and the Chorley area. Numbers dwindled rapidly after the end of February, but 65 remained at Mere Sands until the end of March and 20 until late April; there were 45 at Grizedale during April.

It is suspected that a proportion of late autumn migrants flying over coastal watchpoints may be Common Redpolls but there are as yet no ringing recoveries to resolve this either way.

BM.
This species account was sponsored by Towneley Hall Art Gallery and Museum.

ARCTIC REDPOLL

Carduelis hornemanni

Lancashire Category A. (0, 6).

Vagrant from northern Fennoscandia.

Having missed out on previous national influxes of Arctic Redpolls, Lancashire made up lost ground during the record-breaking winter of 1995/96 during which almost 400 records were ultimately accepted nationally.

Our first accepted record was of a male at Rowley Lake in Burnley on 29 December 1995. It was found by Peter Grice in the company of two Lesser and seven Mealy Redpolls – a proportion which was roughly matched elsewhere – feeding in birches and on grass and weed seeds. A number of birds were claimed from this site up to the end of 1995 and 'at least' two were subsequently accepted by the BBRC.

The remaining records came hot on the heels of the first with two at Skelmersdale on 1 January 1996, one of which remained there until at least the 3rd. A male was also found at Mere Sands Wood on 1 January 1996 and remained there until at least 23 March; another of uncertain sex and age was present on 27 March.

Arctic Redpoll, Mere Sands Wood, March 1996. (Steve Young)

Thus, by the end of the winter the county total had moved from zero to six. Far more than this had been considered as 'probables' or 'possibles' and in a more normal year might have been followed up more closely. It is assumed that all records related to the sub-species *exilipes* since the national influx in 1995/96 was predominantly if not entirely of that race, but none was sub-specifically identified in Lancashire.

None has been recorded since, although a couple of 'possibles' have been reported.

SJW, MJ.
This species account was sponsored by Jonathan Fenton.

CROSSBILL

Loxia curvirostra

Lancashire Category A.

Rare breeder; uncommon passage migrant and winter visitor from continental Europe.

The large Crossbill populations of Fennoscandia and north Russia, normally resident and dispersive, occasionally erupt southward and westward, impelled by an exceptional breeding season and/or a poor spruce-seed crop. These movements normally begin in early summer and may continue through the autumn; in such years varying numbers pass through or stay to winter in Britain, leading to widespread nesting attempts, often successful, in the following spring. Most of the colonies thus established tend to be small and temporary but some have persisted and expanded.

In Lancashire this pattern of periodic invasion and subsequent localised breeding appears to be of long-standing. Mitchell described the Crossbill as an irregular autumn and winter visitor which had occurred in most parts of the county between July and March; he considered that occasional nesting was likely, although this had not been confirmed. Oakes recorded notable influxes in 1888, 1893 and 1909, but his claim of successful breeding at Hutton, near Preston in 1887 was discounted by Spencer (1973). Oakes noted that breeding had also been reported, but not confirmed, in the Ainsdale-Formby pinewoods in 1917 and during 1930-32, and Spencer considered that Crossbills had nested there at least once between 1953 and 1973, and might well be permanent residents of the county, albeit in very small numbers.

Since the 1960s extensive conifer plantations in upland areas, particularly in the Gisburn Forest and elsewhere in east Lancashire, in Rossendale and on the West Pennine Moors have reached maturity, greatly increasing the area of suitable Crossbill nesting habitat, and successive invasions over the last 40 years have been followed by an increasing incidence of confirmed or probable breeding. Whether a permanent, self-sustaining Crossbill population has yet been established, however, is open to question.

The most notable irruptions in recent decades were in 1962, 1966, 1976, 1985, 1990, 1997, 2002 and 2005, but at least a few Crossbills have been recorded annually since the mid-1970s. During influx years small, and occasionally sizeable, flocks are typically widespread in suitable habitat from June or July onwards. As one might expect, numbers tend to be higher in upland areas than in the south-west or the Fylde, but, as in Oakes's time, the Ainsdale-Formby pinewoods often attract significant gatherings. Among the more noteworthy counts are 40-50 on Longridge Fell in July 1962, 50 at Ainsdale in July 1976, 67 in Gisburn Forest in June 1985, 100 in Delph Plantations in September 1990 and a similar number over Darwen Moor edge on 27 October of the same year.

Male Crossbill, Freshfield Dune Heath, March 2006. (Steve Young)

The largest and most widespread irruption to date took place from mid-June 1997; most flocks had moved out of the county by mid-July but Crossbills were recorded in at least 28 locations between 15 June and 5 July, including 50 at Ainsdale on 25 June, 130 in the Marshaw-Tower Lodge area of Bowland on the 27th and up to 100 near Belmont on 1 July. A conservative estimate yields a total of at least a thousand birds during this main influx period. Following the invasion of summer 2002 there were up to 70 on Beacon Fell in August-September and at Stocks Reservoir in November, when 40 were also present at Longridge Fell and Higher Thrushgill; parties of up to 20 Crossbills remained in several upland conifer plantations until March 2003. The 2005 influx began early with 15 at Prescot Reservoirs on 12 May followed by a small but steady stream of new arrivals throughout the county from June to October. Double-figure counts were reported at a dozen or so sites and the largest concentration was 50 or so at Ainsdale at the end of December.

Breeding records have been concentrated in, but are by no means confined to, seasons immediately following years of significant influx. At least one pair attempted nesting at Formby Point in 1967, a group of six including three juveniles at Longridge Fell on 27 May 1978 was strongly suggestive of local breeding, and juveniles were seen in the Gisburn Forest in spring 1985 and 1986. Nesting was also considered probable at Calf Hey, Rossendale in 1985 and breeding by two pairs was confirmed there in the following year. At least one pair bred in Delph Plantations in 1986 and five pairs were confirmed there and in Entwistle Plantations in 1987, when two pairs also bred at Knowsley Park and one at Lytham Hall. At least two family parties were recorded in the Gisburn Forest in 1991, and during 1992-95 nesting by one or more pairs was confirmed or judged likely at Earnsdale Reservoir, Beacon Fell, Ainsdale NNR, Haslingden Grane (up to six pairs in 1995), Crawshawbooth and Belmont. Crossbills bred again at Haslingden in 1998 and 2002 and there were single pairs in the Trough of Bowland in 1999 and at Stocks Reservoir in 2003. Birds have been seen during the breeding season at various West Pennine sites in most recent years without confirmation of breeding. The Lancashire Atlas estimated an average county total of approximately five pairs during 1997-2000.

Crossbills are scarce and irregular spring and autumn migrants at coastal watchpoints. During the 1990 irruption several small overflying parties were recorded at Heysham and on the Fylde coast, including twelve at Fairhaven on 26 August, eight there on 15 October, and another eight at Heysham on the 26th; a flock of 14 passed over Heysham on 28 September 1991 and three flew north-west there, out to sea, on 3 April 1996. In most years since then at least a few coastal migrants have been reported, including five at Rossall Point on 1 November 2001, 23 at Heysham on 12 September 2002, seven at Lytham on 17 March 2002, five at Marshside on 23 April 2003 and 20 over Seaforth on 31 October 2005. There have been no ringing recoveries.

BM, RW.
This species account was sponsored by Sam Forde.

COMMON ROSEFINCH

Carpodacus erythrinus

Lancashire Category A. (0, 3).

Vagrant from central and eastern Europe.

A first-winter bird was trapped and ringed by Tom Wilmer and Pete Marsh at Heysham in the last hour of daylight on 29 September 1992 but was not seen after its release. The second followed quickly when a female or first-winter was seen at Jenny Brown's Point, Silverdale on 10 October 1992.

The latest was a most unexpected record of an adult male during the breeding season. It was found at Jackhouse Reservoir, Oswaldtwistle on 18 June 1999 and remained until the 21st. Although there was no sign of any female, the timing of the record and its frequent singing led to its publication in the Lancashire Atlas, which was being compiled at the time, as a 'possible breeding' record.

First-summer male Common Rosefinch, Pilling, May 2007. (Chris Batty)

SJW, MJ.
This species account was sponsored by Tom Wilmer.

BULLFINCH

Pyrrhula pyrrhula

Lancashire Category A.

Common resident breeder.

A general population increase in Britain in the 1950s and 1960s was followed by a sustained decline from the mid-1970s, attributed in part to agricultural intensification, in particular to the removal of old, dense hedgerows much favoured for nesting by Bullfinches. The British population declined by 57% between 1970 and 2001 (CBC) but seems to have stabilised since 1994 (BBS).

Mitchell had little to say about the Bullfinch's range beyond that birds were 'very evenly distributed; nowhere common as a breeding species, there being seldom above two or three pairs in any one district'. Oakes considered breeding to be widespread in the Ribble and Lune Valleys and increasing at Grimsargh and St. Michael's-on-Wyre, but knew of no convincing evidence of nesting south of the 'Parbold-Rivington area' and considered it a rarity near the coast. Spencer (1973) reported a marked increase in the population, in line with the national trend, from the late 1950s, although Bullfinches remained local breeders in the Fylde and south of the Ribble.

The Lancashire range changed little at the 10km square level between 1968-72 and 1997-2000, when birds were located in 287 tetrads (31%) and the population was estimated at 1,800 pairs. However, extensions in distribution were widely reported until the early 1980s.

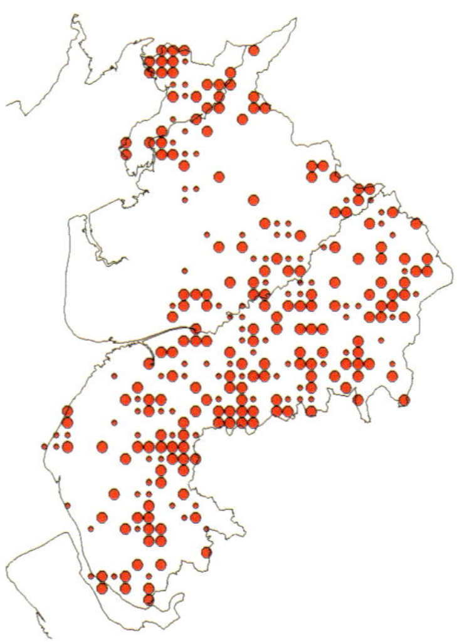

Breeding distribution of Bullfinch, 1997-2000. (Large dots: confirmed. Small dots: possible)

In the Fylde Bullfinches bred in 1971 at Blackpool for the first time since 1930 and became resident in the Lytham area from 1972; continuing increases were recorded in both coastal and inland areas of the Fylde until about 1980. Since then the decline has been dramatic; the 1997-2000 Breeding Atlas located pairs only in the Ingol area, at the south-eastern edge of the peninsula.

The main breeding outpost in Rossendale prior to the mid-1970s was in the Irwell Valley; subsequent expansion up the Irwell brought breeding pairs to Rawtenstall and Stacksteads and along the Limy to Crawshawbooth, and by 1981 the species was breeding in most suitable habitat in Rossendale. There has, however, been a substantial contraction in range since the mid-1980s, although the Bullfinch population appears to have stabilised at a relatively low level in more recent years, and nesting was recorded at five localities in 2003.

Tony Disley

Bullfinch numbers have remained generally robust in the long-established stronghold areas of north and east Lancashire, where the species is widely-distributed in the Lune and Wyre Valleys and along the Ribble and its tributaries, with little long-term change in status reported; only the higher, largely treeless fell country is without breeding Bullfinches. Around 18 pairs have bred annually at Leighton Moss since the mid-1970s, while at nearby Warton Crag between eight and 18 pairs bred annually between 1989 and 2005.

The species also breeds in most suitable habitat in the Chorley area and West Pennine Moors, and on the eastern edge of the south-west mosslands from Rufford, Mere Sands Wood and Parbold to Skelmersdale. It is also well represented in parts of north Merseyside, particularly south Liverpool. In the rest of the coastal south-west, however, apart from a small but thriving population in the dunes between Formby Point and Birkdale, Bullfinches breed only very locally. According to Smith (1963) the Formby population originated from birds caught by a fruit grower in East Anglia and released at Ainsdale in 1962; Bullfinches had been extremely rare on the Sefton coast previously.

Outside the breeding season Lancashire Bullfinches appear to be fairly sedentary; of thirteen recoveries of birds ringed in the county eleven were local and the other two were caught in northern England. Some small-scale dispersal does occur although parties rarely exceed a dozen birds. Thirty-two in Lumb Vale, Rossendale in November 1965, 42 in a young plantation near Nelson in December 1970, 23 at Belmont in December 1983 with 18 there in January 1999, and up to 50 daily at Leighton Moss in winter during the late 1980s and early 1990s are noteworthy. More recently, 18 at Rishton in January 1995, eleven at Lee Green Reservoir, Burnley in February 1999 and 15 at Sunnyhurst Woods, Darwen in January 2003 are among the highest counts recorded.

On occasion the species' partiality to heather seeds produces small incursions into untypical habitat, as in the case of seven birds at the summit of Grindleton Fell in February 1985 and eight at 400m altitude at Wayoh Reservoir in February 1998. A more conventional attraction to garden feeders has become widely evident since the early 1990s, with sunflower seeds in particular favoured; a winter survey in the Chorley area recorded Bullfinches in 50% of gardens in 2002-03.

Bullfinches are occasionally recorded, usually in very small numbers, at coastal migration watchpoints, mainly in October and November, less regularly in late March and April. One or two were seen annually at Heysham in late autumn during the late 1970s and early 1980s, but the species has occurred less frequently since then: eleven moved south there on 19 October 1985, five in early November 1987 and nine in October-November 1994; fifteen, nearly all first-winter females, were trapped between 19 and 27 October 1997. Marton Mere recorded its first Bullfinch on 21 October 2001, when one was also trapped at Heysham, and odd migrants have also been recorded at Marshside, including three in a heavy fall during a rainstorm on 12 April 1993.

Oakes cited two possible occurrences of the much larger northern and central European nominate race, a male at Towneley, Burnley on 4 January 1931 and a pair at Wennington in the Lune Valley during March 1944; two males were also reported from Formby Point on 20 November 1967. Spencer (1973) considered that the likelihood of northern Bullfinches reaching Lancashire in winter was quite high.

A massive invasion of continental Bullfinches into northern Britain began on 10 October 2004 (Pennington & Meek 2006), the first birds reaching Lancashire on the 28th when one flew over Heysham. Further records followed: two at Stocks Reservoir on 31 October; one at Aldcliffe on 21 November and singles at Quernmore and Wennington on 11 & 12 December. In 2005 a female was at Aldcliffe on 3 January and up to four northern birds remained at Stocks Reservoir until at least 3 March. These birds were mainly distinguished by their unusual 'toy trumpet' calls and, at the time of writing, their racial/population identity has not been resolved (Wright 2005).

BM, RW.
This species account was sponsored by David S. Pilling.

HAWFINCH

Coccothraustes coccothraustes

Rare breeder. Lancashire Category A.

Rare resident breeder.

Hawfinches favour mature broadleaved woodland, parkland and large gardens where there is a wide range of suitable seed-bearing trees, particularly cherry, hornbeam, yew, and beech. Such habitat is not abundant in Lancashire and is virtually absent in the east and on the coastal plain. They are very secretive and easily overlooked, nesting being particularly difficult to prove; nevertheless, it is unlikely that the current county population exceeds ten pairs.

Mitchell considered the Hawfinch to be local in distribution, mentioning records from Claughton, Goosnargh, Leagram, Whalley, near Chorley, and at Worden Hall. Some increase appears to have occurred towards the end of the nineteenth century and their presence was noted by Oakes at Silverdale, Carnforth, Lancaster, Wennington, Hornby, several sites in the Ribble Valley near Preston, between Ribchester and Dinckley, Sabden, Burnley, four sites in the Chorley area, near Lytham and at Carleton, Blackpool. Hawfinches are also known to have bred at Witton Park around 1880-1900 and at Woodfold Park, Blackburn in the 1920s (Oakes & Battersby 1939).

The species is now seen most regularly in the limestone woodlands around Silverdale, where they were known from at least eleven sites in 1979 and breeding was confirmed or considered probable in three tetrads during 1997-2000. Woodwell is the favoured place for birders to watch them although the population there appears to have been declining a little for the past 20 years

Tony Disley

or so, with three pairs breeding in 1983 and peak counts of eleven individuals in 1992, seven in 2002 and just three in 2005. Birds may be encountered almost anywhere in this area with Gaitbarrows the next best site, and irregular sightings at Leighton Moss as recently as 1999. Most records relate to single-figure groups, 25 in beeches at Challon Hall and Eaves Wood in January and February 1989 and up to 41 near Gaitbarrows on 6-7 February 1991 were quite remarkable and perhaps included influxes from south Cumbria where the species is more common.

Small numbers may also still occur in the Lune Valley – most likely at Crook O' Lune and near Caton and Hornby – but none has been reported for several years. Five or six were recorded over the Snab, opposite Hornby, on 28 June 1964 but most recent sightings have been of single birds. There have also been isolated reports from Quernmore, Littledale, Barnacre and Dolphinholme; a pair was observed prospecting for nest sites at Williamson Park, Lancaster on 17 April 1979.

The only other area where Hawfinches have been seen regularly in recent years is between Witton Country Park and Pleasington Old Hall, near Blackburn. Most records are of fewer than five individuals, usually during the period December to March, though in 1985 there were regular sightings until 22 June. In the 1990s as many as ten birds were recorded on occasion but only a single pair was seen in 2003 and just one bird in 2004 and 2005. The decline was also well recorded at Brindle Lodge, Hoghton, where ten or more were recorded in October 1978 and seven in March 1980, declining to just one or two by 1988 (L. Knowles *pers. comm.*); one pair bred in this area in 1997. There have also been occasional records elsewhere in the Darwen Valley, including Walton-le-Dale, Woodfold Park, Ramsgreave and Sunnyhurst Wood, Darwen.

Small numbers bred in the lower Ribble Valley from at least the 1960s until at least 1987, mainly in the area around Brockholes, Red Scar, Cuerden Hall, Broughton, Penwortham and Samlesbury. A rare instance of confirmed breeding was a pair with young at Red Scar Wood on 20 June 1978. Elsewhere in the Ribble Valley there have been isolated records from Alston and Mitton Woods.

Records further east almost certainly involve wandering rather than local birds. These include a remarkable flock of 15 in the Clitheroe area on 2 December 1965, singles in Burnley on 28 October 1973 and 3 November 2000, one at Stocks Reservoir on 15 January 1979 and up to three at Brierfield, between Burnley and Nelson, from 30 October 2002 into 2003. Similarly, eight to ten at Whitewell in February 1987 are unlikely to have been local residents; the occurrence of continental immigrants cannot be ruled out (Migration Atlas).

Elsewhere in Lancashire the Hawfinch is very rare, with only three records from Rossendale, including a pair at Crawshawbooth in April 1974. A pair bred at Duxbury Wood, Chorley in 1982 and 1984 and there have been occasional reports from there since including an adult and juvenile together in August 1988, an adult and two juveniles in July 1994 and up to three in 1995. Other breeding season records include a pair that bred in Lytham in 1953, two at Mere Brow in May 1970 and a female at Savick Brook on 10 July 1997. Singles at Lytham on 31 March 1954 and 25 March 1959 may also have been breeding birds.

Most other records probably relate to birds dispersing from northern England or possibly longer-distance migrants, including singles at Formby Point on 9 August 1964 (which remains the only record anywhere in north Merseyside), Mere Sands Wood in September 1985, Happy Mount Park, Morecambe on 10 October 1993, Heysham on 20 October 1995 and 15 October 2003, in a Leyland garden in mid-November 1998 and at Martin Mere on 26 October 2005. Recent Fylde records, the first since 1959, were of singles flying east over Marton Mere on 22 October 2002, two at Fluke Hall, Pilling on 21 December 2002, two over Marton Mere and Fairhaven, and one over St. Anne's, on 14 October 2003.

SJW, RW.
This species account was sponsored by Bill Berry.

BLACKPOLL WARBLER

Dendroica striata

Lancashire Category A. (0, 1).

Vagrant from North America.

A male in full breeding plumage, Lancashire's first North American warbler of any species, spent the day at Seaforth Nature Reserve on 2 June 2000. It was located by song by Chris Sharratt, its identity confirmed by Steve White, on a still, damp, overcast morning in a small thicket of alder and willow trees. It sang continually until mid-afternoon, when it became less active as the rain intensified and was seen going to roost in a willow at dusk, having been watched by more than 400 people, but had disappeared by dawn the next day.

Male Blackpoll Warbler, Seaforth Nature Reserve, June 2000. (Steve Young)

The Seaforth bird was the 37th record in Britain and Ireland but the first to occur in spring – almost all others have occurred in October with a handful in late September.

Blackpoll Warblers winter in South America, breeding across Alaska and Canada, south and east to New England, and are known to undertake long migratory journeys across the sea, making them candidates for weather-induced vagrancy. How many make it across the Atlantic under their own power and how many are ship-assisted cannot be known; this one had almost certainly hitched a lift. Blackpoll Warblers are relatively late migrants but, even so, the June date perhaps suggests that this may have been a first-summer, although it showed no signs of immaturity.

SJW.
This species account was sponsored by Chris Sharratt.

OVENBIRD

Seiurus aurocapillus

Lancashire Category D.

On 4 January 1969 a wing of this North American warbler was picked up on the tideline at Formby by Reg Wagstaffe, Curator of Liverpool Museum (*British Birds* 63: 289). It was not admitted to the British list by the BOURC as there was no evidence that it been alive within the British recording area.

SJW.

SONG SPARROW

Melospiza melodia

Lancashire Category A. (0, 1).

Vagrant from North America.

The first of a trio of North American passerines recorded at Seaforth in the closing decade of the twentieth century was found in the early afternoon of 15 October 1994 by Andy Pryce and Tim Vaughan. It was first seen on top of a skip-load of old tyres close to the scrap metal yard to the west of the reserve. For an hour it moved energetically around this area, feeding in rough grass but occasionally perching on a fence, singing with gusto and finally allowing confirmation of its identity and ageing as a first-winter.

It took some time to organise public access across operational industrial land and only a handful of local birdwatchers managed to see the bird that day. By late afternoon it had settled in an area of sea club-rush on the edge of the saltwater lagoon, periodically emerging to feed in the open.

Arrangements were made for what turned out to be Lancashire's largest ever 'twitch' the following morning. Before dawn the next day a large queue had formed at the dock gates, held back by rather bemused Port Police officers. It had been a quiet autumn on the Scilly Isles and birders fled the islands en masse. What followed at Seaforth had more in common with a football match than birdwatching, due in part to the enormous attendance of at least 2,000 and in part to the 'terraced' viewing facilities overlooking the pumping station outfall where the bird fed on sea mayweed seeds.

No access was possible the following day but the bird was still present in the same area although it failed to give anything more than brief views when flushed. It was not seen subsequently.

This was the eight record of Song Sparrow in Europe and the seventh for Britain, but it was only the second on the mainland – the previous being at Spurn in 1964. The Seaforth bird is the only accepted autumn record but one was reportedly on board the *Mauretania* when it docked in Southampton on 14 October 1962.

First-winter Song Sparrow, Seaforth Nature Reserve, 16 October 1994. (Alan Tate)

SJW.

This species account was sponsored by Andy Pryce.

WHITE-CROWNED SPARROW

Zonotrichia leucophrys

Lancashire Category A. (0, 1).

Vagrant from North America.

Barely a year after the arrival of the Song Sparrow, Lancashire's second North American passerine arrived at the same site. It was found in the morning of 2 October 1995 by Chris Sharratt in the rubble mounds at Seaforth in loose association with a large fall of Meadow Pipits. Initially it provided only brief glimpses but a combination of face pattern and long tail pointed to one of the American sparrows. It was a further frustrating 90 minutes before the bird showed again in flight and another half an hour elapsed before it was relocated at close range on the ground, when its identity was resolved by Andy Pryce and the bird aged as a first-winter.

The bird continued to range widely over the eastern end of the reserve for some time before eventually settling down in the sandy rubble mounds. It fed energetically on evening primrose and sea mayweed seeds, pursued at a respectful distance by small groups of birdwatchers. About 400 people managed to see it before it went to roost at dusk, but a large crowd the following morning was disappointed and the bird was not seen again.

First-winter White-crowned Sparrow, Seaforth Nature Reserve, 2 October 1995. (Steve Young)

This was the third record in Britain, the two previous both occurred in May 1977, on Fair Isle on the 15th and at Hornsea Mere, Yorkshire on the 22nd. In addition, there have been two documented reports of birds on board ships: on the *Nova Scotia* off Ireland when bound for Liverpool in June 1948, and on the *Queen Elizabeth II* in Southampton Water on 26 September 1988.

SJW.

This species account was sponsored by Chris Sharratt.

DARK-EYED JUNCO

Junco hyemalis

Lancashire Category A. (0, 1).

Vagrant from North America.

Merseyside made it three years in a row for North American passerines when this first record for the county turned up on 29 April 1996 on the Finnegan family's suburban bird table in Thornton on the outskirts of Crosby, just a few kilometres from the coast and the Seaforth Docks.

It was first seen early in the morning and photographed before the finders had to leave for work. At this stage its identity was unknown and it was thought to be an escaped exotic but a later skim through a field guide quickly revealed the truth. One can imagine the frustration of knowing there is a British rarity in your back garden while you're stuck at work! Fortunately, the bird was present again for a hour in the early evening and returned for a final visit at 7 p.m. but by the time other local birders arrived it had disappeared and was not seen subsequently.

Dark-eyed Junco, Thornton, Merseyside, 29 April 1996. (Dave Finnegan)

This was the 19th record of Dark-eyed Junco in Britain and Ireland and the first for north-west England. The following year another appeared in suburban Chester, remaining there from 15 December 1997 to 19 April 1998.

More than three-quarters of all British records have occurred during April and May, often at bird tables. The species breeds throughout much of North America but the eastern, nominate race, 'Slate-coloured Junco' – to which this record refers – is confined to the north-eastern USA, Alaska and most of Canada. Migratory populations head north early in spring with the main passage in southern Canada occurring from late March to early April, a month earlier than most 'warblers'.

SJW.

This species account was sponsored by Dr. Alan Fielding.

LAPLAND BUNTING

Calcarius lapponicus

Lancashire Category A. (2, c.200).

Uncommon passage migrant and winter visitor from Fennoscandia and possibly from Greenland.

Mitchell published details of four birds either shot or captured between 1833 and 1882; Oakes was not satisfied with the authenticity of two of these but believed a first-winter shot on Whitemoss, Middleton in November 1865, and a male trapped at Formby and kept in captivity during winter 1881/82 were probably valid records. He added just one other, at Ainsdale on 19 February 1938 amongst a flock of Skylarks; Spencer (1977) mentioned a report of two on Worsthorne Moor in the late 1940s.

No more were reported until singles on Lytham Moss on 6 March and 24 November 1963, and another at Lea Marsh, Preston on 11 October 1964. The first multiple sighting was of four at Hundred End on 2 April 1967, with a male staying until the 9th.

Records multiplied rapidly by the end of the 1960s and Lapland Buntings have been recorded in every year since 1967 with the exception of 1982, 1992, 1996 and 2003; the county total now stands at around 100 records involving over 200 birds.

Total sightings averaged just under five a year between 1963 and 2005 and, although there are significant differences between years, there has been no clear trend up or down throughout this period.

The majority of records have been of singles, occasionally up to three, but several larger groups have occurred. By far the largest was a flock of 31 at Crossens in January 1980, four of which remained until 1 March. The same site also held four from 2 October 1980 to 1 January 1981, and six were at nearby Marshside on 24 December 1986. Four to six were on Lytham shore on 31 December 1974, four on Fleetwood Golf Course on 3 October 1993, and seven to eleven at Fleetwood on 10 January 1994.

Lapland Buntings are relatively late migrants and the earliest arrivals have been at Marton Mere on 23 September 1977 and at Seaforth on the same date in 1990. Most have arrived in October (Figure 1) but new birds have been found in roughly equal numbers throughout November and December, and into January (January totals in Figure 1 include the exceptional 31 at Crossens in 1980). Around a fifth of autumn records in recent years have been of overflying birds, identified by call. More than three-quarters have been seen on just one day, presumably on their way further south.

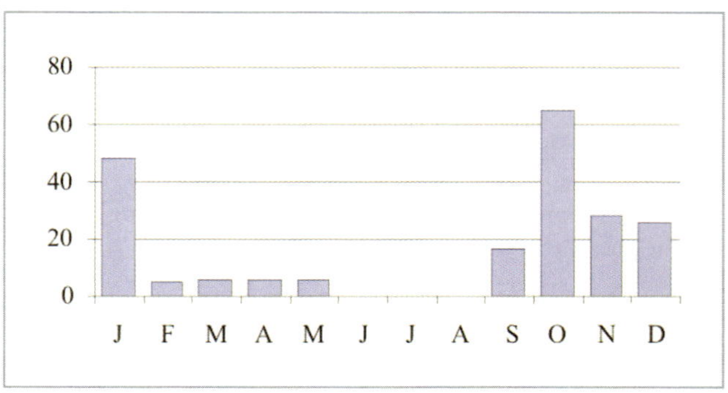

Figure 1. Monthly totals of Lapland Buntings in Lancashire, 1963-2005.

Wintering birds have all been on saltmarshes or coastal grasslands. In some years occasional birds have lingered into March or even April and there have been three May records with the latest on the 8th – at Cabin Hill NNR in 1974, Hightown in 1985 and Formby in 1989.

Lapland Bunting, Crosby Marine Park, April 2005. (Steve Young)

There have been just eight records away from the coast since the 1940 record on Worsthorne Moor: singles at Kirkby Moss on 12 December 1972; Crown Point, Burnley on 19 January 1985; Nutshaw Hill, Clowbridge on 6 October 1993; Whinney Hill, Altham on 19 October 1997; Upper Coldwell Reservoir on 29 September 2002; one over Caton Moor on 4 October 2002 with four there two days later; and one near Ormskirk on 15 November 2005.

It is widely assumed that the majority of British records relate to the nominate race from Scandinavia but, although there are no confirmed records of birds from Greenland or North America, the occurrence of occasional Nearctic *subcalcaratus*, particularly on the west coast, seems likely (BWP). Some late September Lancashire records have coincided with others on the west coast and have occurred prior to arrivals on the east coast. This, and weather conditions when some 'fly-overs' have been recorded, suggests a possible Greenland origin for earlier birds and perhaps a Scandinavian origin for later arrivals.

SJW, RW.

This species account was sponsored by Andy Bunting.

SNOW BUNTING

Plectrophenax nivalis

Lancashire Category A.

Fairly common winter visitor from Iceland.

The Snow Bunting is a fairly common winter visitor to sparsely vegetated habitats on hill and moorland summits and along strandlines and dunes on the coast. On average, about 120 birds were seen annually between 1983 and 2005 but there have been large variations between years (Figure 1). However, Snow Buntings are prone to wandering during the winter and some duplication of records is likely.

Exceptional influxes of 350 occurred in 1984, 228 in 1997 and 211 in 2004. Overall, numbers have shown no significant trend over the past 20 years but more have been reported from inland sites since the mid-1990s, while coastal records have shown a moderate decline. Whether this is the result of a genuine change in winter distribution, more intensive recording on the fell tops or increased disturbance on beaches is a matter for speculation.

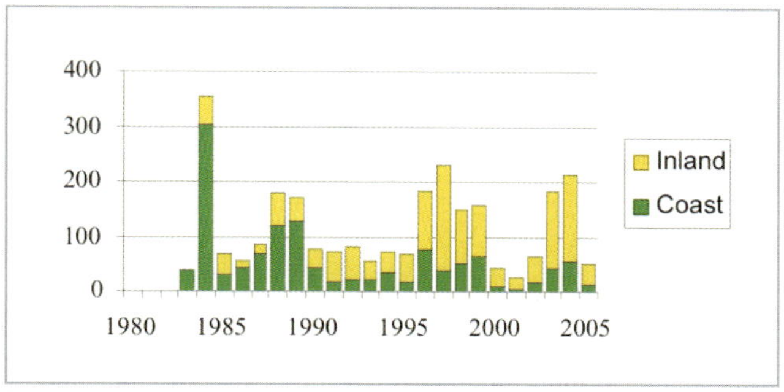

Figure 1. Estimated total numbers of Snow Buntings in Lancashire, 1983-2005.

Earlier large influxes included what remains the record county flock of 200 at Hundred End on 8 February 1929 and, during the harsh winter in February 1963, flocks of 60-70 in the Rossall area and 80+ on Lytham Moss. In December 1959 there were about 60 around Morecambe Bay, nine at Fairhaven, 'scores' between Crossens and Banks in small scattered parties, about 40 at Ainsdale, seven at Formby and small numbers near Waterfoot, Rossendale, until the end of December. The 1984 influx was particularly notable for some large groups in north Lancashire, with parties of 60 and 25 in the Carnforth area and 50 on Clougha Fell. Elsewhere that year there were 73 in the Rossall area and 60 at Crossens.

Snow Buntings may be found anywhere along the coast, but most frequently on the Fylde and Merseyside shores and the Ribble marshes. Large flocks outside the main influx years include 23 at Ainsdale in November 1966, 49 at Crossens in January 1971, 57 at Seaforth/Crosby Marine Park in December 1975, 24 at Fleetwood in January 1988 and 22 at Fairhaven in December 1996.

Upland flocks tend to be concentrated on the bare, highest tops and are often considerably larger than on the coast. Pendle Hill is amongst the best-watched sites and birds are recorded there in most winters with flocks of 30 or more fairly regular and largest counts of 70 in January 1997 and 80 in December 2003. Snow Buntings occur less frequently and in smaller numbers at several Rossendale locations, with high counts of 50 on Cowpe Moss in November 1988 and at scattered sites in February 1999, and 30 at Top o' Leach in December 1996.

Other upland sites appear to be used less regularly, but many may simply be under-recorded. Significant counts include 29 on Anglezarke Moor in January 1980, 30 at Crown Point, Burnley in February 1997 and 18 on Hameldon Hill in December 1997. Other double-figure flocks have been recorded at a number of other locations, including parts of Bowland (e.g. 15 at Ward's Stone in November 1996 and 50-60 on Musden Head Moor on 26 December 2004), Longridge Fell, Weets Moor near Barnoldswick, the Coldwell-Thursden area north-east of Burnley, Cliviger and above Belmont. Lowland sightings are very rare inland, but have occurred in the Ribble Valley area, north-east Lancashire and the south-west, with a maximum of five birds at Balderstone on 6 December 1966.

The earliest autumn record was on 2 September 1979 near Turn in Rossendale but there are only two other September records, in 1983 on the 25th at Clifton Marsh and 1992 on the 27th at Pilling Lane Ends. Most early records are of singles on the coast from about mid-October; they rarely linger. A flock of 12-15 near Trawden on 21 October 1993 was both a high count for the time of year and also an early inland record.

Male Snow Bunting, Seaforth Nature Reserve, April 2004. (Steve Young)

Most turn up during the period November to January, with the earliest often passing quickly through. Autumn passage was especially noticeable at Heysham in 1989, when a total of 64 moved through between 30 October and 26 November with a peak of 25 on 19 November. Arrivals between December and February are sometimes attributable to cold-weather movements. Many winter flocks stay at the same location throughout the winter, gradually decreasing in numbers during February and early March after which only occasional single-figure groups are recorded. The largest March count was, remarkably, over 100 birds on playing fields at Bootle, Merseyside on 3 March 1960. Upland flocks may be particularly long-stayers, for example groups were recorded on Pendle Hill from 16 December 1990 until 25 March 1991 and from 20 November 1991 until 8 March 1992 and in Rossendale from 28 November 1959 until early March 1960.

Most April records relate to single birds and most are probably migrants from further south, often moulting into breeding plumage. Only a handful have been seen after mid-April, including one at Lytham on 8 May 1963, one at Formby on 7 May 1972 with four there on 4 May 1989, and one on Pendle Hill on 12 May 1980.

Ringing recoveries in Scotland suggest that the majority of British wintering Snow Buntings are of the Icelandic race *insulae* but birds resembling the Siberian and Nearctic race *nivalis* are also thought to occur in some numbers. Our only ringing recovery, a male found dead in Litherland near Seaforth in January 1990 which had been ringed at Sandwich Bay, Kent in November 1988, sheds no light on the origins of Lancashire's birds.

SJW, RW.

This species account was sponsored by Valerie Rushworth.

YELLOWHAMMER

Emberiza citrinella

Lancashire Category A.

Fairly common resident breeder.

Along with so many predominantly farmland species, the Yellowhammer underwent a major decline in its breeding population and reduction of its Lancashire range during the final quarter of the twentieth century, mirroring the national trend which saw numbers fall by 56% between 1973 and 1998. Locally as nationally, a range of changes in agricultural practices are implicated in this decline, principally the switch to autumn sowing of cereals and the loss of winter stubbles, and the removal of hedgerows.

In Mitchell's day the species bred 'numerously almost everywhere', whilst Oakes described it as 'common in most districts, but rare in parts of the Lune Valley and the coastal districts of Lytham and Crosby'. The national atlas survey of 1968-72 located Yellowhammers in 47 (90%) 10 km squares in Lancashire but by 1988-91 this had fallen to 36 squares (70%). The Lancashire Atlas survey of 1997-2000 was the first comprehensive examination of Yellowhammer distribution and revealed the extent of its decline. Birds were located in 34 10km squares in just 232 (25%) of the county's tetrads with an estimated breeding population of around 1,000 pairs. Virtually all of these are found in a roughly 10km-wide belt extending from St. Helens in the south to Over Wyre in the north; Yellowhammers are almost entirely absent from east and north Lancashire.

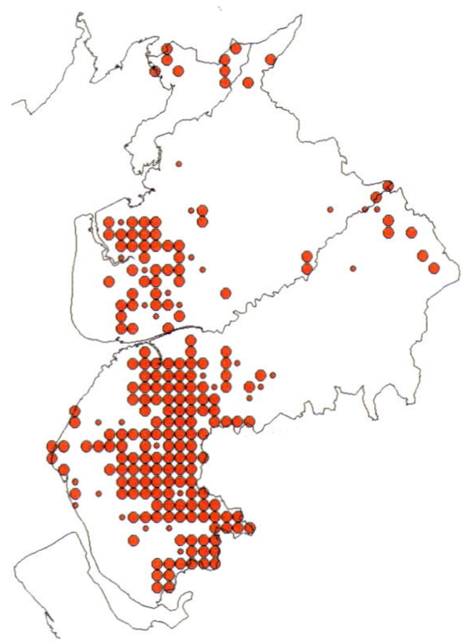

Breeding distribution of Yellowhammer, 1997-2000. (Large dots: confirmed. Small dots: possible)

The main strongholds occur south of the Ribble on the mosslands now under arable cultivation, with areas of West Lancashire in the vicinity of Martin Mere, Skelmersdale, Kirkby and St. Helens close to the border with Greater Manchester holding the highest densities. Numbers have undoubtedly declined since the mid-1980s even within this central belt but what is most noticeable is the fragmentation of breeding areas and local extinctions on its edges, particularly in the Fylde and around the Liverpool conurbation. Moderate numbers breed Over Wyre where they may be increasing as a result of supplementary winter feeding, but no Yellowhammers are found close to the Fylde coast, though they bred just inland at Marton Mere in the 1950s. Only a handful hang on in the Sefton coast dunes, where numbers declined from a dozen or so pairs in the mid-1980s to four or five by 1999 and perhaps only one or two by 2003.

The species finally disappeared from former sites at White Coppice and Withnell by 2000, although small numbers can still be found in the south of the Chorley area, for example at Adlington and Hic Bibi. Although never very common in the lowland parts of the Ribble Valley, it would now appear to be completely absent with none at the last major site of Lower Penwortham since four pairs nested in 1990. Breeding was also reported from Walton-le-Dale in 1990, but not subsequently.

Male Yellowhammer, Eagland Hill, Wyre, January 2006. (Mike Malpass)

There has been a long decline in east Lancashire since the early 1960s. In the Burnley area four out of 19 breeding sites were abandoned between 1960 and 1976 (Hornby 1994). A survey of the area between Blackburn and Burnley in 1966 revealed a total of 51 singing males at 31 sites but by the mid-1990s Stainscomb Clough was the only remaining site with three singing males in 1995; a lone male was all that was left here by 1997 and it was last seen in 2000. Birds were also present during 1997-2000 in nine tetrads close to the county boundary in an area between Wycoller, Colne and Paythorne but none has been seen there subsequently. Yellowhammers have always been uncommon in Rossendale, with most records along the Irwell around Stubbins. A small spread was noted in the 1960s as far as Lumb Vale and Townsendfold, but none has been reported since 1983.

A considerable decline became apparent in north Lancashire from the 1970s. A survey of 123 tetrads in 1977, replicated in 1988-91, found a reduction from 14 probable pairs to just three, while in the Lancaster district as a whole the breeding range declined from 26 tetrads in 1988-91 to 11 in 1997-2000. These were almost all in the Warton Crag-Silverdale area and in the upper Lune Valley towards Kirkby Lonsdale. Further south, a small population still persisted in the Grizedale-Nicky Nook area in 1997. None has been recorded during the breeding season in the LDBWS area since 2003.

The decline in the breeding fortunes of the Yellowhammer has been matched by an equal, and perhaps more evident, decline during the winter months. In north Lancashire mixed flocks of Yellowhammers and finches were a regular sight during the 1950s and large flocks used to be attracted to the grain in the pheasant pens at Leighton Moss, with peaks of 140 in 1978 and 120 in 1986. Numbers fell to just five or ten by the mid-1990s, partly due to 'cleaner' pheasant feeding methods but also reflecting the shrinking local population. Numbers at the Allen Hide grain field also declined from about 40 in 1987 to no more than five by 1995. The only winter records in north Lancashire since 2003 have been two sightings at Wennington and occasional passage records at Heysham.

In the Ribble Valley area flocks of up to 40 were occasionally reported during the 1960s and early 1970s, with the largest being 75 on Whalley Nab on 29 January 1973. Double-figure counts had become exceptional by the late 1980s, and even rarer in the 1990s. A site at Walton-le-Dale which held a flock of about 20 in 1983 had only two a decade later, although there was an unusually high count of 45 at Cuerden Valley Park on 18 September 1991.

The largest winter flocks are found in the south-west and Fylde. The highest published counts of 250 at Churchtown Moss on 24 January 1981 and 230 at Ashurst Beacon, near Skelmersdale in late December 1988 are never remotely matched nowadays. The highest counts in West Lancashire and Merseyside since the mid-1990s were 50 on Kirkby Moss in March 1996, 50 at Upholland in February 2000 and 50 at Reed's Moss, St. Helens in December 2002. Over Wyre feeding station counts have included 55 in December 1998 and 80 in January 2005.

Yellowhammers are extremely sedentary; nationally, 70% of adults winter within 5 km of their breeding territories. Five out of seven Lancashire ringing recoveries have involved movements of less than 4 km, but two longer movements have been recorded: one of 66 km from Blackburn to Cheshire and one of 35 km from Carnforth to Poulton-le-Fylde.

Unsurprisingly, few are seen on migration or wintering outside of the breeding range. Occasional singles have been seen moving south at Fairhaven and rather more at Heysham, where the species was recorded in most years between 1995 and 2002 during October and November with a peak of five records in 1996. Seaforth and Crosby Marine Park recorded up to four during the same period, also in October and November. Whether such records refer to local dispersal or longer-distance migration is not known.

SJW, RW.

This species account was sponsored by R. Wilson.

[CIRL BUNTING]

Emberiza cirlus

The status of the Cirl Bunting in Lancashire is uncertain. Mitchell published one undated record in our present recording area of a pair breeding at Formby but Oakes considered this report to be unsatisfactory. He did, however, accept six records between 1940 and 1946, mostly in the Brindle area of Chorley in the breeding season and including three nesting pairs. However, in turn, Spencer (1973) found that none of these were completely satisfactory, basing his view to a large extent on his own examination of field notes of a bird in Burnley in 1944.

Another report in suburban Liverpool in June 1947 was published in the 29th Lancashire and Cheshire Fauna Committee Report with the comment 'a drawing left no doubt about the identification'. It was, however, not listed by Oakes and the reported presence of such a rare species in a city garden in the middle of the breeding season does not inspire confidence. Hardy published two records: a nesting attempt at Lower Copthurst near Blackburn, identified on the basis of an addled egg, and a singing male in Knowsley Park in 1965 (Hardy 1979). A final published claim was of three at Formby Point on 16 October 1951.

None of these records is sufficiently documented to enable a proper review and a question mark hangs over whether Cirl Buntings have ever occurred in Lancashire. The species did not colonise Britain until the nineteenth century and only slowly extended its breeding range, being largely confined to southern England but reaching its furthest extent in North Wales, before shrinking back to the south-west from about the 1940s (New Atlas). Although isolated breeding attempts in Lancashire during the 1940s cannot be ruled out absolutely, they cannot be regarded as proven. British Cirl Buntings are extremely sedentary but some continental birds are migratory, so a genuine record of an overshooting spring or 'reverse' autumn migrant is possible – but a record of three together in autumn at a known Yellowhammer breeding site would require more substantial documentation than is presently available.

SJW.

ORTOLAN BUNTING

Emberiza hortulana

Lancashire Category A. (0, 9).

Vagrant from southern Europe.

None was reported in our present recording area until 1952, when one was seen by Nelson Harwood on Lytham Moss on 28 October. There were a further eight records between 1970 and 1990 but none since. Three of these have been in autumn and all involved female/first-winter birds: at Fairhaven on 12 October 1970, Marshside on 31 October 1973 and Heysham Harbour on 30 September 1979. The remainder were in spring: males at Formby on 6 May 1973 and 29 April 1978, at Ainsdale NNR on 8 June 1983, a female at Rossall School on 9 May 1984 and another male at Warton Marsh on 1 June 1990.

SJW, MJ.

This species account was sponsored by Steve Riley.

LITTLE BUNTING

Emberiza pusilla

Lancashire Category A. (0, 3).

Vagrant from Siberia or Fennoscandia.

The Little Bunting was dropped from the list of species considered by the BBRC in 1982 but it remains a major rarity in Lancashire. The first was found by Laurence Eccles on the site of the present Heysham Power Station and Nature Reserve on 30 March 1957. It was a further 36 years before the next was found. This was trapped and ringed in Gillar's Wood, St. Helens, close to Eccleston Mere on 26 December 1993 but after a few days moved to agricultural land nearby. It associated with Reed Buntings and other seed-eaters, including St. Helens' first Lapland Bunting, and was viewed by birdwatchers from a small housing estate, whose welcoming residents became quite proud of their visitor. It remained in the area until at least 19 March 1994.

Little Bunting, St. Helens, January 1994. (Steve Young)

Remarkably, another bird was found soon after at Jameson Road Tip, Fleetwood on 9 January 1994, where it remained until 24 March. Like the St. Helens bird it was sometimes quite elusive as it established a fairly large feeding circuit but with patience most county listers managed to connect with one or other of these birds.

SJW, MJ.

This species account was sponsored by the Fylde Bird Club.

REED BUNTING

Emberiza schoeniclus

Lancashire Category A.

Common resident breeder.

The Lancashire Atlas survey recorded Reed Buntings in just over half of all Lancashire tetrads and it remains a fairly common breeding species almost everywhere that wetland habitats are found. Breeding sites vary from the large wetland reserves of Leighton Moss and Martin Mere, through saltmarsh and dune slacks, to reed-fringed reservoirs, lakes, ponds and ditches.

The breeding population is estimated at around 2,000 pairs, roughly 1% of the UK total. The national population suffered a more than 50% decline between the 1970s and 1990s but increased from this low point by 30% between 1994 and 2005 (BBS).

Data from several Lancashire sites reflect this early decline but without conclusive evidence of recent recovery. The county stronghold at Leighton Moss regularly held 100-130 pairs from 1964-88 but numbers had fallen to 48 pairs by 1999 and 33 in 2002. Ringing totals during the breeding season at Leighton Moss tell a similar story, with a relatively constant effort maintained over the years the number trapped fell from 259 in 1976 to 88 in 2002. The Marshside population has shown a similar decline, from 20 pairs in 1984 to seven in 2004. Numbers at Martin Mere, however, have almost doubled over the past decade as a result of reedbed creation, from 25 pairs in 1990 to 51 in 2002 and 40 in 2004.

The main sites have never supported a very high proportion of the county's breeding birds and Reed Buntings are not a species whose fate turns upon what happens in nature reserves; they are very much birds of the wider countryside. The results of two Waterways Bird Survey transects probably give a more representative picture of their fortunes. The 22km stretch of the River Lune from Crook O'Lune to Leck Beck supported 42 pairs in 1978; this fell to 28 pairs in 1979 after a harsh winter and has never recovered, fluctuating between 8 and 18 pairs from 1983 to 1993 and five to ten pairs between 1994 and 2003. Further south, numbers on 4.5 km of the Leeds-Liverpool Canal between Tarleton and Rufford declined from 16 pairs in 1990 to about six in 1997.

The highest densities away from nature reserves occur on the south-west mosslands, where they inhabit the vegetated ditches that form the field boundaries, Over Wyre north to the Lune, and on the West Pennine Moors, where numbers have increased with rush encroachment on in-bye fields up to 325m (and some as high as 390m) above sea level. The Sefton Coast dunes continue to support good populations as do the saltmarshes of the Ribble, Wyre, Lune and upper Morecambe Bay. Even relatively small habitat patches may regularly attract birds, for example two small ponds at Witton Park have seen unbroken occupation since at least the 1950s. Increasing use of oilseed rape fields for nesting was noted from the mid-1990s and by 2005 this had become the overwhelmingly preferred habitat in many areas of the south-west mosses, holding out hope of some recovery in numbers there.

The undoubted general population decline is not yet reflected in changes in range which appears to have remained virtually unchanged for more than 100 years. Mitchell described the Reed Bunting as 'common, though irregularly distributed' and Oakes concurred, writing that it was 'common....but rather locally distributed owing to its association with special types of habitat'.

Reed Buntings nested in all of Lancashire's 10 km squares between 1968-72 and 1997-2000 when they were found in 478 (51%) tetrads and the population was estimated at 2,000 pairs. More than two-thirds of occupied tetrads occur in the western lowlands with the largest clusters south of the Ribble, but the distribution is also fairly continuous on the West Pennine Moors. They are very thinly distributed in east Lancashire and are largely absent from Bowland and many other upland areas although in times of higher population, as in the mid-1970s, some moved into less favourable habitats on higher moorland.

Reed Buntings are relatively sedentary and few if any British birds leave our shores. However, many upland areas are deserted after the breeding season and clear-cut passage migrants are seen most years at the main coastal watchpoints of Heysham, Rossall, Fairhaven and Seaforth. This movement takes place between late August and mid-November but usually peaks from late September through October. Seasonal visible migration totals of 100 or more are not uncommon at each of these sites, for example 120 were logged going south over Heysham between 31 August and 31 October 1998. Day-tallies are usually in single figures but counts in the range of 20-40 are reasonably regular. However, in 2004 an exceptional passage at Fairhaven totalled 267 on 17 days between 1 September and 2 November with maxima of 51 on 29 September and 15 October and 56 on 8 October.

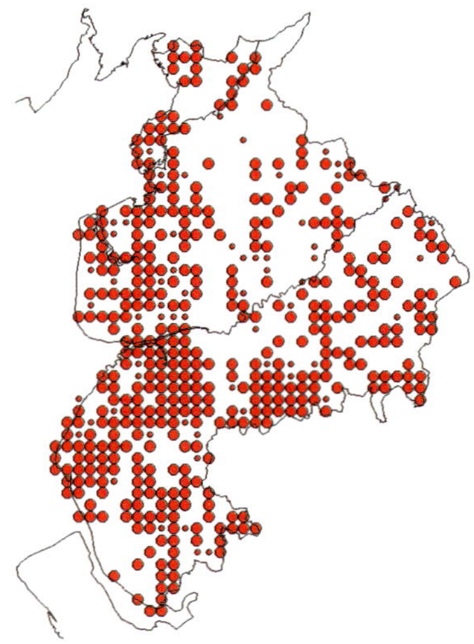

Breeding distribution of Reed Bunting, 1997-2000. (Large dots: confirmed. Small dots: possible)

As in Mitchell's day, birds are scarce during the winter months in most upland areas, most records relating to low single figures. An exception is on the West Pennine Moors where many remain feeding on the seed of purple moor-grass, for example 60 at Belmont Reservoir in October 2003 and up to 70 in two flocks on moorland above Belmont at 330m above sea level in November/December 2003. Winter flocks exceeding 20 are exceptional in the east, the highest reported being 30 at Sheddon Clough, Burnley in December 1989, 20-30 at Rowley Lake in February and December 1990, 45 at Belmont in December 1999, 40 at Grey Heights in Rossendale in December 2000 and 50 at Swinden Reservoir in winter 2001/02.

Reed Buntings were first noted at peanut-feeders in Lancashire during the 1960s and the habit became more widespread during the 1980s. Rather oddly, it was reported mostly from the east of the county where sometimes quite large numbers have been seen, including 40 in the Darwen area in December 1986. The farmland supplementary feeding stations Over Wyre have begun to attract significant numbers, a site maximum of ten in 2002 rising to 87 in 2005.

The largest winter numbers occur in the lowland areas of the west and south-west, mostly along the coast but also on the mosslands. Flock size and overall numbers have declined significantly since about the mid-1970s, before which flocks of 250 or so were seen fairly regularly. Unprecedented numbers occurred on the outer Ribble in November and December 1976, when an estimated 1,500 were feeding on the saltmarshes, particularly on *Spartina*. Flocks of 100 or more were still being recorded annually until about 1984, with an exceptional 250 at Lytham during the winter of 1982/83. Significant numbers still winter on coastal wetlands in Morecambe Bay and the Lune, Wyre, Ribble and Mersey Estuaries but three-figure counts are now very rarely recorded, the most recent being 100 at Cockersands in December 2000 and 200 at Cockerham in February 2001.

Male Reed Bunting, Marton Mere, May 2004. (Steve Young)

Few large wintering flocks have been reported on farmland in recent years except where supplementary feeding takes place – 50 near Rufford in February 1999 and 28 in a stubble field in Preesall in March 1999 being exceptions – but night-time roosts sometimes congregate in reedbeds. Numbers have declined significantly at Marton Mere from 80 in 1966 to a peak of 24 in 1997. Other recent reports include 42 at Mere Brow in February 1997, 27 at Hic Bibi in December 1996 and 50-70 at Mere Sands Wood between 1997 and 2000.

The return to upland areas occurs mainly between mid-February and late March, 200 at Belmont in March 1976 being quite exceptional even for the mid-1970s. Coastal passage migrants are much scarcer in spring than in autumn but the same sites regularly register single-figure day-counts with 15 at Seaforth on 1 April 1990 at the top of the range.

Recoveries of birds ringed or found in Lancashire confirm that most make only small movements between breeding and wintering quarters, the majority being recovered within 10 km of the ringing site. Nevertheless, 17 out of 116 moved more than 100km, indicating that a significant proportion of the population is migratory. Four of these involved juveniles ringed in the breeding season in Lancashire and recovered the following winter in Devon (2), Dorset and Surrey. Add to these two ringed in winter in Shropshire, one in Worcestershire and one in Nottinghamshire that were recovered in summer in Lancashire, together with one ringed in March in Lancashire and recovered the next month in Cumbria, and a picture emerges of a small north-south migration within Britain, which perhaps accounts for the majority of our coastal migrants. However, it is known that a small proportion of the highly migratory Scandinavian populations also visit Britain on passage, and the control of a first-winter male at Mere Sands Wood in March 1999 that had been ringed as a juvenile in Rogaland, Norway, nearly 800 km to the north-east, indicates that some of our wintering and/or passage birds are indeed of Scandinavian origin.

SJW, RW.

This species account was sponsored by Mark Champion and Berwyn Morris.

RED-HEADED BUNTING

Emberiza bruniceps

Lancashire Category D.

No record of Red-headed Bunting has been accepted onto the British list. This colourful species used to be imported in large numbers into the country and was a common cage bird, but this trade declined from the 1980s and the escape likelihood has also probably declined. The BBRC is currently carrying out a review of the most recent records and it is possible that the species will ultimately be admitted to Category A of the British list.

Eric Hardy published the first record in Lancashire, a male paired with a Reed Bunting at Formby on 1 July 1970. Further males were seen at Freckleton on 9 August 1979, Heysham on 12 May 1982 and Seaforth on 12 July 1990. This was followed by yet another male with a mixed flock of finches, sparrows and buntings in stubble fields at Little Crosby on 1 August 1998. This is the only Lancashire record being reviewed by the BBRC and may perhaps eventually become the official first for the county.

Male Red-headed Bunting, Little Crosby, August 1998. (Steve Young)

SJW.

BLACK-HEADED BUNTING

Emberiza melanocephala

Lancashire Category A. (0, 1).

Vagrant from south-eastern Europe.

Our only record was found during the afternoon of 19 June 2002 by Chris Fyles in his back garden in Birkdale, Southport. First seen as a flash of bright yellow in an apple tree, it soon revealed its identity and flew to seed-feeders just 20 metres away. Several other observers arrived before long and it performed at close range for 40 minutes or so before flying off. It reappeared briefly that day and was again on the feeders for a few minutes on the 21st and 22nd.

It was an adult male in full breeding plumage, showing no signs of wear. The record was accepted by the BBRC as the 156th British record. Black-headed Buntings have an unusual east-west migration pattern and arrive late in spring on breeding grounds in the Caucasus, Turkey and south-east Europe, usually not before the end of April. More than 60% of British records have been in spring, the great majority between the second week of May and the third week of June, and spring records have a more westerly bias than those in autumn. Although a proportion of British records are likely to be escapes, the Birkdale bird fits well with the national pattern of late spring records and was probably an overshooting migrant.

Male Black-headed Bunting, Southport, 19 June 2002. (Field sketch, Barry McCarthy)

SJW.
This species account was sponsored by Chris Fyles

CORN BUNTING

Emberiza calandra

Lancashire Category A.

Common resident breeder.

Lancashire remains a stronghold for Corn Buntings, a species, which like so many of our farmland birds, has shown a more than 50% national decline in numbers over the past 25 years and 32% between 1994 and 2005 (BBS). Its distribution in the county is closely tied to areas of grain production, especially barley, on the north Merseyside, West Lancashire, Ribble and Fylde mosslands. The most northerly breeders in 1997-2000 were in the Thurnham area, south of the Lune, and the eastern edge of their range in central Lancashire was in the Lostock Hall area. South of the Ribble, the breeding range is more or less continuous on farmland, at least at the tetrad level, although the species is absent from many areas of St. Helens. The distribution is rather more patchy, however, in the Fylde.

During the Lancashire Atlas survey Corn Buntings were found to be breeding in 176 tetrads, or roughly 20% of the county. A comparison, based upon proven breeding in 10 km squares, showed a decline from 36 squares in 1968-72 to 20 in 1997-2000, indicating a 40% reduction in range over the past three decades. The Fylde Atlas survey of 1988-91 located birds in 54-70 tetrads but by 1997-2000 this had fallen to 33.

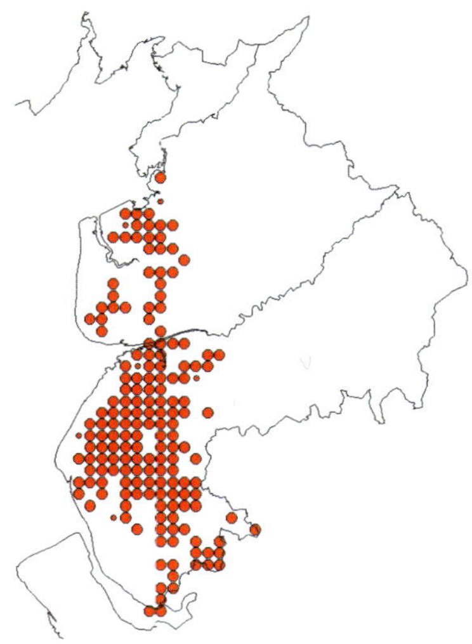

Breeding distribution of Corn Bunting, 1997-2000. (Large dots: confirmed. Small dots: possible)

The main northern breeding site used to be on the Lune Estuary between Overton and Sunderland Point to the west and Stodday and Aldcliffe to the east but this population has been in decline since the 1980s and only a handful of birds remain. Ten pairs bred at Sunderland Point in 1984 but all had gone by the early 1990s. Further north, there were isolated singing males at Warton, Carnforth and Nether Kellet until at least 1981 and occasional single pairs in the Lancaster-Slyne-Halton area between 1985 and 1991, but none since.

Small numbers were present in east Lancashire up to the mid-1970s, perhaps relict populations from the days up to 1950s when oats were grown in this area. One or two singing males were present at Woodfold Park, Blackburn throughout the 1950s, six pairs bred near Balderstone Hall, Ribchester in 1968 and up to three pairs in the Briercliffe-Thursden-Worsthorne area from 1966-74. The most recent records in the Preston area were at Walton-le-Dale where five or six pairs bred in 1984 but only one pair in 1985, and then only the occasional male until the last report in 1993. There has only been one Rossendale record, two near Haslingden on 1 August 1971. Exceptionally, one was in song at Roddlesworth on the edge of the West Pennine Moors in July 1976.

The Corn Bunting's heartland seems to have changed little since the nineteenth century; both Mitchell and Oakes described it as commonest in the south-west, while Oakes noted an increase in range into the Fylde in the middle of the twentieth century as grassland was turned over to arable. However, there has been a noticeable decline at Lytham Moss since the 1990s and a contraction of range in the Blackpool area. Corn Buntings remain relatively common in central areas of the Fylde, however, and particularly north of the Wyre where recent provision of winter grain has helped to stem and perhaps reverse the decline. The range has contracted dramatically at the edge of the south-west mosses too, for example about 20 pairs on Banks Marsh in the late 1970s had become extinct by the late 1980s.

Corn Bunting, south-west mosslands. (Mike McKavett)

With their very diverse mating systems, breeding Corn Buntings are not easy to census. The Lancashire Atlas estimated a county population of 1,200 'pairs' in 1997-2000, based on counts of singing males which were uprated according to the results of intensive surveys in West Lancashire and the Fylde. Over the whole of the range, breeding densities averaged about six pairs per tetrad (1.5 pairs per square kilometre) but were at least double this on the south-west mosslands, where the squares SD30, 31, 40 and 41 support about 75% of the county total.

Distribution in winter mirrors that of the breeding season, with the largest numbers and most frequent sightings in south-west Lancashire, Merseyside and the Fylde. Prior to the mid-1980s flocks of up to 200 were seen regularly and there were also reports of large roosts, the largest being 1,000 at Mere Brow in mid-February 1980. The size of feeding congregations depends to a large extent upon the concentration of food resources but also gives some indication of overall numbers. Flocks of 100 or more were reported regularly during the early 1990s, including 280 on the Altcar Withins in March 1991, but have become much scarcer. Since 1995 almost all three-figure counts have been in north Fylde, most recently mainly on various supplementary feeding stations; these have included 166 in 1995, 194 in 2002 and 294 in 2004. Birds appear to be more dispersed in the south-west, and 106 at Plex Moss in 1994 and 100 at White Moss, Skelmersdale in 1997 are the largest recent counts. Corn Buntings are rather taken for granted throughout the mosses and are probably seriously under-reported, but flocks of 50 or more have been noted regularly from Croston, Holmeswood, Skelmersdale, Rainford, St. Helens, south Liverpool, Little Crosby and the Formby and Southport mosslands.

Sightings at any distance from the breeding haunts are very rare, the most surprising being five at Foulridge Reservoir on 31 October 1992. Small numbers of migrants were seen flying south over Fairhaven in autumn in the mid-1980s when the Fylde breeding population was larger. Numbers wintering on the Sefton coast dunes have been best documented at Crosby Marine Park, where numbers fell from 40-50 in the mid-1990s to less than ten in the first years of this century.

Marton Mere supported a regular winter and spring roost of up to 130 in Reed Canary-grass during at least 1994 -95. There have been irregular spring sightings at various other coastal sites, including small numbers between Fleetwood and Hightown in early May 1985, but whether these refer to true migrants or birds simply moving back from local wintering areas is uncertain. Our single ringing recovery was a bird retrapped in winter on its presumed breeding grounds six years after ringing, a ripe old age for any small passerine.

SJW, RW.

This species account was sponsored by F. Ian Lee and in memory of Colin Antrobus.

ESCAPES & BIRDS OF UNKNOWN PROVENANCE

BLACK SWAN *Cygnus atratus*
Recorded almost annually since at least 1980 in all seasons, mostly near the coast. Numbers increased throughout the 1990s to a peak of nine in 2000. There has been no definite evidence of breeding in the county but juveniles have been seen occasionally.

EMPEROR GOOSE *Anser canagica*
Five were at Stocks Reservoir with four Barnacle Geese in July to September 1991 and three were at Marton Mere on 18 July 2000. No evidence of breeding.

BAR-HEADED GOOSE *Anser indicus*
There have been one to four records almost annually since at least 1980, scattered throughout the county. No evidence of breeding.

SWAN GOOSE *Anser cygnoides*
Up to three were at Anglezarke Reservoir in 1986 and singles at Marton Mere in 1991, Ribchester in 1995, Clifton Marsh and Stanley Park, Blackpool on and off all year from 2000 to 2004. Two were at Rivington Reservoir throughout 2001 to 2005 and this or another pair was at Brockholes Quarry in 2003 and 2004.

BLUE-WINGED GOOSE *Cyanochen cyanopterus*
One was at Mere Sands Wood during April and May 1987.

RED-BREASTED GOOSE *Branta ruficollis*
An adult was with feral Greylags at Eccleston Mere on 14 August 1997, moving on the 26th to Martin Mere where it associated with feral Barnacles before joining up with Pink-footed Geese; it was last seen on 8 November.

Between 2003 and 2006 what was perhaps the same bird commuted with feral Barnacles between Knowsley Park and various St. Helens sites, where it summered, and Martin Mere in winter, occasionally wandering further afield with wild Pink-footed Geese. In its first winter it excited considerable national attention but enthusiasm gradually waned.

A different bird was at Wayoh Reservoir in early December 2003 and singles flew over Blackpool on 9 January 2005 and Seaforth the next day.

AUSTRALIAN SHELDUCK *Tadorna tadornoides*
One was at Hest Bank in October 1981 and a male was paired with a Shelduck at Arkholme in 1977.

PARADISE SHELDUCK *Tadorna variegata*
One was on the Lancaster Canal at Bolton-le-Sands on 18 April 2002.

CAPE SHELDUCK *Tadorna cana*
A male was on the Ribble during autumn 1975-77 with another there during 1999. One, possibly a hybrid, was at Seaforth on 18 March 2005 and a female at Martin Mere during November 2005.

FULVOUS WHISTLING-DUCK *Dendrocygna bicolor*
One was on the Leeds-Liverpool Canal in 1996 and two free-flying birds were at Martin Mere on 27 June 1999. Most recently, a full-winged adult was at Hundred End on 20 June 2005.

MUSCOVY DUCK *Cairina moschata*
Almost certainly under-reported. Recent records include three at Wayoh Reservoir during 1995, one near Belmont in 1997 and 1998, a pair attempting to breed at Pine Lake in 2002, up to two on the Leeds-Liverpool Canal in Burnley from 2003 to 2005 and five at Stanley Park, Blackpool throughout 2003, declining to three in 2004.

WOOD DUCK *Aix sponsa*
Up to 25 unpinioned birds were at Martin Mere during the late 1970s and early 1980s, occasionally wandering to other sites. There have been up to four records a year since at least 1982, including three together at Mere Sands Wood during 2004. A pair was introduced to Birkacre, Chorley in 2000 but both fell to predators by July 2001. A pair was on the River Yarrow at Croston on 14 May and 20 October 2002; other pair(s) were seen during October 2002 at Mere Sands Wood and Garth Prison, Leyland. There was no evidence of breeding until one pair raised several young at Mere Sands Wood in 2006.

RINGED TEAL *Callonetta leucophrys*
A pair was at Pilling in 2000 and at Stanley Park, Blackpool and other Fylde sites from 2001 to 2004 with one surviving to 2005. A male was on a pond in Read on 2 December 2004 and on the neighbouring River Calder from 8-12 December. Finally, one was at Martin Mere on 5 November 2005.

CHILOE WIGEON *Anas sibilatrix*

Free-flying singles were at Mitton on 5 November 1995, Dockacres in February-March 1997, Marton Mere in 1999-2000, Marshside in December 2000, Leighton Moss in August 2001, Martin Mere in March 2003, Mere Sands Wood in October 2003 and Myerscough Quarry from 28 March to 14 April 2004. A pinioned pair was on the Lune at Arkholme during May-June 2000.

WHITE-CHEEKED PINTAIL *Anas bahamensis*

Singles were at Mere Sands Wood on 8 June 1992, Seaforth on 21 August 1992, Marshside on 20 April 1994, Pilling-Preesall in May to August 1997 and Preesall on 11 March 2000. A wing-clipped female was on the Lune at Greta Foot on 7 June 2000.

CAPE TEAL *Anas capensis*

One was at Seaforth on at least 19 June 1986 before moving to Martin Mere on the 23rd. Another was on Fairhaven Lake during August 2005.

CINNAMON TEAL *Anas cyanoptera*

There have been at least four records of males and one or two females. This species is sometimes suggested as a potential vagrant but dates and locations all point to captive origin: a male at Holden Wood Reservoir on 19 May & 1 June 1993 and presumably the same on the River Irwell near Townsendfold from 1993-1995 and Clowbridge Reservoir in 1995; a first-winter male at Martin Mere on 19-26 September 1994; a female at Freckleton Naze pool on 12 August 1995; this or another female near Marton Mere during 2001-2002, paired with a Shoveler in 2002 at least; and a male near Marton Mere from 1998 to 2000 (narrowly missing out on the female!).

CHESTNUT TEAL *Anas castanea*

One was in Sefton Park, Liverpool during summer 2000.

AUSTRALASIAN SHOVELER *Anas rynchotis*

One was at Marshside during spring 1983.

COMB DUCK *Sarkidiornis melanotos*

A bird described as an 'odd thing that resembled a female Comb Duck' was with 192 Pink-footed Geese on Aldcliffe Marsh on 20 March 2004, and perhaps the same female was at Mere Sands Wood on 13 April 2004.

BAER'S POCHARD *Aythya baeri*

Two were at Martin Mere on 7 May 1977 and there were regular sightings of escapes from Blackpool Zoo at Marton Mere during the late 1970s, where a female bred with a Common Pochard and was seen with ten ducklings on 16 July 1980.

REDHEAD *Aythya americana*

A colour-ringed bird was on Eccleston Mere on 4 May 1996, subsequently moving to Budworth Mere in Cheshire.

CANVASBACK *Aythya valisineria*

A male in eclipse plumage was reported at Seaforth on 23-26 July 1988 and other males were at Martin Mere in early 1996 and 2001. None was submitted to the BBRC and question marks hang over the identification of all of them.

WHITE-HEADED DUCK *Oxyura leucocephala*

An unringed, fully-winged juvenile was at Martin Mere on 1-3 October 1999.

NORTHERN BOBWHITE *Colinus virginianus*

A number were released in the Formby dunes in 1962 and 1963 in an unsuccessful attempt to establish them.

CHUKAR *Alectoris chukar*

Before the practice was stopped in the early 1990s, Chukar and Chukar x Red-legged Partridge hybrids were frequently released and seen in many parts of the county. Sightings decreased rapidly after 1992, with reports from only four sites in 1995 and the last recorded were three pure Chukar on Plex Moss in 1996 and hybrids reported from Quernmore in 1997.

Fourteen at Seaforth in October 1989 were assumed to have been released from a ship berthing in the Liverpool docks; some were seen the length of the Liverpool waterfront for at least two years but they probably never bred successfully. The most recent record was one 'singing' at Seaforth on 1 March 2004, presumably also ship-assisted.

GOLDEN PHEASANT *Chrysolophus pictus*

There have been very many introductions/escapes throughout the county but there is no evidence that any of them have ever become self-sustaining. The largest and most long-standing group is at Lytham Hall, where nine males and a female were seen in 2002.

LADY AMHERST'S PHEASANT *Chrysolophus amherstiae*

Single males were in the Liverpool docks in May-June 1999 and in gardens at Clitheroe and in the Allsprings area of Great Harwood in autumn 2001. A male and female were on Rawcliffe Moss on 8 October 2005 and, presumably the same female, at nearby Bradshaw Lane on the 24th.

REEVES'S PHEASANT *Syrmaticus reevesii*

Single males were at Brindle Park in 1992, Dunsop Bridge in 1997 and near Fluke Hall in September 2002; three males were at Claughton Hall, Garstang in November 1999 and up to nine males were in the Belmont area from September 2005.

HELMETED GUINEAFOWL *Numida meleagris*

Six were in Orritt's Wood on the south-west mosses in 2002, three of which survived into 2003, declining to two by 2005.

TRAGOPAN sp.

A female was photographed in a Chorley garden during the first week of July 2005.

WHITE PELICAN *Pelecanus onocrotalus*

One found dead on the tideline at Formby Point in November 1966 had escaped from Colwyn Bay Zoo. An adult was at Lytham on 15-17 October 1970.

PINK-BACKED PELICAN *Pelicanus rufescens*

One escaped from Knowsley Safari Park and spent several days on Prescot Reservoirs in September 1999.

LESSER FLAMINGO *Phoeniconaias minor*

One was at Whitemoor Reservoir on 25 May 1980.

CHILEAN FLAMINGO *Phoenicopterus chilensis*

Singles were on the Ribble in the Freckleton area throughout most of the year during 1982-83 and 1988, at Stocks Reservoir on 5 May 1990, Hightown in December 1993, Dockacres in March 1996 and Martin Mere on 25 July 2002.

DEMOISELLE CRANE *Anthropoides virgo*

One was on fields by the River Cocker at Cockerham on 21-26 October 1967, having been seen previously on the Kent Estuary in Cumbria. One escaped from Blackpool Zoo and was seen at Marton Mere on 9 September 1986.

SACRED IBIS *Threskiornis aethiopicus*

One was on farmland for several months near Colne in 1999 before being found dead in September. The specimen is now in Fleetwood Museum.

BALD IBIS or SOUTHERN BALD IBIS *Geronticus eremita or G. calvus*

One escaped from Blackpool Zoo in 2001 and was seen at Marton Mere during May that year. Another made a bid for freedom from the same site in October 2002 and was found wandering on Blackpool Promenade and taken into care in Rochdale, where the local press and TV got rather overexcited about it.

BUFF-NECKED IBIS *Theristicus caudatus*

One that had been seen at several sites in Cheshire and Lancashire in 1993 was finally captured at Halsall on 11 May, when it was taken into care and returned to its owner – but it soon escaped again and was back in Lancashire in June.

(AMERICAN) BLACK VULTURE *Coragyps atratus*

One was at Abbey Village, near Chorley in late October to early November 2003.

BALD EAGLE *Haliaeetus leucocephalus*

One that had escaped in Yorkshire was in the Blackburn-Clitheroe area in 1996.

HARRIS'S HAWK *Parabuteo unicintus*

One was seen regularly near Preston in May 1995, at one point nest-building. Other singles were at Belmont in March to May 1997, Duxbury Wood, Chorley in May to June 1998, Hurst Green in April to June 2000, Dockacres on 20 March 2001, Lytham Moss on 24 September 2001, with Buzzards in the Langden Valley in April 2002, at Lytham on 14 November 2004 and in May 2005, in the Belmont area during March and April 2005 likely to have been the same as one in Darwen in late April and Winmarleigh Moss on 3 July 2005.

RED-TAILED HAWK *Buteo jamaicensis*

One was at large in the Sefton Coast pinewoods from at least 1998 to 2005; it was not viewed favourably by those Formby residents who witnessed it regularly taking Red Squirrels in their gardens. Another was at Prescot Reservoirs on 22 February 1998.

SAKER *Falco cherrug*

Large, escaped falconers' birds are seen fairly regularly especially in the lowlands and are generally reported as Sakers, but many are likely to be hybrids. One definitely pure Saker escaped from North Wales and took up residence in the Liverpool docks in 2001; it was recaptured by its owner but escaped again and was back in the docks throughout 2002 and until 2005.

LANNER *Falco biarmicus*

Singles were reported at Rossall on 6 November 1978, Hambleton in January 1998 and Martin Mere in 1999.

LAUGHING DOVE *Streptopelia senegalensis*

One was in Blackpool from August to October 1988 and again in 1989 to January 1990.

BLUE-FACED HONEYEATER *Entomyzon cyanotis*

One was at Warton Bank on at least 7-14 October 2001.

BUDGERIGAR *Melopsittacus undulatus*

Records have been published for only six years since 1980 but budgies are undoubtedly one of our commonest escaped cage birds.

ALEXANDRINE PARAKEET *Psittacula eupatria*

A pair was released at Fazakerley, north Liverpool, probably in 1994, and bred successfully in at least 1997 and 1998; the last was seen in 2000.

PLUM-HEADED PARAKEET *Psittacula cyanocephala*

One was at Lower Hodder Wood in 1980.

MONK PARAKEET *Myiopsitta monachus*

One was in a Chorley garden on 1 April 2002 and remained in the neighbourhood until the autumn. Another was in a Crosby garden during the second week of March 2004.

WHITE-EYED PARAKEET *Aratinga leucophthalmus*

One was at Warton, Fylde throughout 2005.

CRIMSON ROSELLA *Platycercus elegans*

Singles were at Crawley Cross Farm on 17-22 June 2001 and on Darwen Moor on 11 May 2003.

YELLOW ROSELLA *Platycercus flaveolus*

One was at Southport Marine Lake on 4 June 2005.

EASTERN ROSELLA *Platycercus eximius*

One was near Sandhills Station in north Liverpool on 25 May 2004.

COCKATIEL *Nyphicus hollandicus*

Up to seven have been recorded annually during the summer months since at least 1982. A unusual mass breakout resulted in four arriving at Martin Mere on 12 May 2004.

Cockatiels seem to bring out the worst in some birds; two have been seen being killed – by a Herring Gull at Blackpool and Common Terns at Seaforth.

SENEGAL PARROT *Poicephalus senegalus*

One was at Formby in 1997.

EAGLE OWL *Bubo bubo*

Singles were in Kirkby on 23 May 1992, Edenfield, Rossendale on 27 December 1997, Walton, Liverpool on 19 July 2002 and Stanley Park, Blackpool on 8 April 2004.

One at Sollom on 31 August 2005 had escaped from Garth Prison, Leyland after it had been loaned as a deterrent to other birds! One wearing jesses in the Dunsop Valley on 27 October 2005 may have been the same bird and seems likely to have been the female that laid a clutch of infertile eggs in Bowland in 2006.

SNOWY OWL *Nyctea scandiaca*

A male was seen by several observers at Crown Point, Burnley on 17 March 2004; it proved to be an escape from Gibfield Farm, half a mile away.

RIVER CHAT (WHITE-CROWNED REDSTART) *Chaimarrornis leucocephalus*

A male frequented the River Calder at Burnley from late October 1971 to at least the year's end.

RED-BILLED LEOTHRIX (PEKIN ROBIN) *Leothrix lutea*

Singles were seen in the Albert Dock, Liverpool in the late 1970s and at Marton Mere on 14 May 1992.

CHINESE BABAX *Babax lanceolatus*

One was in a garden at Tarleton from June 2003 to the end of the year.

WHITE-CROWNED (BLACK) WHEATEAR *Oenanthe leucopyga*

An adult was at Fazakerley Reedbed, Liverpool on 17 October 2002.

BLACK-BREASTED THRUSH *Turdus dissimilis*

One was in an Earby garden from November 1999 to 13 February 2000.

NORTHERN CARDINAL *Cardinalis cardinalis*

A male was at Lower Clough Farm, Langho on 17 July 1975.

SCALY-BREASTED MUNIA *Lonchura punctulata*

Singles were at MMWWT in 2000 and in a garden at Hundred End during October 2004.

WHITE-HEADED MUNIA *Lonchura maja*

One was in garden at Crossens on 14-20 September 1980.

GREY PLANTAIN-EATER *Crinifer zonurus/piscator*

One described as the East African species *C. zonurus* was in a garden at Tockholes, Darwen on 8 March 2004. What was presumably the same bird, but this time described as the West African *piscator*, was seen on the Beechwood Estate, Blackburn on 10 June 2004.

RED-WHISKERED BULBUL *Pycnonotus jocosus*

One was in song at Belmont on 29 April to 7 May 1993.

PURPLE GLOSSY STARLING *Lamprotornis purpureus*

One was at Marton Mere in August 2000.

VINOUS-BREASTED STARLING *Sturnus burmannicus*

One was with Starlings at Lower Bottin Farm, Worsthorne in late June 2002.

HILL MYNA *Gracula sp.*

Singles were at Heysham on 25 October 1992 and Delph Reservoir throughout most of 2004 into 2005.

VILLAGE WEAVER *Ploceus cucullatus*

One was at Altcar Rifle Ranges on 29 April 1999 and a male was with Greenfinches at Marshside on 4 October 2005.

RED-BILLED QUELEA *Quelea quelea*

Singles were at Colne on 7 September 1981 and on a bird table at Pilling in October 1999.

ZEBRA FINCH *Poephilla or Taeniopygia guttata*

Singles were at Seaforth in August 1991 and Martin Mere in June 1993.

RED BISHOP sp. *Euplectes sp.*

One was in the Heysham area from late August to early December 2003.

ORANGE-CHEEKED WAXBILL *Estrilda melopoda*

One was at Marton Mere in September 2000.

YELLOW-HEADED BLACKBIRD *Xanthocephalus xanthocephalus*

A male was in reedbeds at Leighton Moss on 4 -10 August 1964.

STREAKY-HEADED SEED-EATER *Serinus gularis*

One was on garden feeders in Hundred End in the last week of March 2005.

CANARY *Serinus canaria*

Seen fairly regularly at garden feeding stations.

YELLOW-FRONTED CANARY *Serinus mozambicus*

Singles were seen at Ormskirk in August 1997, at Ansdell on 27 July 2003 and Seaforth on 9 August 2003.

TWO-BARRED CROSSBILL *Loxia leucoptera*

One of eight that had been captured on board a Cunard ship in the Bay of Fundy by Donald Dewar in 1855 escaped on arrival in Liverpool (Harrop *et al.* 2007). It was of the North American race *bifasciata*, 'White-winged Crossbill', but, having been held in captivity, does not qualify for acceptance on the British list.

SUDAN GOLDEN SPARROW *Passer luteus*

Singles were at Seaforth on 25 September 1994 and Pilling in June to October 1997.

JAVA SPARROW *Padda oryzivora*

One was at Sefton Meadows Tip on 30 September 1983.

PAINTED BUNTING *Passerina ciris*

One was in a Silverdale garden on at least 2-6 April 1974. The record was originally placed in Category D by the BOURC, but later removed as the bird was considered an almost certain escape.

LAZULI BUNTING *Passerina amoena*

One was in a Bispham garden for two days in late April 1988.

RARE BIRDS IN LANCASHIRE & NORTH MERSEYSIDE, 2006-2007

The following rare and scarce birds have been recorded in the county since the end of 2005 up until mid-October 2007. Only records adjudicated by either the British Birds Rarities Committee or the Lancashire Records Committee have been included.

They include two species not previously seen in Lancashire: Black Scoter and White-tailed Lapwing (Plover), bringing the county total to 350 species (336 Category A, 7 Category B and 7 Category C).

Male Black Scoter, Jenny Brown's Point, May 2007. (Jim Beattie)

Adult White-tailed Lapwing, Eric Morecambe complex, June 2007. (Chris Batty)

LESSER SCAUP *Aythya affinis*
A male was on the Dockacres complex and Leighton Moss from 14 September to 22 October 2006.

RING-NECKED DUCK *Aythya collaris*
A male was on Rivington and Anglezarke Reservoirs from 20 November to 7 December 2006.

BLACK SCOTER *Melanitta americana*
A male was found near the Eric Morecambe complex on 16 May 2007 and released at Jenny Brown's Point. The first record in Lancashire.

SOOTY SHEARWATER *Puffinus griseus*
One was seen off Formby Point on 19 September 2006.

NIGHT HERON *Nycticorax nycticorax*
A first-summer was at Galgate from 9 to 12 May 2006.

BLACK STORK *Ciconia nigra*
Singles were seen flying over Marshside on 8 June 2006, Liverpool on 15 June 2006 and the M65 near Preston on 2 May 2007.

GREAT WHITE EGRET *Ardea alba*
Singles were at the Eric Morecambe Complex from 27 August to at least mid-October 2007, and Marshside from 30 August to 4 September 2007.

GLOSSY IBIS *Plegadis falcinellus*
One was at Martin Mere, Brockholes Quarry, Pilling, Newton Marsh, Marshside and various other sites from 1 October 2006 until at least mid-October 2007.

ROUGH-LEGGED BUZZARD *Buteo lagopus*
One was on Banks Marsh on 4 November 2006.

SPOTTED CRAKE *Porzana porzana*
Singles were at Martin Mere on 28 to 31 July 2006, Marton Mere on 19 September 2006 and Marshside on 12 to 14 August 2007.

COMMON CRANE *Grus grus*
Four flew south over Haweswater, Lancaster, Rainford and Liverpool on 28 January 2006, two flew south over Leighton Moss on 29 March 2006, and one was at Chipping on 25 to 28 May 2007.

BLACK-WINGED STILT *Himantopus himantopus*
Three arrived at Martin Mere on 5 May 2006 with a pair staying to breed unsuccessfully; last seen on 23 June.

STONE CURLEW *Burhinus oedicnemus*
One was at Knott End on 14 to 15 April 2007

WHITE-TAILED LAPWING *Vanellus leucurus*
An adult was at the Eric Morecambe Complex and Leighton Moss on 10 to 17 June 2007. It was the first for Lancashire, and had been seen previously at Caelaverock in Dumfries & Galloway.

TEMMINCK'S STINT *Calidris temminckii*
One was on Alston Reservoirs on 26 to 27 May 2007.

WHITE-RUMPED SANDPIPER *Calidris fuscicollis*
An adult was at Seaforth and Crosby Shore on 22 to 26 July 2007.

BROAD-BILLED SANDPIPER *Limicola falcinellus*
An adult was at Cockersand on 15 to 17 May 2006.

LESSER YELLOWLEGS *Tringa flavipes*
An adult was at the Eric Morecambe Complex and Leighton Moss on 24 to 27 July 2007.

RED-NECKED PHALAROPE *Phalaropus lobatus*
Females were at Marshside on 29 May 2006 and Martin Mere on 4 to 7 June 2007.

LAUGHING GULL *Larus atricilla*
Adults were at Marton Mere on 9 to 17 April 2006, and Stodday on 19 August 2006.

RING-BILLED GULL *Larus delawarensis*
An adult was at Seaforth and Crosby from 2005 to 6 March 2006, a second-winter there from 2005 to 27 March 2006 and a first-winter from 29 June 2006 to 11 May 2007. An adult was on the River Wyre from 12 to 20 October 2006 and 22 January 2007, Myerscough Quarry on 28 March 2007 and Glasson on 27 April 2007.

CASPIAN TERN *Hydroprogne caspia*
One was at Knott End on 2 July 2007.

HOOPOE *Upupa epops*
Singles were on Fleetwood Golf Course on 27 April 2006 and in garden at Hutton on 19 April 2007.

WRYNECK *Jynx torquilla*
Singles were at Seaforth on 16 to 17 September 2006, Heysham on 23 September 2006 and Kirkham on 8 to 9 September 2007.

RICHARD'S PIPIT *Anthus richardi*
One flew over Fairhaven on 17 October 2006 and one was on Lytham Moss on 24 April 2007.

CETTI'S WARBLER *Cettia cetti*
One was at Marton Mere from at least 11 February to 18 April 2006 and probably the same from 20 October 2006 to 25 March 2007.

PALLAS'S WARBLER *Phylloscopus proregulus*
One was in the Hightown dunes on 19 to 27 December 2006.

LESSER WHITETHROAT *Sylvia curruca*
One, possibly of one the south-eastern races *halimodendri/minula*, was in a Chorley garden in January to early February 2006.

WOODCHAT SHRIKE *Lanius senator*
A female was at Marshside on 20 May 2007.

CHOUGH
A Welsh-ringed first-winter was at Heysham from 18 to 27 September 2007.

COMMON ROSEFINCH *Carpodacus erythrinus*
A first-summer male was in a garden at Pilling on 30 May 2007.

BIBLIOGRAPHY AND REFERENCES

Anon 2006. *Aerial Surveys of Waterbirds in Strategic Windfarm Areas.* Final Report 2004/05. Dept. for Trade & Industry.

Atkinson, D. [c 1976]. *Birdwatching in and around Wycoller: a Visitor's Guide.*

Atkinson, H.W. 1901. *Rossall Flora and Fauna.* Fleetwood.

Atkinson-Willes, G.L. (ed). 1963. *Wildfowl in Great Britain.* London: HMSO.

Baines, D. 1993. Recent trends in Black Grouse numbers. *Game Conservancy Review* 24: 133-135.

Baker, H., Stroud, D.A., Aebischer, NJ, Cranswick, P.A., Gregory, R.D., McSorley, C.A., Noble, D.G. & Rehfisch, M.M. 2006. Population estimates of birds in Great Britain and the United Kingdom. *British Birds* 99: 25-44

Ballance, D.K. 1998. *Birds in Counties: An ornithological bibliography for the counties of England, Wales, Scotland and the Isle of Man.* London.

Banks, R. 1976. Birds of a Blackpool park. *Fylde Nat.* 2: 3-10. Deals with Louie Horrocks Memorial Gardens.

Banks, R. and Davies, C. 2002. *The Birds of St. Helens.* St. Helens Wildlife Recording Group.

Bannon, J.K. 2003. *Birder's Guide to Southport and the Sefton Coast.* Sefton Council Tourism Department, Southport.

Barlow, P. 1992. *Winter Hill to Yellowhammer Lane.* A survey of birds in the Leigh area that includes parts of Lancashire as well as Greater Manchester.

Barnes, J.A.G. 1947. Notes of some birds of Morecambe Bay. *British Birds* 40: 258-261.

Barnes, J.A.G. 1952. The status of the Lesser Black-backed Gull. *British Birds* 45: 3-17

Barnes, J.A.G. 1959. *Check List of the Birds of the Lancaster District.* Lancaster & District Birdwatching Society.

Battersby, E. 1965. List of birds of Accrington Basin. *JANS* 1965: 9-13.

Batty, C. & Lowe, T. 2001. Vagrant Canada Geese in Britain and Ireland. *Birding World* 14: 57-61.

Birkhead, T.R. 1991. *The Magpies.* London: T & D Poyser.

Blackledge, D. 2002. The 2002 breeding season – RSPB Coast Reserves. *Cumbria Bird Club News*: 13 No. 3

Bouldin, L.E. 1959. Survey of House Martin colonies in east Lancashire. *British Birds* 52: 141-149

Bouldin, L.E. 1968. The population of the House Martin *Delichon urbica* in east Lancashire. *Bird Study* 15: 135-146

Briggs, K.B. 1984. The breeding ecology of coastal and inland Oystercatchers in north Lancashire. *Bird Study* 31: 141-147

Brockholes, J.F. 1859-1861. On the birds that nest in the [Liverpool] District. *Proc. Lit. & Phil. Soc. Liverpool XIV*: 115-134, XV: 17-34.

Brown, A. & Grice, P. 2005. *Birds in England.* London: T & D Poyser.

Brown, A.F, Crick, H.Q.P & Stillman, R.A. 1995. The distribution, numbers and breeding ecology of Twite *Acanthis flavirostris* in the southern Pennines of England. *Bird Study* 42: 107-121.

Bruce, N. 1991. *Changes in heather cover on the West Pennine Moors, 1946-1988.* Chorley & District Natural History Society Report 1991: 14-17.

Bunn, D.S., Warburton, A.B. & Wilson, R.D.S. 1982. *The Barn Owl.* Carlton: T & D Poyser.

Byerley, I. 1856. *The Fauna of Liverpool.* London. Expansion of an 1854 paper published in *Proc. Lit. & Phil. Soc. Liverpool VIII*: 10-23.

Calbrade, N., Entwistle, C.A., Smith, A.J. & Spencer, K.G. 2001. Roof assemblies of lapwings and plovers in Britain. *British Birds* 94: 35-38.

Chamberlain, D. and Crick, H.Q.P. 1999. Population declines and reproductive performances of Skylarks *Alauda arvensis* in different regions and habitats of the UK. *Ibis* 141: 38-51.

Charnley, J.R. 1904. *Cockerham Moss, being a short account of a Lancashire gullery.* Lancaster.

Charnley, J.R. 1936. *Vertebrate Fauna of the Blackpool District.* Blackpool. Originally published in Grime, A. (ed.) A Scientific Survey of Blackpool & District.

Charnley, J.R. and Heathcote, W.H. 1909. *The Birds of the Ribble Estuary.* Preston.

Clarke, S.F. 1981. The erratic Stonechat. *The Fylde Naturalist* 7: 27-29.

Clements, R. 2001. The Hobby in Britain: a new population estimate. *British Birds* 94: 402-408.

Clements, R. 2005. Honey-buzzards in Britain. *British Birds* 98: 153-155.

Clutten, W.G. 1923. *Birds of Burnley & District.* Burnley. A species list by Burnley Natural History Society.

Combridge, P., Christie, D.A. & Ferguson-Lees, I.J. 2003. Breeding European Honey-buzzards in Britain. *British Birds* 96: 258-260.

Coveney, J. & Phelan, B. 2001. *Arklow Bank Seabird and Marine Mammal Survey.* Unpublished report to Fehily Timoney & Co.

Coward, T.A. 1910. *A Vertebrate Fauna of Cheshire and Liverpool Bay.* London: Witherby

Coward, T.A. 1919. *Birds of the British Isles and their Eggs.* London.

Coward, T.A. 1930. *Check-list of the Fauna of Lancashire and Cheshire.* Manchester.

Cramp, S. (ed.). [BWP] 1977-1994. *Handbook of the Birds of Europe, the Middle East and North Africa: the Birds of the Western Palearctic.* Nine volumes. Oxford: Oxford University Press.

Cranswick, P.A., Hall, C. & Smith, L. 2004. *All Wales Common Scoter survey: report on 2002/03 work programme.* Wetlands Advisory Service report to Countryside Council for Wales. Contract Science Report No. 615.

Cross, S. 2003. *Wildfowl and Waders of the Mersey Estuary.* In Curtis, M.S. & Baker-Schommer, M. (eds). *The Mersey Estuary: Naturally Ours.* Liverpool Museum. 2003.

Dare, P.J. 1966. The breeding and wintering populations of the Oystercatcher *Himantopus ostralegus* in the British Isles. *Fishery Invest.* London. Series 2, 25.

Davidson, N.C. *et al.* 1991. *Nature Conservation and estuaries in Great Britain.* Nature Conservancy Council, Peterborough.

Davies, J.M. 1997. *The impact of cormorants* (Phalacrocorax carbo L.) *on the lower River Ribble Fishery, Lancashire.* PhD Thesis, Liverpool John Moores University.

Davies, R. 2005. Predation and the profitability of grouse moors. *British Wildlife* 16: 339-347.

Deakin family gamebooks. 3 volumes (1894-1941). Privately held.

Dean, A.R. and Svensson, L. 2005. 'Siberian Chiffchaff' revisited. *British Birds* 98: 396-410.

Dean, T. 1990. *The Natural History of Walney Island.* Faust.

Delacour, J. 1954. *The Waterfowl of the World.* London.

Dementiev, G.P and Gladkov, N.A. 1951. *Birds of the Soviet Union.* Nauka: Moscow.

Deregnaucourt, S., Guyomarc'h, J-C. and Belhamra, M. 2004. Comparision of migratory tendency in European Quail *Coturnix c. coturnix*, domestic Japanese Quail *Coturnix c. japonica* and their hybrids. *Ibis* 147: 25-36

Dobinson, H.M. and Richards, A.J. 1964. The effects of the severe winter of 1962/63 on birds in Britain. *British Birds* 57: 373-434.

Doherty, P. 1992. Letter to the editor regarding Icterine Warblers breeding in Yorkshire. *British Birds* 85: 247

Dunstan, S. & White, S.J. 2001. Honey Buzzards In Lancashire and North Merseyside during Autumn 2000. *Lancashire Bird Report 2000.*

Dunstan, S. 2004. Water Pipits on the north Ribble Marshes at Warton Bank. *Lancashire Bird Report 2003.*

Dunstan, S. & Guy, P. (eds.). 2000. *Fylde Breeding Bird Atlas 1986 to 1990.* Fylde Bird Club.

Eades, R.A. 1976. Notes on the distribution and feeding of Little Gulls at sea in Liverpool Bay. *Seabird Report* 6: 115-121

Eaton, M.A., Noble, D.G.,Cranswick, P.A., Carter, N., Wotton, S., Ratcliffe, N., Wilson, A., Hilton, G.M. & Gregory, R.D. 2004. *The State of the UK's Birds, 2003.* Sandy. BTO, RSPB & WWT.

Edmunds, M., Mitcham, T. & Morries, G. (eds.). 2004. *Wildlife of Lancashire: exploring the natural history of Lancashire, Manchester and North Merseyside.* Lancaster. Lancashire Wildlife Trust, Carnegie Publishing.

Feltham M.J., Davies, J.M., Wilson, B.R., Holden, T., Cox, I.G., Harvey, J.P. & Britton, J.R. 1999. Case studies of the impacts of fish-eating birds on inland fisheries in England and Wales. *Contract No. VC0106. Report to the Ministry of Agriculture, Fisheries and Food.* 212 pp + annexes.

Felton, C. 1966. Check list of birds and their ecology on the South-West dunes and shore. *Merseyside Naturalists Association. NW Bird Report.* 1963-66: 54-67.

Fitter, R.S.R. 1959. *The Ark in our Midst: The story of the introduced animals of Britain.* Collins.

Forshaw, W.D. 1978-2006. *Annual reports on wild geese and swans in Lancashire.* Unpublished.

Forshaw, W.D. 1982. History of the Pink-Footed Goose in Lancashire. *Lancashire Bird Report* 1981.

Forshaw, W.D. 1983. Numbers, distribution and behaviour of Pink-footed Geese in Lancashire. *Wildfowl* 34: 64-76. Wildfowl Trust, Slimbridge.

Forshaw, W.D. 1998. *Numbers, distribution and behaviour of Pink-footed Geese in Lancashire: an overview of the last twenty years, 1978-1998.* Unpublished

Fox, A.D. 1988. Breeding status of the Gadwall in Britain and Ireland. *British Birds* 84: 51-66

Fox, A.D. and Mitchell, C.R. 1988. Migration and seasonal distribution of Gadwall in Britain and Ireland: a preliminary assessment. *Wildfowl* 39: 145-152

Fraser, P.A. & Rogers, M.J. 2005. Report on scarce migrant birds in Britain in 2002. *British Birds* 98: 73-88.

Fuller, R.J., Noble, D.G., Smith, K.W. and Vanhinsbergh, D. 2005. Recent declines in populations of woodland birds in Britain: a review of possible causes. *British Birds* 98: 116-143.

Furness, R.W. 1987, *The Skuas.* Calton: T & A.D. Poyser.

Gerard, J. 1894. *Stonyhurst College.* Belfast. Contains list of birds on pp 281-281 thought to be by Thomas Altham.

Gibbons, D.W., Reid, J.B. & Chapman, R.A. 1993. *The New Atlas of Breeding Birds in Britain and Ireland: 1988-1991.* London: T & A.D. Poyser.

Gladstone, H.S. 1930. *Record bags & shooting records.* London.

Gooch, S., Baillie, S. & Birkhead, T.R. 1991. The impact of Magpies *Pica pica* on songbird populations. *Journal of Applied Ecology* 28: 1068-1086.

Gray, A.J. *et. al.* 1991. *River Wyre – the ecological effects of a tidal barrage.* Wareham.

Greenhalgh, M.E. 1967. The Ruff in Lancashire. *Naturalist* 903: 117-118.

Greenhalgh, M.E. 1968. The autumn migration of waders through the Inner Ribble Marshes, Lancashire. *Naturalist* 908: 79-84.

Greenhalgh, M.E. 1969a. The breeding of the Oystercatcher in northwest England. *Naturalist* 909: 43-47.

Greenhalgh, M.E. 1969b. The populations of Redshank and Dunlin on saltmarshes in northwest England. *Bird Study* 16: 63-64.

Greenhalgh, M.E. 1971. The breeding bird communities of Lancashire saltmarshes. *Bird Study* 18: 199-212.

Greenhalgh, M.E. 1972. The breeding population of the Oystercatcher in northern England, 1971. *Naturalist* 921: 49-51.

Greenhalgh, M.E. 1973/4. The breeding birds of an overgrown canal. *Nature in Lancashire* 4: 20-23. Rufford Branch of Leeds-Liverpool Canal.

Greenhalgh, M.E. 1973a. Black-tailed Godwits on the Ribble Estuary in autumn. *Wader Study Group Bulletin* 8: 8-9.

Greenhalgh, M.E. 1973b. A comparison of breeding success of the Oystercatcher between inland and coastal areas in N.W. England. *Naturalist* 926: 87-88.

Greenhalgh, M.E. 1974. Population growth and breeding success in a saltmarsh Common Tern colony. *Naturalist* 931: 121-129

Greenhalgh, M.E. 1975a. Aspects of the ecology of an increasing Black-headed Gull colony. *Naturalist* 933: 43-51.

Greenhalgh, M.E. 1975b. The breeding birds of the Ribble Estuary salt-marshes. *Nature in Lancashire* 5: 11-19.

Greenhalgh, M.E. 1975c. *Wildfowl of the Ribble Estuary*. Sevenoaks.

Greenhalgh, M.E. 2004. Early records of Polecat, Red Kites and Grass Snakes in North Merseyside. *Lancashire & Cheshire Fauna Society Report* 105: 14-15.

Greenhalgh, M.E. and Greenhalgh, P.A. 1970. Glaucous and Iceland Gulls in Lancashire. *Naturalist* 914: 93-94.

Greenhalgh, M.E. and Greenhalgh, P.A. 1971. The Ruff as a winter visitor to Lancashire. *Nature in Lancashire* 2: 34-35.

Greenoak, F. 1997. *British birds, their folklore, names & literature*. London.

Guest J.P., Elphick, D., Hunter, J.S.A. & Norman, D. 1992. *The Breeding Bird Atlas of Cheshire & Wirral*. Cheshire and Wirral Ornithological Society.

Hagemeijer, W.J.M. and Blair, M.J. 1997. *The European Breeding Bird Atlas*. London: T & A.D. Poyser.

Hale, W.G. 1955. Observations on the winter populations of the Blackbird (*Turdus merula* L.) and the Song-thrush (*Turdus ericetorum* Turton) in a northern habitat. *The North Western Naturalist*. Sept-Dec 1955: 324-337.

Hancock, M., Baines, D., Gibbons, D., Etheridge, B. & Shepherd, M. 1999. The status of Black Grouse in Britain. *Bird Study* 46: 1-15.

Hardy, E. 1941. *The Birds of the Liverpool Area*. Arbroath.

Hardy, E. 1979. *Birdwatching in Lancashire*. Clapham.

Hardy, E. (ed.). *North West Bird Reports 1958-1983*. Merseyside Naturalists Association.

Harrison, K. (ed.). 1995. *An Atlas of Breeding Birds of Lancaster and District*. Lancaster & District Birdwatching Society.

Harrison, K. (ed.) 2000. *Checklist of the Birds of Lancaster & District, 1989-1999*. Lancaster & District Birdwatching Society.

Harrison, T.H. and Hollom, P.A.D. 1932. The Great Crested Grebe Enquiry 1931. *British Birds* 26: 62-92, 102-131, 142-155, 174-195.

Harrop, A.H.J, Knox, A,G. & McGowan, R.Y. 2007. Britain's first Two-barred Crossbill. *British Birds* 100: 650-657

Harting, J.E. 1872. British Heronries. *The Zoologist* 7: 3261-3272

Harting, J.E. 1873. Appendix to British Heronries. *The Zoologist* 8: 3404-3407

Harwood, N. 1953-4. Bird notes from the Fylde coast. *NW Naturalist* NSII: 184-190.

Harwood, N. 1955. Bird movements on the north side of the Ribble Estuary, 1954. *NW Naturalist* 26, 68-75.

Hayhow, S.J. 1996. Sociable Plover *Chettusia gregaria* in Lancashire – Britain's first record. *Lancashire Bird Report* 1995.

Hémery, G. & Jouanin, C. 1988. 'Statut et origine géographique des populations de pétrel culblanc (*Oceanodroma leucorhoa leucorhoa*) présentes dans le Golfe de Gascogne.' *Alauda* 56: 238–245.

Higson, D. 1909. *Seafowl Shooting Sketches*. Preston. Based on articles published by the author in *Shooting Times* and *The Preston Herald*, mainly about fowling on the Ribble Estuary.

Hirons, G. & Linsley, M. 1989. Counting Woodcock. *Game Conservancy Annual Review* 20: 47-48.

Holden, T.H. and Britcliffe, W. 1904. List of local birds found within a ten-mile radius of Burnley Town Hall. *J. Burnley Lit. & Phil. Soc.* 21.

Holder, F.W. & Wagstaffe, R. 1930a. The migrations of the Bar-tailed Godwit as observed on the South Lancashire coast. *British Birds* 23: 318-323.

Holder, F.W. & Wagstaffe, R. 1930b. Notes from the south Lancashire coast. *British Birds* 23, 50-56.

Holder, F.W. 1920a. Bird notes from the south Lancashire dunes. *Lancashire & Cheshire Naturalist*, Nov./Dec. 1920: 111-118.

Holder, F.W. 1920b. Yellow-legged Herring-Gull *Larus cachinnans*, Pallas, in Lancashire. *Lancashire & Cheshire Naturalist* Nov./Dec. 1920: 46.

Holland, P., Spence, I. & Sutton, T. 1984. *Breeding Birds in Greater Manchester*. Manchester Ornithological Society.

Hollom, P.A.D. 1959. The Great Crested Grebe Sample Census 1946-1955. *Bird Study* 6: 1-7.

Holloway, S. 1996. *The Historical Atlas of Breeding Birds in Britain and Ireland*, 1875-1900. London: T. & A.D. Poyser,

Holt, J. 1795. *General view of the agriculture of the county of Lancaster*. David & Charles Reprints 1969.

Hornby, H.P. 1924. *The Birds of St Michaels*. St Michaels-on-Wyre. An 11 page list of the birds in the museum.

Hornby, P. 1994. *A Members Guide, Species by Species, to Assist Record Keeping and Reporting*. East Lancashire Ornithologists Club.

Howard, R.J. and Mitchell, F.S. 1888. *The Birds of Stonyhurst*. Market Weighton. First published without authors' names in *Stonyhurst Magazine* July 1888: 208-221. A slim volume of the birds within ten miles of Stonyhurst.

Hudson, P.J. 1986. *Red Grouse - the biology & management of a wild gamebird*. Game Conservancy.

Hudson, P.J. 1992. *The Grouse in Space and Time – the population biology of a managed gamebird*. Game Conservancy.

Hudson, R. 1965. The spread of the Collared Dove in Britain and Ireland. *British Birds* 58: 105-139.
Hudson, R. 1972. Collared Doves in Britain and Ireland during 1965-70. *British Birds* 65: 139-155.
Inglis, I.R., Isaacson, A.J., Thearle, R.J.P. & Westwood, N.J. 1990. The effects of changing agricultural practice upon Woodpigeon *Columba palumbus* numbers. *Ibis* 132: 262-272.
Jackson, D. 1980. Birds of the Hyndburn District. *JANS* 10: 35-46.
Jackson, D. 1981. Rare and unusual bird species recorded in the Hyndburn area. *JANS* 11: 11-14.
Jones, M. 1975. Marton Mere: a report on its origins, natural history and conservation. *Fylde Nat.* 1: 3-16.
Jones, M. 1978. Birds of the Fylde – a systematic list to December 1975. *Fylde Nat.* 4: 3-44.
Jones, M. 1984. Canada Geese occurring with wintering Pink-Footed Geese in Lancashire. *Lancashire Bird Report* 1983.
Kaiser, M. J., Galanidi, M., Showler, D. A., Elliott, A. J., Caldow, R. W. G., Rees, E. I. S., Stillman R. A. & Sutherland W. J. 2006. Distribution and behaviour of Common Scoter *Melanitta nigra* relative to prey resources and environmental parameters. *Ibis* 148: 110-128
Kehoe, C. 1992. A possible Ring-billed Gull x Common Gull. *Birding World* 5: 312-313.
Kehoe, C. 2004. An Odd Quail at Plex Moss. *Lancashire Bird Report* 2003.
Kirby, J.S. & Smith, P.H. 1992/3. Comparison of winter foraging activity of Pochard and Tufted Duck at Seaforth, Merseyside. Lancashire *Wildlife Journal* 2/3: 7-16.
Kirby, J.S., Cross, S., Taylor, J.E. & Wolfenden, I.H. 1988. The distribution and abundance of waders wintering on the Alt Estuary, Merseyside, England. *Wader Study Group Bulletin* 54: 23-28.
Lack, D. 1986. *The Atlas of Wintering Birds in Britain and Ireland.* Calton: T & A.D. Poyser.
Langston, R.H.W., Smith, T., Brown, A.F., Eaton, M.A. & Gregory, R.D. 2006. The status of breeding Twite *Carduelis flavirostris* in the UK. *Bird Study* 53: 55-63.
Lassey, P.A. & Greenhalgh. M.E. 1969. Age ratios of Little Gulls on passage in Lancashire. *British Birds* 62: 382-386
Lassey, P.A. 1968. *The Birds of the South Lancashire Dunes and the factors influencing their migrations.* Unpublished manuscript.
Leafloor, J.O., Ankey, C.D & Rusch, D.H. 1998. Environmental effects on body size of Canada Geese. *Auk* 115:26-33.
Leeming, R. 1985. The Jay *Garrulus glandarius* in the Fylde: winter 1983-84. *Fylde Bird Report* 1984.
Leigh, C. 1700. *The Natural History of Lancashire, Cheshire, and the Peak District in Derbyshire.* Oxford.
Leslie, A.S. (Ed) 1912. *The Grouse in health and disease.* Popular edition. London.
Lever, C. 1977. *The Naturalized Animals of the British Isles.* Hutchinson
Liggett, C. 1995. Bewick's and Whooper Swans in the Ribble/Martin Mere Area. *Lancashire Bird Report 1994.*
Lloyd, C., Tasker, M.L. and Partridge, K. 1991. *The Status of Seabirds in Britain and Ireland. London*: T & A.D. Poyser,
Lovat, Lord. 1911. *The Grouse in Health and in Disease* - The final report of the Committee of Inquiry on Grouse Disease – Vols. 1 & 2. Smith, Elder & Co. London.
Lunn, J. 1991. The diet of Short-eared Owls on a lowland Lancashire Moss. *Lancashire Wildlife Journal* 1: 46-48.
Maclean, N., Collinson, M. & Newell, R.G. 2005. Taxonomy for birders: a beginner's guide to DNA and species problems. *British Birds* 98: 512-537.
Madden, B. & Ruttledge, R.F. 1993. Little Gulls in Ireland 1970-1991. *Irish Birds* 5: 23-34
Madge, S.C. and Alsopp, K. 1978. Recent reports. *British Birds* 71: 606-608
Marquiss, M. 1981. *The Goshawk in Britain - its provenance and current status.* In Kenwood, R.E. & Lindsay, M. *Understanding the Goshawk.* Oxford. International Association for Falconry.
Marsh, P.J. & Marsh, R. (eds.). 1989. *A Checklist of the Birds of Lancaster & District: with reference to 1979-1988.* Lancaster & District Birdwatching Society.
Martin, S.J. & Rhodes, R.W. 1995. Breeding waders in the West Pennine Moors. *Chorley & District Natural History Society Report.* 1995: 54 – 72.
Martin, S.J. 1991. Red grouse: A historical digest of its changing status on the north Bolton moors. *Chorley & District Natural History Society Report* 1991: 18-19.
Martin, S.J. 1993. *Survey of breeding birds at Roddlesworth Plantations.* Unpublished report to United Utilities.
Martin, S.J. 2007. The fall and rise of the Belmont gullery: A tale of past persecution, a recent population explosion and a conservation dilemma. *Lancashire Bird Report* 2006.
Martin, S.J. and Rhodes, R.W. 1995. *Breeding waders on the West Pennine Moors: a five-year appraisal of breeding waders around Belmont, Lancashire, 1990-1994.* Unpublished report to North West Water.
Mather, J.R. 1986. *The Birds of Yorkshire.* London: Croom Helm.
Mawby, F.J. 1989. The Spring Migration of Waders on the Ribble and Alt Estuaries during 1984 & 1985. *Lancashire Bird Report* 1988.
May, H.D. 1971. Birds of Botany Bay Wood. *Nature in Lancashire* 2: 46-56.
McCarthy, B. 1999. Seawatching in Lancashire. *Lancashire Bird Report 1999.*
McCarthy, B. 2001. *Birds of Marshside.* Maghull: Hobby Publications.
McGhie, H.A., Brown, A.F., Reed, S., & Bates, S.M. 1994. Aspects of the breeding ecology of Twite in the south Pennines. *English Nature Research Report No. 118.* Peterborough: English Nature.
McGough, P. 2002. *Birds of Marton Mere Local Nature Reserve.* Poulton-le-Fylde.

McNicholl, E.D. (ed). 1883. *A Handbook for Southport.* Robert Johnson & Co., Southport.
Mead, C. 2000. *The status of the nation's birds.* Whittet Books, Stowmarket.
Melling, T. & White, S.J. 2000. The Plight of Lancashire's Twite. *Lancashire Bird Report 1999.*
Messenger, D. & White, S.J. 1991. *Results of spring censuses of Little Gulls in north-west England and north Wales.* Unpublished. Lancashire Trust for Nature Conservation, Bamber Bridge.
Messenger, D. 1993. Spring passage of Little Gulls across northern England. *British Birds* 86: 397-406
Miller, G.C. 1948. *Hoghton Tower.* Preston. Contains bird notes to the area around Hoghton Tower.
Millward, R. 1955. *Lancashire: an illustrated essay on the history of the landscape.* Hodder and Stoughton.
Mitchell, F.S. 1885. *The Birds of Lancashire.* London.
Mitchell, F.S. 1892. *The Birds of Lancashire.* 2nd edition edited by H. Saunders. London.
Mitchell, P.I., Newton, S.F., Ratcliffe, N. and Dunn, T.E. 2004. *Seabird Populations of Britain and Ireland.* London: T & AD Poyser.
Morgan, P.G.D. 1985. *Birds of the Preston Area from 1943 to 1984.* Preston.
Morries, G. 1986. *Lancashire woodland heritage: an introduction based on the county woodland survey.* Lancashire County Council.
Murton, R.K., Westwood, N.J. & Isaacson, A.J. 1964. The feeding habits of the wood-pigeon, *Columba palumbus*, stock dove C. *oenas* and turtle dove *Streptopelia turtur. Ibis* 106: 174-188.
Oakes, C. 1948. *A Bird-Watcher in Lancashire.* London.
Oakes, C. 1953. *The Birds of Lancashire.* Edinburgh & London.
Oakes, C. and Battersby, E. 1939. *The Birds of East Lancashire.* Burnley.
Ogilvie, M.A. 2000. Rare Breeding Birds in the UK in 1999. *British Birds* 93: 358-393
Ogilvie, M.A. 2002. Rare Breeding Birds in the UK in 2000. *British Birds* 95: 542-582
Ogilvie, M.A. 2003. Rare Breeding Birds in the UK in 2001. *British Birds* 96:10
Olsen, K.M. and Larsson, H. 2004. *Gulls of Europe, Asia and North America.* London: Christopher Helm.
Pack, D. [c1981] *The Bird Life of Sunnyhurst Wood.* Blackburn.
Parker, C.K. 1928. *Rossendale Birds.* Bacup.
Parkinson, W. 1905. Our birds. In *Accrington Naturalists' & Antiquarian Soc. Souvenir, 1885-1905.* Accrington.
Parslow, J. 1973. *Breeding birds of Britain and Ireland.* Berkhamstead: T. & A.D. Poyser.
Pennington, D.D. 1918. *Catalogue of Birds in the Collection of D.D. Pennington.* Southport.
Percy, R. 1986. *Debrett's book of game-cards.* London.
Prater, A.J. 1981. *Estuary Birds of Britain and Ireland.* Calton: Poyser.
Prestt, I. and Mills, D.H. 1966. A census of Great Crested Grebes in Britain in 1965. *Bird Study* 13: 163-203
Pritchard, D.E., Housden, S.E., Mudge, G.P., Galbraith, C.A. and Pienkowski M W (eds.) 1992. *Important Bird Areas in the UK including the Channel Islands and the Isle of Man.* RSPB, English Nature, Countryside Council for Wales, Scottish Natural Heritage and Joint Nature Conservation Committee.
Pyefinch, R. and Golborn, P. 2001. *Atlas of the Breeding Birds of Lancashire and North Merseyside.* Liverpool: Hobby Publications for Lancashire & Cheshire Fauna Society.
Quinn, J.L. and Kirby, J.S. 1992. *An ornithological evaluation of North West Water's Reservoirs.* 2 vols. Slimbridge. Deals with the county's reservoirs.
Raine, A.F., Sowter, D.J., Brown, A.F. & Sutherland, W.J. In prep [1]. Natal philopatry and movement of Twite *Carduelis flavirostris* in the South Pennines.
Raine, A.F., Sowter, D.J., Brown, A.F. & Sutherland, W.J. In prep [2]. Migration patterns of two populations of Twite *Carduelis flavirostris* in Britain.
Raines, F.R. 1848. *The Journal of Nicholas Assheton of Downham in the County of Lancaster.* The Chetham Society.
Ratcliffe, D. 1997. *The Raven.* London: Poyser.
Rebecca, G.W. and Bainbridge, I. P. 1998. The breeding status of the Merlin *Falco columbarius* in 1993-94. *Bird Study* 45: 172-187.
Rehfisch, M.M., Austin, G.E., Armitage, M., Atkinson, P., Holloway, S.J., Musgrove, A.J. & Pollitt, M.S. 2003. Numbers of wintering waterbirds in Great Britain and the Isle of Man (1994/95–1998/99): II. Coastal waders (Charadrii). *Biological Conservation* 112: 329-341.
Riddiough. 1812. Letters to Lord Derby. Manuscripts. Liverpool Museum.
Rigby D.J. 1992. *Martin Mere Refuge Report 1991/92.* Slimbridge: Wildfowl & Wetlands Trust.
Roberts, J. & White, S.J. 2006. An exceptionally large movement of Redwings across north-west England in October 2004. *British Birds* 99: 60-66
Ruxton, J. 1973. *Wildfowl of Morecambe Bay.* Sevenoaks.
Salmon, M.A. 2000. *The Aurelian Legacy.* Colchester.
Saunders, H. 1888. *Manual of British Birds.* London.
Scott, P. 1939. *Wild Chorus.* Country Life, London.
Sharrock, J.T.R. 1976. *The Atlas of Breeding Birds in Britain and Ireland.* Berkhamstead: T & A.D. Poyser.
Shorrock, H. 1971. Pink-footed Geese in Lancashire. *Nature in Lancashire* 2: 30-33.

Sibley, D. 2000. *The North American Field Guide*. Sussex: Pica Press.

Simm, I.M.W., Gregory, R.D., Hancock, M.H. & Brown, A.F. 2005. Recent changes in the abundance of British upland breeding birds. *Bird Study* 52: 261-275

Skaife, J. 1838. On the ornithology of Blackburn and the North of Lancashire. *Mag. Nat. Hist II*: 426-433, 524-531.

Slade, P. [1980s] *Birds of Marton Mere*. Fylde Bird Club.

Slater, P. 2001. Breeding ecology of a suburban population of Woodpigeons *Columba palumbus* in northwest England. *Bird Study* 48: 361-366.

Smith, H.E. 1865-1866. Notabilia of the archaeology and natural history of the Mersey District during three years 1863-5: Ornithology and oology. *Trans. Hist. Soc. Lancashire & Cheshire* II: 235-252.

Smith, P.H. & Forshaw, W.D. 1988. Occurrence of "Russian" Bean Geese in Lancashire/Merseyside. *British Birds* 81, 68-70.

Smith, P.H. 1974. The Little Gull in Lancashire. *Lapwing* 1: 4-5. Lancashire Trust for Nature Conservation.

Smith, P.H. 1987. The changing status of Little Gulls *Larus minutus* in north Merseyside, England. *Seabird* 10: 12-21

Smith, P.H. 1999. *The Sands of Time. An introduction to the sand-dunes of the Sefton Coast.* National Museums & Galleries on Merseyside, Liverpool.

Smith, P.H. and Greenhalgh, M.E. 1977. A four-year census of wading birds on the Ribble Estuary, Lancashire/Merseyside. *Bird Study* 24: 243-258.

Smith, R. 1963. The Breeding Birds of the Formby District. Unpublished manuscript.

Smith, S., Harradine, J. & Bateley, J. 1995. *Farmers, Woodpigeons and Woodpigeon Shooting*. Wrexham: British Association for Shooting and Conservation.

Sowter, D. 2002-2004. *The Tarnbrook Fell Gullery Reports*. Unpublished.

Sowter, D. 2004. The Lancashire Twite Mystery Solved. *Greater Manchester Bird Report 2003.*

Spencer, K.G. 1953. *The Lapwing in Britain.* London: Brown.

Spencer, K.G. 1961. *Bird Distribution in East Lancashire: A bibliographical survey, with some notes on the writers concerned.* North West Naturalists' Union.

Spencer, K.G. 1965a. A history of the non-domestic doves and pigeons in Lancashire during the past century. *Naturalist* 893: 48-50.

Spencer, K.G. 1965b. A survey of Lancashire names for birds. *J. Lancashire Dialect Soc.* 14.

Spencer, K.G. 1965c. An early reference to Black Grouse in Yorkshire. *Naturalist* 893: 50

Spencer, K.G. 1968. Birds, in Caul, R. (ed), *The Natural History of the Burnley Area.* Burnley. An updated version, edited by E. Halsall, The Countryside Around Us: A Natural History of East Lancashire was published in 1989.

Spencer, K.G. 1973. *The Status and Distribution of Birds in Lancashire.* Burnley.

Spencer, K.G. 1977. *The Status and Distribution of Birds in the Burnley Area.* Burnley.

Spencer, K.G. 1998. Rooftop assemblies of Lapwings. *East Lancashire Ornithologists Club Annual Report* 1997: 59-60.

Steeden, D. & Steeden, J. 1982. Rookeries of the Fylde. *The Fylde Naturalist* 8: 2-12.

Steeden, D. & Steeden, J. 1984. Rookeries of the Fylde: a further note. *The Fylde Naturalist* 9: 34.

Steele, J. 2006. Do we know what British 'soft-plumaged petrels' are? *British Birds* 99: 404-419

Stott, M., Callion, J., Kinley, I., Raven, C. & Roberts, J. (eds.) 2002. *The Breeding Birds of Cumbria: A tetrad atlas 1997-2001.* Cumbria Bird Club.

Svensson, L. 1992. *Identification Guide to European Passerines.* Stockholm.

Tapper, S. (ed.) 1999. *A question of balance. Game animals & their role in the British countryside.* Game Conservancy.

Tasker, M.L., Webb A., Hall A.J., Pienkowski M.W. & Langslow D.R. 1987. *Seabirds in the North Sea.* Nature Conservancy Council, Peterborough.

Taylor, A. 1913. *Birds of a County Palatine.* London. Birds around Whalley and Ribble/Calder.

Thorpe, J.P. & A.M. Sapsford. 1992. Population structure of Goldcrests *Regulus regulus* caught on migration at the Calf of Man Bird Observatory in 1989. *Ringing & Migration* 19: 7-12

Toms, M. 1997-2004. *The Bird Table.*

Trobe, W.M. 1990. *The Merlin.* Brighton: Oriel Stringer.

Tucker, G.M. and Heath, M.F. 1994. *Birds in Europe: their Conservation Status.* Birdlife International, Cambridge.

Tyler, S.J. and Ormerod, S.J. 1994. *The Dippers.* London: T. & A.D. Poyser.

Vinicombe, K.E. & Harrop, A.H.J. 1999. Ruddy Shelducks in Britain and Ireland, 1986-94. *British Birds* 92: 225-255

Wagstaffe R. and Holder, F.W. 1927-8. Notes from the South Lancashire Coast. *British Birds* 21: 190-194.

Wagstaffe, R. 1926. The ducks and wading birds of Southport. *The North Western Naturalist* 1: 196-201.

Wagstaffe, R. 1927. *Birds of the Southport Pier and Marine Lake.* Southport.

Wagstaffe, R. 1932. Birds of the South West Lancashire Coast. 23rd report, *Southport Society of Natural Science*, 15-16.

Wagstaffe, R. 1935. The birds of Southport and district with notes on their distribution and status. *Report of the Southport Scientific Society* 4, 105-126.

Walsh, J.F. 1987. Coal Tit Movements in the Fylde, Autumn 1985. *Lancashire Bird Report 1986.*

Walsh, JF. 2002. Jay movements in the Fylde in autumn 2001. *Fylde Bird Report 2001*: 76-80.

Walsh, J.F. & Blacow, L.G. 2002. *Breeding Bird Survey 2002 of Lytham Hall Country Park. Fylde Bird Club Report to Lancashire County Council.*

Ward, E. 1989. Rossendale Birds. Burnley. A second edition, subtitled A Millennium Update, was published in 2002.

Ward, E. 1992. The Hile, Rossendale CBC Study. Lancashire Bird Report 1991.

Wernham, C.V., Toms, M.P., Marchant, J.H. Clark, J.A., Siriwardena, G.M. & Baillie, S.R. (eds.). 2002. The Migration Atlas: Movements of the Birds of Britain and Ireland. London: BTO/T&D Poyser.

Wheeler, E.C. 1954. Some Observations on the Terneries of Southport and District. *North Western Naturalist* 2: 31-36

White, S.J. 1995. Aspects of behaviour of Little Gulls *Larus minutus* at a spring migration staging site in Liverpool, England. Unpublished MSc. thesis, University of Liverpool.

White, S.J. 2001. The Common Scoters of Liverpool Bay. *Lancashire Bird Report 2000.*

White, S.J. 2003a. Lapwing Survey of Lancashire and North Merseyside, 2002-2003. *Lancashire Bird Report 2002.*

White, S.J. 2003b. The Distribution and Population Size of House Sparrows in Urban North Merseyside, 2001-2002. *Lancashire Bird Report 2002.*

White, S.J. 2005. The Skelmersdale chiffchaff, 18 April to 2 May 2004. *Lancashire Bird Report 2004.*

White, S.J. and Kehoe, C. 1993. *A survey of breeding birds on Heald Moor.* Unpublished report to Lancashire County Council.

White, S.J. and Kehoe, C. 2001. Difficulties in determining the age of Common Terns in the field. *British Birds* 94: 268-277.

White, S.J. and Smith, P.H. 2003. The Gulls and Terns of the Mersey Estuary. In Curtis, M.S. & Baker-Schommer, M. (eds). *The Mersey Estuary: Naturally Ours* (2nd edition). Liverpool Museum.

Williams, T.S. 1936. Bird life round Formby. Observations on wild duck. *North Western Naturalist* 11: 17-20.

Williams, T.S. 1943. Bird Life of the Formby District. *North Western Naturalist* 17: 179-188

Wilson, A.M. and Vickery, J.A. 2003. Wet grassland waders in decline. *BTO News* No. 247.

Wilson, A.M. and Vickery, J.A. 2005. Decline in Yellow Wagtail *Motacilla flava flavissima* breeding on lowland wet grassland in England and Wales between 1982 and 2002. *Bird Study* 52: 88-92

Wilson, J. 1972. Recent changes in the status of some Lancashire birds. *Nature in Lancashire* 3: 41-43.

Wilson, J. 1973. Wader populations of Morecambe Bay. *Bird Study* 20, 9-23.

Wilson, J. 1974. *The Birds of Morecambe Bay.* Milnthorpe: Clapham. 2nd edition 1988.

Wilson, J. 1978. The breeding bird community of willow scrub at Leighton Moss, Lancashire. *Bird Study* 25: 239-244.

Wilson, J. 1993. Colonisation by Bearded Tits of Leighton Moss, Lancashire. *British Birds* 86: 352-358.

Wilson, J. 1999. The colonisation of Marsh Harriers of Leighton Moss RSPB Reserve. *The Birds of Lancaster & District* 40: 52-53.

Wilson, J. 2002. The Decline of Bearded Tits at Leighton Moss in 2001. *Lancashire Bird Report 2001.*

Wilson, J. 2004. Rookery censuses in the Society's area 1975-2002. *The Birds of Lancaster & District 2002, Annual report* 44. 97-98.

Wilson, J. 2004. The Status of Greylag Geese in North Lancashire. *Lancashire Bird Report 2003.*

Wilson, J. and Marsh, P.J. 1987. Birds on pp 153-188 in Robinson, N.A. & Pringle, A.W. *Morecambe Bay: an assessment of present ecological knowledge.* Lancaster.

Wilson, J. and Peach W. 2006. Impact of an exceptional winter flood on the population dynamics of bearded tits *Panurus biarmacus. Animal Conservation* 9: 463-473

Wilson, J. and Thomas, M. 1972. *A Guide to the Birds and Flowers of the Silverdale-Arnside Area including Leighton Moss RSPB Reserve.* Silverdale.

Wilson, R.D.S. [c.1977] *Birds of Witton Country Park, Blackburn.*

Witherby, H.F. *et al.* 1938-1941. *The Handbook of British Birds.* London.

Woolfall, S.J. 1992. *The importance of the Wyre Estuary for bird populations in relation to the proposed Wyre barrage.* Thetford.

Wotton, S.R., Langston, R.H.W. & Gregory, R.D. 2002. The breeding status of the Ring Ouzel *Turdus torquatus* in the UK in 1999. *Bird Study* 49: 26-34

Wright, J. 2005. 'Northern/Eastern' Bullfinches in Lancashire, 2004. *Lancashire Bird Report 2004.*

Wrigley, J. 1892. *Notes on the Bird Life of Formby, Liverpool.* An update of his MS in Liverpool Central Library, *Notes on the Natural History of Formby* (1883).

Wynn, R.B, Yésou, P. & Josey, S. 2005. The changing status of the Balearic Shearwater *Puffinus mauretanicus* in northwest European waters: relationships to sea surface temperature, phytoplankton concentrations and fish abundance. *Proceedings of the International Manx Shearwater Workshop. www.cbo.org.uk*

GAZETTEER OF BIRDWATCHING SITES IN LANCASHIRE AND NORTH MERSEYSIDE

Site	Grid Ref	Town / Area
Abbey Village (Rake Brook) Reservoir	SD647223	West Pennine Moors
Abbeystead Fell	SD552576	Forest of Bowland
Abbeystead Reservoir	SD560540	Forest of Bowland
Ainsdale Sands National Nature Reserve	SD290105	Sefton Coast
Aldcliffe Marsh	SD455608	Lune Estuary
Allen Pool (Eric Morecambe complex)	SD475730	Morecambe Bay
Allsprings	SD734334	Great Harwood
Alston Reservoirs	SD608368	Longridge
Alston Woods	SD607334	Longridge
Altcar Rifle Ranges	SD290045	Sefton Coast
Altcar Withins	SD340050	South-west Mosses
Altham Bridge	SD774331	River Calder
Anglezarke Moor	SD640175	West Pennine Moors
Anglezarke Reservoir	SD615165	West Pennine Moors
Arkholme	SD587715	Lune Valley
Arley Reservoir	SD586113	Chorley
Arm Hill	SD346463	Wyre Estuary
Ashurst's Beacon	SD501079	Skelmersdale
Astley Park	SD575182	Chorley
Aughton Woods	SD543663	Lune Valley
Avenham Park	SD543284	Preston
Babydoc	SD514733	Dockacres complex
Bank End	SD440526	Lune Estuary
Bank Houses	SD431530	Lune Estuary
Banks Marsh	SD395238	Ribble Marshes
Barnaby's Sands	SD350461	Wyre Estuary
Barnacre Moor	SD530477	Garstang
Barnacre Reservoir	SD526478	Garstang
Barrow Lodge	SD741382	Clitheroe
Barrow Scout	SD478434	Silverdale
Barrowford Reservoir	SD868400	Colne
Bartle Pools	SD490336	Preston
Bazil Point	SD437567	Lune Estuary
Beacon Country Park	SD506065	Skelmersdale
Beacon Fell Country Park	SD573426	Longridge
Beatrix Fell	SD663525	Forest of Bowland
Belmont Reservoir	SD672170	West Pennine Moors
Bickerstaffe Moss	SD435025	South-west Mosses
Billinge Hill	SD523016	St. Helens
Billinge Hill & Wood	SD656280	Blackburn
Billinge Wood, Euxton	SD531181	Yarrow Valley
Birkacre	SD573150	Yarrow Valley
Birkdale Dunes	SD310140	Sefton Coast
Birkett Fell	SD675485	Forest of Bowland
Bispham Marsh	SD329403	Blackpool
Black Coppice/Stronstrey Bank	SD618183	West Pennine Moors
Black Moss Reservoirs	SD824413	Barley
Blea Tarn Reservoir	SD493585	Lancaster
Bleadale	SD605495	Forest of Bowland
Bleasdale Moors	SD565481	Garstang
Bloe Greet	SD701583	Forest of Bowland
Blundellsands Dunes	SD299010	Sefton Coast
Boilton Wood	SD582314	Preston
Bold (Collier's) Moss	SJ545940	St Helens
Boulsworth Hill	SD925355	Trawden
Bourbles Pit	SD376477	Over Wyre
Bradford Fell	SD725477	Forest of Bowland
Brennand Fell	SD635554	Forest of Bowland
Brennand Valley	SD653534	Forest of Bowland
Bretherton Eyes	SD466195	South-west Mosses
Brockholes Quarry	SD585307	Preston
Burbo Bank	SJ280980	Liverpool Bay
Burholme	SD660485	Forest of Bowland
Burn Fell	SD678531	Forest of Bowland
Burn Moor, Blacko	SD848432	Colne
Burnslack Fell	SD623463	Forest of Bowland
Burrow's Marsh	SD355450	Wyre Estuary
Cabin Hill NNR	SD282052	Sefton Coast
Calder Fell	SD558487	Garstang
Calder Foot	SD710371	Whalley
Calf Hey Reservoir	SD753224	Rossendale
Cant Clough Reservoir	SD897308	Burnley
Carnforth Marsh	SD469721	Morecambe Bay
Carnforth Slag Tips (Cote Stones)	SD486719	Morecambe Bay
Carr House Green Common, Inskip	SD474373	Preston
Carr Mill Dam	SJ525985	St. Helens
Carr Wood, Great Altcar	SD345047	South-west Mosses
Catchdale Moss	SJ480960	St. Helens
Catlow Fell	SD708599	Forest of Bowland
Caton Moor	SD576636	Lune Valley
Catshaw Fell	SD555511	Forest of Bowland
CEGB Pools	SD335460	Fleetwood
Champion Moor	SD745525	Forest of Bowland
Childwall Woods	SJ413886	Liverpool
Churchtown Moss	SD383185	South-west Mosses
Clifton Marsh	SD465285	Ribble Marshes
Cliviger Gorge	SD8728	Burnley
Clough Bottom Reservoir	SD847268	Burnley
Clougha Pike	SD547595	Forest of Bowland
Clowbridge Reservoir	SD887282	Burnley
Coal Clough wind farm	SD894285	Burnley
Cockerham Marsh	SD435518	Lune Estuary
Cockerham Moss	SD443486	Over Wyre
Cockersand	SD426536	Lune Estuary
Coldwell Reservoirs	SD905363	
Colloway Marsh	SD452586	Lune Estuary
Common Bank	SD564174	Yarrow Valley
Conder Green	SD460557	Lune Estuary
Conder Pool	SD455558	Lune Estuary
Copperworks Wood	SD569170	Yarrow Valley
Coppull Moor / Chisnall	SD552135	Chorley
Cowm Reservoir	SD880190	Rossendale
Cowpe Moss	SD842193	Rossendale
Cowpe Reservoir	SD842201	Rossendale
Cranberry Moss	SD710192	South Pennines
Cringlebarrow Wood	SD497753	Silverdale
Croasdale	SD700552	Forest of Bowland
Croasdale Fell	SD675569	Forest of Bowland
Crosby Marine Park and Lake	SJ314975	Sefton Coast
Cross of Greet Bridge	SD703590	Forest of Bowland

Site	Grid Ref	Town / Area
Crossens Marsh	SD365215	Ribble Marshes
Croston Big Wood	SD497177	South-west Mosses
Croston Marsh	SD482186	South-west Mosses
Croston Moss	SD480170	South-west Mosses
Crown Point	SD849287	Burnley
Croxteth Country Park	SJ410945	Liverpool
Cuerden Valley Park	SD565238	Bamber Bridge
Darwen Moor	SD680200	West Pennine Moors
Dean Clough Reservoir	SD715331	Great Harwood
Dean Wood, Rivington	SD629153	West Pennine Moors
Deeply Vale	SD825146	Edenfield
Deerplay Moor	SD866274	South Pennines
Deerstones	SD787394	Clitheroe
Delph Plantations	SD698165	West Pennine Moors
Delph Reservoir	SD700165	West Pennine Moors
Dilworth Reservoir	SD615383	Longridge
Dingle Reservoir	SD693147	West Pennine Moors
Dockacres Gravel Pits (Borwick Waters)	SD520723	Dockacres complex
Downholland Moss	SD335090	South-west Mosses
Dunkenshaw Fell	SD585575	Forest of Bowland
Dunsop Bridge	SD659501	Forest of Bowland
Dunsop Fell	SD679548	Forest of Bowland
Dunsop Valley	SD655500	Forest of Bowland
Duxbury Woods	SD584152	Yarrow Valley
Eagland Hill	SD432453	Over Wyre
Earnsdale Reservoir	SD670222	Darwen
Easington Fell	SD728493	Forest of Bowland
Eaves Wood	SD468762	Silverdale
Eccleston Delph	SD518150	Chorley
Eccleston Mere	SJ482949	Prescot
Ellel Grange	SD481538	Lancaster
Ellerbeck	SD585140	Yarrow Valley
Emmott Moor	SD953403	Trawden
Entwistle Plantations	SD705175	West Pennine Moors
Eric Morecambe complex	SD475730	Morecambe Bay
E-shaped pond, Bretherton	SD486198	South-west Mosses
Ewood Bridge Sewage Farm	SD794205	Haslingden
Fair Oak Fell	SD625475	Forest of Bowland
Fairhaven Dunes	SD335274	Fylde Coast
Fairhaven Lake	SD340273	Fylde Coast
Fairsnape Fell	SD592469	Forest of Bowland
Farington Moss	SD525241	South-west Mosses
Fazakerley Reedbed	SJ388965	Liverpool
Fazakerley Woods	SJ379968	Liverpool
Fishmoor Reservoir	SD697262	Blackburn
Fleagarth Wood	SD470745	Silverdale
Fleetwood Marine Lake	SD324482	Fleetwood
Fleetwood Marsh	SD335460	Fleetwood
Fluke Hall, Pilling	SD393499	Morecambe Bay
Folly Clough	SD817259	Rossendale
Folly Tip	SD814257	Rossendale
Formby Hall	SD311101	South-west Mosses
Formby Moss	SD310074	South-west Mosses
Formby Point	SD270070	Sefton Coast
Foulridge Reservoirs	SD894414	Colne
Freckleton Naze	SD435272	Ribble Marshes
Freshfield (Formby Point)	SD270070	Sefton Coast
Freshfield Dune Heath	SD298092	Sefton Coast
Gaitbarrows NNR	SD482774	Lancaster
Garston Shore	SJ400834	Liverpool
Gisburn Forest	SD745567	Forest of Bowland
Glasson Dock	SD445562	Lune Estuary
Glasson Marsh	SD437558	Lune Estuary
Granny's Bay, Fairhaven	SD344273	Ribble Estuary
Great Plumpton Sidings	SD385335	Kirkham
Greta Foot	SD600727	Lune Valley
Grey Heights Wood	SD613717	West Pennine Moors
Grimsargh Reservoir	SD590346	Preston
Grindleton Fell	SD740480	Forest of Bowland
Grisedale Wood	SD487744	Silverdale
Guide Reservoir	SD702259	Blackburn
Habergham Eaves	SD807336	Burnley
Hackensall Wood	SD350476	Over Wyre
Hale Duck Decoy (Cheshire)	SJ478827	Liverpool
Halsall Moss	SD350120	South-west Mosses
Halstead Fell	SD740605	Forest of Bowland
Hambleton Marsh	SD365415	Wyre Estuary
Hameldon Common	SD788296	Accrington
Hapton Scout	SD807293	South Pennines
Harden Moor	SD811165	Rossendale
Hare Appletree Fell	SD545583	Forest of Bowland
Hareden Fell	SD620492	Forest of Bowland
Harrisend Fell	SD536500	Forest of Bowland
Harrop Fold	SD745494	Forest of Bowland
Hasgill Fell	SD715599	Forest of Bowland
Haskayne Cutting	SD357089	South-west Mosses
Haslingden Grane	SD746227	Rossendale
Haslingden Moor	SD756242	Rossendale
Haweswater	SD477766	Lancaster
Hawthornthwaite Fell	SD575515	Forest of Bowland
Heald Moor	SD885265	Burnley
Healey Nab	SD606183	West Pennine Moors
Heapey Lodges	SD610194	West Pennine Moors
Heaton Marsh	SD583594	Lune Estuary
Heckenhurst Reservoir	SD868329	Burnley
Hesketh Golf Course	SD353190	Sefton Coast
Hesketh Out Marsh	SD415255	Ribble Marshes
Hesketh Park	SD348182	Southport
Hest Bank	SD466666	Morecambe Bay
Heysham Moss	SD423603	Morecambe Bay
Heysham Nature Reserve	SD407601	Morecambe Bay
Hic Bibi	SD567126	Chorley
High Bullough Reservoir, Anglezarke	SD619169	West Pennine Moors
Salter Fell	SD638595	Forest of Bowland
Higher Hill	SD835184	Rossendale
Higher Hodder Bridge	SD697411	Forest of Bowland
Hightown Dunes	SD299025	Sefton Coast
Hodder Bank Fell	SD675493	Forest of Bowland
Hoddlesden Moss	SD726211	South Pennines
Hoghton Bottoms	SD626270	Chorley
Hoghton Tower	SD624264	Chorley
Holcombe Moor	SD766184	Rossendale
Holden Wood Reservoir	SD771224	Rossendale
Hundred End, Banks Marsh	SD415227	Ribble Marshes
Hurst Green	SD688374	Longridge
Hurstwood Reservoir	SD887316	Burnley
Hutton Marsh	SD454273	Ribble Marshes
Hyles Moor	SD805525	Forest of Bowland
ICI Pool	SD333453	Fleetwood
Ince Blundell Woods	SD330028	South-west Mosses
Jackhouse Reservoir	SD742260	Oswaldtwistle
Jameson Road Tip	SD336456	Fleetwood
Jenny Brown's Point	SD460735	Morecambe Bay
Jumbles Reservoir	SD735146	West Pennine Moors
Kemple End	SD690405	Longridge Fell
Kirkby Moss	SJ445983	South-west Mosses

Site	Grid Ref	Town / Area
Knowles Wood, Heskin	SD517156	Chorley
Knowsley Park	SJ450950	Liverpool
Lamb Hill Fell	SD685589	Forest of Bowland
Langden Valley	SD630510	Forest of Bowland
Lea Green Flash and Tip	SJ503920	St. Helens
Lea Marsh	SD481292	Ribble Marshes
Lead Mines Clough	SD632165	West Pennine Moors
Leagram Hall	SD624442	Chipping
Leck Beck	SD646779	Lune Valley
Leck Fell	SD670786	Lune Valley
Lee Green Reservoir	SD880337	South Pennines
Leighton Moss	SD485752	Morecambe Bay
Lever Park, Rivington	SD630138	West Pennine Moors
Lightfoot Green	SD513340	Preston
Limbrick	SD605164	Yarrow Valley
Little Crosby Estate	SD323015	South-west Mosses
Lomeshaye Marsh	SD847377	Nelson
Longridge Fell	SD640396	Longridge
Longton Brickpits	SD481251	Ribble Marshes
Longton Marsh	SD450263	Ribble Marshes
Longton Moss	SD515245	South-west Mosses
Longworth Clough	SD694153	West Pennine Moors
Lord's Lot Wood	SD545707	Lune Valley
Lower Burgh Meadow, Chorley	SD575155	Yarrow Valley
Lower Healey Lodges	SD599182	West Pennine Moors
Lowerhouse Lodges	SD806328	Burnley
Lytham Hall	SD356280	South Fylde
Lytham Moss	SD340305	South Fylde
Lytham St Anne's Nature Reserve	SD308302	Fylde Coast
Mallowdale Fell	SD625588	Forest of Bowland
Marshaw Fell	SD606526	Forest of Bowland
Marshside	SD355205	Ribble Marshes
Martholme Sewage Works	SD757333	Great Harwood
Martholme Viaduct	SD752338	Great Harwood
Martin Mere	SD425144	South-west Mosses
Marton Mere	SD343353	Blackpool
Mawdesley Moss	SD482158	South-west Mosses
Mere Brow Leisure Lakes	SD410179	South-west Mosses
Mere Sands Wood	SD447157	South-west Mosses
Middleton Industrial Estate	SD417590	Morecambe Bay
Mitton Hall	SD718386	Whalley
Mitton Wood	SD713377	Whalley
Moor Piece	SD695448	Bashall Eaves
Mossborough Hall	SJ463976	South-west Mosses
Mount Park	SD333482	Fleetwood
Much Hoole Moss	SD497226	South-west Mosses
Musbury Tor	SD771207	Rossendale
Musden Head Moor	SD756200	Rossendale
Myerscough Quarry	SD506388	Preston
Mythop	SD358348	Blackpool
Nab Wood	SD590320	Preston
Newton Lake	SJ595958	Newton-le-Willows
Newton Marsh	SD450291	Ribble Marshes
Nickey Nook	SD523488	Garstang
Nuck's Wood	SD419168	South-west Mosses
Oakenclough Fell	SD555474	Forest of Bowland
Ogden Reservoir	SD763227	Rossendale
Oglet Bay	SJ447818	Liverpool
Old Coach Road	SJ458975	South-west Mosses
Old Hollow Farm, Banks Marsh	SD391227	Ribble Marshes
Oswaldtwistle Moor	SD743245	South Pennines
Otterspool	SJ370861	Liverpool

Site	Grid Ref	Town / Area
Out Rawcliffe	SD403418	Over Wyre
Oxcliffe Marsh	SD446613	Lune Estuary
Parbold Hill	SD507106	Ormskirk
Parrox Hall	SD360478	Over Wyre
Parsonage Reservoir	SD700320	Blackburn
Paythorne Moor	SD835535	Gisburn
Pendle Hill	SD805414	Clitheroe
Pickup Bank Reservoir	SD720236	Over Wyre
Pilling Lane Ends	SD415495	Morecambe Bay
Pilling Marsh	SD410496	Morecambe Bay
Pine Lake	SD513721	Dockacres complex
Pleasington NR	SD645271	Blackburn
Plex Moss	SD340105	South-west Mosses
Plock Wood, Chorley	SD575158	Yarrow Valley
Plunge Valley	SD807193	Rossendale
Potts Wood	SD495727	Carnforth
Preesall Flashes	SD361470	Over Wyre
Preesall Sands	SD370497	Morecambe Bay
Prescot Reservoirs	SJ470938	Prescot
Preston Dock	SD515298	Preston
Quernmore	SD520590	Lancaster
Rawcliffe Moss	SD412441	Over Wyre
Ream Hills	SD368342	Blackpool
Red Bridge, Bretherton	SD465188	South-west Mosses
Red Lea Reservoir, Abbey Village	SD644233	West Pennine Moors
Red Moss	SD842276	Rossendale
Red Scar Wood	SD585321	Preston
Reed's Moss, Rainford	SJ477987	South-west Mosses
Rimrose Valley	SJ330985	Crosby
Rishton Reservoir	SD714300	Blackburn
Rivington Moor	SD650145	West Pennine Moors
Rivington Reservoirs	SD624140	West Pennine Moors
Roddlesworth Plantations	SD660210	West Pennine Moors
Roeburndale	SD608655	Lune Valley
Rossall Point	SD312476	Fylde Coast
Rowley Lake	SD860330	Burnley
Saddle Fell	SD612470	Forest of Bowland
Sand Villa	SD436505	Over Wyre
Sands Lake, Ainsdale	SD301130	Sefton Coast
Sankey Valley Park	SJ555950	St. Helens
Scarisbrick Hall	SD392127	South-west Mosses
Scorton (Street Bridge) Gravel Pits	SD515520	Garstang
Scout Moor	SD825194	Rossendale
Seaforth Nature Reserve	SJ315970	Sefton Coast
Sefton Meadows	SD350025	South-west Mosses
Sefton Park	SJ378875	Liverpool
Shard Bridge	SD367409	Wyre Estuary
Shedden Clough	SD894296	Burnley
Shell Flat	SD24	Liverpool Bay
Short Clough Reservoir	SD813250	Rossendale
Silverdale Moss	SD472774	Silverdale
Simonswood Moss	SJ445985	South-west Mosses
Skerton Weir	SD481633	Lancaster
Skippool Creek	SD357410	Wyre Estuary
Skirden Beck	SD781481	Forest of Bowland
Slipper Hill Reservoir	SD875420	Foulridge
Sollom Moss	SD445190	South-west Mosses
Southport Marine Lake	SD335180	Sefton Coast
Spade Mill Reservoir	SD618375	Longridge
Spring Wood, Heskin	SD525158	Chorley
Springs Reservoir	SD690146	West Pennine Moors
Stacksteads Tip	SD852208	Rossendale

Site	Grid Ref	Town / Area
Stake House Fell	SD558499	Forest of Bowland
Stalmine Moss	SD396455	Over Wyre
Stanley Park	SD360330	Blackpool
Stanworth Woods	SD645244	Blackburn
Staple Oak Fell	SD645518	Forest of Bowland
Stiperden Moor	SD910288	South Pennines
Stocks Reservoir	SD730560	Forest of Bowland
Stodday	SD462587	Lune Estuary
Street Bridge Gravel Pits	SD517520	Garstang
Stubbins Wood	SD620341	Longridge
Sunderland Point	SD423552	Lune Estuary
Sunnyhurst Hey Reservoir	SD676219	Darwen
Sunnyhurst Woods	SD678228	Darwen
Swinden Reservoirs	SD887334	South Pennines
Sykes Fell	SD609500	Forest of Bowland
Tarnbrook Fell	SD605571	Forest of Bowland
The Hile	SD850230	Rossendale
The Snab	SD565680	Lune Valley
Thievely Pike	SD871271	South Pennines
Thievely Scout, Cliviger	SD882274	South Pennines
Thornton ICI Reservoir	SD340445	Fleetwood
Thrushgill Wood, Gressingham	SD579706	Lune Valley
Tockholes (Roddlesworth) Plantations	SD660210	West Pennine Moors
Todderstaffe Hall	SD365366	South Fylde
Top o' Leach	SD852195	South Pennines
Towneley Park	SD852307	Burnley
Townsendfold	SD803219	Rossendale
Tun Brook Wood	SD594329	Preston
Turton & Entwistle Reservoir	SD720175	West Pennine Moors
Turton Moor	SD685182	West Pennine Moors
Twin Lakes, Croston	SD483191	South-west Mosses
Twiston Moor, Pendle	SD825430	Clitheroe
Ulnes Walton	SD496208	Chorley
Waddington Fell	SD715471	Forest of Bowland
Walverden Reservoir	SD872365	Nelson
Walves Reservoir	SD747151	Rossendale
Wardley's Creek	SD366427	Wyre Estuary
Ward's Reservoir	SD670158	West Pennine Moors
Ward's Stone	SD585585	Forest of Bowland
Warton Bank	SD402274	Ribble Marshes
Warton Crag	SD493728	Carnforth
Warton Marsh	SD390270	Ribble Marshes
Water Sheddles Reservoir	SD9638	Trawden
Waterfoot	SD832219	Rawtenstall
Watson Road Park	SD313335	Blackpool
Wayoh Reservoir	SD733167	West Pennine Moors
Weeton	SD384347	South Fylde
Weets Hill	SD858449	Barnoldswick
Whalley Nab	SD723344	Whalley
Wheelton Moor	SD627196	West Pennine Moors
Wheelton Plantation (Heather Lea Wood), Brinscall	SD627207	West Pennine Moors
Whin Scar Clough	SD843310	Burnley
Whinney Hill Tip	SD757305	Accrington
White Coppice	SD619191	West Pennine Moors
White Moor	SD870440	Barnoldswick
White Moor Reservoir	SD878432	Foulridge
White Moss, Skelmersdale	SD475047	South-west Mosses
Whitendale Fell	SD663564	Forest of Bowland
Whitewell Bottom	SD836237	Rossendale
Whittle Pike	SD825189	Rossendale
Whitton Country Park	SD656276	Blackburn

Site	Grid Ref	Town / Area
Wilkinson's Gravel Pit	SD366481	Over Wyre
Williamson Park	SD489612	Lancaster
Winder Wood, Roeburndale	SD598636	Forest of Bowland
Windy Harbour	SD387404	Wyre Estuary
Winmarleigh Moss	SD443476	Over Wyre
Winter Hill	SD658152	West Pennine Moors
Withnell Fold Flash	SD613238	Chorley
Withnell Fold Nature Reserve	SD637225	Chorley
Withnell Moor	SD645205	West Pennine Moors
Witton Country Park	SD657270	Blackburn
Wood End Sewage Works	SD827352	Burnley
Woodfold Park	SD638289	Blackburn
Woodvale Airfield (Freshfield Dune Heath)	SD298092	Sefton Coast
Woodwell	SD463744	Lancaster
Worden Park	SD536212	Leyland
Worsthorne Moor	SD895304	South Pennines
Wrightington Lakes	SD534107	Standish
Wycoller	SD932394	Trawden
Wyre Light	SD325513	Fylde Coast
Wyreside Fisheries, Scorton	SD516523	Garstang
Yarrow Reservoir, Rivington	SD625156	West Pennine Moors
Yarrow Valley Park	SD572150	Yarrow Valley
Yealand Hall Allotment	SD490762	Silverdale

INDEX